THE ECONOMICS OF MONEY, BANKING, AND FINANCIAL MARKETS

FIFTH CANADIAN EDITION

THE ECONOMICS
OF MONEY, BANKING,
AND FINANCIAL MARKETS

FIFTH CANADIAN EDITION

FREDERIC S. MISHKIN
COLUMBIA UNIVERSITY

APOSTOLOS SERLETIS
UNIVERSITY OF CALGARY

PEARSON

Toronto

Vice-President, Editorial Director: Gary Bennett
Editor-in-Chief: Nicole Lukach
Acquisitions Editor: Claudine O'Donnell
Sponsoring Editor: Jen Parks
Marketing Manager: Leigh-Anne Graham
Supervising Developmental Editor: Madhu Ranadive
Developmental Editor: Rebecca Ryoji
Project Manager: Sarah Lukaweski
Manufacturing Coordinator: Jane Schell
Production Editor: Carrie Fox
Copy Editor: Susan Bindernagel
Proofreader: Stephanie Fysh
Project Coordination and Editorial Services: Electronic Publishing Services Inc., NYC
Electronic Page Makeup: Jouve
Permissions Researcher: Tom Wilcox, PreMediaGlobal
Art Director: Julia Hall
Cover Designer: Anthony Leung
Interior Designer: Anthony Leung
Cover Image: Masterfile

10 9 8 7 6 5 4 3 2 1 [EB]

Library and Archives Canada Cataloguing in Publication
Mishkin, Frederic S.
The economics of money, banking and financial markets / Frederic S. Mishkin, Apostolos Serletis.
— 5th Canadian ed.

Includes bibliographical references and index.
ISBN 978-0-321-78570-1

1. Finance—Textbooks.   2. Money—Textbooks.   3. Banks and banking—Textbooks.
I. Serletis, Apostolos, 1954- II. Title.

HG173.M58 2013   332   C2012-905239-6

9780321785701

Brief Contents

Contents

Contents on the Web

The following updated chapter and appendices are available on our Companion Website at MyEconLab.

WEB CHAPTER
The *ISLM* Model   MyEconLab

Preview

Keynes's Fixed Price Level Assumption and
the *IS* Curve
    The *LM* Curve
    Equilibrium in the Market for Money: The *LM* Curve

ISLM Approach to Aggregate Output and
Interest Rates

Factors That Cause the *LM* Curve to Shift

Changes in Equilibrium Level of the
Interest Rate and Aggregate Output
    Response to a Change in Monetary Policy
    Response to a Change in Fiscal Policy

Application The Economic Stimulus
Act of 2008 in the United States

Effectiveness of Monetary Versus Fiscal Policy
    Monetary Policy Versus Fiscal Policy:
        The Case of Complete Crowding Out

Application Targeting
Money Supply Versus Interest Rates

ISLM Model in the Long Run

Summary

Questions and Applied Problems

Web Exercises

Web References

APPENDIX TO WEB CHAPTER
Algebra of the *ISLM* Model

Basic Closed-Economy *ISLM* Model
    IS and *LM* Curves
    Solution of the Model
    Implications

Open-Economy *ISLM* Model

Implications

Web Appendices

Chapter 4: Measuring Interest-Rate Risk: Duration

Chapter 5: Models of Asset Pricing

Chapter 5: Applying the Asset Market Approach
to a Commodity Market: The Case of Gold

Chapter 5: Loanable Funds Framework

Chapter 7: Evidence on the Efficient Market
Hypothesis

Chapter 10: Banking Crises Throughout the World

Chapter 13: Measuring Bank Performance

Chapter 13: Nonbanking Financial Institutions and
Duration Analysis

Chapter 16: The Bank of Canada's Balance
Sheet and the Monetary Base

Chapter 16: The M2+ Money Multiplier

Chapter 18: Monetary Targeting

Chapter 20: The Canadian Balance of Payments

Chapter 21: The Baumol-Tobin and the Tobin
Mean-Variance Models of the Demand for Money

Chapter 21: Empirical Evidence on the
Demand for Money

Chapter 24: The Effects of Macroeconomic
Shocks on Asset Prices

Chapter 24: Aggregate Demand and Supply:
A Numerical Example

Chapter 24: The Algebra of the Aggregate
Demand and Supply Model

Chapter 24: The Taylor Principle
and Inflation Stability

Chapter 27: Evaluating Empirical Evidence:
The Debate over the Importance of
Money in Economic Fluctuations

Mini-Cases

Preface

Hallmarks

Although this text has undergone a major revision, it retains the basic hallmarks that have made it the best-selling textbook on money and banking over the past four editions:

- A unifying, analytic framework that uses a few basic economic principles to organize students' thinking about the structure of financial markets, the foreign exchange markets, financial institution management, and the role of monetary policy in the economy
- A careful, step-by-step development of models (an approach found in the best principles of economics textbooks), which makes it easier for students to learn
- The complete integration of an international perspective throughout the text
- A thoroughly up-to-date treatment of the latest developments in monetary theory
- Special features called "Financial News" to encourage reading of financial newspapers
- An applications-oriented perspective with numerous applications and special-topic boxes that increase students' interest by showing them how to apply theory to real-world examples

What's New in the Fifth Canadian Edition

In addition to the expected updating of all data whenever possible, there is major new material in every part of the text.

Revised Chapter 9: Financial Crises

The previous edition of this textbook contained a new chapter on financial crises, including the most recent one. It was written, however, before the global financial crisis was over. Now with the perspective of a couple of years after the crisis, we have been able to improve this chapter substantially, first, by completely reorganizing the chapter to tell a more coherent story and second, by adding new sections, such as the run on the shadow banking system. In addition, we have added new boxes on the process of securitization, collateralized debt obligations (CDOs), Ireland and the financial crisis, and the Greek sovereign debt crisis. The material in this chapter continues to be very exciting for students. Indeed, students continue to be more engaged with this material.

Compelling New Material on the Global Financial Crisis Throughout the Text

The aftermath of the global financial crisis of 2007–2009 has led to ongoing changes in the structure of the financial system and the way central banks operate. This has required the addition of many timely new sections, applications, and boxes throughout the rest of the book.

- A new box on Ireland and the 2007–2009 financial crisis (Chapter 9)
- A new box on Greece and the European sovereign debt crisis (Chapter 9)
- A new box on Canada and the 2007–2009 financial crisis (Chapter 9)

- A new box on the Basel Accord and the global financial crisis (Chapter 10)
- A new box on credit default swaps on Greek debt (Chapter 12)
- A new box on the U.S. money supply during the 2007–2009 crisis (Chapter 16)
- A new section on nonconventional monetary policy tools (Chapter 17)
- A new section on monetary policy tools by the Fed and the ECB (Chapter 17)
- A new box on price-level targeting versus inflation-rate targeting (Chapter 17)
- A new section on lessons for monetary policy strategy from the global financial crisis (Chapter 18)
- A new application on the U.S. fiscal stimulus package of 2009 (Chapter 22)
- A new box on the zero lower bound and nonconventional policy (Chapter 23)
- A new application on autonomous monetary policy easing in Canada at the onset of the global financial crisis (Chapter 23)
- A new application on negative supply shocks in Canada (Chapter 24)
- A new application on positive supply shocks in Canada (Chapter 24)
- A new application on negative supply and demand shocks in the United States and the 2007–2009 financial crisis (Chapter 24)
- A new application on the United Kingdom and the 2007–2009 financial crisis (Chapter 24)
- A new application on China and the 2007–2009 financial crisis (Chapter 24)
- A new application on quantitative (credit) easing in response to the global financial crisis (Chapter 25)
- A new box on the activist/nonactivist debate over the Obama fiscal stimulus package in the United States (Chapter 25)
- A new application on the effects of three oil price shocks on the Canadian economy (Chapter 26)
- A new application on credibility and the Bank of Canada's victory over inflation (Chapter 26)

Additional New Material on Financial Markets and Institutions and Monetary Policy

There have also been changes in financial markets and institutions in recent years that have not been directly related to the global subprime financial crisis, and we have added the following new material to keep the text current:

- A new section on why the efficient market hypothesis does not imply that financial markets are efficient (Chapter 7)
- A new box on the securitization process (Chapter 9)
- A new box on collateralized debt obligations (CDOs) (Chapter 9)
- A new section on the monetary policy tools in Canada (Chapter 17)
- A new section on the policy trilemma (Chapter20)
- A new application on the Zimbabwean hyperinflation (Chapter 21)
- A new box on the demise of monetary targeting in Switzerland (Chapter 26)
- A new box on the political business cycle (Chapter 26)
- A new application on a tale of three oil price shocks (Chapter 26)

A Dynamic Approach to Monetary Theory

In past editions, we have used the *ISLM* model and a static aggregate demand and supply (*AD/AS*) framework, in which the price level is on the vertical axis in *AD/AS* diagrams to discuss monetary theory. Over the years, we have found it more and more difficult to teach with this framework because it does not emphasize the dynamic interaction of inflation with economic activity, which is what modern monetary theory is all about. In this edition, we have completely rewritten Chapters 22 to 26 to develop a powerful, dynamic aggregate demand and supply model that highlights the interaction of inflation and economic activity by putting inflation on the vertical axis in the *AD/AS* diagram.

We build the dynamic *AD/AS* model step-by-step in Chapters 22 to 24.

- Chapter 22 develops the first building block of the aggregate demand and supply model, the *IS curve*.

- Chapter 23 describes how monetary policymakers set real interest rates with the *monetary policy (MP) curve*, which describes the relationship between inflation and real interest rates. It then uses the *MP* curve to derive the dynamic aggregate demand curve.

- Chapter 24 derives the short- and long-run aggregate supply curves and then puts all of them together with the aggregate demand curve to develop the dynamic aggregate demand and supply model. This model is then put to use with numerous applications analyzing business cycle fluctuations in Canada and in foreign countries.

The dynamic *AD/AS* model is then used to conduct a modern treatment of monetary policy in Chapters 25 and 26.

- Chapter 25 examines the theory of monetary policy and enables students to understand how monetary policymakers can respond to shocks to the economy in order to stabilize both inflation and economic activity.

- Chapter 26 looks at the role of expectations in monetary policy and discusses such issues as the Lucas critique, the rules versus discretion debate, and the role of credibility in producing good policy outcomes.

In addition, we have revised Chapter 21 to make it more dynamic by emphasizing the link between the demand for money, quantity theory, and inflation.

The Interaction of Finance and Monetary Theory

In the aftermath of the global financial crisis, monetary theory has been challenged by critics as being inadequate because in the past it has not given a prominent role to finance in economic fluctuations. In response, economists are now focusing on the link from finance to economic fluctuations in recent research, but this has not yet been reflected in textbooks. This book is the first textbook that we know of that responds to the challenges raised by critics of monetary theory by bringing finance directly into the aggregate demand and supply model at the outset. Barriers to the efficient functioning of financial markets from asymmetric information problems, known as financial frictions, are treated as one of the key factors affecting aggregate demand when this concept is first discussed. Then the impact of increases in financial frictions, as occurred during the global financial crisis, are easy to analyze using the aggregate demand and supply model. By emphasizing the interaction of finance and monetary theory, this book greatly enhances the realism of the aggregate demand and supply model, increasing the relevance of the analysis in the monetary theory part of the book.

End-of-Chapter Questions and Applied Problems

Because students best learn by doing, in this edition we have substantially expanded the number of end-of-chapter questions and problems for each chapter. We have also added a new type of problem under the heading of "Applied Problems." These problems are more analytical and applied and so give the student more hands-on practice applying the economic concepts in the text.

Chapters, Appendices, and Mini-Cases on the Web

The MyEconLab website that accompanies this book (**www.myeconlab.com**) is an essential resource for additional content.

The web chapter for the fifth Canadian edition of *The Economics of Money, Banking, and Financial Markets* is Web Chapter 1: The *ISLM* Model.

The web appendices include

Chapter 4:	Measuring Interest-Rate Risk: Duration
Chapter 5:	Models of Asset Pricing
Chapter 5:	Applying the Asset Market Approach to a Commodity Market: The Case of Gold
Chapter 5:	Loanable Funds Framework
Chapter 7:	Evidence on the Efficient Market Hypothesis
Chapter 10:	Banking Crises Throughout the World
Chapter 13:	Measuring Bank Performance
Chapter 13:	Nonbanking Financial Institutions and Duration Analysis
Chapter 16:	The Bank of Canada's Balance Sheet and the Monetary Base
Chapter 16:	The M2+ Money Multiplier
Chapter 18:	Monetary Targeting
Chapter 20:	The Canadian Balance of Payments
Chapter 21:	The Baumol-Tobin and the Tobin Mean-Variance Models of the Demand for Money
Chapter 21:	Empirical Evidence on the Demand for Money
Chapter 24:	The Effects of Macroeconomic Shocks on Asset Prices
Chapter 24:	Aggregate Demand and Supply: A Numerical Example
Chapter 24:	The Algebra of the Aggregate Demand and Supply Model
Chapter 24:	The Taylor Principle and Inflation Stability
Chapter 27:	Evaluating Empirical Evidence: The Debate over the Importance of Money in Economic Fluctuations

Mini-cases available on MyEconLab include

Chapter 4:	Interest Rates, Bond Yields, and Duration
Chapter 5:	The Behaviour of Interest Rates
Chapter 6:	Yield Curve Hypotheses and the Effects of Economic Events
Chapter 7:	Adaptive Expectations, Rational Expectations, and Optimal Forecasts
Chapter 11:	The Changing Landscape for Domestic and Global Financial Markets
Chapter 13:	Bank Performance Analysis

Chapter 13:   Calculating and Comparing Gap, Duration, and Risk-Management Alternatives

Chapter 19:   The Foreign Exchange Market and Financial Derivatives

Instructors can either use these web appendices and mini-cases in class to supplement the material in the textbook or recommend them to students who want to expand their knowledge of the money and banking field. The answers to the web mini-cases are available in the Instructor's Manual.

Flexibility and Modularity

In using previous editions, adopters, reviewers, and survey respondents have continually praised this text's flexibility and modularity, that is, the ability to pick and choose which chapters to cover and in what order to cover them. Flexibility and modularity are especially important in the money and banking course because there are as many ways to teach this course as there are instructors. To satisfy the diverse needs of instructors, the text achieves flexibility as follows:

- Core chapters provide the basic analysis used throughout the book, and other chapters or sections of chapters can be used or omitted according to instructor preferences. For example, Chapter 2 introduces the financial system and basic concepts such as transaction costs, adverse selection, and moral hazard. After covering Chapter 2, the instructor may decide to give more detailed coverage of financial structure by assigning Chapter 8, or may choose to skip Chapter 8 and take any of a number of different paths through the book.

- The text also allows instructors to cover the most important issues in monetary theory and policy without having to do detailed development of the *IS*, *MP*, and *AD* curves in Chapters 22 and 23. Instructors who want to teach a more complete treatment of monetary theory would make use of these chapters.

- Part VII on monetary theory can easily be taught before Part IV of the book in order to give students a deeper understanding of the rationale for monetary policy.

- Chapter 27 on the transmission mechanisms of monetary policy can be taught at many different points in the course—either with Part IV of the book when monetary policy is discussed or with Chapter 22 or Chapter 24 when the concept of aggregate demand is developed. It could be taught at the end of the book as a special topic.

- The internationalization of the text through marked international sections within chapters, as well as through complete separate chapters on the foreign exchange market and the international monetary system, is comprehensive yet flexible. Although many instructors will teach all the international material, others will not. Instructors who want less emphasis on international topics can easily skip Chapter 19 on the foreign exchange market and Chapter 20 on the international financial system and monetary policy. The international sections within chapters are self-contained and can be omitted with little loss of continuity.

To illustrate how this book can be used for courses with varying emphases, several course outlines are suggested for a semester teaching schedule. More detailed information about how the text can be used flexibly in your course is available in the Instructor's Manual.

- *General Money and Banking Course:* Chapters 1–5, 10–13, 17, 18, 24–25, with a choice of 6 of the remaining 14 chapters.
- *General Money and Banking Course with an International Emphasis:* Chapters 1–5, 10–13, 17–20, 24–25, with a choice of 4 of the remaining 12 chapters.
- *Financial Markets and Institutions Course:* Chapters 1–14, with a choice of 7 of the remaining 13 chapters.
- *Monetary Theory and Policy Course:* Chapters 1–5, 15–18, 21–26, with a choice of 4 of the remaining 12 chapters.

Pedagogical Aids

In teaching theory or its applications, a textbook must be a solid motivational tool. To this end, we have incorporated a wide variety of pedagogical features to make the material easy to learn:

1. **Previews** at the beginning of each chapter tell students where the chapter is heading, why specific topics are important, and how they relate to other topics in the book.
2. **Applications**, numbering around 50, demonstrate how the analysis in the book can be used to explain many important real-world situations.
3. **Financial News boxes** introduce students to relevant news articles and data that are reported daily in the press and explain how to read them.
4. **Inside the Central Bank boxes** give students a feel for what is important in the operation and structure of central banks.
5. **Global boxes** include interesting material with an international focus.
6. **FYI boxes** highlight dramatic historical episodes, interesting ideas, and intriguing facts related to the subject matter.
7. **Key statements** are important points set in boldface italic type so that students can easily find them for later reference.
8. **Graphs** with captions, numbering more than 150, help students clearly understand the interrelationship of the variables plotted and the principles of analysis.
9. **Summary** at the end of each chapter list the main points covered.
10. **Key terms** are important words or phrases, boldface when they are defined for the first time and listed by page number at the end of the chapter.
11. **End-of-chapter questions and problems**, numbering more than 600, help students learn the subject matter by applying economic concepts.
12. **Web Exercises** encourage students to collect information from online sources or use online resources to enhance their learning experience.
13. **Web Sources** report the Web URL source of the data used to create the many tables and charts.
14. **Web References** point the student to websites that provide information or data that supplement the text material.
15. **Glossary** at the back of the book provides definitions of all the key terms.

An Easier Way to Teach: Supplements to Accompany the Fifth Canadian Edition

The Economics of Money, Banking, and Financial Markets, Fifth Canadian Edition, includes the most comprehensive program of supplements of any money, banking, and financial markets textbook. These items are available to qualified domestic adopters but in some cases may not be available to international adopters.

MyEconLab

MyEconLab is the premier online assessment and tutorial system, pairing rich online content with innovative learning tools. The MyEconLab course for the Fifth Canadian Edition of *The Economics of Money, Banking, and Financial Markets* includes online versions of end-of-chapter Questions and Applied Problems from the text as well as additional questions for further study, which can be easily assigned and automatically graded.

STUDENTS AND MYECONLAB   This online homework and tutorial system puts students in control of their own learning through a suite of study and practice tools correlated with the online, interactive version of the textbook and other media tools. Within MyEconLab's structured environment, students practise what they learn, test their understanding, and then pursue a study plan that MyEconLab generates for them based on their performance on practice tests.

INSTRUCTORS AND MYECONLAB   MyEconLab provides flexible tools that allow instructors to easily and effectively customize online course materials to suit their needs. Instructors can create and assign tests, quizzes, or homework assignments. MyEconLab saves time by automatically grading all questions and tracking results in an online grade book. MyEconLab can even grade assignments that require students to draw a graph.

After registering for MyEconLab, instructors have access to downloadable supplements such as an instructor's manual, PowerPoint lecture notes, and the test bank. The test bank can also be used within MyEconLab, giving instructors ample material from which they can create assignments.

Additional MyEconLab features include

- *Animated Figures.* Key figures from the textbook are presented in step-by-step animations with audio explanations of the action. There is an animation icon printed in the text to indicate which key text figures have an accompanying animation on the MyEconLab.

- *Mishkin Interviewed on the Financial Crisis.* Watch video footage from a recent interview with one of the authors.

- *CANSIM Data.* CANSIM data are available for relevant text questions in the Resources section of MyEconLab.

- *Answers to Questions and Applied Problems.* Check your understanding of Questions and Applied Problems by viewing the solutions on MyEconLab.

- *Mini-Cases.* Online mini-cases are available for select chapters in the text. Each mini-case includes a unique Economics scenario and associated questions that provide real-life context for key chapter concepts.

- *Web Appendices.* Online Appendices include additional information to supplement core chapter concepts and theories.

- *Economics News: The Reader.* Access additional readings associated with each part in the text that apply chapter concepts to the real-world scenarios.

- *Economics and Finance: News You Can Use.* Visit our Canadian Economics and Finance: News You Can Use blog to access up-to-date articles and analysis about recent news events that impact economics in Canada and the world.

- *Audio Chapter Summaries:* Students can review key chapter concepts by listening to audio versions of the chapter summaries. Each of the available audio summaries is noted with an icon in the text. ((•

For more information and to register, please visit **www.myeconlab.com**.

Additional Instructor Resources

1. **Instructor's Manual** Prepared by the authors, the Instructor's Manual provides conventional elements such as sample course outlines, chapter outlines, and answers to questions and problems in the text.

2. **PowerPoint® Slides** A complete set of slides that are specifically designed for the textbook is available electronically.

3. **TestGen** The computerized test bank allows the instructor to produce exams efficiently. This product consists of multiple-choice and short-answer questions and offers editing capabilities. It is available in Windows and Macintosh versions.

4. **Test Item File in Word** This test bank includes all the questions from the TestGen version in Microsoft Word format.

5. **Image Library** This library contains .gif or .jpg versions of figures from the textbook.

Additional Student Resources

1. **Technology Specialists** Pearson's Technology Specialists work with faculty and campus course designers to ensure that Pearson technology products, assessment tools, and online course materials are tailored to meet your specific needs. This highly qualified team is dedicated to helping schools take full advantage of a wide range of educational resources by assisting in the integration of a variety of instructional materials and media formats. Your local Pearson Education sales representative can provide you with more details on this service program.

2. **CourseSmart** is a new way for instructors and students to access textbooks online anytime from anywhere. With thousands of titles across hundreds of courses, CourseSmart helps instructors choose the best textbook for their class and give their students a new option for buying the assigned textbook as a lower cost eTextbook. For more information, visit **www.coursesmart.com**.

Acknowledgments

This book is the result of efforts by many people. We are extremely grateful to Claudine O'Donnell, Acquisitions Editor; Jen Parks, Sponsoring Editor; Rebecca Ryoji, Developmental Editor; Sarah Lukaweski, Project Manager; Susan Bindernagel, Copy Editor; Therese Trainor, MyEconLab Content Development Author; and the many others at Pearson Canada who have contributed to the completion of this edition.

We are also grateful to all of the many people who commented on various chapters of the book, made valuable suggestions, and kindly provided us with data. We would particularly like to thank the following reviewers whose comments on the manuscript contributed to the development of this edition:

Ramesh Bhardwaj, George Brown College

Suzanne Iskander, Humber ITAL and Guelph Humber University

Michael Ho, University of Toronto

Frank Ingold, George Brown College

Dan Otchere, Concordia University

Narine Grigoryan, Camosun College

Alison Coffin, Memorial University

Duane Rockerbie, University of Lethbridge

Although we have done our best to make this edition as complete and error free as possible, as most of you know, perfection is impossible. We would greatly appreciate any suggestions for improvement. Please send your comments to serletis@ucalgary.ca.

Frederic S. Mishkin
Apostolos Serletis
2013

About the Authors

Frederic S. Mishkin is the Alfred Lerner Professor of Banking and Financial Institutions at the Graduate School of Business, Columbia University. He is also a Research Associate at the National Bureau of Economic Research and past president of the Eastern Economics Association. Since receiving his Ph.D. from the Massachusetts Institute of Technology in 1976, he has taught at the University of Chicago, Northwestern University, Princeton University, and Columbia. He has also received an honorary professorship from the People's (Renmin) University of China. From 1994 to 1997, he was Executive Vice President and Director of Research at the Federal Reserve Bank of New York and an associate economist of the Federal Open Market Committee of the Federal Reserve System. From September 2006 to August 2008, he was a member (governor) of the Board of Governors of the Federal Reserve System.

Professor Mishkin's research focuses on monetary policy and its impact on financial markets and the aggregate economy. He is the author of more than fifteen books, including *Financial Markets and Institutions*, Sixth Edition (Addison-Wesley, 2009); *Monetary Policy Strategy* (MIT Press, 2007); *The Next Great Globalization: How Disadvantaged Nations Can Harness Their Financial Systems to Get Rich* (Princeton University Press, 2006); *Inflation Targeting: Lessons from the International Experience* (Princeton University Press, 1999); *Money, Interest Rates, and Inflation* (Edward Elgar, 1993); and *A Rational Expectations Approach to Macroeconometrics: Testing Policy Ineffectiveness and Efficient Markets Models* (University of Chicago Press, 1983). In addition, he has published more than 150 articles in such journals as *American Economic Review, Journal of Political Economy, Econometrica, Quarterly Journal of Economics, Journal of Finance,* and *Journal of Monetary Economics.*

Professor Mishkin has served on the editorial board of *American Economic Review* and has been an associate editor at *Journal of Business and Economic Statistics,* the *Journal of Applied Econometrics,* and *Journal of Money, Credit and Banking;* he also served as the editor of the Federal Reserve Bank of New York's *Economic Policy Review.* He is currently an associate editor (member of the editorial board) at six academic journals, including *Macroeconomics and Monetary Economics Abstracts; Journal of International Money and Finance; International Finance; Finance India; Economic Policy Review;* and *Emerging Markets, Finance and Trade.* He has been a consultant to the Board of Governors of the Federal Reserve System, the World Bank, and the International Monetary Fund, as well as to many central banks throughout the world. He was also a member of the International Advisory Board to the Financial Supervisory Service of South Korea and an adviser to the Institute for Monetary and Economic Research at the Bank of Korea. Professor Mishkin was a Senior Fellow at the Federal Deposit Insurance Corporation's Center for Banking Research and was an academic consultant to and served on the Economic Advisory Panel of the Federal Reserve Bank of New York.

Apostolos Serletis is Professor of Economics and Finance at the University of Calgary. Since receiving his Ph.D. from McMaster University in 1984, he has held visiting appointments at the University of Texas at Austin, the Athens University of Economics and Business, and the Research Department of the Federal Reserve Bank of St. Louis.

Professor Serletis' teaching and research interest focus on monetary and financial economics, macroeconometrics, and nonlinear and complex dynamics. He is the author of twelve books, including *Principles of Economics* (First Canadian Edition), with R. Glenn Hubbard, Anthony Patrick O'Brien, and Jason Childs (Pearson forthcoming), *Macroeconomics: A Modern Approach* (First Canadian Edition), with Robert J. Barro (Nelson 2010), *The Demand for Money: Theoretical and Empirical Approaches* (Springer 2007), *Financial Markets and Institutions: Canadian Edition*, with Frederic S. Mishkin and Stanley G. Eakins (Addison-Wesley 2004), and *The Theory of Monetary Aggregation*, co-edited with William A. Barnett (Elsevier 2000). In addition, he has published over 200 articles in such journals as the *Journal of Economic Literature, Journal of Monetary Economics, Journal of Money, Credit, and Banking, Journal of Econometrics, Journal of Applied Econometrics, Journal of Business and Economic Statistics, Macroeconomic Dynamics, Journal of Banking and Finance, Journal of Economic Dynamics and Control, Economic Inquiry, Canadian Journal of Economics*, and *Studies in Nonlinear Dynamics and Econometrics*.

Professor Serletis is Associate Editor of two academic journals, *Macroeconomic Dynamics* and *Energy Economics*. He is also a member of the editorial board at two journals, the *Journal of Economic Asymmetries* and the *Journal of Economic Studies*. He is listed in a variety of directories, including *Who's Who in Economics* and *Who's Who in the World*.

THE ECONOMICS OF MONEY, BANKING, AND FINANCIAL MARKETS

FIFTH CANADIAN EDITION

Introduction

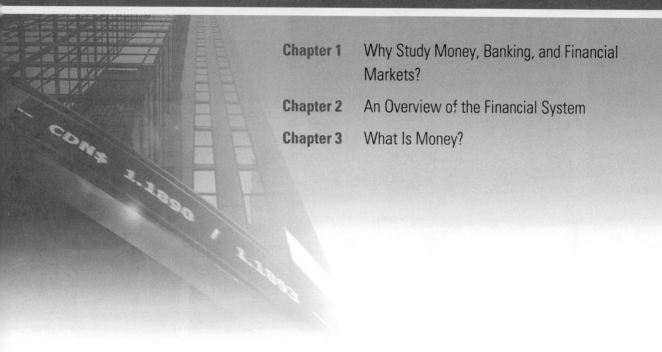

Crisis and Response: Global Financial Crisis and Its Aftermath

The global financial crisis that started in the United States in August 2007 was the result of a credit-driven, asset-price bubble in the U.S. housing market. When that bubble burst, the value of mortgage-backed securities held by financial institutions plummeted. The crisis ended up bringing down the financial system, which led not only to an economic downturn and a rise in unemployment in the United States, but also to a global recession. Governments around the world worked on full-scale banking bailouts and rescue packages adding up to trillions of dollars. However, even with these aggressive actions to stabilize the financial system, four years after the crisis economies throughout the world were still experiencing problems and the finances of many governments were in tatters.

The global financial crisis and its aftermath demonstrate the importance of banks and the financial system to economic well-being and the major role of money in the economy. Part I of this book provides an introduction to the study of money, banking, and financial markets. Chapter 1 outlines a road map of the book and discusses why it is so worthwhile to study the field of money, banking, and financial markets. Chapter 2 provides a general overview of the financial system. Chapter 3 then explains what money is and how it is measured.

CHAPTER 1

Why Study Money, Banking, and Financial Markets?

LEARNING OBJECTIVES

After studying this chapter you should be able to

1. outline what is involved in the study of financial markets (such as bonds, stocks, and foreign exchange markets)

2. identify what it means to study financial institutions (i.e., banks, insurance companies, mutual funds)

3. describe why money is a major influence on inflation, business cycles, and interest rates

PREVIEW

On the evening news, you hear that the Bank of Canada is raising the overnight interest rate by one-half of a percentage point. What effect might this have on the interest rate of an automobile loan when you finance your purchase of a sleek new sports car? Does it mean that a house will be more or less affordable in the future? Will it make it easier or harder for you to get a job next year?

This book provides answers to these and other questions by examining how financial markets (such as those for bonds, stocks, and foreign exchange) and financial institutions (chartered banks, trust and mortgage loan companies, credit unions and *caisses populaires*, insurance companies, mutual fund companies, and other institutions) work and by exploring the role of money in the economy. Financial markets and institutions not only affect your everyday life but also involve flows of billions of dollars of funds through our economy, which in turn affect business profits, the production of goods and services, and even the economic well-being of countries other than Canada. What happens to financial markets, financial institutions, and money is of great concern to politicians and can even have a major impact on elections. The study of money, banking, and financial markets will reward you with an understanding of many exciting issues. In this chapter we provide a road map of the book by outlining these issues and exploring why they are worth studying.

Why Study Financial Markets?

Part II of this book focuses on **financial markets**, markets in which funds are transferred from people who have an excess of available funds to people who have a shortage. Financial markets such as bond and stock markets are crucial to promoting greater economic efficiency by channelling funds from people who do not have a productive use for them to those who do. Well-functioning financial markets are a key factor in producing high economic growth and poorly performing financial markets are one reason that many countries in the world remain desperately poor. Activities in financial markets also have direct effects on personal wealth, the behaviour of businesses and consumers, and the cyclical performance of the economy.

The Bond Market and Interest Rates

A **security** (also called a *financial instrument*) is a claim on the issuer's future income or **assets** (any financial claim or piece of property that is subject to ownership). A **bond** is a debt security that promises to make payments periodically for a specified period of time.[1] The bond market is especially important to economic activity because it enables corporations and governments to borrow to finance their activities and because it is where interest rates are determined. An **interest rate** is the cost of borrowing or the price paid for the rental of funds (usually expressed as a percentage of the rental of $100 per year). There are many interest rates in the economy—mortgage interest rates, car loan rates, and interest rates on many different types of bonds.

Interest rates are important on a number of levels. On a personal level, high interest rates could deter you from buying a house or a car because the cost of financing it would be high. Conversely, high interest rates could encourage you to save because you can earn more interest income by putting aside some of your earnings as savings. On a more general level, interest rates have an impact on the overall health of the economy because they affect not only consumers' willingness to spend or save but also businesses' investment decisions. High interest rates, for example, may cause a corporation to postpone building a new plant that would ensure more jobs.

Because changes in interest rates have important effects on individuals, financial institutions, businesses, and the overall economy, it is important to explain fluctuations in interest rates that have been substantial over the past twenty years. For example, the interest rate on three-month Treasury bills peaked at over 20% in August 1981. This interest rate then fell to a low of less than 3% in 1997, rose to near 5% in the late 1990s, fell to a low of 2% in the early 2000s, rose to above 4% by 2007, only to fall close to zero in 2008 and remain around 1% since then.

Because different interest rates have a tendency to move in unison, economists frequently lump interest rates together and refer to "the" interest rate. As Figure 1-1 shows, however, interest rates on several types of bonds can differ substantially. The interest rate on three-month Treasury bills, for example, fluctuates more than the other interest rates and is lower on average. The interest rate on long-term corporate bonds is higher on average than the other interest rates, and the spread between it and the other rates fluctuates over time.

In Chapter 2 we study the role of bond markets in the economy, and in Chapters 4 through 6 we examine what an interest rate is, how the common movements in interest rates come about, and why the interest rates on different bonds vary.

The Stock Market

A **common stock** (typically just called a *stock*) represents a share of ownership in a corporation. It is a security that is a claim on the earnings and assets of the corporation. Issuing stock and selling it to the public is a way for corporations to raise

---

[1]The definition of *bond* used throughout this book is the broad one in common use by academics, which covers short-term as well as long-term debt instruments. However, some practitioners in financial markets use the word *bond* only to describe specific long-term debt instruments such as corporate bonds or Canada bonds.

FIGURE 1-1 Interest Rates on Selected Bonds, 1977–2012

Although different interest rates have a tendency to move in unison, they do often differ substantially and the spreads between them fluctuate.

Note: Shaded areas represent recessions.

Source: Statistics Canada CANSIM II Series V122531, V122544, and V122518.

funds to finance their activities. The stock market, in which claims on the earnings of corporations (shares of stock) are traded, is the most widely followed financial market in almost every country that has one (that's why it is often called simply "the market"). A big swing in the prices of shares in the stock market is always a big story on the evening news. People often speculate on where the market is heading and get very excited when they can brag about their latest "big killing," but they become depressed when they suffer a big loss. The attention the market receives can probably be best explained by one simple fact: it is a place where people get rich—and poor—quickly.

As Figure 1-2 indicates, stock prices are extremely volatile. After the market rose in the 1980s, on "Black Monday," October 19, 1987, it experienced the worst one-day drop in its entire history, with the S&P/TSX Composite Index falling by 11%. From then until 2000, the stock market experienced one of the great bull markets in its history, with the S&P/TSX climbing to a peak of over 11 000. With the collapse of the high-tech bubble in 2000, the stock market fell sharply, dropping by over 40% by late 2002. It then rose to an all-time high above the 14 000 level in early 2008, only to fall close to 8000 early in 2009, but recovered again to close to 14 000 by early 2011. These considerable fluctuations in stock prices affect the size of people's wealth and, as a result, may affect their willingness to spend.

The stock market is also an important factor in business investment decisions because the price of shares affects the amount of funds that can be raised by selling newly issued stock to finance investment spending. A higher price for a firm's shares allows the firm to raise a larger amount of funds that can be used to buy production facilities and equipment.

In Chapter 2 we examine the role that the stock market plays in the financial system, and we return to the issue of how stock prices behave and respond to information in the marketplace in Chapter 7.

FIGURE 1-2 Stock Prices as Measured by the S&P/TSX Composite Index, 1956–2012

Stock prices are extremely volatile.

Source: Statistics Canada CANSIM II Series V122620.

Why Study Financial Institutions and Banking?

Part III of this book focuses on financial institutions and the business of banking. Banks and other financial institutions are what make financial markets work. Without them, financial markets would not be able to move funds from people who save to people who have productive investment opportunities. Thus they play a crucial role in the economy.

Structure of the Financial System

The financial system is complex, comprising many different types of private-sector financial institutions, including banks, insurance companies, mutual funds, finance companies, and investment banks, all of which are heavily regulated by the government. If an individual wanted to make a loan to Bombardier or Research In Motion, for example, they would not go directly to the president of the company and offer a loan. Instead, they would lend to such companies indirectly through **financial intermediaries**, institutions that borrow funds from people who have saved and in turn make loans to others.

Why are financial intermediaries so crucial to well-functioning financial markets? Why do they extend credit to one party but not to another? Why do they usually write complicated legal documents when they extend loans? Why are they the most heavily regulated businesses in the economy?

We answer these questions in Chapter 8 by developing a coherent framework for analyzing financial structure in Canada and in the rest of the world.

Financial Crises

At times, the financial system seizes up and produces **financial crises**, major disruptions in financial markets that are characterized by sharp declines in asset prices and failures of many financial and nonfinancial firms. Financial crises have been a feature of capitalist economies for hundreds of years and are typically followed by the worst business-cycle downturns. Starting in August of 2007, the United States economy was hit by the worst financial disruption since the Great Depression. Defaults in subprime residential mortgages led to major losses in financial institutions, producing not only numerous bank failures, but also the demise of Bear Stearns and Lehman Brothers, two of the largest investment banks in the United States. Chapter 9 discusses why these crises occur and how they can do so much damage to the economy.

Banks and Other Financial Institutions

Banks are financial institutions that accept deposits and make loans. Included under the term *banks* are firms such as chartered banks, trust and mortgage loan companies, and credit unions and *caisses populaires*. Banks are the financial intermediaries that the average person interacts with most frequently. A person who needs a loan to buy a house or a car usually obtains it from a local bank. Most Canadians keep a large proportion of their financial wealth in banks in the form of chequing accounts, savings accounts, or other types of bank deposits. Because banks are the largest financial intermediaries in our economy, they deserve the most careful study. However, banks are not the only important financial institutions. Indeed, in recent years, other financial institutions such as insurance companies, finance companies, pension funds, mutual funds, and investment banks have been growing at the expense of banks, and so we need to study them as well.

In Chapter 11 we look at the banking industry, examine how the competitive environment has changed in the industry and learn why some financial institutions have been growing at the expense of others. In Chapter 10 we extend the economic analysis from Chapter 8 to understand why bank regulation takes the form it does and what can go wrong in the regulatory process. In Chapter 12 we identify the differences between banks and nonbank financial institutions and explain the regulation of nonbank financial institutions in the context of adverse selection and moral hazard problems.

In Chapter 13 we examine how banks and other financial institutions manage their assets and liabilities to make profits. Because the economic environment for banks and other financial institutions has become increasingly risky, these institutions must find ways to manage risk. How they manage risk with financial derivatives is the topic of Chapter 14.

Financial Innovation

Financial innovation, the development of new financial products and services, can be an important force for good by making the financial system more efficient. Unfortunately, as we will see in Chapter 9, financial innovation can have a dark side: it can lead to devastating financial crises, such as the one we have recently experienced. In Chapter 11 we study why and how financial innovation takes place, with particular emphasis on how the dramatic improvements in information technology have led to new financial products and the ability to deliver financial services electronically, in what has become known as **e-finance**. We also study financial innovation because it shows us how creative thinking on the part of financial institutions can lead to higher profits but can sometimes result in financial disasters. By seeing how and why financial institutions have been creative in the past, we obtain a better grasp of how they may be creative in the future. This knowledge provides us with useful clues about how the financial system may change over time and will help keep our knowledge about banks and other financial institutions from becoming obsolete.

Why Study Money and Monetary Policy?

Money is defined as anything that is generally accepted in payment for goods or services or in the repayment of debts. Money is linked to changes in economic variables that affect all of us and are important to the health of the economy. The final two parts of the book examine the role of money in the economy.

Money and Business Cycles

In 1981–1982, total production of goods and services (called **aggregate output**) in the economy fell and the number of people out of work rose to close to 12% of the labour force. After 1982, the economy began to expand rapidly, and by 1989, the **unemployment rate** (the percentage of the available labour force unemployed) had declined to 7.5%. In 1990, the eight-year expansion came to an end, and the economy began to decline again, with unemployment rising above 11%. The economy bottomed out in 1991, and the subsequent recovery has been the longest in Canadian history, with unemployment rates falling to around 6% in 2008 before rising to over 8% in early 2009 in the aftermath of the global financial crisis.

Why did the economy undergo such pronounced fluctuations? Evidence suggests that money plays an important role in generating **business cycles**, the upward and downward movement of aggregate output produced in the economy. Business cycles affect all of us in immediate and important ways. When output is rising, for example, it is easier to find a good job; when output is falling, finding a good job might be difficult. Figure 1-3 shows the movements of the rate of money growth from 1968 to 2012, with the shaded areas representing **recessions**, periods of declining aggregate output. What we see is that the rate of money growth has declined before almost every recession, indicating that changes in money might be a driving force behind business-cycle fluctuations. However, not every decline in the rate of money growth is followed by a recession.

We explore how money and monetary policy might affect aggregate output in Chapters 21 through 27, where we study **monetary theory**, the theory that relates the quantity of money and monetary policy to changes in aggregate economic activity and inflation.

Money and Inflation

Twenty years ago, the movie you may have paid $13 to see last week would have set you back only a couple of dollars. In fact, for $13 you could probably have had dinner, seen the movie, and bought yourself a big bucket of hot buttered popcorn.

FIGURE 1-3 Money Growth (M2++ (Gross) Annual Rate) and the Business Cycle in Canada, 1968–2011

Although money growth has declined before every recession, not every decline in the rate of money growth is followed by a recession. Shaded areas represent recessions.

Source: Statistics Canada CANSIM II Series V41552801.

FIGURE 1-4 Aggregate Price Level and the Money Supply in Canada, 1968–2011

From 1960 to 2011, the price level has increased more than sixfold.

Source: Statistics Canada CANSIM II Series V1997756 and V41552801.

As shown in Figure 1-4, which illustrates the movement of average prices in the Canadian economy from 1968 to 2011, the prices of most items are quite a bit higher now. The average price of goods and services in an economy is called the **aggregate price level** or, more simply, the *price level* (a more precise definition is found in the Web Appendix to this chapter). **Inflation**, a continual increase in the price level, affects individuals, businesses, and the government. It is generally regarded as an important problem to be solved and is often at the top of political and policymaking agendas. To solve the inflation problem, we need to know something about its causes.

What explains inflation? One clue to answering this question is found in Figure 1-4. As we can see, the price level and the **money supply** generally move closely together. These data seem to indicate that a continuing increase in the money supply might be an important factor in causing the continuing increase in the price level that we call inflation.

Further evidence that inflation may be tied to continuing increases in the money supply is found in Figure 1-5. For a number of countries, it plots the average **inflation rate** (the rate of change of the price level, usually measured as a percentage change per year) from 2000 to 2010 against the average rate of money growth over the same period. As you can see, a positive association exists between inflation and the growth rate of the money supply: the countries with the highest inflation rates are also the ones with the highest money growth rates. Turkey, Ukraine, and Zambia, for example, experienced high inflation during this period, and their rates of money growth were high. By contrast, Canada, Sweden, and the United States had low inflation rates over the same period, and their rates of money growth were low. Such evidence led Milton Friedman, a Nobel laureate in economics, to make the famous statement "Inflation is always and everywhere a monetary phenomenon."[2] We look at money's role in creating inflation in Chapters 21 and 25.

Money and Interest Rates

In addition to other factors, money plays an important role in the interest-rate fluctuations that are of such great concern to businesses and consumers. Figure 1-6 shows the changes in the interest rate on long-term Canada bonds and the rate

[2]Milton Friedman, *Dollars and Deficits* (Upper Saddle River, NJ: Prentice Hall, 1968), 39.

FIGURE 1-5 Average Inflation Rate Versus Average Rate of Money Growth for Selected
Countries, 2000–2010

There is a positive association between the 10-year averages of inflation and the growth rate of the
money supply: the countries with the highest inflation rates are also the ones with the highest money
growth rates.

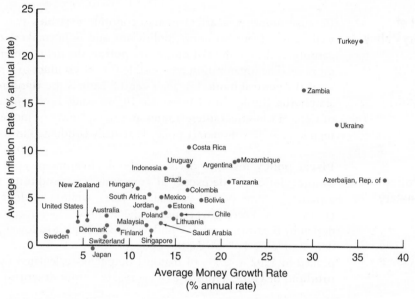

Source: Based on International Financial Statistics, www.imfstatistics.org/imf.

FIGURE 1-6 M2++ (Gross) Money Growth (Over 12 Months) and Interest Rates (Long-Term Government of
Canada Bonds), 1977–2012

As the money growth rate fell in the 1980s and 1990s, the long-term bond rate fell with it. However, the relationship between
money growth and interest rates has been less clear-cut since 2000.

Source: Statistics Canada CANSIM II Series V41552801 and V122544.

of money growth. As the money growth rate rose in the late 1970s, the long-term bond rate rose with it. However, the relationship between money growth and interest rates has been less clear-cut since 1980. We analyze the relationship between money and interest rates when we examine the behaviour of interest rates in Chapter 5.

Conduct of Monetary Policy

Because money can affect many economic variables that are important to the well-being of our economy, politicians and policymakers throughout the world care about the conduct of **monetary policy**, the management of money and interest rates. The organization responsible for the conduct of a nation's monetary policy is the **central bank**. Canada's central bank is the **Bank of Canada** (also called simply **the Bank**). In Chapters 15–18, we study how central banks like the Bank of Canada can affect interest rates and the quantity of money in the economy and then look at how monetary policy is actually conducted in Canada and elsewhere.

Fiscal Policy and Monetary Policy

Fiscal policy involves decisions about government spending and taxation. A **budget deficit** is the excess of government expenditures over tax revenues for a particular time period (typically a year), while a **budget surplus** arises when tax revenues exceed government expenditures. The government must finance any deficit by borrowing, while a budget surplus leads to a lower government debt burden. As Figure 1-7 shows, the budget deficit, relative to the size of our economy, peaked in 1992 at 8.7% of national output (as calculated by the **gross domestic product,** or GDP, a measure of aggregate output described in the Web Appendix

FIGURE 1-7 Government Budget Surplus or Deficit as a Percentage of Gross Domestic Product, 1961–2011

The budget deficit, relative to the size of the Canadian economy, has fluctuated a lot over the years, rising to close to 9% of GDP in 1993 and falling subsequently so there were budget surpluses from 1997 to 2008, only to rise subsequently with budget deficits rising to over 3% of GDP by 2009.

Source: Statistics Canada CANSIM II Series V498316, V498326, and V498086.

to this chapter). Since then, the budget deficit at first declined and the budget actually went into surplus from 1997 to 2008. In the aftermath of the 2007–2009 global financial crisis the budget has swung back again into deficit, with recent deficits exceeding 3% of GDP. Budget deficits have been the subject of bitter battles between Canadian politicians. Some argue that deficits increase the national debt and make us vulnerable to increases in world interest rates. They propose to cut government spending to pay down the debt and to reduce taxes. Others argue that the ability to issue public debt allows the government to smooth taxes and inflation over time.

You may have seen or heard statements in newspapers or on TV that budget surpluses are a good thing while deficits are undesirable. We explore the accuracy of such claims in Chapters 9 and 20 by seeing how budget deficits might lead to a financial crisis, as they did in Argentina in 2001. In Chapter 21, we examine why deficits might result in a higher rate of money growth, a higher rate of inflation, and higher interest rates.

Why Study International Finance?

The globalization of financial markets has accelerated at a rapid pace in recent years. Financial markets have become increasingly integrated throughout the world, with Canadian companies often borrowing in foreign financial markets and foreign companies borrowing in Canadian financial markets. Banks and other financial institutions have become increasingly international and often have operations in many countries throughout the world. Part VI of this book explores the foreign exchange market and the international financial system.

The Foreign Exchange Market

For funds to be transferred from one country to another, they have to be converted from the currency in the country of origin (say, dollars) into the currency of the country to which they are going (say, euros). The **foreign exchange market** is where this conversion takes place and it is instrumental in moving funds between countries. It is also important because it is where the **foreign exchange rate**, the price of one country's currency in terms of another's, is determined.

Because the foreign exchange rate is the relative price of two national currencies, there are two ways of quoting an exchange rate: either as the amount of domestic currency that can be purchased with a unit of foreign currency or as the amount of foreign currency that can be purchased with a unit of domestic currency. Throughout this book, we always use the latter quoting convention—that is, we express the exchange rate as units of foreign currency per Canadian dollar. In these terms, when the exchange rate increases so that a Canadian dollar buys more units of foreign currency, we say that the Canadian dollar has had an **appreciation**. A decline in the exchange rate is associated with a **depreciation** of the Canadian dollar.

Figure 1-8 shows the exchange rate for the Canadian dollar from 1971 to 2012 in terms of the U.S. dollar. The exchange rate is defined as the U.S. dollar price of one Canadian dollar. Clearly, the exchange rate has experienced four long swings over this period. The first is a 30.8% depreciation from January 1973 to February 1986; the second is a 26.0% appreciation from February 1986 to January 1992; the third is a 26.7% depreciation from January 1992 to October 2002; and the fourth is a 54% appreciation from October 2002 to December 2011.

FIGURE 1-8 Exchange Rate for the Canadian Dollar, 1971–2012

The value of the Canadian dollar relative to the United States dollar has fluctuated substantially over the years.

Source: Statistics Canada CANSIM II Series V37426.

What have these fluctuations in the exchange rate meant to the Canadian public and businesses? A change in the exchange rate has a direct effect on Canadian consumers because it affects the cost of foreign goods. In particular, a weaker dollar leads to more expensive foreign goods, makes vacationing abroad more expensive, and raises the cost of indulging your desire for imported delicacies. When the value of the dollar drops, Canadians decrease their purchases of foreign goods and increase their consumption of domestic goods (such as travel within Canada).

Conversely, a strong dollar means that Canadian goods exported abroad will cost more in foreign countries and foreigners will buy fewer of them. Exports of steel, for example, declined sharply when the dollar strengthened in the late 1980s.

A strong dollar benefited Canadian consumers by making foreign goods cheaper but hurt Canadian businesses and eliminated some jobs by cutting both domestic and foreign sales of their products. The increase in the value of the dollar since 2002 has had a similar effect: it has made foreign goods less expensive but has made Canadian businesses less competitive. Fluctuations in the foreign exchange markets have major consequences in the Canadian economy.

In Chapter 19 we study how exchange rates are determined in the foreign exchange market in which dollars are bought and sold for foreign currencies.

The International Financial System

The tremendous increase in capital flows between countries means that the international financial system has a growing impact on domestic economies. Whether a country fixes its exchange rate to that of another is an important determinant of how monetary policy is conducted. Whether there are capital controls that restrict mobility of capital across national borders has a large effect on domestic financial systems and the performance of the economy. What role international financial institutions such as the International Monetary Fund should play in the international financial system is very controversial. All of these issues are explored in Chapter 20.

How We Will Study Money, Banking, and Financial Markets

This text stresses the economic way of thinking by developing a unifying framework to study money, banking, and financial markets. This analytic framework uses a few basic economic concepts to organize your thinking about the determination of asset prices, the structure of financial markets, bank management, and the role of money in the economy. It encompasses the following basic concepts:

- A simplified approach to the demand for assets
- The concept of equilibrium
- Basic supply and demand to explain behaviour in financial markets
- The search for profits
- An approach to financial structure based on transaction costs and asymmetric information
- Aggregate supply and demand analysis

The unifying framework used in this text will keep your knowledge from becoming obsolete and make the material more interesting. It will enable you to learn what *really* matters without having to memorize a mass of dull facts that you will forget soon after the final exam. This framework will also provide you with the tools to understand trends in the financial marketplace and in variables such as interest rates, exchange rates, inflation, and aggregate output.

To help you understand and apply the unifying analytic framework, simple models are constructed in which the variables held constant are carefully delineated, each step in the derivation of the model is clearly and carefully laid out, and the models are then used to explain various phenomena by focusing on changes in one variable at a time, holding all other variables constant.

To reinforce the models' usefulness, this text uses case studies, applications, and special-interest boxes to present evidence that supports or casts doubts on the theories being discussed. This exposure to real-life events and empirical data should dissuade you from thinking that all economists make abstract assumptions and develop theories that have little to do with actual behaviour.

To function better in the real world outside the classroom, you must get into the lifelong habit of regularly following the financial news that appears in leading financial publications such as *The Globe and Mail: Report on Business* and the *National Post: Financial Post*. To help and encourage you to read the financial section of the newspaper, this text contains a set of special boxed inserts titled "Financial News" that contain actual columns and data from the media that appear daily or periodically. These boxes give you the detailed information and definitions you need to evaluate the data being presented. In addition to these applications, this text also contains over 500 end-of-chapter problems that ask you to apply the analytic concepts you have learned to other real-world issues.

Exploring the Web

The Internet has become an extremely valuable and convenient resource for financial research. We emphasize the importance of this tool in several ways. First, wherever we utilize the web to find information to build the charts and tables that appear throughout the text, we include the source site's URL. These sites often contain additional information and are updated frequently. Second, we have added Web Exercises to the end of each chapter. These exercises prompt you to visit sites related to the chapter and work with real-time data and information. We have also provided Web References on the MyEconLab that accompanies this book that list the URLs of sites related to the material being discussed. Visit these sites to further explore a topic you find of particular interest.

Collecting and Graphing Data

The following sample Web Exercise is especially important because it demonstrates how to export data from a website into Microsoft Excel for further analysis. We suggest you work through this problem on your own so that you will be able to perform this activity when prompted in subsequent Web Exercises.

Sample Web Exercise

You have been hired by Risky Ventures Ltd. as a consultant to help the company analyze interest rate trends. Your employers are initially interested in determining the historical relationship between short-term interest rates. The biggest task you must immediately undertake is collecting market interest-rate data. You know the best source of this information is the web.

1. You decide that your best indicators of short-term interest rates are the bank rate, the one-month bankers' acceptances rate, and the three-month prime corporate rate. Your first task is to gather historical data. Go to www.bankofcanada.ca and select "Rates and Statistics" and then "Canadian Interest Rates." The site should look like the screen shown on page 15.

2. Although you have located an accurate source of historical interest-rate data, getting it onto a spreadsheet will be very tedious. You recall that Excel (Microsoft Excel) will let you convert text data into columns. Begin by indicating that you want to display the data in CSV format, sorted by date. Under the monthly series frequency, click on "V122530," "V122504," and "V122491," specify dates by choosing the start and end dates, and click on "Get Rates." A new screen should appear with a link to download the CSV data to your computer.

3. You now want to analyze the interest rates by graphing them. Use Excel to open the CSV file you downloaded. Click on the Chart Wizard icon on the toolbar (or Insert/Chart). Select "Scatter Diagram" and choose any type of scatter diagram that connects the dots. Let the Excel wizard take you through the steps of completing the graph.

Concluding Remarks

The topic of money, banking, and financial markets is an exciting field that directly affects your life—interest rates influence earnings on your savings and the payments on loans you may seek on a car or a house, and monetary policy may affect your job prospects and the prices of goods in the future. Your study of money, banking, and financial markets will introduce you to many of the controversies about the conduct of economic policy that are hotly debated in the political arena and will help you gain a clearer understanding of economic phenomena you hear about in the news media. The knowledge you gain will stay with you and benefit you long after your course is done.

Source: Bank of Canada, www.bankofcanada.ca/rates/interest-rates/canadian-interest-rates/.

MyEconLab   MyEconLab is an online homework and tutorial system that puts you in control of your own learning with study and practice tools directly correlated to this chapter's content. Visit MyEconLab to explore the following resources:

- The Questions and Applied Problems are all available in the Study Plan on MyEconLab for further practice. You will also find the answers to all of the Questions and Applied Problems in the Student Resources section of your MyEconLab.

MyEconLab also features Additional Readings, Videos, Glossary Flashcards, Audio Chapter Summaries, Economics News Feeds, Animations, and many additional tools to help you master key concepts from the text.

((• SUMMARY

MyEconLab
Audio Summary

1. Activities in financial markets have direct effects on individuals' wealth, the behaviour of businesses, and the efficiency of our economy. Three financial markets deserve particular attention: the bond market (where interest rates are determined), the stock market (which has a major effect on people's wealth and on firms' investment decisions), and the foreign exchange market (because fluctuations in the foreign exchange rate have major consequences for the Canadian economy).

2. Banks and other financial institutions channel funds from people who might not put them to productive use to people who can do so and thus play a crucial role in improving

the efficiency of the economy. When the financial system seizes up and produces a financial crisis, financial firms fail, which causes severe damage to the economy.

3. Money appears to have a major influence on inflation, business cycles, and interest rates. Because these economic variables are so important to the health of the economy, we need to understand how monetary policy is and should be conducted. We also need to study government fiscal policy because it can be an influential factor in the conduct of monetary policy.

4. This textbook stresses the economic way of thinking by developing a unifying analytic framework for the study of money, banking, and financial markets using a few basic economic principles. This textbook also emphasizes the interaction of theoretical analysis and empirical data.

KEY TERMS

aggregate output, p. 7
aggregate price level, p. 8
appreciation, p. 11
asset, p. 3
Bank of Canada (the Bank), p. 10
banks, p. 6
bond, p. 3
budget deficit, p. 10
budget surplus, p. 10
business cycles, p. 7
central bank, p. 10

common stock, p. 3
depreciation, p. 11
e-finance, p. 6
financial crises, p. 5
financial innovation, p. 6
financial intermediaries, p. 5
financial markets, p. 2
fiscal policy, p. 10
foreign exchange market, p. 11
foreign exchange rate, p. 11
gross domestic product, p. 10

inflation, p. 8
inflation rate, p. 8
interest rate, p. 3
monetary policy, p. 10
monetary theory, p. 7
money, p. 6
money supply, p. 8
recession, p. 7
security, p. 3
unemployment rate, p. 7

QUESTIONS

1. What is the typical relationship between interest rates on three-month Treasury bills, long-term Canada bonds, and BBB corporate bonds?

2. What effect might a fall in stock prices have on business investment?

3. What effect might a rise in stock prices have on consumers' decisions to spend?

4. Why are financial markets important to the health of the economy?

5. What was the main cause of the global financial crisis that began in 2007?

6. What is the basic activity of banks?

7. What are the other important financial intermediaries in the economy other than banks?

8. Can you think of any financial innovation in the past 10 years that has affected you personally? Has it made you better off or worse off? Why?

9. Has the inflation rate in Canada increased or decreased in the past few years? What about interest rates?

10. If history repeats itself and we see a decline in the rate of money growth, what might you expect to happen to

    a. real output?
    b. the inflation rate?
    c. interest rates?

11. When interest rates decrease, how might businesses and consumers change their economic behaviour?

12. Is everybody worse off when interest rates rise?

13. Why do managers of financial institutions care so much about the activities of the Bank of Canada?

14. How does the current size of the Canadian budget deficit compare to the time period since 1960?

15. How does a fall in the value of the pound sterling affect British consumers?

16. How does an increase in the value of the pound sterling affect Canadian businesses?

17. How can changes in foreign exchange rates affect the profitability of financial institutions?

18. Looking at Figure 1-8, in which years would you have chosen to visit the Canadian Rockies rather than the Grand Canyon in Arizona?

19. When the dollar is worth more in relation to currencies of other countries, are you more likely to buy Canadian-made or foreign-made jeans? Are Canadian companies that manufacture jeans happier when the dollar is strong or when it is weak? What about a Canadian company that is in the business of importing jeans into Canada?

20. Much of the Canadian government debt is held as Canada bonds and bills by foreign investors. How do fluctuations in the dollar exchange rate affect the value of that debt held by foreigners?

APPLIED PROBLEMS

CANSIM Questions

21. The following table lists monthly foreign exchange rates between the U.S. dollar and the Canadian dollar (in $/US$) for 2011 (this is CANSIM II series V37426).

January	0.993845
February	0.987555
March	0.976591
April	0.958215
May	0.967976
June	0.97675
July	0.9553
August	0.982836
September	1.0026
October	1.019825
November	1.025819
December	1.023785

   a. Which month would have been the best month to convert Canadian dollars into U.S. dollars? Which month would have been the worst?
   b. Did the Canadian dollar appreciate or depreciate in 2011?
   c. What was the percentage appreciation or depreciation of the Canadian dollar?
   d. If you convert the monthly observations into an annual observation (by taking the arithmetic average), how representative will the annual observation be of the exchange rate during 2011?

22. The following table lists monthly stock prices in Canada as measured by the S&P/TSX Composite Index (this is CANSIM II series V122620) for 2011.

January	13551.99
February	14136.5
March	14116.1
April	13944.79
May	13802.88
June	13300.87
July	12945.63
August	12768.7
September	11623.84
October	12252.06
November	12204.11
December	11955.09

   a. Which month would have been the worst month to buy the index?
   b. What was the percentage decline in the index from January to December?

WEB EXERCISES

1. In this exercise we will practise collecting data from the web and graphing it using Excel. Use the example on page 14 as a guide. Go to **www.forecasts.org/data/index.htm**, click on "Stock Index Data" at the top of the page, and then choose the U.S. Stock Indices—Monthly option. Finally, choose the Dow Jones Industrial Average option.

   a. Move the data into an Excel spreadsheet.
   b. Using the data from part (a), prepare a graph. Use the graphing wizard to properly label your axes.

2. In Web Exercise 1 you collected and graphed the Dow Jones Industrial Average. This same site reports forecast values of the DJIA. Go to **www.forecasts.org**. Click on the "Dow Jones Industrials" link under "6 Month Forecasts" in the far left column.

   a. What is the Dow forecast to be in six months?
   b. What percentage increase is forecast for the next six months?

Defining Aggregate Output, Income, the Price Level, and the Inflation Rate

Because these terms are used so frequently throughout the text, we need to have a clear understanding of the definitions of *aggregate output, income,* the *price level,* and the *inflation rate.*

Aggregate Output and Income

The most commonly reported measure of aggregate output, the **gross domestic product (GDP)**, is the market value of all final goods and services produced in a country during the course of the year. This measure excludes two sets of items that at first glance you might think it would include. Purchases of goods that have been produced in the past, whether a Rembrandt painting or a house built 20 years ago, are not counted as part of GDP, nor are purchases of stocks or bonds. None of these enter into GDP because they are not goods and services produced during the course of the year. Intermediate goods, which are used up in producing final goods and services, such as the sugar in a chocolate bar or the energy used to produce steel, are also not counted separately as part of GDP. Because the value of the final goods already includes the value of the intermediate goods, to count them separately would be to count them twice.

Aggregate income, the total income of *factors of production* (land, labour, and capital) from producing goods and services in the economy during the course of the year, is best thought of as being equal to aggregate output. Because the payments for final goods and services must eventually flow back to the owners of the factors of production as income, income payments must equal payments for final goods and services. For example, if the economy has an aggregate output of $10 trillion, total income payments in the economy (aggregate income) are also $10 trillion.

Real Versus Nominal Magnitudes

When the total value of final goods and services is calculated using current prices, the resulting GDP measure is referred to as *nominal GDP.* The word *nominal* indicates that values are measured using current prices. If all prices doubled but actual production of goods and services remained the same, nominal GDP would double even though people would not enjoy the benefits of twice as many goods and services. As a result, nominal variables can be misleading measures of economic well-being.

A more reliable measure of economic production expresses values in terms of prices for an arbitrary base year, currently 2002. GDP measured with constant prices is referred to as *real GDP,* the word *real* indicating that values are measured in terms of fixed prices. Real variables thus measure the quantities of goods and services and do not change because prices have changed, but rather only if actual quantities have changed.

A brief example will make the distinction clearer. Suppose that you have a nominal income of $30 000 in 2013 and that your nominal income was $15 000 in 2002. If all prices doubled between 2002 and 2013, are you better off? The answer is no: although your income has doubled, your $30 000 buys you only the same amount of goods because prices have also doubled. A real income measure indicates that your income in terms of the goods it can buy is the same. Measured in 2002 prices, the $30 000 of nominal income in 2013 turns out to be only $15 000 of real income. Because your real income is actually the same in the two years, you are no better or worse off in 2013 than you were in 2002.

Because real variables measure quantities in terms of real goods and services, they are typically of more interest than nominal variables. In this text, discussion of aggregate output or aggregate income always refers to real measures (such as real GDP).

Aggregate Price Level

In this chapter, we defined the aggregate price level as a measure of average prices in the economy. Three measures of the aggregate price level are commonly encountered in economic data. The first is the *GDP deflator,* which is defined as nominal GDP divided by real GDP. Thus, if 2013 nominal GDP is $10 trillion but 2013 real GDP in 2002 prices is $9 trillion,

$$\text{GDP deflator} = \frac{\$10 \text{ trillion}}{\$9 \text{ trillion}} = 1.11$$

The GDP deflator equation indicates that, on average, prices have risen 11% since 2002. Typically, measures of the price level are presented in the form of a price index, which expresses the price level for the base year (in our example, 2002) as 100. Thus the GDP deflator for 2013 would be 111.

Another popular measure of the aggregate price level (which officials in the Bank of Canada frequently focus on) is the *PCE deflator,* which is similar to the GDP deflator and is defined as nominal personal consumption expenditures (PCE) divided by real PCE.

The measure of the aggregate price level that is most frequently reported in the press is the *consumer price index* (CPI). The CPI is measured by pricing a "basket" of goods and services bought by a typical urban household. If, over the course of the year, the cost of this basket of goods and services rises from $500 to $600, the CPI has risen by 20%. The CPI is also expressed as a price index with the base year equal to 100.

The CPI, the PCE deflator, and the GDP deflator measures of the price level can be used to convert or deflate a nominal magnitude into a real magnitude. This is accomplished by dividing the nominal magnitude by the price index. In our example, in which the GDP deflator for 2013 is 1.11 (expressed as an index value of 111), real GDP for 2013 equals

$$\frac{\$10 \text{ trillion}}{1.11} = \$9 \text{ trillion in 2002 prices}$$

which corresponds to the real GDP figure for 2013 assumed earlier.

Growth Rates and the Inflation Rate

The media often talk about the economy's growth rate, and particularly the growth rate of real GDP. A growth rate is defined as the percentage change in a variable, i.e.,

$$\text{growth rate} = \frac{x_t - x_{t-1}}{x_{t-1}} \times 100$$

where t indicates today and $t-1$ a year earlier.

For example, if real GDP grew from \$9 trillion in 2013 to \$9.5 trillion in 2014, then the GDP growth rate for 2014 would be 5.6%:

$$\text{GDP growth rate} = \frac{\$9.5 \text{ trillion} - \$9 \text{ trillion}}{\$9 \text{ trillion}} \times 100 = 5.6\%$$

The inflation rate is defined as the growth rate of the aggregate price level. Thus, if the GDP deflator rose from 111 in 2013 to 113 in 2014, the inflation rate using the GDP deflator would be 1.8%:

$$\text{inflation rate} = \frac{113 - 111}{111} \times 100 = 1.8\%$$

If the growth rate is for a period less than one year, it is usually reported on an annualized basis; that is, it is converted to the growth rate over a year's time, assuming that the growth rate remains constant. For GDP, which is reported quarterly, the annualized growth rate would be approximately four times the percentage change in GDP from the previous quarter. For example, if GDP rose $\frac{1}{2}$% from the first quarter of 2013 to the second quarter of 2013, then the annualized GDP growth rate for the second quarter of 2013 would be reported as 2% ($= 4 \times \frac{1}{2}$%). (A more accurate calculation would be 2.02%, because a precise quarterly growth rate should be compounded on a quarterly basis.)

CHAPTER 2

An Overview of the Financial System

LEARNING OBJECTIVES

After studying this chapter you should be able to

1. summarize the basic function performed by financial markets
2. explain why financial markets are classified as debt and equity markets, primary and secondary markets, exchanges and over-the-counter markets, and money and capital markets
3. describe the principal money market and capital market instruments
4. express why the government regulates financial markets and financial intermediaries (i.e., chartered banks, trust and loan companies, credit unions and *caisses populaires,* insurance companies, mutual fund companies, and other institutions)

PREVIEW

Inez the Inventor has designed a low-cost robot that cleans house (even does windows), washes the car, and mows the lawn, but she has no funds to put her wonderful invention into production. Walter the Widower has plenty of savings, which he and his wife accumulated over the years. If Inez and Walter could get together so that Walter could provide funds to Inez, Inez's robot would see the light of day, the economy would be better off, and we would have cleaner houses, shinier cars, and more beautiful lawns.

Financial markets (bond and stock markets) and financial intermediaries (banks, insurance companies, pension funds) have the basic function of getting people like Inez and Walter together by moving funds from those who have a surplus of funds (Walter) to those who have a shortage of funds (Inez). More realistically, when Apple invents a better iPod, it may need funds to bring it to market. Similarly, when a local government needs to build a road or a school, it may need more funds than local property taxes provide. Well-functioning financial markets and financial intermediaries are crucial to economic health.

To study the effects of financial markets and financial intermediaries on the economy, we need to acquire an understanding of their general structure and operation. In this chapter, we learn about the major financial intermediaries and the instruments that are traded in financial markets as well as how these markets are regulated.

This chapter presents an overview of the fascinating study of financial markets and institutions. We return to a more detailed treatment of the regulation, structure, and evolution of the financial system in Chapters 8 through 13.

Function of Financial Markets

Financial markets perform the essential economic function of channelling funds from households, firms, and governments who have saved surplus funds by spending less than their income to those who have a shortage of funds because they wish to spend more than they earn. This function is shown schematically in Figure 2-1. Those who have saved and are lending funds, the lender-savers, are at the left, and those who must borrow funds to finance their spending, the borrower-spenders, are at the right. The principal lender-savers are households, but business enterprises and the government (particularly provincial and local government), as well as foreigners and their governments, sometimes also find themselves with excess funds and so lend them out. The most important borrower-spenders are businesses and the government (particularly the federal government), but households and foreigners also borrow to finance their purchases of cars, furniture, and houses. The arrows show that funds flow from lender-savers to borrower-spenders via two routes.

In *direct finance* (the route at the bottom of Figure 2-1), borrowers borrow funds directly from lenders in financial markets by selling them *securities* (also called *financial instruments*), which are claims on the borrower's future income or assets. Securities are assets for the person who buys them but **liabilities** (IOUs or debts) for the individual or firm that sells (issues) them. For example, if Research In Motion (RIM) needs to borrow funds to pay for a new factory to manufacture new products, it might borrow the funds from savers by selling them *bonds*, debt securities that promise to make payments periodically for a specified period of time, or *stocks*, securities that entitle the owners to a share of the company's profits and assets.

FIGURE 2-1 Flows of Funds Through the Financial System

The arrows show that funds flow from lender-savers to borrower-spenders via two routes: *direct finance*, in which borrowers borrow funds directly from financial markets by selling securities, and *indirect finance*, in which a financial intermediary borrows funds from lender-savers and then uses these funds to make loans to borrower-spenders.

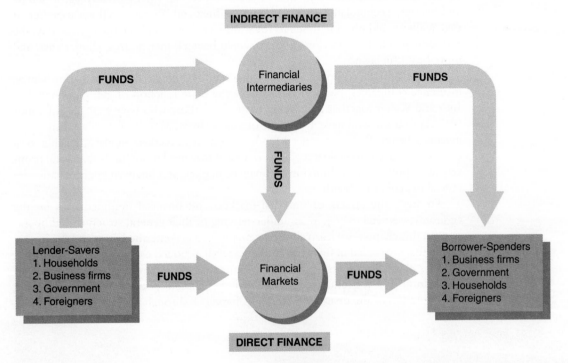

Why is this channelling of funds from savers to spenders so important to the economy? The answer is that the people who save are frequently not the same people who have profitable investment opportunities available to them, the entrepreneurs. Let's first think about this on a personal level. Suppose that you have saved $1000 this year, but no borrowing or lending is possible because there are no financial markets. If you do not have an investment opportunity that will permit you to earn income with your savings, you will just hold on to the $1000 and will earn no interest. However, Carl the Carpenter has a productive use for your $1000: he can use it to purchase a new tool that will shorten the time it takes him to build a house, thereby earning him an extra $200 per year. If you could get in touch with Carl, you could lend him the $1000 at a rental fee (interest) of $100 per year, and both of you would be better off. You would earn $100 per year on your $1000, instead of the zero amount that you would earn otherwise, while Carl would earn $100 more income per year (the $200 extra earnings per year minus the $100 rental fee for the use of the funds).

In the absence of financial markets, you and Carl the Carpenter might never get together. You would both be stuck with the status quo, and both of you would be worse off. Without financial markets, it is hard to transfer funds from a person who has no investment opportunities to one who has them; financial markets are thus essential to promoting economic efficiency.

The existence of financial markets is beneficial even if someone borrows for a purpose other than increasing production in a business. Say that you are recently married, have a good job, and want to buy a house. You earn a good salary, but because you have just started to work, you have not saved much. Over time you would have no problem saving enough to buy the house of your dreams, but by then you would be too old to get full enjoyment from it. Without financial markets, you are stuck; you cannot buy the house and must continue to live in your tiny apartment.

If a financial market were set up so that people who had built up savings could lend you the funds to buy the house, you would be more than happy to pay them some interest in order to own a home while you are still young enough to enjoy it. Then, over time, you would pay back your loan. If this loan could occur, you would be better off, as would the persons who made you the loan. They would now earn some interest, whereas they would not if the financial market did not exist.

Now we can see why financial markets have such an important function in the economy. They allow funds to move from people who lack productive investment opportunities to people who have such opportunities. Financial markets are critical for producing an efficient allocation of capital, which contributes to higher production and efficiency for the overall economy. Indeed, as we will explore in Chapter 9, when financial markets break down during financial crises, as they did during the recent global financial crisis, severe economic hardship results, which can even lead to dangerous political instability.

Well-functioning financial markets also directly improve the well-being of consumers by allowing them to time their purchases better. They provide funds to young people to buy what they need and can eventually afford without forcing them to wait until they have saved up the entire purchase price. Financial markets that are operating efficiently improve the economic welfare of everyone in the society.

Structure of Financial Markets

Now that we understand the basic function of financial markets, let's look at their structure. The following descriptions of several categorizations of financial markets illustrate essential features of these markets.

Debt and Equity Markets

A firm or an individual can obtain funds in a financial market in two ways. The most common method is to issue a debt instrument, such as a bond or a mortgage, which is a contractual agreement by the borrower to pay the holder of the instrument fixed dollar amounts at regular intervals (interest and principal payments) until a specified date (the maturity date), when a final payment is made. The **maturity** of a debt instrument is the number of years (term) until that instrument's expiration date. A debt instrument is **short-term** if its maturity is less than a year and **long-term** if its maturity is 10 years or longer. Debt instruments with a maturity between one and 10 years are said to be **intermediate-term**.

The second method of raising funds is by issuing **equities**, such as common stock, which are claims to share in the net income (income after expenses and taxes) and the assets of a business. If you own one share of common stock in a company that has issued one million shares, you are entitled to one-millionth of the firm's net income and one-millionth of the firm's assets. Equities often make periodic payments (**dividends**) to their holders and are considered long-term securities because they have no maturity date. In addition, owning stock means that you own a portion of the firm and thus have the right to vote on issues important to the firm and to elect its directors.

The main disadvantage of owning a corporation's equities rather than its debt is that an equity holder is a *residual claimant*; that is, the corporation must pay all its debt holders before it pays its equity holders. The advantage of holding equities is that equity holders benefit directly from any increases in the corporation's profitability or asset value because equities confer ownership rights on the equity holders. Debt holders do not share in this benefit because their dollar payments are fixed. We examine the pros and cons of debt versus equity instruments in more detail in Chapter 8, which provides an economic analysis of financial structure.

Primary and Secondary Markets

A **primary market** is a financial market in which new issues of a security, such as a bond or a stock, are sold to initial buyers by the corporation or government agency borrowing the funds. A **secondary market** is a financial market in which securities that have been previously issued can be resold.

The primary markets for securities are not well known to the public because the selling of securities to initial buyers often takes place behind closed doors. An important financial institution that assists in the initial sale of securities in the primary market is the **investment bank**. It does this by **underwriting** securities: it guarantees a price for a corporation's securities and then sells them to the public.

The Toronto Stock Exchange (TSX) and the TSX Venture Exchange, in which previously issued stocks are traded, are the best-known examples of Canadian secondary markets, although the bond markets, in which previously issued bonds of major corporations and the Canadian government are bought and sold, actually have a larger trading volume. Other examples of secondary markets are foreign exchange markets, futures markets, and options markets. Securities brokers and dealers are crucial to a well-functioning secondary market. **Brokers** are agents of investors who match buyers with sellers of securities; **dealers** link buyers and sellers by buying and selling securities at stated prices.

When an individual buys a security in the secondary market, the person who has sold the security receives money in exchange for the security, but the corporation that issued the security acquires no new funds. A corporation acquires new funds only when its securities are first sold in the primary market. Nonetheless, secondary markets serve two important functions. First, they make it easier to sell these financial instruments to raise cash; that is, they make the financial instruments more **liquid**. The increased liquidity of these instruments then makes them more desirable and thus easier for the issuing firm to sell in the primary market.

Second, they determine the price of the security that the issuing firm sells in the primary market. The investors that buy securities in the primary market will pay the issuing corporation no more than the price they think the secondary market will set for this security. The higher the security's price in the secondary market, the higher will be the price that the issuing firm will receive for a new security in the primary market and hence the greater the amount of financial capital it can raise. Conditions in the secondary market are therefore the most relevant to corporations issuing securities. It is for this reason that books like this one, which deal with financial markets, focus on the behaviour of secondary markets rather than that of primary markets.

Exchanges and Over-the-Counter Markets

Secondary markets can be organized in two ways. One is to organize **exchanges**, where buyers and sellers of securities (or their agents or brokers) meet in one central location to conduct trades. The Toronto Stock Exchange for stocks and ICE Futures Canada (a subsidiary of IntercontinentalExchange) for commodities (wheat, oats, barley, and other agricultural commodities) are examples of organized exchanges. The Montreal Exchange (ME) is another example of an organized exchange, offering a range of equity, interest rate, and index derivative products.

The other method of organizing a secondary market is to have an **over-the-counter (OTC) market**, in which dealers at different locations who have an inventory of securities stand ready to buy and sell securities "over the counter" to anyone who comes to them and is willing to accept their prices. Because over-the-counter dealers are in computer contact and know the prices set by one another, the OTC market is very competitive and not very different from a market with an organized exchange.

Many common stocks are traded over the counter, although a majority of the largest corporations have their shares traded at organized stock exchanges. The Canadian government bond market, by contrast, is set up as an over-the-counter market. Dealers establish a "market" in these securities by standing ready to buy and sell Canadian government bonds. Other over-the-counter markets include those that trade other types of financial instruments such as negotiable certificates of deposit, overnight funds, and foreign exchange.

Money and Capital Markets

Another way of distinguishing between markets is on the basis of the maturity of the securities traded in each market. The **money market** is a financial market in which only short-term debt instruments (generally those with original maturity of less than one year) are traded; the **capital market** is the market in which longer-term debt (generally those with original maturity of one year or greater) and equity instruments are traded. Money market securities are usually more widely traded than longer-term securities and so tend to be more liquid. In addition, as we will see in Chapter 4, short-term securities have smaller fluctuations in prices than long-term securities, making them safer investments. As a result, corporations and banks actively use the money market to earn interest on surplus funds that they expect to have only temporarily. Capital market securities, such as stocks and long-term bonds, are often held by financial intermediaries such as insurance companies and pension funds, which have more certainty about the amount of funds they will have available in the future.

Financial Market Instruments

To complete our understanding of how financial markets perform the important role of channelling funds from lender-savers to borrower-spenders, we need to examine the securities (instruments) traded in financial markets. We first focus on the instruments traded in the money market and then turn to those traded in the capital market.

Money Market Instruments

Because of their short terms to maturity, the debt instruments traded in the money market undergo the least price fluctuations and so are the least risky investments. The money market has undergone great changes in the past three decades, with the amount of some financial instruments growing at a far more rapid rate than others.

The principal money market instruments are listed in Table 2-1, along with the amount outstanding at the end of 1980, 1990, 2000, and 2010. The *National Post: Financial Post* reports money market rates in its "Bond Yields and Rates" column (see the Financial News: Money Market Rates box on page 28).

GOVERNMENT OF CANADA TREASURY BILLS   These short-term debt instruments of the Canadian government are issued in 1-, 3-, 6-, and 12-month maturities to finance the federal government. They pay a set amount at maturity and have no interest payments, but they effectively pay interest by initially selling at a discount, that is, at a price lower than the set amount paid at maturity. For instance, you might pay $9600 in May 2013 for a one-year Treasury bill that can be redeemed in May 2014 for $10 000.

Treasury bills are the most liquid of all the money market instruments because they are the most actively traded. They are also the safest of all money market instruments because there is almost no possibility of **default**, a situation in which the party issuing the debt instrument (the federal government, in this case) is unable to make interest payments or pay off the amount owed when the instrument matures. The federal government is always able to meet its debt obligations, because it can raise taxes to pay off its debts. Treasury bills are held mainly by banks, although households, corporations, and other financial intermediaries hold small amounts.

CERTIFICATES OF DEPOSIT   A *certificate of deposit* (CD) is a debt instrument sold by a bank to depositors that pays annual interest of a given amount and at maturity pays back the original purchase price. CDs are often negotiable, meaning that they can be traded, and in bearer form (called **bearer deposit notes**), meaning that the buyer's name is recorded neither in the issuer's books nor on the security itself. These negotiable CDs are issued in multiples of $100 000 and with maturities of 30 to 365 days, and can be resold in a secondary market, thus offering the purchaser both yield and liquidity.

TABLE 2-1   Principal Money Market Instruments

Type of Instrument	Amount Outstanding ($ Millions)			
	1980	**1990**	**2000**	**2010**
Treasury Bills				
Government of Canada	13 709	113 654	76 633	150 830
Provincial governments	905	12 602	17 541	33 858
Municipal governments	113	514	188	873
Short-Term Paper				
Commercial paper	2555	12 971	24 330	11 221

Source: Statistics Canada Cansim II series V37377, V122256, V122257, and V122652.

Chartered banks also issue non-negotiable CDs. That is, they cannot be sold to someone else and cannot be redeemed from the bank before maturity without paying a substantial penalty. Non-negotiable CDs are issued in denominations ranging from $5000 to $100 000 and with maturities of one day to five years. They are also known as **term deposit receipts** or **term notes**.

CDs are also an extremely important source of funds for trust and mortgage loan companies. These institutions issue CDs under a variety of names; for example, DRs (Deposit Receipts), GTCs (Guaranteed Trust Certificates), GICs (Guaranteed Investment Certificates), and GIRs (Guaranteed Investment Receipts).

COMMERCIAL PAPER   *Commercial paper* is an unsecured short-term debt instrument issued in either Canadian dollars or other currencies by large banks and well-known corporations, such as Bank of Montreal and Bombardier. Because commercial paper is unsecured, only the largest and most creditworthy corporations issue commercial paper. The interest rate the corporation is charged reflects the firm's level of risk. The interest rate on commercial paper is low relative to those on other corporate fixed-income securities and slightly higher than rates on Government of Canada Treasury bills.

Sales finance companies also issue short-term promissory notes known as **finance paper**. Finance and commercial paper are issued in minimum denominations of $50 000 and in maturities of 30 to 365 days for finance paper and 1 to 365 days for commercial paper. Most finance and commercial paper is issued on a discounted basis. Chapter 11 discusses why the commercial paper market has had such tremendous growth.

REPURCHASE AGREEMENTS   *Repurchase agreements*, or *repos*, are effectively short-term loans (usually with a maturity of less than two weeks) for which Treasury bills serve as *collateral*, an asset that the lender receives if the borrower does not pay back the loan. Repos are made as follows: A large corporation, such as Bombardier, may have some idle funds in its bank account, say $1 million, which it would like to lend for a week. Bombardier uses this excess $1 million to buy Treasury bills from a bank, which agrees to repurchase them the next week at a price slightly above Bombardier's purchase price. The effect of this agreement is that Bombardier makes a loan of $1 million to the bank and holds $1 million of the bank's Treasury bills until the bank repurchases the bills to pay off the loan. Repurchase agreements are now an important source of bank funds. The most important lenders in this market are large corporations.

OVERNIGHT FUNDS   These are typically overnight loans by banks to other banks. The *overnight funds* designation is somewhat confusing, because these loans are not made by the federal government or by the Bank of Canada, but rather by banks to other banks. One reason why a bank might borrow in the overnight funds market is that it might find it does not have enough settlement deposits at the Bank of Canada. It can then borrow these balances from another bank with excess settlement balances.

The overnight market is very sensitive to the credit needs of the deposit-taking institutions, so the interest rate on overnight loans, called the **overnight interest rate**, is a closely watched barometer of the tightness of credit market conditions in the banking system and the stance of monetary policy. When it is high, it indicates that the banks are strapped for funds, whereas when it is low, banks' credit needs are low.

FINANCIAL NEWS

Money Market Rates

The Globe and Mail and the *National Post* publish daily a listing of interest rates on many different financial instruments. In the *National Post: Financial Post*, this listing can be found in the "Bond Yields and Rates" column.

The interest rates in the "Bond Yields and Rates" column that are discussed most frequently in the media are as follows:

Bank rate: The interest rate charged by the Bank of Canada on loans made to members of the Canadian Payments Association.

Overnight money market (financing) rate: A measure of the collateralized overnight rate compiled by the Bank of Canada.

Prime rate: The base interest rate on corporate bank loans, an indicator of the cost of business borrowing from banks.

Treasury bill rates: The interest rates on Government of Canada Treasury bills, an indicator of general interest rate movements.

Selected U.S. interest rates: Selected U.S. interest rates such as Treasury bill rates, commercial paper rates, the discount rate, the prime rate, and the federal funds rate. These are indicators of general interest rate movements in the United States.

London interbank offer rate (or *Libor*): The British Bankers' Association average of interbank rates for dollar deposits in the London market.

Capital Market Instruments

Capital market instruments are debt and equity instruments with maturities of greater than one year. They have far wider price fluctuations than money market instruments and are considered to be fairly risky investments. The principal capital market instruments are listed in Table 2-2, which shows the amount outstanding at the end of 1980, 1990, 2000, and 2010.

STOCKS   *Stocks* are equity claims on the net income and assets of a corporation. Aggregate Canadian Market Capitalization was US$2.28 trillion at the end of 2010. The amount of new stock issues in any given year is typically quite small—less than 1% of the total value of shares outstanding. Individuals hold around half of the value of stocks; pension funds, mutual funds, and insurance companies hold the rest.

TABLE 2-2   Principal Capital Market Instruments

Type of Instrument	Amount Outstanding ($ Billions)			
	1980	1990	2000	2010
Corporate stocks (market value)	42.9	109.4	239.4	369.1
Residential mortgages	91.9	245.3	431.2	995.1
Corporate bonds	29.8	72.3	184.8	324.4
Government of Canada securities (marketable)	27.9	124.6	301.9	344.3
Bank commercial loans	58.7	102.6	132.2	167.4
Consumer loans	43.6	95.6	202.9	463.5
Nonresidential and farm mortgages	15.1	56.1	50.2	82.8

Source: Statistics Canada Cansim II series V122642, V122746, V122640, V37378 V122631, V122707, V122656, V122657, V122658, V122659, and V800015, and the authors' calculations.

MORTGAGES AND MORTGAGE-BACKED SECURITIES   **Mortgages** are loans to households or firms to purchase housing, land, or other real structures, where the structure or land serves as collateral for the loans. The mortgage market is the largest debt market in Canada, with the amount of residential mortgages (used to purchase residential housing) outstanding more than tenfold the amount of commercial and farm mortgages. Mortgages are provided by financial institutions such as chartered banks, trust and mortgage loan companies, credit unions and *caisses populaires*, pension funds, and life insurance companies. However in recent years, a growing amount of the funds for mortgages have been provided by **mortgage-backed securities**, a bond-like debt instrument which is backed by a bundle of individual mortgages, whose interest and principal payments are collectively paid to the holders of the security. As we will see in Chapter 9, mortgage-backed securities and more complicated variants (CDOs) have become notorious because they played a key role in promoting the recent global financial crisis.

Banks and life insurance companies provide the majority of non-residential and farm mortgages. The federal government also plays an active role in the mortgage market via the Canada Mortgage and Housing Corporation (CMHC), which provides funds to the mortgage market by selling bonds and using the proceeds to buy mortgages.

CORPORATE BONDS   These are long-term bonds issued by corporations with very strong credit ratings. The typical *corporate bond* sends the holder an interest payment twice a year and pays off the face value when the bond matures. Some corporate bonds, called *convertible bonds*, have the additional feature of allowing the holder to convert them into a specified number of shares of stock at any time up to the maturity date. This feature makes convertible bonds more desirable to prospective purchasers than regular bonds, and allows the corporation to reduce its interest payments, because these bonds can increase in value if the price of the stock appreciates sufficiently. Because the outstanding amount of both convertible and nonconvertible bonds for any given corporation is small, they are not nearly as liquid as other securities such as Government of Canada bonds.

Although the size of the corporate bond market is substantially smaller than that of the stock market, the volume of new corporate bonds issued each year is substantially greater than the volume of new stock issues. Thus the behaviour of the corporate bond market is probably far more important to a firm's financing decisions than the behaviour of the stock market. The principal buyers of corporate bonds are life insurance companies; pension funds and households are other large holders.

GOVERNMENT OF CANADA BONDS   Intermediate-term bonds (those with initial maturities from 1 to 10 years) and long-term bonds (those with initial maturities greater than 10 years) are issued by the federal government to finance its deficit. Because they are the most widely traded bonds in Canada, they are the most liquid security traded in the capital market. They are held by the Bank of Canada, banks, households, and foreign investors.

These debt instruments are issued in either bearer or registered form and in denominations of $1000, $5000, $25 000, $100 000, and $1 million. In the case of **registered bonds**, the name of the owner appears on the bond certificate and is also recorded at the Bank of Canada. Some issues have the additional **call** (or **redemption**) feature of allowing them to be "called" on specified notice (usually 30 to 60 days).

CANADA SAVINGS BONDS   These are nonmarketable bonds issued by the Government of Canada and sold each year from early October through to April 1. *Canada Savings Bonds* (CSBs) are floating-rate bonds, available in denominations from

$100 to $10 000 and offered exclusively to individuals, estates, and specified trusts. They are issued as registered bonds and can be purchased from financial institutions or through payroll savings plans.

CSBs are different from all other bonds issued by the Government of Canada in that they do not rise or fall in value, like other bonds do. They have the valuable option of being redeemable at face value plus accrued interest, at any time prior to maturity, by being presented at any financial institution. In October 1998 the Government of Canada introduced another type of bond that is similar to CSBs—Canada Premium Bonds (CPBs). CPBs offer a slightly higher coupon rate than the CSBs but can be redeemed only once a year, on the anniversary of the issue date and during the month after that date.

PROVINCIAL AND MUNICIPAL GOVERNMENT BONDS   Provincial and municipal governments also issue bonds to finance expenditures on schools, roads, and other large programs. The securities issued by provincial governments are referred to as **provincial bonds** or **provincials** and those issued by municipal governments as **municipal bonds** or **municipals**—the securities issued by the federal government are referred to as **Canadas**. Provincials and municipals are denominated in either domestic currency or foreign currencies, mostly U.S. dollars, Swiss francs, and Japanese yen. They are mainly held by trusteed pension plans, social security funds (predominantly the Canada Pension Plan), and foreigners.

GOVERNMENT AGENCY SECURITIES   These are long-term bonds issued by various government agencies such as the Ontario Municipal Improvement Corporation and the Alberta Municipal Financing Corporation to assist municipalities to finance such items as mortgages, farm loans, or power-generating equipment. The provincial governments guarantee many of these securities. They function much like Canadas, provincials, and municipals and are held by similar parties.

CONSUMER AND BANK COMMERCIAL LOANS   These loans to consumers and businesses are made principally by banks, but in the case of consumer loans, also by finance companies.

Internationalization of Financial Markets

The growing internationalization of financial markets has become an important trend. Before the 1980s, U.S. financial markets were much larger than financial markets outside the United States, but in recent years the dominance of U.S. markets has been disappearing (see the Global box Are U.S. Capital Markets Losing Their Edge?).

The extraordinary growth of foreign financial markets has been the result of both large increases in the pool of savings in foreign countries such as Japan and the deregulation of foreign financial markets, which has enabled foreign markets to expand their activities. Canadian corporations and banks are now more likely to tap international capital markets to raise needed funds, and Canadian investors often seek investment opportunities abroad. Similarly, foreign corporations and banks raise funds from Canadians, and foreigners have become important investors in Canada. A look at international bond markets and world stock markets will give us a picture of how this globalization of financial markets is taking place.

International Bond Market, Eurobonds, and Eurocurrencies

The traditional instruments in the international bond market are known as **foreign bonds**. Foreign bonds are sold in a foreign country and are denominated in that country's currency. For example, if the German automaker Porsche sells a bond in Canada denominated in Canadian dollars, it is classified as a foreign bond. Foreign

GLOBAL

Are U.S. Capital Markets Losing Their Edge?

Over the past few decades, the United States lost its international dominance in a number of manufacturing industries, including automobiles and consumer electronics, as other countries became more competitive in global markets. Recent evidence suggests that financial markets are now undergoing a similar trend: just as Ford and General Motors have lost global market share to Toyota and Honda, U.S. stock and bond markets recently have seen their share of sales of newly issued corporate securities slip. The London and Hong Kong stock exchanges now handle a larger share of initial public offerings (IPOs) of stock than does the New York Stock Exchange, which had been by far the dominant exchange in terms of IPO value before 2000. Furthermore, the number of stocks listed on U.S. exchanges has been falling, while stock listings abroad have been growing rapidly: listings outside the United States are now about 10 times greater than in the United States. Likewise, the portion of new corporate bonds issued worldwide that are initially sold in U.S. capital markets has fallen below the share sold in European debt markets. Why do corporations that issue new securities to raise capital now conduct more of this business in financial markets in Europe and Asia? Among the factors contributing to this trend are quicker adoption of technological innovation by foreign financial markets, tighter immigration controls in the United States following the terrorist attacks in 2001, and perceptions that listing on American exchanges will expose foreign securities issuers to greater risks of lawsuits. Many people see burdensome financial regulation as the main cause, however, and point specifically to the Sarbanes-Oxley Act of 2002. The U.S. Congress passed this act after a number of accounting scandals involving U.S. corporations and the accounting firms that audited them came to light. Sarbanes-Oxley aims to strengthen the integrity of the auditing process and the quality of information provided in corporate financial statements. The costs to corporations of complying with the rules and procedures are high, especially for smaller firms, but largely avoidable if firms choose to issue their securities in financial markets outside the United States. For this reason, there is much support for revising Sarbanes-Oxley to lessen its alleged harmful effects and induce more securities issuers back to United States financial markets. However, there is not conclusive evidence to support the view that Sarbanes-Oxley is the main cause of the relative decline of U.S. financial markets and therefore in need of reform.

Discussion of the relative decline of U.S. financial markets and debate about the factors that are contributing to it likely will continue.

bonds have been an important instrument in the international capital market for centuries. In fact, a large percentage of U.S. railroads built in the nineteenth century were financed by sales of foreign bonds in Britain.

A more recent innovation in the international bond market is the **Eurobond**, a bond denominated in a currency other than that of the country in which it is sold—for example, a bond issued by a Canadian corporation that is denominated in Japanese yen and sold in Germany. Currently, over 80% of the new issues in the international bond market are Eurobonds, and the market for these securities has grown very rapidly.

A variant of the Eurobond is **Eurocurrencies**, which are foreign currencies deposited in banks outside the home country. The most important of the Eurocurrencies are **Eurodollars**, which are U.S. dollars deposited in foreign banks outside the United States or in foreign branches of U.S. banks. Because these short-term deposits earn interest, they are similar to short-term Eurobonds. Canadian banks borrow Eurodollar deposits from other banks or from their own foreign branches, and Eurodollars are now an important source of funds for Canadian banks.

Note that the name of the European currency, the euro, can create some confusion about the terms Eurobond, Eurocurrencies, and Eurodollars. A Eurobond is

FINANCIAL NEWS

Foreign Stock Market Indexes

The foreign stock market indexes discussed most frequently in the media are:

Dow Jones Industrial Average (DJIA): An index of the 30 largest publicly traded corporations in the United States maintained by the Dow Jones Corporation.

S&P 500: An index of 500 of the largest companies traded in the United States maintained by Standard & Poor's.

Nasdaq Composite: An index for all the stocks that trade on the Nasdaq stock market, where most of the technology stocks in the United States are traded.

FTSE 100: An index the 100 most highly *capitalized* U.K. companies listed on the London Stock Exchange.

DAX: An index of the 30 largest German companies trading on the Frankfurt Stock Exchange.

CAC 40: An index of the largest 40 French companies traded on Euronext Paris.

Hang Seng: An index of the largest companies traded on the Hong Kong stock markets.

Straits Times: An index of the largest 30 companies traded on the Singapore Exchange.

These indexes are reported daily in newspapers and Internet sites such as **www.finance.yahoo.com**.

---

typically not a bond that is denominated in euros. A bond denominated in euros is called a Eurobond only if *it is sold outside the countries that have adopted the euro.* Similarly, Eurodollars have nothing to do with euros, but are instead U.S. dollars deposited in banks outside the United States.

World Stock Markets

Until recently, the U.S. stock market was by far the largest in the world, but stock markets in other countries have been growing in importance. Now the United States is not always number one: in the mid-1980s, the value of stocks traded in Japan had at times exceeded the value of stocks traded in the United States. The increased interest in foreign stocks has prompted the development in Canada of mutual funds that specialize in trading in foreign stock markets. Canadian investors now pay attention not only to the Canadian stock market but also to stock price indexes for foreign stock markets such as the Dow Jones Industrial Average (New York), the Nikkei 300 (Tokyo), and the Financial Times Stock Exchange (FTSE) 100 Indexes (London).

The internationalization of financial markets is having profound effects on Canada. Foreigners not only are providing funds to corporations in Canada but are also helping finance the federal government. Without these foreign funds, the Canadian economy would have grown far less rapidly in the last 20 years. The internationalization of financial markets is also leading the way to a more integrated world economy in which flows of goods and technology between countries are more commonplace. In later chapters, we will encounter many examples of the important roles that international factors play in our economy.

Function of Financial Intermediaries: Indirect Finance

As shown in Figure 2-1 (page 22), funds can move from lenders to borrowers by a second route, called *indirect finance,* because it involves a financial intermediary that stands between the lender-savers and the borrower-spenders and helps transfer funds from one to the other. A financial intermediary does this by borrowing funds from the lender-savers and then using these funds to make loans to borrower-spenders. For example, a bank might acquire funds by issuing a liability to the public (an asset

GLOBAL

The Importance of Financial Intermediaries Relative to Securities Markets: An International Comparison

Patterns of financing corporations differ across countries, but one key fact emerges. Studies of Italy, Germany, and France show that when businesses go looking for funds to finance their activities, they usually obtain them indirectly through financial intermediaries and not directly from securities markets.* Even in Canada and the United States, which have the most developed securities markets in the world, loans from financial intermediaries are far more important for corporate finance than securities markets are. The countries that have made the least use of securities markets are Germany and Japan; in these two countries, financing from financial intermediaries has been almost 10 times greater than that from securities markets. However, after the deregulation of Japanese securities markets in

recent years, the share of corporate financing by financial intermediaries has been declining relative to the use of securities markets in the major developed countries, including Canada, the United States, Great Britain, and Japan.

Although the dominance of financial intermediaries over securities markets is clear in all countries, the relative importance of bond versus stock markets differs widely across countries. In the United States, the bond market is far more important as a source of corporate finance. On average, the amount of new financing raised using bonds is 10 times the amount using stocks. By contrast, countries such as France and Italy make more use of equities markets than of the bond markets to raise capital.

*See, for example, Colin Mayer, "Financial Systems, Corporate Finance, and Economic Development," in *Asymmetric Information, Corporate Finance, and Investment*, ed. R. Glenn Hubbard (Chicago: University of Chicago Press, 1990), 307–332.

for the public) in the form of savings deposits. It might then use the funds to acquire an asset by making a loan to Canadian Pacific (CP) or by buying a Canadian Pacific bond in the financial market. The ultimate result is that funds have been transferred from the public (the lender-savers) to Canadian Pacific (the borrower-spender) with the help of the financial intermediary (the bank).

The process of indirect finance using financial intermediaries, called **financial intermediation**, is the primary route for moving funds from lenders to borrowers. Indeed, although the media focus much of their attention on securities markets, particularly the stock market, financial intermediaries are a far more important source of financing for corporations than securities markets are. This is true not only for Canada but for other industrialized countries as well (see the Global box). Why are financial intermediaries and indirect finance so important in financial markets? To answer this question, we need to understand the role of transaction costs, risk sharing, and information costs in financial markets.

Transaction Costs

Transaction costs, the time and money spent in carrying out financial transactions, are a major problem for people who have excess funds to lend. As we have seen, Carl the Carpenter needs $1000 for his new tool, and you know that it is an excellent investment opportunity. You would like to lend him the funds, but to protect your investment, you have to hire a lawyer to write up the loan contract that specifies how much interest Carl will pay you, when he will make these interest payments, and when he will repay you the $1000. Obtaining the contract will cost you $500. When you include this transaction cost for making the loan, you realize that you can't earn enough from the deal (you spend $500 to make perhaps $100) and reluctantly tell Carl that he will have to look elsewhere.

This example illustrates that small savers like you or potential borrowers like Carl might be frozen out of financial markets and thus be unable to benefit from them. Can anyone come to the rescue? Financial intermediaries can.

Financial intermediaries can substantially reduce transaction costs because they have developed expertise in lowering costs and because their large size allows them to take advantage of **economies of scale**, the reduction in transaction costs per dollar of transactions as the size (scale) of transactions increases. For example, a bank knows how to find a good lawyer to produce an airtight loan contract, and this contract can be used over and over again in its loan transactions, thus lowering the legal cost per transaction. Instead of a loan contract (which may not be all that well written) costing $500, a bank can hire a top-flight lawyer for $5000 to draw up an airtight loan contract that can be used for 2000 loans at a cost of $2.50 per loan. At a cost of $2.50 per loan, it now becomes profitable for the financial intermediary to lend Carl the $1000.

Because financial intermediaries are able to reduce transaction costs substantially, they make it possible for you to provide funds indirectly to people like Carl with productive investment opportunities. In addition, a financial intermediary's low transaction costs mean that it can provide its customers with **liquidity services**, services that make it easier for customers to conduct transactions. For example, banks provide depositors with chequing accounts that enable them to pay their bills easily. In addition, depositors can earn interest on chequing and savings accounts and yet still convert them into goods and services whenever necessary.

Risk Sharing

Another benefit made possible by the low transaction costs of financial institutions is that they can help reduce the exposure of investors to **risk**, that is, uncertainty about the returns investors will earn on assets. Financial intermediaries do this through **risk sharing**: they create and sell assets with risk characteristics that people are comfortable with, and the intermediaries then use the funds they acquire by selling these assets to purchase other assets that may have far more risk. Low transaction costs allow financial intermediaries to share risk at low cost, enabling them to earn a profit on the spread between the returns they earn on risky assets and the payments they make on the assets they have sold. This process of risk sharing is also sometimes referred to as **asset transformation**, because, in a sense, risky assets are turned into safer assets for investors.

Financial intermediaries also promote risk sharing by helping individuals to diversify and thereby lower the amount of risk to which they are exposed. **Diversification** entails investing in a collection (**portfolio**) of assets whose returns do not always move together, with the result that overall risk is lower than for individual assets. (*Diversification* is another name for the old adage that "you shouldn't put all your eggs in one basket.") Low transaction costs allow financial intermediaries to do this by pooling a collection of assets into a new asset and then selling it to individuals.

Asymmetric Information: Adverse Selection and Moral Hazard

The presence of transaction costs in financial markets explains, in part, why financial intermediaries and indirect finance play such an important role in financial markets. An additional reason is that in financial markets, one party often does not know enough about the other party to make accurate decisions. This inequality is called **asymmetric information**. For example, a borrower who takes out a loan usually has better information about the potential returns and risk associated with the investment projects for which the funds are earmarked than the lender does. Lack of information creates problems in the financial system on two fronts: before the transaction is entered into and after.

Adverse selection is the problem created by asymmetric information *before* the transaction occurs. Adverse selection in financial markets occurs when the potential borrowers who are the most likely to produce an undesirable (*adverse*) outcome—the bad credit risks—are the ones who most actively seek out a loan and are thus most likely to be selected. Because adverse selection makes it more likely that loans might be made to bad credit risks, lenders may decide not to make any loans even though there are good credit risks in the marketplace.

To understand why adverse selection occurs, suppose that you have two aunts to whom you might make a loan—Aunt Sheila and Aunt Louise. Aunt Louise is a conservative type who borrows only when she has an investment she is quite sure will pay off. Aunt Sheila, by contrast, is an inveterate gambler who has just come across a get-rich-quick scheme that will make her a millionaire if she can just borrow $1000 to invest in it. Unfortunately, as with most get-rich-quick schemes, there is a high probability that the investment won't pay off and that Aunt Sheila will lose the $1000.

Which of your aunts is more likely to call you to ask for a loan? Aunt Sheila, of course, because she has so much to gain if the investment pays off. You, however, would not want to make a loan to her because there is a high probability that her investment will turn sour and she will be unable to pay you back.

If you knew both your aunts very well—that is, if your information were not asymmetric—you wouldn't have a problem because you would know that Aunt Sheila is a bad risk and so you would not lend to her. Suppose, though, that you don't know your aunts well. You are more likely to lend to Aunt Sheila than to Aunt Louise because Aunt Sheila would be hounding you for the loan. Because of the possibility of adverse selection, you might decide not to lend to either of your aunts, even though there are times when Aunt Louise, who is an excellent credit risk, might need a loan for a worthwhile investment.

Moral hazard is the problem created by asymmetric information *after* the transaction occurs. Moral hazard in financial markets is the risk (*hazard*) that the borrower might engage in activities that are undesirable (*immoral*) from the lender's point of view because they make it less likely that the loan will be paid back. Because moral hazard lowers the probability that the loan will be repaid, lenders may decide that they would rather not make a loan.

As an example of moral hazard, suppose that you made a $1000 loan to another relative, Uncle Melvin, who needs the money to purchase a computer so he can set up a business inputting students' term papers. Once you have made the loan, however, Uncle Melvin is more likely to slip off to the track and play the horses. If he bets on a 20-to-1 long shot and wins with your money, he is able to pay you back your $1000 and live high off the hog with the remaining $19 000. But if he loses, as is likely, you don't get paid back, and all he has lost is his reputation as a reliable, upstanding uncle. Uncle Melvin therefore has an incentive to go to the track because his gains ($19 000) if he bets correctly may be much greater than the cost to him (his reputation) if he bets incorrectly. If you knew what Uncle Melvin was up to, you would prevent him from going to the track, and he would not be able to increase the moral hazard. However, because it is hard for you to keep informed about his whereabouts—that is, because information is asymmetric—there is a good chance that Uncle Melvin will go to the track and you will not get paid back. The risk of moral hazard might therefore discourage you from making the $1000 loan to Uncle Melvin, even if you were sure that you would be paid back if he used it to set up his business.

The problems created by adverse selection and moral hazard are an important impediment to well-functioning financial markets. Again, financial intermediaries can alleviate these problems.

With financial intermediaries in the economy, small savers can provide their funds to the financial markets by lending these funds to a trustworthy intermediary, say, the Honest John Bank, which in turn lends the funds out either by making loans or by buying securities such as stocks or bonds. Successful financial intermediaries have higher earnings on their investments than small savers because they are better equipped than individuals to screen out good from bad credit risks, thereby reducing losses due to adverse selection. In addition, financial intermediaries have high earnings because they develop expertise in monitoring the parties they lend to, thus reducing losses due to moral hazard. The result is that financial intermediaries can afford to pay lender-savers interest or provide substantial services and still earn a profit.

As we have seen, financial intermediaries play an important role in the economy because they provide liquidity services, promote risk sharing, and solve information problems, thereby allowing small savers and borrowers to benefit from the existence of financial markets. The success of financial intermediaries performing this role is evidenced by the fact that most Canadians invest their savings with them and obtain loans from them. Financial intermediaries play a key role in improving economic efficiency because they help financial markets channel funds from lender-savers to people with productive investment opportunities. Without a well-functioning set of financial intermediaries, it is very hard for an economy to reach its full potential. We will explore further the role of financial intermediaries in the economy in Part III.

Economies of Scope and Conflicts of Interest

Another reason why financial intermediaries play such an important role in the economy is that by providing multiple financial services to their customers, such as offering them bank loans or selling their bonds for them, they can also achieve **economies of scope**; that is, they can lower the cost of information production for each service by applying one information resource to many different services. A bank, for example, can evaluate how good a credit risk a corporation is when making a loan to the firm, which then helps the bank decide whether it would be easy to sell the bonds of this corporation to the public.

Although the presence of economies of scope may substantially benefit financial institutions, it also creates potential costs in terms of **conflicts of interest**. Conflicts of interest are a type of moral hazard problem that arise when a person or institution has multiple objectives (interests) and, as a result, has conflicts between those objectives. Conflicts of interest are especially likely to occur when a financial institution provides multiple services. The potentially competing interests of those services may lead an individual or firm to conceal information or disseminate misleading information. We care about conflicts of interest because a substantial reduction in the quality of information in financial markets increases asymmetric information problems and prevents financial markets from channelling funds into the most productive investment opportunities. Consequently, the financial markets and the economy become less efficient.

Types of Financial Intermediaries

We have seen why financial intermediaries play such an important role in the economy. Now we look at the principal financial intermediaries and how they perform the intermediation function. They fall into three categories: depository institutions (banks and near banks), contractual savings institutions, and investment intermediaries. Table 2-3 provides a guide to the discussion of the financial intermediaries

TABLE 2-3 Primary Assets and Liabilities of Financial Intermediaries

Type of Intermediary	Primary Liabilities (Sources of Funds)	Primary Assets (Uses of Funds)
Depository Institutions (Banks)		
Chartered banks	Deposits	Loans, mortgages, government bonds
Trust and loan companies	Deposits	Mortgages
Credit unions and *caisses populaires*	Deposits	Mortgages
Contractual Savings Institutions		
Life insurance companies	Premiums from policies	Corporate bonds and mortgages
Property and casualty insurance companies	Premiums from policies	Corporate bonds and stocks
Pension funds	Retirement contributions	Corporate bonds and stocks
Investment Intermediaries		
Finance companies	Finance paper, stocks, bonds	Consumer and business loans
Mutual funds	Shares	Stocks and bonds
Money market mutual funds	Shares	Money market instruments

that fit into these three categories by describing their primary liabilities (sources of funds) and assets (uses of funds). The relative size of these intermediaries in Canada is indicated in Table 2-4.

Depository Institutions (Banks)

Depository institutions (which for simplicity we refer to as *banks* throughout this text) are financial intermediaries that accept deposits from individuals and institutions and make loans. The study of money and banking focuses special attention on this group of financial institutions because they are involved in the creation of deposits, an important component of the money supply. These institutions include chartered banks and the so-called near banks: trust and loan companies, and credit unions and *caisses populaires*.

CHARTERED BANKS These financial intermediaries raise funds primarily by issuing chequable deposits (deposits on which cheques can be written), savings deposits (deposits that are payable on demand but do not allow their owner to write cheques), and term deposits (deposits with fixed terms to maturity). They then use these funds to make commercial, consumer, and mortgage loans and to buy Canadian government securities and provincial and municipal bonds. There are 77 chartered banks in Canada, and as a group they are the largest financial intermediary and have the most diversified portfolios (collections) of assets.

TRUST AND LOAN COMPANIES These depository institutions obtain funds primarily through chequable and nonchequable savings deposits, term deposits, guaranteed investment certificates, and debentures. In the past, these institutions were constrained in their activities and mostly made mortgage loans for residential housing. Over time, these restrictions have been loosened so that the distinction between these depository institutions and chartered banks has blurred. These intermediaries have become more alike and are now more competitive with each other.

TABLE 2-4   Relative Shares of Financial Institutions and Pension Plans Regulated by OSFI (as of March 31, 2010)

Type of Intermediary	Number	Total Assets (in Millions)	Percentage (%)
Chartered Banks			
Domestic	22	2 662 874	67.47
Foreign bank subsidiaries	25	145 302	3.68
Foreign bank branches	30	65 434	1.66
Trust and Loan Companies			
Bank-owned	30	243 074	6.16
Other	36	52 510	1.33
Cooperative Credit Associations	6	23 360	0.59
Life Insurance Companies			
Canadian-incorporated	45	484 425	12.27
Foreign branches	39	14 483	0.37
Fraternal Benefit Societies			
Canadian-incorporated	10	6642	0.17
Foreign branches	7	2064	0.05
Property and Casualty Insurance Companies			
Canadian-incorporated	95	89 950	2.28
Foreign branches	92	33 686	0.85
Pension Plans	1 398	123 000	3.12
Total		3 946 804	100.00

Source: OSFI Annual Report 2009–2010.

CREDIT UNIONS AND *CAISSES POPULAIRES* (CUCPs)   Credit unions and *caisses populaires* are very small cooperative lending institutions organized around a particular group: union members, employees of a particular firm, and so forth. They acquire funds from deposits and primarily make mortgage and consumer loans.

Contractual Savings Institutions

Contractual savings institutions, such as insurance companies and pension funds, are financial intermediaries that acquire funds at periodic intervals on a contractual basis. Because they can predict with reasonable accuracy how much they will have to pay out in benefits in the coming years, they do not have to worry as much as depository institutions about losing funds. As a result, the liquidity of assets is not as important a consideration for them as it is for depository institutions, and they tend to invest their funds primarily in long-term securities such as corporate bonds, stocks, and mortgages.

LIFE INSURANCE COMPANIES   Life insurance companies, numbering 94, insure people against financial hazards following a death and sell annuities (annual income payments upon retirement). They acquire funds from the premiums that people pay to keep their policies in force and use them mainly to buy corporate bonds and mortgages. They also purchase stocks but are restricted in the amount that they can hold. Currently, with about $500 billion of assets, they are among the largest of the contractual savings institutions.

PROPERTY AND CASUALTY (P&C) INSURANCE COMPANIES These companies, numbering 187, insure their policyholders against loss from theft, fire, and accidents. They are very much like life insurance companies, receiving funds through premiums for their policies, but they have a greater possibility of loss of funds if major disasters occur. For this reason, they use their funds to buy more liquid assets than life insurance companies do. Their largest holding of assets is government bonds and debentures; they also hold corporate bonds and stocks.

PENSION FUNDS AND GOVERNMENT RETIREMENT FUNDS Private pension funds and provincial and municipal retirement funds provide retirement income in the form of annuities to employees who are covered by a pension plan. Funds are acquired by contributions from employers and/or from employees, who either have a contribution automatically deducted from their paycheques or contribute voluntarily. The largest asset holdings of pension funds are corporate bonds and stocks. The establishment of pension funds has been actively encouraged by the federal government both through legislation requiring pension plans and through tax incentives to encourage contributions.

Investment Intermediaries

This category of financial intermediaries includes finance companies, mutual funds, and money market mutual funds.

FINANCE COMPANIES Finance companies raise funds by selling commercial paper (a short-term debt instrument) and by issuing stocks and bonds. They lend these funds to consumers, who make purchases of such items as furniture, automobiles, and home improvements, and to small businesses. Some finance companies are organized by a parent corporation to help sell its product. For example, Ford Credit makes loans to consumers who purchase Ford automobiles.

MUTUAL FUNDS These financial intermediaries acquire funds by selling shares to many individuals and use the proceeds to purchase diversified portfolios of stocks and bonds. Mutual funds allow shareholders to pool their resources so that they can take advantage of lower transaction costs when buying large blocks of stocks or bonds. In addition, mutual funds allow shareholders to hold more diversified portfolios than they otherwise would. Shareholders can sell (redeem) shares at any time, but the value of these shares will be determined by the value of the mutual fund's holdings of securities. Because these fluctuate greatly, the value of mutual fund shares will too; therefore, investments in mutual funds can be risky.

MONEY MARKET MUTUAL FUNDS These financial institutions have the characteristics of mutual funds but also function to some extent as depository institutions because they offer deposit-type accounts. Like most mutual funds, they sell shares to acquire funds that are then used to buy money market instruments that are both safe and very liquid. The interest on these assets is paid out to shareholders.

Regulation of the Financial System

The financial system is among the most heavily regulated sectors of the Canadian economy. The government regulates financial markets for three main reasons: to increase the information available to investors, to ensure the soundness of the financial system,

TABLE 2-5 Principal Regulatory Agencies of the Canadian Financial System

Regulatory Agency	Subject of Regulation	Nature of Regulations
Provincial securities and exchange commissions	Organized exchanges and financial markets	Requires disclosure of information and restricts insider trading
Bank of Canada	Chartered banks, TMLs, and CUCPs	Examines the books of the deposit-taking institutions and coordinates with the federal agencies that are responsible for financial institution regulation: OSFI and CDIC
Office of the Superintendent of Financial Institutions Canada (OSFI)	All federally regulated chartered banks, TMLs, CUCPs, life insurance companies, P&C insurance companies, and pension plans	Sets capital adequacy, accounting, and board-of-directors responsibility standards; conducts bank audits and coordinates with provincial securities commissions
Canada Deposit Insurance Corporation (CDIC)	Chartered banks, TMLs, CUCPs	Provides insurance of up to $100 000 for each depositor at a bank, examines the books of insured banks, and imposes restrictions on assets they can hold
Québec Deposit Insurance Board	TMLs and credit cooperatives in Québec	Similar role to the CDIC
Canadian Life and Health Insurance Compensation Corporation (CompCorp)	Life insurance companies	Compensates policyholders if the issuing life insurance company goes bankrupt
P&C Insurance Compensation Corporation (PACIC)	Property and casualty insurance companies	Compensates policyholders if the issuing P&C insurance company goes bankrupt

and to improve control of monetary policy. We will examine how these three reasons have led to the present regulatory environment. As a study aid, the principal regulatory agencies of the Canadian financial system are listed in Table 2-5.

Increasing Information Available to Investors

Asymmetric information in financial markets means that investors may be subject to adverse selection and moral hazard problems that may hinder the efficient operation of financial markets. Risky firms or outright crooks may be the most eager to sell securities to unwary investors, and the resulting adverse selection problem may keep investors out of financial markets. Furthermore, once an investor has bought a security, thereby lending money to a firm, the borrower may have incentives to engage in risky activities or to commit outright fraud. The presence of this moral hazard problem may also keep investors away from financial markets. Government regulation can reduce adverse selection and moral hazard problems in financial markets and increase their efficiency by increasing the amount of information available to investors.

Provincial securities commissions, the most significant being the Ontario Securities Commission (OSC), administer provincial acts requiring corporations issuing securities to disclose certain information about their sales, assets, and earnings to the public and restrict trading by the largest stockholders in the corporation. By requiring disclosure of this information and by discouraging insider trading, which could be used to manipulate security prices, regulators hope that investors will be better informed and be protected from abuses in financial markets. Indeed, in recent years, the OSC has been particularly active in prosecuting people involved in insider trading in Canada's largest stock exchange, the Toronto Stock Exchange.

Ensuring the Soundness of Financial Intermediaries

Asymmetric information can lead to the widespread collapse of financial intermediaries, referred to as a **financial panic**. Because providers of funds to financial intermediaries may not be able to assess whether the institutions holding their funds are sound or not, if they have doubts about the overall health of financial intermediaries they may want to pull their funds out of both sound and unsound institutions. The possible outcome is a financial panic that produces large losses for the public and causes serious damage to the economy. To protect the public and the economy from financial panics, the government has implemented various types of regulations.

RESTRICTIONS ON ENTRY Provincial banking and insurance commissions, the Bank of Canada, and the Office of the Superintendent of Financial Institutions (OSFI), an agency of the federal government, have created tight regulations governing who is allowed to set up a financial intermediary. Individuals or groups that want to establish a financial intermediary, such as a bank or an insurance company, must obtain a charter from the provincial or federal government. Only if they are upstanding citizens with impeccable credentials and a large amount of initial funds will they be given a charter.

DISCLOSURE There are stringent reporting requirements for financial intermediaries. Their bookkeeping must follow certain strict principles, their books are subject to periodic inspection, and they must make certain information available to the public.

RESTRICTIONS ON ASSETS AND ACTIVITIES There are restrictions on what financial intermediaries are allowed to do and what assets they can hold. Before you put your funds into a chartered bank or some other such institution, you would want to know that your funds are safe and that the financial intermediary will be able to meet its obligations to you. One way of doing this is to restrict the financial intermediary from engaging in certain risky activities. Another way to limit a financial intermediary's risk behaviour is to restrict it from holding certain risky assets, or at least from holding a greater quantity of these risky assets than is prudent. For example, chartered banks and other depository institutions are not allowed to hold common stock because stock prices experience substantial fluctuations. Insurance companies are allowed to hold common stock, but their holdings cannot exceed a certain fraction of their total assets.

DEPOSIT INSURANCE The government can insure people's deposits so that they do not suffer any financial loss if the financial intermediary that holds these deposits fails. The most important government agency that provides this type of insurance is the Canada Deposit Insurance Corporation (CDIC), created by an act of Parliament in 1967. It insures each depositor at a member deposit-taking financial institution up to a loss of $100 000 per account. Except for certain wholesale branches of foreign banks, credit unions, and some provincial institutions, all deposit-taking financial institutions in Canada are members of the CDIC. All CDIC members make contributions into the CDIC fund, which are used to pay off depositors in the case of a bank's failure. The Québec Deposit Insurance Board, an organization similar to CDIC and set up at the same time as CDIC, provides insurance for TMLs and credit cooperatives in Québec.

LIMITS ON COMPETITION   Politicians have often declared that unbridled competition among financial intermediaries promotes failures that will harm the public. Although the evidence that competition has this effect is extremely weak, provincial and federal governments at times have imposed restrictive regulations. For example, from 1967 to 1980 the entry of foreign banks into Canadian banking was prohibited. Since 1980, however, the incorporation of foreign bank subsidiaries has been regulated, but Canada still ranks low with respect to the degree of competition from foreign banks.

In later chapters we will look more closely at government regulation of financial markets and will see whether it has improved their functioning.

Financial Regulation Abroad

Not surprisingly, given the similarity of the economic systems here and in the United States, Japan, and the nations of Western Europe, financial regulation in these countries is similar to financial regulation in Canada. The provision of information is improved by requiring corporations issuing securities to report details about assets and liabilities, earnings, and sales of stock, and by prohibiting insider trading. The soundness of intermediaries is ensured by licensing, periodic inspection of financial intermediaries' books, and the provision of deposit insurance.

The major differences between financial regulation in Canada and abroad relate to bank regulation. In the past, for example, the United States was the only industrialized country to subject banks to restrictions on branching, which limited banks' size and restricted them to certain geographic regions. These restrictions were abolished by legislation in 1994. U.S. and Canadian banks are also the most restricted in the range of assets they may hold. Banks in other countries frequently hold shares in commercial firms; in Japan and Germany, those stakes can be sizable.

MyEconLab   MyEconLab is an online homework and tutorial system that puts you in control of your own learning with study and practice tools directly correlated to this chapter's content. Visit MyEconLab to explore the following resources:

- The Questions and Applied Problems are all available in the Study Plan on MyEconLab for further practice. You will also find the answers to all of the Questions and Applied Problems in the Student Resources section of your MyEconLab.

MyEconLab also features Additional Readings, Videos, Glossary Flashcards, Audio Chapter Summaries, Economics News Feeds, Animations, and many additional tools to help you master key concepts from the text.

SUMMARY

MyEconLab
Audio Summary

1. The basic function of financial markets is to channel funds from savers who have an excess of funds to spenders who have a shortage of funds. Financial markets can do this either through direct finance, in which borrowers borrow funds directly from lenders by selling them securities, or through indirect finance, which involves a financial intermediary that stands between the lender-savers and the borrower-spenders and helps transfer funds from

one to the other. This channelling of funds improves the economic welfare of everyone in the society. Because they allow funds to move from people who have no productive investment opportunities to those who have such opportunities, financial markets contribute to economic efficiency. In addition, channelling of funds directly benefits consumers by allowing them to make purchases when they need them most.

2. Financial markets can be classified as debt and equity markets, primary and secondary markets, exchanges and over-the-counter markets, and money and capital markets.

3. The principal money market instruments (debt instruments with maturities of less than one year) are Treasury bills, certificates of deposit, commercial paper, repurchase agreements, overnight funds, and Eurodollars. The principal capital market instruments (debt and equity instruments with maturities greater than one year) are stocks, mortgages, corporate bonds, Canadian government securities, Canada Savings Bonds, government agency securities, provincial and municipal government bonds, and consumer and bank commercial loans.

4. An important trend in recent years is the growing internationalization of financial markets. Eurobonds, which are denominated in a currency other than that of the country in which they are sold, are now the dominant security in the international bond market. Eurodollars, which are dollars deposited in foreign banks, are an important source of funds for Canadian banks.

5. Financial intermediaries are financial institutions that acquire funds by issuing liabilities and in turn use those funds to acquire assets by purchasing securities or making loans. Financial intermediaries play an important role in the financial system because they reduce transaction costs, allow risk sharing, and solve problems created by adverse selection and moral hazard. As a result, financial intermediaries allow small savers and borrowers to benefit from the existence of financial markets, thereby increasing the efficiency of the economy. However, the economies of scope that help make financial intermediaries successful can lead to conflicts of interest that make the financial system less efficient.

6. The principal financial intermediaries fall into three categories: (a) banks—chartered banks, trust and loan companies, and credit unions and *caisses populaires*; (b) contractual savings institutions—life insurance companies, property and casualty insurance companies, and pension funds; and (c) investment intermediaries—finance companies, mutual funds, and money market mutual funds.

7. The government regulates financial markets and financial intermediaries for three main reasons: to increase the information available to investors, to ensure the soundness of the financial system, and to improve control of monetary policy. Regulations include requiring disclosure of information to the public, restrictions on who can set up a financial intermediary, restrictions on what assets financial intermediaries can hold, and the provision of deposit insurance.

KEY TERMS

adverse selection, p. 35

asset transformation, p. 34

asymmetric information, p. 34

bearer deposit notes, p. 26

brokers, p. 24

call (redemption), p. 29

Canadas, p. 30

capital market, p. 25

conflicts of interest, p. 36

dealers, p. 24

default, p. 26

diversification, p. 34

dividends, p. 24

economies of scale, p. 34

economies of scope, p. 36

equities, p. 24

Eurobond, p. 31

Eurocurrencies, p. 31

Eurodollars, p. 31

exchanges, p. 25

finance paper, p. 27

financial intermediation, p. 33

financial panic, p. 41

foreign bonds, p. 30

intermediate-term, p. 24

investment bank, p. 24

liabilities, p. 22

liquid, p. 24

liquidity services, p. 34

long-term, p. 24

maturity, p. 24

money market, p. 25

moral hazard, p. 35

mortgage-backed securities, p. 29

mortgages, p. 29

municipal bonds (municipals), p. 30

over-the-counter (OTC) market, p. 25

overnight interest rate, p. 27

portfolio, p. 34

primary market, p. 24

provincial bonds (provincials), p. 30

registered bonds, p. 29

risk, p. 34

risk sharing, p. 34

secondary market, p. 24

short-term, p. 24

term deposit receipts (term notes), p. 27

transaction costs, p. 33

underwriting, p. 24

QUESTIONS

1. If I can buy a car today for $5000 and it is worth $10 000 in extra income next year to me because it enables me to get a job as a travelling salesman, should I take out a loan from Larry the Loan Shark at a 90% interest rate if no one else will give me a loan? Will I be better or worse off as a result of taking out this loan? Can you make a case for legalizing loan-sharking?

2. Some economists suspect that one of the reasons that economies in developing countries grow so slowly is that they do not have well-developed financial markets. Does this argument make sense?

3. Why is a share of Air Canada common stock an asset for its owner and a liability for Air Canada?

4. If you suspect that a company will go bankrupt next year, which would you rather hold, bonds issued by the company or equities issued by the company? Why?

5. "Because corporations do not actually raise any funds in secondary markets, they are less important to the economy than primary markets." Is this statement true, false, or uncertain?

6. For each of the following money market instruments, describe who issues the debt:
   a. Treasury bills
   b. Certificates of deposit
   c. Commercial paper
   d. Repurchase agreement
   e. Overnight funds

7. What is the difference between a *mortgage* and a *mortgage-backed security*?

8. The U.S. economy borrowed heavily from the British in the nineteenth century to build a railroad system. Why did this make both countries better off?

9. A significant number of European banks held large amounts of assets as mortgage-backed securities derived from the U.S. housing market, which crashed after 2006. How does this demonstrate both a benefit and a cost to the internationalization of financial markets?

10. How does risk sharing benefit both financial intermediaries and private investors?

11. How can the adverse selection problem explain why you are more likely to make a loan to a family member than to a stranger?

12. One of the factors contributing to the global financial crisis of 2007–2009 was the widespread issuance of sub-prime mortgages. How does this demonstrate adverse selection?

13. Why do loan sharks worry less about moral hazard in connection with their borrowers than some other lenders do?

14. If you are an employer, what kinds of moral hazard problems might you worry about with your employees?

15. If there were no asymmetry in the information that a borrower and a lender had, could there still be a moral hazard problem?

16. "In a world without information costs and transaction costs, financial intermediaries would not exist." Is this statement true, false, or uncertain? Explain your answer.

17. Why might you be willing to make a loan to your neighbour by putting funds in a savings account earning a 5% interest rate at the bank and having the bank lend her the funds at a 10% interest rate rather than lend her the funds yourself?

18. How do conflicts of interest make the asymmetric information problem worse?

19. How can the provision of several types of financial services by one firm be both beneficial and problematic?

20. If you were going to get a loan to purchase a new car, which financial intermediary would you use: a credit union, a pension fund, or an investment bank?

21. Why would a life insurance company be concerned about the financial stability of major corporations or the health of the housing market?

22. In 2008, as a financial crisis began to unfold in the United States, the FDIC raised the limit on insured losses to bank depositors from $100 000 per account to $250 000 per account. How would this help stabilize the financial system?

APPLIED PROBLEMS

23. Suppose you have just inherited $10 000 and are considering the following options to invest the money to maximize your return:

   Option 1: Put the money in an interest bearing chequing account, which earns 2%. The CDIC insures the account against bank failure.

   Option 2: Invest the money in a corporate bond, with a stated return of 5%, but there is a 10% chance the company could go bankrupt.

   Option 3: Loan the money to one of your friends' roommates, Mike, at an agreed-upon interest rate of 8%, but you believe there is a 7% chance that Mike will leave town without repaying you.

   Option 4: Hold the money in cash and earn zero return.

   a. If you are risk neutral (that is, neither seek out or shy away from risk), which of the four options should you choose to maximize your expected return? (Hint: to calculate the *expected return* of an outcome, multiply the probability of an event occurring by the outcome of that event.)

b. Suppose Option 3 is your only possibility. If you could pay your friend $100 to find out extra information about Mike that would indicate with certainty whether he will leave town without paying or not, would you pay the $100? What does this say about the value of better information about risk?

WEB EXERCISES

1. One of the single best sources of information about financial institutions is the financial data produced by the OSFI. Go to **www.osfi-bsif.gc.ca**, click on "Banks" and then "Financial Data–Banks," and answer the following questions.

   a. What percentage of assets do domestic chartered banks hold in loans? What percentage of assets are held in mortgage loans?

   b. What percentage of assets do trust companies hold in mortgage loans?

   c. What percentage of assets do cooperatives hold in mortgage loans and in consumer loans?

2. The most famous financial market in the world is the New York Stock Exchange. Go to **www.nyse.com**.

   a. What is the mission of the NYSE?

   b. Firms must pay a fee to list their shares for sale on the NYSE. What would be the fee for a firm with five million common shares outstanding?

CHAPTER 3

What Is Money?

LEARNING OBJECTIVES

After studying this chapter you should be able to

1. describe the meaning of the word *money*

2. distinguish among the three primary functions of money: a medium of exchange, a unit of account, and a store of value

3. illustrate how information technology has paved the way for e-money, e-banking, and e-commerce

4. explain money measurement matters

PREVIEW

If you lived in Canada before the creation of the central bank (the Bank of Canada) in 1935, your money might have consisted primarily of gold and silver coins and paper notes, called banknotes, issued by private banks. Today, you use not only coins and dollar bills as means of payment, but also cheques written on accounts held at banks, credit cards, debit cards, stored-value cards, and electronic cash. Money has been different things at different times, but it has always been important to people and to the economy.

To understand the effects of money on the economy, we must understand exactly what money is. In this chapter we develop precise definitions by exploring the functions of money, looking at why and how it promotes economic efficiency, tracing how its forms have evolved over time, and examining how money is currently measured.

Meaning of Money

As the word *money* is used in everyday conversation, it can mean many things, but to economists it has a very specific meaning. To avoid confusion, we must clarify how economists' use of the word *money* differs from conventional usage.

Economists define money as anything that is generally accepted in payment for goods or services or in the repayment of debts. Currency, consisting of dollar bills and coins, clearly fits this definition and is one type of money. When most people talk about money, they're talking about **currency** (paper money and coins). If, for example, someone comes up to you and says, "Your money or your life," you should quickly hand over all your currency rather than ask, "What exactly do you mean by 'money'?"

To define money merely as currency is much too narrow for economists. Because cheques are also accepted as payment for purchases, chequing account deposits are considered money as well. An even broader definition of money is often needed because other items such as savings deposits can in effect function as money if they can be quickly and easily converted into currency or chequing account deposits. As you can see, there is no single, precise definition of money or the money supply, even for economists.

To complicate matters further, the word *money* is frequently used synonymously with *wealth*. When people say, "Joe is rich—he has an awful lot of money," they probably mean that Joe not only has a lot of currency and a high balance in his chequing account but also has stocks, bonds, four cars, three houses, and a yacht. Thus while "currency" is too narrow a definition of money, this other popular usage is much too broad. Economists make a distinction between money in the form of currency, demand deposits, and other items that are used to make purchases, and **wealth**, the total collection of pieces of property that serve to store value. Wealth includes not only money but also other assets such as bonds, common stock, art, land, furniture, cars, and houses.

People also use the word *money* to describe what economists call *income*, as in the sentence "Sheila would be a wonderful catch; she has a good job and earns a lot of money." **Income** is a flow of earnings per unit of time. Money, by contrast, is a stock: it is a certain amount at a given point in time. If someone tells you that he has an income of $1000, you cannot tell whether he earned a lot or a little without knowing whether this $1000 is earned per year, per month, or even per day. But if someone tells you that she has $1000 in her pocket, you know exactly how much this is.

Keep in mind that the money discussed in this book refers to anything that is generally accepted in payment for goods and services or in the repayment of debts and is distinct from income and wealth.

Functions of Money

Whether money is shells or rocks or gold or paper, it has three primary functions in any economy: as a medium of exchange, as a unit of account, and as a store of value. Of the three functions, its function as a medium of exchange is what distinguishes money from other assets such as stocks, bonds, and houses.

Medium of Exchange

In almost all market transactions in our economy, money in the form of currency or cheques is a **medium of exchange**; it is used to pay for goods and services. The use of money as a medium of exchange promotes economic efficiency by eliminating much of the time spent in exchanging goods and services. To see why, let's look at a barter economy, one without money, in which goods and services are exchanged directly for other goods and services.

Take the case of Ellen the Economics Professor, who can do just one thing well: give brilliant economics lectures. In a barter economy, if Ellen wants to eat, she must find a farmer who not only produces the food she likes but also wants to learn economics. As you might expect, this search will be difficult and time-consuming, and Ellen may spend more time looking for such an economics-hungry farmer than she will teaching. It is even possible that she will have to quit lecturing and go into farming herself. Even so, she may still starve to death.

The time spent trying to exchange goods or services is called a transaction cost. In a barter economy, transaction costs are high because people have to satisfy a "double coincidence of wants"—they have to find someone who has a good or service they want and who also wants the good or service they have to offer.

Let's see what happens if we introduce money into Ellen-the-Economics-Professor's world. Ellen can teach anyone who is willing to pay money to hear her lecture. She can then go to any farmer (or his representative at the supermarket) and buy the food she needs with the money she has been paid. The problem of the double coincidence of wants is avoided and Ellen saves a lot of time, which she may spend doing what she does best: teaching.

As this example shows, money promotes economic efficiency by eliminating much of the time spent exchanging goods and services. It also promotes efficiency by allowing people to specialize in what they do best. Money is therefore essential in an economy: it is a lubricant that allows the economy to run more smoothly by lowering transaction costs, thereby encouraging specialization and the division of labour.

The need for money is so strong that almost every society beyond the most primitive invents it. For a commodity to function effectively as money, it has to meet several criteria: (1) It must be easily standardized, making it simple to ascertain its value; (2) it must be widely accepted; (3) it must be divisible so that it is easy to "make change"; (4) it must be easy to carry; and (5) it must not deteriorate quickly. Forms of money that have satisfied these criteria have taken many unusual forms throughout human history, ranging from wampum (strings of beads), used by Native Americans, to tobacco and whiskey, used by the early American colonists, to cigarettes, used in prisoner-of-war camps during World War II. The diversity of forms of money that have been developed over the years is as much a testament to the inventiveness of the human race as the development of tools and language. See, for example, the FYI box Money in a Prisoner-of-War Camp and Modern Prisons.

Unit of Account   The second role of money is to provide a **unit of account**; that is, it is used to measure value in the economy. We measure the value of goods and services in terms of money, just as we measure weight in terms of kilograms or distance in terms of

---

FYI

Money in a Prisoner-of-War Camp and Modern Prisons

An extremely entertaining article on the development of money in a prisoner-of-war camp during World War II is R. A. Radford's "The Economic Organization of a P.O.W. Camp."* He describes his experience with the economy of a German prisoner-of-war camp where cigarettes had become the primary medium of exchange, with most prices expressed in units of cigarettes.

Cigarettes have also been used as currency in prisons in the United States and other countries in much the same way. Recently, however, with the enactment of a ban on smoking (and therefore the prohibition of the cigarette pack) in federal prisons in the United States, a substitute currency has evolved: pouches of mackerel—in prison lingo, "macks."

In particular, inmates in modern federal prisons in the United States get credits in their commissary accounts from prison jobs, which pay about 40 cents per hour, and use these credits to buy goods such as food and toiletries from the commissary. Prisoners are not allowed to possess cash, but they have developed a substitute medium of exchange by using their commissary account credits to buy macks, which they then use as currency. That is, they use macks to pay for gambling debts and to buy goods and services from other prisoners, such as haircuts and shoeshines. Macks are a good substitute for the U.S. dollar because they each cost about US$1.

Economica 12 (November 1945): 189–201.

kilometres. To see why this function is important, let's look again at a barter economy where money does not perform this function. If the economy has only three goods, say, peaches, economics lectures, and movies, then we need to know only three prices to tell us how to exchange one for another: the price of peaches in terms of economics lectures (that is, how many economics lectures you have to pay for a peach), the price of peaches in terms of movies, and the price of economics lectures in terms of movies.

If there were 10 goods, we would need to know 45 prices in order to exchange one good for another; with 100 goods, we would need 4950 prices; and with 1000 goods, 499 500 prices.[1]

Imagine how hard it would be in a barter economy to shop at a supermarket with 1000 different items on its shelves, having to decide whether chicken or fish is a better buy if the price of a kilogram of chicken were quoted as 4 kilograms of butter and the price of a kilogram of fish as 8 kilograms of tomatoes. To make it possible to compare prices, the tag on each item would have to list up to 999 different prices, and the time spent reading them would result in very high transaction costs.

The solution to the problem is to introduce money into the economy and have all prices quoted in terms of units of that money, enabling us to quote the price of economics lectures, peaches, and movies in terms of, say, dollars. If there were only three goods in the economy, this would not be a great advantage over the barter system because we would still need three prices to conduct transactions. But for 10 goods we now need only 10 prices; for 100 goods, 100 prices; and so on. At the 1000-good supermarket, there are now only 1000 prices to look at, not 499 500!

We can see that using money as a unit of account reduces transaction costs in an economy by reducing the number of prices that need to be considered. The benefits of this function of money grow as the economy becomes more complex.

Store of Value

Money also functions as a **store of value**; it is a repository of purchasing power over time. A store of value is used to save purchasing power from the time income is received until the time it is spent. This function of money is useful because most of us do not want to spend our income immediately upon receiving it but rather prefer to wait until we have the time or the desire to shop.

Money is not unique as a store of value; any asset, whether money, stocks, bonds, land, houses, art, or jewellery, can be used to store wealth. Many such assets have advantages over money as a store of value: they often pay the owner a higher interest rate than money, experience price appreciation, and deliver services such as providing a roof over one's head. If these assets are a more desirable store of value than money, why do people hold money at all?

The answer to this question relates to the important economic concept of **liquidity**, the relative ease and speed with which an asset can be converted into a medium of exchange. Liquidity is highly desirable. Money is the most liquid asset of all because it is the medium of exchange; it does not have to be converted into anything else in order to make purchases. Other assets involve transaction costs when they are converted

---

[1]The formula for telling us the number of prices we need when we have N goods is the same formula that tells us the number of pairs when there are N items. It is

$$\frac{N(N-1)}{2}$$

In the case of 10 goods, for example, we would need

$$\frac{10(10-1)}{2} = \frac{90}{2} = 45$$

into money. When you sell your house, for example, you have to pay a brokerage commission (usually 5% to 7% of the sales price), and if you need cash immediately to pay some pressing bills, you might have to settle for a lower price in order to sell the house quickly. The fact that money is the most liquid asset, then, explains why people are willing to hold it even if it is not the most attractive store of value.

How good a store of value money is depends on the price level, because its value is fixed in terms of the price level. A doubling of all prices, for example, means that the value of money has dropped by half; conversely, a halving of all prices means that the value of money has doubled. During a period of high inflation, when the price level is increasing rapidly, money loses value rapidly, and people will be more reluctant to hold their wealth in this form. This is especially true during periods of extreme inflation, known as **hyperinflation**, in which the inflation rate exceeds 50% per month.

Hyperinflation occurred in Germany after World War I, with inflation rates sometimes exceeding 1000% per month. By the end of the hyperinflation in 1923, the price level had risen to more than 30 billion times what it had been just two years before. The quantity of money needed to purchase even the most basic items became excessive. There are stories, for example, that near the end of the hyperinflation, a wheelbarrow of cash would be required to pay for a loaf of bread. Money was losing its value so rapidly that workers were paid and given time off several times during the day to spend their wages before the money became worthless. No one wanted to hold on to money, and so the use of money to carry out transactions declined and barter became more and more dominant. Transaction costs skyrocketed, and as we would expect, output in the economy fell sharply.

Evolution of the Payments System

We can obtain a better picture of the functions of money and the forms it has taken over time by looking at the evolution of the **payments system**, the method of conducting transactions in the economy. The payments system has been evolving over centuries, and with it the form of money. At one point, precious metals such as gold were used as the principal means of payment and were the main form of money. Later, paper assets such as cheques and currency began to be used in the payments system and viewed as money. Where the payments system is heading has an important bearing on how money will be defined in the future.

Commodity Money

To obtain perspective on where the payments system is heading, it is worth exploring how it has evolved. For any object to function as money, it must be universally acceptable; everyone must be willing to take it in payment for goods and services. An object that clearly has value to everyone is a likely candidate to serve as money, and a natural choice is a precious metal such as gold or silver. Money made up of precious metals or another valuable commodity is called **commodity money**, and from ancient times until several hundred years ago commodity money functioned as the medium of exchange in all but the most primitive societies. The problem with a payments system based exclusively on precious metals is that such a form of money is very heavy and is hard to transport from one place to another. Imagine the holes you'd wear in your pockets if you had to buy things only with coins! Indeed, for large purchases such as a house, you'd have to rent a truck to transport the money payment.

Fiat Money

The next development in the payments system was paper currency (pieces of paper that function as a medium of exchange). Initially, paper currency embodied a promise that it was convertible into coins or into a quantity of precious metal. However, currency has evolved into **fiat money**, paper currency decreed by governments as legal tender (meaning that legally it must be accepted as payment for debts) but not convertible into coins or precious metals. Paper currency has the advantage of being much lighter than coins or precious metals, but it can be accepted as a medium of exchange only if there is some trust in the authorities who issue it and printing has reached a sufficiently advanced stage that counterfeiting is extremely difficult. Because paper currency has evolved into a legal arrangement, countries can change the currency that they use at will. Indeed, this is what many European countries did when they abandoned their currencies for the euro in 2002.

Major drawbacks of paper currency and coins are that they are easily stolen and can be expensive to transport because of their bulk if there are large amounts. To combat this problem, another step in the evolution of the payments system occurred with the development of modern banking: the invention of cheques.

Cheques

A cheque is an instrument from you to your bank used to transfer money from your account to someone else's account when she deposits the cheque. Cheques allow transactions to take place without the need to carry around large amounts of currency. The introduction of cheques was a major innovation that improved the efficiency of the payments system. Frequently, payments made back and forth cancel each other; without cheques, this would involve the movement of a lot of currency. With cheques, payments that cancel each other can be settled by cancelling the cheques, and no currency need be moved. The use of cheques thus reduces the transportation costs associated with the payments system and improves economic efficiency. Another advantage of cheques is that they can be written for any amount up to the balance in the account, making transactions for large amounts much more easily. Cheques are advantageous in that loss from theft is greatly reduced, and they provide convenient receipts for purchases.

There are, however, two problems with a payments system based on cheques. First, it takes time to get cheques from one place to another, a particularly serious problem if you are paying someone in a different location who needs to be paid quickly. In addition, if you have a chequing account, you know that it usually takes several business days before a bank will allow you to make use of the funds from a cheque you have deposited. If your need for cash is urgent, this feature of paying by cheque can be frustrating. Second, all the paper shuffling required to process cheques is costly.

Electronic Payment

The development of inexpensive computers and the spread of the Internet now make it cheap to pay bills electronically. In the past, you had to pay your bills by mailing a cheque, but now banks provide websites that allow you to log on, make a few clicks, and thereby transmit your payment electronically. Not only do you save the cost of the stamp, but paying bills becomes (almost) a pleasure, requiring little effort. Electronic payment systems provided by banks now even spare you the step of logging on to pay bills. Instead, recurring bills can be automatically deducted from your bank account. Estimated cost savings when a bill is paid electronically rather than by cheque exceed one dollar. Electronic payment is thus becoming far more common in Canada and the United States.

E-Money

Electronic payment technology can not only substitute for cheques, but can substitute for cash, as well, in the form of **electronic money** (or **e-money**), money that exists only in electronic form. The first form of e-money was the debit card. Debit cards, which look like credit cards, enable customers to purchase goods and services by electronically transferring funds directly from their bank accounts to a merchant's account. Debit cards are used in many of the same places that accept credit cards and are now often becoming faster to use than cash. At most supermarkets, for example, you can swipe your debit card through the card reader at the checkout station, press some buttons, and the amount of your purchases is deducted from your bank account. Most banks and credit card companies such as Visa and MasterCard issue debit cards, and your ATM card typically can function as a debit card.

A more advanced form of e-money is the stored-value card. The simplest form of stored-value card is purchased for a preset dollar amount that the consumer pays up front, like a prepaid phone card. The more sophisticated stored-value card is known as a **smart card**. It contains a computer chip that allows it to be loaded with digital cash from the owner's bank account whenever needed. In Asian countries such as Japan and South Korea, cellphones now have a smart card feature that raises the expression "pay by phone" to a new level. Smart cards can be loaded from ATMs, personal computers with a smart card reader, or specially equipped telephones.

A third form of electronic money is often referred to as **e-cash**, which is used on the Internet to purchase goods or services. A consumer gets e-cash by setting up an account with a bank that has links to the Internet and then has the e-cash transferred to her PC. When she wants to buy something with e-cash, she surfs to a store on the web and clicks the "buy" option for a particular item, whereupon the e-cash is automatically transferred from her computer to the merchant's computer. The merchant can then have the funds transferred from the consumer's bank account to his before the goods are shipped.

Given the convenience of e-money, you might think that we would move quickly to a cashless society in which all payments are made electronically. However, this hasn't happened, as discussed in the FYI box Are We Headed for a Cashless Society?

FYI

Are We Headed for a Cashless Society?

Predictions of a cashless society have been around for decades, but they have not come to fruition. For example, *Business Week* predicted in 1975 that electronic means of payment "would soon revolutionize the very concept of money itself," only to reverse itself several years later. Pilot projects in recent years with smart cards to convert consumers to the use of e-money have not been a success. Mondex, one of the widely touted, early stored-value cards, launched in Britain in 1995, is used only on a few British university campuses. In Germany and Belgium, millions of people carry bank cards with computer chips embedded in them that enable them to make use of e-money, but very few use them. Why has the movement to a cashless society been so slow in coming?

Although e-money might be more convenient and may be more efficient than a payment system based on paper, several factors work against the disappearance of the paper system. First, it is very expensive to set up the computer, card reader, and telecommunications networks necessary to make electronic money the dominant form of payment.

Second, electronic means of payment raise security and privacy concerns. We often hear media reports that an unauthorized hacker has been able to access a computer database and to alter information stored there. Because this is not an uncommon occurrence, unscrupulous persons might be able to access bank accounts in electronic payment systems and steal funds by moving them from someone else's accounts into their own. The prevention of this type of fraud is no easy task, and a whole new field of computer science has developed to cope with security issues. A further concern is that the use of electronic means of payment leaves an electronic trail that contains a large amount of personal data on buying habits. There are worries that government, employers, and marketers might be able to access these data, thereby encroaching on our privacy.

The conclusion from this discussion is that, although the use of e-money will surely increase in the future, to rephrase Mark Twain, "the reports of cash's death are greatly exaggerated."

Measuring Money

The definition of money as anything that is generally accepted in payment for goods and services tells us that money is defined by people's behaviour. What makes an asset money is that people believe it will be accepted by others when making payment. As we have seen, many different assets have performed this role over the centuries, ranging from gold to paper currency to chequing accounts. For that reason, this behavioural definition does not tell us exactly what assets in our economy should be considered money. To measure money, we need a precise definition that tells us exactly what assets should be included.

The Bank of Canada's Monetary Aggregates

The Bank of Canada (the Bank), the central banking authority responsible for monetary policy in Canada, has conducted many studies on how to measure money. The problem of measuring money has become especially crucial because extensive financial innovation has produced new types of assets that might properly belong in a measure of money.

Since 1980, the Bank of Canada has modified its measures of money several times. More recently, financial innovation and the removal of reserve requirements have made it difficult to distinguish between demand and notice deposits and prompted the Bank of Canada to terminate a number of money aggregate time series and replace them with alternative series that do not rely on the distinction between demand and notice deposits. Moreover, the new measures include private-sector **float** (funds in transit between the time a cheque is deposited and the time the payment is settled) because of the declining importance of float. Recently, the Bank of Canada settled on the following measures of the money supply, which are also referred to as **monetary aggregates** (also shown in Table 3-1).

THE M1+ AND M1++ DEFINITIONS OF THE MONEY SUPPLY   Panel (a) of Figure 3-1 illustrates the narrow definitions of the money supply in Canada. The narrowest definition is called **M1+**. It includes

1. *Currency,* which is all the paper money and coins that are in circulation, where "in circulation" means not held by banks or the government. Surprisingly, there is close to $1500 cash in the hands of each person in Canada and more than US$2000 in the hands of each person in the United States (see the FYI box Where Are All the Dollars?).
2. The value of all chequable deposits at chartered banks, trust and mortgage loans companies (TMLs), and credit unions and *caisses populaires* (CUCPs).

These assets are all extremely liquid because they can be turned into cash quickly at very little cost. A broader definition of the money supply is **M1++**. As panel (a) of Figure 3-1 shows, M1++ includes everything that is in M1+, plus all nonchequable deposits at chartered banks, TMLs, and CUCPs.

THE M2, M2+, AND M2++ DEFINITIONS OF THE MONEY SUPPLY   As panel (b) of Figure 3-1 shows, the **M2** monetary aggregate includes currency, personal deposits at chartered banks, non-personal demand and notice deposits at chartered banks, and fixed-term deposits. The **M2+** aggregate includes everything that is in M2, plus deposits at TMLs, deposits at CUCPs, life insurance company individual annuities, personal deposits at government-owned savings institutions, and money market mutual funds. The **M2++** is the broadest definition of the money supply in Canada and includes everything that is in M2+, plus Canada Savings Bonds and other retail debt instruments and non-money market mutual funds.

TABLE 3-1   Measures of Monetary Aggregates and Their Components

Asset	M1+	M1++	M2	M2+	M2++	M3
Currency outside banks	✓	✓	✓	✓	✓	✓
Personal deposits at chartered banks			✓	✓	✓	✓
Non-personal demand and notice deposits at chartered banks			✓	✓	✓	✓
Fixed-term deposits			✓	✓	✓	✓
Deposits at trust and mortgage loan companies (TMLs)				✓	✓	
Deposits at credit unions and *caisses populaires* (CUCPs)				✓	✓	
Life insurance company individual annuities				✓	✓	
Personal deposits at government-owned savings institutions				✓	✓	
Money market mutual funds				✓	✓	
Canada Savings Bonds and other retail instruments					✓	
Non-money market mutual funds					✓	
All chequable deposits at chartered banks, TMLs, and CUCPs	✓	✓				
All nonchequable deposits at chartered banks, TMLs, and CUCPs		✓				
Non-personal term deposits at chartered banks						✓
Foreign currency deposits of residents at chartered banks						✓

Notes: Monetary aggregates exclude interbank deposits and include continuity adjustments. In January 2007, the monetary aggregates were redefined to reflect (i) the elimination of demand deposits and (ii) the inclusion of private-sector float.

FIGURE 3-1 Definitions of the Money Supply

(a) Components of M1+ and M1++

Currency outside banks

All chequable deposits at chartered banks
Deposits at trust and mortgage loan companies (TMLs)
Deposits at credit unions and *caisses populaires* (CUCPs)

M1+

All nonchequable deposits at chartered banks, TMLs, and CUCPs

M1++

(b) Components of M2, M2+, and M2++

Currency outside banks

Personal deposits at chartered banks
Non-personal demand and notice deposits at chartered banks
Fixed-term deposits

M2

Deposits at trust and mortgage loan companies (TMLs)
Deposits at credit unions and *caisses populaires* (CUCPs)
Life insurance company individual annuities
Personal deposits at government-owned savings institutions
Money market mutual funds

M2+

Canada Savings Bonds and other retail instruments
Non-money market mutual funds

M2++

(c) Components of M3

Currency outside banks

Personal deposits at chartered banks
Non-personal demand and notice deposits at chartered banks
Fixed-term deposits

M2

Non-personal term deposits at chartered banks
Foreign currency deposits of residents at chartered banks

M3

THE M3 DEFINITION OF THE MONEY SUPPLY   Another definition of the money supply is called **M3**. As panel (c) of Figure 3-1 shows, M3 includes everything that is in M2, plus non-personal term deposits at chartered banks and foreign currency deposits of residents at chartered banks. The non-personal term deposits are held by provincial and municipal governments, corporations, and institutions, and also include deposits held by one bank with another, known as interbank deposits. The foreign currency deposits are mostly denominated in U.S. dollars.

FYI

Where Are All the Dollars?

The close to $1500 currency per person in Canada and over US$2000 of U.S. currency per person in the United States are surprisingly large numbers. Currency is bulky, can be easily stolen, and pays no interest, so it doesn't make sense for most of us to hold a lot of it. Do you know anyone who carries $1500 in their pockets? We have a puzzle: where are all these dollars and who is holding them?

One group that holds a lot of dollars is criminals. If you were engaged in illegal activity, you would not conduct your transactions with cheques because they are traceable and therefore a potentially powerful piece of evidence against you. This is why Tony Soprano had so much cash in his backyard.

Some businesses also like to hold a lot of cash because if they operate as a cash business, which makes their transactions less traceable, they can avoid declaring income on which they would have to pay taxes.

The other group that holds Canadian and (to a larger extent) U.S. dollars is foreigners. In many countries, people do not trust their own currency because they often experience high inflation, which erodes the value of their currency; these people hold dollars as a hedge against this inflation risk. Lack of trust in the ruble, for example, has led Russians to hold enormous amounts of U.S. dollars. In fact, over half the quantity of U.S. dollars are held abroad.

Notice that the M2 and M3 monetary aggregates do not include deposits with trust and mortgage loan companies and credit unions and *caisses populaires*.

Because we cannot be sure which of the monetary aggregates is the true measure of money, it is logical to wonder if their movements closely parallel one another. If they do, then using one monetary aggregate to predict future economic performance and to conduct policy will be the same as using another, and the fact that we are not sure of the appropriate definition of money for a given policy decision is not too costly. However, if the monetary aggregates do not move together, then what one monetary aggregate tells us is happening to the money supply might be quite different from what another monetary aggregate would tell us. The conflicting stories might present a confusing picture that would make it hard for policymakers to decide on the right course of action.

Figure 3-2 plots the growth rates of M2, M1++, and M2++ from 1969 to 2012. The growth rates of these three aggregates do tend to move together. Yet some glaring discrepancies exist in the movements of these aggregates. The average growth rate of money in the 1970s was 14.2% according to M2, 11.9% according to M1++,

FIGURE 3-2 Growth Rates of M2, M1++, and M2++, 1969–2012

Timing of the rise and fall of growth rates is roughly similar. There are, however, periods when they move in opposite directions, providing conflicting recommendations about the course of monetary policy.

Source: Statistics Canada CANSIM II Series V41552796, V37152, V41552801.

and 15% according to M2++. The average monetary growth rate in the 1990s was 3.6% according to M2, 2.7% according to M1++, and 6.6% according to M2++. Thus, the different measures of money tell a very different story about the course of monetary policy.

From the data in Figure 3-2, you can see that obtaining a single precise, correct measure of money does seem to matter and that it does make a difference which monetary aggregate policymakers and economists choose as the true measure of money.

Money as a Weighted Aggregate

The measures of the money supply listed in Table 3-1 make black-and-white decisions about whether a given asset is money by including it or excluding it. In addition, these measures are simple-sum indices in which all monetary components are assigned a constant and equal (unitary) weight. This index is M in

$$M = x_1 + x_2 + \ldots + x_n$$

where x_1 is one of the n monetary components of the monetary aggregate M. This summation index implies that all monetary components contribute equally to the money total and it views all components as dollar-for-dollar perfect substitutes. Such an index, there is no question, represents an index of the stock of nominal monetary wealth, but cannot, in general, represent a valid structural economic variable for the services of the quantity of money.

Over the years, there has been a steady stream of attempts at properly weighting monetary components within a simple-sum aggregate. With no theory, however, any weighting scheme is questionable. Recently, attention has been focused on the gains that can be achieved by a rigorous use of microeconomic theory, aggregation theory, and index number theory. This new approach to monetary aggregation led to the construction of weighted monetary aggregates.[2] These aggregates represent a viable and theoretically appropriate alternative to the simple-sum aggregates. Moreover, recent research indicates that these new measures of money seem to predict inflation and the business cycle somewhat better than more conventional measures.[3]

---

[2]William Barnett, Douglas Fisher, and Apostolos Serletis, "Consumer Theory and the Demand for Money," in *Journal of Economic Literature* 30 (1992): 2086–2119, provide a state-of-the-art survey of this literature. See also William Barnett and Apostolos Serletis, *The Theory of Monetary Aggregation* (Amsterdam: North-Holland, 2000), and Apostolos Serletis, *The Demand for Money: Theoretical and Empirical Approaches,* 2nd edition (Springer, 2007).

[3]See, for example, Apostolos Serletis and Terence E. Molik, "Monetary Aggregates and Monetary Policy," in *Money, Monetary Policy, and Transmission Mechanisms* (Ottawa: Bank of Canada, 2000): 103–135.

MyEconLab MyEconLab is an online homework and tutorial system that puts you in control of your own learning with study and practice tools directly correlated to this chapter's content. Visit MyEconLab to explore the following resources:

- The Questions and Applied Problems are all available in the Study Plan on MyEconLab for further practice. You will also find the answers to all of the Questions and Applied Problems in the Student Resources section of your MyEconLab.

- CANSIM data are available for relevant CANSIM questions in the Student Resources section of your MyEconLab.

MyEconLab also features Additional Readings, Videos, Glossary Flashcards, Audio Chapter Summaries, Economics News Feeds, Animations, and many additional tools to help you master key concepts from the text.

((• SUMMARY

MyEconLab
Audio Summary

1. To economists, the word *money* has a different meaning from *income* or *wealth*. Money is anything that is generally accepted as payment for goods or services or in the repayment of debts.

2. Money serves three primary functions: as a medium of exchange, as a unit of account, and as a store of value. Money as a medium of exchange avoids the problem of double coincidence of wants that arises in a barter economy, lowers

transaction costs, and encourages specialization and the division of labour. Money as a unit of account reduces the number of prices needed in the economy, which also reduces transaction costs. Money also functions as a store of value but performs this role poorly if it is rapidly losing value due to inflation.

3. The payments system has evolved over time. Until several hundred years ago, the payments system in all but the most primitive societies was based primarily on precious metals. The introduction of paper currency lowered the cost of transporting money. The next major advance was the introduction of cheques, which lowered transaction costs still further. We are currently moving toward an electronic payments system in which paper is eliminated and all transactions are handled by computers. Despite the potential efficiency of such a system, obstacles are slowing the movement to the chequeless society and the development of new forms of electronic money.

4. The Bank of Canada has defined six different measures of the money supply—M1+, M1++, M2, M2+, M2++, and M3. These measures are not equivalent and do not always move together, so they cannot be used interchangeably by policymakers. Obtaining the precise, correct measure of money does seem to matter and has implications for the conduct of monetary policy.

KEY TERMS

commodity money, p. 50

currency, p. 46

e-cash, p. 52

electronic money (e-money), p. 51

fiat money, p. 50

float, p. 53

hyperinflation, p. 50

income, p. 47

liquidity, p. 49

M1+, p. 53

M1++, p. 53

M2, p. 53

M2+, p. 53

M2++, p. 53

M3, p. 55

medium of exchange, p. 47

monetary aggregates, p. 53

payments system, p. 50

smart card, p. 52

store of value, p. 49

unit of account, p. 48

wealth, p. 47

QUESTIONS

1. Why is simply counting currency an inadequate measure of money?

2. In prison, cigarettes are sometimes used among inmates as a form of payment. How is it possible for cigarettes to solve the "double coincidence of wants" problem, even if a prisoner does not smoke?

3. There are three goods produced in an economy by three individuals:

Good	Producer
Apples	Orchard owner
Bananas	Banana grower
Chocolate	Chocolatier

   If the orchard owner likes only bananas, the banana grower likes only chocolate, and the chocolatier likes only apples, will any trade between these three persons take place in a barter economy? How will introducing money into the economy benefit these three producers?

4. Why did cavemen not need money?

5. Most of the time it is quite difficult to separate the three functions of money. Money performs its three functions at all times, but sometimes we can stress one in particular. For each of the following situations, identify which function of money is emphasized.

   a. Brooke accepts money in exchange for performing her daily tasks at her office, since she knows she can use that money to buy goods and services.

   b. Tim wants to calculate the relative value of oranges and apples, and therefore checks the price per pound of each of these goods quoted in currency units.

   c. Maria is currently pregnant. She expects her expenditures to increase in the future and decides to increase the balance in her savings account.

6. In Brazil, a country that underwent a rapid inflation before 1994, many transactions were conducted in U.S. dollars rather than in reals, the domestic currency. Why?

7. Was money a better store of value in Canada in the 1950s than it was in the 1970s? Why or why not? In which period would you have been more willing to hold money?

8. Why have some economists described money during a hyperinflation as a "hot potato" that is quickly passed from one person to another?

9. Why were people in Canada in the nineteenth century sometimes willing to be paid by cheque rather than with gold, even though they knew that there was a possibility that the cheque might bounce?

10. In ancient Greece, why was gold a more likely candidate than wine for use as money?

11. If you use an online payment system such as PayPal to purchase goods or services on the Internet, does this affect the M1+ money supply, M2+ money supply, both, or neither? Explain.

12. Rank the following assets from most liquid to least liquid:
    a. Chequing account deposits
    b. Houses
    c. Currency
    d. Automobile
    e. Savings deposits
    f. Common stock

13. Which of the Bank of Canada's measures of the monetary aggregates—M2+ or M2—is composed of the most liquid assets? Which is the largest measure?

14. It is not unusual to find a business that displays a sign "no personal cheques, please." Based on this observation, comment on the relative degree of liquidity of a chequing account and currency.

15. For each of the following assets, indicate which of the monetary aggregates (M1+ and M2+) includes them:
    a. Currency
    b. Money market mutual funds
    c. Canada Savings Bonds
    d. Chequable deposits

16. Assume that you are interested in earning some return on idle balances you usually keep in your chequing account and decide to buy some money market mutual funds shares by writing a cheque. Comment on the effect of your action (everything else the same) on M1+ and M2+.

17. In a weighted monetary aggregate, which of the following assets would probably receive the highest weights? Which would receive the lowest weights?
    a. Currency
    b. Savings account deposits
    c. Foreign currency deposits
    d. Canada Savings Bonds

18. Suppose that a researcher discovers that a measure of the total amount of debt in the Canadian economy over the past 20 years was a better predictor of inflation and the business cycle than M1+ or M2. Does this discovery mean that we should define money as equal to the total amount of debt in the economy?

APPLIED PROBLEMS

19. Look up the M1+, M1++, M2, M2+, M2++, and M3 numbers in the Bank of Canada Banking and Financial Statistics for the most recent one-year period. Have their growth rates been similar? What implications do their growth rates have for the conduct of monetary policy?

20. Which of the Bank of Canada's measures of the monetary aggregates, M1+, M1++, M2, M2+, M2++, or M3, is composed of the most liquid assets? Which is the largest measure?

CANSIM Questions

21. Go to the CANSIM data available in the Student Resources section of your MyEconLab website and download monthly data since 1970 on the M2 (gross) monetary aggregate (series V41552796).
    a. What is the average money growth rate over the entire period?
    b. Calculate the average monetary growth rate and its standard deviation over each of the last four decades.
    c. Which decade had the lowest money growth? The highest?
    d. Which decade had the lowest money growth volatility? The highest?

WEB EXERCISES

1. Go to **www.bankofcanada.ca** and click on "Rates and Statistics" and then "Summary of key monetary policy variables."
    a. What has been the growth rate in M1+, M1++, and M2++ over the last 12 months?
    b. From what you know about the state of the economy, does this seem expansionary or restrictive?

2. Go to **www.bankofcanada.ca** and click on "Monetary Policy." Select one policy on which the Bank of Canada has a written policy. Write a one-paragraph summary of this policy.

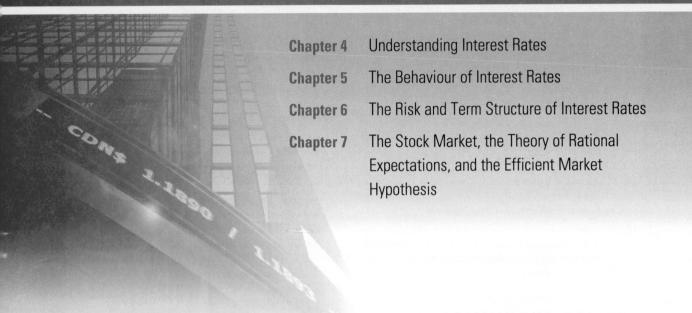

Crisis and Response: Credit Market Turmoil and the Stock Market Crash in October 2008

The financial crisis that started during the summer of 2007 in the United States began snowballing as the value of mortgage-backed securities on financial institutions' balance sheets plummeted. A "flight to quality" drove three-month Treasury bill rates down to almost zero, which had last happened during the Great Depression of the 1930s. Credit spreads—an indicator of risk—shot through the roof, with the U.S. Treasury bill to Eurodollar rate (TED) spread going from around 40 basis points (0.40 percentage points) before the financial crisis started to over 450 basis points in mid-October, the highest value in its history. After earlier sharp declines, the stock market crashed further, with the week beginning on October 6, 2008, showing the worst weekly decline in history.

The recent financial crisis illustrates how volatile financial markets can be. This volatility hit financial consumers directly with difficulty getting loans, falling home values, declining retirement account values, and jobs in jeopardy. How can policy respond to disruptions in financial markets? We begin addressing this question by examining the inner workings of financial markets, particularly interest rate dynamics. Chapter 4 explains what an interest rate is, and the relationship between interest rates, bond prices, and returns. Chapter 5 examines how the overall level of interest rates is determined. In Chapter 6, we extend the analysis of the bond market to explain changes in credit spreads and the relationship of long-term to short-term interest rates. Chapter 7 looks at the role of expectations in the stock market and what drives stock prices.

CHAPTER 4

Understanding Interest Rates

LEARNING OBJECTIVES

After studying this chapter you should be able to

1. detail the present value concept and the meaning of the term *interest rate*

2. discern among the ways of measuring the interest rate: the yield to maturity, the current yield, and the yield on a discount basis

3. illustrate how bond prices and interest rates are negatively related: when interest rates rise, bond prices fall, and vice versa

4. explain the difference between nominal and real interest rates

5. assess the difference between interest rates and rates of return

PREVIEW

Interest rates are among the most closely watched variables in the economy. Their movements are reported almost daily by the news media because they directly affect our everyday lives and have important consequences for the health of the economy. They affect personal decisions such as whether to consume or save, whether to buy a house, and whether to purchase bonds or put funds into a savings account. Interest rates also affect the economic decisions of businesses and households, such as whether to use their funds to invest in new equipment for factories or to save their money in a bank.

Before we can go on with the study of money, banking, and financial markets, we must understand exactly what the phrase *interest rate* means. In this chapter we see that a concept known as the *yield to maturity* is the most accurate measure of interest rates; the yield to maturity is what economists mean when they use the term *interest rate*. We discuss how the yield to maturity is measured. We'll also see that a bond's interest rate does not necessarily indicate how good an investment the bond is because what it earns (its rate of return) does not necessarily equal its interest rate. Finally, we explore the distinction between real interest rates, which are adjusted for inflation, and nominal interest rates, which are not.

Although learning definitions is not always the most exciting of pursuits, it is important to read carefully and understand the concepts presented in this chapter. Not only are they continually used throughout the remainder of this text, but a firm grasp of these terms will give you a clearer understanding of the role that interest rates play in your life as well as in the general economy.

Measuring Interest Rates

Different debt instruments have very different streams of cash payments to the holder (known as **cash flows**) with very different timing. Thus we first need to understand how we can compare the value of one kind of debt instrument with another before we see how interest rates are measured. To do this, we make use of the concept of *present value*.

Present Value

The concept of **present value** (or **present discounted value**) is based on the common-sense notion that a dollar paid to you one year from now is less valuable to you than a dollar paid to you today: this notion is true because you can deposit a dollar in a savings account that earns interest and have more than a dollar in one year. Economists use a more formal definition, as explained in this section.

Let's look at the simplest kind of debt instrument, which we will call a **simple loan**. In this loan, the lender provides the borrower with an amount of funds (called the *principal*) that must be repaid to the lender at the *maturity date*, along with an additional payment for the interest. For example, if you made your friend, Jane, a simple loan of $100 for one year, you would require her to repay the principal of $100 in one year's time along with an additional payment for interest—say, $10. In the case of a simple loan like this one, the interest payment divided by the amount of the loan is a natural and sensible way to measure the interest rate. This measure of the so-called *simple interest rate, i,* is

$$i = \frac{\$10}{\$100} = 0.10 = 10\%$$

If you made this $100 loan, at the end of the year you would have $110, which can be rewritten as

$$\$100 \times (1 + 0.10) = \$110$$

If you then lent out the $110, at the end of the second year you would have

$$\$110 \times (1 + 0.10) = \$121$$

or, equivalently,

$$\$100 \times (1 + 0.10) \times (1 + 0.10) = \$100 \times (1 + 0.10)^2 = \$121$$

Continuing with the loan again, you would have at the end of the third year

$$\$121 \times (1 + 0.10) = \$100 \times (1 + 0.10)^3 = \$133$$

Generalizing, we can see that at the end of n years, your $100 would turn into

$$\$100 (1 + i)^n$$

The amounts you would have at the end of each year by making the $100 loan today can be seen in the following timeline:

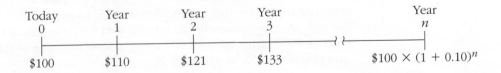

This timeline immediately tells you that you are just as happy having $100 today as having $110 a year from now (of course, as long as you are sure that Jane will pay you back). Or that you are just as happy having $100 today as having $121 two years from now, or $133 three years from now, or $100 \times (1 + 0.10)^n$ n years from now. The timeline tells us that we can also work backward from future amounts to the present: for example, $133 = $100 \times (1 + 0.10)^3$ three years from now is worth $100 today, so that

$$\$100 = \frac{\$133}{(1 + 0.10)^3}$$

APPLICATION

How to Use Your Financial Calculator

The same answer can be obtained by using a financial calculator. Assuming that you have the Texas Instruments calculator (A BA-35 Solar calculator was used for this calculation. Other TI financial calculators available include BAII Plus Professional, BAII Plus, and BA 20 Profit Manager), set it in the "FIN" mode by pressing the "MODE" key until the word "FIN" appears on the screen, and clear it by pushing the "2nd" key and then the "CE/C" key.

1. Enter 133 and push the "FV" key
2. Enter 10 and push the "%*i*" key
3. Enter 3 and push the "N" key
4. Enter 0 and push the "PMT" key
5. You want to solve for the present value, so push the "CPT" key and then the "PV" key

The answer is 99.9249.

The process of calculating today's value of dollars received in the future, as we have done above, is called *discounting the future*. We can generalize this process by writing today's (present) value of $100 as *PV*, writing the future cash flow (payment) of $133 as *CF*, and replacing 0.10 (the 10% interest rate) with *i*. This leads to the following formula:

$$PV = \frac{CF}{(1 + i)^n} \tag{1}$$

Intuitively, what Equation 1 tells us is that if you are promised $1 of cash flow for certain ten years from now, this dollar would not be as valuable to you as $1 is today because if you had the $1 today, you could invest it and end up with more than $1 in 10 years.

The concept of present value is extremely useful, because it allows us to figure out today's value (price) of a credit market instrument at a given simple interest rate, *i*, by just adding up the individual present values of all the future payments received. This information allows us to compare the value of two instruments with very different timing of their payments.

APPLICATION

Simple Present Value

What is the present value of $250 to be paid in two years if the interest rate is 15%?

Solution

The present value would be $189.04. Using Equation 1:

$$PV = \frac{CF}{(1 + i)^n}$$

where

$CF =$ cash flow in two years $= \$250$
$i =$ annual interest rate $\quad= 0.15$
$n =$ number of years $\quad\quad= 2$

Thus

$$PV = \frac{\$250}{(1 + 0.15)^2} = \frac{\$250}{1.3225} = \$189.04$$

To solve using a financial calculator (such as the Texas Instruments BA-35 Solar calculator):

1. Enter 250 and push the "FV" key
2. Enter 15 and push the "%*i*" key
3. Enter 2 and push the "N" key
4. Enter 0 and push the "PMT" key
5. Push the "CPT" key and then the "PV" key

The answer is 189.0359.

APPLICATION

How Much Is That Jackpot Worth?

Assume that you just hit the $20 million jackpot in a lottery, which promises you a payment of $1 million for the next 20 years. You are clearly excited, but have you really won $20 million?

Solution

No, not in the present-value sense. In today's dollars, that $20 million is worth a lot less. If we assume an interest rate of 10% as in the earlier examples, the first payment of $1 million is clearly worth $1 million today, but the next payment next year is only worth $1 million$/(1 + 0.10) = \$909\ 091$, a lot less than $1 million. The following year the payment is worth $1 million$/(1 + 0.10)^2 = \$826\ 446$ in today's dollars, and so on. When you add all these up, they come to $9.4 million. You are still pretty excited (who wouldn't be?), but because you understand the concept of present value, you recognize that you are the victim of false advertising. You didn't really win $20 million, but instead won less than half as much.

Four Types of Credit Market Instruments

In terms of the timing of their cash flow payments, there are four basic types of credit market instruments:

1. A simple loan, which we have already discussed, in which the lender provides the borrower with an amount of funds that must be repaid to the lender at the maturity date along with an additional payment for the interest. Many money market instruments are of this type: for example, commercial loans to businesses.

2. A **fixed-payment loan** (which is also called a **fully amortized loan**) in which the lender provides the borrower with an amount of funds, which must be repaid by making the same payment every period (such as a month) consisting of part of the principal and interest for a set number of years. For example, if you borrowed $1000, a fixed-payment loan might require you to pay $126 every year for 25 years. Installment loans (such as auto loans) and mortgages are frequently of the fixed-payment type.

3. A **coupon bond** pays the owner of the bond a fixed interest payment (coupon payment) every year until the maturity date, when a specified final amount (**face value** or **par value**) is repaid. The coupon payment is so named because the bondholder used to obtain payment by clipping a coupon off the bond and sending it to the bond issuer, who then sent the payment to the holder. Nowadays, it is no longer necessary to send in coupons to receive these payments. A coupon bond with $1000 face value, for example, might pay you a coupon payment of $100 per year for 10 years and at the maturity date repay you the face value amount of $1000. (The face value of a bond is usually in $1000 increments.)

   A coupon bond is identified by three pieces of information. First is the corporation or government agency that issues the bond. Second is the maturity date of the bond. Third is the bond's **coupon rate**, the dollar amount of the yearly coupon payment expressed as a percentage of the face value of the bond. In our example, the coupon bond has a yearly coupon payment of $100 and a face value of $1000. The coupon rate is then $100/$1000 = 0.10, or 10%. Canada bonds and corporate bonds are examples of coupon bonds.

4. A **discount bond** (also called a **zero-coupon bond**) is bought at a price below its face value (at a discount), and the face value is repaid at the maturity date. Unlike a coupon bond, a discount bond does not make any interest payments; it just pays off the face value. For example, a discount bond with a face value of $1000 might be bought for $900 and in a year's time the owner would be repaid the face value of $1000. Canadian government Treasury bills and long-term zero-coupon bonds are examples of discount bonds.

These four types of instruments require payments at different times: simple loans and discount bonds make payment only at their maturity dates, whereas fixed-payment loans and coupon bonds have payments periodically until maturity.

How would you decide which of these instruments provides you with more income? They all seem so different because they make payments at different times. To solve this problem, we use the concept of present value to provide us with a procedure for measuring interest rates on these different types of instruments.

Yield to Maturity   Of the several common ways of calculating interest rates, the most important is the **yield to maturity**, the interest rate that equates the present value of cash flow payments received from a debt instrument with its value today.[1] Because the concept behind the calculation of yield to maturity makes good economic sense, economists consider it the most accurate measure of interest rates.

To understand yield to maturity better, we now look at how it is calculated for the four types of credit market instruments. In all these examples, the key to understanding the calculation of the yield to maturity is equating today's value of the debt instrument with the present value of all of its future cash flows.

SIMPLE LOAN   Using the concept of present value, the yield to maturity on a simple loan is easy to calculate. For the one-year loan we discussed, today's value is $100, and the payments in one year's time would be $110 (the repayment of $100 plus the interest payment of $10). We can use this information to solve for the yield to maturity i by recognizing that the present value of the future payments must equal today's value of a loan.

APPLICATION

Yield to Maturity on a Simple Loan

If Pete borrows $100 from his sister and next year she wants $110 back from him, what is the yield to maturity on this loan?

Solution   The yield to maturity on the loan is 10%.

$$PV = \frac{CF}{(1 + i)^n}$$

where

PV = amount borrowed   = $100
CF = cash flow in one year = $110
n = number of years   = 1

Thus

$$\$100 = \frac{\$110}{(1 + i)}$$

$$(1 + i)\,\$100 = \$110$$

$$(1 + i) = \frac{\$110}{\$100}$$

$$i = 1.10 - 1 = 0.10 = 10\%$$

Today 0		Year 1
$100		$110
	$i = 10\%$	

---

[1]In other contexts, it is also called the *internal rate of return*.

To find the yield to maturity using a financial calculator:

1. Enter 100 and push the "PV" key
2. Enter 110 and push the "FV" key
3. Enter 1 and push the "N" key
4. Enter 0 and push the "PMT" key
5. Push the "CPT" key and then the "%*i*" key

The answer is 10.

This calculation of the yield to maturity should look familiar because it equals the interest payment of $10 divided by the loan amount of $100; that is, it equals the simple interest rate on the loan. An important point to recognize is that *for simple loans, the simple interest rate equals the yield to maturity.* Hence the same term *i* is used to denote both the yield to maturity and the simple interest rate.

FIXED-PAYMENT LOAN   Recall that this type of loan has the same cash flow payment every period throughout the life of the loan. On a fixed-rate mortgage, for example, the borrower makes the same payment to the bank every month until the maturity date, when the loan will be completely paid off. To calculate the yield to maturity for a fixed-payment loan, we follow the same strategy we used for the simple loan—we equate today's value of the loan with its present value. Because the fixed-payment loan involves more than one cash flow payment, the present value of the fixed-payment loan is calculated as the sum of the present values of all payments (using Equation 1).

In the case of our earlier example, the loan is $1000 and the yearly cash flow payment is $126 for the next 25 years. The present value is calculated as follows: at the end of one year there is a $126 payment with a *PV* of $126/(1 + *i*); at the end of two years there is another $126 payment with a *PV* of $126/(1 + *i*)^2; and so on until at the end of the 25th year, the last payment of $126 with a *PV* of $126/(1 + *i*)^{25} is made. Making today's value of the loan ($1000) equal to the sum of the present values of all the yearly payments gives us

$$\$1000 = \frac{\$126}{1 + i} + \frac{\$126}{(1 + i)^2} + \frac{\$126}{(1 + i)^3} + \cdots + \frac{\$126}{(1 + i)^{25}}$$

More generally, for any fixed-payment loan,

$$LV = \frac{FP}{1 + i} + \frac{FP}{(1 + i)^2} + \frac{FP}{(1 + i)^3} + \cdots + \frac{FP}{(1 + i)^n} \tag{2}$$

where

LV = loan value
FP = fixed yearly payment
n = number of years until maturity

For a fixed-payment loan amount, the fixed yearly payment and the number of years until maturity are known quantities, and only the yield to maturity is not. So we can solve this equation for the yield to maturity *i*. Because this calculation is not easy, many pocket calculators have programs that allow you to find *i* given the loan's numbers for

LV, *FP*, and *n*. For example, in the case of the 25-year loan with yearly payments of $126, the yield to maturity that solves Equation 2 is 12%. Real estate brokers always have a pocket calculator that can solve such equations so that they can immediately tell the prospective house buyer exactly what the yearly (or monthly) payments will be if the house purchase is financed by taking out a mortgage.

APPLICATION

Yield to Maturity on a Fixed-Payment Loan

You decide to purchase a new home and need a $100 000 mortgage. You take out a loan from the bank that has an interest rate of 7%. What is the yearly payment to the bank to pay off the loan in 20 years?

Solution

The yearly payment to the bank is $9439.29.

$$LV = \frac{FP}{1+i} + \frac{FP}{(1+i)^2} + \frac{FP}{(1+i)^3} + \cdots + \frac{FP}{(1+i)^n}$$

FP = fixed payment

where

LV = loan value amount = $100 000
i = annual interest rate = 0.07
n = number of years = 20

Thus

$$\$100\,000 = \frac{FP}{1+0.07} + \frac{FP}{(1+0.07)^2} + \frac{FP}{(1+0.07)^3} + \cdots + \frac{FP}{(1+0.07)^{20}}$$

To find the yearly payment for the loan using a financial calculator:

1. Enter 100 000 and push the "PV" key
2. Enter 0 and push the "FV" key
3. Enter 20 and push the "N" key
4. Enter 7 and push the "%*i*" key
5. Push the "CPT" and "PMT" keys

The answer is 9439.29.

COUPON BOND   To calculate the yield to maturity for a coupon bond, follow the same strategy used for the fixed-payment loan: equate today's value of the bond with its present value. Because coupon bonds also have more than one cash flow payment, the present value of the bond is calculated as the sum of the present values of all the coupon payments plus the present value of the final payment of the face value of the bond.

The present value of a $1000-face-value bond with 10 years to maturity and yearly coupon payments of $100 (a 10% coupon rate) can be calculated as follows: at the end of one year, there is a $100 coupon payment with a *PV* of $100/(1 + *i*);

at the end of the second year, there is another $100 coupon payment with a PV of $\$100/(1 + i)^2$; and so on until, at maturity, there is a $100 coupon payment with a PV of $\$100/(1 + i)^{10}$ plus the repayment of the $1000 face value with a PV of $\$1000/(1 + i)^{10}$. Setting today's value of the bond (its current price, denoted by P) equal to the sum of the present values of all the cash flow payments for this bond gives

$$P = \frac{\$100}{1 + i} + \frac{\$100}{(1 + i)^2} + \frac{\$100}{(1 + i)^3} + \cdots + \frac{\$100}{(1 + i)^{10}} + \frac{\$1000}{(1 + i)^{10}}$$

More generally, for any coupon bond,[2]

$$P = \frac{C}{1 + i} + \frac{C}{(1 + i)^2} + \frac{C}{(1 + i)^3} + \cdots + \frac{C}{(1 + i)^n} + \frac{F}{(1 + i)^n} \tag{3}$$

where

P = price of coupon bond
C = yearly coupon payment
F = face value of the bond
n = years to maturity date

In Equation 3, the coupon payment, the face value, the years to maturity, and the price of the bond are known quantities, and only the yield to maturity is not. Hence we can solve this equation for the yield to maturity i. Just as in the case of the fixed-payment loan, this calculation is not easy, so business-oriented pocket calculators have built-in programs that solve this equation for you.

APPLICATION

Yield to Maturity on a Coupon Bond

Find the price of a 10% coupon bond with a face value of $1000, a 12.25% yield to maturity, and eight years to maturity.

Solution

To solve using the Texas Instruments BA-35 Solar calculator:

1. Enter 1000 and push the "FV" key
2. Enter 8 and push the "N" key
3. Enter 12.25 and push the "%i" key
4. Enter 100 and push the "PMT" key
5. Push the "CPT" and "PV" keys

The answer is 889.1977.

---

[2]Most coupon bonds actually make coupon payments on a semi-annual basis rather than once a year as assumed here. The effect on the calculations is only very slight and will be ignored here.

Table 4-1 shows the yields to maturity calculated for several bond prices. Three interesting facts emerge:

1. When the coupon bond is priced at its face value, the yield to maturity equals the coupon rate.

2. The price of a coupon bond and the yield to maturity are negatively related; that is, as the yield to maturity rises, the price of the bond falls. As the yield to maturity falls, the price of the bond rises.

3. The yield to maturity is greater than the coupon rate when the bond price is below its face value.

These three facts are true for any coupon bond and are really not surprising if you think about the reasoning behind the calculation of the yield to maturity. When you put $1000 in a bank account with an interest rate of 10%, you can take out $100 every year and you will be left with the $1000 at the end of 10 years. This is similar to buying the $1000 bond with a 10% coupon rate analyzed in Table 4-1, which pays a $100 coupon payment every year and then repays $1000 at the end of 10 years. If the bond is purchased at the par value of $1000, its yield to maturity must equal 10%, which is also equal to the coupon rate of 10%. The same reasoning applied to any coupon bond demonstrates that if the coupon bond is purchased at its par value, the yield to maturity and the coupon rate must be equal.

It is straightforward to show that the bond price and the yield to maturity are negatively related. As i, the yield to maturity, rises, all denominators in the bond price formula must necessarily rise. Hence a rise in the interest rate as measured by the yield to maturity means that the price of the bond must fall. Another way to explain why the bond price falls when the interest rate rises is that a higher interest rate implies that the future coupon payments and final payment are worth less when discounted back to the present; hence the price of the bond must be lower.

The third fact, that the yield to maturity is greater than the coupon rate when the bond price is below its par value, follows directly from facts one and two. When the yield to maturity equals the coupon rate, then the bond price is at the face value, and when the yield to maturity rises above the coupon rate, the bond price necessarily falls and so must be below the face value of the bond.

There is one special case of a coupon bond that is worth discussing because its yield to maturity is particularly easy to calculate. This bond is called a **consol** or a **perpetuity**; it is a perpetual bond with no maturity date and no repayment of principal that makes fixed coupon payments of C forever. Consols were first sold by the British Treasury during the Napoleonic Wars and are still traded today; they are

TABLE 4-1   Yields to Maturity on a 10% Coupon-Rate Bond Maturing in 10 Years (Face Value = $1000)

Price of Bond ($)	Yield to Maturity (%)
1200	7.13
1100	8.48
1000	10.00
900	11.75
800	13.81

quite rare, however, in Canadian capital markets. The formula in Equation 3 for the price of the consol P simplifies to the following:[3]

$$P_c = \frac{C}{i_c}$$ (4)

where

P_c = price of the perpetuity (consol)
C = yearly payment
i_c = yield to maturity of the perpetuity (consol)

One nice feature of perpetuities is that you can immediately see that as i_c goes up, the price of the bond falls. For example, if a perpetuity pays \$100 per year forever and the interest rate is 10%, its price will be \$1000 = \$100/0.10. If the interest rate rises to 20%, its price will fall to \$500 = \$100/0.20. We can also rewrite this formula as

$$i_c = \frac{C}{P_c}$$ (5)

The formula in Equation 5, which describes the calculation of the yield to maturity for a perpetuity, also provides a useful approximation for the yield to maturity on coupon bonds. When a coupon bond has a long term to maturity (say, 20 years or more), it is very much like a perpetuity, which pays coupon payments forever. This is because the cash flows more than 20 years in the future have such small present discounted values that the value of a long-term coupon bond is very close to the value of a perpetuity with the same coupon rate. Thus i_c in Equation 5 will be very close to the yield to maturity for any long-term bond. For this reason, i_c, the yearly coupon payment divided by the price of the security, has been given the name **current yield** and is frequently used as an approximation to describe interest rates on long-term bonds.

DISCOUNT BOND The yield-to-maturity calculation for a discount bond is similar to that for the simple loan. Let us consider a discount bond such as a one-year Canadian Treasury bill, which pays off a face value of \$1000 in one year's time.

---

[3]The bond price formula for a consol is

$$P = \frac{C}{1 + i} + \frac{C}{(1 + i)^2} + \frac{C}{(1 + i)^3} + \cdots$$

which can be written as

$$P = C(x + x^2 + x^3 + \cdots)$$

in which $x = 1/(1 + i)$. The formula for an infinite sum is

$$1 + x + x^2 + x^3 + \cdots = \frac{1}{1 - x} \text{ for } x < 1$$

and so

$$P = C\left(\frac{1}{1 - x} - 1\right) = C\left(\frac{1}{1 - 1/(1 + i)} - 1\right)$$

which by suitable algebraic manipulation becomes

$$P = C\left(\frac{1 + i}{i} - \frac{i}{i}\right) = \frac{C}{i}$$

APPLICATION

Yield to Maturity on a Perpetuity

What is the yield to maturity on a bond that has a price of $2000 and pays $100 annually forever?

Solution

The yield to maturity would be 5%.

$$i_c = \frac{C}{P_c}$$

where

C = yearly payment   = $100
P_c = price of perpetuity (consol) = $2000

Thus

$$i_c = \frac{\$100}{\$2000}$$

$$i_c = 0.05 = 5\%$$

To solve using the Texas Instruments BA-35 Solar calculator:

1. Enter 2000 and push the "PV" key
2. Enter 0 and push the "FV" key
3. Enter 999 (to approximate an infinite number of payments) and push the "N" key
4. Enter 100 and push the "PMT" key
5. Push the "CPT" and "%i" keys

The answer is 5.

If the current purchase price of this bill is $900, then equating this price to the present value of the $1000 received in one year, using Equation 1 (page 63), gives

$$\$900 = \frac{\$1000}{1 + i}$$

and solving for i,

$$(1 + i) \times \$900 = \$1000$$
$$\$900 + \$900i = \$1000$$
$$\$900i = \$1000 - \$900$$
$$i = \frac{\$1000 - \$900}{\$900} = 0.111 = 11.1\%$$

More generally, for any one-year discount bond, the yield to maturity can be written as

$$i = \frac{F - P}{P} \qquad (6)$$

where

F = face value of the discount bond
P = current price of the discount bond

CHAPTER 4 *Understanding Interest Rates* **73**

In other words, the yield to maturity equals the increase in price over the year, $F - P$, divided by the initial price P. In normal circumstances, investors earn positive returns from holding these securities and so they sell at a discount, meaning that the current price of the bond is below the face value. Therefore, $F - P$ should be positive, and the yield to maturity should be positive as well. However, this is not always the case, as recent extraordinary events in Japan indicate (see the Global box Negative T-Bill Rates? It Can Happen).

An important feature of this equation is that it indicates that for a discount bond, the yield to maturity is negatively related to the current bond price. This is the same conclusion that we reached for a coupon bond. For example, Equation 6 shows that a rise in the bond price from $900 to $950 means that the bond will have a smaller increase in its price at maturity, and the yield to maturity falls from 11.1% to 5.3%. Similarly, a fall in the yield to maturity means that the price of the discount bond has risen.

SUMMARY The concept of present value tells you that a dollar in the future is not as valuable to you as a dollar today because you can earn interest on this dollar. Specifically, a dollar received n years from now is worth only $\$1/(1 + i)^n$ today. The present value of a set of future cash flow payments on a debt instrument equals the sum of the present values of each of the future payments. The yield to maturity for an instrument is the interest rate that equates the present value of the future payments on that instrument to its value today. Because the procedure for calculating yield to maturity is based on sound economic principles, this is the measure that economists think most accurately describes the interest rate.

Our calculations of the yield to maturity for a variety of bonds reveal the important fact that *current bond prices and interest rates are negatively related: when the interest rate rises, the price of the bond falls, and vice versa.*

The Distinction Between Interest Rates and Returns

Many people think that the interest rate on a bond tells them all they need to know about how well off they are as a result of owning it. If Irving the Investor thinks he is better off when he owns a long-term bond yielding a 10% interest rate and the interest rate rises to 20%, he will have a rude awakening: as we will see shortly, if he has to sell the bond, Irving has lost his shirt! How well a person does by holding a bond or any other security over a particular time period is accurately measured by the **return**, or, in more precise terminology, the **rate of return**. The concept of *return* discussed here is extremely important because it is used continually throughout this book and understanding it will make the material presented later in the book easier to follow. For any security, the rate of return is defined as the payments to the owner plus the change in its value, expressed as a fraction of its purchase price. To make this definition clearer, let us see what the return would look like for a $1000-face-value coupon bond with a coupon rate of 10% that is bought for $1000, held for one year, and then sold for $1200. The payments to the owner are the yearly coupon payments of $100, and the change in its value is $1200 – $1000 = $200. Adding these together and expressing them as a fraction of the purchase price of $1000 gives us the one-year holding-period return for this bond:

$$\frac{\$100 + \$200}{\$1000} = \frac{\$300}{\$1000} = 0.30 = 30\%$$

You may have noticed something quite surprising about the return that we have just calculated: it equals 30%, yet as Table 4-1 (page 70) indicates, initially the yield to maturity was only 10%. This demonstrates that ***the return on a bond will not necessarily equal the yield to maturity on that bond.*** We now see that the distinction between interest rate and return can be important, although for many securities the two may be closely related.

More generally, the return on a bond held from time t to time $t + 1$ can be written as

$$RET = \frac{C + P_{t+1} - P_t}{P_t} \tag{7}$$

where

RET = return from holding the bond from time t to time $t + 1$
P_t = price of the bond at time t
P_{t+1} = price of the bond at time $t + 1$
C = coupon payment

APPLICATION

Calculating the Rate of Return

Solution

What would the rate of return be on a bond bought for $1000 and sold one year later for $800? The bond has a face value of $1000 and a coupon rate of 8%.

The rate of return on the bond for holding it one year is −12%.

$$RET = \frac{C + P_{t+1} - P_t}{P_t}$$

where

$$C = \text{coupon payment} = \$1000 \times 0.08 = \$80$$
$$P_{t+1} = \text{price of the bond one year later} = \$800$$
$$P_t = \text{price of the bond today} = \$1000$$

Thus

$$RET = \frac{\$80 + (\$800 - \$1000)}{\$1000} = \frac{-\$120}{\$1000} = -0.12 = -12\%$$

A convenient way to rewrite the return formula in Equation 8 is to recognize that it can be split into two separate terms:

$$RET = \frac{C}{P_t} + \frac{P_{t+1} - P_t}{P_t}$$

The first term is the current yield i_c (the coupon payment over the purchase price):

$$\frac{C}{P_t} = i_c$$

The second term is the **rate of capital gain**, or the change in the bond's price relative to the initial purchase price:

$$\frac{P_{t+1} - P_t}{P_t} = g$$

where g = rate of capital gain. Equation 8 can then be rewritten as

$$RET = i_c + g \tag{8}$$

which shows that the return on a bond is the current yield i_c plus the rate of capital gain g. This rewritten formula illustrates the point we just discovered. Even for a

APPLICATION

Calculating the Rate of Capital Gain

Calculate the rate of capital gain or loss on a 10-year zero-coupon bond for which the interest rate has increased from 10% to 20%. The bond has a face value of $1000.

Solution   The rate of capital gain or loss is −49.7%.

$$g = \frac{P_{t+1} - P_t}{P_t}$$

where

$$P_{t+1} = \text{price of the bond one year from now} = \frac{\$1000}{(1 + 0.20)^9} = \$193.81$$

$$P_t = \text{price of the bond today} = \frac{\$1000}{(1 + 0.10)^{10}} = \$385.54$$

Thus

$$g = \frac{\$193.81 - \$385.54}{\$385.54}$$

$$g = -0.497 = -49.7\%$$

bond for which the current yield i_c is an accurate measure of the yield to maturity, the return can differ substantially from the interest rate. Returns will differ from the interest rate especially if there are sizable fluctuations in the price of the bond that produce substantial capital gains or losses.

To explore this point even further, let's look at what happens to the returns on bonds of different maturities when interest rates rise. Table 4-2 calculates the one-year return using Equation 8 on several 10%-coupon-rate bonds all purchased at par when interest rates on all these bonds rise from 10% to 20%. Several key findings in this table are generally true of all bonds:

- The only bond whose return equals the initial yield to maturity is one whose time to maturity is the same as the holding period (see the last bond in Table 4-2).
- A rise in interest rates is associated with a fall in bond prices, resulting in capital losses on bonds whose terms to maturity are longer than the holding period.
- The more distant a bond's maturity, the greater the size of the percentage price change associated with an interest-rate change.
- The more distant a bond's maturity, the lower the rate of return that occurs as a result of the increase in the interest rate.
- Even though a bond has a substantial initial interest rate, its return can turn out to be negative if interest rates rise.

At first it frequently puzzles students (as it puzzles poor Irving the Investor) that a rise in interest rates can mean that a bond has been a poor investment. The trick to understanding this is to recognize that a rise in the interest rate means that the price of a bond has fallen. A rise in interest rates therefore means that a capital loss has occurred, and if this loss is large enough, the bond can be a poor investment indeed. For example, we see in Table 4-2 that the bond that has 30 years to maturity when purchased has a capital loss of 49.7% when the interest rate rises from 10% to 20%. This loss is so large that it exceeds the current yield of 10%, resulting in a negative return (loss) of 39.7%. If Irving does not sell the bond, his capital loss is often referred to as a "paper loss." This is a loss nonetheless, because if he had not bought

TABLE 4-2	One-Year Returns on Different-Maturity 10%-Coupon-Rate Bonds When Interest Rates Rise from 10% to 20%				
(1) Years to Maturity When Bond Is Purchased	**(2)** Initial Current Yield (%)	**(3)** Initial Price ($)	**(4)** Price Next Year* ($)	**(5)** Rate of Capital Gain (%)	**(6)** Rate of Return (2 + 5) (%)
30	10	1000	503	−49.7	−39.7
20	10	1000	516	−48.4	−38.4
10	10	1000	597	−40.3	−30.3
5	10	1000	741	−25.9	−15.9
2	10	1000	917	−8.3	+1.7
1	10	1000	1000	0.0	+10.0

*Calculated with a financial calculator using Equation 3.

this bond and had instead put his money in the bank, he would now be able to buy more bonds at their lower price than he presently owns.

Maturity and the Volatility of Bond Returns: Interest-Rate Risk

The finding that the prices of longer-maturity bonds respond more dramatically to changes in interest rates helps explain an important fact about the behaviour of bond markets: *prices and returns for long-term bonds are more volatile than those for shorter-term bonds*. Price changes of +20% and –20% within a year, with corresponding variations in returns, are common for bonds more than 20 years away from maturity.

We now see that changes in interest rates make investments in long-term bonds quite risky. Indeed, the riskiness of an asset's return that results from interest-rate changes is so important that it has been given a special name, **interest-rate risk**.[4] Dealing with interest-rate risk is a major concern of managers of financial institutions and investors, as we will see in later chapters.

Although long-term debt instruments have substantial interest-rate risk, short-term debt instruments do not. Indeed, bonds with a maturity that is as short as the holding period have no interest-rate risk.[5] We see this for the coupon bond at the bottom of Table 4-2, which has no uncertainty about the rate of return because it equals the yield to maturity, which is known at the time the bond is purchased. The key to understanding why there is no interest-rate risk for any bond whose time to maturity matches the holding period is to recognize that (in this case) the price at the end of the holding period is already fixed at the face value. The change in interest rates can then have no effect on the price at the end of the holding period for these bonds, and the return will therefore be equal to the yield to maturity known at the time the bond is purchased.[6]

---

[4]Interest-rate risk can be quantitatively measured using the concept of duration. This concept and how it is calculated are discussed in an appendix to this chapter, which can be found on this book's MyEconLab.

[5]The statement that there is no interest-rate risk for any bond whose time to maturity matches the holding period is literally true only for discount bonds and zero-coupon bonds that make no intermediate cash payments before the holding period is over. A coupon bond that makes an intermediate cash payment before the holding period is over requires that this payment be reinvested. Because the interest rate at which this payment can be reinvested is uncertain, there is some uncertainty about the return on this coupon bond even when the time to maturity equals the holding period. However, the riskiness of the return on a coupon bond from reinvesting the coupon payments is typically quite small, and so the basic point that a coupon bond with a time to maturity equalling the holding period has very little risk still holds true.

[6]In the text, we are assuming that all holding periods are short and equal to the maturity on short-term bonds and are thus not subject to interest-rate risk. However, if an investor's holding period is longer than the term to maturity of the bond, the investor is exposed to a type of interest-rate risk called *reinvestment risk*. Reinvestment risk occurs because the proceeds from the short-term bond need to be reinvested at a future interest rate that is uncertain.

To understand reinvestment risk, suppose that Irving the Investor has a holding period of two years and decides to purchase a $1000 one-year bond at face value and will then purchase another one at the end of the first year. If the initial interest rate is 10%, Irving will have $1100 at the end of the year. If the interest rate rises to 20%, as in Table 4-2, Irving will find that buying $1100 worth of another one-year bond will leave him at the end of the second year with $1100 × (1 + 0.20) = $1320. Thus Irving's two-year return will be ($1320 – $1000)/$1000 = 0.32 = 32%, which equals 14.9% at an annual rate. In this case, Irving has earned more by buying the one-year bonds than if he had initially purchased the two-year bond with an interest rate of 10%. Thus when Irving has a holding period that is longer than the term to maturity of the bonds he purchases, he benefits from a rise in interest rates. Conversely, if interest rates fall to 5%, Irving will have only $1155 at the end of two years: $1100 × (1 + 0.05). Thus his two-year return will be ($1155 – $1000)/$1000 = 0.155 = 15.5%, which is 7.5% at an annual rate. With a holding period greater than the term to maturity of the bond, Irving now loses from a fall in interest rates.

We have thus seen that when the holding period is longer than the term to maturity of a bond, the return is uncertain because the future interest rate when reinvestment occurs is also uncertain—in short, there is reinvestment risk. We also see that if the holding period is longer than the term to maturity of the bond, the investor benefits from a rise in interest rates and is hurt by a fall in interest rates.

Summary   The return on a bond, which tells you how good an investment it has been over the holding period, is equal to the yield to maturity in only one special case: when the holding period and the maturity of the bond are identical. Bonds whose term to maturity is longer than the holding period are subject to interest-rate risk: changes in interest rates lead to capital gains and losses that produce substantial differences between the return and the yield to maturity known at the time the bond is purchased. Interest-rate risk is especially important for long-term bonds, where the capital gains and losses can be substantial. This is why long-term bonds are not considered to be safe assets with a sure return over short holding periods.

The Distinction Between Real and Nominal Interest Rates

So far in our discussion of interest rates, we have ignored the effects of inflation on the cost of borrowing. What we have up to now been calling the interest rate makes no allowance for inflation, and it is more precisely referred to as the **nominal interest rate**. We distinguish it from the **real interest rate**, the interest rate that is adjusted by subtracting expected changes in the price level (inflation) so that it more accurately reflects the true cost of borrowing. This interest rate is more precisely referred to as the *ex ante real interest rate* because it is adjusted for *expected* changes in the price level. The *ex ante* real interest rate is most important to economic decisions, and typically it is what economists mean when they make reference to the "real" interest rate. The interest rate that is adjusted for *actual* changes in the price level is called the *ex post real interest rate*. It describes how well a lender has done in real terms after the fact.

The real interest rate is more accurately defined by the *Fisher equation*, named for Irving Fisher, one of the great monetary economists of the twentieth century. The Fisher equation states that the nominal interest rate i equals the real interest rate r plus the expected rate of inflation π^e.[7]

$$i = r + \pi^e \tag{9}$$

Rearranging terms, we find that the real interest rate equals the nominal interest rate minus the expected inflation rate:

$$r = i - \pi^e \tag{10}$$

To see why this definition makes sense, let us first consider a situation in which you have made a one-year simple loan with a 5% interest rate ($i = 5\%$) and you expect the price level to rise by 3% over the course of the year ($\pi^e = 3\%$). As a result of making the loan, at the end of the year you expect to have 2% more in **real terms**,

---

[7]A more precise formulation of the Fisher equation is

$$i = r + \pi^e + (r \times \pi^e)$$

because

$$1 + i = (1 + r)(1 + \pi^e) = 1 + r + \pi^e + (r \times \pi^e)$$

and subtracting 1 from both sides gives us the first equation. For small values of r and π^e, the term $r \times \pi^e$ is so small that we ignore it, as in the text.

that is, in terms of real goods and services you can buy. In this case, the interest rate you expect to earn in terms of real goods and services is 2%; that is,

$$r = 5\% - 3\% = 2\%$$

as indicated by the Fisher equation.

APPLICATION

Calculating Real Interest Rates

What is the real interest rate if the nominal interest rate is 8% and the expected inflation rate is 10% over the course of a year?

Solution

The real interest rate is –2%. Although you will be receiving 8% more dollars at the end of the year, you will be paying 10% more for goods. The result is that you will be able to buy 2% fewer goods at the end of the year, and you will be 2% worse off in real terms.

$$r = i - \pi^e$$

where

$$i = \text{nominal interest rate} = 0.08$$
$$\pi^e = \text{expected inflation rate} = 0.10$$

Thus

$$r = 0.08 - 0.10 = -0.02 = -2\%$$

As a lender, you are clearly less eager to make a loan in this case because in terms of real goods and services you have actually earned a negative interest rate of 2%. By contrast, as the borrower, you fare quite well because at the end of the year, the amounts you will have to pay back will be worth 2% less in terms of goods and services—you as the borrower will be ahead by 2% in real terms. *When the real interest rate is low, there are greater incentives to borrow and fewer incentives to lend.*

A similar distinction can be made between nominal returns and real returns. Nominal returns, which do not allow for inflation, are what we have been referring to as simply "returns." When inflation is subtracted from a nominal return, we have the real return, which indicates the amount of extra goods and services that can be purchased as a result of holding the security.

The distinction between real and nominal interest rates is important because the real interest rate, which reflects the real cost of borrowing, is likely to be a better indicator of the incentives to borrow and lend. It appears to be a better guide to how people will be affected by what is happening in credit markets. Figure 4-1, which presents estimates from 1953 to 2011 of the real and nominal interest rates on three-month U.S. Treasury bills, shows us that nominal and real rates often do not move together. (This is also true for nominal and real interest rates in Canada and the rest of the world.) By the standard of nominal interest rates, you would have thought that credit market conditions were tight in this period because it was expensive to borrow. However, the estimates of the real

FIGURE 4-1 Real and Nominal Interest Rates (Three-Month Treasury Bills), 1953–2011

Sources: Nominal rates from www.federalreserve.gov/releases/H15. The real rate is constructed using the procedure outlined in Frederic S. Mishkin, "The Real Interest Rate: An Empirical Investigation," *Carnegie-Rochester Conference Series on Public Policy* 15 (1981): 151–200. These procedures involve estimating expected inflation as a function of past interest rates, inflation, and time trends and then subtracting the expected inflation measure from the nominal interest rate.

rates indicate that you would have been mistaken. In real terms, the cost of borrowing was actually quite low.[8]

Formerly, real interest rates in Canada were not observable; only nominal rates were reported. This all changed on December 10, 1991, when the government of Canada began to issue **indexed bonds**, whose interest and principal payments are adjusted for changes in the price level (see the FYI box With Real Return Bonds, Real Interest Rates Have Become Observable in Canada).

---

[8]Because most interest income in Canada is subject to income taxes, the true earnings in real terms from holding a debt instrument are not reflected by the real interest rate defined by the Fisher equation but rather by the *after-tax real interest rate*, which equals the nominal interest rate *after income tax payments have been subtracted*, minus the expected inflation rate. For a person facing a 30% tax rate, the after-tax interest rate earned on a bond yielding 10% is only 7% because 30% of the interest income must be paid to Revenue Canada. Thus the after-tax real interest rate on this bond when expected inflation is 5% equals 2% (= 7% − 5%). More generally, the after-tax real interest rate can be expressed as

$$i(1 - \tau) - \pi^e$$

where τ = the income tax rate.

This formula for the after-tax real interest rate also provides a better measure of the effective cost of borrowing for many corporations in Canada because in calculating income taxes, they can deduct interest payments on loans from their income. Thus if you face a 30% tax rate and take out a business loan with a 10% interest rate, you are able to deduct the 10% interest payment and thus lower your business taxes by 30% of this amount. Your after-tax nominal cost of borrowing is then 7% (10% minus 30% of the 10% interest payment), and when the expected inflation rate is 5%, the effective cost of borrowing in real terms is again 2% (= 7% − 5%).

As the example (and the formula) indicates, after-tax real interest rates are always below the real interest rate defined by the Fisher equation. For a further discussion of measures of after-tax real interest rates, see Frederic S. Mishkin, "The Real Interest Rate: An Empirical Investigation," *Carnegie-Rochester Conference Series on Public Policy* 15 (1981): 151–200.

FYI

With Real Return Bonds, Real Interest Rates Have Become Observable in Canada

On December 10, 1991, the Canadian government issued coupon bonds whose coupon payment and face value are indexed to the Consumer Price Index (CPI). These securities are known as *Real Return Bonds* and are designed to provide investors with a known real return if held to maturity. Other countries such as the United Kingdom, Australia, and Sweden also issue similar indexed securities, and the U.S. Treasury joined the group in January 1997, by issuing TIPS (Treasury Inflation Protection Securities).

These indexed securities have successfully acquired a niche in the bond market, enabling governments to raise more funds. In addition, because their interest and principal payments are adjusted for changes in the price level, the interest rate on these bonds provides a direct measure of a real interest rate. These indexed bonds are very useful to policymakers, especially monetary policymakers, because by subtracting their interest rate from a nominal interest rate on a nonindexed bond, they generate more insight into expected inflation, a valuable piece of information.

For example, on December 22, 2011, the interest rate on long-term Canada bonds was 2.5%, while that on the long-term Real Return Bond was 0.48%. Thus, the implied expected inflation rate, derived from the difference between these two rates, was 2.02%. The private sector finds the information provided by Real Return Bonds very useful: many financial institutions routinely publish the expected Canadian inflation rate derived from these bonds.

APPLICATION

Calculating the Principal and Coupon Payment of Real Return Bonds

Consider a real return bond with a face value of $1000 and a coupon yield of 2%. Calculate the principal and coupon payment after one year if the inflation rate is 3%.

Solution

After a year, to account for inflation, the principal will be increased by 3%, from $1000 to $1030. The coupon yield is still 2%, but applies to the new principal of $1030, instead of $1000. Hence, the coupon payment will be $0.02 \times \$1030 = \$20.60$.

MyEconLab

MyEconLab is an online homework and tutorial system that puts you in control of your own learning with study and practice tools directly correlated to this chapter's content. Visit MyEconLab to explore the following resources:

- The Questions and Applied Problems are all available in the Study Plan on MyEconLab for further practice. You will also find the answers to all of the Questions and Applied Problems in the Student Resources section of your MyEconLab.
- CANSIM data are available for relevant CANSIM questions in the Student Resources section of your MyEconLab.
- Visit the Student Resources section of MyEconLab to access the following mini-case for this chapter: Mini-Case 4.1: Interest Rates, Bond Yields, and Duration.
- Visit the Student Resources section of MyEconLab to access the following appendix for this chapter: Appendix 4.1: Measuring Interest-Rate Risk: Duration.

MyEconLab also features Additional Readings, Videos, Glossary Flashcards, Audio Chapter Summaries, Economics News Feeds, Animations, and many additional tools to help you master key concepts from the text.

SUMMARY

1. The yield to maturity, which is the measure that most accurately reflects the interest rate, is the interest rate that equates the present value of future payments of a debt instrument with its value today. Application of this principle reveals that bond prices and interest rates are negatively related: when the interest rate rises, the price of the bond must fall, and vice versa.

2. The return on a security, which tells you how well you have done by holding this security over a stated period of time, can differ substantially from the interest rate as measured by the yield to maturity. Long-term bond prices have substantial fluctuations when interest rates change and thus bear interest-rate risk. The resulting capital gains and losses can be large, which is why long-term bonds are not considered to be safe assets with a sure return.

3. The real interest rate is defined as the nominal interest rate minus the expected rate of inflation. It is a better measure of the incentives to borrow and lend than the nominal interest rate, and it is a more accurate indicator of the tightness of credit market conditions than the nominal interest rate.

KEY TERMS

cash flows, p. 62

consol (perpetuity), p. 70

coupon bond, p. 65

coupon rate, p. 65

current yield, p. 71

discount bond (zero-coupon bond), p. 65

face value (par value), p. 65

fixed-payment loan (fully amortized loan), p. 65

indexed bond, p. 80

interest-rate risk, p. 77

nominal interest rate, p. 78

present value (present discounted value), p. 62

present value, p. 62

rate of capital gain, p. 75

real interest rate, p. 78

real terms, p. 78

return (rate of return), p. 74

simple loan, p. 62

yield to maturity, p. 66

QUESTIONS

1. Would a dollar tomorrow be worth more to you today when the interest rate is 20%, or when it is 10%?

2. Write down the formula that is used to calculate the yield to maturity on a 20-year 10% coupon bond with $1000 face value that sells for $2000.

3. To pay for college, you have just taken out a $1000 government loan that makes you pay $126 per year for 25 years. However, you don't have to start making these payments until you graduate from college two years from now. Why is the yield to maturity necessarily less than 12% (this is the yield to maturity on a normal $1000 fixed-payment loan in which you pay $126 per year for 25 years)?

4. Is it better for bondholders when the yield to maturity increases or decreases?

5. A financial adviser has just given you the following advice: "Long-term bonds are a great investment because their interest rate is over 20%." Is the financial adviser necessarily right?

6. If mortgage rates rise from 5% to 10% but the expected rate of increase in housing prices rises from 2% to 9%, are people more or less likely to buy houses?

7. When is the current yield a good approximation to the yield to maturity?

8. Why would a government choose to issue a perpetuity, which requires payments forever, instead of a terminal loan, such as a fixed payment loan, discount bond, or coupon bond?

9. Under what conditions will a discount bond have a negative nominal interest rate? Is it possible for a coupon bond or a perpetuity to have a negative nominal interest rate?

10. True or false: With a discount bond, the return on a bond is equal to the rate of capital gain.

11. If there is a decline in interest rates, which would you rather be holding, long-term bonds or short-term bonds? Why? Which type of bond has the greater interest-rate risk?

12. Interest rates were lower in the mid-1980s than they were in the late 1970s, yet many economists have commented that real interest rates were actually much higher in the mid-1980s than in the late 1970s. Does this make sense? Do you think that these economists are right?

13. Retired persons often have much of their wealth placed in savings accounts and other interest-bearing investments, and complain whenever interest rates are low. Do they have a valid complaint?

APPLIED PROBLEMS

14. If the interest rate is 10%, what is the present value of a security that pays you $1100 next year, $1210 the year after, and $1331 the year after that?

15. Calculate the present value of a $1000 discount bond with five years to maturity if the yield to maturity is 6%.

16. A lottery claims its grand prize is $10 million, payable over five years at $2 000 000 per year. If the first payment is made immediately, what is this grand prize really worth? Use an interest rate of 6%.

17. What is the yield to maturity on a $1000-face-value discount bond maturing in one year that sells for $800?

18. What is the yield to maturity on a simple loan for $1 million that requires a repayment of $2 million in five years' time?

19. Which $1000 bond has the higher yield to maturity, a 20-year bond selling for $800 with a current yield of 15% or a one-year bond selling for $800 with a current yield of 5%?

20. Consider a bond with a 4% annual coupon and a face value of $1000. Complete the following table.

Years to Maturity	Yield to Maturity	Current Price
2	2%	
2	4%	
3	4%	
5	2%	
5	6%	

What relationships do you observe between years to maturity, yield to maturity, and the current price?

21. Consider a coupon bond that has a $1000 par value and a coupon rate of 10%. The bond is currently selling for $1044.89 and has two years to maturity. What is the bond's yield to maturity?

22. What is the price of a perpetuity that has a coupon of $50 per year and a yield to maturity of 2.5%? If the yield to maturity doubles, what will happen to its price?

23. Property taxes in a particular district are 4% of the purchase price every year. If you just purchased a $250 000 home, what is the present value of all the future property tax payments? Assume that the house remains worth $250 000 forever, property tax rates never change, and a 6% interest rate is used for discounting.

24. A $1000-face-value bond has a 10% coupon rate, its current price is $960, and is expected to increase to $980 next year. Calculate the current yield, the rate of capital gain, and the rate of return.

25. Assume you just deposited $1000 into a bank account. The current real interest rate is 2%, and inflation is expected to be 6% over the next year. What nominal rate would you require from the bank over the next year? How much money will you have at the end of one year? If you are saving to buy a fancy bicycle that currently sells for $1050, will you have enough to buy it?

CANSIM Questions

26. Go to the CANSIM data available in the Student Resources section of your MyEconLab website and download monthly data since 1953 for the three-month T-bill rate (series V122541) and the total consumer price index (series V41690973).

    a. What is the average year-over-year inflation rate, using the formula
    $$\pi_t = 100 \times (P_t - P_{t-12})/P_{t-12}$$
    b. What is the average T-bill rate?
    c. Assume that the expected inflation rate is the same as the actual inflation rate (a restrictive assumption!) and calculate the average real interest rate, r.

27. Go to the CANSIM data available in the Student Resources section of your MyEconLab website and download monthly data (from November 1991 to December 2011) for the interest rate on long-term Canada Real Return Bonds (series V122553). This is a direct measure of the real interest rate.

    a. What is the mean real interest rate over the sample period?
    b. What is its standard deviation? (The standard deviation is the square root of the variance.)

WEB EXERCISES

1. Go to **www.bankofcanada.ca/rates/interest-rates** and click on "Canadian bonds."

    a. Compare the short-term nominal interest rate to the long-term nominal interest rate. Which is greater?
    b. Compare the long-term nominal interest rate to the long-term real interest rate. Which appears to be greater?

2. Investigate the data on interest rates available from the Bank of Canada at **www.bankofcanada.ca**. Answer the following questions.

    a. What is the difference in the interest rates on 10-year and two-year bonds?
    b. What is the difference in the interest rate on long-term Government of Canada bonds and Real Return Bonds?
    c. What is the difference in the interest rate on long-term Government of Canada bonds and corporate bonds?

CHAPTER 5

The Behaviour of Interest Rates

LEARNING OBJECTIVES

After studying this chapter you should be able to

1. describe how the demand and supply analysis for bonds provides one theory of how nominal interest rates are determined

2. explain how the demand and supply analysis for money, known as the liquidity preference framework, provides an alternative theory of interest-rate determination

3. outline the factors that cause interest rates to change

4. characterize the effects of monetary policy on interest rates: the liquidity effect, the income effect, the price-level effect, and the expected-inflation effect

PREVIEW

In the early 1950s, nominal interest rates on three-month Treasury bills were about 1% at an annual rate; by 1981, they had reached over 20%; in the early 2000s they fell below 2%, rose to 5% in 2007, and then fell close to zero in 2008. What explains these substantial fluctuations in interest rates? One reason we study money, banking, and financial markets is to provide some answers to this question.

In this chapter we examine how the overall level of nominal interest rates (which we refer to as simply "interest rates") is determined and what factors influence their behaviour. We learned in Chapter 4 that interest rates are negatively related to the price of bonds, so if we can explain why bond prices change, we can also explain why interest rates fluctuate. We make use of supply and demand analysis for markets for bonds and money to examine how interest rates change.

In order to derive a demand curve for assets like money or bonds, the first step in our analysis, we must first understand what determines the demand for these assets. We do this by examining *portfolio theory,* an economic theory that outlines criteria that are important when deciding how much of an asset to buy. Armed with this theory, we can then go on to derive the demand curve for bonds or money. After deriving supply curves for these assets, we develop the concept of market equilibrium, the point at which the quantity supplied equals the quantity demanded. Then we use this model to explain changes in equilibrium interest rates.

Because interest rates on different securities tend to move together, in this chapter we will act as if there is only one type of security and one interest rate in the entire economy. In the following chapter, we expand our analysis to look at why interest rates on different types of securities differ.

Determinants of Asset Demand

Before going on to our supply and demand analysis of the bond market and the market for money, we must first understand what determines the quantity demanded of an asset. Recall that an asset is a piece of property that is a store of value. Items such as money, bonds, stocks, art, land, houses, farm equipment, and manufacturing machinery are all assets. Facing the question of whether to buy and hold an asset or whether to buy one asset rather than another, an individual must consider the following factors:

1. **Wealth**, the total resources owned by the individual, including all assets
2. **Expected return** (the return expected over the next period) on one asset relative to alternative assets
3. **Risk** (the degree of uncertainty associated with the return) on one asset relative to alternative assets
4. **Liquidity** (the ease and speed with which an asset can be turned into cash) relative to alternative assets.

Wealth

When we find that our wealth has increased, we have more resources available with which to purchase assets, and so, not surprisingly, the quantity of assets we demand increases. Therefore, the effect of changes in wealth on the quantity demanded of an asset can be summarized as follows: ***holding everything else constant, an increase in wealth raises the quantity demanded of an asset.***

Expected Return

In Chapter 4 we saw that the return on an asset (such as a bond) measures how much we gain from holding that asset. When we make a decision to buy an asset, we are influenced by what we expect the return on that asset to be. If a Bell Canada bond, for example, has a return of 15% half the time and 5% the other half of the time, its expected return (which you can think of as the average return) is 10% (= 0.5 × 15% + 0.5 × 5%).[1] If the expected return on the Bell bond rises relative to expected returns on alternative assets, holding everything else constant, then it becomes more desirable to purchase it, and the quantity demanded increases. This can occur in either of two ways: (1) when the expected return on the Bell bond rises while the return on an alternative asset—say, stock in TD Canada Trust—remains unchanged or (2) when the return on the alternative asset, the TD Canada Trust stock, falls while the return on the Bell bond remains unchanged. To summarize, ***an increase in an asset's expected return relative to that of an alternative asset, holding everything else unchanged, raises the quantity demanded of the asset.***

Risk

The degree of risk or uncertainty of an asset's returns also affects the demand for the asset. Consider two assets, stock in Fly-by-Night Airlines and stock in Feet-on-the-Ground Bus Company. Suppose that Fly-by-Night stock has a return of 15% half the time and 5% the other half of the time, making its expected return 10%, while stock in Feet-on-the-Ground has a fixed return of 10%. Fly-by-Night stock has

---

[1]If you are interested in finding out more information on how to calculate expected returns, as well as standard deviations of returns that measure risk, you can look at an appendix to this chapter that describes models of asset pricing on this book's MyEconLab. This appendix also describes how diversification lowers the overall risk of a portfolio and has a discussion of systematic risk and basic asset pricing models such as the capital asset pricing model and arbitrage pricing theory.

uncertainty associated with its returns and so has greater risk than stock in Feet-on-the-Ground, whose return is a sure thing.

A *risk-averse* person prefers stock in Feet-on-the-Ground (the sure thing) to Fly-by-Night stock (the riskier asset), even though the stocks have the same expected return, 10%. By contrast, a person who prefers risk is a *risk preferrer* or *risk lover*. Most people are risk-averse, especially in their financial decisions: everything else being equal, they prefer to hold the less-risky asset. Hence, **holding everything else constant, if an asset's risk rises relative to that of alternative assets, its quantity demanded will fall.**

Liquidity

Another factor that affects the demand for an asset is how quickly it can be converted into cash at low cost—its liquidity. An asset is liquid if the market in which it is traded has depth and breadth; that is, if the market has many buyers and sellers. A house is not a very liquid asset because it may be hard to find a buyer quickly; if a house must be sold to pay off bills, it might have to be sold for a much lower price. And the transaction costs in selling a house (broker's commissions, lawyer's fees, and so on) are substantial. A Canadian government Treasury bill, by contrast, is a highly liquid asset. It can be sold in a well-organized market where there are many buyers, so it can be sold quickly at low cost. **The more liquid an asset is relative to alternative assets, holding everything else unchanged, the more desirable it is, and the greater will be the quantity demanded.**

Theory of Portfolio Choice

All the determining factors we have just discussed can be assembled into the **theory of portfolio choice**, which tells us how much of an asset people want to hold in their portfolio. It states that, holding all of the other factors constant:

1. The quantity demanded of an asset is positively related to wealth.
2. The quantity demanded of an asset is positively related to its expected return relative to alternative assets.
3. The quantity demanded of an asset is negatively related to the risk of its returns relative to alternative assets.
4. The quantity demanded of an asset is positively related to its liquidity relative to alternative assets.

These results are summarized in Table 5-1.

TABLE 5-1 Response of the Quantity of an Asset Demanded to Changes in Income or Wealth, Expected Returns, Risk, and Liquidity		
Variable	**Change in Variable**	**Change in Quantity Demanded**
Wealth	↑	↑
Expected return relative to other assets	↑	↑
Risk relative to other assets	↑	↓
Liquidity relative to other assets	↑	↑

Note: Only increases (↑) in the variables are shown. The effect of decreases in the variables on the change in demand would be the opposite of those indicated in the rightmost column.

Supply and Demand in the Bond Market

Our first approach to the analysis of interest-rate determination looks at supply and demand in the bond market to see how the price of bonds is determined. With our understanding of how interest rates are measured from the previous chapter, we then recognize that each bond price is associated with a particular level of interest rates. Specifically, the negative relationship between bond prices and interest rates means that when we see that the bond price rises, the interest rate falls (or vice versa).

The first step in the analysis is to obtain a bond **demand curve**, which shows the relationship between the quantity demanded and the price when all other economic variables are held constant (that is, values of other variables are taken as given). You may recall from previous economics courses that the assumption that all other economic variables are held constant is called *ceteris paribus,* which means "other things being equal" in Latin.

Demand Curve

To clarify our analysis, let us consider the demand for one-year discount bonds, which make no coupon payments but pay the owner the $1000 face value in a year. If the holding period is one year, then, as we saw in Chapter 4, the return on the bonds is known absolutely and is equal to the interest rate as measured by the yield to maturity. This means that the expected return on this bond is equal to the interest rate i, which, using Equation 6 from Chapter 4 (page 72), is

$$i = RET^e = \frac{F - P}{P}$$

where

$i =$ interest rate $=$ yield to maturity

$RET^e =$ expected return

$F =$ face value of the discount bond

$P =$ initial purchase price of the discount bond

This formula shows that a particular value of the interest rate corresponds to each bond price. If the bond sells for $950, the interest rate and expected return is

$$\frac{\$1000 - \$950}{\$950} = 0.053 = 5.3\%$$

At this 5.3% interest rate and expected return corresponding to a bond price of $950, let us assume that the quantity of bonds demanded is $100 billion, which is plotted as point A in Figure 5-1.

At a price of $900, the interest rate and expected return are

$$\frac{\$1000 - \$900}{\$900} = 0.111 = 11.1\%$$

Because the expected return on these bonds is higher, with all other economic variables (such as income, expected returns on other assets, risk, and liquidity) held constant, the quantity demanded of bonds will be higher as predicted by portfolio theory. Point B in Figure 5-1 shows that the quantity of bonds demanded at the price of $900 has risen to $200 billion. Continuing with this reasoning, if the bond price is $850 (interest rate and expected return = 17.6%), the quantity of bonds demanded (point C) will be greater than at point B. Similarly, at the lower prices of $800 (interest rate = 25%) and $750 (interest rate = 33.3%), the quantity of bonds demanded will be even higher (points D and E). The curve B^d, which connects these points, is the demand curve for bonds. It has the usual downward slope, indicating that at

MyEconLab
Animation

FIGURE 5-1 Supply and Demand for Bonds

Equilibrium in the bond market occurs at point C, the intersection of the demand curve B^d and the bond supply curve B^s. The equilibrium price is $P^* = \$850$, and the equilibrium interest rate is $i^* = 17.6\%$.

lower prices of the bond (everything else being equal), the quantity demanded is higher.[2]

Supply Curve

An important assumption behind the demand curve for bonds in Figure 5-1 is that all other economic variables besides the bond's price and interest rate are held constant. We use the same assumption in deriving a **supply curve**, which shows the relationship between the quantity supplied and the price when all other economic variables are held constant.

When the price of the bonds is $750 (interest rate = 33.3%), point F shows that the quantity of bonds supplied is $100 billion for the example we are considering. If the price is $800, the interest rate is the lower rate of 25%. Because at this interest rate it is now less costly to borrow by issuing bonds, firms will be willing to borrow more through bond issues, and the quantity of bonds supplied is at the higher level of $200 billion (point G). An even higher price of $850, corresponding to a lower interest rate of 17.6%, results in a larger quantity of bonds supplied of $300 billion (point C). Higher prices of $900 and $950 result in even greater quantities of bonds supplied (points H and I). The B^s curve, which connects these points, is the supply curve for bonds. It has the usual upward slope found in supply curves, indicating that as the price increases (everything else being equal), the quantity supplied increases.

---

[2]Note that although our analysis indicates that the demand curve is downward-sloping, it does not imply that the curve is a straight line. For ease of exposition, however, we will draw demand curves and supply curves as straight lines.

Market Equilibrium

In economics, **market equilibrium** occurs when the amount that people are willing to buy (*demand*) equals the amount that people are willing to sell (*supply*) at a given price. In the bond market, this is achieved when the quantity of bonds demanded equals the quantity of bonds supplied:

$$B^d = B^s \tag{1}$$

In Figure 5-1, equilibrium occurs at point C, where the demand and supply curves intersect at a bond price of $850 (interest rate of 17.6%) and a quantity of bonds of $300 billion. The price of $P^* = \$850$, where the quantity demanded equals the quantity supplied, is called the *equilibrium* or *market-clearing* price. Similarly, the interest rate of $i^* = 17.6\%$ that corresponds to this price is called the *equilibrium* or *market-clearing interest rate.*

The concepts of market equilibrium and equilibrium price or interest rate are useful because there is a tendency for the market to head toward them. We can see that it does in Figure 5-1 by first looking at what happens when we have a bond price that is above the equilibrium price. When the price of bonds is set too high, at, say, $950, the quantity of bonds supplied at point I is greater than the quantity of bonds demanded at point A. A situation like this, in which the quantity of bonds supplied exceeds the quantity of bonds demanded, is called a condition of **excess supply**. Because people want to sell more bonds than others want to buy, the price of the bonds will fall, and this is why the downward arrow is drawn in the figure at the bond price of $950. As long as the bond price remains above the equilibrium price, there will continue to be an excess supply of bonds, and the price will continue to fall. This will stop only when the price has reached the equilibrium price of $850, where the excess supply of bonds will be eliminated.

Now let's look at what happens when the price of bonds is below the equilibrium price. If the price of the bonds is set too low, say at $750, the quantity demanded at point E is greater than the quantity supplied at point F. This is called a condition of **excess demand**. People now want to buy more bonds than others are willing to sell, and so the price of bonds will be driven up. This is illustrated by the upward arrow drawn in the figure at the bond price of $750. Only when the excess demand for bonds is eliminated by the price rising to the equilibrium level of $850 is there no further tendency for the price to rise.

We can see that the concept of equilibrium price is a useful one because it indicates where the market will settle. Because each price on the vertical axis of Figure 5-1 shows a corresponding interest rate value, the same diagram also shows that the interest rate will head toward the equilibrium interest rate of 17.6%. When the interest rate is below the equilibrium interest rate, as it is when it is at 5.3%, the price of the bond is above the equilibrium price, and there will be an excess supply of bonds. The price of the bond then falls, leading to a rise in the interest rate toward the equilibrium level. Similarly, when the interest rate is above the equilibrium level, as it is when it is at 33.3%, there is excess demand for bonds, and the bond price will rise, driving the interest rate back down to the equilibrium level of 17.6%.

Supply and Demand Analysis

Our Figure 5-1 is a conventional supply and demand diagram with price on the left vertical axis and quantity on the horizontal axis. Because the interest rate that corresponds to each bond price is also marked on the vertical axis, this diagram allows us to read the equilibrium interest rate, giving us a model that describes the determination of interest rates. It is important to recognize that a supply and demand diagram like Figure 5-1 can be drawn for *any* type of bond because the interest rate and price of a bond are *always* negatively related for any type of bond, whether a discount bond or a coupon bond.

An important feature of the analysis here is that supply and demand are always in terms of *stocks* (amounts at a given point in time) of assets, not in terms of *flows*. The **asset market approach** for understanding behaviour in financial markets—which emphasizes stocks of assets rather than flows in determining asset prices—is now the dominant methodology used by economists because correctly conducting analyses in terms of flows is very tricky, especially when we encounter inflation.[3]

Changes in Equilibrium Interest Rates

We will now use the supply and demand framework for bonds to analyze why interest rates change. To avoid confusion, it is important to make the distinction between *movements along* a demand (or supply) curve and *shifts in* a demand (or supply) curve. When quantity demanded (or supplied) changes as a result of a change in the price of the bond (or, equivalently, a change in the interest rate), we have a *movement along* the demand (or supply) curve. The change in the quantity demanded when we move from point A to B to C in Figure 5-1, for example, is a movement along a demand curve. A *shift in* the demand (or supply) curve, by contrast, occurs when the quantity demanded (or supplied) changes *at each given price* (or *interest rate*) of the bond in response to a change in some other factor besides the bond's price or interest rate. When one of these factors changes, causing a shift in the demand or supply curve, there will be a new equilibrium value for the interest rate.

In the following pages we will look at how the supply and demand curves shift in response to changes in variables, such as expected inflation and wealth, and what effects these changes have on the equilibrium value of interest rates.

Shifts in the Demand for Bonds

The theory of portfolio choice, which we developed at the beginning of the chapter, provides a framework for deciding what factors cause the demand curve for bonds to shift. These factors include changes in four parameters:

1. Wealth
2. Expected returns on bonds relative to alternative assets
3. Risk of bonds relative to alternative assets
4. Liquidity of bonds relative to alternative assets

To see how a change in each of these factors (holding all other factors constant) can shift the demand curve, let us look at some examples. (As a study aid, Table 5-2 summarizes the effects of changes in these factors on the bond demand curve.)

WEALTH   When the economy is growing rapidly in a business cycle expansion and wealth is increasing, the quantity of bonds demanded at each bond price (or interest rate) increases, as shown in Figure 5-2. To see how this works, consider point B on the initial demand curve for bonds B_1^d. With higher wealth, the quantity of bonds demanded at the same price must rise, to point B'. Similarly, the higher wealth causes the quantity demanded at the same bond price to rise to point D'. Continuing with this

---

[3]The asset market approach developed in the text is useful in understanding not only how interest rates behave but also how any asset price is determined. An appendix to this chapter, which is on this book's MyEconLab, shows how the asset market approach can be applied to understanding the behaviour of commodity markets, in particular, the gold market. The analysis of the bond market that we have developed here has another interpretation using a different terminology and framework involving the supply and demand for loanable funds. This loanable funds framework is discussed in an appendix to this chapter, which is also on MyEconLab.

| **TABLE 5-2** | Factors That Shift the Demand Curve for Bonds | | |

Variable	Change in Variable	Change in Quantity Demanded at Each Bond Price	Shift in Demand Curve
Wealth	↑	↑	P → B_1^d B_2^d B
Expected interest rate	↑	↓	P ← B_2^d B_1^d B
Expected inflation	↑	↓	P ← B_2^d B_1^d B
Riskiness of bonds relative to other assets	↑	↓	P ← B_2^d B_1^d B
Liquidity of bonds relative to other assets	↑	↑	P → B_1^d B_2^d B

Note: Only increases (↑) in the variables are shown. The effect of decreases in the variables on the change in demand would be the opposite of those indicated in the remaining columns.

reasoning for every point on the initial demand curve B_1^d, we can see that the demand curve shifts to the right from B_1^d to B_2^d as is indicated by the arrows.

The conclusion we have reached is that in a business cycle expansion with growing wealth, the demand for bonds rises and the demand curve for bonds shifts to the right. Using the same reasoning, in a recession, when income and wealth are falling, the demand for bonds falls, and the demand curve shifts to the left.

MyEconLab
Animation

FIGURE 5-2 Shift in the Demand Curve for Bonds

When the demand for bonds increases, the demand curve shifts to the right as shown.

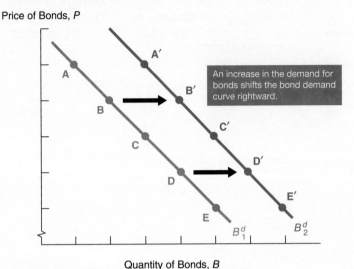

Another factor that affects wealth is the public's propensity to save. If households save more, wealth increases and, as we have seen, the demand for bonds rises and the demand curve for bonds shifts to the right. Conversely, if people save less, wealth and the demand for bonds will fall and the demand curve shifts to the left.

EXPECTED RETURNS   For a one-year discount bond and a one-year holding period, the expected return and the interest rate are identical, so nothing besides today's interest rate affects the expected return.

For bonds with maturities of greater than one year, the expected return may differ from the interest rate. For example, we saw in Chapter 4, Table 4-2 (page 76), that a rise in the interest rate on a long-term bond from 10% to 20% would lead to a sharp decline in price and a very negative return. Hence, if people begin to think that interest rates will be higher next year than they had originally anticipated, the expected return today on long-term bonds will fall, and the quantity demanded will fall at each interest rate. ***Higher expected interest rates in the future lower the expected return for long-term bonds, decrease the demand, and shift the demand curve to the left.***

By contrast, a revision downward of expectations of future interest rates would mean that long-term bond prices would be expected to rise more than originally anticipated, and the resulting higher expected return today would raise the quantity demanded at each bond price and interest rate. ***Lower expected interest rates in the future increase the demand for long-term bonds and shift the demand curve to the right*** (as in Figure 5-2).

Changes in expected returns on other assets can also shift the demand curve for bonds. If people suddenly became more optimistic about the stock market and began to expect higher stock prices in the future, both expected capital gains and expected returns on stocks would rise. With the expected return on bonds held constant, the expected return on bonds today relative to stocks would fall, lowering the demand for bonds and shifting the demand curve to the left.

A change in expected inflation is likely to alter expected returns on physical assets (also called *real assets*) such as automobiles and houses, which affects the demand for bonds. An increase in expected inflation, say, from 5% to 10%, will lead to higher prices on cars and houses in the future and hence higher nominal capital gains. The resulting rise in the expected returns today on these real assets will lead to a fall in the expected return on bonds relative to the expected return on real assets today and thus cause the demand for bonds to fall. Alternatively, we can think of the rise in expected inflation as lowering the real interest rate on bonds, and the resulting decline in the relative expected return on bonds causes the demand for bonds to fall. *An increase in the expected rate of inflation lowers the expected return for bonds, causing their demand to decline and the demand curve to shift to the left.*

RISK   If prices in the bond market become more volatile, the risk associated with bonds increases, and bonds become a less attractive asset. *An increase in the riskiness of bonds causes the demand for bonds to fall and the demand curve to shift to the left.*

Conversely, an increase in the volatility of prices in another asset market, such as the stock market, would make bonds more attractive. *An increase in the riskiness of alternative assets causes the demand for bonds to rise and the demand curve to shift to the right* (as in Figure 5-2).

LIQUIDITY   If more people started trading in the bond market and as a result it became easier to sell bonds quickly, the increase in their liquidity would cause the quantity of bonds demanded at each interest rate to rise. *Increased liquidity of bonds results in an increased demand for bonds, and the demand curve shifts to the right* (see Figure 5-2). *Similarly, increased liquidity of alternative assets lowers the demand for bonds and shifts the demand curve to the left.* The reduction of brokerage commissions for trading common stocks that occurred when the fixed-rate commission structure was abolished in 1975, for example, increased the liquidity of stocks relative to bonds, and the resulting lower demand for bonds shifted the demand curve to the left.

Shifts in the Supply of Bonds

Certain factors can cause the supply curve for bonds to shift, among them:

1. Expected profitability of investment opportunities
2. Expected inflation
3. Government activities

We will look at how the supply curve shifts when each of these factors changes (all others remaining constant). (As a study aid, Table 5-3 summarizes the effects of changes in these factors on the bond supply curve.)

EXPECTED PROFITABILITY OF INVESTMENT OPPORTUNITIES   The more profitable plant and equipment investments that a firm expects it can make, the more willing it will be to borrow in order to finance these investments. When the economy is growing rapidly, as in a business cycle expansion, investment opportunities that are expected to be profitable abound, and the quantity of bonds supplied at any given bond price will increase (see Figure 5-3). *Therefore, in a business cycle expansion, the supply of bonds increases, and the supply curve shifts to the right. Likewise, in a recession, when there are far fewer expected profitable investment opportunities, the supply of bonds falls and the supply curve shifts to the left.*

EXPECTED INFLATION   As we saw in Chapter 4, the real cost of borrowing is more accurately measured by the real interest rate, which equals the (nominal) interest rate minus the expected inflation rate. For a given interest rate (and bond price), when expected inflation increases, the real cost of borrowing falls; hence the quantity of bonds supplied increases at any given bond price. *An increase in expected inflation causes the supply of bonds to increase and the supply curve to shift to the right* (see Figure 5-3).

TABLE 5-3   Factors That Shift the Supply Curve of Bonds

Variable	Change in Variable	Change in Quantity Supplied at Each Bond Price	Shift in Supply Curve
Profitability of investments	↑	↑	
Expected inflation	↑	↑	
Government deficit	↑	↑	

Note: Only increases (↑) in the variables are shown. The effect of decreases in the variables on the change in supply would be the opposite of those indicated in the remaining columns.

FIGURE 5-3 Shift in the Supply Curve for Bonds

When the supply of bonds increases, the supply curve shifts to the right.

MyEconLab
Animation

Price of Bonds, *P*

An increase in the supply of bonds shifts the bond supply curve rightward.

Quantity of Bonds, *B*

GOVERNMENT BUDGET   The activities of the government can influence the supply of bonds in several ways. The Canadian government issues bonds to finance government deficits, the gap between the government's expenditures and its revenues. When these deficits are large, the government sells more bonds, and the quantity of bonds supplied at each bond price increases. ***Higher government deficits increase the supply of bonds and shift the supply curve to the right*** (see Figure 5-3). ***On the other hand, government surpluses, as have occurred in recent years, decrease the supply of bonds and shift the supply curve to the left.***

Provincial and municipal governments and other government agencies also issue bonds to finance their expenditures, and this can also affect the supply of bonds. We will see in later chapters that the conduct of monetary policy involves the purchase and sale of bonds, which in turn influences the supply of bonds.

We now can use our knowledge of how supply and demand curves shift to analyze how the equilibrium interest rate can change. The best way to do this is to pursue several applications that are particularly relevant to our understanding of how monetary policy affects interest rates. In going through these applications, keep two things in mind:

1. When you examine the effect of a variable change, remember that we are assuming that all other variables are unchanged; that is, we are making use of the *ceteris paribus* assumption.

2. Remember that the interest rate is negatively related to the bond price, so when the equilibrium bond price rises, the equilibrium interest rate falls. Conversely, if the equilibrium bond price moves downward, the equilibrium interest rate rises.

APPLICATION

Changes in the Interest Rate Due to Expected Inflation: The Fisher Effect

We have already done most of the work to evaluate how a change in expected inflation affects the nominal interest rate in that we have already analyzed how a change in expected inflation shifts the supply and demand curves. Figure 5-4 shows the effect on the equilibrium interest rate of an increase in expected inflation.

Suppose that expected inflation is initially 5% and the initial supply and demand curves B_1^s and B_1^d intersect at point 1, where the equilibrium bond price is P_1. If expected inflation rises to 10%, the expected return on bonds relative to real assets falls for any given bond price and interest rate. As a result, the demand for bonds falls, and the demand curve shifts to the left from B_1^d to B_2^d. The rise in expected inflation also shifts the supply curve. At any given bond price and interest rate, the real cost of borrowing has declined, causing the quantity of bonds supplied to increase, and the supply curve shifts to the right, from B_1^s to B_2^s.

When the demand and supply curves shift in response to the change in expected inflation, the equilibrium moves from point 1 to point 2, the intersection of B_2^d and B_2^s. The equilibrium bond price has fallen from P_1 to P_2, and because the bond price is negatively related to the interest rate, this means that the interest rate has risen. Note that Figure 5-4 has been drawn so that the equilibrium quantity of bonds remains the same for both point 1 and point 2. However, depending on the size of the shifts in the supply and demand curves, the equilibrium quantity of bonds could either rise or fall when expected inflation rises.

MyEconLab
Animation

FIGURE 5-4 Response to a Change in Expected Inflation

When expected inflation rises, the supply curve shifts from B_1^s to B_2^s, and the demand curve shifts from B_1^d to B_2^d. The equilibrium moves from point 1 to point 2, with the result that the equilibrium bond price falls from P_1 to P_2 and the equilibrium interest rate rises.

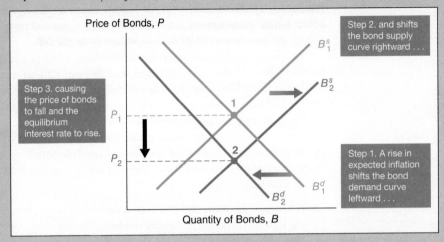

Our supply and demand analysis has led us to an important observation: ***when expected inflation rises, interest rates will rise***. This result has been named the **Fisher effect**, after Irving Fisher, the economist who first pointed out the relationship of expected inflation to interest rates. The accuracy of this prediction is shown in Figure 5-5 for the United States. The interest rate on three-month U.S. Treasury bills has usually moved along with the expected inflation rate. Consequently, it is understandable that many economists recommend that inflation must be kept low if we want to keep interest rates low.

FIGURE 5-5 Expected Inflation and Interest Rates (Three-Month Treasury Bills), 1953–2011

The interest rate on three-month Treasury bills and the expected inflation rate generally move together, as the Fisher effect predicts.

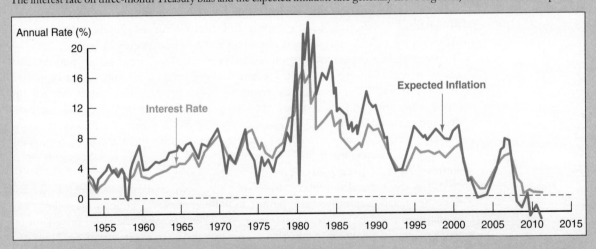

Source: Expected inflation calculated using procedures outlined in Frederic S. Mishkin, "The Real Interest Rate: An Empirical Investigation," *Carnegie-Rochester Conference Series on Public Policy 15* (1981): 151–200. These procedures involve estimating expected inflation as a function of past interest rates, inflation, and time trends.

APPLICATION

Changes in the Interest Rate Due to a Business Cycle Expansion

Figure 5-6 analyzes the effects of a business cycle expansion on interest rates. In a business cycle expansion, the amount of goods and services being produced in the economy rises, so national income increases. When this occurs, businesses will be more willing to borrow because they are likely to have many profitable investment opportunities for which they need financing. Hence, at a given bond price, the quantity of bonds that firms want to sell (that is, the supply of bonds) will increase. This means that in a business cycle expansion, the supply curve for bonds shifts to the right (see Figure 5-6) from B_1^s to B_2^s.

Expansion in the economy will also affect the demand for bonds. As the business cycle expands, wealth is likely to increase, and the theory of portfolio choice tells us that the demand for bonds will rise as well. We see this in Figure 5-6, where the demand curve has shifted to the right, from B_1^d to B_2^d.

Given that both the supply and demand curves have shifted to the right, we know that the new equilibrium reached at the intersection of B_2^d and B_2^s must also move to the right. However, depending on whether the supply curve shifts more than the demand curve or vice versa, the new equilibrium interest rate can either rise or fall.

The supply and demand analysis used here gives us an ambiguous answer to the question of what will happen to interest rates in a business cycle expansion. The figure has been drawn so that the shift in the supply curve is greater than the shift in the demand curve, causing the equilibrium bond price to fall to P_2, leading to a rise in the equilibrium interest rate. The reason the figure has been drawn so that a business cycle expansion and a rise in income lead to a higher interest rate is that this is the outcome we actually see in

FIGURE 5-6 Response to a Business Cycle Expansion

MyEconLab
Animation

In a business cycle expansion, when income and wealth are rising, the demand curve shifts rightward from B_1^d to B_2^d. If the supply curve shifts to the right more than the demand curve, as in this figure, the equilibrium bond price moves down from P_1 to P_2, and the equilibrium interest rate rises.

FIGURE 5-7   Business Cycles and Interest Rates (Three-Month Treasury Bills), 1962–2012

Shaded areas indicate periods of recession. The interest rate tends to rise during business cycle expansions and fall during recessions.

Source: Statistics Canada CANSIM II Series V122531.

the data. Figure 5-7 plots the movement of the interest rate on three-month Treasury bills from 1962 to 2012 and indicates when the business cycle is undergoing recessions (shaded areas). As you can see, the interest rate tends to rise during business cycle expansions and fall during recessions, which is what the supply and demand diagram in Figure 5-6 indicates.

APPLICATION

Explaining Low Japanese Interest Rates

In the 1990s and early 2000s, Japanese interest rates became the lowest in the world. Indeed, in November 1998, an extraordinary event occurred: interest rates on Japanese six-month Treasury bills turned slightly negative (see Chapter 4). Why did Japanese rates drop to such low levels?

In the late 1990s, Japan experienced a prolonged recession, which was accompanied by deflation, a negative inflation rate. Using these facts, analysis similar to that used in the preceding application explains the low Japanese interest rates.

Negative inflation caused the demand for bonds to rise because the expected return on real assets fell, thereby raising the relative expected return on bonds and in turn causing the demand curve to shift to the right. The negative inflation also raised the real interest rate and therefore the real cost of borrowing for any given nominal rate, thereby causing the supply of bonds to contract and the supply curve to shift to the left. The outcome was then exactly the opposite of that graphed in Figure 5-4 (page 96): the rightward shift of the demand curve and leftward shift of the supply curve led to a rise in the bond price and a fall in interest rates.

The business cycle contraction and the resulting lack of investment opportunities in Japan also led to lower interest rates by decreasing the supply of bonds and shifting the supply curve to the left. Although the demand curve also would shift to the left because wealth decreased during the business cycle contraction, we have seen in the preceding application that the demand curve would shift less than the supply curve. Thus, the bond price rose and interest rates fell (the opposite outcome to that in Figure 5-6, page 97).

Usually, we think that low interest rates are a good thing because they make it cheap to borrow. But the Japanese example shows that just as there is a fallacy in the adage "You can never be too rich or too thin" (maybe you can't be too rich, but you can certainly be too thin and do damage to your health), there is a fallacy in always thinking that lower interest rates are better. In Japan, the low, and even negative, interest rates were a sign that the Japanese economy was in real trouble, with falling prices and a contracting economy. Only when the Japanese economy returns to health will interest rates rise back to more normal levels.

Supply and Demand in the Market for Money: The Liquidity Preference Framework

Instead of determining the equilibrium interest rate using the supply of and demand for bonds, an alternative model developed by John Maynard Keynes, known as the **liquidity preference framework**, determines the equilibrium interest rate in terms of the supply of and demand for money. Although the two frameworks look different, the liquidity preference analysis of the market for money is closely related to the loanable funds framework of the bond market.[4]

The starting point of Keynes's analysis is his assumption that there are two main categories of assets that people use to store their wealth: money and bonds. Therefore, total wealth in the economy must equal the total quantity of bonds plus money in the economy, which equals the quantity of bonds supplied B^s plus the quantity of money supplied M^s. The quantity of bonds B^d and money M^d that people want to hold and thus demand must also equal the total amount of wealth, because people cannot purchase more assets than their available resources allow. The conclusion is that the quantity of bonds and money supplied must equal the quantity of bonds and money demanded:

$$B^s + M^s = B^d + M^d \tag{2}$$

Collecting the bond terms on one side of the equation and the money terms on the other, this equation can be rewritten as

$$B^s - B^d = M^d - M^s \tag{3}$$

The rewritten equation tells us that if the market for money is in equilibrium ($M^s = M^d$), the right-hand side of Equation 3 equals zero, implying that $B^s = B^d$, meaning that the bond market is also in equilibrium.

Thus it is the same to think about determining the equilibrium interest rate by equating the supply and demand for bonds or by equating the supply and demand for money. In this sense, the liquidity preference framework, which analyzes the market for money, is equivalent to a framework analyzing supply and demand in the bond market. In practice, the approaches differ because, by assuming that there are only two kinds of assets, money and bonds, the liquidity preference approach implicitly ignores any effects on interest rates that arise from changes in the expected returns

[4]Note that the term *market for money* refers to the market for the medium of exchange, money. This market differs from the *money market* referred to by finance practitioners, which is the financial market in which short-term debt instruments are traded.

on real assets such as automobiles and houses. In most instances, however, both frameworks yield the same predictions.

The reason that we approach the determination of interest rates with both frameworks is that the bond supply and demand framework is easier to use when analyzing the effects from changes in expected inflation, whereas the liquidity preference framework provides a simpler analysis of the effects from changes in income, the price level, and the supply of money.

Because the definition of money that Keynes used includes currency (which earns no interest) and chequing account deposits (which in his time typically earned little or no interest), he assumed that money has a zero rate of return. Bonds, the only alternative asset to money in Keynes's framework, have an expected return equal to the interest rate i.[5] As this interest rate rises (holding everything else unchanged), the expected return on money falls relative to the expected return on bonds, and as the theory of portfolio choice tells us, this causes the demand for money to fall.

We can also see that the demand for money and the interest rate should be negatively related by using the concept of **opportunity cost**, the amount of interest (expected return) sacrificed by not holding the alternative asset—in this case, a bond. As the interest rate on bonds, i, rises, the opportunity cost of holding money rises, and so money is less desirable and the quantity of money demanded must fall.

Figure 5-8 shows the quantity of money demanded at a number of interest rates, with all other economic variables, such as income and the price level, held constant. At an interest rate of 25%, point A shows that the quantity of money demanded is $100 billion. If the interest rate is at the lower rate of 20%, the opportunity cost of

FIGURE 5-8 Equilibrium in the Market for Money

Equilibrium in the market for money occurs at point C, the intersection of the money demand curve M^d and the money supply curve M^s. The equilibrium interest is $i^* = 15\%$.

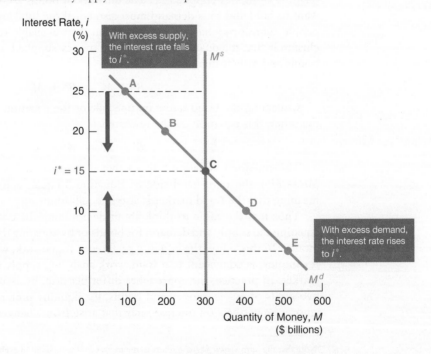

---

[5]Keynes did not actually assume that the expected returns on bonds equalled the interest rate but rather argued that they were closely related. This distinction makes no appreciable difference in our analysis.

money is lower, and the quantity of money demanded rises to $200 billion, as indicated by the move from point A to point B. If the interest rate is even lower, the quantity of money demanded is even higher, as is indicated by points C, D, and E. The curve M^d connecting these points is the demand curve for money, and it slopes downward.

At this point in our analysis, we will assume that a central bank controls the amount of money supplied at a fixed quantity of $300 billion, so the supply curve for money M^s in the figure is a vertical line at $300 billion. The equilibrium where the quantity of money demanded equals the quantity of money supplied occurs at the intersection of the supply and demand curves at point C, where

$$M^d = M^s \tag{4}$$

The resulting equilibrium interest rate is at $i^* = 15\%$.

We can again see that there is a tendency to approach this equilibrium by first looking at the relationship of money demand and supply when the interest rate is above the equilibrium interest rate. When the interest rate is 25%, the quantity of money demanded at point A is $100 billion, yet the quantity of money supplied is $300 billion. The excess supply of money means that people are holding more money than they desire, so they will try to get rid of their excess money balances by trying to buy bonds. Accordingly, they will bid up the price of bonds, and as the bond price rises, the interest rate will fall toward the equilibrium interest rate of 15%. This tendency is shown by the downward arrow drawn at the interest rate of 25%.

Likewise, if the interest rate is 5%, the quantity of money demanded at point E is $500 billion, but the quantity of money supplied is only $300 billion. There is now an excess demand for money because people want to hold more money than they currently have. To try to obtain more money, they will sell their only other asset—bonds—and the price will fall. As the price of bonds falls, the interest rate will rise toward the equilibrium rate of 15%. Only when the interest rate is at its equilibrium value will there be no tendency for it to move further, and the interest rate will settle to its equilibrium value.

Changes in Equilibrium Interest Rates

Analyzing how the equilibrium interest rate changes using the liquidity preference framework requires that we understand what causes the demand and supply curves for money to shift.

Shifts in the Demand for Money

In Keynes's liquidity preference analysis, two factors cause the demand curve for money to shift: income and the price level.

INCOME EFFECT   In Keynes's view, there were two reasons why income would affect the demand for money. First, as an economy expands and income rises, wealth increases and people will want to hold more money as a store of value. Second, as the economy expands and income rises, people will want to carry out more transactions using money, with the result that they will also want to hold more money. The conclusion is that *a higher level of income causes the demand for money at each interest rate to increase and the demand curve to shift to the right.*

PRICE-LEVEL EFFECT   Keynes took the view that people care about the amount of money they hold in real terms, that is, in terms of the goods and services that it can buy. When the price level rises, the same nominal quantity of money is no longer as valuable; it cannot be used to purchase as many real goods or services. To restore their holdings of money in real terms to their former level, people will want to hold a greater nominal quantity of money, so *a rise in the price level causes the demand for money at each interest rate to increase and the demand curve to shift to the right.*

**Shifts in the
Supply of
Money**

We will assume that the supply of money is completely controlled by the central bank, which in Canada is the Bank of Canada. (Actually, the process that determines the money supply is substantially more complicated, involving banks, depositors, and borrowers from banks. We will study it in more detail later in the book.) For now, all we need to know is that **an increase in the money supply engineered by the Bank of Canada will shift the supply curve for money to the right.**

APPLICATION

Changes in the Equilibrium Interest Rate Due to Changes in Income, the Price Level, or the Money Supply

To see how the liquidity preference framework can be used to analyze the movement of interest rates, we will again look at several applications that will be useful in evaluating the effect of monetary policy on interest rates. In going through these applications, remember to use the *ceteris paribus* assumption: when examining the effect of a change in one variable, hold all other variables constant. (As a study aid, Table 5-4 summarizes the shifts in the demand and supply curves for money.)

TABLE 5-4   Factors That Shift the Demand for and Supply of Money

Variable	Change in Variable	Change in Money Demand (M^d) or Supply (M^s) at Each Interest Rate	Change in Interest Rate	
Income	↑	M^d ↑	↑	
Price level	↑	M^d ↑	↑	
Money supply	↑	M^s ↑	↓	

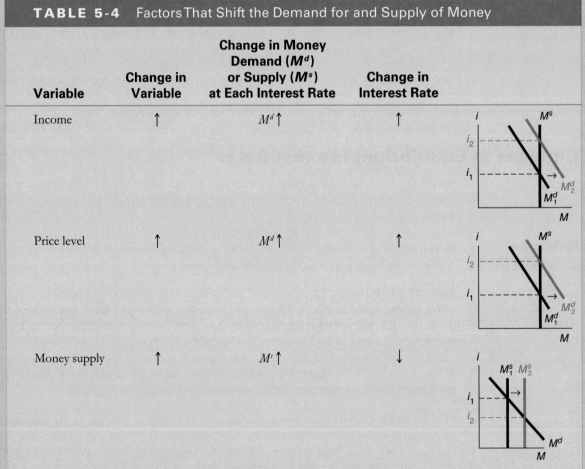

Note: Only increases (↑) in the variables are shown. The effect of decreases in the variables on the change in demand would be the opposite of those indicated in the remaining columns.

Changes in Income	When income is rising during a business cycle expansion, we have seen that the demand for money will rise, as shown in Figure 5-9 by the shift rightward in the demand curve from M_1^d to M_2^d. The new equilibrium is reached at point 2 at the intersection of the M_2^d curve with the money supply curve M^s. As you can see, the equilibrium interest rate rises from i_1 to i_2. The liquidity preference framework thus generates the conclusion that ***when income is rising during a business cycle expansion (holding other economic variables constant), interest rates will rise.*** This conclusion is unambiguous when contrasted to the conclusion reached about the effects of a change in income on interest rates using the bond supply and demand framework.

Changes in the Price Level	When the price level rises, the value of money in terms of what it can purchase is lower. To restore their purchasing power in real terms to its former level, people will want to hold a greater nominal quantity of money. A higher price level shifts the demand curve for money to the right from M_1^d to M_2^d (see Figure 5-9). The equilibrium moves from point 1 to point 2, where the equilibrium interest rate has risen from i_1 to i_2, illustrating that ***when the price level increases, with the supply of money and other economic variables held constant, interest rates will rise.***

Changes in the Money Supply	An increase in the money supply due to an expansionary monetary policy by the Bank of Canada implies that the supply curve for money shifts to the right. As is shown in Figure 5-10 by the movement of the supply curve from M_1^s to M_2^s, the equilibrium moves from point 1 down to point 2, where the M_2^s supply curve intersects with the demand curve M^d and the equilibrium interest rate has fallen from i_1 to i_2. ***When the money supply increases (everything else remaining equal), interest rates will decline.***[6]

FIGURE 5-9 Response to a Change in Income or the Price Level

In a business cycle expansion, when income is rising, or when the price level rises, the demand curve shifts from M_1^d to M_2^d. The supply curve is fixed at $M^s = M$. The equilibrium interest rate rises from i_1 to i_2.

---

[6]This same result can be generated using the supply and demand for bonds framework.

FIGURE 5-10 Response to a Change in the Money Supply

When the money supply increases, the supply curve shifts from M_1^s to M_2^s and the equilibrium interest rate falls from i_1 to i_2.

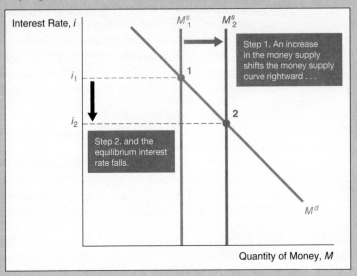

APPLICATION

Money and Interest Rates

The liquidity preference analysis in Figure 5-10 seems to lead to the conclusion that an increase in the money supply will lower interest rates. This conclusion has important policy implications because it has frequently caused politicians to call for a more rapid growth of the money supply in order to drive down interest rates.

But is this conclusion that money and interest rates should be negatively related correct? Might there be other important factors left out of the liquidity preference analysis in Figure 5-10 that would reverse this conclusion? We will provide answers to these questions by applying the supply and demand analysis we have used in this chapter to obtain a deeper understanding of the relationship between money and interest rates.

Milton Friedman, a Nobel laureate in economics, has raised an important criticism of the conclusion that a rise in the money supply lowers interest rates. He acknowledges that the liquidity preference analysis is correct and calls the result—that an increase in the money supply (*everything else remaining equal*) lowers interest rates—the *liquidity effect*. However, he views the liquidity effect as merely part of the story: an increase in the money supply might not leave "everything else equal" and will have other effects on the economy that may make interest rates rise. If these effects are substantial, it is entirely possible that when the money supply rises, interest rates too may rise.

We have already laid the groundwork to discuss these other effects because we have shown how changes in income, the price level, and expected inflation affect the equilibrium interest rate.

1. *Income Effect.* Because an increasing money supply is an expansionary influence on the economy, it should raise national income and wealth. Both the liquidity

preference and bond supply and demand frameworks indicate that interest rates will then rise (see Figures 5-6 on page 97 and 5-9 on page 103). Thus ***the income effect of an increase in the money supply is a rise in interest rates in response to the higher level of income.***

2. *Price-Level Effect.* An increase in the money supply can also cause the overall price level in the economy to rise. The liquidity preference framework predicts that this will lead to a rise in interest rates. So ***the price-level effect from an increase in the money supply is a rise in interest rates in response to the rise in the price level.***

3. *Expected-Inflation Effect.* The higher inflation rate that results from an increase in the money supply also affects interest rates by affecting the expected inflation rate. Specifically, an increase in the money supply may lead people to expect a higher price level in the future—hence the expected inflation rate will be higher. The supply and demand for bonds framework has shown us that this increase in expected inflation will lead to a higher level of interest rates. Therefore, ***the expected-inflation effect of an increase in the money supply is a rise in interest rates in response to the rise in the expected inflation rate.***

At first glance it might appear that the price-level effect and the expected-inflation effect are the same thing. They both indicate that increases in the price level induced by an increase in the money supply will raise interest rates. However, there is a subtle difference between the two, and this is why they are discussed as two separate effects.

Suppose that there is a one-time increase in the money supply today that leads to a rise in prices to a permanently higher level by next year. As the price level rises over the course of this year, the interest rate will rise via the price-level effect. Only at the end of the year, when the price level has risen to its peak, will the price-level effect be at a maximum.

The rising price level will also raise interest rates via the expected-inflation effect because people will expect that inflation will be higher over the course of the year. However, when the price level stops rising next year, inflation and the expected inflation rate will return to zero. Any rise in interest rates as a result of the earlier rise in expected inflation will then be reversed. We thus see that in contrast to the price-level effect, which reaches its greatest impact next year, the expected-inflation effect will have its smallest impact (zero impact) next year. The basic difference between the two effects, then, is that the price-level effect remains even after prices have stopped rising, whereas the expected-inflation effect disappears.

An important point is that the expected-inflation effect will persist only as long as the price level continues to rise. As we will see in our discussion of monetary theory in subsequent chapters, a one-time increase in the money supply will not produce a continually rising price level; only a higher rate of money supply growth will. Thus a higher rate of money supply growth is needed if the expected-inflation effect is to persist.

Does a Higher Rate of Growth of the Money Supply Lower Interest Rates?

We can now put together all the effects we have discussed to help us decide whether our analysis supports the politicians who advocate a greater rate of growth of the money supply when they feel that interest rates are too high. Of all the effects, only the liquidity effect indicates that a higher rate of money growth will cause a decline in interest rates. In contrast, the income, price-level, and expected-inflation effects indicate that interest rates will rise when money growth is higher. Which of these effects are largest, and how quickly do they take effect? The answers are critical in determining whether interest rates will rise or fall when money supply growth is increased.

Generally, the liquidity effect from the greater money growth takes effect immediately because the rising money supply leads to an immediate decline in the equilibrium interest rate. The income and price-level effects take time to work because it takes time for the increasing money supply to raise the price level and income, which in turn raise interest rates. The expected-inflation effect, which also raises interest rates, can be slow or fast, depending on whether people adjust their expectations of inflation slowly or quickly when the money growth rate is increased.

Three possibilities are outlined in Figure 5-11; each shows how interest rates respond over time to an increased rate of money supply growth starting at time T.

FIGURE 5-11 Response over Time to an Increase in Money Supply Growth

Each panel shows how interest rates respond over time to an increased rate of money supply growth, starting at time T.

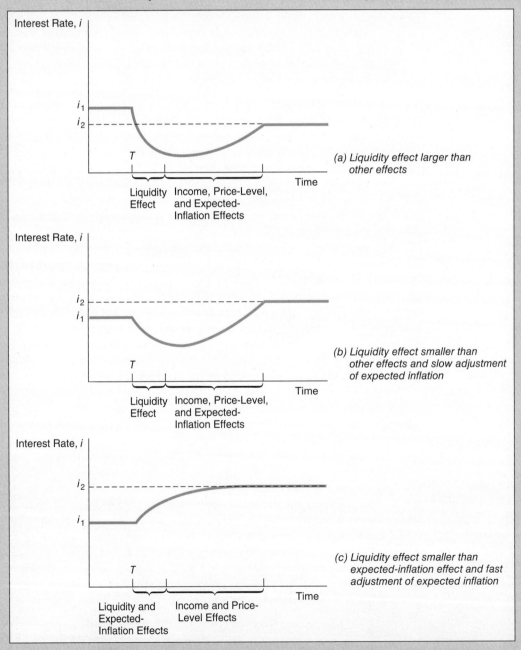

Panel (a) shows a case in which the liquidity effect dominates the other effects so that the interest rate falls from i_1 at time T to a final level of i_2. The liquidity effect operates quickly to lower the interest rate, but as time goes by the other effects start to reverse some of the decline. Because the liquidity effect is larger than the others, however, the interest rate never rises back to its initial level.

Panel (b) has a smaller liquidity effect than the other effects, with the expected-inflation effect operating slowly because expectations of inflation are slow to adjust upward. Initially, the liquidity effect drives down the interest rate. Then the income, price-level, and expected-inflation effects begin to raise it. Because these effects are dominant, the interest rate eventually rises above its initial level to i_2. In the short run, lower interest rates result from increased money growth, but eventually they end up climbing above the initial level.

Panel (c) has the expected-inflation effect dominating as well as operating rapidly because people quickly raise their expectations of inflation when the rate of money growth increases. The expected-inflation effect begins immediately to overpower the liquidity effect, and the interest rate immediately starts to climb. Over time, as the income and price-level effects start to take hold, the interest rate rises even higher, and the eventual outcome is an interest rate that is substantially above the initial interest rate. The result shows clearly that increasing money supply growth is not the answer to reducing interest rates; rather, money growth should be reduced in order to lower interest rates!

An important issue for economic policymakers is which of these three scenarios is closest to reality. If a decline in interest rates is desired, then an increase in money supply growth is called for when the liquidity effect dominates the other effects, as in panel (a). A decrease in money growth is appropriate if the other effects dominate the liquidity effect and expectations of inflation adjust rapidly, as in panel (c). If the other effects dominate the liquidity effect but expectations of inflation adjust only slowly, as in panel (b), then whether you want to increase or decrease money growth depends on whether you care more about what happens in the short run or the long run.

Which scenario does the evidence support? The relationship of interest rates and money growth from 1968 to 2012 is plotted in Figure 5-12. When the rate of money supply growth began to climb in the late 1970s, interest rates rose, indicating that

FIGURE 5-12 Money Growth (M2, Annual Rate) and Interest Rates (Three-Month Treasury Bills), 1968–2012

Source: Statistics Canada CANSIM II Series V122531 and V41552796.

the price-level, income, and expected-inflation effects dominated the liquidity effect. By the early 1980s, interest rates reached levels unprecedented in the post–World War II period, as did the rate of money supply growth.

The scenario depicted in panel (a) of Figure 5-11 seems doubtful, and the case for lowering interest rates by raising the rate of money growth is much weakened. Looking back at Figure 5-5 (page 96), which shows the relationship between interest rates and expected inflation, you should not find this too surprising. The rise in the rate of money supply growth in the 1960s and 1970s is matched by a large rise in expected inflation, which would lead us to predict that the expected-inflation effect would be dominant. It is the most plausible explanation for why interest rates rose in the face of higher money growth. However, Figure 5-12 does not really tell us which one of the two scenarios, panel (b) or panel (c) of Figure 5-11, is more accurate. It depends critically on how fast people's expectations about inflation adjust. However, research using more sophisticated methods than just looking at a graph like Figure 5-12 indicates that increased money growth temporarily lowers short-term interest rates.

MyEconLab is an online homework and tutorial system that puts you in control of your own learning with study and practice tools directly correlated to this chapter's content. Visit MyEconLab to explore the following resources:

- The Questions and Applied Problems are all available in the Study Plan on MyEconLab for further practice. You will also find the answers to all of the Questions and Applied Problems in the Student Resources section of your MyEconLab.
- CANSIM data are available for relevant CANSIM questions in the Student Resources section of your MyEconLab.
- Visit the Student Resources section of MyEconLab to access the following mini-case for this chapter: Mini-Case 5.1: The Behaviour of Interest Rates.
- Visit the Student Resources section of MyEconLab to access the following appendices for this chapter: Appendix 5.1: Models of Asset Pricing; Appendix 5.2: Applying the Asset Market Approach to a Commodity Market: The Case of Gold; and Appendix 5.3: Loanable Funds Framework.

MyEconLab also features Additional Readings, Videos, Glossary Flashcards, Audio Chapter Summaries, Economics News Feeds, Animations, and many additional tools to help you master key concepts from the text.

SUMMARY

((•
MyEconLab
Audio Summ

1. The theory of portfolio choice tells us that the quantity demanded of an asset is (a) positively related to wealth, (b) positively related to the expected return on the asset relative to alternative assets, (c) negatively related to the riskiness of the asset relative to alternative assets, and (d) positively related to the liquidity of the asset relative to alternative assets.

2. The supply and demand analysis for bonds provides one theory of how interest rates are determined. It predicts that interest rates will change when there is a change in demand because of changes in income (or wealth), expected returns, risk, or liquidity or when there is a change in supply because of changes in the attractiveness of investment opportunities, the real cost of borrowing, or government activities.

3. An alternative theory of how interest rates are determined is provided by the liquidity preference framework, which

analyzes the supply of and demand for money. It shows that interest rates will change when there is a change in the demand for money because of changes in income or the price level or when there is a change in the supply of money.

4. There are four possible effects of an increase in the money supply on interest rates: the liquidity effect, the income effect, the price-level effect, and the expected-inflation effect. The liquidity effect indicates that a rise in money supply growth will lead to a decline in interest rates; the other effects work in the opposite direction. The evidence seems to indicate that the income, price-level, and expected-inflation effects dominate the liquidity effect such that an increase in money supply growth leads to higher rather than lower interest rates.

KEY TERMS

asset market approach, p. 90

demand curve, p. 87

excess demand, p. 89

excess supply, p. 89

expected return, p. 85

Fisher effect, p. 96

liquidity, p. 85

liquidity preference framework, p. 99

market equilibrium, p. 89

opportunity cost, p. 100

risk, p. 85

supply curve, p. 88

theory of portfolio choice, p. 86

wealth, p. 85

QUESTIONS

1. Explain why you would be more or less willing to buy a share of Research In Motion (RIM) stock in the following situations:
   a. Your wealth falls.
   b. You expect the stock to appreciate in value.
   c. The bond market becomes more liquid.
   d. You expect gold to appreciate in value.
   e. Prices in the bond market become more volatile.

2. Explain why you would be more or less willing to buy a house under the following circumstances:
   a. You just inherited $100 000.
   b. Real estate commissions fall from 6% of the sales price to 5% of the sales price.
   c. You expect Research In Motion (RIM) stock to double in value next year.
   d. Prices in the stock market become more volatile.
   e. You expect housing prices to fall.

3. Explain why you would be more or less willing to buy gold under the following circumstances:
   a. Gold again becomes acceptable as a medium of exchange.
   b. Prices in the gold market become more volatile.
   c. You expect inflation to rise, and gold prices tend to move with the aggregate price level.
   d. You expect interest rates to rise.

4. Explain why you would be more or less willing to buy long-term Air Canada bonds under the following circumstances:
   a. Trading in these bonds increases, making them easier to sell.
   b. You expect a bear market in stocks (stock prices are expected to decline).
   c. Brokerage commissions on stocks fall.
   d. You expect interest rates to rise.
   e. Brokerage commissions on bonds fall.

5. What would happen to the demand for Rembrandt paintings if the stock market underwent a boom? Why?

6. "The more risk-averse people are, the more likely they are to diversify." Is this statement true, false, or uncertain? Explain your answer.

7. "No one who is risk-averse will ever buy a security that has a lower expected return, more risk, and less liquidity than another security." Is this statement true, false, or uncertain? Explain your answer.

8. What effect will a sudden increase in the volatility of gold prices have on interest rates?

9. How might a sudden increase in people's expectations of future real estate prices affect interest rates?

10. Explain what effect a large federal deficit should have on interest rates.

11. In the aftermath of the global economic crisis that started to take hold in 2008, Canadian government budget deficits increased, yet interest rates on Canada bonds fell sharply, and stayed low for quite some time. Does this make sense? Why or why not?

12. Will there be an effect on interest rates if brokerage commissions on stocks fall? Explain your answer.

13. The governor of the Bank of Canada announces in a press conference that he will fight the higher inflation rate with a new anti-inflation program. Predict what will happen to interest rates if the public believes him.

14. Predict what will happen to interest rates if the public suddenly expects a large increase in stock prices.

15. Predict what will happen to interest rates if prices in the bond market become more volatile.

16. Would fiscal policymakers ever have reason to worry about potentially inflationary conditions? Why or why not?

17. Why should a rise in the price level (but not in expected inflation) cause interest rates to rise when the nominal money supply is fixed?

18. If the next governor of the Bank of Canada has a reputation for advocating an even slower rate of money growth than the current governor, what will happen to interest rates? Discuss the possible resulting situations.

19. M1 money growth in the United States was about 16% in 2008, 7% in 2009, and 9% in 2010. Over the same time period, the yield on three-month Treasury bills fell from almost 3% to close to 0%. Given these high rates of money growth, why did interest rates fall, rather than increase? What does this say about the income, price-level, and expected-inflation effects?

APPLIED PROBLEMS

20. Suppose you visit with a financial adviser, and you are considering investing some of your wealth in one of three investment portfolios: stocks, bonds, or commodities. Your financial adviser provides you with the following table, which gives the probabilities of possible returns from each investment:

Stocks	
Probability	**Return**
0.25	12%
0.25	10%
0.25	8%
0.25	6%

Bonds	
Probability	**Return**
0.6	10%
0.4	7.50%

Commodities	
Probability	**Return**
0.2	20%
0.25	12%
0.25	6%
0.25	4%
0.05	0%

   a. Which investment should you choose to maximize your expected return: stocks, bonds, or commodities?
   b. If you are risk-averse and had to choose between the stock or the bond investments, which would you choose? Why?

21. An important way in which the Bank of Canada decreases the money supply is by selling bonds to the public. Using a supply and demand analysis for bonds, show what effect this action has on interest rates. Is your answer consistent with what you would expect to find with the liquidity preference framework?

22. Using both the liquidity preference framework and the supply and demand for bonds framework, show why interest rates are procyclical (rising when the economy is expanding and falling during recessions).

23. Using both the supply and demand for bonds and liquidity preference frameworks, show what the effect is on interest rates when the riskiness of bonds rises. Are the results the same in the two frameworks?

24. The demand curve and supply curve for one-year discount bonds with a face value of $1000 are represented by the following equations:

$$B^d: \text{Price} = -0.6 \text{ Quantity} + 1140$$
$$B^s: \text{Price} = \text{Quantity} + 700$$

   a. What is the expected equilibrium price and quantity of bonds in this market?
   b. Given your answer to part (a), what is the expected interest rate in this market?

25. The demand curve and supply curve for one-year discount bonds with a face value of $1000 are represented by the following equations:

$$B^d: \text{Price} = -0.6 \text{ Quantity} + 1140$$
$$B^s: \text{Price} = \text{Quantity} + 700$$

Suppose that, as a result of monetary policy actions, the Bank of Canada sells 80 of its bonds that it holds. Assume that bond demand and money demand are held constant.

   a. How does the Bank of Canada policy affect the bond supply equation?
   b. Calculate the effect on the equilibrium interest rate in this market, as a result of the Bank of Canada action.

CANSIM Question

26. Go to the CANSIM data available in the Student Resources section of your MyEconLab website and download monthly data from 1962:1 to 2011:12 for the three-month T-bill rate (series V122531).

   a. What is the average nominal interest rate, i_t?

   b. Calculate the change in i_t.
   $$\Delta i_t = i_{t+1} - i_t.$$
   What is the average change? The average standard deviation?

WEB EXERCISES

1. One of the largest single influences on the level of interest rates is inflation. There are a number of sites that report inflation over time. Go to **www.bankofcanada .ca/rates/price-indexes/cpi** and review the data. What has the average rate of inflation been since 2000? What year had the lowest level of inflation? What year had the highest level of inflation?

2. Increasing prices erode the purchasing power of the dollar. It is interesting to calculate how much goods would have cost at some point in the past after adjusting for inflation. Click on **www.bankofcanada.ca/rates/related/ inflation-calculator/**. What is the cost today of a car that cost $10 000 the year that you were born?

3. One of the points made in this chapter is that inflation erodes investment returns. Go to **www.money chimp.com/articles/econ/inflation_calculator.htm** and review how changes in inflation alter your real return. What happens to the difference between the adjusted value of an investment compared to its inflation-adjusted value as

    a. inflation increases?
    b. the investment horizon lengthens?
    c. expected returns increase?

CHAPTER 6

The Risk and Term Structure of Interest Rates

LEARNING OBJECTIVES

After studying this chapter you should be able to

1. describe how default risk, liquidity, and tax considerations affect interest rates

2. explain how interest rates on bonds with different maturities are related by applying the expectations theory, the segmented markets theory, and the liquidity premium theory

3. predict the movement of short-term interest rates in the future using the yield curve

PREVIEW

In our supply and demand analysis of interest-rate behaviour in Chapter 5, we examined the determination of just one interest rate. Yet we saw earlier that there are enormous numbers of bonds on which the interest rates can and do differ. In this chapter we complete the interest-rate picture by examining the relationship of the various interest rates to one another. Understanding why they differ from bond to bond can help businesses, banks, insurance companies, and private investors decide which bonds to purchase as investments and which ones to sell.

We first look at why bonds with the same term to maturity have different interest rates. The relationship among these interest rates is called the **risk structure of interest rates**, although risk and liquidity both play a role in determining the risk structure. A bond's term to maturity also affects its interest rate, and the relationship among interest rates on bonds with different terms to maturity is called the **term structure of interest rates**. In this chapter we examine the sources and causes of fluctuations in interest rates relative to one another and look at a number of theories that explain these fluctuations.

Risk Structure of Interest Rates

Figure 6-1 shows the yields to maturity for several categories of long-term bonds from 1990 to 2012. It shows us two important features of interest-rate behaviour for bonds of the same maturity: interest rates on different categories of bonds differ from one another in any given year, and the spread (or difference) between the interest rates varies over time. The interest rates on corporate bonds, for example, are above those on Canada bonds and provincial bonds. In addition, the spread between the interest rates on corporate bonds and Canada bonds is very large during

FIGURE 6-1 Long-Term Bond Yields, 1978–2012

Interest rates on different categories of bonds differ from one another in any given year, and the spread (or difference) between the interest rates varies over time.

Source: Statistics Canada CANSIM II Series V122544, V122517, and V122518.

the 1980–1982 and 1990–1991 recessions, is smaller during the mid-1990s, and then widens again afterwards. What factors are responsible for these phenomena?

Default Risk   One attribute of a bond that influences its interest rate is its **risk of default**, which occurs when the issuer of the bond is unable or unwilling to make interest payments when promised or pay off the face value when the bond matures. A corporation suffering big losses might be more likely to suspend interest payments on its bonds. The default risk on its bonds would therefore be quite high. By contrast, Canadian government bonds have usually been considered to have no default risk because the federal government can always increase taxes to pay off its obligations. Bonds like these with no default risk are called **default-free bonds**. The spread between the interest rates on bonds with default risk and default-free bonds, called the **risk premium**, indicates how much additional interest people must earn in order to be willing to hold that risky bond. Our supply and demand analysis of the bond market in Chapter 5 can be used to explain why a bond with default risk always has a positive risk premium and why the higher the default risk is, the larger the risk premium will be.

To examine the effect of default risk on interest rates, let us look at the supply and demand diagrams for the default-free (Canadian government) and corporate long-term bond markets in Figure 6-2. To make the diagrams somewhat easier to read, let's assume that initially corporate bonds have the same default risk as Canada bonds. In this case, these two bonds have the same attributes (identical risk and maturity); their equilibrium prices and interest rates will initially be equal ($P_1^c = P_1^T$ and $i_1^c = i_1^T$), and the risk premium on corporate bonds ($i_1^c - i_1^T$) will be zero.

If the possibility of a default increases because a corporation begins to suffer large losses, the default risk on corporate bonds will increase, and the expected return on these bonds will decrease. In addition, the corporate bond's return will be more uncertain. The theory of portfolio choice predicts that because the expected return on the corporate bond falls relative to the expected return on the default-free

FIGURE 6-2 Response to an Increase in Default Risk on Corporate Bonds

Initially $P_1^c = P_1^T$ and the risk premium is zero. An increase in default risk on corporate bonds shifts the demand curve from D_1^c to D_2^c. Simultaneously, it shifts the demand curve for Canada bonds from D_1^T to D_2^T. The equilibrium price for corporate bonds falls from P_1^c to P_2^c, and the equilibrium interest rate on corporate bonds rises to i_2^c. In the Canada market, the equilibrium bond price rises from P_1^T to P_2^T, and the equilibrium interest rate falls to i_2^T. The brace indicates the difference between i_2^c and i_2^T, the risk premium on corporate bonds. (Note that because P_2^c is lower than P_2^T, i_2^c is greater than i_2^T.)

(a) Corporate bond market

(b) Default-free (Canada) bond market

Canada bond while its relative riskiness rises, the corporate bond is less desirable (holding everything else equal), and demand for it will fall. Another way of thinking about this is that if you were an investor, you would want to hold (demand) a smaller amount of corporate bonds. The demand curve for corporate bonds in panel (a) of Figure 6-2 then shifts to the left, from D_1^c to D_2^c.

At the same time, the expected return on default-free Canada bonds increases relative to the expected return on corporate bonds while their relative riskiness declines. The Canada bonds thus become more desirable, and demand rises, as shown in panel (b) by the rightward shift in the demand curve for these bonds from D_1^T to D_2^T.

As we can see in Figure 6-2, the equilibrium price for corporate bonds falls from P_1^c to P_2^c, and since the bond price is negatively related to the interest rate, the equilibrium interest rate on corporate bonds rises to i_2^c. At the same time, however, the equilibrium price for the Canada bonds rises from P_1^T to P_2^T and the equilibrium interest rate falls to i_2^T. The spread between the interest rates on corporate and default-free bonds—that is, the risk premium on corporate bonds—has risen from zero to $i_2^c - i_2^T$. We can now conclude that ***a bond with default risk will always have a positive risk premium, and an increase in its default risk will raise the risk premium.***

Because default risk is so important to the size of the risk premium, purchasers of bonds need to know whether a corporation is likely to default on its bonds. This information is provided by **credit-rating agencies**, investment advisory firms that rate the quality of corporate and municipal bonds in terms of the probability of default. Credit-rating agencies have become very controversial in recent years because of the role they played in the global financial crisis of 2007–2009 (see the FYI box Conflicts of Interest at Credit-Rating Agencies and the Global Financial Crisis).

Table 6-1 provides the ratings and their description for the four largest credit-rating agencies in Canada: Dominion Bond Rating Service (DBRS), Standard & Poor's Corporation (S&P), Moody's Investor Service, and Fitch Ratings. Bonds with

TABLE 6-1 Bond Ratings by DBRS, Moody's, Standard & Poor's, and Fitch

Rating				
DBRS	**Moody's**	**S&P**	**Fitch**	**Definitions**
AAA	Aaa	AAA	AAA	Prime Maximum Safety
AA high	Aa1	AA+	AA+	High Grade High Quality
AA	Aa2	AA	AA	
AA low	Aa3	AA−	AA−	
A high	A1	A+	A+	Upper Medium Grade
A	A2	A	A	
A low	A3	A−	A−	
BBB high	Baa1	BBB+	BBB+	Lower Medium Grade
BBB	Baa2	BBB	BBB	
BBB low	Baa3	BBB−	BBB−	
BB high	Ba1	BB+	BB+	Noninvestment Grade
BB	Ba2	BB	BB	Speculative
BB low	Ba3	BB−	BB−	
B high	B1	B+	B+	Highly Speculative
B	B2	B	B	
B low	B3	B−	B−	
CCC	Caa1	CCC+	CCC	Substantial Risk
CC	Caa2	CCC	—	In Poor Standing
C	Caa3	CCC−	—	
—	Ca	—	—	Extremely Speculative
—	C	—	—	May Be in Default
—	—	—	DDD	Default
—	—	—	DD	—
D	—	D	D	

relatively low risk of default are called *investment-grade* securities and have a rating of BBB and above. Bonds with ratings below BBB have higher default risk and have been aptly dubbed speculative-grade or **junk bonds**. Because these bonds always have higher interest rates than investment-grade securities, they are also referred to as high-yield bonds. Investment-grade securities whose rating has fallen to junk levels are referred to as **fallen angels**.

Next let's look back at Figure 6-1 and see if we can explain the relationship between interest rates on corporate and Canada bonds. Corporate bonds always have higher interest rates than Canada bonds because they always have some risk of default, whereas Canada bonds do not. Because corporate bonds have a greater default risk than Canada bonds, their risk premium is greater, and the corporate bond rate therefore always exceeds the Canada bond rate. We can use the same analysis to explain the huge jump in the risk premium on corporate bond rates during the 1980–1982, 1990–1991, and 2000 recessions. The recession periods saw a very high rate of business failures and defaults. As we would expect, these factors led to a substantial increase in default risk for bonds issued by vulnerable corporations, and the risk premium for corporate bonds reached unprecedented high levels.

FYI

Conflicts of Interest at Credit-Rating Agencies and the Global Financial Crisis

Debt ratings play a major role in the pricing of debt securities and in the regulatory process. Conflicts of interest arose for credit-rating agencies in the years running up to the global financial crisis when they advised clients on how to structure complex financial instruments that paid out cash flows from subprime mortgages. At the same time, they were rating these identical products, leading to the potential for severe conflicts of interest. Specifically, the large fees they earned from advising clients on how to structure products that they were rating meant they did not have sufficient incentives to make sure their ratings were accurate.

When housing prices began to fall and subprime mortgages began to default in the United States, it became crystal clear that the ratings agencies had done a terrible job of assessing the risk in the subprime products they had helped to structure. Many AAA-rated products had to be downgraded over and over again until they reached junk status. The resulting massive losses on these assets were one reason why so many financial institutions who were holding them got into trouble. Indeed, some commentators have cited credit credit-rating agencies as among the chief villains that should be blamed for the occurrence of the global financial crisis.

APPLICATION

The Global Financial Crisis and the BBB-Treasury Spread in the United States

Starting in August 2007, the collapse of the subprime mortgage market in the United States led to large losses in American financial institutions (which will be discussed more extensively in Chapter 9). As a consequence of the subprime collapse, many investors began to doubt the financial health of corporations with low credit ratings, such as BBB, and even the reliability of the ratings themselves. The perceived increase in default risk for BBB bonds made them less desirable at any given interest rate, decreased the quantity demanded, and shifted the demand curve for BBB bonds to the left. As shown in panel (a) of Figure 6-2, the interest rate on BBB bonds should have risen, which is indeed what happened. Interest rates on BBB bonds rose by 280 **basis points** (2.80 percentage points) from 6.63% at the end of July 2007 to 9.43% at the most virulent stage of the global financial crisis in mid-October 2008. But the increase in perceived default risk for BBB bonds in October 2008 made default-free U.S. Treasury bonds relatively more attractive and shifted the demand curve for these securities to the right—an outcome described by some analysts as a "flight to quality." Just as our analysis predicts in Figure 6-2, interest rates on U.S. Treasury bonds fell by 80 basis points, from 4.78% at the end of July 2007 to 3.98% in mid-October 2008. The spread between interest rates on BBB and Treasury bonds rose by 360 basis points from 1.85% before the crisis to 5.45% afterward.

Liquidity

Another attribute of a bond that influences its interest rate is its liquidity. As we learned in Chapter 5, a liquid asset is one that can be quickly and cheaply converted into cash if the need arises. The more liquid an asset is, the more desirable it is (holding everything else constant). Canada bonds are the most liquid of all long-term bonds because they are so widely traded that they are the easiest to sell quickly and the cost of selling them is low. Corporate bonds are not as liquid because fewer bonds for any one corporation are traded; thus it can be costly to sell these bonds in an emergency because it may be hard to find buyers quickly.

How does the reduced liquidity of corporate bonds affect their interest rates relative to the interest rate on Canada bonds? We can use supply and demand analysis with the same figure that was used to analyze the effect of default risk, Figure 6-2, to show that the lower liquidity of corporate bonds relative to Canada bonds increases the spread between the interest rates on these two bonds. Let us start the analysis by assuming that initially corporate and Canada bonds are equally liquid and all their other attributes are the same. As shown in Figure 6-2, their equilibrium prices and interest rates will initially be equal: $P_1^c = P_1^T$ and $i_1^c = i_1^T$. If the corporate bond becomes less liquid than the Canada bond because it is less widely traded, then (as the theory of portfolio choce indicates) demand for it will fall, shifting its demand curve from D_1^c to D_2^c, as in panel (a). The Canada bond now becomes relatively more liquid in comparison with the corporate bond, so its demand curve shifts rightward from D_1^T to D_2^T, as in panel (b). The shifts in the curves in Figure 6-2 show that the price of the less liquid corporate bond falls and its interest rate rises, while the price of the more liquid Canada bond rises and its interest rate falls.

The result is that the spread between the interest rates on the two bond types has risen. Therefore, the differences between interest rates on corporate bonds and Canada bonds (that is, the risk premiums) reflect not only the corporate bond's default risk but its liquidity too. This is why a risk premium is more accurately a "risk and liquidity premium," but convention dictates that it be called a *risk premium*.

Income Tax Considerations

In Canada, coupon payments on fixed-income securities are taxed as ordinary income in the year they are received. In some other countries, however, certain government bonds are not taxable. In the United States, for example, interest payments on municipal bonds are exempt from federal income taxes, and these bonds have had lower interest rates than U.S. Treasury bonds for at least 40 years. How does taxation affect the interest rate on bonds?

Let us imagine that you have a high enough income to put you in the 40% income tax bracket, where for every extra dollar of income you have to pay 40 cents to the government. If you own a $1000-face-value taxable bond that sells for $1000 and

APPLICATION

Tax-Exempt Versus Taxable Bonds

Suppose you had the opportunity to buy either a tax-exempt bond or a taxable bond, both of which have a face value and purchase price of $1000. Assume both bonds have identical risk. The tax-exempt bond has coupon payments of $60 and a coupon rate of 6%. The taxable bond has coupon payments of $80 and an interest rate of 8%. Which bond would you choose to purchase, assuming a 40% tax rate?

Solution

You would choose to purchase the tax-exempt bond because it will earn you $60 in coupon payments and an interest rate after taxes of 6%. In this case, you pay no taxes on the $60 coupon payments and earn 6% after taxes. However, you have to pay taxes on taxable bonds. You will keep only 60% of the $80 coupon payment because the other 40% goes to taxes. Therefore, you receive $48 of the coupon payment and have an interest rate of 4.8% after taxes. Buying the tax-exempt bond would yield you higher earnings.

has a coupon payment of $100, you get to keep only $60 of the payment after taxes. Although the bond has a 10% interest rate, you actually earn only 6% after taxes.

Suppose, however, that you put your savings into a $1000-face-value tax-exempt bond that sells for $1000 and pays only $80 in coupon payments. Its interest rate is only 8%, but because it is a tax-exempt security, you pay no taxes on the $80 coupon payment, so you earn 8% after taxes. Clearly, you earn more on the tax-exempt bond, so you are willing to hold the bond even though it has a lower interest rate than the taxable bond. Notice that the tax-exempt status of a bond becomes a significant advantage when income tax rates are very high.

Summary

In general, the risk structure of interest rates (the relationship among interest rates on bonds with the same maturity) is explained by three factors: default risk, liquidity, and the income tax treatment of the bond's interest payments. As a bond's default risk increases, the risk premium on that bond (the spread between its interest rate and the interest rate on a default-free Canadian government bond) rises. The greater liquidity of Canada bonds also explains why their interest rates are lower than interest rates on less liquid bonds. If a bond has a favourable tax treatment, as do municipal bonds in the United States, whose interest payments are exempt from federal income taxes, its interest rate will be lower.

Term Structure of Interest Rates

We have seen how risk, liquidity, and tax considerations (collectively embedded in the risk structure) can influence interest rates. Another factor that influences the interest rate on a bond is its term to maturity: bonds with identical risk, liquidity, and tax characteristics may have different interest rates because the time remaining to maturity is different. A plot of the yields on bonds with differing terms to maturity but the same risk, liquidity, and tax considerations is called a **yield curve**, and it describes the term structure of interest rates for particular types of bonds, such as government bonds. The Financial News box shows a yield curve for Government of Canada securities. Yield curves can be classified as upward-sloping, flat, and downward-sloping (the last sort is often referred to as an **inverted yield curve**). When yield curves slope upward, as in the Financial News box, the long-term interest rates are above the short-term interest rates; when yield curves are flat, short- and long-term interest rates are the same; and when yield curves are inverted, long-term interest rates are below short-term interest rates. Yield curves can also have more complicated shapes in which they first slope up and then down, or vice versa. Why do we usually see upward slopes of the yield curve?

Besides explaining why yield curves take on different shapes at different times, a good theory of the term structure of interest rates must explain the following three important empirical facts:

1. As we see in Figure 6-3, interest rates on bonds of different maturities move together over time.

2. When short-term interest rates are low, yield curves are more likely to have an upward slope; when short-term interest rates are high, yield curves are more likely to slope downward and be inverted.

3. Yield curves almost always slope upward, like the yield curves in the Financial News box.

Three theories have been put forward to explain the term structure of interest rates, that is, the relationship among interest rates on bonds of different maturities reflected in yield curve patterns: (1) the expectations theory, (2) the segmented markets theory, and (3) the liquidity premium theory, each of which is described in the

FINANCIAL NEWS

Yield Curves

Many newspapers and Internet sites such as **www.finance.yahoo.com** publish a daily plot of the yield curve for government securities. An example for December 22, 2011, is presented here. The numbers on the vertical axis indicate the interest rate for the Government of Canada securities, with the maturity given on the horizontal axis with "m" denoting month and "y" denoting year.

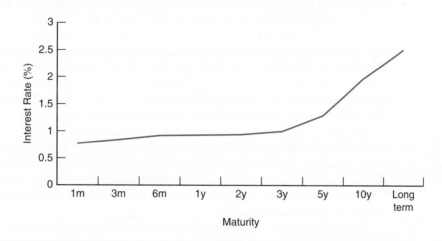

FIGURE 6-3 Movements over Time of Interest Rates on Government of Canada Bonds with Different Maturities, 1962–2012

Interest rates on bonds with different maturities move together over time.

Source: Statistics Canada CANSIM II Series V122531, V122485, and V122487.

following sections. The expectations theory does a good job of explaining the first two facts on our list but not the third. The segmented markets theory can explain fact 3 but not the other two facts, which are well explained by the expectations theory. Because each theory explains facts that the others cannot, a natural way to seek a better understanding of the term structure is to combine features of both theories, which leads us to the liquidity premium theory, which can explain all three facts.

If the liquidity premium theory does a better job of explaining the facts and is hence the most widely accepted theory, why do we spend time discussing the other two theories? There are two reasons. First, the ideas in these two theories provide the groundwork for the liquidity premium theory. Second, it is important to see how economists modify theories to improve them when they find that the predicted results are inconsistent with the empirical evidence.

Expectations Theory

The **expectations theory** of the term structure states the following commonsense proposition: the interest rate on a long-term bond will equal an average of short-term interest rates that people expect to occur over the life of the long-term bond. For example, if people expect that short-term interest rates will be 10% on average over the coming five years, the expectations theory predicts that the interest rate on bonds with five years to maturity will be 10% too. If short-term interest rates were expected to rise even higher after this five-year period so that the average short-term interest rate over the coming 20 years is 11%, then the interest rate on 20-year bonds would equal 11% and would be higher than the interest rate on five-year bonds. We can see that the explanation provided by the expectations theory for why interest rates on bonds of different maturities differ is that short-term interest rates are expected to have different values at future dates.

The key assumption behind this theory is that buyers of bonds do not prefer bonds of one maturity over another, so they will not hold any quantity of a bond if its expected return is less than that of another bond with a different maturity. Bonds that have this characteristic are said to be *perfect substitutes*. What this means in practice is that if bonds with different maturities are perfect substitutes, the expected return on these bonds must be equal.

To see how the assumption that bonds with different maturities are perfect substitutes leads to the expectations theory, let us consider the following two investment strategies:

1. Purchase a one-year bond, and when it matures in one year, purchase another one-year bond.
2. Purchase a two-year bond and hold it until maturity.

APPLICATION

Expectations Theory

The current interest rate on a one-year bond is 9%, and you expect the interest rate on the one-year bond next year to be 11%. What is the expected return over the two years? What interest rate must a two-year bond have to equal the two one-year bonds?

Solution

The expected return over the two years will average 10% per year ([9% + 11%]/2 = 10%). The bondholder will be willing to hold both the one- and two-year bonds only if the expected return per year of the two-year bond equals 10%. Therefore, the interest rate on the two-year bond must equal 10%, the average interest rate on the two one-year bonds. Graphically, we have

Because both strategies must have the same expected return if people are holding both one- and two-year bonds, the interest rate on the two-year bond must equal the average of the two one-year interest rates.

We can make this argument more general. For an investment of $1, consider the choice of holding, for two periods, a two-period bond or two one-period bonds. Using the definitions

i_t = today's (time t) interest rate on a one-period bond

i_{t+1}^e = interest rate on a one-period bond expected for next period (time $t+1$)

i_{2t} = today's (time t) interest rate on the two-period bond

the expected return over the two periods from investing $1 in the two-period bond and holding it for the two periods can be calculated as

$$(1 + i_{2t})(1 + i_{2t}) - 1 = 1 + 2i_{2t} + (i_{2t})^2 - 1 = 2i_{2t} + (i_{2t})^2$$

After the second period, the $1 investment is worth $(1 + i_{2t})(1 + i_{2t})$. Subtracting the $1 initial investment from this amount and dividing by the initial $1 investment gives the rate of return calculated in the above equation. Because $(i_{2t})^2$ is extremely small—if $i_{2t} = 10\% = 0.10$, then $(i_{2t})^2 = 0.01$—we can simplify the expected return for holding the two-period bond for the two periods to

$$2i_{2t}$$

With the other strategy, in which one-period bonds are bought, the expected return on the $1 investment over the two periods is

$$(1 + i_t)(1 + i_{t+1}^e) - 1 = 1 + i_t + i_{t+1}^e + i_t(i_{t+1}^e) - 1 = i_t + e_{t+1}^e + i_t(i_{t+1}^e)$$

This calculation is derived by recognizing that after the first period, the $1 investment becomes $1 + i_t$, and this is reinvested in the one-period bond for the next period, yielding an amount $(1 + i_t)(1 + i_{t+1}^e)$. Then, subtracting the $1 initial investment from this amount and dividing by the initial investment of $1 gives the expected return for the strategy of holding one-period bonds for the two periods. Because $i_t(i_{t+1}^e)$ is also extremely small—if $i_t = i_{t+1}^e = 0.10$, then $i_t(i_{t+1}^e) = 0.01$—we can simplify this to

$$i_t + i_{t+1}^e$$

Both bonds will be held only if these expected returns are equal, that is, when

$$2i_{2t} = i_t + e_{t+1}^e$$

Solving for i_{2t} in terms of the one-period rates, we have

$$i_{2t} = \frac{i_t + i_{t+1}^e}{2} \tag{1}$$

which tells us that the two-period rate must equal the average of the two one-period rates. Graphically, this can be shown as

We can conduct the same steps for bonds with a longer maturity so that we can examine the whole term structure of interest rates. Doing so, we will find that the interest rate of i_{nt} on an n-period bond must equal

$$i_{nt} = \frac{i_t + i^e_{t+1} + i^e_{t+2} + \cdots + i^e_{t+(n-1)}}{n} \qquad (2)$$

Equation 2 states that the *n*-period interest rate equals the average of the one-period interest rates expected to occur over the *n*-period life of the bond. This is a restatement of the expectations theory in more precise terms.[1]

APPLICATION

Expectations Theory and the Yield Curve

The one-year interest rate over the next five years is expected to be 5%, 6%, 7%, 8%, and 9%. Given this information, what are the interest rates on a two-year bond and a five-year bond? Explain what is happening to the yield curve.

Solution

The interest rate on the two-year bond would be 5.5%.

$$i_{nt} = \frac{i_t + i^e_{t+1} + i^e_{t+2} + \cdots + i^e_{t+(n-1)}}{n}$$

where

i_t = year 1 interest rate = 5%
i^e_{t+1} = year 2 interest rate = 6%
n = number of years   = 2

Thus

$$i_{2t} = \frac{5\% + 6\%}{2} = 5.5\%$$

The interest rate on the five-year bond would be 7%.

$$i_{nt} = \frac{i_t + i^e_{t+1} + i^e_{t+2} + \cdots + i^e_{t+(n-1)}}{n}$$

where

i_t = year 1 interest rate = 5%
i^e_{t+1} = year 2 interest rate = 6%
i^e_{t+2} = year 3 interest rate = 7%
i^e_{t+3} = year 4 interest rate = 8%
i^e_{t+4} = year 5 interest rate = 9%
n = number of years   = 5

Thus

$$i_{5t} = \frac{5\% + 6\% + 7\% + 8\% + 9\%}{5} = 7.0\%$$

Using the same equation for the one-, three-, and four-year interest rates, you will be able to verify the one-year to five-year rates as 5.0%, 5.5%, 6.0%, 6.5%, and 7.0%, respectively. The rising trend in short-term interest rates produces an upward-sloping yield curve along which interest rates rise as maturity lengthens.

---

[1]The analysis here has been conducted for discount bonds. Formulas for interest rates on coupon bonds would differ slightly from those used here but would convey the same principle.

The expectations theory is an elegant theory that explains why the term structure of interest rates (as represented by yield curves) changes at different times. When the yield curve is upward-sloping, the expectations theory suggests that short-term interest rates are expected to rise in the future, as we have seen in our numerical example. In this situation, in which the long-term rate is currently above the short-term rate, the average of future short-term rates is expected to be higher than the current short-term rate, which can occur only if short-term interest rates are expected to rise. This is what we see in our numerical example. When the yield curve is inverted (slopes downward), the average of future short-term interest rates is expected to be below the current short-term rate, implying that short-term interest rates are expected to fall, on average, in the future. Only when the yield curve is flat does the expectations theory suggest that short-term interest rates are not expected to change, on average, in the future.

The expectations theory also explains fact 1, that interest rates on bonds with different maturities move together over time. Historically, short-term interest rates have had the characteristic that if they increase today, they will tend to be higher in the future. Hence, a rise in short-term rates will raise people's expectations of future short-term rates. Because long-term rates are the average of expected future short-term rates, a rise in short-term rates will also raise long-term rates, causing short- and long-term rates to move together.

The expectations theory also explains fact 2, that yield curves tend to have an upward slope when short-term interest rates are low and are inverted when short-term rates are high. When short-term rates are low, people generally expect them to rise to some normal level in the future, and the average of future expected short-term rates is high relative to the current short-term rate. Therefore, long-term interest rates will be substantially above current short-term rates, and the yield curve would then have an upward slope. Conversely, if short-term rates are high, people usually expect them to come back down. Long-term rates would then drop below short-term rates because the average of expected future short-term rates would be below current short-term rates and the yield curve would slope downward and become inverted.[2]

The expectations theory is an attractive theory because it provides a simple explanation of the behaviour of the term structure, but unfortunately it has a major shortcoming: it cannot explain fact 3, that yield curves usually slope upward. The typical upward slope of yield curves implies that short-term interest rates are usually expected to rise in the future. In practice, short-term interest rates are just as likely to fall as they are to rise, and so the expectations theory suggests that the typical yield curve should be flat rather than upward-sloping.

Segmented Markets Theory

As the name suggests, the **segmented markets theory** of the term structure sees markets for different-maturity bonds as completely separate and segmented. The interest rate for each bond with a different maturity is then determined by the supply of and demand for that bond with no effects from expected returns on other bonds with other maturities.

---

[2]The expectations theory explains another important fact about the relationship between short-term and long-term interest rates. As you can see looking back at Figure 6-3, short-term interest rates are more volatile than long-term rates. If interest rates are *mean-reverting*—that is, if they tend to head back down after they are at unusually high levels or go back up when they are at unusually low levels—then an average of these short-term rates must necessarily have lower volatility than the short-term rates themselves. Because the expectations theory suggests that the long-term rate will be an average of future short-term rates, it implies that the long-term rate will have lower volatility than short-term rates.

The key assumption in the segmented markets theory is that bonds of different maturities are not substitutes at all, so the expected return from holding a bond of one maturity has no effect on the demand for a bond of another maturity. This theory of the term structure is at the opposite extreme to the expectations theory, which assumes that bonds of different maturities are perfect substitutes.

The argument for why bonds of different maturities are not substitutes is that investors have very strong preferences for bonds of one maturity but not for another, so they will be concerned with the expected returns only for bonds of the maturity they prefer. This might occur because they have a particular holding period in mind, and if they match the maturity of the bond to the desired holding period, they can obtain a certain return with no risk at all.[3] (We have seen in Chapter 4 that if the term to maturity equals the holding period, the return is known for certain because it equals the yield exactly, and there is no interest-rate risk.) For example, people who have a short holding period would prefer to hold short-term bonds. Conversely, if you were putting funds away for your young child to go to college, your desired holding period might be much longer, and you would want to hold longer-term bonds.

In the segmented markets theory, differing yield curve patterns are accounted for by supply and demand differences associated with bonds of different maturities. If, as seems sensible, investors have short desired holding periods and generally prefer bonds with shorter maturities that have less interest-rate risk, the segmented markets theory can explain fact 3, that yield curves typically slope upward. Because in the typical situation the demand for long-term bonds is relatively lower than that for short-term bonds, long-term bonds will have lower prices and higher interest rates, and hence the yield curve will typically slope upward.

Although the segmented markets theory can explain why yield curves usually tend to slope upward, it has a major flaw in that it cannot explain facts 1 and 2. Because it views the market for bonds of different maturities as completely segmented, there is no reason for a rise in interest rates on a bond of one maturity to affect the interest rate on a bond of another maturity. Therefore, it cannot explain why interest rates on bonds of different maturities tend to move together (fact 1). Second, because it is not clear how demand and supply for short- versus long-term bonds change with the level of short-term interest rates, the theory cannot explain why yield curves tend to slope upward when short-term interest rates are low and to be inverted when short-term interest rates are high (fact 2).

Because each of our two theories explains empirical facts that the other cannot, a logical step is to combine the theories, which leads us to the liquidity premium and preferred habitat theories.

Liquidity Premium and Preferred Habitat Theories

The **liquidity premium theory** of the term structure states that the interest rate on a long-term bond will equal an average of short-term interest rates expected to occur over the life of the long-term bond plus a liquidity premium (also referred to as a *term premium*) that responds to supply and demand conditions for that bond.

The liquidity premium theory's key assumption is that bonds of different maturities are substitutes, which means that the expected return on one bond *does* influence the expected return on a bond of a different maturity, but it allows investors to prefer

---

[3]The statement that there is no uncertainty about the return if the term to maturity equals the holding period is literally true only for a discount bond. For a coupon bond with a long holding period, there is some risk because coupon payments must be reinvested before the bond matures. Our analysis here is thus being conducted for discount bonds. However, the gist of the analysis remains the same for coupon bonds because the amount of this risk from reinvestment is small when coupon bonds have the same term to maturity as the holding period.

one bond maturity over another. In other words, bonds of different maturities are assumed to be substitutes but not perfect substitutes. Investors tend to prefer shorter-term bonds because these bonds bear less interest-rate risk. For these reasons, investors must be offered a positive liquidity premium to induce them to hold longer-term bonds. Such an outcome would modify the expectations theory by adding a positive liquidity premium to the equation that describes the relationship between long- and short-term interest rates. The liquidity premium theory is thus written as

$$i_{nt} = \frac{i_t + i_{t+1}^e + i_{t+2}^e + \cdots + i_{t+(n-1)}^e}{n} + l_{nt} \tag{3}$$

where l_{nt} = the liquidity (term) premium for the n-period bond at time t, which is always positive and rises with the term to maturity of the bond, n.

Closely related to the liquidity premium theory is the **preferred habitat theory**, which takes a somewhat less direct approach to modifying the expectations hypothesis but comes up with a similar conclusion. It assumes that investors have a preference for bonds of one maturity over another, a particular bond maturity (preferred habitat) in which they prefer to invest. Because they prefer bonds of one maturity over another, they will be willing to buy bonds that do not have the preferred maturity (habitat) only if they earn a somewhat higher expected return. Because investors are likely to prefer the habitat of short-term bonds to that of longer-term bonds, they are willing to hold long-term bonds only if they have higher expected returns. This reasoning leads to the same Equation 3 implied by the liquidity premium theory with a term premium that typically rises with maturity.

The relationship between the expectations theory and the liquidity premium and preferred habitat theories is shown in Figure 6-4. There we see that because the liquidity premium is always positive and typically grows as the term to maturity increases, the yield curve implied by the liquidity premium theory is always above the yield curve implied by the expectations theory and generally has a steeper slope. (Note that for simplicity we are assuming that the expectations theory yield curve is flat.)

FIGURE 6-4 The Relationship Between the Liquidity Premium (Preferred Habitat) and Expectations Theories

Because the liquidity premium is always positive and grows as the term to maturity increases, the yield curve implied by the liquidity premium and preferred habitat theories is always above the yield curve implied by the expectations theory and has a steeper slope. Note that the yield curve implied by the expectations theory is drawn under the scenario of unchanging future one-year interest rates.

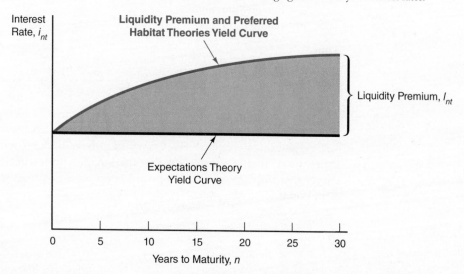

APPLICATION

Liquidity Premium Theory

Let's suppose that the one-year interest rate over the next five years is expected to be 5%, 6%, 7%, 8%, and 9%. Investors' preferences for holding short-term bonds have the liquidity premiums for one-year to five-year bonds as 0%, 0.25%, 0.5%, 0.75%, and 1.0%, respectively. What is the interest rate on a two-year bond and a five-year bond? Compare these findings with the answer in the previous Application dealing with the pure expectations theory.

Solution

The interest rate on the two-year bond would be 5.75%.

$$i_{nt} = \frac{i_t + i^e_{t+1} + i^e_{t+2} + \cdots + i^e_{t+(n-1)}}{n} + l_{nt}$$

where

$$i_t = \text{year 1 interest rate} = 5\%$$
$$i^e_{t+1} = \text{year 2 interest rate} = 6\%$$
$$l_{2t} = \text{liquidity premium} = 0.25\%$$
$$n = \text{number of years} = 2$$

Thus

$$i_{2t} = \frac{5\% + 6\%}{2} + 0.25\% = 5.75\%$$

The interest rate on the five-year bond would be 8%.

$$i_{nt} = \frac{i_t + i^e_{t+1} + i^e_{t+2} + \cdots + i^e_{t+(n-1)}}{n} + l_{nt}$$

where

$$i_t = \text{year 1 interest rate} = 5\%$$
$$i^e_{t+1} = \text{year 2 interest rate} = 6\%$$
$$i^e_{t+2} = \text{year 3 interest rate} = 7\%$$
$$i^e_{t+3} = \text{year 4 interest rate} = 8\%$$
$$i^e_{t+4} = \text{year 5 interest rate} = 9\%$$
$$l_{5t} = \text{liquidity premium} = 1\%$$
$$n = \text{number of years} = 5$$

Thus

$$i_{5t} = \frac{5\% + 6\% + 7\% + 8\% + 9\%}{5} + 1\% = 8.0\%$$

If you did similar calculations for the one-, three-, and four-year interest rates, the one-year to five-year interest rates would be as follows: 5.0%, 5.75%, 6.5%, 7.25%, and 8.0%, respectively. Comparing these findings with those for the pure expectations theory, we can see that the liquidity preference theory produces yield curves that slope more steeply upward because of investors' preferences for short-term bonds.

Let's see if the liquidity premium and preferred habitat theories are consistent with all three empirical facts we have discussed. They explain fact 1, that interest rates on different-maturity bonds move together over time: a rise in short-term interest rates indicates that short-term interest rates will, on average, be higher in the future, and the first term in Equation 3 then implies that long-term interest rates will rise along with them.

They also explain why yield curves tend to have an especially steep upward slope when short-term interest rates are low and to be inverted when short-term rates are high (fact 2). Because investors generally expect short-term interest rates to rise to some normal level when they are low, the average of future expected short-term rates will be high relative to the current short-term rate. With the additional boost of a positive liquidity premium, long-term interest rates will be substantially above current short-term rates, and the yield curve would then have a steep upward slope. Conversely, if short-term rates are high, people usually expect them to come back down. Long-term rates would then drop below short-term rates because the average of expected future short-term rates would be so far below current short-term rates that despite positive liquidity premiums, the yield curve would slope downward.

The liquidity premium and preferred habitat theories explain fact 3, which states that yield curves typically slope upward, by recognizing that the liquidity premium rises with a bond's maturity because of investors' preferences for short-term bonds. Even if short-term interest rates are expected to stay the same on average in the future, long-term interest rates will be above short-term interest rates, and yield curves will typically slope upward. How can the liquidity premium and preferred habitat theories explain the occasional appearance of inverted yield curves if the liquidity premium is positive? It must be that at times short-term interest rates are expected to fall so much in the future that the average of the expected short-term rates is well below the current short-term rate. Even when the positive liquidity premium is added to this average, the resulting long-term rate will still be below the current short-term interest rate.

As our discussion indicates, a particularly attractive feature of the liquidity premium and preferred habitat theories is that they tell you what the market is predicting about future short-term interest rates just from the slope of the yield curve. A steeply rising yield curve, as in panel (a) of Figure 6-5, indicates that short-term interest rates are expected to rise in the future. A moderately steep yield curve, as in panel (b), indicates that short-term interest rates are not expected to rise or fall much in the future. A flat yield curve, as in panel (c), indicates that short-term rates are expected to fall moderately in the future. Finally, an inverted yield curve, as in panel (d), indicates that short-term interest rates are expected to fall sharply in the future.

The Predictive Power of the Yield Curve

People often think that the slope of the yield curve can be used to forecast future short-term interest rates. The yield curve has this practical use only if it is determined by the expectations theory of the term structure that views long-term interest rates as equalling the average of future short-term interest rates. If, however, there are liquidity (term) premiums in the term structure, then it will be difficult to extract a reliable forecast of future short-term interest rates without good measures of these premiums.

In the 1980s, researchers examining the term structure of interest rates questioned whether the slope of the yield curve provides information about movements of future short-term interest rates. They found that the spread between long- and short-term interest rates does not always help predict future short-term interest rates, a finding that may stem from substantial fluctuations in the liquidity (term) premium for long-term bonds. More recent research using more discriminating tests

FIGURE 6-5 Yield Curves and the Market's Expectations of Future Short-Term Interest Rates According to the Liquidity Premium (Preferred Habitat) Theory

A steeply rising yield curve, as in panel (a) of Figure 6-5, indicates that short-term interest rates are expected to rise in the future. A moderately steep yield curve, as in panel (b), indicates that short-term interest rates are not expected to rise or fall much in the future. A flat yield curve, as in panel (c), indicates that short-term rates are expected to fall moderately in the future. Finally, an inverted yield curve, as in panel (d), indicates that short-term interest rates are expected to fall sharply in the future.

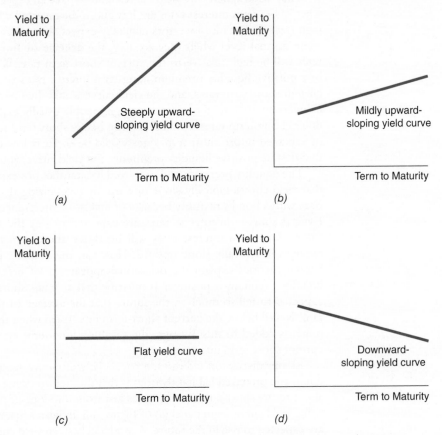

now favours a different view. It shows that the term structure contains quite a bit of information for the very short run (over the next several months) and the long run (over several years) but is unreliable at predicting movements in interest rates over the intermediate term (the time in between). Research also finds that the yield curve helps forecast future inflation and business cycles (see the FYI box).

Summary

The liquidity premium and preferred habitat theories are the most widely accepted theories of the term structure of interest rates because they explain the major empirical facts about the term structure so well. They combine the features of both the expectations theory and the segmented markets theory by asserting that a long-term interest rate will be the sum of a liquidity (term) premium and the average of the short-term interest rates that are expected to occur over the life of the bond.

The liquidity premium and preferred habitat theories explain the following facts: (1) Interest rates on bonds of different maturities tend to move together over time, (2) yield curves usually slope upward, and (3) when short-term interest rates are low, yield curves are more likely to have a steep upward slope, whereas when short-term interest rates are high, yield curves are more likely to be inverted.

The theories also help us predict the movement of short-term interest rates in the future. A steep upward slope of the yield curve means that short-term rates are expected to rise, a mild upward slope means that short-term rates are expected to remain the same, a flat slope means that short-term rates are expected to fall moderately, and an inverted yield curve means that short-term rates are expected to fall sharply.

FYI

The Yield Curve as a Forecasting Tool for Inflation and the Business Cycle

Because the yield curve contains information about future expected interest rates, it should also have the capacity to help forecast inflation and real output fluctuations. To see this, recall from Chapter 5 that rising interest rates are associated with economic booms and falling interest rates with recessions. When the yield curve is either flat or downward sloping, it suggests that future short-term interest rates are expected to fall and, therefore, that the economy is more likely to enter a recession. Indeed, the yield curve is found to be an accurate predictor of the business cycle.

In Chapter 4, we also learned that a nominal interest rate is composed of a real interest rate and expected inflation, implying that the yield curve contains information about the future path of nominal interest rates and future inflation. A steep yield curve predicts a future increase in inflation, while a flat or downward-sloping yield curve forecasts a future decline in inflation.

The ability of the yield curve to forecast business cycles and inflation is one reason why the slope of the yield curve is part of the toolkit of many economic forecasters and is often viewed as a useful indicator of the stance of monetary policy, with a steep yield curve indicating loose policy and a flat or downward-sloping yield curve indicating tight policy.

APPLICATION

Interpreting Yield Curves, 1990–2012

Figure 6-6 illustrates several yield curves that have appeared for Canadian government bonds in recent years. What do these yield curves tell us about the public's expectations of future movements of short-term interest rates?

The inverted yield curve that occurred in January 1990 indicated that short-term interest rates were expected to decline sharply in the future. In order for longer-term interest rates with their positive liquidity premium to be well below the short-term interest rate, short-term interest rates must be expected to decline so sharply that their average is far below the current short-term rate. Indeed, the public's expectations of sharply lower short-term interest rates evident in the yield curve were realized soon after January 1990; by March 1991, three-month Treasury bill rates had declined from over 12% to less than 9%.

The upward-sloping yield curve in January 2011 indicates that short-term interest rates would climb in the future. The long-term interest rate is above the short-term interest rate when short-term interest rates are expected to rise because their average plus the liquidity premium will be above the current short-term rate. The moderately upward-sloping yield curve in September 1986 indicates that short-term interest rates were expected neither to rise nor to fall in the near future. In this case, their average remains the same as the current short-term rate, and the positive liquidity premium for longer-term bonds explains the moderate upward slope of the yield curve.

FIGURE 6-6 Yield Curves for Government of Canada Bonds

Yield curves for Government of Canada bonds for different dates from 1986 to 2012.

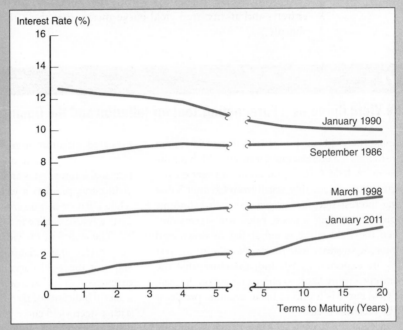

Source: Statistics Canada CANSIM II Series V122531, V122532, V122533, V122538, V122539, V122540, V122543, and V122544, and the authors' calculations.

APPLICATION

Using the Term Structure to Forecast Interest Rates

Interest-rate forecasts are extremely important to managers of financial institutions because future changes in interest rates have a significant impact on the profitability of their institutions. Furthermore, interest-rate forecasts are needed when managers of financial institutions have to set interest rates on loans that are promised to customers in the future. Our discussion of the term structure of interest rates has indicated that the slope of the yield curve provides general information about the market's prediction of the future path of interest rates. For example, a steeply upward-sloping yield curve indicates that short-term interest rates are predicted to rise in the future, and a downward-sloping yield curve indicates that short-term interest rates are predicted to fall. However, a financial institution manager needs much more specific information on interest-rate forecasts than this. Here we show how the manager of a financial institution can generate specific forecasts of interest rates using the term structure.

To see how this is done, let's start the analysis using the approach we took in developing the expectations theory. Recall that because bonds of different maturities are considered perfect substitutes, we assumed that the expected return over two periods from investing $1 in a two-period bond, which is $(1 + i_{2t})(1 + i_{2t}) - 1$, must equal the expected return from investing \$1 in one-period bonds, which is $(1 + i_t)(1 + i_{t+1}^e) - 1$. This is shown graphically as follows:

In other words,

$$(1 + i_t)(1 + i_{t+1}^e) - 1 = (1 + i_{2t})(1 + i_{2t}) - 1$$

Through some tedious algebra we can solve for i_{t+1}^e:

$$i_{t+1}^e = \frac{(1 + i_{2t})^2}{1 + i_t} - 1 \tag{4}$$

This measure of i_{t+1}^e is called the **forward rate** because it is the one-period interest rate that the pure expectations theory of the term structure indicates is expected to prevail one period in the future. To differentiate forward rates derived from the term structure from actual interest rates that are observed at time t, we call these observed interest rates **spot rates**.

Going back to the Application Expectations Theory and the Yield Curve (p. 122), which we used to discuss the expectations theory earlier in this chapter, at time t the one-year interest rate is 5% and the two-year rate is 5.5%. Plugging these numbers into Equation 4 yields the following estimate of the forward rate one period in the future:

$$i_{t+1}^e = \frac{(1 + 0.055)^2}{1 + 0.05} - 1 = 0.06 = 6\%$$

Not surprisingly, this 6% forward rate is identical to the expected one-year interest rate one year in the future. This is exactly what we should find, as our calculation here is just another way of looking at the pure expectations theory.

We can also compare holding the three-year bond against holding a sequence of one-year bonds, which reveals the following relationship:

$$(1 + i_t)(1 + i_{t+1}^e)(1 + i_{t+2}^e) - 1 = (1 + i_{3t})(1 + i_{3t})(1 + i_{3t}) - 1$$

And plugging in the estimate for i_{t+1}^e derived in Equation 4, we can solve for i_{t+2}^e:

$$i_{t+2}^e = \frac{(1 + i_{3t})^3}{(1 + i_{2t})^2} - 1$$

Continuing with these calculations, we obtain the general solution for the forward rate n periods into the future:

$$i_{t+n}^e = \frac{(1 + i_{n+1t})^{n+1}}{(1 + i_{nt})^n} - 1 \tag{5}$$

Our discussion indicated that the expectations theory is not entirely satisfactory because investors must be compensated with liquidity premiums to induce them to hold longer-term bonds. Hence, we need to modify our analysis, as we did when discussing the liquidity premium theory, by allowing for these liquidity premiums in estimating predictions of future interest rates.

Recall from the discussion of those theories that because investors prefer to hold short-term rather than long-term bonds, the n-period interest rate differs from that indicated by the pure expectations theory by a liquidity premium of ℓ_{nt}. So to allow for liquidity premiums, we need merely subtract ℓ_{nt} from i_{nt} in our formula to derive i^e_{t+n}:

$$i^e_{t+n} = \frac{(1 + i_{n+1t} - \ell_{n+1t})^{n+1}}{(1 + i_{nt} - \ell_{nt})^n} - 1 \tag{6}$$

This measure of i^e_{t+n} is referred to, naturally enough, as the *adjusted forward-rate forecast*. In the case of i^e_{t+1}, Equation 6 produces the following estimate:

$$i^e_{t+1} = \frac{(1 + i_{2t} - \ell_{2t})^2}{1 + i_t} - 1$$

Using the example from the Liquidity Premium Theory Application on page 126, at time t the ℓ_{2t} liquidity premium is 0.25%, $\ell_{1t} = 0$, the one-year interest rate is 5%, and the two-year interest rate is 5.75%. Plugging these numbers into our equation yields the following adjusted forward-rate forecast for one period in the future:

$$i^e_{t+1} = \frac{(1 + 0.0575 - 0.0025)^2}{1 + 0.05} - 1 = 0.06 = 6\%$$

which is the same as the expected interest rate used in the Application on expectations theory, as it should be.

Our analysis of the term structure thus provides managers of financial institutions with a fairly straightforward procedure for producing interest-rate forecasts. First they need to estimate ℓ_{nt}, the values of the liquidity premiums for various n. Then they need merely apply the formula in Equation 6 to derive the market's forecasts of future interest rates.

APPLICATION

Forward Rate

A customer asks a bank if it would be willing to commit to making the customer a one-year loan at an interest rate of 8% one year from now. To compensate for the costs of making the loan, the bank needs to charge one percentage point more than the expected interest rate on a Canada bond with the same maturity if it is to make a profit. If the bank manager estimates the liquidity premium to be 0.4%, and the one-year Canada bond rate is 6% and the two-year bond rate is 7%, should the manager be willing to make the commitment?

Solution

The bank manager is unable to make the loan because at an interest rate of 8%, the loan is likely to be unprofitable to the bank.

$$i^e_{t+n} = \frac{(1 + i_{n+1t} - \ell_{n+1t})^{n+1}}{(1 + i_{nt} - \ell_{nt})^n} - 1$$

where

$i_{n+1t} = $ two-year bond rate $= 0.07$
$\ell_{n+1t} = $ liquidity premium $= 0.004$
$i_{nt} = $ one-year bond rate $= 0.06$
$\ell_{1t} = $ liquidity premium $= 0$
$n = $ number of years $= 1$

Thus

$$i_{t+1}^e = \frac{(1 + 0.07 - 0.004)^2}{1 + 0.06} - 1 = 0.072 = 7.2\%$$

The market's forecast of the one-year Canada bond rate one year in the future is therefore 7.2%. Adding the 1% necessary to make a profit on the one-year loan means that the loan is expected to be profitable only if it has an interest rate of 8.2% or higher.

MyEconLab

MyEconLab is an online homework and tutorial system that puts you in control of your own learning with study and practice tools directly correlated to this chapter's content. Visit MyEconLab to explore the following resources:

- The Questions and Applied Problems are all available in the Study Plan on MyEconLab for further practice. You will also find the answers to all of the Questions and Applied Problems in the Student Resources section of your MyEconLab.

- CANSIM data are available for relevant CANSIM questions in the Student Resources section of your MyEconLab.

- Visit the Student Resources section of MyEconLab to access the following mini-case for this chapter: Mini-Case 6.1: Yield Curve Hypotheses and the Effects of Economic Events.

MyEconLab also features Additional Readings, Videos, Glossary Flashcards, Audio Chapter Summaries, Economics News Feeds, Animations, and many additional tools to help you master key concepts from the text.

((• SUMMARY

MyEconLab
dio Summary

1. Bonds with the same maturity will have different interest rates because of three factors: default risk, liquidity, and tax considerations. The greater a bond's default risk, the higher its interest rate relative to other bonds; the greater a bond's liquidity, the lower its interest rate; and bonds with tax-exempt status will have lower interest rates than they otherwise would. The relationship among interest rates on bonds with the same maturity that arises because of these three factors is known as the risk structure of interest rates.

2. Three theories of the term structure provide explanations of how interest rates on bonds with different terms to maturity are related. The expectations theory views long-term interest rates as equalling the average of future short-term interest rates expected to occur over the life of the bond. By contrast, the segmented markets theory treats the determination of interest rates for each bond's maturity as the outcome of supply and demand in that market only. Neither of these theories

by itself can explain the fact that interest rates on bonds of different maturities move together over time and that yield curves usually slope upward.

3. The liquidity premium (preferred habitat) theory combines the features of the other two theories, and by so doing is able to explain the facts just mentioned. It views long-term interest rates as equalling the average of future short-term interest rates expected to occur over the life of the bond plus a liquidity premium. This theory allows us to infer the market's expectations about the movement of future short-term interest rates from the yield curve. A steeply upward-sloping curve indicates that future short-term rates are expected to rise; a mildly upward-sloping curve, that short-term rates are expected to stay the same; a flat curve, that short-term rates are expected to decline slightly; and an inverted yield curve, that a substantial decline in short-term rates is expected in the future.

KEY TERMS

basis point, p. 116

credit-rating agencies, p. 114

default-free bonds, p. 113

expectations theory, p. 120

fallen angels, p. 115

forward rate, p. 131

inverted yield curve, p. 118

junk bonds, p. 115

liquidity premium theory, p. 124

QUESTIONS

1. If junk bonds are "junk," why would investors buy them?

2. Which should have the higher risk premium on its interest rates, a corporate bond with a Moody's BBB rating or a corporate bond with a C rating? Why?

3. Why do Canadian Treasury bills have lower interest rates than large-denomination negotiable bank CDs?

4. In the fall of 2008, AIG, the largest insurance company in the world at the time, was at risk of defaulting due to the severity of the global financial crisis. As a result, the U.S. government stepped in to support AIG with large capital injections and an ownership stake. How would this affect the yield and risk premium on AIG corporate debt, if at all?

5. Risk premiums on corporate bonds are usually *anticyclical*; that is, they decrease during business cycle expansions and increase during recessions. Why is this so?

6. "If bonds of different maturities are close substitutes, their interest rates are more likely to move together." Is this statement true, false, or uncertain? Explain your answer.

7. The Canadian government offers some of its debt as Real Return Bonds, in which the price of bonds is adjusted for inflation over the life of the debt instrument. Real Return Bonds are traded on a much smaller scale than nominal Canada bonds of equivalent maturity. What can you conclude about the liquidity premium between Real Return Bonds and nominal Canada bonds?

8. Predict what will happen to interest rates on a corporation's bonds if the federal government guarantees today that it will pay creditors if the corporation goes bankrupt in the future. What will happen to the interest rates on Canada bonds?

9. Predict what would happen to the risk premiums on corporate bonds if brokerage commissions were lowered in the corporate bond market.

10. During 2008, the difference in yield (the *yield spread*) between three-month AA-rated financial commercial paper and three-month AA-rated nonfinancial commercial paper steadily increased from its usual level of close to zero, spiking to over a full percentage point at its peak in October 2008. What explains this sudden increase?

11. If the income tax exemption on U.S. municipal bonds were abolished, what would happen to the interest rates on these bonds? What effect would the change have on interest rates on U.S. Treasury securities?

12. Prior to 2008, mortgage lenders in the United States required a house inspection to assess its value, and often used the same one or two inspection companies in the same geographical market. Following the collapse of the housing market in 2008, mortgage lenders required a house inspection, but this was arranged through a third party. How does this illustrate a conflict of interest similar to the role that credit-rating agencies played in the global financial crisis?

13. "Using the expectations theory of the term structure, it is better to invest in one-year bonds, reinvested over two years, than to invest in a two-year bond, if interest rates on one-year bonds are expected to be the same in both years." Is this statement true, false, or uncertain?

14. If bond investors decide that 30-year bonds are no longer as desirable an investment, predict what will happen to the yield curve, assuming (a) the expectations theory of the term structure holds and (b) the segmented markets theory of the term structure holds.

15. Suppose the interest rates on one-, five-, and 10-year Canada bonds are currently 3%, 6%, and 6%, respectively. Investor A chooses to hold only one-year bonds and Investor B is indifferent between holding five- and 10-year bonds. How can you explain the behaviours of Investors A and B?

16. If a yield curve looks like the one shown in the figure below, what is the market predicting about the movement of future short-term interest rates? What might the yield curve indicate about the market's predictions for the inflation rate in the future?

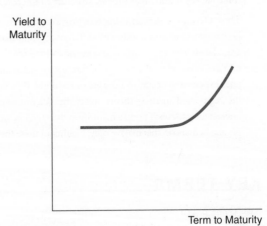

17. If a yield curve looks like the one shown in the figure below, what is the market predicting about the movement of future short-term interest rates? What might the yield curve indicate about the market's predictions for the inflation rate in the future?

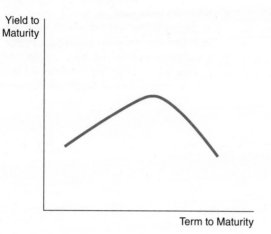

18. If yield curves, on average, were flat, what would this say about the liquidity (term) premiums in the term structure? Would you be more or less willing to accept the expectations theory?

19. If the yield curve suddenly became steeper, how would you revise your predictions of interest rates in the future?

20. If expectations of future short-term interest rates suddenly fell, what would happen to the slope of the yield curve?

21. Suppose that the Bank of Canada made an announcement that it would purchase up to $300 billion of longer-term Canada securities over the following six months. What effect might this policy have on the yield curve?

APPLIED PROBLEMS

22. In 2010 and 2011, the government of Greece risked defaulting on its debt due to a severe budget crisis. Show, using bond market graphs, the effect on the risk premium between Canadian government debt and comparable maturity Greek debt.

23. Assuming that the expectations theory is the correct theory of the term structure, calculate the interest rates in the term structure for maturities of one to five years, and plot the resulting yield curves for the following paths of one-year interest rates over the next five years:

    a. 5%, 7%, 7%, 7%, 7%
    b. 5%, 4%, 4%, 4%, 4%

    How would your yield curves change if people preferred shorter-term bonds over longer-term bonds?

24. Assuming that the expectations theory is the correct theory of the term structure, calculate the interest rates in the term structure for maturities of one to five years, and plot the resulting yield curves for the following paths of one-year interest rates over the next five years:

    a. 5%, 6%, 7%, 6%, 5%
    b. 5%, 4%, 3%, 4%, 5%

    How would your yield curves change if people preferred shorter-term bonds over longer-term bonds?

25. The table below shows current and expected future one-year interest rates, as well as current interest rates on multi-year bonds. Use the table to calculate the liquidity premium for each multi-year bond.

Year	1-Year Bond Rate	Multi-Year Bond Rate
1	2%	2%
2	3%	3%
3	4%	5%
4	6%	6%
5	7%	8%

CANSIM Questions

26. Go to the CANSIM data available in the Student Resources section of your MyEconLab website and download monthly data from January 1976 to December 2011 on the three-month T-bill rate (series V122531) and the interest rate on long-term Canada bonds (series V122544).

    a. Calculate the mean and standard deviation as well as the maximum and minimum values for each series over the sample period.

    b. Which were the worst and best years in terms of interest rates?

WEB EXERCISES

1. Go to **www.bloomberg.com** and click on "Market Data" and then "Rates & Bonds" to find information about the yield curve in Australia, Brazil, Germany, Hong Kong, Japan, the United Kingdom, and the United States. What does each of these yield curves tell us about the public's expectations of future movements of short-term interest rates?

2. Investment companies attempt to explain to investors the nature of the risk the investor incurs when buying shares in their mutual funds. For example, Vanguard (a U.S. company) carefully explains interest-rate risk and offers alternative funds with different interest-rate risks. Go to **http://flagship.vanguard.com/ VGApp/hnw/FundsStocksOverview**.

   a. Select the bond fund you would recommend to an investor who has very low tolerance for risk and a short investment horizon. Justify your answer.

   b. Select the bond fund you would recommend to an investor who has very high tolerance for risk and a long investment horizon. Justify your answer.

CHAPTER 7

The Stock Market, the Theory of Rational Expectations, and the Efficient Market Hypothesis

LEARNING OBJECTIVES

After studying this chapter you should be able to

1. illustrate how stocks are valued as the present value of dividends
2. determine how information in the market affects asset prices: the theory of efficient capital markets, according to which current asset prices fully reflect all available information

PREVIEW

Rarely does a day go by that the stock market isn't a major news item. We have witnessed huge swings in the stock market in recent years. The 1990s were an extraordinary decade for stocks: the S&P/TSX Composite in Canada and the Dow Jones and S&P 500 indexes in the United States increased more than 400%, while the tech-laden Nasdaq index rose more than 1000%. By early 2000 these indexes had reached record highs. Unfortunately, the good times did not last. Starting in March 2000, the stock market began to decline and many investors lost their shirts. The S&P/TSX crashed, falling by more than 40% through March 2003. After subsequently rising over 120%, the stock market crashed again during the global financial crisis, falling by over 40% from its peak in the fall of 2007. Starting in 2009, the stock market recovered quickly, rising by more than 50% by 2011.

Because so many people invest in the stock market and the price of stocks affects the ability of people to retire comfortably, the market for stocks is undoubtedly the financial market that receives the most attention and scrutiny. In this chapter, we look first at how this important market works.

We begin by discussing the fundamental theories that underlie the valuation of stocks. These theories are critical to understanding the forces that cause the value of stocks to rise and fall minute by minute and day by day. Once we have learned the methods for stock valuation, we need to explore how expectations about the market affect its behaviour. We do so by examining the *theory of rational expectations*, which has more general implications for how markets in other securities besides stocks operate. When this theory is applied to financial markets, the outcome is the *efficient market hypothesis*. The theory of rational expectations is also central to debates about the conduct of monetary policy, to be discussed in Chapter 26.

Computing the Price of Common Stock

Common stock is the principal way that corporations raise equity capital. Holders of common stock own an interest in the corporation consistent with the percentage of outstanding shares owned. This ownership interest gives **shareholders**—those who hold stock in a corporation—a bundle of rights. The most important are the right to vote and to be the **residual claimant** of all funds flowing into the firm (known as **cash flows**), meaning that the shareholder receives whatever remains after all other claims against the firm's assets have been satisfied. Shareholders are paid dividends from the net earnings of the corporation. **Dividends** are payments made periodically, usually every quarter, to shareholders. The board of directors of the firm sets the level of the dividend, usually upon the recommendation of management. In addition, the shareholder has the right to sell the stock.

One basic principle of finance is that the value of any investment is found by computing the value today of all cash flows the investment will generate over its life. For example, a commercial building will sell for a price that reflects the net cash flows (rents – expenses) it is projected to have over its useful life. Similarly, we value common stock as the value in today's dollars of all future cash flows. The cash flows a shareholder might earn from stock are dividends, the sales price, or both. To develop the theory of stock valuation, we begin with the simplest possible scenario: you buy the stock, hold it for one period to get a dividend, and then sell the stock. We call this the *one-period valuation model*.

The One-Period Valuation Model

Suppose that you have some extra money to invest for one year. After a year, you will need to sell your investment to pay tuition. After watching the financial news on TV, you decide that you want to buy Royal Bank stock. You call your broker and find that Royal Bank is currently selling for $50 per share and pays $1.25 per year in dividends. The analyst on the financial news predicts that the stock will be selling for $60 in one year. Should you buy this stock?

To answer this question, you need to determine whether the current price accurately reflects the analyst's forecast. To value the stock today, you need to find the present discounted value of the expected cash flows (future payments) using the formula $PV = CF(1 + i)n$ in Equation 1 of Chapter 4 (page 63). Note that in this equation, the discount factor used to discount the cash flows is the required return on investments in equity rather than the interest rate. The cash flows consist of one dividend payment plus a final sales price. When these cash flows are discounted back to the present, the following equation computes the current price of the stock:

$$P_0 = \frac{Div_1}{(1 + k_e)} + \frac{P_1}{(1 + k_e)} \tag{1}$$

where P_0 = the current price of the stock; the zero subscript refers to time period zero, or the present

Div_1 = the dividend paid at the end of year

k_e = the required return on investments in equity

P_1 = the price at the end of the first period; the assumed sales price of the stock

The Generalized Dividend Valuation Model

Using the same concept, the one-period dividend valuation model can be extended to any number of periods: the value of stock is the present value of all future cash flows. The only cash flows that an investor will receive are dividends and a final sales

APPLICATION

Stock Valuation

To see how Equation 1 works, let's compare the price of the Royal Bank stock given the figures reported above. You will need to know the required return on equity to find the present value of the cash flows. Since a stock is more risky than a bond, you will require a higher return than that offered in the bond market. Assume that after careful consideration you decide that you would be satisfied to earn 12% on the investment.

Solution

Putting the numbers into Equation 1 yields the following:

$$P_0 = \frac{\$1.25}{1 + 0.12} + \frac{\$60}{1 + 0.12} = \$1.12 + \$53.57 = \$54.69$$

Based on your analysis, you find that the stock is worth $54.69. Since the stock is currently available for $50 per share, you would choose to buy it. Why is the stock selling for less than $54.69? It may be because other investors place a different risk on the cash flows or estimate the cash flows to be less than you do.

price when the stock is ultimately sold in period *n*. The generalized multi-period formula for stock valuation can be written as

$$P_0 = \frac{D_1}{(1 + k_e)^1} + \frac{D_2}{(1 + k_e)^2} + \cdots + \frac{D_n}{(1 + k_e)^n} + \frac{P_n}{(1 + k_e)^n} \tag{2}$$

If you tried to use Equation 2 to find the value of a share of stock, you would soon realize that you must first estimate the value the stock will have at some point in the future before you can estimate its value today. In other words, you must find P_n in order to find P_0. However, if P_n is far in the future, it will not affect P_0. For example, the present value of a share of stock that sells for $50 seventy-five years from now using a 12% discount rate is just one cent [$50/(1.12^{75}) = \$0.01$]. This reasoning implies that the current value of a share of stock can be calculated as simply the present value of the future dividend stream. The **generalized dividend model** is rewritten in Equation 3 without the final sales price:

$$P_0 = \sum_{t=1}^{\infty} \frac{D_t}{(1 + k_e)^t} \tag{3}$$

Consider the implications of Equation 3 for a moment. The generalized dividend model says that the price of stock is determined only by the present value of the dividends and that nothing else matters. Many stocks do not pay dividends, so how is it that these stocks have value? *Buyers of the stock expect that the firm will pay dividends someday.* Most of the time a firm institutes dividends as soon as it has completed the rapid growth phase of its life cycle.

The generalized dividend valuation model requires that we compute the present value of an infinite stream of dividends, a process that could be difficult, to say the least. Therefore, simplified models have been developed to make the calculations easier. One such model is the **Gordon growth model**, which assumes constant dividend growth.

The Gordon Growth Model

Many firms strive to increase their dividends at a constant rate each year. Equation 4 rewrites Equation 3 to reflect this constant growth in dividends:

$$P_0 = \frac{D_0 \times (1 + g)^1}{(1 + k_e)^1} + \frac{D_0 \times (1 + g)^2}{(1 + k_e)^2} + \cdots + \frac{D_0 \times (1 + g)^\infty}{(1 + k_e)^\infty} \tag{4}$$

where

D_0 = the most recent dividend paid
g = the expected constant growth rate in dividends
k_e = the required return on an investment in equity

Equation 4 has been simplified using algebra to obtain Equation 5.[1]

$$P_0 = \frac{D_0 \times (1 + g)}{(k_e - g)} = \frac{D_1}{(k_e - g)} \tag{5}$$

This model is useful for finding the value of stock, given a few assumptions:

1. *Dividends are assumed to continue growing at a constant rate forever.* Actually, as long as they are expected to grow at a constant rate for an extended period of time, the model should yield reasonable results. This is because errors about distant cash flows become small when discounted to the present.

2. *The growth rate is assumed to be less than the required return on equity, k_e.* Myron Gordon, in his development of the model, demonstrated that this is a reasonable assumption. In theory, if the growth rate were faster than the rate demanded by holders of the firm's equity, in the long run the firm would grow impossibly large.

APPLICATION

Stock Valuation, Constant Growth

To see how Equation 5 works, let's compute the current market price of Coca-Cola stock, assuming dividends grow at a constant rate of 10.95%, $D_0 = \$1.00$, and the required return is 13%.

---

[1]To generate Equation 5 from Equation 4, first multiply both sides of Equation 4 by $(1 + k_e)/(1 + g)$ and subtract Equation 4 from the result. This yields

$$\frac{P_0 \times (1 + k_e)}{(1 + g)} - P_0 = D_0 - \frac{D_0 \times (1 + g)^\infty}{(1 + k_e)^\infty}$$

Assuming that k_e is greater than g, the term on the far right will approach zero and can be dropped. Thus, after factoring P_0 out of the left-hand side,

$$P_0 \times \left[\frac{1 + k_e}{1 + g} - 1 \right] = D_0$$

Next, simplify by combining terms to

$$P_0 \times \frac{(1 + k_e) - (1 + g)}{1 + g} = D_0$$

$$P_0 = \frac{D_0 \times (1 + g)}{(k_e - g)} = \frac{D_1}{(k_e - g)}$$

Solution

$$P_0 = \frac{D_0 \times (1 + g)}{k_e - g}$$

$$P_0 = \frac{\$1.00 \times (1.1095)}{0.13 - 0.1095}$$

$$P_0 = \frac{\$1.1095}{0.0205} = \$54.12$$

Coca-Cola stock should sell for $54.12 if the assumptions regarding the constant growth rate and required return are correct.

Price-Earnings Valuation Method

Theoretically, the best method of stock valuation is the dividend valuation approach. Sometimes, however, it is difficult to apply. If a firm is not paying dividends or has a very erratic growth rate, the results may not be satisfactory. Other approaches to stock valuation are sometimes applied. Among the more popular is the price-earnings ratio.

The **price-earnings ratio (PE)** is a widely watched measure of how much the market is willing to pay for $1 of earnings from a firm. A high PE has two interpretations:

1. A higher than average PE may mean that the market expects earnings to rise in the future. This would return the PE to a more normal level.

2. A high PE may alternatively indicate that the market feels the firm's earnings are very low risk and is therefore willing to pay a premium for them.

The PE ratio can be used to estimate the value of a firm's stock. Note that algebraically the product of the PE ratio times expected earnings is the firm's stock price.

$$\frac{P}{E} \times E = P \tag{6}$$

Firms in the same industry are expected to have similar PE ratios in the long run. The value of a firm's stock can be found by multiplying the average industry PE times the expected earnings per share.

APPLICATION

Stock Valuation, PE Ratio Approach

The average industry PE ratio for restaurants similar to Applebee's, a pub-restaurant chain, is 23. What is the current price of Applebee's if earnings per share are projected to be $1.13?

Solution

Using Equation 6 and the data given we find

$$P_0 = P/E \times E$$

$$P_0 = 23 \times \$1.13 = \$25.99$$

The PE ratio approach is especially useful for valuing privately held firms and firms that do not pay dividends. The weakness of the PE approach to valuation is that by using an industry average PE ratio, firm-specific factors that might contribute to a long-term PE ratio above or below the average are ignored in the analysis. A skilled analyst will adjust the PE ratio up or down to reflect unique characteristics of a firm when estimating its stock price.

How the Market Sets Stock Prices

Suppose you went to an auto auction. The cars are available for inspection before the auction begins, and you find a little Mazda Miata that you like. You test-drive it in the parking lot and notice that it makes a few strange noises, but you decide that you would still like the car. You decide $5000 would be a fair price that would allow you to pay some repair bills should the noises turn out to be serious. You see that the auction is ready to begin, so you go in and wait for the Miata to enter.

Suppose there is another buyer who also spots the Miata. He test-drives the car and recognizes that the noises are simply the result of worn brake pads that he can fix himself at a nominal cost. He decides that the car is worth $7000. He also goes in and waits for the Miata to enter.

Who will buy the car and for how much? Suppose only the two of you are interested in the Miata. You begin the bidding at $4000. He ups your bid to $4500. You bid your top price of $5000. He counters with $5100. The price is now higher than you are willing to pay, so you stop bidding. The car is sold to the more informed buyer for $5100.

This simple example raises a number of points. First, the price is set by the buyer willing to pay the highest price. The price is not necessarily the highest price the asset could fetch, but it is incrementally greater than what any other buyer is willing to pay. Second, the market price will be set by the buyer who can take best advantage of the asset. The buyer who purchased the car knew that he could fix the noise easily and cheaply. Because of this he was willing to pay more for the car than you were. The same concept holds for other assets. For example, a piece of property or a building will sell to the buyer who can put the asset to the most productive use.

Finally, the example shows the role played by information in asset pricing. Superior information about an asset can increase its value by reducing its risk. When you consider buying a stock, there are many unknowns about the future cash flows. The buyer who has the best information about these cash flows will discount them at a lower interest rate than will a buyer who is very uncertain.

Now let us apply these ideas to stock valuation. Suppose that you are considering the purchase of stock expected to pay a $2 dividend next year. Market analysts expect the firm to grow at 3% indefinitely. You are uncertain about both the constancy of the dividend stream and the accuracy of the estimated growth rate. To compensate yourself for this uncertainty (risk), you require a return of 15%.

Now suppose Jennifer, another investor, has spoken with industry insiders and feels more confident about the projected cash flows. Jennifer requires only a 12% return because her perceived risk is lower than yours. Bud, on the other hand, is dating the CEO of the company. He knows with more certainty what the future of the firm actually is, and thus requires only a 10% return.

What are the values each investor will give to the stock? Applying the Gordon growth model yields the following stock prices:

Investor	Discount Rate	Stock Price
You	15%	$16.67
Jennifer	12%	$22.22
Bud	10%	$28.57

You are willing to pay $16.67 for the stock. Jennifer would pay up to $22.22, and Bud would pay $28.57. The investor with the lowest perceived risk is willing to pay the most for the stock. If there were no other traders but these three, the market price would be between $22.22 and $28.57. If you already held the stock, you would sell it to Bud.

APPLICATION

Monetary Policy and Stock Prices

Stock market analysts tend to hang on every word that the governor of the Bank of Canada utters because they know that an important determinant of stock prices is monetary policy. But how does monetary policy affect stock prices?

The Gordon growth model in Equation 5 tells us how. Monetary policy can affect stock prices in two ways. First, when the Bank of Canada lowers interest rates, the return on bonds (an alternative asset to stocks) declines, and investors are likely to accept a lower required rate of return on an investment in equity (k_e). The resulting decline in k_e would lower the denominator in the Gordon growth model (Equation 5), lead to a higher value of P_0, and raise stock prices. Furthermore, a lowering of interest rates is likely to stimulate the economy, so that the growth rate in dividends, g, is likely to be somewhat higher. This rise in g also causes the denominator in Equation 5 to fall, which also leads to a higher P_0 and a rise in stock prices.

As we will see in Chapter 26, the impact of monetary policy on stock prices is one of the key ways in which monetary policy affects the economy.

APPLICATION

The Global Financial Crisis and the Stock Market

The subprime financial crisis in the United States that started in August 2007 led to one of the worst bear markets in the last 50 years. Our analysis of stock price valuation, again using the Gordon growth model, can help us understand how this event affected stock prices.

The subprime financial crisis had a major negative impact on the economy, leading to a downward revision of the growth prospects for companies, thus lowering the dividend growth rate (g) in the Gordon model. The resulting increase in the denominator in Equation 5 would lead to a decline in P_0 and hence a decline in stock prices.

Increased uncertainty for the economy and the widening credit spreads resulting from the subprime crisis also raised the required return on investment in equity. A higher k_e also led to an increase in the denominator in Equation 5, a decline in P_0, and a general fall in stock prices.

In the early stages of the global financial crisis, the decline in growth prospects and credit spreads were moderate and so, as the Gordon model predicts, the stock market decline was also moderate. However, when the crisis entered a particularly virulent stage in October of 2008, credit spreads shot through the roof, the economy tanked, and, as the Gordon model predicts, the stock market crashed. From its peak in October 2007 (high of S&P/TSX of 14625) to the bottom in February 2009 (S&P/TSX low of 8123) the market lost 45% of its value.

We thus see that the players in the market, bidding against each other, establish the market price. When new information is released about a firm, expectations change, and with them, prices change. New information can cause changes in expectations about the level of future dividends or the risk of those dividends. Since market participants are constantly receiving new information and revising their expectations, it is reasonable that stock prices are constantly changing as well.

The Theory of Rational Expectations

The analysis of stock price evaluation we have outlined in the previous section depends on people's expectations—especially of cash flows. Indeed, it is difficult to think of any sector in the economy in which expectations are not crucial; this is why it is important to examine how expectations are formed. We do so by outlining the *theory of rational expectations,* currently the most widely used theory to describe the formation of business and consumer expectations.

In the 1950s and 1960s, economists regularly viewed expectations as formed from past experience only. Expectations of inflation, for example, were typically viewed as being an average of past inflation rates. This view of expectation formation, called **adaptive expectations**, suggests that changes in expectations will occur slowly over time as past data change. So if inflation had formerly been steady at a 5% rate, expectations of future inflation would be 5% too. If inflation rose to a steady rate of 10%, expectations of future inflation would rise toward 10%, but slowly: In the first year, expected inflation might rise only to 6%; in the second year, to 7%; and so on.

Adaptive expectations have been faulted on the grounds that people use more information than just past data on a single variable to form their expectations of that variable. Their expectations of inflation will almost surely be affected by their predictions of future monetary policy as well as by current and past monetary policy. In addition, people often change their expectations quickly in the light of new information. To meet these objections to adaptive expectations, John Muth developed an alternative theory of expectations, called **rational expectations**, which can be stated as follows: ***Expectations will be identical to optimal forecasts (the best guess of the future) using all available information.***[2]

What exactly does this mean? To explain it more clearly, let's use the theory of rational expectations to examine how expectations are formed in a situation that most of us encounter at some point in our lifetimes: our drive to work. Suppose that when Joe Commuter travels when it is not rush hour, it takes an average of 30 minutes for his trip. Sometimes it takes him 35 minutes, other times 25 minutes, but the average non-rush-hour driving time is 30 minutes. If, however, Joe leaves for work during the rush hour, it takes him, on average, an additional 10 minutes to get to work. Given that he leaves for work during the rush hour, the best guess of the driving time—the **optimal forecast**—is 40 minutes.

If the only information available to Joe before he leaves for work that would have a potential effect on his driving time is that he is leaving during the rush hour, what does rational expectations theory allow you to predict about Joe's expectations of his driving time? Since the best guess of his driving time using all available information is 40 minutes, Joe's expectation should also be the same. Clearly, an expectation of 35 minutes would not be rational, because it is not equal to the optimal forecast, the best guess of the driving time.

---

[2]John Muth, "Rational Expectations and the Theory of Price Movements," *Econometrica* 29 (1961): 315–335.

Suppose that the next day, given the same conditions and the same expectations, it takes Joe 45 minutes to drive because he hits an abnormally large number of red lights, and the day after that he hits all the lights right and it takes him only 35 minutes. Do these variations mean that Joe's 40-minute expectation is irrational? No, an expectation of 40 minutes' driving time is still a rational expectation. In both cases, the forecast is off by five minutes, so the expectation has not been perfectly accurate. However, the forecast does not have to be perfectly accurate to be rational—it need only be the *best possible* given the available information; that is, it has to be correct *on average*, and the 40-minute expectation meets this requirement. Since there is bound to be some randomness in Joe's driving time regardless of driving conditions, an optimal forecast will never be completely accurate.

The example makes the following important point about rational expectations: Even though a rational expectation equals the optimal forecast using all available information, a prediction based on it may not always be perfectly accurate.

What if an item of information relevant to predicting driving time is unavailable or ignored? Suppose that on Joe's usual route to work there is an accident that causes a two-hour traffic jam. If Joe has no way of ascertaining this information, his rush-hour expectation of 40 minutes' driving time is still rational, because the accident information is not available to him for incorporation into his optimal forecast. However, if there was a radio or TV traffic report about the accident that Joe did not bother to listen to or heard but ignored, his 40-minute expectation is no longer rational. In light of the availability of this information, Joe's optimal forecast should have been two hours and 40 minutes.

Accordingly, there are two reasons why an expectation may fail to be rational:

1. People might be aware of all available information but find it takes too much effort to make their expectation the best guess possible.

2. People might be unaware of some available relevant information, so their best guess of the future will not be accurate.

Nonetheless, it is important to recognize that if an additional factor is important but information about it is not available, an expectation that does not take account of it can still be rational.

Formal Statement of the Theory

We can state the theory of rational expectations somewhat more formally. If X stands for the variable that is being forecast (in our example, Joe Commuter's driving time), X^e for the expectation of this variable (Joe's expectation of his driving time), and X^{of} for the optimal forecast of X using all available information (the best guess possible of his driving time), the theory of rational expectations then simply says:

$$X^e = X^{of} \tag{7}$$

That is, the expectation of X equals the optimal forecast using all available information.

Rationale Behind the Theory

Why do people try to make their expectations match their best possible guess of the future using all available information? The simplest explanation is that it is costly for people not to do so. Joe Commuter has a strong incentive to make his expectation of the time it takes him to drive to work as accurate as possible. If he underpredicts his driving time, he will often be late to work and risk being fired. If he overpredicts, he will, on average, get to work too early and will have given up sleep or leisure time unnecessarily. Accurate expectations are desirable, and there are strong incentives for people to try to make them equal to optimal forecasts by using all available information.

The same principle applies to businesses. Suppose that an appliance manufacturer—say, General Electric—knows that interest-rate movements are important to the sales of appliances. If GE makes poor forecasts of interest rates, it will earn less profit, because it might produce either too many appliances or too few. There are strong incentives for GE to acquire all available information to help it forecast interest rates and use the information to make the best possible guess of future interest-rate movements.

The incentives for equating expectations with optimal forecasts are especially strong in financial markets. In these markets, people with better forecasts of the future get rich. The application of the theory of rational expectations to financial markets (where it is called the **efficient market hypothesis** or the **theory of efficient capital markets**) is thus particularly useful.

Implications of the Theory

Rational expectations theory leads to two commonsense implications for the forming of expectations that are important in the analysis of both the stock market and the aggregate economy:

1. *If there is a change in the way a variable moves, the way in which expectations of this variable are formed will change as well.* This tenet of rational expectations theory can be most easily understood through a concrete example. Suppose that interest rates move in such a way that they tend to return to a "normal" level in the future. If today's interest rate is high relative to the normal level, an optimal forecast of the interest rate in the future is that it will decline to the normal level. Rational expectations theory would imply that when today's interest rate is high, the expectation is that it will fall in the future.

   Suppose now that the way in which the interest rate moves changes so that when the interest rate is high, it stays high. In this case, when today's interest rate is high, the optimal forecast of the future interest rate, and hence the rational expectation, is that it will stay high. Expectations of the future interest rate will no longer indicate that the interest rate will fall. The change in the way the interest-rate variable moves has therefore led to a change in the way that expectations of future interest rates are formed. The rational expectations analysis here is generalizable to expectations of any variable. Hence, when there is a change in the way any variable moves, the way in which expectations of this variable are formed will change too.

2. *The forecast errors of expectations will on average be zero and cannot be predicted ahead of time.* The forecast error of an expectation is $X - X^e$, the difference between the realization of a variable X and the expectation of the variable; that is, if Joe Commuter's driving time on a particular day is 45 minutes and his expectation of the driving time is 40 minutes, the forecast error is five minutes.

   Suppose that in violation of the rational expectations tenet, Joe's forecast error is not, on average, equal to zero; instead, it equals five minutes. The forecast error is now predictable ahead of time because Joe will soon notice that he is, on average, five minutes late for work and can improve his forecast by increasing it by five minutes. Rational expectations theory implies that this is exactly what Joe will do because he will want his forecast to be the best guess possible. When Joe has revised his forecast upward by five minutes, on average, the forecast error will equal zero so that it cannot be predicted ahead of time. Rational expectations theory implies that forecast errors of expectations cannot be predicted.

The Efficient Market Hypothesis: Rational Expectations in Financial Markets

While the theory of rational expectations was being developed by monetary economists, financial economists were developing a parallel theory of expectation formation in financial markets. It led them to the same conclusion as that of the rational expectations theorists: expectations in financial markets are equal to optimal forecasts using all available information.[3] Although financial economists gave their theory another name, calling it the *efficient market hypothesis*, in fact their theory is just an application of rational expectations to the pricing of not only stocks but other securities.

The efficient market hypothesis is based on the assumption that prices of securities in financial markets fully reflect all available information. You may recall from Chapter 4 that the rate of return from holding a security equals the sum of the capital gain on the security (the change in the price), plus any cash payments, divided by the initial purchase price of the security:

$$R = \frac{P_{t+1} - P_t + C}{P_t} \tag{8}$$

where
$$R = \text{rate of return on the security held from time } t \text{ to } t + 1 \text{ (say,}$$
the end of 2010 to the end of 2011)
$$P_{t+1} = \text{price of the security at time } t + 1, \text{ the end of the holding period}$$
$$P_t = \text{price of the security at time } t, \text{ the beginning of the holding period}$$
$$C = \text{cash payment (coupon or dividend payments) made in the}$$
period t to $t + 1$

Let's look at the expectation of this return at time t, the beginning of the holding period. Because the current price P_t and the cash payment C are known at the beginning, the only variable in the definition of the return that is uncertain is the price next period, P_{t+1}.[4] Denoting the expectation of the security's price at the end of the holding period as P_{t+1}^e, the expected return R^e is

$$R^e = \frac{P_{t+1}^e - P_t + C}{P_t}$$

The efficient market hypothesis also views expectations of future prices as equal to optimal forecasts using all currently available information. In other words, the market's expectations of future securities prices are rational, so that

$$P_{t+1}^e = P_{t+1}^{of}$$

which in turn implies that the expected return on the security will equal the optimal forecast of the return:

$$R^e = R^{of} \tag{9}$$

Unfortunately, we cannot observe either R^e or P_{t+1}^e, so the rational expectations equations by themselves do not tell us much about how the financial market behaves.

----

[3]The development of the efficient market hypothesis was not wholly independent of the development of rational expectations theory, in that financial economists were aware of Muth's work.

[4]There are cases where C might not be known at the beginning of the period, but that does not make a substantial difference to the analysis. We would in that case assume that not only price expectations but also the expectations of C are optimal forecasts using all available information.

However, if we can devise some way to measure the value of R^e, these equations will have important implications for how prices of securities change in financial markets.

The supply and demand analysis of the bond market developed in Chapter 5 shows us that the expected return on a security (the interest rate, in the case of the bond examined) will have a tendency to head toward the equilibrium return that equates the quantity demanded to the quantity supplied. Supply and demand analysis enables us to determine the expected return on a security with the following equilibrium condition: The expected return on a security R^e equals the equilibrium return R^*, which equates the quantity of the security demanded to the quantity supplied; that is,

$$R^e = R^* \tag{10}$$

The academic field of finance explores the factors (risk and liquidity, for example) that influence the equilibrium returns on securities. For our purposes, it is sufficient to know that we can determine the equilibrium return and thus determine the expected return with the equilibrium condition.

We can derive an equation to describe pricing behaviour in an efficient market by using the equilibrium condition to replace R^e with R^* in the rational expectations equation (Equation 9). In this way, we obtain:

$$R^{of} = R^* \tag{11}$$

APPLICATION

The Efficient Market Hypothesis

Suppose that a share of Microsoft had a closing price yesterday of $90, but new information was announced after the market closed that caused a revision in the forecast of the price next year to go to $120. If the annual equilibrium return on Microsoft is 15%, what does the efficient market hypothesis indicate the price will go to today when the market opens? (Assume that Microsoft pays no dividends.)

Solution   The price would rise to $104.35 after the opening.

$$R^{of} = \frac{P^{of}_{t+1} - P_t + C}{P_t} = R^*$$

where

R^{of} = optimal forecast of the return = 15% = 0.15
R^* = equilibrium return = 15% = 0.15
P^{of}_{t+1} = optimal forecast of price next year = $120
P_t = price today after opening
C = cash (dividend) payment = 0

Thus

$$0.15 = \frac{\$120 - P_t}{P_t}$$

$$P_t \times 0.15 = \$120 - P_t$$

$$P_t(1.15) = \$120$$

$$P_t = \$104.35$$

This equation tells us that *current prices in a financial market will be set so that the optimal forecast of a security's return using all available information equals the security's equilibrium return*. Financial economists state it more simply: in an efficient market, a security's price fully reflects all available information.

Rationale Behind the Theory

To see why the efficient market hypothesis makes sense, we make use of the concept of **arbitrage**, in which market participants (*arbitrageurs*) eliminate **unexploited profit opportunities** (i.e., returns on a security that are larger than what is justified by the characteristics of that security). There are two types of arbitrage, *pure arbitrage*, in which the elimination of unexploited profit opportunities involves no risk, and the type of arbitrage we discuss here in which the arbitrageur takes on some risk when eliminating the unexploited profit opportunities.

To see how arbitrage leads to the efficient market hypothesis, suppose that, given its risk characteristics, the normal return on a security—say, Nexen common stock—is 10% at an annual rate, and its current price P_t is lower than the optimal forecast of tomorrow's price P_{t+1}^{of}, so that the optimal forecast of the return at an annual rate is 50%, which is greater than the equilibrium return of 10%. We are now able to predict that, on average, Nexen's return would be abnormally high, so that there is no unexploited profit opportunity. Knowing that, on average, you can earn such an abnormally high rate of return on Nexen because $R^{of} > R^*$, you would buy more, which would in turn drive up its current price P_t relative to the expected future price P_{t+1}^{of}, thereby lowering R^{of}. When the current price had risen sufficiently so that R^{of} equals R^* and the efficient market condition (Equation 11) is satisfied, the buying of Nexen will stop, and the unexploited profit opportunity will have disappeared.

Similarly, a security for which the optimal forecast of the return is 5% and the equilibrium return is 10% ($R^{of} < R^*$) would be a poor investment, because, on average, it earns less than the equilibrium return. In such a case, you would sell the security and drive down its current price relative to the expected future price until R^{of} rose to the level of R^* and the efficient market condition is again satisfied. What we have shown can be summarized as follows:

$$R^{of} > R^* \rightarrow P_t\uparrow \rightarrow R^{of}\downarrow$$

$$R^{of} < R^* \rightarrow P_t\downarrow \rightarrow R^{of}\uparrow$$

until

$$R^{of} = R^*$$

Another way to state the efficient market condition is this: *in an efficient market, all unexploited profit opportunities will be eliminated*.

An extremely important factor in this reasoning is that *not everyone in a financial market must be well informed about a security or have rational expectations for its price to be driven to the point at which the efficient market condition holds*. Financial markets are structured so that many participants can play. As long as a few (often referred to as "smart money") keep their eyes open for unexploited profit opportunities, they will eliminate the profit opportunities that appear, because in so doing, they make a profit. The efficient market hypothesis makes sense, because it does not require everyone in a market to be cognizant of what is happening to every security.

APPLICATION

Practical Guide to Investing in the Stock Market

The efficient market hypothesis has numerous applications to the real world.[5] It is especially valuable because it can be applied directly to an issue that concerns many of us: how to get rich (or at least not get poor) in the stock market. A practical guide to investing in the stock market, which we develop here, provides a better understanding of the use and implications of the efficient market hypothesis.

How Valuable Are Published Reports by Investment Advisers?

Suppose you have just read in the financial news that investment advisers are predicting a boom in oil stocks because an oil shortage is developing. Should you proceed to withdraw all your hard-earned savings from the bank and invest them in oil stocks?

The efficient market hypothesis tells us that when purchasing a security, we cannot expect to earn an abnormally high return, a return greater than the equilibrium return.

Information in newspapers and in the published reports of investment advisers is readily available to many market participants and is already reflected in market prices. So acting on this information will not yield abnormally high returns, on average. As we have seen, the empirical evidence for the most part confirms that recommendations from investment advisers cannot help us outperform the general market. Indeed, as the FYI box Should You Hire an Ape as Your Investment Adviser? suggests, human investment advisers in San Francisco do not on average even outperform an orangutan!

Probably no other conclusion is met with more skepticism by students than this one when they first hear it. We all know or have heard of somebody who has been successful in the stock market for a period of many years. We wonder, "How could someone be so consistently successful if he or she did not really know how to predict when returns would be abnormally high?" The following story, reported in the press, illustrates why such anecdotal evidence is not reliable.

A get-rich-quick artist invented a clever scam. Every week, he wrote two letters. In letter A, he would pick team A to win a particular football game, and in letter B, he would pick the opponent, team B. A mailing list would then be separated into two groups, and he would send letter A to the people in one group and letter B to the people in the other. The following week he would do the same thing but would send these letters only to the group who had received the first letter with the correct prediction. After doing this for ten games, he had a small cluster of people who had received letters predicting the correct winning team for every game. He then mailed a final letter to them, declaring that since he was obviously an expert predictor of the outcome of football games (he had picked winners ten weeks in a row) and since his predictions were profitable for the recipients who bet on the games, he would continue to send his predictions only if he were paid a substantial amount of money. When one of his clients figured out what he was up to, the con man was prosecuted and thrown in jail!

What is the lesson of the story? Even if no forecaster is an accurate predictor of the market, there will always be a group of consistent winners. A person who has done well regularly in the past cannot guarantee that he or she will do well in the future. Note that there will also be a group of persistent losers, but you rarely hear about them because no one brags about a poor forecasting record.

---

[5]The empirical evidence on the efficient market hypothesis is discussed in an appendix to this chapter on this book's MyEconLab.

Should You Be Skeptical of Hot Tips?

Suppose your broker phones you with a hot tip to buy stock in the Happy Feet Corporation (HFC) because it has just developed a product that is completely effective in curing athlete's foot. The stock price is sure to go up. Should you follow this advice and buy HFC stock?

The efficient market hypothesis indicates that you should be skeptical of such news. If the stock market is efficient, it has already priced HFC stock so that its expected return will equal the equilibrium return. The hot tip is not particularly valuable and will not enable you to earn an abnormally high return.

You might wonder, though, if the hot tip is based on new information and would give you an edge on the rest of the market. If other market participants have gotten this information before you, the answer is no. As soon as the information hits the street, the unexploited profit opportunity it creates will be quickly eliminated. The stock's price will already reflect the information, and you should expect to realize only the equilibrium return. But if you are one of the first to gain the new information, it can do you some good. Only then can you be one of the lucky ones who, on average, will earn an abnormally high return by helping eliminate the profit opportunity by buying HFC stock.

Do Stock Prices Always Rise When There Is Good News?

If you follow the stock market, you might have noticed a puzzling phenomenon: when good news about a stock, such as a particularly favourable earnings report, is announced, the price of the stock frequently does not rise. The efficient market hypothesis and the **random-walk** behaviour of stock prices explain this phenomenon.

Because changes in stock prices are unpredictable, when information is announced that has already been expected by the market, the stock price will remain unchanged. The announcement does not contain any new information that should lead to a change in stock prices. If this were not the case and the announcement led to a change in stock prices, it would mean that the change was predictable. Because that is ruled out in an efficient market, *stock prices will respond to announcements only when the information being announced is new and unexpected.* If the news is expected, there will be no stock price response. This is exactly what the evidence we described earlier, which shows that stock prices reflect publicly available information, suggests will occur.

Sometimes an individual stock price declines when good news is announced. Although this seems somewhat peculiar, it is completely consistent with the workings of an efficient market. Suppose that although the announced news is good, it is not as good as expected. HFC's earnings may have risen 15%, but if the market expected earnings to rise by 20%, the new information is actually unfavourable, and the stock price declines.

Efficient Market Prescription for the Investor

What does the efficient market hypothesis recommend for investing in the stock market? It tells us that hot tips, investment advisers' published recommendations, and technical analysis—all of which make use of publicly available information—cannot help an investor outperform the market. Indeed, it indicates that anyone without better information than other market participants cannot expect to beat the market. So what is an investor to do?

The efficient market hypothesis leads to the conclusion that such an investor (and almost all of us fit into this category) should not try to outguess the market by constantly buying and selling securities. This process does nothing but boost the income of brokers, who earn commissions on each trade.[6] Instead, the investor

---

[6]The investor may also have to pay Canada Revenue Agency (CRA) capital gains taxes on any profits that are realized when a security is sold—an additional reason why continual buying and selling does not make sense.

should pursue a "buy-and-hold" strategy—purchase stocks and hold them for long periods of time. This will lead to the same returns, on average, but the investor's net profits will be higher, because fewer brokerage commissions will have to be paid.

It is frequently a sensible strategy for a small investor, whose costs of managing a portfolio may be high relative to its size, to buy into a mutual fund rather than individual stocks. Because the efficient market hypothesis indicates that no mutual fund can consistently outperform the market, an investor should not buy into one that has high management fees or that pays sales commissions to brokers, but rather should purchase a no-load (commission-free) mutual fund that has low management fees.

As we have seen, the evidence indicates that it will not be easy to beat the prescription suggested here, although some of the anomalies to the efficient market hypothesis suggest that an extremely clever investor (which rules out most of us) may be able to outperform a buy-and-hold strategy.

FYI

Should You Hire an Ape as Your Investment Adviser?

The *San Francisco Chronicle* came up with an amusing way of evaluating how successful investment advisers are at picking stocks. They asked eight analysts to pick five stocks at the beginning of the year and then compared the performance of their stock picks to those chosen by Jolyn, an orangutan living at Marine World/Africa USA in Vallejo, California.

Consistent with the results found in the "Investment Dartboard" feature of the *Wall Street Journal*, Jolyn beat the investment advisers as often as they beat her. Given this result, you might be just as well off hiring an orangutan as your investment adviser as you would be hiring a human being!

Why the Efficient Market Hypothesis Does Not Imply That Financial Markets Are Efficient

Many financial economists take the efficient market hypothesis one step further in their analysis of financial markets. Not only do they believe that expectations in financial markets are rational—that is, equal to optimal forecasts using all available information—but they also add the condition that prices in financial markets reflect the true fundamental (intrinsic) value of the securities. In other words, all prices are always correct and reflect **market fundamentals** (items that have a direct impact on future income streams of the securities) and so financial markets are efficient.

This stronger view of market efficiency has several important implications in the academic field of finance. First, it implies that in an efficient capital market, one investment is as good as any other because the securities' prices are correct. Second, it implies that a security's price reflects all available information about the intrinsic value of the security. Third, it implies that security prices can be used by managers of both financial and nonfinancial firms to assess their cost of capital (cost of financing their investments) accurately and hence that security prices can be used to help them make the correct decisions about whether a specific investment is worth making. This stronger version of market efficiency is a basic tenet of much analysis in the finance field.

The efficient markets hypothesis may be misnamed, however. It does not imply the stronger view of market efficiency, but rather just that prices in markets like the stock market are unpredictable. Indeed, as the following application suggests, the existence of market crashes and **bubbles**, in which the prices of assets rise well above their fundamental values, cast serious doubt on the stronger view that financial markets are efficient, but provide less of an argument against the basic lessons of the efficient markets hypothesis.

APPLICATION

What Do Stock Market Crashes Tell Us About the Efficient Market Hypothesis and the Efficiency of Financial Markets?

On October 19, 1987, dubbed "Black Monday," the Dow Jones Industrial Average declined more than 20%, the largest one-day decline in U.S. history. The collapse of the high-tech companies' share prices from their peaks in March 2000 caused the heavily tech-laden Nasdaq index to fall from around 5000 in March 2000 to around 1500 in 2001 and 2002, for a decline of well over 60%. These stock crashes have caused many economists to question the validity of efficient market hypothesis. They do not believe that a rational marketplace could have produced such a massive swing in share prices. To what degree should these stock market crashes make us doubt the validity of the efficient market hypothesis?

Nothing in efficient markets theory rules out large changes in stock prices. A large change in stock prices can result from new information that produces a dramatic decline in optimal forecasts of the future valuation of firms. However, economists are hard-pressed to come up with fundamental changes in the economy that can explain the Black Monday and tech crashes. One lesson from these crashes is that factors other than market fundamentals probably have an effect on asset prices. Indeed, as we will explore in Chapters 8 and 9, there are good reasons to believe that there are impediments to financial markets working well. Hence, these crashes have convinced many economists that the stronger version of market efficiency, which states that asset prices reflect the true fundamental (intrinsic) value of securities, is incorrect. They attribute a large role in determination of stock and other asset prices to market psychology and to the institutional structure of the marketplace. However, nothing in this view contradicts the basic reasoning behind rational expectations or the efficient market hypothesis—that market participants eliminate unexploited profit opportunities. Even though stock market prices may not always solely reflect market fundamentals, as long as market crashes are unpredictable, the basic lessons of efficient markets theory hold.

However, other economists believe that market crashes and bubbles suggest that there may be unexploited profit opportunities and that the efficient market hypothesis might be fundamentally flawed. The controversy over the efficient markets hypothesis continues.

Behavioural Finance

Doubts about the efficiency of financial markets, triggered by the stock market crash of 1987, led to a new field of study, **behavioural finance**, which applies concepts from other social sciences like anthropology, sociology, and, particularly, psychology to understand the behaviour of securities prices.[7]

As we have seen, the efficient market hypothesis assumes that unexploited profit opportunities are eliminated by "smart money" market participants. But can smart money dominate ordinary investors so that financial markets are efficient? Specifically, the efficient market hypothesis suggests that smart money participants sell when a stock price goes up irrationally, with the result that the stock falls back down to a price that is justified by fundamentals.

For this to occur, however, smart money must be able to engage in **short sales:** that is, they borrow stock from brokers and then sell it in the market, with the hope that they earn a profit by buying the stock back again ("covering the short") after it has fallen in price. However, work by psychologists suggests that people are subject to loss aversion: that is, they are more unhappy when they suffer losses than they are happy from making gains. Short sales can result in losses far in excess of an investor's initial investment if the stock price climbs sharply above the price at which the short sale is made (and losses have the possibility of being unlimited if the stock price climbs to astronomical heights).

Loss aversion can thus explain an important phenomenon: very little short selling actually takes place. Short selling may also be constrained by rules restricting it because it seems unsavoury for someone to make money from another person's misfortune. That there is so little short selling can explain why stock prices sometimes get overvalued. Not enough short selling can take place by smart money to drive stock prices back down to their fundamental value.

Psychologists have also found that people tend to be overconfident in their own judgments. As a result, investors tend to believe that they are smarter than other investors. Because investors are willing to assume that the market typically doesn't get it right, they trade on their beliefs and not pure facts. This theory can explain why securities markets have such a large trading volume, something that the efficient market hypothesis does not predict.

Overconfidence and social contagion (fads) provide an explanation for stock market bubbles. When stock prices go up, investors attribute their profits to their intelligence and talk up the stock market. This word-of-mouth enthusiasm and the media then can produce an environment in which even more investors think stock prices will rise in the future. The result is a positive feedback loop in which prices continue to rise, producing a speculative bubble, which finally crashes when prices get too far out of line with fundamentals.[8]

The field of behavioural finance is a young one, but it holds out hope that we might be able to explain some features of securities markets' behaviour that are not well explained by the efficient market hypothesis.

---

[7]Surveys of this field can be found in Hersh Shefrin, *Beyond Greed and Fear: Understanding of Behavioral Finance and the Psychology of Investing* (Boston: Harvard Business School Press, 2000); Andrei Shleifer, *Inefficient Markets* (Oxford: Oxford University Press, 2000); and Robert J. Shiller, "From Efficient Market Theory to Behavioral Finance," Cowles Foundation Discussion Paper No. 1385 (October 2002).

[8]See Robert J. Shiller, *Irrational Exuberance* (New York: Broadway Books, 2001).

MyEconLab MyEconLab is an online homework and tutorial system that puts you in control of your own learning with study and practice tools directly correlated to this chapter's content. Visit MyEconLab to explore the following resources:

- The Questions and Applied Problems are all available in the Study Plan on MyEconLab for further practice. You will also find the answers to all of the Questions and Applied Problems in the Student Resources section of your MyEconLab.
- CANSIM data is available for relevant CANSIM questions in the Student Resources section of your MyEconLab.
- Visit the Student Resources section of MyEconLab to access the following mini-case for this chapter: Mini-Case 7.1: Adaptive Expectations, RationalExpectations, and Optimal Forecasts.
- Visit the Student Resources section of MyEconLab to access the following appendix for this chapter: Appendix 7.1: Evidence on the Efficient Market Hypothesis.

MyEconLab also features Additional Readings, Videos, Glossary Flashcards, Audio Chapter Summaries, Economics News Feeds, Animations, and many additional tools to help you master key concepts from the text.

SUMMARY

EconLab
o Summary

1. Stocks are valued as the present value of future dividends. Unfortunately, we do not know very precisely what these dividends will be. This uncertainty introduces a great deal of error to the valuation process. The Gordon growth model is a simplified method of computing stock value that depends on the assumption that the dividends are growing at a constant rate forever. Given our uncertainty regarding future dividends, this assumption is often the best we can do.

2. The interaction among traders in the market is what actually sets prices on a day-to-day basis. The trader that values the security the most (either because of less uncertainty about the cash flows or because of greater estimated cash flows) will be willing to pay the most. As new information is released, investors will revise their estimates of the true value of the security and will either buy or sell it depending upon how the market price compares to their estimated valuation. Because small changes in estimated growth rates or required return result in large changes in price, it is not surprising that the markets are often volatile.

3. The efficient market hypothesis states that current security prices will fully reflect all available information because, in an efficient market, all unexploited profit opportunities are eliminated. The elimination of unexploited profit opportunities, necessary for a financial market to be efficient, does not require that all market participants be well informed.

4. The efficient market hypothesis indicates that hot tips, investment advisers' published recommendations, and technical analysis cannot help an investor outperform the market. The prescription for investors is to pursue a buy-and-hold strategy—purchase stocks and hold them for long periods of time. Empirical evidence generally supports these implications of the efficient market hypothesis in the stock market.

5. The existence of market crashes and bubbles have convinced many economists that the stronger version of market efficiency, which states that asset prices reflect the true fundamental (intrinsic) value of securities, is not correct. It is far less clear that these crashes show that the efficient market hypothesis is wrong. Even if the stock market were driven by factors other than fundamentals, these crashes do not clearly demonstrate that many of the basic lessons of the efficient market hypothesis are no longer valid, as long as these crashes could not have been predicted.

6. The new field of behavioural finance applies concepts from other social sciences like anthropology, sociology, and particularly psychology to understand the behaviour of securities prices. Loss aversion, overconfidence, and social contagion can explain why trading volume is so high, stock prices get overvalued, and speculative bubbles occur.

KEY TERMS

QUESTIONS

1. What basic principle of finance can be applied to the valuation of any investment asset?

2. What are the two main sources of cash flows for a shareholder? How reliably can these cash flows be estimated? Compare the problem of estimating stock cash flows to estimating bond cash flows. Which security would you predict to be more volatile?

3. Some economists think that central banks should try to prick bubbles in the stock market before they get out of hand and cause later damage when they burst. How can monetary policy be used to prick a bubble? Explain how it can do this using the Gordon growth model.

4. If monetary policy becomes more transparent about the future course of interest rates, how would that affect stock prices, if at all?

5. "Forecasters' predictions of inflation are notoriously inaccurate, so their expectations of inflation cannot be rational." Is this statement true, false, or uncertain? Explain your answer.

6. "Any time it is snowing when Joe Commuter gets up in the morning, he misjudges how long it will take him to drive to work. When it is not snowing, his expectations of the driving time are perfectly accurate. Considering that it snows only once every 10 years where Joe lives, Joe's expectations are almost always perfectly accurate." Are Joe's expectations rational? Why or why not?

7. If a forecaster spends hours every day studying data to forecast interest rates but his expectations are not as accurate as predicting that tomorrow's interest rates will be identical to today's interest rate, are his expectations rational?

8. "If stock prices did not follow a random walk, there would be unexploited profit opportunities in the market." Is this statement true, false, or uncertain? Explain your answer. (Review Web Appendix for Chapter 7 on MyEconLab to answer this question.)

9. Suppose that increases in the money supply lead to a rise in stock prices. Does this mean that when you see that the money supply has had a sharp increase in the past week, you should go out and buy stocks? Why or why not?

10. If the public expects a corporation to lose $5 per share this quarter and it actually loses $4, which is still the largest loss in the history of the company, what does the efficient market hypothesis say will happen to the price of the stock when the $4 loss is announced?

11. If you read in *The Globe and Mail* that the "smart money" on Bay Street expects stock prices to fall, should you follow that lead and sell all your stocks?

12. If your broker has been right in her five previous buy and sell recommendations, should you continue listening to her advice?

13. Can a person with rational expectations expect the price of a share of Google to rise by 10% in the next month?

14. "If most participants in the stock market do not follow what is happening to the monetary aggregates, prices of common stocks will not fully reflect information about them." Is this statement true, false, or uncertain? Explain your answer.

15. "An efficient market is one in which no one ever profits from having better information than the rest." Is this statement true, false, or uncertain? Explain your answer.

16. If higher money growth is associated with higher future inflation, and if announced money growth turns out to be extremely high but is still less than the market expected, what do you think would happen to long-term bond prices?

17. "Foreign exchange rates, like stock prices, should follow a random walk." Is this statement true, false, or uncertain? Explain your answer. (Review Web Appendix for Chapter 7 on MyEconLab to answer this question.)

18. Can we expect the value of the dollar to rise by 2% next week if our expectations are rational?

19. "Human fear is the source of stock market crashes, so these crashes indicate that expectations in the stock market cannot be rational." Is this statement true, false, or uncertain? Explain your answer.

20. In the late 1990s, as information technology rapidly advanced and the Internet widely developed, stock markets soared, peaking in early 2001. Later that year, these markets began to unwind, and then crash, with many commentators identifying the previous few years as a "stock market bubble." How might it possible for this episode to be a bubble, but still adhere to the efficient markets hypothesis?

21. Why might the efficient markets hypothesis be less likely to hold when fundamentals suggest stocks should be at a lower level?

APPLIED PROBLEMS

22. Compute the price of a share of stock that pays a $1 per year dividend and that you expect to be able to sell in one year for $20, assuming you require a 15% return.

23. After careful analysis, you have determined that a firm's dividends should grow at 7% on average in the foreseeable future. The firm's last dividend was $3. Compute the current price of this stock, assuming the required return is 18%.

24. The current price of a stock is $65.88. If dividends are expected to be $1 per share for the next five years, and the

required return is 10%, then what should the price of the stock be in 5 years when you plan to sell it? If the dividend and required return remain the same, and the stock price is expected to increase by $1 five years from now, does the current stock price also increase by $1? Why or why not?

25. A company has just announced a 3-for-1 stock split, effective immediately. Prior to the split, the company had a market value of $5 billion with 100 million shares outstanding. Assuming that the split conveys no new information about the company, what is the value of the company, the number of shares outstanding, and price per share after the split? If the actual market price immediately following the split is $17.00 per share, what does this tell us about market efficiency?

CANSIM Questions

26. Go to the CANSIM data available in the Student Resources section of your MyEconLab website and download monthly data from January 1956 to December 2011 on the S&P TSX Composite Index (series V122620).

    a. Calculate the mean and standard deviation as well as the maximum and minimum values for this series.

    b. Which were the worst and best years in terms of the stock market?

WEB EXERCISES

1. Visit **www.forecasts.org/data/index.htm**. Click on "Stock Index Data" at the very top of the page. Now choose "U.S. Stock Indices—Monthly." Review the indexes for the DJIA, the S&P 500, and the Nasdaq composite. Which index appears most volatile? In which index would you have rather invested in 1985 if the investment had been allowed to compound until now?

2. The Internet is a great source of information on stock prices and stock price movements. Yahoo! Finance is a great source for stock market data. Go to **http://finance.yahoo.com** and click on "DOW" (near the top of the page) to view current data on the Dow Jones Industrial Average. Click on the chart to manipulate the different variables. Change the time range and observe the stock trend over various intervals. Have stock prices been going up or down over the last day, week, three months, and year?

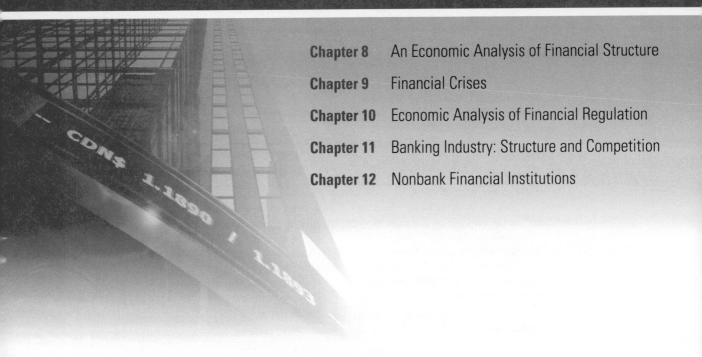

PART III
Financial Institutions

Crisis and Response: Bailout Packages in the Trillions of Dollars

In response to the global financial crisis, governments and central banks around the world departed significantly from their traditional policy tools and introduced new facilities, pouring trillions of dollars into financial institutions. In the United States, for example, the House of Representatives passed the Emergency Economic Stabilization Act on October 3, 2008. This stunning $700 billion bailout package sought to promote recovery from the financial crisis by authorizing the U.S. Treasury to purchase troubled mortgage assets from struggling financial institutions. To calm fears further, the Act raised the federal deposit insurance limit from $100 000 to $250 000.

The initial bill was voted down on September 29 when constituents flooded their representatives with complaints about bailing out the greedy Wall Street executives behind the crisis. The debate in the United States pitted Wall Street against Main Street: bailing out financial institutions was seen as being in opposition to helping struggling homeowners. How could injecting capital into the financial system help those fearful of losing their job or, worse yet, suddenly without work?

The central role of financial institutions in the working of the economy—the focus of Part III—was overlooked. Banks and other financial institutions make financial markets work by moving funds from people who save to people who have productive investment opportunities. That bank branch on Main Street was not going to be able to lend freely to a small business owner or recent university graduate looking to fund a new car purchase until capital once again flowed.

The global financial crisis highlights how the financial system changes over time, be it from financial innovations or hard lessons from crises such as the one at hand. Chapter 8 analyzes financial structure in Canada and in the rest of the world. In Chapter 9, we develop a framework to understand the dynamics of financial crises—and focus in particular on the red-hot global crisis of 2007–2009. In Chapter 10, we extend the economic analysis developed in Chapter 8 to understand the motivations for bank regulation and we examine the pitfalls in the regulatory process. Chapter 11 examines the development of the Canadian banking system over time and the growing internationalization of banking. In Chapter 12, we look at the business of nonbank financial institutions.

CHAPTER 8

An Economic Analysis of Financial Structure

LEARNING OBJECTIVES

After studying this chapter you should be able to

1. depict how asymmetric information results in adverse selection and moral hazard problems that interfere with the efficient functioning of financial markets

2. express how government regulation, the private production and sale of information, and financial intermediaries can lessen, but cannot eliminate, asymmetric information problems

PREVIEW   A healthy and vibrant economy requires a financial system that moves funds from people who save to people who have productive investment opportunities. But how does the financial system make sure that your hard-earned savings get channelled to Paula the Productive Investor rather than to Benny the Bum?

This chapter answers that question by providing an economic analysis of how our financial structure is designed to promote economic efficiency. The analysis focuses on a few simple but powerful economic concepts that enable us to explain features of our financial system such as why financial contracts are written as they are and why financial intermediaries are more important than securities markets for getting funds to borrowers. The analysis also demonstrates the important link between the financial system and the performance of the aggregate economy, which is the subject of the last part of the text.

Basic Facts About Financial Structure Throughout the World

The financial system is complex in structure and function throughout the world. It includes many different types of institutions: banks, insurance companies, mutual funds, stock and bond markets, and so on—all of which are regulated by government. The financial system channels billions of dollars per year from savers to people with productive investment opportunities. If we take a close look at financial structure all over the world, we find eight basic facts, some of which are quite surprising, that we need to explain in order to understand how the financial system works.

FIGURE 8-1   Sources of External Funds for Nonfinancial Businesses: A Comparison of Canada with Germany, Japan, and the United States

The data are for the 1970–2002 period for Canada and for the 1970–2000 period for Germany, Japan, and the United States. The *Bank Loans* category is made up primarily of loans from depository institutions; *Nonbank Loans* is composed primarily of loans by other financial intermediaries; the *Bonds* category includes marketable debt securities such as corporate bonds and commercial paper; and *Stock* consists of new issues of new equity (stock market shares).

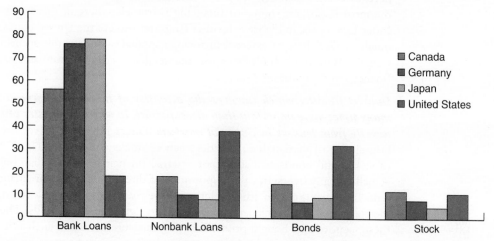

Sources: Andreas Hackethal and Reinhard H. Schmidt, "Financing Patterns: Measuring Concepts and Empirical Results," Johann Wolfgang Goethe-Universitat Working Paper No. 125, January 2004; and Apostolos Serletis and Karl Pinno, "Corporate Financing in Canada," *Journal of Economic Asymmetries* 3 (2006); 1–20.

The bar chart in Figure 8-1 shows how Canadian businesses financed their activities using external funds (those obtained from outside the business itself) in the period 1970–2002 and compares the Canadian data to those of Germany, Japan, and the United States.

Now let us explore the eight facts.

1. ***Stocks are not the most important source of external financing for businesses.*** Because so much attention in the media is focused on the stock market, many people have the impression that stocks are the most important sources of financing for Canadian corporations. However, as we can see from the bar chart in Figure 8-1, the stock market accounted for only a small fraction of the external financing of businesses in the 1970–2002 period: 12%.[1] Similarly small figures apply in the other countries presented in Figure 8-1 as well. Why is the stock market less important than other sources of financing in Canada and other countries?

---

[1]The 12% figure for the percentage of external financing provided by stocks is based on the flows of external funds to corporations. However, this flow figure is somewhat misleading, because when a share of stock is issued, it raises funds permanently, whereas when a bond is issued, it raises funds only temporarily until they are paid back at maturity. To see this, suppose that a firm raises $1000 by selling a share of stock and another $1000 by selling a $1000 one-year bond. In the case of the stock issue, the firm can hold on to the $1000 it raised this way, but to hold on to the $1000 it raised through debt, it has to issue a new $1000 bond every year. If we look at the flow of funds to corporations over a 33-year period, as in Figure 8-1, the firm will have raised $1000 with a stock issue only once in the 33-year period, while it will have raised $1000 with debt 33 times, once in each of the 33 years. Thus it will look as though debt is 33 times more important than stocks in raising funds, even though our example indicates that they are actually equally important for the firm.

2. *Issuing marketable debt and equity securities is not the primary way in which businesses finance their operations.* Figure 8-1 shows that bonds are a more important source of financing than stocks in Canada (15% versus 12%). However, stocks and bonds combined (27%), which make up the total share of marketable securities, still supply less than one-third of the external funds corporations need to finance their activities. The fact that issuing marketable securities is not the most important source of financing is true elsewhere in the world as well. Indeed, as we see in Figure 8-1, other countries (except the United States) have a much smaller share of external financing supplied by marketable securities than Canada. Why don't businesses use marketable securities more extensively to finance their activities?

3. *Indirect finance, which involves the activities of financial intermediaries, is many times more important than direct finance, in which businesses raise funds directly from lenders in financial markets.* Direct finance involves the sale to households of marketable securities such as stocks and bonds. The 27% share of stocks and bonds as a source of external financing for Canadian businesses actually greatly overstates the importance of direct finance in our financial system. In general, only a small fraction of newly issued corporate bonds, commercial paper, and stocks are sold directly to Canadian households. The rest of these securities are bought primarily by financial intermediaries such as insurance companies, pension funds, and mutual funds. Because in most countries marketable securities are an even less important source of finance than in Canada, direct finance is also far less important than indirect finance in the rest of the world. Why are financial intermediaries and indirect finance so important in financial markets? In recent years, indirect finance has been declining in importance. Why is this happening?

4. *Financial intermediaries, particularly banks, are the most important source of external funds used to finance businesses.* As we can see in Figure 8-1, the primary source of external funds for businesses throughout the world are loans made by banks and other nonbank financial intermediaries such as insurance companies, pension funds, and finance companies (56% in the United States, but over 70% in Japan, Germany, and Canada). In other industrialized countries, bank loans are the largest category of sources of external finance and so the data suggest that banks in these countries have the most important role in financing business activities. In developing countries, banks play an even more important role in the financial system than they do in the industrialized countries. What makes banks so important to the workings of the financial system? Although banks remain important, their share of external funds for businesses has been declining in recent years. What is driving their decline?

5. *The financial system is among the most heavily regulated sectors of the economy.* The financial system is heavily regulated in Canada and all other developed countries. Governments regulate financial markets primarily to promote the provision of information, and to ensure the soundness (stability) of the financial system. Why are financial markets so extensively regulated throughout the world?

6. *Only large, well-established corporations have easy access to securities markets to finance their activities.* Individuals and smaller businesses that are not well established are less likely to raise funds by issuing marketable securities. Instead, they most often obtain their financing from banks. Why do only large, well-known corporations find it easier to raise funds in securities markets?

7. ***Collateral is a prevalent feature of debt contracts for both households and businesses.*** **Collateral** is property that is pledged to a lender to guarantee payment in the event that the borrower is unable to make debt payments. Collateralized debt (also known as **secured debt** to contrast it with **unsecured debt**, such as credit card debt, which is not collateralized) is the predominant form of household debt and is widely used in business borrowing as well. The majority of household debt in Canada consists of collateralized loans: your automobile is collateral for your auto loan, and your house is collateral for your mortgage. Commercial and farm mortgages, for which property is pledged as collateral, make up one-quarter of borrowing by nonfinancial businesses; corporate bonds and other bank loans also often involve pledges of collateral. Why is collateral such an important feature of debt contracts?

8. ***Debt contracts typically are extremely complicated legal documents that place substantial restrictions on the behaviour of the borrower.*** Many students think of a debt contract as a simple IOU that can be written on a single piece of paper. The reality of debt contracts is far different, however. In all countries, bond or loan contracts typically are long legal documents with provisions (called **restrictive covenants**) that restrict and specify certain activities that the borrower can engage in. Restrictive covenants are not just a feature of debt contracts for businesses; for example, personal automobile loan and home mortgage contracts have covenants that require the borrower to maintain sufficient insurance on the automobile or house purchased with the loan. Why are debt contracts so complex and restrictive?

As you may recall from Chapter 2, an important feature of financial markets is that they have substantial transaction and information costs. An economic analysis of how these costs affect financial markets provides us with explanations of the eight facts, which in turn provide us with a much deeper understanding of how our financial system works. In the next section, we examine the impact of transaction costs on the structure of our financial system. Then we turn to the effect of information costs on financial structure.

Transaction Costs

Transaction costs are a major problem in financial markets. An example will make this clear.

How Transaction Costs Influence Financial Structure

Say you have $500 you would like to invest, and you think about investing in the stock market. Because you have only $500, you can buy only a small number of shares. Even if you use online trading, your purchase is so small that the brokerage commission for buying the stock you picked will be a large percentage of the purchase price of the shares. If instead you decide to buy a bond, the problem is even worse because the smallest denomination for some bonds you might want to buy is as much as $10 000 and you do not have that much to invest. You are disappointed and realize that you will not be able to use financial markets to earn a return on your hard-earned savings. You can take some consolation, however, in the fact that you are not alone in being stymied by high transaction costs. This is a fact of life for many of us.

You also face another problem because of transaction costs. Because you have only a small amount of funds available, you can make only a restricted number of investments, because a large number of small transactions would result in very high transaction costs. That is, you have to put all your eggs in one basket, and your inability to diversify will subject you to a lot of risk.

How Financial Intermediaries Reduce Transaction Costs

This example of the problems posed by transaction costs and the example outlined in Chapter 2 when legal costs kept you from making a loan to Carl the Carpenter illustrate that small savers like you are frozen out of financial markets and are unable to benefit from them. Fortunately, financial intermediaries, an important part of the financial structure, have evolved to reduce transaction costs and allow small savers and borrowers to benefit from the existence of financial markets.

ECONOMIES OF SCALE   One solution to the problem of high transaction costs is to bundle the funds of many investors together so that they can take advantage of *economies of scale,* the reduction in transaction costs per dollar of investment as the size (scale) of transactions increases. Bundling investors' funds together reduces transaction costs for each individual investor. Economies of scale exist because the total cost of carrying out a transaction in financial markets increases only a little as the size of the transaction grows. For example, the cost of arranging a purchase of 10 000 shares of stock is not much greater than the cost of arranging a purchase of 50 shares of stock.

The presence of economies of scale in financial markets helps explain why financial intermediaries developed and have become such an important part of our financial structure. The clearest example of a financial intermediary that arose because of economies of scale is a mutual fund. A *mutual fund* is a financial intermediary that sells shares to individuals and then invests the proceeds in bonds or stocks. Because it buys large blocks of stocks or bonds, a mutual fund can take advantage of lower transaction costs. These cost savings are then passed on to individual investors after the mutual fund has taken its cut in the form of management fees for administering their accounts. An additional benefit for individual investors is that a mutual fund is large enough to purchase a widely diversified portfolio of securities. The increased diversification for individual investors reduces their risk, thus making them better off.

Economies of scale are also important in lowering the costs of things such as computer technology that financial institutions need to accomplish their tasks. Once a large mutual fund has invested a lot of money in setting up a telecommunications system, for example, the system can be used for a huge number of transactions at a low cost per transaction.

EXPERTISE   Financial intermediaries also arise because they are better able to develop expertise to lower transaction costs. Their expertise in computer technology enables them to offer customers convenient services like being able to call a toll-free number for information on how well their investments are doing and to write cheques on their accounts.

An important outcome of a financial intermediary's low transaction costs is the ability to provide its customers with *liquidity services,* services that make it easier for customers to conduct transactions. Some money market mutual funds, for example, not only pay shareholders high interest rates, but also allow them to write cheques for convenient bill-paying.

Asymmetric Information: Adverse Selection and Moral Hazard

The presence of transaction costs in financial markets explains in part why financial intermediaries and indirect finance play such an important role in financial markets (fact 3). To understand financial structure more fully, however, we turn to the role of information in financial markets.

Asymmetric information—one party's having insufficient knowledge about the other party involved in a transaction to make accurate decisions—is an important aspect of financial markets. For example, managers of a corporation know whether they are honest or have better information about how well their business is doing than the shareholders do. The presence of asymmetric information leads to adverse selection and moral hazard problems, which were introduced in Chapter 2.

Adverse selection is an asymmetric information problem that occurs *before* the transaction occurs: potential bad credit risks are the ones who most actively seek out loans. Thus the parties who are the most likely to produce an undesirable outcome are the ones most likely to want to engage in the transaction. For example, big risk takers or outright crooks might be the most eager to take out a loan because they know that they are unlikely to pay it back. Because adverse selection increases the chances that a loan might be made to a bad credit risk, lenders may decide not to make any loans even though there are good credit risks in the marketplace.

Moral hazard arises *after* the transaction occurs: the lender runs the risk that the borrower will engage in activities that are undesirable from the lender's point of view because they make it less likely that the loan will be paid back. For example, once borrowers have obtained a loan, they may take on big risks (which have possible high returns but also run a greater risk of default) because they are playing with someone else's money. Because moral hazard lowers the probability that the loan will be repaid, lenders may decide that they would rather not make a loan.

The analysis of how asymmetric information problems affect economic behaviour is called **agency theory**. We will apply this theory here to explain why financial structure takes the form it does, thereby explaining the facts described at the beginning of the chapter.

The Lemons Problem: How Adverse Selection Influences Financial Structure

A particular characterization of how the adverse selection problem interferes with the efficient functioning of a market was outlined in a famous article by Nobel Prize winner George Akerlof. It is called the "lemons problem" because it resembles the problem created by lemons in the used-car market.[2] Potential buyers of used cars are frequently unable to assess the quality of the car; that is, they can't tell whether a particular used car is a car that will run well or a lemon that will continually give them grief. The price that a buyer pays must therefore reflect the *average* quality of the cars in the market, somewhere between the low value of a lemon and the high value of a good car.

The owner of a used car, by contrast, is more likely to know whether the car is a peach or a lemon. If the car is a lemon, the owner is more than happy to sell it at the price the buyer is willing to pay, which, being somewhere between the value of a lemon and a good car, is greater than the lemon's value. However, if the car is a peach, the owner knows that the car is undervalued at the price the buyer is willing to pay, and so the owner may not want to sell it. As a result of this adverse selection,

[2]George Akerlof, "The Market for 'Lemons': Quality, Uncertainty and the Market Mechanism," *Quarterly Journal of Economics* 84 (1970): 488–500. Two important papers that have applied the lemons problem analysis to financial markets are Stewart Myers and N. S. Majluf, "Corporate Financing and Investment Decisions When Firms Have Information That Investors Do Not Have," *Journal of Financial Economics* 13 (1984): 187–221, and Bruce Greenwald, Joseph E. Stiglitz, and Andrew Weiss, "Information Imperfections in the Capital Market and Macroeconomic Fluctuations," *American Economic Review* 74 (1984): 194–199.

few good used cars will come to the market. Because the average quality of a used car available in the market will be low and because few people want to buy a lemon, there will be few sales. The used-car market will function poorly, if at all.

Lemons in the Stock and Bond Markets

A similar lemons problem arises in securities markets, that is, the debt (bond) and equity (stock) markets. Suppose that our friend Irving the Investor, a potential buyer of securities such as common stock, can't distinguish between good firms with high expected profits and low risk and bad firms with low expected profits and high risk. In this situation, Irving will be willing to pay only a price that reflects the *average* quality of firms issuing securities—a price that lies between the value of securities from bad firms and the value of those from good firms. If the owners or managers of a good firm have better information than Irving and *know* that they are a good firm, they know that their securities are undervalued and will not want to sell them to Irving at the price he is willing to pay. The only firms willing to sell Irving securities will be bad firms (because his price is higher than the securities are worth). Our friend Irving is not stupid; he does not want to hold securities in bad firms, and hence he will decide not to purchase securities in the market. In an outcome similar to that in the used-car market, this securities market will not work very well because few firms will sell securities in it to raise capital.

The analysis is similar if Irving considers purchasing a corporate debt instrument in the bond market rather than an equity share. Irving will buy a bond only if its interest rate is high enough to compensate him for the average default risk of the good and bad firms trying to sell the debt. The knowledgeable owners of a good firm realize that they will be paying a higher interest rate than they should, and so they are unlikely to want to borrow in this market. Only the bad firms will be willing to borrow, and because investors like Irving are not eager to buy bonds issued by bad firms, they will probably not buy any bonds at all. Few bonds are likely to sell in this market, and so it will not be a good source of financing.

The analysis we have just conducted explains fact 2—why marketable securities are not the primary source of financing for businesses in any country in the world. It also partly explains fact 1—why stocks are not the most important source of financing for Canadian businesses. The presence of the lemons problem keeps securities markets such as the stock and bond markets from being effective in channelling funds from savers to borrowers.

Tools to Help Solve Adverse Selection Problems

In the absence of asymmetric information, the lemons problem goes away. If buyers know as much about the quality of used cars as sellers so that all involved can tell a good car from a bad one, buyers will be willing to pay full value for good used cars. Because the owners of good used cars can now get a fair price, they will be willing to sell them in the market. The market will have many transactions and will do its intended job of channelling good cars to people who want them.

Similarly, if purchasers of securities can distinguish good firms from bad, they will pay the full value of securities issued by good firms, and good firms will sell their securities in the market. The securities market will then be able to move funds to the good firms that have the most productive investment opportunities.

PRIVATE PRODUCTION AND SALE OF INFORMATION   The solution to the adverse selection problem in financial markets is to eliminate asymmetric information by furnishing people supplying funds with full details about the individuals or firms seeking to finance their investment activities. One way to get this material to saver-lenders is to have private companies collect and produce information that distinguishes good from bad firms and then sell it. In Canada, companies such as Standard & Poor's and the Dominion Bond Rating Service gather information on firms' balance sheet positions and investment activities, publish these data, and sell them to subscribers (individuals, libraries, and financial intermediaries involved in purchasing securities).

The system of private production and sale of information does not completely solve the adverse selection problem in securities markets, however, because of the so-called **free-rider problem**. The free-rider problem occurs when people who do not pay for information take advantage of the information that other people have paid for. The free-rider problem suggests that the private sale of information will be only a partial solution to the lemons problem. To see why, suppose that you have just purchased information that tells you which firms are good and which are bad. You believe that this purchase is worthwhile because you can make up the cost of acquiring this information, and then some, by purchasing the securities of good firms that are undervalued. However, when our savvy (free-riding) investor Irving sees you buying certain securities, he buys right along with you, even though he has not paid for any information. If many other investors act as Irving does, the increased demand for the undervalued good securities will cause their low price to be bid up immediately to reflect the securities' true value. Because of all these free riders, you can no longer buy the securities for less than their true value. Now because you will not gain any profits from purchasing the information, you realize that you never should have paid for this information in the first place. If other investors come to the same realization, private firms and individuals may not be able to sell enough of this information to make it worth their while to gather and produce it. The weakened ability of private firms to profit from selling information will mean that less information is produced in the marketplace, and so adverse selection (the lemons problem) will still interfere with the efficient functioning of securities markets.

GOVERNMENT REGULATION TO INCREASE INFORMATION   The free-rider problem prevents the private market from producing enough information to eliminate all the asymmetric information that leads to adverse selection. Could financial markets benefit from government intervention? The government could, for instance, produce information to help investors distinguish good from bad firms and provide it to the public free of charge. This solution, however, would involve the government in releasing negative information about firms, a practice that might be politically difficult. A second possibility (and one followed by Canada and most governments throughout the world) is for the government to regulate securities markets in a way that encourages firms to reveal honest information about themselves so that investors can determine how good or bad the firms are. In Canada, government regulation exists that requires firms selling securities to have independent **audits**, in which accounting firms certify that the firm adheres to standard accounting principles and discloses information about sales, assets, and earnings. Similar regulations are found in other countries. However, disclosure requirements do not always work well, as the recent collapse of Enron and accounting scandals at other corporations, such as WorldCom and Parmalat (an Italian company) suggest (see the FYI box The Enron Implosion).

The asymmetric information problem of adverse selection in financial markets helps explain why financial markets are among the most heavily regulated sectors in the economy (fact 5). Government regulation to increase information for investors is needed to reduce the adverse selection problem, which interferes with the efficient functioning of securities (stock and bond) markets.

FYI

The Enron Implosion

Until 2001, Enron Corporation, a firm that specialized in trading in the energy market, appeared to be spectacularly successful. It had a quarter of the energy-trading market and was valued as high as US$77 billion in August 2000 (just a little over a year before its collapse), making it the seventh-largest corporation in the United States at that time. Toward the end of 2001, however, Enron came crashing down. In October 2001, Enron announced a third-quarter loss of US$618 million and disclosed accounting "mistakes." The U.S. SEC then engaged in a formal investigation of Enron's financial dealings with partnerships led by its former finance chief. It became clear that Enron was engaged in a complex set of transactions by which it was keeping substantial amounts of debt and financial contracts off its balance sheet. These transactions enabled Enron to hide its financial difficulties. Despite securing as much

as US$1.5 billion of new financing from JPMorgan Chase and Citigroup, the company was forced to declare bankruptcy in December 2001, making it the largest bankruptcy in U.S. history.

The Enron collapse illustrates that government regulation can lessen asymmetric information problems but cannot eliminate them. Managers have tremendous incentives to hide their companies' problems, making it hard for investors to know the true value of the firm.

The Enron bankruptcy not only increased concerns in financial markets about the quality of accounting information supplied by corporations, but it also led to hardship for many of the former employees who found that their pensions had become worthless. Outrage against executives at Enron was high, and several were indicted, convicted, and sent to jail.

Although government regulation lessens the adverse selection problem, it does not eliminate it. Even when firms provide information to the public about their sales, assets, or earnings, they still have more information than investors: there is a lot more to knowing the quality of a firm than statistics can provide. Furthermore, bad firms have an incentive to make themselves look like good firms because this would enable them to fetch a higher price for their securities. Bad firms will slant the information they are required to transmit to the public, thus making it harder for investors to sort out the good firms from the bad.

FINANCIAL INTERMEDIATION   So far we have seen that private production of information and government regulation to encourage provision of information lessen but do not eliminate the adverse selection problem in financial markets. How, then, can the financial structure help promote the flow of funds to people with productive investment opportunities when there is asymmetric information? A clue is provided by the structure of the used-car market.

An important feature of the used-car market is that most used cars are not sold directly by one individual to another. An individual considering buying a used car might pay for privately produced information by subscribing to a magazine like *Consumer Reports* to find out if a particular make of car has a good repair record. Nevertheless, reading *Consumer Reports* does not solve the adverse selection problem because even if a particular make of car has a good reputation, the specific car someone is trying to sell could be a lemon. The prospective buyer might also bring the used car to a mechanic for a once-over. But what if the prospective buyer doesn't know a mechanic who can be trusted or if the mechanic charges a high fee to evaluate the car?

Because these roadblocks make it hard for individuals to acquire enough information about used cars, most used cars are not sold directly by one individual to another. Instead, they are sold by an intermediary, a used-car dealer who purchases used cars from individuals and resells them to other individuals. Used-car dealers produce information in the market by becoming experts in determining whether a car is a peach or a lemon. Once they know that a car is good, they can sell it with some form of a guarantee: either a guarantee that is explicit, such as a warranty, or an implicit guarantee in which they stand by their reputation for honesty. People are more likely to purchase a used car because of a dealer's guarantee, and the dealer is able to make a profit on the production of information about automobile quality by being able to sell the used car at a higher price than the dealer paid for it. If dealers purchase and then resell cars on which they have produced information, they avoid the problem of other people free-riding on the information they produced.

Just as used-car dealers help solve adverse selection problems in the automobile market, financial intermediaries play a similar role in financial markets. A financial intermediary such as a bank becomes an expert in producing information about firms so that it can sort out good credit risks from bad ones. Then it can acquire funds from depositors and lend them to the good firms. Because the bank is able to lend mostly to good firms, it is able to earn a higher return on its loans than the interest it has to pay to its depositors. The resulting profit that the bank earns allows it to engage in this information production activity.

An important element in the bank's ability to profit from the information it produces is that it avoids the free-rider problem by primarily making private loans rather than by purchasing securities that are traded in the open market. Because a private loan is not traded, other investors cannot watch what the bank is doing and bid up the loan's price to the point that the bank receives no compensation for the information it has produced. The bank's role as an intermediary that holds mostly nontraded loans is the key to its success in reducing asymmetric information in financial markets.

Our analysis of adverse selection indicates that financial intermediaries in general, and banks in particular because they hold a large fraction of nontraded loans, should play a greater role in moving funds to corporations than securities markets do. Our analysis thus explains facts 3 and 4: why indirect finance is so much more important than direct finance and why banks are the most important source of external funds for financing businesses.

Another important fact that is explained by the analysis here is the greater importance of banks in the financial systems of developing countries. As we have seen, when the quality of information about firms is better, asymmetric information problems will be less severe, and it will be easier for firms to issue securities. Information about private firms is harder to collect in developing countries than in industrialized countries; therefore, the smaller role played by securities markets leaves a greater role for financial intermediaries such as banks. A corollary of this analysis is that as information about firms becomes easier to acquire, the role of banks should decline. A major development in the past thirty years has been huge improvements in information technology. Thus the analysis here suggests that the lending role of financial institutions such as banks should have declined, and this is exactly what has occurred.

Our analysis of adverse selection also explains fact 6, which questions why large firms are more likely to obtain funds from securities markets, a direct route, rather than from banks and financial intermediaries, an indirect route. The better known a corporation is, the more information about its activities is available in the marketplace. Thus it is easier for investors to evaluate the quality of the corporation and determine whether it is a good firm or a bad one. Because investors have fewer worries about adverse selection with well-known corporations, they will be willing to invest directly in their securities. Our adverse selection analysis thus suggests that there should be a pecking order for firms that can issue securities. Hence we have an explanation for fact 6: The larger and more established a corporation is, the more likely it will be to issue securities to raise funds.

COLLATERAL AND NET WORTH   Adverse selection interferes with the functioning of financial markets only if a lender suffers a loss when a borrower is unable to make loan payments and thereby defaults. Collateral, property promised to the lender if the borrower defaults, reduces the consequences of adverse selection because it reduces the lender's losses in the event of a default. If a borrower defaults on a loan, the lender can sell the collateral and use the proceeds to make up for the losses on the loan. For example, if you fail to make your mortgage payments, the lender can take title to your house, auction it off, and use the receipts to pay off the loan. Lenders are thus more willing to make loans secured by collateral, and borrowers are willing to supply collateral because the reduced risk for the lender makes it more likely they will get the loan in the first place and perhaps at a better loan rate. The presence of adverse selection in credit markets thus provides an explanation for why collateral is an important feature of debt contracts (fact 7).

   Net worth (also called **equity capital**), the difference between a firm's assets (what it owns or is owed) and its liabilities (what it owes), can perform a similar role to collateral. If a firm has a high net worth, then even if it engages in investments that cause it to have negative profits and so defaults on its debt payments, the lender can take title to the firm's net worth, sell it off, and use the proceeds to recoup some of the losses from the loan. In addition, the more net worth a firm has in the first place, the less likely it is to default because the firm has a cushion of assets that it can use to pay off its loans. Hence when firms seeking credit have high net worth, the consequences of adverse selection are less important and lenders are more willing to make loans. This analysis lies behind the often-heard lament, "Only the people who don't need money can borrow it!"

Summary

So far we have used the concept of adverse selection to explain seven of the eight facts about financial structure introduced earlier: the first four emphasize the importance of financial intermediaries and the relative unimportance of securities markets for the financing of corporations; the fifth, that financial markets are among the most heavily regulated sectors of the economy; the sixth, that only large, well-established corporations have access to securities markets; and the seventh, that collateral is an important feature of debt contracts. In the next section we will see that the other asymmetric information concept of moral hazard provides additional reasons for the importance of financial intermediaries and the relative unimportance of securities markets for the financing of corporations, the prevalence of government regulation, and the importance of collateral in debt contracts. In addition, the concept of moral hazard can be used to explain our final fact (fact 8) of why debt contracts are complicated legal documents that place substantial restrictions on the behaviour of borrowers.

How Moral Hazard Affects the Choice Between Debt and Equity Contracts

Moral hazard is the asymmetric information problem that occurs after the financial transaction takes place, when the seller of a security may have incentives to hide information and engage in activities that are undesirable for the purchaser of the security. Moral hazard has important consequences for whether a firm finds it easier to raise funds with debt than with equity contracts.

Moral Hazard in Equity Contracts: The Principal– Agent Problem

Equity contracts, such as common stock, are claims to a share in the profits and assets of a business. Equity contracts are subject to a particular type of moral hazard called the **principal–agent problem**. When managers own only a small fraction of the firm they work for, the shareholders who own most of the firm's equity (called the *principals*) are not the same people as the managers of the firm, who are the *agents* of the owners. This separation of ownership and control involves moral hazard in that the managers in control (the agents) may act in their own interest rather than in the interest of the shareholder-owners (the principals) because the managers have less incentive to maximize profits than the shareholder-owners do.

To understand the principal–agent problem more fully, suppose that your friend Steve asks you to become a silent partner in his ice-cream store. The store requires an investment of $10 000 to set up and Steve has only $1000. So you purchase an equity stake (shares) for $9000, which entitles you to 90% of the ownership of the firm, while Steve owns only 10%. If Steve works hard to make tasty ice cream, keeps the store clean, smiles at all the customers, and hustles to wait on tables quickly, after all expenses (including Steve's salary), the store will have $50 000 in profits per year, of which Steve receives 10% ($5000) and you receive 90% ($45 000).

But if Steve doesn't provide quick and friendly service to his customers, uses the $50 000 in income to buy artwork for his office, and even sneaks off to the beach while he should be at the store, the store will not earn any profit. Steve can earn the additional $5000 (his 10% share of the profits) over his salary only if he works hard and forgoes unproductive investments (such as art for his office). Steve might decide that the extra $5000 just isn't enough to make him want to expend the effort to be a good manager; he might decide that it would be worth his while only if he earned an extra $10 000. If Steve feels this way, he does not have enough incentive to be a good manager and will end up with a beautiful office, a good tan, and a store that doesn't show any profits. Because the store won't show any profits, Steve's decision not to act in your interest will cost you $45 000 (your 90% of the profits if he had chosen to be a good manager instead).

The moral hazard arising from the principal–agent problem might be even worse if Steve were not totally honest. Because his ice-cream store is a cash business, Steve has the incentive to pocket $50 000 in cash and tell you that the profits were zero. He now gets a return of $50 000, and you get nothing.

Further indications that the principal–agent problem created by equity contracts can be severe are provided by recent corporate scandals in corporations such as Enron and Tyco International, in which managers have been accused of diverting funds for personal use. Besides pursuing personal benefits, managers might also pursue corporate strategies (such as the acquisition of other firms) that enhance their personal power but do not increase the corporation's profitability.

The principal–agent problem would not arise if the owners of a firm had complete information about what the managers were up to and could prevent wasteful expenditures or fraud. The principal–agent problem, which is an example of moral hazard, arises only because a manager, like Steve, has more information about his activities than the shareholder does—that is, there is asymmetric information. The principal–agent problem would also not arise if Steve alone owned the store and there were no separation of ownership and control. If this were the case, Steve's hard work and avoidance of unproductive investments would yield him a profit (and extra income) of $50 000, an amount that would make it worth his while to be a good manager.

Tools to Help Solve the Principal– Agent Problem

PRODUCTION OF INFORMATION: MONITORING You have seen that the principal– agent problem arises because managers have more information about their activities and actual profits than shareholders do. One way for shareholders to reduce this moral hazard problem is for them to engage in a particular type of information production, the monitoring of the firm's activities: auditing the firm frequently and checking on what the management is doing. The problem is that the monitoring process can be expensive in terms of time and money, as reflected in the name economists give it, **costly state verification**. Costly state verification makes the equity contract less desirable, and it explains, in part, why equity is not a more important element in our financial structure.

As with adverse selection, the free-rider problem decreases the amount of information production that would reduce the moral hazard (principal–agent) problem. In this example, the free-rider problem decreases monitoring. If you know that other shareholders are paying to monitor the activities of the company you hold shares in, you can take a free ride on their activities. Then you can use the money you save by not engaging in monitoring to vacation on a Caribbean island. If you can do this, though, so can other shareholders. Perhaps all the shareholders will go to the islands, and no one will spend any resources on monitoring the firm. The moral hazard problem for shares of common stock will then be severe, making it hard for firms to issue them to raise capital (providing an explanation for fact 1).

GOVERNMENT REGULATION TO INCREASE INFORMATION   As with adverse selection, the government has an incentive to try to reduce the moral hazard problem created by asymmetric information, which provides another reason why the financial system is so heavily regulated (fact 5). Governments everywhere have laws to force firms to adhere to standard accounting principles that make profit verification easier. They also pass laws to impose stiff criminal penalties on people who commit the fraud of hiding and stealing profits. However, these measures can only be partly effective. Catching this kind of fraud is not easy; fraudulent managers have the incentive to make it very hard for government agencies to find or prove fraud.

FINANCIAL INTERMEDIATION   Financial intermediaries have the ability to avoid the free-rider problem in the face of moral hazard, and this is another reason why indirect finance is so important (fact 3). One financial intermediary that helps reduce the moral hazard arising from the principal–agent problem is the **venture capital firm**. Venture capital firms pool the resources of their partners and use the funds to help budding entrepreneurs start new businesses. In exchange for the use of the venture capital, the firm receives an equity share in the new business. Because verification of earnings and profits is so important in eliminating moral hazard, venture capital firms usually insist on having several of their own people participate as members of the managing body of the firm, the board of directors, so that they can keep a close watch on the firm's activities. When a venture capital firm supplies start-up funds, the equity in the firm is not marketable to anyone *but* the venture capital firm. Thus other investors are unable to take a free ride on the venture capital firm's verification activities. As a result of this arrangement, the venture capital firm is able to garner the full benefits of its verification activities and is given the appropriate incentives to reduce the moral hazard problem.

Venture capital firms have been important in the development of the high-tech sector in Canada and the United States, which has resulted in job creation, economic growth, and increased international competitiveness.

DEBT CONTRACTS   Moral hazard arises with an equity contract, which is a claim on profits in all situations, whether the firm is making or losing money. If a contract could be structured so that moral hazard would exist only in certain situations, there would be a reduced need to monitor managers, and the contract would be more attractive than the equity contract. The debt contract has exactly these attributes because it is a contractual agreement by the borrower to pay the lender *fixed* dollar amounts at periodic intervals. When the firm has high profits, the lender receives the contractual payments and does not need to know the exact profits of the firm. If the managers are hiding profits or are pursuing activities that are personally beneficial but don't increase profitability, the lender doesn't care as long as these activities do not interfere with the ability of the firm to make its debt payments on time. Only when the firm cannot meet its debt payments, thereby being in a state of default, is there a need for the lender to verify the state of the firm's profits. Only in this situation do lenders involved in debt contracts need to act more like equity holders; now they need to know how much income the firm has in order to get their fair share.

The less frequent need to monitor the firm, and thus a lower cost of state verification, helps explain why debt contracts are used more frequently than equity contracts to raise capital. The concept of moral hazard thus helps explain fact 1, why stocks are not the most important source of financing for businesses.[3]

How Moral Hazard Influences Financial Structure in Debt Markets

Even with the advantages just described, debt contracts are still subject to moral hazard. Because a debt contract requires the borrowers to pay out a fixed amount and lets them keep any profits above this amount, the borrowers have an incentive to take on investment projects that are riskier than the lenders would like.

For example, suppose that because you are concerned about the problem of verifying the profits of Steve's ice-cream store, you decide not to become an equity partner. Instead, you lend Steve the $9000 he needs to set up his business and have a debt contract that pays you an interest rate of 10%. As far as you are concerned, this is a surefire investment because there is a strong and steady demand for ice cream in your neighbourhood. However, once you give Steve the funds, he might use them for purposes other than you intended. Instead of opening up the ice-cream store, Steve might use your $9000 loan to invest in chemical research equipment because he thinks he has a 1-in-10 chance of inventing a diet ice cream that tastes every bit as good as the premium brands but has no fat or calories.

Obviously, this is a very risky investment, but if Steve is successful, he will become a multimillionaire. He has a strong incentive to undertake the riskier investment with your money because the gains to him would be so large if he succeeded. You would clearly be very unhappy if Steve used your loan for the riskier investment because if he were unsuccessful, which is highly likely, you would lose most, if not all, of the money you loaned him. And if he were successful, you wouldn't share in his success—you would still get only a 10% return on the loan because the principal and interest payments are fixed. Because of the potential moral hazard (that Steve might use your money to finance a very risky venture), you would probably not make the loan to Steve, even though an ice-cream store in the neighbourhood is a good investment that would provide benefits for everyone.

Tools to Help Solve Moral Hazard in Debt Contracts

NET WORTH AND COLLATERAL   When borrowers have more at stake because their net worth (the difference between their assets and liabilities) or the collateral they have pledged to the lender is high, the risk of moral hazard—the temptation to act in a manner that lenders find objectionable—will be greatly reduced because the borrowers themselves have a lot to lose. Let's return to Steve and his ice-cream business.

---

[3]Another factor that encourages the use of debt contracts rather than equity contracts is our tax laws. Debt interest payments are a deductible expense for Canadian firms, whereas dividend payments to equity shareholders are not.

Suppose that the cost of setting up either the ice-cream store or the research equipment is $100 000 instead of $10 000. So Steve needs to put $91 000 of his own money into the business (instead of $1000) in addition to the $9000 supplied by your loan. Now if Steve is unsuccessful in inventing the no-calorie nonfat ice cream, he has a lot to lose, the $91 000 of net worth ($100 000 in assets minus the $9000 loan from you). He will think twice about undertaking the riskier investment and is more likely to invest in the ice-cream store, which is more of a sure thing. Hence when Steve has more of his own money (net worth) in the business, you are more likely to make him the loan.

Similarly, if you have pledged your house as collateral, you are less likely to go to Las Vegas and gamble away your earnings that month because you might not be able to make your mortgage payments and might lose your house.

One way of describing the solution that high net worth and collateral provides to the moral hazard problem is to say that it makes the debt contract **incentive-compatible**; that is, it aligns the incentives of the borrower with those of the lender. The greater the borrower's net worth and collateral pledged, the greater the borrower's incentive to behave in the way that the lender expects and desires, the smaller the moral hazard problem in the debt contract, and the easier it is for the firm or household to borrow. Conversely, when the borrower's net worth and collateral is lower, the moral hazard problem is greater, and it is harder to borrow.

MONITORING AND ENFORCEMENT OF RESTRICTIVE COVENANTS   As the example of Steve and his ice-cream store shows, if you could make sure that Steve doesn't invest in anything riskier than the ice-cream store, it would be worth your while to make him the loan. You can ensure that Steve uses your money for the purpose *you* want it to be used for by writing provisions (restrictive covenants) into the debt contract that restrict his firm's activities. By monitoring Steve's activities to see whether he is complying with the restrictive covenants and enforcing the covenants if he is not, you can make sure that he will not take on risks at your expense. Restrictive covenants are directed at reducing moral hazard either by ruling out undesirable behaviour or by encouraging desirable behaviour. There are four types of restrictive covenants that achieve this objective:

1. *Covenants to discourage undesirable behaviour.* Covenants can be designed to lower moral hazard by keeping the borrower from engaging in the undesirable behaviour of undertaking risky investment projects. Some covenants mandate that a loan can be used only to finance specific activities, such as the purchase of particular equipment or inventories. Others restrict the borrowing firm from engaging in certain risky business activities, such as purchasing other businesses.

2. *Covenants to encourage desirable behaviour.* Restrictive covenants can encourage the borrower to engage in desirable activities that make it more likely that the loan will be paid off. One restrictive covenant of this type requires the breadwinner in a household to carry life insurance that pays off the mortgage upon that person's death. Restrictive covenants of this type for businesses focus on encouraging the borrowing firm to keep its net worth high because higher borrower net worth reduces moral hazard and makes it less likely that the lender will suffer losses. These restrictive covenants typically specify that the firm must maintain minimum holdings of certain assets relative to the firm's size.

3. *Covenants to keep collateral valuable.* Because collateral is an important protection for the lender, restrictive covenants can encourage the borrower to keep the collateral in good condition and make sure that it stays in the possession of the borrower. This is the type of covenant ordinary people encounter most often. Automobile loan contracts, for example, require the car owner to maintain a minimum amount of collision and theft insurance and prevent the sale of the car unless the loan is paid

off. Similarly, the recipient of a home mortgage must have adequate insurance on the home and must pay off the mortgage when the property is sold.

4. ***Covenants to provide information.*** Restrictive covenants also require a borrowing firm to provide information about its activities periodically in the form of quarterly financial statements, thereby making it easier for the lender to monitor the firm and reduce moral hazard. This type of covenant may also stipulate that the lender has the right to audit and inspect the firm's books at any time.

We now see why debt contracts are often complicated legal documents with numerous restrictions on the borrower's behaviour (fact 8): debt contracts require complicated restrictive covenants to lower moral hazard.

FINANCIAL INTERMEDIATION   Although restrictive covenants help reduce the moral hazard problem, they do not eliminate it completely. It is almost impossible to write covenants that rule out *every* risky activity. Furthermore, borrowers may be clever enough to find loopholes in restrictive covenants that make them ineffective.

Another problem with restrictive covenants is that they must be monitored and enforced. A restrictive covenant is meaningless if the borrower can violate it knowing that the lender won't check up or is unwilling to pay for legal recourse. Because monitoring and enforcement of restrictive covenants are costly, the free-rider problem arises in the debt securities (bond) market just as it does in the stock market. If you know that other bondholders are monitoring and enforcing the restrictive covenants, you can free-ride on their monitoring and enforcement. But other bondholders can do the same thing, so the likely outcome is that not enough resources are devoted to monitoring and enforcing the restrictive covenants. Moral hazard therefore continues to be a severe problem for marketable debt.

As we have seen before, financial intermediaries, particularly banks, have the ability to avoid the free-rider problem as long as they primarily make private loans. Private loans are not traded, so no one else can free-ride on the intermediary's monitoring and enforcement of the restrictive covenants. The intermediary making private loans thus receives the benefits of monitoring and enforcement and will work to shrink the moral hazard problem inherent in debt contracts. The concept of moral hazard has provided us with additional reasons why financial intermediaries play a more important role in channelling funds from savers to borrowers than marketable securities do, as described in facts 3 and 4.

Summary

The presence of asymmetric information in financial markets leads to adverse selection and moral hazard problems that interfere with the efficient functioning of those markets. Tools to help solve these problems involve the private production and sale of information, government regulation to increase information in financial markets, the importance of collateral and net worth to debt contracts, and the use of monitoring and restrictive covenants. A key finding from our analysis is that the existence of the free-rider problem for traded securities such as stocks and bonds indicates that financial intermediaries, particularly banks, should play a greater role than securities markets in financing the activities of businesses. Economic analysis of the consequences of adverse selection and moral hazard has helped explain the basic features of our financial system and has provided solutions to the eight facts about our financial structure outlined at the beginning of this chapter.

To help you keep track of the tools that help solve asymmetric information problems, Table 8-1 provides a listing of the asymmetric information problems and tools that can help solve them. In addition, it lists how these tools and asymmetric information problems explain the eight facts of financial structure described at the beginning of the chapter.

TABLE 8-1   Asymmetric Information Problems and Tools to Solve Them

Asymmetric Information Problem	Tools to Solve It	Explains Fact Number
Adverse selection	Private production and sale of information	1, 2
	Government regulation to increase information	5
	Financial intermediation	3, 4, 6
	Collateral and net worth	7
Moral hazard in equity contracts (principal–agent problem)	Production of information: monitoring	1
	Government regulation to increase information	5
	Financial intermediation	3
	Debt contracts	1
Moral hazard in debt contracts	Collateral and net worth	6, 7
	Monitoring and enforcement of restrictive covenants	8
	Financial intermediation	3, 4

Note: List of facts:

1. Stocks are not the most important source of external financing.
2. Marketable securities are not the primary source of finance.
3. Indirect finance is more important than direct finance.
4. Banks are the most important source of external funds.
5. The financial system is heavily regulated.
6. Only large, well-established firms have access to securities markets.
7. Collateral is prevalent in debt contracts.
8. Debt contracts have numerous restrictive covenants.

APPLICATION

Financial Development and Economic Growth

Recent research has found that an important reason why many developing countries or ex-communist countries like Russia (which are referred to as *transition countries*) experience very low rates of growth is that their financial systems are underdeveloped (a situation referred to as *financial repression*).[4] The economic analysis of financial structure helps explain how an underdeveloped financial system leads to a low state of economic development and economic growth.

The financial systems in developing and transition countries face several difficulties that keep them from operating efficiently. As we have seen, two important tools used to help solve adverse selection and moral hazard problems in credit markets

---

[4]See World Bank, *Finance for Growth: Policy Choices in a Volatile World* (World Bank and Oxford University Press, 2001) for a survey of the literature linking economic growth to financial development and a list of additional references.

are collateral and restrictive covenants. In many developing countries, the system of property rights (the rule of law, constraints on government expropriation, absence of corruption) functions poorly, making it hard to make effective use of these two tools. In these countries, bankruptcy procedures are often extremely slow and cumbersome. For example, in many countries, creditors (holders of debt) must first sue the defaulting debtor for payment, which can take several years, and then once a favourable judgment has been obtained, the creditor has to sue again to obtain title to the collateral. The process can take in excess of five years, and by the time the lender acquires the collateral, it may have been neglected and thus have little value. In addition, governments often block lenders from foreclosing on borrowers in politically powerful sectors such as agriculture. Where the market is unable to use collateral effectively, the adverse selection problem will be worse because the lender will need even more information about the quality of the borrower in order to screen out a good loan from a bad one. The result is that it will be harder for lenders to channel funds to borrowers with the most productive investment opportunities. There will be less productive investment and hence a slower-growing economy. Similarly, a poorly developed or corrupt legal system may make it extremely difficult for lenders to enforce restrictive covenants. Thus they may have a much more limited ability to reduce moral hazard on the part of borrowers and so will be less willing to lend. Again the outcome will be less productive investment and a lower growth rate for the economy. The importance of an effective legal system in promoting economic growth suggests that lawyers play a more positive role in the economy than we give them credit for.

Governments in developing and transition countries often use their financial systems to direct credit to themselves or to favoured sectors of the economy by setting interest rates at artificially low levels for certain types of loans, by creating so-called development finance institutions to make specific types of loans, or by directing existing institutions to lend to certain entities. As we have seen, private institutions have an incentive to solve adverse selection and moral hazard problems and lend to borrowers with the most productive investment opportunities. Governments have less incentive to do so because they are not driven by the profit motive and so their directed credit programs may not channel funds to sectors that will produce high growth for the economy. The outcome is again likely to result in less-efficient investment and slower growth.

In addition, banks in many developing and transition countries are owned by their governments. Again because of the absence of the profit motive, these **state-owned banks** have little incentive to allocate their capital to the most productive uses. Not surprisingly, the primary loan customer of these state-owned banks is often the government, which does not always use the funds wisely.

We have seen that government regulation can increase the amount of information in financial markets to make them work more efficiently. Many developing and transition countries have an underdeveloped regulatory apparatus that retards the provision of adequate information to the marketplace. For example, these countries often have weak accounting standards, making it very hard to ascertain the quality of a borrower's balance sheet. As a result, asymmetric information problems are more severe, and the financial system is severely hampered in channelling funds to the most productive uses.

The institutional environment of a poor legal system, weak accounting standards, inadequate government regulation, and government intervention through directed credit programs and state ownership of banks all help explain why many countries stay poor while others grow richer.

APPLICATION

Is China a Counter-Example to the Importance of Financial Development?

Although China appears to be on its way to becoming an economic powerhouse, its financial development is still in its early stages. The country's legal system is weak, so financial contracts are difficult to enforce, while accounting standards are lax, so high-quality information about creditors is hard to find. Regulation of the banking system is still in its formative stages, and the banking sector is dominated by large state-owned banks. Yet China has had one of the highest growth rates in the world over the last twenty years. How has China been able to grow so rapidly given its low level of financial development?

As noted above, China is in an early state of development with a per capita income that is still less than US$10 000, one-fifth that in Canada. With an extremely high savings rate averaging around 40% over the last two decades, it has been able to rapidly build up its capital stock and shift a massive pool of underutilized labour from the subsistence agriculture sector into higher-productivity activities that use capital. Even though available savings have not been allocated to their most productive uses, the huge increase in capital, when combined with the gains in productivity from moving labour out of low-productivity subsistence agriculture, has been enough to produce high growth.

As China gets richer, however, this strategy is unlikely to work. The Soviet Union provides a graphic example. In the 1950s and 60s, the Soviet Union had many similarities to China. It had high growth fuelled by a high savings rate, a massive buildup of capital, and shifts of a large pool of underutilized labour from subsistence agriculture to manufacturing. During this high-growth phase, the Soviet Union was unable to develop the institutions to allocate capital efficiently. As a result, once the pool of subsistence labourers was used up, the Soviet Union's growth slowed dramatically and it was unable to keep up with the West. Today no one considers the Soviet Union to have been an economic success story, and its inability to develop the institutions necessary to sustain financial development and growth was an important reason for the demise of this once superpower.

To move into the next stage of development, China will need to allocate its capital more efficiently, and to do this it has to improve its financial system. The Chinese leadership is well aware of this challenge: The government has announced that state-owned banks are being put on the path to privatization. In addition, the government is engaged in legal reform to make financial contracts more enforceable. New bankruptcy law is being developed so that lenders have the ability to take over the assets of firms that default on their loan contracts. Whether the Chinese government will be successful in developing a first-rate financial system, thereby enabling China to join the ranks of developed countries, is a big question mark.

MyEconLab

MyEconLab is an online homework and tutorial system that puts you in control of your own learning with study and practice tools directly correlated to this chapter's content. Visit MyEconLab to explore the following resources:

- The Questions and Applied Problems are all available in the Study Plan on MyEconLab for further practice. You will also find the answers to all of the Questions and Applied Problems in the Student Resources section of your MyEconLab.

MyEconLab also features Additional Readings, Videos, Glossary Flashcards, Audio Chapter Summaries, Economics News Feeds, Animations, and many additional tools to help you master key concepts from the text.

SUMMARY

1. There are eight basic facts about financial structure throughout the world. The first four emphasize the importance of financial intermediaries and the relative unimportance of securities markets for the financing of corporations; the fifth recognizes that financial markets are among the most heavily regulated sectors of the economy; the sixth states that only large, well-established corporations have access to securities markets; the seventh indicates that collateral is an important feature of debt contracts; and the eighth presents debt contracts as complicated legal documents that place substantial restrictions on the behaviour of borrowers.

2. Transaction costs freeze many small savers and borrowers out of direct involvement with financial markets. Financial intermediaries can take advantage of economies of scale and are better able to develop expertise to lower transaction costs, thus enabling savers and borrowers to benefit from the existence of financial markets.

3. Asymmetric information results in two problems: adverse selection, which occurs before the transaction, and moral hazard, which occurs after the transaction. Adverse selection refers to the fact that bad credit risks are the ones most likely to seek loans, and moral hazard refers to the risk of the borrower's engaging in activities that are undesirable from the lender's point of view.

4. Adverse selection interferes with the efficient functioning of financial markets. Tools to help reduce the adverse selection problem include private production and sale of information, government regulation to increase information, financial intermediation, and collateral and net worth. The free-rider problem occurs when people who do not pay for information take advantage of information that other people have paid for. This problem explains why financial intermediaries, particularly banks, play a more important role in financing the activities of businesses than securities markets do.

5. Moral hazard in equity contracts is known as the principal–agent problem because managers (the agents) have less incentive to maximize profits than shareholders (the principals). The principal–agent problem explains why debt contracts are so much more prevalent in financial markets than equity contracts. Tools to help reduce the principal–agent problem include monitoring, government regulation to increase information, and financial intermediation.

6. Tools to reduce the moral hazard problem in debt contracts include net worth, monitoring and enforcement of restrictive covenants, and financial intermediaries.

KEY TERMS

agency theory, p. 165

audits, p. 167

collateral, p. 163

costly state verification, p. 172

free-rider problem, p. 167

incentive-compatible, p. 174

net worth (equity capital), p. 170

principal–agent problem, p. 171

restrictive covenants, p. 163

secured debt, p. 163

state-owned banks, p. 177

unsecured debt, p. 163

venture capital firm, p. 172

QUESTIONS

1. For each of the following countries, identify the single most important (largest) and least important (smallest) source of external funding: United States; Germany; Japan; Canada. Comment on the similarities and differences between the countries' funding sources.

2. How can economies of scale help explain the existence of financial intermediaries?

3. Describe two ways in which financial intermediaries help lower transaction costs in the economy.

4. Why are financial intermediaries willing to engage in information collection activities when investors in financial instruments may be unwilling to do so?

5. Suppose you go to a bank intending to buy a certificate of deposit with your savings. Explain why you would not offer a loan to the next individual who applies for a car loan at your local bank at a higher interest rate than the bank pays on certificates of deposit (but lower than the rate the bank charges for car loans).

6. Wealthy people often worry that others will seek to marry them only for their money. Is this a problem of adverse selection?

7. Do you think the lemons problem would be more severe for stocks traded on the Toronto Stock Exchange or those traded over the counter? Explain.

8. Would you be more willing to lend to a friend if she put all of her life savings into her business than you would if she had not done so? Why?

9. What specific procedures do financial intermediaries use to reduce asymmetric information problems in lending?

10. What steps can the government take to reduce asymmetric information problems and help the financial system function more smoothly and efficiently?

11. How can asymmetric information problems lead to a bank panic?

12. In December 2001, Argentina announced it would not honour its sovereign (government-issued) debt. Many investors were left holding Argentinean bonds now priced at a fraction of their former value. A few years later Argentina announced it would pay back 25% of the face value of its debt. Comment on the effects of information asymmetries on government bond markets. Do you think investors are currently willing to buy bonds issued by the government of Argentina?

13. How does the free-rider problem aggravate adverse selection and moral hazard problems in financial markets?

14. Would moral hazard and adverse selection still arise in financial markets if information were not asymmetric? Explain.

15. How do standardized accounting principles help financial markets work more efficiently?

16. Which firms are most likely to use bank financing rather than to issue bonds or stocks to finance their activities? Why?

17. How can the existence of asymmetric information provide a rationale for government regulation of financial markets?

18. The more collateral there is backing a loan, the less the lender has to worry about adverse selection." Is this statement true, false, or uncertain? Explain your answer.

19. Explain how the separation of ownership and control in Canadian corporations might lead to poor management.

20. Many policymakers in developing countries have proposed to implement systems of deposit insurance like the one that exists in Canada. Explain why this might create more problems than solutions in the financial system of developing countries.

21. Gustavo is a young doctor who lives in a country with a relatively inefficient legal and financial system. When Gustavo applied for a mortgage, he found that banks usually required collateral for up to 300% of the amount of the loan. Explain why banks might require that much collateral in such a financial system. Comment on the consequences for such a system for economic growth.

APPLIED PROBLEMS

For problems 22–25, use the fact that the expected value of an event is a probability weighted average, or the sum of each probable outcome multiplied by the probability of the event occurring.

22. You are in the market for a used car. At a used car lot, you know that the blue book value for the cars you are looking at is between $20 000 and $24 000. If you believe the dealer knows *as much* about the car as you, how much are you willing to pay? Why? Assume that you only care about the expected value of the car you buy and that the car values are symmetrically distributed.

23. Refer to Problem 22 above. Now, you believe the dealer knows *more* about the cars than you. How much are you willing to pay? Why? How can this be resolved in a competitive market?

24. You wish to hire Ron to manage your Alberta operations. The profits from the operations depend partially on how hard Ron works, as follows.

	Probabilities	
	Profit = $10 000	Profit = $50 000
Lazy	60%	40%
Hard worker	20%	80%

If Ron is lazy, he will surf the Internet all day, and he views this as a zero-cost opportunity. However, Ron would view working hard as a "personal cost" valued at $1000. What fixed percentage of the profits should you offer Ron? Assume Ron only cares about his expected payment less any "personal cost."

25. You own a house worth $400 000 that is located on a river. If the river floods moderately, the house will be completely destroyed. This happens about once every 50 years. If you build a seawall, the river would have to flood heavily to destroy your house, which only happens about once every 200 years. What would be the annual premium for an insurance policy that offers full insurance? For a policy that only pays 75% of the home value, what are your expected costs with and without a seawall? Do the different policies provide an incentive to be safer (i.e., to build the seawall)?

WEB EXERCISES

1. In this chapter we discuss the lemons problem and its effect on the efficient functioning of a market. This theory was initially developed by George Akerlof. Go to **www.nobelprize.org/nobel_prizes/economics/laureates/2001/#**. This site reports that Akerlof, Spence, and Stiglitz were awarded the Nobel Prize in Economics in 2001 for their work. Read this report down through the section on George Akerlof. Summarize his research ideas in one page.

CHAPTER 9

Financial Crises

LEARNING OBJECTIVES

After studying this chapter you should be able to

1. discuss the factors that lead to financial crises
2. explain how increases in adverse selection and moral hazard cause financial crises
3. discuss the global financial crisis of 2007–2009, which led to a number of banking crises around the world and a decline in global economic activity

PREVIEW   Financial crises are major disruptions in financial markets characterized by sharp declines in asset prices and firm failures. Beginning in August 2007, defaults in the subprime mortgage market (for borrowers with weak credit records) sent a shudder through the financial markets, leading to the worst financial crisis since the Great Depression. In Congressional testimony, Alan Greenspan, former Chairman of the Fed, described the financial crisis as a "once-in-a-century credit tsunami." Wall Street firms and commercial banks suffered hundreds of billions of dollars of losses. Households and businesses found they had to pay higher rates on their borrowings—and it was much harder to get credit. All over the world, stock markets crashed, with the S&P/TSX market falling by more than 40% from its peak. Many financial firms, including commercial banks, investment banks, and insurance companies, went belly up.

Why did this financial crisis occur? Why have financial crises been so prevalent throughout U.S. history, as well as in so many other countries, and what insights do they provide on the current crisis? Why are financial crises almost always followed by severe contractions in economic activity? We will examine these questions in this chapter by developing a framework to understand the dynamics of financial crises. Building on Chapter 8, we make use of agency theory, the economic analysis of the effects of asymmetric information (adverse selection and moral hazard) on financial markets and the economy, to see why financial crises occur and why they have such devastating effects on the economy. We will then apply the analysis to explain the course of events in a number of past financial crises throughout the world, including the most recent global financial crisis.

What Is a Financial Crisis?

In the previous chapter we saw that a well-functioning financial system solves asymmetric information problems (moral hazard and adverse selection) so that capital is allocated to its most productive uses. These asymmetric information problems that act as a barrier to efficient allocation of capital are often described by economists as **financial frictions**. When financial frictions increase, financial markets are less capable of channelling funds efficiently from savers to households and firms with productive investment opportunities, with the result that economic activity declines. A **financial crisis** occurs when information flows in financial markets experience a particularly large disruption, with the result that financial frictions increase sharply and financial markets stop functioning. Then economic activity will collapse.

Dynamics of Financial Crises in Advanced Economies

As earth-shaking and headline-grabbing as the most recent financial crisis was, it was only one of a number of financial crises that have hit industrialized countries like Canada and the United States over the years. These experiences have helped economists uncover insights into present-day economic turmoil.

Financial crises in advanced economies have progressed in two and sometimes three stages. To understand how these crises have unfolded, refer to Figure 9-1, which traces the stages and sequence of financial crises in advanced economies.

Stage One: Initiation of Financial Crisis

Financial crises can begin in several ways: mismanagement of financial liberalization/innovation, asset-price booms and busts, or a general increase in uncertainty caused by failures of major financial institutions.

MISMANAGEMENT OF FINANCIAL INNOVATION/LIBERALIZATION   The seeds of a financial crisis are often sown when an economy introduces new types of loans or other financial products, known as **financial innovation**, or when countries engage in **financial liberalization**, the elimination of restrictions on financial markets and institutions. In the long run, financial liberalization promotes financial development and encourages a well-run financial system that allocates capital efficiently. However, financial liberalization has a dark side: in the short run, it can prompt financial institutions to go on a lending spree, called a **credit boom**. Unfortunately, lenders may not have the expertise, or the incentives, to manage risk appropriately in these new lines of business. Even with proper management, credit booms eventually outstrip the ability of institutions—and government regulators—to screen and monitor credit risks, leading to overly risky lending.

Government safety nets, such as deposit insurance, weaken market discipline and increase the moral hazard incentive for banks to take on greater risk than they otherwise would. Because lender-savers know that government-guaranteed insurance protects them from losses, they will supply even undisciplined banks with funds. Banks and other financial institutions can make risky, high-interest loans to borrower-spenders. They will walk away with nice profits if the loans are repaid, and rely on government deposit insurance, funded by taxpayers, if borrower-spenders default. Without proper monitoring, risk taking grows unchecked.

Eventually, losses on loans begin to mount, and the value of the loans (on the asset side of the balance sheet) falls relative to liabilities, thereby driving down the net worth (capital) of banks and other financial institutions. With less capital, these financial institutions cut back on their lending to borrower-spenders, a process called **deleveraging**. Furthermore, with less capital, banks and other financial institutions

FIGURE 9-1 Sequence of Events in Financial Crises in Advanced Economies

The solid arrows trace the sequence of events during a typical financial crisis; the dotted arrows show the additional set of events that occur if the crisis develops into a debt deflation. The sections separated by the dashed horizontal lines show the different stages of a financial crisis.

STAGE ONE Initiation of Financial Crisis

Deterioration in Financial Institutions' Balance Sheets ← Asset-Price Decline   Increase in Uncertainty

Adverse Selection and Moral Hazard Problems Worsen and Lending Contracts

STAGE TWO Banking Crisis

Economic Activity Declines

Banking Crisis

Adverse Selection and Moral Hazard Problems Worsen and Lending Contracts

Economic Activity Declines

STAGE THREE Debt Deflation

Unanticipated Decline in Price Level

Adverse Selection and Moral Hazard Problems Worsen and Lending Contracts

Economic Activity Declines

█ Factors Causing Financial Crises   ██ Consequences of Changes in Factors

become riskier, causing lender-savers and other potential lenders to these institutions to pull out their funds. Fewer funds mean fewer loans to fund productive investments and a credit freeze: the lending boom turns into a lending crash.

When financial institutions stop collecting information and making loans, financial frictions rise, limiting the financial system's ability to address the asymmetric information problems of adverse selection and moral hazard (as shown in the arrow pointing from the first factor, "Deterioration in Financial Institutions' Balance Sheets," in the top row of Figure 9-1). As loans become scarce, borrower-spenders are no longer able to fund their productive investment opportunities and they decrease their spending, causing economic activity to contract.

ASSET-PRICE BOOM AND BUST   Prices of assets such as equity shares and real estate can be driven by investor psychology (dubbed "irrational exuberance" by Alan Greenspan when he was chairman of the Federal Reserve) well above their **fundamental economic values**, that is, their values based on realistic expectations of the assets' future income streams. The rise of asset prices above their fundamental economic values is an **asset-price bubble**. Examples of asset-price bubbles are the tech stock market bubble of the late 1990s and the recent housing price bubble in the United States that we will discuss later in this chapter. Asset-price bubbles are often also driven by credit booms, in which the large increase in credit is used to fund purchases of assets, thereby driving up their price.

When the bubble bursts and asset prices realign with fundamental economic values, stock and real estate prices tumble, companies see their net worth (the difference between their assets and their liabilities) decline, and the value of collateral they can pledge drops. Now these companies have less at stake because they have less "skin in the game" and so they are more likely to make risky investments because they have less to lose, the problem of moral hazard. As a result, financial institutions tighten lending standards for borrower-spenders and lending contracts (as shown by the downward arrow pointing from the second factor, "Asset-Price Decline," in the top row of Figure 9-1).

The asset-price bust also causes a decline in the value of financial institutions' assets, thereby causing a decline in their net worth and hence a deterioration in their balance sheets (shown by the arrow from the second factor to the first factor in the top row of Figure 9-1), which causes them to deleverage, steepening the decline in economic activity.

INCREASE IN UNCERTAINTY   Canadian financial crises have usually began in periods of high uncertainty, such as just after the start of a recession, a crash in the stock market, or the failure of a major financial institution. The failure of major financial institutions (such as Bear Stearns, Lehman Brothers, and AIG in 2008 in the United States), is a particularly important source of heightened uncertainty that features prominently in financial crises. Examples in Canadian history are the Bank of Upper Canada in 1866, the Home Bank in 1923, and the bank panic of 1879. With information hard to come by in a period of high uncertainty, financial frictions increase, reducing lending and economic activity (as shown by the arrow pointing from the last factor, "Increases in Uncertainty," in the top row of Figure 9-1).

Stage Two: Banking Crisis

Deteriorating balance sheets and tougher business conditions lead some financial institutions into insolvency, when net worth becomes negative. Unable to pay off depositors or other creditors, some banks go out of business. If severe enough, these factors can lead to a **bank panic**, in which multiple banks fail simultaneously. The source of the contagion is asymmetric information. In a panic, depositors, fearing for the safety of their deposits (in the absence of or with limited amounts of deposit insurance) and not knowing the quality of banks' loan portfolios, withdraw their deposits to the point that the banks fail. Uncertainty about the health of the banking system in general can lead to runs on banks, both good and bad, which will force banks to sell off assets quickly to raise the necessary funds. These **fire sales** of assets may cause their prices to decline so much that the bank becomes insolvent, even if the resulting contagion can then lead to multiple bank failures and a full-fledged bank panic.

With fewer banks operating, information about the creditworthiness of borrower-spenders disappears. Increasingly severe adverse selection and moral hazard problems in financial markets deepen the financial crisis, causing declines in asset prices and the failure of firms throughout the economy who lack funds for productive investment opportunities. Figure 9-1 represents this progression in the stage two portion. Bank panics were a feature of all Canadian financial crises during the nineteenth and twentieth centuries, occurring in 1866, 1879, 1923, and 1930–1933. Bank panics were also a feature of all U.S. financial crises until World War II, occurring every 20 years or so in 1819, 1837, 1857, 1873, 1884, 1893, 1907, and 1930–33.

Eventually, public and private authorities shut down insolvent firms and sell them off or liquidate them. Uncertainty in financial markets declines, the stock market recovers, and balance sheets improve. Financial frictions diminish and the financial crisis subsides. With the financial markets able to operate well again, the stage is set for an economic recovery.

Stage Three: Debt Deflation

If, however, the economic downturn leads to a sharp decline in the price level, the recovery process can be short-circuited. In stage three in Figure 9-1, **debt deflation** occurs when a substantial unanticipated decline in the price level sets in, leading to a further deterioration in firms' net worth because of the increased burden of indebtedness.

In economies with moderate inflation, which characterizes most advanced countries, many debt contracts with fixed interest rates are typically of fairly long maturity, 10 years or more. Because debt payments are contractually fixed in nominal terms, an unanticipated decline in the price level raises the value of borrowing firms' liabilities in real terms (increases the burden of the debt) but does not raise the real value of borrowing firms' assets. The borrowing firm's net worth in real terms (the difference between assets and liabilities in real terms) thus declines.

To better understand how this decline in net worth occurs, consider what happens if a firm in 2013 has assets of $100 million (in 2013 dollars) and $90 million of long-term liabilities, so that it has $10 million in net worth (the difference between the value of assets and liabilities). If the price level falls by 10% in 2014, the real value of the liabilities would rise to $99 million in 2013 dollars, while the real value of the assets would remain unchanged at $100 million. The result would be that real net worth in 2013 dollars would fall from $10 million to $1 million ($100 million minus $99 million).

The substantial decline in real net worth of borrowers from a sharp drop in the price level causes an increase in adverse selection and moral hazard problems facing lenders. Lending and economic activity decline for a long time. The most significant financial crisis that displayed debt deflation was the Great Depression, the worst economic contraction in history.

APPLICATION

The Mother of All Financial Crises: The Great Depression in the United States

With our framework for understanding financial crises in place, we are prepared to analyze how a financial crisis unfolded during the Great Depression and how it led to the worst economic downturn in U.S. history.

FIGURE 9-2 Stock Prices During the Great Depression Period

Stock prices in the United States crashed in 1929, falling by 40% by the end of 1929, and then continued to fall to only 10% of their peak value by 1932.

Source: Dow Jones Industrial Average (DJIA). Global Financial Data, www.globalfinancialdata.com/index_tabs. php?action=detailedinfo&id=1165.

Stock Market Crash

In 1928 and 1929, prices doubled in the U.S. stock market. Federal Reserve officials viewed the stock market boom as excessive speculation. To curb it, they pursued a tightening of monetary policy to raise interest rates to limit the rise in stock prices. The Federal Reserve got more than it bargained for when the stock market crashed in October 1929, falling by 40% by the end of 1929, as shown in Figure 9-2.

Bank Panics

By the middle of 1930, stocks recovered almost half of their losses and credit market conditions stabilized. What might have been a normal recession turned into something far worse, however, when severe droughts in the Midwest led to a sharp decline in agricultural production, with the result that farmers could not pay back their bank loans. The resulting defaults on farm mortgages led to large loan losses on bank balance sheets in agricultural regions. The weakness of the economy and the banks in agricultural regions in particular prompted substantial withdrawals from banks, building to a full-fledged panic in November and December 1930, with the stock market falling sharply. For more than two years, the Federal Reserve sat idly by through one bank panic after another, the most severe spate of panics in U.S. history. After what would be the era's final panic in March 1933, President Franklin Delano Roosevelt declared a bank holiday, a temporary closing of all banks. "The only thing we have to fear is fear itself," Roosevelt told the nation. The damage was done, however, and more than one-third of U.S. commercial banks had failed.

Continuing Decline in Stock Prices

Stock prices kept falling. By mid-1932, stocks had declined to 10% of their value at the 1929 peak (as shown in Figure 9-2), and the increase in uncertainty from the unsettled business conditions created by the economic contraction worsened adverse selection and moral hazard problems in financial markets. With a greatly reduced number of financial intermediaries still in business, adverse selection and moral hazard problems intensified even further. Financial markets struggled to channel funds to borrower-spenders with productive investment opportunities. As our analysis predicts, the amount of outstanding commercial loans fell by half

FIGURE 9-3 Credit Spreads During the Great Depression in the United States

Credit spreads (the difference between rates on Baa corporate bonds and U.S. Treasury bonds) rose sharply during the Great Depression.

Source: Federal Reserve Bank of St. Louis FRED database, http://research.stlouisfed.org/fred2/categories/22.

from 1929 to 1933, and investment spending collapsed, declining by 90% from its 1929 level.

A manifestation of the rise in financial frictions was that lenders began charging businesses much higher interest rates to protect themselves from credit losses. The resulting rise in the **credit spread**—the difference between the interest rate on loans to households and businesses and the interest rate on completely safe assets that are sure to be paid back, such as U.S. Treasury securities—is shown in Figure 9-3, which displays the difference between interest rates on corporate bonds with a Baa (medium-quality) credit rating and similar-maturity Treasury bonds. (Note the credit spread is closely related to the risk premium discussed in Chapter 5.)

Debt Deflation

The ongoing deflation that started in 1930 eventually led to a 25% decline in the U.S. price level. This deflation short-circuited the normal recovery process that occurs in most recessions. The huge decline in prices triggered a debt deflation in which net worth fell because of the increased burden of indebtedness borne by firms and households. The decline in net worth and the resulting increase in adverse selection and moral hazard problems in the credit markets led to a prolonged economic contraction in which unemployment rose to 25% of the labour force. The financial crisis in the Great Depression was the worst ever experienced in the United States, which explains why the economic contraction was also the most severe ever experienced by that nation.

International Dimensions

Although the Great Depression started in the United States, it was not just a U.S. phenomenon. Bank panics in the United States also spread to the rest of the world, and the contraction of the U.S. economy sharply decreased the demand for foreign goods. The worldwide depression caused great hardship, with millions upon millions of people out of work, and the resulting discontent led to the rise of fascism and World War II. The consequences of the Great Depression financial crisis were disastrous.

APPLICATION

The Global Financial Crisis of 2007–2009

Most economists thought that financial crises of the type experienced during the Great Depression were a thing of the past for advanced countries like Canada and the United States. Unfortunately, the financial crisis that engulfed the world in 2007–2009 proved them wrong.

Causes of the 2007–2009 Financial Crisis

We begin our look at the subprime financial crisis in the United States that was the underlying driving force behind the global financial crisis of 2007–2009. We examine three central factors that caused the U.S. subprime financial crisis: financial innovation in mortgage markets, agency problems in mortgage markets, and the role of asymmetric information in the credit-rating process.

FINANCIAL INNOVATION IN THE MORTGAGE MARKETS   Before 2000, only the most credit-worthy (prime) borrowers could obtain residential mortgages; however, advances in computer technology and new statistical techniques, known as data mining, led to enhanced, quantitative evaluation of the credit risk for a new class of risky residential mortgages. Households with credit records could now be assigned a numerical credit score that would predict how likely they would be to default on their loan payments. In addition, by lowering transactions costs, computer technology enabled the bundling together of smaller loans (like mortgages) into standard debt securities, a process known as **securitization** (discussed in the FYI box The Process of Securitization). These factors made it possible for banks to offer **subprime mortgages** to borrowers with less-than-stellar credit records.

The ability to cheaply quantify the default risk of the underlying high-risk mortgages and bundle them in a standardized debt security called **mortgage-backed securities** provided a new source of financing for these mortgages. Financial innovation didn't stop there. **Financial engineering**, the development of new, sophisticated financial instruments, led to **structured credit products** that pay out income streams from a collection of underlying assets, designed to have particular risk characteristics that appeal to investors with differing preferences. The most notorious of these products were collateralized debt obligations (CDOs) (discussed in the FYI box Collatoralized Debt Obligations).

FYI

The Process of Securitization

Traditionally, when a bank made a loan to a household or a business, it kept the loan and collected the payments until the loan was paid off. The bank could not resell the loan in the secondary market as, for example, shares of stock issued by Air Canada can be bought and sold on the Toronto Stock Exchange. That is, the loan was not a **security**, because it could not be bought and sold in a financial market.

In the 1970s, the process of securitization began. It involves the creation of a secondary market in which otherwise illiquid financial assets (such as residential mortgages, auto loans, and credit card receivables) are bundled together and are bought and sold in financial markets, just as government and corporate bonds are.

The securitization process is outlined below.

Figure 9-6 shows how in this process banks make loans to households and businesses and bundle these loans together into securities that are then sold to investors. In fact, banks bundle together a portfolio of loans with varying small denominations (often less than $100 000), divide the portfolio of loans into standardized amounts, and then sell the claims to these interest and principal payments to third parties as securities.

The standardized amounts of these securitized loans make them liquid securities, and the fact that they are made up of a bundle of loans helps diversify risk, making them desirable.

Figure 9-7 shows that banks collect the interest and principal payments on the original loans in the bundle, and after charging a fee, "pass them through" (pay them out) to the investors who bought the securities.

FIGURE 9-6 Securitizing a Loan

FIGURE 9-7 The Flow of Payments on a Securitized Loan

AGENCY PROBLEMS IN THE MORTGAGE MARKETS The mortgage brokers that originated the loans often did not make a strong effort to evaluate whether the borrower could pay off the loan, since they would quickly sell (distribute) the loans to investors in the form of mortgage-backed securities. Indeed, in some cases mortgage brokers would even extend loans that they knew were beyond the capability of the borrower to pay back. This **originate-to-distribute** business model was exposed to *principal–agent (agency) problems* of the type discussed in Chapter 8, in which the mortgage brokers acted as agents for investors (the principals) but did not have the investors' best interests at heart. Once the mortgage broker earns his or her fee, why should the broker care if the borrower makes good on his or her payment? The more volume the broker originates, the more he or she makes.

Not surprisingly, adverse selection became a major problem. Risk-loving investors lined up to obtain loans to acquire houses that would be very profitable if housing prices

FYI

Collateralized Debt Obligations (CDOs)

The creation of a collateralized debt obligation involves a corporate entity called a *special purpose vehicle (SPV)* that buys a collection of assets such as corporate bonds and loans, commercial real estate bonds, and mortgage-backed securities. The SPV then separates the payment streams (cash flows) from these assets into a number of buckets that are referred to as tranches. The highest-rated tranches, called super senior tranches, are the ones that are paid off first and so have the least risk. The super senior CDO is a bond that pays out these cash flows to investors, and because it has the least risk, it also has the lowest interest rate. The next bucket of cash flows, known as the senior tranche, is paid out next; the senior CDO has a little more risk and pays a higher interest rate. The next tranche of payment streams, the mezzanine tranche of the CDO, is paid out after the super senior and senior tranches and so it bears more risk and has an even higher interest rate. The lowest tranche of the CDO is the equity tranche; this is the first set of cash flows that are not paid out if the underlying assets go into default and stop making payments. This tranche has the highest risk and is often not traded.

If all of this sounds complicated, it is. There were even CDO^2s and CDO^3s that sliced and diced risk even further, paying out the cash flows from CDOs to CDO^2s and from CDO^2s to CDO^3s. Although financial engineering has the potential benefit of creating products and services that match investors' risk appetites, it also has a dark side. Structured products like CDOs, CDO^2s, and CDO^3s can get so complicated that it can be hard to value cash flows of the underlying assets for a security or to determine who actually owns these assets. Indeed, at a speech given in October 2007, Ben Bernanke, the chairman of the Federal Reserve, joked that he "would like to know what those damn things are worth." In other words, the increased complexity of structured products can actually reduce the amount of information in financial markets, thereby worsening asymmetric information in the financial system and increasing the severity of adverse selection and moral hazard problems.

went up, knowing they could "walk away" if housing prices went down. The principal–agent problem also created incentives for mortgage brokers to encourage households to take on mortgages they could not afford, or to commit fraud by falsifying information on a borrower's mortgage applications in order to qualify them for mortgages. Compounding this problem was lax regulation of originators, who were not required to disclose information to borrowers that would have helped them assess whether they could afford the loans.

The agency problems went even deeper. Commercial and investment banks, which were earning large fees by underwriting mortgage-backed securities and structured credit products like CDOs, also had weak incentives to make sure that the ultimate holders of the securities would be paid off. Large fees from writing financial insurance contracts called **credit default swaps,** which provide payments to holders of bonds if they default, also drove units of insurance companies like AIG to write hundreds of billions of dollars' worth of these risky contracts.

ASYMMETRIC INFORMATION AND CREDIT-RATING AGENCIES   Credit-rating agencies, who rate the quality of debt securities in terms of the probability of default, were another contributor to asymmetric information in financial markets. The rating agencies advised clients on how to structure complex financial instruments, like CDOs, at the same time they were rating these identical products. The rating agencies were thus subject to conflicts of interest because the large fees they earned from advising clients on how to structure products they were rating meant that they did not have sufficient incentives to make sure their ratings were accurate. The result was wildly inflated ratings that enabled the sale of complex financial products that were far riskier than investors recognized.

Effects of the 2007–2009 Financial Crisis

Consumers and businesses alike suffered as a result of the 2007–2009 financial crisis. The impact of the crisis was most evident in five key areas: the U.S. residential housing market, financial institutions' balance sheets, the shadow banking system, global financial markets, and the headline-grabbing failures of major firms in the financial industry.

RESIDENTIAL HOUSING PRICES: BOOM AND BUST   Aided by liquidity from huge cash inflows into the United States from countries like China and India and by low interest rates on residential mortgages, the subprime mortgage market took off after the recession ended in the United States in 2001. By 2007, it had become over a trillion-dollar market. The development of the subprime mortgage market was lauded by economists and politicians alike because it led to a "democratization of credit" and helped raise U.S. home ownership rates to the highest levels in history. The asset-price boom in housing, which took off after the 2000–2001 recession was over, also helped stimulate the growth of the subprime mortgage market. High housing prices meant that subprime borrowers could refinance their houses with even larger loans when their homes appreciated in value. With housing prices rising, subprime borrowers were also unlikely to default because they could always sell their house to pay off the loan, making investors happy because the securities backed by cash flows from subprime mortgages had high returns. The growth of the subprime mortgage market, in turn, increased the demand for houses and so fueled the boom in housing prices, resulting in a housing price bubble. A highly controversial issue is whether the Federal Reserve was to blame for the housing price bubble.

As housing prices rose and profitability for mortgage originators and lenders was high, the underwriting standards for subprime mortgages fell to lower and lower standards. High-risk borrowers were able to obtain mortgages, and the amount of the mortgage relative to the value of the house, the loan-to-value ratio, rose. Borrowers were often able to get piggyback, second, and third mortgages on top of their original 80% loan-to-value mortgage, so that they had to put almost no money down. When asset prices rise too far out of line with fundamentals—in the case of housing, how much housing costs if purchased relative to the cost of renting it, or the cost of houses relative to households' median income—they must come down. Eventually, the housing price bubble burst. With housing prices falling after their peak in 2006, the rot in the financial system began to be revealed. The decline in housing prices led to many subprime borrowers finding that their mortgages were "underwater"—that is, the value of the house fell below the amount of the mortgage. When this happened, struggling homeowners had tremendous incentives to walk away from their homes and just send the keys back to the lender. Defaults on mortgages shot up sharply, eventually leading to millions of mortgages in foreclosure.

DETERIORATION OF FINANCIAL INSTITUTIONS' BALANCE SHEETS   The decline in U.S. housing prices led to rising defaults on mortgages. As a result, the value of mortgage-backed securities and CDOs collapsed, leaving banks and other financial institutions with a lower value of assets and thus a decline in net worth. With weakened balance sheets, these banks and other financial institutions began to deleverage, selling off assets and restricting the availability of credit to both households and businesses. With no one else able to step in to collect information and make loans, the reduction in bank lending meant that financial frictions increased in financial markets.

RUN ON THE SHADOW BANKING SYSTEM   The sharp decline in the value of mortgages and other financial assets triggered a run on the **shadow banking system**, composed of hedge funds, investment banks, and other nondepository financial firms, which are not as tightly regulated as banks. Funds from shadow banks flowed through the financial system and for many years supported the issuance of low interest-rate mortgages and auto loans.

These securities were funded primarily by **repurchase agreements (repos)**, short-term borrowing that, in effect, uses assets like mortgage-backed securities as collateral. Rising concern about the quality of a financial institution's balance sheet led lenders to require larger amounts of collateral, known as **haircuts**. For example, if a borrower took out a $100 million loan in a repo agreement, it might have to post $105 million of mortgage-backed securities as collateral, and the haircut would then be 5%.

With rising defaults on mortgages, the value of mortgage-backed securities fell, which then led to a rise in haircuts. At the start of the crisis, haircuts were close to zero, but they eventually rose to nearly 50%. The result was that the same amount of collateral would allow financial institutions to borrow only half as much. Thus, to raise funds, financial institutions had to engage in fire sales and sell off their assets very rapidly. Because selling assets quickly requires lowering their price, the fire sales led to a further decline in financial institutions' asset values. This decline lowered the value of collateral further, raising haircuts and thereby forcing financial institutions to scramble even more for liquidity. The result was similar to the run on the banking system that occurred during the Great Depression in the United States, causing massive delever-aging that resulted in a restriction of lending and a decline in economic activity.

The decline in asset prices in the stock market (which fell by over 50% from October 2007 to March 2009, as shown in Figure 9-4) and the more than 30% drop in residential house prices, along with the fire sales resulting from the run on the shadow banking system, weakened both firms' and households' balance sheets. This worsening of financial frictions manifested itself in widening credit spreads, caus-ing higher costs of credit for households and businesses and tighter lending stan-dards. The resulting decline in lending meant that both consumption expenditure and investment fell, causing the economy to contract.[1]

FIGURE 9-4 Stock Prices and the Financial Crisis of 2007–2009

Stock prices in the United States fell by 50% from October 2007 to March 2009.

Source: Dow Jones Industrial Average (DJIA). Global Financial Data, www.globalfinancialdata.com/index_tabs. php?action=detailedinfo&id=1165.

---

[1] During this period there was also a substantial supply shock because oil and other commodity prices rose sharply until the summer of 2008, but then fell precipitously thereafter. We discuss the aggregate demand and supply analy-sis of the impact of this supply shock in Chapter 24.

GLOBAL FINANCIAL MARKETS   Although the problem originated in the United States, the wake-up call for the financial crisis came from Europe, a sign of how extensive the globalization of financial markets had become. After Fitch and Standard & Poor's announced ratings downgrades on mortgage-backed securities and CDOs totalling more than $10 billion, on August 7, 2007, a French investment house, BNP Paribas, suspended redemption of shares held in some of its money market funds, which had sustained large losses. The run on the shadow banking system began, only to become worse and worse over time. Despite huge injections of liquidity into the financial system by central banks around the world, banks began to horde cash and were unwilling to lend to each other. The drying up of credit led to the first major bank failure in the United Kingdom in over 100 years, when Northern Rock, which had relied on short-term borrowing in the repo market rather than deposits for its funding, collapsed in September 2007. A string of other European financial institutions then failed as well. Particularly hard hit were countries like Ireland, which up until this crisis was seen as one of the most successful countries in Europe with a very high rate of economic growth (see the Global box Ireland and the 2007–2009 Financial Crisis). European countries actually experienced a more severe economic downturn than did the United States (see the Global box The Greek Sovereign Debt Crisis).

FAILURE OF HIGH-PROFILE FIRMS   The impact of the financial crisis on firm balance sheets forced major players in the financial markets to take drastic action. In March 2008, Bear Stearns, the fifth-largest investment bank in the United States, which had invested heavily in subprime-related securities, had a run on its repo funding and was forced to sell

GLOBAL

Ireland and the 2007–2009 Financial Crisis

From 1995 to 2007, Ireland had one of the highest economic growth rates in the world, with real GDP growing at an average annual rate of 6.3%. As a result, Ireland earned the title the "Celtic Tiger," and it became one of Europe's wealthiest nations, with more Mercedes owners per capita than even Germany. But behind the scenes, soaring real estate prices and a boom in mortgage lending were laying the groundwork for a major financial crisis that hit in 2008, sending the Irish economy into a severe recession.

Irish banks eased loan standards, offering to cover a greater share of housing costs and at longer terms. As in the United States, a housing price bubble got underway, with Irish home values rising even more rapidly, doubling once between 1995 and 2000, and then again from 2000 to 2007. By 2007, residential construction reached 13% of GDP, twice the average of other wealthy nations, with Irish banks increasing their mortgage loans by 25% a year.

With the onset of the financial crisis in late 2007, home prices collapsed—falling nearly 20%, among the steepest housing price declines in the world. Irish banks were particularly vulnerable because of their exposure to mortgage markets and because they had funded their balance sheet expansions through short-term borrowing in the repo market. The combination of tighter funding and falling asset prices led to large losses, and in October 2008, the Irish government guaranteed all deposits. By early 2009, the government had nationalized one of the three largest banks and injected capital into the other two. Banks remained weak, with the government announcing a plan to shift "toxic" bank assets into a government-funding vehicle.

The financial crisis in Ireland triggered a painful recession, among the worst in modern Irish history. Unemployment rose from 4.5% before the crisis to 12.5%, while GDP levels tumbled by more than 10%. Tax rolls thinned, and losses in the banking sector continued to escalate, leading to an astronomical government budget deficit of over 30% of GDP in 2010. In dire straights, Ireland suffered the humiliation of having to be bailed out by the European Union and the IMF.

GLOBAL

The Greek Sovereign Debt Crisis

The global financial crisis and recession of 2007–2009 caused big problems for a number of European countries, particularly Greece, Ireland, Portugal, Spain, and Italy. To deal with the recession, these countries increased government spending and paid for the resulting government budget deficits by issuing sovereign debt—by **sovereign debt** we mean bonds issued by a government. By the spring of 2010, they had issued so much debt that investors began doubting government ability to make the interest and principal payments on the debt. This led to a wave of downgrading of government bonds by the credit-rating agencies and to a number of **sovereign debt crises** in Europe, most notably that of Greece.

The Greek debt crisis has not led to actual default because of two bailout packages by the European Commission, the International Monetary Fund, and the European Central Bank, together described by the slang term "troika." In exchange for the aid

packages, Greece is required to implement an austerity package, reducing government spending and raising taxes, even though doing so results in protests from unions and other interest groups. The country is also required to implement a number of structural and economic reforms to make the economy competitive.

Whether the worst of the Greek debt crisis is over and Greece survives as a modern and prosperous European state will depend on the Greek government's ability to restructure and modernize its economy, including the primitive tax-collection system and the irrational pension system. So far, the actions taken by the troika have been designed to help Greece and also to prevent euro zone debt contagion. If Greece leaves the euro and starts issuing drachmas, the destabilizing effects on the European banking system will potentially threaten the survival of the euro as the common currency of the 17 member countries of the European monetary union.

itself to J.P. Morgan for less than 5% of what it was worth just a year earlier. To broker the deal, the Federal Reserve had to take over $30 billion of Bear Stearns's hard-to-value assets. In July, Fannie Mae and Freddie Mac, the two privately owned government-sponsored enterprises that together insured over $5 trillion of mortgages or mortgage-backed assets, were propped up by the U.S. Treasury and the Federal Reserve after suffering substantial losses from their holdings of subprime securities. In early September 2008, they were then put into conservatorship (in effect, run by the government).

On Monday, September 15, 2008, after suffering losses in the subprime market, Lehman Brothers, the fourth-largest investment bank by asset size with over $600 billion in assets and 25 000 employees, filed for bankruptcy, making it the largest bankruptcy filing in U.S. history. The day before, Merrill Lynch, the third-largest investment bank, who also suffered large losses on its holding of subprime securities, announced its sale to Bank of America for a price 60% below its value a year earlier. On Tuesday, September 16, AIG, an insurance giant with assets of over $1 trillion, suffered an extreme liquidity crisis when its credit rating was downgraded. It had written over $400 billion of insurance contracts (credit default swaps) that had to make payouts on possible losses from subprime mortgage securities. The Federal Reserve then stepped in with an $85 billion loan to keep AIG afloat (with total government loans later increased to $173 billion).

Height of the 2007–2009 Financial Crisis

The financial crisis reached its peak in September 2008 after the U.S. House of Representatives, fearing the wrath of constituents who were angry about bailing out Wall Street, voted down a $700 billion bailout package proposed by the Bush administration. The Emergency Economic Stabilization Act finally passed nearly a week later. The stock market crash accelerated, with the week beginning October 6, 2008, showing the worst weekly decline in U.S. history. Credit spreads went through

FIGURE 9-5 Credit Spreads and the 2007–2009 Financial Crisis in the United States

Credit spreads (the difference between rates on Baa corporate bonds and U.S. Treasury bonds) rose by more than 4 percentage points (400 basis points) during the crisis. Debate over the bailout package and the stock market crash caused credit spreads to peak in December 2008.

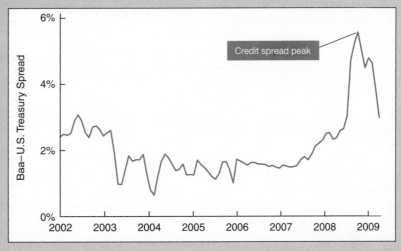

Source: Federal Reserve Bank of St. Louis FRED database; http://research.stlouisfed.org/fred2/categories/22.

the roof over the next three weeks, with the spread between Baa corporate bonds (just above investment grade) and U.S. Treasury bonds going to over 5.5 percentage points (550 basis points), as illustrated by Figure 9-5.

The impaired financial markets and surging interest rates faced by borrower-spenders led to sharp declines in consumer spending and investment. Real GDP declined sharply, falling at a 1.3% annual rate in the third quarter of 2008 and then at a 5.4% and 6.4% annual rate in the next two quarters. The unemployment rate shot up, going over the 10% level in late 2009. The recession that started in December 2007 became the worst economic contraction in the United States since World War II and, as a result, is now referred to as the "Great Recession."

Government Intervention and the Recovery

Although the recession produced by the global financial crisis was very severe, the economic contraction was far smaller in magnitude than during the Great Depression because of massive interventions by governments to prop up financial markets and stimulate the economy.

The Federal Reserve took extraordinary actions to contain the crisis involving both monetary policy to stimulate the economy and liquidity provision to support orderly functioning of financial markets. In addition, the U.S. government engaged in massive bailouts with over $150 billion of loans to AIG and the **Troubled Asset Relief Program (TARP)**, the most important provision of the Bush administration's Economic Recovery Act passed in October 2008, which authorized the U.S. Treasury to spend $700 billion purchasing subprime mortgage assets from troubled financial institutions or to inject capital into these institutions—the route actually followed. In addition, the Act raised the federal deposit insurance limit temporarily from $100 000 to $250 000 in order to limit withdrawals from banks. Shortly thereafter, the FDIC put in place a guarantee for certain debt newly issued by banks, and the Treasury guaranteed for a year money market mutual fund shares at par value. Similarly European governments conducted massive bailouts, which were in excess of $10 trillion, in order to prop up their banking systems (see the Global box Worldwide Government Bailouts During the 2007–2009 Financial Crisis).

GLOBAL

Worldwide Government Bailouts During the 2007–2009 Financial Crisis

The spreading bank failures in Europe in the fall of 2008 led to massive bailouts of financial institutions: The Netherlands, Belgium, and Luxembourg injected $16 billion to prop up Fortis, a major European bank; the Netherlands injected $13 billion into ING, a banking and insurance giant; Germany provided a $50 billion rescue package for Hypo Real Estate Holdings; and Iceland took over its three largest banks after its banking system collapsed. Ireland's government guaranteed all the deposits of its commercial banks as well as interbank lending, as did Greece. Spain implemented a bailout package similar to that of the United States to buy up to 50 billion euros ($70 billion) of assets in its banks in order to encourage them to lend.

The U.K. Treasury set up a bailout plan with a similar price tag to that of the U.S. Treasury's plan of 400 billion pounds ($699 billion). It guaranteed 250 billion pounds of bank liabilities, added 100 billion pounds to a facility that swaps these assets for government bonds, and allowed the U.K. government to buy up to 50 billion pounds of equity stakes in British banks. Bailout plans to the tune of over $100 billion in South Korea, $200 billion in Sweden, $400 billion in France, and $500 billion in Germany, all of which guaranteed the debt of their banks as well as injecting capital into them, then followed. Both the scale of these bailout packages and the degree of international coordination was unprecedented.

Fiscal stimulus to stimulate the economy was another key piece of the U.S. government's response to the crisis. In February 2008, the U.S. Congress passed the Bush administration's Economic Stimulus Act of 2008, which gave one-time tax rebates of $78 billion by sending $600 cheques to individual taxpayers. Shortly after coming to office, the Obama administration proposed and got passed the American Recovery and Reinvestment Act of 2009, a much bigger $787 billion fiscal stimulus package which, to this day, is highly controversial.

With the government bailouts, the Federal Reserve's extraordinary actions, and fiscal stimulus, starting in March 2009 a bull market in stocks got under way (see Figure 9-4) and credit spreads began to fall (Figure 9-5). With the recovery in financial markets, the U.S. economy started to recover, but unfortunately, the pace of recovery has been slow.

APPLICATION

Canada and the 2007–2009 Financial Crisis

In Canada, the early symptom of the U.S. subprime crisis was the freezing of the asset-backed commercial paper (ABCP) market in August 2007. It caused a sharp decrease in liquidity in short-term Canadian credit markets, including the overnight interbank market and the overnight repurchase market. In order to restore confidence and liquidity in the ABCP market, and prevent significant write-offs for banks that would have reduced their capital and raised concerns about their solvency, market participants reached an agreement, known as the Montreal Accord, to restructure the frozen ABCP market and minimize the costs to the Canadian taxpayer. (See the FYI box Canada's Asset-Backed Commercial Paper Crisis for more details.)

FYI

Canada's Asset-Backed Commercial Paper Crisis

As we noted in Chapter 2, commercial paper is short-term, unsecured debt issued by corporations, typically for financing accounts receivable and inventories. Asset-backed commercial paper, like traditional commercial paper, is also a short-term security (with a maturity that is typically less than nine months). It is issued by conduits (that is, bankruptcy-remote Special Purpose Vehicles), but instead of being an unsecured promissory note, is backed by physical assets such as mortgages, trade receivables, credit card receivables, automobile loans and leases, and other types of assets. Because of this backing, the quality of the ABCP depends on the underlying securities and thus ABCP could be very risky. For example, if there are negative developments in the underlying markets, the risk of ABCP will increase and investors will switch out of ABCP and into safer money market instruments such as traditional commercial paper, bankers' acceptances, and Treasury bills. As a result, conduits will not be able to roll over their ABCP and will face a liquidity crunch.

The ABCP market in Canada expanded very rapidly from the 1990s to 2007. As at July 31, 2007, the size of the Canadian ABCP market was $115 billion (equal to about 32.5% of the Canadian money market), of which $80 billion was bank-sponsored and $35 billion was non-bank-sponsored. At the same time, the ABCP market in the United States was approximately US$1.2 trillion, equal to about 50% of the U.S. commercial paper market. Bank-sponsored ABCP conduits are invested in "plain vanilla" assets such as residential mortgages and credit card receivables. Non-bank-sponsored ABCP conduits are invested in structured finance assets such as collateralized debt obligations (CDOs) and subprime mortgages. Canadian banks are involved in the distribution of ABCP and also provide liquidity back-stop facilities to non-bank-sponsored ABCP conduits under the so-called general market disruption clause.

In August of 2007, investors in the Canadian ABCP market declined to roll over maturing notes because of concerns about exposure to the U.S. subprime mortgage sector in the underlying assets. As a result, the market was divided into those ABCP conduits that could honour their obligations (bank-sponsored) and those that could not honour their obligations (non-bank-sponsored).

In the case of bank-sponsored ABCP, the Big Six banks took back onto their balance sheets significant amounts of their own sponsored ABCP. Moreover, valuation and fair-value issues led to significant write-downs in the fourth quarter of 2007 and the first quarter of 2008. In the case of non-bank-sponsored ABCP, a number of conduits faced significant liquidity shortages, seeking liquidity funding support from their liquidity providers (banks). However, major liquidity providers denied requests for liquidity support, arguing that the "general market disruption" clause was not met. They interpreted the clause to mean that the majority of the conduits in the entire Canadian ABCP market would need to be unable to roll over before a liquidity provider had to step in. As a result, the Canadian non-bank-sponsored ABCP market froze and investors, including Québec's huge pension fund, *Caisse de dépôt et placement du Québec*, Alberta's ATB Financial, the National Bank of Canada, and about 2000 individual small investors, had their cash frozen in non-bank-sponsored ABCP.

At the time, the Bank of Canada indicated that it would not accept ABCP as collateral for loans to banks and that a solution from participants in the ABCP market was deemed to be appropriate. As a result, major market participants, including non-bank-sponsored ABCP conduits, institutional investors, liquidity providers (ABN AMRO Group, HSBC, Deutsche Bank, Merrill Lynch, Barclays Capital), and the Affected Trusts, reached an agreement on August 16, 2007, known as the Montreal Accord. Under the Montreal Accord, investors agreed to a standstill period (initially 60 days, to October 16, 2007, extended three times to February 22, 2008), with the objective of restructuring the frozen ABCP into long-term floating rate notes with maturities matching the maturities of the underlying assets in the conduits. However, the agreement had to be renegotiated again 16 months later, in December 2008, with the participation of the federal government and three provinces (Ontario, Québec, and Alberta), where publicly owned institutions held over $30 billion of frozen non-bank-sponsored ABCP. Small investors (holding less than $1 million of the paper) were fully paid out in cash by the brokerage firms that had sold them the paper, whereas the larger investors were given bonds.

The ABCP crisis in Canada was managed well although the final cost of the restructuring was in excess of $200 million in fees, with the big investors footing the bill.

Subprime Mortgages in Canada

The subprime mortgage crisis in the United States dominated news headlines, but there is also the Canadian version of subprime mortgages. High-risk, long-term (40-year), zero-down mortgages proliferated in Canada in 2007 and 2008 after the Conservative government opened up the Canadian mortgage market to big U.S. players in its first budget in May of 2006. This created the Canadian version of subprime mortgages. How did Canadian regulators allow the entry into Canada of U.S.-style subprime mortgages?

The Canadian mortgage insurance market is the second largest and one of the most lucrative mortgage insurance markets in the world. For over 50 years, since revisions in the National Housing Act and the Bank Act in 1954 allowed chartered banks to make insured mortgage loans, the business of mortgage insurance was mainly the domain of the Canada Mortgage and Housing Corporation (CMHC). CMHC insured the mortgages of those home buyers that could not make a 25% down payment, charging them an insurance premium, with the federal government backing the CMHC's insurance policies with a 100% federal guarantee.

For many years, U.S. insurance companies had conducted orchestrated lobbying of Canada's Department of Finance and Office of the Superintendent of Financial Institutions. In May 2006, the government allowed big U.S. players such as AIG to enter the Canadian mortgage insurance market and also committed to guarantee their business up to $200 billion. In February of 2006, in an attempt to protect its business in anticipation of the entry of the big U.S. insurers, CMHC announced that it would insure 30-year mortgages. Two weeks later, Genworth Mortgage Insurance Co., the Canadian mortgage subsidiary of the U.S. conglomerate General Electric and the only other (private) mortgage insurer in Canada at that time (with an estimated market share of about 30%), announced that it would insure 35-year mortgages. By October of 2006, AIG, CMHC, and Genworth were competing in the Canadian mortgage insurance market by insuring 40-year mortgages.

In response to the subprime meltdown in the United States, the Canadian government banned subprime mortgages in Canada in the summer of 2008. Although there are currently no publicly available figures, it is estimated that more than half of the total new mortgages approved by Canadian financial institutions during this period (worth over $50 billion) were risky, 40-year mortgages, and that 10% of these mortgages (worth over $10 billion) were taken out with zero money down.

More recently, on June 21st, 2012, Jim Flaherty, the finance minister, tightened several regulations for real estate lending, his fourth round of tightening in four years. The most significant regulatory changes are as follows: the maximum amortization period for a mortgage will now be 25 years, down from 30; refinancing a home will be allowed only up to 80% of its value, down from 85%; and homebuyers will have to demonstrate their housing costs are no more than 39% of their gross household income. In addition, Canada's banking regulator, the Office of the Superintendent of Financial Institutions (OSFI), has placed a loan-to-value limit of 65% on borrowing against home equity.

Why Canada's Banking System Is the Envy of the World

Canadian banks also had their problems during the recent turbulent financial conditions. Their shares fell by almost 50% and some of them experienced huge losses in derivatives trading; for example, CIBC lost $2.1 billion in derivatives trading in 2008. However, while governments in the United States and Europe have been working on full-scale banking bailouts and rescue packages (in the trillions of dollars), the Canadian government did not have to bail out any banks.

One reason that Canada's banks have fared better than banks in other countries is the structure of the Canadian mortgage market. Unlike banks in the United States that sold the bulk of their mortgages, banks in Canada held a large proportion of their mortgages on their balance sheets. This practice gave Canadian banks an incentive to make sure that their mortgage loans were good loans. In addition, law in

Canada allows banks to go after other assets when a consumer walks away from a mortgage, thereby making it difficult for consumers to do so.

Another reason is that Canada's big banks have been more conservative in their lending and acquisition practices in comparison with major banks around the world. Also, Canada's top banking regulator, the Office of the Superintendent of Financial Institutions (OSFI), has been more conservative than banking regulators in the United States and Europe. For example, at the beginning of the financial crisis, Canada's banks had higher capital requirements than their global peers. As a result, they had stronger reserves to cushion potential losses. Although this conservative regulatory regime enabled Canadian banks to withstand the financial crisis better than banks in other countries, it has been argued that it makes the Canadian banking sector less competitive because of the lower leverage and a lower rate of return on capital than in other jurisdictions.

Moreover, the activities of Canada's banks are well diversified and are not limited to traditional retail banking. In particular, the federal government's decision in the late 1980s to allow banks to acquire investment brokers on Bay Street and to engage in the mutual fund and insurance businesses created a more diversified financial services marketplace for Canada's banks. In addition, these arm's-length institutions are subject to the same strict rules and regulations as the banks, unlike investment dealers in the United States that had been subject to very relaxed and minimal regulation from the Securities and Exchange Commission.

Overall, in the aftermath of the global economic meltdown, Canada's banking system has been viewed as the soundest in the world. In fact, many countries around the world are now considering Canadian-style reforms of their financial markets.

Dynamics of Financial Crises in Emerging Market Economies

Before the financial crisis of 2007–2009, economists looked abroad for recent examples of financial crises. **Emerging market economies**, economies in an earlier stage of market development that have recently opened up to the flow of goods, services, and capital from the rest of the world, are particularly vulnerable. With the opening up of their economies to markets, emerging market countries have been no stranger to devastating financial crises in recent years. The dynamics of financial crises in emerging market economies have many of the same elements as those found in the United States, but with some important differences. Figure 9-8 outlines the key stages and sequence of events in financial crises in these economies that we will address in this section.

Stage One: Initiation of Financial Crisis

Crises in advanced economies can be triggered by a number of different factors. But in emerging market countries, financial crises develop along two basic paths: either the mismanagement of financial liberalization and globalization or severe fiscal imbalances. The first path of mismanagement of financial liberalization/globalization is the most common culprit, precipitating the crises in Mexico in 1994 and many East Asian crises in 1997.

PATH A: MISMANAGEMENT OF FINANCIAL LIBERALIZATION/GLOBALIZATION As in the United States during the subprime financial crisis of 2007–2009, the seeds of a financial crisis in emerging market countries are often sown when countries liberalize their financial systems. Countries liberalize by eliminating restrictions on financial institutions and markets domestically and opening up their economies to flows of capital and financial firms from other nations, a process called **financial globalization**. Countries often begin the process with solid fiscal policy. In the run-up to crisis, Mexico had a budget

FIGURE 9-8 Sequence of Events in Emerging Market Financial Crises

The arrows trace the sequence of events during a financial crisis. The sections separated by the dashed horizontal lines show the different stages of a financial crisis.

deficit of only 0.7% of GDP, a number to which most advanced countries would aspire. The countries in East Asia even ran budget surpluses before their crises struck.

It is often said that emerging market financial systems have a weak "credit culture," with ineffective screening and monitoring of borrowers and lax government supervision of banks. Lending booms that accompany financial liberalization in emerging-market nations are typically marked by especially risky lending practices, sowing the seeds for enormous loan losses down the road. The financial globalization process adds fuel to the fire because it allows domestic banks to borrow abroad. Banks pay high interest rates to attract foreign capital and so can rapidly increase their lending. The capital inflow is further stimulated by government policies that fix the value of the domestic currency to the U.S. dollar, which provides foreign investors a sense of comfort.

Just as in advanced countries like Canada, the lending boom ends in a lending crash. Significant loan losses emerge from long periods of risky lending, weakening bank balance sheets and prompting banks to cut back on lending. The deterioration in bank balance sheets has an even greater negative impact on lending and economic activity than in advanced countries, which tend to have sophisticated securities markets and large nonbank financial sectors that can pick up the slack when banks falter. So as banks stop lending, no other players are available to solve adverse selection and moral hazard problems, and financial frictions increase (as shown by the arrow pointing from the first factor in the top row of Figure 9-8).

The story told so far suggests that a lending boom and crash are inevitable outcomes of financial liberalization and globalization in emerging market countries, but this is not the case. They occur only when an institutional weakness prevents the nation from successfully navigating the liberalization/globalization process. More specifically, if prudential regulation and supervision to limit excessive risk taking were strong, the lending boom and bust would not happen. Why are regulation and supervision typically weak? The answer is the principal–agent problem, discussed in the previous chapter, which encourages powerful domestic business interests to pervert the financial liberalization process. Politicians and prudential supervisors are ultimately agents for voters-taxpayers (principals)—that is, the goal of politicians and prudential supervisors is, or should be, to protect the taxpayers' interest. Taxpayers almost always bear the cost of bailing out the banking sector if losses occur.

Once financial markets have been liberalized, however, powerful business interests that own banks will want to prevent the supervisors from doing their job properly, and so prudential supervisors may not act in the public interest. Powerful business interests who contribute heavily to politicians' campaigns are often able to persuade politicians to weaken regulations that restrict their banks from engaging in high-risk/high-payoff strategies. After all, if bank owners achieve growth and expand bank lending rapidly, they stand to make a fortune. If the bank gets in trouble, though, the government is likely to bail it out and the taxpayer foots the bill. In addition, these business interests can also make sure that the supervisory agencies, even in the presence of tough regulations, lack the resources to effectively monitor banking institutions or to close them down.

Powerful business interests also have acted to prevent supervisors from doing their job properly in advanced countries. The weak institutional environment in emerging market countries adds to the perversion of the financial liberalization process. In emerging market economies, business interests are far more powerful than they are in advanced economies, where a better-educated public and a free press monitor (and punish) politicians and bureaucrats who are not acting in the public interest. Not surprisingly, then, the cost to society of the principal–agent problem we have been describing here is particularly high in emerging market economies.

PATH B: SEVERE FISCAL IMBALANCES   The financing of government spending can also place emerging market economies on a path toward financial crisis. The financial crisis in Argentina in 2001–2002 is of this type; other crises—for example, in Russia in 1998, Ecuador in 1999, and Turkey in 2001—have some elements of this type of crisis, as well.

When Willie Sutton, a famous bank robber, was asked why he robbed banks, he answered, "Because that's where the money is." Governments in emerging market countries sometimes have the same attitude. When they face large fiscal imbalances and cannot finance their debt, they often cajole or force banks to purchase government debt. Investors who lose confidence in the ability of the government to repay this debt unload the bonds, which causes their prices to plummet. Banks that hold this debt then face a big hole on the asset side of their balance sheets, with a huge decline in their net worth. With less capital, these institutions will have fewer resources to lend and lending will decline. The situation can even be worse if the decline in bank capital leads to a bank panic, in which many banks fail at the same time. The result of severe fiscal imbalances is therefore a weakening of the banking system, which leads to a worsening of adverse selection and moral hazard problems (as shown by the arrow from the first factor in stage two of Figure 9-8).

ADDITIONAL FACTORS   Other factors also often play a role in the first stage in crises. For example, another precipitating factor in some crises (e.g., the Mexican crisis) was a rise in interest rates from events abroad, such as a tightening of U.S. monetary policy. As we saw in Chapter 8, individuals and firms with the riskiest investment projects are those who are willing to pay the highest interest rates. Hence, when interest rates rise, good credit risks are less likely to want to borrow, whereas bad credit risks are still willing to borrow. Because of the resulting increase in adverse selection, lenders will no longer want to make loans.

Increases in interest rates can also have a part in promoting a financial crisis through their effect on **cash flow**, the difference between cash receipts and expenditures. A firm with sufficient cash flow can finance its projects internally, and no asymmetric information is present because it knows how good its own projects are. (Indeed, most businesses fund their investments with internal funds.) An increase in interest rates, and therefore in household and firm interest payments, decreases their cash flow. With less cash flow, the firm has fewer internal funds and must raise funds from an external source, say, a bank, which does not know the firm as well as its owners or managers. How can the bank be sure that the firm will invest in safe projects and not take on big risks and then be unlikely to pay back the loan? Because of this increased adverse selection and moral hazard, the bank may choose not to lend firms, even those with good risks, the money to undertake potentially profitable investments. Thus, increases in interest rates abroad that raise domestic interest rates increase financial frictions (as shown by the arrow from the second factor in the top row of Figure 9-8).

Because asset markets are not as large in emerging market countries as they are in advanced countries, they play a less prominent role in financial crises. Asset-price declines in the stock market do, nevertheless, decrease the net worth of firms and so increase adverse selection problems. Less collateral is available for lenders to seize and moral hazard problems are increased because, given their decreased net worth, the owners of the firm have less to lose if they engage in riskier activities than they did before the crisis. Asset-price declines can therefore worsen adverse selection and moral hazard problems directly and also indirectly by causing a deterioration in banks' balance sheets from asset writedowns (as shown by the arrow pointing from the third factor in the first row of Figure 9-8).

As in advanced countries, when an emerging market economy is in a recession or a prominent firm fails, people become more uncertain about the returns on investment projects. In emerging market countries, notoriously unstable political systems are another source of uncertainty. When uncertainty increases, it becomes hard for lenders to screen out good credit risks from bad and to monitor the activities of firms to whom they have loaned money, again worsening adverse selection and moral hazard problems (as shown by the arrow pointing from the last factor in the first row of Figure 9-8).

Stage Two: Currency Crisis

As the effects of any or all of the factors at the top of the diagram in Figure 9-8 build on each other, participants in the foreign exchange market sense an opportunity: They can make huge profits if they bet on a depreciation of the currency. A currency that is fixed against the U.S. dollar now becomes subject to a **speculative attack**, in which speculators engage in massive sales of the currency. As currency sales flood the market, supply far outstrips demand, the value of the currency collapses, and a currency crisis ensues (see the stage two section of Figure 9-8). High interest rates abroad, increases in uncertainty, and falling asset prices all play a role. The deterioration in bank balance sheets and severe fiscal imbalances, however, are the two key factors that trigger speculative attacks and plunge the economies into a full-scale, vicious downward spiral of currency crisis, financial crisis, and meltdown.

DETERIORATION OF BANK BALANCE SHEETS TRIGGERS CURRENCY CRISES When banks and other financial institutions are in trouble, governments have a limited number of options. Defending their currencies by raising interest rates should encourage capital inflows. If the government raises interest rates, banks must pay more to obtain funds. This increase in costs decreases bank profitability, which may lead them to insolvency. Thus, when the banking system is in trouble, the government and central bank are now between a rock and a hard place: if they raise interest rates too much, they will destroy their already weakened banks and further cripple their economy. It they don't, they can't maintain the value of their currency.

Speculators in the market for foreign currency recognize the troubles in a country's financial sector and realize that when the government's ability to raise interest rates and defend the currency is so costly the government is likely to give up and allow the currency to depreciate. They will seize an almost sure-thing bet because the currency can only go downward in value. Speculators engage in a feeding frenzy and sell the currency in anticipation of its decline, which will provide them with huge profits. These sales rapidly use up the country's holdings of reserves of foreign currency because the country has to sell its reserves to buy the domestic currency and keep it from falling in value. Once the country's central bank has exhausted its holdings of foreign currency reserves, the cycle ends. It no longer has the resources to intervene in the foreign exchange market and must let the value of the domestic currency fall: That is, the government must allow a devaluation.

SEVERE FISCAL IMBALANCES TRIGGER CURRENCY CRISES   We have seen that severe fiscal imbalances can lead to a deterioration of bank balance sheets, and so can help produce a currency crisis along the lines described immediately above. Fiscal imbalances can also directly trigger a currency crisis. When government budget deficits spin out of control, foreign and domestic investors begin to suspect that the country may not be able to pay back its government debt and so will start pulling money out of the country and selling the domestic currency. Recognition that the fiscal situation is out of control thus results in a speculative attack against the currency, which eventually results in its collapse.

Stage Three: Full-Fledged Financial Crisis

In contrast to most advanced economies that typically denominate debt in domestic currency, emerging market economies denominate many debt contracts in foreign currency (dollars), while their assets are denominated in domestic currency, leading to what is known as **currency mismatch**. An unanticipated depreciation or devaluation of the domestic currency (for example, pesos) in emerging market countries increases the debt burden of domestic firms in terms of domestic currency. That is, it takes more pesos to pay back the dollarized debt. Because most firms price the goods and services they produce in domestic currency, the firms' assets do not rise in value in terms of pesos, while the debt does. Depreciation of the domestic currency increases the value of debt relative to assets, and the firm's net worth declines. The decline in net worth then increases the adverse selection and moral hazard problems described earlier. The rise in financial frictions, in turn, leads to a decline in investment and economic activity (as shown by the stage three section of Figure 9-8).

We now see how the institutional structure of debt markets in emerging market countries interacts with currency devaluations to propel the economies into full-fledged financial crises. A currency crisis, with its resulting depreciation of the currency, leads to a deterioration of firms' balance sheets, which sharply increases financial frictions. Economists often call a concurrent currency crisis and financial crisis the "twin crises."

The collapse of a currency also can result in higher inflation. The central banks in most emerging market countries, in contrast to those in advanced countries, have little credibility as inflation fighters. Thus, a sharp depreciation of the currency after a currency crisis leads to immediate upward pressure on import prices. A dramatic rise in both actual and expected inflation will likely follow. The resulting increase in interest payments causes reductions in firms' cash flow, which lead to increased adverse selection and moral hazard problems because firms are now more dependent on external funds to finance their investment. This asymmetric information analysis suggests that the resulting increase in financial frictions leads to a reduction in investment and economic activity.

As shown in Figure 9-8, further deterioration in the economy occurs. The collapse in economic activity and the deterioration of cash flow and of firm and household balance sheets mean that many debtors are no longer able to pay off their debts, resulting in substantial losses for banks. Sharp rises in interest rates also have a negative effect on banks' profitability and balance sheets. Even more problematic for the banks is the sharp increase in the value of their foreign currency-denominated liabilities after the devaluation. Thus, bank balance sheets are squeezed from both sides—the value of their assets falls as the value of their liabilities rises.

Under these circumstances, the banking system will often suffer a banking crisis in which many banks are likely to fail. The banking crisis and the contributing factors in the credit markets explain a further worsening of adverse selection and moral hazard problems and a further collapse of lending and economic activity in the aftermath of the crisis.

APPLICATION

Financial Crises in Mexico, 1994–1995; East Asia, 1997–1998; and Argentina, 2001–2002

When emerging market countries opened up their markets to the outside world in the 1990s, they had high hopes that globalization would stimulate economic growth and eventually make them rich. Instead of leading to high economic growth and reduced poverty, however, many of them experienced financial crises that were every bit as devastating as the Great Depression had been in the United States and other advanced economies.

The most dramatic of these crises were the Mexican crisis, which started in 1994; the East Asian crisis, which started in July 1997; and the Argentine crisis, which started in 2001. We now apply the asymmetric information analysis of the dynamics of financial crises to explain why a developing country can shift dramatically from a path of high growth before a financial crisis—as was true in Mexico and particularly the East Asian countries of Thailand, Malaysia, Indonesia, the Philippines, and South Korea—to a sharp decline in economic activity.[2]

Before their crises, Mexico and the East Asian countries had achieved a sound fiscal policy. The East Asian countries ran budget surpluses, and Mexico ran a

---

[2] This application does not examine four other crises, those in Russia, Brazil, Ecuador, and Turkey. Russia's financial crisis in August 1998 can also be explained with the asymmetric information story here, but it is more appropriate to view it as a symptom of a wider breakdown in the economy. The Brazilian crisis in January 1999 has features of a more traditional balance-of-payments crisis (see Chapter 20) rather than a financial crisis. Ecuador's crisis of 1999 and the Turkish crisis of 2001 have features of both types of emerging market financial crises discussed in the application, with mismanagement of financial liberalization/globalization and severe fiscal imbalances playing prominent roles.

budget deficit of less than 1% of GDP, a number that most advanced countries, including Canada, would be thrilled to have today. The key precipitating factor driving these crises was the deterioration in banks' balance sheets because of increasing loan losses. When financial markets in these countries were liberalized and opened to foreign capital markets in the early 1990s, a lending boom ensued. Bank credit to the private nonfinancial business sector accelerated sharply, with lending expanding at 15–30% per year. Because of weak supervision by bank regulators, aided and abetted by powerful business interests and a lack of expertise in screening and monitoring borrowers at banking institutions, losses on loans began to mount, causing an erosion of banks' net worth (capital). As a result of this erosion, banks had fewer resources to lend. This lack of lending led to a contraction of economic activity along the lines outlined in the previous section.

In contrast to Mexico and the East Asian countries, Argentina had a well-supervised banking system, and a lending boom did not occur before the crisis. The banks were in surprisingly good shape before the crisis, even though a severe recession had begun in 1998. This recession led to declining tax revenues and a widening gap between expenditures and taxes. The subsequent severe fiscal imbalances were so large that the government had trouble getting both citizens and foreigners to buy enough of its bonds, so it coerced banks into absorbing large amounts of government debt. Investors soon lost confidence in the ability of the Argentine government to repay this debt. The price of the debt plummeted, leaving big holes in banks' balance sheets. This weakening helped lead to a decline in lending and a contraction of economic activity, as in Mexico and East Asia.

Another precipitating factor in the Mexican and Argentine (but not East Asian) financial crises was a rise in interest rates abroad. Before the Mexican crisis, in February 1994, and before the Argentine crisis, in mid-1999, the Federal Reserve began a cycle of raising the federal funds rate to head off inflationary pressures. Although the Fed's monetary policy actions were successful in keeping U.S. inflation in check, they put upward pressure on interest rates in both Mexico and Argentina. The rise in interest rates in Mexico and Argentina directly added to increased adverse selection and moral hazard problems in their financial markets. As discussed earlier, it was more likely that the parties willing to take on the most risk would seek loans, and the higher interest payments led to a decline in firms' cash flow.

Also, stock market declines and increases in uncertainty initiated and contributed to full-blown financial crises in Mexico, Thailand, South Korea, and Argentina. (The stock market declines in Malaysia, Indonesia, and the Philippines, on the other hand, occurred simultaneously with the onset of these crises.) The Mexican economy was hit by political shocks in 1994 (specifically, the assassination of the ruling party's presidential candidate, Luis Colosio, and an uprising in the southern state of Chiapas) that created uncertainty, whereas the ongoing recession increased uncertainty in Argentina. Right before their crises, Thailand and South Korea experienced major failures of financial and nonfinancial firms that increased general uncertainty in financial markets.

As we have seen, an increase in uncertainty and a decrease in net worth as a result of a stock market decline promotes financial frictions. It becomes harder to screen out good from bad borrowers. The decline in net worth decreases the value of firms' collateral and increases their incentives to make risky investments because there is less equity to lose if the investments are unsuccessful. The increase in uncertainty and stock market declines that occurred before the crises, along with the deterioration in banks' balance sheets, worsened adverse selection and moral hazard problems and made the economies ripe for a serious financial emergency.

At this point, full-blown speculative attacks developed in the foreign exchange market, plunging these countries into a full-scale crisis. With the Colosio assassination, the Chiapas uprising, and the growing weakness in the banking sector, the Mexican peso came under attack. Even though the Mexican central bank intervened in the foreign exchange market and raised interest rates sharply, it was unable to stem the attacks and was forced to devalue the peso on December 20, 1994. In the case of Thailand, concerns about the large current account deficit and weakness in the Thai financial system—culminating with the failure of a major finance company, Finance One—led to a successful speculative attack. The Thai central bank was forced to allow the baht to depreciate in July 1997. Soon thereafter, speculative attacks developed against the other countries in the region, leading to the collapse of the Philippine peso, the Indonesian rupiah, the Malaysian ringgit, and the South Korean won. In Argentina, a full-scale banking panic began in October–November 2001. This, along with realization that the government was going to default on its debt, also led to a speculative attack on the Argentine peso, resulting in its collapse on January 6, 2002.

The institutional structure of debt markets in Mexico and East Asia now interacted with currency devaluations to propel the economies into full-fledged financial crises. Because so many firms in these countries had debt denominated in foreign currencies like the U.S. dollar and the yen, depreciation of their currencies resulted in increases in their indebtedness in domestic currency terms, even though the value of their assets remained unchanged. When the peso lost half its value by March 1995 and the Thai, Philippine, Malaysian, and South Korean currencies lost between one-third and one-half of their value by the beginning of 1998, firms' balance sheets took a big negative hit, causing a dramatic increase in adverse selection and moral hazard problems. This negative shock was especially severe for Indonesia and Argentina, which saw the value of their currencies fall by more than 70%, resulting in insolvency for firms with substantial amounts of debt denominated in foreign currencies.

The collapse of currencies also led to a rise in actual and expected inflation in these countries. Market interest rates rose sky-high (to around 100% in Mexico and Argentina). The resulting increase in interest payments caused reductions in household and firm cash flows. A feature of debt markets in emerging market countries, like those in Mexico, East Asia, and Argentina, is that debt contracts have very short durations, typically less than one month. Thus the rise in short-term interest rates in these countries made the effect on cash flow and hence on balance sheets substantial. As our asymmetric information analysis suggests, this deterioration in households' and firms' balance sheets increased financial frictions, making domestic and foreign lenders even less willing to lend.

Consistent with the theory of financial crises outlined in this chapter, the sharp decline in lending helped lead to a collapse of economic activity, with real GDP growth falling sharply. Further deterioration in the economy occurred because the collapse in economic activity and the deterioration in the cash flow and balance sheets of both firms and households worsened banking crises. Many firms and households were no longer able to pay off their debts, resulting in substantial losses for the banks. Even more problematic for the banks were their many short-term liabilities denominated in foreign currencies. The sharp increase in the value of these liabilities after the devaluation led to a further deterioration in the banks' balance sheets. Under these circumstances, the banking system would have collapsed in the absence of a government safety net—as it did in the United States during the Great Depression. With the assistance of the International Monetary Fund, these countries were in some cases able to protect depositors and avoid a bank panic. However, given the loss of bank capital and the need for the government to intervene to prop up the banks, the banks' ability to lend was nevertheless sharply curtailed. As we have seen, a banking crisis of this type hinders the ability of the banks to lend and also makes adverse selection and moral hazard problems worse in financial markets, because banks are less capable of playing their traditional financial intermediation role. The banking crisis, along with other factors that increased adverse selection and moral hazard problems in the credit markets of Mexico, East Asia, and Argentina, explains the collapse of lending and hence economic activity in the aftermath of the crisis.

Following their crises, Mexico began to recover in 1996, whereas the crisis countries in East Asia tentatively began their recovery in 1999, with a stronger recovery later. Argentina was still in a severe depression in 2003, but subsequently the economy bounced back. In all these countries, the economic hardship caused by financial crises was tremendous. Unemployment rose sharply, poverty increased substantially, and even the social fabric of the society was stretched thin. For example, after the financial crises, Mexico City and Buenos Aires became crime-ridden, and Indonesia experienced waves of ethnic violence.

MyEconLab   MyEconLab is an online homework and tutorial system that puts you in control of your own learning with study and practice tools directly correlated to this chapter's content. Visit MyEconLab to explore the following resources:

- The Questions are all available in the Study Plan on MyEconLab for further practice. You will also find the answers to all of the Questions in the Student Resources section of your MyEconLab.

MyEconLab also features Additional Readings, Videos, Glossary Flashcards, Audio Chapter Summaries, Economics News Feeds, Animations, and many additional tools to help you master key concepts from the text.

((• SUMMARY

EconLab
Summary

1. A financial crisis occurs when a particularly large disruption to information flows occurs in financial markets, with the result that financial frictions increase sharply, thereby rendering financial markets incapable of channeling funds to households and firms with productive investment opportunities, and causing a sharp contraction in economic activity.

2. Financial crises can start in advanced countries like Canada and the United States in several possible ways: mismanagement of financial liberalization/innovation, asset-price booms and busts, or a general increase in uncertainty when major financial institutions fail. The result is a substantial increase in adverse selection and moral hazard problems that lead to a contraction of lending and a decline in economic activity. The worsening business conditions and deterioration in bank balance sheets then triggers the second stage of the crisis, the simultaneous failure of many banking institutions: a banking crisis. The resulting decrease in the number of banks causes a loss of their information capital, leading to a further decline of lending and a spiralling down of the economy. In some instances, the resulting economic downturn leads to a sharp slide

in prices, which increases the real liabilities of firms and households and therefore lowers their net worth, leading to a debt deflation. The further decline in borrowers' net worth worsens adverse selection and moral hazard problems, so that lending, investment spending, and aggregate economic activity remain depressed for a long time.

3. The most significant financial crisis in history, which led to the Great Depression, involved several stages: a stock market crash, bank panics, worsening of asymmetric information problems, and finally a debt deflation.

4. The global financial crisis of 2007–2009 was triggered by mismanagement of financial innovations in the United States involving subprime residential mortgages and the bursting of a housing price bubble. The crisis spread globally, with substantial deterioration in banks' and other financial institutions' balance sheets, a run on the shadow banking system, and the failure of many high-profile firms.

5. The 2007–2009 financial crisis did not lead to a depression because of aggressive central bank actions around the world and worldwide government intervention through bailouts of financial institutions.

6. Financial crises in emerging market countries develop along two basic paths: one involving the mismanagement of financial liberalization/globalization, which weakens bank balance sheets, and the other involving severe fiscal imbalances. Both lead to a speculative attack on the currency, and eventually to a currency crisis in which the value of domestic currency sharply declines. This decline causes a sharp rise in the debt burden of domestic firms, which leads to a decrease in firms' net worth, as well as increases in inflation and interest rates. Adverse selection and moral hazard problems then worsen, leading to a collapse of lending and economic activity. The worsening economic conditions and increases in interest rates result in substantial losses for banks, leading to a banking crisis, which further depresses lending and aggregate economic activity.

7. The financial crises in Mexico in 1994–1995, East Asia in 1997–1998, and Argentina in 2001–2002 led to great economic hardship and weakened the social fabric of these countries.

KEY TERMS

asset-price bubble, p. 184

bank panic, p. 184

cash flow, p. 202

credit boom, p. 182

credit default swaps, p. 190

credit spread, p. 187

currency mismatch, p. 203

debt deflation, p. 185

deleveraging, p. 182

emerging market economies, p. 199

financial crisis, p 182

financial engineering, p. 188

financial frictions, p. 182

financial globalization, p. 199

financial innovation, p. 182

financial liberalization, p. 182

fire sales, p. 184

fundamental economic values, p. 184

haircuts, p. 192

mortgage-backed securities, p. 188

originate-to-distribute model, p. 189

repurchase agreements (repos), p. 192

securitization, p. 188

security, p. 188

shadow banking system, p. 191

sovereign debt, p. 194

sovereign debt crisis, p. 194

speculative attack, p. 202

structured credit products, p. 188

subprime mortgages, p. 188

Troubled Asset Relief Program (TARP), p. 195

QUESTIONS

1. How does the concept of asymmetric information help to define a financial crisis?

2. How can a bursting of an asset-price bubble in the stock market help trigger a financial crisis?

3. How does an unanticipated decline in the price level cause a drop in lending?

4. How can a decline in real estate prices cause deleveraging and a decline in lending?

5. How do a deterioration in balance sheets of financial institutions and the simultaneous failures of these institutions cause a decline in economic activity?

6. How does a general increase in uncertainty as a result of a failure of a major financial institution lead to an increase in adverse selection and moral hazard problems?

7. Why do credit spreads rise significantly during a financial crisis?

8. How can government fiscal imbalances lead to a financial crisis?

9. How can financial liberalizations lead to financial crises?

10. What role do weak financial regulation and supervision play in causing financial crises?

11. Describe two similarities and two differences between the United States' experiences during the Great Depression and the financial crisis of 2007–2009.

12. What do you think prevented the financial crisis of 2007–2009 from becoming a depression?

13. What technological innovations led to the development of the subprime mortgage market?

14. Why is the originate-to-distribute business model subject to the principal–agent problem?

15. "Financial engineering always leads to a more efficient financial system." Is this statement true, false, or uncertain?

16. How did a decline in housing prices help trigger the subprime financial crisis in the United States starting in 2007?

17. What is the shadow banking system, and why is it an important part of the 2007–2009 financial crisis?

18. Why would haircuts on collateral increase sharply during a financial crisis? How would this lead to fire sales on assets?

19. What similarities exist between experiences in the United States and in Ireland during the 2007–2009 financial crisis?

20. When can a decline in the value of a country's currency exacerbate adverse selection and moral hazard problems? Why?

21. Why do debt deflations occur in advanced countries, but not in emerging market countries?

22. How can opening up to capital flows from abroad lead to a financial crisis?

23. Why does the "twin crises" phenomenon of currency and banking crises occur in emerging market countries?

24. How can a currency crisis lead to higher interest rates?

25. How can a deterioration in bank balance sheets lead to a currency crisis?

26. What was the Canadian experience during the 2007–2009 financial crisis?

WEB EXERCISES

1. This chapter discusses how an understanding of adverse selection and moral hazard can help us better understand financial crises. The greatest financial crisis faced by the United States was the Great Depression of 1929–1933. Go to **www.amatecon.com/greatdepression.html**. This site contains a brief discussion of the factors that led to the Great Depression. Write a one-page summary explaining how adverse selection and moral hazard contributed to the Great Depression.

2. Go to the International Monetary Fund's Financial Crisis page at **www.imf.org/external/np/exr/key/finstab. htm**. Report on the most recent three countries that the IMF has given emergency loans in response to a financial crisis. According to the IMF, what caused the crisis in each country?

3. One of the countries hardest hit by the global financial crisis of 2008 was Iceland. Go to **http://assets.opencrs. com/rpts/RS22988_20081120.pdf** and summarize the causes and events that led to the crisis in Iceland.

CHAPTER 10

Economic Analysis of Financial Regulation

LEARNING OBJECTIVES

After studying this chapter you should be able to

1. explain bank regulation in the context of asymmetric information problems

2. characterize how the CDIC handles failed banks and detail recent CDIC developments

3. outline the banking crises that have occurred in Canada and other countries throughout the world

PREVIEW

As we have seen in the previous chapters, the financial system is among the most heavily regulated sectors of the economy, and banks are among the most heavily regulated of financial institutions. In this chapter we develop an economic analysis of why regulation of the financial system takes the form it does.

Unfortunately, the regulatory process may not always work very well, as evidenced by the recent global financial crisis. Here we also use our economic analysis of financial regulation to explain the worldwide crises in banking and how the regulatory system can be reformed to prevent future disasters.

Asymmetric Information and Financial Regulation

In earlier chapters we have seen how asymmetric information, the fact that different parties in a financial contract do not have the same information, leads to adverse selection and moral hazard problems that have an important impact on our financial system. The concepts of asymmetric information, adverse selection, and moral hazard are especially useful in understanding why government has chosen the form of financial regulation we see in Canada and in other countries. There are 10 basic categories of financial regulation: the government safety net, restrictions on asset holdings, capital requirements, prompt corrective action, chartering and examination, assessment of risk management, disclosure requirements, consumer protection, restrictions on competition, and macroprudential supervision.

Government Safety Net

As we saw in Chapter 8, financial intermediaries, like banks, are particularly well suited to solving adverse selection and moral hazard problems because they make private loans that help avoid the free-rider problem. However, this solution to the free-rider problem creates another asymmetric information problem, because depositors lack information about the quality of these private loans. This asymmetric information problem leads to several reasons why the financial system might not function well.

BANK PANICS AND THE NEED FOR DEPOSIT INSURANCE   Before the CDIC started operations in 1967, a **bank failure** (in which a bank is unable to meet its obligations to pay its depositors and other creditors and so must go out of business) meant that depositors would have to wait to get their deposit funds until the bank was liquidated (until its assets had been turned into cash); at that time, they would be paid only a fraction of the value of their deposits. Unable to learn if bank managers were taking on too much risk or were outright crooks, depositors would be reluctant to put money in the bank, thus making financial institutions less viable. Depositors' lack of information about the quality of bank assets can lead to bank panics, which, as we saw in Chapter 9, can have serious harmful consequences for the economy. To see this, consider the following situation. There is no deposit insurance, and an adverse shock hits the economy. As a result of the shock, 5% of the banks have such large losses on loans that they become insolvent (have a negative net worth and so are bankrupt). Because of asymmetric information, depositors are unable to tell whether their bank is a good bank or one of the 5% that are insolvent. Depositors at bad *and* good banks recognize that they may not get back 100 cents on the dollar for their deposits and will want to withdraw them. Indeed, because banks operate on a "sequential service constraint" (a first-come, first-served basis), depositors have a very strong incentive to show up at the bank first because if they are last in line, the bank may have run out of funds and they will get nothing. Uncertainty about the health of the banking system in general can lead to runs on banks both good and bad, and the failure of one bank can hasten the failure of others (referred to as the *contagion effect*). If nothing is done to restore the public's confidence, a bank panic can ensue.

A government safety net for depositors can short-circuit runs on banks and bank panics, and by providing protection for the depositor, it can overcome reluctance to put funds in the banking system. One form of the safety net is deposit insurance, a guarantee such as that provided by the Canada Deposit Insurance Corporation (CDIC) in which depositors are paid off in full on the first $100 000 they have deposited in the bank no matter what happens to the bank. With fully insured deposits, depositors don't need to run to the bank to make withdrawals—even if they are worried about the bank's health—because their deposits will be worth 100 cents on the dollar no matter what.

The CDIC uses two primary methods to handle a failed bank. In the first, called the *payoff method,* the CDIC allows the bank to fail and pays off deposits up to the $100 000 insurance limit (with funds acquired from the insurance premiums paid by the banks that have bought CDIC insurance). After the bank has been liquidated, the CDIC lines up with other creditors of the bank and is paid its share of the proceeds from the liquidated assets. Typically, when the payoff method is used, account holders with deposits in excess of the $100 000 limit get back more than 90 cents on the dollar, although the process can take several years to complete.

In the second method, called the *purchase and assumption method,* the CDIC reorganizes the bank, typically by finding a willing merger partner who assumes (takes over) all of the failed bank's liabilities so that no depositor or other creditor loses a penny. The CDIC often sweetens the pot for the merger partner by providing it with subsidized loans or by buying some of the failed bank's weaker loans. The net effect of the purchase and assumption method is that the CDIC has guaranteed *all* of a bank's deposits, not just those under the $100 000 limit.

In recent years, government deposit insurance has been growing in popularity and has spread to many countries throughout the world. Whether this trend is desirable is discussed in the Global box The Spread of Government Deposit Insurance Throughout the World: Is It a Good Thing?

OTHER FORMS OF THE GOVERNMENT SAFETY NET   Deposit insurance is not the only form of government safety net. In other countries, governments have often stood ready to provide support to domestic banks facing runs even in the absence of explicit deposit insurance. Furthermore, banks are not the only financial intermediaries that can pose a systemic threat to the financial system, as our discussion of financial crises in Chapter 9 has illustrated. When financial institutions are very large or highly interconnected with other financial institutions or markets, their failure has the potential to bring down the entire financial system. Indeed, as we saw in Chapter 9, this is exactly what happened in the United States when Bear Stearns and Lehman Brothers, two investment banks, and AIG, an insurance company, got into trouble during the global financial crisis in 2008.

One way governments provide support is through lending from the central bank to troubled institutions, as the Bank of Canada did during the recent financial crisis (more on this in Chapter 17). This form of support is often referred to as the "lender of last resort" role of the central bank. In other cases, funds are provided directly to troubled institutions as was done by the government of Canada through the Canada Mortgage and Housing Corporation (CMHC), by the U.S. Treasury, and by other governments in 2008 during the most virulent phase of the global financial

GLOBAL

The Spread of Government Deposit Insurance Throughout the World: Is It a Good Thing?

Government deposit insurance has taken off throughout the world because of growing concern about the health of banking systems, particularly after the increasing number of banking crises in recent years (documented at the end of the chapter). Has this spread of deposit insurance been a good thing? Has it helped improve the performance of the financial system and prevent banking crises?

The answer seems to be no under many circumstances. Research at the World Bank has found that on average, the adoption of explicit government deposit insurance is associated with less banking sector stability and a higher incidence of banking crises.* Furthermore, on average it seems to retard financial development. However, the negative effects of deposit insurance appear only in countries with weak institutional environments: an absence of rule of law, ineffective regulation and supervision of the financial sector, and high corruption. This is exactly what might be expected because, as we will see later in this chapter, a strong institutional environment is needed to limit the moral hazard incentives for banks to engage in the excessively risky behaviour encouraged by deposit insurance. The problem is that developing a strong institutional environment may be very difficult to achieve in many emerging-market countries. This leaves us with the following conclusion: adoption of deposit insurance may be exactly the wrong medicine for promoting stability and efficiency of banking systems in emerging-market countries.

*See World Bank, *Finance for Growth: Policy Choices in a Volatile World* (Oxford: World Bank and Oxford University Press, 2001).

crisis. Governments also take over (nationalize) troubled institutions and guarantee that all creditors will be repaid their loans in full.

MORAL HAZARD AND THE GOVERNMENT SAFETY NET   Although a government safety net can help protect depositors and other creditors and prevent or ameliorate financial crises, it is a mixed blessing. The most serious drawback of the government safety net stems from moral hazard, the incentives of one party to a transaction to engage in activities detrimental to the other party. Moral hazard is an important concern in insurance arrangements in general because the existence of insurance provides increased incentives for taking risks that might result in an insurance payoff. For example, some drivers who have automobile collision insurance with a low deductible might be more likely to drive recklessly, because if they get into an accident, the insurance company pays most of the costs for damage and repairs.

Moral hazard is a prominent concern in government arrangements to provide a safety net. With a safety net, depositors or creditors know that they will not suffer losses if a financial institution fails, so they do not impose the discipline of the marketplace on financial institutions by withdrawing funds when they suspect that the financial institution is taking on too much risk. Consequently, financial institutions with a government safety net have an incentive to take on greater risks than they otherwise would, with taxpayers paying the bill if the bank subsequently goes belly up. Financial institutions have been given the following bet: "Heads I win, tails the taxpayer loses."

ADVERSE SELECTION AND THE GOVERNMENT SAFETY NET   A further problem with a government safety net like deposit insurance arises because of adverse selection, the fact that the people who are most likely to produce the adverse outcome insured against (bank failure) are those who most want to take advantage of the insurance. For example, bad drivers are more likely than good drivers to take out automobile collision insurance with a low deductible. Because depositors and creditors protected by a government safety net have little reason to impose discipline on financial institutions, risk-loving entrepreneurs might find the financial industry a particularly attractive one to enter—they know that they will be able to engage in highly risky activities. Even worse, because protected depositors and creditors have so little reason to monitor the financial institution's activities, without government intervention outright crooks might also find finance an attractive industry for their activities because it is easy for them to get away with fraud and embezzlement.

"TOO BIG TO FAIL"   The moral hazard created by a government safety net and the desire to prevent financial failures has presented financial regulators with a particular quandary. Because the failure of a very large financial institution makes it more likely that a major financial disruption will occur, financial regulators are naturally reluctant to allow a big institution to fail and cause losses to its depositors and creditors.

One problem with the too-big-to-fail policy is that it increases the moral hazard incentives for big banks. If the CDIC were willing to close a bank using the payoff method, paying depositors only up to the $100 000 limit, large depositors with more than $100 000 would suffer losses if the bank failed. Thus they would have an incentive to monitor the bank by examining the bank's activities closely and pulling their money out if the bank were taking on too much risk. To prevent such a loss of deposits, the bank would be more likely to engage in less risky activities. However, once large depositors know that a bank is too big to fail, they have no incentive to monitor the bank and pull out their deposits when it takes on too much risk: no matter what the bank does, large depositors will not suffer any losses. The result of the too-big-to-fail policy is that big banks might take on even greater risks, thereby making bank failures more likely.

Similarly, the too-big-to-fail policy increases the moral hazard incentives for non-bank financial institutions that are extended a government safety net. Knowing that the financial institution will get bailed out, creditors have little incentive to monitor the institution and pull their money out when the institution is taking on excessive risk. As a result, large or interconnected financial institutions will be more likely to engage in high-risk activities, making it more likely that a financial crisis will occur.

FINANCIAL CONSOLIDATION AND THE GOVERNMENT SAFETY NET   Financial consolidation has been proceeding at a rapid pace, leading to both larger and more complex financial organizations. Financial consolidation poses two challenges to financial regulation because of the existence of the government safety net. First, the increased size of financial institutions as a result of financial consolidation increases the too-big-to-fail problem, because there will now be more large institutions whose failure exposes the financial system to systemic (system-wide) risk. Thus more financial institutions are likely to be treated as too big to fail, and the increased moral hazard incentives for these large institutions to take on greater risk can then increase the fragility of the financial system. Second, financial consolidation of banks with other financial services firms means that the government safety net may be extended to new activities such as securities underwriting, insurance, or real estate activities, as occurred in the United States during the global financial crisis. This increases incentives for greater risk taking in these activities that can also weaken the fabric of the financial system. Limiting the moral hazard incentives for the larger, more complex financial organizations that have arisen as a result of recent changes in legislation will be one of the key issues facing financial regulators in the aftermath of the global financial crisis.

Restrictions on Asset Holdings

As we have seen, the moral hazard associated with a government safety net encourages too much risk taking on the part of financial institutions. Financial regulations that restrict asset holdings are directed at minimizing this moral hazard, which can cost the taxpayers dearly.

Even in the absence of a government safety net, financial institutions still have the incentive to take on too much risk. Risky assets may provide a financial institution with higher earnings when they pay off; but if they do not pay off and the institution fails, depositors are left holding the bag. If depositors and creditors were able to monitor the institution easily by acquiring information on its risk-taking activities, they would immediately withdraw their funds if the institution were taking on too much risk. To prevent such a loss of funds, the institution would be more likely to reduce its risk-taking activities. Unfortunately, acquiring information on an institution's activities to learn how much risk the institution is taking can be a difficult task. Hence, most depositors and creditors are incapable of imposing discipline that might prevent financial institutions from engaging in risky activities. A strong rationale for government regulation to reduce risk taking on the part of financial institutions therefore existed even before the establishment of deposit insurance.

Because banks are most prone to panics, they are subjected to strict regulations to restrict their holding of risky assets such as common stocks. Bank regulations also promote diversification, which reduces risk by limiting the amount of loans given in particular categories or to individual borrowers. With the extension of the government safety net during the global financial crisis, it is likely that nonbank financial institutions (to be discussed in detail in Chapter 12) may face greater restrictions on their holdings of risky assets. There is a danger, however, that these restrictions may become so onerous that the efficiency of the financial system will be impaired.

Capital Requirements

Government-imposed capital requirements are another way of minimizing moral hazard at financial institutions. When a financial institution is forced to hold a large amount of equity capital, the institution has more to lose if it fails and is thus more likely to pursue lower-risk activities. In addition, as will be illustrated in Chapter 13, capital functions as a cushion when bad shocks occur, making it less likely that a financial institution will fail, thereby directly adding to the safety and soundness of financial institutions.

Capital requirements for banks take two forms. The first type is based on the **leverage ratio**, the amount of capital divided by the bank's total assets. To be classified as well capitalized, a bank's leverage ratio must exceed 5%; a lower leverage ratio, especially one below 3%, triggers increased regulatory restrictions on the bank.

In the past decade, regulators in Canada and the rest of the world have become increasingly worried about banks' holdings of risky assets and about the increase in banks' **off-balance-sheet activities**, activities that involve trading financial instruments and generating income from fees, which do not appear on bank balance sheets but nevertheless expose banks to risk. An agreement among banking officials from industrialized nations has set up the **Basel Committee on Bank Supervision** (because it meets under the auspices of the Bank for International Settlements in Basel, Switzerland), which has implemented the **Basel Accord** that deals with a second type of capital requirement: risk-based capital requirements. The Basel Accord, which required that banks hold as capital at least 8% of their risk-weighted assets, has been adopted by more than 100 countries, including Canada and the United States. Assets and off-balance-sheet activities were allocated into four categories, each with a different weight to reflect the degree of credit risk. The first category carried a zero weight and included items that have little default risk, such as reserves and government securities issued by the Organisation for Economic Co-operation and Development (OECD)—industrialized countries. The second category has a 20% weight and includes claims on banks in OECD countries. The third category has a weight of 50% and includes municipal bonds and residential mortgages. The fourth category has the maximum weight of 100% and includes debts to consumers and corporations. Off-balance-sheet activities are treated in a similar manner by assigning a credit-equivalent percentage that converts them to on-balance-sheet items to which the appropriate risk weight applies, and there are minimum capital requirements for risks in banks' trading accounts.

Over time, limitations of the Basel Accord have become apparent, because the regulatory measure of bank risk as stipulated by the risk weights can differ substantially from the actual risk the bank faces. This has resulted in what is known as **regulatory arbitrage**, a practice in which banks keep on their books assets that have the same risk-based capital requirements but are relatively risky, such as a loan to a company with a very low credit rating, while taking off their books low-risk assets such as a loan to a company with a very high credit rating. The Basel Accord could thus lead to increased risk taking, the opposite of its intent. To address these limitations, the Basel Committee on Bank Supervision came up with a new capital accord, often referred to as Basel 2, but in the aftermath of the global financial crisis it developed an even newer accord, which the media has dubbed "Basel 3." These accords are described in the Global box Where Is the Basel Accord Heading After the Global Financial Crisis?

Prompt Corrective Action

If the amount of a financial institution's capital falls to low levels, there are two serious problems. First, the bank is more likely to fail because it has a smaller capital cushion if it suffers loan losses or other asset writedowns. Second, with less capital, a financial institution has less "skin in the game" and is therefore more likely to take on excessive risks. In other words, the moral hazard problem becomes more severe, making it more likely that the institution will fail and the taxpayer will be left holding the bag. To prevent this, the CDIC adopted prompt corrective action provisions that require the CDIC to intervene earlier and more vigorously when a bank gets into trouble (see the Application Evaluating CDIC and Other Proposed Reforms of the Banking Regulatory System on page 229).

Financial Supervision: Chartering and Examination

Overseeing who operates financial institutions and how they are operated, referred to as **financial supervision** or **prudential supervision**, is an important method for reducing adverse selection and moral hazard in the financial industry. Because financial institutions can be used by crooks or overambitious entrepreneurs to engage in highly speculative activities, such undesirable people would be eager to run a financial institution. Chartering financial institutions is one method for preventing this adverse selection problem; through chartering, proposals for new institutions are screened to prevent undesirable people from controlling them.

Regular on-site examinations, which allow regulators to monitor whether an institution is complying with capital requirements and restrictions on asset holdings, also function to limit moral hazard. Bank examiners give banks a *CAMELS rating* (the acronym is based on the six areas assessed: capital adequacy, asset quality, management, earnings, liquidity, and sensitivity to market risk). With this information about a bank's activities, regulators can enforce regulations by taking such formal actions as *cease and desist orders* to alter the bank's behaviour or even close a bank if its CAMELS rating is sufficiently low. Actions taken to reduce moral hazard by restricting banks from taking on too much risk help reduce the adverse selection problem further, because with less opportunity for risk taking, risk-loving entrepreneurs will be less likely to be attracted to the banking industry. Note that the methods regulators use to cope with adverse selection and moral hazard have their counterparts in private financial markets (see Chapters 8 and 9). Chartering is similar to the screening of potential borrowers, regulations restricting risky asset holdings are similar to restrictive covenants that prevent borrowing firms from engaging in risky investment activities, capital requirements act like restrictive covenants that require minimum amounts of net worth for borrowing firms, and regular examinations are similar to the monitoring of borrowers by lending institutions.

A chartered bank obtains a charter either by an Act of Parliament or through application to the minister of finance, who has the authority to issue a charter. To obtain a charter, the people planning to organize the bank must submit an application that shows how they plan to operate the bank. In evaluating the application, the regulatory authority looks at whether the bank is likely to be sound by examining the quality of the bank's intended management, the likely earnings of the bank, and the amount of the bank's initial capital. Moreover, the chartering agency typically explores the issue of whether the community needs a new bank. Often a new bank charter would not be granted if existing banks in a community would be hurt by its presence. Today this anticompetitive stance (justified by the desire to prevent bank failures of existing banks) is no longer as strong.

Once a bank has been chartered, it is required to file periodic (usually quarterly) *call reports* that reveal the bank's assets and liabilities, income and dividends, ownership, foreign exchange operations, and other details. The bank is also subject to examination by the bank regulatory agencies to ascertain its financial condition at least once a year. To avoid duplication of effort, the three federal agencies work together and usually accept each other's examinations. This means that, typically, chartered banks are examined by the OSFI, the CDIC, and the Bank of Canada.

GLOBAL

Where Is the Basel Accord Heading After the Global Financial Crisis?

Starting in June 1999, the Basel Committee on Banking Supervision released several proposals to reform the original 1988 Basel Accord. These efforts have culminated in what bank supervisors refer to as Basel 2, which is based on three pillars:

1. Pillar 1 links capital requirements for large, internationally active banks more closely to three types of actual risk: market risk, credit risk, and operational risk. It does so by specifying many more categories of assets with different risk weights in its standardized approach. Alternatively, it allows sophisticated banks to pursue an internal ratings-based approach that permits banks to use their own models of credit risk.

2. Pillar 2 focuses on strengthening the supervisory process, particularly in assessing the quality of risk management in financial institutions and evaluating whether these institutions have adequate procedures to determine how much capital they need.

3. Pillar 3 focuses on improving market discipline through increased disclosure of details about banks' credit exposures, amounts of reserves and capital, officials who control the banks, and the effectiveness of their internal rating systems.

Although Basel 2 made great strides toward limiting excessive risk taking by internationally active banking institutions, it greatly increases the complexity of the accord. The document describing the original Basel Accord was 26 pages, while the final draft of Basel 2 exceeded 500 pages. The original timetable called for the completion of the final round of consultation by the end of 2001, with the new rules taking effect by 2004.

However, criticism from banks, trade associations, and national regulators led to several postponements. The final draft was not published until June 2004; Basel 2 started to be implemented at the end of 2007 by the "Big Six" internationally active banks in Canada, and at the beginning of 2008 by European banks. American banks submitted plans for compliance with Basel 2 in 2008, but full implementation did not occur until 2009. Only the dozen or so largest U.S. banks are subject to

Basel 2; all others will be allowed to use a simplified version of the standards it imposes.

The global financial crisis, however, revealed many limitations of the new accord. First, Basel 2 did not require banks to have sufficient capital to weather the financial disruption during this period. Second, risk weights in the standardized approach are heavily reliant on credit ratings, which proved to be so unreliable in the run-up to the financial crisis. Third, Basel 2 is very procyclical. That is, it demands that banks hold less capital when times are good, but more when times are bad, thereby exacerbating credit cycles. Because the probability of default and expected losses for different classes of assets rises during bad times, Basel 2 may require more capital at exactly the time when capital is most short. This has been a particularly serious concern in the aftermath of the global financial crisis. As a result of this crisis, banks' capital balances eroded, leading to a cutback on lending that was a big drag on the economy. Basel 2 made this cutback in lending even worse, doing even more harm to the economy. Fourth, Basel 2 did not focus sufficiently on the dangers of a possible drying up of liquidity, which brought financial institutions down during the financial crisis.

As a result of these limitations, in 2010 the Basel Committee developed a new accord, Basel 3. It beefs up capital standards by not only raising them substantially, but improving the quality of the capital; makes them less procyclical by raising capital requirements in good times and lowering them in bad; makes new rules on the use of credit ratings; and requires financial institutions to have more stable funding so they are better able to withstand liquidity shocks. Measures to achieve these objectives are highly controversial because there are concerns that tightening up capital standards might cause banks to restrict their lending, which would make it harder for economies throughout the world to recover from the recent deep recession. Basel 3 is being implemented slowly over time, with the target for full implementation extending out to the end of 2019. Whether Basel 3 will be fully implemented by that date and be successful in restraining risk taking is highly uncertain.

Bank examinations are conducted by bank examiners, who study a bank's books to see whether it is complying with the rules and regulations that apply to its holdings of assets. If a bank is holding securities or loans that are too risky, the bank examiner can force the bank to get rid of them. If a bank examiner decides that a loan is unlikely to be repaid, the examiner can force the bank to declare the loan worthless (to write off the loan, which reduces the bank's capital). If, after examining the bank, the examiner feels that it does not have sufficient capital or has engaged in dishonest practices, the bank can be declared a "problem bank" and will be subject to more frequent examinations.

Assessment of Risk Management

Traditionally, on-site examinations have focused primarily on assessment of the quality of a financial institution's balance sheet at a point in time and whether it complies with capital requirements and restrictions on asset holdings. Although the traditional focus is important for reducing excessive risk taking by financial institutions, it is no longer felt to be adequate in today's world, in which financial innovation has produced new markets and instruments that make it easy for financial institutions and their employees to make huge bets easily and quickly. In this new financial environment, a financial institution that is healthy at a particular point in time can be driven into insolvency extremely rapidly from trading losses, as forcefully demonstrated by the failure of Barings in 1995 (discussed in Chapter 13). Thus an examination that focuses only on a financial institution's position at a point in time may not be effective in indicating whether it will, in fact, be taking on excessive risk in the near future.

This change in the financial environment for financial institutions has resulted in a major shift in thinking about the prudential supervisory process throughout the world. Bank examiners, for example, are now placing far greater emphasis on evaluating the soundness of a bank's management processes with regard to controlling risk. This shift in thinking is now reflected in a new focus on risk management in the guidelines to examiners on trading and derivatives activities. Now bank examiners focus on four elements of sound risk management: (1) the quality of oversight provided by the board of directors and senior management, (2) the adequacy of policies and limits for all activities that present significant risks, (3) the quality of the risk measurement and monitoring systems, and (4) the adequacy of internal controls to prevent fraud or unauthorized activities on the part of employees.

This shift toward focusing on management processes is also reflected in recent guidelines adopted by the Canadian bank regulatory authorities to deal with interest-rate risk. These guidelines require the bank's board of directors to establish interest-rate risk limits, appoint officials of the bank to manage this risk, and monitor the bank's risk exposure. The guidelines also require that senior management of a bank develop formal risk-management policies and procedures to ensure that the board of directors' risk limits are not violated and to implement internal controls to monitor interest-rate risk and compliance with the board's directives. Particularly important is the implementation of **stress tests**, which calculate losses under dire scenarios and the need for more capital, or **value-at-risk (VaR)** calculations, which measure the size of the loss on a trading portfolio that might happen 1% of the time. In addition to these guidelines, bank examiners will continue to consider interest-rate risk in deciding a bank's capital requirements.

Disclosure Requirements

The free-rider problem described in Chapter 8 indicates that individual depositors and creditors will not have enough incentive to produce private information about the quality of a financial institution's assets. To ensure that there is better information in the marketplace, regulators can require that financial institutions adhere to certain standard accounting principles and disclose a wide range of information that helps the market assess the quality of an institution's portfolio and the amount of its exposure to risk. More public information about the risks incurred by financial institutions and the quality of their portfolios can better enable shareholders, creditors, and depositors to evaluate and monitor financial institutions and so act as a deterrent to excessive risk taking.

Disclosure requirements are a key element of financial regulation. Basel 2 puts a particular emphasis on disclosure requirements with one of its three pillars focusing on increasing market discipline by mandating increased disclosure of credit exposure, amount of reserves, and capital. Provincial securities commissions, the most significant being the Ontario Securities Commission (OSC), also impose disclosure requirements on all corporations, including financial institutions, that issue publicly traded securities. In addition, Basel 2 has required financial institutions to provide additional disclosure regarding their off-balance-sheet positions and more information about how they value their portfolios.

Regulation to increase disclosure is needed to limit incentives to take on excessive risk, and it also improves the quality of information in the marketplace so that investors can make informed decisions, thereby improving the ability of financial markets to allocate capital to its most productive uses. The efficiency of markets is assisted by the OSC's disclosure requirements mentioned above, as well as its regulation of brokerage firms, mutual funds, exchanges, and credit-rating agencies to ensure that they produce reliable information and protect investors. Bill 198, introduced by the Ontario government in October 2002 in response to the Sarbanes-Oxley Act in the United States, took disclosure of information even further by increasing the incentives to produce accurate audits of corporate income statements and balance sheets, and put in place regulations to limit conflicts of interest in the financial services industry.

Particularly controversial in the wake of the global financial crisis is the move to **mark-to-market accounting** (also called **fair-value accounting**), in which assets are valued on the balance sheet at what they could sell for in the market (see the FYI box Mark-to-Market Accounting and the Global Financial Crisis).

Consumer Protection

The existence of asymmetric information also suggests that consumers may not have enough information to protect themselves fully. Consumer protection regulation has taken several forms. First is "truth in lending," which requires all lenders, not just banks, to provide information to consumers about the cost of borrowing including a standardized interest rate (called the *annual percentage rate,* or *APR*) and the total finance charges on the loan. Legislation also requires creditors, especially credit card issuers, to provide information on the method of assessing finance charges and requires that billing complaints be handled quickly.

The subprime mortgage crisis in the United States and Canada's short experiment with subprime lending have illustrated the need for greater consumer protection because so many borrowers ended up taking out loans that they could not understand and which were well beyond their means to repay. The result was millions of foreclosures, with many households losing their homes. Because weak consumer protection regulation played a prominent role in this crisis, there have been increasing demands to beef up this regulation, not only in the United States but in other countries as well, as is discussed in the FYI box The Subprime Mortgage Crisis and Consumer Protection Regulation.

Restrictions on Competition

Increased competition can also increase moral hazard incentives for financial institutions to take on more risk. Declining profitability as a result of increased competition could tip the incentives of financial institutions toward assuming greater risk in an effort to maintain former profit levels. Thus governments in many countries have instituted regulations to protect financial institutions from competition. These regulations have taken different forms in the past, one being preventing nonbank institutions from competing with banks by engaging in banking business.

Although restricting competition propped up the health of banks, restrictions on competition also had serious disadvantages: they led to higher charges to consumers and decreased the efficiency of financial institutions, which did not have to compete as vigorously. Thus, although the existence of asymmetric information provided a rationale for anticompetitive regulations, it did not mean that they would be beneficial. Indeed, in recent years, the impulse of governments in industrialized countries to restrict competition has been waning.

Macroprudential Versus Microprudential Supervision

Before the global financial crisis, the regulatory authorities engaged in **microprudential supervision**, which is focused on the safety and soundness of *individual* financial institutions. Microprudential supervision looks at each individual institution separately and assesses the riskiness of its activities and whether it complies with disclosure requirements. Most importantly, it checks whether that institution satisfies capital *ratios* and, if not, engages in prompt corrective action to force the institution to either raise its capital ratios or the supervisor closes it down, along the lines we have discussed above.

The discussion of the global financial crisis in Chapter 9 shows that a focus on microprudential supervision is not enough to prevent financial crises. The run on the shadow banking system illustrates how the problems of one financial institution can harm other otherwise healthy financial institutions. When the troubled financial institution is forced to engage in fire sales and sell off assets to meet target capital ratios or haircut requirements, this leads to a decline in asset values. This decline in asset values then causes other institutions to engage in fire sales, leading to a rapid deleveraging process and a systemic crisis. In situations like this, even institutions that would normally be healthy and have high capital ratios may find themselves in trouble.

The global financial crisis has therefore made it clear that there is a need for **macroprudential supervision**, which focuses on the safety and soundness of the financial system *in the aggregate*. Rather than focus on the safety and soundness of individual institutions, macroprudential supervision seeks to mitigate system-wide fire sales and deleveraging by assessing the overall capacity of the financial system to avoid them. In addition, because many institutions that were well capitalized faced liquidity shortages and found that their access to short-term funding was cut off, macroprudential supervision focuses not only on capital adequacy as a whole but on on whether the financial system has sufficient liquidity.

Macroprudential policies can take several forms. In the run up to the global financial crisis, there was a so-called **leverage cycle**, in which there was a feedback loop from a boom in issuing credit, which led to higher asset prices that led to higher capital buffers at financial institutions, that supported further lending in the context of unchanging capital requirements, which then raised asset prices further, and so on; in the bust, the value of the capital dropped precipitously, leading to a cut in lending. To short-circuit this leverage cycle, macroprudential policies would make capital requirements countercyclical; that is, they would be adjusted upward during a boom and downward during a bust. In addition, during the upward swing in the leverage cycle, macroprudential policies might involve forcing financial institutions to tighten credit standards or even direct limits on the growth of credit. In the downward swing, macroprudential supervison might be needed to force the banking system as a whole to raise an aggregate amount of new capital so that banks would not curtail lending in order to reduce the level of their assets and raise capital ratios. To assure that financial institutions have enough liquidity, macroprudential policies could require that financial institutions have a sufficiently low *net stable funding ratio* (NSFR), which is the percentage of the institution's short-term funding to total funding. Macroprudential policies of the type discussed here are being considered as part of the Basel 3 framework but have not yet been completely worked out.

Summary

Asymmetric information analysis explains what types of financial regulations are needed to reduce moral hazard and adverse selection problems in the financial system. However, understanding the theory behind regulation does not mean

---

FYI

Mark-to-Market Accounting and the Global Financial Crisis

The controversy over mark-to-market accounting has made accounting a hot topic. Mark-to-market accounting was made standard practice in the accounting industry in the United States in 1993. U.S. Generally Accepted Accounting Principles (GAAP) established a number of ways for measuring fair value, depending on whether a financial instrument is traded on an active market or in the absence of an active market. Canadian GAAP are similar to U.S. GAAP, as well as to standards in effect in those countries (approximately 110) that have adopted a set of global standards, known as International Financial Reporting Standards (IFRS), developed by the International Accounting Standards Board (IASB).

The rationale behind mark-to-market accounting is that market prices provide a better basis for estimating the true value of assets, and hence capital, in the firm. Before mark-to-market accounting, firms relied on the traditional historical-cost (book value) basis in which the value of an asset is set at its initial purchase price. The problem with historical-cost accounting is that changes in the value of assets and liabilities because of changes in interest rates or default are not reflected in the calculation of the firm's equity capital. Yet changes in the market value of assets and liabilities—and hence changes in the market value of equity capital—are what indicate if a firm is in good shape, or, alternatively, if it is getting into trouble and may therefore be more susceptible to moral hazard.

Mark-to-market accounting, however, is subject to a major flaw. At times markets stop working, as occurred during the global financial crisis. The price of an asset sold at a time of financial distress does not reflect its fundamental value. That is, the fire-sale liquidation value of an asset

can at times be well below the present value of its expected future cash flows.

Many people, particularly bankers, criticized mark-to-market accounting during the global financial crisis, claiming that it was an important factor driving the crisis. They claim that the seizing up of the markets led to market prices being well below fundamental values. Since mark-to-market accounting requires that the financial firms' assets be marked down in value, this markdown creates a shortfall in capital that leads to a cutback in lending, which causes a further deterioration in asset prices, which in turn causes a further cutback in lending. The resulting adverse feedback loop can then make a financial crisis even worse. Although the criticisms of mark-to-market accounting have some validity, some of the criticism by bankers is self-serving. The criticism was made only when asset values were falling, when mark-to-market accounting was painting a bleaker picture of banks' balance sheets, as opposed to when asset prices were booming and it made banks' balance sheets look very good.

In the aftermath of the global financial crisis, the criticisms of mark-to-market accounting led the International Accounting Standards Board to form an advisory panel to enhance its guidance on valuing financial instruments in inactive markets in times of crisis. Moreover, in the United States there was a Congressional focus on fair-value accounting that resulted in a provision in the Emergency Economic Stabilization Act of 2008 that required the SEC, in consultation with the Federal Reserve and the U.S. Treasury, to submit a study of mark-to-market accounting applicable to financial institutions. Who knew that accounting could get even politicians worked up!

FYI

The Subprime Mortgage Crisis and Consumer Protection Regulation

Because of the principal–agent problem inherent in the originate-to-distribute model for subprime mortgages discussed in Chapter 9, there were weak incentives for mortgage originators, typically mortgage brokers who were virtually unregulated, to ensure that subprime borrowers had the ability to pay back their loans. After all, mortgage brokers earned large fees from mortgage originators, even if sometime down the road the borrowers defaulted on their loan and lost their homes. With these incentives, mortgage brokers weakened their underwriting standards, leading to subprime mortgage products such as "no-doc loans," more pejoratively referred to as "liar loans," in which borrowers did not have to produce documentation about their assets or income. A particularly infamous variant of no-doc loans was dubbed the "NINJA loan," because it was issued to borrowers with No Income, No Job, and No Assets.

Mortgage brokers also had incentives to saddle households with very complicated mortgage products borrowers could not understand and which they couldn't afford to pay. In some cases, mortgage brokers even engaged in fraud by falsifying information on borrowers' mortgage applications in order to qualify them for mortgage loans.

Lax consumer protection regulation was an important factor in producing the subprime mortgage crisis in the United States. Mortgage originators were not required to disclose information to borrowers that would have helped them better understand complicated mortgage products and whether they could afford to repay them. Outrage over the surge of foreclosures in the United States has been an important stimulus for new regulation to provide better information to mortgage borrowers and to ban unfair and deceptive practices.

that regulation and supervision of the financial system are easy in practice. Getting regulators and supervisors to do their job properly is difficult for several reasons. First, financial institutions have strong incentives to avoid existing regulations by exploiting loopholes. Thus, regulation applies to a moving target: regulators are continually playing cat-and-mouse with financial institutions—financial institutions think up clever ways to avoid regulations, which then lead regulators to modify their regulation activities. Regulators continually face new challenges in a dynamically changing financial system—and unless they can respond rapidly to change, they may not be able to keep financial institutions from taking on excessive risk. This problem can be exacerbated if regulators and supervisors do not have the resources or expertise to keep up with clever people in financial institutions seeking to circumvent the existing regulations.

Financial regulation and supervision are difficult for two other reasons. In the regulation and supervision game, the devil is in the details. Subtle differences in the details may have unintended consequences; unless regulators get the regulation and supervision just right, they may be unable to prevent excessive risk taking. In addition, regulated firms may lobby politicians to lean on regulators and supervisors to go easy on them. For all these reasons, there is no guarantee that regulators and supervisors will be successful in promoting a healthy financial system. These same problems bedevil financial regulators in other countries, as the Global box International Financial Regulation indicates. Indeed, as we will see, financial regulation and supervision have not always worked well, leading to banking crises throughout the world.

Because so many laws regulating the financial system have been passed in Canada, it is hard to keep track of them all. As a study aid, Table 10-1 lists the major financial legislation in the twentieth century and its key provisions.

TABLE 10.1 Major Financial Legislation in Canada

Bank of Canada Act (1934)

Created the Bank of Canada following the recommendations of the Macmillan Commission

Bank Act of 1936

Prohibited banks from issuing banknotes

Imposed reserve requirements on depository institutions to be held with the Bank of Canada

Bank Act of 1954

Increased reserve requirements on depository institutions

Allowed chartered banks to offer mortgages issued under the National Housing Act

Canada Deposit Insurance Corporation Act (1967)

Created the CDIC to insure deposits with all federally chartered banks and near banks

Bank Act of 1967

Removed the 6% loan interest rate ceiling

Restricted foreign competition

Imposed secondary reserve requirements on depository institutions

Put chartered banks and near banks on equal footing regarding mortgage lending

Bank Act of 1981

Created the Canadian Payments Association to operate the national payments system and plan its development

Lowered reserve requirements on Canadian-dollar deposits

Increased competition by introducing a less complicated procedure for obtaining a licence to operate as a bank

Allowed foreign banks to establish subsidiaries in Canada, subject to reciprocal treatment of Canadian banks

Extended banks' business powers to include financial leasing, factoring, and data processing

Redesigned corporate clauses to ensure consistency between the Bank Act and the Canada Business Corporations Act

Provided a simpler incorporation method for new banks (letters patent) while retaining incorporation through a special Act of Parliament

Office of the Superintendent of Financial Institutions Act (1987)

Created the OSFI to succeed two separate federal regulatory bodies (the Department of Insurance and the Inspector General of Banks) in the supervision of financial institutions

Financial Institutions and Deposit Insurance System Amendment Act (1987)

Allowed chartered banks to own investment banking subsidiaries, thereby initiating the merging of the four pillars

Savings and Credit Union Act of the Province of Québec (1988)

Set rules for credit unions, federations, and confederations, with specific reference to the Mouvement Desjardins

Bank Act of 1992

Comprehensive banking law

Allowed chartered banks to own trust companies

(continued)

TABLE 10-1 (continued)

Allowed trust companies to make commercial loans

Made provisions for the phasing out of reserve requirements

Set rules regarding the supervisory role of the Bank of Canada and the OSFI with respect to chartered banks

Reset the "sunset" clause from 10 years to 5 years to address the changing Canadian financial services marketplace

Cooperative Credit Associations Act (1992)

Replaced the Cooperative Credit Association Act of 1952–1953 and set rules for federally chartered credit unions

Followed the same format as the Bank Act

Insurance Companies Act (1992)

Replaced the Canadian and British Insurance Companies Act and the Foreign Insurance Companies Act, both passed in 1932

Set rules for life insurance companies and property and casualty (P&C) insurance companies

Allowed insurance companies to own Schedule II chartered banks

Followed the same format as the Bank Act

Trust and Loan Companies Act (1992)

Replaced the Trust Companies Act and the Loan Companies Act, both passed in 1914

Set rules for federally incorporated Trust and Mortgage Loan Companies (TMLs) and provincially incorporated TMLs reporting to the OSFI

Required large, formerly closely held TMLs to become 35% widely held

Followed the same format as the Bank Act

Bank Act of 1997

Yielded minor changes because the government was waiting for the recommendations of the MacKay Task Force

Bank Act Reform of 2001

Set new ownership rules

Established a process for reviewing mergers involving large banks

Allowed bank financial groups to organize under a holding company structure

Allowed greater flexibility for bank involvement in the information technology area

Allowed non-deposit-taking financial institutions access to the payments and clearance systems

Financial System Review Act (FSRA) of March 29, 2012

Amendments to the Bank Act and other associated statutes

The 1980s Canadian Banking Crisis

The period from 1923 (when the Home Bank failed) to 1985 was one in which the failure of Canadian chartered banks was thought to be impossible. During the same period, failures of deposit-taking financial institutions in the United States were averaging about 20 a year. In the mid-1980s, however, the situation in Canada changed dramatically with the failure of two chartered banks and the financial difficulties of a large number of other financial institutions. Why did this happen? How did a stable banking system that seemed to be working well find itself in trouble?

Early Stage of the Crisis

The story starts with the oil boom in western Canada in the 1970s. It led to the creation of several western banks, including two Alberta-based Schedule I banks, the Canadian Commercial Bank and the Northland Bank, both formed in 1975. Unfortunately, the managers of these banks did not have the expertise that would have enabled them to manage risk appropriately; they excessively concentrated on a few borrowers in western Canada and placed a large percentage of their total loans in real estate.

The existence of deposit insurance increased moral hazard for the Canadian Commercial and Northland banks, because insured depositors had little incentive to keep the banks from taking on too much risk. Regardless of how much risk the banks were taking, deposit insurance guaranteed that depositors would not suffer any losses.

Canadian Commercial and Northland pursued rapid growth and took on risky projects, attracting the necessary funds by issuing large-denomination certificates of deposit with high interest rates. Without deposit insurance, high interest rates would not have induced depositors to provide the high-rolling banks with funds

GLOBAL

International Financial Regulation

Because asymmetric information problems in the banking industry are a fact of life throughout the world, financial regulation in other countries is similar to that in Canada. Financial institutions are chartered and supervised by government regulators, just as they are in Canada. Disclosure requirements for financial institutions and corporations issuing securities are similar in other developed countries. Deposit insurance is also a feature of the regulatory systems in most other countries, although its coverage is different than in Canada and is intentionally not advertised. We have also seen that capital requirements are in the process of being standardized across countries with agreements like the Basel Accord. Accounting and financial reporting are also in the process of being standardized across countries by moving to IFRS, a set of global standards developed by the IASB.

Particular problems in financial regulation occur when financial institutions operate in many countries and thus can readily shift their business from one country to another. Financial regulators closely examine the domestic operations of financial institutions in their country, but they often do not have the knowledge or ability to keep a close watch on operations in other countries, either by domestic institutions' foreign affiliates or by foreign institutions with domestic branches. In addition, when a financial institution operates in many countries, it is not always clear which national

regulatory authority should have primary responsibility for keeping the institution from engaging in overly risky activities.

The difficulties inherent in international financial regulation were highlighted by the collapse of the Bank of Credit and Commerce International (BCCI). BCCI, which was operating in more than 70 countries including the United States and the United Kingdom, was supervised by Luxembourg, a tiny country unlikely to be up to the task. When massive fraud was discovered, the Bank of England closed BCCI down, but not before depositors and shareholders were exposed to huge losses. Cooperation among regulators in different countries and standardization of regulatory requirements provide potential solutions to the problems of international financial regulation. The world has moved in this direction through agreements like the Basel Accord and oversight procedures announced by the Basel Committee in July 1992, which require a bank's worldwide operations to be under the scrutiny of a single home-country regulator with enhanced powers to acquire information on the bank's activities. Also, the Basel Committee ruled that regulators in other countries can restrict the operations of a foreign bank if they feel that it lacks effective oversight. Whether agreements of this type will solve the problem of international financial regulation in the future is an open question.

because of the realistic expectation that they might not get the funds back. But with deposit insurance, the government was guaranteeing that the deposits were safe, so depositors were more than happy to make deposits in the Canadian Commercial and Northland banks with the higher interest rates.

As already noted, the managers of Canadian Commercial and Northland did not have the required expertise to manage risk in the permissive atmosphere of western Canada. Even if the required expertise was available initially, rapid credit growth may have outstripped the available information resources of the banking institution, resulting in excessive risk taking. Also, the lending boom meant that the activities of Canadian Commercial and Northland were expanding in scope and were becoming more complicated, requiring an expansion of regulatory resources to monitor these activities appropriately. Unfortunately, regulators of chartered banks at the Inspector General of Banks (the predecessor of the Office of the Superintendent of Financial Institutions) had neither the expertise nor the resources that would have enabled them to sufficiently monitor the activities of Canadian Commercial and Northland. Given the lack of expertise in both the banks and the Inspector General of Banks, the weakening of the regulatory apparatus, and the moral hazard incentives provided by deposit insurance, it is no surprise that Canadian Commercial and Northland took on excessive risks, which led to huge losses on bad loans.

In addition, the incentives of moral hazard were increased dramatically by a historical accident: the combination of sharp increases in interest rates from late 1979 until 1981 and a severe recession in 1981–1982, both of which were engineered by the Federal Reserve in the United States to bring down inflation. The sharp rise in interest rates produced rapidly rising costs of funds for the banks that were not matched by higher earnings on their principal asset, long-term residential mortgages (whose rates had been fixed at a time when interest rates were far lower). The 1981–1982 recession and a collapse in the prices of energy and farm products hit the economy of Alberta very hard. As a result, there were defaults on many loans. Losses for Canadian Commercial and Northland mounted and the banks had negative net worths and were thus insolvent by the beginning of 1985.

Later Stage of the Crisis: Regulatory Forbearance

At this point, a logical step might have been for the regulators—the Bank of Canada and the Inspector General of Banks—to close the insolvent banks. Instead, the regulators adopted a stance of **regulatory forbearance**: they refrained from exercising their regulatory right to put the insolvent Canadian Commercial Bank and Northland Bank out of business.

There were two main reasons why the Bank of Canada and the Inspector General of Banks opted for regulatory forbearance. First, the CDIC did not have sufficient funds in its insurance fund to close the insolvent banks and pay off their deposits. Second, because bureaucrats do not like to admit that their own agency is in trouble, the regulators preferred to sweep their problems under the rug in the hope that they would go away.

When Canadian Commercial and Northland were declared insolvent in September of 1985, rumours of financial trouble caused many large depositors to withdraw large deposits from the Bank of British Columbia, Mercantile Bank, and Continental Bank. By the time Mercantile was acquired by the National Bank of Canada, Bank of British Columbia by the Hongkong Bank of Canada, and Continental by Lloyds Bank of Canada (a subsidiary of a U.K.-based banking powerhouse), the Bank of Canada had lent over $5 billion.

The loss of public confidence in the Canadian banking system led to the financial reforms of 1987–1992 (see Table 10-1) and the consolidating of financial institution supervision under the Office of the Superintendent of Financial Institutions.

CDIC Developments

The Canada Deposit Insurance Corporation (CDIC) insures each depositor at member institutions up to a loss of $100 000 per account. All federally incorporated financial institutions and all provincially incorporated trust and mortgage loan companies are members of the CDIC. Insurance companies, credit unions, *caisses populaires,* and investment dealers are not eligible for CDIC membership; the Québec Deposit Insurance Board (QDIB) insures provincially incorporated financial institutions in Québec, and the other provinces have deposit insurance corporations that insure the deposits of credit unions in their jurisdiction, on terms similar to the CDIC's.

The CDIC is allowed to insure only deposits in Canadian currency and payable in Canada; foreign currency deposits, such as accounts in U.S. dollars, are not insured. Moreover, not all deposits and investments offered by CDIC member institutions are insurable. Insurable deposits include savings and chequing accounts, term deposits with a maturity date of less than five years, money orders and drafts, certified drafts and cheques, and traveller's cheques. The CDIC does not insure term deposits with an initial maturity date of more than five years, Treasury bills, bonds and debentures issued by governments and corporations (including the chartered banks), or investments in stocks, mutual funds, and mortgages.

The primary rationale for deposit insurance is protecting depositors from bank insolvency and thus ensuring financial stability. Deposit insurance could also promote competition among financial institutions by removing barriers to entry for new deposit-taking institutions. In the absence of deposit insurance, it is difficult for new banks to attract deposits. Most depositors, for example, are not capable of making appropriate risk calculations to assess the risk of a new bank. Those depositors would tend to place their deposits in banks that are considered too big to fail, thereby producing significant barriers to entry and unfair disadvantages for small new entrants. By insuring deposits at all deposit-taking financial institutions, the CDIC effectively removes barriers to entry for new deposit takers.

Differential Premiums

Until recently, CDIC premium revenue was not tied to the risk profile of financial institutions; the premium rate was the same for all deposit-taking institutions, irrespective of their risk profile. For example, in the 1998–1999 fiscal year, the flat-rate insurance premium was 1/6 of 1%, or 0.1667%, meaning that each deposit-taking financial institution paid an insurance premium of close to 17 cents per $100. This was one of the reasons that the Big Six, represented by the Canadian Bankers Association, vigorously opposed the establishment of the CDIC in 1967; it was argued that deposit insurance would be a subsidy to small banks paid by the big banks.

Over the years, the Canadian Bankers Association strongly promoted the reform of the Canadian deposit insurance system. As a result, the CDIC developed the Differential Premiums By-law, which came into effect for the premium year beginning May 1, 1999. The bylaw undergoes regular reviews and has been amended a number of times. The important feature of this legislation is its implicit, prompt corrective action provisions, which require the CDIC to intervene earlier and more vigorously when a bank gets into trouble. CDIC member institutions are now classified into four premium groups based on their risk profile. An institution's risk profile is determined using a variety of quantitative and qualitative criteria, including capital adequacy, profitability, asset concentration, income volatility, regulatory ratings, and adherence to CDIC's Standards of Sound Business and Financial Practices, with capital adequacy dominating the criteria, accounting for 20% of the score.

Under the new system, the premium rates for CDIC member institutions are those shown in Table 10-2; they vary from 2 cents to 22 cents per $100. Group 1, classified as "best," is well-capitalized banks that significantly exceed minimum requirements. On the other hand, banks in group 4, classified as "worst," are significantly (and perhaps critically) undercapitalized and the insurance premium that they pay is 22 basis points, the maximum allowed under the CDIC Act. In addition, for group 4 banks, the CDIC is required to take prompt corrective actions such as requiring them to submit a capital restoration plan, restrict their asset growth, and seek regulatory approval to open new branches or develop new lines of business. Today, over 90% of CDIC member institutions are classified in categories 1 and 2, but as in other countries, the premium category and related supervisory information applicable to individual CDIC members are confidential.

Opting Out

Another interesting recent development is the Opting-Out By-law that came into effect on October 15, 1999. This legislation permits Schedule III banks that accept primarily wholesale deposits (defined as $150 000 or more) to opt out of CDIC membership and therefore to operate without deposit insurance. The new legislation, however, includes provisions to protect depositors who hold deposits eligible for CDIC protection. In particular, it requires an opted-out bank to inform all depositors, by posting notices in its branches, that their deposits will not be protected by the CDIC, and not to charge any early withdrawal penalties for depositors who choose to withdraw.

Probably the most important feature of the opting-out legislation is its minimization of CDIC exposure to uninsured deposits. This represents a significant departure from past practices, when the CDIC showed generosity to uninsured depositors. For example, in the Canadian Commercial and Northland failures of the mid-1980s, the CDIC paid 100 cents on the dollar to all depositors, both insured and uninsured. By compensating only the insured depositors rather than all depositors, the opting-out legislation increases the incentives of uninsured depositors to monitor the risk-taking activities of banks, thereby reducing moral hazard risk.

TABLE 10-2 Premium Structure and Rates for CDIC Member Institutions in 2011	
Premium Category	**Premium Rate (as a Percentage of Insured Deposits)**
1	1/36 of 1%, or 0.02778
2	1/18 of 1%, or 0.05556
3	1/9 of 1%, or 0.11111
4	2/9 of 1%, or 0.22222

Source: CDIC website: www.cdic.ca.

APPLICATION

Evaluating CDIC and Other Proposed Reforms of the Banking Regulatory System

The new system of risk-based premiums and opting-out rules is a major step in reformulating the financial regulatory system. How well will it work to solve the adverse selection and moral hazard problems of the bank regulatory system? Let's use the analysis in the chapter to evaluate the new legislation to answer this question.

Limits on the Scope of Deposit Insurance

CDIC's reductions of the scope of deposit insurance by limiting insurance to insured deposits might have increased the incentives for uninsured depositors to monitor banks and to withdraw funds if the bank were taking on too much risk. Because banks might now fear the loss of deposits when they engage in risky activities, they might have less incentive to take on too much risk.

Although the cited new elements of deposit insurance strengthen the incentive of depositors to monitor banks, some critics would take these limitations on the scope of deposit insurance even further. Some suggest that deposit insurance should be eliminated entirely or should be reduced in amount from the current $100 000 limit to, say, $20 000 or $10 000. Another proposed reform would institute a system of **coinsurance** in which only a percentage of a deposit, say, 90%, would be covered by insurance. In this system, the insured depositor would suffer a percentage of the losses along with the deposit insurance agency. Because depositors facing a lower limit on deposit insurance or coinsurance would suffer losses if the bank went broke, they would have an incentive to monitor the bank's activities.

However, other experts do not believe that depositors are capable of monitoring banks and imposing discipline on them. The basic problem with reducing the scope of deposit insurance even further is that banks would be subject to runs, sudden withdrawals by nervous investors. Such runs could by themselves lead to bank failures. In addition to protecting individual depositors, the purpose of deposit insurance is to prevent a large number of bank failures, which would lead to an unstable banking system and an unstable economy. From this perspective, deposit insurance has been a resounding success. Bank panics, in which there are simultaneous failures of many banks and consequent disruption of the financial system, have not occurred since deposit insurance was established.

Eliminating the too-big-to-fail policy altogether would also cause some of the same problems that would occur if deposit insurance were eliminated or reduced: the probability of bank panics would increase. If a bank were allowed to fail, the repercussions in the financial system might be immense. Other banks with a correspondent relationship with the failed bank (those that have deposits at the bank in exchange for services) would suffer large losses and might fail in turn, leading to full-scale panic. In addition, the problem of liquidating the big bank's loan portfolio might create a major disruption in the financial system.

Prompt Corrective Action

The prompt corrective action provisions of CDIC should also substantially reduce incentives for bank risk taking and reduce taxpayer losses. CDIC uses a carrot-and-stick approach to get banks to hold more capital. If they are well capitalized, they receive better ratings and are placed in a better premium rate category (see Table 10-2); if their capital ratio falls, they are subject to more and more onerous regulation. Increased bank capital reduces moral hazard for the bank because the bank now has more to lose if it fails and so is less likely to take on too much risk. In addition, encouraging banks to hold more capital reduces potential losses for the CDIC because increased bank capital is a cushion that makes bank failure less likely.

Prompt corrective action, which requires regulators to intervene early when bank capital begins to fall, is a serious attempt to reduce the principal–agent problem for politicians and regulators. With prompt corrective action provisions, regulators no longer have the option of regulatory forbearance, which, as we have seen, can greatly increase moral hazard incentives for banks.

Risk-Based Insurance Premiums

Under the Differential Premiums By-law, banks deemed to be taking on greater risk, in the form of lower capital or riskier assets, are subjected to higher insurance premiums, as can be seen in Table 10-2. Risk-based insurance premiums consequently reduce the moral hazard incentives for banks to take on higher risk. In addition, the fact that risk-based premiums drop as the bank's capital increases encourages the banks to hold more capital, which has the benefits already mentioned.

One problem with risk-based premiums is that the scheme for determining the amount of risk the bank is taking may not be very accurate. For example, it might be hard for regulators to determine when a bank's loans are risky. Some critics have also pointed out that the classification of banks by such measures as the Basel risk-based capital standard solely reflects credit risk and does not take sufficient account of interest-rate risk. The regulatory authorities, however, are encouraged to modify existing risk-based standards to include interest-rate risk.

Other CDIC Provisions

CDIC's requirements that regulators perform frequent bank examinations and member institutions file a Standards report at least once a year are necessary for monitoring banks' compliance with bank capital requirements and asset restrictions. As the Canadian Commercial and Northland debacles illustrate, frequent supervisory examinations of banks are necessary to keep them from taking on too much risk or committing fraud. Similarly, beefing up the ability of the regulators to monitor foreign banks might help dissuade international banks from engaging in these undesirable activities.

The stricter and more burdensome reporting requirements for banks have the advantage of providing more information to regulators to help them monitor bank activities. However, these reporting requirements have been criticized by banks, which claim that the requirements make it harder to lend to small businesses. As a result, the CDIC developed the Modernized Standards By-law, adopted in early 2001, which enables the CDIC to determine the frequency of a member institution's reporting based on its categorization under the Differential Premiums By-law.

The Modernized Standards By-law allows CDIC discretion in examining the performance of problem member institutions. Under the new regime, well-capitalized, category 1 banks will be required to file a Standards report every five years. However, banks in categories 3 and 4 may be subjected to special examination at any time, the cost of which will be chargeable to the institution. The Modernized Standards By-law, in addition to increasing the regulatory supervision of problem banks, also increases the accountability of the CDIC. Moreover, it decreases the incentives of banks to take on excessive risk and increases their incentives to hold capital.

Other Proposed Changes in Banking Regulations

REGULATORY CONSOLIDATION   The current bank regulatory system in Canada has financial institutions supervised by three federal agencies: the Bank of Canada, the Office of the Superintendent of Financial Institutions, and the CDIC. Critics of this system of multiple regulatory agencies with overlapping jurisdictions believe it creates a system that is too complex and too costly because it is rife with duplication. For example, although the CDIC has no direct supervisory role, its Standards of Sound Business and Financial Practices overlap with those of the OSFI.

The MacKay Task Force, named after its chairman Harold MacKay and set up by the government in 1996 to review the financial services sector and propose a framework for its future, considered whether the CDIC and the OSFI should be amalgamated. Although the task force recommended that the regulator (OSFI) and the insurer (CDIC) should not be combined in a single institution, it proposed that the CDIC's mandate be amended to remove the overlap with the OSFI's mandate.

Overall Evaluation

The recent CDIC developments appear to be an important step in the right direction because they increase the incentives for banks to hold capital and decrease their incentives to take on excessive risk. However, more could be done to improve the incentives for banks to limit their risk taking. Yet eliminating deposit insurance and the too-big-to-fail policy altogether may be going too far because these proposals might make the banking system too prone to a banking panic.

Banking Crises Throughout the World

Because misery loves company, it may make you feel better to know that Canada was not alone in suffering banking crises even before the global financial crisis of 2007–2009. Indeed, as Table 10-3 and Figure 10-1 illustrate, banking crises are very common and many of them have been substantially worse than the one Canada experienced in the 1980s.

"Déjà Vu All Over Again"

In the banking crises in different countries, history keeps repeating itself. The parallels between banking crisis episodes in various countries are remarkable, creating a feeling of déjà vu. They all started with financial liberalization or innovation with weak bank regulatory systems and a government safety net. Although financial liberalization is generally a good thing because it promotes competition and can make a financial system more efficient, it can lead to an increase in moral hazard, with more risk taking on the part of banks if there is lax regulation and supervision; the result can then be banking crises.[1]

However, the banking crisis episodes listed in Table 10-3 do differ in that deposit insurance has not played an important role in many of the countries experiencing banking crises. For example, the size of the Japanese equivalent of the CDIC, the Deposit Insurance Corporation, was so tiny that it did not play a prominent role in the banking system and exhausted its resources almost immediately with the first bank failures. This example indicates that deposit insurance is not to blame for some of these banking crises. However, what is common to all the countries discussed here is the existence of a government safety net, in which the government stood ready to bail out banks whether deposit insurance was an important feature of the regulatory environment or not. It is the existence of a government safety net, and not deposit insurance per se, that increases moral hazard incentives for excessive risk taking on the part of banks.

---

[1]An appendix to this chapter on this book's MyEconLab discusses many of the episodes of banking crises listed in Table 10-3 in more detail.

TABLE 10-3   The Cost of Rescuing Banks in a Number of Countries

Country	Date	Cost as a Percentage of GDP
1980–2003		
Indonesia	1997–2001	57
Argentina	1980–1982	55
Thailand	1997–2000	44
Chile	1981–1985	43
Turkey	2000–2001	32
South Korea	1997–1998	31
Israel	1977	30
Ecuador	1998–2002	22
Mexico	1994–1996	19
China	1998	18
Malaysia	1997–1999	16
Philippines	1997–2001	13
Brazil	1994–1998	13
Finland	1991–1995	13
Argentina	2001–2003	10
Jordan	1989–1991	10
Hungary	1991–1995	10
Czech Republic	1996–2000	7
Sweden	1991–1995	4
United States	1988	4
Norway	1991–1993	3
2007–2009		
Iceland	2007–2009	13
Ireland	2007–2009	8
Luxembourg	2007–2009	8
Netherlands	2007–2009	7
Belgium	2007–2009	5
United Kingdom	2007–2009	5
United States	2007–2009	4
Germany	2007–2009	1

Sources: Luc Laeven and Fabian Valencia, "Resolution of Banking Crises: The Good, the Bad and the Ugly," IMF Working Paper No. WP/10/46 (June 2010).

FIGURE 10-1 Banking Crises Throughout the World Since 1970

Systemic
banking crises

Episodes of
nonsystemic
banking crises

No crises

Insufficient
information

Source: Data from Gerard Caprio and Daniela Klingebiel, "Episodes of Systemic and Borderline Financial Crises" mimeo., World Bank, October 1999; Luc Laeven and Fabian Valencia, "Resolution of Banking Crises: The Good, the Bad and the Ugly," IMF Working Paper No. WP/10/46 (June 2010).

The Global Financial Crisis and Future Regulation

The recent global financial crisis has led to banking crises throughout the world, and it is too soon to tell how large the costs of rescuing the banks will be as a result of this episode (which is why they are not listed in Table 10-3). Given the size of the bailouts and the nationalization of so many financial institutions, the system of financial regulation is undergoing dramatic changes. Here we discuss several areas where regulation may be heading in the future.

CAPITAL REQUIREMENTS Regulation and supervision of financial institutions to ensure that they have enough capital to cope with the amount of risk they take are likely to be strengthened. Given the risks they were taking before the recent financial crisis, banks and investment banks did not have enough capital relative to their assets and their risky activities. Similarly, the capital at AIG was not sufficient to cover the high risk it was taking by issuing credit insurance. Capital requirements will almost surely be beefed up for all of these institutions. Banks' sponsoring of structured investment vehicles (SIVs), which were supposedly off balance sheet but came back on the balance sheet once the SIVs got into trouble, indicate that some off-balance-sheet activities should be treated as though they are on the balance sheet, and this will be a focus of future regulation. In addition, because of the too-big-to-fail problem, **systemically important financial institutions** are likely to take on more risk, and so regulators and the Basel Committee are considering regulations to increase capital requirements for these firms. Capital requirements are also likely to be adjusted to increase in booms and decrease in busts so that they become more countercyclical in order to restrain the boom-and-bust cycle in credit markets.

COMPENSATION   As we saw in Chapter 8, the high fees and executive compensation that have so outraged the public created incentives for the financial industry to push out securities that turned out to be much riskier than advertised and proved to be disastrous. Regulators are closely studying regulations to modify compensation in the financial services industry to reduce risk taking. For example, regulators are in the process of issuing requirements that bonuses be paid out for a number of years after they have been earned and only if the firm has remained in good health. Such "clawbacks" will encourage employees to reduce the riskiness of their activities so that they are more likely to be paid these bonuses in the future.

CREDIT-RATING AGENCIES   Regulations to restrict conflicts of interest at credit rating agencies and to give them greater incentives to provide reliable ratings have already been strengthened in the aftermath of the 2007–2009 financial crisis, but even more is likely to be done. The inaccurate ratings provided by credit rating agencies helped promote risk taking throughout the financial system and led to investors not having the information they needed to make informed choices about their investments. The reliance on credit ratings in the Basel 2 capital requirements may also have to be rethought, given the poor performance of credit rating agencies in recent years.

THE DANGER OF OVERREGULATION   As a result of the 2007–2009 financial crisis, the world of financial regulation will never be the same. Although it is clear that more regulation is needed to prevent such a crisis from ever occurring again, there is a substantial danger that too much or poorly designed regulation could hamper the efficiency of the financial system. If new regulations choke off financial innovation that can benefit both households and businesses, economic growth in the future will suffer.

MyEconLab   MyEconLab is an online homework and tutorial system that puts you in control of your own learning with study and practice tools directly correlated to this chapter's content. Visit MyEconLab to explore the following resources:

- The Questions and Applied Problems are all available in the Study Plan on MyEconLab for further practice. You will also find the answers to all of the Questions and Applied Problems in the Student Resources section of your MyEconLab.

- Visit the Student Resources section of MyEconLab to access the following appendix for this chapter: Appendix 10.1: Banking Crises Throughout the World.

MyEconLab also features Additional Readings, Videos, Glossary Flashcards, Audio Chapter Summaries, Economics News Feeds, Animations, and many additional tools to help you master key concepts from the text.

SUMMARY

1. The concepts of asymmetric information, adverse selection, and moral hazard help explain the 10 types of financial regulation that we see in Canada and other countries: the government safety net, restrictions on asset holdings, capital requirements, prompt corrective action, chartering and examination, assessment of risk management, disclosure requirements, consumer protection, restrictions on competition, and macroprudential policies.

2. Because of financial innovation, deregulation, and a set of historical accidents, adverse selection and moral hazard problems increased in the 1980s and resulted in huge losses for the Canadian banking industry and for taxpayers.

MyEconL
Audio Sum

3. The Canadian deposit insurance system has recently been reformed by the introduction of the differential premiums and opting-out by-laws. The former is designed to increase the incentive for banks to hold capital and the latter aims to decrease their incentive to take on excessive risk.

4. The parallels between the banking crisis episodes that have occurred in countries throughout the world are striking, indicating that similar forces are at work.

KEY TERMS

bank failure, p. 211

Basel Accord, p. 215

Basel Committee on Bank Supervision, p. 215

coinsurance, p. 229

fair-value accounting, p. 219

financial supervision (prudential supervision), p. 216

leverage cycle, p. 220

leverage ratio, p. 215

macroprudential supervision, p. 220

mark-to-market accounting, p. 219

microprudential supervision, p. 220

off-balance-sheet activities, p. 215

regulatory arbitrage, p. 215

regulatory forbearance, p. 226

stress tests, p. 218

systemically important financial institutions, p. 233

value-at-risk (VaR), p. 218

QUESTIONS

1. Why are deposit insurance and other types of government safety nets important to the health of the economy?

2. If casualty insurance companies provided fire insurance without any restrictions, what kind of adverse selection and moral hazard problems might result?

3. Do you think that eliminating or limiting the amount of deposit insurance would be a good idea? Explain your answer.

4. How could higher deposit insurance premiums for banks with riskier assets benefit the economy?

5. What are the costs and benefits of a too-big-to-fail policy?

6. What types of bank regulations are designed to reduce moral hazard problems? Will they completely eliminate the moral hazard problem?

7. Why does imposing bank capital requirements on banks help limit risk taking?

8. At the height of the global financial crisis in October 2008, the U.S. Treasury forced nine of the largest U.S. banks to accept capital injections in exchange for non-voting ownership stock, even though some of the banks did not need the capital and did not want to participate. What could be the rationale for doing this?

9. What special problem do off-balance-sheet activities present to bank regulators, and what have they done about it?

10. What are some of the limitations to the Basel and Basel 2 Accords? How does the Basel 3 Accord attempt to address these limitations?

11. How does bank chartering reduce adverse selection problems? Will it always work?

12. Why has the trend in bank supervision moved away from a focus on capital requirements to a focus on risk management?

13. How do disclosure requirements help limit excessive risk taking by banks?

14. Suppose Universal Bank holds $100 million in assets, which are composed of the following:

Desired Reserves:	$10 million
Excess Reserves:	$5 million
Mortgage Loans:	$20 million
Corporate Bonds:	$15 million
Stocks:	$25 million
Commodities:	$25 million

a. Do you think it is a good idea for Universal Bank to hold stocks, corporate bonds, and commodities as assets? Why or why not?

b. If the housing market suddenly crashed, would Universal Bank be better off with a mark-to-market accounting system or a historical-cost system?

c. If the price of commodities suddenly increased sharply, would Universal Bank be better off with a mark-to-market accounting system or a historical-cost system?

d. What do your answers to (b) and (c) tell you about the tradeoffs between the two accounting systems?

15. Why might more competition in financial markets be bad? Would restrictions on competition be better? Why or why not?

16. Why is it a good idea for macroprudential policies to require countercyclical capital requirements?

17. How does the process of financial innovation impact the effectiveness of macroprudential regulation?

18. How can the 1980s Canadian banking crisis be blamed on the principal–agent problem?

19. Why are there consumer protection provisions in recent regulations designed to strengthen the financial system?

20. Why is it important for the Canadian government to have resolution authority?

APPLIED PROBLEMS

21. Consider a failing bank. A deposit of $350 000 is worth how much if the CDIC uses the *payoff method*? The *purchase-and-assumption* method? Which is more costly to taxpayers?

22. Consider a bank with the following balance sheet:

Assets		Liabilities	
Desired Reserves	$8 million	Chequable Deposits	$100 million
Excess Reserves	$3 million	Bank Capital	$6 million
T-bills	$45 million		
Commercial Loans	$50 million		

The bank makes a loan commitment for $10 million to a commercial customer. Calculate the bank's capital ratio before and after the agreement. Calculate the bank's risk-weighted assets before and after the agreement.

Problems 23 through 25 relate to a sequence of transactions at Oldhat Financial.

23. Oldhat Financial started its first day of operations with $9 million in capital. $130 million in chequable deposits are received. The bank makes a $25 million commercial loan and lends another $50 million in mortgages, with the following terms: 200 standard 30-year, fixed-rate mortgages with a nominal annual rate of 5.25% each for $250 000.

Assume that desired reserves are 8%.

a. What does the bank balance sheet look like? Ignore any loan loss reserves.

b. How well-capitalized is the bank?

c. Calculate the risk-weighted assets and risk-weighted capital ratio after Oldhat's first day.

24. Early the next day the bank invests $50 million of its excess reserves in commercial loans. Later that day, terrible news hits the mortgage markets, and mortgage rates jump to 13%, implying a present value of its current mortgage holdings of $124 798 per mortgage. Bank regulators force Oldhat to sell its mortgages to recognize the fair market value. What does Oldhat's balance sheet look like? How do these events affect its capital position?

25. In order to avoid insolvency, regulators decide to provide the bank with $25 million in bank capital. However, the bad news about the mortgages is featured in the local newspaper, causing a bank run. As a result, $30 million in deposits is withdrawn. Show the effects of the capital injection and bank run on the balance sheet. Was the capital injection enough to stabilize the bank? If the bank regulators decide that the bank needs a capital ratio of 10% to prevent further runs on the bank, how much of an additional capital injection would be required to reach a 10% capital ratio?

WEB EXERCISES

1. Go to **www.cdic.ca** and click on "International Work." Write an essay summarizing how globalization and international financial integration affect Canada's financial sector safety net.

2. Go to **www.fdic.gov/regulations/laws/important/**. This site reports on the most significant pieces of legislation affecting U.S. banks since the 1800s. Summarize the most recently enacted bank regulation listed on this site.

CHAPTER 11

Banking Industry: Structure and Competition

LEARNING OBJECTIVES

After studying this chapter you should be able to

1. chronicle the historical development of the Canadian banking industry and its current structure

2. describe the globalization of banking, the international activities of Canadian banks, and the role of foreign banks in Canada

3. differentiate between chartered banks and near banks (i.e., trust and loan companies and credit unions and *caisses populaires*)

4. assess why financial-sector legislation is expected to lead to larger and increasingly complex financial groups engaging in a full gamut of financial activities

PREVIEW

The operations of individual banks (how they acquire, use, and manage funds to make a profit) are roughly similar throughout the world. In all countries, banks are financial intermediaries in the business of earning profits. When you consider the structure and operation of the banking industry as a whole, however, Canada is in a class by itself, with a comparatively concentrated banking industry and small financial institutions. Unlike the United States, where there are over 7000 commercial banks, over 1200 savings and loan associations, 400 mutual savings banks, and over 8000 credit unions, Canada has six large commercial banks, commonly called chartered banks, that typically dominate the banking industry.[1]

Is fewer better? Does it mean that the Canadian banking system is more stable and competitive and therefore more economically efficient and sound than banking systems in other countries? What in the Canadian economic and political system explains this small number of banking institutions? In this chapter we try to answer these questions by examining the historical trends in the banking industry and its overall structure.

We start by examining the historical development of the banking system and how financial innovation has increased the competitive environment for the banking industry and is causing fundamental changes in it. We then go on to look at the chartered banking industry in detail and then discuss the near-banking industry, which includes trust and loan companies and credit unions and *caisses populaires*. We spend more time on chartered banks because they are by far the largest depository institutions, accounting for over two-thirds of the deposits in the banking system. In

---

[1]Commercial banks in Canada are called chartered banks because they can be established only by charter granted either in a special act of the federal Parliament or by the minister of finance.

addition to looking at our domestic banking system, we also examine forces behind the growth in international banking to see how it has affected us in Canada.

Historical Development of the Canadian Banking System

The modern Canadian banking industry began with the creation of the Bank of Montreal in 1817 by nine merchants in Montreal. Initially, the Bank of Montreal was without statutory authority, but a charter was approved by the legislature of Lower Canada and confirmed by royal assent in 1822. Meanwhile, other banks opened for business, and the Canadian banking industry was off and running; the Bank of New Brunswick received royal assent in 1820 and the Chartered Bank of Upper Canada in York (Toronto) in 1821. (As a study aid, Figure 11-1 provides a timeline of the most important dates in the history of Canadian commercial banking before World War II.)

All these banks were authorized to issue notes (redeemable in specie, essentially British or American gold or silver coins, on demand), receive deposits, and lend for commercial purposes only; no bank was allowed to lend funds on mortgages, land, or real property. There were, however, some differences between the charters of these banks. For example, the terms of the charter of the Bank of New Brunswick followed the banking tradition of New England. The charter of the Bank of Montreal almost duplicated the terms governing the First Bank of the United States (see the FYI box The Dual Banking System in the United States), which had elements of both a private and a **central bank**, a government institution

FIGURE 11-1   Timeline of the Early History of Commercial Banking in Canada

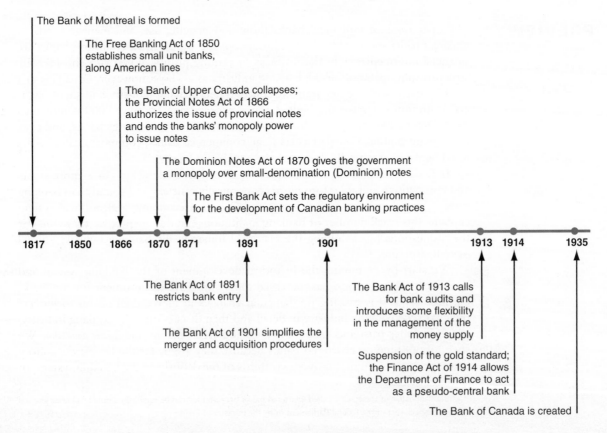

that has responsibility for the amount of money and credit supplied in the economy as a whole. Also, the Bank of New Brunswick had to submit regular annual statements to the government and was not allowed to open **branches** (additional offices for the conduct of banking operations), whereas the Bank of Montreal had to provide statements only on request and was allowed to open branches in any part of Upper or Lower Canada.

The Free Banking Experiment

Until 1850, no national currency existed in Canada, and banks obtained funds primarily by issuing *banknotes* (currency circulated by the banks that could be redeemed for gold). No banks failed, but because banking regulations were extremely lax, banks regularly experienced substantial declines in bank capital due to business failures; their banknotes tended to become scarce. The government tried various schemes to guarantee the provision of stable money, including the issuing of its own notes, but it was significantly influenced by the concept of **free banking**, implemented in New York in 1837. This system, as the name suggests, permitted the organization of a bank by any group that met certain established criteria concerning the amount of equity capital and maintenance of reserves.

The Free Banking Act was passed in Canada in 1850, with the purpose of facilitating the entry of small unit banks along American lines. It allowed the establishment of a bank, without a legislative charter, by any group that met the lax requirements set out in the free banking legislation. Under this legislation, the minimum amount of net worth to organize a bank was $100 000, branching was not allowed, and although the banknotes of the free banks were untaxed, the amount of note issue was limited to the amount of government debt held by the banks. The move to free banking was a step in the right direction, but Canada's experience with free banking was a failure. It did not lead to the establishment of a large number of new banks;

FYI

The Dual Banking System in the United States

The modern commercial banking industry in the United States began when the Bank of North America was chartered in Philadelphia in 1782. A major controversy involving the U.S. banking industry in its early years was whether the federal government or the states should charter banks. The Federalists, particularly Alexander Hamilton, advocated greater centralized control of banking and federal chartering of banks. Their efforts led to the creation in 1791 of the First Bank of the United States.

Until 1863, all commercial banks in the United States were chartered by the banking commission of the state in which each operated. No national currency existed, and banks obtained funds primarily by issuing banknotes (currency circulated by the banks that could be redeemed for gold).

Because banking regulations were extremely lax in many states, banks regularly failed due to fraud or lack of sufficient bank capital; their banknotes became worthless. To eliminate the abuses of the state-chartered banks (called **state banks**), the National Bank Act of 1863 (and subsequent amendments to it) created a new banking system of federally chartered banks (called **national banks**). This legislation was originally intended to dry up sources of funds to state banks by imposing a prohibitive tax on their banknotes while leaving the banknotes of the federally chartered banks untaxed. The state banks cleverly escaped extinction by acquiring funds through deposits.

As a result, today the United States has a **dual banking system** in which banks supervised by the federal government and banks supervised by the states operate side by side.

only five new banks were established, two of which soon failed, and the other three converted to legislative charters.

The restriction on branching and the issue of banknotes based on government debt, rather than on commercial loans, were blamed for the failure of Canada's free banking experiment. The most important factor, however, was the fact that the option of a legislative charter was still available, unlike the situation in the United States, where the provision of a legislative charter was simultaneously abolished in those states where free banking was established. In Canada, free banking, with its restrictive provisions, particularly the restriction on branches and the less liberal provision for note issue, proved to be less profitable than banking under legislative charters.

In 1850, there were 15 chartered banks in Canada: eight in Central Canada and seven in what was to become Atlantic Canada. From 1850 until Confederation in 1867, and except for a short period after 1857, the Canadian provinces experienced an economic expansion and thirty new banks were established. However, 11 of these failed or closed their doors for other reasons, leaving 34 chartered banks with a total of 127 branches at the end of 1867.

The Provincial Notes Act, 1866

In the years before Confederation, governments were anxious about the chartered banks' control of the note issue. They believed that the best way to protect the public from some of the consequences of bank failures would be to separate the currency of the country from the banking interests. In 1860, Alexander Galt, finance minister of the Province of Canada, proposed the substitution of a government-issued paper currency for banknotes. His proposal, however, was defeated by his critics, especially the chartered banks, for obvious reasons: the substitution of interest-free government debt for interest-free bank debt would have directly reduced their profits.

In the midst of a minor financial crisis in 1866, with the collapse of the Bank of Upper Canada (Canada's first chartered bank failure), the proponents of government-issued paper money finally achieved their objective with the enactment of the Provincial Notes Act. The Act authorized the issue of provincial notes, which, because of their legal reserve status, could be substituted for specie. With the cooperation of the Bank of Montreal, which had become the government's fiscal agent in 1864 by replacing the Bank of Upper Canada, the banks began to hold the new currency, thereby surrendering their power to issue notes.

The Dominion Notes Act, 1870

Canada was created by the Constitution (formerly the British North America Act) in 1867. The Act granted the new federal government of Canada exclusive jurisdiction over all matters pertaining to currency and banking, and the first problem to be tackled was the issue of paper money. With the failure in 1867 of the Chartered Bank of Canada (the second chartered bank failure in Canadian history), the Dominion Notes Act was passed in 1870. The Act confirmed the rights of banks to issue banknotes on their own credit, but restricted to large-denomination (over $5) notes, thereby giving the government a monopoly over small-denomination ($1 and $2) notes, the Dominion notes.

Although the Dominion Notes Act of 1870 did not set any reserve requirements, it required banks to hold at least half of their reserves in Dominion notes, thereby giving the government a share of the profits from the issuance of money, which is called **seigniorage**. The Dominion notes themselves were fractionally backed by gold, and in this sense the Dominion Notes Act of 1870 confirmed that Canada would operate under the **gold standard**, meaning that its currency was convertible directly into gold.

Canada operated under the gold standard, keeping its currency backed by and convertible into gold, until World War I. During the years 1870–1935, Dominion notes increased in importance, but they never accounted for a major fraction of currency in circulation. They were superseded, together with the banknotes, by Bank of Canada notes, soon after the creation of the Bank of Canada (Canada's central bank) in 1935.

The First Bank Act, 1871

The first Bank Act came into effect in 1871. It was to be revised every 10 years, in light of experience and changing conditions; this "sunset" clause effectively ensured that governments over the years paid periodic attention to banking reform. The Bank Act set the regulatory environment for Canadian chartered banks and for the future development of Canadian banking practices.

The Act continued the legislative chartering of banks, with each charter running for a 10-year period, then to be reviewed and renewed. New banks had to meet minimum capital requirements: $100 000 paid up before they opened for business against a total of $500 000. The banks' note issue continued to be restricted to large-denomination (over $5) notes and limited to the amount of their paid-up capital plus reserves. There were no reserve requirements, but one-third of a bank's cash reserves were required to be in the form of Dominion notes.

The Act continued the prohibition against mortgage lending and real estate loans, but it reinforced the commercial nature of banking by allowing banks to make loans on the security of most kinds of merchandise. Also, for the greater security of the public, bank shareholders were liable for double the amount of their subscription. Finally, each bank was required to submit a detailed statement to the government on a monthly basis, but there was no provision for government inspection or audit.

The Bank Act, 1881–1913

A depression followed Confederation and lasted from 1873 to 1879. During the depression years, the banks were hard hit and 13 bank failures (four in 1878, five in 1887, and another four in 1890) wiped out the savings of many noteholders. To prevent future losses from such failures, the early decennial revisions of the Bank Act, in 1881, 1891, 1901, and 1913 (postponed since 1911), were intended to provide better protection for the holders of banknotes, but the Act was not substantially changed.

In particular, in the Bank Act revision of 1891, the capital requirement was increased to $250 000 paid up, thereby restricting entry into the industry. The proportion of Dominion notes in bank cash reserves was increased to 40%, and the notes of a failed bank were made a first charge against its assets in the event of liquidation. Moreover, in the Bank Act revision of 1891, a Bank Circulation Redemption Fund was created, each bank contributing an amount equal to 5% of its average note circulation, to insure noteholders against loss.

In the years between mid-1890 and the outbreak of World War I, the Canadian economy experienced a phenomenal economic expansion. While bank entry was restrained (due to the increase in capital requirements in the Bank Act of 1891), the Bank Act revision of 1901 simplified the merger and acquisition procedures by requiring only approval of Cabinet; previously, a special Act of Parliament was required for all mergers. As a result of these legislative changes, 13 mergers took place before the end of 1914, relative to only six in the previous 33-year period, and the number of banks declined from 41 in 1890 to 22 in 1914. Over the same period, however, the number of bank branches increased from 426 to over 3000.

Another important legislative change occurred in the 1913 revision of the Bank Act. The Act called for a *bank audit*: annual, independent verification of the financial statements of the banks, with the results distributed to the shareholders and the minister of finance. The objective was to limit adverse selection and moral hazard problems that had increased over the years and been found to be the cause of a number of bank failures, particularly the failure of the Farmers Bank in 1910.

An additional noteworthy change was the excess circulation provision that introduced some flexibility in the management of the money supply. The economic expansion in the period after mid-1890 caused banknote issues to reach the ceiling that the Bank Act of 1871 had fixed at the amount of paid-up capital plus reserves. The banks did not increase their capital (and thus their note-issuing capacity), producing a shortage of currency. In order to achieve expansion in the money supply with the growth of economic activity, the Bank Act of 1913 allowed for the issuing of banknotes in excess of a bank's paid-up capital plus reserves.

The Finance Act, 1914

At the end of July 1914, less than a year after the revision of the Bank Act in 1913, World War I looked more and more inescapable. Canada's established banking legislation appeared to be inadequate and the immediate problem was to preserve the stability and liquidity of the financial system. Panic had taken hold, with depositors converting their money into gold for hoarding, and the banks and the government being concerned about their ability to convert money into gold on demand, since their gold reserves were a small fraction of their combined monetary liabilities. In light of these developments, on August 3, 1914, the government suspended the convertibility of Dominion notes and banknotes into gold, thereby ending the gold standard that had emerged over 40 years earlier in 1870. The gold standard was re-established in 1926 and suspended again in 1929, when the Great Depression hit the world.

A major legislative change, following the suspension of the gold standard, was the Finance Act of 1914. Patterned on the episode of 1907, during which banks could obtain cash reserves from the Department of Finance to prevent bank runs (which were triggered by bank failures in the United States), the Finance Act allowed the Department of Finance to act as a **lender of last resort**, that is, to provide Dominion notes to banks (on the pledge of approved securities) when no one else would, thereby preventing bank and financial panics. The Finance Act foreshadowed the increased flexibility in the management of the money supply that was provided by the Bank of Canada in 1935. We will examine in detail the economic forces that led to the creation of the Bank of Canada in Chapter 15.

Financial Innovation and the Growth of the "Shadow Banking System"

Although banking institutions are still the most important financial institutions in the Canadian economy, in recent years the traditional banking business of making loans that are funded by deposits has been in decline. Some of this business has been replaced by the **shadow banking system**, in which bank lending has been replaced by lending via the securities markets.

To understand how the banking industry has evolved over time, we must first understand the process of financial innovation, which has transformed the entire financial system. Like other industries, the financial industry is in business to earn profits by selling its products. If a soap company perceives that there is a need in the marketplace for a laundry detergent with fabric softener, it develops a product to fit the need. Similarly, to maximize their profits, financial institutions develop new products to satisfy their own needs as well as those of their customers; in other words, innovation—which can be extremely beneficial to the economy—is driven by the desire to get (or stay) rich. This view of the innovation process leads to the following simple analysis: *a change in the financial environment will stimulate a search by financial institutions for innovations that are likely to be profitable*.

Starting in the 1960s, individuals and financial institutions operating in financial markets were confronted with drastic changes in the economic environment: inflation and interest rates climbed sharply and became harder to predict, a situation that changed demand conditions in financial markets. The rapid advance in computer technology changed supply conditions. In addition, financial regulations became more burdensome. Financial institutions found that many of the old ways of doing business were no longer profitable; the financial services and products they had been offering to the public were not selling. Many financial intermediaries found that they were no longer able to acquire funds with their traditional financial instruments, and without these funds they would soon be out of business. To survive in the new economic environment, financial institutions had to research and develop new products and services that would meet customer needs and prove profitable, a process referred to as **financial engineering**. In their case, necessity was the mother of innovation.

Our discussion of why financial innovation occurs suggests that there are three basic types of financial innovation: responses to changes in demand conditions, responses to changes in supply conditions, and avoidance of regulations. These three motivations often interact in producing particular financial innovations. Now that we have a framework for understanding why financial institutions produce innovations, let's look at examples of how financial institutions in their search for profits have produced financial innovations of the three basic types.

Responses to Changes in Demand Conditions: Interest-Rate Volatility

The most significant change in the economic environment that altered the demand for financial products in recent years has been the dramatic increase in the volatility of interest rates. In the 1950s, the interest rate on three-month Treasury bills fluctuated between 1.0% and 5.5%; in the 1970s, it fluctuated between 3% and 14%; in the 1980s, it ranged from 7% to over 20%. Large fluctuations in interest rates lead to substantial capital gains or losses and greater uncertainty about returns on investments. Recall that the risk that is related to the uncertainty about interest-rate movements and returns is called *interest-rate risk,* and high volatility of interest rates, such as we saw in the 1970s and 1980s, leads to a higher level of interest-rate risk.

We would expect the increase in interest-rate risk to increase the demand for financial products and services that could reduce that risk. This change in the economic environment would thus stimulate a search for profitable innovations by financial institutions that meet this new demand and would spur the creation of new financial instruments that help lower interest-rate risk. Two examples of financial innovations that appeared in the 1970s confirm this prediction: the development of adjustable-rate mortgages and financial derivatives.

ADJUSTABLE-RATE MORTGAGES   Like other investors, financial institutions find that lending is more attractive if interest-rate risk is lower. They would not want to make a mortgage loan at a 10% interest rate and two months later find that they could obtain 12% in interest on the same mortgage. To reduce interest-rate risk, financial institutions began to issue adjustable-rate mortgages, that is, mortgage loans on which the interest rate changes when a market interest rate (usually the Treasury bill rate) changes. Initially, an adjustable-rate mortgage might have a 5% interest rate. In six months, this interest rate might increase or decrease by the amount of the increase or decrease in, say, the six-month Treasury bill rate, and the mortgage payment would change. Because adjustable-rate mortgages allow mortgage-issuing institutions to earn higher interest rates on mortgages when market rates rise, profits are kept higher during these periods.

This attractive feature of adjustable-rate mortgages has encouraged mortgage-issuing institutions to issue adjustable-rate mortgages with lower initial interest rates than on conventional fixed-rate mortgages, making them popular with many households. However, because the mortgage payment on an adjustable-rate mortgage can increase, many households continue to prefer fixed-rate mortgages. Hence, both types of mortgages are widespread.

FINANCIAL DERIVATIVES   Given the greater demand for the reduction of interest-rate risk, commodity exchanges such as the Chicago Board of Trade recognized that if they could develop a product that would help investors and financial institutions to protect themselves from, or to **hedge**, interest-rate risk, then they could make profits by selling this new instrument. **Futures contracts**, in which the seller agrees to provide a certain standardized commodity to the buyer on a specific future date at an agreed-on price, had been around for a long time. Officials at the Chicago Board of Trade realized that if they created futures contracts in financial instruments, which are called **financial derivatives** because their payoffs are linked to (i.e., derived from) previously issued securities, they could be used to hedge risk. Thus, in 1975, financial derivatives were born.

Responses to Changes in Supply Conditions: Information Technology

The most important source of the changes in supply conditions that stimulate financial innovation has been the improvement in computer and telecommunications technology. This technology, called *information technology,* has had two effects. First, it has lowered the cost of processing financial transactions, making it profitable for financial institutions to create new financial products and services for the public. Second, it has made it easier for investors to acquire information, thereby making it easier for firms to issue securities. The rapid developments in information technology have resulted in many new financial products and services that we examine here.

BANK CREDIT AND DEBIT CARDS   Credit cards have been around since well before World War II. Many individual stores (such as, for example, Sears and the Bay) institutionalized charge accounts by providing customers with credit cards that allowed them to make purchases at these stores without cash. Nationwide credit cards were not established until after World War II, when Diners Club developed one to be used in restaurants. Similar credit card programs were started by American Express and Carte Blanche, but because of the high cost of operating these programs, cards were issued only to selected persons and businesses that could afford expensive purchases.

A firm issuing credit cards earns income from loans it makes to credit card holders and from payments made by stores on credit card purchases (a percentage of the purchase price, say, 5%). A credit card program's costs arise from loan defaults, stolen cards, and the expense involved in processing credit card transactions.

Seeing the success of Diners Club, American Express, and Carte Blanche, bankers wanted to share in the profitable credit card business. Several chartered banks attempted to expand the credit card business to a wider market in the 1950s, but the cost per transaction of running these programs was so high that their early attempts failed.

In the late 1960s, improved computer technology lowered the transaction costs for providing credit card services and made the bank credit card programs more profitable. The banks tried to enter this business again, and this time their efforts led to the creation of two successful bank credit card programs: Visa and MasterCard. These programs have become phenomenally successful. Indeed, bank credit cards have been so profitable that nonfinancial institutions such as Sears (which launched the Discover card), General Motors, and Walmart have also entered the credit card business. Consumers have benefited because credit cards are more widely accepted than cheques to pay for purchases (particularly abroad), and they allow consumers to take out loans more easily.

The success of bank credit cards led these institutions to come up with a new financial innovation, *debit cards*. Debit cards often look just like credit cards and can be used to make purchases in an identical fashion. However, in contrast to credit cards, which extend the purchaser a loan that does not have to be paid off immediately, a debit card purchase is immediately deducted from the card holder's bank account. Debit cards depend even more on low costs of processing transactions, because their profits are generated entirely from the fees paid by merchants on debit card purchases at their stores. Debit cards have grown increasingly popular in recent years.

ELECTRONIC BANKING   The wonders of modern computer technology have also enabled banks to lower the cost of bank transactions by having customers interact with electronic banking (e-banking) facility rather than with a human being. One important form of an e-banking facility is the **automated teller machine (ATM)**, an electronic machine that allows customers to get cash, make deposits, transfer funds from one account to another, and check balances. The ATM has the advantage that it does not have to be paid overtime and never sleeps, thus being available for use 24 hours a day. Not only does this result in cheaper transactions for the bank, it also provides more convenience for the customer. Because of their low cost, ATMs can be put at locations other than a bank or its branches, further increasing customer convenience. The low cost of ATMs has meant that they have sprung up everywhere. Furthermore, it is now as easy to get foreign currency from an ATM when you are travelling in Europe as it is to get cash from your local bank.

With the drop in the cost of telecommunications, banks developed another financial innovation, *home banking*. It is now cost-effective for banks to set up an electronic banking facility in which the bank's customer is linked up with the bank's computer to carry out transactions by using either a telephone or a personal computer. Now a bank's customers can conduct many of their bank transactions without ever leaving the comfort of home. The advantage for the customer is the convenience of home banking, while banks find that the cost of transactions is substantially less than having the customer come to the bank.

With the decline in the price of personal computers and their increasing presence in the home, we have seen a further innovation in the home banking area, the appearance of a new type of banking institution, the **virtual bank**, a bank that has no physical location but rather exists only in cyberspace. In 1995, Security First Network Bank, based in Atlanta but now owned by Royal Bank of Canada, became the first virtual bank, offering an array of banking services on the Internet—accepting chequing account and savings deposits, selling certificates of deposit, issuing ATM cards, providing bill-paying facilities, and so on. The virtual bank thus takes home banking one step further, enabling the customer to have a full set of banking services at home 24 hours a day. In 1996, Bank of America and Wells Fargo entered the virtual banking market, to be followed by many others, with Bank of America now being the largest Internet bank in the United States. Will virtual banking be the predominant form of banking in the future (see the Global box Will "Clicks" Dominate "Bricks" in the Banking Industry?)?

JUNK BONDS   Before the advent of computers and advanced telecommunications, it was difficult to acquire information about the financial situation of firms that might want to sell securities. Because of the difficulty in screening out bad from good credit risks, the only firms that were able to sell bonds were very well-established corporations that had high credit ratings.[2] Before the 1980s, then, only corporations that could issue bonds with ratings of BBB or above could raise funds by selling newly issued bonds. Some firms that had fallen on bad times, so-called *fallen angels*, had previously issued long-term corporate bonds that now had ratings that had fallen below BBB, bonds that were pejoratively dubbed "junk bonds."

With the improvement in information technology in the 1970s, it became easier for investors to acquire financial information about corporations, making it easier to screen out bad from good credit risks. With easier screening, investors were more willing to buy long-term debt securities from less well-known corporations with lower credit ratings. With this change in supply conditions, we would expect that some smart individual would pioneer the concept of selling new public issues of junk bonds, not for fallen angels but for companies that had not yet achieved investment-grade status. This is exactly what Michael Milken of Drexel Burnham Lambert, an investment-banking firm, started to do in 1977. Junk bonds became an important factor in the corporate bond market. Although there was a sharp slowdown in activity in the junk bond market after Milken was indicted for securities law violations in 1989, it heated up again in the 1990s and 2000s.

COMMERCIAL PAPER MARKET   Recall that *commercial paper* is a short-term debt security issued by large banks and corporations. The commercial paper market has undergone tremendous growth since 1970, with commercial paper being one of the fastest-growing money market instruments.

GLOBAL

Will "Clicks" Dominate "Bricks" in the Banking Industry?

With the advent of virtual banks ("clicks") and the convenience they provide, a key question is whether they will become the primary form in which banks do their business, eliminating the need for physical bank branches ("bricks") as the main delivery mechanism for banking services. Indeed, will stand-alone Internet banks be the wave of the future?

The answer seems to be no. Internet-only banks have had disappointing revenue growth and profits. The result is that pure online banking has not been the success that proponents had hoped for. Why has Internet banking been a disappointment?

There are several strikes against Internet banking. First, bank depositors want to know that their savings are secure, so are reluctant to put their money into new institutions without a long track record. Second, customers worry about the security of their online transactions and whether their transactions will truly be kept private. Traditional banks are viewed as being more secure and trustworthy in terms of releasing private information. Third, customers may prefer services provided by physical branches. For example, banking customers seem to prefer to purchase long-term savings products face to face. Fourth, Internet banking still has run into technical problems—server crashes, slow connections over phone lines, mistakes in conducting transactions—that will probably diminish over time as technology improves.

The wave of the future thus does not appear to be pure Internet banks. Instead it looks like "clicks and bricks" will be the predominant form of banking, in which online banking is used to complement the services provided by traditional banks. Nonetheless, the delivery of banking services is undergoing massive changes, with more and more banking services delivered over the Internet and the number of physical bank branches likely to decline in the future.

---

[2]The discussion of adverse selection problems in Chapter 8 provides a more detailed analysis of why only well-established firms with high credit ratings were able to sell securities.

CHAPTER 11 *Banking Industry: Structure and Competition* **247**

Improvements in information technology also help provide an explanation for the rapid rise of the commercial paper market. We have seen that the improvement in information technology made it easier for investors to screen out bad from good credit risks, thus making it easier for corporations to issue debt securities. Not only did this make it easier for corporations to issue long-term debt securities as in the junk bond market, but it also meant that they could raise funds by issuing short-term debt securities such as commercial paper more easily. Many corporations that used to do their short-term borrowing from banks now frequently raise short-term funds in the commercial paper market instead.

The development of money market mutual funds has been another factor in the rapid growth in the commercial paper market. Because money market mutual funds need to hold liquid, high-quality, short-term assets such as commercial paper, the growth of assets in these funds has created a ready market in commercial paper. The growth of pension and other large funds that invest in commercial paper has also stimulated the growth of this market.

SECURITIZATION An important example of a financial innovation arising from improvements in both transaction and information technology is securitization, one of the most important financial innovations in the past two decades, which played an especially prominent role in the development of the subprime mortgage market in the mid-2000s. **Securitization** is the process of transforming otherwise illiquid financial assets (such as residential mortgages, auto loans, and credit card receivables), which have typically been the bread and butter of banking institutions, into marketable capital market securities. As we have seen, improvements in the ability to acquire information have made it easier to sell marketable capital market securities. In addition, with low transaction costs because of improvements in computer technology, financial institutions find that they can cheaply bundle together a portfolio of loans (such as mortgages) with varying small denominations (often less than $100 000), collect the interest and principal payments on the mortgages in the bundle, and then "pass them through" (pay them out) to third parties. By dividing the portfolio of loans into standardized amounts, the financial institution can then sell the claims to these interest and principal payments to third parties as securities. The standardized amounts of these securitized loans make them liquid securities, and the fact that they are made up of a bundle of loans helps diversify risk, making them desirable. The financial institution selling the securitized loans makes a profit by servicing the loans (collecting the interest and principal payments and paying them out) and charging a fee to the third party for this service.

Avoidance of Existing Regulations

The process of financial innovation we have discussed so far is much like innovation in other areas of the economy: it occurs in response to changes in demand and supply conditions. However, because the financial industry is more heavily regulated than other industries, government regulation is a much greater spur to innovation in this industry. Government regulation leads to financial innovation by creating incentives for firms to skirt regulations that restrict their ability to earn profits. Edward Kane, an economist at Boston College, describes this process of avoiding regulations as "loophole mining." The economic analysis of innovation suggests that when the economic environment changes such that regulatory constraints are so burdensome that large profits can be made by avoiding them, loophole mining and innovation are more likely to occur.

Two sets of regulations have seriously restricted the ability of banks (especially in the United States) to make profits: reserve requirements that force banks to keep a certain fraction of their deposits as reserves (deposits in the Federal Reserve System) and restrictions on the interest rates that can be paid on deposits. For the following reasons, these regulations have been major forces behind financial innovation.

1. *Reserve requirements.* Although in Canada reserve requirements were phased out in the Bank of Canada Act in 1992, banks in the United States are still subject to reserve requirements. The key to understanding why reserve requirements led to financial innovation is to recognize that they act, in effect, as a tax on deposits. Because up until 2008 the Fed did not pay interest on reserves, the opportunity cost of holding them was the interest that a bank could otherwise have earned by lending the reserves out. For each dollar of deposits, reserve requirements therefore imposed a cost on the bank equal to the interest rate, i, that could be earned if the reserves could be lent out, times the fraction of deposits required as reserves, r_r. The cost of $i \times r_r$ imposed on the bank was just like a tax on bank deposits of $i \times r_r$ per dollar of deposits.

   It is a great tradition to avoid taxes if possible, and banks also play this game. Just as taxpayers look for loopholes to lower their tax bills, banks seek to increase their profits by mining loopholes and by producing financial innovations that allow them to escape the tax on deposits imposed by reserve requirements.

2. *Restrictions on interest paid on deposits.* Canadian banks have never been subject to deposit rate ceilings. In the United States, however, until 1980, legislation prohibited banks in most states from paying interest on chequing account deposits, and through **Regulation Q**, the Fed set maximum limits on the interest rate that could be paid on time deposits. To this day, banks in the United States are not allowed to pay interest on corporate chequing accounts. The desire to avoid these **deposit rate ceilings** also led to financial innovations.

   If market interest rates rose above the maximum rates that banks paid on time deposits under Regulation Q, depositors withdrew funds from banks to put them into higher-yielding securities. This loss of deposits from the banking system restricted the amount of funds that banks could lend (called **disintermediation**) and thus limited bank profits. Banks had an incentive to get around deposit rate ceilings because by so doing, they could acquire more funds to make loans and earn higher profits.

We can now look at how the desire to avoid restrictions on interest payments and the tax effect of reserve requirements in the United States led to two important financial innovations.

MONEY MARKET MUTUAL FUNDS   Money market mutual funds issue shares that are redeemable at a fixed price (usually $1). For example, if you buy 5000 shares for $5000, the money market fund uses these funds to invest in short-term money market securities (Treasury bills, certificates of deposit, commercial paper) that provide you with interest payments. Although money market fund shares effectively function as deposits that earn interest, they are not legally deposits and so are not insured by the CDIC.

In the United States, money market mutual funds also offer chequing privileges, effectively functioning as chequing account deposits that earn interest. For this reason, money market mutual funds in that country have experienced extraordinary growth since 1970, when they first appeared. Currently, their assets are around US$3 trillion. As consumers shift to mutual funds, deposit-taking financial institutions (throughout the world) risk losing a low-cost source of funds.

The first money market mutual fund was created by two Wall Street mavericks, Bruce Bent and Henry Brown, in 1970. In a supreme irony, risky investments by a money market mutual fund founded by Bruce Brent almost brought down the money market mutual fund industry during the subprime financial crisis in 2008 (see the FYI box Bruce Bent and the Money Market Mutual Fund Panic of 2008).

SWEEP ACCOUNTS Another innovation that enables banks in the United States to avoid the "tax" from reserve requirements is the **sweep account**. In this arrangement, any balances above a certain amount in a corporation's chequing account at the end of a business day are "swept out" of the account and invested in overnight securities that pay interest. Because the "swept out" funds are no longer classified as chequable deposits, they are not subject to reserve requirements and thus are not "taxed." They also have the advantage that they allow banks in effect to pay interest on these chequing accounts, which otherwise is not allowed under existing regulations. Because sweep accounts have become so popular, they have lowered the amount of required reserves to the degree that most banking institutions do not find reserve requirements binding: in other words, they voluntarily hold more reserves than they are required to.

The financial innovations of sweep accounts and money market mutual funds are particularly interesting because they were stimulated not only by the desire to avoid a costly regulation, but also by a change in supply conditions—in this case, information technology. Without low-cost computers to process inexpensively the additional transactions required by these innovations, they would not have been profitable and therefore would not have been developed. Technological factors often combine with other incentives, such as the desire to get around a regulation, to produce innovation.

FYI

Bruce Bent and the Money Market Mutual Fund Panic of 2008

Bruce Bent, one of the originators of money market mutual funds, almost brought down the industry during the subprime financial crisis in the fall of 2008. Mr. Bent told his shareholders in a letter written in July 2008 that the fund was managed on a basis of "unwavering discipline focused on protecting your principal." He also wrote the U.S. Securities and Exchange Commission in September 2007, "When I first created the money market fund back in 1970, it was designed with the tenets of safety and liquidity." He added that these principles had "fallen to the wayside as portfolio managers chased the highest yield and compromised the integrity of the money fund." Alas, Bent did not follow his own advice, and his fund, the Reserve Primary Fund, bought risky assets so that its yield was higher than the industry average.

When Lehman Brothers went into bankruptcy on September 15, 2008, the Reserve Primary Fund, with assets of over $60 billion, was caught holding the bag on $785 million of Lehman's debt, which then had to be marked down to zero. The resulting losses meant that on September 16, Bent's fund could no longer afford to redeem its shares at the par value of $1, a situation known as "breaking the buck." Bent's shareholders began to pull their money out of the fund, causing it to lose 90% of its assets.

The fear that this could happen to other money market mutual funds led to a classic panic in which shareholders began to withdraw their funds at an alarming rate. The whole money market mutual fund industry looked like it could come crashing down. To prevent this, the Federal Reserve and the U.S. Treasury rode to the rescue on September 19, 2008. The Fed set up a facility to make loans to purchase commercial paper from money market mutual funds so they could meet the demands for redemptions from their investors. The U.S. Treasury then put in a temporary guarantee for all money market mutual fund redemptions and the panic subsided.

Not surprisingly, given the extension of a government safety net to the money market mutual fund industry, there are calls to regulate this industry more heavily. The money market mutual fund industry will never be the same.

Financial Innovation and the Decline of Traditional Banking

The traditional financial intermediation role of banking has been to make long-term loans and fund them by issuing short-term deposits, a process of asset transformation commonly referred to as "borrowing short and lending long." Here we examine how financial innovations have created a more competitive environment for the banking industry, causing the industry to change dramatically, with its traditional banking business going into decline.

To understand why traditional banking business has declined in size, we need to look at how the financial innovations described earlier have caused banks to suffer declines in their cost advantages in acquiring funds—that is, on the liabilities side of their balance sheet—while at the same time they have lost income advantages on the assets side of their balance sheet. The simultaneous decline of cost and income advantages has resulted in reduced profitability of traditional banking and an effort by banks to leave this business and engage in new and more profitable activities.

DECLINE IN COST ADVANTAGES IN ACQUIRING FUNDS (LIABILITIES)   Until 1980, banks were paying low interest rates on chequable deposits. This worked to the banks' advantage because their major source of funds was chequable deposits. Unfortunately, this cost advantage for banks did not last. The rise in inflation from the late 1960s on led to higher interest rates, which made investors more sensitive to yield differentials on different assets. The result was the *disintermediation* process, in which people began to take their money out of banks, with their low interest rates on both chequable and time deposits, and began to seek out higher-yielding investments. Also, as we have seen, at the same time, financial innovation led to money market mutual funds, which put the banks at an even further disadvantage because depositors could now obtain chequing-account-like services while earning high interest on their money market mutual fund accounts. One manifestation of these changes in the financial system was that the low-cost source of funds, chequable deposits, declined dramatically in importance for banks.

DECLINE IN INCOME ADVANTAGES ON USES OF FUNDS (ASSETS)   Banks have also been hit by a decline in income advantages on the assets side from the financial innovations we discussed earlier—junk bonds, securitization, and the rise of the commercial paper market. The resulting loss of income advantages for banks relative to these innovations has resulted in a loss of market share and has led to the growth of the shadow banking system, which has made use of these innovations to enable borrowers to bypass the traditional banking system.

We have seen that improvements in information technology have made it easier for firms to issue securities directly to the public. This has meant that instead of going to banks to finance short-term credit needs, many of the banks' best business customers now find it cheaper to go instead to the commercial paper market for funds.

The emergence of the junk bond market has eaten into banks' loan business. Improvements in information technology have made it easier for corporations to sell their bonds to the public directly, thereby bypassing banks. Although well-established companies started taking this route in the 1970s, now lower-quality corporate borrowers are using banks less often because they have access to the junk bond market.

We have also seen that improvements in computer technology have led to securitization, whereby illiquid financial assets such as bank loans and mortgages are transformed into marketable securities. Computers enable other financial institutions to originate loans because they can now accurately evaluate credit risk with statistical methods, while computers have lowered transaction costs, making it possible to bundle these loans and sell them as securities. When default risk can be easily evaluated with computers, banks no longer have an advantage in making loans. Without their former advantages, banks have lost loan business to other financial institutions even though the banks themselves are involved in the process of securitization.

BANKS' RESPONSES   Canadian banks have sought to maintain former profit levels by pursuing new off-balance-sheet activities that are more profitable. They have, in effect, embraced the shadow banking system. This strategy, however, has generated concerns about what are proper activities for banks. Nontraditional bank activities can be riskier, and therefore result in excessive risk taking by banks. Indeed, they led to a substantial weakening of bank balance sheets during the subprime financial crisis, as was discussed in Chapter 9.

The decline of banks' traditional business has thus meant that the banking industry has been driven to seek out new lines of business. This could be beneficial because by so doing, banks can keep vibrant and healthy. Indeed, bank profitability was high up until 2007, and nontraditional, off-balance-sheet activities played an important role in the high bank profits. However, the new directions in banking have led to increased risk taking, and thus the decline in traditional banking has required regulators to be more vigilant. It also poses new challenges for bank regulators, who as we saw in Chapter 10 must now be far more concerned about banks' off-balance sheet activities.

DECLINE OF TRADITIONAL BANKING IN OTHER INDUSTRIALIZED COUNTRIES
Forces similar to those in Canada and the United States have been leading to the decline of traditional banking in other industrialized countries. The loss of banks' monopoly power over depositors has occurred outside Canada and the United States as well. Financial innovation and deregulation are occurring worldwide and have created attractive alternatives for both depositors and borrowers. In Japan, deregulation opened a wide array of new financial instruments to the public, causing a disintermediation process similar to that in Canada and the United States. In European countries, innovations have steadily eroded the barriers that have traditionally protected banks from competition.

In other countries, banks also face increased competition from the expansion of securities markets and the growth of the shadow banking system. Both financial deregulation and fundamental economic forces in other countries have improved the availability of information in securities markets, making it easier and less costly for firms to finance their activities by issuing securities rather than going to banks. Further, even in countries where securities markets have not grown, banks have still lost loan business because their best corporate customers have had increasing access to foreign and offshore capital markets, such as the Eurobond market. In smaller economies, like Australia, which still do not have well-developed corporate bond or commercial paper markets, banks have lost loan business to international securities markets.

In addition, the same forces that drove the securitization process in Canada and the United States have been at work in other countries and have undercut the profitability of traditional banking in these countries as well. Canada and the United States have not been unique in seeing their banks face a more difficult competitive environment. Thus, although the decline of traditional banking occurred earlier in North America than elsewhere, the same forces have caused a decline in traditional banking in other countries.

Structure of the Canadian Chartered Banking Industry

As of September 2012, there were 78 banks in Canada with over 8000 branches and over 257 000 employees. As Table 11-1 indicates, however, the six largest chartered banks, the Royal Bank of Canada, Canadian Imperial Bank of Commerce (CIBC), Bank of Montreal, Scotiabank, TD Canada Trust, and the National Bank of Canada, together hold over 90% of the assets in the industry.

TABLE 11-1   Canadian Banks (as of July 31, 2011)

Bank	Date of establishment	Assets ($ millions)	Percentage (%) of bank assets
The Big Six			
RBC Financial Group	1869	730 569	22.40
Canadian Imperial Bank of Commerce	1961	362 578	11.12
BMO Financial Group	1822	476 556	14.61
Scotiabank	1832	567 688	17.41
TD Bank Financial Group	1955	664 812	20.39
National Bank of Canada	1980	153 313	4.70
Big Six Subtotal		2 955 516	90.63
Laurentian Bank of Canada	1987	24 082	0.74
Canadian Western Bank	1988	13 996	0.43
Eight Domestic Banks Subtotal		2 993 594	91.80
Other Banks			
Domestic Banks		33 962	1.04
Foreign Banks		233 593	7.16
Total		3 261 149	100.00

Source: OSFI web site at www.osfi-bsif.gc.ca. Reprinted with permission.

Schedule I, Schedule II, and Schedule III Banks

The Big Six, together with the Laurentian Bank of Canada, the Canadian Western Bank, and another 24 domestic banks, are Canada's **Schedule I banks**. The remaining 54 banks are **Schedule II banks** (foreign bank subsidiaries, controlled by eligible foreign institutions) and **Schedule III banks** (foreign bank branches of foreign institutions).

Until 1981, foreign banks were not allowed to operate in Canada and there was no distinction between Schedule I and Schedule II banks. The 1981 revisions to the Bank Act focused on introducing more competition into the Canadian financial services industry. Domestic Canadian banks became Schedule I banks and subsidiaries of foreign banks became Schedule II banks.

Schedule I and Schedule II banks have identical powers; the only difference between them is the ownership structure permitted. In particular, according to current ownership policy, all Schedule I banks must be widely held: no individual can own more than 10% of any class of shares. Schedule II banks, however, are exceptions to this rule, if small. In fact, there are three categories of exception. The first exception is that widely held foreign banks can own 100% of a Canadian bank subsidiary. The second exception is that a Schedule II bank may have a significant shareholder (more than 10%) for up to 10 years after chartering, as a transition measure to becoming a Schedule I bank. The third exception, introduced in the 1992 revision of the Bank Act, is that any widely held and regulated Canadian financial institution, other than a bank, may own 100% of a bank. In the case of large Schedule II banks (those with over $5 billion in equity capital), the same widely held ownership rule that applies to Schedule I banks applies.

With the 2001 Bank Act Reform (to be discussed in detail later in this chapter), a foreign bank may enter the Canadian banking industry as either a Schedule II or a Schedule III bank. The difference between Schedule II and Schedule III banks is that a Schedule II bank is a Canadian subsidiary of a foreign bank whereas a Schedule III bank is a foreign bank allowed to branch directly into Canada, under certain restrictions (to be discussed later in the chapter).

Competition and Technology

Although Canada has a small number of banks relative to other countries, Canadians enjoy one of the most dynamic and competitive financial services industries. Besides chartered banks, there are over 4000 financial institutions providing financial services. These include trust and loan companies, credit unions and *caisses populaires,* government savings institutions, insurance companies, pension funds, mutual funds, and investment dealers.

New technology and the Internet have also helped in the development of a more competitive and innovative banking system in Canada. They have enabled new entrants to come into the Canadian financial services market and provide increased competition to the Big Six. For example, ING Bank of Canada, a Canadian banking subsidiary of a major Netherlands banking and insurance conglomerate, and Citizens Bank of Canada, a subsidiary of Vancouver City Savings Credit Union, are virtual banks offering an array of banking services on the Internet. In addition, U.S. credit card banks, such as MBNA and Capital One Financial Corporation, are now offering specialized credit card products in Canada, and some of the largest banks in the United States provide loans to Canadian small businesses from the United States.

Moreover, the 2001 changes to bank ownership laws encouraged the establishment of new banks. For example, Canadian Tire established a banking subsidiary (Canadian Tire Bank), as has Loblaws (President's Choice Bank). Western Financial Group, a holding company for a network of insurance agencies, created Bank West, and the Wheaton Group, a chain of car dealerships, launched a new bank called General Bank of Canada. In addition, a large number of private-sector competitors (for example, General Motors Acceptance Corporation, Ford Credit, GE Capital Group, CIT Group, and Dell Financial Services) participate in Canada's financial services market and offer similar products and services as Canada's banks, including credit cards, residential and commercial mortgages, equipment leasing, and motor vehicle financing.

Comparison with the United States

The structure of the commercial banking industry in Canada, although similar to that in many other industrialized countries, is radically different from that in the United States. There are approximately 7000 commercial banks in the United States, far more than in any other country in the world. Japan, for example, has fewer than 100 commercial banks—a mere fraction of the number of banks in the United States, even though its economy and population are half the size of the United States—and, as already noted, Canada has 78 banks. Moreover, as Table 11-2 indicates, the United States has an extraordinary number of small banks; 40% of its commercial banks have less than US$100 million in assets, and the 10 largest U.S. banks (listed in Table 11-3) together hold just over 50% of the assets in the industry.

The presence of so many commercial banks in the United States reflects past regulations that restricted the ability of these financial institutions to open branches. The result was that many small banks stayed in existence because a large bank capable of driving them out of business was often restricted from opening a branch nearby. Indeed, it was often easier for a U.S. bank to open a branch in a foreign country than to open one in another state in the United States! In fact, most industries in the United States have far fewer firms than the commercial banking industry. For

TABLE 11-2   Size Distribution of Insured Commercial Banks, March 30, 2011

Assets	Number of Banks	Share of Banks (%)	Share of Assets Held (%)
Less than $100 million	2 328	35.7	1.9
$100 million–$1 billion	3 693	56.6	11.5
$1 billion–$10 billion	423	6.5	12.8
More than $10 billion	86	1.3	73.9
Total	6 530	100.00	100.00

Source: www2.fdic.gov/qbp/2008sep/cb4.html.

TABLE 11-3   Ten Largest U.S. Banks, June 30, 2011

Bank	Assets ($ millions)	Share of All Commercial Bank Assets (%)
1. J.P. Morgan Chase	1 723 460	15.14
2. Bank of America Corp.	1 451 387	13.75
3. Citibank	1 161 359	10.20
4. Wells Fargo	1 093 030	9.60
5. U.S. Bank	305 969	2.69
6. PNC	251 221	2.21
7. Bank of NY Mellon	200 249	1.70
8. HSBC USA	197 545	1.69
9. FIA Card Service	188 639	1.66
10. TD Bank	175 145	1.54
Total	6 743 005	59.25

Source: www.federalreserve.gov/releases/h8/20081229.

example, Microsoft dominates the computer software industry and General Motors, Ford, Chrysler, Toyota, and Honda dominate the automobile industry.

Does the large number of banks in the commercial banking industry in the United States and the absence of a few dominant firms suggest that commercial banking is more competitive than other industries? Advocates of restrictive state branching regulations in the United States argued that regulations foster competition by keeping so many banks in business. But the existence of large numbers of banks in the United States should be seen as an indication of a *lack* of competition, *not* the presence of vigorous competition. Inefficient banks were able to remain in business because their customers could not find a conveniently located branch of another bank.

**Response to
Branching
Restrictions in the
United States**

An important feature of the U.S. banking industry is that competition can be repressed by regulation but not completely quashed. As we saw earlier in the chapter, the existence of restrictive regulation stimulates financial innovations that get around these regulations in the banks' search for profits. Regulations restricting branching have stimulated similar economic forces and have promoted the development of two financial innovations: bank holding companies and automated teller machines.

BANK HOLDING COMPANIES A **bank holding company** is a corporation that owns several different companies. This form of corporate ownership has important advantages for banks in that it has allowed them to circumvent restrictive branching regulations, because the holding company can own a controlling interest in several banks even if branching is not permitted. Furthermore, a bank holding company can engage in other activities related to banking, such as the provision of investment advice, data processing and transmission services, leasing, credit card services, and servicing of loans in other states.

The growth of the bank holding companies in the United States has been dramatic over the past three decades. Today bank holding companies own almost all large banks, and more than 90% of all commercial bank deposits are held in banks owned by holding companies.

AUTOMATED TELLER MACHINES Another financial innovation that avoided the restrictions on branching is the automated teller machine (ATM). Banks realized that if they did not own or rent the ATM but instead let it be owned by someone else and paid for each transaction with a fee, the ATM would probably not be considered a branch of the bank and thus would not be subject to branching regulations. This is exactly what the regulatory agencies and courts in most states in the United States concluded. Because they enable banks to widen their markets, a number of these shared facilities (such as Cirrus and NYCE) have been established nationwide. Furthermore, even when an ATM is owned by a bank, states typically have special provisions that allow wider establishment of ATMs than is permissible for traditional "brick and mortar" branches.

As we saw earlier in the chapter, avoiding regulation was not the only reason for the development of the ATM. The advent of cheaper computer and telecommunications technology enabled banks to provide ATMs at low cost, making them a profitable innovation. This example further illustrates that technological factors often combine with incentives such as the desire to avoid restrictive regulations, like branching restrictions, to produce financial innovations.

Competition Across All Four Pillars

Another important feature of the structure of the banking industry in Canada until recently was the separation of the banking and other financial services industries—such as securities, insurance, and real estate. Regulations enforced the separation of institutions according to their core financial service, and only four distinct types of financial services were identified: banking, brokerage, trusts, and insurance. This approach to regulation by institution (versus regulation by function) has been known as the **four-pillar approach**. The separation of the four pillars prohibited chartered banks from engaging in insurance and real estate activities. In turn, it prevented investment banks and insurance companies from engaging in commercial banking activities and thus protected banks from competition.

Convergence

In recent years, however, financial markets have opened up and Canada's traditional four-pillar system has changed. Despite the prohibitions in the legislation, the pursuit of profits and financial innovation stimulated both banks and other financial institutions to bypass the intent of the legislation and encroach on each other's traditional territory. For example, credit unions long offered insurance to their members and brokerage firms engaged in the traditional banking business of issuing deposit instruments with the development of money market mutual funds and cash management accounts.

Not surprisingly, the regulatory barriers between banking and other financial services markets have been coming down in response to these forces. Before the 1950s, for example, legislation allowed chartered banks to make loans for commercial purposes only and prohibited them from making residential mortgage loans. It was only after the 1967 revision of the Bank Act that banks were allowed to make conventional residential mortgage loans, thereby directly competing with trust and loan companies and credit unions and *caisses populaires*.

In the 1980s, the Bank Act was amended to allow Canadian and foreign financial institutions to own up to 100% of securities firms. Moreover, the 1990s revisions to the Bank Act allowed cross-ownership via subsidiaries between financial institutions. Chartered banks, for example, can either buy independent investment dealers or expand on their own into capital raising, brokerage, and other securities activities. As a result, the Big Six now dominate the investment banking industry through their investment brokerage subsidiaries; they hold about a 70% share in the business.

As a result of these recent legislative changes, Canada's traditional four pillars of financial services—banking, brokerage, trusts, and insurance—have now converged into a single financial services marketplace. Similar trends are also appearing in the United States as old rules and laws are overturned. With the merger in 1998 of Citicorp (the second-largest bank in the United States) and Travelers Group (an insurance company that also owned the third-largest securities firm in the country, Salomon Smith Barney), the Gramm-Leach-Bliley Financial Services Modernization Act of 1999 overturned the Glass-Steagall separation of the banking and securities industries. This allowed securities firms and insurance companies to purchase banks and banks to underwrite insurance and securities and engage in real estate activities.

Not surprisingly, the advent of the web and improved computer technology is another factor driving bank consolidation. Economies of scale have increased because large upfront investments are required to set up many information technology platforms for financial institutions. To take advantage of these economies of scale, banks have needed to get bigger, and this development has led to additional consolidation. Information technology has also been increasing economies of scope, the ability to use one resource to provide many different products and services. For example, details about the quality and creditworthiness of firms not only inform decisions about whether to make loans to them, but also can be useful in determining at what price their shares should trade. Similarly, once you have marketed one financial product to an investor, you probably know how to market another. Business people describe economies of scope by saying that there are "synergies" between different lines of business, and information technology is making these synergies more likely. The result is that consolidation is taking place not only to make financial institutions bigger, but also to increase the combination of products and services they can provide. This consolidation has had two consequences. First, different types of financial intermediaries are encroaching on each other's territory, making them more alike. Second, consolidation has led to the development of what has been named **large, complex banking organizations**.

Implications for Financial Consolidation

As we have seen, recent legislation has stimulated consolidation of the banking industry. The financial consolidation process will even further speed up in the future, because the way is now open to consolidation in terms not only of the number of banking institutions, but also across financial service activities. Given that

FYI

The Subprime Financial Crisis and the Demise of Large, Free-Standing Investment Banks

Although the move toward bringing financial service activities into larger, complex banking organizations was inevitable after the demise of Glass-Steagall, no one expected it to occur as rapidly as it did in 2008. Over a six-month period from March to September of 2008, all five of the largest free-standing investment banks in the United States ceased to exist in their old form. When Bear Stearns, the fifth-largest investment bank, revealed its large losses from investments in subprime mortgage securities, it had to be bailed out by the Federal Reserve in March 2008; the price it paid was a forced sale to J.P. Morgan for less than one-tenth what it had been worth only a year or so before. The Bear Stearns bailout made it clear that the government safety net had been extended to investment banks. The tradeoff is that investment banks will be subject to more regulation, along the lines for commercial banks, in the future.

Next to go was Lehman Brothers, the fourth-largest investment bank, which declared bankruptcy on September 15, 2008. Only one day before, Merrill Lynch, the third-largest investment bank, which also suffered large losses on its holdings of subprime securities, announced its sale to Bank of America for less than half of its year-earlier price. Within a week Goldman Sachs and Morgan Stanley, the first- and second-largest investment banks, both of which had smaller exposure to subprime securities, nevertheless saw the writing on the wall. They realized that they would soon become regulated on a similar basis and decided to become bank holding companies so they could access insured deposits, a more stable funding base.

It was the end of an era. Large, free-standing investment banking firms in the United States are now a thing of the past.

information technology is increasing economies of scope, mergers of banks with other financial service firms like that of Citicorp and Travelers in the United States should become increasingly common, and more mega-mergers are likely to be on the way. Banking institutions are becoming not only larger, but also increasingly complex organizations, engaging in the full gamut of financial service activities. The trend toward larger and more complex banking organizations was accelerated by the subprime financial crisis of 2007–2008 (see the FYI box The Subprime Financial Crisis and the Demise of Large, Free-Standing Investment Banks).

Separation of Banking and Other Financial Services Industries Throughout the World

Not many other countries in the aftermath of the Great Depression followed the lead of Canada and the United States in separating the banking and other financial services industries. In fact, in the past this separation was the most prominent difference between banking regulation in Canada and the United States versus regulation in other countries. Around the world, there are three basic frameworks for the banking and securities industries.

The first framework is *universal banking,* which exists in Germany, the Netherlands, and Switzerland. It provides no separation at all between the banking and securities industries. In a universal banking system, commercial banks provide a full range of banking, securities, real estate, and insurance services, all within a single legal entity. Banks are allowed to own sizable equity shares in commercial firms, and often they do.

The *British-style universal banking system,* the second framework, is found in the United Kingdom and countries with close ties to it, such as Australia, Canada, and now the United States. The British-style universal bank engages in securities underwriting, but it differs from the German-style universal bank in three ways: separate legal subsidiaries are more common, bank equity holdings of commercial firms are less common, and combinations of banking and insurance firms are less common.

The third framework features some legal separation of the banking and other financial services industries, as in Japan. A major difference between British-style and Japanese banking systems is that Japanese banks are allowed to hold substantial equity stakes in commercial firms, whereas British-style universal banks cannot. Although the banking and securities industries are legally separated in Japan under Section 65 of the Japanese Securities Act, commercial banks are increasingly being allowed to engage in securities activities and are thus becoming more like British-style universal banks.

The Near Banks: Regulation and Structure

Not surprisingly, the regulation and structure of the near banks (trust and loan companies and credit unions and *caisses populaires*) closely parallel the regulation and structure of the chartered banking industry.

Trust Companies

Over the years, the Bank Acts have denied to chartered banks the power to function as corporate **trustees** (or fiduciaries). Unlike the situation in the United States, legislators in Canada reasoned that deposit-taking financial institutions might face a conflict of interest if they were to act as both financial fiduciaries and banks. So trust companies were established, under a variety of provincial and federal laws, and specialized in the provision of fiduciary services. As financial fiduciaries, trust companies administer estates, trusts, and agencies (i.e., assets that belong to someone else), for a fee, and under conditions prescribed in a contract.

Over the years, the structure of the trust industry has changed significantly and today trusts offer similar services to banks (i.e., deposit-taking, loans) as well as fiduciary services. Moreover, over the years the Bank Acts have allowed regulated federal financial institutions (domestic chartered banks and life insurance companies) to own trust companies, thereby providing fiduciary services indirectly through their subsidiaries. As a result, and with the acquisition of Canada Trust (Canada's largest trust company) by the Toronto Dominion Bank in early 2000, trust companies now constitute a relatively small market segment.

Loan Companies

The development of trust companies was paralleled by the growth of loan companies. The concept of loan companies came from the building societies in the United Kingdom (during the early part of the nineteenth century), whose purpose was to enable members to acquire land, build homes, or develop farms. Today's loan companies take deposits and primarily make residential mortgage loans. They do not act as trustees, unless they are licensed specifically for that purpose. Over the years, the loan companies together with the trust companies formed the second pillar of the traditional financial services industry in Canada. However, as you saw in this chapter, financial innovation, competition, and regulatory evolution significantly changed the competitive position of financial institutions in recent years.

Trust and loan companies operate under a charter issued by either the federal government or one of the provincial governments. Federally incorporated trust and loan companies come under the federal Trust and Loan Companies Act and are regulated and supervised by OSFI. They must also register in all of the provinces in which they operate and must conform to the regulations of those provinces. In the case of trust companies, the fiduciary component of their business is only subject to provincial legislation, even if the company is federally incorporated. Deposit insurance for trust and loan companies outside Québec is provided by the CDIC (up to $100 000 per account). The Québec Deposit Insurance Board

(QDIB) insures deposits for Québec trust and loan companies on terms similar to the CDIC's.

Trust and loan companies are funded almost entirely by chequable and nonchequable savings deposits, term deposits, guaranteed investment certificates, and debentures; together, they account for about 80% of the balance sheet. Their risk asset portfolio is made up mostly by residential mortgages and personal loans; together they account for about 60% of assets. The low-risk assets are largely in short-term paper and Canadian bonds.

Cooperatives: Credit Unions and *Caisses Populaires*

Cooperatives are small lending institutions organized around a particular group of individuals with a common bond (union members or employees of a particular firm). Alphonse Desjardins formed Canada's first cooperative bank in 1900 in Québec, and it was based on the cooperative movements in Europe, which, among other things, stressed the provision of credit to the "little man." Today, there are two cooperative financial systems in Canada: the *caisses populaires* system in Québec and the credit union system in other parts of the country.

There are about 1000 credit unions and *caisses populaires* in Canada, with almost 11 million members and more than 60 000 employees, offering products and services ranging from mortgages and car loans to credit lines and automated teller machines. Because their members share a common goal, credit unions and *caisses populaires* are typically quite small; most are about the size of a single bank branch and hold less than $10 million of assets, with the largest being VanCity Savings, with assets over $15 billion. The credit unions and *caisses populaires* are established under provincial legislation and are non–profit-seeking financial institutions. Unlike the shareholder-owned chartered banks that accept deposits from and lend funds to the general public, the cooperative banks accept deposits (shares) from and lend funds only to their members. Members have voting rights and elect a board of directors, which determines the union's lending and investment policies.

As member-owned, independent financial firms, credit unions and *caisses populaires* constitute an alternative financial system, different from the profit-seeking banking system. They have also developed their own set of institutions, including central banking and deposit insurance arrangements. In particular, each province has a central credit union, owned by the member credit unions, providing financial services to individual credit unions. All central credit unions outside Québec are members of the Credit Union Central of Canada (CUCC), also known as Canadian Central. The Canadian Central serves as the third tier for the credit union movement; it coordinates various functions and provides cheque-clearing services for all provincial central credit unions.

In Québec, *caisses populaires* are assembled under a single federation, the Fédération des caisses Desjardins du Québec, which has a similar structure to the provincial central credit unions in the rest of Canada but with considerably broader regulatory responsibilities. The federation dominates retail and corporate financial intermediation in Québec. It owns a major P&C insurance group, Desjardins General Insurance; a life and health insurance company, Desjardins Financial Security; a venture capital firm, Desjardins Venture Capital; and an investment dealer and discount brokerage, Desjardins Securities and Disnat. It also owns Caisse Centrale Desjardins, which functions as a central bank, as the CUCC does for the rest of Canada.

Credit unions and *caisses populaires* are not directly covered by the CDIC. However, each provincial government has an agency, commonly called a stabilization fund, which has a line of credit with the provincial treasury and provides deposit guarantees for credit unions. Deposits in New Brunswick and Prince Edward Island are insured up to $60 000 per account, in Ontario and British Columbia up to $100 000, in Nova Scotia and Newfoundland and Labrador up to $250 000, and in Alberta, Saskatchewan, and Manitoba there are no limits on the amount of coverage provided. In Québec, the Québec Deposit Insurance Board, the same provincial government agency that insures deposits in other deposit-taking financial institutions in Québec, also provides deposit guarantees for *caisses populaires,* on terms similar to the CDIC's.

The main source of funds of credit unions and *caisses populaires* is deposits—they account for almost 80% of liabilities—followed by members' equity (about 6% of liabilities). Their asset portfolio is made up largely by residential and nonresidential mortgages (close to 55% of the balance sheet) and cash loans to members (about 13%). Low-risk assets, such as cash and deposits (primarily with central credit unions) also represent a significant proportion of the balance sheet (close to 15%). The rest of the balance sheet consists of fixed assets, and shares in central credit unions.

Government Savings Institutions

In addition to the near banks (trust and loan companies and credit unions and *caisses populaires*), there are some government-operated deposit-taking institutions, such as the Alberta Treasury Branches (ATB) Financial.

The province of Alberta established Treasury branches back in 1938 in response to Albertans' needs in remote areas. Today, there are 165 branches in 242 communities across the province operating in three target markets: individual financial services, agricultural operations, and independent business. ATB Financial (with assets in excess of $26 billion) is funded almost entirely by demand, notice, and fixed-term deposits, and its risk asset portfolio is made up largely of residential mortgages and personal, commercial, and agricultural loans.

International Banking

Canadian banks have a well-developed presence in the global financial services marketplace, which varies among the individual institutions. From its inception, for example, the Bank of Montreal found some of its best opportunities in international operations and was soon joined by the Canadian Imperial Bank of Commerce and the Bank of Nova Scotia. The spectacular growth in international banking can be explained by three factors.

First is the rapid growth in international trade and multinational (worldwide) corporations that has occurred in recent years. When Canadian firms operate abroad, they need banking services in foreign countries to help finance international trade. For example, they might need a loan in a foreign currency to operate a factory abroad. And when they sell goods abroad, they need to have a bank exchange the foreign currency they have received for their goods into Canadian dollars. Although these firms could use foreign banks to provide them with these international banking services, many of them prefer to do business with the Canadian banks with which they have established long-term relationships and that understand Canadian business customs and practices. As international trade has grown, international banking has grown with it.

Second, Canadian banks have been able to earn substantial profits by being very active in global investment banking, in which they underwrite foreign securities. They also sell insurance abroad, and they derive substantial profits from these investment banking and insurance activities.

Third, Canadian banks have wanted to tap into the large pool of Eurocurrencies—currencies deposited in banks outside the home country. To understand the structure of Canadian banking overseas, let us first look at the Eurocurrencies market, an important source for international banking.

Eurocurrencies Market

The most important of the Eurocurrencies are Eurodollars, which originated after World War II with U.S.-dollar deposits in European banks. They were created when deposits in accounts in the United States were transferred to a bank outside the United States and were kept in the form of U.S. dollars. For example, if Rolls-Royce PLC deposits a US$1 million cheque, written on an account at an American bank, in its bank in London—specifying that the deposit be payable in U.S. dollars—$1 million in Eurodollars is created.[3] More than 90% of Eurodollar deposits are time deposits, more than half of them certificates of deposit with maturities of 30 days or more. The total amount of Eurodollars outstanding is in excess of US$5 trillion, making the Eurodollar market (which was born in an ironic way—see the Global box Ironic Birth of the Eurodollar Market) one of the most important financial markets in the world economy.

Although most offshore deposits are denominated in U.S. dollars, some are also denominated in other currencies. Collectively, these offshore deposits are referred to as Eurocurrencies. A Canadian-dollar-denominated deposit held in London, for example, is called a Euro Canadian dollar, and a Japanese yen–denominated deposit held in London is called a Euroyen. Why would companies such as Rolls-Royce want to hold Eurocurrencies? First, some currencies are widely used in international trade, so Rolls-Royce might want to hold deposits in these currencies to conduct its international transactions. Second, Eurocurrencies are "offshore" deposits—they are held in countries that will not subject them to regulations such as reserve requirements or restrictions (called *capital controls*) on taking the deposits outside the country.

The main centre of the Eurocurrencies market is London, a major international financial centre for hundreds of years. Eurocurrencies are also held outside Europe in locations that provide offshore status to these deposits—for example, Singapore, the Bahamas, and the Cayman Islands.

The minimum transaction in the Eurocurrencies market is typically $1 million, and approximately 75% of Eurocurrency deposits are held by banks. Plainly, you and I are unlikely to come into direct contact with Eurocurrencies. The Eurocurrencies market is, however, an important source of funds to Canadian banks. Rather than using an intermediary and borrowing all the deposits from foreign banks, Canadian banks decided that they could earn higher profits by opening their own branches abroad to attract these deposits. Consequently, the Eurocurrencies market has been an important stimulus to Canadian banking overseas.

GLOBAL

Ironic Birth of the Eurodollar Market

One of capitalism's great ironies is that the Eurodollar market, one of the most important financial markets used by capitalists, was fathered by the Soviet Union. In the early 1950s, during the height of the Cold War, the Soviets had accumulated a substantial amount of dollar balances held by banks in the United States. Because the Russians feared that the U.S. government might freeze these assets in the United States, they wanted to move the deposits to Europe, where they would be safe from expropriation. (This fear was not unjustified—consider the U.S. freeze on Iranian assets in 1979 and Iraqi assets in 1990.) However, they also wanted to keep the deposits in dollars so that they could be used in their international transactions. The solution to the problem was to transfer the deposits to European banks but to keep the deposits denominated in dollars. When the Soviets did this, the Eurodollar was born.

---

[3]Note that the bank in London keeps the $1 million on deposits at the American bank, so the creation of Eurodollars has not caused a reduction in the amount of bank deposits in the United States.

Canadian Banking Overseas

Canadian banks have been present in international financial markets for over 100 years, providing services to Canadians and multinational businesses. The international presence of the Big Six varies among the individual institutions. In particular, the Bank of Montreal, the Canadian Imperial Bank of Commerce, and TD Canada Trust have a significant presence in the United States, whereas Scotiabank has established a presence in South America, and the Royal Bank in Europe and Asia.

During the 1970s and early 1980s a large proportion of the banks' foreign lending was in **sovereign loans**; loans to foreign governments and their agencies in the less developed countries (LDCs), particularly Mexico, Brazil, Venezuela, Argentina, and Chile. Most of this activity in international lending was unregulated, with near disastrous consequences. One example is the international debt crisis, which had its origin in the oil price shocks of the 1970s. In particular, the 1973–1974 increase in the price of oil was a bonanza for some oil-exporting countries like Mexico but a disaster for oil-importing countries like Brazil, which had to either cut their living standards or borrow massively abroad in order to pay their higher oil bills. At the time, real interest rates were very low (in fact negative) and the oil importers couldn't resist the temptation to borrow abroad.

At the same time, the oil exporters were depositing huge sums in banks and as a result the banks were lending not only to the oil-importing countries but also to the oil-exporting countries, because the latter had large oil reserves and seemed like good credit risks. The banks underestimated the **indebtedness** of these countries—the total amount these countries had borrowed from banks—and, as a result, were severely punished in the early 1980s when the recession hit and real interest rates increased significantly. With Argentina, Brazil, Mexico, and Peru threatening to default on their loans, the banks had two choices: to reschedule their loans and make more loans to these countries (to enable them to pay the interest on the debt) or to declare these countries in default and acknowledge large losses on their balance sheets. The banks chose to make more loans, because in many cases the losses would have been large enough to destroy them.

As a result of their lending experience in Latin America, the Big Six have withdrawn from certain countries and focused more of their international activities in the United States. Moreover, the international activities of Canadian banking organizations are now regulated primarily by OSFI.

Foreign Banks in Canada

The growth in international trade not only has encouraged Canadian banks to open offices overseas but also has encouraged foreign banks to establish offices in Canada. Foreign banks have been extremely successful in Canada. Over the past 20 years, since the 1981 revision to the Bank Act, globally prominent foreign banks have set up and expanded banking subsidiaries in Canada. Foreign banks are a highly fragmented group and currently hold about 7% of total Canadian bank assets, with HSBC Bank Canada (the former Hongkong and Shanghai Banking Corp.) enjoying a national market share of over 3%. It should be noted, however, that these institutions target specific groups, achieving a higher representation within their target groups than their national share would suggest. For example, HSBC, the largest of the Schedule II banks, enjoys a strong presence and success in the Chinese communities of British Columbia and Ontario.

Foreign banks may enter the Canadian financial services industry as either Schedule II or Schedule III banks. As already noted, Schedule II banks don't have to be widely held if small. If, however, their equity capital exceeds $1 billion, then at least 35% of it must be widely held. In the case that their equity capital exceeds $5 billion, then the same widely held ownership rule applies as for Schedule I banks. The major difference between Schedule II and Schedule III banks is that Schedule III banks can branch directly into Canada, following authorization by the minister of finance,

TABLE 11-4 Ten Largest Banks in the World, 2011	
Bank	**Assets (US$ millions)**
1. BNP Paribas SA, France	2 675 627
2. Deutsche Bank AG, Germany	2 551 727
3. Barclays PLC, U.K.	2 326 004
4. Credit Agricole SA, France	2 133 810
5. Industrial and Commercial Bank of China, China	2 043 861
6. The Royal Bank of Scotland Group PLC, U.K.	2 020 790
7. The Bank of Tokyo-Mitsubishi UFJ Ltd, Japan	1 644 768
8. China Construction Bank Corp, China	1 641 683
9. JP Morgan-Chase NA, U.S.	1 621 621
10. Bank Santander, Spain	1 590 560

Source: http://topforeignstocks.com/2008/07/25/the-top-10-banks-in-the-world-2008/.

whereas Schedule II banks can add branches to their initial branch only with ministerial approval. However, Schedule III banks cannot take retail deposits (i.e., deposits less than $150 000) and, as a result, have the advantage of not being subject to regulations that apply to full-service banks (such as requirements for CDIC insurance). Given that most Schedule II banks do little retail deposit gathering, it is likely that in the future many Schedule II banks will become Schedule III banks.

The internationalization of banking, both by Canadian banks going abroad and by foreign banks entering Canada, has meant that financial markets throughout the world have become more integrated. As a result, there is a growing trend toward international coordination of bank regulation, one example of which is the 1988 Basel Accord to standardize minimum capital requirements in industrialized countries, discussed in Chapter 10. Financial market integration has also encouraged bank consolidation abroad, culminating in the creation of the first trillion-dollar bank with the merger of the Industrial Bank of Japan, Dai-Ichi Kangyo Bank, and Fuji Bank in 2002. Another development has been the importance of foreign banks in international banking. As is shown in Table 11-4, in 2011, the 10 largest banking groups in the world were foreign. The implication of this financial market integration for the operation of our economy is examined further in Chapter 20 when we discuss the international financial system in more detail.

The 2001 Bank Act Reform

We have seen that fundamental structural changes make possible new financial products and services, increasing the competitive environment in the financial services industry and changing the financial intermediation role of banking at Internet speed. It is against this backdrop of phenomenal change that the federal government introduced legislation reforming the policy framework of the Canadian financial services sector.[4] This legislation took effect in October of 2001 and is known as **Bank Act Reform**.

---

[4]Since 1992, the practice of reviewing legislation governing Canada's chartered banks has been extended to reviewing legislation governing all federal financial institutions.

In what follows we provide an overview of the key elements of the new regulatory environment for financial institutions that has the potential to dramatically change the face of competition in Canada's financial services marketplace. As you will see, the new laws establish the regulatory framework to accelerate changes already taking place throughout the Canadian and world economies and introduce new opportunities for strategic alliances and partnerships, with the objective of fostering more competition and providing more innovative products and services to Canadians.

Bank Holding Companies

Before Bank Act Reform, the organizational structure of Canada's bank financial groups was based on the "bank-as-parent" model, where all banking functions and all subsidiaries of the bank are subject to the same regulation. Under the new legislation, bank financial groups have the option of organizing themselves under a holding company.[5] A holding company is a corporation that owns several different companies. For example, under a holding company structure, a bank financial group may have a banking subsidiary, an insurance subsidiary, a securities subsidiary, and another subsidiary for its unregulated businesses.

Most developed countries permit holding company structures, and the growth of holding companies has been dramatic over the past three decades. Today, in the United States, for example, holding companies own almost all large banks, and over 90% of all commercial bank deposits are held in banks owned by holding companies. In fact, the Gramm-Leach-Bliley Act of 1999 modernized the holding company rules in the United States (which had been in place since 1956) to allow a new and more flexible holding company model—the financial holding company.

The holding company form of corporate ownership has important advantages for bank financial groups in that (1) it allows them to engage in other activities related to banking, such as the provision of investment advice, data processing and transmission services, leasing, and credit card services; (2) a holding company structure allows for lighter regulation throughout the bank financial group because certain activities (those not involving retail deposit-taking and insurance) can be undertaken by less regulated, non–bank-affiliated companies held by the holding company parent rather than the regulated operating bank; and (3) the holding company model provides bank financial groups increased flexibility to achieve economies of scale and scope through strategic partnerships, alliances, and joint ventures.[6]

The big advantage of the new regime for establishing holding companies is that financial groups will be able to move parts of their heavily regulated business into less-regulated affiliates under a common holding company. The holding company, however, would be a viable option for financial groups if the transition to a holding company would be tax-neutral and without increased costs or regulatory burdens. If, for example, additional taxes or heavier regulation were to arise as a result of a restructuring into a holding company, then the holding company option wouldn't be feasible. For this reason, the new legislation also provides a set of transitional rules to address unintended cost consequences that would be triggered by the transition to a holding company.

---

[5]The new legislation introduced a holding company regime for Canada's insurance companies as well. Under the legislation, insurance holding companies are required to have an investment in at least one life insurance company and are regulated under the Insurance Companies Act. Bank holding companies are regulated under the Bank Act and are required to have an investment in at least one bank.

[6]Recently, for example, the British-based banking group HSBC entered into a joint venture with the U.S.-based securities dealer Merrill Lynch, to create a global online banking and investment company, called Merrill Lynch HSBC.

Permitted Investments

A second item of the 2001 legislation pertains to the type of investments federally regulated financial institutions are allowed to make. At present, there is a restrictive list of activities beyond banking that banks, for example, can get involved in. The new legislation, however, provides greater flexibility for bank involvement in the information technology area (and, in particular, the Internet and wireless technology). It permits bank financial groups to establish and operate information services entities utilizing recent advances in Internet and wireless banking and voice recognition technologies.

New information technologies are critical to the ability of Canadian banks and insurance companies to provide new financial products and services and adapt to the changing marketplace. Although bank and insurance company involvement in the information technology area is subject to regulation, the new permitted investment regime will enhance the ability of banks and insurance companies to pursue strategic alliances and joint ventures and will further accelerate the technological advances that are already taking place and revolutionize the financial services sector.

Ownership Rules

A third policy measure that can significantly change the face of competition in Canada's financial services marketplace is the new ownership regime that enables investors to take a greater equity interest in widely held bank financial groups, by expanding the definition of "widely held." In particular, the 2001 legislation increased the limit (that was in place since 1967) a single shareholder can own of a widely held financial institution (either a bank holding company or a bank subsidiary under the holding company) from 10% of any class of shares to 20% of voting shares and 30% of nonvoting shares. The new legislation, however, does not permit a single shareholder to own more than 10% of both a bank holding company and a bank subsidiary under the holding company at the same time. Moreover, acquisitions of more than 10% are subject to approval by the minister of finance based on a "fit and proper person" test.

The new legislation also includes a three-tiered ownership regime. Small banks (those with equity capital under $1 billion) don't have to be widely held and can be wholly owned (have one particular investor own 100% of their shares).

Medium-sized banks (and bank holding companies) with shareholders' equity between $1 billion and $5 billion can be closely held provided that there is a 35% public float (that is, they could have a single shareholder own up to 65% of their shares). Large banks (and bank holding companies), those with shareholders' equity in excess of $5 billion, are required to be widely held.

The new ownership regime, together with other provisions in the legislation, such as the lowering of the capital needed to create a bank from $10 million to $5 million and the allowance of domestic and foreign commercial enterprises (such as department stores and grocery chains) to establish small and medium-sized banks, will fundamentally change Canada's financial sector.

The CP Act and Access to the Payments and Clearance System

Before the 2001 financial-sector legislation, membership in the Canadian Payments Association (CPA), a nonprofit organization formed in 1980 by an Act of Parliament to operate Canada's payments systems, was limited to the Bank of Canada and the deposit-taking financial institutions—chartered banks, trust and loan companies, and credit unions and *caisses populaires*. The 2001 legislation introduced some important changes for the Canadian Payments Association and also renamed the Canadian Payments Association Act to Canadian Payments Act (CP Act).

In particular, the CP Act extends eligibility for membership in the Canadian Payments Association—and therefore access to Canada's two domestic payments systems, the Large Value Transfer System (LVTS) and the Automated Clearing

Settlement System (ACSS), both to be discussed in detail in Chapter 17—to non–deposit-taking financial institutions, such as life insurance companies, securities dealers, and money market mutual funds. This regulatory change will significantly affect Canada's financial services sector, since it will allow these organizations to provide bank-like services, such as chequing accounts and debit cards, without being banks, thereby directly competing with banks, trust and loan companies, and credit unions and *caisses populaires*.

Expanding access to the payments and clearance system, by allowing non–deposit-taking financial institutions to participate, will further accelerate the process of the blurring of distinction between deposit-taking and non–deposit-taking financial institutions. As already noted, this process started in 1987, when securities dealers were allowed to own banks, and was reinforced by the 1992 federal financial reforms that permitted cross-ownership of financial institutions.

Merger Review Policy

The government has also issued a statement establishing a process for reviewing mergers involving large banks—banks like the Bank of Montreal and CIBC—with shareholder equity in excess of $5 billion. By doing so, the government acknowledges that mergers are a legitimate business option that should be available to Canadian bank financial groups. The bank merger review process, however, unlike those in other countries such as the United States and the United Kingdom, is political, having Parliament directly involved in it.

Under the new merger review policy, the merger partners are required to submit a public interest impact assessment (PIIA), covering various effects of the merger, such as the impact on the structure and competition of the banking industry, branch closures, and job losses. The merger proposal would then be submitted to the House of Commons Standing Committee on Finance and the Standing Senate Committee on Banking, Trade, and Commerce for consideration and public hearings. Each of these committees will report to the minister of finance, who would make these reports public, together with a report from the Competition Bureau on the competitive aspects of the proposed merger and a report from OSFI on the prudential aspects of the proposed merger. The minister of finance will decide whether the proposed merger will be allowed to proceed.

The government has also indicated that it will not allow mergers between large banks and large demutualized life insurance companies such as Manulife and Sun Life. We would note, however, that in other countries such as Australia, Germany, the Netherlands, Switzerland, the United Kingdom, and the United States, mergers of banks, insurance companies, and other financial services providers are not prohibited.

The National Financial Services OmbudService

Another recent significant achievement is the creation of a National Financial Services OmbudService (NFSO), which began operations on July 1, 2002. This service has been created, with the support of the federal and provincial governments, by the banking sector (through the Canadian Bankers Association), the insurance sector (through the Insurance Bureau of Canada and the Canadian Life and Health Association of Canada), and the securities sector (through the Investment Dealers Association of Canada, the Mutual Funds Dealers Association, and the Investment Funds Institute of Canada). The NFSO provides Canadian consumers and small businesses access to dispute-resolution services regarding their dealings with financial institutions.

The creation of the NFSO has been viewed as a first step towards building a national regulatory system and eliminating the overlaps among the many federal, provincial, and territorial departments and agencies that currently regulate the different industries of the Canadian financial services sector.

Implications for the Canadian Banking Industry

A bank holding company structure (as an alternative to the current "bank-as-parent" structure), new ownership rules, expanded permitted investments, expanded access to the payments and clearance system, and a transparent merger review policy offer new opportunities for strategic alliances and joint ventures that have the potential to reshape the Canadian financial services marketplace. These developments, together with new information technologies, make possible new financial products and services and a more vibrant and dynamic market for financial services.

As we have seen, the 1991 federal financial reforms have stimulated consolidation of the Canadian banking industry. The financial consolidation process has further been sped up by the 2001 legislation, because the way is now open to both mergers and acquisitions, and strategic alliances, partnerships, and joint ventures. As already noted, bank financial groups will become not only larger, but also increasingly complex organizations, engaging in a full gamut of financial activities.

MyEconLab MyEconLab is an online homework and tutorial system that puts you in control of your own learning with study and practice tools directly correlated to this chapter's content. Visit MyEconLab to explore the following resources:

- The Questions are all available in the Study Plan on MyEconLab for further practice. You will also find the answers to all of the Questions in the Student Resources section of your MyEconLab.
- Visit the Student Resources section of MyEconLab to access the following mini-case for this chapter: Mini-Case 11.1: The Changing Landscape for Domestic and Global Financial Markets.

MyEconLab also features Additional Readings, Videos, Glossary Flashcards, Audio Chapter Summaries, Economics News Feeds, Animations, and many additional tools to help you master key concepts from the text.

SUMMARY

1. The history of banking in Canada has left us with a small number of banks chartered by the federal government. Multiple agencies regulate chartered banks: the Office of the Superintendent of Financial Institutions (OSFI), the Bank of Canada, and the Canada Deposit Insurance Corporation (CDIC).

2. The Big Six (the Royal Bank of Canada, Canadian Imperial Bank of Commerce, Bank of Montreal, Scotiabank, TD Canada Trust, and the National Bank of Canada) together with the Desjardins institutions dominate the deposit-taking industry in Canada.

3. In the United States there is a dual banking system, with commercial banks chartered by the states and the federal government. Restrictive state-branching regulations that prohibited branching across state lines led to a large number of small commercial banks in the United States. The large number of commercial banks in the United States reflects the past *lack* of competition, not the presence of vigorous competition.

4. A change in the economic environment will stimulate financial institutions to search for financial innovations. Changes in demand conditions, especially the rise in interest-rate risk; changes in supply conditions, especially improvements in information technology; and the desire to avoid costly regulations have been major driving forces behind financial innovation. Financial innovation has caused banks to suffer declines in cost advantages in acquiring funds and in income advantages on their assets. The resulting squeeze has hurt profitability in banks' traditional line of business and has led to a decline in traditional banking.

5. The regulation and structure of the near banks (trust and loan companies and credit unions and *caisses populaires*) parallel closely the regulation and structure of the chartered banks. Federally incorporated near banks are regulated and supervised by OSFI. They must also register in all the provinces in which they do business and must conform to the regulations of those provinces.

6. With the rapid growth of world trade since 1960, international banking has grown dramatically. Canadian banks engage in international banking activities by opening branches abroad and owning controlling interests in foreign banks. Foreign banks operate in Canada by owning a subsidiary Canadian bank or by operating branches or agency offices in Canada.

7. Until 1981, foreign banks were not allowed to operate in Canada. Today, we have 54 foreign bank subsidiaries and branches, operating as Schedule II and III banks. They have the same powers as the domestic banks but differ in the ownership structure permitted. That is, all Schedule I banks must be widely held, whereas Schedule II and III banks can be closely held if small.

8. The 2001 Bank Act Reform introduced a bank holding company structure, new ownership rules, expanded access to the payments and clearance system, and new opportunities for strategic alliances and joint ventures. These changes are reshaping the financial services marketplace in Canada by making it easier to introduce new financial products and services and increasing the competitive environment in the industry.

KEY TERMS

automated teller machine (ATM), p. 245

Bank Act Reform, p. 263

bank holding companies, p. 255

branches, p. 239

central bank, p. 238

deposit rate ceiling, p. 248

disintermediation, p. 248

dual banking system, p. 239

financial derivatives, p. 244

financial engineering, p. 243

four-pillar approach, p. 255

free banking, p. 239

futures contracts, p. 244

gold standard, p. 240

hedge, p. 244

indebtedness, p. 262

large, complex banking organizations, p. 256

lender of last resort, p. 242

national banks, p. 239

Regulation Q, p. 248

Schedule I banks, p. 252

Schedule II banks, p. 252

Schedule III banks, p. 252

securitization, p. 247

seigniorage, p. 240

shadow banking system, p. 242

sovereign loans, p. 262

state banks, p. 239

sweep account, p. 249

trustees, p. 258

virtual bank, p. 245

QUESTIONS

1. Describe how the 2001 Bank Act Reform attempted to introduce more competiton in Canada's financial services marketplace.

2. Which regulatory agency has the primary responsibility for supervising the following categories of financial institutions?
   a. chartered banks
   b. trust and loan companies
   c. credit unions and *caisses populaires*

3. "The commercial banking industry in Canada is less competitive than the commercial banking industry in the United States because in Canada only a few large banks dominate the industry, while in the United States there are around 7000 commercial banks." Is this statement true, false, or uncertain? Explain your answer.

4. How did new technology cause banks' traditional lending activities to decline in balance-sheet importance?

5. Contrast the activities of a Schedule I bank, a Schedule II bank, a trust company, and a credit union.

6. Explain how sovereign loans in the 1970s and early 1980s caused problems for the Big Six.

7. Explain how the early development of chartered banks in Canada differed from the development of commercial banks in the United States.

8. What incentives do Canadian regulatory agencies have to encourage the establishment of foreign banks in Canada?

9. Explain how securitization can be used to change illiquid assets into liquid assets.

10. If the bank at which you keep your chequing account is owned by Saudi Arabians, should you worry that your deposits are less safe than if Canadians owned the bank?

11. What are the essential differences between chartered banks, trust and loan companies, and credit unions and *caisses populaires*?

12. Why have banks been losing cost advantages in acquiring funds in recent years?

13. "If inflation had not risen in the 1960s and 1970s, the banking industry might be healthier today." Is this statement true, false, or uncertain? Explain your answer.

14. Why have banks been losing income advantages on their assets in recent years?

15. "The invention of the computer is the major factor behind the decline of the banking industry." Is this statement true, false, or uncertain? Explain your answer.

WEB EXERCISES

1. Go to the Canadian Bankers Association website at **www.cba.ca** and search for an article called "Automated Banking Machine Market in Canada." Write a short essay on ABM transactions in Canada and bank access points. According to the trends, does the public appear to have more or less access to banking facilities?

2. Despite the regulations that protect banks from failure, some do fail. Go to **www2.fdic.gov/hsob/index.asp**. Select the tab labelled "Failures and Assistance Transactions." How many bank failures occurred in the United States during the most recent complete calendar year? What were the total assets held by the banks that failed? How many U.S. banks failed in 1937?

WEB REFERENCES

www.osfi-bsif.gc.ca

Visit this website to gather statistics on the Canadian banking industry.

www.fdic.gov/index.html

Visit this website to gather statistics on the banking industry in the United States.

CHAPTER 12

Nonbank Finance

LEARNING OBJECTIVES

After studying this chapter you should be able to

1. identify the difference between banks and nonbank financial institutions (insurance companies, pension funds, finance companies, mutual funds, and investment banks

2. explain the regulation of nonbank financial institutions in the context of asymmetric information problems

3. report how recent financial-sector legislation is expected to lead to larger and increasingly complex financial groups, engaging in a full gamut of financial activities

PREVIEW

Banking is not the only type of financial intermediation you are likely to encounter. You might decide to purchase insurance, take out an installment loan, or buy a share of stock. In each of these transactions you will be engaged in nonbank finance and will deal with nonbank financial institutions. In our economy, nonbank finance also plays an important role in channelling funds from lender-savers to borrower-spenders. Furthermore, the process of financial innovation we discussed in Chapter 11 has increased the importance of nonbank finance and is blurring the distinction between different financial institutions. This chapter examines in more detail how institutions engaged in nonbank finance operate, how they are regulated, and recent trends in nonbank finance.

Insurance

Every day we face the possibility of the occurrence of certain catastrophic events that could lead to large financial losses. A spouse's earnings might disappear due to death or illness; a car accident might result in costly repair bills or payments to an injured party. Because financial losses from crises could be large relative to our financial resources, we protect ourselves against them by purchasing insurance coverage that will pay a sum of money if catastrophic events occur. Life insurance companies sell policies that provide income if a person dies, is incapacitated by illness, or retires. Property and casualty companies specialize in policies that pay for losses incurred as a result of accidents, fire, or theft.

Life Insurance

As you can see in Table 12-1, there are currently 84 life insurance companies in Canada (45 Canadian-incorporated and 39 branches of foreign-owned companies), which are organized as either stock companies or mutuals. Shareholders own stock companies; mutuals are technically similar to credit unions, owned by the policyholders. Prior to 1999, half of the life insurance companies in Canada were organized as mutuals. In 1999, however, many of the large mutual life insurance companies started a process called **demutualization**, and have now converted to stock companies.

Life insurance company regulation is the responsibility of OSFI and Assuris, formerly known as the Canadian Life and Health Insurance Compensation Corporation (CompCorp). OSFI regulation is primarily prudential, directed at sales practices, the provision of adequate liquid assets to cover losses, and restrictions on the amount of risky assets (such as common stock) the companies can hold. In other words, OSFI performs the same oversight functions as it does for banks and near banks. Assuris has no regulatory role in overseeing individual life insurance companies. It is a federally incorporated private, nonprofit corporation established and funded by the Canadian life and health insurance industry to provide liability insurance to policyholders: it compensates policyholders if the issuing company goes bankrupt.

Because death rates for the population as a whole are predictable with a high degree of certainty, life insurance companies can accurately predict what their payouts to policyholders will be in the future. Consequently, they hold long-term assets that are not particularly liquid—corporate bonds (about 50% of assets) and commercial mortgages (15% of assets) as well as some corporate stock. Actuarial liabilities make up about 70% of the liabilities of the Canadian life insurance industry. These are the present values of expected claims of policyholders.

There are two basic classes of life insurance, distinguished by the way they are sold: individual life insurance and group life insurance. **Individual life insurance**, as its name implies, is sold one policy at a time, whereas **group life insurance** is sold

TABLE 12-1 Relative Shares of OSFI-Regulated Financial Intermediary Assets (as at March 31, 2010)

Financial Institution Company	Number of Companies	Total assets ($ millions)	Percentage (%)
Insurance Companies			
Life Insurance	84	498 908	12.63
Property and Casualty	187	123 636	3.13
Fraternal Benefit Societies	17	8 706	0.22
Pension Plans	1 398	123 000	3.11
Depository Institutions			
Banks	77	2 873 610	72.74
Trust and Loan Companies	66	295 584	7.48
Cooperative Associations	7	27 095	0.69
Total	1 836	3 950 539	100.00

Source: Office of the Superintendent of Financial Institutions Canada, OSFI Annual Report 2009–2010, www.osfi-bsif.gc.ca/app/DocRepository/1/RA/0708/eng/index_e.html.

to a group of people under a single policy. There are two principal forms of individual life insurance policies: **permanent life insurance** (such as the traditional whole-life insurance) and **temporary life insurance** (such as term insurance). Permanent life insurance policies have a constant premium throughout the life of the policy. In the early years of the policy, the size of this premium exceeds the amount needed to insure against death because the probability of death is low. Thus the policy builds up a cash value in its early years, but in later years the cash value declines because the constant premium falls below the amount needed to insure against death, the probability of which is now higher. The policyholder can borrow against the cash value of the permanent life policy or can claim it by cancelling the policy. For this reason, permanent insurance is also called **endowment insurance**.

Term insurance, by contrast, has a premium that is matched every year to the amount needed to insure against death during the period of the term (such as one year or five years). As a result, term policies have premiums that rise over time as the probability of death rises (or level premiums with a decline in the amount of death benefits). Term policies have no cash value and thus, in contrast to permanent life policies, provide insurance only, with no savings aspect.

Beginning in the mid-1970s, life insurance companies began to restructure their business to become managers of assets for pension funds. Now more than half of the assets managed by life insurance companies are for pension funds and not for life insurance. Insurance companies have also begun to sell investment vehicles for retirement such as **annuities**, arrangements whereby the customer pays an annual premium in exchange for a future stream of annual payments beginning at a set age, say, 65, and continuing until death.

Property and Casualty Insurance

There are 187 property and casualty (P&C) or "general" insurance companies in Canada (see Table 12-1), and about 27% of the industry, measured by assets held, is foreign-controlled. Most property and casualty insurance companies in Canada are federally registered and subject to regulation by OSFI and the Property and Casualty Insurance Compensation Corporation (PACICC). PACICC was set up in 1988 and performs the same role for property and casualty companies as Assuris does for life insurance companies. Some lines of P&C insurance, for example auto insurance, are also subject to provincial laws and regulations.

Property insurance covers losses of real property, and casualty insurance protects against legal liability exposures. Although property and casualty insurance companies have seen a slight increase in their share of total financial intermediary assets since 1960, in recent years they have not fared well, and insurance rates have skyrocketed. With the high interest rates in the 1970s, insurance companies had high investment income that enabled them to keep insurance rates low. Since then, however, investment income has fallen with the decline in interest rates, while the growth in lawsuits involving property and casualty insurance and the explosion in amounts awarded in such cases have produced substantial losses for companies.

To return to profitability, insurance companies have raised their rates dramatically—sometimes doubling or even tripling premiums—and have refused to provide coverage for some people. They have also campaigned actively for limits on insurance payouts, particularly for medical malpractice. In the search for profits, insurance companies are also branching out into uncharted territory by insuring the payment of interest on corporate bonds and mortgage-backed securities. One worry is that the insurance companies may be taking on excessive risk in order to boost their profits. One result of the concern about the health of the property and casualty insurance industry is that insurance regulators have proposed new rules that would impose capital requirements on these companies based on the riskiness of their assets and operations.

The investment policies of these companies are affected by the fact that property losses are very uncertain. In fact, because property losses are more uncertain than the death rate in a population, these insurers are less able to predict how much they will have to pay policyholders than life insurance companies are. Natural disasters such as the ice storm of 1998 and the Calgary hailstorm of 1991 exposed the property and casualty insurance companies to billions of dollars of losses.[1] Therefore, property and casualty insurers hold more liquid assets than life insurers: cash, due and accrued investment income, money market instruments, and receivables amount to over a third of their assets, and most of the remainder is held in bonds, debentures, and stocks. Their largest liability relates to unpaid claims and adjustment expenses, followed by unearned premiums (premiums representing the unexpired part of policies).

Property and casualty insurance companies will insure against losses from almost any type of event, including fire, theft, negligence, malpractice, earthquakes, and automobile accidents. If a possible loss being insured is too large for any one firm, several firms may join together to write a policy in order to share the risk. Insurance companies may also reduce their risk exposure by obtaining **reinsurance**. Reinsurance allocates a portion of the risk to another company in exchange for a portion of the premium and is particularly important for small insurance companies. You can think of reinsurance as insurance for the insurance company. The most famous risk-sharing operation is Lloyd's of London, an association in which different insurance companies can underwrite a fraction of an insurance policy. Lloyd's of London has claimed that it will insure against any contingency—for a price.

Credit Insurance

In recent years, insurance companies have also entered into the business of supplying credit insurance. There are two ways they have done this.

CREDIT DEFAULT SWAPS One way insurance companies can in effect provide credit insurance is by selling a traded derivative called a **credit default swap (CDS)**, in which the seller is required to make a payment to the holder of the CDS if there is a *credit event* for that instrument such as a bankruptcy or downgrading of the firm's credit rating. (Credit derivatives are discussed more extensively in Chapter 14.) Issuing a CDS is thus tantamount to providing insurance on the debt instrument because, just like insurance, it makes a payment to the holder of the CDS when there is a negative credit event (see the FYI box Credit Default Swaps on Greek Debt). Major insurance companies have entered the CDS market in recent years, sometimes to their great regret (see the FYI box The AIG Blowup).

MONOLINE INSURANCE Another way of providing credit insurance is to supply it directly, just as with any insurance policy. However, insurance regulations do not allow property/casualty insurance companies, life insurance companies, or insurance companies with multiple lines of business to underwrite credit insurance. **Monoline insurance companies**, which specialize in credit insurance alone, are therefore the only insurance companies that are allowed to provide insurance that guarantees the timely repayment of bond principal and interest when a debt issuer defaults. These insurance companies have become particularly important in the municipal bond market, where they insure a large percentage of these securities. When a municipal

---

[1]For example, the freezing rains of January 1998 triggered about 840 000 insurance claims. As a result, Canadian P&C insurers paid out over $1.44 billion. Similar disasters in the United States, such as the Los Angeles earthquake in 1994, Hurricane Katrina, which devasted New Orleans in 2005, Hurricane Ike, which devastated Galveston in 2008, and the September 11, 2001, destruction of the World Trade Center, exposed the U.S. property and casualty insurance companies to billions of dollars of losses.

FYI

Credit Default Swaps on Greek Sovereign Debt

The sovereign debt crisis in the euro area that started in early 2010 raised doubts about the sustainability of the finances of a number of European countries. For example, after it was revealed that the Greek government had lied about its budget finances, Greece's deficit grew so large in 2010 that it could not raise funds at reasonable interest rates, and it looked likely it would default on its debt. This increase in credit (or default) risk was reflected in credit default swap spreads. For example, if on

September 20, 2011, you were holding €10 million of Greek government bonds and wanted to buy protection against the Greek government defaulting on its bonds over the next five years, you would have to pay 5,737 basis points; 1 basis point on credit default swaps protecting €10 million is equivalent to €1000.

This means that on September 20, 2011, it cost €5.737 million (plus some annual fee) to insure €10 million of Greek debt for five years.

FYI

The AIG Blowup

American International Group, better known as AIG, was a trillion-dollar insurance giant and before 2008 was one of the 20 largest companies in the world. A small separate unit, AIG's Financial Products division, went into the credit default swap business in a big way, insuring over US$400 billion of securities, of which US$57 billion were debt securities backed by subprime mortgages. Lehman Brothers' troubles and eventual bankruptcy on September 15, 2008, revealed that subprime securities were worth much less than they were being valued at, and investors came to the realization that AIG's losses, which had already been substantial in the first half of the year, could bankrupt the company. Lenders to AIG then pulled back with a vengeance, and AIG could not raise enough capital to stay afloat.

On September 16, the Federal Reserve and the U.S. Treasury decided to rescue AIG because its failure was deemed potentially catastrophic for

the financial system. Banks and mutual funds were large holders of AIG's debt, plus the bankruptcy of AIG would have rendered all the credit default swaps it had sold worthless, thereby imposing huge losses on financial institutions that had bought them. The Federal Reserve set up an US$85 billion credit facility (with the total loan from the Fed and the government increased to US$173 billion) to provide liquidity to AIG. The rescue did not come cheap, however: AIG was charged a very high interest rate on the loans from the Fed, and the government was given the rights to an 80% stake in the company if it survived. Maurice Greenberg, the former CEO of the company, described the government's actions as a "nationalization" of AIG.

Insurance companies have never been viewed as posing a risk to the financial system as a whole. Because the problems at AIG nearly brought down the U.S. financial system, this view is no longer tenable. The insurance industry will never be the same.

security with a lower credit rating, say an A rating, has an insurance policy from a monoline insurer, it takes on the credit rating of the monoline insurer, say AAA. This lowers the interest cost for the municipality and so makes it worthwhile for the municipality to pay premiums for this insurance policy. Of course, to do this, the monoline insurers need to have a very high credit rating.

The New Legislative Framework

As noted in Chapter 11, in 2001 the government passed legislation reforming the regulatory framework governing Canada's financial services sector. The new legislation allows demutualized life and health insurance companies to restructure under a holding company structure, to enter into joint ventures and strategic alliances, and to access the Canadian payments and clearance systems, in an attempt to bring the sector in line with the banking sector. However, the new legislation does not allow mergers involving large banks and large demutualized life and health insurance companies. Moreover, the new legislation requires that large life and health insurance companies (those with equity over $5 billion) be widely held, in the sense that an individual or firm cannot own more than 20% of the voting shares. Small demutualized companies (those with equity under $1 billion) are eligible to be closely held.

APPLICATION

Insurance Management

Insurance, like banking, is the financial intermediation business of transforming one type of asset into another for the public. Insurance providers use the premiums paid on policies to invest in assets such as bonds, stocks, mortgages, and other loans; the earnings from these assets are then used to pay out claims on the policies. In effect, insurers transform assets such as bonds, stocks, and loans into insurance policies that provide a set of services (for example, claim adjustments, savings plans, friendly insurance agents). If the insurer's production process of asset transformation efficiently provides its customers with adequate insurance services at low cost and if it can earn high returns on its investments, it will make profits; if not, it will suffer losses.

The economic concepts of adverse selection and moral hazard discussed in Chapter 8 also apply to the lending activities of insurers. Here we apply the adverse selection and moral hazard concepts to explain many management practices specific to insurance.

In the case of an insurance policy, moral hazard arises when the existence of insurance encourages the insured party to take risks that increase the likelihood of an insurance payoff. For example, a person covered by burglary insurance might not take as many precautions to prevent a burglary because the insurance company will reimburse most of the losses if a theft occurs. Adverse selection holds that the people most likely to receive large insurance payoffs are the ones who will want to purchase insurance the most. For example, a person suffering from a terminal disease would want to take out the biggest life and medical insurance policies possible, thereby exposing the insurance company to potentially large losses. Both adverse selection and moral hazard can result in large losses to insurance companies because they lead to higher payouts on insurance claims. Lowering adverse selection and moral hazard to reduce these payouts is therefore an extremely important goal for insurance companies, and this goal explains the insurance practices we will discuss here.

Information Collection and Screening

To reduce adverse selection, insurance providers try to screen out good insurance risks from poor ones. Effective information collection procedures are therefore an important principle of insurance management.

When you apply for auto insurance, the first thing your insurance agent does is ask you questions about your driving record (number of speeding tickets and accidents), the type of car you are insuring, and certain personal matters (age, marital status). If you are applying for life insurance, you go through a similar grilling, but you are asked even more personal questions about such things as your health, smoking habits, and drug and alcohol use. The life insurer even orders a medical evaluation (usually done by an independent company) that involves taking blood and urine samples. Just as a bank calculates a credit score to evaluate a potential borrower, the insurer uses the information you provide to allocate you to a risk class—a statistical estimate of how likely you are to have an insurance claim.

Based on this information, the insurer can decide whether to accept you for the insurance or to turn you down because you pose too high a risk and thus would be an unprofitable customer.

Risk-Based Premiums

Charging insurance premiums on the basis of how much risk a policyholder poses for the insurance provider is a time-honoured principle of insurance management. Adverse selection explains why this principle is so important to insurance company profitability.

To understand why an insurance provider finds it necessary to have risk-based premiums, let's consider an example of risk-based insurance premiums that at first glance seems unfair. Harry and Sally, both college students with no accidents or speeding tickets, apply for auto insurance. Normally, Harry will be charged a much higher premium than Sally. Insurance companies do this because young males have a much higher accident rate than young females. Suppose, though, that one insurer did not base its premiums on a risk classification but rather just charged a premium based on the average combined risk for males and females. Then Sally would be charged too much and Harry too little. Sally could go to another insurer and get a lower rate, while Harry would sign up for the insurance. Because Harry's premium isn't high enough to cover the accidents he is likely to have, on average the insurer would lose money on Harry. Only with a premium based on a risk classification, so that Harry is charged more, can the insurance company make a profit.[2]

Restrictive Provisions

Restrictive provisions in policies are an insurance management tool for reducing moral hazard. Such provisions discourage policyholders from engaging in risky activities that make an insurance claim more likely. For example, life insurers have provisions in their policies that eliminate death benefits if the insured person commits suicide within the first two years that the policy is in effect. Restrictive provisions may also require certain behaviour on the part of the insured. A company renting motor scooters may be required to provide helmets for renters in order to be covered for any liability associated with the rental. The role of restrictive provisions is not unlike that of restrictive covenants on debt contracts described in Chapter 8. Both serve to reduce moral hazard by ruling out undesirable behaviour.

Prevention of Fraud

Insurance providers also face moral hazard because an insured person has an incentive to lie to the insurer and seek a claim even if the claim is not valid. For example, a person who has not complied with the restrictive provisions of an insurance contract may still submit a claim. Even worse, a person may file claims for events that did not actually occur. Thus an important management principle for insurance providers is conducting investigations to prevent fraud so that only policyholders with valid claims receive compensation.

Cancellation of Insurance

Being prepared to cancel policies is another insurance management tool. Insurers can discourage moral hazard by threatening to cancel a policy when the insured person engages in activities that make a claim more likely. If your auto insurance company makes it clear that coverage will be cancelled if you get too many speeding tickets, you will be less likely to speed.

---

[2]Note that the example here is in fact the lemons problem described in Chapter 8.

Deductibles

The **deductible** is the fixed amount by which the insured's loss is reduced when a claim is paid off. A $250 deductible on an auto policy, for example, means that if you suffer a loss of $1000 because of an accident, the insurer will pay you only $750. Deductibles are an additional management tool that helps insurance companies reduce moral hazard. With a deductible, you experience a loss along with the insurer when you make a claim. Because you also stand to lose when you have an accident, you have an incentive to drive more carefully. A deductible thus makes a policyholder act more in line with what is profitable for the insurer; moral hazard has been reduced. And because moral hazard has been reduced, the insurance provider can lower the premium by more than enough to compensate the policyholder for the existence of the deductible. Another function of the deductible is to eliminate the administrative costs of handling small claims by forcing the insured to bear these losses.

Coinsurance

When a policyholder shares a percentage of the losses along with the insurer, their arrangement is called **coinsurance**. For example, some medical insurance plans provide coverage for 80% of medical bills, and the insured person pays 20% after a certain deductible has been met. Coinsurance works to reduce moral hazard in exactly the same way that a deductible does. A policyholder who suffers a loss along with the insurer has less incentive to take actions, such as going to a specialist unnecessarily, that involve higher claims. Coinsurance is thus another useful management tool for insurance providers.

Limits on the Amount of Insurance

Another important principle of insurance management is that there should be limits on the amount of insurance provided, even though a customer is willing to pay for more coverage. The higher the insurance coverage, the more the insured person can gain from risky activities that make an insurance payoff more likely and hence the greater the moral hazard. For example, if Zelda's car were insured for more than its true value, she might not take proper precautions to prevent its theft, such as making sure that the key is always removed or putting in an alarm system. If it were stolen, she would come out ahead because the excessive insurance payment would allow her to buy an even better car. By contrast, when the insurance payments are lower than the value of her car, she will suffer a loss if it is stolen and will thus take precautions to prevent this from happening. Insurance providers must always make sure that their coverage is not so high that moral hazard leads to large losses.

Summary

Effective insurance management requires several practices: information collection and screening of potential policyholders, risk-based premiums, restrictive provisions, prevention of fraud, cancellation of insurance, deductibles, coinsurance, and limits on the amount of insurance. All of these practices reduce moral hazard and adverse selection by making it harder for policyholders to benefit from engaging in activities that increase the amount and likelihood of claims. With smaller benefits available, the poor insurance risks (those who are more likely to engage in the activities in the first place) see less benefit from the insurance and are thus less likely to seek it out.

Pension Funds

In performing the financial intermediation function of asset transformation, pension funds provide the public with another kind of protection: income payments on retirement. Employers, unions, or private individuals can set up pension plans, which acquire funds through contributions paid in by the plan's participants or their employees. Pension plans have grown in importance in recent years, with their share of total financial intermediary assets rising significantly. Federal tax policy has been a major factor behind the rapid growth of pension funds because employer contributions to employee pension plans are tax-deductible. Furthermore, tax policy has also encouraged employee contributions to pension funds by making them tax-deductible as well and enabling self-employed individuals to open up their own tax-sheltered pension plans.

Because the benefits paid out of the pension fund each year are highly predictable, pension funds invest in long-term securities, with the bulk of their asset holdings in bonds, stocks, and long-term mortgages. The key management issues for pension funds revolve around asset management. Pension fund managers try to hold assets with high expected returns and to lower risk through diversification. The investment strategies of pension plans have changed radically over time. In the aftermath of World War II, most pension fund assets were held in government bonds. However, the strong performance of stocks in the 1950s and 1960s afforded pension plans higher returns, causing them to shift their portfolios into stocks, currently on the order of over 50% of their assets. As a result, pension plans now have a much stronger presence in the stock market.

Although the purpose of all pension plans is the same, they can differ in a number of attributes. First is the method by which payments are made: if the benefits are determined by the contributions into the plan and their earnings, the pension is a **defined-contribution plan**; if future income payments (benefits) are set in advance (usually based on the highest average salary and the number of years of pensionable service), the pension is a **defined-benefit plan**. In the case of a defined-benefit plan, a further attribute is related to how the plan is funded. A defined-benefit plan is **fully funded** if the contributions into the plan and their earnings over the years are sufficient to pay out the defined benefits when they come due. If the contributions and earnings are not sufficient, the plan is **underfunded**. For example, if Jane Brown contributes $100 per year into her pension plan (at the beginning of each year) and the interest rate is 10%, after 10 years the contributions and their earnings would be worth $1753.[3] If the defined benefit on her pension plan pays her $1753 or less after 10 years, the plan is fully funded because her contributions and earnings will fully pay for this payment. But if the defined benefit is $2000, the plan is underfunded because her contributions and earnings do not cover this amount.

A second characteristic of pension plans is their *vesting*, the length of time that a person must be enrolled in the pension plan (by being a member of a union or an employee of a company) before being entitled to receive benefits. Typically, firms require that an employee work two years for the company before being vested and

---

[3]The $100 contributed in year 1 would be worth $100 $(1 + 0.10)10$ = $259.37 at the end of 10 years; the $100 contributed in year 2 would be worth $100 $(1 + 0.10)9$ = $235.79; and so on until the $100 contributed in year 10 would be worth $100 $(1 + 0.10)$ = $110. Adding these together, we get the total value of these contributions and their earnings at the end of 10 years:

$$\$259.37 + \$235.79 + \$214.36 + \$194.87 + \$177.16$$
$$+ \ \$161.05 + \$146.41 + \$133.10 + \$121.00 + \$110.00 = \$1753.11$$

qualifying to receive pension benefits; if the employee leaves the firm before the two years are up, either by quitting or being fired, all rights to benefits are lost.

Public Pension Plans

The most important government-administered pension plan is the Old Age Security (OAS) program, which also includes the Guaranteed Income Supplement (GIS) and Spouse's Allowance (SPA) programs. The OAS guarantees a minimum income to all Canadians aged 65 and over and in some cases also pays income to persons before age 65. In particular, it makes monthly flat payments (out of federal government revenues) to retired or disabled workers or their surviving spouses.

Other government-administered pension plans are the Canada Pension Plan (CPP) and in Quebec the Quebec Pension Plan (QPP), both established in 1966 and intended for persons who hold a job. They are supported by contributions from employees and their employers and cover almost all workers in Canada (the participation of workers aged 18 and over is compulsory). The accumulated funds of the CPP are managed by an investment board, called the CPP Investment Board, and those of the QPP are managed by the Caisse de dépôt et placement du Québec.

When the government pension plans were established, the federal government intended to operate them like private pension plans. However, unlike private pension plans, benefits are typically paid out from current contributions, not tied closely to a participant's past contributions. This "pay-as-you-go" system led to a massive underfunding. The problems of the public pension plans could become worse in the future because of the growth in the number of retired people relative to the working population. The government has been grappling with the problems of the public pension plans for years, but the prospect of a huge bulge of new retirees has resulted in calls for radical surgery (see the FYI box Should Public Pension Plans Be Privatized?). In 1999, for example, the CPP was given authority to sharply increase contribution rates from 5.6% in 1999 to 9.9% in 2003. It was also given the authority to invest its accumulated assets in the market in order to earn a higher return so that future increases in contribution levels will not be needed.

Private Pension Plans

Private pension plans are voluntary, employer-sponsored plans, with the contributions usually shared between employer and employee. They are registered with the federal or a provincial pension regulatory authority as well as with the Canada Revenue Agency (CRA) for tax purposes. They are also known in Canada as Registered Pension Plans (RPPs).

Trusteed pension plans account for the majority of registered pension plans in Canada. Typically, a pension plan sponsor (such as a government or private-sector employer) will hire a bank, a life insurance company, or a pension fund manager to manage the fund for the benefit of the plan members. The largest trusteed pension funds in Canada are the Ontario Teachers' Pension Plan Board and the Ontario Municipal Employees' Retirement Board. Among the largest pension fund managers are the Caisse de dépôt et placement du Québec and Royal Trust, a subsidiary of the Royal Bank.

Many private pension plans are underfunded because they plan to meet their pension obligations out of current earnings when the benefits come due. As long as companies have sufficient earnings, underfunding creates no problems, but if not, they may not be able to meet their pension obligations. Because of potential problems caused by corporate underfunding, mismanagement, fraudulent practices, and other abuses of private pension funds, these funds are heavily regulated. As with insurance companies, the regulatory system governing pension funds is split between OSFI and provincial superintendents of pensions. Pension funds administered for people working in businesses that are federal in scope (for example, railways, air transport, telecommunications, and banking) are the responsibility of OSFI.

FYI

Should Public Pension Plans Be Privatized?

In recent years, public confidence in the public pension plans has reached a new low. Some surveys suggest that young people have more confidence in the existence of flying saucers than they do in the government's promise to pay them their public pension plan benefits. Without some overhaul of the system, public pension plans will not be able to meet their future obligations. The government has set up advisory commissions and has been holding hearings to address this problem.

Currently, the assets of the public pension plans, which reside in trust funds, are all invested in government securities. Because stocks and corporate bonds have higher returns than government securities, many proposals to save the public pension plans suggest investing part of the trust fund in corporate securities and thus partially privatizing the systems.

Suggestions for privatization take three basic forms:

1. *Government investment of trust fund assets in corporate securities.* This plan has the advantage of possibly improving the trust funds' overall return, while minimizing transaction costs because it exploits the economies of scale of the trust funds. Critics warn that government ownership of private assets could lead to increased government intervention in the private sector.

2. *Shift of trust fund assets to individual accounts that can be invested in private assets.* This option has the advantage of possibly increasing the return on investments and does not involve the government in the ownership of private assets. However, critics warn that it might expose individuals to greater risk and to transaction costs on individual accounts that might be very high because of the small size of many of these accounts.

3. *Individual accounts in addition to those in the trust funds.* This option has advantages and disadvantages similar to those of option 2 and may provide more funds to individuals at retirement. However, some increase in contributions would be required to fund these accounts.

Whether some privatization of the public pension plans occurs is an open question. In the short term, public pension plan reform is likely to involve an increase in contributions, a reduction in benefits, or both. For example, under the 1997 changes to the CPP Act, the percentage of liabilities of CPP that are funded is expected to increase from the current 8% to 20% by 2018.

However, most trusteed pension funds are registered under provincial acts. These acts and regulations tend to be similar across provinces. They establish minimum standards for the reporting and disclosure of information, set rules for vesting and the degree of underfunding, and place restrictions on investment practices.

Provincial and local governments and the federal government, like private employers, have also set up pension plans for their employees. These plans are almost identical in operation to private pension plans and hold similar assets. Underfunding of the plans is also prevalent, and some investors in municipal bonds worry that it may lead to future difficulties in the ability of provincial and local governments to meet their debt obligations.

Personal Pension Plans

An alternative to both public pension plans and private pension plans is **personal pension plans**. These are the Registered Retirement Savings Plans (RRSPs) that Canadians set up with financial institutions. They provide tax-sheltered, self-financed retirement funds. Upon retirement, an RRSP must be converted into an annuity or a Registered Retirement Income Fund (RRIF) that provides taxable annuity payments. Since RRIFs are less popular than annuities, which may only be offered by insurance companies, the insurance industry has benefited from the introduction of the RRSP.

Another way to set money aside for retirement is the Tax-Free Savings Account (TFSA), introduced by the federal government in 2009. Unlike RRSP contributions, TFSA contributions are not tax-deductible. However, the amount contributed as well as the income earned in the account is tax-free when it is withdrawn.

Finance Companies

Finance companies acquire funds by issuing commercial paper or stocks and bonds or borrowing from banks, and they use the proceeds to make loans (often for small amounts) that are particularly well suited to consumer and business needs. The financial intermediation process of finance companies can be described by saying that they borrow in large amounts but often lend in small amounts—a process quite different from that of banking institutions, which collect deposits in small amounts and then often make large loans. Renamed in 1998, finance companies became known as *nondepository credit intermediaries* under the industry classification system.

A key feature of finance companies is that although they lend to many of the same customers that borrow from banks, they are virtually unregulated compared to chartered banks and near banks. Provinces regulate the maximum amount they can loan to individual consumers and the terms of the debt contract, but there are no restrictions on branching, the assets they hold, or how they raise their funds. The lack of restrictions enables finance companies to tailor their loans to customer needs better than banking institutions can.

There are three types of finance companies: sales, consumer, and business.

1. *Sales finance companies* are owned by a particular retailing or manufacturing company and make loans to consumers to purchase items from that company. Sales finance companies compete directly with banks for consumer loans and are used by consumers because loans can frequently be obtained faster and more conveniently at the location where an item is purchased.

2. *Consumer finance companies* make loans to consumers to buy particular items such as furniture or home appliances, to make home improvements, or to help refinance small debts. Consumer finance companies are separate corporations or are owned by banks. Typically, these companies charge higher interest rates and make loans to consumers who cannot obtain credit from other sources.

3. *Business finance companies* provide specialized forms of credit to businesses by making loans and purchasing accounts receivable (bills owed to the firm) at a discount; this provision of credit is called *factoring*. For example, a dressmaking firm might have outstanding bills (accounts receivable) of $100 000 owed by the retail stores that have bought its dresses. If this firm needs cash to buy 100 new sewing machines, it can sell its accounts receivable for, say, $90 000 to a finance company, which is now entitled to collect the $100 000 owed to the firm. Besides factoring, business finance companies also specialize in leasing equipment (such as railroad cars, jet planes, and computers), which they purchase and then lease to businesses for a set number of years.

Securities Market Operations

The smooth functioning of securities markets, in which bonds and stocks are traded, involves several financial institutions, including securities brokers and dealers, investment banks, and organized exchanges. None of these institutions were included in our list of financial intermediaries in Chapter 2 because they do not perform the intermediation function of acquiring funds by issuing liabilities and then using the funds to acquire financial assets. Nonetheless, they are important in the process of channelling funds from savers to spenders and can be thought of as "financial facilitators."

First, however, we must recall the distinction between primary and secondary securities markets discussed in Chapter 2. In a primary market, new issues of a security are sold to buyers by the corporation or government agency borrowing the funds. A secondary market then trades the securities that have been sold in the primary market (and so are secondhand). *Investment banks* (also called investment dealers) assist in the initial sale of securities in the primary market; *securities brokers* and *dealers* assist in the trading of securities in the secondary markets, some of which are organized into exchanges.

Investment Banking

When a corporation wishes to borrow (raise) funds, it normally hires the services of an investment banker to help sell its securities. Despite its name, an investment banker is not a banker in the ordinary sense; that is, it is not engaged in financial intermediation that takes in deposits and then lends them out. The top investment bankers in Canada are subsidiaries of the Big Six Canadian banks and they are known as RBC Capital Markets, TD Securities, Scotia Capital, CIBC World Markets, BMO Nesbitt Burns, and National Bank Financial.

Investment bankers assist in the sale of securities as follows. First, they advise the corporation on whether it should issue bonds or stock. If they suggest that the corporation issue bonds, investment bankers give advice on what the maturity and interest payments on the bonds should be. If they suggest that the corporation should sell stock, they give advice on what the price should be. This is fairly easy to do if the firm has prior issues currently selling in the market, called **seasoned issues**. However, when a firm issues stock for the first time in what is called an **initial public offering (IPO)**, it is more difficult to determine what the correct price should be. All the skills and expertise of the investment banking firm then need to be brought to bear to determine the most appropriate price. IPOs have become very important in the Canadian economy, because they are a major source of financing for Internet companies, which became all the rage on Bay Street in the late 1990s. Not only have IPOs helped these companies to acquire capital to substantially expand their operations, but they have also made the original owners of these firms very rich. Many a nerdy 20- to 30-year-old became an instant millionaire when his stake in his Internet company was given a high valuation after the initial public offering of shares in the company. However, with the bursting of the tech bubble in 2000, many of them lost much of their wealth when the value of their shares came tumbling down to earth.

When the corporation decides which kind of financial instrument it will issue, it offers them to **underwriters**—investment bankers that guarantee the corporation a price on the securities and then sell them to the public. If the issue is small, only one investment-banking firm underwrites it (usually the original investment banking firm hired to provide advice on the issue). If the issue is large, several investment-banking firms form a syndicate to underwrite the issue jointly, thus limiting the risk that any one investment bank must take. The underwriters sell the securities to the general public by contacting potential buyers, such as banks and insurance companies, directly and by placing advertisements in newspapers like the *National Post* and *The Globe and Mail*.

The activities of investment bankers and the operation of primary markets are heavily regulated by the provinces and the federal government. The Ontario Securities Commission (OSC), for example, is responsible for administering the Ontario Securities Act, Canada's first provincial securities act, passed in 1945. Other provinces and territories have generally tended to follow Ontario's lead and passed Securities Acts regulating investment banking and the trading of securities. Canada doesn't have a Securities Act, but portions of the Criminal Code of Canada specifically apply to securities trading.

Securities Brokers and Dealers

Securities brokers and dealers conduct trading in secondary markets. Brokers act as agents for investors in the purchase or sale of securities. Their function is to match buyers with sellers, a function for which they are paid brokerage commissions. In contrast to brokers, dealers link buyers and sellers by standing ready to buy and sell securities at given prices. Therefore, dealers hold inventories of securities and make their living by selling these securities for a slightly higher price than they paid for them—that is, on the "spread" between the asked price and the bid price. This can be a high-risk business because dealers hold securities that can rise or fall in price; in recent years, several firms specializing in bonds have collapsed. Brokers, by contrast, are not as exposed to risk because they do not own the securities involved in their business dealings.

Brokerage firms engage in all three securities market activities, acting as brokers, dealers, and investment bankers. That is, the same investment banks that handle the sale of securities in the primary markets also are involved in the retail business of trading for clients on the stock exchanges. However, the provinces and the federal government regulate the investment banking operation of the firms and also restrict brokers and dealers from misrepresenting securities and from trading on *insider information,* nonpublic information known only to the management of a corporation.

Organized Exchanges

As discussed in Chapter 2, secondary markets can be organized either as over-the-counter markets, in which trades are conducted using dealers, or as organized exchanges, in which trades are conducted in one central location. The largest of the organized stock exchanges in Canada is the Toronto Stock Exchange, owned and operated by the TMX Group. It was established in 1852 and today boasts the third most active stock exchange in North America, after the New York Stock Exchange (NYSE) and Nasdaq. The TMX Group also encompasses the TSX Venture Exchange and (since 2008) the Montréal Exchange, which provides interest-rate derivatives trading and clearing, index derivatives trading and clearing, and equity derivatives trading and clearing.

Organized stock exchanges actually function as a hybrid of an auction market (in which buyers and sellers trade with each other in a central location) and a dealer market (in which dealers make the market by buying and selling securities at given prices). Securities are traded on the floor of the exchange with the help of a special kind of dealer-broker called a **specialist**. A specialist matches buy and sell orders submitted at the same price and so performs a brokerage function. However, if buy and sell orders do not match up, the specialist buys stocks or sells from a personal inventory of securities, in this manner performing a dealer function. By assuming both functions, the specialist maintains orderly trading of the securities for which he or she is responsible.

The growing internationalization of capital markets has encouraged another trend in securities trading. Increasingly, Canadian companies are being listed on U.S. stock exchanges, and the markets are moving toward trading stocks internationally, 24 hours a day.

Mutual Funds

Mutual funds are financial intermediaries that pool the resources of many small investors by selling them shares and using the proceeds to buy securities. Through the asset transformation process of issuing shares in small denominations and buying large blocks of securities, mutual funds can take advantage of volume discounts on brokerage commissions and purchase diversified holdings (portfolios) of securities. Mutual funds allow the small investor to obtain the benefits of lower transaction costs in purchasing securities and to take advantage of the reduction of risk by diversifying the portfolio of securities held. Many mutual funds are run by brokerage firms, but others are run by banks or independent investment advisers such as Fidelity or Investors Group.

Mutual funds are primarily held by households (around 80%), with the rest held by financial institutions and nonfinancial businesses. They have seen a large increase in their market share since 1980, due primarily to the booming stock market during the 1990s. Another source of growth has been mutual funds that specialize in debt instruments, which first appeared in the 1970s. Before 1970, mutual funds invested almost solely in common stocks. Funds that purchase common stocks may specialize even further and invest solely in foreign securities or in specialized industries, such as energy or high technology. Funds that purchase debt instruments may specialize further in corporate, government, or municipal bonds or in long-term or short-term securities.

The growing importance of mutual funds and pension funds, known as **institutional investors**, has resulted in their controlling a large share of total financial sector assets. Thus institutional investors are the predominant players in the stock markets, with over 70% of the total daily volume in the stock market due to their trading. Increased ownership of stocks has also meant that institutional investors have more clout with corporate boards, often forcing changes in leadership or in corporate policies. Particularly controversial in recent years has been a type of institutional investor called **sovereign wealth funds**, state-owned investment funds that invest in foreign assets (see the FYI box Sovereign Wealth Funds: Are They a Danger?).

Mutual funds are structured in two ways. The more common structure is an **open-end fund**, from which shares can be redeemed at any time at a price that is tied to the asset value of the fund. Mutual funds also can be structured as a **closed-end fund**, in which a fixed number of nonredeemable shares are sold at an initial offering and are then traded like a common stock. The market price of these shares fluctuates with the value of the assets held by the fund. In contrast to the open-end fund, however, the price of the shares may be above or below the value of the assets held by the fund, depending on factors such as the liquidity of the shares or the quality of the management. The greater popularity of the open-end funds is explained by the greater liquidity of their redeemable shares relative to that of the nonredeemable shares of closed-end funds.

Originally, shares of most open-end mutual funds were sold by salespeople (usually brokers) who were paid a commission. Since this commission is paid at the time of purchase and is immediately subtracted from the redemption value of the shares, these funds are called **load funds**. Most mutual funds are currently **no-load funds**; they are sold directly to the public with no sales commissions. In both types of funds, the managers earn their living from management fees paid by the shareholders. These fees amount to approximately 0.5% of the asset value of the fund per year.

Mutual funds are regulated by a variety of agencies. As securities distributed by investment dealers and financial advisers, they fall within provincial jurisdiction. As services provided by financial institutions, they fall under the Bank Act, Trust and Loan Companies Act, and Insurance Companies Act, and are the responsibility of OSFI. Moreover, each mutual fund is a member of a self-regulating organization such as the Investment Industry Association of Canada and the Mutual Fund Dealers Association of Canada (MFDA). Regulations require periodic disclosure of information on these funds to the public and restrictions on the methods of soliciting business.

FYI

Sovereign Wealth Funds: Are They a Danger?

Sovereign wealth funds have been around a long time: The first, the Kuwait Investment Authority, was established in 1953. When governments accumulate a substantial amount of foreign exchange earnings, as has happened in oil-rich countries, they often recognize that these earnings would be better put into investments in foreign countries rather than kept at home. The largest sovereign wealth funds are the Abu Dhabi Investment Authority, Government Pension Fund of Norway, Government of Singapore Investment Corporation, Kuwait Investment Authority, China Investment Corporation, the Stabilization Fund of the Russian Federation, and Singapore's Temasek Holdings. Canada's Alberta Heritage Savings Trust Fund, established in 1976, is a small fund with about $15 billion of assets under management. In 2011, there were about 50 sovereign wealth funds with estimated assets under management close to $5 trillion, representing about 3% of global assets.

Up until recently these funds have been relatively uncontroversial because they were comparatively small and primarily invested in government bonds issued by industrialized countries. In recent years, however, they have grown in size and, in the search for higher returns, invest in a much broader set of assets. This shift in size and focus has led to serious concerns about them in industrialized countries.

One concern is that as the size of these funds increases, they may play a more important role in asset markets, and since some of them are very large—the Abu Dhabi fund has close to $1 trillion of assets—the decision of one fund to pull out of a particular asset market could cause market instability. Sovereign wealth funds also raise national security issues, because they might use their investments for political purposes. They might buy up strategically important industries or use their clout to get political concessions. This is a particular concern because the governments of Russia, China, and Arab countries control many of the largest of these funds. A third concern is that many of these funds, with the exception of the Norwegian fund, provide very little information about their operations and the assets in which they invest.

Although sovereign wealth funds do pose some dangers, they are probably overplayed. Xenophobia often plays well in politics, and foreign purchase of domestic assets is often prevented under the banner of national security in order to protect domestic companies from unwanted takeovers. The lack of transparency for some of these large funds is a serious problem, however. This is why organizations like the International Monetary Fund (IMF) and the Organisation for Economic Co-operation and Development (OECD) proposed rules to increase the amount of information these funds disclose to the markets.

Money Market Mutual Funds

An important addition to the family of mutual funds resulting from the financial innovation process described in earlier chapters is the *money market mutual fund*. Recall that this type of mutual fund invests in short-term debt (money market) instruments of very high quality, such as Treasury bills, commercial paper, and bank certificates of deposit. There is some fluctuation in the market value of these securities, but because their maturity is typically less than six months, the change in the market value is small enough that these funds allow their shares to be redeemed at a fixed value. (Changes in the market value of the securities are figured into the interest paid out by the fund.)

Hedge Funds

Hedge funds are a special type of investment fund, with estimated assets of more than $1 trillion. Hedge funds have received considerable attention recently due to the shock to the financial system resulting from the near collapse of Long-Term Capital Management, once one of the most important hedge funds (see the FYI box

The Long-Term Capital Management Debacle). Well-known hedge funds in the United States include Moore Capital Management and the Quantum group of funds associated with George Soros. Investors in hedge funds, who are limited partners, give their money to managing (general) partners to invest on their behalf. Several features distinguish hedge funds from mutual funds. Hedge funds have a minimum investment requirement between $100 000 and $20 million, with the typical minimum investment being $1 million. Long-Term Capital Management required a $10 million minimum investment. In the United States, federal law limits hedge funds to have no more than 99 investors (limited partners) who must have steady annual incomes of $200 000 or more or a net worth of $1 million, excluding their homes. These restrictions are aimed at allowing hedge funds to be largely unregulated, on the theory that the rich can look out for themselves. Many of the hedge funds are located offshore to escape regulatory restrictions.

Hedge funds also differ from traditional mutual funds in that they usually require that investors commit their money for long periods of time, often several years. The purpose of this requirement is to give managers breathing room to pursue long-run

---

FYI

The Long-Term Capital Management Debacle

Long-Term Capital Management (LTCM) was a hedge fund with a star cast of managers, including 25 Ph.D.s, two Nobel Prize winners in economics (Myron Scholes and Robert Merton), a former vice-chairman of the Federal Reserve System (David Mullins), and one of Wall Street's most successful bond traders (John Meriwether). It made headlines in September 1998 because its near collapse roiled markets and required a private rescue plan organized by the Federal Reserve Bank of New York.

The experience of Long-Term Capital demonstrates that hedge funds are far from risk-free, despite their use of market-neutral strategies. Long-Term Capital got into difficulties when it thought that the high spread between prices on long-term Treasury bonds and long-term corporate bonds was too high, and bet that this "anomaly" would disappear and the spread would narrow. In the wake of the collapse of the Russian financial system in August 1998, investors increased their assessment of the riskiness of corporate securities and, as we saw in Chapter 6, the spread between corporates and Treasuries rose rather than narrowed as Long-Term Capital had predicted. The result was that Long-Term Capital took big losses on its positions, eating up much of its equity position.

By mid-September, Long-Term Capital was unable to raise sufficient funds to meet the demands of its creditors. With Long-Term Capital facing the potential need to liquidate its portfolio of $80 billion in securities and more than $1 trillion of notional value in derivatives, the Federal Reserve Bank of New York stepped in on September 23 and organized a rescue plan with its creditors. The Fed's rationale for stepping in was that a sudden liquidation of Long-Term Capital's portfolio would create unacceptable systemic risk. Tens of billions of dollars of illiquid securities would be dumped on an already jittery market, causing potentially huge losses to numerous lenders and other institutions. The rescue plan required creditors, banks, and investment banks to supply an additional $3.6 billion of funds to Long-Term Capital in exchange for much tighter management control of funds and a 90% reduction in the managers' equity stake. In the middle of 1999, John Meriwether began to wind down the fund's operations.

Even though no public funds were expended, the Fed's involvement in organizing the rescue of Long-Term Capital was highly controversial. Some critics argue that the Fed intervention increased moral hazard by weakening discipline imposed by the market on fund managers because future Fed interventions of this type would be expected. Others think that the Fed's action was necessary to prevent a major shock to the financial system that could have provoked a financial crisis. The debate on whether the Fed should have intervened is likely to go on for some time.

strategies. Hedge funds also typically charge large fees to investors. The typical fund charges a 2% annual fee on the assets it manages plus 20% of profits.

The term *hedge fund* is highly misleading, because the word "hedge" typically indicates strategies to avoid risk. As the near failure of Long-Term Capital illustrates, despite their name, these funds can and do take big risks. Many hedge funds engage in what are called "market-neutral" strategies where they buy a security, such as a bond, that seems cheap and sell an equivalent amount of a similar security that appears to be overvalued. If interest rates as a whole go up or down, the fund is hedged because the decline in value of one security is matched by the rise in value of the other. However, the fund is speculating on whether the spread between the prices on the two securities moves in the direction predicted by the fund managers. If the fund bets wrong, it can lose a lot of money, particularly if it has leveraged up its positions—that is, has borrowed heavily against these positions so that its equity stake is small relative to the size of its portfolio. When Long-Term Capital was rescued, it had a leverage ratio of 50 to 1; that is, its assets were 50 times larger than its equity, and even before it got into trouble, it was leveraged 20 to 1.

In the wake of the near collapse of Long-Term Capital, many U.S. politicians have called for regulation of these funds. However, because these funds operate offshore in places like the Cayman Islands and are outside U.S. jurisdiction, they would be extremely hard to regulate. What regulators can do is ensure that banks and investment banks have clear guidelines on the amount of lending they can provide to hedge funds and require that these institutions get the appropriate amount of disclosure from hedge funds as to the riskiness of their positions.

Private Equity and Venture Capital Funds

Another type of investment fund is the **private equity fund**, which makes long-term investments in companies that are not traded in public markets and has a similar structure to hedge funds. In a private equity fund, investors who are limited partners (e.g., high-wealth individuals, pension funds, financial institutions, and university endowments) place their money with the managing (general) partners who make the private equity investments. Private equity funds are of two types. **Venture capital funds** make investments in new startup businesses, often in the technology industry. **Capital buyout funds** instead make investments in established businesses, and in many cases, buy publicly traded firms through a so-called **leveraged buyout (LBO)**, in which the publicly traded firm is taken private by buying all of its shares, while financing the purchase by increasing the leverage (debt) of the firm.

Private equity has several advantages over investing in publicly traded companies. First, private companies are not subject to controversial and costly regulations. Second, managers of private companies do not feel under pressure to produce immediate profits, as do those at publicly traded companies, and thus can manage their company with their eyes on longer-term profitability. Third, because private equity funds give managers of these companies larger stakes in the firm than is usually the case in publicly traded corporations, they have greater incentives to work hard to maximize the value of the firm. Fourth, private equity overcomes the free-rider problem that we discussed in Chapter 8. In contrast to publicly traded companies, which have a diverse set of owners who are happy to free-ride off of each other, venture capital and capital buyout funds are able to garner almost all the benefits of monitoring the firm and therefore have incentives to make sure the firm is run properly.

In both venture capital and capital buyout funds, once the startup or the purchased company is successful, the fund earns its returns by either selling the firm to another company or selling it off to the public through an initial public offering (IPO). The managing partners of private equity funds are well compensated for their activities: Like hedge funds, they typically earn around a 2% fee for management of the equity fund investments and earn 20% of the profits, which is called **carried interest**.

Both venture capital and capital buyout funds have been highly profitable. Venture capital firms have been an especially important driver of economic growth in recent years because they have funded so many successful high-tech firms, including Apple Computer, Cisco Systems, Microsoft, and Sun Microsystems.

Government Financial Intermediation

The government has become involved in financial intermediation in two basic ways: by supplying government guarantees for private loans and by setting up credit agencies that directly engage in financial intermediation.

Crown Finance Companies

To promote housing and community development, in 1946 the government created the Canada Mortgage and Housing Corporation (CMHC) to provide funds to the mortgage market by borrowing from the federal government and also from the private sector by issuing mortgage-backed securities. The CMHC is not a bank; it doesn't take deposits and is not governed by the Bank Act, but as a financial intermediary makes direct loans and investments primarily for social housing.

Agriculture is another area in which government financial intermediation plays an important role. Farm Credit Canada (FCC), headquartered in Regina, was set up as a Crown corporation in 1959 and is the successor of the Canadian Farm Loan Board, which was established in 1927 to help Canadian farmers. It makes direct loans to new and established farmers for any agricultural or farm-related operation, including the purchase of land, equipment, and livestock. It sources its funds directly from the federal government.

To stimulate the export of Canadian goods and services, Export Development Canada (EDC) was established in 1969 as the successor to the Export Credits Insurance Corporation, which dated from 1944. The EDC is a Crown corporation wholly owned by the Canadian government. With its head office in Ottawa, the EDC provides loans to Canadian exporters to finance the working capital buildup associated with international trade. It also provides intermediate-term, low-interest-rate loans to foreign concerns for the purchase of Canadian goods, equipment, and services.

To promote and assist in the establishment and development of business enterprises in Canada, in 1995 the government created the Business Development Bank of Canada (BDC), headquartered in Montreal. It is the successor to the Federal Business Development Bank (FBDB), which had been set up in 1975 to succeed the Industrial Development Bank (IDB), which dated from 1944. Prior to 2008, the BDC issued its own short- and long-term debt in domestic and foreign financial markets and used the proceeds to make loans to small and medium-sized businesses. Since 2008, the BDC has been funded directly from the federal government.

Government-Sponsored Enterprises in the United States

The U.S. government has also created a number of government agencies that provide funds, either directly or indirectly, to the mortgage market. Three agencies—the Government National Mortgage Association (GNMA, or "Ginnie Mae"), the Federal National Mortgage Association (FNMA, or "Fannie Mae"), and the Federal Home Loan Mortgage Corporation (FHLMC, or "Freddie Mac")—provide funds to the U.S. mortgage market by selling bonds and using the proceeds to buy mortgages or mortgage-backed securities. Except for Ginnie Mae, which is a federal agency and thus is an entity of the U.S. government (like CMHC, FCC, EDC, and BDC are in Canada), the other agencies, known as **government-sponsored enterprises (GSEs)**, are federally sponsored agencies that function as private corporations with close ties to the government. Although the U.S. government does not explicitly back the debt of the GSEs, as is the case for government-sponsored Treasury bonds, in practice the federal government in the United States has not allowed a default on their securities.

Unfortunately, the implicit government backing of GSE debt leads to moral hazard problems similar to those that led to financial crises discussed in Chapter 9. Because the U.S. government in effect guarantees GSE debt, market discipline to limit excessive risk taking by GSEs is quite weak. The GSEs therefore have incentives to take on excessive risk, and this is exactly what they have done in the United States, with the taxpayer left holding the bag. The recent bailout of Fannie Mae and Freddie Mac by the U.S. government involved US$200 billion of government funds (see the FYI box The Subprime Financial Crisis and the Bailout of Fannie Mae and Freddie Mac).

FYI

The Subprime Financial Crisis and the Bailout of Fannie Mae and Freddie Mac

Because it encouraged excessive risk taking, the peculiar structure of Fannie Mae and Freddie Mac—private companies sponsored by the U.S. government—was an accident waiting to happen. Earlier editions of this textbook, as well as many economists, predicted exactly what came to pass: a government bailout of both companies, with huge potential losses for American taxpayers.

When there is a government safety net for financial institutions, there needs to be appropriate government regulation and supervision to make sure these institutions do not take on excessive risk. Fannie and Freddie were given a federal regulator and supervisor, the Office of Federal Housing Oversight (OFHEO), as a result of legislation in 1992, but this regulator was quite weak with only a limited ability to rein them in. The outcome was not surprising: These GSEs had strong incentives to resist effective regulation and supervision because it would cut into their profits. This is exactly what they did: Fannie and Freddie were legendary for their lobbying machine in the U.S. Congress. Between 1998 and 2008, Fannie and Freddie jointly spent over US$170 million on lobbyists, and from 2000 to 2008, they and their employees made over US$14 million of political campaign contributions.

With a weak regulator and strong incentives to take on risk, Fannie and Freddie grew like crazy, and by 2008 had purchased or were guaranteeing over US$5 trillion in mortgages or mortgage-backed securities. The accounting scandals might have even pushed them to take on more risk. In the 1992 legislation, Fannie and Freddie had been given a mission to promote affordable housing. What better way to do this than to purchase subprime mortgages or mortgage-backed securities

(discussed in Chapter 9)? The accounting scandals made this motivation even stronger because they weakened the political support for Fannie and Freddie, giving them even greater incentives to please the U.S. Congress and support affordable housing through the purchase of these assets. By the time the subprime financial crisis hit in force, they had over US$1 trillion of subprime assets on their books. Furthermore, they had extremely low ratios of capital relative to their assets: indeed, their capital ratios were far lower than for other financial institutions like commercial banks.

By 2008, after many subprime mortgages went into default, Fannie and Freddie had booked large losses. Their small capital buffer meant that they had little cushion to withstand these losses, and investors started to pull their money out. With Fannie and Freddie playing such a dominant role in mortgage markets, the U.S. government could not afford to have them go out of business because this would have had a disastrous effect on the availability of mortgage credit, which would have had further devastating effects on the housing market. With bankruptcy imminent, the U.S. Treasury stepped in with a pledge to provide up to US$200 billion of taxpayer money to the companies if needed. The sad saga of Fannie Mae and Freddie Mac illustrates how dangerous it was for the U.S. government to set up GSEs that were exposed to a classic conflict-of-interest problem: They were supposed to serve two masters. As publicly traded corporations, they were expected to maximize profits for their shareholders, but as government agencies, they were obliged to work in the interests of the public. In the end, neither the public nor the shareholders were well served.

SUMMARY

((•
MyEconL
Audio Sum

1. Insurance providers, which are regulated by OSFI and the provinces, acquire funds by selling policies that pay out benefits if catastrophic events occur. Property and casualty insurance companies hold more liquid assets than life insurance companies, because of greater uncertainty regarding the benefits they will have to pay out. All insurers face moral hazard and adverse selection problems that explain the use of insurance management tools, such as information collection and screening of potential policyholders, risk-based premiums, restrictive provisions, prevention of fraud, cancellation of insurance, deductibles, coinsurance, and limits on the amount of insurance.

2. Pension plans provide income payments to people when they retire after contributing to the plans for many years. Pension funds have experienced very rapid growth as a result of encouragement by federal tax policy and now play an important role in the stock market. Many pension plans are underfunded, which means that in future years they will have to pay out higher benefits than the value of their contributions and earnings. The problem of underfunding is especially acute for public pension plans such as the CPP and QPP.

3. Finance companies raise funds by issuing commercial paper and stocks and bonds and use the proceeds to make loans that are particularly suited to consumer and business needs. Virtually unregulated in comparison to chartered banks and near banks, finance companies have been able to tailor their loans to customer needs very quickly and have grown rapidly.

4. Investment bankers assist in the initial sale of securities in primary markets, whereas securities brokers and dealers assist in the trading of securities in the secondary markets, some of which are organized into exchanges. The provinces and the federal government regulate the financial institutions in the securities markets and ensure that adequate information reaches prospective investors.

5. Mutual funds sell shares and use the proceeds to buy securities. Open-end funds issue shares that can be redeemed at any time at a price tied to the asset value of the firm. Closed-end funds issue nonredeemable shares, which are traded like common stock. They are less popular than open-end funds because their shares are not as liquid. Money market mutual funds hold only short-term, high-quality securities, allowing shares to be redeemed at a fixed value.

6. Hedge funds are a special type of investment fund. Investors in hedge funds, who are limited partners, give money to managing (general) partners to invest on their behalf. They have large minimum investments and usually require that investors commit their money for long periods of time.

7. Private equity funds make long-term investments in companies that are not traded publicly and are of two types: venture capital funds, which make investments in startups, and capital buyout funds, which make investments in established companies, often taking publicly traded firms private.

8. To provide credit to residential housing and agriculture, stimulate the export of Canadian goods and services, and assist in the development of business enterprises, the government created a number of Crown corporations, such as CMHC, FCC, EDC, and BDC.

9. The U.S. government has also created a number of government agencies. Particularly important are government-sponsored enterprises (GSEs), which are federally sponsored agencies that function as private corporations with close ties to the government. Because the U.S. government provides an implicit guarantee for GSE debt, market discipline to limit excessive risk taking by GSEs is weak. The resulting moral hazard problem has led to major taxpayer bailouts, especially the recent bailout of Fannie Mae and Freddie Mac, which involved US$200 billion of government funds.

KEY TERMS

annuities, p. 272

brokerage firms, p. 283

capital buyout funds, p. 287

carried interest, p. 288

closed-end fund, p. 284

coinsurance, p. 277

credit default swap (CDS), p. 273

deductible, p. 277

defined-benefit plan, p. 278

QUESTIONS

1. If death rates were to become less predictable than they are, how would life insurance companies change the types of assets they hold?

2. Why do property and casualty insurance companies have large holdings of liquid assets but life insurance companies do not?

3. Why are all defined-contribution pension plans fully funded?

4. How can favourable tax treatment of pension plans encourage saving?

5. "In contrast to private pension plans, government pension plans are rarely underfunded." Is this statement true, false, or uncertain? Explain your answer.

6. What explains the widespread use of deductibles in insurance policies?

7. Why might insurance companies restrict the amount of insurance a policyholder can buy?

8. Why are restrictive provisions a necessary part of insurance policies?

9. If you needed to take out a loan, why might you first go to your local bank rather than to a finance company?

10. Explain why shares in closed-end mutual funds typically sell for less than the market value of the stocks they hold.

11. Why might you buy a no-load mutual fund instead of a load fund?

12. Why can a money market mutual fund allow its shareholders to redeem shares at a fixed price but other mutual funds cannot?

13. Why might government loan guarantees be a high-cost way for the government to subsidize certain activities?

14. If you like to take risks, would you rather be a dealer, a broker, or a specialist? Why?

15. Is investment banking a good career for someone who is afraid of taking risks? Why or why not?

16. How do hedge funds differ from mutual funds?

17. How do private equity funds escape the free-rider problem?

18. What are the four advantages of private equity funds?

19. How have GSEs in the United States exposed taxpayers to large losses?

WEB EXERCISES

1. The Office of the Superintendent of Financial Institutions (OSFI) maintains extensive data on insurers. Go to **www.osfi-bsif.gc.ca** and click on "Life Insurance Companies & Fraternals" and then on "Financial Data—Life Insurance Companies."

   a. Do life insurance companies make more mortgage loans than they invest in bonds and debentures?

   b. Which type of asset has grown most rapidly over the last five years?

   c. Repeat (a) and (b) for property and casualty insurers.

2. OSFI also maintains extensive data on nondepository credit intermediaries (known as finance companies). Go to its website at the address in Exercise 1, locate the data, and answer the following questions.

   a. Do finance companies make more personal loans than business loans?

   b. Do they borrow more from the money market than the bond market?

   c. Which type of asset has grown most rapidly over the last five years?

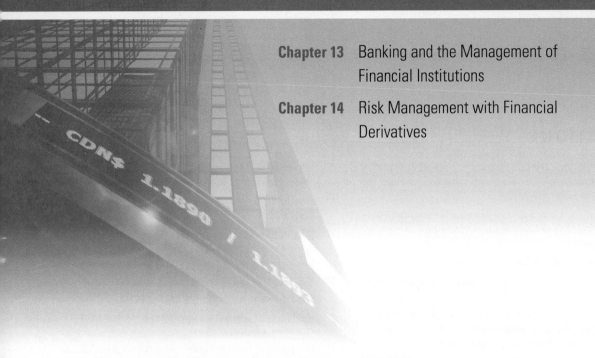

PART IV

The Management of Financial Institutions

Chapter 13 Banking and the Management of Financial Institutions

Chapter 14 Risk Management with Financial Derivatives

Crisis and Response: Canadian Banks Are the World's Best

During the subprime financial crisis, the value of mortgage-backed securities held by financial institutions plummeted and governments in the United States and Europe worked on full-scale banking bailouts and rescue packages in the trillions of dollars. Canada, however, did not have to bail out any banks, although Canadian banks also had their problems. Their shares fell by almost 50% and some of them experienced huge losses; for example, the CIBC suffered writedowns in excess of $6 billion in 2008 because of significant exposure to the U.S. capital and real estate markets.

One reason Canadian banks have done much better than their U.S. and European counterparts is because Canada's banking regulator, the Office of the Superintendent of Financial Institutions (OSFI), has been more conservative than banking regulators in other countries. As a result, Canadian banks have lower leverage and more conservative lending and acquisition practices. In fact, in the aftermath of the Great Recession, Canada's banking system has been viewed as the soundest in the world, with many countries considering Canadian-style reforms of their financial markets.

Managing banks is not an easy task, and the global financial crisis highlights that it has become even more difficult because of increased complexity in the financial services marketplace. In Chapter 13 we look at the business and process of banking and in Chapter 14 we study financial derivatives and how managers of financial institutions use derivatives to manage different types of risk.

CHAPTER 13

Banking and the Management of Financial Institutions

LEARNING OBJECTIVES

After studying this chapter you should be able to

1. outline a bank's sources and uses of funds
2. specify how banks make profits by accepting deposits and making loans
3. discuss how bank managers manage credit risk and interest-rate risk
4. explain gap analysis and duration analysis
5. illustrate how off-balance-sheet activities affect bank profits

PREVIEW   Because banking plays such a major role in channelling funds to borrowers with productive investment opportunities, this financial activity is important in ensuring that the financial system and the economy run smoothly and efficiently. In Canada and other countries, banks (depository institutions) provide loans to businesses, help us finance our postsecondary educations or the purchase of a new car or home, and provide us with services such as chequing and savings accounts. Managing banks, however, has never been an easy task, and recently it has become even more difficult because of greater complexity and uncertainty in the economic environment. Asset prices and interest rates have become much more volatile, resulting in substantial fluctuations in profits and in the value of assets and liabilities held by financial institutions.

In this chapter, we examine how banking is conducted to earn the highest profits possible, how and why banks make loans, how they acquire funds and manage their assets and liabilities (debts), and how they earn income. We also examine how banks cope with credit risk, the risk arising because borrowers may default on their obligations, and, with interest-rate risk, the risk arising from fluctuations in interest rates.

Although we focus on commercial banking, because this is the most important financial intermediary activity, many of the same principles are applicable to other types of financial intermediation.

The Bank Balance Sheet

To understand how banking works, we start by looking at the bank **balance sheet**, a list of the bank's assets and liabilities. As the name implies, this list balances; that is, it has the characteristic that

$$\text{Total assets} = \text{total liabilities} + \text{capital}$$

A bank's balance sheet is also a list of its *sources* of bank funds (liabilities) and *uses* to which the funds are put (assets). Banks obtain funds by borrowing and by issuing other liabilities such as deposits. They then use these funds to acquire assets such as securities and loans. Banks make profits by earning an interest rate on their holdings of securities and loans that is higher than the expenses on their liabilities. The balance sheet of all banks in Canada, as of October 31, 2011, appears in Table 13-1.

Liabilities

A bank acquires funds by issuing (selling) liabilities such as deposits, which are the *sources of funds* the bank uses. The funds obtained from issuing liabilities are used to purchase income-earning assets. Banks have three main sources of funds: deposits, borrowings, and equity. Table 13-1 shows that deposits make about 65% of bank liabilities, borrowings 29%, and equity 6%.

DEMAND AND NOTICE DEPOSITS   Demand deposits are payable on demand; that is, if a depositor shows up at the bank and requests payment by making a withdrawal, the bank must pay the depositor immediately. Similarly, if a person who receives a cheque written on an account from a bank presents that cheque at the bank, the bank must pay the funds out immediately (or credit them to that person's account). Notice deposits are more important as a source of funds for the banks than are demand deposits. Although notice deposits have a notice requirement in the contractual agreement with the client, the banks rarely enforce this clause, and so in fact most notice deposits are really just like demand deposits in this sense.

Demand deposits and notice deposits are bank accounts that allow the owner to write cheques to third parties. Table 13-1 shows that this category of chequable deposits is an important low-cost source of bank funds, making up close to 32% of bank liabilities. Once, chequable deposits were the most important source of bank

TABLE 13-1   Balance Sheet of All Banks in Canada (items as a percentage of the total, October 31, 2011)

Assets (Uses of Funds)*		Liabilities (Sources of Funds)	
Reserves and cash items	5.01	Demand and notice deposits	32.53
Securities	24.58	Fixed-term deposits	32.79
Loans		Advances from the Bank of Canada	0.01
Non-mortgage loans	34.02	Borrowings	28.84
Mortgages	20.00	Bank capital	5.83
Other assets	16.39		
Total	100.00	Total	100.00

* In order of decreasing liquidity

Source: OSFI website, www.osfi-bsif.gc.ca.

funds, but with the appearance of new, more attractive financial instruments, the share of chequable deposits in total bank liabilities has shrunk over time.

A chequable deposit is an asset for the depositor because it is part of his or her wealth. Conversely, because the depositor can withdraw from an account funds that the bank is obligated to pay, chequable deposits are a liability for the bank.

They are usually the lowest-cost source of bank funds because depositors are willing to forgo some interest in order to have access to a liquid asset that can be used to make purchases. The bank's costs of maintaining chequable deposits include interest payments and the costs incurred in servicing these accounts—processing and storing cancelled cheques, preparing and sending out monthly statements, providing efficient tellers (human or otherwise), maintaining an impressive building and conveniently located branches, and advertising and marketing to entice customers to deposit their funds with a given bank.

FIXED-TERM DEPOSITS Fixed-term deposits are the primary source of bank funds (almost 33% of bank liabilities in Table 13-1). Owners (retail customers, small- and medium-sized businesses, large corporations, governments, and other financial institutions) cannot write cheques on fixed-term deposits, but the interest rates are usually higher than those on chequable deposits. There are two main types of fixed-term deposits: savings accounts and time deposits (also called *certificates of deposit*, or *CDs*).

Savings accounts were once the most common type of fixed-term deposit. In these accounts, to which funds can be added or from which funds can be withdrawn at any time, transactions and interest payments are recorded in a monthly statement or in a small book (the passbook) held by the owner of the account.

Time deposits have a fixed maturity length, ranging from several months to over five years, and have substantial penalties for early withdrawal (the forfeiture of several months' interest). Small-denomination time deposits (deposits of less than $100 000) are less liquid for the depositor than passbook savings, earn higher interest rates, and are a more costly source of funds for the banks.

Large-denomination time deposits (CDs) are available in denominations of $100 000 or over and are typically bought by corporations or other banks. Large-denomination CDs are negotiable; like bonds, they can be resold in a secondary market before they mature. For this reason, negotiable CDs are held by corporations, money market mutual funds, and other financial institutions as alternative assets to Treasury bills and other short-term bonds. Since 1964, when they first appeared in Canada, negotiable CDs have become an important source of bank funds.

BORROWINGS Banks obtain funds by borrowing from the Bank of Canada, other banks, and corporations. Borrowings from the Bank of Canada are called **overdraft loans** (also known as **advances**). Banks also borrow reserves overnight in the overnight market from other banks and financial institutions. Banks borrow funds overnight to have enough **settlement balances** at the Bank of Canada to facilitate the clearing of cheques and other transfers (these clearing and settlement processes will be investigated in detail in Chapter 17). Other sources of borrowed funds are loan arrangements with corporations (such as repurchase agreements) and borrowings of Eurodollars (deposits denominated in dollars residing in foreign banks or foreign branches of Canadian banks). Borrowings have become a more important source of bank funds over time: in 1960, they made up only a small fraction of bank liabilities; currently, they are close to 29% of bank liabilities.

BANK CAPITAL The final category on the liabilities side of the balance sheet is bank capital, the bank's net worth, which equals the difference between total assets and liabilities (close to 6% of total bank assets in Table 13-1). The funds are raised by selling new equity (stock) or from retained earnings. Bank capital is a cushion against a drop in the value of its assets, which could force the bank into insolvency (having liabilities in excess of assets, meaning that the bank can be forced into liquidation).

Assets

A bank uses the funds that it has acquired by issuing liabilities to purchase income-earning assets. Bank assets are thus naturally referred to as *uses of funds*, and the interest payments earned on them are what enable banks to make profits.

RESERVES   All banks hold some of the funds they acquire as deposits in an account at the Bank of Canada, in the form of settlement balances. **Reserves** are these settlement balances plus currency that is physically held by banks (called **vault cash** because it is stored in bank vaults overnight). Although Canadian banks are not required to hold reserves in some proportion to their deposits (Canada removed all such legal requirements in June 1994) and there is a requirement of zero settlement balances with the Bank of Canada at the end of each banking day, banks hold some reserves, which we call **desired reserves**.

Banks hold reserves because of their desire to manage their own short-term liquidity requirements and respond to predictable clearing drains and predictable across-the-counter and automated banking machine drains. Moreover, banks hold reserves in order to meet unpredictable and potentially large withdrawals by their liability holders. The risk that net cash withdrawals might be negative is known as **banker's risk**, and from the perspective of this risk, banks hold reserves to meet unpredictable cash and clearing drains. We will refer to the fraction of deposits banks hold in the form of reserves as the **desired reserve ratio**.

CASH ITEMS IN PROCESS OF COLLECTION   Suppose that a cheque written on an account at another bank is deposited in your bank and the funds for this cheque have not yet been received (collected) from the other bank. The cheque is classified as a cash item in process of collection, and it is an asset for your bank because it is a claim on another bank for funds that will be paid within a few days. Items in process of collection are also called **items in transit** or **bank float**.

DEPOSITS AT OTHER BANKS   Many small banks hold deposits in larger banks in exchange for a variety of services, including cheque collection, foreign exchange transactions, and help with securities purchases. These deposits are known as **interbank deposits**.

Collectively, reserves, cash items in process of collection, and deposits at other banks are referred to as cash items. In Table 13-1 they constitute close to 5% of total assets, and their importance has been shrinking over time: in 1960, for example, they accounted for over 20% of total assets.

SECURITIES   A bank's holdings of securities are an important income-earning asset: securities (made up entirely of debt instruments for commercial banks because banks are not allowed to hold stock) account for about 25% of bank assets in Table 13-1. These securities can be classified into three categories: Government of Canada, provincial and municipal securities, and other securities. The Government of Canada securities are the most liquid because they can be easily traded and converted into cash with low transaction costs. Because of their high liquidity, short-term Canadian government securities (such as Treasury bills) are called **secondary reserves**.

Provincial and municipal government securities are desirable for banks to hold primarily because provincial and municipal governments are more likely to do business with banks that hold their securities. Provincial and municipal government and other securities are less marketable (hence less liquid) and are also riskier than Government of Canada securities, primarily because of default risk: there is some possibility that the issuer of the securities may not be able to make its interest payments or pay back the face value of the securities when they mature.

LOANS Banks make their profits primarily by issuing loans. In Table 13-1, some 54% of bank assets are in the form of loans, and in recent years they have generally produced more than half of bank revenues. A loan is a liability for the individual or corporation receiving it but an asset for a bank because it provides income to the bank. Loans are typically less liquid than other assets because they cannot be turned into cash until the loan matures. If the bank makes a one-year loan, for example, it cannot get its funds back until the loan comes due in one year. Loans also have a higher probability of default than other assets. Because of the lack of liquidity and higher default risk, the bank earns its highest return on loans.

As you can see in Table 13-1, the largest categories of loans for banks are non-mortgage loans (commercial and industrial loans made to businesses, consumer loans, and interbank loans) and mortgages. The balance sheet in Table 13-1 shows that non-mortgage loans exceed mortgage loans (34% versus 20% of bank assets). This is so because a larger portion of the foreign activities of Canadian banks is in corporate loans rather than mortgages. In fact, the major difference in the balance sheets of the various depository institutions is primarily the type of loan they specialize in. Trust and mortgage loan companies and credit unions and *caisses populaires*, for example, specialize in residential mortgages.

OTHER ASSETS Bankers' acceptances and the physical capital (bank buildings, computers, and other equipment) owned by the banks are included in this category.

Basic Banking

Before proceeding to a more detailed study of how a bank manages its assets and liabilities in order to make the highest profit, you should understand the basic operation of a bank.

In general terms, banks make profits by selling liabilities with one set of characteristics (a particular combination of liquidity, risk, size, and return) and using the proceeds to buy assets with a different set of characteristics. This process is often referred to as *asset transformation*. For example, a savings deposit held by one person can provide the funds that enable the bank to make a mortgage loan to another person. The bank has, in effect, transformed the savings deposit (an asset held by the depositor) into a mortgage loan (an asset held by the bank). Another way this process of asset transformation is described is to say that the bank "borrows short and lends long" because it makes long-term loans and funds them by issuing short-dated deposits.

The process of transforming assets and providing a set of services (cheque clearing, record keeping, credit analysis, and so forth) is like any other production process in a firm. If the bank produces desirable services at low cost and earns substantial income on its assets, it earns profits; if not, the bank suffers losses.

To make our analysis of the operation of a bank more concrete, we use a tool called a **T-account**. In this case we will use it like a simplified balance sheet, with lines in the form of a T, that lists only the changes that occur in balance sheet items starting from some initial balance sheet position.

The key characteristic of banks is their ability to buy assets by issuing their own deposit liabilities. Suppose that the First Bank has found some profitable loans that it wants to add to its portfolio. It makes a loan in the amount of $100 to a business and credits the business's chequable deposit in that amount. The business accepts the First Bank's deposit liabilities because they have the characteristic of being the medium of exchange and are accepted as money by others. The T-accounts for the First Bank and the business look like these:

First Bank				Business			
Assets		Liabilities		Assets		Liabilities	
Loans	+$100	Chequable deposits	+$100	Chequable deposits	+$100	Bank loans	+$100

Note that the transaction is simply an exchange of assets and liabilities, with no change in the net worth of both the First Bank and the business. The bank's act of making a new loan to the business increases chequable deposits, and thus the money supply, by the amount of the loan. Note, however, that the bank's objective is not to create deposits and increase the money supply: *the bank is in the business of making a profit for its shareholders and the creation of deposits occurs as a byproduct of the bank's financing decisions.*

Acquiring income-producing assets is not the only way in which the First Bank can create new chequable deposits. Let's say that Jane Brown has heard that the First Bank provides excellent service, so she opens a chequing account with a $100 bill. She now has a $100 chequable deposit at the bank, which shows up as a $100 liability on the bank's balance sheet. The bank now puts her $100 bill into its vault so that the bank's assets rise by the $100 increase in vault cash. The T-account for the bank looks like this:

First Bank			
Assets		Liabilities	
Vault cash	+$100	Chequable deposits	+$100

Because vault cash is also part of the bank's reserves, we can rewrite the T-account as follows:

Assets		Liabilities	
Reserves	+$100	Chequable deposits	+$100

Note that Jane Brown's opening of a chequing account leads to *an increase in the bank's reserves equal to the increase in chequable deposits.*

If Jane had opened her account with a $100 cheque written on an account at another bank, say, the Second Bank, we would get the same result. The initial effect on the T-account of the First Bank is as follows:

Assets		Liabilities	
Cash items in process of collection	+$100	Chequable deposits	+$100

Chequable deposits increase by $100 as before, but now the First Bank is owed $100 by the Second Bank. This asset for the First Bank is entered in the T-account as $100 of cash items in process of collection because the First Bank will now try to collect the funds that it is owed. It could go directly to the Second Bank and ask for payment of the funds, but if the two banks are in separate provinces, that would be a time-consuming and costly process. Instead, the First Bank deposits the cheque in its account at the Bank of Canada, and the Bank of Canada collects the funds from the Second Bank. The result is that the Bank of Canada transfers $100 of reserves from the Second Bank to the First Bank, and the final balance sheet positions of the two banks are as follows:

First Bank				**Second Bank**			
Assets		Liabilities		Assets		Liabilities	
Reserves	+$100	Chequable deposits	+$100	Reserves	−$100	Chequable deposits	−$100

The process initiated by Jane Brown can be summarized as follows: when a cheque written on an account at one bank is deposited in another, the bank receiving the deposit gains reserves equal to the amount of the cheque, while the bank on which the cheque is written sees its reserves fall by the same amount. Therefore, ***when a bank receives additional deposits, it gains an equal amount of reserves; when it loses deposits, it loses an equal amount of reserves.***

Now that you understand how banks gain and lose reserves, we can examine how a bank rearranges its balance sheet to make a profit when it experiences a change in its deposits. Let's return to the situation when the First Bank has just received the extra $100 of chequable deposits. As you know, the bank wants to keep a certain fraction of its chequable deposits as reserves. If the fraction (the desired reserve ratio) is 10%, the First Bank's desired reserves have increased by $10, and we can rewrite its T-account as follows:

First Bank			
Assets		Liabilities	
Desired reserves	+$10	Chequable deposits	+$100
Excess reserves	+$90		

Let's see how well the bank is doing as a result of the additional chequable deposits. While reserves earn little interest, servicing the extra $100 of chequable deposits is costly because the bank must keep records, pay tellers, pay for cheque clearing, and so forth. The bank is making a loss! The situation is even worse if the bank makes interest payments on the deposits. If it is to make a profit, the bank must put to productive use all or part of the $90 of excess reserves it has available.

One way to do this is to invest in securities. The other is to make loans; as we have seen, loans account for approximately 70% of the total value of bank assets (uses of funds). Because lenders are subject to the asymmetric information problems of adverse selection and moral hazard (discussed in Chapter 8), banks take steps to reduce the incidence and severity of these problems. Bank loan officers evaluate potential borrowers using what are called the "five Cs"—character, capacity (ability to repay), collateral, conditions (in the local and national economies), and capital (net worth)—before they agree to lend. (A more detailed discussion of the methods banks use to reduce the risk involved in lending appears later in this chapter.)

Let us assume that the bank chooses not to hold any excess reserves but to make loans instead. Assuming that the bank gives up its cash directly, the T-account then looks like this:

Assets		Liabilities	
Desired reserves	+$10	Chequable deposits	+$100
Loans	+$90		

The bank is now making a profit because it holds short-term liabilities such as chequable deposits and uses the proceeds to buy longer-term assets such as loans with higher interest rates. As mentioned earlier, this process of asset transformation is frequently described by saying that banks are in the business of "borrowing short and lending long." For example, if the loans have an interest rate of 10% per year, the bank earns $9 in income from its loans over the year. If the $100 of chequable deposits is in an account with a 5% interest rate and it costs another $3 per year to service the account, the cost per year of these deposits is $8. The bank's profit on the new deposits is then $1 per year, plus any interest that is paid on reserves.

General Principles of Bank Management

Now that you have some idea of how a bank operates, let's look at how a bank manages its assets and liabilities in order to earn the highest possible profit. The bank manager has four primary concerns. The first is to make sure that the bank has enough ready cash to pay its depositors when there are **deposit outflows**, that is, when deposits are lost because depositors make withdrawals and demand payment. To keep enough cash on hand, the bank must engage in **liquidity management**, the acquisition of sufficiently liquid assets to meet the bank's obligations to depositors. Second, the bank manager must pursue an acceptably low level of risk by acquiring assets that have a low rate of default and by diversifying asset holdings (**asset management**). The third concern is to acquire funds at low cost (**liability management**). Finally, the manager must decide the amount of capital the bank should maintain and then acquire the needed capital (**capital adequacy management**).

To understand bank and other financial institution management fully, we must go beyond the general principles of bank asset and liability management described next and look in more detail at how a financial institution manages its assets. The two sections following this one provide an in-depth discussion of how a financial institution manages **credit risk**, the risk arising because borrowers may default, and how it manages **interest-rate risk**, the riskiness of earnings and returns on bank assets that result from interest-rate changes.

Liquidity Management and the Role of Reserves

Let us see how a typical bank, the First Bank, can deal with deposit outflows that occur when its depositors withdraw cash from chequing or savings accounts or write cheques that are deposited in other banks. In the example that follows, we assume that the bank has ample excess reserves and that all deposits have the same desired reserve ratio of 10% (the bank wants to keep 10% of its time and chequable deposits as reserves). Suppose that the First Bank's initial balance sheet is as follows:

Assets		Liabilities	
Reserves	$20 million	Deposits	$100 million
Loans	$80 million	Bank capital	$ 10 million
Securities	$10 million		

The bank's desired reserves are 10% of $100 million, or $10 million. Given that it holds $20 million of reserves, the First Bank has excess reserves of $10 million. If a deposit outflow of $10 million occurs, the bank's balance sheet becomes

Assets		Liabilities	
Reserves	$10 million	Deposits	$90 million
Loans	$80 million	Bank capital	$10 million
Securities	$10 million		

The bank loses $10 million of deposits *and* $10 million of reserves, but because its desired reserves are now 10% of only $90 million ($9 million), its reserves still exceed this amount by $1 million. In short, *if a bank has ample reserves, a deposit outflow does not necessitate changes in other parts of its balance sheet*.

The situation is quite different when a bank holds insufficient reserves. Let's assume that instead of initially holding $10 million in excess reserves, the First Bank makes additional loans of $10 million, so that it holds no excess reserves. Its initial balance sheet would be

Assets		Liabilities	
Reserves	$10 million	Deposits	$100 million
Loans	$90 million	Bank capital	$ 10 million
Securities	$10 million		

When it suffers the $10 million deposit outflow, its balance sheet becomes

Assets		Liabilities	
Reserves	$ 0 million	Deposits	$90 million
Loans	$90 million	Bank capital	$10 million
Securities	$10 million		

After $10 million has been withdrawn from deposits and hence reserves, the bank has a problem: its desired reserves are 10% of $90 million, or $9 million, but it has no reserves! To eliminate this shortfall, the bank has four basic options. One is to acquire reserves to meet a deposit outflow by borrowing them from other banks in the overnight market or by borrowing from corporations.[1] If the First Bank acquires the $9 million shortfall in reserves by borrowing it from other banks or corporations, its balance sheet becomes

Assets		Liabilities	
Reserves	$ 9 million	Deposits	$90 million
Loans	$90 million	Borrowings	$ 9 million
Securities	$10 million	from other	
		banks or	
		corporations	
		Bank capital	$10 million

---

[1]One way that the First Bank can borrow from other banks and corporations is by selling negotiable certificates of deposit. This method for obtaining funds is discussed in the section on liability management.

The cost of this activity is the interest rate on these loans, such as the overnight interest rate.

A second alternative is for the bank to sell some of its securities to help cover the deposit outflow. For example, it might sell $9 million of its securities and deposit the proceeds with the Bank of Canada, resulting in the following balance sheet:

Assets		Liabilities	
Reserves	$ 9 million	Deposits	$90 million
Loans	$90 million	Bank capital	$10 million
Securities	$ 1 million		

The bank incurs some brokerage and other transaction costs when it sells these securities. The Government of Canada securities that the bank holds are very liquid, so the transaction costs of selling them are quite modest. However, the other securities the bank holds are less liquid, and the transaction costs can be appreciably higher.

A third way that the bank can meet a deposit outflow is to acquire reserves by borrowing from the Bank of Canada. In our example, the First Bank could leave its security and loan holdings the same and borrow $9 million in advances from the Bank of Canada. Its balance sheet would be

Assets		Liabilities	
Reserves	$ 9 million	Deposits	$90 million
Loans	$90 million	Advances from	$ 9 million
Securities	$10 million	the Bank of Canada	
		Bank capital	$10 million

The cost associated with advances from the Bank of Canada is the interest rate that must be paid to the Bank of Canada (called the **bank rate**).

Finally, a bank can acquire the $9 million of reserves to meet the deposit outflow by reducing its loans by this amount and depositing the $9 million it then receives with the Bank of Canada, thereby increasing its reserves by $9 million. This transaction changes the balance sheet as follows:

Assets		Liabilities	
Reserves	$ 9 million	Deposits	$90 million
Loans	$81 million	Bank capital	$10 million
Securities	$10 million		

The First Bank is once again in good shape because its $9 million of reserves satisfies the (desired) reserve requirement.

However, this process of reducing its loans is the bank's costliest way of acquiring reserves when there is a deposit outflow. If the First Bank has numerous short-term loans renewed at fairly short intervals, it can reduce its total amount of loans outstanding fairly quickly by *calling in* loans—that is, by not renewing some loans when they come due. Unfortunately for the bank, this is likely to antagonize the customers whose loans are not being renewed because they have not done anything to deserve such treatment. Indeed, they are likely to take their business elsewhere in the future, a very costly consequence for the bank.

A second method for reducing its loans is for the bank to sell them off to other banks. Again, this is very costly because other banks do not personally know the customers who have taken out the loans and so may not be willing to buy the loans at their full value (this is just the lemons adverse selection problem discussed in Chapter 8).

The foregoing discussion explains why banks hold reserves even though loans or securities earn a higher return. When a deposit outflow occurs, holding reserves allows the bank to escape the costs of (1) borrowing from other banks or corporations, (2) selling securities, (3) borrowing from the Bank of Canada, or (4) calling in or selling off loans. ***Reserves are insurance against the costs associated with deposit outflows. The higher the costs associated with deposit outflows, the more reserves banks will want to hold.***

Just as you and I would be willing to pay an insurance company to insure us against a casualty loss such as the theft of a car, a bank is willing to pay the cost of holding reserves (the opportunity cost, the earnings forgone by not holding income-earning assets such as loans or securities) to insure against losses due to deposit outflows. Because reserves, like insurance, have a cost, banks also take other steps to protect themselves; for example, they might shift their holdings of assets to more liquid securities (secondary reserves).

Asset Management

Now that you understand why a bank has a need for liquidity, we can examine the basic strategy a bank pursues in managing its assets. To maximize its profits, a bank must simultaneously seek the highest returns possible on loans and securities, reduce risk, and make adequate provisions for liquidity by holding liquid assets. Banks try to accomplish these three goals in four basic ways.

First, banks try to find borrowers who will pay high interest rates and are unlikely to default on their loans. They seek out loan business by advertising their borrowing rates and by approaching corporations directly to solicit loans. It is up to the bank's loan officer to decide if potential borrowers are good credit risks who will make interest and principal payments on time (i.e., to engage in screening to reduce the adverse selection problem). Typically, banks are conservative in their loan policies; the default rate is usually less than 1%. It is important, however, that banks not be so conservative that they miss out on attractive lending opportunities that earn high interest rates.

Second, banks try to purchase securities with high returns and low risk. Third, in managing their assets, banks must attempt to lower risk by diversifying. They accomplish this by purchasing many different types of assets (short- and long-term, Government of Canada, and municipal bonds) and approving many types of loans to a number of customers. Banks that have not sufficiently sought the benefits of diversification often come to regret it later. For example, banks that had overspecialized in making loans to energy companies, real estate developers, or farmers suffered huge losses in the 1980s with the slump in energy, property, and farm prices. Indeed, some of these banks (e.g., the Canadian Commercial Bank and the Northland Bank) went broke because they had "put too many eggs in one basket."

Finally, the bank must manage the liquidity of its assets so that it can pay depositors when there are deposit outflows without bearing huge costs. This means that it will hold liquid securities even if they earn a somewhat lower return than other assets. In addition, it will want to hold government securities so that even if a deposit outflow forces some costs on the bank, these will not be terribly high. Again, it is not wise for a bank to be too conservative. If it avoids all costs associated with deposit outflows by holding only reserves, the bank suffers losses because reserves earn little interest, while the bank's liabilities are costly to maintain. The bank must balance its desire for liquidity against the increased earnings that can be obtained from less liquid assets such as loans.

Liability Management

Before the 1960s, liability management was a staid affair: for the most part, banks took their liabilities as fixed and spent their time trying to achieve an optimal mix of assets. There were two main reasons for the emphasis on asset management. First, a large part of the sources of bank funds was obtained through demand deposits that did not pay any interest. Thus banks could not actively compete with one another for these deposits, and so their amount was effectively a given for an individual bank. Second, because the markets for making overnight loans between banks were not well developed, banks rarely borrowed from other banks to meet their reserve needs.

Starting in the 1960s, however, large banks (called **money centre banks**) began to explore ways in which the liabilities on their balance sheets could provide them with reserves and liquidity. This led to an expansion of overnight loan markets, such as the federal funds market in the United States and the overnight funds market in Canada, and the development of new financial instruments such as negotiable CDs (first developed in 1961), which enabled money centre banks to acquire funds quickly.[2]

This new flexibility in liability management meant that banks could take a different approach to bank management. They no longer needed to depend on chequable deposits as the primary source of bank funds and as a result no longer treated their sources of funds (liabilities) as given. Instead, they aggressively set target goals for their asset growth and tried to acquire funds (by issuing liabilities) as they were needed.

For example, today, when a money centre bank finds an attractive loan opportunity, it can acquire funds by selling a negotiable CD. Or if it has a reserve shortfall, funds can be borrowed from another bank in the overnight market without incurring high transaction costs. The overnight market can also be used to finance loans. Because of the increased importance of liability management, most banks now manage both sides of the balance sheet together in an *asset–liability management (ALM) committee.*

The emphasis on liability management explains some of the important changes over the past three decades in the composition of banks' balance sheets. While negotiable CDs and bank borrowings have greatly increased in importance as a source of bank funds in recent years, chequable deposits have decreased in importance. Newfound flexibility in liability management and the search for higher profits have also stimulated banks to increase the proportion of their assets held in loans, which earn higher income.

Capital Adequacy Management

Banks have to make decisions about the amount of capital they need to hold for three reasons. First, bank capital helps prevent *bank failure,* a situation in which the bank cannot satisfy its obligations to pay its depositors and other creditors and so goes out of business. Second, the amount of capital affects returns for the owners (equity holders) of the bank. Third, a minimum amount of bank capital (bank capital requirements) is required by regulatory authorities.

---

[2] Because small banks are not as well known as money centre banks and so might be a higher credit risk, they find it harder to raise funds in the negotiable CD market. Hence, they do not engage nearly as actively in liability management.

HOW BANK CAPITAL HELPS PREVENT BANK FAILURE   Let's consider two banks with identical balance sheets, except that the High Capital Bank has a ratio of capital to assets of 10% while the Low Capital Bank has a ratio of 4%.

High Capital Bank				Low Capital Bank			
Assets		Liabilities		Assets		Liabilities	
Reserves	$10 million	Deposits	$90 million	Reserves	$10 million	Deposits	$96 million
Loans	$90 million	Bank capital	$10 million	Loans	$90 million	Bank capital	$ 4 million

Suppose that both banks got caught up in the euphoria of the real estate market in 2006 and 2007, only to find that $5 million of their real estate loans became worthless. When these bad loans are written off (valued at zero), the total value of assets declines by $5 million. As a consequence, bank capital, which equals total assets minus liabilities, also declines by $5 million. The balance sheets of the two banks now look like this:

High Capital Bank				Low Capital Bank			
Assets		Liabilities		Assets		Liabilities	
Reserves	$10 million	Deposits	$90 million	Reserves	$10 million	Deposits	$96 million
Loans	$85 million	Bank capital	$ 5 million	Loans	$85 million	Bank capital	−$1 million

The High Capital Bank takes the $5 million loss in stride because its initial cushion of $10 million in capital means that it still has a positive net worth (bank capital) of $5 million after the loss. The Low Capital Bank, however, is in big trouble. The value of its assets has fallen below its liabilities, and its net worth is now –$1 million. Because the bank has a negative net worth, it is insolvent: it does not have sufficient assets to pay off all holders of its liabilities. When a bank becomes insolvent, government regulators close the bank, its assets are sold off, and its managers are fired. Since the owners of the Low Capital Bank will find their investment wiped out, they would clearly have preferred the bank to have had a large enough cushion of bank capital to absorb the losses, as was the case for the High Capital Bank. We therefore see an important rationale for a bank to maintain a sufficient level of capital: *a bank maintains bank capital to lessen the chance that it will become insolvent*.

HOW THE AMOUNT OF BANK CAPITAL AFFECTS RETURNS TO EQUITY HOLDERS
Because owners of a bank must know whether their bank is being managed well, they need good measures of bank profitability. A basic measure of bank profitability is the **return on assets** (**ROA**), the net profit after taxes per dollar of assets:

$$ROA = \frac{\text{net profit after taxes}}{\text{assets}}$$

The return on assets provides information on how efficiently a bank is being run, because it indicates how much profit is generated on average by each dollar of assets.

However, what the bank's owners (equity holders) care about most is how much the bank is earning on their equity investment. This information is provided by the other basic measure of bank profitability, the **return on equity** (**ROE**), the net profit after taxes per dollar of equity capital:

$$ROE = \frac{\text{net profit after taxes}}{\text{equity capital}}$$

There is a direct relationship between the return on assets (which measures how efficiently the bank is run) and the return on equity (which measures how well the owners are doing on their investment). This relationship is determined by the **equity multiplier (EM)**, the amount of assets per dollar of equity capital:

$$EM = \frac{\text{assets}}{\text{equity capital}}$$

To see this, we note that

$$\frac{\text{net profit after taxes}}{\text{equity capital}} = \frac{\text{net profit after taxes}}{\text{assets}} \times \frac{\text{assets}}{\text{equity capital}}$$

which, using our definitions, yields

$$ROE = ROA \times EM \qquad (1)$$

The formula in Equation 1 tells us what happens to the return on equity when a bank holds a smaller amount of capital (equity) for a given amount of assets. As we have seen, the High Capital Bank initially has $100 million of assets and $10 million of equity, which gives it an equity multiplier of 10 (= $100 million/$10 million). The Low Capital Bank, by contrast, has only $4 million of equity, so its equity multiplier is higher, equalling 25 (= $100 million/$4 million). Suppose that these banks have been equally well run so that they both have the same return on assets, 1%. The return on equity for the High Capital Bank equals 1% $\times$ 10 = 10%, while the return on equity for the Low Capital Bank equals 1% $\times$ 25 = 25%. The equity holders in the Low Capital Bank are clearly a lot happier than the equity holders in the High Capital Bank because they are earning more than twice as high a return. We now see why owners of a bank may not want it to hold a lot of capital. ***Given the return on assets, the lower the bank capital, the higher the return for the owners of the bank.***

TRADE-OFF BETWEEN SAFETY AND RETURNS TO EQUITY HOLDERS   We now see that bank capital has benefits and costs. Bank capital benefits the owners of a bank in that it makes their investment safer by reducing the likelihood of bankruptcy. But bank capital is costly because the higher it is, the lower will be the return on equity for a given return on assets. In determining the amount of bank capital, managers must decide how much of the increased safety that comes with higher capital (the benefit) they are willing to trade off against the lower return on equity that comes with higher capital (the cost).[3]

In more uncertain times, when the possibility of large losses on loans increases, bank managers might want to hold more capital to protect the equity holders. Conversely, if they have confidence that loan losses won't occur, they might want to reduce the amount of bank capital, have a high equity multiplier, and thereby increase the return on equity.

BANK CAPITAL REQUIREMENTS   Banks also hold capital because they are required to do so by regulatory authorities. Because of the high costs of holding capital for the reasons just described, bank managers often want to hold less bank capital relative to assets than is required by the regulatory authorities. In this case, the amount of bank capital is determined by the bank capital requirements.

---

[3]Managers of financial institutions also need to know how well their banks are doing at any point in time. A Web Appendix to this chapter discusses how bank performance is measured, and is available on this book's MyEconLab.

APPLICATION

Strategies for Managing Bank Capital

Suppose that as the manager of the First Bank, you have to make decisions about the appropriate amount of bank capital. Looking at the balance sheet of the bank, which like the High Capital Bank has a ratio of bank capital to assets of 10 ($10 million of capital and $100 million of assets), you are concerned that the large amount of bank capital is causing the return on equity to be too low. You conclude that the bank has a capital surplus and should increase the equity multiplier to increase the return on equity. What should you do?

To lower the amount of capital relative to assets and raise the equity multiplier, you can do any of three things: (1) you can reduce the amount of bank capital by buying back some of the bank's stock; (2) you can reduce the bank's capital by paying out higher dividends to its shareholders, thereby reducing the bank's retained earnings; or (3) you can keep bank capital constant but increase the bank's assets by acquiring new funds, say, by issuing CDs and then seeking out loan business or purchasing more securities with these new funds. Because you think that it would enhance your position with the shareholders, you decide to pursue the second alternative and raise the dividend on the First Bank stock.

Now suppose that the First Bank is in a similar situation to the Low Capital Bank and has a ratio of bank capital to assets of 4%. You now worry that the bank is short on capital relative to assets because it does not have a sufficient cushion to prevent bank failure. To raise the amount of capital relative to assets, you now have the following three choices: (1) you can raise capital for the bank by having it issue equity (common stock); (2) you can raise capital by reducing the bank's dividends to shareholders, thereby increasing retained earnings that it can put into its capital account; or (3) you can keep capital at the same level but reduce the bank's assets by making fewer loans or by selling off securities and then using the proceeds to reduce its liabilities. Suppose that raising bank capital is not easy to do at the current time because capital markets are tight or because shareholders will protest if their dividends are cut. Then you might have to choose the third alternative and decide to shrink the size of the bank.

In the aftermath of the subprime mortgage crisis in the United States, many banks experienced capital shortfalls and had to restrict asset growth, as you might have had to do if the First Bank were short of capital. The important consequences of this for the credit markets are discussed in the Application that follows.

APPLICATION

How a Capital Crunch Caused a Credit Crunch During the Global Financial Crisis

The dramatic slowdown in the growth of credit in the wake of the financial crisis starting in 2007 triggered a "credit crunch" in which credit was hard to get. As a result, the performance of the economy in 2008 and 2009 was very poor. What caused the credit crunch?

Our analysis of how a bank manages its capital indicates that the 2008–2009 credit crunch was caused, at least in part, by the capital crunch, in which shortfalls of bank capital led to slower credit growth.

As we discussed in the previous chapter, there was a major boom and bust in the U.S. housing market that led to huge losses for banks around the world from their holdings of securities backed by U.S. residential mortgages. In addition, banks had to take back onto their balance sheets many of the structured investment vehicles (SIVs) they had sponsored. The losses that reduced bank capital, along with the need for more capital to support the assets coming back onto their balance sheets, led to capital shortfalls: banks had to either raise new capital or restrict asset growth by cutting back on lending. Banks did raise some capital but with the growing weakness of the world economy, raising new capital was extremely difficult, so banks also chose to tighten their lending standards and reduce lending. Both of these helped produce a weak economy in 2008 and 2009.

Managing Credit Risk

As seen in the earlier discussion of general principles of asset management, banks and other financial institutions must make successful loans that are paid back in full (and so subject the institution to little credit risk) if they are to earn high profits. The economic concepts of adverse selection and moral hazard discussed in Chapters 2 and 8 provide a framework for understanding the principles that financial institutions have to follow to reduce credit risk and make successful loans.

Adverse selection in loan markets occurs because bad credit risks (those most likely to default) are the ones who usually line up for loans—in other words, those who are most likely to produce an *adverse* outcome are the most likely to be *selected*. Borrowers with very risky investment projects have much to gain if their projects are successful, and so they are the most eager to obtain loans. Clearly, however, they are the least desirable borrowers because of the greater possibility that they will be unable to pay back their loans.

Moral hazard is a problem in loan markets because borrowers may have incentives to engage in activities that are undesirable from the lender's point of view. In such situations, it is more likely that the lender will be exposed to the *hazard* of default. Once borrowers have obtained a loan, they are more likely to invest in high-risk investment projects—projects that pay high returns to the borrowers if successful. The high risk, however, makes it less likely that they will be able to pay the loan back.

To be profitable, financial institutions must overcome the adverse selection and moral hazard problems that make loan defaults more likely. The attempts of financial institutions to solve these problems help explain a number of principles for managing credit risk: screening and monitoring, establishment of long-term customer relationships, loan commitments, collateral and compensating balance requirements, and credit rationing.

Screening and Monitoring

Asymmetric information is present in loan markets because lenders have less information about the investment opportunities and activities of borrowers than borrowers do. This situation leads to two information-producing activities by financial institutions: screening and monitoring.

SCREENING   Adverse selection in loan markets requires that financial institutions screen out the bad credit risks from the good ones so that loans will be profitable to them. To accomplish effective screening, lenders must collect reliable information from prospective borrowers. Effective screening and information collection together form an important principle of credit risk management.

When you apply for a consumer loan (such as a car loan or a mortgage to purchase a house), the first thing you are asked to do is fill out forms that elicit a great deal of information about your personal finances. You are asked about your salary, bank accounts, other assets (such as cars, insurance policies, and furnishings), and your outstanding loans; your record of loan, credit card, and charge account repayments; and the number of years you've worked and who your employers have been. You also are asked personal questions such as your age, marital status, and number of children. The lender uses this information to evaluate how good a credit risk you are by calculating your credit score, a statistical measure derived from your answers that predicts whether you are likely to have trouble making your loan payments. Deciding on how good a risk you are cannot be entirely scientific, so the lender must also use judgment. A loan officer, whose job is to decide whether you should be given the loan, might call your employer or talk to some of the personal references you supplied. The officer might even make a judgement based on your demeanour or your appearance (this is why most people dress neatly and conservatively when they go to a bank to apply for a loan).

The process of screening and collecting information is similar when a financial institution makes a business loan. It collects information about the company's profits and losses (income) and about its assets and liabilities. The lender also has to evaluate the likely future success of the business. So in addition to obtaining information on such items as sales figures, a loan officer might ask questions about the company's future plans, the purpose of the loan, and the competition in the industry. The officer might even visit the company to obtain a first-hand look at its operations. The bottom line is that, whether for personal or business loans, bankers and other financial institutions need to be nosy.

SPECIALIZATION IN LENDING   One puzzling feature of bank lending is that a bank often specializes in lending to local firms or to firms in particular industries, such as energy. In one sense, this behaviour appears surprising because it means that the bank is not diversifying its portfolio of loans and is therefore exposing itself to more risk. But from another perspective, such specialization makes perfect sense. The adverse selection problem requires that banks screen out bad credit risks. It is easier for a bank to collect information about local firms and determine their creditworthiness than to collect similar information on firms that are far away. Similarly, by concentrating its lending on firms in specific industries, the bank becomes more knowledgeable about these industries and is therefore better able to predict which firms will be able to make timely payments on their debt.

MONITORING AND ENFORCEMENT OF RESTRICTIVE COVENANTS   Once a loan has been made, the borrower may have an incentive to engage in risky activities that make it less likely that the loan will be repaid. To reduce this moral hazard, financial institutions must adhere to the principle for managing credit risk that a lender should write provisions (restrictive covenants) into loan contracts that prevent borrowers from engaging in overly risky activities. By monitoring borrowers' activities to see whether they are complying with the restrictive covenants and by enforcing the covenants if they are not, lenders can make sure that borrowers are not taking on risks at the institution's expense. The need for banks and other financial institutions to engage in screening and monitoring explains why they spend so much money on auditing and information-collecting activities.

Long-Term Customer Relationships

An additional way for banks and other financial institutions to obtain information about borrowers is through long-term customer relationships, another important principle of credit risk management.

If a prospective borrower has had a chequing or savings account or other loans with a bank over a long period of time, a loan officer can look at past activity in the accounts and learn quite a bit about the borrower. The balances in the chequing and savings accounts tell the banker how liquid the potential borrower is and at what time of year the borrower has a strong need for cash. A review of the cheques the borrower has written reveals the borrower's suppliers. If the borrower has borrowed previously from the bank, the bank has a record of the loan payments. Thus, long-term customer relationships reduce the costs of information collection and make it easier to screen out bad credit risks.

The need for monitoring by lenders adds to the importance of long-term customer relationships. If the borrower has borrowed from the bank before, the bank has already established procedures for monitoring that customer. Therefore, the costs of monitoring long-term customers are lower than those for new customers.

Long-term relationships benefit the customers as well as the bank. A firm with a previous relationship will find it easier to obtain a loan at a low interest rate because the bank has an easier time determining if the prospective borrower is a good credit risk and incurs fewer costs in monitoring the borrower.

A long-term customer relationship has another advantage for the bank. No bank can think of every contingency when it writes a restrictive covenant into a loan contract; there will always be risky borrower activities that are not ruled out. However, what if a borrower wants to preserve a long-term relationship with a bank because it will be easier to get future loans at low interest rates? The borrower then has incentive to avoid risky activities that would upset the bank, even if restrictions on these risky activities are not specified in the loan contract. Indeed, if a bank doesn't like what a borrower is doing even when the borrower isn't violating any restrictive covenants, it has some power to discourage the borrower from such activity: the bank can threaten not to let the borrower have new loans in the future. Long-term customer relationships therefore enable banks to deal with even unanticipated moral hazard contingencies.

Loan Commitments

Banks also create long-term relationships and gather information by issuing **loan commitments** to commercial customers. A loan commitment is a bank's commitment (for a specified future period of time) to provide a firm with loans up to a given amount at an interest rate that is tied to some market interest rate. The majority of commercial and industrial loans are made under the loan commitment arrangement. The advantage for the firm is that it has a source of credit when it needs it. The advantage for the bank is that the loan commitment promotes a long-term relationship, which in turn facilitates information collection. In addition, provisions in the loan commitment agreement require that the firm continually supply the bank with information about the firm's income, asset and liability position, business activities, and so on. A loan commitment arrangement is a powerful method for reducing a bank's costs for screening and information collection.

Collateral and Compensating Balances

Collateral requirements for loans are important credit risk management tools. Collateral, which is property promised to the lender as compensation if the borrower defaults, lessens the consequences of adverse selection because it reduces the lender's losses in the case of a loan default. It also reduces moral hazard, because the borrower has more to lose from a default. If a borrower defaults on a loan, the lender can sell the collateral and use the proceeds to make up for its losses on the loan. One particular form of collateral required when a bank makes commercial loans is called **compensating balances**: a firm receiving a loan must keep a required minimum amount of funds in a chequing account at the bank. For example, a business getting a $10 million loan may be required to keep compensating balances of at least $1 million in its chequing account at the bank. The $1 million in compensating balances can be taken by the bank to make up some of the losses on the loan if the borrower defaults.

Besides serving as collateral, compensating balances help increase the likelihood that a loan will be paid off. They do this by helping the bank monitor the borrower and consequently reduce moral hazard. Specifically, by requiring the borrower to use a chequing account at the bank, the bank can observe the firm's cheque payment practices, which may yield a great deal of information about the borrower's financial condition. For example, a sustained drop in the borrower's chequing account balance may signal that the borrower is having financial trouble, or account activity may suggest that the borrower is engaging in risky activities; perhaps a change in suppliers means that the borrower is pursuing new lines of business. Any significant change in the borrower's payment procedures is a signal to the bank that it should make inquiries. Compensating balances therefore make it easier for banks to monitor borrowers more effectively and are consequently another important credit risk management tool.

Credit Rationing

Another way in which financial institutions deal with adverse selection and moral hazard is through **credit rationing**: refusing to make loans even though borrowers are willing to pay the stated interest rate or even a higher rate. Credit rationing takes two forms. The first occurs when a lender refuses to make a loan of *any amount* to a borrower, even if the borrower is willing to pay a higher interest rate. The second occurs when a lender is willing to make a loan but restricts the size of the loan to less than the borrower would like.

At first you might be puzzled by the first type of credit rationing. After all, even if the potential borrower is a credit risk, why doesn't the lender just extend the loan but at a higher interest rate? The answer is that adverse selection prevents this solution. Individuals and firms with the riskiest investment projects are exactly those that are willing to pay the highest interest rates. If a borrower took on a high-risk investment and succeeded, the borrower would become extremely rich. But a lender wouldn't want to make such a loan precisely because the credit risk is high; the likely outcome is that the borrower will *not* succeed and the lender will not be paid back. Charging a higher interest rate just makes adverse selection worse for the lender; that is, it increases the likelihood that the lender is lending to a bad credit risk. The lender would therefore rather not make any loans at a higher interest rate; instead, it would engage in the first type of credit rationing and would turn down loans.

Financial institutions engage in a second type of credit rationing to guard against moral hazard: they grant loans to borrowers, but not loans as large as the borrowers want. Such credit rationing is necessary because the larger the loan, the greater the benefits from moral hazard. If a bank gives you a $1000 loan, for example, you are likely to take actions that enable you to pay it back because you don't want to hurt your credit rating for the future. However, if the bank lends you $10 million, you are more likely to fly off to Rio to celebrate. The larger your loan, the greater your incentives to engage in activities that make it less likely that you will repay the loan. Because more borrowers repay their loans if the loan amounts are small, financial institutions ration credit by providing borrowers with smaller loans than they seek.

Managing Interest-Rate Risk

With the increased volatility of interest rates that occurred in the 1980s, banks and other financial institutions became more concerned about their exposure to interest-rate risk, the riskiness of earnings and returns that is associated with changes in interest rates. To see what interest-rate risk is all about, let's take a look at the balance sheet of the First Bank:

First Bank			
Assets		**Liabilities**	
Rate-sensitive assets	$20 million	Rate-sensitive liabilities	$50 million
Variable-rate and		Variable-rate CDs	
short-term loans			
Short-term securities			
Fixed-rate assets	$80 million	Fixed-rate liabilities	$50 million
Reserves		Chequable deposits	
Long-term loans		Savings deposits	
Long-term securities		Long-term CDs	
		Equity capital	

A total of $20 million of its assets are rate-sensitive, with interest rates that change frequently (at least once a year), and $80 million of its assets are fixed-rate, with interest rates that remain unchanged for a long period (over a year). On the liabilities side, the First Bank has $50 million of rate-sensitive liabilities and $50 million of fixed-rate liabilities. Suppose that interest rates rise by 5 percentage points on average, from 10% to 15%. The income on the assets increases by $1 million (= 5% × $20 million of rate-sensitive assets), while the payments on the liabilities increase by $2.5 million (= 5% × $50 million of rate-sensitive liabilities). The First Bank's profits now decline by $1.5 million (= $1 million − $2.5 million). Conversely, if interest rates fall by 5 percentage points, similar reasoning tells us that the First Bank's profits increase by $1.5 million. This example illustrates the following point: *if a bank has more rate-sensitive liabilities than assets, a rise in interest rates will reduce bank profits and a decline in interest rates will raise bank profits.*

Gap Analysis

One simple and quick approach to measuring the sensitivity of bank income to changes in interest rates is **gap analysis** (also called **income gap analysis**), in which the amount of rate-sensitive liabilities is subtracted from the amount of rate-sensitive assets. This calculation, *GAP*, can be written as

$$GAP = RSA - RSL \tag{2}$$

where

$$RSA = \text{rate-sensitive assets}$$
$$RSL = \text{rate-sensitive liabilities}$$

In our example, the bank manager calculates *GAP* to be

$$GAP = \$20 \text{ million} - \$50 \text{ million} = -\$30 \text{ million}$$

Multiplying *GAP* times the change in the interest rate immediately reveals the effect on bank income:

$$\Delta I = GAP \times \Delta i \tag{3}$$

where

$$\Delta I = \text{change in bank income}$$
$$\Delta i = \text{change in interest rates}$$

APPLICATION

Gap Analysis

Using the −$30-million gap calculated using Equation 2, what is the change in income if interest rates rise by 1%?

Solution   The change in income is −$300 000:

$$\Delta I = GAP \times \Delta i$$

where

$$GAP = RSA - RSL \qquad = -\$30 \text{ million}$$
$$\Delta i = \text{change in interest rate} = 0.01$$

Thus

$$\Delta I = -\$30 \text{ million} \times 0.01 = -\$300\,000$$

The analysis we just conducted is known as *basic gap analysis*, and it suffers from the problem that many of the assets and liabilities that are not classified as rate-sensitive have different maturities. One refinement to deal with this problem, the *maturity bucket approach*, is to measure the gap for several maturity subintervals, called *maturity buckets*, so that effects of interest-rate changes over a multi-year period can be calculated. The second refinement, called *standardized gap analysis*, accounts for the differing degrees of rate sensitivity for different rate-sensitive assets and liabilities.

Duration Analysis

The gap analysis we have examined so far focuses only on the effect of interest-rate changes on income. Clearly, owners and managers of banks care not only about the effect of changes in interest rates on income but also about the effect of changes in interest rates on the market value of the net worth of the bank.[4]

An alternative method for measuring interest-rate risk, called **duration analysis**, examines the sensitivity of the market value of the bank's net worth to changes in interest rates. Duration analysis is based on Macaulay's concept of *duration*, which measures the average lifetime of a security's stream of payments (described in the Web Appendix to Chapter 4). Recall that duration is a useful concept because it provides a good approximation, particularly when interest-rate changes are small, of the sensitivity of a security's market value to a change in its interest rate using the following formula:

$$\%\Delta P = -DUR \times \frac{\Delta i}{1 + i} \tag{4}$$

where

$$\%\Delta P = (P_{t+1} - P_t)/P_t = \text{percentage change in market value of security}$$
$$DUR = \text{duration}$$
$$i = \text{interest rate}$$

---

[4]Note that accounting net worth is calculated on a historical-cost (book-value) basis, meaning that the value of assets and liabilities is based on their initial price. However, book-value net worth does not give a complete picture of the true worth of a firm; the market value of net worth provides a more accurate measure. This is why duration gap analysis focuses on what happens to the market value of net worth, and not on book value, when interest rates change.

After having determined the duration of all assets and liabilities on the bank's balance sheet, the bank manager could use this formula to calculate how the market value of each asset and liability changes when there is a change in interest rates and then calculate the effect on net worth. There is, however, an easier way to go about doing this, derived from the basic fact about duration we learned in the Web Appendix to Chapter 4: duration is additive; that is, the duration of a portfolio of securities is the weighted average of the durations of the individual securities, with the weights reflecting the proportion of the portfolio invested in each. What this means is that the bank manager can figure out the effect that interest-rate changes will have on the market value of net worth by calculating the average duration for assets and for liabilities and then using those figures to estimate the effects of interest-rate changes.

To see how a bank manager would do this, let's return to the balance sheet of the First Bank. Suppose that the average duration of its assets is three years (that is, the average lifetime of the stream of payments is three years), while the average duration of its liabilities is two years. In addition, the First Bank has $100 million of assets and, say, $90 million of liabilities, so its bank capital is 10% of assets. With a 5-percentage-point increase in interest rates, the market value of the bank's assets falls by 15% ($= -5\% \times 3$ years), a decline of $15 million on the $100 million of assets. However, the market value of the liabilities falls by 10% ($= -5 \times 2$ years), a decline of $9 million on the $90 million of liabilities. The net result is that the net worth (the market value of the assets minus the liabilities) has declined by $6 million, or 6% of the total original asset value. Similarly, a 5-percentage-point decline in interest rates increases the net worth of the First Bank by 6% of the total asset value.

APPLICATION

Duration Analysis

Suppose that a bank's average duration of assets is 2.70 years and its average duration of liabilities is 1.03 years. The bank manager wants to know what happens when interest rates rise from 10% to 11%. The total asset value is $100 million, and the total liability value is $95 million. Use Equation 4 to calculate the change in the market value of the assets and liabilities.

Solution

With a total asset value of $100 million, the market value of assets falls by $2.5 million ($100 million $\times$ 0.025 = $2.5 million).

$$\%\Delta P = -DUR \times \frac{\Delta i}{1 + i}$$

where

DUR = duration $\qquad\qquad\qquad\qquad$ = 2.70

Δi = change in interest rate = $0.11 - 0.10$ = 0.01

i = interest rate $\qquad\qquad\qquad\qquad$ = 0.10

Thus

$$\%\Delta P = -2.70 \times \frac{0.01}{1 + 0.10} = -0.025 = -2.5\%$$

With total liabilities of $95 million, the market value of liabilities falls by $0.9 million ($95 million $\times$ 0.009 = $-$0.9 million).

$$\%\Delta P = -DUR \times \frac{\Delta i}{1 + i}$$

where

$$DUR = \text{duration} \qquad\qquad\qquad = 1.03$$
$$\Delta i = \text{change in interest rate} = 0.11 - 0.10 = 0.01$$
$$i = \text{interest rate} \qquad\qquad\qquad = 0.10$$

Thus

$$\%\Delta\text{P} = -1.03 \times \frac{0.01}{1 + 0.10} = -0.009 = -0.9$$

The result is that the net worth of the bank would decline by \$1.6 million ($-\$2.5$ million $-$ [$-\$0.9$ million] $= -\$2.5$ million $+ \$0.9$ million $= -\$1.6$ million).

The bank manager could have gotten to the answer even more quickly by first calculating what is called a duration gap, which is defined as follows:

$$DUR_{gap} = DUR_a - \left(\frac{L}{A} \times DUR_l\right) \tag{5}$$

where

$$DUR_a = \text{average duration of assets}$$
$$DUR_l = \text{average duration of liabilities}$$
$$L = \text{market value of liabilities}$$
$$A = \text{market value of assets}$$

Then, to estimate what will happen if interest rates change, the bank manager uses the DUR_{gap} calculation in Equation 4 to obtain the change in the market value of net worth as a percentage of total assets. In other words, the change in the market value of net worth as a percentage of assets is calculated as

$$\frac{\Delta NW}{A} = -DUR_{gap} \times \frac{\Delta i}{1 + i} \tag{6}$$

APPLICATION

Duration Gap Analysis

Based on the information provided in the previous Application, use Equation 5 to determine the duration gap for the First Bank and then use Equation 6 to determine the change in the market value of net worth as a percentage of assets if interest rates rise from 10% to 11%.

Solution

The duration gap for First Bank is 1.72 years.

$$DUR_{gap} = DUR_a - \left(\frac{L}{A} \times DUR_l\right)$$

where

$$DUR_a = \text{average duration of assets} \qquad = 2.70$$
$$L = \text{market value of liabilities} \qquad = 95$$
$$A = \text{market value of assets} \qquad = 100$$
$$DUR_l = \text{average duration of liabilities} = 1.03$$

Thus

$$DUR_{gap} = 2.70 - \left(\frac{95}{100} \times 1.03 \right) = 1.72 \text{ years}$$

Hence, a rise in interest rates from 10% to 11% would lead to a change in the market value of net worth as a percentage of assets of -1.6%:

$$\frac{\Delta NW}{A} = -DUR_{gap} \times \frac{\Delta i}{1 + i}$$

where

$$
\begin{aligned}
DUR_{gap} &= \text{duration gap} & &= 1.72 \\
\Delta i &= \text{change in interest rate} = 0.11 - 0.10 &&= 0.01 \\
i &= \text{interest rate} & &= 0.10
\end{aligned}
$$

Thus

$$\frac{\Delta NW}{A} = -1.72 \times \frac{0.01}{1 + 0.10} = -0.016 = -1.6$$

With assets totalling $100 million, this Application indicates a fall in the market value of net worth of $1.6 million, which is the same figure that we found in the previous Application.

As our example makes clear, both gap analysis and duration analysis indicate that First Bank will suffer if interest rates rise, but will gain if they fall. Duration analysis and gap analysis are thus useful tools for telling a financial institution manager the institution's degree of exposure to interest-rate risk.[5]

APPLICATION

Strategies for Managing Interest-Rate Risk

Suppose that as the manager of the First Bank, you have done a duration and gap analysis for the bank as discussed in the text. Now you need to decide which alternative strategies you should pursue to manage the interest-rate risk.

If you firmly believe that interest rates will fall in the future, you may be willing to take no action because you know that the bank has more rate-sensitive liabilities than rate-sensitive assets and so will benefit from the expected interest-rate decline. However, you also realize that the First Bank is subject to substantial interest-rate risk because there is always a possibility that interest rates will rise rather than fall. What should you do to eliminate this interest-rate risk? One thing you could do is to shorten the duration of the bank's assets to increase their rate sensitivity. Alternatively, you could lengthen the duration of the liabilities. By this adjustment

---

[5]Gap analysis and duration analysis apply equally to other financial institutions. A second Web Appendix to this chapter applies gap and duration analyses to a nonbank financial institution; it can be found on the book's MyEconLab.

of the bank's assets and liabilities, the bank's income will be less affected by interest-rate swings.

One problem with eliminating the First Bank interest-rate risk by altering the balance sheet is that doing so might be very costly in the short run. The bank may be locked into assets and liabilities of particular durations because of where its expertise lies. Fortunately, recently developed financial instruments known as *financial derivatives*—financial forwards and futures, options, and swaps—can help the bank reduce its interest-rate risk exposure but do not require that the bank rearrange its balance sheet.

Off-Balance-Sheet Activities

Although asset and liability management has traditionally been the major concern of banks, in the more competitive environment of recent years banks have been aggressively seeking out profits by engaging in off-balance-sheet activities. **Off-balance-sheet activities** involve trading financial instruments and generating income from fees and loan sales, activities that affect bank profits but do not appear on bank balance sheets. Indeed, off-balance-sheet activities have been growing in importance for banks: the income from these activities as a percentage of assets has nearly doubled since 1980.

Loan Sales

One type of off-balance-sheet activity that has grown in importance in recent years involves income generated by loan sales. A **loan sale**, also called a *secondary loan participation*, involves a contract that sells all or part of the cash stream from a specific loan so that it no longer is an asset on the bank's balance sheet. Banks earn profits by selling loans for an amount slightly greater than the amount of the original loan. Because the high interest rate on these loans makes them attractive, institutions are willing to buy them even though the higher price means that they earn a slightly lower interest rate than the original interest rate on the loan, usually on the order of 0.15 percentage points.

Generation of Fee Income

Another type of off-balance-sheet activity involves the generation of income from fees that banks receive for providing specialized services to their customers, such as making foreign exchange trades on a customer's behalf, servicing a mortgage-backed security by collecting interest and principal payments and then paying them out, guaranteeing debt securities such as banker's acceptances (by which the bank promises to make interest and principal payments if the party issuing the security cannot), and providing backup lines of credit. There are several types of backup lines of credit. The most important is the loan commitment, under which for a fee the bank agrees to provide a loan at the customer's request, up to a given dollar amount, over a specified period of time. Credit lines are also now available to bank depositors with "overdraft privileges"—these bank customers can write cheques in excess of their deposit balances and, in effect, write themselves a loan.

Off-balance-sheet activities involving guarantees of securities and backup credit lines increase the risk a bank faces. Even though a guaranteed security does not appear on a bank balance sheet, it still exposes the bank to default risk: if the issuer of the security defaults, the bank is left holding the bag and must pay off the security's owner. Backup credit lines also expose the bank to risk because the bank may be forced to provide loans when it does not have sufficient liquidity or when the borrower is a very poor credit risk.

Banks also earn fees by creating financial instruments like the structured investment vehicles (SIVs) mentioned in Chapter 9 and selling them off to investors. However, as became clear during the global financial crisis, when they decline in value, many of these financial instruments have to be taken back onto the balance sheet of the bank sponsoring them, because to do otherwise would severely damage the reputation of the bank. Even though these financial instruments at first appear to be off-balance-sheet, in reality they are back on the balance sheet if they are subject to large losses. To their regret, banks ended up taking large losses on these financial instruments during the global financial crisis, indicating that these off-balance-sheet vehicles exposed banks to just as much risk as if they had been part of the balance sheet at the outset.

Trading Activities and Risk-Management Techniques

We have already mentioned that banks' attempts to manage interest-rate risk led them to trading in financial futures, options for debt instruments, and interest-rate swaps. Banks engaged in international banking also conduct transactions in the foreign exchange market. All transactions in these markets are off-balance-sheet activities because they do not have a direct effect on the bank's balance sheet. Although bank trading in these markets is often directed toward reducing risk or facilitating other bank business, banks also try to outguess the markets and engage in speculation. This speculation can be a very risky business and indeed has led to bank insolvencies, the most dramatic being the failure of Barings, a British bank, in 1995.

Trading activities, although often highly profitable, are dangerous because they make it easy for financial institutions and their employees to make huge bets quickly. A particular problem for management of trading activities is that the principal–agent problem, discussed in Chapter 8, is especially severe. Given the ability to place large bets, a trader (the agent), whether she trades in bond markets, in foreign exchange markets, or in financial derivatives, has an incentive to take on excessive risks: if her trading strategy leads to large profits, she is likely to receive a high salary and bonuses, but if she takes large losses, the financial institution (the principal) will have to cover them. As the Barings Bank failure in 1995 so forcefully demonstrated, a trader subject to the principal–agent problem can take an institution that is quite healthy and drive it into insolvency very fast (see the Global box Barings, Daiwa, Sumitomo, and Société Générale: Rogue Traders and the Principal–Agent Problem).

To reduce the principal–agent problem, managers of financial institutions must set up internal controls to prevent debacles like the one at Barings. Such controls include complete separation of the people in charge of trading activities from those in charge of the bookkeeping for trades. In addition, managers must set limits on the total amount of traders' transactions and on the institution's risk exposure. Managers must also scrutinize risk assessment procedures using the latest computer technology. One such method involves the value-at-risk approach. In this approach, the institution develops a statistical model with which it can calculate the maximum loss that its portfolio is likely to sustain over a given time interval, dubbed the "value at risk," or VaR. For example, a bank might estimate that the maximum loss it would be likely to sustain over one day with a probability of 1 in 100 is $1 million; the $1 million figure is the bank's calculated value at risk. Another approach is called "stress testing." In this approach, a manager determines what would happen if a doomsday scenario occured; that is, she looks at the losses the institution would sustain if an unusual combination of bad events occurred. With the value-at-risk approach and stress testing, a financial institution can assess its risk exposure and take steps to reduce it.

Regulators have become concerned about the increased risk that banks are facing from their off-balance-sheet activities, and, as we saw in Chapter 10, are encouraging banks to pay increased attention to risk management. In addition, the Bank for International Settlements is developing additional bank capital requirements based on value-at-risk calculations for a bank's trading activities.

GLOBAL

Barings, Daiwa, Sumitomo, and Société Générale: Rogue Traders and the Principal–Agent Problem

The demise of Barings, a venerable British bank over a century old, is a sad morality tale of how the principal–agent problem operating through a rogue trader can take a financial institution that has a healthy balance sheet one month and turn it into an insolvent tragedy the next.

In July 1992, Nick Leeson, Barings's new head clerk at its Singapore branch, began to speculate on the Nikkei, the Japanese version of the Dow Jones index. By late 1992, Leeson had suffered losses of US$3 million, which he hid from his superiors by stashing the losses in a secret account. He even fooled his superiors into thinking he was generating large profits, thanks to a failure of internal controls at his firm that allowed him to execute trades on the Singapore exchange *and* oversee the bookkeeping of those trades. (As anyone who runs a cash business, such as a bar, knows, there is always a lower likelihood of fraud if more than one person handles the cash. Similarly for trading operations, you never mix management of the back room with management of the front room; this principle was grossly violated by Barings's management.)

Things didn't get better for Leeson, who by late 1994 had losses exceeding US$250 million. In January and February 1995, he bet the bank. On January 17, 1995, the day of the earthquake in Kobe, Japan, he lost US$75 million, and by the end of the week had lost more than US$150 million. When the stock market declined on February 23, leaving him with a further loss of US$250 million, he called it quits and fled Singapore. Three days later, he turned himself in at the Frankfurt airport. By the end of his wild ride, Leeson's losses, US$1.3 billion in all, ate up Barings's capital and caused the bank to fail. Leeson was subsequently convicted and sent to jail in Singapore for his activities. He was released in 1999 and apologized for his actions.

Our asymmetric information analysis of the principal–agent problem explains Leeson's behaviour and the danger of Barings's management lapse. By letting Leeson control both his own trades and the back room, it increased asymmetric information because it reduced the principal's (Barings's) knowledge about Leeson's trading activities. This lapse increased the moral hazard incentive for him to take risks at the bank's expense, as he was now less likely to be caught. Furthermore, once he had experienced large losses, he had even greater incentives to take on even higher risk because if his bets worked out, he could reverse his losses and keep in good standing with the company, whereas if his bets soured, he had little to lose since he was out of a job anyway. Indeed, the bigger his losses, the more he had to gain by placing bigger bets, which explains the escalation of the amount of his trades as his losses mounted. If Barings's managers had understood the principal–agent problem, they would have been more vigilant at finding out what Leeson was up to, and the bank might still be here today.

Unfortunately, Nick Leeson is no longer a rarity in the rogue traders' billionaire club, those who have lost more than US$1 billion. Over 11 years, Toshihide Iguchi, an officer in the New York branch of Daiwa Bank, also had control of both the bond trading operation and the back room, and he racked up US$1.1 billion in losses over the period. In July 1995, Iguchi disclosed his losses to his superiors, but the management of the bank did not disclose them to its regulators. The result was that Daiwa was slapped with a US$340 million fine and the bank was thrown out of the country by U.S. bank regulators. Yasuo Hamanaka is also a member of the billionaire club. In July 1996, he topped Leeson's and Iguchi's record, losing US$2.6 billion for his employer, the Sumitomo Corporation, one of Japan's top trading companies. Jerome Kerriel's loss for his bank, Société Générale, in January 2008 set the all-time record for a rogue trader: his unauthorized trades cost the bank US$7.2 billion.

The moral of these stories is that management of firms engaged in trading activities must reduce the principal–agent problem by closely monitoring their traders' activities, or the rogues' gallery will continue to grow.

MyEconLab MyEconLab is an online homework and tutorial system that puts you in control of your own learning with study and practice tools directly correlated to this chapter's content. Visit MyEconLab to explore the following resources:

- The Questions and Applied Problems are all available in the Study Plan on MyEconLab for further practice. You will also find the answers to all of the Questions and Applied Problems in the Student Resources section of your MyEconLab.
- Visit the Student Resources section of MyEconLab to access the following mini-cases for this chapter: Mini-Case 13.1: Bank Performance Analysis; Mini-Case 13.2: Calculating and Comparing Gap, Duration, and Risk Management Alternatives.
- Visit the Student Resources section of MyEconLab to access the following appendices for this chapter: Appendix 13.1: Measuring Bank Performance; Appendix 13.2: Nonbanking Financial Institutions and Duration Analysis.

MyEconLab also features Additional Readings, Videos, Glossary Flashcards, Audio Chapter Summaries, Economics News Feeds, Animations, and many additional tools to help you master key concepts from the text.

SUMMARY

MyEconL
Audio Sum

1. The balance sheet of commercial banks can be thought of as a list of the sources and uses of bank funds. The bank's liabilities are its sources of funds, which include chequable deposits, time deposits, advances from the Bank of Canada, borrowings from other banks and corporations, and bank capital. The bank's assets are its uses of funds, which include cash reserves, cash items in process of collection, deposits at other banks, securities, loans, and other assets (mostly physical capital).

2. Banks make profits through the process of asset transformation: they borrow short (accept deposits) and lend long (make loans). When a bank takes in additional deposits, it gains an equal amount of reserves; when it pays out deposits, it loses an equal amount of reserves.

3. Although more liquid assets tend to earn lower returns, banks still desire to hold them. Specifically, banks hold reserves because they provide insurance against the costs of a deposit outflow. Banks manage their assets to maximize profits by seeking the highest returns possible on loans and securities while at the same time trying to lower risk and making adequate provisions for liquidity. Although liability management was once a staid affair, large (money centre) banks now actively seek out sources of funds by issuing liabilities such as negotiable CDs or by actively borrowing from other banks and corporations. Banks manage the amount of capital they hold to prevent bank failure and to meet bank capital requirements set by the regulatory authorities. However, they do not want to hold too much capital because by so doing they will lower the returns to equity holders.

4. The concepts of adverse selection and moral hazard explain the origin of many credit risk management principles involving loan activities, including screening and monitoring, development of long-term customer relationships, loan commitments, collateral, compensating balances, and credit rationing.

5. With the increased volatility of interest rates that occurred in recent years, financial institutions became more concerned about their exposure to interest-rate risk. Gap and duration analyses tell a financial institution if it has fewer rate-sensitive assets than liabilities (in which case a rise in interest rates will reduce income and a fall in interest rates will raise it) or more rate-sensitive assets than liabilities (in which case a rise in interest rates will raise income and a fall in interest rates will reduce it). Financial institutions can manage interest-rate risk by modifying their balance sheets and by making use of new financial instruments.

6. Off-balance-sheet activities consist of trading financial instruments and generating income from fees and loan sales, all of which affect bank profits but are not visible on bank balance sheets. Because these off-balance-sheet activities expose banks to increased risk, bank management must pay particular attention to risk assessment procedures and internal controls to restrict employees from taking on too much risk.

KEY TERMS

asset management, p. 300

balance sheet, p. 294

bank rate, p. 302

banker's risk, p. 296

capital adequacy management, p. 300

compensating balance, p. 310

credit rationing, p. 311

credit risk, p. 300

deposit outflows, p. 300

desired reserve ratio, p. 296

desired reserves, p. 296

duration analysis, p. 313

equity multiplier (EM), p. 306

gap analysis (income gap analysis), p. 312

interbank deposits, p. 296

interest-rate risk, p. 300

items in transit (bank float), p. 296

liability management, p. 300

liquidity management, p. 300

loan commitments, p. 310

loan sale, p. 317

money centre banks, p. 304

Off-balance sheet activities, p. 317

overdraft loans (advances), p. 295

reserves, p. 296

return on assets (*ROA*), p. 305

return on equity (*ROE*), p. 305

secondary reserves, p. 296

settlement balances, p. 295

T-account, p. 297

vault cash, p. 296

QUESTIONS

1. Why might a bank be willing to borrow funds from other banks at a higher rate than it can borrow from the Bank of Canada?

2. Rank the following bank assets from most to least liquid:

   a. Commercial loans

   b. Securities

   c. Reserves

   d. Physical capital

3. The bank you own has the following balance sheet:

Assets		Liabilities	
Reserves	$ 75 million	Deposits	$500 million
Loans	$525 million	Bank capital	$100 million

   If the bank suffers a deposit outflow of $50 million with a desired reserve ratio on deposits of 10%, what actions should you take?

4. If a deposit outflow of $50 million occurs, which balance sheet would a bank rather have initially, the balance sheet in Question 3 or the following balance sheet? Why?

Assets		Liabilities	
Reserves	$100 million	Deposits	$500 million
Loans	$500 million	Bank capital	$100 million

5. Why has the development of overnight loan markets made it more likely that banks will hold fewer excess reserves?

6. If the bank you own has no excess reserves and a sound customer comes in asking for a loan, should you automatically turn the customer down, explaining that you don't have any excess reserves to lend out? Why or why not? What options are available for you to provide the funds your customer needs?

7. If a bank finds that its *ROE* is too low because it has too much bank capital, what can it do to raise its *ROE*?

8. If a bank is falling short of meeting its capital requirements by $1 million, what three things can it do to rectify the situation?

9. Why do equity holders care more about *ROE* than about *ROA*?

10. If a bank doubles the amount of its capital and *ROA* stays constant, what will happen to *ROE*?

11. What are the benefits and costs for a bank when it decides to increase the amount of its bank capital?

12. Why is being nosy a desirable trait for a banker?

13. A bank almost always insists that the firms it lends to keep compensating balances at the bank. Why?

14. If the president of a bank told you that the bank was so well run that it has never had to call in loans, sell securities, or borrow as a result of a deposit outflow, would you be willing to buy stock in that bank? Why or why not?

15. "Because diversification is a desirable strategy for avoiding risk, it never makes sense for a bank to specialize in making specific types of loans." Is this statement true, false, or uncertain? Explain your answer.

16. If you are a banker and expect interest rates to rise in the future, would you want to make short-term or long-term loans?

17. "Bank managers should always seek the highest return possible on their assets." Is this statement true, false, or uncertain? Explain your answer.

18. Why has noninterest income been growing as a source of bank operating income?

APPLIED PROBLEMS

19. Using the T-accounts of the First Bank and the Second Bank, describe what happens when Jane Brown writes a $50 cheque on her account at the First Bank to pay her friend Joe Green, who in turn deposits the cheque in his account at the Second Bank.

20. What happens to reserves at the First Bank if one person withdraws $1000 of cash and another person deposits $500 of cash? Use T-accounts to explain your answer.

Questions 21 and 22 relate to the first month's operations of NewBank.

21. NewBank started its first day of operations with $6 million in capital. $100 million in chequable deposits is received. The bank makes a $25 million commercial loan and another $25 million in mortgages. If desired reserves are 8%, what does the bank balance sheets look like? Ignore any loan loss reserves.

22. NewBank decides to invest $45 million in 30-day T-bills. The T-bills are currently trading at $4986.70 (including commissions) for a $5000-face-value instrument. How many do they purchase? What does the balance sheet look like?

23. X-Bank reported an *ROE* of 15% and an *ROA* of 1%. How well capitalized is this bank?

24. Suppose that you are the manager of a bank whose $100 billion of assets have an average duration of four years and whose $90 billion of liabilities have an average duration of six years. Conduct a duration analysis for the bank, and show what will happen to the net worth of the bank if interest rates rise by 2 percentage points. What actions could you take to reduce the bank's interest-rate risk?

25. Suppose that you are the manager of a bank that has $15 million of fixed-rate assets, $30 million of rate-sensitive assets, $25 million of fixed-rate liabilities, and $20 million of rate-sensitive liabilities. Conduct a gap analysis for the bank, and show what will happen to bank profits if interest rates rise by 5 percentage points. What actions could you take to reduce the bank's interest-rate risk?

WEB EXERCISES

1. It is relatively easy to find up-to-date information on banks because of their extensive reporting requirements. Go to **www.osfi-bsif.gc.ca**. This site is sponsored by the Office of the Superintendent of Financial Institutions Canada (OSFI). You will find balance sheet data on domestic banks as well as on foreign bank subsidiaries.

   a. Have bank loans been increasing or decreasing over the last few years?

   b. Has bank capital been increasing? How does it compare to the figure reported in Table 13-1 (p. 294)?

2. Table 13-1 reports the balance sheet of all commercial banks based on aggregate data found in the OSFI's website. Compare this table to the balance sheet information reported (under Financial Highlights) by CIBC at **www.cibc.com/ca/inside-cibc/fin-highlights.html**. Does CIBC have more or less of its portfolio in loans than the average Canadian bank?

CHAPTER 14

Risk Management with Financial Derivatives

LEARNING OBJECTIVES

After studying this chapter you should be able to

1. distinguish among forwards, futures, options, swaps, and credit derivatives
2. discuss the success of the financial derivatives market
3. explain how managers of financial institutions use financial derivatives to manage interest-rate and foreign exchange risk
4. outline the dangers of derivatives

PREVIEW

Starting in the 1970s and increasingly in the 1980s and 1990s, the world became a riskier place for financial institutions. Swings in interest rates widened, and the bond and stock markets went through some episodes of increased volatility. As a result of these developments, managers of financial institutions have become more concerned with reducing the risk their institutions face. Given the greater demand for risk reduction, the process of financial innovation came to the rescue by producing new assets that help financial institution managers manage risk better. These instruments, called **financial derivatives**, have payoffs that are linked to previously issued securities and are extremely useful risk reduction tools.

In this chapter we look at the most important financial derivatives that managers of financial institutions use to reduce risk: forward contracts, financial futures, options, and swaps. We examine not only how markets for each of these financial derivatives work but also how each can be used by financial institutions to manage risk. We also study financial derivatives because they have become an important source of profits for financial institutions, particularly larger banks.

Hedging

Financial derivatives are effective in reducing risk because they enable financial institutions to **hedge**, that is, engage in a financial transaction that reduces or eliminates risk. When a financial institution has bought an asset, it is said to have taken a **long position**, and this exposes the institution to risk if the returns on the asset are uncertain. Conversely, if it has sold an asset that it has agreed to deliver to another party at a future date, it is said to have taken a **short position**, and this can also expose the institution to risk. Financial derivatives can be used to reduce risk by invoking the following basic principle of hedging: *hedging risk involves engaging in a financial transaction that offsets a long position by taking an additional short position, or offsets a short position by taking an additional long position.* In other words, if a financial institution has bought a security and has therefore taken a long position, it conducts a hedge by contracting to sell that security (take a short position) at some future date. Alternatively, if it has taken a short position by selling a security that it needs to deliver at a future date, then it conducts a hedge by contracting to buy that security (take a long position) at a future date. We first look at how this principle can be applied using forward contracts.

Forward Contracts and Markets

Forward contracts are agreements by two parties to engage in a financial transaction at a future (forward) point in time. Here we focus on forward contracts that are linked to debt instruments, called **interest-rate forward contracts**; later in the chapter we discuss forward contracts for foreign currencies.

Interest-Rate Forward Contracts

Interest-rate forward contracts involve the future sale (or purchase) of a debt instrument and have several dimensions: (1) specification of the actual debt instrument that will be delivered at a future date, (2) amount of the debt instrument to be delivered, (3) price (interest rate) on the debt instrument when it is delivered, and (4) date on which delivery will take place. An example of an interest-rate forward contract might be an agreement for the First Bank to sell to the Rock Solid Insurance Company, one year from today, $5 million face value of the 6s of 2030 Canada bonds (coupon bonds with a 6% coupon rate that mature in 2030) at a price that yields the same interest rate on these bonds as today's, say, 6%. Because Rock Solid will buy the securities at a future date, it has taken a long position, while the First Bank, which will sell the securities, has taken a short position.

APPLICATION

Hedging with Interest-Rate Forward Contracts

Why would the First Bank want to enter into this forward contract with Rock Solid Insurance Company in the first place?

To understand, suppose that you are the manager of the First Bank and have previously bought $5 million of the 6s of 2030 Canada bonds. The bonds are currently selling at par value, so their yield to maturity is also 6%. Because these are long-term bonds, you recognize that you are exposed to substantial interest-rate risk. If interest rates rise in the future, the price of these bonds will fall and result in a substantial capital loss that may cost you your job. How do you hedge this risk?

Knowing the basic principle of hedging, you see that your long position in these bonds must be offset by a short position with a forward contract. That is, you need to contract to sell these bonds at a future date at the current par value price. As a result you agree with another party, in this case, Rock Solid Insurance Company, to sell it the $5 million of the 6s of 2030 Canada bonds at par one year from today. By entering into this forward contract, you have successfully hedged against interest rate risk. By locking in the future price of the bonds, you have eliminated the price risk you face from interest-rate changes.

Why would Rock Solid Insurance Company want to enter into the forward contract with the First Bank? Rock Solid expects to receive premiums of $5 million in one year's time that it will want to invest in the 6s of 2030, but worries that interest rates on these bonds will decline between now and next year. By using the forward contract, it is able to lock in the 6% interest rate on the Canada bonds that will be sold to it by the First Bank.

Pros and Cons of Forward Contracts

The advantage of forward contracts is that they can be as flexible as the parties involved want them to be. This means that an institution like the First Bank may be able to hedge completely the interest-rate risk for the exact security it is holding in its portfolio, just as it has in our example.

However, forward contracts suffer from two problems that severely limit their usefulness. The first is that it may be very hard for an institution like the First Bank to find another party (called a *counterparty*) to make the contract with. There are brokers to facilitate the matching up of parties like the First Bank with the Rock Solid Insurance Company, but few institutions may want to engage in a forward contract specifically for the 6s of 2030. This means that it may prove impossible to find a counterparty when a financial institution like the First Bank wants to make a specific type of forward contract. Furthermore, even if the First Bank finds a counterparty, it may not get as high a price as it wants because there may not be anyone else to make the deal with. A serious problem for the market in interest-rate forward contracts, then, is that it may be difficult to make the financial transaction or that it will have to be made at a disadvantageous price; in the parlance of financial economists, this market suffers from a *lack of liquidity*. (Note that this use of the term *liquidity* when it is applied to a market is somewhat broader than its use when it is applied to an asset. For an asset, liquidity refers to the ease with which the asset can be turned into cash; for a market, liquidity refers to the ease of carrying out financial transactions.)

The second problem with forward contracts is that they are subject to default risk. Suppose that in one year's time, interest rates rise so that the price of the 6s of 2030 falls. The Rock Solid Insurance Company might then decide that it would like to default on the forward contract with the First Bank, because it can now buy the bonds at a lower price. Or perhaps Rock Solid may not have been rock solid after all, and may have gone bust during the year, and is no longer available to complete the terms of the forward contract. Because no outside organization is guaranteeing the contract, the only recourse is for the First Bank to go to the courts to sue Rock Solid, but this process will be costly. Furthermore, if Rock Solid is already bankrupt, the First Bank will suffer a loss; the bank can no longer sell the 6s of 2030 at the price it had agreed with Rock Solid, but instead will have to sell at a price well below that, because the price of these bonds has fallen.

The presence of default risk in forward contracts means that parties to these contracts must check each other out to be sure that the counterparty is both financially sound and likely to be honest and live up to its contractual obligations. Because this type of investigation is costly and because all the adverse selection and moral hazard problems discussed in earlier chapters apply, default risk is a major barrier to the use of interest-rate forward contracts. When the default risk problem is combined with a lack of liquidity, we see that these contracts may be of limited usefulness to financial institutions. Although there is a market for interest-rate forward contracts, particularly in Canada and mortgage-backed, it is not nearly as large as the financial futures market, to which we turn next.

Financial Futures Contracts and Markets

Given the default risk and liquidity problems in the interest-rate forward market, another solution to hedging interest-rate, stock market, and foreign exchange risks was needed. This solution was provided by the development of financial futures contracts by the Chicago Board of Trade starting in 1975.

Financial futures are classified as (1) interest-rate futures, (2) stock index futures, and (3) currency futures. In Canada, such contracts are traded on the Montréal Exchange (ME), which maintains active markets in short- and long-term Canada bond futures and stock index futures. In what follows, we discuss interest-rate and stock index futures. Later in the chapter, we also discuss currency futures.

Interest-Rate Futures Contracts

An **interest-rate futures contract** is similar to an interest-rate forward contract in that it specifies that a financial instrument must be delivered by one party to another on a stated future date. However, it differs from an interest-rate forward contract in several ways that overcome some of the liquidity and default problems of forward markets.

To understand what interest-rate futures contracts are all about, let's look at one of the most widely traded futures contracts, that for 10-year Canada bonds, which are traded on the Montréal Exchange.

The contract value is for $100 000 face value of bonds. Prices are quoted in points, with each point equal to $1000, and the smallest change in price is one hundredth of a point ($10). This contract specifies that the bonds to be delivered must have at least 10 years to maturity at the delivery date. If the Canada bonds delivered to settle the futures contract have a coupon rate different from (say) the 6% specified in the futures contract, the amount of bonds to be delivered is adjusted to reflect the difference in value between the delivered bonds and the 6% coupon bond. In line with the terminology used for forward contracts, parties who have bought a futures contract and thereby agreed to buy (take delivery of) the bonds are said to have taken a *long position*, and parties who have sold a futures contract and thereby agreed to sell (deliver) the bonds have taken a *short position*.

To make our understanding of this contract more concrete, let's consider what happens when you buy or sell one of these Canada bond futures contracts. Let's say that on January 1, you sell one $100 000 March contract at a price of 115 (that is, $115 000). By selling this contract, you agree to deliver $100 000 face value of the long-term Canada bonds to the contract's counterparty at the end of March for $115 000. By buying the contract at a price of 115, the buyer has agreed to pay $115 000 for the $100 000 face value of bonds when you deliver them at the end of March. If interest rates on long-term bonds rise so that when the contract matures at the end of March the price of these bonds has fallen to 110 ($110 000 per $100 000 of face value), the buyer of the contract will have lost $5000 because he or she paid $115 000 for the bonds but can sell them only for the market price of $110 000. But you, the seller of the contract, will have gained $5000 because you can now sell the bonds to the buyer for $115 000 but have to pay only $110 000 for them in the market.

It is even easier to describe what happens to the parties who have purchased futures contracts and those who have sold futures contracts if we recognize the following fact: *at the expiration date of a futures contract, the price of the contract is the same as the price of the underlying asset to be delivered.* To see why this is the case, consider what happens on the expiration date of the March contract at the end of March when the price of the underlying $100 000-face-value Canada bond is 110 ($110 000). If the futures contract is selling below 110, say, at 109, a trader can buy the contract for $109 000, take delivery of the bond, and immediately sell it for $110 000, thereby earning a quick profit of $1000. Because earning this profit involves no risk, it is a great deal that everyone would like to get in on. That means that everyone will try to buy the contract, and as a result, its price will rise. Only when the price rises to 110 will the profit opportunity cease to exist and the buying pressure disappear. Conversely, if the price of the futures contract is above 110, say, at 111, everyone will want to sell the contract. Now the sellers get $111 000 from selling the futures contract but have to pay only $110 000 for the Canada bonds that they must deliver to the buyer of the contract, and the $1000 difference is their profit. Because this profit involves no risk, traders will continue to sell the futures contract until its price falls back down to 110, at which price there are no longer any profits to be made. The elimination of riskless profit opportunities in the futures market is referred to as **arbitrage**, and it guarantees that the price of a futures contract at expiration equals the price of the underlying asset to be delivered.[1]

The fact that a futures contract at expiration equals the price of the underlying asset makes it even easier to see who profits and who loses from such a contract when interest rates change. When interest rates have risen so that the price of the Canada bond is 110 on the expiration day at the end of March, the March Canada bond futures contract will also have a price of 110. Thus if you bought the contract for 115 in January, you have a loss of 5 points, or $5000 (5% of $100 000). But if you sold the futures contract at 115 in January, the decline in price to 110 means that you have a profit of 5 points, or $5000.

APPLICATION

Hedging with Interest-Rate Futures

First Bank can also use interest-rate futures to hedge the interest-rate risk on its holdings of $5 million of the 6s of 2030 (Canada bonds with a 6% coupon rate that mature in 2030).

To see how, suppose that in March 2013, the 6s of 2030 are the long-term bonds that would be delivered in the Montréal Exchange's Canada bond futures contract expiring one year in the future, in March 2014. Also suppose that the interest rate on these bonds is expected to remain at 6% over the next year, so that both the 6s of 2030 and the futures contract are selling at par (i.e., the $5 million of bonds is selling for $5 million and the $100 000 futures contract is selling for $100 000). The basic principle of hedging indicates that you, as the manager of First Bank, need to offset the long position in these bonds with a short position, so you have to sell the futures contract. But how many contracts should you sell? The number of contracts required to hedge the interest-rate risk is found by dividing the amount of the asset to be hedged by the dollar value of each contract, as is shown in Equation 1.

$$NC = VA/VC \qquad (1)$$

where

NC = number of contracts for the hedge
VA = value of the asset
VC = value of each contract

---

[1] In actuality, futures contracts sometimes set conditions for delivery of the underlying assets that cause the price of the contract at expiration to differ slightly from the price of the underlying assets. Because the difference in price is extremely small, we ignore it in this chapter.

Given that the 6s of 2030 are the long-term bonds that would be delivered in the Montréal Exchange's Canada bond futures contract expiring one year in the future and that the interest rate on these bonds is expected to remain at 6% over the next year, so that both the 6s of 2030 and the futures contract are selling at par, how many contracts must First Bank sell to remove its interest-rate exposure from its $5 million holdings of the 6s of 2030?[2]

Since $VA = \$5$ million and $VC = \$100\ 000$,

$$NC = \$5 \text{ million}/\$100\ 000 = 50$$

You therefore hedge the interest-rate risk by selling 50 of the Canada bond futures contracts.

Now suppose that over the next year, interest rates increase to 8% due to an increased threat of inflation. The value of the 6s of 2030 that the First Bank is holding will then fall to $4 039 640 in March 2014.[3] Thus, the loss from the long position in these bonds is $960 360, as shown below:

Value in March 2014 @ 8% interest rate	$4 039 640
Value in March 2013 @ 6% interest rate	−$5 000 000
Loss	−$ 960 360

However, the short position in the 50 futures contracts that obligate you to deliver $5 million of the 6s of 2030 in March 2014 has a value equal to $4 039 640, the value of the $5 million of bonds after the interest rate has risen to 8%. Yet when you sold the futures contract, the buyer was obligated to pay you $5 million on the maturity date. Thus the gain from the short position on these contracts is also $960 360:

Amount paid to you in March 2014, agreed in March 2013	$5 000 000
Value of bonds delivered in March 2014 @ 8% interest rate	−$4 039 640
Gain	$ 960 360

Therefore, the net gain for the First Bank is zero, showing that the hedge has been conducted successfully.

The hedge just described is called a **micro hedge** because the financial institution is hedging the interest-rate risk for a specific asset it is holding. A second type of hedge that financial institutions engage in is called a **macro hedge**, in which the hedge is for the institution's entire portfolio. For example, if a bank has more rate-sensitive liabilities than assets, a rise in interest rates will cause the value of the bank to decline. By selling interest-rate future contracts that will yield a profit when interest rates rise, the bank can offset the losses on its overall portfolio from an interest-rate rise and thereby hedge its interest-rate risk.

---

[2] In the real world, designing a hedge is somewhat more complicated than the example here because the bond that is most likely to be delivered might not be a 6s of 2030.

[3] The value of the bonds can be calculated using a financial calculator as follows: $FV = \$5\ 000\ 000$, $PMT = \$300\ 000$, $I = 8\%$, $N = 19$, $PV = \$4\ 039\ 640$.

Organization of Trading in Financial Futures Markets

Financial futures contracts are traded on organized exchanges such as the Chicago Board of Trade, the Chicago Mercantile Exchange, the Montréal Exchange, the London International Financial Futures Exchange, and the Marché à Terme International de France. These futures exchanges are highly competitive with one another, and each

TABLE 14-1 Widely Traded Financial Futures Contracts in the United States

Type of Contract	Contract Size	Open Interest, May 2011
Interest-Rate Contracts		
Treasury bonds	$100 000	740 953
Treasury notes	$100 000	1 973 136
Five-year Treasury notes	$100 000	1 555 969
Two-year Treasury notes	$200 000	1 046 815
Thirty-day Fed funds rate	$5 million	751 787
Eurodollar	$4 million	10 202 720
Stock Index Contracts		
Standard & Poor's 500 Index	$250 × index	332 153
Standard & Poor's MIDCAP 400	$500 × index	1 721
Nasdaq 100	$100 × index	18 137
Nikkei 225 Stock Average	$5 × index	46 773
Currency Contracts		
Yen	12 500 000 yen	95 929
Euro	125 000 euros	270 101
Canadian dollar	100 000 Canadian $	125 654
British pound	100 000 pounds	108 085
Swiss franc	125 000 francs	67 713
Mexican peso	500 000 new pesos	142 530

Source: CME Group: www.cmegroup.com/market-data/volume-open-interest/ and click on "CME Group Open Interest Report."

organization tries to design contracts and set rules that will increase the amount of futures trading on its exchange. The exchanges are also regulated to ensure that prices in the market are not being manipulated. Listed in Table 14-1 are the most widely traded financial futures contracts in the United States, along with their contract size and the number of contracts outstanding, called **open interest**, for March 2011.

Given the globalization of other financial markets in recent years, it is not surprising that increased international competition has been occurring in financial futures markets as well.

The Globalization of Financial Futures Markets

Because futures exchanges in the United States were the first to develop financial futures, they dominated the trading of financial futures in the early 1980s. For example, in 1985, all of the top 10 futures contracts were traded on exchanges in the United States. With the rapid growth of financial futures markets and the resulting high profits made by the American exchanges, exchanges in other countries saw a profit opportunity and began to enter the business. By the 1990s, Eurodollar contracts traded on the London International Financial Futures Exchange, Japanese government bond contracts and Euroyen contracts traded on the Tokyo Stock Exchange, French government bond contracts traded on the Marché à Terme International de France (now Euronext), and Nikkei 225 contracts traded on the Osaka Securities Exchange all became among the most widely traded futures contracts in the world.

International competition has also spurred knockoffs of the most popular financial futures contracts initially developed in the United States. These contracts traded on financial futures exchanges in other countries are virtually identical to those traded in the United States and have the advantage that they can be traded when the American exchanges are closed. The movement to 24-hour-a-day trading in financial futures has been further stimulated by the development of the Globex electronic trading platform, which allows traders throughout the world to trade futures even when the exchanges are not officially open. Financial futures trading has thus become completely internationalized, and competition between U.S. and foreign exchanges is now intense.

Explaining the Success of Futures Markets

There are several differences between financial futures and forward contracts and in the organization of their markets that help explain why financial futures markets such as those for Canada bonds have been so successful.

Several features of futures contracts were designed to overcome the liquidity problem inherent in forward contracts. The first feature is that, in contrast to forward contracts, the quantities delivered and the delivery dates of futures contracts are standardized, making it more likely that different parties can be matched up in the futures market, thereby increasing the liquidity of the market. In the case of the 10-year Canada bond futures contract, the quantity delivered is $100 000 face value of bonds, and the delivery dates are set to be the last business day of March, June, September, and December. The second feature is that after the futures contract has been bought or sold, it can be traded (bought or sold) again at any time until the delivery date. In contrast, once a forward contract is agreed on, it typically cannot be traded. The third feature is that in a futures contract, not just one specific type of Canada bond is deliverable on the delivery date, as in a forward contract. Instead, any Canada bond that matures in more than 10 years and is not callable for 10 years is eligible for delivery. Allowing continuous trading also increases the liquidity of the futures market, as does the ability to deliver a range of Canada bonds rather than one specific bond.

Another reason why futures contracts specify that more than one bond is eligible for delivery is to limit the possibility that someone might corner the market and "squeeze" traders who have sold contracts. To corner the market, someone buys up all the deliverable securities so that investors with a short position cannot obtain from anyone else the securities that they contractually must deliver on the delivery date. As a result, the person who has cornered the market can set exorbitant prices for the securities that investors with a short position must buy to fulfill their obligations under the futures contract. The person who has cornered the market makes a fortune, but investors with a short position take a terrific loss. Clearly, the possibility that corners might occur in the market will discourage people from taking a short position and might therefore decrease the size of the market. By allowing many different securities to be delivered, the futures contract makes it harder for anyone to corner the market, because a much larger amount of securities would have to be purchased to establish the corner. Corners are a concern to both regulators and the organized exchanges that design futures contracts.

Trading in the futures market has been organized differently from trading in forward markets to overcome the default risk problems arising in forward contracts. In both types, for every contract there must be a buyer who is taking a long position and a seller who is taking a short position. However, the buyer and seller of a futures contract make their contract not with each other but with the clearinghouse associated with the futures exchange. This setup means that the buyer of the futures contract does not need to worry about the financial health or trustworthiness of the seller, or vice versa, as in the forward market. As long as the clearinghouse is financially solid, buyers and sellers of futures contracts do not have to worry about default risk.

To make sure that the clearinghouse is financially sound and does not run into financial difficulties that might jeopardize its contracts, buyers or sellers of futures contracts must put an initial deposit, called a **margin requirement**, of perhaps $2000 per Canada bond contract into a margin account kept at their brokerage firm. Futures contracts are then **marked to market** every day. What this means is that at the end of every trading day, the change in the value of the futures contract is added to or subtracted from the margin account. Suppose that after buying the Canada bond contract at a price of 115 on Wednesday morning, its closing price at the end of the day, the *settlement price*, falls to 114. You now have a loss of 1 point, or $1000, on the contract, and the seller who sold you the contract has a gain of 1 point, or $1000. The $1000 gain is added to the seller's margin account, making a total of $3000 in that account, and the $1000 loss is subtracted from your account, so you now only have $1000 in your account. If the amount in this margin account falls below the maintenance margin requirement (which can be the same as the initial requirement but is usually a little less), the trader is required to add money to the account. For example, if the maintenance margin requirement is also $2000, you would have to add $1000 to your account to bring it up to $2000. Margin requirements and marking to market make it far less likely that a trader will default on a contract, thus protecting the futures exchange from losses.

A final advantage that futures markets have over forward markets is that most futures contracts do not result in delivery of the underlying asset on the expiration date, whereas forward contracts do. A trader who sold a futures contract is allowed to avoid delivery on the expiration date by making an offsetting purchase of a futures contract. Because the simultaneous holding of the long and short positions means that the trader would in effect be delivering the bonds to itself, under the exchange rules the trader is allowed to cancel both contracts. Allowing traders to cancel their contracts in this way lowers the cost of conducting trades in the futures market relative to the forward market in that a futures trader can avoid the costs of physical delivery, which is not so easy with forward contracts.

APPLICATION

Hedging Foreign Exchange Risk

As we discussed in Chapter 1, foreign exchange rates have been highly volatile in recent years. The large fluctuations in exchange rates subject financial institutions and other businesses to significant foreign exchange risk because they generate substantial gains and losses. Luckily for financial institution managers, the financial derivatives discussed in this chapter—forward and financial futures contracts—can be used to hedge foreign exchange risk.

To understand how financial institution managers manage foreign exchange risk, let's suppose that in January, the First Bank's customer Frivolous Luxuries, Inc. is due a payment of 10 million euros in two months for $14 million worth of goods it has just sold in Germany. Frivolous Luxuries is concerned that if the value of the euro falls substantially from its current value of $1.40, the company might suffer a large loss because the 10 million euro payment will no longer be worth $14 million. So Sam, the CEO of Frivolous Luxuries, calls up his friend Mona, the manager of the First Bank, and asks her to hedge this foreign exchange risk for his company. Let's see how the bank manager does this using forward and financial futures contracts.

Hedging Foreign Exchange Risk with Forward Contracts

Forward markets in foreign exchange have been highly developed by commercial banks and investment banking operations that engage in extensive foreign exchange trading and so are widely used to hedge foreign exchange risk. Mona knows that she can use this market to hedge the foreign exchange risk for Frivolous Luxuries. Such a hedge is quite straightforward for her to execute. Because the payment of euros in two months means that at that time Sam would hold a long position in euros, Mona knows that the basic principle of hedging indicates that she should offset this long position by a short position. Thus, she just enters a forward contract that obligates her to sell 10 million euros two months from now in exchange for dollars at the current forward rate of $1.40 per euro.[4]

Hedging Foreign Exchange Risk with Futures Contracts

In two months, when her customer receives the 10 million euros, the forward contract ensures that it is exchanged for dollars at an exchange rate of $1.40 per euro, thus yielding $14 million. No matter what happens to future exchange rates, Frivolous Luxuries will be guaranteed $14 million for the goods it sold in Germany. Mona calls up her friend Sam to let him know that his company is now protected from any foreign exchange movements, and he thanks her for her help.

As an alternative, Mona could have used the currency futures market to hedge the foreign exchange risk. In this case, she would see that the Chicago Mercantile Exchange has a euro contract with a contract amount of 125 000 euros and a price of $1.40 per euro. To do the hedge, Mona must sell euros as with the forward contract, to the tune of $14 million of the March futures. How many of the Chicago Mercantile Exchange March euro contracts must Mona sell in order to hedge the 10 million euro payment due in March?

Using Equation 1 with

$$VA = 10 \text{ million euros}$$
$$VC = 125\,000 \text{ euros}$$

we have

$$NC = 10 \text{ million}/125\,000 = 80$$

Thus, Mona can hedge the 10 million euros by selling 80 of the CME euro contracts. Given the $1.40 per euro price, the sale of the contract yields $80 \times 125\,000$ euros = $14 million. The futures hedge thus again enables her to lock in the exchange rate for Frivolous Luxuries so that it gets its payment of $14 million.

One advantage of using the futures market is that the contract size of 125 000 euros, worth $175 000, is quite a bit smaller than the minimum size of a forward contract, which is usually $1 million or more. However, in this case, the bank manager is making a large enough transaction that she can use either the forward or the futures market. Her choice depends on whether the transaction costs are lower in one market than in the other. If the First Bank is active in the forward market, that market would probably have the lower transaction costs, but if First Bank rarely deals in foreign exchange forward contracts, the bank manager may do better by sticking with the futures market.

---

[4]The forward exchange rate will probably differ slightly from the current spot rate of $1.40 per euro because the interest rates in Europe and Canada may not be equal. In that case, as we will see in Chapter 19, the future expected exchange rate will not equal the current spot rate and neither will the forward rate. However, since interest differentials have typically been less than 6% at an annual rate (1% bimonthly), the expected appreciation or depreciation of the euro over a two-month period has always been less than 1%. Thus the forward rate is always close to the current spot rate, and so our assumption in the example that the forward rate and the spot rate are the same is a reasonable one.

Stock Index Futures

As we have seen, interest rate futures markets can be useful in hedging interest-rate risk. However, financial institution managers, particularly those who manage mutual funds, pension funds, and insurance companies, also worry about **stock market risk**, the risk that occurs because stock prices fluctuate. Stock index futures were developed in 1982 to meet the need to manage stock market risk, and they have become among the most widely traded of all futures contracts. The futures trading in stock price indexes is now controversial because critics assert that it has led to substantial increases in market volatility.

Stock Index Futures Contracts

To understand stock index futures contracts, let's look at the Standard & Poor's 500 Index futures contract, the most widely traded stock index futures contract in North America. (The S&P 500 Index measures the value of 500 of the most widely traded stocks in the United States.) Stock index futures contracts differ from most other financial futures contracts in that they are settled with a cash delivery rather than with the delivery of a security. Cash settlement gives these contracts the advantage of a high degree of liquidity and also rules out the possibility of anyone cornering the market. In the case of the S&P 500 Index contract, at the final settlement date, the cash delivery due is US$250 times the index, so if the index is at 1000 on the final settlement date, $250 000 would be the amount due. The price quotes for this contract are also quoted in terms of index points, so a change of 1 point represents a change of $250 in the contract's value.

To understand what all this means, let's look at what happens when you buy or sell this futures contract. Suppose that on January 1, you sell one March contract at a price of 1000 (that is, $250 000). By selling the contract, you agree to a delivery amount due of $250 times the S&P 500 Index on the expiration date at the end of March. By buying the contract at a price of 1000, the buyer has agreed to pay $250 000 for the delivery amount due of $250 times the S&P 500 Index at the expiration date at the end of March. If the stock market falls so that the S&P 500 Index declines to 900 on the expiration date, the buyer of the contract will have lost $25 000 because he or she has agreed to pay $250 000 for the contract but has a delivery amount due of $225 000 (900 × $250). But you, the seller of the contract, will have a profit of $25 000 because you agreed to receive a $250 000 purchase price for the contract but have a delivery amount due of only $225 000. Because the amounts payable and due are netted out, only $25 000 will change hands; you, the seller of the contract, will receive $25 000 from the buyer.

APPLICATION

Hedging with Stock Index Futures

Solution

Financial institution managers can use stock index futures contracts to reduce stock market risk.

Suppose that in March 2013, Mort, the portfolio manager of the Rock Solid Insurance Company, has a portfolio of stocks valued at $100 million that moves percentagewise one-for-one with the S&P Index. Suppose also that the March 2014 S&P 500 Index contracts are currently selling at a price of 1000. How many of these contracts should Mort sell so that he hedges the stock market risk of this portfolio over the next year?

Because Mort is holding a long position, using the basic principle of hedging, he must offset it by taking a short position in which he sells S&P futures. To calculate the number of contracts he needs to sell, he uses Equation 1.

$$VA = \$100 \text{ million}$$
$$VC = \$250 \times 1000 = \$250\,000$$

Thus

$$NC = \$100 \text{ million}/\$250\,00 = 400$$

Mort's hedge therefore involves selling 400 S&P March 2014 futures contracts.

If the S&P Index falls 10% to 900, the $100 million portfolio will suffer a $10 million loss. At the same time, however, Mort makes a profit of $100 \times \$250 = \$25\,000$ per contract because he agreed to be paid $250 000 for each contract at a price of 1000, but at a price of 900 on the expiration date, he has a delivery amount of only $225 000 ($900 \times \$250$). Multiplied by 400 contracts, the $25 000 profit per contract yields a total profit of $10 million. The $10 million profit on the futures contract exactly offsets the loss on Rock Solid's stock portfolio, so Mort has been successful in hedging the stock market risk.

Why would Mort be willing to forgo profits when the stock market rises? One reason is that he might be worried that a bear market was imminent, so he wants to protect Rock Solid's portfolio from the coming decline (and so protect his job).

Options

Another vehicle for hedging interest-rate, foreign exchange, and stock market risk involves the use of options on assets. **Options** are contracts that give the purchaser the option, or *right*, to buy or sell the underlying asset at a specified price, called the **exercise price** or **strike price**, within a specific period of time (the *term to expiration*). The seller (sometimes called the *writer*) of the option is *obligated* to buy or sell the asset to the purchaser if the owner of the option exercises the right to sell or buy. These option contract features are important enough to be emphasized: the *owner* or buyer of an option does not have to exercise the option; he or she can let the option expire without using it. Hence the *owner* of an option is *not obligated* to take any action but rather has the *right* to exercise the contract if he or she so chooses. The *seller* of an option, by contrast, has no choice in the matter; he or she *must* buy or sell the asset if the owner exercises the option.

Because the right to buy or sell an asset at a specified price has value, the owner of an option is willing to pay an amount for it called a **premium**. There are two types of option contracts: **American options** can be exercised *at any time up to* the expiration date of the contract, and **European options** can be exercised only *on* the expiration date.

Option contracts written on individual stocks are called **stock options**, and such options have existed for a long time. However, option contracts can also be written on assets. Options on financial futures called **financial futures options** or, more commonly, **futures options**, were developed in 1982 and have become the most widely traded option contracts.

You might wonder why option contracts are more likely to be written on financial futures than on underlying financial instruments such as bonds. As you saw earlier in the chapter, at the expiration date, the price of the futures contract and of the deliverable debt instrument will be the same because of arbitrage. So it would seem that investors should be indifferent about having the option written on the asset or on the futures contract. However, financial futures contracts have been so well designed that their markets are often more liquid than the markets in the underlying assets. Investors would rather have the option contract written on the more liquid instrument, in this case the futures contract. That explains why the most popular futures options are written on many of the same futures contracts listed in Table 14-1.

In Canada, the regulation of option markets is the responsibility of the Canadian Derivatives Clearing Corporation (CDCC), a firm that is jointly owned by Canada's stock exchanges. The regulation of U.S. option markets is split between the Securities and Exchange Commission (SEC), which regulates stock options, and the Commodity Futures Trading Commission (CFTC), which regulates futures options. Regulation focuses on ensuring that writers of options have enough capital to make good on their contractual obligations and on overseeing traders and exchanges to prevent fraud and ensure that the market is not being manipulated.

Stock Options

To understand option contracts more fully, let's first discuss stock options (options on individual stocks) before we turn to the more complicated futures options (that is, options on financial futures).

PROFITS AND LOSSES ON CALLS   A **call option** is a contract that gives the owner the right (but not the obligation) to *buy* a stock (from the option writer) at the exercise price within a specific period of time. Since a call represents an option to buy, the purchase of a call is undertaken if the price of the underlying stock is expected to go up. The buyer of a call is said to be **long in a call** and the writer of a call is said to be **short in a call**. The buyer of a call option will have to pay a premium, called a **call premium**, in order to get the writer to sign the contract and assume the risk.

To illustrate the profitability of a call option, suppose you hold a European call option on an equity security with an exercise price of X (say $100) and a call premium of (say $5), as shown in Figure 14-1. If at the expiration date the price of the

FIGURE 14-1 Profits from Buying and Writing a Call Option

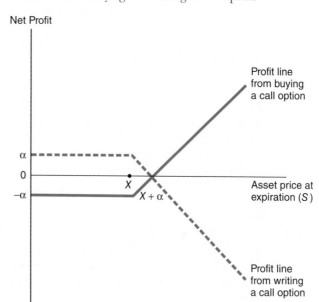

underlying asset, S, is less than X, the call will not be exercised, resulting in a loss of the premium. At a price above X, the call will be exercised. In particular, at a price between X and $X + \alpha$, the gain would be insufficient to cover the cost of the premium, while at a price above $X + \alpha$ the call will yield a net profit. In fact, at a price above $X + \alpha$, each \$1 rise in the price of the asset will cause the profit of the call option to increase by \$1.

The payoff function from writing the call option is the mirror image of the payoff function from buying the call and is represented by the dashed line in Figure 14-1. Note that the writer of the call receives the call premium up front and must stand ready to sell the underlying asset to the buyer of the call at the exercise price X, if the buyer exercises the option to buy.

In general, the value of a call option C at expiration with asset price S (at that time) and exercise price X is

$$C = \max (0, S - X)$$

In other words, the value of a call option at maturity (also known as the **intrinsic value**) is the difference between the current asset price and the exercise price, $S - X$, or zero, whichever is greater. If the stock price happens to be greater than the exercise price ($S > X$), the call is said to be **in the money**, and the owner will exercise it for a net profit of $C - \alpha$. If the asset price happens to be less than the exercise price ($S < X$), the call is said to be **out of the money** and will expire worthless. A call with $S = X$ is said to be **at the money** or **trading at par**.

PROFIT AND LOSSES ON PUTS   As already noted, a second type of option contract is the put option. A **put option** is a contract that gives the owner the right (but not the obligation) to *sell* an asset (to the option writer) at the specified exercise price within a specific period of time. As a put represents an option to sell rather than buy, it is worth buying a put when the price of the underlying asset is expected to fall. As with calls, the buyer of a put is said to be **long in a put** and the writer of a put is said to be **short in a put**. Also, as with calls, the buyer of a put option will have to pay a premium, called a **put premium**, in order to get the writer to sign the contract and assume the risk.

The solid line in Figure 14-2 illustrates the profit line from buying a put with an exercise price of X and a premium of β. At a price of X or higher, the put will not be exercised, resulting in a loss of the premium. At a price below $X - \beta$, the put is sufficiently deep in the money to cover the option premium and yield a net profit. In fact, between $X - \beta$ and X, the put will be exercised, but the gain is insufficient to cover the cost of the premium.

The payoff function from writing a put is the mirror image of that from buying a put and is represented by the dashed line in Figure 14-2. As with writing a call, the writer of a put receives the put premium β up front and must sell the asset underlying the option if the buyer of the put exercises the option to sell.

In general, the value of a put option P at the expiration date with exercise price X and asset price S (at that time) is

$$P = \max (X - S, 0)$$

That is, the value of a put at maturity is the difference between the exercise price of the option and the price of the asset underlying the option, $X - S$, or zero, whichever is greater. If the stock price happens to be greater than the exercise price ($S > X$), the put is said to be out of the money and will expire worthless. If the asset price happens to be less than the exercise price ($S < X$), the put is said to be in the money and the owner will exercise it for a net profit of $P - \beta$. If $S = X$, the put is said to be at the money.

FIGURE 14-2 Profits from Buying and Writing a Put Option

Remembering which is a call option and which is a put option is not always easy. To keep them straight, just remember that having a *call* option to *buy* an asset is the same as having the option to *call in* the asset for delivery at a specified price. Having a *put* option to *sell* an asset is the same as having the option to *put up* an asset for the other party to buy.

Futures Options

To understand option contracts on financial futures, let's examine the option on a June Canada bond futures contract. If you buy this futures contract at a price of 115 (that is, $115 000), you have agreed to pay $115 000 for $100 000 face value of long-term Canada bonds when they are delivered to you at the end of June. If you sold this futures contract at a price of 115, you agreed, in exchange for $115 000, to deliver $100 000 face value of the long-term Canada bonds at the end of June. An option contract on the Canada bond futures contract has several key features: (1) it has the same expiration date as the underlying futures contract; (2) it is an American option and so can be exercised at any time before the expiration date; and (3) the premium (price) of the option is quoted in points that are the same as in the futures contract, so each point corresponds to $1000. If, for a premium of $2000, you buy one call option contract on the June Canada bond contract with an exercise price of 115, you have purchased the right to buy (call in) the June Canada bond futures contract for a price of 115 ($115 000 per contract) at any time through the expiration date of this contract at the end of June. Similarly, when for $2000 you buy a put option on the June Canada bond contract with an exercise price of 115, you have the right to sell (put up) the June Canada bond futures contract for a price of 115 ($115 000 per contract) at any time until the end of June.

Futures option contracts are somewhat complicated, so to explore how they work and how they can be used to hedge risk, let's first examine how profits and losses on the call option on the June Canada bond futures contract occur. In February, our old friend Irving the Investor buys, for a $2000 premium, a call option on the $100 000 June Canada bond futures contract with a strike price of 115. (We assume that if Irving exercises the option, it is on the expiration date at the end of June and not before.) On the expiration date at the end of June, suppose that the underlying Canada bond for the futures contract has a price of 110. Recall that on the expiration date, arbitrage forces the price of the futures contract to be the same as the price of the underlying bond, so it too has a price of 110 on the expiration date at the end of June. If Irving exercises the call option and buys the futures contract at an exercise price of 115, he will lose money by buying at 115 and selling at the lower market price of 110. Because Irving is smart, he will not exercise the option, but he will be out the $2000 premium he paid. In such a situation, in which the price of the underlying financial instrument is below the exercise price, a call option is said to be "out of the money." At the price of 110 (less than the exercise price), Irving thus suffers a loss on the option contract of the $2000 premium he paid. This loss is plotted as point A in panel (a) of Figure 14-3.

On the expiration date, if the price of the futures contract is 115, the call option is "at the money," and Irving is indifferent whether he exercises his option to buy the futures contract or not, since exercising the option at 115 when the market price is also at 115 produces no gain or loss. Because he has paid the $2000 premium, at the price of 115 his contract again has a net loss of $2000, plotted as point B.

If the futures contract instead has a price of 120 on the expiration day, the option is "in the money," and Irving benefits from exercising the option: he would buy the futures contract at the exercise price of 115 and then sell it for 120, thereby earning a 5% gain ($5000 profit) on the $100 000 Canada bond futures contract. Because

FIGURE 14-3 Profits and Losses on Options Versus Futures Contracts

The futures contract is the $100 000 June Canada bond contract, and the option contracts are written on this futures contract with an exercise price of 115. Panel (a) shows the profits and losses for the buyer of the call option and the buyer of the futures contract, and panel (b) shows the profits and losses for the buyer of the put option and the seller of the futures contract.

(a) *Profit or loss for buyer of call option and buyer of futures*

(b) *Profit or loss for buyer of put option and seller of futures*

Irving paid a $2000 premium for the option contract, however, his net profit is $3000 ($5000 − $2000). The $3000 profit at a price of 120 is plotted as point C. Similarly, if the price of the futures contract rose to 125, the option contract would yield a net profit of $8000 ($10 000 from exercising the option minus the $2000 premium), plotted as point D. Plotting these points, we get the kinked profit curve for the call option that we see in panel (a).

Suppose that instead of purchasing the futures *option* contract in February, Irving decides to buy the $100 000 June Canada bond *futures* contract at the price of 115. If the price of the bond on the expiration day at the end of June declines to 110, meaning that the price of the futures contract also falls to 110, Irving suffers a loss of 5 percentage points, or $5000. The loss of $5000 on the futures contract at a price of 110 is plotted as point A′ in panel (a). At a price of 115 on the expiration date, Irving would have a zero profit on the futures contract, plotted as point B′. At a price of 120, Irving would have a profit on the contract of 5 percentage points, or $5000 (point C′), and at a price of 125, the profit would be 10 percentage points, or $10 000 (point D′). Plotting these points, we get the linear (straight-line) profit curve for the futures contract that appears in panel (a).

Now we can see the major difference between a futures contract and an option contract. As the profit curve for the futures contract in panel (a) indicates, the futures contract has a linear profit function: profits grow by an equal dollar amount for every point increase in the price of the underlying asset. By contrast, the kinked profit curve for the option contract is nonlinear, meaning that profits do not always grow by the same amount for a given change in the price of the underlying asset. The reason for this nonlinearity is that the call option protects Irving from having losses that are greater than the amount of the $2000 premium. In contrast, Irving's loss on the futures contract is $5000 if the price on the expiration day falls to 110, and if the price falls even further, Irving's loss will be even greater. This insurance-like feature of option contracts explains why their purchase price is referred to as a premium. Once the underlying asset's price rises above the exercise price, however, Irving's profits grow linearly. Irving has given up something by buying an option rather than a futures contract. As we see in panel (a), when the price of the underlying asset rises above the exercise price, Irving's profits are always less than that on the futures contract by exactly the $2000 premium he paid.

Panel (b) plots the results of the same profit calculations if Irving buys not a call but a put option (an option to sell) with an exercise price of 115 for a premium of $2000 and if he sells the futures contract rather than buying one. In this case, if on the expiration date the Canada bond futures have a price above the 115 exercise price, the put option is "out of the money." Irving would not want to exercise the put option and then have to sell the futures contract he owns as a result of exercising the put option at a price below the market price and lose money. He would not exercise his option, and he would be out only the $2000 premium he paid. Once the price of the futures contract falls below the 115 exercise price, Irving benefits from exercising the put option because he can sell the futures contract at a price of 115 but can buy it at a price below this. In such a situation, in which the price of the underlying asset is below the exercise price, the put option is "in the money," and profits rise linearly as the price of the futures contract falls. The profit function for the put option illustrated in panel (b) of Figure 14-3 is kinked, indicating that Irving is protected from losses greater than the amount of the premium he paid. The profit curve for the sale of the futures contract is just the negative of the profit for the futures contract in panel (a) and is therefore linear.

Panel (b) of Figure 14-3 confirms the conclusion from panel (a) that profits on option contracts are nonlinear but profits on futures contracts are linear.

Two other differences between futures and option contracts must be mentioned. The first is that the initial investment on the contracts differs. As we saw earlier in the chapter, when a futures contract is purchased, the investor must put up a fixed amount, the margin requirement, in a margin account. But when an option contract is purchased, the initial investment is the premium that must be paid for the contract. The second important difference between the contracts is that the futures contract requires money to change hands daily when the contract is marked to market, whereas the option contract requires money to change hands only when it is exercised.

APPLICATION

Hedging with Futures Options

Solution

Earlier in the chapter, we saw how the First Bank could hedge the interest-rate risk on its $5 million holdings of 6s of 2030 by selling $5 million of Canada bond futures (50 contracts). A rise in interest rates and the resulting fall in bond prices and bond futures contracts would lead to profits on the bank's sale of the futures contracts that would exactly offset the losses on the 6s of 2030 the bank is holding.

As panel (b) of Figure 14-3 (p. 338) suggests, an alternative way for the manager to protect against a rise in interest rates and hence a decline in bond prices is to buy $5 million of put options written on the same Canada bond futures. As long as the exercise price is not too far from the current price as in panel (b), the rise in interest rates and decline in bond prices will lead to profits on the futures and the futures put options, profits that will offset any losses on the $5 million of Canada bonds.

The one problem with using options rather than futures is that the First Bank will have to pay premiums on the options contracts, thereby lowering the bank's profits in order to hedge the interest-rate risk. Why might the bank manager be willing to use options rather than futures to conduct the hedge? The answer is that the option contract, unlike the futures contract, allows the First Bank to gain if interest rates decline and bond prices rise. With the hedge using futures contracts, the First Bank does not gain from increases in bond prices because the profits on the bonds it is holding are offset by the losses from the futures contracts it has sold. However, as panel (b) of Figure 14-3 indicates, the situation when the hedge is conducted with put options is quite different: Once bond prices rise above the exercise price, the bank does not suffer additional losses on the option contracts. At the same time, the value of the Canada bonds the bank is holding will increase, thereby leading to a profit for the bank. Thus using options rather than futures to conduct the micro hedge allows the bank to protect itself from rises in interest rates but still allows the bank to benefit from interest-rate declines (although the profit is reduced by the amount of the premium).

Similar reasoning indicates that the bank manager might prefer to use options to conduct a macro hedge to immunize the entire bank portfolio from interest-rate risk. Again, the strategy of using options rather than futures has the disadvantage that the First Bank has to pay the premiums on these contracts up front. By contrast, using options allows the bank to keep the gains from a decline in interest rates (which will raise the value of the bank's assets relative to its liabilities) because these gains will not be offset by large losses on the option contracts.

In the case of a macro hedge, there is another reason why the bank might prefer option contracts to futures contracts. Profits and losses on futures contracts can cause accounting problems for banks because such profits and losses are not allowed to be offset by unrealized changes in the value of the rest of the bank's portfolio. Consider the case when interest rates fall. If First Bank sells futures contracts to conduct the macro hedge, then when interest rates fall and the prices of the Canada bond futures contracts rise, it will have large losses on these contracts. Of course, these losses are offset by unrealized profits in the rest of the bank's portfolio, but the bank is not allowed to offset these losses in its accounting statements. So even though the macro hedge is serving its intended purpose of immunizing the bank's portfolio from interest-rate risk, the bank would experience large accounting losses when interest rates fall. Indeed, bank managers have lost their jobs when perfectly sound hedges with interest-rate futures have led to large accounting losses. Not surprisingly, bank managers might shrink from using financial futures to conduct macro hedges for this reason.

Futures options, however, can come to the rescue of the managers of banks and other financial institutions. Suppose that First Bank conducted the macro hedge by buying put options instead of selling Canada bond futures. Now if interest rates fall and bond prices rise well above the exercise price, the bank will not have large losses on the option contracts because it will just decide not to exercise its options. The bank will not suffer the accounting problems produced by hedging with financial futures. Because of the accounting advantages of using futures options to conduct macro hedges, option contracts have become important to financial institution managers as tools for hedging interest-rate risk.

Factors Affecting the Prices of Option Premiums

Several interesting facts can be noted about how the premiums on option contracts are priced. First, when the strike (exercise) price for a contract is set at a higher level, the premium for the call option is lower and the premium for the put option is higher. For example, in going from a contract with a strike price of 112 to one with 115, the premium for a call option for the month of March might fall from 1 45/64 to 16/64, and the premium for the March put option might rise from 19/64 to 1 54/64.

Our understanding of the profit function for option contracts illustrated in Figure 14-3 helps explain this fact. As we saw in panel (a), a higher price for the underlying asset (in this case a Canada bond futures contract) relative to the option's exercise price results in higher profits on the call (buy) option. Thus, the lower the strike price, the higher the profits on the call option contract and the greater the premium that investors like Irving are willing to pay. Similarly, we saw in panel (b) that a higher price for the underlying asset relative to the exercise price lowers profits on the put (sell) option, so that a higher strike price increases profits and thus causes the premium to increase.

Second, as the period of time over which the option can be exercised (the term to expiration) gets longer, the premiums for both call and put options rise. For example, at a strike price of 112, the premium on the call option might increase from 1 45/64 in March to 1 50/64 in April and to 2 28/64 in May. Similarly, the premium on a put option might increase from 19/64 in March to 1 43/64 in April and to 2 22/64 in May. The fact that premiums increase with the term to expiration is also explained by the nonlinear profit function for option contracts. As the term to expiration lengthens, there is a greater chance that the price of the underlying asset will be very high or very low by the expiration date. If the price becomes very high and goes well above the exercise price, the call (buy) option will yield a high profit, but if the price becomes very low and goes well below the exercise price, the losses will be small because the owner of the call option will simply decide not to exercise the option. The possibility of greater variability of the underlying asset as the term to expiration lengthens raises profits on average for the call option.

Similar reasoning tells us that the put (sell) option will become more valuable as the term to expiration increases because the possibility of greater price variability of the underlying financial instrument increases as the term to expiration increases. The greater chance of a low price increases the chance that profits on the put option will be very high. But the greater chance of a high price does not produce substantial losses for the put option because the owner will again just decide not to exercise the option.

Another way of thinking about this reasoning is to recognize that option contracts have an element of "heads, I win; tails, I don't lose too badly." The greater variability of where the prices might be by the expiration date increases the value of both kinds of options. Since a longer term to the expiration date leads to greater variability of where the prices might be by the expiration date, a longer term to expiration raises the value of the option contract.

The reasoning that we have just developed also explains another important fact about option premiums. When the volatility of the price of the underlying asset is great, the premiums for both call and put options will be higher. Higher volatility of prices means that for a given expiration date, there will again be greater variability of where the prices might be by the expiration date. The "heads, I win; tails, I don't lose too badly" property of options then means that the greater variability of possible prices by the expiration date increases average profits for the option and thus increases the premium that investors are willing to pay.

Summary

Our analysis of how profits on options are affected by price movements for the underlying asset leads to the following conclusions about the factors that determine the premium on an option contract:

1. The higher the strike price, everything else being equal, the lower the premium on call (buy) options and the higher the premium on put (sell) options.
2. The greater the term to expiration, everything else being equal, the higher the premiums for both call and put options.
3. The greater the volatility of prices of the underlying instrument, everything else being equal, the higher the premiums for both call and put options.

The results we have derived here appear in more formal models, such as the Black-Scholes model, which analyze how the premiums on options are priced. You might study such models in other finance courses.

Swaps

In addition to forwards, futures, and options, financial institutions use one other important financial derivative to manage risk. **Swaps** are financial contracts that obligate each party to the contract to exchange (swap) a set of payments (not assets) it owns for another set of payments owned by another party. Swaps are of two basic kinds. **Currency swaps** involve the exchange of a set of payments in one currency for a set of payments in another currency. **Interest-rate swaps** involve the exchange of one set of interest payments for another set of interest payments, all denominated in the same currency. We focus on interest-rate swaps.

FIGURE 14-4 Interest-Rate Swap Payments

In this swap arrangement, with a notional principal of $1 million and a term of 10 years, First Trust pays a fixed rate of 7% $1 million to the Friendly Finance Company, which in turn agrees to pay the one-year Treasury bill rate plus 1% $1 million to First Trust.

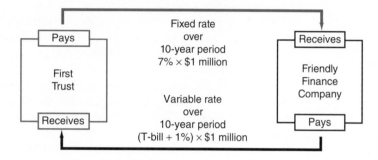

Interest-Rate Swap Contracts	Interest-rate swaps are an important tool for managing interest-rate risk, and they first appeared in the United States in 1982 when there was an increase in the demand for financial instruments that could be used to reduce interest-rate risk. The most common type of interest-rate swap (called the *plain vanilla swap*) specifies (1) the interest rate on the payments that are being exchanged; (2) the type of interest payments (variable or fixed-rate); (3) the amount of **notional principal**, which is the amount on which the interest is being paid; and (4) the time period over which the exchanges continue to be made. There are many other more complicated versions of swaps, including forward swaps and swap options (called *swaptions*), but here we will look only at the plain vanilla swap. Figure 14-4 illustrates an interest-rate swap between First Trust and the Friendly Finance Company. First Trust agrees to pay Friendly Finance a fixed rate of 7% on $1 million of notional principal for the next 10 years, and Friendly Finance agrees to pay First Trust the one-year Treasury bill rate plus 1% on $1 million of notional principal for the same period. Thus, as shown in Figure 14-4, every year First Trust would be paying the Friendly Finance Company 7% on $1 million while Friendly Finance would be paying First Trust the one-year T-bill rate plus 1% on $1 million.

APPLICATION

Hedging with Interest-Rate Swaps

You might wonder why these two parties find it advantageous to enter into this swap agreement. The answer is that it may help both of them hedge interest-rate risk.

Suppose that First Trust, which tends to borrow short-term and then lend long-term in the mortgage market, has $1 million less of rate-sensitive assets than it has of rate-sensitive liabilities. As we learned in Chapter 13, this situation means that as interest rates rise, the rise in the cost of funds (liabilities) is greater than the rise in interest payments it receives on its assets, many of which are fixed-rate. The result of rising interest rates is thus a shrinking of First Trust's net interest margin and a decline in its profitability. As we saw in Chapter 13, to avoid this interest-rate risk, the manager of First Trust would like to convert $1 million of its fixed-rate assets into $1 million of rate-sensitive assets, in effect making rate-sensitive assets equal to rate-sensitive liabilities, thereby eliminating the gap. This is exactly what happens when she engages in the interest-rate swap. By taking $1 million of its fixed-rate income and exchanging it for $1 million of rate-sensitive Treasury bill income, she has converted income on $1 million of fixed-rate assets into income on $1 million of rate-sensitive assets. Now when interest rates increase, the rise in rate-sensitive income on its assets exactly matches the rise in the rate-sensitive cost of funds on its liabilities, leaving the net interest margin and bank profitability unchanged.

The manager of the Friendly Finance Company, which issues long-term bonds to raise funds and uses them to make short-term loans, finds that he is in exactly the opposite situation to First Trust: he has $1 million more of rate-sensitive assets than of rate-sensitive liabilities. He is therefore concerned that a fall in interest rates, which will result in a larger drop in income from its assets than the decline in the cost of funds on its liabilities, will cause a decline in profits. By doing the interest-rate swap, the manager eliminates this interest-rate risk because he has converted $1 million of rate-sensitive income into $1 million of fixed-rate income. Now the manager of the Friendly Finance Company finds that when interest rates fall, the decline in rate-sensitive income is smaller and so is matched by the decline in the rate-sensitive cost of funds on its liabilities, leaving profitability unchanged.

Advantages of Interest-Rate Swaps

To eliminate interest-rate risk, both First Trust and the Friendly Finance Company could have rearranged their balance sheets by converting fixed-rate assets into rate-sensitive assets, and vice versa, instead of engaging in an interest-rate swap. However, this strategy would have been costly for both financial institutions for several reasons. The first is that financial institutions incur substantial transaction costs when they rearrange their balance sheets. Second, different financial institutions have informational advantages in making loans to certain customers who may prefer certain maturities. Thus, adjusting the balance sheet to eliminate interest-rate risk may result in a loss of these informational advantages, which the financial institution is unwilling to give up. Interest-rate swaps solve these problems for financial institutions because in effect they allow the institutions to convert fixed-rate assets into rate-sensitive assets without affecting the balance sheet. Large transaction costs are avoided, and the financial institutions can continue to make loans where they have an informational advantage.

We have seen that financial institutions can also hedge interest-rate risk with other financial derivatives such as futures contracts and futures options. Interest-rate swaps have one big advantage over hedging with these other derivatives: they can be written for very long horizons, sometimes as long as 20 years, whereas financial futures and futures options typically have much shorter horizons, not much more than a year. If a financial institution needs to hedge interest-rate risk for a long horizon, financial futures and option markets may not do it much good. Instead it can turn to the swap market.

Disadvantages of Interest-Rate Swaps

Although interest-rate swaps have important advantages that make them very popular with financial institutions, they also have disadvantages that limit their usefulness. Swap markets, like forward markets, can suffer from a lack of liquidity. Let's return to looking at the swap between First Trust and the Friendly Finance Company. As with a forward contract, it might be difficult for First Trust to link up with the Friendly Finance Company to arrange the swap. In addition, even if First Trust could find a counterparty like the Friendly Finance Company, it might not be able to negotiate a good deal because it couldn't find any other institution to negotiate with.

Swap contracts also are subject to the same default risk that we encountered for forward contracts. If interest rates rise, the Friendly Finance Company would love to get out of the swap contract, because the fixed-rate interest payments it receives are less than it could get in the open market. It might then default on the contract, exposing First Trust to a loss. Alternatively, the Friendly Finance Company could go bust, meaning that the terms of the swap contract would not be fulfilled.

Financial Intermediaries in Interest-Rate Swaps

As we have just seen, financial institutions do have to be aware of the possibility of losses from a default on swaps. As with a forward contract, each party to a swap must have a lot of information about the other party to make sure that the contract is likely to be fulfilled. The need for information about counterparties and the liquidity problems in swap markets could limit the usefulness of these markets. However, when informational and liquidity problems crop up in a market, financial intermediaries come to the rescue. That is exactly what happens in swap markets. Intermediaries such as investment banks and especially large banks have the ability to acquire information cheaply about the creditworthiness and reliability of parties to swap contracts and are also able to match up parties to a swap. Hence, large banks and investment banks have set up swap markets in which they act as intermediaries.

Credit Derivatives

In recent years, a new type of derivative has come on the scene to hedge credit risk. Like other derivatives, **credit derivatives** offer payoffs on previously issued securities, but ones that bear credit risk. In the past 10 years, the markets in credit derivatives have grown at an outstanding pace and the notional amounts of these derivatives now number in the trillions of dollars. These credit derivatives take several forms.

Credit Options

Credit options work just like the options discussed earlier in the chapter: for a fee, the purchaser gains the right to receive profits that are tied either to the price of an underlying security or to an interest rate. Suppose you buy $1 million of General Motors bonds but worry that a potential slowdown in the sale of SUVs might lead a credit-rating agency to *downgrade* (lower the credit rating on) GM bonds. As we saw in Chapter 6, such a downgrade would cause the price of GM bonds to fall. To protect yourself, you could buy an option for, say, $15 000 to sell the $1 million of bonds at a strike price that is the same as the current price. With this strategy, you would not suffer any losses if the value of the GM bonds declined because you could exercise the option and sell them at the price you paid for them. In addition, you would be able to reap any gains that occurred if GM bonds rose in value.

The second type of credit option ties profits to changes in an interest rate such as a credit spread (the interest rate on the average bond with a particular credit rating minus the interest rate on default-free bonds such as those issued by the Canadian goverment). Suppose that your company, which has a BBB credit rating, plans to issue $10 million of one-year bonds in three months and expects to have a credit spread of 1 percentage point (i.e., it will pay an interest rate that is 1 percentage point higher than the one-year T-bill rate). You are concerned that the market might start to think that BBB companies in general will become riskier in the coming months. If this were to happen by the time you are ready to issue your bonds in three months, you would have to pay a higher interest rate than the 1 percentage point in excess of the T-bill rate and your cost of issuing the bonds would increase. To protect yourself against these higher costs, you could buy for, say, $20 000, a credit option on $10 million of BBB bonds that would pay you the difference between the average BBB credit spread in the market minus the 1 percentage point credit spread on $10 million. If the credit spread jumps to 2 percentage points, you would receive $100 000 from the option (= [2% − 1%] × $10 million), which would exactly offset the $100 000 higher interest costs from the 1-percentage-point higher interest rate you would have to pay on your $10 million of bonds.

Credit Swaps

Suppose you manage a bank in Calgary called Oil Drillers' Bank (ODB), which specializes in lending to a particular industry in your local area, oil drilling companies. Another bank, Potato Farmers' Bank (PFB), specializes in lending to potato farmers in Charlottetown. Both ODB and PFB have a problem because their loan portfolios are not sufficiently diversified. To protect ODB against a collapse in the oil market, which would result in defaults on most of its loans made to oil drillers, you could reach an agreement to have the loan payments on, say, $100 million worth of your loans to oil drillers paid to the PFB in exchange for PFB paying you the loan payments on $100 million of its loans to potato farmers. Such a transaction, in which risky payments on loans are swapped for each other, is called a **credit swap**. As a result of this swap, ODB and PFB have increased their diversification and lowered the overall risk of their loan portfolios because some of the loan payments to each bank are now coming from a different type of loan.

Another form of credit swap is, for arcane reasons, called a *credit default swap*, although it functions more like insurance. With a credit default swap, one party who wants to hedge credit risk pays a fixed payment on a regular basis, in return for a contingent payment that is triggered by a credit event such as the bankruptcy of a particular firm or the downgrading of the firm's credit rating by a credit rating agency. For example, you could use a credit default swap to hedge the $1 million of General Motors bonds that you are holding by arranging to pay an annual fee of $1000 in exchange for a payment of $10 000 if the GM bonds' credit rating is lowered. If a credit event happens and GM's bonds are downgraded so that their price falls, you will receive a payment that will offset some of the loss you suffer if you sell the bonds at this lower price.

Credit-Linked Notes

Another type of credit derivative, the **credit-linked note**, is a combination of a bond and a credit option. Just like any corporate bond, the credit-linked note makes periodic coupon (interest) payments and a final payment of the face value of the bond at maturity. If a key financial variable specified in the note changes, however, the issuer of the note has the right (option) to lower the payments on the note. For example, General Motors could issue a credit-linked note that pays a 5% coupon rate, with the specification that if a national index of SUV sales falls by 10%, then GM has the right to lower the coupon rate by 2 percentage points to 3%. In this way, GM can lower its risk because when it is losing money as SUV sales fall, it can offset some of these losses by making smaller payments on its credit-linked notes.

APPLICATION

Lessons from the Global Financial Crisis: When Are Financial Derivatives Likely to Be a Worldwide Time Bomb?

Although financial derivatives can be useful in hedging risk, the AIG blowup discussed in Chapter 12 illustrates that they can pose a real danger to the financial system. Indeed, Warren Buffett warned about the dangers of financial derivatives by characterizing them as "financial weapons of mass destruction." Particularly scary are the notional amounts of derivatives contracts—more than $500 trillion worldwide. What does the recent global financial crisis tell us about when financial derivatives are likely to be a time bomb that could bring down the world financial system?

Two major concerns surround financial derivatives. The first is that financial derivatives allow financial institutions to increase their leverage; that is, these institutions can in effect hold an amount of the underlying asset that is many times greater than the amount of money they have had to put up. Increasing their leverage enables them to take huge bets, which, if they are wrong, can bring down the institution. This is exactly what AIG did, to its great regret, when it plunged into the credit default swap (CDS) market. Even more of a problem was that AIG's speculation in the CDS market had the potential to bring down the whole financial system. An important lesson from the subprime financial crisis is that having one player take huge positions in a derivatives market is highly dangerous.

A second concern is that banks have holdings of huge notional amounts of financial derivatives, particularly interest-rate and currency swaps, that greatly exceed the amount of bank capital, and so these derivatives expose the banks to serious risk of failure. Banks are indeed major players in the financial derivatives markets, particularly in the interest-rate and currency swaps market, where our earlier analysis has shown that they are the natural market-makers because they can act as intermediaries between two counterparties who would not make the swap without their involvement. However, looking at the notional amount of interest-rate and currency swaps at banks gives a very misleading picture of their risk exposure. Because banks act as intermediaries in the swap markets, they are typically exposed only to credit risk—a default by one of their counterparties. Furthermore, these swaps, unlike loans, do not involve payments of the notional amount but rather the much smaller payments that are based on the notional amounts. For example, in the case of a 7% interest rate, the payment is only $70 000 for a $1 million swap. Estimates of the credit exposure from swap contracts indicate that they are on the order of only 1% of the notional value of the contracts and that credit exposure at banks from derivatives is generally less than a quarter of their total credit exposure from loans. Banks' credit exposures from their derivative positions are thus not out of line with other credit exposures they face. Indeed, during the recent subprime financial crisis, in which the financial system was put under great stress, derivatives exposure at banks was not a serious problem.

The conclusion is that recent events indicate that financial derivatives pose serious dangers to the financial system, but some of these dangers have been overplayed. The biggest danger occurs in trading activities of financial institutions, and this is particularly true for credit derivatives, as was illustrated by AIG's activities in the CDS market. As discussed in Chapter 10, regulators have been paying increased attention to this danger and are continuing to develop new disclosure requirements and regulatory guidelines for how derivatives trading should be done. Of particular concern is the need for financial institutions to disclose their exposure in derivatives contracts, so that regulators can make sure that a large institution is not playing too large a role in these markets and does not have too large an exposure to derivatives relative to its capital, as was the case for AIG. Another concern is that derivatives, particularly credit derivatives, need to have a better clearing mechanism so that the failure of one institution does not bring down many others whose net derivatives positions are small, even though they have many offsetting positions. Better clearing could be achieved either by having these derivatives traded in an organized exchange like a futures market, or by having one clearing organization net out trades.

The credit risk exposure posed by interest-rate derivatives, by contrast, seems to be manageable with standard methods of dealing with credit risk, both by managers of financial institutions and the institutions' regulators.

New regulations for derivatives markets are sure to come in the wake of the global financial crisis. The industry has also had a wake-up call as to where the dangers in derivatives products might lie. Now, the hope is that any time bomb arising from derivatives can be defused with appropriate effort on the part of markets and regulators.

MyEconLab MyEconLab is an online homework and tutorial system that puts you in control of your own learning with study and practice tools directly correlated to this chapter's content. Visit MyEconLab to explore the following resources:

- The Questions and Applied Problems are all available in the Study Plan on MyEconLab for further practice. You will also find the answers to all of the Questions and Applied Problems in the Student Resources section of your MyEconLab.

MyEconLab also features Additional Readings, Videos, Glossary Flashcards, Audio Chapter Summaries, Economics News Feeds, Animations, and many additional tools to help you master key concepts from the text.

SUMMARY

MyEcon
Audio Sum

1. Interest-rate forward contracts, which are agreements to sell a debt instrument at a future (forward) point in time, can be used to hedge interest-rate risk. The advantage of forward contracts is that they are flexible, but the disadvantages are that they are subject to default risk and their market is illiquid.

2. A financial futures contract is similar to an interest-rate forward contract in that it specifies that a debt instrument must be delivered by one party to another on a stated future date. However, it has advantages over a forward contract in that it is not subject to default risk and is more liquid. Forward and futures contracts can be used by financial institutions to hedge (protect) against interest-rate risk.

3. Stock index futures are financial futures whose underlying financial instrument is a stock market index. Stock index futures can be used to hedge stock market risk by reducing systematic risk in portfolios or by locking in stock prices.

4. An option contract gives the purchaser the right to buy (call option) or sell (put option) a security at the exercise (strike) price within a specific period of time. The profit function for options is nonlinear—profits do not always grow by the same amount for a given change in the price of the underlying asset. The nonlinear profit function for options explains why their value (as reflected by the premium paid for them) is negatively related to the exercise price for call options, positively related to the exercise price for put options, positively related to the term to expiration for both call and put options, and positively related to the volatility of the prices of the underlying asset for both call and put options. Financial institutions use futures options to hedge interest-rate risk in a similar fashion to the way they use financial futures and forward contracts. Futures options may be preferred for macro hedges because they suffer from fewer accounting problems than financial futures.

5. Interest-rate swaps involve the exchange of one set of interest payments for another set of interest payments and have default risk and liquidity problems similar to those of forward contracts. As a result, interest-rate swaps often involve intermediaries such as large banks and investment banks that make a market in swaps. Financial institutions find that interest-rate swaps are useful ways to hedge interest-rate risk. Interest-rate swaps have one big advantage over financial futures and options: they can be written for very long horizons.

6. Credit derivatives are a new type of derivative that offer payoffs on previously issued securities that have credit risk. These derivatives—credit options, swaps, and credit-linked notes—can be used to hedge credit risk.

7. There are two major concerns about the dangers of derivatives: they allow financial institutions to more easily increase their leverage and take big bets (by effectively enabling them to hold a larger amount of the underlying assets than the amount of money put down), and they expose financial institutions to large credit risks because the huge notional amounts of derivative contracts greatly exceed the capital of these institutions. The second danger seems to be overplayed, but the danger from increased leverage using derivatives is very real, as events in the subprime financial crisis revealed.

KEY TERMS

American option, p. 334

arbitrage, p. 327

at the money (trading at par), p. 336

call option, p. 335

call premium, p. 335

credit derivatives, p. 345

credit-linked note, p. 346

credit options, p. 345

credit swap, p. 346

currency swaps, p. 342

European option, p. 334

exercise price (strike price), p. 334

financial derivatives, p. 323

financial futures, p. 326

financial futures option (futures option), p. 334

forward contracts, p. 324

hedge, p. 323

in-the-money option, p. 336

interest-rate forward contracts, p. 324

interest-rate futures contract, p. 326

interest-rate swaps, p. 342

intrinsic value, p. 336

long in a call, p. 335

long in a put, p. 336

long position, p. 323

macro hedge, p. 328

margin requirement, p. 331

marked to market, p. 331

micro hedge, p. 328

notional principal, p. 343

open interest, p. 329

options, p. 334

out-of-the-money option, p. 336

premium, p. 334

put option, p. 336

put premium, p. 336

short in a call, p. 335

short in a put, p. 336

short position, p. 323

stock market risk, p. 333

stock options, p. 334

swaps, p. 342

QUESTIONS

1. Explain why greater volatility or a longer term to maturity leads to a higher premium on both call and put options.

2. Why does a lower strike price imply that a call option will have a higher premium and a put option a lower premium?

APPLIED PROBLEMS

3. If the pension fund you manage expects to have an inflow of $120 million six months from now, what forward contract would you seek to enter into to lock in current interest rates?

4. If the portfolio you manage is holding $25 million of 8s of 2030 Canada bonds with a price of 110, what forward contract would you enter into to hedge the interest-rate risk on these bonds over the coming year?

5. If at the expiration date, the deliverable Canada bond is selling for 101 but the Canada bond futures contract is selling for 102, what will happen to the futures price? Explain your answer.

6. If you buy a $100 000 June Canada bond contract for 108 and the price of the deliverable Canada bond at the expiration date is 102, what is your profit or loss on the contract?

7. Suppose that the pension you are managing is expecting an inflow of funds of $100 million next year and you want to make sure that you will earn the current interest rate of 8% when you invest the incoming funds in long-term bonds. How would you use the futures market to do this?

8. How would you use the options market to accomplish the same thing as in Problem 7? What are the advantages and disadvantages of using an options contract rather than a futures contract?

9. If you buy a put option on a $100 000 Canada bond futures contract with an exercise price of 95 and the price of the Canada bond is 120 at expiration, is the contract in the money, out of the money, or at the money? What is your profit or loss on the contract if the premium was $4000?

10. Suppose that you buy a call option on a $100 000 Canada bond futures contract with an exercise price of 110 for a premium of $1500. If on expiration the futures contract has a price of 111, what is your profit or loss on the contract?

11. If the finance company you manage has a gap of +$5 million (rate-sensitive assets greater than rate-sensitive liabilities by $5 million), describe an interest-rate swap that would eliminate the company's income gap.

12. If the bank you manage has a gap of –$42 million, describe an interest-rate swap that would eliminate the bank's income risk from changes in interest rates.

13. If your company has a payment of 200 million euros due one year from now, how would you hedge the foreign exchange risk in this payment with a 125 000 euro futures contract?

14. If your company has to make a 10 million euro payment to a German company three months from now, how would you hedge the foreign exchange risk in this payment with a 125 000 euro futures contract?

15. Suppose that your company will be receiving 30 million euros six months from now and the euro is currently selling for 1.4 Canadian dollars. If you want to hedge the foreign exchange risk in this payment, what kind of forward contract would you want to enter into?

16. A swap agreement calls for Rocky Industries to pay interest annually based on a rate of 2% over the one-year T-bill rate, currently 3%. In return, Rocky Industries receives interest at a rate of 4% on a fixed-rate basis. The notional principal for the swap is $100 000. What is Rocky's net interest for the year after the agreement?

WEB EXERCISES

1. The following site can be used to demonstrate how the features of an option affect the option's prices. Go to **www.option-price.com/index.php**. What happens to the price of an option under each of the following situations:

a. The strike price increases.
b. Interest rates increase.
c. Volatility increases.
d. The time until the option matures increases.

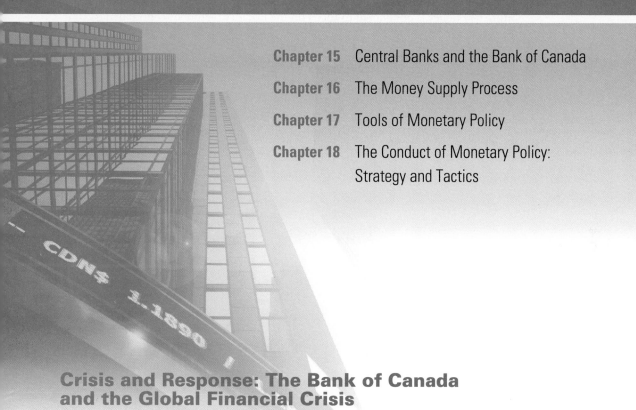

PART V

Central Banking and the Conduct of Monetary Policy

Crisis and Response: The Bank of Canada and the Global Financial Crisis

The onset of the subprime financial crisis in August 2007 was a curve ball for central banks around the world. The global financial crisis, described by former Federal Reserve Chairman Alan Greenspan as a "once-in-a-century credit tsunami," had the potential to devastate the world economy.

The Bank of Canada resolved to come to the rescue of the Canadian economy. Starting in September of 2007, the Bank of Canada enacted monetary policy at a rapid rate by reducing the overnight interest rate. Specifically, the Bank lowered the overnight rate target in December by 25 basis points (0.25 percentage points) from 4.50% to 4.25%, and eventually drove the overnight rate target down to 0.25% by April of 2009.

At the same time, the Bank of Canada implemented large liquidity injections into the credit markets to try to get them lending again. Over the course of the crisis, the Bank broadened its provision of liquidity to the financial system well outside of its traditional lending to depository institutions. The number of new Bank of Canada instruments over the course of the crisis spawned a whole new terminology, including term PRAs, quantitative easing, and credit easing, making the Bank of Canada sound like the military with code-named initiatives and weapons. Like the military, the Bank of Canada was fighting a war, although its weapons were financial rather than physical.

The recent global financial crisis has demonstrated the importance of central banks like the Bank of Canada to the health of the financial system and the economy. Chapter 15 outlines what central banks are trying to achieve, what motivates them, and how they are set up. Chapter 16 describes how the money supply is determined. In Chapter 17, we look at the tools that central banks like the Bank of Canada have at their disposal and how they use them. Chapter 18 extends the discussion of how monetary policy is conducted to focus on the broader picture of central banks' strategies and tactics.

CHAPTER 15

Central Banks and the Bank of Canada

LEARNING OBJECTIVES

After studying this chapter you should be able to

1. classify the institutional structure of the Bank of Canada as well as four of the most important foreign central banks

2. identify the Bank of Canada's functions and degree of independence and specify the arguments for and against an independent central bank

3. describe the relationship between central bank independence and macroeconomic performance

PREVIEW

Among the most important players in financial markets throughout the world are central banks, the government authorities in charge of monetary policy. Central banks' actions affect interest rates, the amount of credit, and the money supply, all of which have direct impacts not only on financial markets but also on aggregate output and inflation. To understand the role that central banks play in financial markets and the overall economy, we need to understand how these organizations work. Who controls central banks and determines their actions? What motivates their behaviour? Who holds the reins of power?

In this chapter, we look at the institutional structure of major central banks, and focus particularly on the Bank of Canada, Canada's central bank, often just called the Bank. We start by examining the elements of the Bank of Canada's institutional structure that determine where the true power within the Bank of Canada lies. By understanding who makes the decisions, we will have a better idea of how they are made. We then examine what explains central bank behaviour and whether it is a good idea to make central banks independent by insulating them from politicians. Finally, we look at the structure and independence of other major central banks, particularly the Federal Reserve System in the United States—the most important central bank in the world—and the European Central Bank. With this context in place, we will be prepared to comprehend the actual conduct of monetary policy described in the following chapters.

Origins of the Bank of Canada

The devastation of the Great Depression was of fundamental importance in the creation of the Bank of Canada. From 1929 to 1933, Canadian real GDP fell by almost 30% and the unemployment rate increased sevenfold from less than 3% to close to 20%. The Great Depression not only involved the largest decline in the level of economic activity in the history of Canada, but was also followed by an extremely slow recovery. Being such a cataclysmic event, the Great Depression contributed to significant changes in government policy, including fiscal policy, monetary policy, banking policy, and international policy.

In particular, as the depth of the Great Depression was blamed on the operation of the monetary system, in 1933 the federal Conservative government established a royal commission to study the problems of the Great Depression. Based on a recommendation of the royal commission, Parliament passed the Bank of Canada Act in 1934 and the newly founded Bank of Canada started operations on March 11, 1935. By this time, most other countries already had a central bank (see the Global box Establishment of Selected Central Banks). Although the primary motivation for the formation of the Bank of Canada was economic (or monetary), other motives within the government included the need for Canada to reflect its growing political independence from Britain and the need to coordinate its international economic policy.

Initially the Bank of Canada was a private institution but was nationalized in 1938, so it is now a national institution with headquarters in Ottawa. The Bank also has regional offices in Toronto (for Ontario), Vancouver (for British Columbia and the Yukon), Calgary (for the Prairies, Northwest Territories, and Nunavut), Montréal (for Quebec), and Halifax (for Atlantic Canada), and in 2002 the Bank also established a post in New York to enhance communication with the world's largest financial community. Unlike a private bank that operates in pursuit of profit, the Bank of Canada is responsible for the country's monetary policy and for the regulation of Canada's deposit-based financial institutions.

GLOBAL

Establishment of Selected Central Banks

Canada did not have a central bank for almost the first 70 years after Confederation. By the time the Bank of Canada began operations in 1935, most other countries already had a central bank. In fact, as you can see in the table, Sweden and the United Kingdom created their central banks back in the seventeenth century. These early central banks, however, were initially privately owned and gradually evolved into modern publicly owned central banks.

Country	Year Central Bank Was Established
Sweden	1656
United Kingdom	1694
France	1800
Belgium	1850
Germany	1875
Japan	1882
Italy	1893
Switzerland	1905
United States	1913
Canada	1935

Source: Forrest H. Capie, Terence C. Mills, and Geoffrey E. Wood, "Central Bank Dependence and Inflation Performance: An Exploratory Data Analysis," in *Varieties of Monetary Reform: Lessons and Experiences on the Road to Monetary Union,* ed. Pierre L. Siklos (Dordrecht, The Netherlands: Kluwer Academic Publishers, 1994), 95–132. Reprinted with permission of the publisher.

Formal Structure of the Bank of Canada

The overall responsibility for the operation of the Bank of Canada rests with a **Board of Directors**, which consists of 15 members—the governor, the senior deputy governor, the deputy minister of finance, and 12 outside directors. The Board appoints the governor and senior deputy governor with the government's approval, for a renewable term of seven years. The outside directors are appointed by the minister of finance, with Cabinet approval, for a three-year term, and they are required to come from all regions of Canada representing a variety of occupations with the exception of banking. The governor of the Bank is the chief executive officer and chairman of the Board of Directors. Currently, the governor of the Bank of Canada is Mark Carney (see the Inside the Central Bank box The Political Environment and the Bank of Canada). On November 26, 2012, however, it was announced that Mark Carney was appointed as Governor of the Bank of England to serve a five-year term effective July 1, 2013. His successor was not known at the time of writing.

In 1994 the Board of Directors made some changes in the internal organization of the Bank. Most prominently the Board established a new senior decision-making authority within the Bank called the **Governing Council**. The council is chaired by the governor and is composed of the senior deputy governor and four deputy governors. Since this change, the six members of the Governing Council of the Bank collectively assume responsibility for the Bank's quarterly *Monetary Policy Report*, published in January, April, July, and October. This system of "collective responsibility" ensures that the Bank's governor is not personally identified with the Bank's policy.

The Functions of the Bank of Canada

In the words of the preamble of the Bank of Canada Act, the functions of the Bank of Canada are

> to regulate credit and currency in the best interests of the economic life of the nation, to control and protect the external value of the national monetary unit and to mitigate by its influence fluctuations in the general level of production, trade, prices and employment, so far as may be possible within the scope of monetary action, and generally to promote the economic and financial welfare of Canada.

INSIDE THE CENTRAL BANK — The Political Environment and the Bank of Canada

Since the inception of the Bank of Canada there have been eight governors:

1935–1954, Graham Towers
1955–1961, James Coyne
1961–1973, Louis Rasminsky
1973–1987, Gerald Bouey
1987–1994, John Crow
1994–2000, Gordon Thiessen
2001–2007, David Dodge
2008–2013, Mark Carney
2013–   , Not known at the time of writing

It is interesting to note that during the same period, Canadians went to the polls more than 20 times to elect a federal government. The Bank of Canada is not completely independent from the government. For example, the government can directly influence the Bank by not renewing the governor's appointment when it expires, as the Liberal government did in 1994 when it didn't renew the appointment of John Crow, who was appointed by the Conservative government in 1987.

This is a vague mandate, leaving a lot of room for interpretation. To explore this subject, we discuss four main areas of responsibility of the Bank of Canada as they are mentioned in the Bank's webpage:

- currency
- funds management
- financial system and
- monetary policy

Currency

Before the creation of the Bank of Canada, the federal government and the early banks issued notes designed to circulate as currency. The day it began operations, the Bank replaced the outstanding issue of federal government notes and provision was also made for the gradual removal of notes issued by banks. By 1945 the Bank had a monopoly over note issue. Although the original Bank Act required the Bank to redeem its notes in gold, this provision was never used. In fact, it was removed with the 1967 revision of the Bank Act, thereby providing the Bank with unlimited powers to issue legal tender.

The Bank also conducts ongoing research, working closely with private-sector partnerships and note-issuing authorities in other countries, in order to improve cost-effectiveness, increase the durability of bank notes, and reduce counterfeiting. In its role as provider of paper money, the Bank's overall objective is to preserve the integrity and safety of Canadian currency in the most economical and efficient manner possible.

Funds Management

In its role as the federal government's fiscal agent, the Bank of Canada provides debt-management services for the federal government such as advising on borrowings, managing new debt offerings, and servicing outstanding debt. Before 1995 these services were provided for all of the federal government's debt. In 1995, however, a special agency of the Department of Finance was created, known as Canada Investment and Savings, to be responsible for the federal government's debt held by individuals, commonly known as retail debt.

Canada Investment and Savings handles Government of Canada securities such as Canada Savings Bonds, Treasury bills, and marketable bonds, and is also responsible for the development of new investment products and marketing initiatives. The Bank of Canada, however, continues to be responsible for all of the government's securities after they are issued, administering millions of bondholder accounts and making payments on behalf of the federal government for interest and debt redemption.

In its role as fiscal agent, the Bank of Canada also manages the government's foreign exchange reserves held by the **Exchange Fund Account** of the Department of Finance. In particular, the Bank assists the Department of Finance in investing these foreign reserves and in borrowing when necessary to maintain an adequate level of reserves. The Bank also engages in international financial transactions, on behalf of the government, in order to influence exchange rates. (We discuss the Bank's foreign exchange interventions more formally in Chapter 20.)

Financial System

The Bank of Canada serves as the lender of last resort if a deposit-taking financial institution faces a liquidity crisis. Because of its unique power to create base money, the Bank can ease the liquidity problems of any financial institution by extending advances, and therefore deter bank runs and panics. **Base money** (also called **monetary base**) consists of the monetary liabilities of the central bank and, as you will see in the next chapter, is an important part of the money supply, because changes in it lead to multiple changes in the money supply. Of course, lender-of-last-resort lending is closely coordinated with the two federal regulatory agencies that are set up specifically to regulate financial institutions—the Office of the Superintendent of Financial Institutions Canada and the Canada Deposit Insurance Corporation.[1] Moreover, such lending is done judiciously, explicitly considering the effects on other financial institutions, the money supply, and government policy.

The Bank of Canada also plays a central role in Canada's national payments system (to be discussed in some detail in Chapter 17). This is essentially an electronic system that clears and settles payments and transactions including securities and foreign exchange, currently handling 15 times our gross domestic product per year. Although this system is operated by the Canadian Payments Association, federal legislation that came into force in 1996 gave the Bank explicit responsibility for the regulatory oversight of this system. The Bank's main concern is whether problems that affect one participant in the clearing and settlement system will spread to other participants.

Finally, the Bank of Canada acts as the holder of deposit accounts of the federal government, the directly clearing members of the Canadian Payments Association, international organizations such as the International Monetary Fund, and other central banks. As the federal government's banker, the Bank is also responsible for the government's operating accounts. In this role, as you will see in Chapter 17, the Bank shifts government balances between the government's transactions account with the Bank and the government's non-transactions accounts with the banks, using twice-daily auctions of government term deposits.

Monetary Policy

The Bank of Canada employs such tools as **open market buyback operations** (the purchase and sale of government securities that affect both interest rates and the amount of reserves in the banking system) and, to a lesser extent, the shifting of government balances between it and the directly clearing members of the Canadian Payments Association to implement changes in the money supply. The Bank's ultimate objective is to keep inflation low. The Bank has a staff of professional economists, which provides economic analysis that the Board of Directors uses in making its decisions (see the Inside the Central Bank box Role of the Bank's Research Staff).

The Bank's goal of low inflation is closely related to the goal of steady economic growth, because businesses are more likely to invest in capital equipment to increase productivity and economic growth when inflation is low. Low inflation is also desirable because it protects the purchasing power of pensioners and those on fixed incomes.

Although the Bank determines monetary policy, in the following section you will learn that the ultimate responsibility for policy rests with the government, since it is the government that must answer to Parliament. This system of "joint responsibility" dates back to 1967 when the Bank of Canada Act was amended to give responsibility for monetary policy to the government.

---

[1] The Office of the Superintendent of Financial Institutions Canada was created in 1987 to succeed the Department of Insurance and the Inspector General of Banks, whereas the Canada Deposit Insurance Corporation was created by an act of Parliament in 1967 to insure deposits, currently up to $100 000 per account, of member deposit-taking institutions.

INSIDE THE CENTRAL BANK

Role of the Bank's Research Staff

The Bank of Canada is the largest employer of economists in Canada. What do all these economists do?

The most important task of the Bank's economists is to follow the incoming data from government agencies and private-sector organizations on the economy and provide guidance to policymakers on where the economy may be heading and what the impact of monetary policy actions on the economy might be. Moreover, the Bank's economists maintain large econometric models (models whose equations are estimated with statistical procedures) that help them produce forecasts of the national economy, and brief the governor and the senior management of the Bank on their forecasts for the Canadian economy.

Because of the increased influence of developments in foreign countries on the Canadian economy, the research staff produces reports on the major foreign economies. They also conduct research on developments in the foreign exchange market because of its growing importance in the monetary policy process and to support the activities of the Bank's foreign exchange desk.

Staff economists also engage in basic research on the effects of monetary policy on output and inflation, developments in the labour markets, international trade, international capital markets, banking and other financial institutions, financial markets, and regional economy, among other topics. This research is published widely in academic journals and in Bank of Canada publications. Bank of Canada publications, such as the *Annual Report* (published in March each year), the *Bank of Canada Review* (published quarterly), the *Financial System Review* (published in June and December), the *Bank of Canada Banking and Financial Statistics* (published monthly), and the *Monetary Policy Report* (published quarterly) are good sources of supplemental material for money and banking students.

Another important activity of the research staff is in the public education area. Staff economists are called on frequently to make presentations to the public.

How Independent Is the Bank of Canada?

When we look, in the next three chapters, at how the Bank of Canada conducts monetary policy, we will want to know why it decides to take certain policy actions but not others. To understand its actions, we must understand the incentives that motivate the Bank's behaviour. How free is the Bank of Canada from the whims of the government? Do economic, bureaucratic, or political considerations guide it? Is the Bank of Canada truly independent of outside pressures?

Stanley Fischer, who was a professor at MIT and is now governor of the Bank of Israel, has defined two different types of independence of central banks: **instrument independence**, the ability of the central bank to set monetary policy instruments, and **goal independence**, the ability of the central bank to set the goals of monetary policy. Unlike the U.S. Federal Reserve and the European Central Bank, which have both types of independence and are remarkably free of political pressures that influence other government agencies, the Bank of Canada has instrument independence but not goal independence.

The Bank of Canada's degree of independence has evolved over time, in part because of changing circumstances, and in part because a clear division of authority was not established in the original Bank of Canada Act. Initially, the Bank of Canada was privately owned, with about 12 000 individual shareholders, and so was largely free of political pressures. It was also free of private interference, because of regulations regarding who could hold how much stock in the Bank. The

Conservative government in office at the time of the Bank's creation believed that the Bank should possess a large share of the responsibility for the development of monetary policy.

Significant changes in the balance of power occurred with the election of a majority Liberal government in the fall of 1935. The Liberals moved the Bank of Canada in the direction of public ownership, culminating in its complete nationalization by 1938. This was done to further isolate the Bank from the pressures of the private system. However, the nationalization of the Bank of Canada did tilt the balance of authority for monetary policy back toward the federal Cabinet and Parliament. The Liberals believed that the Bank of Canada should have discretion in internal management and in implementing monetary policy yet the policies being implemented should be in harmony with the views of the government.

In June 1954, the first governor of the Bank of Canada, Graham Towers, retired after 19 years of service. Graham Towers was replaced by James Coyne (see the Inside the Central Bank box The Political Environment and the Bank of Canada). Like many Canadians at the time, James Coyne was concerned about the level of foreign ownership and the increase in consumer prices during the Korean War. He was convinced that the solution to these problems was a tighter monetary policy stance. A decline in the supply of bank reserves would increase interest rates, thereby raising national savings and reducing Canada's dependence on foreign capital inflows. The tighter monetary policy led to rising unemployment and weak output growth. As a result, the Bank of Canada's policies were criticized by commentary in the popular press and by most of the academic community. In fact, 30 economists signed a letter to the minister of finance calling for Coyne's dismissal.[2]

James Coyne, however, did not change his mind. He was convinced that there was no long-run relationship between inflation and unemployment, despite the publication of a famous paper in 1958 by the British economist A. W. Phillips, showing that higher inflation was typically associated with a lower unemployment rate.[3] Although the Phillips hypothesis attracted widespread support in Canada and was replicated with Canadian data, Coyne was anticipating the pathbreaking work by Milton Friedman and Edmund Phelps on the vertical Phillips curve, to be published 10 years later in 1968.[4] But as a former governor of the Bank of Canada, Gordon Thiessen, put it in a recent speech,

> [t]here was one critical area, however, where Coyne and many other policy analysts, both within and outside the Bank, appear to have been misguided. Those who had questioned the effectiveness of monetary policy in earlier years had failed to appreciate that it was likely to be much stronger than fiscal policy under a flexible exchange rate system, especially when capital was highly mobile. The large capital movements triggered by any change in interest rates would put significant pressure on the exchange rate, amplifying the effects of monetary policy while undercutting the effects of any opposing fiscal policy. Coyne did not realize that, for similar reasons, it was unlikely that a tighter monetary policy would ever raise national savings or reduce foreign investment inflows.[5]

---

[2] See H. S. Gordon, *The Economists Versus the Bank of Canada* (Toronto: The Ryerson Press, 1961): v–vi.

[3] A. W. Phillips, "The Relation Between Unemployment and the Rate of Change of Money Wages in the United Kingdom," *Economica* 24 (1958): 283–299.

[4] Milton Friedman, "The Role of Monetary Policy," *American Economic Review* 58 (1968): 1–17; Edmund Phelps, "Money-Wage Dynamics and Labour Market Equilibrium," *Journal of Political Economy* 76 (1968): 678–711.

[5] Gordon Thiessen, "Can a Bank Change? The Evolution of Monetary Policy at the Bank of Canada 1935–2000," Lecture to the Faculty of Social Science, University of Western Ontario (October 17, 2000).

To avoid accepting blame for this state of affairs, the Liberal government in office reversed its previous stand and disavowed its position that the government was responsible for monetary policy. The government was criticized for this reversal and the new hands-off approach to monetary policy. When the government changed hands on June 10, 1957, and Donald Fleming became the federal minister of finance, the stage was set for a confrontation with the governor of the Bank of Canada, James Coyne. After a long and acrimonious debate, the so-called Coyne Affair was resolved in 1961 with the resignation of Governor Coyne.

On July 24, 1961, Louis Rasminsky accepted the position as the third governor of the Bank of Canada on the condition that the relationship between the government and the Bank of Canada be clearly defined. Soon after he assumed office, he issued a public statement containing two main principles reflecting his views on that relationship

> ... (1) in the ordinary course of events, the Bank has the responsibility for monetary policy, and (2) if the government disapproves of the monetary policy being carried out by the Bank, it has the right and the responsibility to direct the Bank as to the policy which the Bank is to carry out.[6]

A royal commission, whose appointment was partly initiated by the Coyne Affair, accepted Governor Rasminsky's views regarding the relationship between the Bank of Canada and the government. The commission recommended a system of joint responsibility under which the Bank of Canada has considerable autonomy in the conduct of day-to-day monetary policy but the government must accept full responsibility for the policy being followed.

The Bank of Canada Act was amended in 1967 to confirm the joint responsibility system, and this state of affairs regarding monetary policy has generally remained in order to this day. Under this joint responsibility system, the governor of the Bank of Canada and the minister of finance, acting on behalf of the government, consult regularly and, in the event of a serious disagreement over the conduct of monetary policy, the government has the right to override the Bank's decisions. In particular, the minister of finance can issue a directive to the Bank indicating the specific policy changes that the Bank must follow. The directive, however, must be published indicating not only the new policy that the Bank is supposed to undertake but also the period during which it is to apply.

Hence, ultimate responsibility for monetary policy rests with the democratically elected government. However, because of the consequences of issuing a directive, it is unlikely that such a directive would be issued, and none has been issued to date.

The Changing Face of the Bank of Canada

The legislation governing the Bank of Canada's responsibility for monetary policy has remained relatively unchanged since the Bank Act of 1967. Over the past decade, however, the Bank has undertaken a broad range of initiatives and made significant institutional changes to the way it operates. The impetus for change came from the interaction of experience and economic theory, the desire to explain and build confidence in the Bank's actions, and (to a smaller extent) from technological change and globalization.

Clarifying objectives is an important starting point for any successful monetary policy framework. The legislation by which the Bank of Canada is governed does not facilitate a clear understanding of objectives. For example, the preamble to

---

[6]Bank of Canada, *Annual Report*, 1961, p. 3.

legislation governing the Bank refers to multiple, and potentially inconsistent, policy objectives. Over the past few decades, however, the performance of the Canadian economy, together with the evolution of economic theory, led to the view that price stability is the most important goal of monetary policy. As John Crow put it, in his January 1988 Hanson Memorial Lecture at the University of Alberta,

> [t]heory and experience—much of this experience not overly cheerful but certainly instructive—both point to a very clear answer. Monetary policy should be conducted so as to achieve a pace of monetary expansion that promotes stability in the value of money. This means pursuing a policy aimed at achieving and maintaining stable prices.[7]

The Hanson lecture was designed to explicitly identify price stability as the objective of Bank of Canada policy. This message was reinforced on February 26, 1991, through a joint announcement by the governor of the Bank and the minister of finance regarding the establishment of formal inflation targets (to be discussed in detail in Chapter 18). Clearly defined targets can be appealed as an institutional way of improving the macroeconomic outcomes of monetary policy.

The effectiveness of such an institutional framework, however, depends on two fundamental requirements: "independence" and "accountability." Although the Bank of Canada has not been given "goal independence"—the goal of price stability has been set jointly by the Bank and the Department of Finance—over the last decade the Bank placed increased emphasis on its responsibility to achieve the goal of price stability and its greater freedom to take whatever action is needed to do so. This freedom is referred to as "operational" (or "instrument") independence and, although it hasn't been explicitly legislated, it exists in practice. Increased operational independence has also raised the standards for accountability. As already noted, for example, the governor of the Bank has delegated the authority for monetary policy decisions to a committee—the six-member internal Governing Council. Moreover, it has become a de facto standard for the governor to appear before a parliamentary committee following the release of the Bank's *Monetary Policy Report*.

The Bank of Canada has also improved its communications activities by moving towards greater transparency in its operations and objectives. In 1999, for example, the Bank started a twice-yearly *Update* to the *Monetary Policy Report*, both published by the Bank's Governing Council. The *Monetary Policy Report* was published every April and October while the *Update* was published every January and July, giving an account of the Bank's management of monetary policy. Moreover, the Bank has noticeably increased the number of press conferences, press releases, and speeches, and also reorganized its regional offices in 1996–1997 with the objective of improving communication, transparency, and its assessment of economic conditions across Canada. For example, the Bank's regional offices, by maintaining contact with provincial governments, industries, and the general public, present quarterly "grassroots" assessments of current and prospective economic developments to the Bank's Governing Council—information that complements economic projections prepared by the Bank's staff. Finally, the Bank of Canada maintains a comprehensive website (at **www.bankofcanada.ca**) to disseminate information regarding financial statistics, publications, the transmission of monetary policy, and Bank-related material.[8]

---

[7]John Crow, "The Work of Canadian Monetary Policy," The Eric J. Hanson Memorial Lecture, University of Alberta, Edmonton, Alberta. *Bank of Canada Review* (1988): 3–17.

[8]An inside view of how the Bank interacts with the public and the politicians can be found in John Crow, *Making Money: An Insider's Perspective on Finance, Politics, and Canada's Central Bank* (Toronto: John Wiley, 2002).

The direction taken in the recent evolution of the monetary policy framework in Canada has been heavily influenced by the role that the institutional monetary structure plays in influencing the monetary conduct.[9] As the Bank's former governor, Gordon Thiessen, put it in his October 17, 2000, speech to the Faculty of Social Science of the University of Western Ontario,

> [t]he Bank tries to work with the markets, rather than against them, to avoid surprising them with unexpected actions. Greater transparency facilitates the policy-transmission process by conditioning market expectations, and helps avoid unnecessary confusion about the reasons for our actions.[10]

From Opaqueness to Accountability and Transparency

The Bank of Canada did not release information regarding its guidelines or resulting consequences during the 1960s and 1970s. As a general rule, the Bank wanted to remain nontransparent, keeping its monetary policy approaches secret. The use of multiple instruments and goals, vague statements about its policies, and moral suasion with banks, resulted in an unnecessary level of secrecy. Due to this instrument and goal opaqueness, the public was not able to question or comprehend the Bank's actions, allowing the accountability of the Bank of Canada to deteriorate.

Over the past decade, however, the Bank of Canada has rejected multiple policy instruments by adopting the overnight interest rate as the centrepiece of its monetary policy implementation and by focusing on an explicit inflation-control target. The goal of the Bank's current monetary policy is to keep the inflation rate within a target range of 1% to 3%, with the midpoint of the inflation target range, 2%, being the most desirable outcome; the 1% to 3% target range for inflation applies until the end of 2016. By announcing a target overnight interest rate, establishing planned dates for policy changes, and implementing the Governing Council for making decisions and disclosing information, the Bank of Canada has moved towards greater accountability and transparency.

The Bank's move toward accountability and transparency was motivated by a number of recent trends in society and the economy. For example, the shift from fixed to flexible exchange rates removed an obstacle to openness. The experience with inflation in the 1970s and the recession in the early 1980s allowed the Bank of Canada to reconsider its analysis of inflation and its costs. In addition, economic comprehension about interest rates, developments about targets and inflation, and greater openness in the government also contributed to the accountability and transparency of the Bank of Canada.[11]

Should the Bank of Canada Be Independent?

As we have seen, the Bank of Canada is probably the most independent government agency in Canada. Every few years, the question arises whether the independence given to the Bank of Canada should be curtailed. Politicians who strongly oppose a Bank policy often want to bring it under their supervision in order to impose a policy more to their liking. Should the Bank of Canada be independent, or would we be better off with a central bank under the control of the government?

---

[9] For a discussion of similar changes implemented by other central banks around the world, see Graydon Paulin, "The Changing Face of Central Banking in the 1990s," *Bank of Canada Review* (Summer 2000): 3–13.

[10] Gordon Thiessen, "Can a Bank Change? The Evolution of Monetary Policy at the Bank of Canada 1935–2000." Lecture to the Faculty of Social Science, University of Western Ontario (October 17, 2000).

[11] For more details regarding the Bank's recent move toward openness and accountability, see John Chant, "The Bank of Canada: Moving Towards Transparency," *Bank of Canada Review* (Spring 2003): 5–13. Also, regarding Canada's experience with central banking, see Michael D. Bordo and Angela Redish, "70 Years of Central Banking: The Bank of Canada in an International Context, 1935–2005," *Bank of Canada Review* (Winter 2005–2006): 7–14, and David Laidler, "Free Banking and the Bank of Canada," *Bank of Canada Review* (Winter 2005–2006): 15–24.

The Case for Independence

The strongest argument for an independent Bank of Canada rests on the view that subjecting the Bank to more political pressures would impart an inflationary bias to monetary policy. In the view of many observers, politicians in a democratic society are shortsighted because they are driven by the need to win their next election. With this as the primary goal, they are unlikely to focus on long-run objectives, such as promoting a stable price level. Instead, they will seek short-run solutions to problems, like high unemployment and high interest rates, even if the short-run solutions have undesirable long-run consequences. For example, we saw in Chapter 5 that high money growth might lead initially to a drop in interest rates but might cause an increase later as inflation heats up. Would a Bank of Canada under the control of the government be more likely to pursue a policy of excessive money growth when interest rates are high, even though it would eventually lead to inflation and even higher interest rates in the future? The advocates of an independent central bank say yes. They believe that a politically insulated central bank is more likely to be concerned with long-run objectives and thus be a defender of a sound dollar and a stable price level.

A variation on the preceding argument is that the political process in Canada could lead to a **political business cycle**, in which just before an election, expansionary policies are pursued to lower unemployment and interest rates. After the election, the bad effects of these policies—high inflation and high interest rates—come home to roost, requiring contractionary policies that politicians hope the public will forget before the next election. Although the issue has not been completely settled, research indicates that there is no credible evidence that such a political business cycle exists in Canada (see the FYI box Economics and Politics).

FYI

Economics and Politics

Recent politico-institutional approaches to the theory of economic policy emphasize the incentives of rational and maximizing policymakers in explaining movements in macroeconomic variables. Central to this perspective is the general assumption that policymakers respond to incentives and constraints just like the rest of the economic agents. As a consequence, the actual policies of government give rise to political cycles, which on the basis of the primary motivational force involved are distinguished into opportunistic and partisan cycles.

In opportunistic (or electoral) business cycle models, politicians maximize their popularity or their probability of re-election by following pre-election expansionary fiscal policies in order to please the fiscally knowledgeable voters. As a consequence, their actual policies give rise to **electoral business cycles**, that is, persistent cyclical patterns of key policy and target variables across electoral terms, regardless of the political orientation of the incumbent government. In particular, models of opportunistic cycles predict pre-election high growth and low unemployment, increasing inflation around the election time, and a post-election contraction, regardless of the political party in power.

In the more accepted partisan cycle models, politicians are ideological; that is, they represent the interests of different pressure groups and, when in office, follow policies that are favourable to their supporting groups. For example, the left-wing parties pursue expansionary policies in order to reduce unemployment, while the right-wing parties tend to induce post-election contractions in economic performance in order to reduce inflation. The outcome, therefore, is **partisan business cycles**, that is, systematic and permanent differences in macroeconomic outcomes that differ by political party.

Work by Apostolos Serletis and Panos Afxentiou of the University of Calgary indicates that there is no credible evidence that such a political business cycle exists in Canada.[12]

[12]Apostolos Serletis and Panos C. Afxentiou, "Electoral and Partisan Cycle Regularities in Canada," *Canadian Journal of Economics* 31 (1998): 28–46.

Putting the Bank of Canada under the control of the government is also considered dangerous because the Bank can be used to facilitate government financing of large budget deficits by its purchases of government bonds in the open market. Such open market purchases by the Bank of Canada increase the money supply and lead to inflation. Government pressure on the Bank of Canada to "help out" might lead to a more inflationary bias in the economy. An independent Bank of Canada is better able to resist this pressure from the government.

Another argument for Bank of Canada independence is that control of monetary policy is too important to leave to politicians, a group that has repeatedly demonstrated a lack of expertise at making hard decisions on issues of great economic importance, such as reducing the budget deficit or reforming the banking system. Another way to state this argument is in terms of the principal–agent problem discussed in Chapters 8, 9, and 10. Both the Bank of Canada and politicians are agents of the public (the principals), and as we have seen, both politicians and the Bank of Canada have incentives to act in their own interest rather than in the interest of the public. The argument supporting Bank of Canada independence is that the principal–agent problem is worse for politicians than for the Bank of Canada because politicians have fewer incentives to act in the public interest.

Indeed, some politicians may prefer to have an independent Bank of Canada, which can be used as a public scapegoat to take some of the heat off their backs. It is possible that a politician who in private opposes an inflationary monetary policy will be forced to support such a policy in public for fear of not being re-elected. An independent Bank of Canada can pursue policies that are politically unpopular yet in the public interest.

The Case Against Independence

Proponents of a Bank of Canada under the control of the government argue that it is undemocratic to have monetary policy (which affects almost everyone in the economy) controlled by an elite group responsible to no one. The current lack of de facto accountability of the Bank of Canada has serious consequences: if the Bank performs badly, there is no provision for replacing members (as there is with politicians). True, the Bank of Canada needs to pursue long-run objectives, but elected government officials vote on long-run issues also (foreign policy, for example). If we push the argument further that policy is always performed better by elite groups like the Bank of Canada, we end up with such conclusions as the Canada Revenue Agency should set tax policies with no oversight from the government. Would you advocate this degree of independence for the Canada Revenue Agency?

The public holds government responsible for the economic well-being of the country, yet it lacks control over the government agency that may well be the most important factor in determining the health of the economy. In addition, to achieve a cohesive program that will promote economic stability, monetary policy must be coordinated with fiscal policy (management of government spending and taxation). Only by placing monetary policy under the control of the politicians who also control fiscal policy can these two policies be prevented from working at cross-purposes.

There is no consensus on whether Bank of Canada independence is a good thing, although public support for independence of the central bank seems to have been growing in both Canada and abroad. As you might expect, people who like the Bank's policies are more likely to support its independence, while those who dislike its policies advocate a less independent Bank of Canada.

Global Central Bank Independence and Macroeconomic Performance

We have seen that advocates of **central bank independence** believe that macroeconomic performance will be improved by making the central bank more independent. Empirical evidence seems to support this conjecture: when central banks are ranked from least independent to most independent, inflation performance is found to be the best for countries with the most independent central banks. Although a more independent central bank appears to lead to a lower inflation rate, this is not achieved at the expense of poorer real economic performance. Countries with independent central banks are no more likely to have high unemployment or greater output fluctuations than countries with less independent central banks.

Explaining Central Bank Behaviour

One view of government bureaucratic behaviour is that bureaucracies serve the public interest (this is the *public interest view*). Yet some economists have developed a theory of bureaucratic behaviour that suggests other factors that influence how bureaucracies operate. The *theory of bureaucratic behaviour* suggests that the objective of a bureaucracy is to maximize its own welfare, just as a consumer's behaviour is motivated by the maximization of personal welfare and a firm's behaviour is motivated by the maximization of profits. The welfare of a bureaucracy is related to its power and prestige. Thus this theory suggests that an important factor affecting a central bank's behaviour is its attempt to increase its power and prestige.

What predictions does this view of a central bank like the Bank of Canada suggest? One is that the Bank of Canada will fight vigorously to preserve its autonomy, a prediction verified time and time again as the Bank of Canada has continually counterattacked attempts to control its functions. Another prediction is that the Bank of Canada will try to avoid conflict with powerful groups that might threaten to curtail its power and reduce its autonomy. The Bank's behaviour may take several forms. One possible factor explaining why the Bank is sometimes slow to increase interest rates and thus smooth out their fluctuations is that it wishes to avoid a conflict with the government over increases in interest rates.

The theory of bureaucratic behaviour seems applicable to the Bank of Canada's actions, but we must recognize that this view of the Bank of Canada as being solely concerned with its own self-interest is too extreme. Maximizing one's welfare does not rule out altruism. (You might give generously to a charity because it makes you feel good about yourself, but in the process you are helping a worthy cause.) The Bank of Canada is surely concerned that it conducts monetary policy in the public interest. However, much uncertainty and disagreement exist over what monetary policy should be.[13] When it is unclear what is in the public interest, other motives may influence the Bank's behaviour. In these situations, the theory of bureaucratic behaviour may be a useful guide to predicting what motivates the Bank of Canada and other central banks.

---

[13] One example of the uncertainty over how best to conduct monetary policy was discussed in Chapter 3: economists are not sure how to measure money. So even if economists agreed that controlling the quantity of money is the appropriate way to conduct monetary policy (a controversial position, as we will see in later chapters), the Bank of Canada cannot be sure which monetary aggregate it should control.

Structure and Independence of Foreign Central Banks

In contrast to the Bank of Canada, which is a centralized unit owned by the government, central banks in other industrialized countries have a more decentralized structure. Here we examine the structure and degree of independence of four of the most important foreign central banks: the Federal Reserve System of the United States, the European Central Bank, the Bank of England, and the Bank of Japan.

Federal Reserve System

Of all the central banks in the world, the **Federal Reserve System** of the United States (also called simply **the Fed**) probably has the most unusual structure. It includes the following entities: the **Board of Governors of the Federal Reserve System**, the **Federal Reserve Banks**, the **Federal Open Market Committee (FOMC)**, the Federal Advisory Council, and around 2500 member commercial banks. Figure 15-1 outlines the relationships of these entities to one another and to the three policy tools of the Fed—open market operations, the discount rate (the U.S. equivalent of the bank rate in Canada), and reserve requirements.

FIGURE 15-1 Structure and Responsibility for Policy Tools in the Federal Reserve System

The relationships of the Federal Reserve banks, the Board of Governors of the Federal Reserve System, and the FOMC to the three policy tools of the Fed (open market operations, the discount rate, and reserve requirements). Dashed lines indicate that the FOMC "advises" on the setting of reserve requirements and the discount rate.

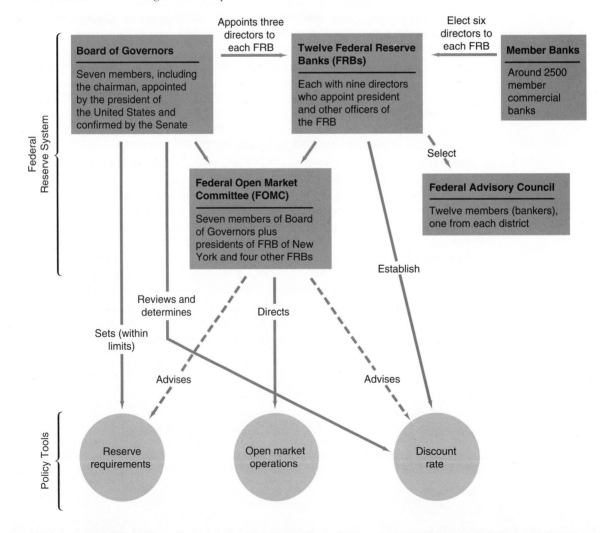

BOARD OF GOVERNORS OF THE FEDERAL RESERVE SYSTEM   At the head of the Federal Reserve System is the seven-member Board of Governors, headquartered in Washington, D.C. Each governor is appointed by the president of the United States and confirmed by the Senate. To limit the president's control over the Fed and insulate the Fed from other political pressures, the governors can serve one nonrenewable 14-year term plus part of another term, with one governor's term expiring every other January. The chairman of the Board of Governors is chosen from among the seven governors and serves a four-year term. It is expected that once a new chairman is chosen, the old chairman resigns from the Board of Governors, even if there are many years left to his or her term as a governor.

FEDERAL RESERVE BANKS   Each of the 12 Federal Reserve districts has one main Federal Reserve bank, which may have branches in other cities in the district. The locations of these districts, the Federal Reserve banks, and their branches are shown in Figure 15-2. The three largest Federal Reserve banks in terms of assets are those of New York, Chicago, and San Francisco—combined they hold more than 50% of the assets (discount loans, securities, and other holdings) of the Federal Reserve System. The New York bank, with around one-quarter of the assets, is the most important of the Federal Reserve banks (see the Inside the Central Bank box The Special Role of the Federal Reserve Bank of New York).

FEDERAL OPEN MARKET COMMITTEE (FOMC)   The 12 Federal Reserve banks and the Board of Governors are actively involved in decisions concerning the conduct of monetary policy. In particular, all seven governors are voting members of the FOMC, together with the president of the Federal Reserve Bank of New York

FIGURE 15-2   Federal Reserve System

The locations of the Federal Reserve districts, the Federal Reserve banks, and their branches.

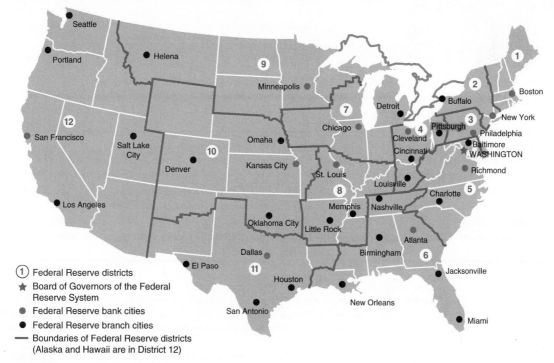

- ① Federal Reserve districts
- ★ Board of Governors of the Federal Reserve System
- ● Federal Reserve bank cities
- ● Federal Reserve branch cities
- — Boundaries of Federal Reserve districts (Alaska and Hawaii are in District 12)

Source: Federal Reserve *Bulletin*.

and presidents of four other Federal Reserve banks. The FOMC usually meets eight times a year (about every six weeks) and makes decisions regarding the conduct of monetary policy in the United States and the setting of the policy interest rate, the **federal funds rate**, the interest rate on overnight loans from one bank to another. Indeed, the FOMC is often referred to as "the Fed" in the press: for example, when the media say that the Fed is meeting, they actually mean that the FOMC is meeting.

HOW INDEPENDENT IS THE FED?   The Federal Reserve appears to be remarkably free of the political pressures that influence other government agencies in the United States. Yet it is still subject to the influence of the president of the United States, since the president appoints members to the Board of Governors. The power of the United States president in appointing members to the Board of Governors is limited, however. Because the term of the chairman of the Board of Governors is not necessarily concurrent with that of the president of the United States, a president may have to deal with a chairman of the Board of Governors appointed by a previous administration. Alan Greenspan, for example, was appointed chairman in 1987 by President Ronald Reagan and was reappointed to another term by another Republican president, George Bush, in 1992. When Bill Clinton, a Democrat, became president in 1993, Greenspan had several years left to his term. Clinton was put under tremendous pressure to reappoint Greenspan when his term expired and did so in 1996 and again in 2000, even though Greenspan is a Republican.[14] George W. Bush, a Republican, then reappointed Greenspan in 2004.

You can see that the Federal Reserve has extraordinary independence for a government agency. Nonetheless, the Fed is not free from political pressures. Indeed, to understand the Fed's behaviour, we must recognize that public support for the actions of the Federal Reserve plays a very important role.[15]

INSIDE THE CENTRAL BANK   **The Special Role of the Federal Reserve Bank of New York**

The Federal Reserve Bank of New York plays a special role in the Federal Reserve System for several reasons. First, its district contains many of the largest commercial banks in the United States, the safety and soundness of which are paramount to the health of the U.S. financial system. The Federal Reserve Bank of New York conducts examinations of bank holding companies and state-chartered member banks in its district, making it the supervisor of some of the most important financial institutions in the U.S.

financial system. Not surprisingly, given this responsibility, the bank supervision group is one of the largest units of the New York Fed and is by far the largest bank supervision group in the Federal Reserve System.

The second reason for the New York Fed's special role is its active involvement in the bond and foreign exchange markets. The New York Fed houses the open market desk, which conducts open market operations—the purchase and sale of bonds—that determine the amount of

---

[14] Similarly, William McChesney Martin Jr., the chairman from 1951 to 1970, was appointed by President Truman (Dem.) but was reappointed by Presidents Eisenhower (Rep.), Kennedy (Dem.), and Nixon (Rep.). Also Paul Volcker, the chairman from 1979 to 1987, was appointed by President Carter (Dem.) but was reappointed by President Reagan (Rep.).

[15] An inside view of how the Fed interacts with the public and the politicians can be found in Bob Woodward, *Maestro: Greenspan's Fed and the American Boom* (New York: Simon and Schuster, 2000).

reserves in the banking system. Because of this involvement in the Treasury securities market, as well as its walking-distance location near the New York and American Stock Exchanges, the officials at the Federal Reserve Bank of New York are in constant contact with the major financial markets in the United States. In addition, the Federal Reserve Bank of New York houses the foreign exchange desk, which conducts foreign exchange interventions on behalf of the Federal Reserve System and the U.S. Treasury. Its involvement in these financial markets means that the New York Fed is an important source of information on what is happening in U.S. and foreign financial markets, particularly during crisis periods, such as the recent subprime meltdown, as well as a liaison between officials in the Federal Reserve System and private participants in the markets.

The third reason for the Federal Reserve Bank of New York's prominence is that it is the only Federal Reserve bank to be a member of the Bank for International Settlements (BIS).

Thus the president of the New York Fed, along with the chairman of the Board of Governors, represents the Federal Reserve System in its regular monthly meetings with other major central bankers at the BIS. This close contact with foreign central bankers and interaction with foreign exchange markets means that the New York Fed has a special role in international relations, both with other central bankers and with private market participants. Adding to its prominence in international circles is that the New York Fed is the repository for more than US$100 billion of the world's gold, an amount greater than the gold at Fort Knox.

Finally, the president of the Federal Reserve Bank of New York is the only permanent member of the FOMC among the Federal Reserve bank presidents, serving as the vice-chairman of the committee. Thus he and the chairman and vice-chairman of the Board of Governors are the three most important officials in the Federal Reserve System.

European Central Bank

Until recently, the Federal Reserve had no rivals in terms of importance in the central banking world. However, this situation changed in January 1999 with the startup of the European Central Bank (ECB)—the central bank of the 17 euro area countries—which now conducts monetary policy for countries that are members of the European Monetary Union. These countries, taken together, have a population that exceeds that in the United States and a GDP comparable to that of the United States. The Maastricht Treaty, which established the ECB and the **European System of Central Banks (ESCB)**, patterned these institutions after the Federal Reserve, in that central banks for each country (referred to as *National Central Banks*, or *NCBs*) have a similar role to that of the Federal Reserve Banks. The European Central Bank and the national central banks of the countries that have adopted the euro are referred to as the **Eurosystem**. The Eurosystem excludes the central banks of the European Union countries that have not yet adopted the euro. The Eurosystem should not be confused with the European System of Central Banks, the term used to refer to the European Central Bank and the national central banks of all 27 European Union (EU) member countries—when all EU member countries adopt the euro, the Eurosystem and the European System of Central Banks will become one entity.

The European Central Bank, which is housed in Frankfurt, Germany, has an Executive Board that is similar in structure to the Board of Governors of the Federal Reserve; it is made up of the president, the vice president, and four other members, who are appointed to eight-year, nonrenewable terms. The Governing Council, which comprises the Executive Board and the presidents of the National Central Banks, is similar to the FOMC and makes the decisions on monetary policy. While the presidents of the National Central Banks are appointed by their countries' respective governments, the members of the Executive Board are appointed by a committee consisting of the heads of state of all the countries that are part of the European Monetary Union.

DIFFERENCES BETWEEN THE EUROPEAN SYSTEM OF CENTRAL BANKS AND THE FEDERAL RESERVE SYSTEM　In the popular press, the European System of Central Banks is usually referred to as the European Central Bank (ECB), even though it would be more accurate to refer to it as the Eurosystem, just as it would be more accurate to refer to the Federal Reserve System rather than the Fed. Although the structure of the Eurosystem is similar to that of the Federal Reserve System, some important differences distinguish the two. First, the budgets of the Federal Reserve Banks are controlled by the Board of Governors, while the National Central Banks control their own budgets *and* the budget of the ECB in Frankfurt. The ECB in the Eurosystem therefore has less power than does the Board of Governors in the Federal Reserve System. Second, the monetary operations of the Eurosystem are conducted by all the National Central Banks in each country, so monetary operations are not centralized as they are in the Federal Reserve System. Third, in contrast to the Federal Reserve, the ECB is not involved in supervision and regulation of financial institutions; these tasks are left to the individual countries in the European Monetary Union.

GOVERNING COUNCIL　Just as there is a focus on meetings of the FOMC in the United States, there is a similar focus in Europe on meetings of the Governing Council, which meets monthly at the ECB in Frankfurt to make decisions on monetary policy. Currently, 17 countries are members of the European Monetary Union, and the head of each of the 17 National Central Banks has one vote in the Governing Council; each of the six Executive Board members has one vote. In contrast to FOMC meetings, which staff from both the Board of Governors and individual Federal Reserve Banks attend, only the 21 members of the Governing Council attend the meetings with no staff present.

The Governing Council has decided that although its members have the legal right to vote, no formal vote is actually taken; instead the Council operates by consensus. One reason the Governing Council has decided not to take votes is because of worries that the casting of individual votes might lead to heads of National Central Banks supporting a monetary policy that would be appropriate for their individual countries but not necessarily for the countries in the European Monetary Union as a whole. This problem is less severe for the Federal Reserve: although Federal Reserve Bank presidents do live in different regions of the country, all have the same nationality and are more likely to take a national view in monetary policy decisions rather than a regional view.

Just as the Federal Reserve releases the FOMC's decision on the setting of the policy interest rate (the federal funds rate) immediately after the meeting is over, the ECB does the same after the Governing Council meeting concludes (announcing the target for a similar short-term interest rate for interbank loans). However, whereas the Fed simply releases a statement about the setting of the monetary policy instruments, the ECB goes further by having a press conference in which the president and vice president of the ECB take questions from the news media. Holding such a press conference so soon after the meeting is tricky because it requires the president and vice president to be quick on their feet in dealing with the press. The first president of the ECB, Willem F. Duisenberg, put his foot in his mouth at some of these press conferences, and the ECB came under some sharp criticism. His successor, Jean-Claude Trichet, a more successful communicator, encountered fewer problems in this regard. Mario Draghi, an Italian economist and banker, succeeded Jean-Claude Trichet as president of the ECB on November 1, 2011.

Although currently only 16 countries in the European Monetary Union have representation on the Governing Council, this situation is likely to change in the future. Three more countries in the European Community already qualify for entering the European Monetary Union: the United Kingdom, Sweden, and Denmark. Six other countries in the European Community (the Czech Republic, Estonia, Hungary, Latvia, Lithuania, and Poland) might enter the European Monetary Union once they qualify, which may not be too far in the future. The possible expansion of membership in the Eurosystem presents a particular dilemma. The current size of the Governing Council (21 voting members) is substantially larger than the FOMC (12 voting members). Many commentators have wondered whether the Governing Council is already too unwieldy—a situation that would get considerably worse as more countries join the European Monetary Union. To deal with this potential problem, the Governing Council has decided on a complex system of rotation, somewhat like that for the FOMC, in which National Central Banks from the larger countries will vote more often than National Central Banks from smaller countries.

HOW INDEPENDENT IS THE ECB?   Although the Federal Reserve is a highly independent central bank, the Maastricht Treaty, which established the Eurosystem, has made the latter the most independent central bank in the world. Like the Board of Governors, the members of the Executive Board have long terms (eight years), while heads of National Central Banks are required to have terms at least five years long. Like the Fed, the Eurosystem determines its own budget, and the governments of the member countries are not allowed to issue instructions to the ECB. These elements of the Maastricht Treaty make the ECB highly instrument-independent.

The Maastricht Treaty specifies that the overriding, long-term goal of the ECB is price stability, which means that the goal for the Eurosystem is more clearly specified than it is for the Federal Reserve System. However, the Maastricht Treaty did not specify exactly what "price stability" means. The Eurosystem has defined the quantitative goal for monetary policy to be an inflation rate slightly less than 2%, so from this perspective, the ECB is slightly less goal-independent than the Fed. The Eurosystem is, however, much more goal-independent than the Federal Reserve System in another way: the Eurosystem's charter cannot be changed by legislation; it can be changed only by revision of the Maastricht Treaty—a difficult process, because *all* signatories to the treaty must agree to accept any proposed change.

Bank of England

Founded in 1694, the Bank of England is one of the oldest central banks. The Bank Act of 1946 gave the government statutory authority over the Bank of England. The Court (equivalent to a board of directors) of the Bank of England is made up of the governor and two deputy governors, who are appointed for five-year terms, and 16 nonexecutive directors, who are appointed for three-year terms.

Until 1997, the Bank of England was the least independent of the central banks examined in this chapter because the decision to raise or lower interest rates resided not within the Bank of England but with the Chancellor of the Exchequer (the equivalent of the Canadian minister of finance). All of this changed when a new Labour government came to power in May 1997 and the Chancellor of the Exchequer, Gordon Brown, made a surprise announcement that the Bank of England would henceforth have the power to set interest rates. However, the Bank was not granted total instrument independence: the government can overrule the Bank and set rates "in extreme economic circumstances" and "for a limited period." Nonetheless, as in Canada, because overruling the Bank would be so public and is supposed to occur only in highly unusual circumstances and for a limited time, it is likely to be a rare occurrence.

Because the United Kingdom is not a member of the European Monetary Union, the Bank of England makes its monetary policy decisions independently from the European Central Bank. The decision to set interest rates resides in the Monetary Policy Committee, made up of the governor, two deputy governors, two members appointed by the governor after consultation with the chancellor (normally central bank officials), plus four outside economic experts appointed by the chancellor. (Surprisingly, two of the four outside experts initially appointed to this committee were not British citizens—one was Dutch and the other American, and some later appointments have also not been British citizens.) The inflation target for the Bank of England is set by the Chancellor of the Exchequer, so the Bank of England has as much goal independence as the Bank of Canada, but is less goal-independent than the Fed.

Bank of Japan

The Bank of Japan (Nippon Ginko) was founded in 1882 during the Meiji Restoration. Monetary policy is determined by the Policy Board, which is composed of the governor, two vice-governors, and six outside members appointed by the cabinet and approved by the parliament, all of whom serve for five-year terms.

Until recently, the Bank of Japan was not formally independent of the government, with the ultimate power residing with the Ministry of Finance. However, the new Bank of Japan Law, which took effect in April 1998 and was the first major change in the powers of the Bank of Japan in 55 years, has changed this. In addition to stipulating that the objective of monetary policy is to attain price stability, the law granted greater instrument and goal independence to the Bank of Japan. Before this, the government had two voting members on the Policy Board, one from the Ministry of Finance and the other from the Economic Planning Agency. Now the government may send two representatives from these agencies to board meetings, but they no longer have voting rights, although they do have the ability to request delays in monetary policy decisions. In addition, the Ministry of Finance lost its authority to oversee many of the operations of the Bank of Japan, particularly the right to dismiss senior officials. However, the Ministry of Finance continues to have control over the part of the Bank's budget that is unrelated to monetary policy, which might limit its independence to some extent.

The Trend Toward Greater Independence

As our survey of the structure and independence of the major central banks indicates, in recent years we have been seeing a remarkable trend toward increasing independence. It used to be that the Federal Reserve was substantially more independent than almost all other central banks, with the exception of those in Germany and Switzerland. Now the newly established European Central Bank is far more independent than the Fed, and greater independence has been granted to central banks like the Bank of England and the Bank of Japan, putting them more on a par with the Fed, as well as to central banks in such diverse countries as New Zealand, Sweden, and the euro nations. Both theory and experience suggest that more independent central banks produce better monetary policy, thus providing an impetus for this trend.

SUMMARY

yEconLab
io Summary

1. The Bank of Canada was created by an act of Parliament in 1934 and began operations on March 11, 1935. Initially it was privately owned but became a Crown corporation in 1938.

2. The overall responsibility for the operation of the Bank of Canada rests with a Board of Directors, consisting of the governor, the senior deputy governor, the deputy minister of finance, and twelve outside directors. The Bank's governor is the chief executive officer and chairman of the Board of Directors.

3. Although on paper the Bank of Canada is an arm of the government, in practice the Bank has more independence than the Bank of Canada Act suggests.

4. The Bank of Canada is more independent than most agencies of the Canadian government, but it is still subject to political pressures. The theory of bureaucratic behaviour indicates that one factor driving the Bank's behaviour is its attempt to increase its power and prestige. This view explains many of the Bank's actions, although the agency may also try to act in the public interest.

5. The case for an independent Bank of Canada rests on the view that curtailing the Bank's independence and subjecting it to more political pressures would impart an inflationary bias to monetary policy. An independent Bank of Canada can afford to take the long view and not respond to short-run problems that will result in expansionary monetary policy and a political business cycle. The case against an independent Bank of Canada holds that it is undemocratic to have monetary policy (so important to the public) controlled by an elite group that is not accountable to the public. An independent Bank of Canada also makes the coordination of monetary and fiscal policy difficult.

6. The Federal Reserve System was created in 1913 to lessen the frequency of bank panics. Because of public hostility to

central banks and the centralization of power, the Federal Reserve System was created with many checks and balances to diffuse power.

7. The formal structure of the Federal Reserve System consists of 12 regional Federal Reserve banks, around 2500 member commercial banks, the Board of Governors of the Federal Reserve System, the Federal Open Market Committee, and the Federal Advisory Council.

8. Although on paper the Federal Reserve appears to be decentralized, in practice it has come to function as a unified central bank controlled by the Board of Governors, especially the board's chairman.

9. The European Central Bank is the central bank of the euro area—a common currency area, currently consisting of 17 countries: Austria, Belgium, Cyprus, Estonia, Finland, France, Germany, Greece, Ireland, Italy, Luxembourg, Malta, the Netherlands, Portugal, Slovakia, Slovenia, and Spain. The ECB is based in Frankfurt, Germany, and came into being on January 1, 1999.

10. The Eurosystem is the term used to refer to the European Central Bank and the national central banks of the 17 countries that have adopted the euro. The Eurosystem excludes the central banks of the European Union countries that have not yet adopted the euro. These countries continue to pursue national monetary policies and have no input into the decisions related to the single monetary policy for the euro area.

11. The European System of Central Banks (ESCB) is the term used to refer to the European Central Bank and the national central banks of all 27 European Union (EU) member countries—when all EU member countries adopt the euro, the Eurosystem and the European System of Central Banks will become one entity.

KEY TERMS

base money (monetary base), p. 356

Board of Directors, p. 355

Board of Governors of the Federal Reserve System, p. 366

central bank independence, p. 365

electoral business cycles, p. 363

European System of Central Banks (ESCB), p. 369

Eurosystem, p. 369

Exchange Fund Account, p. 356

federal funds rate, p. 368

Federal Open Market Committee (FOMC), p. 366

Federal Reserve Banks, p. 366

Federal Reserve System (the Fed), p. 366

goal independence, p. 358

Governing Council, p. 355

instrument independence, p. 358

open market buyback operations, p. 357

partisan business cycles, p. 363

political business cycle, p. 363

QUESTIONS

1. What political realities might explain the creation of the Bank of Canada in 1934?

2. In what ways can the government influence the conduct of monetary policy?

3. Who is responsible for monetary policy in Canada?

4. Do you think that the seven-year renewable term for the governor of the Bank of Canada effectively insulates the Bank from political pressure?

5. How did the "Coyne Affair" motivate the current system of joint responsibility for monetary policy?

6. Over time, which entities have gained power in the conduct of monetary policy in Canada and which have lost power? Why do you think this has happened?

7. "The strongest argument for an independent Bank of Canada rests on the view that subjecting the Bank of Canada to more political pressures would impart an inflationary bias to monetary policy." Is this statement true, false, or uncertain? Explain your answer.

8. The Bank of Canada is the most independent of all Canadian government agencies. What is the main difference between it and other government agencies that explains its greater independence?

9. How can the government directly influence the Bank of Canada?

10. How is the responsibility for monetary policy shared in the Eurosystem?

11. "The theory of bureaucratic behaviour indicates that the Bank of Canada never operates in the public interest." Is this statement true, false, or uncertain? Explain your answer.

12. Why might eliminating the Bank's independence lead to a more pronounced political business cycle?

13. "The independence of the Bank of Canada leaves it completely unaccountable for its actions." Is this statement true, false, or uncertain? Explain your answer.

14. "The independence of the Bank of Canada has meant that it takes the long view and not the short view." Is this statement true, false, or uncertain? Explain your answer.

15. Why did Canada show little interest in the establishment of a central bank during the first 60 or so years of Confederation?

WEB EXERCISES

1. Go to **www.bankofcanada.ca** and click on "About the Bank." Choose "Management and Corporate Governance." Write a short essay about the diversity of the 12 outside directors of the Bank of Canada's Board of Directors.

2. Go to **www.federalreserve.gov** and click on "About The Fed." Then click on "The Federal Reserve System" and then on "Structure." According to the Federal Reserve, what is the most important responsibility of the Board of Governors?

3. Go to the above site and click on "Monetary Policy." Then click on "Reports" and then choose "Beige Book." According to the summary of the most recently published book, is the U.S. economy weakening or recovering?

WEB REFERENCES

www.federalreserve.gov
The website for the Federal Reserve.

www.ecb.int
The website for the European Central Bank.

www.bankofengland.co.uk
The website for the Bank of England.

www.boj.or.jp/en/
The website for the Bank of Japan.

CHAPTER 16

The Money Supply Process

LEARNING OBJECTIVES

After studying this chapter you should be able to

1. characterize the framework for the implementation of monetary policy in Canada (the LVTS, the target and the operating band for the overnight interest rate, and the Bank of Canada's standing liquidity facilities)

2. explain the market for reserves and the channel/corridor system for setting the overnight interest rate in Canada

3. identify the Bank of Canada's approach to monetary policy and the tools of policy (open market operations, settlement balances management, and Bank of Canada lending)

PREVIEW

As we saw in Chapter 5 and will see in later chapters on monetary theory, movements in the money supply affect interest rates and inflation and thus affect us all. Because of its far-reaching effects on economic activity, it is important to understand how the money supply is determined. Who controls it? What causes it to change? How might control of it be improved? In this and subsequent chapters, we answer these questions by providing a detailed description of the *money supply process*, the mechanism that determines the level of the money supply.

Because deposits at banks are by far the largest component of the money supply, learning how these deposits are created is the first step in understanding the money supply process. This chapter provides an overview of how the banking system creates deposits, and describes the basic principles of the money supply, needed as a foundation for later chapters.

Three Players in the Money Supply Process

The "cast of characters" in the money supply story is as follows:

1. The *central bank*—the government agency that oversees the banking system and is responsible for the conduct of monetary policy; in Canada, the Bank of Canada

2. *Banks* (depository institutions)—the financial intermediaries that accept deposits from individuals and institutions and make loans: commercial banks, trust and loan companies, and credit unions

3. *Depositors*—individuals and institutions that hold deposits in banks

Of the three players, the central bank—the Bank of Canada—is the most important. The Bank's conduct of monetary policy involves actions that affect its balance sheet (holdings of assets and liabilities), to which we turn now.

The Bank of Canada's Balance Sheet

The operation of the Bank of Canada and its monetary policy involve actions that affect its balance sheet, its holdings of assets and liabilities. Here we discuss a simplified balance sheet that includes just four items that are essential to our understanding of the money supply process.

Bank of Canada	
Assets	Liabilities
Securities	Currency in circulation
Loans to financial institutions	Reserves

Liabilities

The two liabilities on the balance sheet, currency in circulation and reserves, are often referred to as the *monetary liabilities* of the Bank of Canada. They are an important part of the money supply story, because increases in either or both will lead to an increase in the money supply (everything else being constant). The sum of the Bank's monetary liabilities (currency in circulation and reserves) and the Canadian Mint's monetary liabilities coins in circulation is called the **monetary base**. When discussing the monetary base, we will focus only on the monetary liabilities of the Bank of Canada because the monetary liabilities of the Canadian Mint account for a very small fraction of the base.

1. *Notes in circulation.* The Bank of Canada issues notes (those blue, purple, green, red, and brown pieces of paper in your wallet that say "Bank of Canada"). The Bank of Canada notes in circulation is the amount of these notes that is in the hands of the public and the depository institutions. Coins issued by the Canadian Mint are not a liability of the Bank of Canada. The coins and Bank of Canada notes that we use in Canada today are collectively known as *currency*.

   Bank of Canada notes are IOUs from the Bank to the bearer and are also liabilities, but unlike most liabilities, they promise to pay back the bearer solely with Bank of Canada notes; that is, they pay off IOUs with other IOUs. Accordingly, if you bring a $100 bill to the Bank of Canada and demand payment, you will receive two $50s, five $20s, ten $10s, or twenty $5 bills.

   People are more willing to accept IOUs from the Bank of Canada than from you or me because Bank of Canada notes are a recognized medium of exchange; that is, they are accepted as a means of payment and so function as *money*.

   Unfortunately, neither you nor I can convince people that our IOUs are worth anything more than the paper they are written on.[1]

---

[1] The notes item on our balance sheet refers only to notes in circulation—that is, the amount in the hands of the public. Notes that have been printed are not automatically a liability of the Bank. For example, consider the importance of having $1 million of your own IOUs printed up. You give out $100 worth to other people and keep the other $999 900 in your pocket. The $999 900 of IOUs does not make you richer or poorer and does not affect your indebtedness. You care only about the $100 of liabilities from the $100 of circulated IOUs. The same reasoning applies for the Bank of Canada in regard to its notes.

For similar reasons, the currency component of the money supply, no matter how it is defined, includes only currency in circulation. It does not include any additional currency that is not yet in the hands of the public. The fact that currency has been printed but is not circulating means that it is not anyone's asset or liability and thus cannot affect anyone's behaviour. Therefore, it makes sense not to include it in the money supply.

2. *Reserves.* All banks that participate in the Large Value Transfer System (LVTS), to be discussed in detail in Chapter 17, have an account at the Bank of Canada in which they hold deposits (also called **settlement balances**). **Reserves** consist of settlement balances at the Bank of Canada plus currency that is physically held by banks (called *vault cash*, because it is held in bank vaults, cash tills, and automated banking machines). Reserves are assets for the banks but liabilities for the Bank of Canada because the banks can demand payment on them at any time and the Bank of Canada is required to satisfy its obligation by paying Bank of Canada notes. As you will see, an increase in reserves leads to an increase in the level of deposits and hence in the money supply.

As already noted in Chapter 13, Canadian banks are no longer required to hold reserves. Banks, however, hold reserves in order to manage their own short-term liquidity requirements and respond to predictable clearing drains and across-the-counter and automated banking machine drains. We call these reserves prudential or **desired reserves**. For example, banks might desire that for every dollar of deposits, a certain fraction (say, 5 cents) must be held as reserves. This fraction (5%) is called the **desired reserve ratio**. Reserves in excess of the desired amounts are called **excess reserves**.

Assets

The two assets on the Bank of Canada's balance sheet are important for two reasons. First, changes in the asset items lead to changes in reserves and the monetary base, and consequently to changes in the money supply. Second, because these assets (government securities and Bank of Canada loans) earn higher interest rates than the liabilities (currency in circulation, which pays no interest, and reserves), the Bank of Canada makes billions of dollars every year—its assets earn income, and its liabilities cost practically nothing. Although it returns most of its earnings to the federal government, the Bank of Canada does spend some of it on "worthy causes," such as supporting economic research.

1. *Securities.* This category of assets covers the Bank of Canada's holdings of securities issued by the Canadian government and, in unusual circumstances (as discussed in Chapter 17), other securities. As you will see, the primary way the Bank of Canada provides reserves to the banking system is by purchasing securities, thereby increasing its holdings of these assets. An increase in government or other securities held by the Bank of Canada leads to an increase in the money supply.

2. *Loans to financial institutions.* The second way the Bank of Canada can provide reserves to the banking system is by making loans (equivalently, advances) to banks and other financial institutions. For these institutions, the loans they have taken out are referred to as *borrowings from the Bank of Canada* or, alternatively, as *borrowed reserves*. These loans appear as a liability on financial institutions' balance sheets. An increase in loans to financial institutions can also be the source of an increase in the money supply. During normal times, the Bank of Canada makes loans only to banking institutions and the interest rate charged banks for these loans is called the **bank rate**. (As we will discuss in Chapter 17, during the recent financial crisis, the Bank of Canada made loans to other financial institutions.)

Control of the Monetary Base

The *monetary base* (also called **high-powered money**) equals currency in circulation C plus the total reserves in banking system R.[2] The monetary base MB can be expressed as

$$MB = C + R$$

---

[2]Here, currency in circulation includes both Bank of Canada currency (Bank of Canada notes) and Canadian Mint coins.

The Bank of Canada exercises control over the monetary base through its purchases or sales of securities in the open market, called **open market operations**, and through its extension of loans to banks.

Bank of Canada Open Market Operations

The primary way in which the Bank of Canada causes changes in the monetary base is through its open market operations. A purchase of bonds by the Bank of Canada is called an **open market purchase**, and a sale of bonds by the Bank of Canada is called an **open market sale**.

OPEN MARKET PURCHASE FROM A BANK   Suppose that the Bank of Canada purchases $100 million of bonds from banks and pays for them with a cheque for this amount. To understand what occurs as a result of this transaction, we look at *T-accounts*, which list only the changes that occur in balance sheet items, starting from the initial balance sheet position. The bank will either deposit the cheque in its account with the Bank or cash it in for currency, which will be counted as vault cash. Either action means that banks will find themselves with $100 million more reserves and a reduction in its holdings of securities of $100 million. The T-account for the banking system, then, is

Banking System		
Assets		Liabilities
Securities	−$100 m	
Reserves	+$100 m	

The Bank of Canada, meanwhile, finds that its liabilities have increased by the additional $100 million of reserves, while its assets have increased by the $100 million of additional securities that it now holds. Its T-account is

Bank of Canada		
Assets		Liabilities
Securities	+$100 m	Reserves +$100 m

The net result of this open market purchase is that reserves have increased by $100 million, the amount of the open market purchase. Because there has been no change of currency in circulation, the monetary base has also risen by $100 million.

OPEN MARKET PURCHASE FROM THE NONBANK PUBLIC   To understand what happens when there is an open market purchase from the nonbank public, we must look at two cases. First, let's assume that the people or corporations that sell $100 million of bonds to the Bank of Canada deposit the Bank of Canada's cheques in their local banks. The nonbank public's T-account after this transaction is

Nonbank Public		
Assets		Liabilities
Securities	−$100 m	
Chequable deposits	+$100 m	

When banks receive the cheques, they credit depositors' accounts with the $100 million and then deposit the cheques in their account with the Bank of Canada, thereby adding to their reserves. The banking system's T-account becomes

Banking System			
Assets		Liabilities	
Reserves	+$100 m	Chequable deposits	+$100 m

The effect on the Bank of Canada's balance sheet is that it has gained $100 million of securities in its assets column, whereas it has an increase of $100 million of reserves in its liabilities column:

Bank of Canada			
Assets		Liabilities	
Securities	+$100 m	Reserves	+$100 m

As you can see in the above T-account, when the Bank of Canada's cheque is deposited in a bank, the net result of the Bank of Canada's open market purchase from the nonbank public is identical to the effect of its open market purchase from a bank: Reserves increase by the amount of the open market purchase, and the monetary base increases by the same amount.

If, however, the people or corporations selling the bonds to the Bank of Canada cash the Bank of Canada's cheques at a local bank, the effect on reserves is different.[3] This sellers will receive currency of $100 million while reducing holdings of securities by $100 million. The nonbank public's seller's T-account will be

Nonbank Public			
Assets		Liabilities	
Securities	−$100 m		
Currency	+$100 m		

The Bank of Canada now finds that it has exchanged $100 million of currency for $100 million of securities, so its T-account is

Bank of Canada			
Assets		Liabilities	
Securities	+$100 m	Currency in circulation	+$100 m

---

[3]If bond sellers cash cheques at their local banks, the banks' balance sheets will be unaffected, because the $100 million of vault cash that they pay out will be exactly matched by the deposits of the $100 million in cheques at the Bank of Canada. Thus banks' reserves will remain the same, and their T-accounts will not be affected. That is why a T-account for the banking system does not appear here.

The net effect of the open market purchase in this case is that reserves are unchanged, whereas currency in circulation increases by the $100 million of the open market purchase. Thus the monetary base increases by the $100 million amount of the open market purchase, while reserves do not. This contrasts with the situation in which sellers of the bonds deposit the Bank of Canada's cheques in banks; in that case, reserves increase by $100 million, and so does the monetary base.

The analysis reveals that ***the effect of an open market purchase on reserves depends on whether the seller of the bonds keeps the proceeds from the sale in currency or in deposits.*** If the proceeds are kept in currency, the open market purchase has no effect on reserves; if the proceeds are kept as deposits, reserves increase by the amount of the open market purchase.

The effect of an open market purchase on the monetary base, however, is always the same (the monetary base increases by the amount of the purchase) whether the seller of the bonds keeps the proceeds in deposits or in currency. The impact of an open market purchase on reserves is much more uncertain than its impact on the monetary base.

OPEN MARKET SALE   If the Bank of Canada sells $100 million of bonds to banks or the nonbank public, the monetary base will decrease by $100 million. For example, if the Bank sells bonds to individuals who pay for them with currency, the buyers exchange $100 million of currency for $100 million of bonds, and the resulting T-account is

Nonbank Public		
Assets		Liabilities
Securities	+$100 m	
Currency	−$100 m	

The Bank of Canada, for its part, has reduced its holdings of securities by $100 million and has also lowered its monetary liability by accepting the currency as payment for its bonds, thereby reducing the amount of currency in circulation by $100 million:

Bank of Canada		
Assets		Liabilities
Securities	−$100 m	Currency in circulation −$100 m

The effect of the open market sale of $100 million of bonds is to reduce the monetary base by an equal amount, although reserves remain unchanged. Manipulations of T-accounts in cases in which buyers of the bonds are banks or buyers pay for the bonds with cheques written on a chequable deposit account at a local bank lead to the same $100 million reduction in the monetary base, although the reduction occurs because the level of reserves has fallen by $100 million.

The following conclusion can now be drawn from our analysis of open market purchases and sales: ***the effect of open market operations on the monetary base is much more certain than the effect on reserves.*** Therefore, the Bank of Canada can control the monetary base with open market operations more effectively than it can control reserves.

Open market operations can also be done in other assets besides government bonds and have the same effects on the monetary base we have described here.

Although open market operations are the most important monetary policy tool for most central banks around the world, in 1994 the Bank of Canada stopped conducting open market operations in Government of Canada bills and bonds. Since then, the Bank's most common open market operations involve repurchase transactions, either SPRAs or SRAs. More recently, and in response to the subprime financial crisis, the Bank of Canada introduced term PRAs, which are similar to special PRAs. As we will discuss in detail in Chapter 17, the Bank of Canada is currently conducting repurchase transactions to reinforce its operating target—the midpoint of the operating band for the overnight interest rate—and to address liquidity issues at times of financial instability. The Bank, however, neutralizes the effect on settlement balances of SPRAs and SRAs, so that at the end of the day there is no change in the level of settlement balances in the banking system.

Shifts from Deposits into Currency

Even if the Bank of Canada does not conduct open market operations, a shift from deposits to currency will affect the reserves in the banking system. However, such a shift will have no effect on the monetary base, another reason why the Bank of Canada has more control over the monetary base than over reserves.

Let's suppose that during the Christmas season, the public wants to hold more currency to buy gifts and so withdraws $100 million in cash. The effect on the T-account of the nonbank public is

Nonbank Public		
Assets		Liabilities
Chequable deposits	−$100 m	
Currency	+$100 m	

The banking system loses $100 million of deposits and hence $100 million of reserves:

Banking System		
Assets		Liabilities
Reserves −$100 m		Chequable deposits −$100 m

For the Bank of Canada, the public's action means that $100 million of additional currency is circulating in the hands of the public, while reserves in the banking system have fallen by $100 million. The Bank's T-account is

Bank of Canada		
Assets		Liabilities
		Currency in circulation +$100 m
		Reserves −$100 m

The net effect on the monetary liabilities of the Bank of Canada is a wash; the monetary base is unaffected by the public's increased desire for cash. But reserves are affected. Random fluctuations of reserves can occur as a result of random shifts into currency and out of deposits, and vice versa. The same is not true for the monetary base, making it a more stable variable.

Loans to Financial Institutions

In this chapter so far, we have seen how changes in the monetary base occur as a result of open market operations. However, the monetary base is also affected when the Bank of Canada makes a loan to a financial institution. When the Bank of Canada makes a $100 million loan to the First National Bank, the bank is credited with $100 million of reserves from the proceeds of the loan. The effects on the balance sheets of the banking system and the Bank of Canada are illustrated by the following T-accounts:

Banking System				Bank of Canada			
Assets		Liabilities		Assets		Liabilities	
Reserves	+$100 m	Loans (borrowings from the Bank of Canada)	+$100 m	Loans (borrowings from the Bank of Canada)	+$100 m	Reserves	+$100 m

The monetary liabilities of the Bank of Canada have now increased by $100 million, and the monetary base, too, has increased by this amount. However, if a bank pays off a loan from the Bank of Canada, thereby reducing its borrowings from the Bank of Canada by $100 million, the T-accounts of the banking system and the Bank of Canada are as follows:

Banking System				Bank of Canada			
Assets		Liabilities		Assets		Liabilities	
Reserves	−$100 m	Loans (borrowings from the Bank of Canada)	−$100 m	Loans (borrowings from the Bank of Canada)	−$100 m	Reserves	−$100 m

The net effect on the monetary liabilities of the Bank of Canada, and hence on the monetary base, is a reduction of $100 million. We see that the monetary base changes one-for-one with the change in the borrowings from the Bank of Canada.

Other Factors That Affect the Monetary Base

So far in this chapter, it seems as though the Bank of Canada has complete control of the monetary base through its open market operations and loans to financial institutions. However, the world is a little bit more complicated for the Bank of Canada. Two important items that affect the monetary base, but are not controlled by the Bank of Canada, are *float* and *government deposits at the Bank of Canada*. When the Bank of Canada clears cheques for banks, it often credits the amount of the cheque to a bank that has deposited it (increases the bank's reserves) before it debits (decreases the reserves of) the bank on which the cheque is drawn. The resulting temporary net increase in the total amount of reserves in the banking system (and hence in the monetary base) occurring from the Bank of Canada's cheque-clearing process is called **float**. When the government moves deposits from commercial banks to its account at the Bank of Canada, leading to an increase in *government deposits at the Bank of Canada*, it causes a deposit outflow at these banks like that shown in Chapter 13 and thus causes reserves in the banking system and the monetary base to decrease. Thus *float* (affected by random events such as the weather, which influences how quickly cheques are presented for payment) and *government deposits at the Bank of Canada* (determined by the federal government's actions) both affect the monetary base but are not controlled by the Bank of Canada at all.

Overview of the Bank of Canada's Ability to Control the Monetary Base

Our discussion above indicates that two primary features determine the monetary base: open market operations and lending to financial institutions. Whereas the amount of open market purchases or sales is completely controlled by the Bank of Canada's placing orders with dealers in bond markets, the central bank cannot unilaterally determine, and therefore cannot perfectly predict, the amount of borrowings from the Bank of Canada. The Bank of Canada sets the bank rate (interest rate on loans to banks), and then banks make decisions about whether to borrow. The amount of lending, though influenced by the Bank of Canada's setting of the bank rate, is not completely controlled by the Bank of Canada; banks' decisions play a role, too.

Therefore, we might want to split the monetary base into two components: one that the Bank of Canada can control completely and another that is less tightly controlled. The less tightly controlled component is the amount of the base that is created by loans from the Bank of Canada. The remainder of the base (called the **nonborrowed monetary base**) is under the Bank of Canada's control, because it results primarily from open market operations.[4] The nonborrowed monetary base is formally defined as the monetary base minus borrowings from the Bank of Canada, which are referred to as **borrowed reserves**:

$$MB_n = MB - BR$$

where

MB_n = nonborrowed monetary base

MB = monetary base

BR = borrowed reserves from the Bank of Canada

Factors not controlled at all by the Bank of Canada (for example, float and government deposits with the Bank of Canada) undergo substantial short-run variations and can be important sources of fluctuations in the monetary base over time periods as short as a week. However, these fluctuations are usually predictable and so can be offset through open market operations. *Although float and government deposits with the Bank of Canada undergo substantial short-run fluctuations, which complicate control of the monetary base, they do not prevent the Bank of Canada from accurately controlling it*.

Multiple Deposit Creation: A Simple Model

With our understanding of how the Bank of Canada controls the monetary base and how banks operate (Chapter 13), we now have the tools necessary to explain how deposits are created. When the Bank of Canada supplies the banking system with

---

[4]Actually, other items on the Bank of Canada's balance sheet (discussed in the appendix on the website) affect the magnitude of the nonborrowed monetary base. Because their effects on the nonborrowed base relative to open market operations are both small and predictable, these other items do not present the Bank of Canada with difficulties in controlling the nonborrowed base.

$1 of additional reserves, deposits increase by a multiple of this amount—a process called **multiple deposit creation.**

Deposit Creation: The Single Bank

Suppose that the $100 million open market purchase described earlier was conducted with the First National Bank. After the Bank of Canada has bought the $100 million in bonds from the First National Bank, the bank finds that it has an increase in reserves of $100 million. To analyze what the bank will do with these additional reserves, assume that the bank does not want to hold excess reserves because it earns little interest on them. We begin the analysis with the following T-account:

First National Bank		Liabilities
Assets		
Securities	−$100 m	
Reserves	+$100 m	

Because the bank has no increase in its chequable deposits, desired reserves remain the same, and the bank finds that its additional $100 million of reserves means that its excess reserves have risen by $100 million. Let's say that the bank decides to make a loan equal in amount to the $100 million rise in excess reserves. When the bank makes the loan, it sets up a chequing account for the borrower and puts the proceeds of the loan into this account. In this way, the bank alters its balance sheet by increasing its liabilities with $100 million of chequable deposits and at the same time increasing its assets with the $100 million loan. The resulting T-account looks like this:

First National Bank			
Assets		Liabilities	
Securities	−$100 m	Chequable deposits	+$100 m
Reserves	+$100 m		
Loans	+$100 m		

The bank has created chequable deposits by its act of lending. Because chequable deposits are part of the money supply, the bank's act of lending has, in fact, created money.

In its current balance sheet position, the First National Bank still has excess reserves and so might want to make additional loans. However, these reserves will not stay at the bank for very long. The borrowers took out loans not to leave $100 million sitting idle in a chequing account at the First National Bank but to purchase goods and services from other individuals and corporations. When the borrowers make these purchases by writing cheques, the cheques will be deposited at other banks, and the $100 million of reserves will leave the First National Bank. *As a result, a bank cannot safely make a loan for an amount greater than the excess reserves it has before it makes the loan.*

The final T-account of the First National Bank is

	First National Bank		
Assets		Liabilities	
Securities	−$100 m		
Loans	+$100 m		

The increase in reserves of $100 million has been converted into additional loans of $100 at the First National Bank, plus an additional $100 million of deposits that have made their way to other banks. (All the cheques written on accounts at the First National Bank are deposited in banks rather than converted into cash, because we are assuming that the public does not want to hold any additional currency.) Now let's see what happens to these deposits at the other banks.

Deposit Creation: The Banking System

To simplify the analysis, let's assume that the $100 million of deposits created by First National Bank's loan is deposited at Bank A and that this bank and all other banks hold no excess reserves. Bank A's T-account becomes

	Bank A		
Assets		Liabilities	
Reserves	+$100 m	Chequable deposits	+$100 m

If the desired reserve ratio is 10%, this bank will now find itself with a $10 million increase in desired reserves, leaving it $90 million of excess reserves. Because Bank A (like the First National Bank) does not want to hold on to excess reserves, it will make loans for the entire amount. Its loans and chequable deposits will then increase by $90 million, but when the borrowers spend the $90 million of chequable deposits, they and the reserves at Bank A will fall back down by this same amount. The net result is that Bank A's T-account will look like this:

	Bank A		
Assets		Liabilities	
Reserves	+$10 m	Chequable deposits	+$100 m
Loans	+$90 m		

If the money spent by the borrowers to whom Bank A lent the $90 million is deposited in another bank, such as Bank B, the T-account for Bank B will be

	Bank B		
Assets		Liabilities	
Reserves	+$90 m	Chequable deposits	+$100 m

The chequable deposits in the banking system have risen by another $90 million, for a total increase of $190 million ($100 million at Bank A plus $90 million at Bank B). In fact, the distinction between Bank A and Bank B is not necessary to obtain the same result on the overall expansion of deposits. If the borrowers from Bank A write cheques to someone who deposits them at Bank A, the same change in deposits would occur. The T-accounts for Bank B would just apply to Bank A, and its chequable deposits would increase by the total amount of $190 million.

Bank B will want to modify its balance sheet further. It must keep 10% of $90 million ($9 million) as desired reserves and has 90% of $90 million ($81 million) in excess reserves and so can make loans of this amount. Bank B will make loans totaling $81 million to borrowers, who spend the proceeds from the loans. Bank B's T-account will be

Bank B			
Assets		**Liabilities**	
Reserves	+$ 9 m	Chequable deposits	+$90 m
Loans	+$81 m		

The $81 million spent by the borrowers from Bank B will be deposited in another bank (Bank C). Consequently, from the initial $100 million increase of reserves in the banking system, the total increase of chequable deposits in the system so far is $271 million (= 100 m + 90 m + 81 m).

Following the same reasoning, if all banks make loans for the full amount of their excess reserves, further increments in chequable deposits will continue (at Banks C, D, E, and so on), as depicted in Table 16-1. Therefore, the total increase in deposits

TABLE 16-1 Creation of Deposits (assuming a 10% desired reserve ratio and a $100 million increase in reserves)

Bank	Increase in Deposits ($ millions)	Increase in Loans ($ millions)	Increase in Reserves ($ millions)
First National	0.00	100.00	0.00
A	100.00	90.00	10.00
B	90.00	81.00	9.00
C	81.00	72.90	8.10
D	72.90	65.61	7.29
E	65.61	59.05	6.56
F	59.05	53.14	5.91
.	.	.	.
.	.	.	.
.	.	.	.
Total for all banks	1000.00	1000.00	100.00

from the initial $100 million increase in reserves will be $1000 million: the increase is tenfold, the reciprocal of the 10% (0.10) desired reserve ratio.

If the banks choose to invest their excess reserves in securities, the result is the same. If Bank A had taken its excess reserves and purchased securities instead of making loans, its T-account would have looked like this:

Bank A			
Assets		**Liabilities**	
Reserves	+$10 m	Chequable deposits	+$100m
Securities	+$90 m		

When the bank buys $90 million of securities, it writes $90 million in cheques to the sellers of the securities, who in turn deposit the $90 million at a bank such as Bank B. Bank B's chequable deposits increase by $90 million, and the deposit expansion process is the same as before. ***Whether a bank chooses to use its excess reserves to make loans or to purchase securities, the effect on deposit expansion is the same.***

You can now see the difference in deposit creation for the single bank versus the banking system as a whole. Because a single bank can create deposits equal only to the amount of its excess reserves, it cannot by itself generate multiple deposit expansion. A single bank cannot make loans greater in amount than its excess reserves, because the bank will lose these reserves as the deposits created by the loan find their way to other banks. However, the banking system as a whole can generate a multiple expansion of deposits, because when a bank loses its excess reserves, these reserves do not leave the banking system, even though they are lost to the individual bank. So as each bank makes a loan and creates deposits, the reserves find their way to another bank, which uses them to make additional loans and create additional deposits. As you have seen, this process continues until the initial increase in reserves results in a multiple increase in deposits.

The multiple increase in deposits generated from an increase in the banking system's reserves is called the **simple deposit multiplier**.[5] In our example with a 10% desired reserve ratio, the simple deposit multiplier is 10. More generally, the simple deposit multiplier equals the reciprocal of the desired reserve ratio, expressed as a fraction (for example, 10 = 1/0.10), so the formula for the multiple expansion of deposits can be written as follows:

$$\Delta D = \frac{1}{r_d} \times \Delta R \qquad (1)$$

where ΔD = change in total chequable deposits in the banking system
r_d = desired reserve ratio (0.10 in the example)
ΔR = change in reserves for the banking system (100 million in the example)

Deriving the Formula for Multiple Deposit Creation

The formula for the multiple creation of deposits can be derived directly using algebra. We obtain the same answer for the relationship between a change in deposits and a change in reserves.

---

[5]This multiplier should not be confused with the Keynesian multiplier, which is derived through a similar step-by-step analysis. That multiplier relates an increase in income to an increase in investment, whereas the simple deposit multiplier relates an increase in deposits to an increase in reserves.

Our assumption that banks do not hold on to any excess reserves means that the total amount of desired reserves for the banking system DR will equal the total reserves in the banking system R:

$$DR = R$$

The total amount of desired reserves equals the desired reserve ratio r_d times the total amount of chequable deposits D:

$$DR = r_d \times D$$

Substituting r_d for DR in the first equation,

$$r_d \times D = R$$

and dividing both sides of the preceding equation by r_d gives

$$D = \frac{1}{r_d} \times R$$

Taking the change in both sides of this equation and using delta to indicate a change gives

$$\Delta D = \frac{1}{r_d} \times \Delta R$$

which is the same formula for deposit creation found in Equation 1.[6]

This derivation provides us with another way of looking at the multiple creation of deposits, because it forces us to examine the banking system as a whole rather than one bank at a time. For the banking system as a whole, deposit creation (or contraction) will stop only when excess reserves in the banking system are zero; that is, the banking system will be in equilibrium when the total amount of desired reserves equals the total amount of reserves, as seen in the equation $DR = R$. When $r_d \times D$ is substituted for DR, the resulting equation $r_d \times D = R$ tells us how high chequable deposits will have to be for desired reserves to equal total reserves. Accordingly, a given level of reserves in the banking system determines the level of chequable deposits when the banking system is in equilibrium (when $ER = 0$); put another way, the given level of reserves supports a given level of chequable deposits.

In our example, the desired reserve ratio is 10%. If reserves increase by $100 million, chequable deposits must rise by $1000 million for total desired reserves also to increase by $100 million. If the increase in chequable deposits is less than this—say, $900 million—then the increase in desired reserves of $90 million remains below the $100 million increase in reserves, so excess reserves still exist somewhere in the banking system. The banks with the excess reserves will now make additional loans, creating new deposits; this process will continue until all reserves in the system are used up, which occurs when chequable deposits rise by $1000 million.

---

[6]A formal derivation of this formula follows. Using the reasoning in the text, the change in chequable deposits is $100 (= $\Delta R \times 1$) plus $90 $[= \Delta R \times (1 - r_d)]$ plus $81 $[= \Delta R \times (1 - r_d)^2]$ and so on, which can be rewritten as

$$\Delta D = \Delta R \times [1 + (1 - r_d) + (1 - r_d)^2 + (1 - r_d)^3 + \cdots]$$

Using the formula for the sum of an infinite series found in footnote 5 in Chapter 4, this can be rewritten as

$$\Delta D = \Delta R \times \frac{1}{1 - (1 - r_d)} = \frac{1}{r_d} \times \Delta R$$

We can also see this by looking at the T-account of the banking system as a whole (including the First National Bank) that results from this process:

Banking System			
Assets		**Liabilities**	
Securities	−$ 100 m	Chequable deposits	+$1000 m
Reserves	+$ 100 m		
Loans	+$1000 m		

The procedure of eliminating excess reserves by loaning them out means that the banking system (First National Bank and Banks A, B, C, D, and so on) continues to make loans up to the $1000 million amount until deposits have reached the $1000 million level. In this way, $100 million of reserves supports $1000 million (10 times the quantity) of deposits.

Critique of the Simple Model

Our model of multiple deposit creation seems to indicate that the Bank of Canada is able to exercise complete control over the level of chequable deposits by setting the level of reserves. The actual creation of deposits is much less mechanical than the simple model indicates. If proceeds from Bank A's $90 million loan are not deposited but are kept in currency, nothing is deposited in Bank B and the deposit creation process ceases. The total increase in the money supply is now the $90 million increase in currency plus the initial $100 million of deposits created by First National Bank's loans, which were deposited at Bank A, for a total of only $190 million—considerably less than the $1000 million we calculated with the simple model above. Another way of saying this is that currency has no multiple deposit expansion, while deposits do. Thus, if some proceeds from loans are not deposited in banks but instead are used to raise the holdings of currency, less multiple expansion occurs overall, and the money supply will not increase by as much as our simple model of multiple deposit creation tells us.

Another situation ignored in our model is one in which banks do not make loans or buy securities in the full amount of their excess reserves. If Bank A decides to hold on to all $90 million of its excess reserves, no deposits would be made in Bank B, and this would also stop the deposit creation process. The total increase in deposits would be only $100 million, not the $1000 million increase in our example. Hence, if banks choose to hold on to all or some of their excess reserves, the full expansion of deposits predicted by the simple model of multiple deposit creation again does not occur.

Our examples indicate that the Bank of Canada is not the only player whose behaviour influences the level of deposits and therefore the money supply. Depositors' decisions regarding how much currency to hold and banks' decisions regarding the amount of reserves to hold also can cause the money supply to change.

Factors That Determine the Money Supply

Our critique of the simple model shows how we can expand on it to discuss all the factors that affect the money supply. Let's look at changes in each factor in turn, holding all other factors constant.

Changes in the Nonborrowed Monetary Base, MB_n

As shown earlier in the chapter, the Bank of Canada's open market purchases increase the nonborrowed monetary base, and its open market sales decrease it. Holding all other variables constant, an increase in MB_n arising from an open market purchase raises the amount of the monetary base and reserves, so that multiple deposit creation occurs and the money supply increases. Similarly, an open market sale that reduces MB_n shrinks the amount of the monetary base and reserves, thereby causing a multiple contraction of deposits and a decrease in the money supply. We have the following result: ***the money supply is positively related to the nonborrowed monetary base MB_n.***

Changes in Borrowed Reserves, *BR*, from the Bank of Canada

An increase in loans from the Bank of Canada provides additional borrowed reserves, and thereby increases the amount of the monetary base and reserves, so that multiple deposit creation occurs and the money supply expands. If banks reduce the level of their loans from the Bank of Canada, all other variables held constant, the monetary base and amount of reserves would fall, and the money supply would decrease. The result is this: ***the money supply is positively related to the level of borrowed reserves, BR, from the Bank of Canada.***

Changes in the Desired Reserve Ratio, r_d

If the desired reserve ratio on chequable deposits increases while all other variables, such as the monetary base, stay the same, we have seen that multiple deposit expansion is reduced, and hence the money supply falls. If, on the other hand, the desired reserve ratio falls, multiple deposit expansion would be higher and the money supply would rise. We now have the following result: ***the money supply is negatively related to the desired reserve ratio r_d.***

Changes in Currency Holdings

As shown before, chequable deposits undergo multiple expansion, whereas currency does not. Hence, when chequable deposits are converted into currency, holding the monetary base and other variables constant, a switch is made from a component of the money supply that undergoes multiple expansion to one that does not. The overall level of multiple expansion declines and the money supply falls. On the other hand, if currency holdings fall, a switch is made into chequable deposits that undergo multiple deposit expansion, so the money supply would rise. This analysis suggests the following result: ***the money supply is negatively related to currency holdings.***

Changes in Excess Reserves

When banks increase their holdings of excess reserves during anxious or crisis times, those reserves are no longer being used to make loans, causing multiple deposit creation to stop dead in its tracks, resulting in less expansion of the money supply. If, on the other hand, banks chose to hold fewer excess reserves, loans and multiple deposit creation would increase and the money supply would rise. ***The money supply is negatively related to the amount of excess reserves.***

Recall from Chapter 13 that the primary benefit to a bank of holding excess reserves is that they provide insurance against losses due to deposit outflows; that is, they enable the bank experiencing deposit outflows to escape the costs of calling in loans, selling securities, borrowing from the Bank of Canada or other corporations, or bank failure. If banks fear that deposit outflows are likely to increase (that is, if expected deposit outflows increase), they will want more insurance against this possibility and excess reserves will rise.

SUMMARY TABLE 16-1 Money Supply Response

Player	Variable	Change in Variable	Money Supply Response	Reason
Bank of Canada	Nonborrowed monetary base, MB_n	↑	↑	More MB for deposit creation
	Desired reserve ratio, r_d	↑	↓	Less multiple deposit expansion
Banks	Borrowed reserves, BR	↑	↑	More MB for deposit creation
	Excess reserves	↑	↓	Less loans and deposit creation
Depositors	Currency holdings	↑	↓	Less multiple deposit expansion

Note: Only increases (↑) in the variables are shown. The effects of decreases on the money supply would be the opposite of those indicated in the "Money Supply Response" column.

Overview of the Money Supply Process

We now have a model of the money supply process in which all three of the players—the Bank of Canada, depositors, and banks—directly influence the money supply. As a study aid, Summary Table 16-1 charts the money supply response to the five factors discussed above and gives a brief synopsis of the reasoning behind them.

The variables are grouped by the player who is the primary influence behind the variable. The Bank of Canada, for example, influences the money supply by controlling the first two variables. Depositors influence the money supply through their decisions about holdings of currency, while banks influence the money supply with their decisions about borrowings from the Bank of Canada and reserves.

The Money Multiplier

The intuition in the section above is sufficient for you to understand how the money supply process works. For those of you who are more mathematically inclined, we can derive all of the above results using a concept called the **money multiplier**, denoted by m, which tells us how much the money supply changes for a given change in the monetary base. The relationship between the money supply M, the money multiplier, and the monetary base is described by the following equation:

$$M = m \times MB \tag{2}$$

The money multiplier m tells us what multiple of the monetary base is transformed into the money supply. Because the money multiplier is larger than 1, the alternative name for the monetary base, *high-powered money*, is logical: a $1 change in the monetary base leads to more than a $1 change in the money supply.

Deriving the Money Multiplier

Let's assume that the desired holdings of currency C and excess reserves ER grows proportionally with chequable deposits D; in other words, we assume that the ratios of these items to chequable deposits are constants in equilibrium, as the braces in the following expressions indicate:

$$c = \{C/D\} \quad = \text{currency ratio}$$
$$e = \{ER/D\} = \text{excess reserves ratio}$$

We will now derive a formula that describes how the currency ratio desired by depositors, the excess reserves ratio set by banks, and the desired reserve ratio desired by banks affect the multiplier m. We begin the derivation of the model of the money supply with the following equation:

$$R = DR + ER$$

which states that the total amount of reserves in the banking system R equals the sum of desired reserves DR and excess reserves ER. (Note that this equation corresponds to the equilibrium condition $DR = R$ earlier in the chapter, where excess reserves were assumed to be zero.)

The total amount of desired reserves equals the desired reserve ratio r_d times the amount of chequable deposits D:

$$DR = r_d \times D$$

Substituting $r_d \times D$ for DR in the first equation yields an equation that links reserves in the banking system to the amount of chequable deposits and excess reserves they can support:

$$R = (r_d \times D) + ER$$

A key point here is that banks set the desired reserve ratio r_d to less than 1. Thus $1 of reserves can support more than $1 of deposits, and the multiple expansion of deposits can occur.

Let's see how this works in practice. If excess reserves are held at zero ($ER = 0$), the desired reserve ratio is set at $r_d = 0.10$, and the level of chequable deposits in the banking system is $800 billion, then the amount of reserves needed to support these deposits is $80 billion ($= 0.10 \times 800$ billion). The $80 billion of reserves can support 10 times this amount in chequable deposits because multiple deposit creation will occur.

Because the monetary base MB equals currency C plus reserves R, we can generate an equation that links the amount of the monetary base to the levels of chequable deposits and currency by adding currency to both sides of the equation:

$$MB = R + C = (r_d \times D) + ER + C$$

Another way of thinking about this equation is to recognize that it reveals the amount of the monetary base needed to support the existing amounts of chequable deposits, currency, and excess reserves.

To derive the money multiplier formula in terms of the currency ratio $c = \{C/D\}$ and the excess reserves ratio $e = \{ER/D\}$, we rewrite the last equation, specifying C as $c \times D$ and ER as $e \times D$:

$$MB = (r_d \times D) + (e \times D) + (c \times D) = (r_d + e + c) \times D$$

We next divide both sides of the equation by the term inside the parentheses to get an expression linking chequable deposits D to the monetary base MB:

$$D = \frac{1}{r_d + e + c} \times MB \tag{3}$$

Using the M1 definition of the money supply as currency plus chequable deposits ($M = D + C$) and again specifying C as $c \times D$,

$$M = D + (c \times D) = (1 + c) \times D$$

Substituting in this equation the expression for D from Equation 3, we have

$$m = \frac{1 + c}{r_d + e + c} \times MB \qquad (4)$$

We have derived an expression in the form of our earlier Equation 2. As you can see, the ratio that multiplies MB is the money multiplier, which tells how much the money supply changes in response to a given change in the monetary base (high-powered money). The money multiplier m is thus

$$m = \frac{1 + c}{r_d + e + c} \qquad (5)$$

It is a function of the currency ratio set by depositors c, the excess reserves ratio set by banks e, and the desired reserve ratio also set by banks r_d.

Intuition Behind the Money Multiplier

To get a feel for what the money multiplier means, let's construct a numerical example with realistic numbers for the following variables:

$$r_d = \text{desired reserve ratio} = 0.10$$
$$C = \text{currency in circulation} = \$400 \text{ billion}$$
$$D = \text{chequable deposits} = \$800 \text{ billion}$$
$$ER = \text{excess reserves} = \$0.8 \text{ billion}$$
$$M = \text{money supply (M1+)} = C + D = \$1200 \text{ billion}$$

From these numbers we can calculate the values for the currency ratio c and the excess reserves ratio e:

$$c = \frac{\$400 \text{ billion}}{\$800 \text{ billion}} = 0.5$$

$$e = \frac{\$0.8 \text{ billion}}{\$800 \text{ billion}} = 0.001$$

The resulting value of the money multiplier is

$$m = \frac{1 + 0.5}{0.1 + 0.001 + 0.5} = \frac{1.5}{0.601} = 2.5$$

The money multiplier of 2.5 tells us that, given the desired reserve ratio of 10% on chequable deposits and the behaviour of depositors, as represented by $c = 0.5$, and banks, as represented by $e = 0.001$ and $r_d = 0.10$, a \$1 increase in the monetary base leads to a \$2.50 increase in the money supply (M1+).

An important characteristic of the money multiplier is that it is less than the simple deposit multiplier of 10 found earlier in the chapter. The key to understanding this result is to realize that **although there is multiple expansion of deposits, there is no such expansion for currency**. Thus, if some portion of the increase in high-powered money finds its way into currency, this portion does not undergo multiple deposit expansion. In our simple model earlier in the chapter, we did not allow for this possibility, and so the increase in reserves led to the maximum amount of multiple deposit creation. However, in our current model of the money multiplier, the level of currency does rise when the monetary base MB and chequable deposits D increase because c is greater than zero. As previously stated, any increase in *MB* that goes into an increase in currency is not multiplied, so only part of the increase in *MB* is available to support chequable deposits that undergo multiple expansion. The overall level of multiple deposit expansion must be lower, meaning that the increase in *M*, given an increase in *MB*, is smaller than the simple model earlier in the chapter indicated.[7]

Money Supply Response to Changes in the Factors

By recognizing that the monetary base is $MB = MB_n + BR$, we can rewrite Equation 2 as

$$M = m \times (MB_n + BR) \qquad (6)$$

Now we can show algebraically all the results in Summary Table 16-1, which shows the money supply response to the changes in the factors.

As you can see from Equation 6, a rise in MB_n or *BR* raises the money supply *M* by a multiple amount because the money multiplier *m* is greater than one. We can see that a rise in the desired reserve ratio lowers the money supply by calculating what happens to the value of the money multiplier using Equation 5 in our numerical example when r_d increases from 10% to 15% (leaving all other variables unchanged). The money multiplier then falls from 2.5 to

$$m = \frac{1 + 0.5}{0.15 + 0.001 + 0.5} = \frac{1.5}{0.651} = 2.3$$

which, as we would expect, is less than 2.5.

Similarly, we can see in our numerical example that a rise in currency lowers the money supply by calculating what happens to the money multiplier when *c* is raised from 0.50 to 0.75. The money multiplier then falls from 2.5 to

$$m = \frac{1 + 0.75}{0.1 + 0.001 + 0.75} = \frac{1.75}{0.851} = 2.06$$

Finally, we can see that a rise in excess reserves lowers the money supply by calculating what happens to the money multiplier when *e* is raised from 0.001 to 0.005. The money multiplier declines from 2.5 to

$$m = \frac{1 + 0.5}{0.1 + 0.005 + 0.5} = \frac{1.5}{0.605} = 2.48$$

Note that although the excess reserves ratio has risen fivefold, only a small decline has occurred in the money multiplier. This decline is small because in recent years *e* has usually been extremely small, so changes in it have only a minor impact on the money multiplier. However, there have been times, particularly during the Great Depression period and the recent financial crisis in the United States, which we examine in the next two applications, when this ratio was far higher, and its movements had a substantial effect on the money supply and the money multiplier.

---

[7]Another reason the money multiplier is smaller is that *e* is a constant fraction greater than zero, indicating that an increase in *MB* and *D* leads to higher excess reserves. The resulting higher amount of excess reserves means that the amount of reserves used to support chequable deposits will not increase as much as it otherwise would. Hence the increase in chequable deposits and the money supply will be lower, and the money multiplier will be smaller. However, because *e* is often tiny—about 0.001—the impact of this ratio on the money multiplier can be quite small. But there are periods when *e* is much larger and so has a more important role in lowering the money multiplier.

APPLICATION

The Great Depression Bank Panics, 1930–1933, and the Money Supply

We can also use our money supply model to help us understand major movements in the money supply that have occurred in the past. In this application, we use the model to explain the monetary contraction that occurred in the United States during the Great Depression, the worst economic downturn in U.S. history. In Chapter 9, we discussed bank panics and saw that they could harm the economy by making asymmetric information problems more severe in credit markets, as they did during the Great Depression. Here we see that another consequence of bank panics is that they can cause a substantial reduction in the money supply. As we will understand from the chapters on monetary theory later in the text, such reductions can also cause severe damage to the economy.

Figure 16-1 traces the bank crisis during the Great Depression by showing the volume of deposits at failed commercial banks from 1929 to 1933. In their classic book *A Monetary History of the United States, 1867–1960*, Milton Friedman and Anna Schwartz describe the onset of the first banking crisis in late 1930 as follows:

> Before October 1930, deposits of suspended [failed] commercial banks had been somewhat higher than during most of 1929 but not out of line with experience during the preceding decade. In November 1930, they were more than double the highest value recorded since the start of monthly data in 1921. A crop of bank failures, particularly in Missouri, Indiana, Illinois, Iowa, Arkansas, and North

FIGURE 16-1 Deposits of Failed Commercial Banks, 1929–1933

The volume of deposits at failed commercial banks from 1929 to 1933 traces the bank crisis during the Great Depression.

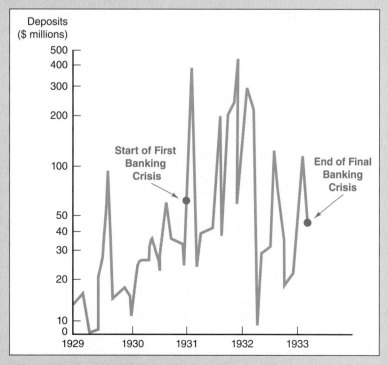

Source: Milton Friedman and Anna Jacobson Schwartz, *A Monetary History of the United States, 1867–1960* (Princeton, NJ: Princeton University Press, 1963), 309.

Carolina, led to widespread attempts to convert demand and time deposits into currency, and also, to a much lesser extent, into postal savings deposits. A contagion of fear spread among depositors, starting from the agricultural areas, which had experienced the heaviest impact of bank failures in the twenties. But failure of 256 banks with $180 million of deposits in November 1930 was followed by the failure of 532 with over $370 million of deposits in December (all figures seasonally unadjusted), the most dramatic being the failure on December 11 of the Bank of United States with over $200 million of deposits. That failure was of especial importance. The Bank of United States was the largest commercial bank, as measured by volume of deposits, ever to have failed up to that time in U.S. history. Moreover, though an ordinary commercial bank, its name had led many at home and abroad to regard it somehow as an official bank, hence its failure constituted more of a blow to confidence than would have been administered by the fall of a bank with a less distinctive name.[8]

The first bank panic, from October 1930 to January 1931, is clearly visible in Figure 16-1 at the end of 1930, when a rise in the amount of deposits at failed banks occurred. Because no deposit insurance was in place at the time (the FDIC wasn't established until 1934), when a bank failed, depositors would receive only partial repayment of their deposits. Therefore, when banks were failing during a bank panic, depositors knew that they would be likely to suffer substantial losses on deposits and thus the expected return on deposits would be negative. The theory of portfolio choice predicts that with the onset of the first bank crisis, depositors would shift their holdings from chequable deposits to currency by withdrawing currency from their bank accounts, and c would rise. Our earlier analysis of the excess reserves ratio suggests that the resulting surge in deposit outflows would cause the banks to protect themselves by substantially increasing their excess reserves ratio e. Both of these predictions are borne out by the data in Figure 16-2. During the first bank panic (October 1930–January 1931) the currency ratio c began to climb. Even more striking is the behaviour of the excess reserves ratio e, which more than doubled from November 1930 to January 1931.

The money supply model predicts that when e and c increase, the money supply will contract. The rise in c results in a decline in the overall level of multiple deposit expansion, leading to a smaller money multiplier and a decline in the money supply, whereas the rise in e reduces the amount of reserves available to support deposits and also causes the money supply to decrease. Thus our model predicts that the rise in e and c after the onset of the first bank crisis would result in a decline in the money supply—a prediction borne out by the evidence in Figure 16-3.

Banking crises continued to occur from 1931 to 1933, and the pattern predicted by our model persisted: c continued to rise, and so did e. By the end of the crises in March 1933, the money supply (M1) had declined by over 25%—by far the largest decline in all of American history—and it coincided with the nation's worst economic contraction (see Chapter 9). Even more remarkable is that this decline occurred despite a 20% rise in the level of the monetary base—which illustrates how important the changes in c and e during bank panics can be in the determination of the money supply. It also illustrates that the Fed's job of conducting monetary policy can be complicated by depositor and bank behaviour.

---

[8]Milton Friedman and Anna Jacobson Schwartz, *A Monetary History of the United States, 1867–1960* (Princeton, NJ: Princeton University Press, 1963), 308–311.

FIGURE 16-2   Excess Reserves Ratio and Currency Ratio, 1929–1933

During the first bank panic (October 1930–January 1931) c began to climb, while e more than doubled from November 1930 to January 1931. Subsequently, the ongoing banking crises led to continuing increases in both c and e.

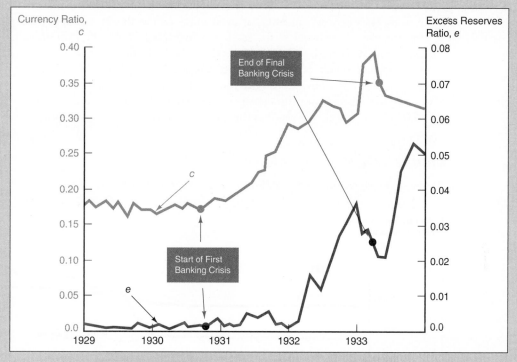

Sources: Federal Reserve *Bulletin*; Milton Friedman and Anna Jacobson Schwartz, *A Monetary History of the United States, 1867–1960* (Princeton, NJ: Princeton University Press, 1963), 333.

FIGURE 16-3   M1 and the Monetary Base, 1929–1933

The rise in e and c after the onset of the first bank crisis led to a decline in the money supply even though the monetary base rose.

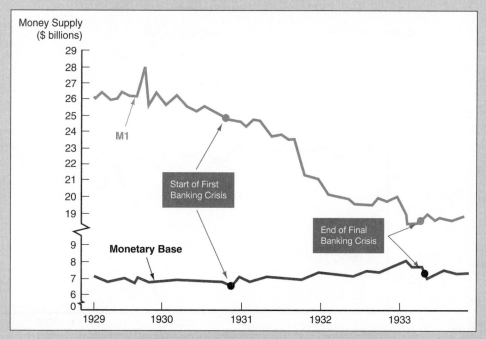

Source: Milton Friedman and Anna Jacobson Schwartz, *A Monetary History of the United States, 1867–1960* (Princeton, NJ: Princeton University Press, 1963), 333.

APPLICATION

The 2007–2009 Financial Crisis and the Money Supply

The previous application shows that the money supply and the monetary base do not always move in tandem. An even more extraordinary example occurred during the recent financial crisis, as shown in Figure 16-4, when the monetary base increased by more than 200% as a result of the Fed's purchase of assets and creation of new lending facilities to stem the financial crisis, while the M1 money supply rose by less than 25%. How does our money supply model explain this?

Figure 16-5 shows the currency ratio c and the excess reserves ratio e for the 2007–2009 period. We see that the currency ratio fell somewhat during this period,

FIGURE 16-4 M1 and the Monetary Base, 2007–2009

The money supply rose by less than 25% despite the increase in the monetary base by over 200%.

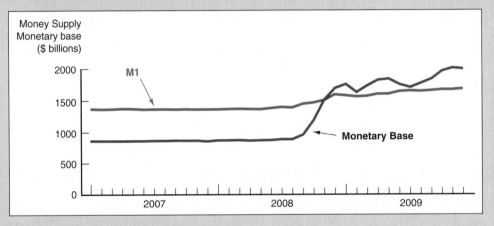

Source: Federal Reserve; www.federalreserve.gov/releases.

FIGURE 16-5 Excess Reserves Ratio and Currency Ratio, 2007–2009

The currency ratio c fell during the crisis, whereas the excess reserves ratio e rose by a factor of over 500.

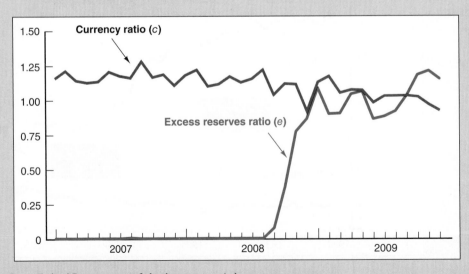

Source: Federal Reserve; www.federalreserve.gov/releases.

which our money supply model suggests would raise the money multiplier and the money supply because it would increase the overall level of deposit expansion. However, the effects of the decline in c were entirely offset by the extraordinary rise in the excess reserves ratio e, which climbed by more than a factor of over 500 during this period. The explanation for this increase in e was that banks were willing to hold the huge increase in excess reserves because they had become costless to hold once the Fed began paying interest on these reserves and this interest rate often exceeded the rate at which the banks could lend them out at in the federal funds market. As our money supply model predicts, the huge increase in e would lower the money multiplier, and so the money supply would expand only slightly, despite the huge increase in the monetary base.

MyEconLab   MyEconLab is an online homework and tutorial system that puts you in control of your own learning with study and practice tools directly correlated to this chapter's content. Visit MyEconLab to explore the following resources:

- The Questions and Applied Problems are all available in the Study Plan on MyEconLab for further practice. You will also find the answers to all of the Questions and Applied Problems in the Student Resources section of your MyEconLab.
- CANSIM data are available for relevant CANSIM questions in the Student Resources section of your MyEconLab.
- Visit the Student Resources section of MyEconLab to access the following appendices for this chapter: Appendix 16.1: The Bank of Canada's Balance Sheet and the Monetary Base; Appendix 16.2: The M2+ Money Multiplier.

MyEconLab also features Additional Readings, Videos, Glossary Flashcards, Audio Chapter Summaries, Economics News Feeds, Animations, and many additional tools to help you master key concepts from the text.

SUMMARY

1. The three players in the money supply process are the central bank, banks (depository institutions), and depositors.

2. Four items in the Bank of Canada's balance sheet are essential to our understanding of the money supply process: the two liability items, currency in circulation and reserves, which together make up the monetary base, and the two asset items, securities and loans to financial institutions.

3. The Bank of Canada controls the monetary base through open market operations and extension of loans to financial institutions and has better control over the monetary base than over reserves. Although float and government deposits with the Bank of Canada undergo substantial short-run fluctuations, which complicate control of the monetary base, they do not prevent the Bank of Canada from accurately controlling it.

4. A single bank can make loans up to the amount of its excess reserves, thereby creating an equal amount of deposits. The banking system can create a multiple expansion of deposits, because as each bank makes a loan and creates deposits, the reserves find their way to another

bank, which uses them to make loans and create additional deposits. In the simple model of multiple deposit creation in which banks do not hold on to excess reserves and the public holds no currency, the multiple increase in chequable deposits (simple deposit multiplier) equals the reciprocal of the desired reserve ratio.

5. The simple model of multiple deposit creation has serious deficiencies. Decisions by depositors to increase their holdings of currency or of banks to hold excess reserves will result in a smaller expansion of deposits than the simple model predicts. All three players—the Bank of Canada, banks, and depositors—are important in the determination of the money supply.

6. The money supply is positively related to the nonborrowed monetary base MB_n, which is determined by open market operations, and the level of borrowed reserves (lending) from the Bank of Canada, BR. The money supply is negatively related to the desired reserve ratio, r_d; holdings of currency; and excess reserves. The model of the money supply process takes into account the behaviour of

all three players in the money supply process: the Bank of Canada, through open market operations; banks, through their decisions to borrow from the Bank of Canada and hold excess reserves; and depositors, through their decisions about holding of currency.

7. The monetary base is linked to the money supply using the concept of the money multiplier, which tells us how much the money supply changes when the monetary base changes.

KEY TERMS

bank rate, p. 377

borrowed reserves, p. 383

desired reserve ratio, p. 377

desired reserves, p. 377

excess reserves, p. 377

float, p. 383

high-powered money, p. 377

monetary base, p. 376

money multiplier, p. 391

multiple deposit creation, p. 384

nonborrowed monetary base, p. 383

open market operations, p. 378

open market purchase, p. 378

open market sale, p. 378

reserves, p. 377

settlement balances, p. 377

simple deposit multiplier, p. 387

QUESTIONS

1. Classify each of these transactions as either an asset, a liability, or neither, for each of the "players" in the money supply process—the Bank of Canada, banks, and depositors.
   a. You get a $10 000 loan from the bank to buy an automobile.
   b. You deposit $400 into your chequing account at the local bank.
   c. The Bank of Canada provides an emergency loan to a bank for $1 000 000.
   d. A bank borrows $500 000 in overnight loans from another bank.
   e. You use your debit card to purchase a meal at a restaurant for $100.

2. The First National Bank receives an extra $100 of reserves but decides not to lend out any of these reserves. How much deposit creation takes place for the entire banking system?

3. Suppose that the Bank of Canada buys $1 million of bonds from the First National Bank. If the First National Bank and all other banks use the resulting increase in reserves to purchase securities only and not to make loans, what will happen to chequable deposits?

4. If a bank depositor withdraws $1000 of currency from an account, what happens to reserves, chequable deposits, and the monetary base?

5. If a bank sells $10 million of bonds to the Bank of Canada to pay back $10 million on the loan it owes, what will be the effect on the level of chequable deposits?

6. If you decide to hold $100 less cash than usual and therefore deposit $100 more cash in the bank, what effect will this have on chequable deposits in the banking system if the rest of the public keeps its holdings of currency constant?

7. "The Bank of Canada can perfectly control the amount of reserves in the system." Is this statement true, false, or uncertain? Explain.

8. "The Bank of Canada can perfectly control the amount of the monetary base, but has less control over the composition of the monetary base." Is this statement true, false, or uncertain? Explain.

9. The Bank of Canada buys $100 million of bonds from the public and there is also a decline in the desired reserve ratio. What will happen to the money supply?

10. Describe how each of the following can affect the money supply: (a) the central bank; (b) banks; and (c) depositors.

11. "The money multiplier is necessarily greater than 1." Is this statement true, false, or uncertain? Explain your answer.

12. What effect might a financial panic have on the money multiplier and the money supply? Why?

13. During the Great Depression years from 1930 to 1933, both the currency ratio c and the excess reserves ratio e rose dramatically in the United States. What effect did these factors have on the money multiplier?

14. In October 2008, the Federal Reserve began paying interest on the amount of excess reserves held by banks. How, if at all, might this affect the multiplier process and the money supply in the United States?

15. The money multiplier declined significantly during the period 1930–1933 and also during the recent financial crisis of 2008–2010. Yet the M1 money supply decreased by 25% in the Depression period but *increased* by more than 20% during the recent financial crisis. What explains the difference in outcomes?

Unless otherwise noted, the following assumptions are made in all questions: The desired reserve ratio on chequable deposits is 10%, banks do not hold any excess reserves, and the public's holdings of currency do not change.

APPLIED PROBLEMS

16. If the Bank of Canada sells $2 million of bonds to the First National Bank, what happens to reserves and the monetary base? Use T-accounts to explain your answer.

17. If the Bank of Canada sells $2 million of bonds to Irving the Investor, who pays for the bonds with a briefcase filled with currency, what happens to reserves and the monetary base? Use T-accounts to explain your answer.

18. If the Bank of Canada lends five banks an additional total of $100 million but depositors withdraw $50 million and hold it as currency, what happens to reserves and the monetary base? Use T-accounts to explain your answer.

19. Using T-accounts, show what happens to chequable deposits in the banking system when the Bank of Canada lends an additional $1 million to the First National Bank.

20. Using T-accounts, show what happens to chequable deposits in the banking system when the Bank of Canada sells $2 million of bonds to the First National Bank.

21. If the Bank of Canada buys $1 million of bonds from the First National Bank, but an additional 10% of any deposit is held as excess reserves, what is the total increase in chequable deposits? (*Hint:* Use T-accounts to show what happens at each step of the multiple expansion process.)

22. If reserves in the banking system increase by $1 billion as a result of Bank of Canada lending to financial institutions of $1 billion, and chequable deposits increase by $9 billion, why isn't the banking system in equilibrium? What will continue to happen in the banking system until equilibrium is reached? Show the T-account for the banking system in equilibrium.

23. If the Bank of Canada reduces reserves by selling $5 million worth of bonds to the banks, what will the T-account of the banking system look like when the banking system is in equilibrium? What will have happened to the level of chequable deposits?

24. If the Bank of Canada sells $1 million of bonds and banks reduce their borrowings from the Bank of Canada by $1 million, predict what will happen to the money supply.

25. Suppose that currency in circulation is $600 billion, the amount of chequable deposits is $900 billion, excess reserves are $15 billion, and the desired ratio is 10%.
    a. Calculate the money supply, the currency deposit ratio, the excess reserve ratio, and the money multiplier.
    b. Suppose the central bank conducts an unusually large open market purchase of bonds held by banks of $1400 billion due to a sharp contraction in the economy. Assuming the ratios you calculated in part (a) are the same, what do you predict will be the effect on the money supply?
    c. Suppose the central bank conducts the same open market purchase as in part (b), except that banks choose to hold all of these proceeds as excess reserves rather than loan them out, due to fear of a financial crisis. Assuming that currency and deposits remain the same, what happens to the amount of excess reserves, the excess reserve ratio, the money supply, and the money multiplier?
    d. Following the financial crisis in 2008 in the United States, the Federal Reserve began injecting the U.S. banking system with massive amounts of liquidity, and at the same time, very little lending occurred. As a result, the M1 money multiplier was below 1 for most of the time from October 2008 through 2011. How does this relate to your answer to part (c)?

CANSIM Questions

26. An important aspect of the money supply process is the money multiplier. Go to the CANSIM data available in the Student Resources section of your MyEconLab website and download Statistics Canada CANSIM II series V37145 (monetary base), V37152 (M1++ (gross)), and V41552801 (M2++ (gross)).
    a. Calculate the M1++ money multiplier. What is its average value over your sample period?
    b. Calculate the M2++ money multiplier. What is its average value?
    c. Compare the two money multipliers.
    d. Does it appear that the money multipliers are increasing or decreasing?

27. Continuing from the previous question, compute the growth rates of M1++ and M2++.
    a. What is the average M1++ growth rate? Its variance?
    b. What is the average M2++ growth rate? Its variance?
    c. Which monetary aggregate is more variable?

WEB EXERCISES

1. An important aspect of the supply of money is bank deposits with the Bank of Canada. Go to **www.osfi-bsif.gc.ca** and locate financial data for banks. This site reports the consolidated balance sheet for all banks.
   a. What is the current level of bank deposits with the Bank of Canada?
   b. What is the change in bank deposits with the Bank of Canada since a year ago?
   c. Based on (a) and (b), does it appear that bank reserves with the Bank of Canada are increasing or decreasing?

2. Go to **www.bankofcanada.ca** and click on "Rates and Statistics," then "Indicators," and then choose "Summary of Key Monetary Policy Variables."
   a. What is the 12-month growth rate of M2 (gross), M1++, and M2++?
   b. What is the change in the 12-month growth rate in M2 (gross), M1++, and M2++ since a year ago?

CHAPTER 17

Tools of Monetary Policy

LEARNING OBJECTIVES

After studying this chapter you should be able to

1. characterize the framework for the implementation of monetary policy in Canada (the LVTS, the target and the operating band for the overnight interest rate, and the Bank of Canada's standing liquidity facilities)

2. explain the market for reserves and the channel/corridor system for setting the overnight interest rate in Canada

3. identify the Bank of Canada's approach to monetary policy and the conventional and nonconventional tools of monetary policy

4. explain how the Federal Reserve and the European Central Bank can use their policy tools to manipulate interest rates and the money supply

PREVIEW

In the chapters describing the structure of the Bank of Canada and the money supply process, we mentioned three policy tools that the Bank can use to manipulate interest rates and the money supply: open market operations, settlement balances management, and Bank of Canada advances. Because the Bank's use of these tools has such an important impact on interest rates and economic activity, it is important to understand how the Bank wields them in practice and how relatively useful each tool is.

In recent years, the Bank of Canada has increased its focus on the **overnight rate**, the interest rate on overnight loans of reserves from one bank to another, as the primary instrument of monetary policy. Since December 2000, the Bank of Canada has announced an overnight rate target eight times throughout the year, an announcement that is watched closely by market participants because it affects interest rates throughout the economy. Thus to fully understand how the Bank's tools are used in the conduct of monetary policy, we must understand their direct effects on the overnight interest rate.

This chapter begins with the institutional framework within which the Bank of Canada conducts monetary policy, followed by a supply and demand analysis of the market for reserves, where the overnight interest rate is determined.

We then go on to look in more detail at the tools of monetary policy—open market operations, settlement balances management, and Bank of Canada lending—to see how they are used in practice.

The Framework for the Implementation of Monetary Policy

The tools used by the Bank of Canada to implement monetary policy are closely linked to the institutional arrangements regarding the clearing and settlement systems in the Canadian economy. Understanding the tools of monetary policy therefore requires that we know the key features of the framework for the implementation of monetary policy. As you will see, this framework has been designed to encourage deposit-taking financial institutions to deal directly with the market, rather than with the Bank of Canada.[1]

The Large Value Transfer System (LVTS)

The core of the Canadian payments system is the **Large Value Transfer System (LVTS)**, introduced by the Canadian Payments Association on February 4, 1999. The LVTS is an electronic, real-time net settlement network, designed to provide immediate finality and settlement to time-critical transactions. In addition to the Bank of Canada, there are 15 **LVTS participants**.[2] A financial institution can participate directly in the LVTS if it is a member of the Canadian Payments Association, uses the SWIFT telecommunications network, maintains a settlement account at the Bank of Canada, and has agreements regarding borrowing from the Bank of Canada and pledging eligible collateral. All other members of the Canadian Payments Association that are not direct participants in the LVTS are able to arrange LVTS payments through the LVTS participants.

The LVTS has been put in place in order to eliminate **systemic risk**—the risk to the entire payments system due to the inability of one financial institution to fulfill its payment obligations in a timely fashion. In fact, each LVTS payment is subject to real-time risk-control tests to confirm that sufficient collateral is available, and is final and irrevocable in real time. In particular, LVTS participants can make a payment only if they have, in real time (right now), either positive settlement balances in their accounts with the Bank of Canada, posted collateral (such as Government of Canada Treasury bills and bonds), or explicit lines of credit with other participants. As a result, the system will settle at the end of each day even in the face of risk and liquidity problems.

Of course, it is not just Canada that is concerned about systemic risk. Real-time settlement systems were implemented by Sweden in 1986, Germany and Switzerland in 1987, Japan in 1988, Italy in 1989, Belgium and the United Kingdom in 1996, and France, Hong Kong, and the Netherlands in 1997. Moreover, the central banks of the G-10 countries, through the Bank for International Settlements, have developed minimum standards for the operation of the global payment network for large-value funds transfers.

In Canada's LVTS, participants know in real time their large-value, wholesale transactions (over $50 000). Although these transactions account for less than 1% of the total number of transactions, they account for about 94% of the value of transactions. For example, the LVTS is used to settle over 20 000 payments daily, with a

---

[1]For more details, see Donna Howard, "A Primer on the Implementation of Monetary Policy in the LVTS Environment," *Bank of Canada Review* (Autumn, 1998): 57–66; Kevin Clinton, "Implementation of Monetary Policy in a Regime with Zero Reserve Requirements," Bank of Canada Working Paper: 97–98; and "The Framework for the Implementation of Monetary Policy in the Large Value Transfer System Environment," Bank of Canada Release, March 31, 1999.

[2]These are the Big Six (Bank of Montreal, Bank of Nova Scotia, Canadian Imperial Bank of Commerce, National Bank of Canada, Royal Bank of Canada, and the Toronto Dominion Bank), Alberta Treasury Branches, Bank of America National Association, BNP Paribas, Caisse centrale Desjardins du Québec, Central Credit Union, HSBC Bank Canada, ING Bank of Canada, Laurentian Bank of Canada, and State Street Bank and Trust Company.

value of over \$185 billion. This information eliminates most of the uncertainty from settlement balance prediction—the largest reason for financial institutions not being able to hit their target settlement balances with the Bank of Canada in the pre-LVTS system. Settlement of payment obligations among LVTS participants takes place, at the end of each banking day, through the transfer of funds in their settlement accounts at the Bank of Canada. The LVTS uses **multilateral netting**, in which only the net credit or debit position of each participant vis-à-vis all other participants is calculated for settlement, thereby reducing the need for a large amount of settlement balances.

Non-LVTS (ACSS) Transactions

Although the LVTS eliminates the uncertainty from daily wholesale settlement balances prediction, there is still a residual stochastic element in settlement balances from non-LVTS paper-based payments items (such as paper cheques, travellers' cheques, gift certificates, and money orders) and electronic payments items (such as pre-authorized debits and fund transfers, direct deposit items, and debit card transactions). Those items are cleared through the Automated Clearing Settlement System (ACSS), an electronic payments system also operated by the Canadian Payments Association, but without the vigorous risk controls of the LVTS. The ACSS aggregates interbank payments and calculates the net amounts to be transferred from and to each participant's settlement account with the Bank of Canada. The Bank completes the settlement the next day (at midday) through the LVTS.

Regarding the smaller value of ACSS settlements, **direct clearers** with positive clearing balances in the ACSS (that is, with net credit positions) receive an interest payment (calculated daily by the Canadian Payments Association, at the Bank of Canada's target overnight interest rate) to cover their cost of crediting their customers' accounts on the business day before receiving funds in settlement. On the other hand, direct clearers with net debit positions in the ACSS make payments (also at the Bank's target overnight interest rate) to offset their benefit of debiting the accounts of their customers on the day before paying funds in settlement. Interest compensation is included in the clearing balances settled at the Bank of Canada using LVTS funds.[3]

The Bank of Canada's Policy Rate

The overnight market in Canada is the key market for finance and monetary policy. This market is very liquid, with a broad range of participants, the most active of which are deposit-taking institutions and their investment dealer affiliates.[4] The interest rate at which participants borrow and lend overnight funds to each other in the money market is called the **overnight interest rate**. This rate is the shortest-term rate available and forms the base of any term structure of interest rates relation.

The Bank of Canada signals its monetary policy stance by announcing a target for the overnight interest rate (the overnight interest rate is known as the **reference rate**). The target for the overnight rate, known as the **policy rate**, is the main tool the Bank uses to conduct monetary policy. This rate refers to collateralized, market-based overnight transactions. The implementation of the stance of monetary policy is more successful when the reference rate is closer to the policy rate; that is, the closer the overnight rate is to the target for the overnight interest rate.

---

[3]There are 11 ACSS direct clearers in addition to the Bank of Canada—the Big Six, Alberta Treasury Branches, Caisse centrale Desjardins du Québec, Central 1 Credit Union, HSBC Bank Canada, and the Laurentian Bank of Canada. Direct clearers maintain a settlement account at the Bank of Canada and participate directly in the ACSS.

[4]See Eugene Lundrigan and Sari Toll, "The Overnight Market in Canada," *Bank of Canada Review* (Winter 1997–1998): 27–42, for details regarding the evolution of the overnight market.

FIGURE 17-1   Operating Band for the Overnight Interest Rate

The Operating Band for the Overnight Interest Rate

The Bank of Canada implements monetary policy by changing the policy rate, in order to influence other short-term interest rates and the exchange rate. In fact, in normal times the Bank's operational objective is to keep the overnight rate within an **operating band** (also known as a *channel* or *corridor*) of 50 basis points (½ of 1%). Recently, however, and in response to the subprime financial crisis, the Bank of Canada temporarily narrowed the operating band for the overnight interest rate to 25 basis points (¼ of 1%).

As Figure 17-1 shows, the upper limit of the operating band defines the bank rate i_b. The bank rate is the interest rate the Bank charges LVTS participants that require an over-draft loan (advance) to cover negative settlement balances on the books of the Bank at the end of the banking day. The lower limit of the operating band is the rate the Bank pays to LVTS participants with positive settlement balances at the end of the day. The midpoint of the operating band is the Bank of Canada's target for the overnight rate, the operating target of the Bank of Canada's monetary policy. When, for example, the operating band is from 1.5% to 2.0%, the bank rate is 2.0%, the rate the Bank pays on deposits to LVTS participants is 1.5%, and the Bank's target for the overnight interest rate is 1.75%.

Since December 2000, the Bank of Canada has operated under a system of eight "fixed" dates throughout the year for announcing any changes to the target and the operating band for the overnight rate, and has reserved the option of acting between the fixed dates in "extraordinary circumstances." Early in the morning (at 9:00 a.m.) on each of the eight announcement dates, the Bank of Canada announces the target and an operating band of 50 basis points for the overnight interest rate (see the FYI box Monetary Policy Implementation in the LVTS Environment).

A similar channel/corridor system for setting the overnight interest rate is also used by other central banks including the Federal Reserve, the European Central Bank, the Bank of Japan, the Bank of England, the Reserve Bank of Australia, and the Reserve Bank of New Zealand.

The Bank of Canada's Standing Facilities

At the end of each banking day, each LVTS participant must bring its settlement balance with the Bank of Canada close to zero. Of course, it can scarcely be expected that LVTS participants will always be successful in ending up with near-zero settlement balances. The Bank of Canada therefore stands ready (with what we call **standing liquidity facilities**) to lend to or borrow from a participant to bring their settlement balances to zero at the end of the banking day. As already noted, participants also know with certainty the rates applicable to positive and negative settlement balances

FYI

Monetary Policy Implementation in the LVTS Environment

In the LVTS environment, the Bank of Canada operates under a system of eight fixed dates throughout the year for announcing, via a press release (at 9:00 a.m.), the target and the operating band for the overnight interest rate. The upper limit of the operating band defines the bank rate at which the Bank provides overdraft loans to LVTS participants at the end of the day and the lower limit is the rate the Bank pays to LVTS participants with positive settlement balances at the end of the day.

The operating band for the overnight rate, reinforced by the Bank's standing liquidity facilities, and a target level of settlement balances (of roughly $50 million) are currently the framework within which the Bank of Canada implements monetary policy. The midpoint of the operating band, the policy rate, is the operating target of the Bank's monetary policy.

In targeting the midpoint of the operating band, the Bank of Canada will intervene in the overnight market at 11:45 a.m. to conduct open market buyback operations at the target overnight interest rate, if required. In particular, the Bank will use SPRAs if overnight funds are traded above the target for the overnight rate and SRAs if overnight funds are traded below the target for the overnight rate. There will be no Bank of Canada intervention in the overnight market if the overnight rate is around the target rate.

To maintain the desired level of settlement balances, the Bank of Canada must neutralize the net impact of its open market buyback operations and of certain federal government and Bank of Canada flows that potentially affect settlement balances. The neutralization is effected through the shifting (transfer) of federal government deposits (balances) between the government's account at the Bank of Canada and the participants in the auction of government cash balances. The shifting is made through the twice-daily auctions of Receiver General (federal government) balances (the first at 9:15 a.m. and the second at 4:15 p.m.).

The LVTS has a pre-settlement trading period of half an hour, at the end of the banking day (6–6:30 p.m.), to permit participating financial institutions to adjust positions with each other (in the overnight market) at a better return than can be achieved at the Bank of Canada's standing facilities. LVTS participants with settlement imbalances at the end of the banking day use the Bank of Canada's standing facilities to bring their settlement balances to the target level. That is, LVTS participants that require an overdraft loan to cover negative settlement balances on the books of the Bank borrow from the Bank at the bank rate. LVTS participants with positive settlement balances at the end of the day earn (during normal times) the bank rate less 50 basis points.

The Market Timetable

9:00 a.m.	Bank of Canada announces changes (if any) to the target and the operating band for the overnight rate
9:15 a.m.	Auction for (federal) government cash balances
11:45 a.m.	Open market buyback operations (if required)
4:15 p.m.	Auction for (federal) government cash balances
6:00 p.m.	Close of LVTS for client transactions
6:00–6:30 p.m.	Pre-settlement period
8:00 p.m. or earlier	Settlement of LVTS balances at the Bank of Canada

Sources: Donna Howard, "A Primer on the Implementation of Monetary Policy in the LVTS Environment," *Bank of Canada Review* (Autumn 1998): 57–66; and "The Framework for the Implementation of Monetary Policy in the Large Value Transfer System Environment," *Bank of Canada Release*, March 31, 1999. Reprinted with permission.

with the Bank of Canada (see the FYI box Monetary Policy Implementation in the LVTS Environment, and Figure 17-1).

To permit participating financial institutions to adjust positions with each other (i.e., reduce the costs of either positive or negative positions), the LVTS has a pre-settlement trading period of half an hour, at the end of the banking day

(6–6:30 p.m.). The purpose of the pre-settlement trading period is to allow LVTS participants to reduce their LVTS positions (which resulted during the day from their own transactions and those of their clients) at interest rates better than those at the Bank of Canada's standing liquidity facilities. That is, to provide a window for those participants with excess positions to trade with those in deficit, at a better return than can be achieved at the Bank's facilities, to the advantage of both. In fact, the typical bid–ask spread on overnight funds in the interbank market has been less than 1/8%. This is significantly less than the spread of 50 basis points between the rate charged on overdrafts and that paid on deposits by the Bank of Canada after settlement of LVTS multilateral positions.

In general, pre-settlement trading among participants will achieve a zero settlement balance for each participant on wholesale transactions. However, if at the end of the settlement day a participant has a negative balance on the books of the Bank of Canada, the deficit will be financed by a collateralized advance at the bank rate. Participants with positive settlement balances at the end of the day are paid interest at the bank rate less 50 basis points (i.e., the bottom of the operating band). Hence, as long as the bank rate is set so that the market bid-ask spread is within the operating band, participants will resolve their nonzero settlement balances among themselves rather than through the Bank of Canada's standing facilities. In fact, in a fully competitive market, participants would be expected to trade at the midpoint of the operating band for the overnight interest rate.

Clearly, the LVTS and the Bank of Canada's standing liquidity facilities have been set up in such a way so as to ensure a determinate demand for settlement balances, treating the costs of deficits and surpluses symmetrically. That is, the cost of holding excess settlement balances (an opportunity cost of 25 basis points) equals the cost of holding deficit levels of settlement balances (a premium of 25 basis points for an overdraft loan). These cost incentives are very important as they encourage banks to target zero settlement balances at the Bank of Canada and in doing so to deal directly with the market rather than to rely on the Bank's automatic standing liquidity facilities.

The Bank of Canada's Implementation of the Operating Band for the Overnight Interest Rate

It is through its lending and taking deposits from LVTS participants that the Bank of Canada implements its target band for the overnight interest rate. ***If the overnight rate increases toward the upper limit of the operating band, then the Bank will lend at the bank rate to put a ceiling on the overnight rate.*** The bank rate is the ceiling on the overnight rate in the money market for LVTS participants, because they are unlikely to borrow overnight funds at a higher interest rate, since they can borrow at the bank rate from the Bank of Canada.

If the overnight rate declines toward the lower limit of the operating band, then the Bank will accept deposits from LVTS participants at the bank rate less 50 basis points, to put a floor on the overnight rate. The bank rate less 50 basis points is the floor on the overnight rate because LVTS participants are unlikely to lend overnight funds at a lower rate, since they can leave funds on deposit at this rate at the Bank of Canada.

The Market for Settlement Balances and the Channel/ Corridor System for Setting the Overnight Interest Rate

The market for settlement balances (reserves) is where the overnight interest rate is determined, and this is why we turn to a supply and demand analysis of this market to analyze how the tools of monetary policy affect the overnight rate. Our analysis of the market for reserves proceeds in a similar fashion to the analysis of the bond market we conducted in Chapter 4 and describes determination of the overnight interest rate in a symmetric channel/corridor system of interest-rate control such as that in Canada, Australia, England, the euro area, and (until spring 2006) New Zealand.

We derive a demand and supply curve for reserves. Then the market equilibrium in which the quantity of reserves demanded equals the quantity of reserves supplied determines the overnight rate, the interest rate charged on the loans of these reserves.

Demand Curve

To derive the demand curve for reserves, we need to ask what happens to the quantity of reserves demanded by banks, holding everything else constant, as the overnight interest rate, i_{or}, changes. Banks in Canada are no longer required to hold reserves determined through government legislation, as it is with banks in the Federal Reserve system in the United States and the European central bank. Canadian banks, however, hold sufficient cash reserves against their deposit liabilities in order to manage their own short-term liquidity requirements, such as, for example, meeting their depositors' day-to-day demand for cash. We call these reserves *desired reserves*. Desired reserves equal the desired reserve ratio, r_d, times the amount of deposits on which reserves are desired.

Reserves in excess of the desired amounts are called *excess reserves*. Excess reserves are insurance against deposit outflows, and the cost of holding these excess reserves is their opportunity cost, the interest rate that could have been earned on lending these reserves out, minus the interest rate that is earned on these reserves, i_{er}, which in Canada equals the bank rate less 50 basis points, $i_{er} = i_b - 0.50$.

When the overnight rate is above the rate paid on excess reserves, i_{er}, as the overnight rate decreases, the opportunity cost of holding excess reserves falls. Holding everything else constant, the quantity of reserves demanded rises. Consequently, the demand curve for reserves, R^d, slopes downward in Figure 17-2 when the overnight rate is above i_{er}. If, however, the overnight rate begins to fall below the interest rate paid on excess reserves i_{er}, banks would not lend in the overnight market at a lower interest rate. Instead, they would just keep on adding to their holdings of excess reserves indefinitely. The result is that the demand curve for reserves, R^d, becomes flat (infinitely elastic) at i_{er} in Figure 17-2.

MyEconLab
Animation

FIGURE 17-2 Equilibrium in the Market for Reserves

Equilibrium occurs at the intersection of the supply curve R^s and the demand curve R^d at point 1 and an overnight interest rate of i_{or}^*.

Supply Curve

The supply of reserves, R^s, can be broken up into two components: the amount of reserves that are supplied by the Bank of Canada's open market operations, called *nonborrowed reserves* (NBR), and the amount of reserves borrowed from the Bank of Canada, called *borrowed reserves* (BR). The primary cost of borrowing from the Bank of Canada is the interest rate the Bank charges on these loans, the bank rate (i_b), which is set at a fixed amount above the overnight rate target and thus changes when the target changes.

Because borrowing overnight funds from other banks is a substitute for borrowing from the Bank of Canada, if the overnight interest rate i_{or} is below the bank rate i_b, then banks will not borrow from the Bank of Canada and borrowed reserves will be zero, because borrowing in the overnight funds market is cheaper. Thus, as long as i_{or} remains below i_b, the supply of reserves will just equal the amount of nonborrowed reserves supplied by the Bank of Canada, NBR, and so the supply curve will be vertical as shown in Figure 17-2. However, as the overnight rate begins to rise above the bank rate, banks would want to keep borrowing more and more at i_b and then lending out the proceeds in the overnight funds market at the higher rate, i_{or}. The result is that the supply curve becomes flat (infinitely elastic) at i_b, as shown in Figure 17-2.

Market Equilibrium

Market equilibrium occurs where the quantity of reserves demanded equals the quantity supplied, $R^d = R^s$. Equilibrium therefore occurs at the intersection of the demand curve R^d and the supply curve R^s at point 1 in Figure 17-2, with an equilibrium overnight interest rate of i_{or}^*. When the overnight interest rate is above the equilibrium rate at i_{or}^2, there are more reserves supplied than demanded (excess supply) and so the overnight rate falls to i_{or}^*, as shown by the downward arrow. When the overnight interest rate is below the equilibrium rate at i_{or}^1, there are more reserves demanded than supplied (excess demand) and so the overnight rate rises as shown by the upward arrow.

APPLICATION

How the Bank of Canada's Operating Procedures Limit Fluctuations in the Overnight Interest Rate

An important advantage of the Bank of Canada's current monetary policy procedures is that they limit fluctuations in the overnight interest rate. We can use our supply and demand analysis of the market for reserves to see why.

Suppose that initially the equilibrium overnight interest rate is at the overnight rate target of i_{or}^* in Figure 17-3. If the demand for reserves has a large unexpected increase, the demand curve would shift to the right to R_2^d, where it now intersects the supply curve for reserves on the flat portion where the equilibrium overnight rate i_{or}^2 equals the bank rate, i_b. No matter how far the demand curve shifts to the right, the equilibrium overnight rate i_{or}^2 will just stay at i_b because borrowed reserves will just continue to increase, matching the increase in demand. Similarly, if the demand for reserves has a large unexpected decrease, the demand curve would shift to the left to R_1^d, and the supply curve intersects the demand curve on its flat portion where the equilibrium overnight rate i_{or}^1 equals the interest rate paid on excess reserves, $i_{er} = i_b - 0.50$. No matter how far the demand curve shifts to the left, the equilibrium overnight interest rate i_{or}^1 will stay at i_{er}, because excess reserves will just keep on increasing so that the quantity demanded of reserves equals the quantity of nonborrowed reserves supplied.

Our analysis therefore shows that the ***Bank of Canada's operating procedures limit the fluctuations of the overnight interest rate to between*** $i_{er} = i_b - 0.50$ ***and*** i_b. If the range between i_{er} and i_b is kept narrow enough, then the fluctuations around the target rate will be small.

A rightward shift in the demand curve for reserves to R_2^d will raise the equilibrium overnight rate to a maximum of $i_{or}^2 = i_b$ while a leftward shift of the demand curve to R_1^d will lower the overnight rate to a minimum of $i_{or}^1 = i_{er}(= i_b - 0.50)$.

FIGURE 17-3 How the Bank of Canada's Operating Procedures Limit Fluctuations in the Overnight Interest Rate

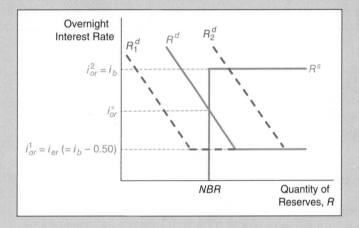

The Bank of Canada's Approach to Monetary Policy

The goal of the Bank of Canada's current monetary policy is to keep the inflation rate within a target range of 1% to 3%, with the midpoint of the inflation target range, 2%, being the most desirable outcome (see also the FYI box Price-Level Targeting Versus Inflation-Rate Targeting). In setting its inflation targets, the Bank

FIGURE 17-4 Inflation Rates and Inflation Targets for Canada, 1980–2011

Canada has significantly reduced the rate of inflation and eventually achieved its inflation targets.

Source: Ben S. Bernanke, Thomas Laubach, Frederic S. Mishkin, and Adam S. Poson, *Inflation Targeting: Lessons from the International Experience* (Princeton, NJ: Princeton University Press, 1999), updates from the same sources, and www.rbnz.govt.nz/statistics/econind/a3/ha3.xls.

of Canada uses the rate of change in the consumer price index (CPI), because it is the most commonly used and understood price measure in Canada. Although the Bank's targets are specified in terms of "headline CPI" (all items), the Bank uses "core CPI," which excludes volatile components such as food, energy, and the effect of indirect taxes, as a measure of the headline rate's trend. Also, defining the inflation targets in terms of ranges provides the Bank of Canada sufficient flexibility to deal with supply shocks beyond those already taken care of by the exclusion of volatile components from core inflation.

Figure 17-4 shows what has happened to the Canadian inflation rate since February 26, 1991, after the Bank's governor and the minister of finance jointly announced a series of declining inflation targets, with a band of plus and minus one percentage point around them. In what follows, we examine the tools used by the Bank of Canada to implement monetary policy, leaving a detailed analysis of the Bank's monetary policy for Chapter 18.

How Monetary Policy Affects the Economy

The Bank of Canada affects interest rates and the level of economic activity by changing the target and operating band for the overnight interest rate. As we saw in Chapter 6, interest rates on different assets tend to move together over time. Hence, changes in the target for the overnight interest rate (and thus the bank rate, i_b) influence other rates, such as the prime rate (the interest rate banks charge to their best customers) and the interest rates on bank deposits and mortgages. These changes in interest rates may also lead to changes in the exchange rate. The level of short-term interest rates and the exchange rate of the Canadian dollar determine the **monetary conditions** in which the economy operates.

The concept of monetary conditions, introduced by the Bank of Canada in its conduct of monetary policy in the early 1990s, focuses on the effect on the economy of both short-term interest rates and the exchange rate. Changes in monetary conditions affect the economy and the Bank's ultimate objective, the inflation rate, only indirectly and are usually felt over a period of several months to several years. This means that the Bank of Canada must always be forward looking in its conduct of monetary policy, anticipating the level of monetary conditions needed today to achieve its ultimate goal of low and stable inflation in the future.

FIGURE 17-5   How the Bank of Canada Keeps the Rate of Inflation from Falling Below the Target Range

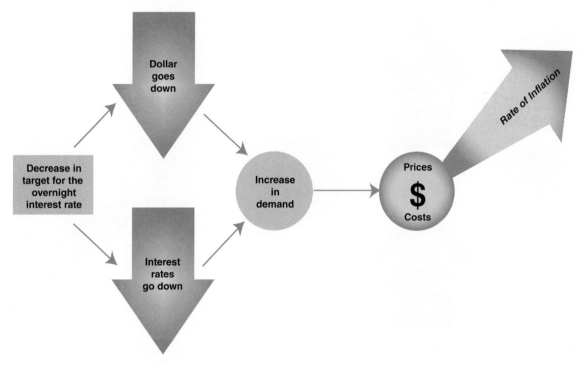

Source: Bank of Canada website: www.bankofcanada.ca. Reprinted with permission.

As an example, suppose that the Bank of Canada expects the economy to slow down and wishes to ease monetary conditions. It lowers the target and operating band for the overnight interest rate.[5] As you can see in Figure 17-5, this reduces interest rates and the value of the dollar and leads to an increase in the supply of money, aggregate demand, and the price level, thereby preventing the inflation rate from falling below the target range of 1% to 3%.

In the opposite case, if the Bank expects the economy to be exceeding its capacity at some point in the future, it raises the operating band in order to prevent inflationary pressures from building. The consequent increase in interest rates and the value of the dollar lead to a decline in the supply of money, aggregate demand, and the price level, thereby preventing the inflation rate from moving above the Bank's target range of 1% to 3%—see Figure 17-6.

Hence, by changing the target and operating band for the overnight rate, the Bank of Canada sends a signal regarding the direction that it would like interest rates and the money supply to take. A rise in the target and operating band, and thus the bank rate, is a signal that the Bank would like to see higher interest rates and less money in the economy. A fall in the target and operating band is a signal that the Bank would like lower interest rates and more money.

Nominal Interest Rates and Monetary Policy

The Bank of Canada uses the *nominal* overnight interest rate as its operating instrument, but as you will learn in Chapter 25, the effects of monetary policy on economic activity stem from how the *real* interest rate, *r*, rather than the nominal interest

---

[5]For example, the Bank might lower the operating band by 25 basis points from 1.5% to 2.0% to 1.25% to 1.75%.

FIGURE 17-6 How the Bank of Canada Keeps the Rate of Inflation from Moving Above the Target Range

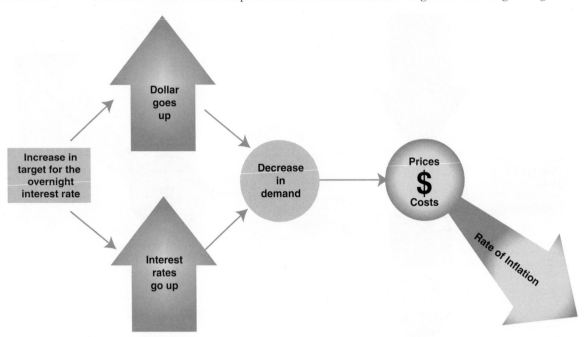

Source: Bank of Canada website: www.bankofcanada.ca. Reprinted with permission.

rate, *i*, affects consumption and investment spending. In fact, the current interest rate targeting approach is based on the belief that it is the real *long-term* interest rate, and not the real short-term interest rate, that affects consumer and business decisions.

How is it that changes in short-term nominal interest rates (such as the Bank of Canada's overnight rate) affect short- and long-term real interest rates? Under the "new Keynesian" assumption of *sticky* prices (that is, under the assumption that prices do not adjust instantaneously to clear the markets), an expansionary monetary policy that lowers the short-term nominal interest rate will also lower the short-term real interest rate, since the aggregate price level adjusts slowly over time and there is not much change in the inflation rate. Moreover, according to the expectations hypothesis of the term structure of interest rates (discussed in detail in Chapter 6), the decline in short-term interest rates will also lead to a decline in long-term interest rates and ultimately to increases in consumer and investment spending.

This transmission mechanism works well even when the short-term nominal interest rate is at or close to zero. With a nominal interest rate of zero, a commitment by the central bank to expansionary monetary policy raises the expected inflation rate, π^e, reduces the real interest rate, *r*, and leads to a rise in aggregate output. Thus, expansionary monetary policy could stimulate spending even when the short-term nominal interest rate is at zero. In fact, this mechanism is the key element in monetarist discussions of why an expansionary monetary policy could have prevented the sharp decline in output in the United States during the Great Depression, why it would have helped the Japanese economy when nominal interest rates fell to near zero in the late 1990s, and why it could help cope with the recent financial crisis and the global economic meltdown.

However, the collapse of stable relationships in financial markets may be causing the term structure of interest rate relationships on which the Keynesian transmission mechanism depends to loosen. For example, the U.S. Federal Reserve raised the target federal funds rate in 17 consecutive meetings from June 2004 to July 2006, from 1% to 5.25%, but long-term interest rates in the United States and around the world declined for most of this period. It has been argued that the reason long-term interest rates did not respond over this period of monetary tightening was the adoption of an inflation-targeting approach to monetary policy by many countries and increased competition from China and India in labour and product markets that contributed to price stability and put downward pressure on long-term interest rates by reducing inflationary expectations.

Similarly, the recent decline in the federal funds rate to its current range of 0% to 0.25% from 5.25% in August of 2007 has not led to the desired decline in long-term interest rates. Why? Because the turmoil in the financial markets has increased risk premiums, thereby keeping long-term nominal interest rates high. Moreover, with collapsing asset prices (stock and real estate prices), there has been an increase in deflationary expectations, which led to a rise in real interest rates. This has the potential to make monetary policy highly contractionary, despite falling short-term nominal interest rates.

Now that we understand how the overnight rate is determined and the Bank of Canada's approach to monetary policy, we can examine how changes in the three tools of monetary policy—open market operations, settlement balances management, and Bank of Canada lending—affect the market for reserves and the equilibrium overnight interest rate.

Open Market Operations

Open market operations are an important monetary policy tool for many central banks around the world, because they are the primary determinants of changes in interest rates and the monetary base, the main source of fluctuations in the money supply. Open market purchases expand bank reserves and the monetary base, thereby lowering short-term interest rates and raising the money supply. Open market sales shrink bank reserves and the monetary base, raising short-term interest rates and lowering the money supply.

The Bank of Canada, however, stopped conducting open market operations in Government of Canada Treasury bills and bonds in 1994, and its most common operations since then have been repurchase transactions with **primary dealers**—the Big Six and the major investment dealers that have signed a Purchase and Resale Agreement with the Bank of Canada. In particular, the Bank uses **special Purchase and Resale Agreements (special PRAs or SPRAs)**, commonly referred to as **repos** or **specials**, as a tool to reduce undesired upward pressure on the overnight interest rate, and **Sale and Repurchase Agreements (SRAs)**, commonly referred to as **reverse repos** or **reverses**, as a tool to reduce undesired downward pressure on the overnight rate.

Let's see how the Bank of Canada uses special PRAs and SRAs in order to reinforce the target for the overnight interest rate during the course of a day.

Special PRAs

Assume that the operating band for the overnight interest rate is 1.5% to 2% and that the Bank of Canada is targeting the overnight rate at the midpoint of the band, at 1.75%. If overnight funds are traded at a rate higher than the target rate of 1.75%, then the Bank of Canada enters into special PRAs, typically at 11:45 a.m. at a price that works out to a 1.75% interest rate, the midpoint of the operating band. That is, the Bank purchases Government of Canada Treasury bills or bonds, with an agreement

FIGURE 17-7 The Mechanics of a Special PRA Operation

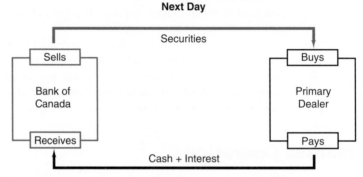

Note: In a special PRA (SPRA), the Bank of Canada buys securities from a primary dealer in exchange for cash and the primary dealer agrees to buy the securities back (repurchase them) the next day at the original price plus interest, regardless of what happens in the market. In that arrangement, the primary dealer gets an overnight collateralized loan and the Bank of Canada gets some interest.

that the seller will repurchase them one business day later (see Figure 17-7 regarding the mechanics of a special PRA).

Since the securities are placed with the Canadian Depository for Securities (CDS), Canada's central securities depository owned and operated by the financial community, the title of the securities changes hands by electronic instruction. The balance sheets of the Bank of Canada and the primary dealers look like this:

Bank of Canada				Primary Dealers			
Assets		Liabilities		Assets		Liabilities	
Government securities	+$100	Settlement balances	+$100	Settlement balances	+$100	SPRAs	+$100

Hence, **special Purchase and Resale Agreements (SPRAs) relieve undesired upward pressure on the overnight interest rate.**

SRAs

If, on the other hand, overnight funds are traded at a rate below the target rate of 1.75%, then the Bank of Canada enters into SRAs, in which the Bank sells government securities and the buyer agrees to sell them back to the Bank one business day later. The balance sheets of the Bank of Canada and the direct clearers now look like this:

Bank of Canada			Primary Dealers		
Assets	Liabilities		Assets		Liabilities
	Settlement balances	−$100	Settlement balances	−$100	
	SRAs	+$100	Government securities	+$100	

Hence, ***Sale and Repurchase Agreements (SRAs) alleviate undesired downward pressure on the overnight financing rate.***

Because the effects on settlement balances of SPRAs and SRAs are reversed on the day the agreement matures, SPRAs and SRAs are actually temporary open market operations. Moreover, as you will see in the next section, because the effects on settlement balances of SPRAs and SRAs are typically neutralized by the end of the day by the Bank of Canada, there is no change at the end of the day in the level of settlement balances in the system.

Advantages of SPRAs and SRAs

The Bank of Canada's repurchase transactions, either special PRAs or SRAs, have several advantages over other tools of monetary policy. They occur at the initiative of the Bank of Canada, which has complete control over their volume, and are easily reversed. Moreover, the Bank of Canada can enter into multiple rounds of open market buyback operations and can also conduct these operations outside of the regular timeframe.

Settlement Balances Management

In addition to targeting the overnight interest rate at the midpoint of the operating band, the Bank of Canada also targets the level of settlement balances in the system. Typically, the target level of settlement balances is announced the previous day. Initially, the Bank targeted a daily level of settlement balances of zero or greater (usually $25 million), but recently, because of pressures on the overnight rate, the Bank made several adjustments to the target level of settlement balances.

However, in targeting the overnight interest rate at the midpoint of the operating band, the Bank of Canada usually neutralizes the impact on settlement balances of any open market buyback operations. For example, the Bank neutralizes special PRA operations, so as not to leave the system in a surplus position at the end of the day, in which case at least one LVTS participant would end up holding positive settlement balances with the Bank of Canada earning the bank rate less 50 basis points, $i_b - 0.50$. Similarly, the Bank of Canada neutralizes SRA operations, so as not to leave the system in a deficit position, in which case at least one LVTS participant would end up holding negative settlement balances with the Bank paying the bank rate, i_b.

Moreover, being the federal government's fiscal agent, the Bank of Canada usually neutralizes the net impact on settlement balances of certain federal government payment flows and Bank of Canada transactions.

The neutralization of the effects of open market buyback operations, public-sector flows on the level of settlement balances, and the adjustment of the level of settlement balances are effected through shifts (transfers) of government deposits (balances) between the government's account at the Bank of Canada and the government's accounts at the LVTS participants. In the pre-LVTS system, government deposit transfers between the government's accounts at banks and its account at the Bank of Canada were effected by the Bank of Canada's daily **drawdowns** (transfers of government deposits from the banks to the Bank of Canada) and **redeposits** (transfers of government deposits from the Bank of Canada to the banks). However, with the instantaneous transfers of funds allowed by the LVTS environment, the drawdown/redeposit mechanism is not a practical tool for government deposit shifting. This is so because the Bank of Canada is not able to debit the government's account with a bank on a day with a net disbursement by the government. In the LVTS environment, the Bank of Canada uses twice-daily auctions of federal government (Receiver General) balances, the first at 9:15 a.m. (which are collateralized) and the second at 4:15 p.m. (which are uncollateralized), when all the flows affecting the Bank of Canada's balance sheet are known. This neutralizes the effect of market buyback operations and of public-sector flows, and also adjusts the level of settlement balances.

Receiver General Auctions

To illustrate the process for neutralizing public sector flows using auctions of Receiver General balances, suppose that there is a net government receipt of $100 (i.e., the government's receipts from the public exceed its payments to the public by $100). Net receipts are drawn on the government's deposits at the LVTS participants, creating claims on the LVTS participants in favour of the Bank of Canada and ultimately reducing settlement balances by an amount equal to the government's net receipts. In the absence of any offsetting transactions by the Bank of Canada, through the workings of supply and demand, a decline in settlement balances will normally cause an increase in the overnight interest rate, as many LVTS participants would have to borrow more to meet their settlement obligations.

However, in targeting the overnight interest rate, the Bank of Canada will neutralize the net government receipt by arranging a net increase of $100 in the government deposit auctions to leave the system unchanged. This procedure results in the following balance sheets for the Bank and the LVTS participants:

Bank of Canada				LVTS Participants			
Assets		Liabilities		Assets		Liabilities	
		Government deposits	−100	Settlement balances	+100	Government deposits	+100
		Settlement balances	+100				

Note that government deposits at the Bank of Canada are reduced by $100 and at the same time the settlement balances of the LVTS participants are increased by $100.

If, instead of a net receipt by the government, there were a net disbursement of $100 (i.e., the government's payments to the public exceed its receipts from the public by $100), then the financial system's settlement balances would increase by the same amount. This would prompt a fall in the overnight interest rate, as many LVTS participants would have to borrow less to meet their settlement obligations. The Bank's neutralization process would prevent a decline in the overnight rate by reducing the banking system's settlement balances. This would involve LVTS transfers of $100 (i.e., the difference between the total amount of government balances maturing and the total amount of government balances auctioned) from the government's accounts at the participating institutions to the government's account at the Bank. This procedure results in the following T-accounts:

Bank of Canada				LVTS Participants			
Assets		Liabilities		Assets		Liabilities	
		Government deposits	+100	Settlement balances	−100	Government deposits	−100
		Settlement balances	−100				

In this case government deposits at the Bank of Canada are increased by $100 and at the same time the clearing balances of the participants are reduced by $100.

Swaps with the Exchange Fund Account

When the Bank of Canada transfers government balances, it usually brings onto its balance sheet Exchange Fund Account assets to back its liabilities. It does so by arranging a swap with the Exchange Fund Account, which holds the country's foreign exchange reserves. This involves a spot purchase and a simultaneous forward sale of foreign exchange. To illustrate the operation, assume that the Bank temporarily buys $100 of foreign currency assets from the Exchange Fund Account. It credits the government's account on its own books and the operation results in the following balance sheets for the Bank and the government:

Bank of Canada				Government of Canada			
Assets		Liabilities		Assets		Liabilities	
Foreign exchange	+100	Government deposits	+100	Exchange Account Fund	−100		
				Deposits at the Bank of Canada	+100		

We see that government deposit balances at the Bank of Canada increase and these balances can then be transferred to participants to increase settlement balances, as we saw earlier.

Although the spot transaction adds to the government deposits at the Bank of Canada and enables the Bank to auction government balances, the forward contract between the Bank and the Exchange Fund Account does not affect the settlement balances of participating financial institutions. The Bank simply sells foreign exchange to the Exchange Fund Account in the future at a price agreed upon today. The advantage to the Bank of Canada of using swap transactions with the Exchange Fund Account is that it can bring a temporary change in the level of settlement balances or respond to some event that the Bank thinks will have a significant but not long-lived effect.

As we will learn in Chapter 20, the foreign exchange reserves held in the Exchange Fund Account can also be used by the Bank of Canada in international financial transactions to prevent undesirable movements in the exchange rate. For example, a Bank of Canada sale of domestic currency and corresponding purchase of foreign assets in the foreign exchange market leads to a gain in international reserves, an increase in the monetary base and the money supply, and a depreciation of the domestic currency. A Bank purchase of domestic currency and corresponding sale of foreign exchange leads to a loss of international reserves, a decline in the monetary base and the money supply, and an appreciation of the domestic currency. We shall discuss such foreign exchange interventions in detail in Chapter 20.

The Target Level of Settlement Balances

In addition to the auctions of Receiver General balances, the Bank of Canada can also adjust the target level of settlement balances if warranted by conditions in the overnight market. That is, the Bank retains the right to adjust the targeted level of settlement balances higher or lower than the typical setting, depending on pressures on the overnight rate.

The Bank of Canada, however, is not always able to completely neutralize special PRA and SRA operations and public sector flows so that the actual level of settlement balances ends up being higher or lower than the target level. However, deviations of the actual level of settlement balances from the target level appear to have insignificant effects on the overnight interest rate the day that they occur, unlike pre-announced changes to the target level of settlement balances, which appear to have a significant effect on the overnight interest rate.

APPLICATION

Monetary Control in the Channel/Corridor System

Suppose that the operating band is 1.5% to 2% and the Bank of Canada expects the economy to exceed its capacity in the near future. To prevent inflationary pressures from building, the Bank wishes to tighten monetary policy by raising the target and operating band by 25 basis points. In one of the eight fixed days for announcing changes to the target and operating band for the overnight rate, the Bank announces, at 9:00 a.m., that it is adjusting the target and operating band up from 1.5% to 2% to 1.75% to 2.25%. From this announcement, LVTS participants know that the bank rate shifts from 2% to 2.25%, the rate on positive settlement balances shifts from 1.5% to 1.75%, and that the Bank of Canada's new target overnight rate, the midpoint of the operating band, shifts from 1.75% to 2%.

Later in the day, at 11:45 a.m., if overnight funds are trading below the target overnight rate (the midpoint of the operating band), the Bank of Canada enters into SRAs to enforce the new target for the overnight rate. That is, it sells government securities to primary dealers, who pay for the securities with settlement balances and agree to sell the securities back to the Bank of Canada on the next business day, at a price that works out to an annual interest rate of 2%—the midpoint of the new operating band. Assuming that the Bank of Canada enters into SRAs in the amount of $100, the T-accounts of the Bank of Canada and the primary dealers will be

Bank of Canada			Primary Dealers		
Assets	Liabilities		Assets		Liabilities
	Settlement balances	−100	Settlement balances	−100	
	SRAs	+100	Government securities	+100	

The clearing banks find that their settlement balances have declined by $100, and because they had not been holding any excess reserves, their holdings of settlement balances are $100 short. Assuming that no other transactions occur during the day, at 4:15 p.m. the Bank of Canada neutralizes the effect on aggregate settlement balances of its issue of SRAs by auctioning off government deposits. The Bank's neutralization process involves auctioning off $100 of government deposits and paying those LVTS participants taking government deposits with settlement balances, bringing the amount of aggregate settlement balances back to zero. The balance sheets of the Bank of Canada and the LVTS participants now look like this:

Bank of Canada			LVTS Participants			
Assets	Liabilities		Assets		Liabilities	
	Settlement balances	+100	Settlement balances	+100	Government securities	+100
	Government deposits	−100				

The Bank of Canada's monetary tightening has been effected through the management of settlement balances, during the course of the day, with no change in the aggregate settlement balances of deposit-taking institutions. As already noted, the change in the overnight rate will influence other interest rates and the level of monetary conditions in which the economy operates.

Bank of Canada Lending

The facility at which banks can borrow reserves from the Bank of Canada is called the **standing lending facility**. The easiest way to understand how the Bank of Canada affects the volume of borrowed reserves is by looking at how the standing lending facility operates.

Operation of the Standing Lending Facility

As already noted, the Bank of Canada offers a lending facility, standing ready to lend (upon presentation of suitable collateral) overnight settlement balances to LVTS participants with negative clearing balances at the end of the business day. The lending rate is the bank rate, denoted by i_b in Figure 17-2 (on page 409), and is 25 basis points higher than the target overnight interest rate, so as to penalize participants for not using the overnight interbank market. LVTS participants know with certainty the lending rate applicable to their negative settlement balances with the Bank of Canada.

To see how the standing lending facility works, let's see what happens if there is a large increase in the demand for reserves. This situation is analyzed in Figure 17-8. Suppose that initially the demand and supply curves for reserves intersect at point 1 so that the overnight rate is at its target level, i_{or}^*. Now the increase in reserves shifts the demand curve to R_2^d and the equilibrium moves to point 2. The result is that borrowed reserves increase from zero to BR and the overnight rate rises to i_b and can rise no further. The standing lending facility has put a ceiling on the overnight interest rate of i_{or}.

FIGURE 17-8   How the Bank of Canada's Standing Facility Puts a Ceiling on the Overnight
Interest Rate

The rightward shift of the demand curve for reserves from R_1^d to R_2^d moves the equilibrium from point
1 to point 2 where $i_{or} = i_b$ and borrowed reserves increase from zero to *BR*.

Lender of Last Resort

In addition to its use as a standing liquidity facility to reinforce the operating band
for the overnight interest rate, Bank of Canada lending is also important in preventing financial panics. In fact, one of the Bank's most important roles is to be
the **lender of last resort** in the Canadian economy.[6] It provides emergency lending
assistance (against eligible collateral) for a maximum period of six months (which
can be extended for periods up to six months as many times as the Bank judges) to
solvent (but illiquid) deposit-taking institutions to prevent bank failures from spin-
ning further out of control, thereby preventing bank and financial panics. The rate
that the Bank normally charges on these loans is the bank rate, although the Bank
has discretion to charge a higher rate. In providing emergency lending assistance,
the Bank always makes a judgment with respect to the trade-off between morally
hazardous behaviour and the costs in terms of financial stability. Last-resort lending is a particularly effective way to provide reserves to the banking system during
a banking crisis because reserves are immediately channelled to the banks that need
them most.

At first glance, it might appear as though the presence of the CDIC, which
insures depositors from losses due to a bank's failure up to a limit of $100 000
per account, would make the lender-of-last-resort function of the Bank of Canada
superfluous. (The CDIC is described in detail in Chapter 10.) There are two reasons
why this is not the case. First, it is important to recognize that the CDIC's insurance fund amounts to a small fraction of the amount of deposits outstanding. If a
large number of bank failures occurred, the CDIC would not be able to cover all the
depositors' losses. Indeed, the failures of deposit-based financial institutions in the
1980s and early 1990s in Canada, described in Chapter 10, led to large losses and a
shrinkage in the CDIC's insurance fund, which reduced the CDIC's ability to cover
depositors' losses. This fact has not weakened the confidence of small depositors in
the banking system because the Bank of Canada has been ready to stand behind the
banks to provide whatever reserves are needed to prevent bank panics. Second, the

---

[6] Regarding the policy framework that governs the Bank of Canada's lender-of-last-resort activities, see Daniel Fred
and Walter Engert, "The Bank of Canada as Lender of Last Resort," *Bank of Canada Review* (Winter 2004–2005).

large-denomination deposits in the banking system are not guaranteed by the CDIC because they exceed the $100 000 limit. A loss of confidence in the banking system could still lead to runs on banks from the large-denomination depositors, and bank panics could still occur despite the existence of the CDIC.

The importance of the Bank of Canada's role as lender of last resort is, if anything, more important today because of the 2007–2009 global financial crisis and economic downturn. Figure 17-9, which shows Bank of Canada advances to members of the Canadian Payments Association, reveals that the Bank of Canada advanced considerable funds in the recent past to financial institutions facing liquidity crises. Unfortunately, the Bank of Canada's lending policy has not always been successful in preventing financial crises. Two examples of the use of the Bank's lending weapon to avoid bank panics are the provisions of huge loans to the Canadian Commercial Bank and the Northland Bank in 1985 (see the Inside the Central Bank box Emergency Lending Assistance to Troubled Banks).

Advantages and Disadvantages of the Bank's Lending Policy

The most important advantage of the Bank of Canada's lending policy is that the Bank can use it to perform its role of lender of last resort and stabilize the financial system in times of stress. Experiences in the 1980s and early 1990s, the Black Monday crash, the terrorist destruction of the World Trade Center, and the recent global financial crisis indicate that this role has become more important in the past couple of decades.

In the past, Bank of Canada advances were used as a tool of monetary policy, with the bank rate changed to affect interest rates and the money supply. However, because the decisions to take out loans are made by banks and are therefore not completely controlled by the Bank of Canada, while open market buyback operations are completely controlled by the Bank of Canada, the use of lending policy to conduct monetary policy has little to recommend it. This is why the Bank of Canada moved to the current channel/corridor system of monetary control in which the bank rate is not used to set the overnight rate, but is only a backup facility to prevent the overnight interest rate from moving outside the operating band.

FIGURE 17-9 Bank of Canada Advances to Members of the Canadian Payments Association, 1975–2011 (in millions of dollars)

INSIDE THE CENTRAL BANK — Emergency Lending Assistance to Troubled Banks

Canadian Commercial and Northland. In 1985, there was public concern over the quality of the assets of two small Alberta-based banks—the Canadian Commercial Bank and the Northland Bank—which had made many bad loans. Larger depositors, whose accounts exceeded the $60 000 limit insured (at that time) by the CDIC, began to withdraw their deposits, and the failure of the banks was imminent. Because the immediate failure of Canadian Commercial and Northland would have had repercussions on other vulnerable banks, the Bank of Canada, under the advice from the Inspector General of Banks (the predecessor of the Office of the Superintendent of Financial Institutions Canada) made extraordinary advances. Total emergency lending assistance amounted to $1.8 billion so that depositors, including the largest, would not suffer any losses.

In doing this, the Bank of Canada was following the precedent established in 1984 by the Federal Reserve's rescue of Continental Illinois National Bank. Continental Illinois had made bad loans (primarily to businesses in the energy industry and to foreign countries), and rumours of financial trouble in early May 1984 caused large depositors to withdraw over US$10 billion of deposits from the bank.

The Federal Deposit Insurance Corporation (FDIC) arranged a rescue effort in July 1984 that culminated in a US$4.5 billion commitment of funds to save the bank. Still, the Fed had to lend Continental Illinois over US$5 billion—making the Bank of Canada's $1.8 billion advances to Canadian Commercial and Northland look like small potatoes! Although Continental Illinois was taken over by the FDIC, the Fed's action prevented further bank failures, and a potential bank panic was averted.

The Bank of Canada, however, was not as successful in preventing a bank crisis. With the failure of Canadian Commercial and Northland, rumours of financial trouble caused many large depositors to withdraw large deposits from the Bank of British Columbia, Mercantile Bank, and Continental Bank. By the time Mercantile was acquired by the National Bank of Canada, the Bank of British Columbia by the Hongkong Bank of Canada, and Continental by Lloyds Bank of Canada, the Bank of Canada had provided emergency lending assistance of more than $5 billion (see Figure 17-9). The loss of public confidence in the Canadian banking system led to the financial reforms of 1987–1992 and the consolidating of financial institution supervision under the Office of the Superintendent of Financial Institutions Canada.

Nonconventional Monetary Policy Tools During the Global Financial Crisis

On April 21, 2009, the Bank of Canada lowered the overnight rate target by 0.25 of a percentage point to 0.25% and also made some changes to its operating framework for the implementation of monetary policy. In particular, the Bank narrowed the operating band for the overnight interest rate to 25 basis points, from 0.25% to 0.5%, with 0.5% being the bank rate and 0.25% being the deposit rate. The Bank also announced that the target for the overnight rate will be the bottom of the operating band (that is, 0.25%) rather than the midpoint of the operating band, thus setting an effective lower bound for the overnight rate.

As the policy rate had reached the effective lower bound, the Bank of Canada had lost its usual ability to signal policy changes via changes in the policy rate. Moreover, with short-term interest rates close to zero, the Bank of Canada had also lost its ability to lower long-term interest rates by lowering short-term interest rates.

For these reasons, many central banks around the world, including the Bank of Japan, the Federal Reserve, and the Bank of England, have departed from the traditional interest-rate targeting approach to monetary policy and are focusing on their balance sheet instead, using quantitative measures of monetary policy. These non-interest-rate tools, known as **nonconventional monetary policy tools**, are designed to deal with the **zero-lower-bound problem**, in which the central bank is unable to lower short-term interest rates further because they have hit a floor of zero or near zero. The Bank of Canada also considered such quantitative measures and has recently identified three alternative instruments that it would consider using in an environment with low short-term (nominal) interest rates: conditional statements about the future path of the policy rate, quantitative easing, and credit easing.

Commitment to Future Policy Actions

Because nominal interest rates cannot fall below zero, the Bank of Canada loses its ability to influence long-term interest rates, using conventional monetary policy tools, when the overnight interest rate is close to zero. In the face of this zero lower bound constraint, to achieve its inflation objectives, the Bank of Canada introduced **conditional statements** about the future path of its policy rate as an alternative monetary policy tool.

The objective of such conditional commitments is to align market expectations of future short-term interest rates with those of the Bank to achieve desirable outcomes in interest rates throughout the term structure.

For example, on April 21, 2009, the Bank of Canada lowered the policy rate by 0.25 of a percentage point to 0.25%, and it also committed to holding the policy rate at 0.25% until the second quarter of 2010, conditional on the outlook for inflation. Such a conditional commitment by the Bank of Canada to keep the policy rate at 25 basis points for a long period was expected to shape market expectations of future short-term interest rates and lower long-term interest rates, since long-term rates are averages of current and expected future short-term interest rates (plus risk premiums). Michael Woodford of Columbia Universiy has referred to such a strategy as **management of expectations**.

Quantitative Easing

Quantitative easing refers to the purchase of financial assets by the central bank through the creation of excess reserves (excess settlement balances in the Canadian case) for banks. This is the same as open market operations, but extends to include private financial assets such as corporate bonds and commercial paper. By buying financial assets, the central bank affects the cost of borrowing by pushing up the price of the purchased assets and reducing their yields. Moreover, by creating excess reserves for banks, the central bank encourages banks to lend more to households and businesses, thereby increasing the level of economic activity.

Quantitative easing is regarded as an unconventional form of monetary policy, very different from interest-rate targeting that central banks and the financial markets around the world have used over the last 20 years. It targets the amount of liquidity provided by the central bank instead of targeting the price of liquidity (as interest-rate targeting does). This policy action might also involve the purchase of government or non-government securities with long terms to maturity, thereby affecting long-term rather than short-term interest rates; conventional open market operations target the short-term interest rate. The Bank of Japan used quantitative easing during the early 2000s, as did the Federal Reserve and the Bank of England during the recent global financial crisis. Quantitative easing, however, is a high-risk monetary policy tool as it runs the risk of going too far, pumping too much money into the economy and possibly creating inflation and even hyperinflation.

To see how quantitative easing works, consider Figure 17-10, which depicts the symmetric corridor system of Figure 17-2, in which the reserve demand is horizontal

FIGURE 17-10 Quantitative Easing in the Channel/Corridor System

at $i_b - 0.50$ and the reserve supply is horizontal at i_b, where both rates are tied to the Bank of Canada's target for the overnight interest rate, i_{or}^*. Initially, the supply curve R_1^s intersects the demand curve R^d in its downward-sloped section at (point 1 and) the target overnight interest rate i_{or}^*.

The central bank can arbitrarily increase the supply of reserves (settlement balances) to undertake expanded asset purchases, shifting its reserve supply schedule from R_1^s to R_2^s. But if it goes beyond a certain point (designated 2 in Figure 17-10), then the overnight interest rate will not equal the central bank's interest rate target, i_{or}^*, but rather the interest rate paid on excess reserves, $i_{er}(= i_b - 0.50)$. Hence, the central bank's ability to arbitrarily choose the quantity of reserves comes at the expense of its ability to enforce its target for the overnight interest rate.

Importantly, however, the central bank can independently choose both the interest rate and the quantity of reserves if it targets the overnight interest rate at the excess reserves rate, i_{er}. In this case, the central bank could supply any amount of reserves without any consequence for the policy rate, which would remain unchanged at i_{er}, since it is bounded from below at i_{er}.

This is exactly what the Bank of Canada did from April 1, 2009, to June 1, 2010, when it lowered the band for the overnight interest rate from 50 basis points to 25 basis points (from ¼% to ½%) and instead of targeting the overnight rate at the midpoint of the band (as it does during normal times), it started targeting it at the bottom of the operating band. On June 1, 2010, the Bank re-established the normal operating band of 50 basis points for the overnight interest rate and started again targeting the overnight rate at the midpoint of the band.

The central bank's ability to arbitrarily choose the quantity of reserves comes at the expense of its ability to enforce its target for the overnight interest rate. If, however, the central bank targets the overnight interest rate at the rate paid on excess reserves, $(i_{er} = i_b - 0.50)$, then it would be able to choose both the overnight interest rate and the quantity of reserves independently.

Credit Easing

Credit easing refers to the purchase of private-sector assets by the central bank in critical markets that are considered important for the effective functioning of the economy. The objective of credit easing is to reduce risky spreads and improve liquidity and trading in these markets, thereby stimulating the level of economic activity. Unlike quantitative easing, which leads to an expansion of settlement balances, the effects of credit easing on settlement balances could be sterilized, for example, by reducing the central bank's holdings of other assets.

The effectiveness of credit easing is judged by reduction in risk premiums and this depends on the substitutability between asset classes. If the degree of substitutability between asset classes is high, any given effect will be transmitted more broadly across assets, but their yields will not be significantly affected, leaving risky spreads unchanged. If, however, the degree of substitutability is low, the effect on the yields of the purchased assets will be greater, although the pass-through to the interest rates on other asset classes will be low. Since the substitutability between asset classes changes over time, the effects of credit easing on credit flows and aggregate demand are likely to be uncertain.

Discretionary Liquidity Operations

Not only can the central bank be a lender of last resort to banks, but it can also play the same role for the financial system as a whole. In fact, under the Bank of Canada Act, under extreme conditions on a financial market or financial system, the Bank of Canada has the authority to provide liquid funds to any (financial or nonfinancial) Canadian or foreign entities, for the purpose of promoting the stability of the financial system. Such central bank intervention can help prevent financial panics that are not triggered by bank failures (see the Inside the Central Bank box Monetary Policy at Times of Crisis).

Recently, central banks around the world have been facing significant challenges in implementing monetary policy because of the financial-market turmoil and the subprime credit crisis in the United States. In response to these challenges, central banks have been improving and refining their financial infrastructures to address turmoil in the financial markets. Although there are differences across countries in institutional arrangements for the conduct of monetary policy,

INSIDE THE CENTRAL BANK   Monetary Policy at Times of Crisis

At times of turmoil in financial markets, central banks face a number of challenges. In the Canadian case, for example, challenges involve keeping the overnight rate near the policy rate, keeping spreads in the term interbank market low by influencing interbank term rates, and deciding how to respond to the potential macroeconomic effects of the crisis by changing the monetary policy stance (that is, the target and operating band for the overnight rate).

Against the backdrop of the recent turmoil in financial markets, the Bank of Canada faced widening spreads and increased volatility in the term interbank market and took extraordinary measures to stabilize the financial system. In its efforts to influence interbank term rates, the Bank introduced term PRAs and increased the frequency and size of its discretionary liquidity operations. Moreover, the Bank expanded its list of

acceptable collateral (for both its standing lending facility as well as for its term PRA operations) to include bank-sponsored asset-backed commercial paper and U.S. Treasuries.

These discretionary liquidity operations do not represent a change in the stance of monetary policy. However, in order to support the Canadian economy, the Bank of Canada, acting in concert with other major central banks, also changed its policy stance by lowering the target and operating band for the overnight interest rate in a series of announcements. In fact, in the first 10 months of 2008 alone, the policy rate was reduced by 300 basis points to 1.5% by the end of 2008 and then to 0.25% by April 2009. Moreover, the Bank is now considering quantitative measures of monetary policy and has identified alternative instruments that it would consider using at the effective lower bound for the overnight interest rate.

most central banks have responded to the recent financial turbulence in a similar fashion, providing liquidity directly to the financial system, called *aggregate system* or *macro liquidity*.

To address market failure and financial instability at times of crisis, central banks rely on discretionary liquidity operations, the maturity of which depends on their objective, independent of the maturity of the reference rate. The Bank of Canada, for example, recently introduced new facilities to address aggregate system liquidity at times of financial instability. In particular, the Bank introduced **term repos**, known in Canada as **term Purchase and Resale Agreements (term PRAs)**, and term securities lending. Let's see how these new facilities are used in providing liquidity to specific markets as opposed to lending directly to banks.

TERM PRAS   Term PRAs are similar to special PRAs (see Figure 17-7) but have a term longer than one business day, typically a term of 28 business days. They are offered to primary dealers and used at times of crisis, when asymmetric information among market participants impairs their ability to buy and sell an asset class or maturity, thereby distorting liquidity premiums in the money market.

For example, against the backdrop of widening spreads and increased volatility in the term interbank market in the second half of 2008, the Bank of Canada announced that it would enter into a series of 28-day PRA transactions, thereby injecting huge amounts of liquidity into the markets. Moreover, the Bank expanded its list of acceptable collateral to include bank-sponsored asset-backed commercial paper and U.S. Treasuries. It also expanded its list of eligible counterparties. In engaging in these trades, the Bank takes securities onto its books in exchange for borrowings from the Bank's standing lending facility.

TERM SECURITIES LENDING   This mechanism is designed to increase the supply of high-quality securities that could be used for collateral by banks. It can also be used to swap less-liquid securities for more liquid securities that the banks are putting up as collateral. It is also designed to partially offset the temporary increase in assets in the Bank's books associated with the term purchase and resale transactions.

Summary

The Bank of Canada and other central banks around the world are switching from the "one tool, one target" mode of operation and are searching for new tools to steer their economies in an environment with interest rates at or near zero. In Canada, the one tool was the overnight interest rate and the target was an inflation rate around 2%. However, with an effective lower bound of 25 basis points for the overnight interest rate, a decoupling of long- and short-term interest rates, and the possibility of a deflationary trap (that is, extremely low nominal interest rates and sustained deflation), the Bank of Canada is now considering new tools to steer the economy.

Monetary Policy Tools of the Federal Reserve and the European Central Bank

Every central bank practises monetary policy somewhat differently and in this section we briefly describe the procedures adopted by the Federal Reserve and the European Central Bank. Understanding monetary policy in the United States and the euro area is very important, because it affects interest rates throughout the world.

Policy Tools of the Federal Reserve

In the United States, according to the Depository Institutions Deregulation and Monetary Control Act of 1980, all depository institutions (including commercial banks, savings and loan associations, mutual savings banks, and credit unions) are subject to the same reserve requirements. In particular, required reserves on all chequable deposits—including non-interest-bearing chequing accounts, NOW accounts, super-NOW accounts, and ATS (automatic transfer savings) accounts—are equal to zero for the first $10.7 million of the bank's chequable deposits, 3% on chequable deposits from $10.7 to $58.8 million, and 10% of the chequable deposits over $58.8 million.[7] The percentage set at 10% can be varied between 8% and 14%, at the Fed's discretion. In extraordinary circumstances, the percentage can be raised as high as 18%.

Like the Bank of Canada and most other central banks, the Federal Reserve offers a lending facility which sets a ceiling on short-term overnight interest rates. In particular, the Fed provides liquidity to the banking system by lending reserves to banks. The Fed's lending of reserves to banks is called **discount window lending** and the interest rate charged banks for these loans is called the **discount rate**, denoted i_d. However, the primary indicator of the stance of monetary policy in the United States is not the discount rate but the **federal funds rate**, i_{ff}, the interest rate on overnight loans of reserves (known as federal funds) that banks trade among themselves. In fact, since February 1994, the Fed announces a federal funds rate target at each FOMC meeting, an announcement that is watched closely by market participants because it affects interest rates throughout the world.

Before 2003, the Fed discouraged banks from borrowing at the discount window, so banks were willing to pay a premium to borrow from other banks in the federal funds market at the federal funds rate. As a result the federal funds rate was usually higher than the discount rate. In 2003, however, the Fed redesigned the architecture of its discount window lending practices and now makes a distinction between *primary credit* discount loans (loans to banks in good condition) and *secondary credit* discount loans (loans to banks that are not in good condition). The interest rate in primary credit discount loans is the discount rate and the Fed now sets the discount rate at 100 basis points (1 percentage point) above its target for the federal funds rate. The secondary credit discount rate is set even higher, at 50 basis points (0.5 percentage points) above the discount rate. Moreover, the Fed stopped discouraging borrowing at the discount window.

For years, the Federal Reserve did not pay interest on reserves. However, during the subprime financial crisis, legislation was passed and changed the institutional structure within which the Fed carries out monetary policy by authorizing the Fed to pay interest on banks' holdings of reserves.

THE MARKET FOR RESERVES IN THE UNITED STATES   The analysis of the market for reserves in the United States proceeds in a similar fashion to the analysis of the market for reserves in Canada depicted in Figure 17-2. The Federal Reserve maintains a two-sided asymmetric corridor system for influencing the federal funds rate as shown in Figure 17-11. The Fed's reserve supply is horizontal at the rate charged by its lending facility, the discount rate i_d, and the bank's reserve demand is horizontal at the interest rate paid by the Fed's deposit facility, i_{er}. Market equilibrium occurs at the intersection of the supply curve R^s and the demand curve R^d at point 1 and a federal funds rate of i_{ff}^*.

---

[7] These figures are for 2011. Each year, the figures are adjusted upward by 80% of the percentage increase in chequable deposits in the United States.

MyEconLab
Animation

FIGURE 17-11 Equilibrium in the Market for Reserves in the United States

Equilibrium occurs at the intersection of the supply curve R^s and the demand curve R^d at point 1 and a federal funds rate of i^*_{ff}.

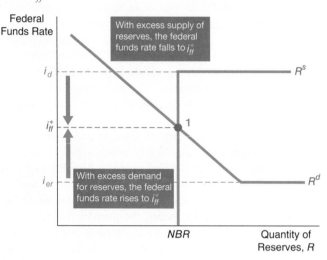

Now that we understand how the federal funds rate is determined, we can examine how changes in the tools of monetary policy—open market operations, discount lending, reserve requirements, and the interest rate paid on reserves—affect the market for reserves and the equilibrium federal funds rate.

OPEN MARKET OPERATIONS   We have already seen that an open market purchase leads to a greater quantity of reserves supplied; this is true at any given federal funds rate because of the higher amount of nonborrowed reserves, which rises from NBR_1 to NBR_2 in panel (a) of Figure 17-12. An open market purchase therefore shifts the supply curve to the right from R^s_1 to R^s_2 and moves the equilibrium from point 1 to point 2, lowering the federal funds rate from i^1_{ff} to i^2_{ff}. The same reasoning implies that an open market sale decreases the quantity of nonborrowed reserves supplied, shifts the supply curve to the left, and causes the federal funds rate to rise. Because this is the typical situation—since the Fed usually keeps the federal funds rate target above the interest rate paid on reserves—the conclusion is that ***an open market purchase causes the federal funds rate to fall, whereas an open market sale causes the federal funds rate to rise***.

However, if the supply curve initially intersects the demand curve on its flat section, as in panel (b) of Figure 17-12, open market operations have no effect on the federal funds rate. To see this, let's again look at an open market purchase that raises the quantity of reserves supplied, which shifts the supply curve from R^s_1 to R^s_2, but now where initially $i^1_{ff} = i_{er}$. The shift in the supply curve moves the equilibrium from point 1 to point 2, but the federal funds rate remains unchanged at i_{er}, because **the interest rate paid on reserves, i_{er}, sets a floor for the federal funds rate.**

DISCOUNT LENDING   The effect of a discount rate change depends on whether the demand curve intersects the supply curve in its vertical section versus its flat section. Panel (a) of Figure 17-13 shows what happens if the intersection occurs on the vertical section of the supply curve so there is no discount lending and borrowed reserves, *BR*, are zero. In this case, when the discount rate is lowered by the Fed from i^1_d to i^2_d, the horizontal section of the supply curve falls, as in R^s_2, but the intersection of the supply and demand curves remains at point 1. Thus, in this case,

FIGURE 17-12 Response to an Open Market Operation

An open market purchase increases nonborrowed reserves and hence the reserves supplied, and shifts the supply curve from R_1^s to R_2^s. In panel (a), the equilibrium moves from point 1 to point 2, lowering the federal funds rate from i_{ff}^1 to i_{ff}^2. In panel (b), the equilibrium moves from point 1 to point 2, but the federal funds rate remains unchanged, $i_{ff}^1 = i_{ff}^2 = i_{er}$.

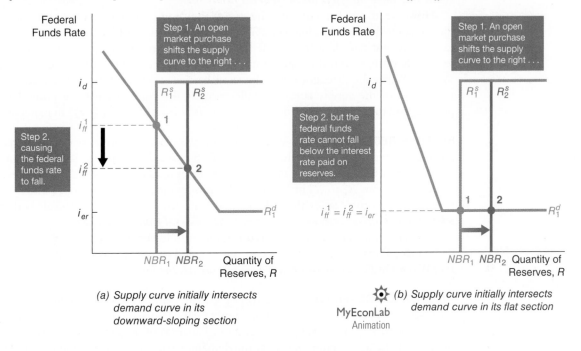

(a) Supply curve initially intersects
demand curve in its
downward-sloping section

(b) Supply curve initially intersects
demand curve in its flat section

MyEconLab
Animation

FIGURE 17-13 Response to a Change in the Discount Rate

In panel (a) when the discount rate is lowered by the Fed from i_d^1 to i_d^2, the horizontal section of the supply curve falls, as in R_2^s, and the equilibrium federal funds rate remains unchanged at i_{ff}^1. In panel (b) when the discount rate is lowered by the Fed from i_d^1 to i_d^2, the horizontal section of the supply curve R_2^s falls, and the equilibrium federal funds rate falls from i_{ff}^1 to i_{ff}^2 as borrowed reserves increase.

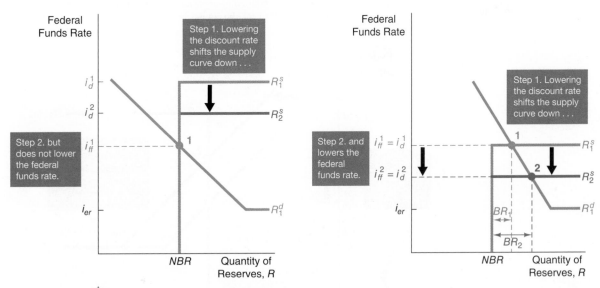

MyEconLab
Animation

(a) No discount lending (BR = 0)

(b) Some discount lending (BR > 0)

there is no change in the equilibrium federal funds rate, which remains at i_{ff}^1. Because this is the typical situation—since the Fed now usually keeps the discount rate above its target for the federal funds rate—the conclusion is that ***most changes in the discount rate have no effect on the federal funds rate***.

However, if the demand curve intersects the supply curve on its flat section, so there is some discount lending (i.e., $BR > 0$), as in panel (b) of Figure 17-13, changes in the discount rate do affect the federal funds rate. In this case, initially discount lending is positive and the equilibrium federal funds rate equals the discount rate, $i_{ff}^1 = i_d^1$. When the discount rate is lowered by the Fed from i_d^1 to i_d^2, the horizontal section of the supply curve R_2^s falls, moving the equilibrium from point 1 to point 2, and the equilibrium federal funds rate falls from i_{ff}^1 to $i_{ff}^2 (= i_d^2)$ in panel (b).

RESERVE REQUIREMENTS   When the required reserve ratio increases, required reserves increase and hence the quantity of reserves demanded increases for any given interest rate. Thus a rise in the required reserve ratio shifts the demand curve to the right from R_1^d to R_2^d in Figure 17-14, moves the equilibrium from point 1 to point 2, and in turn raises the federal funds rate from i_{ff}^1 to i_{ff}^2. The result is that ***when the Fed raises reserve requirements, the federal funds rate rises***.

Similarly, a decline in the required reserve ratio lowers the quantity of reserves demanded, shifts the demand curve to the left, and causes the federal funds rate to fall. ***When the Fed decreases reserve requirements, the federal funds rate falls***.

INTEREST ON RESERVES   The effect of a change in the interest rate the Fed pays on reserves depends on whether the supply curve intersects the demand curve in its downward sloping versus its flat section. Panel (a) of Figure 17-15 shows what happens if the intersection occurs at the demand curve's downward-sloping section where the equilibrium federal funds rate is above the interest rate paid on reserves.

MyEconLab
Animation

FIGURE 17-14 Response to a Change in Required Reserves

When the Fed raises reserve requirements, required reserves increase, which increases the demand for reserves. The demand curve shifts from R_1^d to R_2^d, the equilibrium moves from point 1 to point 2, and the federal fund rate rises from i_{ff}^1 to i_{ff}^2.

FIGURE 17-15 Response to a Change in the Interest Rate on Reserves

In panel (a), when the equilibrium federal funds rate is above the interest rate paid on reserves, a rise in the interest rate from i_{er}^1 to i_{er}^2 raises the horizontal section of the demand curve, as in R_2^d, but the equilibrium federal funds rate remains unchanged at i_{ff}^1. In panel (b), when the equilibrium federal funds rate is at the interest rate paid on reserves, a rise in the interest rate on reserves from i_{er}^1 to i_{er}^2 raises the equilibrium federal funds rate $i_{ff}^1 = i_{er}^1$ to $i_{ff}^2 = i_{er}^2$.

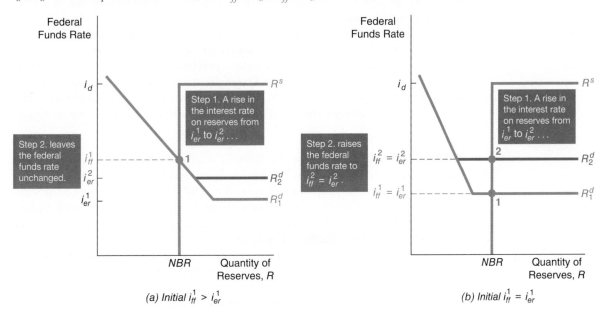

(a) Initial $i_{ff}^1 > i_{er}^1$

(b) Initial $i_{ff}^1 = i_{er}^1$

In this case, when the interest rate on reserves is raised from i_{er}^1 to i_{er}^2, the horizontal section of the demand curve rises, as in R_2^d, but the intersection of the supply and demand curve remains at point 1. However, if the supply curve intersects the demand curve on its flat section where the equilibrium federal funds rate is at the interest rate paid on reserves, as in panel (b) of Figure 17-15, a rise in the interest rate on reserves from i_{er}^1 to i_{er}^2 moves the equilibrium to point 2 where the equilibrium federal funds rate rises from $i_{ff}^1 = i_{er}^1$ to $i_{ff}^2 = i_{er}^2$. **When the federal funds rate is at the interest rate paid on reserves, a rise in the interest rate on reserves raises the federal funds rate.**

Monetary Policy Tools of the European Central Bank

Like the Federal Reserve, the European System of Central Banks (which is usually referred to as the European Central Bank) signals the stance of its monetary policy by setting a **target financing rate**, which in turn sets a target for the **overnight cash rate**. Like the federal funds rate, the overnight cash rate is the interest rate for very short-term interbank loans. The monetary policy tools used by the European Central Bank are similar to those used by the Federal Reserve and involve open market operations, lending to banks, and reserve requirements.

OPEN MARKET OPERATIONS Like the Federal Reserve, the European Central Bank uses open market operations as its primary tool for conducting monetary policy and setting the overnight cash rate at the target financing rate. **Main refinancing operations** are the predominant form of open market operations and are similar to the Fed's repo transactions. They involve weekly **reverse transactions** (purchase or sale of eligible assets under repurchase or credit operations against eligible assets as collateral) that are reversed within two weeks. Credit institutions submit bids, and the European Central Bank decides which bids to accept. Like the Federal Reserve, the European Central Bank accepts the most attractively priced bids and makes purchases or sales to the point where the desired amount of reserves are supplied. In contrast to the Federal Reserve, which conducts open market operations in one location at the Federal Reserve Bank of New York, the European Central Bank decentralizes its open market operations by having them be conducted by the individual national central banks.

A second category of open market operations is the **longer-term refinancing operations**, which are a much smaller source of liquidity for the euro-area banking system and are similar to the Fed's outright purchases or sales of securities. These operations are carried out monthly and typically involve purchases or sales of securities with a maturity of three months. They are not used for signalling the monetary policy stance, but instead are aimed at providing euro-area banks access to longer-term funds.

LENDING TO BANKS   As for the Bank of Canada and the Fed, the next most important tool of monetary policy for the European Central Bank involves lending to banking institutions, which is carried out by the national central banks, just as discount lending in the United States is performed by the individual Federal Reserve Banks. This lending takes place through a standing lending facility called the **marginal lending facility**. There, banks can borrow (against eligible collateral) overnight loans from the national central banks at the **marginal lending rate**, which is set at 100 basis points above the target financing rate. The marginal lending rate provides a ceiling for the overnight market interest rate in the European Monetary Union, just as the bank rate does in Canada and the discount rate in the United States. Just as in the systems in the United States, Canada, Australia, and New Zealand, the Eurosystem has another standing facility, the **deposit facility**, in which banks are paid a fixed interest rate that is 100 basis points below the target financing rate. The pre-specified interest rate on the deposit facility provides a floor for the overnight market interest rate, while the marginal lending rate sets a ceiling. This creates a channel/corridor system as in Canada, New Zealand, and Australia, but with a much wider range of 100 basis points on either side.

RESERVE REQUIREMENTS   Like the Federal Reserve, the European Central Bank imposes reserve requirements such that all deposit-taking institutions are required to hold 2% of the total amount of chequing deposits and other short-term deposits in reserve accounts with national central banks. All institutions that are subject to minimum reserve requirements have access to the European Central Bank's standing lending facilities and participate in open market operations. Like the Federal Reserve, the European Central Bank pays interest on reserves. Consequently, the banks' cost of complying with reserve requirements is low.

MyEconLab   MyEconLab is an online homework and tutorial system that puts you in control of your own learning with study and practice tools directly correlated to this chapter's content. Visit MyEconLab to explore the following resources:

- The Questions and Applied Problems are all available in the Study Plan on MyEconLab for further practice. You will also find the answers to all of the Questions and Applied Problems in the Student Resources section of your MyEconLab.

- CANSIM data are available for relevant CANSIM questions in the Student Resources section of your MyEconLab.

MyEconLab also features Additional Readings, Videos, Glossary Flashcards, Audio Chapter Summaries, Economics News Feeds, Animations, and many additional tools to help you master key concepts from the text.

((·• SUMMARY

EconLab
o Summary

1. The Bank of Canada views the overnight interest rate as the centrepiece of its monetary policy implementation. At 9:00 a.m. on the fixed action date, the Bank announces an operating band of 50 basis points for the overnight rate. The upper limit of the operating band is the bank rate—the rate the Bank charges LVTS participants that require an overdraft loan to cover negative settlement balances. The lower limit is the rate the Bank pays LVTS participants with positive settlement balances.

2. The Bank of Canada targets the value of the overnight interest rate within its operating band, at the midpoint of the band. In doing so, the Bank intervenes in the overnight market using open-market buyback operations at the target rate. If the overnight rate is trading above the target rate, the Bank uses repos in which it purchases Government of Canada securities from primary dealers with an agreement to resell them on the next business day. If the overnight rate is too low relative to the target rate, the Bank uses reverse repos in which it sells Government of Canada securities to primary dealers with an agreement to buy them back on the next day.

3. The Bank uses government deposit shifting to neutralize public-sector flows that affect LVTS participants' settlement balances—this in effect is a cash setting, a cash setting that is typically $25 million. Because its holdings of Government of Canada securities are often much smaller than its monetary liabilities, the Bank brings onto its balance sheet Exchange Fund Account assets to back its liabilities. These amounts are adjusted daily, depending on factors such as the level of financial institution borrowings and/or deposits.

4. In neutralizing the effects of open market buyback operations and of public-sector flows on the level of settlement balances, and also in adjusting the level of settlement balances, the Bank of Canada uses transfers of government deposits (balances) between the government's account at the Bank of Canada and the government's accounts at the LVTS participants. These transfers are effected by twice-daily auctions of federal government (Receiver General) balances, the first at 9:15 a.m. (which are collateralized) and the second at 4:15 p.m. (which are uncollateralized).

5. In normal times, the Bank of Canada relies mainly on its traditional monetary policy tools—standing liquidity facilities (lending and deposit facilities), settlement balances management, and lender-of-last-resort arrangements. At times of crisis, however, to address market failure and financial instability the Bank of Canada relies on discretionary liquidity operations whose maturity depends on their objective, independent of the maturity of the reference rate. For example, the Bank of Canada recently introduced new facilities to address aggregate system liquidity at times of financial instability—term PRAs and term securities lending.

6. A supply and demand analysis of the market for reserves in the United States yields the following results: (1) when the Fed makes an open market purchase or lowers reserve requirements, the federal funds rate declines; or (2) when the Fed makes an open market sale or raises reserve requirements, the federal funds rate rises. Changes in the discount rate may also affect the federal funds rate.

7. The monetary policy tools used by the European Central Bank are similar to those used by the Federal Reserve System and involve open market operations, lending to banks, and reserve requirements. Main financing operations—open market operations in repos that are typically reversed within two weeks—are the primary tool to set the overnight cash rate at the target financing rate. The European Central Bank also operates standing lending facilities that operate to ensure that the overnight cash rate remains within 100 basis points of the target financing rate.

KEY TERMS

credit easing, p. 426

conditional statements, p. 425

deposit facility, p. 434

direct clearers, p. 405

discount rate, p. 429

discount window lending, p. 429

drawdowns, p. 418

federal funds rate, p. 429

Large Value Transfer System (LVTS), p. 404

lender of last resort, p. 422

longer-term refinancing operations, p. 434

LVTS participants, p. 404

main refinancing operations, p. 433

management of expectations, p. 425

marginal lending facility, p. 434

marginal lending rate, p. 434

monetary conditions, p. 412

multilateral netting, p. 405

nonconventional monetary policy tools, p. 425

operating band, p. 406

overnight cash rate, p. 433

overnight interest rate (reference rate), p. 405

overnight rate, p. 403

policy rate, p. 405

primary dealers, p. 415

redeposits, p. 418

repos, p. 415

reverse repos, p. 415

reverse transactions, p. 433

QUESTIONS

1. If government deposits at the Bank of Canada are predicted to increase, what open market operations could be undertaken to neutralize the effect on settlement balances?

2. During the holiday season, when the public's holdings of currency increase, what open market operations typically occur? Why?

3. If the government has just paid for major computer upgrades and as a result its deposits with the Bank of Canada fall, what open market operations could be undertaken?

4. "In the LVTS environment, government deposit shifting is affected by auctions of government balances." Discuss.

5. Most open market operations are currently repurchase agreements. What does this tell us about the likely volume of open market operations relative to dynamic open market operations?

6. "The only way that the Bank of Canada can affect the level of advances is by adjusting the bank rate." Is this statement true, false, or uncertain? Explain your answer.

7. If the Bank of Canada did not administer the operating band, what do you predict would happen to the money supply if the bank rate were several percentage points below the overnight rate?

8. Discuss how the operating band affects interest rates and the money supply in the economy.

9. "Last-resort lending is no longer needed because the presence of the CDIC eliminates the possibility of bank panics." Discuss.

10. The benefits of using last-resort lending to prevent bank panics are straightforward. What are the costs?

11. You often read in the newspaper that the Bank of Canada has just lowered the target overnight rate. Does this signal that the Bank is moving to a more expansionary monetary policy? Why or why not?

12. How can the procyclical movement of interest rates (rising during business cycle expansions and falling during business cycle contractions) lead to a procyclical movement in the money supply as a result of the Bank of Canada's lending policy? Why might this movement of the money supply be undesirable?

13. Explain how SPRAs and SRAs affect the overnight rate.

14. "The channel/corridor system for setting interest rates enables the Bank of Canada to set the overnight rate whatever the demand for reserves, including zero demand." Discuss.

15. Compare the use of open market operations and government deposit shifting to control the money supply, using the following criteria: flexibility, reversibility, effectiveness, and speed of implementation.

APPLIED PROBLEMS

16. If there is a switch from deposits into currency, what happens to the overnight interest rate? Use the supply and demand analysis of the market for reserves to explain your answer.

17. Using the supply and demand analysis of the market for reserves, indicate what happens to the overnight interest rate, borrowed reserves, and nonborrowed reserves holding everything else constant, under the following situations.

    a. The economy is surprisingly strong, leading to an increase in the amount of chequable deposits.

    b. Banks expect an unusually large increase in withdrawals from chequing deposit accounts in the future.

    c. The Bank of Canada raises the target overnight rate.

CANSIM Question

18. Go to the CANSIM data available in the Student Resources section of your MyEconLab website and download daily data since January 1996 for the bank rate (V39078) and the target overnight rate (V39079).

    a. What is the difference between the two series?

    b. Plot the two series.

    c. Calculate the upper and lower bounds of the operating band and plot the time path of the operating band.

    d. What does the time path of the operating band say about the easiness of monetary policy over this period?

WEB EXERCISES

1. Go to **www.bankofcanada.ca** and click on "Media Room" and then "Press Releases." Scroll down and click on the release regarding recent changes in the overnight rate of interest. Summarize the statement in one paragraph. Be sure to note whether the bank rate was increased or decreased. Now review the changes in the operating band for the overnight interest rate in the previous two press releases regarding this issue. Has the stance of monetary policy changed?

2. Refer to Figure 17-1 on page 406. Go to **www.bankof canada.ca** and click on "Rates and Statistics." What is the current overnight rate target? What is the overnight rate? Is the difference between them what you would expect it to be?

WEB REFERENCES

www.bankofcanada.ca/monetary-policy-introduction

This site lists key indicators pertaining to Canadian monetary policy.

www.federalreserve.gov/fomc/fundsrate.htm

This site lists historical federal funds rates and discusses Federal Reserve targets.

CHAPTER 18

The Conduct of Monetary Policy: Strategy and Tactics

LEARNING OBJECTIVES

After studying this chapter you should be able to

1. assess the different types of monetary policy strategy
2. list the advantages and disadvantages of inflation targeting
3. specify the role of a nominal anchor in the conduct of monetary policy
4. outline Bank of Canada policy procedures from a historical perspective

PREVIEW

Getting monetary policy right is crucial to the health of the economy. Overly expansionary monetary policy leads to high inflation, which decreases the efficiency of the economy and hampers economic growth. Monetary policy that is too tight can produce serious recessions in which output falls and unemployment rises. It can also lead to deflation, a fall in the price level, such as occurred in the United States during the Great Depression and in Japan more recently. As we saw in Chapter 9, deflation can be especially damaging to an economy, because it promotes financial instability and can worsen financial crises.

Now that we understand the tools that central banks such as the Bank of Canada use to conduct monetary policy, we can consider how central banks *should* conduct monetary policy. To explore this subject, we start by looking at the goals for monetary policy and then examine one of the most important strategies for the conduct of monetary policy, inflation targeting. We then discuss tactics, that is, the choice and setting of the monetary policy instrument. After examining the strategies and tactics, we can evaluate the Bank of Canada's conduct of monetary policy in the past, with the hope that it will indicate where monetary policy may head in the future.

The Price Stability Goal and the Nominal Anchor

Over the past few decades, policymakers throughout the world have become increasingly aware of the social and economic costs of inflation and more concerned with maintaining a stable price level as a goal of economic policy. Indeed, **price stability**, which central bankers define as low and stable inflation, is increasingly viewed as the most important goal of monetary policy. Price stability is desirable because a rising price level (inflation) creates uncertainty in the economy, and that uncertainty might hamper economic growth. For example, when the overall level of prices is changing, the information conveyed by the prices of goods and services is harder to interpret, which complicates decision making for consumers, businesses, and governments, thereby leading to a less efficient financial system.

Not only do public opinion surveys indicate that the public is hostile to inflation, but a growing body of evidence also suggests that inflation leads to lower economic growth. The most extreme example of unstable prices is *hyperinflation*, such as Argentina, Brazil, Russia, and Zimbabwe have experienced in the recent past. Hyperinflation has proved to be very damaging to the workings of the economy.

Inflation also makes it difficult to plan for the future. For example, it is more difficult to decide how much to put aside to provide for a child's college education in an inflationary environment. Furthermore, inflation can strain a country's social fabric: conflict might result, because each group in the society may compete with other groups to make sure that its income keeps up with the rising level of prices.

The Role of a Nominal Anchor

Because price stability is so crucial to the long-run health of an economy, a central element in successful monetary policy is the use of a **nominal anchor**, a nominal variable such as the inflation rate or the money supply, which ties down the price level to achieve price stability. For example, if a central bank has an explicit target for the inflation rate, say 2%, and takes steps to achieve this target, then the inflation target becomes a nominal anchor. Adherence to a nominal anchor that keeps the nominal variable within a narrow range promotes price stability by directly promoting low and stable inflation expectations. A more subtle reason for a nominal anchor's importance is that it can limit the **time-inconsistency problem**, in which monetary policy conducted on a discretionary, day-by-day basis leads to poor long-run outcomes.

The Time-Inconsistency Problem

The time-inconsistency problem is something we deal with continually in everyday life. We often have a plan that we know will produce a good outcome in the long run, but when tomorrow comes, we just can't help ourselves and we renege on our plan because doing so has short-run gains. For example, we make a New Year's resolution to go on a diet, but soon thereafter we can't resist having one more bite of that rocky road ice cream—and then another bite, and then another bite—and the weight begins to pile back on. In other words, we find ourselves unable to *consistently* follow a good plan over *time*; the good plan is said to be *time-inconsistent* and will soon be abandoned.

Monetary policymakers also face the time-inconsistency problem. They are always tempted to pursue a discretionary monetary policy that is more expansionary than firms or people expect because such a policy would boost economic output (or lower unemployment) in the short run. The best policy, however, is *not* to pursue expansionary policy, because decisions about wages and prices reflect workers' and firms' expectations about policy; when they see a central bank pursuing expansionary policy, workers and firms will raise their expectations about inflation, driving wages and prices up. The rise in wages and prices will lead to higher inflation, but will not result in higher output on average. (We examine this issue more formally in Chapter 26.)

A central bank will have better inflation performance in the long run if it does not try to surprise people with an unexpectedly expansionary policy, but instead keeps inflation under control. However, even if a central bank recognizes that discretionary policy will lead to a poor outcome (high inflation with no gains in output), it still may not be able to pursue the better policy of inflation control, because politicians are likely to apply pressure on the central bank to try to boost output with overly expansionary monetary policy.

A clue to how we should deal with the time-inconsistency problem comes from how-to books on parenting. Parents know that giving in to a child to keep him from acting up will produce a very spoiled child. Nevertheless, when a child throws a tantrum, many parents give him what he wants just to shut him up. Because parents don't stick to their "do not give in" plan, the child expects that he will get what he wants if he behaves badly, so he will throw tantrums over and over again. Parenting books suggest a solution to the time-inconsistency problem (although they don't call it that): parents should set behaviour rules for their children and stick to them.

A nominal anchor is like a behaviour rule. Just as rules help to prevent the time-inconsistency problem in parenting by helping adults resist pursuing the discretionary policy of giving in, a nominal anchor can help prevent the time-inconsistency problem in monetary policy by providing an expected constraint on discretionary policy.

Other Goals of Monetary Policy

Although price stability is the primary goal of most central banks, five other goals are continually mentioned by central bank officials when they discuss the objectives of monetary policy: (1) high employment and output stability, (2) economic growth, (3) stability of financial markets, (4) interest-rate stability, and (5) stability in foreign exchange markets.

High Employment and Output Stability

High employment is a worthy goal for two main reasons: (1) the alternative situation—high unemployment—causes much human misery and (2) when unemployment is high, the economy has both idle workers and idle resources (closed factories and unused equipment), resulting in a loss of output (lower GDP).

Although it is clear that high employment is desirable, how high should it be? At what point can we say that the economy is at full employment? At first, it might seem that full employment is the point at which no worker is out of a job—that is, when unemployment is zero. But this definition ignores the fact that some unemployment, called *frictional unemployment*, which involves searches by workers and firms to find suitable matchups, is beneficial to the economy. For example, a worker who decides to look for a better job might be unemployed for a while during the job search. Workers often decide to leave work temporarily to pursue other activities (raising a family, travel, returning to school), and when they decide to re-enter the job market, it may take some time for them to find the right job.

Another reason that unemployment is not zero when the economy is at full employment is *structural unemployment*, a mismatch between job requirements and the skills or availability of local workers. Clearly, this kind of unemployment is undesirable. Nonetheless, it is something that monetary policy can do little about.

This goal for high employment is not an unemployment level of zero but a level above zero consistent with full employment at which the demand for labour equals the supply of labour. This level is called the **natural rate of unemployment**.

Although this definition sounds neat and authoritative, it leaves a troublesome question unanswered: What unemployment rate is consistent with full employment? In some cases, it is obvious that the unemployment rate is too high. The unemployment rate in excess of 20% during the Great Depression, for example, was clearly far too high. In the early 1960s, on the other hand, policymakers thought that a reasonable goal was 4%, a level that was probably too low, because it led to accelerating inflation. Current estimates of the natural rate of unemployment place it between 4% and 6%, but even this estimate is subject to much uncertainty and disagreement. It is possible, for example, that appropriate government policy, such as the provision of better information about job vacancies or job training programs, might decrease the natural rate of unemployment.

The high employment goal can be thought of in another way. Because the level of unemployment is tied to the level of economic activity in the economy, a particular level of output is produced at the natural rate of unemployment, which naturally enough is referred to as the **natural rate of output** but is more often referred to as **potential output**.

Trying to achieve the goal of high employment thus means that central banks should try to move the level of output toward the natural rate of output. In other words, they should try to stabilize the level of output around its natural rate.

Economic Growth

The goal of steady economic growth is closely related to the high-employment goal because businesses are more likely to invest in capital equipment to increase productivity and economic growth when unemployment is low. Conversely, if unemployment is high and factories are idle, it does not pay for a firm to invest in additional plants and equipment. Although the two goals are closely related, policies can be specifically aimed at promoting economic growth by directly encouraging firms to invest or by encouraging people to save, which provides more funds for firms to invest. In fact, this approach is the stated purpose of *supply-side economics* policies, which are intended to spur economic growth by providing tax incentives for businesses to invest in facilities and equipment and for taxpayers to save more. Active debate continues over what role monetary policy can play in boosting growth.

Stability of Financial Markets

As our analysis in Chapter 9 showed, financial crises can interfere with the ability of financial markets to channel funds to people with productive investment opportunities and lead to a sharp contraction in economic activity. The promotion of a more stable financial system in which financial crises are avoided is thus an important goal for a central bank. Indeed, as we saw in Chapter 15, the Bank of Canada was created to promote financial stability.

Interest-Rate Stability

Interest-rate stability is desirable because fluctuations in interest rates can create uncertainty in the economy and make it harder to plan for the future. Fluctuations in interest rates that affect consumers' willingness to buy houses, for example, make it more difficult for consumers to decide when to purchase a house and for construction firms to plan how many houses to build. A central bank may also want to reduce upward movements in interest rates for the reasons we discussed in Chapter 15: upward movements in interest rates generate hostility toward central banks and lead to demands that their power be curtailed.

The stability of financial markets is also fostered by interest-rate stability, because fluctuations in interest rates create great uncertainty for financial institutions. An increase in interest rates produces large capital losses on long-term bonds and mortgages, losses that can cause the failure of the financial institutions holding them.

Stability in Foreign Exchange Markets

With the increasing importance of international trade to the Canadian economy, the value of the dollar relative to other currencies has become a major consideration for the Bank of Canada. A rise in the value of the dollar makes Canadian industries less competitive with those abroad, and declines in the value of the dollar stimulate inflation in Canada. In addition, preventing large changes in the value of the dollar makes it easier for firms and individuals purchasing or selling goods abroad to plan ahead. Stabilizing extreme movements in the value of the dollar in foreign exchange markets is thus an important goal of monetary policy. In other countries, which are even more dependent on foreign trade, stability in foreign exchange markets takes on even greater importance.

Should Price Stability Be the Primary Goal of Monetary Policy?

In the long run, no inconsistency exists between the price stability goal and the other goals mentioned earlier. The natural rate of unemployment is not lowered by high inflation, so higher inflation cannot produce lower unemployment or more employment in the long run. In other words, there is no long-run trade-off between inflation and employment. In the long run, price stability promotes economic growth as well as financial and interest-rate stability. Although price stability is consistent with the other goals in the long run, in the short run price stability often conflicts with the goals of output stability and interest-rate stability. For example, when the economy is expanding and unemployment is falling, the economy may become overheated, leading to a rise in inflation. To pursue the price stability goal, a central bank would prevent this overheating by raising interest rates, an action that would initially cause output to fall and increase interest-rate instability. How should a central bank resolve this conflict among goals?

Hierarchical Versus Dual Mandates

Because price stability is crucial to the long-run health of the economy, many countries have decided that price stability should be the primary, long-run goal for central banks. For example, the Maastricht Treaty, which created the European Central Bank, states, "The primary objective of the ESCB [European System of Central Banks] shall be to maintain price stability. Without prejudice to the objective of price stability, it shall support the general economic policies in the Community," which include objectives such as "a high level of employment" and "sustainable and non-inflationary growth." Mandates of this type, which put the goal of price stability first, and then say that as long as it is achieved other goals can be pursued, are known as **hierarchical mandates**. They are the directives governing the behaviour of such central banks as the Bank of England, the Bank of Canada, and the Reserve Bank of New Zealand, as well as the European Central Bank.

In contrast, the legislation defining the mission of the Federal Reserve states, "The Board of Governors of the Federal Reserve System and the Federal Open Market Committee shall maintain long-run growth of the monetary and credit aggregates commensurate with the economy's long-run potential to increase production, so as to promote effectively the goals of maximum employment, stable prices, and moderate long-term interest rates." Because, as we learned in Chapter 5, long-term interest rates will be very high if inflation is high, this statement in practice is a **dual mandate** to achieve two coequal objectives: price stability and maximum employment (output stability).

Is it better for an economy to operate under a hierarchical mandate or a dual mandate?

Price Stability as the Primary Long-Run Goal of Monetary Policy

Because no inconsistency exists between achieving price stability in the long run and the natural rate of unemployment, these two types of mandates are not very different *if* maximum employment is defined as the natural rate of employment. In practice, however, a substantial difference between these two mandates could exist, because the public and politicians may believe that a hierarchical mandate puts too much emphasis on inflation control and not enough on stabilizing output.

Because low and stable inflation rates promote economic growth, central bankers have come to realize that price stability should be the primary long-run goal of monetary policy. Nevertheless, because output fluctuations should also be a concern of monetary policy, the goal of price stability should be seen as primary only in the long run. Attempts to keep inflation at the same level in the short run, no matter what, would likely lead to excessive output fluctuations.

As long as price stability is a long-run, but not short-run, goal, central banks can focus on reducing output fluctuations by allowing inflation to deviate from the long-run goal for short periods and, therefore, can operate under a dual mandate. However, if a dual mandate leads a central bank to pursue short-run expansionary policies that increase output and employment without worrying about the long-run consequences for inflation, the time-inconsistency problem may recur. Concerns that a dual mandate might lead to overly expansionary policy is a key reason why central bankers often favour hierarchical mandates in which the pursuit of price stability takes precedence. Hierarchical mandates can also be a problem if they lead to a central bank behaving as what the previous governor of the Bank of England, Mervyn King, has referred to as an "inflation nutter"—that is, a central bank that focuses solely on inflation control, even in the short run, and so undertakes policies that lead to large output fluctuations. The choice of which type of mandate is better for a central bank ultimately depends on the subtleties of how it will work in practice. Either type of mandate is acceptable as long as it operates to make price stability the primary goal in the long run, but not the short run.

Inflation Targeting

The recognition that price stability should be the primary long-run goal of monetary policy and the value of having a nominal anchor to achieve this goal has led to a monetary policy strategy known as inflation targeting. **Inflation targeting** involves several elements: (1) public announcement of medium-term numerical objectives (targets) for inflation; (2) an institutional commitment to price stability as the primary long-run goal of monetary policy and a commitment to achieve the inflation goal; (3) an information-inclusive approach in which many variables (not just monetary aggregates) are used in making decisions about monetary policy; (4) increased transparency of the monetary policy strategy through communication with the public and the markets about the plans and objectives of monetary policymakers; and (5) increased accountability of the central bank for attaining its inflation objectives. New Zealand was the first country to formally adopt inflation targeting in 1990, followed by Canada in 1991, the United Kingdom in 1992, Sweden and Finland in 1993, and Australia and Spain in 1994. Israel, Chile, and Brazil, among others, have also adopted a form of inflation targeting.

Inflation Targeting in New Zealand, Canada, and the United Kingdom

We begin our look at inflation targeting with New Zealand, because it was the first country to adopt it. We then go on to examine the experiences in Canada and the United Kingdom, which were next to adopt this strategy.[1]

NEW ZEALAND   As part of a general reform of the government's role in the economy, the New Zealand parliament passed a new Reserve Bank of New Zealand Act in 1989, which became effective on February 1, 1990. Besides increasing the independence of the central bank, moving it from being one of the least independent to one of the most independent among developed countries, the act committed the Reserve Bank to a sole objective of price stability. The act stipulated that the minister of finance and the governor of the Reserve Bank should negotiate and make public a Policy Targets Agreement, a statement that sets out the targets by which monetary policy performance will be evaluated, specifying numerical target

---

[1]If you are interested in a more detailed discussion of experiences with inflation targeting in these and other countries, see Ben S. Bernanke, Thomas Laubach, Frederic S. Mishkin, and Adam S. Posen, *Inflation Targeting: Lessons from the International Experience* (Princeton, NJ: Princeton University Press, 1999).

ranges for inflation and the dates by which they are to be reached. An unusual feature of the New Zealand legislation is that the governor of the Reserve Bank is held highly accountable for the success of monetary policy. If the goals set forth in the Policy Targets Agreement are not satisfied, the governor is subject to dismissal.

The first Policy Targets Agreement, signed by the minister of finance and the governor of the Reserve Bank on March 2, 1990, directed the Reserve Bank to achieve an annual inflation rate within a 3–5% range. Subsequent agreements lowered the range to 0–2% until the end of 1996, when the range was changed to 0–3% and later to 1–3% in 2002. As a result of tight monetary policy, the inflation rate was brought down from above 5% to below 2% by the end of 1992 (see Figure 18-1, panel a), but at the cost of a deep recession and a sharp rise in unemployment. Since then, inflation has typically remained within the targeted range, with the exception of brief periods in 1995, 2000, and 2008, when it exceeded the range by a small amount. (Under the Reserve Bank Act, the governor could have been dismissed, but after parliamentary debates he retained his job.) Since 1992, New Zealand's growth rate has generally been high, with some years exceeding 5%, and unemployment has come down significantly.

CANADA   On February 26, 1991, a joint announcement by the minister of finance and the governor of the Bank of Canada established formal inflation targets. The target ranges were 2–4% by the end of 1992, 1.5–3.5% by June 1994, and 1–3% by December 1996. After the new government took office in late 1993, the target range was set at 1–3% from December 1995 until December 1998 and has been kept at this level. It was renewed on November 2011 for another five-year term until 2016. Canadian inflation has also fallen dramatically since the adoption of inflation targets, from above 5% in 1991, to a 0% rate in 1995, and to around 2% subsequently (see Figure 18-1, panel b). As was the case in New Zealand, however, this decline was not without cost: unemployment soared to above 10% from 1991 until 1994, but then declined substantially.

UNITED KINGDOM   In October 1992, the United Kingdom adopted an inflation target as its nominal anchor, and the Bank of England began to produce an *Inflation Report*, a quarterly report on the progress being made in achieving that target. The inflation target range was initially set at 1–4% until the next election (spring 1997 at the latest), with the intent that the inflation rate should settle down to the lower half of the range (below 2.5%). In May 1997, the inflation target was set at 2.5% and the Bank of England was given the power to set interest rates henceforth, granting it a more independent role in monetary policy.

Before the adoption of inflation targets, inflation had already been falling in the United Kingdom, with a peak of 9% at the beginning of 1991 and a rate of 4% at the time of adoption (see Figure 18-1, panel c). By the third quarter of 1994, it was at 2.2%, within the intended range. Subsequently, inflation rose, climbing slightly above the 2.5% level by the end of 1995, but then fell and has remained close to the target since then, except for the period from 2008 to 2011. In December 2003, the target was changed to 2.0% for a slightly different measure of inflation. Meanwhile, growth of the U.K. economy was strong until 2008, causing a substantial reduction in the unemployment rate.

Advantages of Inflation Targeting

Because an explicit numerical inflation target increases the accountability of the central bank, inflation targeting has the potential to reduce the likelihood that the central bank will fall into the time-inconsistency trap of trying to expand output and employment in the short run by pursuing overly expansionary monetary policy. A key advantage of inflation targeting is that it can help focus the political debate on what a central

FIGURE 18-1 Inflation Rates and Inflation Targets for New Zealand, Canada, and the United Kingdom, 1980–2011

Inflation-targeting countries have significantly reduced the rate of inflation and eventually have achieved their inflation targets.

Source: Ben S. Bernanke, Thomas Laubach, Frederic S. Mishkin, and Adam S. Poson, *Inflation Targeting: Lessons from the International Experience* (Princeton, NJ: Princeton University Press, 1999), updates from the same sources, and www.rbnz.govt.nz/statistics/econind/a3/ha3.xls.

bank can do in the long run—that is, control inflation—rather than what it cannot do, permanently increase economic growth and the number of jobs through expansionary monetary policy. Thus inflation targeting has the potential to reduce political pressures on the central bank to pursue inflationary monetary policy and thereby to reduce the likelihood of the time-inconsistency problem.

Inflation targeting has the advantage that it is readily understood by the public and is thus highly transparent. Indeed, inflation-targeting regimes put great stress on making policy transparent and on regular communication with the public. Inflation-targeting central banks have frequent communications with the government, some mandated by law and some in response to informal inquiries, and their officials take every opportunity to make public speeches on their monetary policy strategy. Although these techniques are also commonly used in countries that have not adopted inflation targeting, inflation-targeting central banks have taken public outreach a step further: not only do they engage in extended public information campaigns, including the distribution of glossy brochures, but they also publish documents like the Bank of England's *Inflation Report*. The publication of these documents is particularly noteworthy, because they depart from the usual dull-looking, formal reports of central banks and use fancy graphics, boxes, and other eye-catching design elements to engage the public's interest.

The above channels of communication are used by central banks in inflation-targeting countries to explain the following concepts to the general public, financial market participants, and politicians: (1) the goals and limitations of monetary policy, including the rationale for inflation targets; (2) the numerical values of the inflation targets and how they were determined; (3) how the inflation targets are to be achieved, given current economic conditions; and (4) reasons for any deviations from targets. These communications have improved private-sector planning by reducing uncertainty about monetary policy, interest rates, and inflation; they have promoted public debate of monetary policy, in part by educating the public about what a central bank can and cannot achieve; and they have helped clarify the responsibilities of the central bank and of politicians in the conduct of monetary policy.

Another key feature of inflation-targeting regimes is the tendency toward increased accountability of the central bank. Indeed, transparency and communication go hand in hand with increased accountability. The strongest case of accountability of a central bank in an inflation-targeting regime is in New Zealand, where the government has the right to dismiss the Reserve Bank's governor if the inflation targets are breached, even for one quarter. In other inflation-targeting countries, the central bank's accountability is less formalized. Nevertheless, the transparency of policy associated with inflation targeting has tended to make the central bank highly accountable to the public and the government. Sustained success in the conduct of monetary policy as measured against a preannounced and well-defined inflation target can be instrumental in building public support for a central bank's independence and for its policies. This building of public support and accountability occurs even in the absence of a rigidly defined and legalistic standard of performance evaluation and punishment.

The performance of inflation-targeting regimes has been quite good. Inflation-targeting countries seem to have significantly reduced both the rate of inflation and inflation expectations beyond what would likely have occurred in the absence of inflation targets. Furthermore, once down, inflation in these countries has stayed down; following disinflations, the inflation rate in targeting countries has not bounced back up during subsequent cyclical expansions of the economy.

Disadvantages of Inflation Targeting

Critics of inflation targeting cite four disadvantages of this monetary policy strategy: delayed signalling, too much rigidity, the potential for increased output fluctuations, and low economic growth. We look at each in turn and examine the validity of these criticisms.

DELAYED SIGNALLING   Inflation is not easily controlled by the monetary authorities. Furthermore, because of the long lags in the effects of monetary policy, inflation outcomes are revealed only after a substantial lag. Thus an inflation target is unable to send immediate signals to both the public and markets about the stance of monetary policy.

TOO MUCH RIGIDITY   Some economists have criticized inflation targeting because they believe it imposes a rigid rule on monetary policymakers and limits their ability to respond to unforeseen circumstances. However, useful policy strategies exist that are "rule-like" in that they involve forward-looking behaviour that limits policymakers from systematically engaging in policies with undesirable long-run consequences. Such policies avoid the time-inconsistency problem and would best be described as "constrained discretion."

Indeed, inflation targeting can be described exactly in this way. Inflation targeting, as actually practised, is far from rigid and is better described as "flexible inflation targeting." First, inflation targeting does not prescribe simple and mechanical instructions on how the central bank should conduct monetary policy. Rather, it requires the central bank to use all available information to determine which policy actions are appropriate to achieve the inflation target. Unlike simple policy rules, inflation targeting never requires the central bank to focus solely on one key variable. Second, inflation targeting, as practised, contains a substantial degree of policy discretion. Inflation targets have been modified depending on economic circumstances, as we have seen. Moreover, central banks under inflation-targeting regimes have left themselves considerable scope to respond to output growth and fluctuations through several devices.

POTENTIAL FOR INCREASED OUTPUT FLUCTUATIONS   An important criticism of inflation targeting is that a sole focus on inflation may lead to monetary policy that is too tight when inflation is above target and thus may result in larger output fluctuations. Inflation targeting does not, however, require a sole focus on inflation—in fact, experience has shown that inflation targeters display substantial concern about output fluctuations. All the inflation targeters have set their inflation targets above zero.[2] For example, currently, New Zealand, Canada, the United Kingdom, and Sweden set the midpoint of their inflation target at 2%, while Australia has its midpoints at 2.5%.

The decision by inflation targeters to choose inflation targets above zero reflects the concern of monetary policymakers that particularly low inflation can have substantial negative effects on real economic activity. Deflation (negative inflation in which the price level actually falls) is especially to be feared because of the possibility that it may promote financial instability and precipitate a severe economic contraction (as discussed in Chapter 9). The deflation in Japan in recent years has been an important factor in the weakening of the Japanese financial system and economy. Targeting inflation rates of above zero makes periods of deflation less likely. This is one reason why some economists both within and outside Japan have been calling on the Bank of Japan to adopt an inflation target at levels of 2% or higher.

Inflation targeting also does not ignore traditional stabilization goals. Central bankers in inflation-targeting countries continue to express their concern about fluctuations in output and employment, and the ability to accommodate short-run stabilization goals to some degree is built into all inflation-targeting regimes. All inflation-targeting countries have been willing to minimize output declines by gradually lowering medium-term inflation targets toward the long-run goal.

LOW ECONOMIC GROWTH   Another common concern about inflation targeting is that it will lead to low growth in output and employment. Although inflation reduction has been associated with below-normal output during disinflationary phases

---

[2]Consumer price indexes have been found to have an upward bias in the measurement of true inflation, so it is not surprising that inflation targets would be chosen to exceed zero. However, the actual targets have been set to exceed the estimates of this measurement bias, indicating that inflation targeters have decided on targets for inflation that exceed zero even after measurement bias is accounted for.

in inflation-targeting regimes, once low inflation levels were achieved, output and employment returned to levels at least as high as they were before. A conservative conclusion is that once low inflation is achieved, inflation targeting is not harmful to the real economy. Given the strong economic growth after disinflation in many countries (such as Canada and New Zealand) that have adopted inflation targets, a case can be made that inflation targeting promotes real economic growth, in addition to controlling inflation.

Lessons for Monetary Policy Strategy from the Global Financial Crisis

Our discussion of the events during the global financial crisis in previous chapters suggests four basic lessons for economists and policymakers about how the economy works.[3]

1. *Developments in the financial sector have a far greater impact on economic activity than was earlier realized.* Although before the crisis, economists and policymakers generally recognized that financial frictions could play an important role in business cycle fluctuations, as we saw in Chapter 9, the global financial crisis made it abundantly clear that the adverse effects of financial disruptions on economic activity could be far worse than originally anticipated.

2. *The zero lower bound on interest rates can be a serious problem.* As we saw in Chapter 17, the zero lower bound on interest rates has forced central banks to use nonconventional monetary policy tools. Although we have seen that these nonconventional tools can help stimulate the economy, they are more complicated to use than conventional tools and their impact on the economy is more uncertain, so they may be harder to use effectively.

3. *The cost of cleaning up after a financial crisis is very high.* As we saw in Chapter 9, financial crises are followed by deep recessions. But in addition, recoveries from financial crises are very slow. Carmen Reinhart of the Petersen Institute for International Economics and Vincent Reinhart of the American Enterprise Institute have documented that economic growth is significantly lower during the decade following financial crises and unemployment rates stay persistently higher for a decade after crisis episodes. In addition, in the aftermath of financial crises government indebtedness almost always sharply increases and can lead to defaults on government debt, which has become a major concern in Europe in the aftermath of the crisis.[4]

4. *Price and output stability do not ensure financial stability.* Before the recent financial crisis, the common view both in academia and in central banks was that achieving price and output stability would promote financial stability. However, the success of central banks in stabilizing inflation and the decreased volatility of business cycle

---

[3]For a more detailed discussion of the lessons of the global financial crisis for monetary policy strategy, see Frederic S. Mishkin, "Monetary Policy Strategy: Lessons from the Crisis," in Marek Jarocinski, Frank Smets, and Christian Thimann, eds., *Monetary Policy Revisited: Lessons from the Crisis*, Sixth ECB Central Banking Conference (Frankfurt, European Central Bank, 2011), 67–118.

[4]See Carmen M. Reinhart and Vincent R. Reinhart, "After the Fall," *Macroeconomic Challenges: The Decade Ahead*, Federal Reserve Bank of Kansas City Economic Symposium, 2010, manuscript available at www.kansascityfed.org; and Carmen M. Reinhart and Kenneth S. Rogoff, *This Time Is Different: Eight Centuries of Financial Folly* (Princeton, NJ: Princeton University Press, 2009).

fluctuations before 2007, which became known as the Great Moderation, did not protect the economy from financial instability. Indeed, it may have promoted it. The low volatility of both inflation and output fluctuations may have lulled market participants into thinking less risk was present in the economic system than was really the case, leading them to take excessive risks, which helped promote the global financial crisis.

What implications do these lessons have for monetary policy strategy? We first look at how these lessons might affect our thinking about inflation targeting and then on how central banks should respond to asset-price bubbles.

Implications for Inflation Targeting

Earlier in the chapter, we outlined the arguments for inflation targeting, and none of the above lessons contradict these arguments. Although support for the inflation-targeting strategy is not weakened by the lessons from the financial crisis, they do suggest that inflation targeting may need to be more flexible and modified on several dimensions. First, we look at what these lessons might mean for the level of the inflation target.

LEVEL OF THE INFLATION TARGET As our discussion earlier in the chapter indicates, central banks typically have an inflation target around the 2% level. The seriousness of the zero-lower-bound problem raises the question of whether this target level is too low. A controversial paper written by researchers at the IMF, including its chief economist, has suggested that the inflation target might be raised from the 2% to the 4% level.[5] It argues that with expectations of inflation anchored to this target, by lowering the nominal interest rate to zero, the real interest rate, $r = i - \pi^e$, could be decreased to as low as $-4\%(= 0 - 4\%)$, rather than $-2\%(= 0 - 2\%)$, with the 2% inflation target. Conventional monetary policy, which involves manipulating the nominal policy rate, would then be able to become more expansionary when interest rates fell to a floor of zero than it could with the lower inflation target. Another way of stating this is to say that the zero lower bound on the policy rate would be less binding with a higher inflation target.

Although this argument is theoretically sound and raising the inflation target has benefits, we also have to look at its costs. The benefits of a higher inflation target accrue only when the zero-lower-bound problem occurs. Although this was a major problem during the global financial crisis, such episodes have not been very frequent. If the zero-lower-bound problem is rare, then the benefits of a higher inflation target are not very large because they are only available infrequently. However, the costs of higher inflation in terms of the distortions it produces in the economy, mentioned early in the chapter, are ongoing. Thus, although these costs may not be that large in any given year, they add up and may outweigh the intermittent benefits of a higher inflation target when the zero lower bound occurs.

Another problem with a higher inflation target is that the history of inflation suggests that it is more difficult to stabilize the inflation rate at a 4% level than at a 2% level. Once inflation starts to rise above this level, the public is likely to believe that price stability is no longer a credible goal of the central bank, and then the question arises, if a 4% level of inflation is OK, then why not 6%, or 8%, and so on? Indeed, this is what seems to have happened in the 1960s, when economists such as Paul Samuelson and Robert Solow of MIT, both eventual recipients of the Nobel Prize, argued that policymakers should be willing to tolerate higher inflation rates in the

---

[5]Olivier Blanchard, Giovanni Dell'Ariccia, and Paolo Mauro, "Rethinking Monetary Policy," *Journal of Money, Credit and Banking* 42, Issue Supplement S1 (September 2010): 199–217.

4–5% range. But when inflation rose to that level, the policy authorities could not contain it at that level and it kept on rising to double-digit levels by the early 1980s. Getting inflation back down again was very costly. No central banker wants to go through that cycle again, and this is why central bankers have been so hostile to the IMF researchers' suggestion.

FLEXIBILITY OF INFLATION TARGETING   We have seen that inflation targeting as actually practised would be better described as "flexible inflation targeting." However, before the global financial crisis, this flexibility involved allowing some short-run deviations of inflation from the inflation target in order to promote output stability as well as price stability. Two lessons from the crisis—that financial instability can have devastating effects on the economy and that achieving price and output stability does not ensure financial stability—have led to a recognition that central banks need to pay more attention to financial stability not only in designing inflation-targeting regimes, but also in any monetary policy framework, such as the "just do it" approach of the Federal Reserve. Particularly important in this regard is the issue of how central banks should respond to asset-price bubbles, which we discuss immediately below.

How Should Central Banks Respond to Asset-Price Bubbles?

Over the centuries, economies have been periodically subject to **asset-price bubbles**, pronounced increases in asset prices that depart from fundamental values, which eventually burst resoundingly. The story of the global financial crisis, discussed in Chapter 9, indicates how costly these bubbles can be. The bursting of the asset-price bubble in the U.S. housing market brought down the financial system, leading to an economic downturn, a rise in unemployment, disrupted communities, and direct hardship for families forced to leave their homes after foreclosures. The high cost of asset-price bubbles raises the following question: what should central banks do about them? Because asset prices are a central element in how monetary policy affects the economy (the transmission mechanisms of monetary policy discussed in Chapter 27), monetary policy certainly needs to respond to asset prices in order to obtain good outcomes in terms of inflation and output. Hence, the issue of how monetary policy might respond to asset-price movements is not whether it should respond at all, but whether it should respond at a level over and above that called for in terms of the objectives of stabilizing inflation and employment. Another way of defining the issue is whether monetary policy should try to pop, or slow, the growth of potential asset-price bubbles to minimize damage to the economy when these bubbles burst. Alternatively, rather than responding directly to possible asset-price bubbles, should the monetary authorities respond only to the asset-price declines that occur after a bubble bursts, to stabilize both output and inflation? These opposing positions have been characterized as *leaning* against asset-price bubbles versus *cleaning up* after the bubble bursts, and so the debate over what to do about asset-price bubbles has been labelled the "lean versus clean" debate.

WHY CENTRAL BANKS SHOULD NOT TRY TO PRICK ASSET-PRICE BUBBLES BUT SHOULD JUST CLEAN UP AFTER THEY BURST   Under Alan Greenspan, the Federal Reserve in the United States took the position that central banks should not try to prick bubbles, and this became known as the "Greenspan doctrine." His doctrine was based on the following five arguments:

1. Asset-price bubbles are nearly impossible to identify. If central banks or government officials knew that a bubble was in progress, why wouldn't market participants know as well? If so, then a bubble would be unlikely to develop, because market participants would know that prices were getting out of line with

fundamentals. Unless central bank or government officials are smarter than market participants, an unlikely situation given the savvy of especially talented (and high-earning) market participants, they will be unlikely to identify when bubbles of this type are occurring. A strong argument, then, exists for not responding to suspected bubbles.

2. Although some economic analysis suggests that raising interest rates can diminish asset-price increases, raising interest rates may be very ineffective in restraining bubbles, because market participants expect such high rates of return from buying bubble-driven assets. Furthermore, raising interest rates has often been found to cause a bubble to burst more severely, thereby increasing damage to the economy. Another way of saying this is that bubbles are departures from normal behaviour, and it is unrealistic to expect that the usual tools of monetary policy will be effective in abnormal conditions.

3. Many different asset prices exist, and at any one time a bubble may be present in only a fraction of asset markets. Monetary policy actions are a very blunt instrument in such a case, as such actions would be likely to affect asset prices in general, rather than the specific assets that are experiencing a bubble.

4. Monetary policy actions to prick bubbles can have harmful effects on the aggregate economy. If interest rates are raised significantly to curtail a bubble, the economy will slow, people will lose jobs, and inflation can fall below its desirable level. Indeed, as arguments 2 and 3 suggest, the rise in interest rates necessary to prick a bubble may be so high that it can be done only at great cost to workers and the economy. This is not to say that monetary policy should not respond to asset prices per se. The level of asset prices does affect aggregate demand (discussed in Chapter 27) and thus the evolution of the economy. Monetary policy should react to fluctuations in asset prices to the extent that they affect inflation and economic activity.

5. As long as policymakers respond in a timely fashion, by easing monetary policy aggressively after an asset bubble bursts, the harmful effects of a bursting bubble can be kept at a manageable level.

TWO TYPES OF ASSET-PRICE BUBBLES   To understand the response to the argument that central banks should not try to prick bubbles, we first need to ask whether there are different kinds of bubbles that require different types of responses. Asset-price bubbles are of two types: one that is driven by credit and a second that is driven purely by overly optimistic expectations (which Alan Greenspan referred to as "irrational exuberance").

Credit-Driven Bubbles   When a credit boom begins, it can spill over into an asset-price bubble. Easier credit can be used to purchase particular assets and thereby raise their prices. The rise in asset values, in turn, encourages further lending for these assets, either because it increases the value of collateral, making it easier to borrow, or because it raises the value of capital at financial institutions, which gives them more capacity to lend. The lending for these assets can then further increase demand for them and hence raise their prices even more. This feedback loop—in which a credit boom drives up asset prices, which in turn fuels the credit boom, which drives asset prices even higher, and so on—can generate a bubble in which asset prices rise well above their fundamental values.

Credit-driven bubbles are particularly dangerous, as the recent global financial crisis has demonstrated. When asset prices come back down to earth and the bubble bursts, the collapse in asset prices then leads to a reversal of the feedback loop in which loans go sour, lenders cut back on credit supply, the demand for assets declines further, and prices drop even more. These were exactly the dynamics in housing markets during the global financial crisis. Driven by a credit boom in subprime lending, housing prices rose way above fundamental values; but when housing prices crashed, credit shrivelled up and housing prices plummeted.

The resulting losses on subprime loans and securities eroded the balance sheets of financial institutions, causing a decline in credit (deleveraging) and a sharp fall in business and household spending, and therefore in economic activity. As we saw during the global financial crisis, the interaction between housing prices and the health of financial institutions following the collapse of the housing price bubble endangered the operation of the financial system as a whole and had dire consequences for the economy.

Bubbles Driven Solely by Irrational Exuberance Bubbles that are driven solely by overly optimistic expectations, but that are not associated with a credit boom, pose much less risk to the financial system. For example, the bubble in technology stocks in the late 1990s was not fuelled by credit, and the bursting of the tech-stock bubble was not followed by a marked deterioration in financial institutions' balance sheets. The bursting of the tech-stock bubble thus did not have a very severe impact on the economy, and the recession that followed was quite mild. Bubbles driven solely by irrational exuberance are therefore far less dangerous than those driven by credit booms.

THE CASE FOR LEANING VERSUS CLEANING   The recent global financial crisis has clearly demonstrated that the bursting of credit-driven bubbles not only can be extremely costly but also are very hard to clean up. Furthermore, credit-driven bubbles can occur even if price and output stability exists in the period leading up to them. Indeed, as we have seen, price and output stability might actually encourage credit-driven bubbles because they lead market participants to underestimate the amount of risk in the economy. The global financial crisis has therefore provided a much stronger case for leaning against potential bubbles rather than cleaning up afterward.

However, the distinction between the two types of bubbles, one of which (credit-driven) is much more costly than the other, suggests that the lean versus clean debate may have been miscast. Rather than leaning against potential asset-price bubbles, which would include both credit-driven and irrational exuberance-type bubbles, the case is much stronger for leaning against credit booms, which would involve leaning against credit-driven asset-price bubbles, but not asset-price bubbles driven by irrational exuberance. In addition, it is much easier to identify credit booms than asset-price bubbles. When asset-price bubbles are rising rapidly at the same time that credit is booming, the likelihood is greater that asset prices are deviating from fundamentals, because laxer credit standards are driving asset prices upward. In this case, central bank or government officials have a greater likelihood of identifying that a boom is in progress; this was indeed the case during the housing market bubble in the United States because these officials did have information that lenders had weakened lending standards and that credit extension in the mortgage markets was rising at abnormally high rates.

The case for leaning against credit-driven bubbles seems strong, but what policies will be most effective in restraining them?

MACROPRUDENTIAL POLICIES   First, it is important to recognize that the key principle to consider in designing effective policies to lean against credit booms is to curb excessive risk taking. Only when this risk taking is excessive are credit booms likely to develop, and so it is natural to look to prudential regulatory measures to constrain credit booms. Regulatory policy to affect what is happening in credit markets in the aggregate is referred to as macroprudential regulation, and it does seem to be the right tool for reigning in credit-driven bubbles.

Financial regulation and supervision, either by central banks or by other government entities, with the usual elements of a well-functioning prudential regulatory and supervisory system, as described in Chapter 10, can prevent excessive risk taking that can trigger a credit boom, which in turn leads to an asset-price bubble. These elements include adequate disclosure and capital requirements, prompt corrective action, close monitoring of financial institutions' risk management procedures, and close supervision to enforce compliance with regulations. More generally, regulation should focus on preventing leverage cycles. As the global financial crisis demonstrated, the rise in asset prices that accompanied the credit boom resulted in higher capital buffers at financial institutions, supporting further lending in the context of unchanging capital requirements, which led to higher asset prices, and so on; in the bust, the value of the capital dropped precipitously, leading to a cut in lending. Capital requirements that are countercyclical, that is, adjusted upward during a boom and downward during a bust, might help eliminate the pernicious feedback loops that promote credit-driven bubbles.

A rapid rise in asset prices accompanied by a credit boom provides a signal that market failures or poor financial regulation and supervision might be causing a bubble to form. Central banks and other government regulators could then consider implementing policies to rein in credit growth directly or implement measures to make sure credit standards are sufficiently high.

MONETARY POLICY   The fact that the low interest rate policies of central banks, and particularly the Federal Reserve from 2002 to 2005, were followed by excessive risk taking suggests to many that overly easy monetary policy might promote financial instability, as was discussed in Chapter 9. Although it is far from clear that the Federal Reserve is primarily to blame for the housing bubble in the United States, research does suggest that low interest rates can encourage excessive risk taking in what has been called the "risk-taking channel of monetary policy." Low interest rates may increase the incentives for asset managers in financial institutions to search for higher yields and hence increase risk taking. Low interest rates may also increase the demand for assets, raising their prices and leading to increased valuation of collateral, which in turn encourages lenders to lend to riskier borrowers.

The risk-taking channel of monetary policy suggests that monetary policy should be used to lean against credit booms. However, many of the objections to using monetary policy to prick booms are still valid, so wouldn't it be better to use macroprudential supervision to constrain credit booms, leaving monetary policy to focus on price and output stability?

This argument would be quite strong if macroprudential policies were able to do the job. However, there are doubts on this score. Prudential supervision is subject to more political pressure than monetary policy because it affects the bottom line of financial institutions more directly. Thus they have greater incentives to lobby politicians to discourage macroprudential policies that would rein in credit booms, particularly during a credit boom when they are making the most money. In addition, financial institutions are often very good at finding loopholes to avoid regulation, as we discovered in Chapter 11, and so macroprudential supervision may not be effective. The possibility that macroprudential policies may not be implemented sufficiently well to constrain credit booms suggests that monetary policy may have to be used instead.

An important lesson from the global financial crisis is that central banks and other regulators should not have a laissez-faire attitude and let credit-driven bubbles proceed without any reaction. To do this well, however, is indeed a daunting task.

Tactics: Choosing the Policy Instrument

Now that we are familiar with the alternative strategies for monetary policy, let's look at how monetary policy is conducted on a day-to-day basis. Central banks directly control the tools of monetary policy, but knowing the tools and the strategies for implementing a monetary policy does not tell us whether policy is easy or tight. For that, we can observe the **policy instrument** (also called an **operating instrument**), a variable that responds to the central bank's tools and indicates the stance (easy or tight) of monetary policy. A central bank like the Bank of Canada has at its disposal two basic types of policy instruments: reserve aggregates (total reserves, nonborrowed reserves, the monetary base, and the nonborrowed base) and interest rates (overnight interest rate and other short-term interest rates). (Central banks in small countries can choose another policy instrument, the exchange rate, but we leave this topic to Chapter 20.) The policy instrument might be linked to an **intermediate target**, such as a monetary aggregate like M1+ or a long-term interest rate. Intermediate targets stand between the policy instrument and the goals of monetary policy (e.g., price stability, output growth); they are not as directly affected by the tools of monetary policy, but might be more closely linked to the goals of monetary policy. As a study aid, Figure 18-2 shows a schematic of the linkages between the tools of monetary policy, policy instruments, intermediate targets, and the goals of monetary policy.

As an example, suppose the central bank's employment and inflation goals are consistent with a nominal GDP growth rate of 5%. The central bank might believe that the 5% nominal GDP growth rate will be achieved by a 4% growth rate for M1+ (an intermediate target), which will in turn be achieved by a growth rate of 3% for nonborrowed reserves (the policy instrument). Alternatively, the central bank might believe that the best way to achieve its objectives would be to set the overnight interest rate (a policy instrument) at, say, 4%. Can the central bank choose to target both the nonborrowed reserves and the overnight-rate policy instruments at the same time? The answer is no. The application of supply and demand analysis to the market for reserves we developed in Chapter 17 explains why a central bank must choose one or the other.

FIGURE 18-2 Linkages Between Central Bank Tools, Policy Instruments, Intermediate Targets, and Goals of Monetary Policy

The tools of the central bank are used to change the policy instruments to achieve the intermediate target and then the goals of monetary policy.

MyEconLab
Animation

FIGURE 18-3 Result of Targeting on Nonborrowed Reserves

Targeting on nonborrowed reserves of NBR^* will lead to fluctuations in the overnight interest rate between i'_{or} and i''_{or} because of fluctuations in the demand for reserves between $R^{d'}$ and $R^{d''}$.

Let's first see why choosing an aggregate target involves losing control of the interest rate. Figure 18-3 contains a supply and demand diagram for the market for reserves. Although the central bank expects the demand curve for reserves to be at R^{d*}, it fluctuates between $R^{d'}$ and $R^{d''}$ because of changes in banks' desire to hold excess reserves. If the central bank has a nonborrowed reserves target of NBR^* (say, because it has a target growth rate of the money supply of 4%), it expects that the overnight interest rate will be i^*_{or}. However, as the figure indicates, the fluctuations in the reserves demand curve between $R^{d'}$ and $R^{d''}$ will result in a fluctuation in the overnight interest rate between i'_{or} and i''_{or}. Pursuing an aggregate target implies that interest rates will fluctuate.

The supply and demand diagram in Figure 18-4 shows the consequences of an interest-rate target set at i^*_{or}. Again the central bank expects the reserves demand curve to be at R^{d*}, but it fluctuates between $R^{d'}$ and $R^{d''}$ due to unexpected changes in deposits or banks' desire to hold reserves. If the demand curve rises to $R^{d''}$, the overnight interest rate will begin to rise above i^*_{or} and the central bank will engage in open market purchases of bonds until it raises the supply of nonborrowed reserves to NBR'', at which point the equilibrium overnight interest rate is again at i^*_{or}. Conversely, if the demand curve falls to $R^{d'}$ and lowers the overnight interest rate, the central bank would keep making open market sales until nonborrowed reserves fall to NBR'' and the overnight rate returns to i^*_{or}. The central bank's adherence to the interest-rate target thus leads to a fluctuating quantity of nonborrowed reserves and the money supply.

The conclusion from the supply and demand analysis is that interest-rate and reserve (monetary) aggregate targets are incompatible. A central bank can hit one or the other, but not both. Because a choice between them has to be made, we need to examine what criteria should be used to select a policy instrument.

Criteria for Choosing the Policy Instrument

Three criteria apply when choosing a policy instrument: the instrument must be observable and measurable, it must be controllable by the central bank, and it must have a predictable effect on the goals.

OBSERVABILITY AND MEASURABILITY Quick observability and accurate measurement of a policy instrument are necessary because it will be useful only if it

MyEconLab
Animation

FIGURE 18-4 Result of Targeting on the Overnight Interest Rate

Targeting on the interest rate i^*_{or} will lead to fluctuations in nonborrowed reserves between NBR' and NBR'' because of fluctuations in the demand for reserves between $R^{d'}$ and $R^{d''}$.

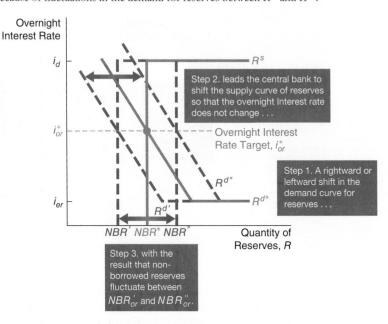

signals the policy stance rapidly. Reserve aggregates like nonborrowed reserves are straightforward to measure, but some lag in reporting of reserve aggregates (a delay of two weeks) exists. Short-term interest rates, like the overnight interest rate, by contrast, not only are easy to measure but also are observable immediately. Thus, it seems that interest rates are more observable and measurable than are reserves and, therefore, are a better policy instrument.

However, as we learned in Chapter 4, the interest rate that is easiest to measure and observe is the nominal interest rate. It is typically a poor measure of the real cost of borrowing, which indicates with more certainty what will happen to the real GDP. This real cost of borrowing is more accurately measured by the real interest rate—that is, the nominal interest rate adjusted for expected inflation $r = i - \pi^e$. Unfortunately, real interest rates are extremely difficult to measure, because we do not have a direct way to measure expected inflation. Given that both interest rates and aggregates have observability and measurability problems, it is not clear whether one should be preferred to the other as a policy instrument.

CONTROLLABILITY   A central bank must be able to exercise effective control over a variable if it is to function as a useful policy instrument. If the central bank cannot control the policy instrument, knowing that it is off track does little good, because the central bank has no way of getting it back on track.

Because of shifts in and out of currency, even reserve aggregates, such as nonborrowed reserves, are not completely controllable. Conversely, the Bank of Canada can control short-term interest rates, such as the overnight interest rate, very tightly. It might appear, therefore, that short-term interest rates would dominate reserve aggregates on the controllability criterion. However, a central bank cannot set short-term real interest rates because it does not have control over expectations of inflation. Once again, a clear-cut case cannot be made that short-term interest rates are preferable to reserve aggregates as a policy instrument, or vice versa.

PREDICTABLE EFFECT ON GOALS The most important characteristic of a policy instrument is that it must have a predictable effect on a goal. If a central bank can accurately and quickly measure the price of tea in China and can completely control its price, what good will that do? The central bank cannot use the price of tea in China to affect unemployment or the price level in its country. Because the ability to affect goals is so critical to the usefulness of any policy instrument, the tightness of the link from reserve or monetary aggregates to goals (output, employment, and inflation) or, alternatively, from interest rates to these goals has been the subject of much research and debate. In recent years, most central banks have concluded that the link between interest rates and goals such as inflation is tighter than the link between aggregates and inflation. For this reason, central banks throughout the world now generally use short-term interest rates as their policy instrument.

Tactics: The Taylor Rule

As we have seen, the Bank of Canada and most other central banks currently conduct monetary policy by setting a target for short-term interest rates like the overnight interest rate. But how should this target be chosen?

John Taylor of Stanford University has come up with an answer, called the **Taylor rule**. The Taylor rule indicates that the overnight interest rate should be set equal to the inflation rate plus an "equilibrium" real overnight interest rate (the real overnight rate that is consistent with full employment in the long run) plus a weighted average of two gaps: (1) an inflation gap, current inflation minus a target rate, and (2) an output gap, the percentage deviation of real GDP from an estimate of its potential (natural rate) level.[6] This rule can be written as follows:

$$\text{Overnight interest rate target} = \text{inflation rate} + \text{equilibrium real overnight rate} + \frac{1}{2}(\text{inflation gap}) + \frac{1}{2}(\text{output gap})$$

Taylor has assumed that the equilibrium real overnight interest rate is 2% and that an appropriate target for inflation would also be 2%, with equal weights of $\frac{1}{2}$ on the inflation and output gaps. For an example of the Taylor rule in practice, suppose that the inflation rate were at 3%, leading to a positive inflation gap of 1% (= 3% − 2%), and real GDP was 1% above its potential, resulting in a positive output gap of 1%. Then the Taylor rule suggests that the overnight interest rate should be set at 6% [= 3% inflation + 2% equilibrium real overnight rate + $\frac{1}{2}$(1% inflation gap) + $\frac{1}{2}$(1% output gap)].

An important feature of the Taylor rule is that the coefficient on the inflation gap, $\frac{1}{2}$, is positive. If the inflation rate rises by 1 percentage point, then the overnight interest target is raised by 1.5 percentage points, and so by more than one-to-one. In other words, a rise in inflation by 1 percentage point leads to a real overnight rate increase of $\frac{1}{2}$ percentage point. The principle that the monetary authorities should raise nominal interest rates by more than the increase in the inflation rate has been named the **Taylor principle**, and it is critical to the success of monetary policy. Suppose the Taylor principle is not followed and nominal rates rise by *less* than the rise in the inflation rate, so that real interest rates *fall* when inflation rises. Serious instability then results because a rise in inflation leads to an effective easing

---

[6]The original formulation of the Taylor rule can be found in John B. Taylor, "Discretion Versus Policy Rules in Practice," *Carnegie-Rochester Conference Series on Public Policy* 39 (1993): 195–214. However, a more intuitive discussion with a historical perspective can be found in John B. Taylor, "A Historical Analysis of Monetary Policy Rules," in *Monetary Policy Rules*, ed. John B. Taylor (Chicago: University of Chicago Press, 1999), 319–341.

of monetary policy, which then leads to even higher inflation in the future. Indeed, this was a feature of monetary policy in the 1970s that led to a loss of the nominal anchor and the era of the so-called "Great Inflation," when inflation rates climbed to double-digit levels. Fortunately, since 1979, the Taylor principle has become a feature of monetary policy, with much happier outcomes on both the inflation and the aggregate output fronts.

The presence of an output gap in the Taylor rule might indicate that the Bank of Canada should care not only about keeping inflation under control but also about minimizing business cycle fluctuations of output around its potential level. Caring about both inflation and output fluctuations is consistent with many statements by Bank of Canada officials that controlling inflation and stabilizing real output are important concerns of the Bank of Canada.

An alternative interpretation of the presence of the output gap in the Taylor rule is that the output gap is an indicator of future inflation, as stipulated in the **Phillips curve theory**. The Phillips curve theory indicates that changes in inflation are influenced by the state of the economy relative to its productive capacity, as well as by other factors.

This productive capacity can be measured by potential GDP, which is a function of the natural rate of unemployment, the rate of unemployment consistent with full employment. A related concept is the **nonaccelerating inflation rate of unemployment** (NAIRU)—the rate of unemployment at which there is no tendency for inflation to change. Simply put, the theory states that when the unemployment rate is above NAIRU with output below potential, inflation will come down, but if it is below NAIRU with output above potential, inflation will rise. Prior to 1995, the NAIRU was thought to reside around 8%. However, with the decline in unemployment to around the 4% level in the late 1990s, with no increase (and even a slight decrease) in inflation, some critics have questioned the value of the Phillips curve theory. Either they claim that it just doesn't work anymore or, alternatively, they believe that great uncertainty exists about the value of NAIRU. The Phillips curve theory is now highly controversial, and critics question whether it should be used as a guide for the conduct of monetary policy.

As Figure 18-5 shows, the Taylor rule does a pretty good, but not perfect, job of describing the Bank of Canada's setting of the overnight interest rate. Does this mean that the Bank of Canada should fire all its economists and put a computer in charge that simply has to compute the Taylor rule setting for the overnight rate? This would certainly save the taxpayers a lot of money. Although the Bank of Canada does not do this, it does make use of the Taylor rule in thinking about

FIGURE 18-5 The Taylor Rule for the Overnight Interest Rate, 1991–2011

The Taylor rule does a pretty good job of describing the Bank of Canada's setting of the overnight interest rate.

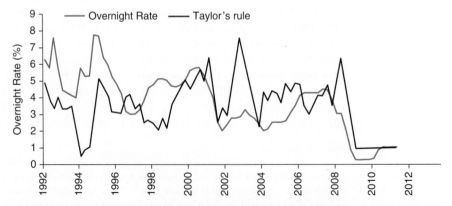

Source: Statistics Canada CANSIM II Series V41690914, V122514, and V1992067, and author's calculations.

how to conduct monetary policy (see the Inside the Central Bank box The Bank of Canada's Use of the Taylor Rule). Given the above reasons, it is no surprise that the Taylor rule does not explain all the movements in the overnight interest rate in Figure 18-5. For this reason, financial institutions hire Bank of Canada watchers, as described in the second Inside the Central Bank box.

INSIDE THE CENTRAL BANK — The Bank of Canada's Use of the Taylor Rule

Why hasn't the Bank of Canada put the overnight interest rate on the Taylor rule on autopilot, guided by a computer? There are several reasons why the Bank of Canada hasn't taken this drastic action. First and foremost, no perfect model of the economy exists, so even the best and brightest economists do not know the current inflation rate and output gap with certainty at any given moment. Since the economy is changing all the time, the Taylor rule coefficients are unlikely to stay constant in any event.

Even if we could determine these rates with certainty, monetary policy is by necessity a forward-looking activity because it takes a long time for monetary policy to affect the economy. Good monetary policy requires that the Bank of Canada forecast where inflation and economic activity are going to be in the future, and then adjust the policy instrument accordingly. The Bank of Canada will therefore look at a much wider range of information than just the current inflation rate and output gap in setting policy, as is done in the Taylor rule. In

other words, the conduct of monetary policy is as much an art as it is a science, requiring both careful analytics and human judgment. The Taylor rule leaves out all the art, and so is unlikely to produce the best monetary policy outcomes. For example, financial crises, such as that which occurred from 2007 to 2009, require complex monetary policy actions because changes in credit spreads (the difference between interest rates on securities with credit risk and those without) may alter how the overnight interest rate affects investment decisions, and therefore economic activity.

The bottom line is that putting monetary policy on autopilot with the Taylor rule with fixed coefficients would be a bad idea. The Taylor rule is, however, useful as a guide to monetary policy. If the setting of the policy instrument is very different from what the Taylor rule suggests, policymakers should ask whether they have a good reason for deviating from this rule. If they don't, then they might be making a mistake.

INSIDE THE CENTRAL BANK — Bank of Canada Watchers

As we have seen, the most important player in the determination of Canadian interest rates is the Bank of Canada. When the Bank of Canada wants to inject reserves into the system, it conducts open market purchases of bonds, which cause bond prices to increase and their interest rates to fall, at least in the short term. If the Bank withdraws reserves from the system, it sells bonds, thereby depressing their price and raising their interest rates. Knowing what actions the Bank of Canada might be taking can thus help investors and financial institutions to predict the future course of interest rates with greater accuracy. Because, as we have seen, changes

in interest rates have a major impact on investors and financial institutions' profits, they are particularly interested in scrutinizing the Bank of Canada's behaviour. To assist in this task, financial institutions hire Bank of Canada watchers, experts on Bank of Canada behaviour who may have worked in the Bank of Canada and so have an insider's view of Bank of Canada operations. A Bank of Canada watcher who can accurately predict the course of monetary policy is a very valuable commodity, and successful Bank of Canada watchers therefore often earn very high salaries, well into the six-figure range and sometimes even higher.

MyEconLab is an online homework and tutorial system that puts you in control of your own learning with study and practice tools directly correlated to this chapter's content. Visit MyEconLab to explore the following resources:

- The Questions and Applied Problems are all available in the Study Plan on MyEconLab for further practice. You will also find the answers to all of the Questions and Applied Problems in the Student Resources section of your MyEconLab.
- Visit the Student Resources section of MyEconLab to access the following appendix for this chapter: Appendix 18.1: Monetary Targeting.

MyEconLab also features Additional Readings, Videos, Glossary Flashcards, Audio Chapter Summaries, Economics News Feeds, Animations, and many additional tools to help you master key concepts from the text.

SUMMARY

1. The six basic goals of monetary policy are price stability (the primary goal), high employment (output stability), economic growth, stability of financial markets, interest-rate stability, and stability in foreign exchange markets.

2. Having a strong nominal anchor is a key element in successful monetary policy. It helps promote price stability by tying down inflation expectations and limiting the time-inconsistency problem, in which monetary policymakers conduct monetary policy in a discretionary way that focuses on short-run objectives but produces poor long-run outcomes.

3. Inflation targeting has several advantages: (1) it enables monetary policy to focus on domestic considerations; (2) it is readily understood by the public and is highly transparent; (3) it increases accountability of the central bank; and (4) it appears to ameliorate the effects of inflationary shocks. It does have some disadvantages, however: (1) inflation is not easily controlled by the monetary authorities, so that an inflation target is unable to send immediate signals to both the public and markets; (2) it might impose a rigid rule on policymakers, although this has not been the case in practice; and (3) a sole focus on inflation may lead to larger output fluctuations, although this has also not been the case in practice.

4. Four lessons can be learned from the global financial crisis: (1) developments in the financial sector have a far greater impact on economic activity than was earlier realized;

(2) the zero lower bound on interest rates can be a serious problem; (3) the cost of cleaning up after a financial crisis is very high; and (4) price and output stability do not ensure financial stability.

5. The lessons from the financial crisis provide an argument for more flexible inflation targeting, possibly with a higher inflation target. The lessons also suggest that there is a case for monetary policy to lean against credit booms but not asset-price bubbles.

6. Because interest-rate and aggregate policy instruments are incompatible, a central bank must choose between them on the basis of three criteria: measurability, controllability, and the ability to affect goal variables predictably. Central banks now typically use short-term interest rates as their policy instrument.

7. The Taylor rule indicates that the overnight interest rate should be set equal to the inflation rate plus an "equilibrium" real overnight rate plus a weighted average of two gaps: (1) an inflation gap, current inflation minus a target rate, and (2) an output gap, the percentage deviation of real GDP from an estimate of its potential (natural rate) level. The output gap in the Taylor rule could represent an indicator of future inflation, as stipulated in the Phillips curve theory. However, this theory is controversial, because high output relative to potential as measured by low unemployment has not seemed to produce higher inflation in recent years.

KEY TERMS

asset-price bubble, p. 450

dual mandate, p. 442

globalization, p. 468

hierarchical mandates, p. 442

inflation targeting, p. 443

intermediate target, p. 454

international policy
    coordination, p. 468

monetarism, p. 463

natural rate of output, p. 441

natural rate of unemployment, p. 440

nominal anchor, p. 439

nonaccelerating inflation rate of
    unemployment (NAIRU), p. 458

operating instrument, p. 454

Phillips curve theory, p. 458

policy instrument, p. 454

potential output, p. 441

price stability, p. 438

Taylor principle, p. 457

Taylor rule, p. 457

time-inconsistency problem, p. 439

QUESTIONS

1. What are the benefits of using a nominal anchor for the conduct of monetary policy?

2. What incentives arise for a central bank to fall into the time-inconsistency trap of pursuing overly expansionary monetary policy?

3. Why would it be problematic for a central bank to have a primary goal of maximizing economic growth?

4. "Since financial crises can impart severe damage to the economy, a central bank's primary goal should be to ensure stability in financial markets." Is this statement true, false, or uncertain? Explain.

5. "A central bank with a dual mandate will achieve lower unemployment in the long run than a central bank with a hierarchical mandate in which price stability takes precedence." Is this statement true, false, or uncertain? Explain.

6. Why is a public announcement of numerical inflation rate objectives important to the success of an inflation-targeting central bank?

7. How does inflation targeting help reduce the time-inconsistency of discretionary policy?

8. What methods have inflation-targeting central banks used to increase communication with the public and increase the transparency of monetary policy making?

9. Why might inflation targeting increase support for the independence of the central bank to conduct monetary policy?

10. "Because inflation targeting focuses on achieving the inflation target, it will lead to excessive output fluctuations." Is this statement true, false, or uncertain? Explain.

11. What are the key advantages and disadvantages of the monetary strategy recently used at the Federal Reserve in which the nominal anchor is only implicit?

12. "The zero lower bound on short-term interest rates is not a problem, since the central bank can just use quantitative easing to lower intermediate and longer-term interest rates instead." Is this statement true, false, or uncertain? Explain.

13. If higher inflation is bad, then why might it be advantageous to have a higher inflation target, rather than a lower target closer to zero?

14. Why aren't most central banks more proactive at trying to use monetary policy to eliminate asset-price bubbles?

15. Why would it be better to *lean* against credit-driven bubbles and *clean* after other types of asset bubbles crash?

16. Under what conditions might a central bank respond to a perceived stock market bubble?

17. Classify each of the following as either a policy instrument or an intermediate target, and explain why.

    a. The 10-year Canada bond rate
    b. The monetary base
    c. M1+
    d. The overnight interest rate

18. "If the demand for reserves did not fluctuate, the Bank of Canada could pursue both a reserves target and an interest-rate target at the same time." Is this statement true, false, or uncertain? Explain.

19. What procedures can the Bank of Canada use to control the overnight interest rate? Why does control of this interest rate imply that the Bank of Canada will lose control of nonborrowed reserves?

20. Compare the monetary base to M1+ on the grounds of controllability and measurability. Which do you prefer as an intermediate target? Why?

21. "Interest rates can be measured more accurately and quickly than reserve aggregates; hence an interest rate is preferred to the reserve aggregates as a policy instrument." Do you agree or disagree? Explain your answer.

22. How can bank behaviour and the Bank of Canada's behaviour cause money supply growth to be procyclical (rising in booms and falling in recessions)?

23. What does the Taylor rule imply that policymakers should do to the overnight interest rate under the following scenarios?

    a. Unemployment rises due to a recession.
    b. An oil price shock causes the inflation rate to rise by 1% and output to fall by 1%.
    c. The economy experiences prolonged increases in productivity growth while actual output growth is unchanged.
    d. Potential output declines while actual output remains unchanged.
    e. The Bank of Canada revises its inflation target down.

APPLIED PROBLEMS

24. If the Bank of Canada has an interest-rate target, why will an increase in the demand for reserves lead to a rise in the money supply? Use a graph of the market for reserves to explain.

25. Since monetary policy changes through the overnight interest rate occur with a lag, policymakers are usually more concerned with adjusting policy according to changes in the forecasted or expected inflation rate, rather than the current inflation rate. In light of this, suppose that monetary policymakers employ the Taylor rule to set the overnight rate, where the inflation gap is defined as the difference between expected inflation and the target inflation rate. Assume that the weights on both the inflation and the output gaps are ½, the equilibrium real overnight rate is 2%, the inflation rate target is 2%, and the output gap is 1%.

   a. If the expected inflation rate is 4%, then at what should the overnight interest rate be set according to the Taylor rule?

   b. Suppose half of Bank of Canada economists forecast inflation to be 3%, and half of Bank of Canada economists forecast inflation to be 5%. If the Bank of Canada uses the average of these two forecasts as its measure of expected inflation, then what should the overnight interest rate be according to the Taylor rule?

   c. Now suppose half of Bank of Canada economists forecast inflation to be 0%, and half forecast inflation to be 8%. If the Bank of Canada uses the average of these two forecasts as its measure of expected inflation, then what should the overnight interest rate be according to the Taylor rule?

   d. Given your answers to (a)–(c) above, do you think it is a good idea for monetary policymakers to use a strict interpretation of the Taylor rule as a basis for setting policy? Why or why not?

WEB EXERCISES

1. Go to **www.bankofcanada.ca**, and click on "About the Bank" and then "What We Do."

   a. Review the Bank of Canada's main functions.
   b. How does the Bank's monetary policy contribute to rising living standards for Canadians?

2. It is possible to access other central bank websites to learn about their structure. One example is the European Central Bank. Go to **www.ecb.int/index.html**. On the ECB home page, locate the current exchange rate between the euro and the U.S. dollar. It was initially set at 1 to 1. What is it now?

3. Many countries have central banks that are responsible for their nation's monetary policy. Go to **www.bis.org/cbanks.htm** and select one of the central banks (for example, Norway). Review that bank's website to determine its policies regarding application of monetary policy. How does this bank's policies compare to those of the Bank of Canada?

Bank of Canada Policy Procedures: Historical Perspective

The well-known adage "the road to hell is paved with good intentions" applies as much to the Bank of Canada as it does to human beings. Understanding a central bank's goals and the strategies it can use to pursue them cannot tell us how monetary policy is actually conducted. To understand the practical results of the theoretical underpinnings, we have to look at how the Bank of Canada has actually conducted policy in the past. This historical perspective not only will show us how our central bank carries out its duties but also will help us interpret the Bank's activities and see where Canadian monetary policy may be heading in the future.

The Early Years

From the end of World War II in 1945 until the early 1970s, the world economy operated under a system of fixed exchange rates, known as the Bretton Woods system (to be discussed in detail in Chapter 20). Initially, Canada opted out of this system, but joined in 1962 and participated with the exchange rate fixed at 92.5 U.S. cents. Even before 1962, Canadian monetary policy had been driven by the goal of maintaining a stable exchange rate with the United States and the Bank of Canada therefore kept short-term interest rates more or less in step with U.S. interest rates. This meant that short-term interest rates, or the differential between U.S. and Canadian rates, were the intermediate target of monetary policy. As a result, inflation rates and interest rates followed generally similar patterns in the two countries (see, for example, Figure 18A).

In 1971, Canada switched to a flexible exchange rate regime, but the Bank of Canada continued to adjust short-term interest rates to keep the foreign exchange and domestic bonds markets functioning smoothly, and paid no attention to the growth rate of money. As a result, monetary policy was quite expansionary in the early 1970s and the inflation rate increased to double digits—in fact, the price level increased by 11% in 1974 compared to only 3% in 1971. By the mid-1970s, there was little doubt that one consequence of the policy of using interest rates as the intermediate target was that the Bank of Canada did not concern itself with the rate of growth of the money supply, as measured by the monetary aggregates.

By the end of this period there was also a wide consensus among central banks around the world that fluctuations in money contained useful information about income and prices. This evidence contributed to the rise of **monetarism**, a theory that emphasizes a steady, predictable rate of growth in the monetary aggregates. It led the Bank of Canada and many other central banks, including the Federal Reserve, the Bank of England, the Bundesbank, the Swiss National Bank, and the Bank of Japan, to adopt key monetary aggregates as the intermediate targets of monetary policy.

FIGURE 18A   Interest Rates (90-Day T-Bills), Canada and the United States, 1941–2011

Canadian and U.S. interest rates tend to move in unison.

Source: Statistics Canada, CANSIM II Series V122541 and Federal Reserve Economic Data (FRED).

Monetary Targeting, 1975–1981

In response to rising inflation in the early 1970s, in 1975 the Bank of Canada introduced a program of "monetary gradualism," under which M1 growth would be controlled within a gradually falling target range (see Table 18A). The change in monetary strategy did not extend to a change in operating procedures—the Bank continued to use an interest rate as its operating target. The idea was to announce (about one year) in advance the target path for the growth of M1 and then adjust policy during the course of the year to make the actual growth rate lie within the target range. The rationale for announcing the monetary policy targets in advance was to influence people's expectations, with the hope that this would help bring down actual inflation faster than otherwise. Moreover, the Bank decided to target M1 because it was the most prominent measure of money with a very stable demand.

As can be seen from Table 18A, the Bank of Canada was successful at keeping actual M1 growth within the target range, and the goal of reducing M1 growth was achieved by the end of the decade. However, the inflation rate accelerated, and by the end of the 1970s, it was almost at the same level as when monetary gradualism was introduced in 1975. What went wrong? Why did the inflation rate remain high? The answers to these questions lie in a series of financial innovations that reduced the demand for M1 balances. In particular, the introduction of new kinds of bank deposit accounts and the development of cash management techniques for corporate accounts motivated individuals and firms to move out of demand deposits—part of M1—into new chequable savings deposits—part of M2. This increased the growth rate of M2 and reduced the growth rate of M1 at the same time that M1 growth was being targeted, thereby rendering what seemed like tight anti-inflationary policy into one that was in fact accommodating inflation.

By 1978, only three years after monetary targeting had begun, the Bank of Canada began to distance itself from this strategy out of concern for the nominal exchange rate, which had been depreciating. In particular, when interest rates in the United States increased sharply in late 1979, the Bank of Canada had to choose between allowing Canadian rates to increase to prevent an outflow of financial capital and

TABLE 18A	Canadian M1 Target Ranges and Actual Growth Rates for 1975–1980		
Announcement Date	Base Period	M1 Growth Target (%)	Outcome (%)
November 1975	April–June 1975	10–15	9.3
August 1976	February–April 1976	8–12	7.7
October 1977	June 1977	7–11	9.3
September 1978	June 1978	6–10	5.1
December 1979	April–June 1979	5–9	5.9
February 1981	August–October 1980	4–8	0.4

Notes: Outcomes are annualized growth rates (%) of seasonally adjusted M1 between the base period and the next announcement of new targets. For example, the outcome corresponding to the November 1975 announcement is the annualized growth rate of M1 between April and June 1975 and August 1976.

Source: Ben Bernanke and Frederic Mishkin, "Central Bank Behaviour and the Strategy of Monetary Policy: Observations from Six Industrialised Countries." *NBER Macroeconomics Annual* (1992): 183–228. Reprinted with permission of the authors.

allowing the exchange rate to depreciate to accommodate the spread in interest rates between the two countries. The Bank responded with an extremely restrictive monetary policy to resist depreciation of the Canadian dollar and the possible inflationary shock from import prices. Not surprisingly, M1 growth was negative in 1981 even though the target range was for growth between 4% and 8% (see Table 18A), and Canadian interest rates increased to unprecedented levels (see Figure 18A). The cost was the very deep 1981–1982 recession, the most severe since the 1930s.

Because of the conflict with exchange rate goals, as well as the uncertainty about M1 as a reliable guide to monetary policy, monetary targeting was formally abandoned in November 1982.

The Checklist Approach, 1982–1988

The period following 1982 was one of groping. With the abandonment of M1 targets, the Bank of Canada switched its focus to a range of broader monetary aggregates, such as M2 and M2+, but no aggregate was found that would be suitable as a guide for conducting monetary policy. As a result, the Bank adopted what came to be called the "checklist" approach to policy, meaning that it looked at a list of factors in order to design and implement monetary policy. The Bank's checklist included the interest rate, the exchange rate, and, with less weight attached to it, the money supply. The goal of monetary policy was inflation containment in the short term and price stability in the long term.

The Bank's anti-inflation policy during the 1982–1988 period can be viewed as one where the interest rate became the operating target and the exchange rate was the intermediate target. Throughout most of the period the Bank targeted interest rates, resisting depreciation of the Canadian dollar (fearing that depreciation would worsen inflation). The Bank's policy, however, had been undertaken against the backdrop of a persistent federal budget deficit that led to higher interest rates, making it difficult for the Bank to control money growth and inflation. In fact inflation had begun to increase again and the Bank of Canada responded with a dramatic reversal of its ad hoc monetary strategy. It announced early in 1988 that short-term issues would henceforth guide policy less and that price stability would be the Bank's long-term objective of monetary policy.

Inflation Targeting, 1989–Present

The adoption of inflation targets in Canada followed a three-year campaign by the Bank of Canada to promote price stability as the long-term goal of monetary policy. Beginning with the Hanson Lecture at the University of Alberta in January 1988, the newly appointed Bank of Canada governor, John Crow, announced that the Bank would subsequently pursue an objective of price stability (or zero inflation).[1] Initially, the policy of zero inflation took the form of a return to the high interest rates of the early 1980s. For example, during 1987 through 1989, interest rates increased and the Canadian dollar appreciated by more than would have normally been expected under previous regimes. The idea was that higher interest rates and a stronger dollar would lower aggregate demand and eventually bring inflation down.

In this most recent attempt at lowering inflation, the Bank of Canada, however, followed a different strategy, by announcing explicit targets for its ultimate goal—the inflation rate—rather than for an intermediate variable such as money growth. In particular, in February 1991 the Bank's governor and the minister of finance jointly announced a series of declining inflation targets, with a band of plus and minus one percentage point around them. The targets were 3% by the end of 1992, falling to 2% by the end of 1995, to remain within a range of 1% to 3% thereafter. The 1% to 3% target range for inflation was renewed in December 1995, in early 1998, May 2001, November 2006, and again in November 2011 to apply until the end of 2016.[2] The midpoint of the current inflation target range, 2%, is regarded as the most desirable outcome.

In setting its inflation targets, the Bank of Canada uses the rate of change in the CPI because of its "headline" quality—it is the most commonly used and understood price measure in Canada. Moreover, the CPI comes out monthly and without revisions, whereas other price indexes, such as the GDP deflator, are frequently revised. Also, because headline CPI (all items) includes volatile components such as food, energy, and the effect of indirect taxes, the Bank of Canada, in order to avoid responses to short-run fluctuations, uses and reports inflation in "core CPI," which excludes volatile components. A core inflation rate is useful in assessing whether trend inflation is on track for the medium term. Thus, although the Bank of Canada targets the headline inflation rate, it uses the core inflation rate as a measure of the headline rate's trend. Also, defining the inflation targets in terms of ranges provides the Bank sufficient flexibility to deal with supply shocks beyond those already taken care of by the exclusion of volatile components from core inflation.

The move to targeting directly a goal of policy rather than an intermediate variable represented a significant shift in Bank of Canada policy procedures. An implication of this change was that the Bank had to broaden its information gathering to include variables containing significant information about future inflation. It has since used the overnight interest rate as the operating target and indicated that a range of monetary aggregates is useful in guiding policy along with an index of

---

[1]Zero inflation should be interpreted as a small positive rate of measured inflation.

[2]The 1995 and 1998 inflation-control agreements between the Bank of Canada and the government had a three-year horizon. However, the 2011 agreement, like the 2006 and 2001 agreements, has a five-year horizon, reflecting the wide acceptance of the targets after over 20 years of operation.

monetary conditions based on interest rates and exchange rates. The main purpose of this index is to capture the two key monetary policy transmission mechanisms in an open economy—the one operating through interest rates and the one operating through exchange rates.

What are the results of Canada's inflation-targeting monetary policy? Figure 18-1 (panel b) on page 445 plots the Canadian inflation rate for each year since 1980 and shows the Bank's target range since 1996. Clearly, inflation has fallen dramatically since the adoption of inflation targets, from above the 5% level in 1991 to a 1% rate in 1998, being most of the time in the lower half of the target range. However, this decline was not without cost: unemployment soared to above the 10% level from 1991 until 1994 but has since fallen. What is difficult to say is whether explicit inflation targets are the only way to achieve good macroeconomic outcomes. As the Bank's former governor, Gordon Thiessen, put it, "It is too early to draw very strong conclusions about the impact of inflation targets on actual economic performance in Canada. We really do require a longer period of time for targets to demonstrate their ability to deal successfully with the peak of an economic upturn without the trend of inflation moving persistently outside the target range."[3]

From Opaqueness to Openness and Accountability

The historical record of the Bank of Canada's conduct of monetary policy reveals that during the 1960s and 1970s, the Bank operated in an environment characterized by instrument and goal opaqueness. The use of multiple instruments and goals tended to shield the Bank from scrutiny and accountability; the public was not able to comprehend the Bank's actions, allowing the accountability of the Bank of Canada to deteriorate.

Over the past decade, however, as John Chant, a former Special Adviser at the Bank of Canada, recently put it, ". . . the Bank of Canada has transformed its conduct of monetary policy by focusing on an explicit inflation-control target, establishing a Governing Council for decision-making, announcing a target overnight interest rate, and adopting fixed action dates for making policy changes."[4] These changes (and in particular the adoption of inflation targets) have moved the Bank away from opaqueness, toward openness and accountability.

Pre-emptive Strikes Against Inflation, Economic Downturns, and Financial Disruptions

The recognition that monetary policy needs to be more forward looking has prompted the Bank of Canada to be more pre-emptive. The Bank has not only engaged in pre-emptive strikes against a rise in inflation, it has acted pre-emptively against negative shocks to aggregate demand and especially to those associated with financial disruptions.

With the onset of the financial crisis in August 2007, the Bank of Canada began to ease policy even in the face of a strong economy with growth close to 3% in the third quarter of 2007, unemployment below 6%, and inflation rising because of

---

[3]Gordon G. Thiessen, "The Canadian Experience with Targets for Inflation Control," *Canadian Public Policy* 24 (1998): 425. For a more detailed discussion of Canada's experience with inflation targets, see Charles Freedman, "Inflation Targeting and the Economy: Lessons from Canada's First Decade," *Contemporary Economic Policy* 19 (2001): 2–19, and Ben Bernanke, Thomas Laubach, Frederic Mishkin, and Adam Posen, *Inflation Targeting: Lessons from the International Experience* (Princeton, NJ: Princeton University Press, 1998).

[4]John Chant, "The Bank of Canada: Moving Towards Transparency," *Bank of Canada Review* (Spring 2003): 5–13.

the increase in energy prices. The potential for the financial disruption to weaken the economy and to produce an adverse feedback loop—in which credit markets would worsen and weaken economic activity, which in turn would further weaken credit markets—encouraged the Bank of Canada to take pre-emptive action, cutting the overnight interest rate by 25 basis points in December of 2007, to 4.25%. Subsequent easing of monetary policy lowered the overnight funds rate to 0.25% by April of 2009. At the same time, the Bank of Canada implemented large liquidity injections into the credit markets to try to get them working again (as discussed in Chapter 17).

These pre-emptive attacks against negative shocks to aggregate demand were particularly successful in the past in keeping economic fluctuations very mild. The magnitude of the financial disruption during the recent financial crisis, however, was so great that the pre-emptive actions by the Bank of Canada were not enough to contain the crisis, and the economy suffered accordingly.

International Considerations

The growing integration and interdependence of national economies (a process known as **globalization**) has brought international considerations to the forefront of Bank of Canada policymaking in recent years. With integrated financial markets, the Bank of Canada's monetary policy is also influenced by developments outside Canada. This is not a bad thing, but requires international policy cooperation to reduce potential disruptions to domestic policymaking and promote greater stability in financial markets. International cooperation has been encouraged by the process of **international policy coordination** (in which countries agree to enact policies cooperatively).

International considerations also played a role in the initiatives recently undertaken by the International Monetary Fund and the Bank for International Settlements, following the G-7 Halifax Summit in 1995, to improve the functioning of international financial markets. These initiatives seek to maximize the benefits of financial globalization, reduce the risks of financial instability that unrestrained capital flows may cause, and develop mechanisms for support in times of financial crisis. For example, the issue of international financial stability played a role in the Federal Reserve's decision to lower the federal funds rate by ¾ of a percentage point in the fall of 1998. Concerns about the potential for worldwide financial crisis in the wake of the collapse of the Russian financial system at that time and weakness in other economies, particularly in Asia, stimulated the Fed to take a dramatic step to calm down markets.

International considerations, although not the primary focus of the Bank of Canada, are also likely to be a major factor in the conduct of Canadian monetary policy in the future.

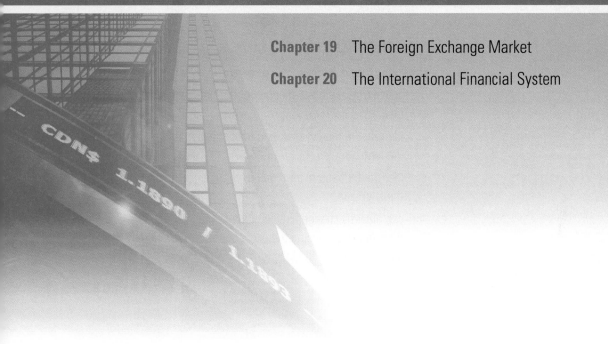

PART VI

International Finance and Monetary Policy

Crisis and Response: Foreign Exchange Market Turmoil and the IMF

From 2002 until 2008, the Canadian dollar steadily increased in value relative to the U.S. dollar. With the credit markets seizing up in September and October of 2008 after the failure of Lehman Bothers, however, the U.S. dollar appreciated sharply. The same "flight to quality" that led investors to step up their purchases of U.S. Treasury securities also led them to want to hold more U.S. dollars, thereby bidding up the U.S. dollar's value relative to other currencies, including the Canadian dollar and the euro.

This good news for the U.S. dollar was often bad news for other currencies. Many countries in Latin America and Eastern Europe found their currencies in free fall. The International Monetary Fund (IMF) stepped in and set up a new lending facility to make loans to distressed countries with fewer strings attached than was true for the IMF's previous lending programs. The IMF started making loans to the tune of billions of dollars. The IMF, which had looked like it was on the sidelines as the global financial crisis spread worldwide, now was moving to front and centre.

The global financial crisis has demonstrated that events that started in the United States have worldwide ramifications and that international financial institutions like the IMF have an important role in responding to make sure that the international financial system continues to work well. Chapter 19 outlines how the foreign exchange market functions and how exchange rates between different countries' currencies are determined. In Chapter 20, we examine how the international financial system operates and how it affects monetary policy.

CHAPTER 19

The Foreign Exchange Market

LEARNING OBJECTIVES

After studying this chapter you should be able to

1. summarize the basic function performed by the foreign exchange market

2. identify the factors that lead to changes in the exchange rate in the long run

3. identify the factors that lead to changes in the exchange rate in the short run

4. explain why changes in the money supply lead to *exchange rate overshooting* (causing the exchange rate to change by more in the short run than in the long run)

PREVIEW In the late 1980s and early 1990s, Canadian businesses became less competitive with their counterparts in the United States; afterward their competitiveness increased. Did this swing in competitiveness occur primarily because Canadian management fell down on the job in the late 1980s and early 1990s and then got its act together afterward? Not really. Canadian business became less competitive in the late 1980s and early 1990s because Canadian dollars became worth more in terms of U.S. dollars, making Canadian goods more expensive relative to U.S. goods. By the late 1990s and early 2000s, the value of the Canadian dollar had fallen appreciably from its highs in the late 1980s, making Canadian goods cheaper and Canadian businesses more competitive.

The price of one currency in terms of another (say, euros per Canadian dollar) is called the **exchange rate**. As you can see in Figure 19-1, exchange rates are highly volatile. The exchange rate affects the economy and our daily lives because when the Canadian dollar becomes more valuable relative to foreign currencies, foreign goods become cheaper for Canadians and Canadian goods become more expensive for foreigners. When the Canadian dollar falls in value, foreign goods become more expensive for Canadians and Canadian goods become cheaper for foreigners.

Fluctuations in the exchange rate also affect both inflation and output, and are an important concern to monetary policymakers. When the Canadian dollar falls in value, the higher prices of imported goods feed directly into a higher price level and inflation. A declining Canadian dollar, which makes Canadian goods cheaper for foreigners, increases the demand for Canadian goods and leads to higher production and output.

We begin our study of international finance by examining the **foreign exchange market**, the financial market where exchange rates are determined.

FIGURE 19-1   Canadian Exchange Rates, 1974–2011

Exchange rates are highly volatile. Note that a decline in these plots means a weakening of the Canadian dollar, and an increase indicates a strengthening of the Canadian dollar.

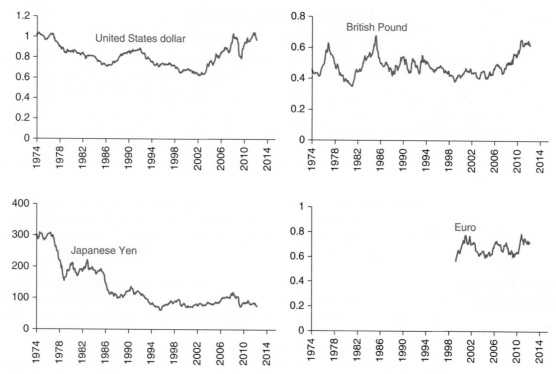

Source: Statistics Canada CANSIM II Series V37426, V37430, V37456, and V21570998.

Foreign Exchange Market

Most countries of the world have their own currencies: Canada has its dollar; the European Monetary Union, its euro; Brazil, its real; and China, its yuan. Trade between countries involves the mutual exchange of different currencies (or, more usually, assets denominated in different currencies). When a Canadian firm buys foreign goods, services, or financial assets, for example, Canadian dollars (typically, assets denominated in Canadian dollars) must be exchanged for foreign currency (assets denominated in the foreign currency).

The trading of currency and assets denominated in particular currencies takes place in the foreign exchange market. Transactions conducted in the foreign exchange market determine the rates at which currencies are exchanged, which in turn determine the cost of purchasing foreign goods and financial assets.

What Are Foreign Exchange Rates?

There are two kinds of exchange rate transactions. The predominant ones, called **spot transactions**, involve the immediate (two-day) exchange of assets. **Forward transactions** involve the exchange of assets at some specified future date. The **spot exchange rate** is the exchange rate for the spot transaction, and the **forward exchange rate** is the exchange rate for the forward transaction.

When a currency increases in value, it experiences **appreciation**; when it falls in value and is worth fewer Canadian dollars, it undergoes **depreciation**. At the beginning of 1999, for example, the euro was valued at 1.76 Canadian dollars, and (as indicated in the Financial News box Foreign Exchange Rates) on December 14, 2011, it

FINANCIAL NEWS

Foreign Exchange Rates

Foreign exchange rates are published daily in newspapers and Internet sites such as www.finance.yahoo.com and www.bloomberg.com. Exchange rates for a currency such as the euro are quoted in two ways: Canadian dollars per unit of domestic currency or domestic currency per Canadian dollar. For example, on December 14, 2011, the euro exchange rate was quoted as $1.34 per euro and

0.74 euros per dollar. Canadians generally would regard the exchange rate with the euro as $1.34 per euro, while Europeans think of it as 0.74 euros per Canadian dollar.

Exchange rates typically are quoted for the spot transaction (the spot exchange rate) and for forward transactions (the forward exchange rate) that will take place one month, three months, and six months in the future.

---

was valued at $1.34. The euro *depreciated* by 23.86%: $(1.34 - 1.76)/1.76 = -23.86\%$. Equivalently, we could say that the Canadian dollar, which went from a value of 0.57 euros per dollar at the beginning of 1999 to a value of 0.74 euros per dollar on December 14, 2011, *appreciated* by 29.82%: $(0.74 - 0.57)/0.57 = 29.82\%$.

Why Are Exchange Rates Important?

Exchange rates are important because they affect the relative price of domestic and foreign goods. The dollar price of French goods to a Canadian is determined by the interaction of two factors: the price of French goods in euros and the euro/dollar exchange rate.

Suppose that Wanda the Winetaster, a Canadian, decides to buy a bottle of 1961 (a very good year) Château Lafite Rothschild to complete her wine cellar. If the price of the wine in France is 1000 euros and the exchange rate is $1.32 to the euro, the wine will cost Wanda $1320 (1000 euros × $1.32/euro).[1] Now suppose that Wanda delays her purchase by two months, at which time the euro has appreciated to $1.50 per euro. If the domestic price of the bottle of Lafite Rothschild remains 1000 euros, its dollar cost will have risen from $1320 to $1500.

The same currency appreciation, however, makes the price of foreign goods in that country less expensive. At an exchange rate of $1.32 per euro, a Dell computer priced at $2000 costs Pierre the Programmer 1515 euros; if the exchange rate increases to $1.50 per euro, the computer will cost him only 1333 euros.

A depreciation of the euro lowers the cost of French goods in Canada but raises the cost of Canadian goods in France. If the euro drops in value to $1.20, Wanda's bottle of Lafite Rothschild will cost her only $1200 instead of $1320, and the Dell computer will cost Pierre 1667 euros rather than 1515.

Such reasoning leads to the following conclusion: *when a country's currency appreciates (rises in value relative to other currencies), the country's goods abroad become more expensive and foreign goods in that country become cheaper (holding domestic prices constant in the two countries). Conversely, when a country's currency depreciates, its goods abroad become cheaper and foreign goods in that country become more expensive.*

Depreciation of a currency makes it easier for domestic manufacturers to sell their goods abroad and makes foreign goods less competitive in domestic markets. From 2002 to 2011, the appreciating Canadian dollar hurt Canadian industries trying

---

[1]Throughout this book we use the symbol $ for the Canadian dollar. We denote the United States dollar using the symbol US$.

to sell more goods, but helped Canadian consumers because foreign goods were less expensive. The price of French wine and cheese and the cost of vacationing abroad fell as a result of the strong Canadian dollar.

How Is Foreign Exchange Traded?

You cannot go to a centralized location to watch exchange rates being determined; currencies are not traded on exchanges such as the Toronto Stock Exchange. Instead, the foreign exchange market is organized as an over-the-counter market in which several hundred dealers (mostly banks) stand ready to buy and sell assets denominated in foreign currencies. Because these dealers are in constant telephone and computer contact, the market is very competitive; in effect, it functions no differently from a centralized market.

An important point to note is that while banks, companies, and governments talk about buying and selling currencies in foreign exchange markets, they do not take a fistful of dollars and sell them for British pound notes. Rather, most trades involve the buying and selling of assets denominated in different currencies. So when we say that a bank is buying euros in the foreign exchange market, what we actually mean is that the bank is buying *assets denominated in euros*. The volume in this market is colossal, exceeding $4 trillion per day.

Trades in the foreign exchange market consist of transactions in excess of $1 million. The market that determines the exchange rates shown in the Financial News box is not where one would buy foreign currency for a trip abroad. Instead, we buy foreign currency in the retail market from dealers such as Thomas Cook or from banks. Because retail prices are higher than wholesale, when we buy foreign exchange, we obtain fewer units of foreign currency per dollar than exchange rates in the Following the Financial News box indicate.

Exchange Rates in the Long Run

Like the price of any good or asset in a free market, exchange rates are determined by the interaction of supply and demand. To simplify our analysis of exchange rates in a free market, we divide it into two parts. First, we examine how exchange rates are determined in the long run; then we use our knowledge of the long-run determinants of the exchange rate to help us understand how they are determined in the short run.

Law of One Price

The starting point for understanding how exchange rates are determined is a simple idea called the **law of one price**: if two countries produce an identical good and transportation costs and trade barriers are very low, the price of the good should be the same throughout the world no matter which country produces it.

Suppose that Canadian steel costs $100 per tonne and identical Japanese steel costs 10 000 yen per tonne. For the law of one price to hold true, the exchange rate between the yen and the dollar must be 100 yen per dollar ($0.01 per yen) so that one tonne of Canadian steel sells for 10 000 yen in Japan (the price of Japanese steel) and one tonne of Japanese steel sells for $100 in Canada (the price of Canadian steel). If the exchange rate were 200 yen to the dollar, Japanese steel would sell for $50 per tonne in Canada or half the price of Canadian steel, and Canadian steel would sell for 20 000 yen per tonne in Japan, twice the price of Japanese steel. Because Canadian steel would be more expensive than Japanese steel in both countries and is identical to Japanese steel, the demand for Canadian steel would go to zero. Given a fixed dollar price for Canadian steel, the resulting excess supply of Canadian steel will be eliminated only if the exchange rate falls to 100 yen per dollar, making the price of Canadian steel and Japanese steel the same in both countries.

Theory of Purchasing Power Parity

One of the most prominent theories of how exchange rates are determined is the **theory of purchasing power parity (PPP)**. It states that exchange rates between any two currencies will adjust to reflect changes in the price levels of the two countries. The theory of PPP is simply an application of the law of one price to national price levels rather than to individual prices. Suppose that the yen price of Japanese steel rises 10% (to 11 000 yen) relative to the dollar price of Canadian steel (unchanged at $100). For the law of one price to hold, the exchange rate must rise to 110 yen to the dollar, a 10% appreciation of the dollar. Applying the law of one price to the price levels in the two countries produces the theory of purchasing power parity, which maintains that if the Japanese price level rises 10% relative to the Canadian price level, the dollar will appreciate by 10%.

Another way of thinking about purchasing power parity is through a concept called the **real exchange rate**, the rate at which domestic goods can be exchanged for foreign goods. In effect, it is the price of domestic goods relative to the price of foreign goods denominated in the domestic currency. For example, if a basket of goods in Toronto costs $50, while the cost of the same basket of goods in Tokyo costs $75 because it costs 7500 yen while the exchange rate is at 100 yen per dollar, then the real exchange rate is 0.66 (= $50/$75). The real exchange rate is below 1.0, indicating that it is cheaper to buy a basket of goods in Canada than in Japan. It is the real exchange rate that indicates whether a currency is relatively cheap or not. Another way of describing PPP is to say that the real exchange rate is always equal to 1.0, so that the purchasing power of the dollar is the same as the purchasing power of other currencies such as the yen or the euro.

As our Canadian/Japanese example demonstrates, the theory of PPP suggests that if one country's price level rises relative to another's, its currency should depreciate (the other country's currency should appreciate). As you can see in Figure 19-2, this prediction is borne out in the long run. Yet, as the same figure indicates, PPP theory often has little predictive power in the short run. So even though PPP theory provides some guidance to the long-run movement of exchange rates, it is not perfect and in the short run is a particularly poor predictor. What explains PPP theory's failure to predict well?

Why the Theory of Purchasing Power Parity Cannot Fully Explain Exchange Rates

The PPP conclusion that exchange rates are determined solely by changes in relative price levels rests on the assumption that all goods are identical in both countries and that transportation costs and trade barriers are very low. When this assumption is true, the law of one price states that the relative prices of all these goods (that is, the relative price level between the two countries) will determine the exchange rate. The assumption that goods are identical may not be too unreasonable for Canadian and Japanese steel, but is it a reasonable assumption for Canadian and Japanese cars? Is a Toyota the equivalent of a Chevrolet?

FIGURE 19-2 Purchasing Power Parity, Canada/United States, 1973–2011

Source: International Financial Statistics and Statistics Canada CANSIM II series V37426.

Because Toyotas and Chevys are obviously not identical, their prices do not have to be equal. Toyotas might be more expensive relative to Chevys and both Canadians and Japanese will still purchase Toyotas. Because the law of one price does not hold for all goods, a rise in the price of Toyotas relative to Chevys will not necessarily mean that the yen must depreciate by the amount of the relative price increase of Toyotas over Chevys.

PPP theory furthermore does not take into account that many goods and services (whose prices are included in a measure of a country's price level) are not traded across borders. Housing, land, and services such as restaurant meals, haircuts, and golf lessons are not traded goods. So even though the prices of these items might rise and lead to a higher price level relative to another country's, there would be little direct effect on the exchange rate.

Factors That Affect Exchange Rates in the Long Run

Our analysis indicates that in the long run, four major factors affect the exchange rate: relative price levels, trade barriers, preferences for domestic versus foreign goods, and productivity. We examine how each of these factors affects the exchange rate while holding the others constant.

The basic reasoning proceeds along the following lines: anything that increases the demand for domestically produced goods that are traded relative to foreign-traded goods tends to appreciate the domestic currency because domestic goods will continue to sell well even when the value of the domestic currency is higher. Similarly, anything that increases the demand for foreign goods relative to domestic goods tends to depreciate the domestic currency because domestic goods will continue to sell well only if the value of the domestic currency is lower. In other words, *if a factor increases the demand for domestic goods relative to foreign goods, the domestic currency will appreciate; if a factor decreases the relative demand for domestic goods, the domestic currency will depreciate*.

RELATIVE PRICE LEVELS   In line with PPP theory, when prices of Canadian goods rise (holding prices of foreign goods constant), the demand for Canadian goods falls and the dollar tends to depreciate so that Canadian goods can still sell well. By contrast, if prices of Japanese goods rise so that the relative prices of Canadian goods fall, the demand for Canadian goods increases, and the dollar tends to appreciate because Canadian goods will continue to sell well even with a higher value of the domestic currency. *In the long run, a rise in a country's price level (relative to the foreign price level) causes its currency to depreciate, and a fall in the country's relative price level causes its currency to appreciate*.

TRADE BARRIERS   Barriers to free trade such as **tariffs** (taxes on imported goods) and **quotas** (restrictions on the quantity of foreign goods that can be imported) can affect the exchange rate. Suppose that Canada increases its tariff or puts a lower quota on Japanese cars. These increases in trade barriers increase the demand for Canadian cars, and the dollar tends to appreciate because Canadian cars will still sell well even with a higher value of the dollar. *Increasing trade barriers cause a country's currency to appreciate in the long run*.

PREFERENCES FOR DOMESTIC VERSUS FOREIGN GOODS   If the Japanese develop an appetite for Canadian goods—say, for Bombardier's high-speed trains and Canadian beef and pork—the increased demand for Canadian goods (exports) tends to appreciate the dollar because the Canadian goods will continue to sell well even at a higher value for the dollar. Likewise, if Canadians decide that they prefer Japanese cars to Canadian cars, the increased demand for Japanese goods (imports) tends to depreciate the dollar. *Increased demand for a country's exports causes its*

TABLE 19-1   Factors That Affect Exchange Rates in the Long Run

Factor	Change in Factor	Response of the Exchange Rate, E*
Domestic price level[†]	↑	↓
Trade barriers	↑	↑
Import demand	↑	↓
Export demand	↑	↑
Productivity[†]	↑	↑

*Units of foreign currency per Canadian dollar: ↑ indicates domestic currency appreciation; ↓, depreciation.
[†]Relative to other countries.
Note: Only increases (↑) in the factors are shown; the effects of decreases in the variables on the exchange rate are the opposite of those indicated in the "Response" column.

currency to appreciate in the long run; conversely, increased demand for imports causes the domestic currency to depreciate.

PRODUCTIVITY   When productivity in a country rises, it tends to rise in domestic sectors that produce traded goods rather than nontraded goods. Higher productivity is therefore associated with a decline in the price of domestically produced traded goods relative to foreign-traded goods. As a result, the demand for domestic traded goods rises, and the domestic currency tends to appreciate. If, however, a country's productivity lags behind that of other countries, its traded goods become relatively more expensive, and the currency tends to depreciate. In the long run, as a country becomes more productive relative to other countries, its currency appreciates.[2]

Our long-run theory of exchange rate behaviour is summarized in Table 19-1. We use the convention that the exchange rate E is quoted so that an appreciation of the currency corresponds to a rise in the exchange rate. In the case of Canada, this means that we are quoting the exchange rate as units of foreign currency per dollar (say, euros per dollar).[3]

Exchange Rates in the Short Run: A Supply and Demand Analysis

We have developed a theory of the long-run behaviour of exchange rates. However, because factors driving long-run changes in exchange rates move slowly over time, if we are to understand why exchange rates exhibit such large changes (sometimes

---

[2]A country might be so small that a change in productivity or the preferences for domestic or foreign goods would have no effect on prices of these goods relative to foreign goods. In this case changes in productivity or changes in preferences for domestic or foreign goods affect the country's income but will not necessarily affect the value of the currency. In our analysis, we are assuming that these factors can affect relative prices and consequently the exchange rate.

[3]Exchange rates can be quoted either as units of foreign currency per domestic currency or alternatively as units of domestic currency per foreign currency. In professional writing, many economists quote exchange rates as units of domestic currency per foreign currency so that an appreciation of the domestic currency is portrayed as a fall in the exchange rate. The opposite convention is used in the text here because it is more intuitive to think of an appreciation of the domestic currency as a rise in the exchange rate.

several percent) from day to day, we must develop a supply and demand analysis of how current exchange rates (spot exchange rates) are determined in the short run.

The key to understanding the short-run behaviour of exchange rates is to recognize that an exchange rate tells us the price at which domestic assets (those denominated in the domestic currency, which includes domestic bank deposits) trade for foreign assets (those denominated in the foreign currency, which includes foreign bank deposits). Because the exchange rate is the price of one asset in terms of another, the natural way to investigate the short-run determination of exchange rates is to use an asset market approach that relies heavily on the theory of portfolio choice developed in Chapter 5. As you will see, however, the long-run determinants of the exchange rate we have just outlined also play an important role in the short-run asset market approach.

In the past, supply and demand approaches to exchange rate determination emphasized the role of import and export demand. The more modern asset market approach used here emphasizes stocks of assets rather than the flows of exports and imports over short periods, because export and import transactions are quite small relative to the amount of domestic and foreign assets at any given time. For example, foreign exchange transactions in Canada each year are well over 25 times greater than the amount of Canadian exports and imports. Thus over short periods such as a year, decisions to hold domestic or foreign assets play a much greater role in exchange rate determination than the demand for exports and imports does.

Supply Curve for Domestic Assets

We start by discussing the supply curve. In this analysis we treat Canada as the home country, so domestic assets are denominated in Canadian dollars. For simplicity, we use euros to stand for any foreign country's currency, so foreign assets are denominated in euros.

The quantity of dollar assets supplied is primarily the quantity of bank deposits, bonds, and equities in Canada and for all practical purposes we can take this amount as fixed with respect to the exchange rate. The quantity supplied at any exchange rate does not change, so the supply curve, S, is vertical, as shown in Figure 19-3.

Demand Curve for Domestic Assets

The demand curve traces out the quantity demanded at each current exchange rate by holding everything else constant, particularly the expected future value of the exchange rate. We write the current exchange rate (the spot exchange rate) as E_t, and the expected exchange rate for the next period as E_{t+1}^e. As the theory of portfolio choice suggests, the most important determinant of the quantity of domestic (dollar) assets demanded is the relative expected return of domestic assets. Let's see what happens as the current exchange rate, E_t, falls.

Suppose we start at point A in Figure 19-3 where the current exchange rate is at E_A. With the future expected value of the exchange rate held constant at E_{t+1}^e, a lower value of the exchange rate, say, at E^*, implies that the dollar is more likely to rise in value, that is appreciate. The greater the expected rise (appreciation) of the dollar, the higher is the relative expected return on dollar (domestic) assets. The theory of portfolio choice then tells us that because dollar assets are now more desirable to hold, the quantity of dollar assets demanded will rise, as is shown by point B in Figure 19-3. If the current exchange rate falls even further to E_C, there is an even higher expected appreciation of the dollar, a higher expected return, and therefore an even greater quantity of dollar assets demanded. This is shown in point C in Figure 19-3. The resulting demand curve, D, which connects these points, is downward-sloping, indicating that at lower current values of the dollar (everything else being equal), the quantity demanded of dollar assets is higher.

MyEconLab
Animation

FIGURE 19-3 Equilibrium in the Foreign Exchange Market

Equilibrium in the foreign exchange market occurs at point B, the intersection of the demand curve D and the supply curve S at an exchange rate of E^*.

Equilibrium in the Foreign Exchange Market

As in the usual supply and demand analysis, the market is in equilibrium when the quantity of dollar assets demanded equals the quantity supplied. In Figure 19-3, equilibrium occurs at point B, the intersection of the demand and supply curves. At point B, the exchange rate is E^*.

Suppose that the exchange rate is at E_A, which is higher than the equilibrium exchange rate of E^*. As we can see in Figure 19-3, the quantity of dollar assets supplied is then greater than the quantity demanded, a condition of excess supply. Given that more people want to sell dollar assets than want to buy them, the value of the dollar will fall. As long as the exchange rate remains above the equilibrium exchange rate, there will continue to be an excess supply of dollar assets, and the dollar will fall in value until it reaches the equilibrium exchange rate of E^*.

Similarly, if the exchange rate is less than the equilibrium exchange rate at E_C, the quantity of dollar assets demanded will exceed the quantity supplied, a condition of excess demand. Given that more people want to buy dollar assets than want to sell them, the value of the dollar will rise until the excess demand disappears and the value of the dollar is again at the equilibrium exchange rate of E^*.

Explaining Changes in Exchange Rates

The supply and demand analysis of the foreign exchange market illustrates how and why exchange rates change.[4] We have simplified this analysis by assuming the amount of dollar assets is fixed: the supply curve is vertical at a given quantity and does not shift. Under this assumption, we need look at only those factors that shift the demand curve for dollar assets to explain how exchange rates change over time.

---

[4]An alternative way to understand how and why exchange rates change is with the the *interest parity condition*, an important concept in international finance that shows the relationship between domestic interest rates, foreign interest rates, and the expected appreciation of the domestic currency. The interest parity condition and how it explains the determination of exchange rates is discussed in an appendix to this chapter.

Shifts in the Demand for Domestic Assets

As we have seen, the quantity of domestic (dollar) assets demanded depends on the relative expected return of dollar assets. To see how the demand curve shifts, we need to determine how the quantity demanded changes, holding the current exchange rate, E_t, constant when other factors change.

For insight into which direction the demand curve shifts, suppose you are an investor who is considering putting funds into domestic (dollar) assets. When a factor changes, decide whether at a given level of the current exchange rate, holding all other variables constant, you would earn a higher or lower expected return on dollar assets versus foreign assets. This decision tells you whether you want to hold more or fewer dollar assets and thus whether the quantity demanded increases or decreases at each level of the exchange rate. Knowing the direction of the change in the quantity demanded at each exchange rate tells you which way the demand curve shifts. In other words, if the relative expected return of dollar assets rises holding the current exchange rate constant, the demand curve shifts to the right. If the relative expected return falls, the demand curve shifts to the left.

DOMESTIC INTEREST RATE, i^D   Suppose that dollar assets pay an interest rate of i^D. When the domestic interest rate on dollar assets i^D rises, holding the current exchange rate E_t and everything else constant, the return on dollar assets increases relative to foreign assets, so people will want to hold more dollar assets. The quantity of dollar assets demanded increases at every value of the exchange rate, as shown by the rightward shift of the demand curve in Figure 19-4 from D_1 to D_2. The new equilibrium is reached at point 2, the intersection of D_2 and S, and the equilibrium exchange rate rises from E_1 to E_2. ***An increase in the domestic interest rate i^D shifts the demand curve for domestic assets, D, to the right and causes the domestic currency to appreciate (E ↑).***

Conversely, if i^D falls, the relative expected return on dollar assets falls, the demand curve shifts to the left, and the exchange rate falls. ***A decrease in the domestic interest rate i^D shifts the demand curve for domestic assets, D, to the left and causes the domestic currency to depreciate (E ↓).***

FIGURE 19-4 Response to an Increase in the Domestic Interest Rate, i^D

MyEconLab
Animation

When the domestic interest rate i^D increases, the relative expected return on domestic (dollar) assets increases and the demand curve shifts to the right. The equilibrium exchange rate rises from E_1 to E_2.

Quantity of Dollar Assets

FIGURE 19-5   Response to an Increase in the Foreign Interest Rate, i^F

When the foreign interest rate i^F increases, the relative expected return on domestic (dollar) assets falls and the demand curve shifts to the left. The equilibrium exchange rate falls from E_1 to E_2.

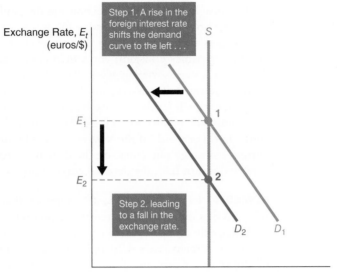

FOREIGN INTEREST RATE, i^F   Suppose that the foreign asset pays an interest rate of i^F. When the foreign interest rate i^F rises, holding the current exchange rate and everything else constant, the return on foreign assets rises relative to dollar assets. Thus the relative expected return on dollar assets falls. Now people want to hold fewer dollar assets, and the quantity demanded decreases at every value of the exchange rate. This scenario is shown by the leftward shift of the demand curve in Figure 19-5 from D_1 to D_2. The new equilibrium is reached at point 2, when the value of the dollar has fallen. Conversely, a decrease in i^F raises the relative expected return on dollar assets, shifts the demand curve to the right, and raises the exchange rate. To summarize, *an increase in the foreign interest rate* $\mathbf{i^F}$ *shifts the demand curve D to the left and causes the domestic currency to depreciate; a fall in the foreign interest rate* $\mathbf{i^F}$ *shifts the demand curve D to the right and causes the domestic currency to appreciate.*

CHANGES IN THE EXPECTED FUTURE EXCHANGE RATE, E^e_{t+1}   Expectations about the future value of the exchange rate play an important role in shifting the current demand curve, because the demand for domestic assets, like the demand for any durable good, depends on the future resale price. Any factor that causes the expected future exchange rate, E^e_{t+1}, to rise increases the expected appreciation of the dollar. The result is a higher relative expected return on dollar assets, which increases the demand for dollar assets at every exchange rate, thereby shifting the demand curve to the right in Figure 19-6 from D_1 to D_2. The equilibrium exchange rate rises to point 2 at the intersection of the D_2 and S curves.

   A rise in the expected future exchange rate, $\mathbf{E^e_{t+1}}$, shifts the demand curve to the right and causes an appreciation of the domestic currency. Using the same reasoning, *a fall in the expected future exchange rate, $\mathbf{E^e_{t+1}}$, shifts the demand curve to the left and causes a depreciation of the currency.*

   Earlier in the chapter we discussed the determinants of the exchange rate in the long run: the relative price level, relative trade barriers, import and export demand,

MyEconLab
Animation

FIGURE 19-6 Response to an Increase in the Expected Future Exchange Rate, E^e_{t+1}

When the expected future exchange rate increases, the relative expected return on domestic (dollar) assets rises and the demand curve shifts to the right. The equilibrium exchange rate rises from E_1 to E_2.

Quantity of Dollar Assets

and relative productivity (refer to Table 19-1). These four factors influence the expected future exchange rate. The theory of purchasing power parity suggests that if a higher Canadian price level relative to the foreign price level is expected to persist, the dollar will depreciate in the long run. A higher expected relative Canadian price level should thus have a tendency to lower E^e_{t+1}, lower the relative expected return on dollar assets, shift the demand curve to the left, and lower the current exchange rate.

Similarly, the other long-run determinants of the exchange rate can influence the relative expected return on dollar assets and the current exchange rate. Briefly, the following changes, all of which increase the demand for domestic goods relative to foreign goods, will raise E^e_{t+1}: (1) expectations of a fall in the Canadian price level relative to the foreign price level; (2) expectations of higher Canadian trade barriers relative to foreign trade barriers; (3) expectations of lower Canadian import demand; (4) expectations of higher foreign demand for Canadian exports; and (5) expectations of higher Canadian productivity relative to foreign productivity. By increasing E^e_{t+1}, all of these changes increase the relative expected return on dollar assets, shift the demand curve to the right, and cause an appreciation of the domestic currency, the dollar.

Recap: Factors That Change the Exchange Rate

Table 19-2 outlines all the factors that shift the demand curve for domestic assets and thereby cause the exchange rate to change. Shifts in the demand curve occur when one factor changes, holding everything else constant, including the current exchange rate. Again, the theory of asset demand tells us that changes in the relative expected return on dollar assets are the source of shifts in the demand curve.

Let's review what happens when each of the seven factors in Table 19-2 changes. Remember that to understand which direction the demand curve shifts, consider what happens to the relative expected return on dollar assets when the factor changes. If the relative expected return rises, holding the current exchange rate constant, the demand curve shifts to the right. If the relative expected return falls, the demand curve shifts to the left.

TABLE 19-2   Factors That Shift the Demand Curve for Domestic Assets and Affect the Exchange Rate

Factor	Change in Factor	Change in Quantity Demanded of Domestic Assets at Each Exchange Rate	Response of Exchange Rate, E_t	
Domestic interest rate, i^D	↑	↑	↑	
Foreign interest rate, i^F	↑	↓	↓	
Expected domestic price level*	↑	↓	↓	
Expected trade barriers*	↑	↑	↑	
Expected import demand	↑	↓	↓	
Expected export demand	↑	↑	↑	
Expected productivity*	↑	↑	↑	

*Relative to other countries.

Note: Only increases (↑) in the factors are shown; the effects of decreases in the variables on the exchange rate are the opposite of those indicated in the "Response" column.

1. When the interest rates on domestic assets i^D rise, the expected return on dollar assets rises at each exchange rate and so the quantity demanded increases. The demand curve therefore shifts to the right, and the equilibrium exchange rate rises, as is shown in the first row of Table 19-2.

2. When the foreign interest rate i^F rises, the return on foreign assets rises, so the relative expected return on dollar assets falls. The quantity demanded of dollar assets then falls, the demand curve shifts to the left, and the exchange rate declines, as in the second row of Table 19-2.

3. When the expected price level is higher, our analysis of the long-run determinants of the exchange rate indicates that the value of the dollar will fall in the future. The expected return on dollar assets thus falls, the quantity demanded declines, the demand curve shifts to the left, and the exchange rate falls, as in the third row of Table 19-2.

4. With higher expected trade barriers, the value of the dollar is higher in the long run and the expected return on dollar assets is higher. The quantity demanded of dollar assets thus rises, the demand curve shifts to the right, and the exchange rate rises, as in the fourth row of Table 19-2.

5. When expected import demand rises, we expect the exchange rate to depreciate in the long run, so the expected return on dollar assets falls. The quantity demanded of dollar assets at each value of the current exchange rate therefore falls, the demand curve shifts to the left, and the exchange rate declines, as in the fifth row of Table 19-2.

6. When expected export demand rises, the opposite occurs because the exchange rate is expected to appreciate in the long run. The expected return on dollar assets rises, the demand curve shifts to the right, and the exchange rate rises, as in the sixth row of Table 19-2.

7. With higher expected domestic productivity, the exchange rate is expected to appreciate in the long run, so the expected return on domestic assets rises. The quantity demanded at each exchange rate therefore rises, the demand curve shifts to the right, and the exchange rate rises, as in the seventh row of Table 19-2.

APPLICATION

Effects of Changes in Interest Rates on the Equilibrium Exchange Rate

Our analysis has revealed the factors that affect the value of the equilibrium exchange rate. Now we use this analysis to take a closer look at the response of the exchange rate to changes in interest rates and money growth.

Changes in domestic interest rates i^D are often cited as a major factor affecting exchange rates. For example, we see headlines in the financial press like this one: "Dollar Recovers as Interest Rates Edge Upward." But is the view presented in this headline always correct?

Not necessarily, because to analyze the effects of interest-rate changes, we must carefully distinguish the sources of the changes. The Fisher equation (Chapter 4) states that a nominal interest rate such as i^D equals the *real* interest rate plus expected inflation: $i = r + \pi^e$. The Fisher equation thus indicates that the interest rate i^D can change for two reasons: either the real interest rate i_r changes or the expected inflation rate π^e changes. The effect on the exchange rate is quite different, depending on which of these two factors is the source of the change in the nominal interest rate.

Suppose that the domestic real interest rate increases so that the nominal interest rate i^D rises while expected inflation remains unchanged. In this case, it is reasonable to assume that the expected appreciation of the dollar will be unchanged because expected inflation is unchanged. In this case, the increase in i^D increases the relative expected return on dollar assets, increases the quantity of dollar assets demanded at each level of the exchange rate, and shifts the demand curve to the right. We end up with the situation depicted in Figure 19-4, which analyzes an increase in i^D, holding everything else constant. Our model of the foreign exchange market produces the following result: *when domestic real interest rates rise, the domestic currency appreciates*.

When the nominal interest rate rises because of an increase in expected inflation, we get a different result from the one shown in Figure 19-4. The rise in expected domestic inflation leads to a decline in the expected appreciation of the dollar, which is typically thought to be larger than the increase in the domestic interest rate i^D. As a result, at any given exchange rate, the relative expected return on domestic (dollar) assets falls, the demand curve shifts to the left, and the exchange rate falls from E_1 to E_2 as shown in Figure 19-7. Our analysis leads to this conclusion: *when domestic interest rates rise due to an expected increase in inflation, the domestic currency depreciates*.

Because this conclusion is completely different from the one reached when the rise in the domestic interest rate is associated with a higher real interest rate, we must always distinguish between *real* and *nominal* measures when analyzing the effects of interest rates on exchange rates.

MyEconLab
Animation

FIGURE 19-7 Effect of a Rise in the Domestic Interest Rate as a Result of an Increase in Expected Inflation

Because a rise in domestic expected inflation leads to a decline in expected dollar appreciation that is larger than the increase in the domestic interest rate, the relative expected return on domestic (dollar) assets falls. The demand curve shifts to the left, and the equilibrium exchange rate falls from E_1 to E_2.

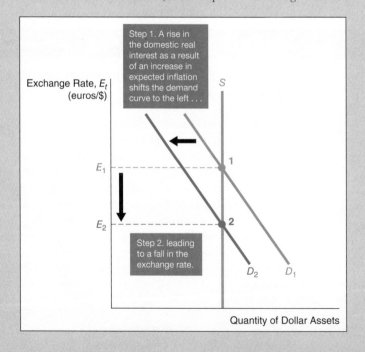

APPLICATION

Why Are Exchange Rates So Volatile?

The high volatility of foreign exchange rates surprises many people. Thirty or so years ago, economists generally believed that allowing exchange rates to be determined in the free market would not lead to large fluctuations in their values. Recent experience has proved them wrong. If we return to Figure 19-1, we see that exchange rates over the 1974–2009 period have been very volatile.

The asset market approach to exchange rate determination that we have outlined in this chapter gives a straightforward explanation of volatile exchange rates. Because expected appreciation of the domestic currency affects the expected return on foreign deposits, expectations about the price level, inflation, trade barriers, productivity, import demand, export demand, and the money supply play important roles in determining the exchange rate. When expectations about any of these variables change, as they do—and often at that—our model indicates that there will be an immediate effect on the expected return on foreign deposits and therefore on the exchange rate. Because expectations on all these variables change with just about every bit of news that appears, it is not surprising that the exchange rate is volatile. Because earlier models of exchange rate behaviour focused on goods markets rather than asset markets, they did not emphasize changing expectations as a source of exchange-rate movements, and so these earlier models could not predict substantial fluctuations in exchange rates. The failure of earlier models to explain volatility is one reason why they are no longer so popular. The more modern approach developed here emphasizes that the foreign exchange market is like any other asset market in which expectations of the future matter. The foreign exchange market, like other asset markets such as the stock market, displays substantial price volatility, and foreign exchange rates are notoriously hard to forecast.

APPLICATION

The Global Financial Crisis and the U.S. Dollar

With the start of the global financial crisis in August 2007, the U.S. dollar began an accelerated decline in value, falling by 9% against the euro until mid-July of 2008, and 6% against a wider basket of currencies. After hitting an all-time low against the euro on July 11, the U.S. dollar suddenly shot upward—by over 20% against the euro by the end of October and 15% against a wider basket of currencies. What is the relationship between the global financial crisis and these large swings in the value of the U.S. dollar?

During 2007, the negative effects of the financial crisis on economic activity were mostly confined to the United States. The Federal Reserve acted aggressively to lower interest rates to counter the contractionary effects, decreasing the federal funds rate target by 325 basis points from September of 2007 to April of 2008. In contrast, other central banks like the ECB did not see the need to lower interest rates, particularly because high energy prices had led to a surge in inflation. The relative expected return on dollar assets thus declined, shifting the demand curve for dollar assets to the left, as in Figure 19-5, leading to a decline in the equilibrium exchange rate. Our analysis of the foreign exchange market thus explains why the early phase of the global financial crisis led to a decline in the value of the dollar.

We now turn to the rise in the value of the U.S. dollar. Starting in the summer of 2008, the effects of the global financial crisis on economic activity began to spread more widely throughout the world. Foreign central banks started to cut interest rates, with the expectation that further rate cuts would follow, as indeed did occur. The expected decline in foreign interest rates then increased the relative expected return of U.S. dollar assets, leading to a rightward shift in the demand curve, and a rise in the value of the U.S. dollar, as shown in Figure 19-4. Another factor driving the U.S. dollar upwards was the "flight to quality" when the global financial crisis reached a particularly virulent stage in September and October. Both Americans and foreigners wanted to put their money in the safest assets possible: U.S. Treasury securities. The resulting increase in the demand for U.S. dollar assets provided an additional reason for the demand curve for U.S. dollar assets to shift out to the right, thereby helping to produce a sharp appreciation of the U.S. dollar.

MyEconLab

MyEconLab is an online homework and tutorial system that puts you in control of your own learning with study and practice tools directly correlated to this chapter's content. Visit MyEconLab to explore the following resources:

- The Questions and Applied Problems are all available in the Study Plan on MyEconLab for further practice. You will also find the answers to all of the Questions and Applied Problems in the Student Resources section of your MyEconLab.
- CANSIM data are available for relevant CANSIM questions in the Student Resources section of your MyEconLab.
- Visit the Student Resources section of MyEconLab to access the following mini-case for this chapter: Mini-Case 19.1: The Foreign Exchange Market and Financial Derivatives.

MyEconLab also features Additional Readings, Videos, Glossary Flashcards, Audio Chapter Summaries, Economics News Feeds, Animations, and many additional tools to help you master key concepts from the text.

SUMMARY

MyEconLa
Audio Summ

1. Foreign exchange rates (the price of one country's currency in terms of another's) are important because they affect the price of domestically produced goods sold abroad and the cost of foreign goods bought domestically.

2. The theory of purchasing power parity suggests that long-run changes in the exchange rate between two countries' currencies are determined by changes in the relative price levels in the two countries. Other factors that affect exchange rates in the long run are tariffs and quotas, import demand, export demand, and productivity.

3. In the short run, exchange rates are determined by changes in the relative expected return on domestic assets, which cause the demand curve to shift. Any factor that changes

the relative expected return on domestic assets will lead to changes in the exchange rate. Such factors include changes in the interest rates on domestic and foreign assets as well as changes in any of the factors that affect the long-run exchange rate and hence the expected future exchange rate. Changes in the money supply lead to exchange rate overshooting, causing the exchange rate to change by more in the short run than in the long run.

4. The asset market approach to exchange rate determination can explain both the volatility of exchange rates and the rise of the dollar in the 1980–1984 period and its subsequent fall.

KEY TERMS

appreciation, p. 471

capital mobility, p. 491

depreciation, p. 471

exchange rate, p. 470

foreign exchange market, p. 470

forward exchange rate, p. 471

forward transaction, p. 471

interest parity condition, p. 489

law of one price, p. 473

quotas, p. 475

real exchange rate, p. 474

spot exchange rate, p. 471

spot transaction, p. 471

tariffs, p. 475

theory of purchasing power parity (PPP), p. 474

QUESTIONS

1. When the euro appreciates, are you more likely to drink Canadian or French wine?

2. "A country is always worse off when its currency is weak (falls in value)." Is this statement true, false, or uncertain? Explain your answer.

3. When the Canadian dollar depreciates, what happens to exports and imports in Canada?

4. If the Japanese price level rises by 5% relative to the price level in Canada, what does the theory of purchasing power parity predict will happen to the value of the Japanese yen in terms of Canadian dollars?

5. If the demand for a country's exports falls at the same time that tariffs on imports are raised, will the country's currency tend to appreciate or depreciate in the long run?

6. When the Bank of Canada conducts an expansionary monetary policy, what happens to the money supply? How does this affect the supply of dollar assets?

7. From 2009 to 2011, the economies of Australia and Switzerland suffered relatively mild effects from the global financial crisis. At the same time, many countries in the euro area were hit hard with high unemployment and burdened with unsustainably high government debts. How should this affect the euro/Swiss franc and euro/Australian dollar exchange rates?

8. In the mid- to late 1970s, the yen appreciated relative to the U.S. dollar even though Japan's inflation rate was higher than the inflation rate in the United States. How can this be explained by an improvement in the productivity of Japanese industry relative to American industry?

9. Suppose the governor of the Bank of Canada announces a new set of reforms which includes a new anti-inflation program. Assuming the announcement is believed by the public, what will happen to the exchange rate for the Canadian dollar?

10. If the British central bank lowers interest rates to reduce unemployment, what will happen to the value of the pound in the short run and the long run?

11. If the Indian government unexpectedly announces that it will be imposing higher tariffs on foreign goods one year from now, what will happen to the value of the Indian rupee today?

12. If nominal interest rates in Canada rise but real interest rates fall, predict what will happen to the Canadian exchange rate.

13. If Canadian auto companies make a breakthrough in automobile technology and are able to produce a car that gets 50 kilometres to the litre, what will happen to the Canadian exchange rate?

14. If Mexicans go on a spending spree and buy twice as much French perfume, Japanese TVs, English sweaters, Swiss watches, and Italian wine, what will happen to the value of the Mexican peso?

15. Through the summer and fall of 2008 as the global financial crisis began to take hold, international financial institutions and sovereign wealth funds significantly increased their purchases of U.S. Treasury securities as a safe haven investment. How should this affect U.S. dollar exchange rates?

16. In March 2009, the Federal Reserve announced a *quantitative easing* program designed to lower intermediate and longer-term interest rates. What effect should this have on the U.S. dollar/euro exchange rate?

APPLIED PROBLEMS

17. A German sports car is selling for 70 000 euros. What is the dollar price in Canada for the German car if the exchange rate is 0.90 euros per dollar?

18. If the Canadian dollar to U.S. dollar exchange rate is 1.28 and the British pound to U.S. dollar exchange rate is 0.62, what must the Canadian dollar to British pound exchange rate be?

19. The New Zealand dollar to U.S. dollar exchange rate is 1.36, and the British pound to U.S. dollar exchange rate is 0.62. If you find that the British pound to New Zealand dollar were trading at 0.49, what would you do to earn a riskless profit?

20. In 1999, the euro was trading at US $0.90 per euro. If the euro is now trading at US $1.16 per euro, what is the

percentage change in the euro's value? Is this an appreciation or depreciation?

21. The Mexican peso is trading at 10 pesos per dollar. If the expected Canadian inflation rate is 2% while the expected Mexican inflation rate is 23% over the next year, given PPP, what is the expected exchange rate in one year?

22. If the price level recently increased by 20% in England while falling by 5% in Canada, how much must the exchange rate change if PPP holds? Assume that the current exchange rate is 0.55 pounds per dollar.

For Problems 23–25, use a graph of the foreign exchange market for dollars to illustrate the effects in each problem.

23. If expected inflation drops in Europe so that interest rates fall there, what will happen to the exchange rate for the Canadian dollar?

24. If the European central bank decides to pursue a contractionary monetary policy to fight inflation, what will happen to the value of the Canadian dollar?

25. If there is a strike in France, making it harder to buy French goods, what will happen to the value of the Canadian dollar?

CANSIM Questions

26. Go to the CANSIM data available in the Student Resources section of your MyEconLab website and download monthly data from January 1974 to December 2011 on the Canadian-dollar-per-U.S.-dollar exchange rate (series V37426), the Canadian-dollar-per-British-pound exchange rate (series V37430), the Canadian-dollar-per-Japanese-yen exchange rate (series V37456),

and the Canadian-dollar-per-euro exchange rate (series V21570998).

Calculate the mean and standard deviation as well as the maximum and minimum values for each series over the sample period.

WEB EXERCISES

1. The Bank of Canada maintains a website that lists the exchange rate between the Canadian dollar and many other currencies. Go to **www.bankofcanada.ca/rates/ exchange/10-year-converter/**. Find the exchange rate between the Canadian dollar and the euro for the past 40 weeks.

    a. What has the percentage change in the euro/dollar exchange rate been in the past 40 weeks?
    b. What has been the annual percentage change in the euro–dollar exchange rate for each year since the euro's introduction?

2. Visit the website of the Bank of Canada, **www. bankofcanada.ca**. Click "Rates and Statistics" and then "Exchange Rates."

    a. What are the fundamental determinants of exchange rates?
    b. What are the different ways that a foreign exchange rate can be quoted?

    c. What is the difference between spot and forward exchange rates?
    d. Go to the CANSIM website at **http://cansim2. statcan.ca/M** and download series V37456 for 2008. Present a time series plot of the yen-per-Canadian-dollar exchange rate. Did the yen appreciate or depreciate in 2008? By how much?

3. International travellers and businesspeople frequently need to accurately convert from one currency to another. It is often easy to find the rate needed to convert the Canadian dollar into another currency. It can be more difficult to find exchange rates between two non-Canadian currencies. Go to **www.xe.com/ucc/full/**. This site lets you convert from any currency into any other currency. How many Lithuanian litas can you currently buy with one Chilean peso?

The Interest Parity Condition

All the results in the text can be derived with a concept that is widely used in international finance. The **interest parity condition** shows the relationship between domestic interest rates, foreign interest rates, and the expected appreciation of the domestic currency. To derive this condition, we examine how expected returns on domestic and foreign assets are compared.

Comparing Expected Returns on Domestic and Foreign Assets

As in the chapter, we treat Canada as the home country, so domestic assets are denominated in dollars. For simplicity, we use euros to stand for any foreign country's currency, so foreign assets are denominated in euros. To illustrate further, suppose that dollar assets pay an interest rate of i^D and do not have any possible capital gains, so that they have an expected return payable in dollars of i^D. Similarly, foreign assets have an interest rate of i^F and an expected return payable in the foreign currency, euros, of i^F. To compare the expected returns on dollar assets and foreign assets, investors must convert the returns into the currency unit they use.

First, let us examine how François the Foreigner compares the returns on dollar assets and foreign assets denominated in his currency, the euro. When he considers the expected return on dollar assets in terms of euros, he recognizes that it does not equal i^D; instead, the expected return must be adjusted for any expected appreciation or depreciation of the dollar. If François expects the dollar to appreciate by 3%, for example, the expected return on dollar assets in terms of euros would be 3% higher than i^D because the dollar is expected to become worth 3% more in terms of euros. Thus, if the interest rate on dollar assets is 4%, with an expected 3% appreciation of the dollar, the expected return on dollar assets in terms of euros is 7%: the 4% interest rate plus the 3% expected appreciation of the dollar. Conversely, if the dollar were expected to depreciate by 3% over the year, the expected return on dollar assets in terms of euros would be only 1%: the 4% interest rate minus the 3% expected depreciation of the dollar.

Writing the current exchange rate (the spot exchange rate) as E_t and the expected exchange rate for the next period as E_{t+1}^e, the expected rate of appreciation of the dollar is $(E_{t+1}^e - E_t)/E_t$. Our reasoning indicates that the expected return on dollar assets R^D in terms of foreign currency can be written as the sum of the interest rate on dollar assets plus the expected appreciation of the dollar.[1]

$$R^D \text{ in terms of euros} = i^D + \frac{E_{t+1}^e - E_t}{E_t}$$

However, François's expected return on foreign assets R^F in terms of euros is just i^F. Thus, in terms of euros, the relative expected return on dollar assets (that is, the difference between the expected return on dollar assets and euro assets) is calculated by subtracting i^F from the expression above to yield

$$\text{Relative } R^D = i^D - i^F + \frac{E_{t+1}^e - E_t}{E_t} \tag{1}$$

As the relative expected return on dollar assets increases, foreigners will want to hold more dollar assets and fewer foreign assets.

Next, let us look at the decision to hold dollar assets versus euro assets from Peter the Canadian's point of view. Following the same reasoning we used to evaluate the decision for François, we know that the expected return on foreign assets R^F in terms of dollars is the interest rate on foreign assets i^F plus the expected appreciation of the foreign currency, equal to minus the expected appreciation of the dollar, $(E_{t+1}^e - E_t)/E_t$

$$R^F \text{ in terms of dollars} = i^F - \frac{E_{t+1}^e - E_t}{E_t}$$

If the interest rate on euro assets is 5%, for example, and the dollar is expected to appreciate by 3%, then the expected return on euro assets in terms of dollars is 2%. Peter earns the 5% interest rate, but he expects to lose 3% because he expects the euro to be worth 3% less in terms of dollars as a result of the dollar's appreciation.

Peter's expected return on the dollar assets R^D in terms of dollars is just i^D. Hence, in terms of dollars, the relative expected return on dollar assets is calculated by subtracting the expression just given from i^D to obtain

$$\text{Relative } R^D = i^D - \left(i^F - \frac{E_{t+1}^e - E_t}{E_t} \right) = i^D - i^F + \frac{E_{t+1}^e - E_t}{E_t}$$

This equation is the same as Equation 1 describing François's relative expected return on dollar assets (calculated in terms of euros). The key point here is that the

---

[1]This expression is actually an approximation of the expected return in terms of euros, which can be more precisely calculated by thinking how a foreigner invests in dollar assets. Suppose that François decides to put one euro into dollar assets. First he buys $1/E_t$ of Canadian dollar assets (recall that E_t, the exchange rate between dollar and euro assets, is quoted in euros per dollar), and at the end of the period he is paid $(1 + i^D)(1/E_t)$ in dollars. To convert this amount into the number of euros he expects to receive at the end of the period, he multiplies this quantity by E_{t+1}^e. François's expected return on his initial investment of one euro can thus be written as $(1 + i^D)(E_{t+1}^e/E_t)$ minus his initial investment of one euro:

$$(1 + i^D)\left(\frac{E_{t+1}^e}{E_t}\right) - 1$$

This expression can be rewritten as

$$i^D\left(\frac{E_{t+1}^e}{E_t}\right) + \frac{E_{t+1}^e - E_t}{E_t}$$

which is approximately equal to the expression in the text because, E_{t+1}^e/E_t is typically close to 1. To see this, consider the example in the text in which $i^D = 0.04; (E_{t+1}^e - E_t)/E_t = 0.03$, so $E_{t+1}^e/E_t = 1.03$. Then François's expected return on dollar assets is $(0.04 \times 1.03) + 0.03 = 0.0712 = 7.12\%$, rather than the 7% reported in the text.

relative expected return on dollar assets is the same—whether it is calculated by François in terms of euros or by Peter in terms of dollars. Thus, as the relative expected return on dollar assets increases, both foreigners and domestic residents respond in exactly the same way—both will want to hold more dollar assets and fewer foreign assets.

Interest Parity Condition

We currently live in a world in which there is **capital mobility**: foreigners can easily purchase Canadian assets, and Canadians can easily purchase foreign assets. If there are few impediments to capital mobility and we are looking at assets that have similar risk and liquidity—say, foreign and Canadian bank deposits—then it is reasonable to assume that the assets are perfect substitutes (that is, equally desirable). When capital is mobile and when assets are perfect substitutes, if the expected return on dollar assets is above that on foreign assets, both foreigners and Canadians will want to hold only dollar assets and will be unwilling to hold foreign assets. Conversely, if the expected return on foreign assets is higher than on dollar assets, both foreigners and Canadians will not want to hold any dollar assets and will want to hold only foreign assets. For existing supplies of both dollar assets and foreign assets to be held, it must therefore be true that there is no difference in their expected returns; that is, the relative expected return in Equation 1 must equal zero. This condition can be rewritten as

$$i^D = i^F - \frac{E^e_{t+1} - E_t}{E_t} \tag{2}$$

This equation, which is called the interest parity condition, states that the domestic interest rate equals the foreign interest rate minus the expected appreciation of the domestic currency. Equivalently, this condition can be stated in a more intuitive way: the domestic interest rate equals the foreign interest rate plus the expected appreciation of the foreign currency. If the domestic interest rate is higher than the foreign interest rate, there is a positive expected appreciation of the foreign currency, which compensates for the lower foreign interest rate. A domestic interest rate of 5% versus a foreign interest rate of 3% means that the expected appreciation of the foreign currency must be 2% (or, equivalently, that the expected depreciation of the dollar must be 2%).

There are several ways to look at the interest parity condition. First, recognize that interest parity means simply that the expected returns are the same on both dollar assets and foreign assets. To see this, note that the left side of the interest parity condition (Equation 2) is the expected return on dollar assets, while the right side is the expected return on foreign assets, both calculated in terms of a single currency, the Canadian dollar. Given our assumption that domestic and foreign assets are perfect substitutes (equally desirable), the interest parity condition is an equilibrium condition for the foreign exchange market. Only when the exchange rate is such that expected returns on domestic and foreign assets are equal—that is, when interest parity holds—investors will be willing to hold both domestic and foreign assets.

With some algebraic manipulation, we can rewrite the interest parity condition in Equation 2 as

$$E_t = \frac{E^e_{t+1}}{i^F - i^D + 1}$$

This equation produces exactly the same results that we find in the supply and demand analysis in the text: if i^D rises, the denominator falls and so E_t rises. If i^F rises, the denominator rises and so E_t falls. If E^e_{t+1} rises, the numerator rises and so E_t rises.

CHAPTER 20

The International Financial System

LEARNING OBJECTIVES

After studying this chapter you should be able to

1. describe central bank intervention in the foreign exchange market and its effects on the money supply and the exchange rate
2. discuss international financial transactions and the balance of payments
3. summarize the arguments for and against capital controls
4. depict the role of the IMF as an international lender of last resort

PREVIEW

As the Canadian economy and the economies of the rest of the world grow more interdependent, a country's monetary policy can no longer be conducted without taking international considerations into account. In this chapter we examine how international financial transactions and the structure of the international financial system affect monetary policy. We also examine the evolution of the international financial system during the past half-century and consider where it may be heading in the future.

Intervention in the Foreign Exchange Market

In Chapter 19 we analyzed the foreign exchange market as if it were a completely free market that responds to all market pressures. Like many other markets, however, the foreign exchange market is not free of government intervention; central banks regularly engage in international financial transactions called **foreign exchange interventions** in order to influence exchange rates. In our current international environment, exchange rates fluctuate from day to day, but central banks attempt to influence their countries' exchange rates by buying and selling currencies. We can use the exchange rate analysis we developed in Chapter 19 to explain the impact of central bank intervention on the foreign exchange market.

Foreign Exchange Intervention and the Money Supply

The first step in understanding how central bank intervention in the foreign exchange market affects exchange rates is to see the impact on the monetary base from a central bank sale in the foreign exchange market of some of its holdings of assets denominated in a foreign currency (called **international reserves**). Suppose that the Bank of Canada decides to sell $1 billion of its foreign assets in exchange for $1 billion of Canadian currency. The Bank's purchase of dollars has two effects. First, it reduces the Bank's holding of international reserves by $1 billion. Second, because the Bank's purchase of currency removes it from the hands of the public, currency in circulation falls by $1 billion. We can see this in the following T-account for the Bank of Canada:

Bank of Canada			
Assets		Liabilities	
Foreign assets (international reserves)	−$1 billion	Currency in circulation	−$1 billion

Because the monetary base is made up of currency in circulation plus reserves, this decline in currency implies that the monetary base has fallen by $1 billion.

If, instead of paying for the foreign assets sold by the Bank of Canada with currency, the persons buying the foreign assets pay for them by cheques written on accounts at domestic banks, then the Bank deducts the $1 billion from the deposit accounts these banks have with the Bank of Canada. The result is that the deposits with the Bank of Canada (reserves) decline by $1 billion, as shown in the following T-account:

Bank of Canada			
Assets		Liabilities	
Foreign assets (international reserves)	−$1 billion	Deposits with the Bank of Canada (reserves)	−$1 billion

In this case, the outcome of the Bank of Canada sale of foreign assets and the purchase of dollar deposits is a $1 billion decline in reserves and, as before, a $1 billion decline in the monetary base, because reserves are also a component of the monetary base.

We now see that the outcome for the monetary base is exactly the same when a central bank sells foreign assets to purchase domestic bank deposits or domestic currency. This is why when we say that a central bank has purchased its domestic currency, we do not have to distinguish whether it actually purchased currency or bank deposits denominated in the domestic currency. We have thus reached an important conclusion: *a central bank's purchase of domestic currency and corresponding sale of foreign assets in the foreign exchange market leads to an equal decline in its international reserves and the monetary base.*

We could have reached the same conclusion by a more direct route. A central bank sale of a foreign asset is no different from an open market sale of a government bond. We learned in our exploration of the money supply process that an open market sale leads to an equal decline in the monetary base; therefore, a sale of foreign assets also leads to an equal decline in the monetary base. By similar reasoning, a central bank purchase of foreign assets paid for by selling domestic currency, like an open market purchase, leads to an equal rise in the monetary base. Thus we reach the following conclusion: *a central bank's sale of domestic currency to purchase foreign assets in the foreign exchange market results in an equal rise in its international reserves and the monetary base.*

The intervention we have just described, in which a central bank allows the purchase or sale of domestic currency to have an effect on the monetary base, is called an **unsterilized foreign exchange intervention**. But what if the central bank does not want the purchase or sale of domestic currency to affect the monetary base? All it has to do is to counter the effect of the foreign exchange intervention by conducting an offsetting open market operation in the government bond market. For example, in the case of a $1 billion purchase of dollars by the Bank of Canada and a corresponding $1 billion sale of foreign assets, which we have seen would decrease the monetary base by $1 billion, the Bank can conduct an open market purchase of $1 billion of government bonds, which would increase the monetary base by $1 billion. The resulting T-account for the foreign exchange intervention and the offsetting open market operation leaves the monetary base unchanged:

Bank of Canada			
Assets		Liabilities	
Foreign assets (international reserves)	−$1 billion	Monetary base (reserves)	0
Government bonds	+$1 billion		

A foreign exchange intervention with an offsetting open market operation that leaves the monetary base unchanged is called a **sterilized foreign exchange intervention**.

Now that we understand that there are two types of foreign exchange interventions, unsterilized and sterilized, let's look at how each affects the exchange rate.

Unsterilized Intervention

Your intuition might lead you to suspect that if a central bank wants to raise the value of the domestic currency, it should buy its currency in the foreign exchange market and sell foreign assets. Indeed, this intuition is correct for the case of an unsterilized intervention.

Recall that in an unsterilized intervention, if the Bank of Canada decides to buy dollars and therefore sells foreign assets in exchange for dollar assets, this works just like an open market sale of bonds to decrease the monetary base. Hence the purchase of dollars leads to a decrease in the money supply, which raises the domestic interest rate and increases the relative expected return on dollar assets. The result is that the demand curve shifts to the right from D_1 to D_2 in Figure 20-1, and the exchange rate rises to E_2.[1]

Our analysis leads us to the following conclusion about unsterilized interventions in the foreign exchange market: *an unsterilized intervention in which domestic currency is bought and foreign assets are sold leads to a fall in international reserves, a fall in the money supply, and an appreciation of the domestic currency.*

---

[1]An unsterilized intervention in which the Bank of Canada sells dollars increases the amount of dollar assets slightly because it leads to an increase in the monetary base while leaving the amount of government bonds in the hands of the public unchanged. The curve depicting the supply of dollar assets would thus shift to the right slightly, which also works toward lowering the exchange rate, yielding the same conclusion derived from Figure 20-1. Because the resulting increase in the monetary base would be only a minuscule fraction of the total amount of dollar assets outstanding, the supply curve would shift by an imperceptible amount. This is why Figure 20-1 is drawn with the supply curve unchanged.

MyEconLab
Animation

FIGURE 20-1   Effect of an Unsterilized Purchase of Dollars and Sale of Foreign Assets

A purchase of dollars and the consequent open market sale of foreign assets decreases the monetary base and the money supply. The resulting fall in the money supply leads to a rise in domestic interest rates, which raises the relative expected return on dollar assets. The demand curve shifts to the right from D_1 to D_2, and the equilibrium exchange rate rises from E_1 to E_2.

The reverse result is found for an unsterilized intervention in which domestic currency is sold and foreign assets are purchased. The sale of domestic currency and purchase of foreign assets (increasing international reserves) works like an open market purchase to increase the monetary base and the money supply. The increase in the money supply lowers the interest rate on dollar assets. The resulting decrease in the relative expected return on dollar assets means that people will buy less dollar assets, so the demand curve shifts to the left and the exchange rate falls. *An unsterilized intervention in which domestic currency is sold and foreign assets are purchased leads to a rise in international reserves, a rise in the money supply, and a depreciation of the domestic currency.*

Sterilized Intervention

The key point to remember about a sterilized intervention is that the central bank engages in offsetting open market operations, so that there is no impact on the monetary base and the money supply. In the context of the model of exchange rate determination we have developed here, it is straightforward to show that a sterilized intervention has almost *no effect* on the exchange rate. A sterilized intervention leaves the money supply unchanged and so has no direct way of affecting interest rates.[2] Because the relative

---

[2]A sterilized intervention changes the amount of foreign securities relative to domestic securities in the hands of the public, called a *portfolio balance effect*. Through this effect, the central bank might be able to affect the interest differential between domestic and foreign assets, which in turn affects the relative expected return of domestic assets. Empirical evidence has not revealed this portfolio balance effect to be significant. However, a sterilized intervention *could* indicate what central banks want to happen to the future exchange rate and so might provide a signal about the course of future monetary policy. In this way a sterilized intervention could lead to shifts in the demand curve for domestic assets and ultimately affect the exchange rate. However, the future change in monetary policy—not the sterilized intervention—is the source of the exchange rate effect. For a further discussion of the signalling and portfolio balance effects and the possible differential effects of sterilized versus unsterilized intervention, see Paul Krugman and Maurice Obstfeld, *International Economics*, 7th ed. (Boston: Addison-Wesley, 2006).

expected return on dollar assets is unaffected, the demand curve would remain at D_1 in Figure 20-1, and the exchange rate would remain unchanged at E_1.

At first it might seem puzzling that a central bank purchase or sale of domestic currency that is sterilized does not lead to a change in the exchange rate. A central bank purchase of domestic currency cannot raise the exchange rate, because with no effect on the domestic money supply or interest rates, any resulting rise in the exchange rate would mean that there would be an excess supply of dollar assets. With more people willing to sell dollar assets than to buy them, the exchange rate would have to fall back to its initial equilibrium level, where the demand and supply curves intersect.

Balance of Payments

Because international financial transactions such as foreign exchange interventions have considerable effects on monetary policy, it is worth knowing how these transactions are measured. The **balance of payments** is a bookkeeping system for recording all receipts and payments that have a direct bearing on the movement of funds between a nation (private sector and government) and foreign countries.

Here we examine the key items in the balance of payments that you often hear about in the media.[3]

The **current account** shows international transactions that involve currently produced goods and services. The difference between merchandise exports and imports, the net receipts from trade, is called the **trade balance**. When imports are greater than exports, as in 2010 by $31.8 billion, we have a trade deficit; if exports are greater than imports, we have a trade surplus.

Additional items included in the current account are the net receipts (cash flows received from abroad minus cash flows sent abroad) from three categories: investment income, service transactions, and unilateral transfers (gifts, pensions, and foreign aid). In 2010, for example, net investment income was minus $16.4 billion for Canada because Canadians received less investment income from abroad than they paid out. Since Canadians made more unilateral transfers to foreign countries than foreigners made to Canada, net unilateral transfers were minus $2.7 billion. The sum of the previous two items plus the trade balance is the current account balance, which in 2010 showed a deficit of $50.9 billion.

Another important item in the balance of payments is the **capital account**, the net receipts from capital transactions. In 2010 the capital account was $4.8 billion, indicating that $4.8 billion more capital came into Canada than left Canada. Another way of saying this is that Canada had a net capital inflow of $4.8 billion.[4] The sum of the current account and the capital account equals the **official reserve transactions balance**, which was minus $44.9 billion in 2010. When economists refer to a surplus or deficit in the balance of payments, they actually mean a surplus or deficit in the official reserve transactions balance.

Because the balance of payments must balance, the official reserve transactions balance, which equals the current account plus the capital account, tells us the net amount of international reserves that must move between governments (as

---

[3]A Web Appendix to this chapter on this book's MyEconLab discusses the Canadian balance of payments in more detail.

[4]Note that the capital account balance number reported above includes a statistical discrepancy item that represents errors due to unrecorded transactions involving smuggling and other capital flows ($1.2 billion in 2010). Many experts believe that the statistical discrepancy item, which keeps the balance of payments in balance, is primarily the result of large hidden capital flows, and this is why it is included in the capital account balance reported above.

represented by their central banks) to finance international transactions. The relationship between the current account, the capital account, and the change in net government international reserves can thus be expressed as

$$\text{Current account} + \text{capital account} = \text{net change in government international reserves}$$

This equation shows us why the current account receives so much attention from economists and the media. The current account balance tells us whether Canada (private sector and government combined) is increasing or decreasing its claims on foreign wealth. A surplus indicates that Canada is increasing its claims on foreign wealth, and thus is increasing its holdings of foreign assets (both good things for Canadians), and a deficit indicates that Canada is reducing its holdings of foreign assets and foreign countries are increasing their claims on Canada.[5]

For example, the rapid growth in the U.S. current account deficit in recent years has raised serious concerns that these large deficits may have negative consequences for the U.S. economy (see the Global box Why the Large U.S. Current Account Deficit Worries Economists).

GLOBAL

Why the Large U.S. Current Account Deficit Worries Economists

The massive U.S. current account deficit in recent years, which in 2011 was 11% of GDP, worries economists for several reasons. First, it indicates that at current exchange rate values, foreigners' demand for U.S. exports is far less than Americans' demand for imports. As we saw in the previous chapter, low demand for U.S. exports and high U.S. demand for imports may lead to a future decline in the value of the U.S. dollar. Some economists estimate that this decline could be very large, with the U.S. dollar depreciating by as much as 50%.

Second, the current account deficit means that foreigners' claims on U.S. assets are growing, and these claims will have to be paid back at some point.

Americans are mortgaging their future to foreigners; when the bill comes due, Americans will be poorer. Furthermore, if Americans have a greater preference for U.S. dollar assets than foreigners do, the movement of American wealth to foreigners could decrease the demand for U.S. dollar assets over time, also causing the U.S. dollar to depreciate.

The hope is that the eventual decline in the U.S. dollar resulting from the large U.S. current account deficit will be a gradual one, occurring over a period of several years. If the decline is precipitous, however, it could potentially disrupt financial markets and hurt the U.S. economy.

Exchange Rate Regimes in the International Financial System

Exchange rate regimes in the international financial system are of two basic types: fixed and floating. In a **fixed exchange rate regime**, the value of a currency is pegged relative to the value of one other currency (called the **anchor currency**), so that the

---

[5]The current account balance can also be viewed as showing by how much total saving exceeds private-sector and government investment in Canada. We can see this by noting that total Canadian saving equals the increase in total wealth held by the Canadian private sector and government. Total investment equals the increase in the Canadian capital stock (wealth physically in Canada). The difference between them is the increase in Canadian claims on foreign wealth.

exchange rate is fixed in terms of the anchor country. In a **floating exchange rate regime**, the value of a currency is allowed to fluctuate against all other currencies. When countries intervene in foreign exchange markets in an attempt to influence their exchange rates by buying and selling foreign assets, the regime is referred to as a **managed float regime** (or a **dirty float**).

In examining past exchange rate regimes, we start with the gold standard of the late nineteenth and early twentieth centuries.

Gold Standard

Before World War I, the world economy operated under the **gold standard**, a fixed exchange rate regime in which most currencies were convertible directly into gold at fixed rates, so exchange rates between countries were also fixed. Canadian dollar bills, for example, could be exchanged for approximately 1/20 ounce of gold. Likewise, the British Treasury would exchange 1/4 ounce of gold for £1. Because a Canadian could convert $20 into 1 ounce of gold, which could be used to buy £4, the exchange rate between the pound and the Canadian dollar was effectively fixed at approximately $5 to the pound. The fixed exchange rates under the gold standard had the important advantage of encouraging world trade by eliminating the uncertainty that occurs when exchange rates fluctuate.

As long as countries abided by the rules under the gold standard and kept their currencies backed by and convertible into gold, exchange rates remained fixed. However, adherence to the gold standard meant that a country had no control over its monetary policy because its money supply was determined by gold flows between countries. Furthermore, monetary policy throughout the world was greatly influenced by the production of gold and gold discoveries. When gold production was low in the 1870s and 1880s, the money supply throughout the world grew slowly and did not keep pace with the growth of the world economy. The result was deflation (falling price levels). Gold discoveries in Alaska and South Africa in the 1890s greatly expanded gold production, causing money supplies to increase rapidly and price levels to rise (inflation) until World War I.

The Bretton Woods System

After World War II, the victors set up a fixed exchange rate system that became known as the **Bretton Woods system**, after the New Hampshire town in which the agreement was negotiated in 1944. The Bretton Woods system was in effect until 1971.

The Bretton Woods agreement created the **International Monetary Fund (IMF)**, headquartered in Washington, D.C., which had 30 original member countries in 1945 and currently has 180. The IMF was given the task of promoting the growth of world trade by setting rules for the maintenance of fixed exchange rates and by making loans to countries that were experiencing balance-of-payments difficulties. As part of its role of monitoring the compliance of member countries with its rules, the IMF also took on the job of collecting and standardizing international economic data.

The Bretton Woods agreement also set up the International Bank for Reconstruction and Development, commonly referred to as the **World Bank**, also headquartered in Washington, D.C., which provides long-term loans to help developing countries build dams, roads, and other physical capital that would contribute to their economic development. The funds for these loans are obtained primarily by issuing World Bank bonds, which are sold in the capital markets of the developed countries. In addition, the General Agreement on Tariffs and Trade (GATT), headquartered in Geneva, was set up to monitor rules for the conduct of trade between countries (tariffs and quotas) and the GATT has evolved into the **World Trade Organization (WTO)**.

Because the United States emerged from World War II as the world's largest economic power, with over half of the world's manufacturing capacity and the greater part of the world's gold, the Bretton Woods system of fixed exchange rates was based on the convertibility of U.S. dollars into gold (for foreign governments and central banks only) at US$35 per ounce. The fixed exchange rates were to be maintained by intervention in the foreign exchange market by central banks in countries besides the United States who bought and sold U.S. dollar assets, which they held as international reserves. The U.S. dollar, which was used by other countries to denominate the assets that they held as international reserves, was called the **reserve currency**. Thus an important feature of the Bretton Woods system was the establishment of the United States as the reserve currency country. Even after the breakup of the Bretton Woods system, the U.S. dollar has kept its position as the reserve currency in which most international financial transactions are conducted. However, with the creation of the euro in 1999, the supremacy of the U.S. dollar may be subject to a serious challenge (see the Global box The Euro's Challenge to the U.S. Dollar).

GLOBAL

The Euro's Challenge to the U.S. Dollar

With the creation of the European Monetary Union and the euro in 1999, the U.S. dollar is facing a challenge to its position as the key reserve currency in international financial transactions. Adoption of the euro increases integration of Europe's financial markets, which could help them rival those in the United States. The resulting increase in the use of euros in financial markets will make it more likely that international transactions are carried out in the euro. The economic clout of the European Union rivals that of the United States; both have a similar share of world GDP (around 20%) and world exports (around 15%). If the European Central Bank can make sure that inflation remains low so that the euro becomes a sound currency, this should bode well for the euro.

However, for the euro to eat into the U.S. dollar's position as a reserve currency, the European Union must function as a cohesive political entity that can exert its influence on the world stage. There are serious doubts on this score, however, particularly with the "no" votes on the European constitution by France and the Netherlands in 2005 and the recent fiscal problems in Greece and elsewhere in the European Union.

Most analysts think it will be a long time before the euro beats out the dollar in international financial transactions.

The fixed exchange rate dictated by the Bretton Woods system was abandoned in 1971, but the fixed exchange rate was only abandoned in 1973. From 1979 to 1990, however, the European Union instituted among its members a fixed exchange rate system, the European Monetary System (EMS). In the *exchange rate mechanism* (ERM) in this system, the exchange rate between any pair of currencies of the participating countries was not supposed to fluctuate outside narrow limits, called the "snake." In practice, all of the countries in the EMS pegged their currencies to the German mark.

How a Fixed Exchange Rate Regime Works

Figure 20-2 shows how a fixed exchange rate regime works in practice by using the supply and demand analysis of the foreign exchange market we learned in the previous chapter. Panel (a) describes a situation in which the domestic currency is fixed relative to an anchor currency at E_{par}, while the demand curve has shifted left to D_1, perhaps because foreign interest rates have risen, thereby lowering the relative expected return of domestic assets. At E_{par}, the exchange rate is now *overvalued*: the demand curve D_1 intersects the supply curve at an exchange rate E_1, which is lower

FIGURE 20-2 Intervention in the Foreign Exchange Market Under a Fixed Exchange Rate Regime

In panel (a), the exchange rate at E_{par} is overvalued. To keep the exchange rate at E_{par} (point 2), the central bank must purchase domestic currency to shift the demand curve to D_2. In panel (b), the exchange rate at E_{par} is undervalued, so the central bank must sell domestic currency to shift the demand curve to D_2 and keep the exchange rate at E_{par} (point 2).

MyEconLa
Animation

(a) Intervention in the case of an
overvalued exchange rate

(b) Intervention in the case of an
undervalued exchange rate

than the fixed (par) value of the exchange rate E_{par}. To keep the exchange rate at E_{par}, the central bank must intervene in the foreign exchange market to purchase domestic currency by selling foreign assets. This action, like an open market sale, means that both the monetary base and the money supply decline, driving up the interest rate on domestic assets, i^D.[6] This increase in the domestic interest rate raises the relative expected return on domestic assets, shifting the demand curve to the right. The central bank will continue purchasing domestic currency until the demand curve reaches D_2 and the equilibrium exchange rate is at E_{par} at point 2 in panel (a).

We have thus come to the conclusion that ***when the domestic currency is overvalued, the central bank must purchase domestic currency to keep the exchange rate fixed, but as a result it loses international reserves.***

Panel (b) in Figure 20-2 describes the situation in which the demand curve has shifted to the right to D_1 because the relative expected return on domestic assets has risen and hence the exchange rate is undervalued: the initial demand curve D_1 intersects the supply curve at exchange rate E_1, which is above E_{par}. In this situation, the central bank must sell domestic currency and purchase foreign assets. This action works like an open market purchase to increase the money supply and lower the interest rate on domestic assets i^D. The central bank keeps selling domestic currency and lowering i^D until the demand curve shifts all the way to D_2, where the equilibrium exchange rate is at E_{par}—point 2 in panel (b). Our analysis thus leads us to the following result: ***when the domestic currency is undervalued, the central bank must sell domestic currency to keep the exchange rate fixed, but as a result it gains international reserves.***

---

[6]Because the exchange rate will continue to be fixed at E_{par}, the expected future exchange rate remains unchanged and so does not need to be addressed in the analysis.

DEVALUATION AND REVALUATION   As we have seen, if a country's currency is overvalued, its central bank's attempts to keep the currency from depreciating will result in a loss of international reserves. If the country's central bank eventually runs out of international reserves, it cannot keep its currency from depreciating, and a **devaluation** must occur, in which the par exchange rate is reset at a lower level.

If, by contrast, a country's currency is undervalued, its central bank's intervention to keep the currency from appreciating leads to a gain of international reserves. As we will see shortly, the central bank might not want to acquire these international reserves, and so it might want to reset the par value of its exchange rate at a higher level (a **revaluation**).

PERFECT CAPITAL MOBILITY   If there is perfect capital mobility—that is, if there are no barriers to domestic residents purchasing foreign assets or foreigners purchasing domestic assets—then a sterilized exchange rate intervention cannot keep the exchange rate at E_{par} because, as we saw earlier in the chapter, the relative expected return of domestic assets is unaffected. For example, if the exchange rate is overvalued, a sterilized purchase of domestic currency will leave the relative expected return and the demand curve unchanged—so pressure for a depreciation of the domestic currency is not removed. If the central bank keeps purchasing its domestic currency but continues to sterilize, it will just keep losing international reserves until it finally runs out of them and is forced to let the value of the currency seek a lower level.

THE POLICY TRILEMMA   One important implication of the foregoing analysis is that a country that ties its exchange rate to an anchor currency of a larger country loses control of its monetary policy. If the larger country pursues a more contractionary monetary policy and decreases its money supply, this would lead to lower expected inflation in the larger country, thus causing an appreciation of the larger country's currency and a depreciation of the smaller country's currency. The smaller country, having locked in its exchange rate to the anchor currency, will now find its currency overvalued and will therefore have to sell the anchor currency and buy its own to keep its currency from depreciating. The result of this foreign exchange intervention will then be a decline in the smaller country's international reserves, a contraction of its monetary base, and thus a decline in its money supply. Sterilization of this foreign exchange intervention is not an option because this would just lead to a continuing loss of international reserves until the smaller country was forced to devalue its currency. The smaller country no longer controls its monetary policy, because movements in its money supply are completely determined by movements in the larger country's money supply.

Our analysis therefore indicates that a country (or monetary union like the Eurozone) can't pursue the following three policies at the same time: (1) free capital mobility, (2) a fixed exchange rate, and (3) an independent monetary policy. Economists call this result the **policy trilemma** (or, more graphically, the **impossible trinity**). Figure 20-3 illustrates the policy trilemma. A country can only choose two of the three options, which are denoted by each side of the triangle. In option 1, a country (or monetary union) chooses to have capital mobility and an independent monetary policy, but not a fixed exchange rate. The Eurozone and the United States have made this choice. Hong Kong and Belize have chosen option 2, in which there is free capital mobility and the exchange rate is fixed, so the country does not have an independent monetary policy. Other countries, like China, have chosen option 3, in which they have a fixed exchange rate and pursue an independent monetary policy, but do not have free capital mobility because they have **capital controls**, restrictions on the free movement of capital across the borders.

FIGURE 20-3 The Policy Trilemma

A country (or monetary union) cannot pursue the following three policies at the same time: (1) free capital mobility, (2) a fixed exchange rate, and (3) an independent monetary policy. Instead, it must choose two of the three policies on each point of the triangle.

APPLICATION

How Did China Accumulate Nearly US$3 Trillion of International Reserves?

By the end of 2011, China had accumulated nearly US$3 trillion of international reserves. How did the Chinese get their hands on this vast amount of foreign assets? After all, China is not yet a rich country.

The answer is that China pegged its exchange rate to the U.S. dollar at a fixed rate of 8.28 yuan (also called *renminbi*) to the U.S. dollar in 1994. Because of China's rapidly growing productivity and an inflation rate that is lower than in the United States, the long-run value of the yuan has increased, leading to a higher relative expected return for yuan assets and a rightward shift of the demand for yuan assets. As a result, the Chinese found themselves in the situation depicted in panel (b) of Figure 20-2, in which the yuan is undervalued. To keep the yuan from appreciating above E_{par} to E_1 in the figure, the Chinese central bank has been engaging in massive purchases of U.S. dollar assets. Today the Chinese government is one of the largest holders of U.S. government bonds in the world.

The pegging of the yuan to the U.S. dollar has created several problems for Chinese authorities. First, the Chinese now own a lot of U.S. assets, particularly U.S. Treasury securities, which have very low returns. Second, the undervaluation of the yuan has meant that Chinese goods are so cheap abroad that many countries have threatened to erect trade barriers against these goods if the Chinese government does not allow an upward revaluation of the yuan. Third, as we learned earlier in the chapter, the Chinese purchase of U.S. dollar assets has resulted in a substantial increase in the Chinese monetary base and money supply, which has the potential to produce high inflation in the future. Because the Chinese authorities have created substantial roadblocks to capital mobility, they have been able to sterilize most of their exchange rate interventions while maintaining the exchange rate peg. Nevertheless, they still worry about inflationary pressures. In July 2005, China finally made its peg somewhat more flexible by letting the value of the yuan rise 2.1% and subsequently allowed it to appreciate at a gradual pace. The central bank also indicated that it would no longer fix the yuan to the U.S. dollar, but would instead maintain its value relative to a basket of currencies. However, in 2008 during the global financial crisis, China reimposed the peg, but then dropped it in June of 2010.

Why did the Chinese authorities maintain this exchange rate peg for so long despite the problems? One answer is that they wanted to keep their export sector humming by keeping the prices of their export goods low. A second answer might be that they wanted to accumulate a large amount of international reserves as a "war chest" that could be sold to buy yuan in the event of a speculative attack against the yuan at some future date. Given the pressure on the Chinese government to further revalue its currency from government officials in the United States and Europe, there are likely to be further adjustments in China's exchange rate policy in the future.

The policy trilemma thus leaves countries with a difficult choice. Do they accept exchange rate volatility (option 1), give up an independent monetary policy (option 2), or restrict capital flows (option 3)?

HOW THE BRETTON WOODS SYSTEM WORKED Under the Bretton Woods system, exchange rates were supposed to change only when a country was experiencing a "fundamental disequilibrium"—that is, large persistent deficits or surpluses in its balance of payments. To maintain fixed exchange rates when countries had balance-of-payments deficits and were losing international reserves, the IMF would loan deficit countries international reserves contributed by other members. As a result of its power to dictate loan terms to borrowing countries, the IMF could encourage deficit countries to pursue contractionary monetary policies that would strengthen their currency or eliminate their balance-of-payments deficits. If the IMF loans were not sufficient to prevent depreciation of a currency, the country was allowed to devalue its currency by setting a new, lower exchange rate.

A notable weakness of the Bretton Woods system was that although deficit countries losing international reserves could be pressured into devaluing their currencies or pursuing contractionary policies, the IMF had no way to force surplus countries to revise their exchange rates upward or pursue more expansionary policies. Particularly troublesome in this regard was the fact that the reserve currency country, the United States, could not devalue its currency under the Bretton Woods system even if the U.S. dollar was overvalued. When the United States attempted to reduce domestic unemployment in the 1960s by pursuing an inflationary monetary policy, a fundamental disequilibrium of an overvalued dollar developed. Because surplus countries were not willing to revise their exchange rates upward, adjustment in the Bretton Woods system did not take place, and the system collapsed in 1971. Attempts to patch up the Bretton Woods system with the Smithsonian Agreement in December 1971 proved unsuccessful, and by 1973, the United States and its trading partners had agreed to allow exchange rates to float.

Managed Float

Although most exchange rates are currently allowed to change daily in response to market forces, central banks have not been willing to give up their option of intervening in the foreign exchange market. Preventing large changes in exchange rates makes it easier for firms and individuals purchasing or selling goods abroad to plan into the future. Furthermore, countries with surpluses in their balance of payments frequently do not want to see their currencies appreciate because it makes their goods more expensive abroad and foreign goods cheaper in their country. Because an appreciation might hurt sales for domestic businesses and increase unemployment, surplus countries have often sold their currency in the foreign exchange market and acquired international reserves.

Countries with balance-of-payments deficits do not want to see their currency lose value because it makes foreign goods more expensive for domestic consumers and can stimulate inflation. To keep the value of the domestic currency high, deficit countries have often bought their own currency exchange in the foreign exchange market and given up international reserves.

The current international financial system is a hybrid of a fixed and a flexible exchange rate system. Rates fluctuate in response to market forces but are not determined solely by them. Furthermore, many countries continue to keep the value of their currency fixed against other currencies, as was the case in the European Monetary System (to be described shortly).

Another important feature of the current system is the continuing de-emphasis of gold in international financial transactions. Not only has the United States suspended convertibility of dollars into gold for foreign central banks, but also since 1970 the IMF has been issuing a paper substitute for gold, called **special drawing rights (SDRs)**. Like gold in the Bretton Woods system, SDRs function as international reserves. Unlike gold, whose quantity is determined by gold discoveries and the rate of production, SDRs can be created by the IMF whenever it decides that there is a need for additional international reserves to promote world trade and economic growth.

The use of gold in international transactions was further de-emphasized by the IMF's elimination of the official gold price in 1975 and the sale of gold by the U.S. Treasury and the IMF to private investors in order to demonetize it. Currently, the price of gold is determined in a free market. Investors who want to speculate in it are able to purchase and sell at will, as are jewellers and dentists who use gold in their businesses.

European Monetary System (EMS)

In March 1979, eight members of the European Economic Community (Germany, France, Italy, the Netherlands, Belgium, Luxembourg, Denmark, and Ireland) set up an exchange rate union, the European Monetary System (EMS), in which they agreed to fix their exchange rates vis-à-vis one another and to float jointly against the U.S. dollar. Spain joined the EMS in June 1989, the United Kingdom in October 1990, and Portugal in April 1992. The EMS created a new monetary unit, the *European currency unit* (ECU), whose value was tied to a basket of specified amounts of European currencies.

The exchange rate mechanism (ERM) of the European Monetary System worked as follows. The exchange rate between every pair of currencies of the participating countries was not allowed to fluctuate outside narrow limits around a fixed exchange rate. (The limits were typically ±2.25% but were raised to ±15% in August 1993.) When the exchange rate between two countries' currencies moved outside these limits, the central banks of both countries were supposed to intervene in the foreign exchange market. If, for example, the French franc depreciated below its lower limit against the German mark, the Bank of France was required to buy francs and sell marks, thereby giving up international reserves. Similarly, the German central bank was also required to intervene to sell marks and buy francs and consequently increase its international reserves. The EMS thus required that intervention be symmetric when a currency fell outside the limits, with the central bank with the weak currency giving up international reserves and the one with the strong currency gaining them. Central bank intervention was also very common even when the exchange rate was within the limits, but in this case, if one central bank intervened, no others were required to intervene as well.

A serious shortcoming of fixed exchange rate systems such as the Bretton Woods system or the European Monetary System is that they can lead to foreign exchange crises involving a "speculative attack" on a currency—massive sales of a weak currency or purchases of a strong currency that cause a sharp change in the exchange rate. In the following application, we use our model of exchange rate determination to understand how the September 1992 exchange rate crisis that rocked the European Monetary System came about.

APPLICATION

The Foreign Exchange Crisis of September 1992

In the aftermath of German reunification in October 1990, the German central bank, the Bundesbank, faced rising inflationary pressures, with inflation having accelerated from below 3% in 1990 to near 5% by 1992. To get monetary growth under control and to dampen inflation, the Bundesbank raised German interest rates to near double-digit levels. Figure 20-4 shows the consequences of these actions by the Bundesbank in the foreign exchange market for British pounds. Note that in the diagram, the pound is the domestic currency and the German mark (deutsche mark, DM, Germany's currency before the advent of the euro in 1999) is the foreign currency.

The increase in German interest rates i^F lowered the relative expected return of British pound assets and shifted the demand curve to D_2 in Figure 20-4. The intersection of the supply and demand curves at point 2 was now below the lower exchange rate limit at that time (2.778 marks per pound, denoted E_{par}). To increase the value of the pound relative to the mark and to restore the mark/pound exchange rate to within the exchange rate mechanism limits, one of two things had to happen. The Bank of England would have to pursue a contractionary monetary policy, thereby raising British interest rates sufficiently to shift the demand curve back to D_1 so that the equilibrium would remain at point 1, where the exchange rate would remain at E_{par}. Alternatively, the Bundesbank would have to pursue an expansionary monetary policy, thereby lowering German interest rates. Lower German interest rates would raise the relative expected return on British assets and shift the demand curve back to D_1 so the exchange rate would be at E_{par}.

The catch was that the Bundesbank, whose primary goal was fighting inflation, was unwilling to pursue an expansionary monetary policy, and the British, who were facing their worst recession in the postwar period, were unwilling to pursue a contractionary monetary policy to prop up the pound. This impasse became clear when, in response to great pressure from other members of the EMS, the Bundesbank was willing to lower its lending rates by only a token amount on September 14 after a speculative attack was mounted on the currencies of the Scandinavian countries. So at some point in the near future, the value of the pound would have to decline to

MyEconLab
Animation

FIGURE 20-4 Foreign Exchange Market for British Pounds in 1992

The realization by speculators that the United Kingdom would soon devalue the pound decreased the relative expected return on British pound assets, resulting in a leftward shift of the demand curve from D_2 to D_3. The result was the need for a much greater purchase of pounds by the British central bank to raise the interest rate so that the demand curve would shift back to D_1 and keep the exchange rate E_{par} at 2.778 German marks per pound.

point 2. Speculators now knew that the depreciation of the pound was imminent. As a result, the relative expected return of the pound fell sharply, shifting the demand curve left to D_3 in Figure 20-4.

As a result of the large leftward shift of the demand curve, there was now a huge excess supply of pound assets at the par exchange rate E_{par}, which caused a massive sell-off of pounds (and purchases of marks) by speculators. The need for the British central bank to intervene to raise the value of the pound now became much greater and required a huge rise in British interest rates. After a major intervention effort on the part of the Bank of England, which included a rise in its lending rate from 10% to 15%, which still wasn't enough, the British were finally forced to give up on September 16: they pulled out of the ERM indefinitely and allowed the pound to depreciate by 10% against the mark.

Speculative attacks on other currencies forced devaluation of the Spanish peseta by 5% and the Italian lira by 15%. To defend its currency, the Swedish central bank was forced to raise its daily lending rate to the astronomical level of 500%! By the time the crisis was over, the British, French, Italian, Spanish, and Swedish central banks had intervened to the tune of US$100 billion; the Bundesbank alone had laid out US$50 billion for foreign exchange intervention. Because foreign exchange crises lead to large changes in central banks' holdings of international reserves and thus significantly affect the official reserve asset items in the balance of payments, these crises are also referred to as **balance-of-payments crises**.

The attempt to prop up the European Monetary System was not cheap for these central banks. It is estimated that they lost US$4 billion to US$6 billion as a result of exchange rate intervention during the crisis. What the central banks lost, the speculators gained. A speculative fund run by George Soros ran up US$1 billion of profits during the crisis, and Citibank traders reportedly made US$200 million. When an exchange rate crisis comes, life can certainly be sweet for exchange rate speculators.

APPLICATION

Recent Foreign Exchange Crises in Emerging-Market Countries: Mexico in 1994, East Asia in 1997, Brazil in 1999, and Argentina in 2002

Major currency crises in emerging-market countries have been a common occurrence in recent years. We can use Figure 20-4 to understand the sequence of events during the currency crises in Mexico in 1994, East Asia in 1997, Brazil in 1999, and Argentina in 2002. To do so, we just need to recognize that United States dollars are the foreign currency, while the domestic currency was either pesos, baht, or reals. (Note that the exchange rate label on the vertical axis would be in terms of U.S. dollars/domestic currency and that the label on the horizontal axis would be the quantity of domestic currency—say, pesos—assets.)

In Mexico in March 1994, political instability (the assassination of the ruling party's presidential candidate) sparked investors' concerns that the peso might be devalued. The result was that the relative expected return on peso assets fell, thus moving the demand curve from D_1 to D_2 in Figure 20-4. In the case of Thailand in May 1997, the large current account deficit and the weakness of the Thai financial system raised similar concerns about the devaluation of the domestic currency, with the same effect on the demand curve. In Brazil in late 1998 and Argentina in 2001, concerns about fiscal situations that could lead to the printing of money to finance the deficit, and thereby raise inflation, also meant that a devaluation was more likely to occur. The concerns thus lowered the relative expected return on domestic assets and shifted the demand curve from D_1 to D_2. In all of these cases, the result was that the intersection of the supply and demand curves was below the pegged value of the domestic currency at E_{par}.

To keep their domestic currencies from falling below E_{par}, these countries' central banks needed to buy the domestic currency and sell U.S. dollars to raise interest rates and shift the demand curve to the right, in the process losing international reserves. At first, the central banks were successful in containing the speculative attacks. However, when more bad news broke, speculators became even more confident that these countries could not defend their currencies. (The bad news was everywhere: in Mexico, there was an uprising in Chiapas and revelations about problems in the banking system; in Thailand, there was a major failure of a financial institution; Brazil had a worsening fiscal situation, along with a threat by a governor to default on his state's debt; and in Argentina, a full-scale bank panic and an actual default on the government debt occurred.) As a result, the relative expected returns on domestic assets fell further, the demand curve moved much farther to the left to D_3, and the central banks lost even more international reserves. Given the stress on the economy from rising interest rates and the loss of reserves, eventually the monetary authorities could no longer continue to defend the currency and were forced to give up and let their currencies depreciate. This scenario happened in Mexico in December 1994, in Thailand in July 1997, in Brazil in January 1999, and in Argentina in January 2002.

Concerns about similar problems in other countries then triggered speculative attacks against them as well. This contagion occurred in the aftermath of the Mexican crisis (jauntily referred to as the "Tequila effect") with speculative attacks on other Latin American currencies, but there were no further currency collapses. In the East Asian crisis, however, fears of devaluation spread throughout the region, leading to a scenario akin to that depicted in Figure 20-4. Consequently, one by one, Indonesia, Malaysia, South Korea, and the Philippines were forced to devalue sharply. Even Hong Kong, Singapore, and Taiwan were subjected to speculative attacks, but because these countries had healthy financial systems, the attacks were successfully averted.

As we saw in Chapter 9, the sharp depreciations in Mexico, East Asia, and Argentina led to full-scale financial crises that severely damaged these countries' economies. The foreign exchange crisis that shocked the European Monetary System in September 1992 cost central banks a lot of money, but the public in European countries were not seriously affected. By contrast, the public in Mexico, Argentina, and the crisis countries of East Asia were not so lucky: the collapse of these currencies triggered by speculative attacks led to the financial crises described in Chapter 9, producing severe depressions that caused hardship and political unrest.

Capital Controls

Because capital flows were an important element in the currency crises in Mexico and East Asia, politicians and some economists have advocated that emerging-market countries avoid financial instability by restricting capital mobility. Are capital controls a good idea?

Controls on Capital Outflows

Capital outflows can promote financial instability in emerging-market countries because when domestic residents and foreigners pull their capital out of a country, the resulting capital outflow forces a country to devalue its currency. This is why recently some politicians in emerging-market countries have found capital controls particularly attractive. For example, Prime Minister Mahathir of Malaysia instituted capital controls in 1998 to restrict outflows in the aftermath of the East Asian crisis.

Although these controls sound like a good idea, they suffer from several disadvantages. First, empirical evidence indicates that controls on capital outflows are seldom effective during a crisis because the private sector finds ingenious ways to evade them and has little difficulty moving funds out of the country. Second, the evidence suggests that capital flight may even increase after controls are put into place because confidence in the government is weakened. Third, controls on capital outflows often lead to corruption, as government officials get paid off to look the other way when domestic residents are trying to move funds abroad. Fourth, controls on capital outflows may lull governments into thinking they do not have to take the steps to reform their financial systems to deal with the crisis, with the result that opportunities to improve the functioning of the economy are lost.

Controls on Capital Inflows

Although most economists find the arguments against controls on capital outflows persuasive, controls on capital inflows receive more support. Supporters reason that if speculative capital cannot come in, then it cannot go out suddenly and create a crisis. Our analysis of the financial crises in East Asia in Chapter 8 provides support for this view by suggesting that capital inflows can lead to a lending boom and excessive risk taking on the part of banks, which then helps trigger a financial crisis.

However, controls on capital inflows have the undesirable feature that they may block from entering a country funds that would be used for productive investment opportunities. Although such controls may limit the fuel supplied to lending booms through capital flows, over time they produce substantial distortions and misallocation of resources as households and businesses try to get around them. Indeed, just as with controls on capital outflows, controls on capital inflows can lead to corruption. There are serious doubts whether capital controls can be effective in today's environment, in which trade is open and where there are many financial instruments that make it easier to get around these controls.

On the other hand, there is a strong case for improving bank regulation and supervision so that capital inflows are less likely to produce a lending boom and encourage excessive risk taking by banking institutions. For example, restricting banks in how fast their borrowing can grow might substantially limit capital inflows. Supervisory controls that focus on the sources of financial fragility, rather than the symptoms, can enhance the efficiency of the financial system rather than hamper it.

The Role of the IMF

The International Monetary Fund was originally set up under the Bretton Woods system to help countries deal with balance-of-payments problems and stay with the fixed exchange rates by lending to deficit countries. When the Bretton Woods system of fixed exchange rates collapsed in 1971, the IMF took on new roles.

The IMF continues to function as a data collector and provides technical assistance to its member countries. Although the IMF no longer attempts to encourage fixed exchange rates, its role as an international lender has become more important recently. This role first came to the fore in the 1980s during the third-world debt crisis, in which the IMF assisted developing countries in repaying their loans. The financial crises in Mexico in 1994–1995 and in East Asia in 1997–1998 led to huge loans by the IMF to these and other affected countries to help them recover from their financial crises and to prevent the spread of these crises to other countries. Then, starting in 2010, the IMF made large loans to Greece, Ireland, and Portugal to help them avoid a default on their government debt. This role, in which the IMF acts like an international lender of last resort to cope with financial instability, is indeed highly controversial.

Should the IMF Be an International Lender of Last Resort?

As we saw in large, industrialized countries, when a financial crisis occurs and the financial system threatens to seize up, domestic central banks can address matters with a lender-of-last-resort operation to limit the degree of instability in the banking system. In emerging markets, however, where the credibility of the central bank as an inflation fighter may be in doubt and debt contracts are typically short-term and in foreign currencies, a lender-of-last-resort operation becomes a double-edged sword—as likely to exacerbate the financial crisis as to alleviate it. For example, when the U.S. Federal Reserve engaged in a lender-of-last-resort operation during the 1987 stock market crash, after the 2001 terrorist destruction of the World Trade Center, and during the global financial crisis, there was almost no sentiment in the markets that there would be substantially higher inflation. However, for a central bank with less inflation-fighting credibility than the Fed, central bank lending to the financial system in the wake of a financial crisis—even under the lender-of-last-resort rhetoric—may well arouse fears of inflation spiralling out of control, causing an even greater currency depreciation and still greater deterioration of balance sheets. The resulting increase in moral hazard and adverse selection problems in financial markets, along the lines discussed in Chapter 9, would only make the financial crisis worse.

Central banks in emerging-market countries therefore have only a very limited ability to successfully engage in a lender-of-last-resort operation. However, liquidity provided by an international lender of last resort does not have these undesirable consequences, and in helping to stabilize the value of the domestic currency it strengthens domestic balance sheets. Moreover, an international lender of last resort may be able to prevent contagion, the situation in which a successful speculative attack on one emerging-market currency leads to attacks on other emerging-market currencies, spreading financial and economic disruption. Since a lender of last resort for emerging-market countries is needed at times, and since it cannot be provided domestically, there is a strong rationale for an international institution to fill this role. Indeed, since Mexico's financial crisis in 1994, the International Monetary Fund and other international agencies have stepped into the lender-of-last-resort role and provided emergency lending to countries threatened by financial instability.

However, support from an international lender of last resort brings risks of its own, especially the risk that the perception it is standing ready to bail out irresponsible financial institutions may lead to excessive risk taking of the sort that makes financial crises more likely. In the Mexican, East Asian, and Irish crises, governments in the crisis countries used IMF support to protect depositors and other creditors of banking institutions from losses. This safety net creates a well-known moral hazard problem because the depositors and other creditors have less incentive to monitor these banking institutions and withdraw their deposits if the institutions are taking on too much risk. The result is that these institutions are encouraged to take on excessive risks. An international lender of last resort must find ways to limit this moral hazard problem, or it can actually make the situation worse. The international lender of last resort can make it clear that it will extend liquidity only to governments that put the proper measures in place to prevent excessive risk taking. In addition, it can reduce the incentives for risk taking by restricting the ability of governments to bail out shareholders and large uninsured creditors of domestic financial institutions. Some critics of the IMF believe that the IMF has not put enough pressure on the governments to which it lends to contain the moral hazard problem.

One problem that arises for international organizations like the IMF engaged in lender-of-last-resort operations is that they know that if they don't come to the rescue, the country will suffer extreme hardship and possible political instability. Politicians in the crisis country may exploit these concerns and engage in a game of chicken with the international lender of last resort: they resist necessary reforms, hoping that the IMF will cave in. Elements of this game were present in the Mexican crisis of 1995 and were also a particularly important feature of the negotiations between the IMF and Indonesia during the Asian crisis.

How Should the IMF Operate?

The IMF would produce better outcomes if it made it clear that it will not play this game. Just as giving in to ill-behaved children may be the easy way out in the short run but supports a pattern of poor behaviour in the long run, some critics worry that the IMF may not be tough enough when confronted by short-run humanitarian concerns. For example, they have been particularly critical of the IMF's lending to the Russian government, which has resisted adopting appropriate reforms to stabilize its financial system.

The IMF has also been criticized for imposing on the East Asian countries so-called austerity programs that focused on tight macroeconomic policies rather than on microeconomic policies to fix the crisis-causing problems in the financial sector. Such programs are likely to increase resistance to IMF recommendations, particularly in emerging-market countries. Austerity programs allow politicians in these countries to label institutions such as the IMF as being anti-growth, rhetoric that helps the politicians mobilize the public against the IMF and avoid doing what they really need to do to reform the financial system in their country. IMF programs that are focused instead on reforms of the financial sector would increase the likelihood that the IMF will be seen as a helping hand in the creation of a more efficient financial system.

An important historical feature of successful lender-of-last-resort operations is that the faster the lending is done, the lower is the amount that actually has to be lent. An excellent example involving the Federal Reserve occurred in the aftermath of the stock market crash on October 19, 1987. At the end of that day, in order to service their customers' accounts, securities firms needed to borrow several billion dollars to maintain orderly trading. However, given the unprecedented developments, banks were nervous about extending further loans to these firms. Upon learning this, the U.S. Federal Reserve engaged in an immediate lender-of-last-resort operation, making it clear that it would provide liquidity to banks making loans to the securities industry. What is striking about this episode is that the extremely quick intervention of the Fed not only resulted in a negligible impact of the stock market crash on the economy, but also meant that the amount of liquidity that the Fed needed to supply to the economy was not very large.

The ability of the Fed to engage in a lender-of-last-resort operation within a day of a substantial shock to the financial system is in sharp contrast to the amount of time it has taken the IMF to supply liquidity during the recent crises. Because IMF lending facilities were originally designed to provide funds after a country was experiencing a balance-of-payments crisis and because the conditions for the loan had to be negotiated, it can take several months before the IMF makes funds available. By this time, the crises can get much worse—and much larger sums of funds may be needed to cope with the crises, often stretching the resources of the IMF. One reason central banks can lend so much more quickly than the IMF is that they have set up procedures in advance to provide loans, with the terms and conditions for this lending agreed upon beforehand. The need for quick provision of liquidity to keep the loan amount manageable argues for similar credit facilities at the international lender of last resort, so that funds can be provided quickly as long as the borrower meets conditions such as properly supervising its banks or keeping budget deficits low.

The flaws in IMF lending programs discussed above led to emerging-market countries avoiding borrowing from the IMF. Countries did not want to be subjected to harsh austerity programs and also were unhappy with IMF delays in disbursing funds during a crisis. As an alternative to the IMF, countries built up substantial cushions of international reserves to deal with balance-of-payments problems on their own. IMF lending therefore shrank to very low levels, even creating a shortfall of revenue for its operations because it was no longer earning income by making loans. The IMF was at risk of becoming irrelevant—until the global financial crisis. With the global financial crisis, the IMF's role as an international lender of last resort returned, as can be seen in the Global box The Global Financial Crisis and the IMF.

The debate on whether the world will be better off with the IMF operating as an international lender of last resort is currently a hot one. Much attention is being focused on making the IMF more effective in performing this role, and redesign of the IMF is at the centre of proposals for a new international financial architecture to help reduce international financial instability.

GLOBAL

The Global Financial Crisis and the IMF

Because financial institutions in emerging-market countries had limited exposure to subprime mortgages, the early stages of the subprime financial crisis had little impact on their economies. However, when the global financial crisis became more virulent in October of 2008, a number of emerging-market countries, as well as Iceland and former communist countries, found that foreigners were pulling funds out of their financial systems, putting not only domestic banks under stress, but also causing a sharp depreciation of their currencies.

The role of the IMF as an international lender of last resort now came to the fore. Toward the end of October, the IMF extended $25 billion in loans to Hungary, $16.5 billion to the Ukraine, and $2 billion to Iceland. These loans stipulated that the countries would have to undergo belt-tightening in order to get their fiscal houses in order.

The IMF recognized, however, that, as the managing director of the IMF, Dominique Strauss-Kahn, put it, "exceptional times call for an exceptional response," and that a new type of lending program was needed to overcome the reluctance of countries to borrow from it during the crisis at hand.

The IMF created a new lending program at the end of October 2008 called the Short-Term Liquidity Facility, with $100 billion of funds. It provides three-month loans to countries whose economies are judged by the IMF to be basically sound, but under stress. These condition-free loans could be disbursed very quickly. In addition, these loans would not have austerity programs attached to them, making them far more attractive to potential borrowing countries.

In 1999, the IMF tried to implement a similar facility called the Contingent Credit Line, but it was unsuccessful because it required preapproval from the IMF, and countries were reluctant to apply for it because doing so might suggest that they were likely to get into trouble. The Short-Term Liquidity Facility and later lending facilities do not require countries to apply for it. The IMF can just determine that a country has access and give them a loan if they need it. It is too soon to determine whether these new lending facilities will overcome some of the criticisms levelled against previous IMF lending programs, but they do appear to be a step in the right direction.

International Considerations and Monetary Policy

Our analysis in this chapter so far has suggested several ways in which monetary policy can be affected by international matters. Awareness of these effects can have significant implications for the way monetary policy is conducted.

Direct Effects of the Foreign Exchange Market on Monetary Policy

When central banks intervene in the foreign exchange market, they acquire or sell off international reserves, and their monetary base is affected. When a central bank intervenes in the foreign exchange market, it gives up some control of its monetary policy. For example, in the early 1970s, the German central bank faced a dilemma. In attempting to keep the German mark from appreciating too much against the U.S. dollar, the Germans acquired huge quantities of international reserves, leading to a rate of money growth that the German central bank considered inflationary.

The Bundesbank could have tried to halt the growth of the money supply by stopping its intervention in the foreign exchange market and reasserting control over its own monetary policy. Such a strategy has a major drawback when the central bank is under pressure not to allow its currency to appreciate: the lower price of imports and higher price of exports as a result of an appreciation in its currency will hurt domestic producers and increase unemployment.

The ability to conduct monetary policy is typically easier when a country's currency is a reserve currency. For example, because the U.S. dollar has been a reserve currency, the U.S. monetary base and money supply have been less affected by developments in the foreign exchange market. As long as other central banks, rather than the Fed, intervene to keep the value of the dollar from changing, U.S. holdings of international reserves are unaffected. However, the central bank of a reserve currency country must worry about a shift away from the use of its currency for international reserves.

Balance-of-Payments Considerations

Under the Bretton Woods system, balance-of-payments considerations were more important than they are under the current managed float regime. When a non–reserve-currency country is running balance-of-payments deficits, it necessarily gives up international reserves. To keep from running out of these reserves, under the Bretton Woods system it had to implement contractionary monetary policy to strengthen its currency. This is exactly what occurred in the United Kingdom before its devaluation of the pound in 1967. When policy became expansionary, the balance of payments deteriorated, and the British were forced to "slam on the brakes" by implementing a contractionary policy. Once the balance of payments improved, policy became more expansionary until the deteriorating balance of payments again forced the British to pursue a contractionary policy. Such on-again, off-again actions became known as a "stop-go" policy, and the domestic instability it created was criticized severely.

Because the United States is a major reserve currency country, it can run large balance-of-payments deficits without losing huge amounts of international reserves. This does not mean, however, that the Federal Reserve is never influenced by developments in the U.S. balance of payments. Current account deficits in the United States suggest that American businesses may be losing some of their ability to compete because the value of the dollar is too high. In addition, large U.S. balance-of-payments deficits lead to balance-of-payments surpluses in other countries, which can in turn lead to large increases in their holdings of international reserves (this was especially true under the Bretton Woods system). Because such increases put a strain on the international financial system and may stimulate world inflation, the Fed worries about U.S. balance-of-payments and current account deficits. To help shrink these deficits, the Fed might pursue a more contractionary monetary policy.

Exchange Rate Considerations

Unlike balance-of-payments considerations, which have become less important under the current managed float system, exchange rate considerations now play a greater role in the conduct of monetary policy. If a central bank does not want to see its currency fall in value, it may pursue a more contractionary monetary policy to raise the domestic interest rate, thereby strengthening its currency. Similarly, if a country experiences an appreciation in its currency, domestic industry may suffer from increased foreign competition and may pressure the central bank to ease monetary policy in order to lower the exchange rate.

To Peg or Not to Peg: Exchange-Rate Targeting as an Alternative Monetary Policy Strategy

In Chapter 18, we discussed several monetary policy strategies that could be followed to promote price stability, including inflation targeting. One other strategy also uses a strong nominal anchor to promote price stability: **exchange-rate targeting** (sometimes referred to as an **exchange-rate peg**).

Targeting the exchange rate is a monetary policy strategy with a long history. It can take the form of fixing the value of the domestic currency to a commodity such as gold, the key feature of the gold standard described earlier in the chapter. More recently, fixed exchange-rate regimes have involved fixing the value of the domestic currency to that of a large, low-inflation country like the United States or Germany (the *anchor country*). Another alternative is to adopt a *crawling target* or *peg*, in which a currency is allowed to depreciate at a steady rate so that the inflation rate in the pegging country can be higher than that of the anchor country.

Advantages of Exchange-Rate Targeting

Exchange-rate targeting has several advantages. First, the nominal anchor of an exchange-rate target directly contributes to keeping inflation under control by tying the inflation rate for internationally traded goods to that found in the anchor country. It does this because the foreign price of internationally traded goods is set by the world market, while the domestic price of these goods is fixed by the exchange-rate target. For example, until 2002 in Argentina the exchange rate for the Argentine peso was exactly one to the U.S. dollar, so that a bushel of wheat traded internationally at five U.S. dollars had its price set at five pesos. If the exchange-rate target is credible (i.e., expected to be adhered to), the exchange-rate target has the added benefit of anchoring inflation expectations to the inflation rate in the anchor country.

Second, an exchange-rate target provides an automatic rule for the conduct of monetary policy that helps mitigate the time-inconsistency problem described in the Web Appendix to Chapter 18. As we saw earlier, an exchange-rate target forces a tightening of monetary policy when there is a tendency for the domestic currency to depreciate or a loosening of policy when there is a tendency for the domestic currency to appreciate, so that discretionary monetary policy is less of an option. The central bank will therefore be constrained from falling into the time-inconsistency trap of trying to expand output and employment in the short run by pursuing overly expansionary monetary policy.

Third, an exchange-rate target has the advantage of simplicity and clarity, which makes it easily understood by the public. A "sound currency" is an easy-to-understand rallying cry for monetary policy. In the past, for example, this aspect was important in France, where an appeal to the "franc fort" (strong franc) was often used to justify tight monetary policy.

Given its advantages, it is not surprising that exchange-rate targeting has been used successfully to control inflation in industrialized countries. Both France and the United Kingdom, for example, successfully used exchange-rate targeting to lower inflation by tying the values of their currencies to the German mark. In 1987, when France first pegged its exchange rate to the mark, its inflation rate was 3%, two percentage points above the German inflation rate. By 1992, its inflation rate had fallen to 2%, a level that can be argued is consistent with price stability, and was even below that in Germany. By 1996, the French and German inflation rates had converged, to a number slightly below 2%. Similarly, after pegging to the German mark in 1990, the United Kingdom was able to lower its inflation rate from 10% to 3% by 1992, when it was forced to abandon the exchange rate mechanism (ERM).

Exchange-rate targeting has also been an effective means of reducing inflation quickly in emerging-market countries. For example, before the devaluation in Mexico in 1994, its exchange-rate target enabled it to bring inflation down from levels above 100% in 1988 to below 10% in 1994.

Disadvantages of Exchange-Rate Targeting

Despite the inherent advantages of exchange-rate targeting, there are several serious criticisms of this strategy. The problem (as we saw earlier in the chapter) is that with capital mobility the targeting country can no longer pursue its own independent monetary policy and use it to respond to domestic shocks that are independent of those hitting the anchor country. Furthermore, an exchange-rate target means that shocks to the anchor country are directly transmitted to the targeting country, because changes in interest rates in the anchor country lead to a corresponding change in interest rates in the targeting country.

A striking example of these problems occurred when Germany was reunified in 1990. In response to concerns about inflationary pressures arising from reunification and the massive fiscal expansion required to rebuild East Germany, long-term German interest rates rose until February 1991 and short-term rates rose until December 1991. This shock to the anchor country in the exchange rate mechanism (ERM) was transmitted directly to the other countries in the ERM whose currencies were pegged to the mark, and their interest rates rose in tandem with those in Germany. Continuing adherence to the exchange-rate target slowed economic growth and increased unemployment in countries such as France that remained in the ERM and adhered to the exchange-rate peg.

A second problem with exchange-rate targets is that they leave countries open to speculative attacks on their currencies. Indeed, one aftermath of German reunification was the foreign exchange crisis of September 1992. As we saw earlier, the tight monetary policy in Germany following reunification meant that the countries in the ERM were subjected to a negative demand shock that led to a decline in economic growth and a rise in unemployment. It was certainly feasible for the governments of these countries to keep their exchange rates fixed relative to the mark in these circumstances, but speculators began to question whether these countries' commitment to the exchange-rate peg would weaken. Speculators reasoned that these countries would not tolerate the rise in unemployment resulting from keeping interest rates high enough to fend off attacks on their currencies.

At this stage, speculators were, in effect, presented with a one-way bet, because the currencies of countries like France, Spain, Sweden, Italy, and the United Kingdom could go in only one direction and depreciate against the mark. Selling these currencies before the likely depreciation occurred gave speculators an attractive profit opportunity with potentially high expected returns. The result was the speculative attack in September 1992. Only in France was the commitment to the fixed exchange rate strong enough so that France did not devalue. The governments in the other countries were unwilling to defend their currencies at all costs and eventually allowed their currencies to fall in value.

The different responses of France and the United Kingdom after the September 1992 exchange rate crisis illustrates the potential cost of an exchange-rate target. France, which continued to peg its currency to the mark and was thus unable to use monetary policy to respond to domestic conditions, found that economic growth remained slow after 1992 and unemployment increased. The United Kingdom, on the other hand, which dropped out of the ERM exchange-rate peg and adopted inflation targeting, had much better economic performance: Economic growth was higher, the unemployment rate fell, and yet its inflation was not much worse than France's.

In contrast to industrialized countries, emerging-market countries (including the transition countries of Eastern Europe) may not lose much by giving up an independent monetary policy when they target exchange rates. Because many emerging-market countries have not developed the political or monetary institutions that allow the successful use of discretionary monetary policy, they may have little to gain from an independent monetary policy, but a lot to lose. Thus they would be better off by, in effect, adopting the monetary policy of a country like the United States through targeting exchange rates than by pursuing their own independent policy. This is one of the reasons that so many emerging-market countries have adopted exchange-rate targeting.

Nonetheless, exchange-rate targeting is highly dangerous for these countries, because it leaves them open to speculative attacks that can have far more serious consequences for their economies than for the economies of industrialized countries. Indeed, the successful speculative attacks in Mexico in 1994, East Asia in 1997, and Argentina in 2002 plunged their economies into full-scale financial crises that devastated their economies.

An additional disadvantage of an exchange-rate target is that it can weaken the accountability of policymakers, particularly in emerging-market countries. Because exchange-rate targeting fixes the exchange rate, it eliminates an important signal that can help constrain monetary policy from becoming too expansionary and thereby limit the time-inconsistency problem. In industrialized countries, particularly in the United States, the bond market provides an important signal about the stance of monetary policy. Overly expansionary monetary policy or strong political pressure to engage in overly expansionary monetary policy produces an inflation scare in which inflation expectations surge, interest rates rise because of the Fisher effect (described in Chapter 5), and there is a sharp decline in long-term bond prices. Because both central banks and the politicians want to avoid this kind of scenario, overly expansionary monetary policy will be less likely.

In many countries, particularly emerging-market countries, the long-term bond market is essentially nonexistent. Under a floating exchange rate regime, however, if monetary policy is too expansionary, the exchange rate will depreciate. In these countries the daily fluctuations of the exchange rate can, like the bond market in Canada and the United States, provide an early warning signal that monetary policy is too expansionary. Just as the fear of a visible inflation scare in the bond market constrains central bankers from pursuing overly expansionary monetary policy and constrains politicians from putting pressure on the central bank to engage in overly expansionary monetary policy, fear of exchange-rate depreciations can make overly expansionary monetary policy, and the time-inconsistency problem, less likely.

The need for signals from the foreign exchange market may be even more acute for emerging-market countries, because the balance sheets and actions of their central banks are not as transparent as they are in industrialized countries. Targeting the exchange rate can make it even harder to ascertain a central bank's policy actions. The public is less able to keep watch on the central bank and the politicians pressuring it, which makes it easier for monetary policy to become too expansionary.

When Is Exchange-Rate Targeting Desirable for Industrialized Countries?

Given the above disadvantages with exchange-rate targeting, when might it be an appropriate strategy?

In industrialized countries, the biggest cost to exchange-rate targeting is the loss of an independent monetary policy to deal with domestic considerations. If an independent domestic monetary policy can be conducted responsibly, this can be a serious cost indeed, as the comparison between the post-1992 experiences of France and the United Kingdom indicates. However, not all industrialized countries have found that they are capable of conducting their own monetary policy successfully, either because the central bank is not independent or because political pressures on the central bank lead to an inflationary bias in monetary policy. In these cases, giving up independent control of domestic monetary policy may not be a great loss, while the gain of having monetary policy determined by a better-performing central bank in the anchor country can be substantial.

Italy provides an example: It was not a coincidence that the Italian public had the most favourable attitude of all those in Europe toward the European Monetary Union. The past record of Italian monetary policy was not good, and the Italian public recognized that having monetary policy controlled by more responsible outsiders had benefits that far outweighed the costs of losing the ability to focus monetary policy on domestic considerations.

A second reason why industrialized countries might find targeting exchange rates useful is that it encourages integration of the domestic economy with its neighbours. Clearly, this was the rationale for long-standing pegging of the exchange rate to the deutsche mark by countries such as Austria and the Netherlands, and the more recent exchange-rate pegs that preceded the European Monetary Union.

To sum up, exchange-rate targeting for industrialized countries is probably not the best monetary policy strategy to control the overall economy unless (1) domestic monetary and political institutions are not conducive to good monetary policy-making or (2) there are other important benefits of an exchange-rate target that have nothing to do with monetary policy.

When Is Exchange-Rate Targeting Desirable for Emerging-Market Countries?

In countries in which political and monetary institutions are particularly weak and that therefore have been experiencing continued bouts of hyperinflation, a characterization that applies to many emerging-market (including transition) countries, exchange-rate targeting may be the only way to break inflationary psychology and stabilize the economy. In this situation, exchange-rate targeting is the stabilization policy of last resort. However, if the exchange-rate targeting regimes in emerging-market countries are not always transparent, they are more likely to break down, often resulting in disastrous financial crises.

Are there exchange-rate strategies that make it less likely that the exchange-rate regime will break down in emerging-market countries? Two such strategies that have received increasing attention in recent years are currency boards and dollarization.

Currency Boards

One solution to the problem of lack of transparency and commitment to the exchange-rate target is the adoption of a **currency board**, in which the domestic currency is backed 100% by a foreign currency (say, U.S. dollars or euros) and in which the note-issuing authority, whether the central bank or the government, establishes a fixed exchange rate to this foreign currency and stands ready to exchange domestic currency for the foreign currency at this rate whenever the public requests it. A currency board is just a variant of a fixed exchange-rate target in which the commitment to the fixed exchange rate is especially strong because the conduct of monetary policy is in effect put on autopilot, taken completely out of the hands of the central bank and the government. In contrast, the typical fixed or pegged exchange rate regime does allow the monetary authorities some discretion in their conduct of monetary policy because they can still adjust interest rates or print money.

A currency board arrangement thus has important advantages over a monetary policy strategy that just uses an exchange-rate target. First, the money supply can expand only when foreign currency is exchanged for domestic currency at the central bank. Thus the increased amount of domestic currency is matched by an equal increase in foreign exchange reserves. The central bank no longer has the ability to print money and thereby cause inflation. Second, the currency board involves a stronger commitment by the central bank to the fixed exchange rate and may therefore be effective in bringing down inflation quickly and in decreasing the likelihood of a successful speculative attack against the currency.

Although they solve the transparency and commitment problems inherent in an exchange-rate target regime, currency boards suffer from some of the same shortcomings: the loss of an independent monetary policy and increased exposure of the economy to shocks from the anchor country, and the loss of the central bank's ability to create money and act as a lender of last resort. Other means must therefore be used to cope with potential banking crises. Also, if there is a speculative attack on a currency board, the exchange of the domestic currency for foreign currency leads to a sharp contraction of the money supply, which can be highly damaging to the economy.

Currency boards have been established in countries such as Hong Kong (1983), Argentina (1991), Estonia (1992), Lithuania (1994), Bulgaria (1997), and Bosnia (1998). Argentina's currency board, which operated from 1991 to 2002 and required the central bank to exchange U.S. dollars for new pesos at a fixed exchange rate of 1 to 1, is one of the most interesting. For more on this subject, see the Global box Argentina's Currency Board.

Dollarization

Another solution to the problems created by a lack of transparency and commitment to the exchange-rate target is **dollarization**, the adoption of a sound currency, like the U.S. dollar, as a country's money. Indeed, dollarization is just another variant of a fixed exchange-rate target with an even stronger commitment mechanism than a currency board provides. A currency board can be abandoned, allowing a change in

GLOBAL

Argentina's Currency Board

Argentina has had a long history of monetary instability, with inflation rates fluctuating dramatically and sometimes surging to beyond 1000% per year. To end this cycle of inflationary surges, Argentina decided to adopt a currency board in April 1991. The Argentine currency board worked as follows: Under Argentina's convertibility law, the peso/U.S. dollar exchange rate was fixed at one to one, and a member of the public could go to the Argentine central bank and exchange a peso for a U.S. dollar, or vice versa, at any time.

The early years of Argentina's currency board looked stunningly successful. Inflation, which had been running at an 800% annual rate in 1990, fell to less than 5% by the end of 1994, and economic growth was rapid, averaging almost 8% per year from 1991 to 1994. In the aftermath of the Mexican peso crisis, however, concern about the health of the Argentine economy resulted in the public pulling money out of the banks (deposits fell by 18%) and exchanging pesos for U.S. dollars, thus causing a contraction of the Argentine money supply. The result was a sharp drop in Argentine economic activity, with real GDP shrinking by more than 5% in 1995 and the unemployment rate jumping above 15%. Only in 1996 did the economy begin to recover.

Because the central bank of Argentina had no control over monetary policy under the currency board system, it was relatively helpless to counteract the contractionary monetary policy stemming from the public's behaviour. Furthermore, because

the currency board did not allow the central bank to create pesos and lend them to the banks, it had very little capability to act as a lender of last resort. With help from international agencies, such as the IMF, the World Bank, and the Inter-American Development Bank, which lent Argentina more than US$5 billion in 1995 to help shore up its banking system, the currency board survived.

However, in 1998 Argentina entered another recession, which was both severe and very long lasting. By the end of 2001, unemployment reached nearly 20%, a level comparable to that experienced in the United States during the Great Depression of the 1930s. The result was civil unrest and the fall of the elected government, as well as a major banking crisis and a default on nearly US$150 billion of government debt. Because the Central Bank of Argentina had no control over monetary policy under the currency board system, it was unable to use monetary policy to expand the economy and get out of its recession. Furthermore, because the currency board did not allow the central bank to create pesos and lend them to banks, it had very little capability to act as a lender of last resort. In January 2002, the currency board finally collapsed and the peso depreciated by more than 70%. The result was the full-scale financial crisis described in Chapter 9, with inflation shooting up and an extremely severe depression. Clearly, the Argentine public is not as enamoured of its currency board as it once was.

the value of the currency, but a change of value is impossible with dollarization: a U.S. dollar bill is always worth one U.S. dollar, whether it is held in the United States or outside of it.

Dollarization has been advocated as a monetary policy strategy for emerging-market countries: it was discussed actively by Argentine officials in the aftermath of the devaluation of the Brazilian real in January 1999 and was adopted by Ecuador in March 2000. Dollarization's key advantage is that it completely avoids the possibility of a speculative attack on the domestic currency (because there is none). (Such an attack is still a danger even under a currency board arrangement.)

Dollarization is subject to the usual disadvantages of an exchange-rate target (the loss of an independent monetary policy, increased exposure of the economy to shocks from the anchor country, and the inability of the central bank to create money and act as a lender of last resort). Dollarization has one additional disadvantage not characteristic of currency boards or other exchange-rate target regimes. Because a country adopting dollarization no longer has its own currency, it loses the revenue that a government receives by issuing money, which is called **seigniorage**. Because governments (or their central banks) do not have to pay interest on their currency, they earn revenue (seigniorage) by using this currency to purchase income-earning assets such as bonds. In the case of the Federal Reserve in the United States, this revenue is usually in excess of US$30 billion per year. If an emerging-market country dollarizes and gives up its currency, it needs to make up this loss of revenue somewhere, which is not always easy for a poor country.

SUMMARY

EconLab
o Summary

1. An unsterilized central bank intervention in which the domestic currency is sold to purchase foreign assets leads to a gain in international reserves, an increase in the money supply, and a depreciation of the domestic currency. Available evidence suggests, however, that sterilized central bank interventions have little long-term effect on the exchange rate.

2. The balance of payments is a bookkeeping system for recording all payments between a country and foreign countries that have a direct bearing on the movement of funds between them. The official reserve transactions balance is the sum of the current account balance plus the items in the capital account. It indicates the amount of international reserves that must be moved between countries to finance international transactions.

3. Before World War I, the gold standard was predominant. Currencies were convertible into gold, thus fixing exchange rates between countries. After World War II, the Bretton Woods system and the IMF were established to promote a fixed exchange rate system in which the U.S. dollar was convertible into gold. The Bretton Woods system collapsed in 1971. We now have an international financial system that has elements of a managed float and a fixed exchange rate system. Some exchange rates fluctuate from day to day, although central banks intervene in the foreign exchange market, while other exchange rates are fixed.

4. Controls on capital outflows receive support because they may prevent domestic residents and foreigners from pulling capital out of a country during a crisis and make devaluation less likely. Controls on capital inflows make sense under the theory that if speculative capital cannot flow in, then it cannot go out suddenly and create a crisis. However, capital controls suffer from several disadvantages: they are seldom effective, they lead to corruption, and they may allow governments to avoid taking the steps needed to reform their financial systems to deal with the crises.

5. The IMF has recently taken on the role of an international lender of last resort. Because central banks in emerging-market countries are unlikely to be able to perform a lender-of-last-resort operation successfully, an international lender of last resort like the IMF is needed to prevent financial instability. However, the IMF's role as an international lender of last resort creates a serious moral hazard problem that can encourage excessive risk taking and make a financial crisis more likely, as refusing to lend may be politically hard to do. In addition, it needs to be able to provide liquidity quickly during a crisis to keep manageable the amount of funds lent.

6. Three international considerations affect the conduct of monetary policy: direct effects of the foreign exchange market on monetary policy, balance-of-payments considerations,

and exchange rate considerations. Inasmuch as the United States has been a reserve currency country in the post–World War II period, U.S. monetary policy has been less affected by developments in the foreign exchange market and its balance of payments than is true for other countries. However, in recent years, exchange rate considerations have been playing a more prominent role in influencing U.S. monetary policy.

7. Exchange-rate targeting has the following advantages as a monetary policy strategy: (1) it directly keeps inflation under control by tying the inflation rate for internationally traded goods to that found in the anchor country to which its currency is pegged; (2) it provides an automatic rule for the conduct of monetary policy that helps mitigate the time-inconsistency problem; and (3) it is simple and clear. Exchange-rate targeting also has serious disadvantages: (1) it results in a loss of independent monetary policy; (2) it leaves the country open to speculative attacks; and (3) it can weaken the accountability of policymakers because the exchange-rate signal is lost. Two strategies that make it less likely that the exchange rate regime will break down are currency boards, in which the central bank stands ready to automatically exchange domestic for foreign currency at a fixed rate, and dollarization, in which a sound currency like the U.S. dollar is adopted as the country's money.

KEY TERMS

anchor currency, p. 497

balance of payments, p. 496

balance-of-payments crisis, p. 506

Bretton Woods system, p. 498

capital account, p. 496

capital controls, p. 501

currency board, p. 517

current account, p. 496

devaluation, p. 501

dollarization, p. 518

exchange-rate peg, p. 513

exchange-rate targeting, p. 513

fixed exchange rate regime, p. 497

floating exchange rate regime, p. 498

foreign exchange interventions, p. 492

gold standard, p. 498

International Monetary Fund (IMF), p. 498

international reserves, p. 492

managed float regime (dirty float), p. 498

official reserve transactions balance, p. 496

policy trilemma (impossible trinity), p. 501

reserve currency, p. 499

revaluation, p. 501

seigniorage, p. 519

special drawing rights (SDRs), p. 504

sterilized foreign exchange intervention, p. 494

trade balance, p. 496

unsterilized foreign exchange intervention, p. 494

World Bank, p. 498

World Trade Organization (WTO), p. 498

QUESTIONS

1. If the Bank of Canada buys dollars in the foreign exchange market but conducts an offsetting open market operation to sterilize the intervention, what will be the impact on international reserves, the money supply, and the exchange rate?

2. If the Bank of Canada buys dollars in the foreign exchange market but does not sterilize the intervention, what will be the impact on international reserves, the money supply, and the exchange rate?

3. For each of the following, identify in which part of the balance-of-payments account it appears (current account, capital account, or net change in international reserves) and whether it is a receipt or a payment.

   a. A British subject's purchase of a share of Johnson & Johnson stock
   b. A Canadian's purchase of an airline ticket from Air France
   c. The Swiss government's purchase of Canada bonds
   d. A Japanese citizen's purchase of Canadian wine
   e. $50 million of foreign aid to Honduras
   f. A loan by a Canadian bank to Mexico
   g. A Canadian bank's borrowing of Eurodollars

4. Why does a balance-of-payments deficit for the United States have a different effect on its international reserves than a balance-of-payments deficit for the Netherlands?

5. How can a large balance-of-payments surplus contribute to the country's inflation rate?

6. Why can balance-of-payments deficits force some countries to implement a contractionary monetary policy?

7. Under the gold standard, if Britain became more productive relative to Canada, what would happen to the money supply in the two countries? Why would the changes in the money supply help preserve a fixed exchange rate between Canada and Britain?

8. What is the exchange rate between dollars and Swiss francs if one dollar is convertible into 1/20 ounce of gold and one Swiss franc is convertible into 1/40 ounce of gold?

9. "Inflation is not possible under the gold standard." Is this statement true, false, or uncertain? Explain your answer.

10. What are some of the disadvantages to China's pegging of the yuan to the U.S. dollar?

11. If a country's par exchange rate was undervalued during the Bretton Woods fixed exchange rate regime, what kind of intervention would that country's central bank be forced to undertake, and what effect would it have on its international reserves and the money supply?

12. "The abandonment of fixed exchange rates after 1973 has meant that countries have pursued more independent monetary policies." Is this statement true, false, or uncertain? Explain your answer.

13. "If a country wants to keep its exchange rate from changing, it must give up some control over its money supply." Is this statement true, false, or uncertain? Explain your answer.

14. Why is it that in a pure flexible exchange rate system, the foreign exchange market has no direct effects on the money supply? Does this mean that the foreign exchange market has no effect on monetary policy?

15. Why did the exchange-rate peg lead to difficulties for the countries in the ERM when German reunification occurred?

16. How can exchange-rate targets lead to a speculative attack on a currency?

17. What are the advantages and disadvantages of having the IMF as an international lender of last resort?

18. How can the long-term bond market help reduce the time-inconsistency problem for monetary policy? Can the foreign exchange market also perform this role?

19. "Balance-of-payments deficits always cause a country to lose international reserves." Is this statement true, false, or uncertain? Explain your answer.

20. How can persistent U.S. balance-of-payments deficits stimulate world inflation?

21. What are the key advantages of exchange-rate targeting as a monetary policy strategy?

22. When is exchange-rate targeting likely to be a sensible strategy for industrialized countries? When is exchange-rate targeting likely to be a sensible strategy for emerging-market countries?

23. What are the advantages and disadvantages of currency boards and dollarization over a monetary policy that just uses an exchange-rate target?

APPLIED PROBLEMS

24. Suppose the Bank of Canada purchases $1 000 000 worth of foreign assets.

    a. If the Bank of Canada purchases the foreign assets with $1 000 000 in currency, show the effect of this open market operation using T-accounts. What happens to the monetary base?
    b. If the Bank of Canada purchases the foreign assets by selling $1 000 000 in T-bills, show the effect of this open market operation using T-accounts. What happens to the monetary base?

25. Suppose the Mexican central bank chose to peg the peso to the U.S. dollar and commit to a fixed peso/dollar exchange rate. Use a graph of the market for peso assets (foreign exchange) to show and explain how the peg must be maintained if a shock in the U.S. economy forces the Federal Reserve to pursue contractionary monetary policy. What does this say about the ability of central banks to address domestic economic problems while maintaining a pegged exchange rate?

CANSIM Questions

26. Visit the website of the Bank of Canada at **www.bankofcanada.ca**. Click on "Rates and Statistics" and then "Exchange Rates."

    a. What is the Canadian-dollar effective exchange rate index (CERI)?
    b. How many foreign countries are included in the index?
    c. What are the weights of the included countries? Which country has the highest weight? Which has the lowest?

    d. Go to the CANSIM data available in the Student Resources section of your MyEconLab website and download series V41589522 (this is a daily series for the Canadian-dollar effective exchange rate index). Did the Canadian dollar appreciate or depreciate in 2011?

WEB EXERCISES

1. Go to **www.bankofcanada.ca/2009/11/speeches/evolution-international-monetary-system/**. Review the speech by Mark Carney, "The Evolution of the International Monetary System." Write a one-page summary that discusses why each monetary standard was dropped in favour of the succeeding one.

2. The International Monetary Fund stands ready to help nations facing monetary crises. Go to **www.imf.org**. Click on the tab labelled "About the IMF." What is the stated purpose of the IMF? How many nations participate and when was it established?

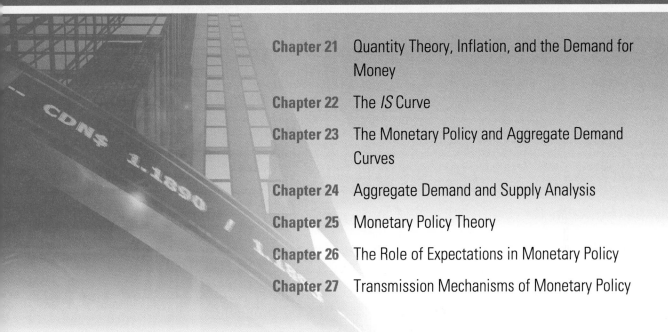

PART VII
Monetary Theory

Crisis and Response: The Perfect Storm of 2007–2009

In 2007 and 2008, the Canadian economy was hit by a perfect storm of formidable shocks. By the end of 2007, oil prices had risen from $60 per barrel at the beginning of the year to $100 and reached a peak of over $140 in July 2008. The oil price shock was both contractionary and inflationary, and as a result led to both higher inflation and unemployment—and many unhappy drivers at gas pumps.

If this supply shock were not bad enough, the global financial crisis hit the economy starting in August 2007 and caused a contraction in both household and business spending. This shock led to a further rise in unemployment, with some weakening of inflationary pressure further down the road.

The result of this perfect storm of adverse shocks was the most severe economic contraction since the Great Depression, with unemployment rising from the 6% level in 2006 and 2007 to over 8% by the end of 2009. Inflation also accelerated from 2.6% in 2007 to over 5% by the middle of 2008, but with the increase in the unemployment rate and the decline of oil and other commodity prices by the fall of 2008, inflation rapidly came back down again.

Although the Bank of Canada's aggressive monetary policy aimed to address the contractionary forces in the economy, the Government of Canada also took action in a coordinated response to the global financial crisis with the Group of 20 (G-20) countries. Although this policy response helped stimulate household spending, it was overwhelmed by the continued worsening of the financial crisis, and the economy went into a tailspin.

The impact of the perfect storm of adverse shocks highlights the need to understand how monetary and other government policies affect inflation and economic activity. Chapter 21 discusses how the quantity theory of money explains inflation in the long run and presents how theories of the demand for money have evolved. Aggregate supply and demand analysis, the basic framework that will enable us to study the effect of monetary policy on output and inflation, is then developed in Chapters 22–25. In Chapter 26, we expand on aggregate supply and demand analysis in order to understand how monetary policy can be used to stabilize the economy and inflation. Chapter 27 outlines the transmission mechanisms through which monetary policy affects the aggregate economy.

CHAPTER 21

Quantity Theory, Inflation, and the Demand for Money

LEARNING OBJECTIVES

After studying this chapter you should be able to

1. describe how theories of the demand for money have evolved
2. describe how the quantity theory of money demand explains inflation in the long run

PREVIEW

In earlier chapters, we spent a lot of time and effort learning what the money supply is, how it is determined, and what part the Bank of Canada plays in it. Now we are ready to explore the role of the money supply and monetary policy in determining inflation and total production of goods and services (aggregate output) in the economy. The study of the effect of money and monetary policy on the economy is called **monetary theory**, and we examine this branch of economics in the chapters of Part 7.

When economists mention *supply*, the word *demand* is sure to follow, and the discussion of money is no exception. The supply of money is an essential building block in understanding how monetary policy affects the economy, because it suggests the factors that influence the quantity of money in the economy. Not surprisingly, another essential part of monetary theory is the demand for money.

After discussing the quantity theory and its link to the demand for money, we delve more deeply into what determines the demand for money. A central question in monetary theory is whether or to what extent the quantity of money demanded is affected by changes in interest rates. Because this issue is crucial to how we view money's effects on aggregate economic activity, we focus on the role of interest rates in the demand for money.

Quantity Theory of Money

Developed by the classical economists in the nineteenth and early twentieth centuries, the quantity theory of money is a theory of how the nominal value of aggregate income is determined. Because it also tells us how much money is held for a given amount of aggregate income, it is a theory of the demand for money. The most important feature of this theory is that it suggests that interest rates have no effect on the demand for money.

Velocity of Money and Equation of Exchange

The clearest exposition of the classical quantity theory approach is found in the work of the American economist Irving Fisher, in his influential book *The Purchasing Power of Money*, published in 1911. Fisher wanted to examine the link between the total quantity of money M (the money supply) and the total amount of spending on final goods and services produced in the economy $P \times Y$, where P is the price level and Y is aggregate output (income). (Total spending $P \times Y$ is also thought of as aggregate nominal income for the economy or as nominal GDP.) The concept that provides the link between M and $P \times Y$ is called the **velocity of money** (often reduced to *velocity*), the average number of times per year (turnover) that a dollar is spent in buying the total amount of goods and services produced in the economy. Velocity V is defined more precisely as total spending $P \times Y$ divided by the quantity of money M:

$$V = \frac{P \times Y}{M} \tag{1}$$

If, for example, nominal GDP $(P \times Y)$ in a year is $2 trillion and the quantity of money (M) is $0.4 trillion, we can calculate velocity to be as follows:

$$V = \frac{\$2 \text{ trillion}}{\$0.4 \text{ trillion}} = 5$$

The value of 5 for velocity means that the average dollar bill is spent five times in purchasing final goods and services in the economy.

By multiplying both sides of this definition by M, we obtain the **equation of exchange**, which relates nominal income to the quantity of money and velocity:

$$M \times V = P \times Y \tag{2}$$

The equation of exchange thus states that the quantity of money multiplied by the number of times that this money is spent in a given year must equal nominal income (the total nominal amount spent on goods and services in that year).[1]

As it stands, Equation 2 is nothing more than an identity—a relationship that is true by definition. It does not tell us, for instance, that when the money supply M changes, nominal income $(P \times Y)$ changes in the same direction; a rise in M, for example, could be offset by a fall in V that leaves $M \times V$ (and therefore $P \times Y$) unchanged. To convert the equation of exchange (an *identity*) into a *theory* of how nominal income is determined requires an understanding of the factors that determine velocity.

DETERMINANTS OF VELOCITY   Irving Fisher reasoned that velocity is determined by the institutions in an economy that affect the way individuals conduct transactions. If people use charge accounts and credit cards to conduct their transactions, as they can today, and consequently use money less often when making purchases, less money is required to conduct the transactions generated by nominal income (M falls relative to $P \times Y$), and velocity $(P \times Y)/M$ will increase. Conversely, if it is

---

[1] Fisher actually first formulated the equation of exchange in terms of the nominal value of transactions in the economy PT:

$$MV_T = PT$$

where P = average price per transaction
T = number of transactions conducted in a year
$V_T = PT/M$ = transactions velocity of money

Because the nominal value of transactions T is difficult to measure, the quantity theory has been formulated in terms of aggregate output Y as follows: T is assumed to be proportional to Y so that $T = vY$, where v is a constant of proportionality. Substituting vY for T in Fisher's equation of exchange yields $MV_T = vPY$, which can be written as Equation 2 in the text, in which $V = V_T/v$.

more convenient for purchases to be paid for with cash, cheques, or debit cards (all of which are money), more money is used to conduct the transactions generated by the same level of nominal income, and velocity will fall. Fisher took the view that the institutional and technological features of the economy would affect velocity only slowly over time, so velocity would normally be reasonably constant in the short run.

DEMAND FOR MONEY   Another way of interpreting Fisher's quantity theory is in terms of the **demand for money**, the quantity of money that people want to hold.

Because the quantity theory of money tells us how much money is held for a given amount of nominal spending, it is, in fact, a theory of the demand for money. To illustrate, let's first divide both sides of the equation of exchange by V to yield the following:

$$M = \frac{1}{V} \times PY$$

When the money market is in equilibrium, money supply equals money demand, so we can replace M in the equation by M^d. In addition, since in the quantity theory of money velocity is assumed to be constant, we can be replace $1/V$ with a constant k. Substituting k for $1/V$ and M^d for M, we can rewrite the equation as

$$M^d = k \times PY \tag{3}$$

Equation 3 tells us that because k is constant, the level of transactions generated by a fixed level of nominal income PY determines the quantity of money M^d that people demand. Therefore Fisher's theory suggests that the demand for money is purely a function of income, and interest rates have no effect on the demand for money.[2]

From the Equation of Exchange to the Quantity Theory of Money

Fisher's view that velocity is fairly constant in the short run, so that $V = \overline{V}$, transforms the equation of exchange into the **quantity theory of money**, which states that nominal income (spending) is determined solely by movements in the quantity of money M.

$$P \times Y = M \times \overline{V} \tag{4}$$

The quantity theory equation above indicates that when the quantity of money M doubles, $M \times \overline{V}$ doubles and so must $P \times Y$, the value of nominal income. To illustrate, let's assume that velocity is 5, nominal income (GDP) is initially $2 trillion, and the money supply is $0.4 trillion. If the money supply doubles to $0.8 trillion, the quantity theory of money tells us that nominal income will double to $4 trillion ($= 5 \times \$0.8$ trillion).

Quantity Theory and the Price Level

Because the classical economists (including Fisher) thought that wages and prices were completely flexible, they believed that the level of aggregate output Y produced in the economy during normal times would remain at the full-employment level. Hence Y in the equation of exchange could also be treated as reasonably constant in the short run and thus assigned a fixed value of $\overline{Y}$ in Equation 4. Dividing both sides of Equation 4 by $\overline{Y}$, we can then write the price level as follows:

$$P = \frac{M \times \overline{V}}{\overline{Y}} \tag{5}$$

---

[2] While Fisher was developing his quantity theory approach to the demand for money, a group of classical economists in Cambridge, England led by Alfred Marshall and A. C. Pigou, came to similar conclusions, although with slightly different reasoning. They derived Equation 3 by recognizing that two properties of money motivate people to hold it: its utility as a medium of exchange and its utility as a store of wealth.

The quantity of money, as represented by Equation 5, implies that if M doubles, P must also double in the short run because $\overline{V}$ and $\overline{Y}$ are constant. In our example, if aggregate output is $2 trillion, velocity is 5, and the money supply is $0.4 trillion, then the price level equals 1.0.

$$P = 1.0 = \frac{\$0.4 \text{ trillion} \times 5}{\$2 \text{ trillion}} = \frac{\$2 \text{ trillion}}{\$2 \text{ trillion}}$$

When the money supply doubles to $0.8 trillion, the price level must also double to 2.0 because

$$P = 2.0 = \frac{\$0.8 \text{ trillion} \times 5}{\$2 \text{ trillion}} = \frac{\$4 \text{ trillion}}{\$2 \text{ trillion}}$$

Classical economists relied on the quantity theory of money to explain movements in the price level. In their view, ***changes in the quantity of money lead to proportional changes in the price level.***

Quantity Theory and Inflation

We now transform the quantity theory of money into a theory of inflation. You might recall from high school math the mathematical fact that the percentage change ($\%\Delta$) of a product of two variables is approximately equal to the sum of the percentage changes of each of these variables. In other words,

$$\text{Percentage Change in } (x \times y) = (\text{Percentage Change in } x) \\ + (\text{Percentage Change in } y)$$

Using this mathematical fact, we can rewrite the equation of exchange as follows:

$$\%\Delta M + \%\Delta V = \%\Delta P + \%\Delta Y$$

Subtracting $\%\Delta Y$ from both sides of the preceding equation, and recognizing that the inflation rate, π, is the growth rate of the price level, that is, $\%\Delta P$,

$$\pi = \%\Delta P = \%\Delta M + \%\Delta V - \%\Delta Y$$

Since we assume velocity is constant, its growth rate is zero, so the quantity theory of money is also a theory of inflation:

$$\pi = \%\Delta M - \%\Delta Y \tag{6}$$

Because the percentage change in a variable at an annual rate is the same as the growth rate in that variable, this equation can also be stated in words: ***the quantity theory of inflation indicates that the inflation rate equals the growth rate of the money supply minus the growth rate of aggregate output.*** For example, if the aggregate output is growing at 3% per year and the growth rate of money is 5%, then inflation is 2% ($= 5\% - 3\%$). If the Bank of Canada increases the money growth rate to 10%, then the quantity theory of inflation in Equation 6 indicates that the inflation rate will rise to 7% ($= 10\% - 3\%$).

APPLICATION

Testing the Quantity Theory of Money

Now that we have fully outlined the quantity theory of money, let's put it to the test with actual data over the long and short runs.

THE QUANTITY THEORY OF MONEY IN THE LONG RUN   The quantity theory of money provides a long-run theory of inflation because it is based on the assumption that wages and prices are flexible. Panel (a) of Figure 21-1 plots 10-year averages of Canadian inflation rates against the 10-year average rate of Canadian money growth (M2) from

1920 through 2000. Because the growth rate of aggregate output Y over 10-year periods does not vary very much, Equation 6 indicates that the 10-year inflation rate should be the 10-year money growth rate minus a constant (the rate of aggregate output growth). Thus a strong positive relationship should exist between inflation and money growth rates—and this relationship is borne out in panel (a) of Figure 21-1. Decades with higher growth rates of the Canadian money supply typically see higher average inflation rates.

FIGURE 21-1 Relation Between Inflation and Money Growth

There is a strong positive association between the average money growth rate and the average inflation rate.

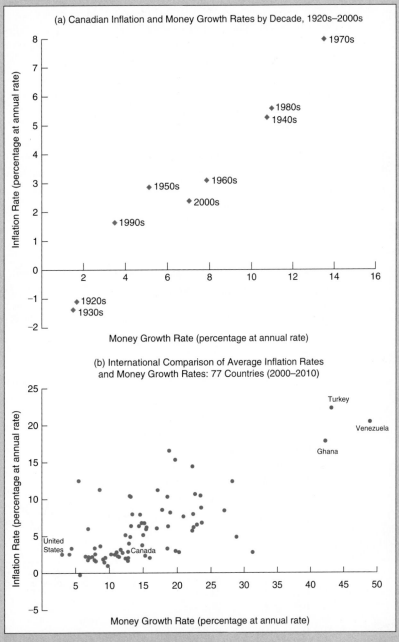

Sources: For panel (a), for 1870 to 1960, M.C. Urquhart, "Canadian Economic Growth 1870–1985," Institute for Economic Research, Queens University: Kingston, Ontario, Discussion Paper No. 734; and since 1961, Statistics Canada CANSIM II series V3860248 and V41552796. For panel (b), International Financial Statistics. International Monetary Fund, http://elibrary-data.imf.org/.

Does the quantity theory also explain differing long-run inflation rates across countries? It certainly does. Panel (b) of Figure 21-1 plots the average inflation rate over the 10-year period from 2000 to 2010 against the 10-year money growth rate for 77 countries. Note that countries with high money growth, such as Turkey, Venezuela, and Ghana, tend to have higher inflation.

THE QUANTITY THEORY OF MONEY IN THE SHORT RUN   Does the quantity theory of money provide a good explanation of short-run inflation fluctuations as well? Figure 21-2 provides evidence on the link between money growth and inflation in the short run by plotting the annual Canadian inflation rate (based on the GDP deflator) from 1971 to 2011 against the annual money growth rate (based on M2++ gross). The money supply lags by two years to allow for the time it takes for changes in money growth to affect inflation. Although the correlation between money growth and inflation on an annual basis is positive and strong, there are many years where money growth is high but inflation is low.

The conclusion is that ***the quantity theory of money is a good theory of inflation in the long run, but not in the short run.*** Another way of stating this conclusion is that Milton Friedman's statement that "inflation is always and everywhere a monetary phenomenon" (mentioned in Chapter 1) is accurate in the long run but is not supported by the data for the short run. This insight tells us that the classical assumption that wages and prices are completely flexible may not be a good assumption for short-run fluctuations in inflation and aggregate output. For this reason, we relax this assumption in the following chapters of the book when we develop models of short-run inflation and output fluctuations.

FIGURE 21-2   Annual Canadian Inflation and Money Growth Rates, 1971–2011

Plots of the annual Canadian inflation rate against the annual money (M2++ gross) growth rate from two years earlier (to allow for lagged effects from money growth to inflation) also support a short-run link between inflation and money growth. There are many years, however, where money growth is high yet inflation is low.

Source: Statistics Canada CANSIM II series V1997756 and V41552801.

Budget Deficits and Inflation

Budget deficits can be an important source of inflationary monetary policy. To see how this could be the case, we need to look at how a government finances its budget deficits.

Government Budget Constraint

Because the government has to pay its bills just as we do, it has a budget constraint. We can pay for our spending in two ways: raise revenue (by working) or borrow. The government also enjoys these two options: raise revenue by levying taxes or go into debt by issuing government bonds. Unlike us, however, it has a third option: the government can create money and use it to pay for the goods and services it buys.

Methods of financing government spending are described by an expression called the **government budget constraint**, which states the following: the government budget deficit *DEF*, which equals the excess of government spending *G* over tax revenue *T*, must equal the sum of the change in the monetary base ΔMB and the change in government bonds held by the public ΔB. Algebraically, this expression can be written as follows:

$$DEF = G - T = \Delta MB + \Delta B \qquad (7)$$

To see what the government budget constraint means in practice, let's look at the case in which the only government purchase is a \$100 million supercomputer. If the government convinces the electorate that such a computer is worth paying for, it will probably be able to raise the \$100 million in taxes to pay for it, and the budget deficit will equal zero. The government budget constraint then tells us that no issue of money or bonds is needed to pay for the computer, because the budget is balanced. If taxpayers think that the supercomputer is too expensive and refuse to pay taxes for it, the budget constraint indicates that the government must pay for it by selling \$100 million of new bonds to the public or by, in effect, printing \$100 million of currency to pay for the computer. In either case, the budget constraint is satisfied. The \$100 million deficit is balanced by the change in the stock of government bonds held by the public ($\Delta B = $ \$100 million) or by the change in the monetary base ($\Delta MB = $ \$100 million).

The government budget constraint thus reveals two important facts: *if the government deficit is financed by an increase in bond holdings by the public, there is no effect on the monetary base and hence on the money supply. But if the deficit is not financed by increased bond holdings by the public, the monetary base and the money supply increase*.

There are several ways to understand why a deficit leads to an increase in the monetary base when the public's bond holdings do not increase. The simplest case is when a government's treasury has the legal right to issue currency to finance its deficit. Financing the deficit is then very straightforward: the government just pays for the spending that is in excess of its tax revenues with new currency. Because this increase in currency adds directly to the monetary base, the monetary base rises and the money supply with it through the process of multiple deposit creation described in Chapter 16.

In Canada, however, and in many other countries, the government does not have the right to issue currency to pay for its bills. In this case, the government must finance its deficit by first issuing bonds to the public to acquire the extra funds to pay its bills. Yet if these bonds do not end up in the hands of the public, the only alternative is that they are purchased by the central bank. For the government bonds not to end up in the hands of the public, the central bank must conduct an open market purchase, which, as we saw in Chapter 16, leads to an increase in the monetary base and in the money supply. This method of financing government spending is called **monetizing the debt** because, as indicated by the two-step process described, government debt issued to finance government spending has been removed from the hands of the public and has been replaced by high-powered money. This method of financing, or the more direct method when a government just issues the currency directly, is also, somewhat inaccurately, referred to as **printing money** because high-powered money (the monetary base) is created in the process. The use of the word *printing* is misleading because what is essential to this method of financing government spending is that the monetary base increases when the central bank conducts open market purchases, just as it would if more currency were put in circulation.

We thus see that a budget deficit can lead to an increase in the money supply if it is financed by the creation of high-powered money. However, because the quantity theory of money explains inflation only in the long run, to produce inflation, the budget deficit must be persistent, that is, last for a substantial period of time. This leads to the following conclusion: *financing a persistent deficit by money creation will lead to a sustained inflation.*

Hyperinflation

The analysis here can be used to explain **hyperinflations**, periods of extremely high inflation of more than 50% per month. Many economies—both poor and developed—have experienced hyperinflation over the past century, but Canada has been spared such turmoil. One of the most extreme examples of hyperinflation throughout world history occurred recently in Zimbabwe in the 2000s, and it is discussed in the Application that follows.

APPLICATION

The Zimbabwean Hyperinflation

We now use our analysis to explain the Zimbabwean hyperinflation that started in the early 2000s.

After the expropriation of farms, which were redistributed to supporters of Robert Mugabe, the president of the country, agricultural output plummeted and, along with it, tax revenue. The result was that the government's expenditures now massively exceeded revenues. The government could have obtained revenues to cover its expenditures by raising taxes, but given the depressed state of the economy, generating revenue in this way was both hard to do and would have been politically unpopular. Alternatively, the government could have tried to finance its expenditure by borrowing from the public, but given the distrust of the government, this was not an option. There was only one route left: the printing press. The government could pay for its expenditures simply by printing more currency (increasing the money supply) and using it to make payments to individuals and businesses. This is exactly what the Zimbabwean government did and the money supply began to increase rapidly.

As predicted by the quantity theory, the surge in the money supply led to a rapidly rising price level. In February 2007, the Reserve Bank of Zimbabwe, the central bank, outlawed price increases on many commodities. Although this tactic has been tried before by governments in countries experiencing hyperinflations, it has never worked: criminalizing inflation cannot stop inflation when the central bank keeps on printing money. In March 2007, the inflation rate hit a record of over 1500%. By 2008, Zimbabwe's official inflation rate was over 2 million percent (but unofficially over 10 million percent). In July 2008, the Zimbabwean central bank issued a new

$100 billion bank note and shortly later issued a $100 trillion dollar bill, the highest denomination dollar note on record. That's a lot of zeros, but don't be too impressed. Although holding one of these bills made you a trillionaire, it could not even buy a bottle of beer. Zimbabwean currency became worth less than toilet paper.

In 2009, the Zimbabwean government allowed the use of foreign currencies like the dollar for all transactions, but the damage had already been done. The hyperinflation wreaked havoc on the economy, and an extremely poor country became even poorer.

Keynesian Theories of Money Demand

In his famous 1936 book *The General Theory of Employment, Interest and Money*, John Maynard Keynes abandoned the quantity theory view that velocity was a constant and developed a theory of money demand that emphasized the importance of interest rates. In his theory of the demand for money, which he called the **liquidity preference theory**, Keynes presented three motives behind the demand for money: the transactions motive, the precautionary motive, and the speculative motive.

Transactions Motive

In the quantity theory approach, individuals are assumed to hold money because it is a medium of exchange that can be used to carry out everyday transactions. Keynes initially accepted the quantity theory view that the transactions component is proportional to income. Later, he and other economists recognized that new methods for payment, referred to as **payment technology**, could also affect the demand for money. For example, credit cards enable consumers to make even very small purchases without needing to hold money. Electronic payments that can be made from investors' brokerage accounts can also reduce money demand. As payment technology advances, the demand for money will be likely to decline relative to income.

Precautionary Motive

Keynes also recognized that people hold money as a cushion against unexpected wants. Suppose that you have been thinking about buying a new Wii entertainment system and now see that it is on sale at 25% off. If you are holding money as a precaution for just such an occurrence, you can immediately buy it. Keynes argued that the precautionary money balances people want to hold would also be proportional to income.

Speculative Motive

Keynes also believed people choose to hold money as a store of wealth, which he called the *speculative motive*. Because the definition of money in Keynes's analysis includes currency (which earns no interest) and chequing account deposits (which typically earn little interest), he assumed that money earns no interest and hence its opportunity cost relative to holding other assets, such as bonds, is the nominal interest rate on bonds, i. As the interest rate i rises, the opportunity cost of money rises (it is more costly to hold money relative to bonds) and the quantity of money demanded falls.

Putting the Three Motives Together

In putting the three motives for holding money balances together into a demand for money equation, Keynes was careful to distinguish between nominal quantities and real quantities. Money is valued in terms of what it can buy. If, for example, all prices in the economy double (the price level doubles), the same nominal quantity of money will only be able to buy half as many goods. Keynes thus reasoned that people want to hold a certain amount of **real money balances** (the quantity of money in real terms). Combining the three motives for holding money balances into a demand for real money balances led to what Keynes called the liquidity preference function, which is written as follows:

$$\frac{M^d}{P} = L(\underset{-}{i}, \underset{+}{Y}) \tag{8}$$

Equation 8 says that the demand for real money balances is negatively related to the nominal interest rate and is positively related to real income.

Later Keynesian economists, such as Nobel Prize winner James Tobin, expanded the analysis and showed that interest rates play a more important role in money demand than even Keynes supposed. They demonstrated that even the transactions and precautionary demand for money would also be negatively related to the interest rate.[3]

An important implication of Keynesian theories of money demand is that velocity is not a constant but will fluctuate with changes in interest rates. To illustrate, we write the liquidity preference function as follows:

$$\frac{P}{M^d} = \frac{1}{L(i,Y)}$$

Multiplying both sides of this equation by Y and recognizing that we can replace M^d by M because they must be equal in money market equilibrium, we solve for velocity:

$$V = \frac{PY}{M} = \frac{Y}{L(i,Y)} \tag{9}$$

We know that the demand for money is negatively related to interest rates; when i goes up, $L(i,Y)$ declines, and therefore velocity rises. Because interest rates have substantial fluctuations, Keynesian theories of the demand for money indicate that velocity has substantial fluctuations as well. Thus Keynesian theories cast doubt on the classical quantity theory view that nominal income is determined primarily by movements in the quantity of money.

Portfolio Theories of Money Demand

Related to Keynes's analysis of the demand for money are so-called portfolio theories of money demand, in which people decide how much of an asset such as money they want to hold as part of their overall portfolio of assets.[4]

Theory of Portfolio Choice and Keynesian Liquidity Preference

In Chapter 5, we developed the theory of portfolio choice, which stated that the demand for an asset is positively related to wealth, expected return relative to other assets, and relative liquidity, whereas it is negatively related to its risk relative to other assets. This theory of portfolio choice can justify the conclusion from the

---

[3]Three famous papers that elaborated on Keynes's approach to the demand for money are as follows: William J. Baumol, "The Transactions Demand for Cash: An Inventory Theoretic Approach," *Quarterly Journal of Economics* 66 (1952): 545–556; James Tobin, "The Interest Elasticity of the Transactions Demand for Cash," *Review of Economics and Statistics* 38 (1956): 241–247; and James Tobin, "Liquidity Preference as Behavior Towards Risk," *Review of Economic Studies* 25 (1958): 65–86. For further discussion of the models in these papers, see the first appendix to this chapter, which can be found on MyEconLab.

[4]This is the approach taken by Milton Friedman in his famous paper "The Quantity Theory of Money: A Restatement," in *Studies in the Quantity Theory of Money*, ed. Milton Friedman (Chicago: University of Chicago Press, 1956), 3–21.

Keynesian liquidity preference function that the demand for real money balances is positively related to income and negatively related to the nominal interest rate.

Because income and wealth tend to move together, when income is higher, wealth is likely to be as well. Hence, higher income means that wealth is higher, and the theory of portfolio choice then indicates that the demand for the money asset will rise and the demand for real money balances will be higher.

As interest rates rise, the expected return for money does not change. However, the return for bonds, an alternative asset, goes up. Thus, although the expected *absolute* return of money did not change, money's expected return *relative* to bonds went down. In other words, as the theory of portfolio choice indicates, higher interest rates make money less desirable, and the demand for real money balances falls.

Other Factors That Affect the Demand for Money

The theory of portfolio choice indicates that other factors besides income and the nominal interest rate can affect the demand for money. We look at each of these in turn.

WEALTH   The theory of portfolio choice posits that as wealth increases, investors have more resources to purchase assets, increasing the demand for money. However, when income is held constant, greater wealth has only a small effect on the demand for money. In general, investors will hold only a small amount of money in their investment portfolio, preferring interest-bearing assets with similar risk and liquidity profiles, such as money market mutual funds, that are not included in measures of money such as M1. Currency and chequable deposits are sometimes said to be **dominated assets**, because investors can hold other assets that pay higher returns and yet are perceived to be just as safe.

RISK   It's hard to imagine an asset less risky than money. Currency will always be accepted, unless there's a revolution and the new government does not accept the old government's currency. And bank deposits are safe as long as deposit insurance exists. In the theory of portfolio choice, however, risk is always measured relative to another asset. Thus, if the stock market becomes more volatile, money can become less risky relative to stocks and demand for it will increase. In addition, although money is extremely safe on a nominal basis, its real return (the nominal return minus expected inflation) can become highly variable when inflation becomes very variable. Higher variability in the real return of money lowers demand for money, as people shift into alternative assets known as **inflation hedges**, whose real returns are less affected than that of money when inflation varies. Popular inflation hedges include Real Return Bonds (discussed in Chapter 4), gold, and real estate.

LIQUIDITY OF OTHER ASSETS   In recent years, financial innovation has led to the development of new liquid assets, such as money market mutual funds or home equity lines of credit, which allow households to write cheques that are backed by their homes. As these alternative assets become more liquid, the relative liquidity of money falls and so the demand for money would fall as well.

Summary

Our analysis of the demand for money using Keynesian and portfolio theories indicates that seven factors affect the demand for money: interest rates, income, payment technology, wealth, riskiness of other assets, inflation risk, and liquidity of other assets. As a study aid, Summary Table 21-1 indicates the response of money demand to changes in each of these factors and gives a brief synopsis of the reasoning behind each response.

SUMMARY TABLE 21-1   Factors That Determine the Demand for Money

Variable	Change in Variable	Money Demand Response	Reason
Interest rates	↑	↓	Opportunity cost of money rises
Income	↑	↑	Higher transactions
Payment technology	↑	↓	Less need for money in transactions
Wealth	↑	↑	More resources to put into money
Risk of other assets	↑	↑	Money relatively less risky and so more desirable
Inflation risk	↑	↓	Money relatively more risky and so less desirable
Liquidity of other assets	↑	↓	Money relatively less liquid and so less desirable

Empirical Evidence for the Demand for Money

Here we examine the empirical evidence for the two key issues that distinguish different theories of money demand and affect their conclusions about whether the quantity of money is the primary determinant of aggregate spending: is the demand for money sensitive to changes in interest rates and is the demand for money function stable over time?[5]

Interest Rates and Money Demand

We have established that if interest rates do not affect the demand for money, velocity is more likely to be constant—or at least predictable—so that the quantity theory view that aggregate spending is determined by the quantity of money is more likely to be true. However, the more sensitive to interest rates the demand for money is, the more unpredictable velocity will be, and the less clear the link between the money supply and aggregate spending will be. Indeed, there is an extreme case of ultrasensitivity of the demand for money to interest rates, called the **liquidity trap**, in which conventional monetary policy has no direct effect on aggregate spending, because a change in the money supply has no effect on interest rates.[6]

The evidence for the interest sensitivity of the demand for money is remarkably consistent. Neither extreme case is supported by the data: in situations in which nominal interest rates have not hit a floor of zero, the demand for money is sensitive to interest rates, and little evidence is present that a liquidity trap has ever existed. However, when nominal interest rates fall to zero, they can go no lower. In this situation, a liquidity trap has occurred because the demand for money is now completely flat. Indeed, exactly this situation has occurred in Canada and the United States in

---

[5] If you are interested in a more detailed discussion of the empirical research on the demand for money, you can find it in a second appendix for this chapter on the Companion Website, MyEconLab.

[6] If the demand for money is ultrasensitive to interest rates, a tiny change in interest rates produces a very large change in the quantity of money demanded. Hence, in this case, the demand for money is completely flat in the supply and demand diagrams of Chapter 5. Therefore, a change in the money supply that shifts the money supply curve to the right or left results in it intersecting the flat money demand curve at the same unchanged interest rate.

recent years, which is why their central banks have had to resort to nonconventional monetary policy.

Stability of Money Demand

If the money demand function, like the one in Equation 8, is unstable and undergoes substantial, unpredictable shifts, as Keynes believed, then velocity is unpredictable, and the quantity of money may not be tightly linked to aggregate spending, as it is in the quantity theory. The stability of the money demand function is also crucial to whether the Bank of Canada should target interest rates or the money supply. If the money demand function is unstable and so the money supply is not closely linked to aggregate spending, then the level of interest rates the Bank of Canada sets will provide more information about the stance of monetary policy than will the money supply.

Until the early 1970s, evidence strongly supported the stability of the money demand function. However, after 1973, the rapid pace of financial innovation, which changed the items that could be used for money, led to substantial instability in estimated money demand functions. The instability of the money demand function calls into question whether our theories and empirical analyses are adequate. It also has important implications for the conduct of monetary policy, because it casts doubt on the usefulness of the money demand function as a tool to provide guidance to policy makers. In particular, because the money demand function has become unstable, velocity is now harder to predict. Monetary policy makers have found that the money supply does not provide reliable information on the future course of the economy, leading them to think of monetary policy in terms of the setting of interest rates. The instability of money demand has thus led to a downgrading of the focus on money supply in the conduct of monetary policy.

MyEconLab   MyEconLab is an online homework and tutorial system that puts you in control of your own learning with study and practice tools directly correlated to this chapter's content. Visit MyEconLab to explore the following resources:

- The Questions and Applied Problems are all available in the Study Plan on MyEconLab for further practice. You will also find the answers to all of the Questions and Applied Problems in the Student Resources section of your MyEconLab.
- CANSIM data are available for relevant CANSIM questions in the Student Resources section of your MyEconLab.
- Visit the Student Resources section of MyEconLab to access the following appendices for this chapter: Appendix 21.1: The Baumol-Tobin and the Tobin Mean-Variance Models of the Demand for Money; Appendix 21.2: Empirical Evidence on the Demand for Money.

MyEconLab also features Additional Readings, Videos, Glossary Flashcards, Audio Chapter Summaries, Economics News Feeds, Animations, and many additional tools to help you master key concepts from the text.

((• SUMMARY

EconLab
Summary

1. The quantity theory of money as expressed by the equation of exchange, $M \times V = P \times Y$, indicates that nominal spending is determined solely by movements in the quantity of money. The quantity theory indicates that (1) changes in the quantity of money lead to proportional changes in the price level, because $P = (M \times \overline{V})/\overline{Y}$, and (2) the inflation rate is the growth rate of the money supply minus the growth rate of aggregate output—that is, $\pi = \%\Delta M - \%\Delta Y$. These implications of the quantity

theory are borne out in the data in the long run, but not the short run.

2. The government budget constraint indicates that a deficit must be financed by either money creation or the issuing of government bonds. That is, $DEF = G - T = \Delta MB + \Delta B$. Combining this fact with the quantity theory indicates that financing a persistent deficit by money creation will lead to a sustained inflation. This analysis helps explain hyperinflations, in which inflation and money

growth go to extremely high levels because of massive budget deficits.

3. John Maynard Keynes suggested three motives for holding money: the transactions motive, the precautionary motive, and the speculative motive. His resulting liquidity preference theory views the transactions and precautionary components of money demand as proportional to income. However, the speculative component of money demand is viewed as sensitive to interest rates as well as to expectations about the future movements of interest rates. This theory, then, implies that velocity is unstable and cannot be treated as a constant.

4. Portfolio theories of money demand indicate that the demand for money is determined not only by interest rates, income, and payment technology, as in the Keynesian analysis, but also by wealth, riskiness of other assets, inflation risk, and liquidity of other assets.

5. Two main conclusions can be reached from the research on the demand for money: The demand for money is sensitive to interest rates, but little evidence exists that it is or has been ultrasensitive (liquidity trap). Since 1973, money demand has been found to be unstable, with the most likely source of the instability being the rapid pace of financial innovation. Because the money demand function is found to be both unstable and sensitive to interest rates, velocity cannot be viewed as constant and is not easily predictable. This situation has led to a downgrading of the focus on money supply and a greater emphasis on interest rates in the conduct of monetary policy.

KEY TERMS

demand for money, p. 527

dominated assets, p. 535

equation of exchange, p. 526

government budget constraint, p. 531

hyperinflations, p. 532

inflation hedges, p. 535

liquidity preference theory, p. 533

liquidity trap, p. 536

monetary theory, p. 525

monetizing the debt, p. 532

payment technology, p. 533

printing money, p. 532

quantity theory of money, p. 527

real money balances, p. 534

velocity of money, p. 526

QUESTIONS

1. How would you expect velocity to typically behave over the business cycle?

2. If velocity and aggregate output are reasonably constant (as the classical economists believed), what happens to the price level when the money supply increases from $1 trillion to $4 trillion?

3. If credit cards were made illegal by government legislation, what would happen to velocity? Explain your answer.

4. "If nominal GDP rises, velocity must rise." Is this statement true, false, or uncertain? Explain your answer.

5. Why would a central bank be concerned about persistent long-term budget deficits?

6. "Persistent budget deficits always lead to higher inflation." Is this statement true, false, or uncertain? Explain your answer.

7. Suppose a new "payment technology" allows individuals to make payments using Canada bonds (i.e., Canada bonds are immediately cashed when needed to make a payment and that balance is transferred to the payee). How do you think this payment technology would affect the transaction components of the demand for money?

8. The use of some payment technologies requires some infrastructure (e.g., merchants need to have access to credit card swiping machines). In most developing countries, this infrastructure is either nonexistent or very costly. Everything else being the same, would you expect the transaction component of the demand for money to be greater or smaller in a developing country than in a rich country?

9. What three motives for holding money did Keynes consider in his liquidity preference theory of the demand for real money balances? On the basis of these motives, what variables did he think determined the demand for money?

10. In many countries, people hold money as a cushion against unexpected needs arising from a variety of potential scenarios (e.g., banking crises, natural disasters, health problems, unemployment) that are not usually covered by insurance markets. Explain the effect of such behaviour on the precautionary component of the demand for money.

11. In Keynes's analysis of the speculative demand for money, what will happen to money demand if people suddenly decide that the normal level of the interest rate has declined? Why?

12. Why is Keynes's analysis of the speculative demand for money important to his view that velocity will undergo substantial fluctuations and thus cannot be treated as constant?

13. According to the portfolio theories of money demand, what are the four factors that determine money demand? What changes in these can increase the demand for money?

14. Explain how the following events will affect the demand for money according to the portfolio theories of money demand:

    a. The economy experiences a business cycle contraction.

    b. Brokerage fees decline, making bond transactions cheaper.

    c. The stock market crashes. (*Hint:* Consider both the increase in stock price volatility following a market crash and the decrease in wealth of shareholders.)

15. Suppose a given country experienced low and stable inflation rates for quite some time, but then inflation picked up and over the past decade has been relatively high and quite unpredictable. Explain how this new inflationary environment would affect the demand for money according to portfolio theories of money demand. What would happen if the government decides to issue inflation-protected securities?

16. Consider the portfolio choice theory of money demand. How do you think the demand for money will be affected during a hyperinflation (i.e., monthly inflation rates in excess of 50%)?

17. Both the portfolio choice and Keynes's theories of the demand for money suggest that as the relative expected return on money falls, demand for it will fall. Why would the portfolio choice approach predict that money demand is unaffected by changes in interest rates? Why did Keynes think that money demand is affected by changes in interest rates?

18. Why does the Keynesian view of the demand for money suggest that velocity is unpredictable?

19. What evidence is used to assess the stability of the money demand function? What does the evidence suggest about the stability of money demand and how has this affected monetary policy making?

20. Suppose that a plot of the values of the money supply, M, and nominal GDP for a given country over 40 years shows that these two variables are very closely related. In particular, a plot of their ratio (nominal GDP/M) yields very stable and easy-to-predict values. On the basis of this evidence, would you recommend the monetary authorities of this country conduct monetary policy by focusing mostly on the money supply rather than on setting interest rates? Explain why.

APPLIED PROBLEMS

21. Suppose the money supply M has been growing at 10% per year, and nominal GDP, PY, has been growing at 20% per year. The data are as follows (in billions of dollars):

	2010	2011	2012
M	100	110	121
PY	1000	1200	1440

    Calculate the velocity in each year. At what rate is velocity growing?

22. Calculate what happens to nominal GDP if velocity remains constant at 5 and the money supply increases from $200 billion to $300 billion.

23. What happens to nominal GDP if the money supply grows by 20% but velocity declines by 30%?

24. If velocity and aggregate output remain constant at $5 and $1000 billion, respectively, what happens to the price level if the money supply declines from $400 billion to $300 billion?

25. Suppose the liquidity preference function is given by

$$L(i,Y) = \frac{Y}{8} - 1000i$$

Calculate velocity for each period, using the money demand equation, along with the following table of values.

	Period 1	Period 2	Period 3	Period 4	Period 5	Period 6	Period 7
Y (in billions)	12 000	12 500	12 250	12 500	12 800	13 000	13 200
Interest rate	0.05	0.07	0.03	0.05	0.07	0.04	0.06

WEB EXERCISES

1. The formula for computing the velocity of money is GDP/*M*, where *M* is a money supply measure. Go to the CANSIM data available in the Student Resources section of your MyEconLab website and download monthly data since 1961 on real GDP (series V41707150), the GDP deflator (series V1997756), and the monetary base (series V37145). Compute the most recent year's velocity of base money and compare it to its level in 2002. Has it risen or fallen? Suggest reasons for its change since that time.

2. Use the data from the previous exercise and also download the three-month T-Bill rate (CANSIM series V122531).

Run a regression of real money balances on a constant, real GDP, and the nominal interest rate.

a. Comment on the fit of the regression.
b. What is the estimated income elasticity of the demand for real money balances? What is the estimated interest rate elasticity?
c. Are your estimates in (b) statistically significant?
d. Is your evidence consistent with the Baumol-Tobin model or with the quantity theory of money?
e. Is the money demand relationship stable?

CHAPTER 22

The *IS* Curve

LEARNING OBJECTIVES

After studying this chapter you should be able to

1. understand the equilibrium relationship between real interest rates and aggregate output, the *IS* curve

2. understand why fluctuations in the level of economic activity occur and how fiscal stimulus packages, like those instituted by most governments around the world during the global financial crisis, affected the economy

PREVIEW   During the Great Depression of the 1930s, aggregate output fell precipitously, with unemployment rising to 30%. Although the recession of 2007–2009 was not as severe, the contraction in economic activity led to unemployment rising to over 8.7%. To understand why these contractions in economic activity occur, economists make use of the concept *aggregate demand,* the total amount of output demanded in the economy. This concept was developed by John Maynard Keynes in his revolutionary book, *The General Theory of Employment, Interest and Money,* published in 1936, in which he argued that short-run changes in aggregate output, such as the decline during the Great Depression, were determined by changes in aggregate demand. The concept of aggregate demand is a central element in the *aggregate demand–aggregate supply (AD/AS) model,* the basic macroeconomic model for explaining short-run fluctuations in aggregate output.

In this chapter, we develop the first building block to understand aggregate demand, the *IS* curve, which describes the relationship between real interest rates and aggregate output when the market for goods and services (more simply referred to as the *goods market*) is in equilibrium. We begin by deriving the *IS* curve and then go on to explain what factors cause the *IS* curve to shift. With our understanding of the *IS* curve, we can examine why fluctuations in economic activity occur and how the U.S. fiscal stimulus package of 2009 affected the American economy. Then in later chapters, we make use of the *IS* curve to understand the role of monetary policy in economic fluctuations.

Planned Expenditure and Aggregate Demand

We start our analysis by discussing the concept of **planned expenditure**, the total amount of spending on domestically produced goods and services that households, businesses, the government, and foreigners want to make. In contrast, *actual expenditure* is the amount that they actually do spend, which equals the total amount of output produced in the economy. Note that all the analysis in this chapter is for expenditure in real terms, that is, in terms of actual physical amounts of goods and services. Keynes viewed **aggregate demand**, the total amount of output demanded in the economy, as being the same as planned expenditure. As we shall see shortly, planned expenditure—and hence aggregate demand—explains the level of aggregate output when the goods market is in equilibrium; that is, when aggregate demand for goods and services is equal to the actual amount of goods and services produced.

The total amount of aggregate demand (planned expenditure) is the sum of four types of spending:

1. **Consumption expenditure** (C), the total demand for consumer goods and services (e.g., hamburgers, iPods, rock concerts, visits to the doctor)
2. **Planned investment spending** (I), the total planned spending by businesses on new physical capital (e.g., machines, computers, factories) plus planned spending on new homes
3. **Government purchases** (G), the spending by all levels of government on goods and services (e.g., aircraft carriers, government workers, red tape), not including transfer payments
4. **Net exports** (NX), the net foreign spending on domestic goods and services, equal to exports minus imports

We represent the total aggregate demand (Y^{ad}) with the following equation:

$$Y^{ad} = C + I + G + NX \tag{1}$$

The Components of Aggregate Demand

To understand what determines aggregate demand (total planned expenditure) in the economy, let's look at each of its components in detail.

Consumption Expenditure

What determines how much you spend on consumer goods and services? Your income is likely the most important factor; if your income rises, you will be willing to spend more. Keynes reasoned similarly that consumption expenditure is related to **disposable income** (denoted by Y_D), the total income available for spending, equal to aggregate output (Y) minus taxes T, ($Y - T$).[1]

CONSUMPTION FUNCTION Keynes called the relationship between disposable income Y_D and consumption expenditure C the **consumption function** and expressed it as follows:

$$C = \overline{C} + mpc \times Y_D \tag{2}$$

Or alternately,

$$C = \overline{C} + mpc \times (Y - T) \tag{3}$$

---

[1]More precisely, taxes T refers to taxes minus net transfers (government payments to households and businesses that are in effect negative taxes). Examples of government transfers are Canada Pension Plan payments or employment insurance payments.

The term $\overline{C}$ stands for **autonomous consumption expenditure**, the amount of consumption expenditure that is **exogenous** (independent of variables in the model, such as disposable income). Autonomous consumption is related to consumers' optimism about their future income and household wealth, which induce consumers to increase spending.

The term *mpc*, the **marginal propensity to consume**, reflects the change in consumption expenditure that results from an additional dollar of disposable income. Keynes assumed that *mpc* was a constant between the values of 0 and 1. If, for example, a $1.00 increase in disposable income leads to an increase in consumption expenditure of $0.60, then *mpc* = 0.6.

Planned Investment Spending

Investment spending is another key component of total expenditure. There are two types of investment: *fixed* and *inventory*. (Note that economist's use of the word *investment* differs from everyday use of the term, as is explained in the FYI box.)

FIXED INVESTMENT **Fixed investment** is planned spending by firms on equipment (machines, computers, airplanes) and structures (factories, office buildings, shopping centres) and planned spending on new residential housing.

INVENTORY INVESTMENT **Inventory investment** is spending by firms on additional holdings of raw materials, parts, and finished goods, calculated as the change in holdings of these items in a given time period—say, a year.

Inventory investment is a much smaller component of investment than fixed investment. We discuss it in detail at this juncture because it plays an important role in the determination of aggregate output. To illustrate, consider the following scenarios:

1. Suppose that Ford Motor Company has 100 000 cars sitting in its factory lots on December 31, 2013, ready to be shipped to dealers. If each car has a wholesale price of $20 000, Ford has an inventory worth $2 billion. If by December 31, 2014, its inventory of cars has risen to 150 000, with a value of $3 billion, its inventory investment in 2014 is $1 billion, the *change* in the level of its inventory over the course of the year ($3 billion minus $2 billion).

2. Now suppose that by December 31, 2014, Ford's inventory of cars has dropped to 50 000 with a value of $1 billion. Its inventory investment in 2014 is now –$1 billion, the *change* in the level of its inventory over the course of the year ($1 billion − $2 billion).

3. Ford may also have additional inventory investment if the level of raw materials and parts that it is holding to produce these cars increases over the course of the year. If on December 31, 2013, it holds $50 million of steel used to produce its cars and on December 31, 2014, it holds $100 million, it has an additional $50 million of inventory investment in 2014.

FYI

Meaning of the Word *Investment*

Economists use the word *investment* somewhat differently than other people do. When noneconomists say that they are making an investment, they are normally referring to the purchase of common stocks or bonds, purchases that do not necessarily involve newly produced goods and services. But when economists speak of investment spending, they are referring to the purchase of *new* physical assets, such as new machines or new houses—purchases that add to aggregate demand.

An important feature of inventory investment is that some inventory investment can be unplanned (in contrast, fixed investment is always planned). Suppose the reason Ford finds itself with an additional $1 billion of cars on December 31, 2014, is that $1 billion fewer of its cars were sold in 2014 than expected. This $1 billion of inventory investment in 2014 was unplanned. In this situation, Ford is producing more cars than it can sell, and it will cut production in order to keep from accumulating unsold goods. Adjusting production to eliminate unplanned inventory investment plays a key role in the determination of aggregate output, as we shall see.

PLANNED INVESTMENT SPENDING AND REAL INTEREST RATES   Planned investment spending, a component of aggregate demand, Y^{ad}, is equal to planned fixed investment plus the amount of inventory investment *planned* by firms. Keynes considered the level of the real cost of borrowing to be a key determinant of planned investment spending.

To understand Keynes's reasoning, we need to recognize that businesses make investments in physical capital (machines and factories) as long as they expect to earn more from the physical capital than the interest cost of a loan to finance the investment. When the real interest rate on borrowing is high, say, at 10%, fewer investments in physical capital will earn more than the 10% cost of borrowed funds, so planned investment spending will be low. When the real interest rate on loans is low, say, 1%, many investments in physical capital will earn more than the 1% interest cost of borrowed funds. Therefore, when the real interest rate on loans and hence the cost of borrowing are low, business firms are more likely to undertake an investment in physical capital, and planned investment spending will increase.

Even if a company has surplus funds and does not need to borrow to undertake an investment in physical capital, its planned investment spending still will be affected by the real interest rate on debt instruments. Instead of investing in physical capital, it could purchase a security, such as a bond. If the real interest rate on this security is high, say, 10%, the opportunity cost (forgone interest earnings) of an investment is high. Planned investment spending will then be low, because the firm would probably prefer to purchase the security and earn the high 10% return than to invest in physical capital. As the real interest rate and the opportunity cost of investing fall, say, to 1%, planned investment spending will increase because investments in physical capital are likely to earn greater income for the firm than the measly 1% the security earns.

PLANNED INVESTMENT AND BUSINESS EXPECTATIONS   Keynes also believed that planned investment spending is heavily influenced by business expectations about the future. Businesses that are optimistic about future profit opportunities are willing to spend more, whereas pessimistic businesses cut back their spending. Thus Keynes posited a component of planned investment spending he called **autonomous investment**, $\bar{I}$, that is completely exogenous and so is unexplained by variables in his model, such as output or interest rates.

Keynes believed that changes in autonomous spending are dominated by these unstable exogenous fluctuations in planned investment spending, which are influenced by emotional waves of optimism and pessimism—factors he labelled "**animal spirits**." His view was coloured by the collapse in investment spending during the Great Depression, which he saw as the primary reason for the economic contraction.

INVESTMENT FUNCTION   Combining Keynes' two factors that drive investment leads to an investment function, which describes how planned investment spending is related to autonomous investment and the real interest cost of borrowing. We write it as follows:

$$I = \bar{I} - dr_c \tag{4}$$

where d is a parameter reflecting how responsive investment is to the real cost of borrowing, which is denoted by r_c.

However, as we learned in Chapter 9, the real cost of borrowing reflects not only the real interest rate on *default-free debt instruments, r,* but also *financial frictions,* denoted by $\bar{f}$, which are additions to the real cost of borrowing because of asymmetric information problems in financial markets. In other words, the real cost of borrowing can be written as follows:

$$r_c = r + \bar{f} \tag{5}$$

Substituting in Equation 4 the real cost of borrowing from Equation 5 yields

$$I = \bar{I} - d(r + \bar{f}) \tag{6}$$

Equation 6 says that investment is positively related to business optimism, as represented by autonomous investment, and is negatively related to the real interest rate and financial frictions.

Net Exports

As with planned investment spending, we can think of net exports as being made up of two components, *autonomous net exports* and the part of net exports that is affected by changes in real interest rates.

REAL INTEREST RATES AND NET EXPORTS   Real interest rates influence the amount of net exports through the **exchange rate**, the price of one currency, say, the dollar, in terms of other currencies, say, the euro.[2] We examined a model that explains the link between the exchange rate and real interest rates in Chapter 19, but here we will only outline the intuition. When Canadian real interest rates rise, Canadian dollar assets earn higher returns relative to foreign assets. People then want to hold more dollars, so they bid up the value of dollars and thereby increase its value relative to other currencies. Thus a rise in Canadian real interest rates leads to a higher value of the dollar.

A rise in the value of the dollar makes Canadian exports more expensive in foreign currencies so foreigners will buy less of them, thereby driving down net exports. It also makes foreign goods less expensive in terms of dollars, so Canadian imports will rise, also causing a decline in net exports. We therefore see that a rise in the real interest rate, which leads to an increase in the value of the dollar, in turn leads to a decline in net exports.

AUTONOMOUS NET EXPORTS   The amount of exports is also affected by the demand by foreigners for domestic goods, while the amount of imports is affected by the demand by domestic residents for foreign goods. For example, if the Chinese have a poor harvest and want to buy more Canadian wheat, Canadian exports will rise. If Canadian consumers discover how good Chilean wine is and want to buy more, then Canadian imports will rise. Thus we can think of net exports as being

---

[2]If the government pegs the exchange rate to another currency so it is fixed, in what is called a *fixed exchange rate regime* (see Chapter 20), then real interest rates do not directly affect net exports as in Equation 5 and $NX = \overline{NX}$. Note also that a rise in income in the domestic economy leads to a rise in spending on imports and thus causes net exports to decline. Adding a response of net exports to domestic income, Y, or taking out the response of net exports to the real interest rates does not change the basic analysis in the chapter but does lead to a slightly different Equation 12 later in the chapter.

determined by real interest rates as well as by a component, **autonomous net exports**, $\overline{NX}$, which is the level of net exports that is treated as exogenous (outside the model).

NET EXPORT FUNCTION   Putting these two components of net exports together leads to a net export function:

$$NX = \overline{NX} - xr \tag{7}$$

where x is a parameter that indicates how net exports respond to the real interest rate. This equation tells us that net exports are positively related to autonomous net exports and are negatively related to the level of real interest rates.

Government Purchases and Taxes

Now we bring the government into the picture. The government affects aggregate demand in two ways: through its purchases and through taxes.

GOVERNMENT PURCHASES   As we saw in the aggregate demand Equation 1, government purchases add directly to aggregate demand. Here we assume that government purchases are also exogenous and write government purchases as follows:

$$G = \overline{G} \tag{8}$$

which says that government purchases are set at a fixed amount $\overline{G}$.

TAXES   The government affects spending through taxes because, as we discussed earlier, disposable income is equal to income minus taxes, $Y - T$, and disposable income affects consumption expenditure. Higher taxes T reduce disposable income for a given level of income and hence cause consumption expenditure to fall. The tax laws in a country like Canada are very complicated, so to keep the model simple, we assume that government taxes are exogenous and are a fixed amount $\overline{T}$:[3]

$$T = \overline{T} \tag{9}$$

Goods Market Equilibrium

Keynes recognized that equilibrium would occur in the economy when the total quantity of output equals the total amount of aggregate demand (planned expenditure). That is,

$$Y = Y^{ad} \tag{10}$$

When this equilibrium condition is satisfied, planned spending for goods and services is equal to the amount that is produced. Producers are able to sell all their output and have no reason to change their production because there is no unplanned inventory investment. This analysis explains why aggregate output goes to a certain level by examining the factors that affect each component of planned spending.

---

[3]For simplicity, we assume here that taxes are unrelated to income. However, because taxes increase with income, we can describe taxes with the following more realistic tax function:

$$T = \overline{T} + tY$$

Using this equation instead of Equation 9 in the derivation of Equation 12 later in the chapter would lead to *mpc* being replaced by *mpc* $(1 - t)$ in Equation 12.

Solving for Goods Market Equilibrium

With our understanding of what drives the components of aggregate demand, we can see how aggregate output is determined by using the aggregate demand Equation 1 to rewrite the equilibrium condition in Equation 10 as follows:

$$Y = C + I + G + NX \tag{11}$$

Aggregate Output = Consumption Expenditure + Planned Investment Spending + Government Purchases + Net Exports

Now we can use our consumption, investment, and net export functions in Equation 3, Equation 6, and Equation 7, along with Equation 8 and Equation 9, to determine aggregate output. Substituting all these equations into the equilibrium condition Equation 11 yields the following:

$$Y = \overline{C} + mpc \times (Y - \overline{T}) + \overline{I} - d(r + \bar{f}) + \overline{G} + \overline{NX} - xr$$

Collecting terms, we can rewrite this equation as follows:

$$Y = \overline{C} + \overline{I} - d\bar{f} + \overline{G} + \overline{NX} + mpc \times Y - mpc \times \overline{T} - (d + x)r$$

Subtracting $mpc \times Y$ from both sides of the equation,

$$Y - mpc \times Y = Y(1 - mpc) = \overline{C} + \overline{I} - d\bar{f} + \overline{G} + \overline{NX} - mpc \times \overline{T} - (d + x)r$$

Then, dividing both sides of the equation by $1 - mpc$, we obtain an equation explaining how to determine aggregate output when the goods market is in equilibrium:[4]

$$Y = [\overline{C} + \overline{I} - d\bar{f} + \overline{G} + \overline{NX} - mpc \times \overline{T}] \times \frac{1}{1 - mpc} - \frac{d + x}{1 - mpc} \times r \tag{12}$$

Deriving the *IS* Curve

We refer to Equation 12 as the **IS curve**, and it shows the relationship between aggregate output and the real interest rate when the goods market is in equilibrium. Equation 12 is made up of two terms. Since mpc is between zero and one, $1/(1 - mpc)$ is positive, so the first term tells us that increases in autonomous consumption, investment, government purchases, or net exports or a decrease in taxes or financial frictions leads to an increase in output at any given real interest rate. In other words, the first term tells us about shifts in the *IS* curve. The second term tells us that an increase in real interest rates results in a decline in output, which is a movement along the *IS* curve.

Understanding the *IS* Curve

To gain a deeper understanding of the *IS* curve, we will proceed in several steps. In this section we begin by looking at the intuition behind the *IS* curve and then discuss a numerical example. Then in the following section, we will outline the factors that shift the *IS* curve.

What the *IS* Curve Tells Us: Intuition

The *IS* curve traces out the points at which the goods market is in equilibrium. For each given level of the real interest rate, the *IS* curve tells us what the aggregate output must be for the goods market to be in equilibrium. As the real interest rate rises, planned investment spending and net exports fall, which in turn lowers aggregate demand; aggregate output must be lower for it to equal aggregate demand and satisfy goods market equilibrium. Hence the *IS* curve is downward-sloping.

---

[4]Note that the term $1/(1 - mpc)$ that multiplies $\overline{G}$ is known as the *expenditure multiplier,* while the term $-mpc/(1 - mpc)$ that multiplies $\overline{T}$ is called the *tax multiplier* and is smaller in absolute value than the expenditure multiplier because $mpc < 1$.

What the *IS* Curve Tells Us: Numerical Example

We can also see what the *IS* curve tells us with the following numerical example, with specific values for the exogenous variables and for the parameters in Equation 12.

$$\overline{C} = \$1.4 \text{ trillion}$$
$$\overline{I} = \$1.2 \text{ trillion}$$
$$\overline{G} = \$3.0 \text{ trillion}$$
$$\overline{T} = \$3.0 \text{ trillion}$$
$$\overline{NX} = \$1.3 \text{ trillion}$$
$$\overline{f} = 1$$
$$mpc = 0.6$$
$$d = 0.3$$
$$x = 0.1$$

With these values, we can rewrite Equation 12 as follows:

$$Y = [1.4 + 1.2 - 0.3 + 3.0 + 1.3 - 0.6 \times 3.0] \times \frac{1}{1 - 0.6} - \frac{0.3 + 0.1}{1 - 0.6} \times r$$

Plugging these values into Equation 12 yields the *IS* curve in Figure 22-1:

$$Y = \frac{4.8}{0.4} - \frac{0.4}{0.4} \times r = 12 - r \tag{13}$$

At a real interest rate $r = 3\%$, equilibrium output $Y = 12 - 3 = \$9$ trillion. We plot this combination of the real interest rate at equilibrium output as point A in Figure 22-1. At a real interest rate of $r = 1\%$, equilibrium output $Y = 12 - 1 = \$11$ trillion,

FIGURE 22-1 The *IS* Curve

The downward-sloping *IS* curve represents points at which the goods market is in equilibrium—for example, points A and B. Notice that output changes as necessary to return to equilibrium. For example, at point G an excess supply of goods exists and firms will cut production, decreasing aggregate output to the equilibrium level at point A. At point H an excess demand for goods exists, so firms will increase production and aggregate output will increase toward the equilibrium level at point B.

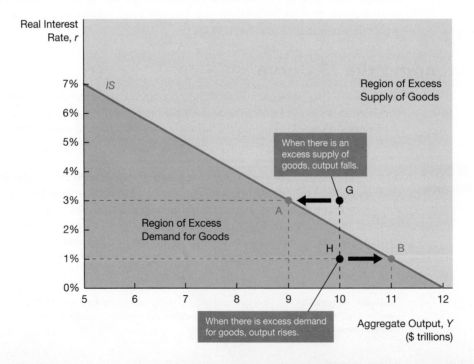

which we plot as point B. The line connecting these points is the *IS* curve and, as you can see, it is downward-sloping.

Why the Economy Heads Toward the Equilibrium

The concept of equilibrium is useful only if there is a tendency for the economy to settle there. Let's first consider what happens if the economy is located to the right of the *IS* curve, where an excess supply of goods exists. In Figure 22-1 at point G, actual output is above aggregate demand, and firms are saddled with unsold inventory. To keep from accumulating unsold goods, firms will continue cutting production. As long as production is above the equilibrium level, output will exceed aggregate demand and firms will continue cutting production, sending aggregate output toward the equilibrium level, as is indicated by the leftward arrow from point G to point A. Only when the economy moves to point A on the *IS* curve will there be no further tendency for output to change.

What happens if aggregate output is below the equilibrium level of output (the area to the left of the *IS* curve), where an excess demand for goods exists? At point H in Figure 22-1, actual output is below aggregate demand, so firms will want to increase production because inventories are declining more than they desire, and aggregate output will increase, as shown by the rightward arrow. When the economy has moved to point B on the *IS* curve, there will again be no further tendency for output to change.

Factors That Shift the *IS* Curve

You have now learned that the *IS* curve describes equilibrium in the goods market—the combinations of the real interest rate and equilibrium output. The *IS* curve shifts whenever change occurs in autonomous factors (factors independent of aggregate output and the real interest rate). Note that a change in the real interest rate that affects equilibrium aggregate output causes only a *movement along* the *IS* curve. A *shift* in the *IS* curve, by contrast, occurs when equilibrium output changes *at each given real interest rate*.

In Equation 12, we identified six candidates as autonomous factors that can shift aggregate demand and hence affect the level of equilibrium output. Although Equation 12 directly tells us how these factors shift the *IS* curve, we will develop some intuition as to how each autonomous factor does so.

Changes in Government Purchases

Let's look at what happens if government purchases rise from $3 trillion to $4 trillion in Figure 22-2. IS_1 represents the same *IS* curve that we developed in Figure 22-1. We determine the equation for IS_2 by inputting the $4 trillion value into Equation 12:

$$Y = [1.4 + 1.2 - 0.3 + 4.0 + 1.3 - 0.6 \times 3.0] \times \frac{1}{1 - 0.6} - r = \frac{5.8}{0.4} - r$$

$$= 14.5 - r$$

On the basis of these results, at a real interest rate of $r = 3\%$, equilibrium output $Y = 14.5 - 3 = \$11.5$ trillion, which we mark as point C on Figure 22-2. At a real interest rate $r = 1\%$, equilibrium output has increased to $Y = 14.5 - 1 = \$13.5$ trillion, which we mark as point D. The increase in government purchases therefore shifts the *IS* curve to the right from IS_1 to IS_2.

An intuitive way to see why an increase in government purchases leads to a rightward shift of the *IS* curve is to recognize that an increase in government purchases causes aggregate demand to increase at any given real interest rate. Since aggregate output equals aggregate demand when the goods market is in equilibrium, *an increase in government purchases that causes aggregate demand to rise also causes equilibrium output to rise, thereby shifting the* **IS** *curve to the right. Conversely, a decline in government purchases causes aggregate demand to fall at any given real interest rate and leads to a leftward shift of the* **IS** *curve.*

FIGURE 22-2 Shift in the *IS* Curve from an Increase in Government Purchases

IS$_1$ represents the *IS* curve we derived in Figure 22-1. *IS*$_2$ reflects a $1.0 trillion increase in government purchases. The increase in government purchases causes aggregate output to rise, shifting the *IS* curve to the right by $2.5 trillion from *IS*$_1$ to *IS*$_2$.

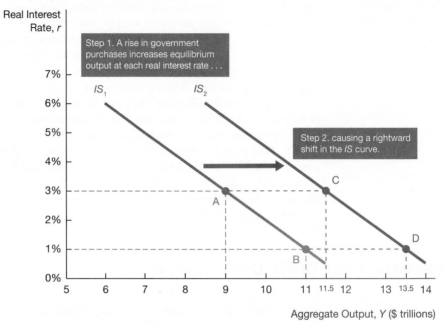

APPLICATION

The Vietnam War Buildup, 1964–1969

The United States' involvement in Vietnam began to escalate in the early 1960s. After 1964, the United States was fighting a full-scale war. Beginning in 1965, the resulting increases in military expenditure raised government purchases. Usually during a period when government purchases are rising rapidly, central banks raise real interest rates to keep the economy from overheating. The Vietnam War period, however, is unusual because the Federal Reserve decided to keep real interest rates constant. Hence, this period provides an excellent example of how policymakers could make use of the *IS* curve analysis to inform policy.

The rise in government purchases would shift the *IS* curve to the right, from *IS*$_{1964}$ to *IS*$_{1969}$ in Figure 22-3. Because the Federal Reserve decided to keep real interest rates constant during this period, at 2%, equilibrium output rose from $3.0 trillion (in 2000 dollars) in 1964 to $3.8 trillion by 1969, with the unemployment rate falling steadily from 5% in 1964 to 3.4% in 1969. However, all was not well for the economy: the increase in government purchases with the real interest rate constant led to an overheating of the economy that eventually resulted in high inflation. (We will discuss the link between an overheating economy and inflation in the coming chapters.)

FIGURE 22-3 Vietnam War Buildup

Beginning in 1965, increases in military spending caused the *IS* curve to shift from IS_{1964} to IS_{1969}. Because the Federal Reserve decided to keep real interest rates constant during this period, at 2%, equilibrium output rose from $3.0 trillion (in 2000 dollars) in 1964 to $3.8 trillion in 1969, setting the stage for an increase in inflation.

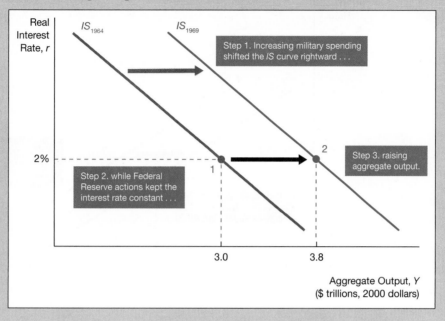

Changes in Taxes   Now let's look at Figure 22-4 to see what happens if the government raises taxes from $3 trillion to $4 trillion. IS_1 represents the same *IS* curve that we developed in Figure 22-1. We determine the equation for IS_2 by inputting the $4 trillion value in Equation 12:

$$Y = [1.4 + 1.2 - 0.3 + 3.0 + 1.3 - 0.6 \times 4.0] \times \frac{1}{1 - 0.6} - r = \frac{4.2}{0.4} - r$$
$$= 10.5 - r$$

At a real interest rate of $r = 3\%$, equilibrium output $Y = 10.5 - 3 = \$7.5$ trillion, which we mark as point E in Figure 22-4. At this real interest rate, equilibrium output has decreased from point A to point E, as shown by the leftward arrow. Similarly, at a real interest rate $r = 1\%$, equilibrium output has decreased to $Y = 10.5 - 1 = \$9.5$ trillion, causing a leftward shift from point B to point F. The *IS* curve shifts to the left, from IS_1 to IS_2, as a result of the increase in taxes.

We then have the following result: ***at any given real interest rate, a rise in taxes causes aggregate demand and hence equilibrium output to fall, thereby shifting the* IS *curve to the left. Conversely, a cut in taxes at any given real interest rate increases disposable income and causes aggregate demand and equilibrium output to rise, shifting the* IS *curve to the right*.

Policymakers use both tax and government purchases policies to stimulate the economy when it enters recessions, as the Application on the next page illustrates.

FIGURE 22-4 Shift in the *IS* Curve from an Increase in Taxes

IS_1 represents the *IS* curve we derived in Figure 22-1. IS_2 reflects a \$1.0 trillion increase in government tax revenue. The increase in taxes decreases aggregate output levels by \$1.5 trillion, shifting the *IS* curve to the left from IS_1 to IS_2.

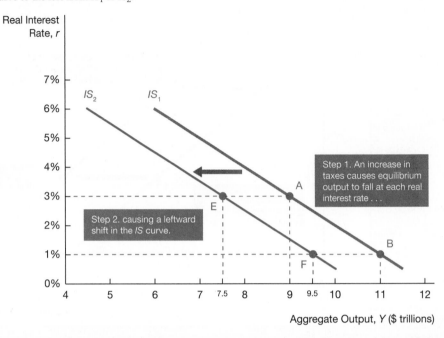

APPLICATION

The Fiscal Stimulus Package of 2009

In the fall of 2008, the U.S. economy was in crisis. By the time the new Obama administration had taken office, the unemployment rate had risen from 4.7% just before the recession began in December 2007 to 7.6% in January 2009. To stimulate the economy, the Obama administration proposed a fiscal stimulus package that, when passed by Congress, included \$288 billion in tax cuts for households and businesses and \$499 billion in increased federal spending, including transfer payments. What does our *IS* curve analysis suggest should have happened to the economy?

As the analysis in Figure 22-2 and Figure 22-4 indicates, these tax cuts and spending increases would increase aggregate demand, thereby raising the equilibrium level of aggregate output at any given real interest rate and so shifting the *IS* curve to the right. Unfortunately, things didn't work out quite as the Obama administration planned. Most of the government purchases did not kick in until after 2010, while the decline in autonomous consumption and investment were much larger than anticipated. The fiscal stimulus was more than offset by weak consumption and investment, with the result that the aggregate demand ended up contracting rather than rising, and the *IS* curve did not shift to the right, as hoped. Despite the good intentions of the fiscal stimulus package, the unemployment rate ended up rising to over 10% in 2009. Without the fiscal stimulus, however, the *IS* curve would likely have shifted further to the left, resulting in even more unemployment.

Changes in Autonomous Spending

As you can see in Equation 12, autonomous consumption, investment, and net exports, $\overline{C}$, $\overline{I}$, and $\overline{NX}$, respectively, all are multiplied by the term $1/(1 - mpc)$ in the same way the $\overline{G}$ term is. Thus an increase in any of these variables has the same impact on the *IS* curve as an increase in government purchases. For this reason, we can lump these variables together as **autonomous spending**, exogenous spending that is unrelated to variables in the model such as output or real interest rates. We look intuitively at how changes in each of these variables affects the *IS* curve in turn.

AUTONOMOUS CONSUMPTION   Suppose that consumers find their wealth has increased when the stock market has boomed or they have become increasingly optimistic about their future income prospects because a positive productivity shock to the economy has occurred. Both of these events are autonomous; that is, they are not affected by the level of the real interest rate. *The resulting rise in autonomous consumption would raise aggregate demand and equilibrium output at any given interest rate, shifting the* **IS** *curve to the right. Conversely, a decline in autonomous consumption expenditure causes aggregate demand and equilibrium output to fall, shifting the* **IS** *curve to the left.*

AUTONOMOUS INVESTMENT SPENDING   Earlier in the chapter, we learned that changes in the real interest rate affect planned investment spending and hence the equilibrium level of output. This change in investment spending merely causes a movement along the *IS* curve and not a shift. An autonomous rise in planned investment spending unrelated to the real interest rate—say, because companies become more confident about investment profitability after the stock market rises—increases aggregate demand. *An increase in autonomous investment spending therefore increases equilibrium output at any given interest rate, shifting the* **IS** *curve to the right. On the other hand, a decrease in autonomous investment spending causes aggregate demand and equilibrium output to fall, shifting the* **IS** *curve to the left.*

AUTONOMOUS NET EXPORTS   An autonomous rise in net exports unrelated to the real interest rate—say, because Canadian-made handbags become more chic than French-made handbags, or because foreign countries have a boom and thus buy more Canadian goods—causes aggregate demand to rise. *An autonomous increase in net exports thus leads to an increase in equilibrium output at any given interest rate and shifts the* **IS** *curve to the right. Conversely, an autonomous fall in net exports causes aggregate demand and equilibrium output to decline, shifting the* **IS** *curve to the left.*

Changes in Financial Frictions

An increase in financial frictions, as occurred during the financial crisis of 2007–2009, raises the real cost of borrowing to firms and hence causes investment spending and aggregate demand to fall. *An increase in financial frictions leads to a decline in equilibrium output at any given real interest rate and shifts the* **IS** *curve to the left. Conversely, a decline in financial frictions causes aggregate demand and equilibrium output to rise, shifting the* **IS** *curve to the right.*

Summary of Factors That Shift the *IS* Curve

As a study aid, Summary Table 22-1 shows how each factor shifts the *IS* curve and the reason the shift occurs. Now that we have a full understanding of the *IS* curve, we can use this building block to examine the relationship between monetary policy and the aggregate demand curve in the following chapter.

TABLE 22.1 Shifts in the *Is* Curve from Autonomous Changes in $\overline{C}, \overline{I}, \overline{G}, \overline{T},$ $\overline{NX}$, and $\overline{f}$

Variable	Change in Variable	Shift in *IS* Curve	Reason
Autonomous consumption expenditure, $\overline{C}$	↑	r ... IS_1 IS_2 Y	$C\uparrow Y\uparrow$
Autonomous investment, $\overline{I}$	↑	r ... IS_1 IS_2 Y	$I\uparrow Y\uparrow$
Government spending, $\overline{G}$	↑	r ... IS_1 IS_2 Y	$G\uparrow Y\uparrow$
Taxes, $\overline{T}$	↑	r ... IS_2 IS_1 Y	$T\uparrow \Rightarrow C\downarrow Y\downarrow$
Autonomous net exports, $\overline{NX}$	↑	r ... IS_1 IS_2 Y	$\overline{NX}\uparrow Y\uparrow$
Financial frictions, $\overline{f}$	↑	r ... IS_2 IS_1 Y	$I\downarrow Y\downarrow$

Note: Only increases (↑) in the variables are shown; the effects of decreases in the variables on aggregate output would be the opposite of those indicated in the last two columns.

MyEconLab   MyEconLab is an online homework and tutorial system that puts you in control of your own learning with study and practice tools directly correlated to this chapter's content. Visit MyEconLab to explore the following resources:

- The Questions and Applied Problems are all available in the Study Plan on MyEconLab for further practice. You will also find the answers to all of the Questions and Applied Problems in the Student Resources section of your MyEconLab.

MyEconLab also features Additional Readings, Videos, Glossary Flashcards, Audio Chapter Summaries, Economics News Feeds, Animations, and many additional tools to help you master key concepts from the text.

SUMMARY

1. Planned expenditure, the total amount of goods demanded in the economy, is the same as aggregate demand, which is the sum of four types of spending: consumption expenditure, planned investment spending, government purchases, and net exports. We represent the total aggregate demand (Y^{ad}) with Equation 1: $Y^{ad} = C + I + G + NX$.

2. Consumption expenditure is described by the consumption function, which indicates that consumption expenditure will rise as disposable income increases. Planned expenditure and hence aggregate demand is negatively related to the real interest rate because a rise in the real interest rate reduces both planned investment spending and net exports. An increase in financial frictions raises the real cost of borrowing and hence lowers investment spending and aggregate demand. The government also affects planned expenditure by increased spending, which directly raises aggregate demand, or by taxes, which indirectly affect aggregate demand by influencing disposable income and hence consumption expenditure.

3. The level of aggregate output when the goods market is in equilibrium is determined by the condition that aggregate output equals aggregate demand.

4. The *IS* curve traces out the combinations of the real interest rate and aggregate output for which the goods market is in equilibrium. The *IS* curve slopes downward because higher real interest rates lower planned investment spending and net exports and so lower equilibrium output.

5. The *IS* curve shifts to the right when there is a rise in autonomous consumption, a rise in autonomous investment, a rise in government purchases, a rise in autonomous net exports, a fall in taxes, or a fall in financial frictions. Movements of these six factors in the opposite direction will shift the *IS* curve to the left.

KEY TERMS

aggregate demand, p. 542

"animal spirits," p. 544

autonomous consumption expenditure, p. 543

autonomous investment, p. 544

autonomous net exports, p. 546

autonomous spending, p. 553

consumption expenditure, p. 542

consumption function, p. 542

disposable income, p. 542

exchange rate, p. 545

exogenous, p. 543

fixed investment, p. 543

government purchases, p. 542

inventory investment, p. 543

IS curve, p. 547

marginal propensity to consume, p. 543

net exports, p. 542

planned expenditure, p. 542

planned investment spending, p. 542

QUESTIONS

1. "When the stock market rises, investment is increasing." Is this statement true, false, or uncertain? Explain your answer.

2. Why is inventory investment counted toward aggregate spending if it isn't actually sold to the final end user?

3. "Since inventories can be costly to hold, firms' planned inventory investment should be zero, and firms should acquire inventory only through unplanned inventory accumulation." Is this statement true, false, or uncertain? Explain your answer.

4. During and in the aftermath of the financial crisis of 2007–2009, planned investment fell substantially, despite significant decreases in the real interest rate. What factors related to the planned investment function could explain this?

5. If households and firms believe the economy will be in a recession in the future, will this necessarily cause a recession, or have any impact on output at all?

6. Why do increases in the real interest rate lead to decreases in net exports, and vice versa?

7. Why does equilibrium output increase as the marginal propensity to consume increases?

8. If firms suddenly become more optimistic about the profitability of investment and planned investment spending rises by $100 billion, while consumers become more pessimistic and autonomous consumer spending falls by $100 billion, what happens to aggregate output?

9. In each of the cases below, what happens to equilibrium output? Briefly explain how it affects the relevant component(s) of planned spending.

   a. The real interest rate rises.

   b. The marginal propensity to consume declines.

   c. Financial frictions increase.

d. Autonomous consumption decreases.

e. Both taxes and government spending decrease by the same amount.

f. The sensitivity of net exports to changes in the real interest rate decreases.

g. The government provides tax incentives for research and development programs for firms.

10. Will aggregate output rise or fall if an increase in autonomous consumer expenditure is matched by an equal increase in taxes?

11. If a change in the interest rate has no effect on planned investment spending or net exports, then what does this imply about the slope of the *IS* curve?

12. Why do companies cut production when they find that their unplanned inventory investment is greater than zero? If they didn't cut production, what effect would this have on their profits? Why?

13. "Firms will increase production when planned investment is less than (actual) total investment." Is this statement true, false, or uncertain? Explain your answer.

14. In each of the cases below, explain whether the *IS* curve shifts to the right or left, does not shift, or is indeterminate in the direction of shift.

a. The real interest rate rises.

b. The marginal propensity to consume declines.

c. Financial frictions increase.

d. Autonomous consumption decreases.

e. Both taxes and government spending decrease by the same amount.

f. The sensitivity of net exports to changes in the real interest rate decreases.

g. The government provides tax incentives for research and development programs for firms.

15. "The fiscal stimulus package of 2009 caused the *IS* curve to shift to the left, since output decreased and unemployment increased after the policies were implemented." Is this statement true, false, or uncertain? Explain your answer.

16. When the central bank reduces its policy interest rate, how, if at all, is the *IS* curve affected? Briefly explain.

17. In its February 18, 2010, edition, *The Wall Street Journal* stated, "The dollar strengthened [. . .] and stocks [. . .] followed suit. The Dow industrials rose 40.43 points, or 0.4%."

a. What effect does the strengthened dollar have on the *IS* curve?

b. What effect does the increase in stock prices have on the *IS* curve?

c. What is the combined effect of these two events on the *IS* curve?

APPLIED PROBLEMS

18. Calculate the value of the consumption function at each level of income in the table below if autonomous consumption = 300, taxes = 200, and *mpc* = 0.9.

Income Y	Disposable Income Y_D	Consumption C
0		
100		
200		
300		
400		
500		
600		

19. Assume that autonomous consumption is $1625 billion and disposable income is $11 500 billion. Calculate consumption expenditure if an increase of $1000 in disposable income leads to an increase of $750 in consumption expenditure.

20. Suppose that Dell Corporation has 20 000 computers in its warehouses on December 31, 2012, ready to be shipped to merchants (each computer is valued at $500). By December 31, 2013, Dell Corporation has 25 000 computers ready to be shipped, each valued at $450.

a. Calculate Dell's inventory on December 31, 2012.

b. Calculate Dell's inventory investment in 2013.

c. What happens to inventory spending during the early stages of an economic recession?

21. If the consumption function is $C = 100 + 0.75Y_D$, $I = 200$, government spending is 200, and net exports are zero, what will be the equilibrium level of output? What happens to aggregate output if government spending rises by 100?

22. If the marginal propensity to consume is 0.75, how much would government spending have to rise to increase output by $1000 billion? How much will taxes need to decrease to increase output by $1000 billion?

23. Assuming both taxes and government spending increase by the same amount, calculate an expression for the effect on equilibrium output.

24. Consider an economy described by the following:

$$\overline{C} = \$3.25 \text{ trillion}$$
$$\overline{I} = \$1.3 \text{ trillion}$$
$$\overline{G} = \$3.5 \text{ trillion}$$
$$\overline{T} = \$3.0 \text{ trillion}$$
$$\overline{NX} = -\$1.0 \text{ trillion}$$
$$\overline{f} = 1$$
$$mpc = 0.75$$
$$d = 0.3$$
$$x = 0.1$$

a. Calculate simplified expressions for the consumption function, investment function, and net export function.
b. Calculate an expression for the *IS* curve.
c. If the real interest rate is $r = 2$, then what is equilibrium output? If $r = 5$, then what is equilibrium output?
d. Draw a graph of the *IS* curve, showing the answers from part (c) above.
e. If government purchases increases to $4.2 trillion, what will happen to equilibrium output at $r = 2$? What happens to equilibrium output at $r = 5$? Show the effect of the increase in government purchases in your graph from part (d).

25. Consider an economy described by the following:

$$\overline{C} = \$4 \text{ trillion}$$
$$\overline{I} = \$1.5 \text{ trillion}$$
$$\overline{G} = \$3.0 \text{ trillion}$$
$$\overline{T} = \$3.0 \text{ trillion}$$
$$\overline{NX} = \$1.0 \text{ trillion}$$
$$\overline{f} = 0$$
$$mpc = 0.8$$
$$d = 0.35$$
$$x = 0.15$$

a. Calculate an expression for the *IS* curve.
b. Assume that the central bank controls the interest rate and sets the interest rate at $r = 4$. What is the equilibrium level of output?
c. Suppose that a financial crisis begins, and $\overline{f}$ increases to $\overline{f} = 3$. What will happen to equilibrium output? If the central bank can set the interest rate, then what should the interest rate be set at to keep output from changing?
d. Suppose that as a result of the financial crisis, in addition to $\overline{f}$ increasing as in part (c), planned autonomous investment decreases to $\overline{I} = \$1.1$ trillion. Will the change in the interest rate by the central bank from part (c) be effective at stabilizing output? If not, what additional monetary or fiscal policy changes could be implemented to stabilize output at the original equilibrium output level in part (b)?

WEB EXERCISES

1. Go to **www.eurmacro.unisg.ch/Tutor/islm.html**. Set the policy instruments to be $G = 80$, $t = 0.20$, $c = 0.75$, $b = 40$. Now increase government spending, *G*, from 80 to 160. How much does the *IS* curve shift horizontally to the right? Why is this amount greater than the increase in *G*? Now increase the marginal propensity to consume, *c*, from 0.75 to 0.90. Which direction does the *IS* curve shift and why? How much does it shift? Now increase the tax rate, *t*, from 0.20 to 0.28. Which direction does the *IS* curve shift and why? How much does it shift?

2. Go to **www.eurmacro.unisg.ch/Tutor/islm.html**. Set the policy instruments to be $G = 80$, $t = 0.20$, $c = 0.75$, $b = 40$. Now increase the sensitivity of investment to the interest rate, *b*, from 40 to 80. What happens to the slope of the *IS* curve? Why?

CHAPTER 23

The Monetary Policy and Aggregate Demand Curves

LEARNING OBJECTIVES

After studying this chapter you should be able to

1. understand why there is a positive relationship between real interest rates and inflation, the *MP* curve

2. illustrate how the *IS* curve and the *MP* curve can be used to derive the aggregate demand curve featured in the aggregate demand and supply framework in the next chapter

PREVIEW

In response to the subprime financial crisis in the United States, the Bank of Canada lowered the target overnight interest rate from 4.5% in August 2007 to 0.25% in April 2009. Moreover, for over a year (from April 1, 2009, to June 1, 2010), the Bank of Canada also lowered the operating band for the overnight interest rate from 50 basis points to 25 basis points, and instead of targeting the overnight interest rate at the midpoint of the operating band (as it does during normal times), it targeted the overnight rate at the bottom of the operating band, at 0.25%, thus setting an effective lower bound for the overnight interest rate.

To see how a monetary policy action like the one above affects the economy, we need to analyze how monetary policy affects aggregate demand. We start this chapter by explaining why monetary policymakers set interest rates to rise when inflation increases, leading to a positive relationship between real interest rates and inflation, which is called the *monetary policy (MP) curve*. Then, using the *MP* curve with the *IS* curve we developed in the previous chapter, we derive the *aggregate demand curve*, a key element in the aggregate demand/aggregate supply model framework used in the rest of this text to discuss short-run economic fluctuations.

The Bank of Canada and Monetary Policy

Central banks throughout the world use a very short-term interest rate as their primary policy tool. In Canada, the Bank of Canada conducts monetary policy via its setting of the overnight interest rate.

As we have seen in Chapter 17, the Bank of Canada controls the overnight rate by varying the settlement balances (reserves) it provides to the banking system. When it provides more reserves, banks have more money to lend to each other, and this excess liquidity causes the overnight rate to fall. When the Bank drains reserves from the banking system, banks have less to lend and the shortage of liquidity leads to a rise in the overnight rate.

The overnight interest is a *nominal* interest rate, but as we learned in the previous chapter it is the *real* interest rate that affects net exports and business spending, thereby determining the level of equilibrium output. How does the Bank of Canada's control of the overnight rate enable it to control the real interest rate, through which monetary policy impacts the economy?

Recall from Chapter 4 that the real interest rate, r, is the nominal interest rate, i, minus expected inflation, π^e.

$$r = i - \pi^e \tag{1}$$

Changes in nominal interest rates can change the real interest rate only if actual and expected inflation remain unchanged in the short run. Because prices typically are slow to move—that is, they are *sticky*—changes in monetary policy will not have an immediate effect on inflation and expected inflation. As a result, **when the Bank of Canada lowers the overnight interest rate, real interest rates fall; and when the Bank of Canada raises the overnight rate, real interest rates rise.**

The Monetary Policy Curve

We have now seen how the Bank of Canada can control real interest rates in the short run. The next step in our analysis is to examine how monetary policy reacts to inflation. The **monetary policy (*MP*) curve** indicates the relationship between the real interest rate the central bank sets and the inflation rate. We can write this curve as follows:

$$r = \bar{r} + \lambda\pi$$

where $\bar{r}$ is the autonomous component of the real interest rate set by the monetary policy authorities, which is unrelated to the current level of the inflation rate, while λ is the responsiveness of the real interest rate to the inflation rate.

To make our discussion of the monetary policy curve more concrete, Figure 23-1 shows an example of a monetary policy curve *MP* in which $\bar{r} = 1.0$ and $\lambda = 0.5$:

$$r = 1.0 + 0.5\pi \tag{2}$$

At point A, where inflation is 1%, the Bank of Canada sets the real interest rate at 1.5%, while at point B, where inflation is 2%, the Bank sets the real interest rate at 2%, and at point C, where inflation is 3%, the Bank of Canada sets the real interest rate at 2.5%. The line going through points A, B, and C is the monetary policy curve *MP*, and it is upward-sloping, indicating that monetary policymakers raise real interest rates when the inflation rate rises.

The Taylor Principle: Why the Monetary Policy Curve Has an Upward Slope

To see why the *MP* curve has an upward slope, we need to recognize that central banks seek to keep inflation stable. To stabilize inflation, monetary policymakers follow the **Taylor principle**, named after John Taylor of Stanford University, in which they raise *nominal* rates by more than any rise in expected inflation so that *real* interest rates rise when there is a rise in inflation, as the *MP* curve suggests.[1] John Taylor and many other researchers have found that monetary policymakers tend to follow the Taylor principle in practice.

---

[1]Note that the Taylor principle differs from the Taylor rule, described in Chapter 18, because it does not provide a rule for how monetary policy should react to conditions in the economy, while the Taylor rule does.

FIGURE 23-1 The Monetary Policy Curve

The upward slope of the *MP* curve indicates that the central bank raises real interest rates when inflation rises because monetary policy follows the Taylor principle.

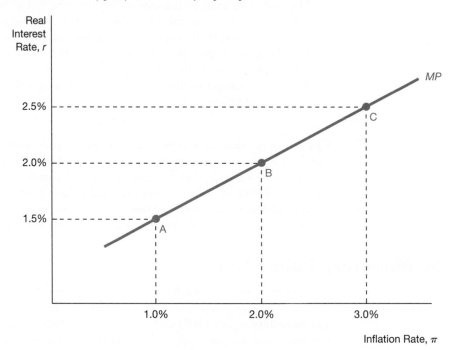

To see why monetary policymakers follow the Taylor principle, in which higher inflation results in higher real interest rates, consider what would happen if monetary policymakers instead allowed the real interest rate to fall when inflation rose. In this case, an increase in inflation would lead to a decline in the real interest rate, which would increase aggregate output, in turn causing inflation to rise further, which would then cause the real interest rate to fall even more, increasing aggregate output. Schematically, we can write this as follows:

$$\pi\uparrow \Rightarrow r\downarrow \Rightarrow Y\uparrow \Rightarrow \pi\uparrow \Rightarrow r\downarrow \Rightarrow Y\uparrow \Rightarrow \pi\uparrow$$

As a result, inflation would continually keep rising and spin out of control. Indeed, this is exactly what happened in the 1970s, when the Bank of Canada did not raise nominal interest rates by as much as inflation rose, so that real interest rates fell. Inflation accelerated to over 10%.[2]

Shifts in the *MP* Curve

In common parlance, the Bank of Canada is said to tighten monetary policy when it raises real interest rates, and to ease it when it lowers real interest rates. It is important, however, to distinguish between changes in monetary policy that shift the monetary policy curve, which we call autonomous changes, and the Taylor principle–driven changes which are reflected as movements along the monetary policy curve, which are called *automatic* adjustments to interest rates.

Central banks may make autonomous changes to monetary policy for various reasons. They may wish to change the inflation rate from its current value. For

[2]In a Web Appendix to Chapter 24 we formally demonstrate the instability of inflation when central banks do not follow the Taylor principle.

example, to lower inflation they could increase $\bar{r}$ by one percentage point, and so raise the real interest rate at any given inflation rate, what we will refer to as an **autonomous tightening of monetary policy**. This autonomous monetary tightening would shift the monetary policy curve upward by one percentage point from MP_1 to MP_2 in Figure 23-2, thereby causing the economy to contract and inflation to fall. Or, the banks may have information above and beyond what is happening to inflation that suggests interest rates must be adjusted to achieve good economic outcomes. For example, if the economy is going into a recession, monetary policymakers would want to lower real interest rates at any given inflation rate, an **autonomous easing of monetary policy**, in order to stimulate the economy and also to prevent inflation from falling. This autonomous easing of monetary policy would result in a downward shift in the monetary policy curve, say, by one percentage point from MP_1 to MP_3 in Figure 23-2.

We contrast these autonomous changes with automatic, Taylor principle–driven changes, a central bank's normal response (also known as an endogenous response) of raising real interest rates when inflation rises. These changes to interest rates do not shift the monetary policy curve, and so cannot be considered autonomous tightening or easing of monetary policy. Instead, they are reflected in movements along the monetary policy curve.

The distinction between autonomous monetary policy changes and movements along the monetary policy curve is illustrated by the monetary policy actions the Bank of Canada took at the onset of the 2007–2009 financial crisis in the fall of 2007.

FIGURE 23-2 Shifts in the Monetary Policy Curve

Autonomous changes in monetary policy, such as when a central bank changes the real interest rate at any given inflation rate, shift the *MP* curve. An autonomous tightening of monetary policy that increases the real interest rate shifts the *MP* curve up to MP_2, whereas an autonomous easing of monetary policy that lowers the real interest rate shifts the *MP* curve down to MP_3.

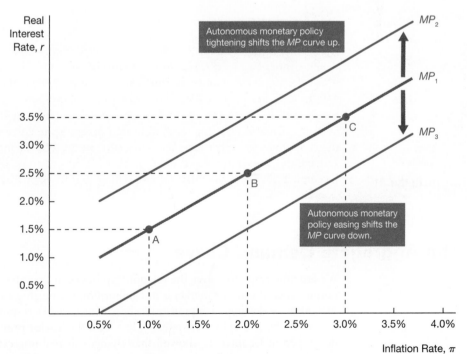

Inflation Rate, π

APPLICATION

Autonomous Monetary Easing at the Onset of the 2007–2009 Financial Crisis

When the financial crisis started in August 2007, inflation was rising and economic growth was quite strong. Yet the Bank of Canada began an aggressive easing, lowering the overnight interest rate as shown in Figure 23-3. What does this tell us about effects on the monetary policy curve?

FIGURE 23-3 The Inflation Rate and the Overnight Interest Rate, 2007–2011

The Bank of Canada began an aggressive autonomous easing of monetary policy in September 2007, bringing down its policy rate, the target overnight interest rate, despite the continuing high inflation.

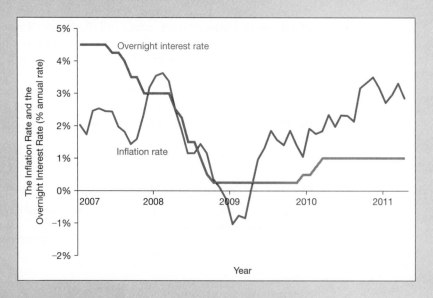

A movement along the *MP* curve would have suggested that the Bank of Canada would continue to keep hiking interest rates because inflation was rising, but instead it did the opposite. The Bank thus shifted the monetary policy curve down from MP_1 to MP_3, as in Figure 23-2. The Bank pursued this autonomous monetary policy easing because the negative shock to the economy from the disruption to financial markets (discussed in Chapter 9) indicated that, despite current high inflation rates, the economy was likely to weaken in the near future and the inflation rate would fall. Indeed, this is exactly what came to pass, with the economy going into recession in December 2007 and the inflation rate falling sharply after August 2008.

The Aggregate Demand Curve

We are now ready to derive the relationship between the inflation rate and aggregate output when the goods market is in equilibrium, the **aggregate demand curve**. The *MP* curve we developed demonstrates how central banks respond to changes in inflation with changes in interest rates, in line with the Taylor principle. The *IS* curve we developed in Chapter 22 showed that changes in real interest rates, in turn, affect equilibrium output. With these two curves, we can now link the quantity of aggregate output demanded with the inflation rate, given the public's expectations of inflation and the stance of monetary policy. The aggregate demand curve is central to the aggregate demand and supply analysis we develop further in the next chapter, which allows us to explain short-run fluctuations in both aggregate output and inflation.

Deriving the Aggregate Demand Curve Graphically

Using the hypothetical *MP* curve from Equation 2, we know that when the inflation rate rises from 1% to 2% to 3%, real interest rates rise from 1.5% to 2% to 2.5%. We plot these points in panel (a) of Figure 23-4 to create the *MP* curve. In panel (b), we graph the *IS* curve described in Equation 13 of Chapter 22 ($Y = 12 - r$). As the real interest rate rises from 1.5% to 2% to 2.5%, the equilibrium moves from point 1 to point 2 to point 3 and aggregate output falls from $10.5 trillion to $10 trillion to $9.5 trillion. In other words, as real interest rates rise, investment and net exports decline, leading to a reduction in aggregate demand. Panels (a) and (b) demonstrate that as inflation rises from 1% to 2% to 3%, the equilibrium moves from point 1 to point 2 to point 3 in panel (c), and aggregate output falls from $10.5 trillion to $10 trillion to $9.5 trillion.

The line that connects the three points in panel (c) is the aggregate demand curve, *AD*, and it indicates the level of aggregate output corresponding to each of the three real interest rates consistent with equilibrium in the goods market for any given inflation rate. The aggregate demand curve has a downward slope, because a higher inflation rate leads the central bank to raise real interest rates, thereby lowering planned spending, and hence lowering the level of equilibrium aggregate output.

By using some algebra (see the FYI box Deriving the Aggregate Demand Curve Algebraically), the *AD* curve in Figure 23-4 can be written numerically as follows:

$$Y = 11 - 0.5\pi \tag{3}$$

Factors That Shift the Aggregate Demand Curve

Movements along the aggregate demand curve describe how the equilibrium level of aggregate output changes when the inflation rate changes. When factors besides the inflation rate change, however, the aggregate demand curve can shift. We first review the factors that shift the *IS* curve, and then consider other factors that shift the *AD* curve.

FIGURE 23-4   Deriving the *AD* Curve

The *MP* curve in panel (a) shows that as inflation rises from 1.5% to 2% to 3.0%, the real interest rate rises from 1.5% to 2.0% to 2.5%. The *IS* curve in panel (b) then shows that higher real interest rates lead to lower planned investment spending, and hence aggregate output falls from $10.5 trillion to $10 trillion to $9.5 trillion. Finally, panel (c) plots the level of equilibrium output corresponding to each of the three inflation rates: the line that connects these points is the *AD* curve, and it is downward-sloping.

(a) MP Curve

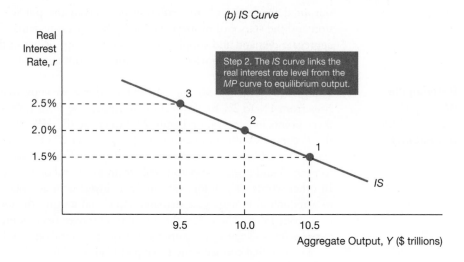

(b) IS Curve

Real Interest Rate, *r*

Step 2. The *IS* curve links the real interest rate level from the *MP* curve to equilibrium output.

2.5%

2.0%

1.5%

IS

9.5   10.0   10.5

Aggregate Output, *Y* ($ trillions)

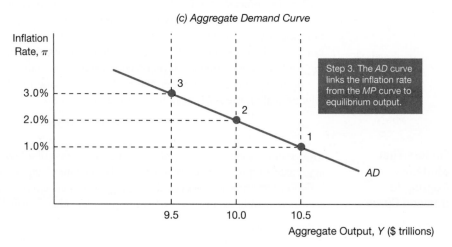

(c) Aggregate Demand Curve

Inflation Rate, *π*

Step 3. The *AD* curve links the inflation rate from the *MP* curve to equilibrium output.

3.0%

2.0%

1.0%

AD

9.5   10.0   10.5

Aggregate Output, *Y* ($ trillions)

SHIFTS IN THE *IS* CURVE   We saw in the previous chapter that six factors cause the *IS* curve to shift. It turns out that the same factors cause the aggregate demand curve to shift as well:

1. Autonomous consumption expenditure

2. Autonomous investment spending

3. Government purchases

4. Taxes

5. Autonomous net exports

6. Financial frictions

We examine how changes in these factors lead to a shift in the aggregate demand curve in Figure 23-5.

Figure 23-5 shows that *any factor that shifts the* **IS** *curve shifts the aggregate demand curve in the same direction*. Therefore, "animal spirits" that encourage a rise in autonomous consumption expenditure or planned investment spending, a rise in government purchases, an autonomous rise in net exports, a fall in taxes, or a decline in financial frictions—all of which shift the *IS* curve to the right—will also shift the aggregate demand curve to the right. Conversely, a fall in autonomous consumption expenditure, a fall in planned investment spending, a fall in government

FIGURE 23-5 Shift in the *AD* Curve from Shifts in the *IS* Curve

At a 2% inflation rate in panel (a), the monetary policy curve indicates that the real interest rate is 2%. An increase in government purchases shifts the *IS* curve to the right in panel (b). At a given inflation rate and real interest rate of 2.0%, equilibrium output rises from $10 trillion to $12.5 trillion, which is shown as a movement from point A_1 to point A_2 in panel (c), shifting the aggregate demand curve to the right from AD_1 to AD_2. Any factor that shifts the *IS* curve shifts the *AD* curve in the same direction.

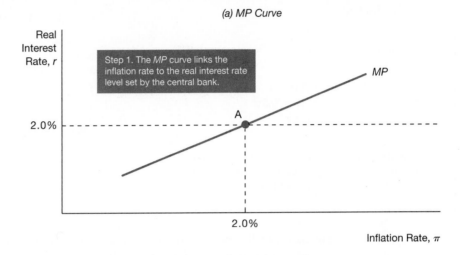

(a) MP Curve

Step 1. The *MP* curve links the inflation rate to the real interest rate level set by the central bank.

(b) IS Curve

Step 2. A rise in government purchases increases equilibrium output, shifting the *IS* curve rightward . . .

(c) Aggregate Demand Curve

Step 3. and shifting the *AD* curve rightward.

FYI

Deriving the Aggregate Demand Curve Algebraically

To derive the numerical AD curve, we start by taking the numerical IS curve, Equation 13, from the previous chapter,

$$Y = 12 - r$$

and then substitute in for r from the numerical MP curve in Equation 2, $r = 1.0 + 0.5\pi$, to yield

$$\begin{aligned} Y &= 12 - (1.0 + 0.5\pi) \\ &= (12 - 1) - 0.5\pi \\ &= 11 - 0.5\pi \end{aligned}$$

as in the text.

Similarly, we can derive a more general version of the AD curve, using the algebraic version of the IS curve from Equation 12 in Chapter 22:

$$Y = [\overline{C} + \overline{I} - d\overline{f} + \overline{G} + \overline{NX} - mpc \times \overline{T}] \\ \times \frac{1}{1 - mpc} - \frac{d + x}{1 - mpc} \times r$$

and then substitute for r from the algebraic MP curve in Equation 1, $r = \overline{r} + \lambda\pi$, to yield the more general AD curve:

$$Y = [\overline{C} + \overline{I} - d\overline{f} + \overline{G} + \overline{NX} - mpc \times \overline{T}] \\ \times \frac{1}{1 - mpc} - \frac{d + x}{1 - mpc} \times (\overline{r} + \lambda\pi) \quad (4)$$

purchases, a fall in net exports, a rise in taxes, or a rise in financial frictions will cause the aggregate demand curve to shift to the left.

SHIFTS IN THE *MP* CURVE   We now examine what happens to the aggregate demand curve when the MP curve shifts. Suppose that the Bank of Canada decides to autonomously tighten monetary policy by raising the real interest rate by one percentage point at any given level of the inflation rate because it is worried about the economy overheating. At an inflation rate of 2.0%, the real interest rate rises from 2.0% to 3.0%, as in Figure 23-6. The MP curve shifts up from MP_1 to MP_2 in panel (a).

FIGURE 23-6   Shifts in the AD Curve from Autonomous Monetary Policy Tightening

Autonomous monetary tightening that raises real interest rates by one percentage point at any given inflation rate shifts the MP curve up from MP_1 to MP_2 in panel (a). With the inflation rate at 2.0%, the higher 3% interest rate results in a movement from point A_1 to A_2 on the IS curve, with output falling from $10 trillion to $9 trillion. This change in equilibrium output leads to movement from point A_1 to point A_2 in panel (c), shifting the aggregate demand curve to the left from AD_1 to AD_2.

(a) MP

(*Continued*)

FIGURE 23-6 *(Continued)*

(b) IS

Step 2. causing movement along the *IS* curve, decreasing equilibrium output . . .

(c) Aggregate Demand

Step 3. and shifting the *AD* curve leftward.

The Zero Lower Bound and Nonconventional Monetary Policy

As policy rates around the world have reached the zero lower bound in recent years, central banks are in a **liquidity trap**, unable to lower them further. Moreover, central banks have lost their usual ability to signal policy changes via changes in the policy rate and to lower long-term interest rates by lowering short-term interest rates.

With the policy rate at the zero lower bound, a decoupling of long- and short-term interest rates, and the possibility of a deflationary trap (that is, extremely low nominal interest rates and sustained deflation), central banks have departed from the traditional interest-rate targeting approach to monetary policy and are now considering new tools to steer their economies. As we discussed in Chapter 17, the Bank of Canada has identified three alternative instruments that it would consider using in an environment with low short-term (nominal) interest rates: forward guidance, quantitative easing, and credit easing. That is, central banks are switching from the "one tool, one target" mode of operation and are searching for new tools to steer their economies in an environment with interest rates at or near zero.

Panel (b) shows that when the inflation rate is at 2.0%, the higher interest rate results in the equilibrium moving from point A_1 to A_2 on the *IS* curve, with output falling from $10 trillion to $9 trillion. The lower output of $9 trillion occurs because the higher real interest leads to a decline in investment and net exports, which lowers aggregate demand. The lower output of $9 trillion then decreases the equilibrium output level from point A_1 to point A_2 in panel (c), and so the *AD* curve shifts to the left from AD_1 to AD_2.

Our conclusion from Figure 23-6 is that ***an autonomous tightening of monetary policy—that is, a rise in the real interest rate at any given inflation rate—shifts the aggregate demand curve to the left. Similarly, an autonomous easing of monetary policy shifts the aggregate demand curve to the right***.

We have now derived and analyzed the aggregate demand curve—an essential element in the aggregate demand and supply framework that we examine in the next chapter. We will use the aggregate demand curve in this framework to determine both aggregate output and inflation, as well as to examine events that cause these variables to change.

MyEconLab   MyEconLab is an online homework and tutorial system that puts you in control of your own learning with study and practice tools directly correlated to this chapter's content. Visit MyEconLab to explore the following resources:

- The Questions and Applied Problems are all available in the Study Plan on MyEconLab for further practice. You will also find the answers to all of the Questions and Applied Problems in the Student Resources section of your MyEconLab.

MyEconLab also features Additional Readings, Videos, Glossary Flashcards, Audio Chapter Summaries, Economics News Feeds, Animations, and many additional tools to help you master key concepts from the text.

SUMMARY

1. When the Bank of Canada lowers the overnight interest rate by providing more liquidity to the banking system, real interest rates fall in the short run; and when the Bank of Canada raises the overnight rate by reducing the liquidity in the banking system, real interest rates rise in the short run.

2. The monetary policy (*MP*) curve shows the relationship between inflation and the real interest rate arising from monetary authorities' actions. Monetary policy follows the Taylor principle, in which higher inflation results in higher real interest rates, as represented by a movement up along the monetary policy curve. An autonomous tightening of monetary policy occurs when monetary policymakers raise the real interest rate at any given inflation rate, resulting in an upward shift in the monetary policy curve. An autonomous easing of monetary policy and a downward shift in the monetary policy curve occurs when monetary policymakers lower the real interest rate at any given inflation rate.

3. The aggregate demand curve tells us the level of equilibrium aggregate output (which equals the total quantity of output demanded) for any given inflation rate. It slopes downward because a higher inflation rate leads the central bank to raise real interest rates, which leads to a lower level of equilibrium output. The aggregate demand curve shifts in the same direction as a shift in the *IS* curve; hence it shifts to the right when government purchases increase, taxes decrease, "animal spirits" encourage consumer and business spending, autonomous net exports increase, or financial frictions decrease. An autonomous tightening of monetary policy—that is, an increase in real interest rates at any given inflation rate—leads to a decline in aggregate demand and the aggregate demand curve shifts to the left.

MyEconLa
Audio Summ

KEY TERMS

aggregate demand curve, p. 562
autonomous easing of monetary policy, p. 561

autonomous tightening of monetary policy, p. 561
liquidity trap, p. 567

monetary policy (*MP*) curve, p. 559
Taylor principle, p. 559

QUESTIONS

1. When the inflation rate increases, what happens to the overnight interest rate? Operationally, how does the Bank of Canada adjust the overnight interest rate?

2. What is the key assumption underlying the Bank of Canada's ability to control the real interest rate?

3. Why is it necessary for the *MP* curve to have an upward slope?

4. If $\lambda = 0$, what does that imply about the relationship between the nominal interest rate and the inflation rate?

5. How does an autonomous tightening or easing of monetary policy by the Bank of Canada affect the *MP* curve?

6. How is an autonomous tightening or easing of monetary policy different from a change in the real interest rate due to a change in the current inflation rate?

7. Suppose that a new Bank of Canada governor is appointed, and his or her approach to monetary policy can be summarized by the following statement: "I care only about increasing employment; inflation has been at very low levels for quite some time; my priority is to ease monetary policy to promote employment." How would you expect the monetary policy curve to be affected, if at all?

8. "The Bank of Canada decreased the overnight interest rate in late 2007, even though inflation was increasing. This demonstrates a violation of the Taylor principle." Is this statement true, false, or uncertain? Explain your answer.

9. What factors affect the slope of the aggregate demand curve?

10. "Autonomous monetary policy is more effective at changing output when λ is higher." Is this statement true, false, or uncertain? Explain your answer.

11. If net exports were not sensitive to changes in the real interest rate, would monetary policy be more—or less—effective in changing output?

12. How does an autonomous tightening or easing of monetary policy by the Bank of Canada affect the aggregate demand curve?

13. For each of the following, describe how (if at all), the *IS* curve, *MP* curve, and *AD* curves are affected.

    a. A decrease in financial frictions.
    b. An increase in taxes, and an autonomous easing of monetary policy.
    c. An increase in the current inflation rate.
    d. A decrease in autonomous consumption.
    e. Firms become more optimistic about the future of the economy.
    f. The new Bank of Canada governor begins to care more about fighting inflation.

14. What would be the effect of an increase in Canadian net exports on the aggregate demand curve? Would an increase in net exports affect the monetary policy curve? Explain why or why not.

15. Why does the aggregate demand curve shift when "animal spirits" change?

16. If government spending increases while taxes are raised to keep the budget balanced, what happens to the aggregate demand curve?

17. Suppose that government spending is increased at the same time that an autonomous monetary policy tightening occurs. What will happen to the position of the aggregate demand curve?

18. "If $\bar{f}$ increases, then the Bank of Canada can keep output constant by reducing the real interest rate by the same amount as the increase in financial frictions." Is this statement true, false, or uncertain? Explain your answer.

APPLIED PROBLEMS

19. Assume the monetary policy curve is given by $r = 1.5 + 0.75\pi$.

    a. Calculate the real interest rate when the inflation rate is 2%, 3%, and 4%.
    b. Draw the graph of the *MP* curve, labelling the points from part (a).
    c. Assume now that the monetary policy curve is $r = 2.5 + 0.75\pi$. Does the new monetary policy curve represent an autonomous tightening or loosening of monetary policy?
    d. Calculate the real interest rate when the inflation rate is 2%, 3%, and 4%, and draw the new *MP* curve showing the shift from part (b).

20. Use an *IS* curve and an *MP* curve to derive graphically the *AD* curve.

21. Suppose the monetary policy curve is given by $r = 1.5 + 0.75\pi$, and the *IS* curve is $Y = 13 - r$.

    a. Calculate an expression for the aggregate demand curve.
    b. Calculate the real interest rate and aggregate output when the inflation rate is 2%, 3%, and 4%.
    c. Draw graphs of the *IS, MP,* and *AD* curves, labelling the points in the appropriate graphs from part (b) above.

22. Consider an economy described by the following:

$$\overline{C} = 4 \text{ trillion}$$
$$\overline{I} = 1.5 \text{ trillion}$$
$$\overline{G} = 3.0 \text{ trillion}$$
$$\overline{T} = 3.0 \text{ trillion}$$
$$\overline{NX} = 1.0 \text{ trillion}$$
$$\overline{f} = 0$$
$$mpc = 0.8$$
$$d = 0.35$$
$$x = 0.15$$
$$\lambda = 0.5$$
$$\overline{r} = 2$$

a. Derive expressions for the *MP* curve and *AD* curve.
b. Calculate the real interest rate and aggregate output when $\pi = 2$ and $\pi = 4$.
c. Draw a graph of the *MP* curve and *AD* curve, indicating the points in part (b) above.

23. Consider an economy described by the following:

$$\overline{C} = 3.25 \text{ trillion}$$
$$\overline{I} = 1.3 \text{ trillion}$$
$$\overline{G} = 3.5 \text{ trillion}$$
$$\overline{T} = 3.0 \text{ trillion}$$
$$\overline{NX} = -1.0 \text{ trillion}$$
$$\overline{f} = 1$$
$$mpc = 0.75$$
$$d = 0.3$$
$$x = 0.1$$
$$\lambda = 1$$
$$\overline{r} = 1$$

a. Derive expressions for the *MP* curve and *AD* curve.
b. Assume that $\pi = 1$. What is the real interest rate, equilibrium level of output, consumption, planned investment, and net exports?
c. Suppose the Bank of Canada increases $\overline{r}$ to $\overline{r} = 2$ Calculate what happens to the real interest rate, equilibrium level of output, consumption, planned investment, and net exports.
d. Considering that output, consumption, planned investment, and net exports all decreased in part (c), why might the Bank choose to increase $\overline{r}$?

24. Consider the economy described in Applied Problem 23.

a. Derive expressions for the *MP* curve and *AD* curve.
b. Assume that $\pi = 2$. What is the real interest rate and equilibrium level of output?
c. Suppose government spending increases to $4 trillion. What happens to equilibrium output?
d. If the Bank of Canada wanted to keep output constant, then what monetary policy change should occur?

25. Suppose the *MP* curve is given as $r = 2 + \pi$, and the *IS* curve is given as $Y = 20 - 2r$.

a. Derive an expression for the *AD* curve, and draw a graph labelling points at $\pi = 0$, $\pi = 4$, and $\pi = 8$.
b. Suppose that λ increases to $\lambda = 2$. Derive an expression for the new *AD* curve, and draw the new *AD* curve using the graph from part (a).
c. What does your answer to part (b) say about the relationship between a central bank's distaste for inflation and the slope of the *AD* curve?

WEB EXERCISES

1. Go to **http://www.bankofcanada.ca/monetary-policy-introduction/**. Review what the Bank of Canada says its goals are for monetary policy. Explain why these are consistent with the Taylor principle.

CHAPTER 24

Aggregate Demand and Supply Analysis

LEARNING OBJECTIVES

After studying this chapter you should be able to

1. interpret the aggregate demand and supply framework for the determination of the inflation rate and aggregate output

2. differentiate between short-run and long-run equilibria in the context of the aggregate demand and supply framework

PREVIEW In earlier chapters, we focused considerable attention on monetary policy, because it touches our everyday lives by affecting the prices of the goods we buy and the quantity of available jobs. In this chapter, we develop a basic tool, aggregate demand and supply analysis, that will enable us to study the effects of monetary policy on output and prices. *Aggregate demand* is the total amount of output demanded at different inflation rates. *Aggregate supply* is the total amount of output that firms in the economy want to sell at different inflation rates. As with the supply and demand analysis from your earlier economics courses, **equilibrium** occurs at the intersection of the aggregate demand and aggregate supply curves.

Aggregate demand and supply analysis will enable us to explore how aggregate output and inflation are determined. (The Financial News box indicates where and how often data on aggregate output and the inflation rate are published.) The analysis will help us interpret not only the past, but also recent episodes in the business cycle, such as the recent severe recession in 2007–2009.

Aggregate Demand

The first building block of aggregate supply and demand analysis is the **aggregate demand curve**, which describes the relationship between the quantity of aggregate output demanded and the inflation rate when all other variables are held constant.

Aggregate demand is made up of four component parts: **consumption expenditure**, the total demand for consumer goods and services; **planned**

FINANCIAL NEWS

Aggregate Output, Unemployment, and Inflation

Newspapers and Internet sites periodically report data that provide information on the level of aggregate output, unemployment, and the price level. Here is a list of the relevant data series, their frequency, and when they are published.

Aggregate Output and Unemployment

Real GDP: Quarterly; published about two months after the end of a quarter.

Industrial production: Monthly. Industrial production is not as comprehensive a measure of aggregate output as real GDP because it measures only manufacturing output: the estimate for the previous month is reported after about two months.

Unemployment rate: Monthly; the estimate for a month is reported two months later.

Price Level

GDP deflator: Quarterly. This comprehensive measure of the price level (described in the Appendix to Chapter 1) is published at the same time as the real GDP data.

Consumer price index (CPI): Monthly. The CPI is a measure of the price level for consumers (also described in the Appendix to Chapter 1); the value for the previous month is published in the third or fourth week of the following month.

Producer price index (PPI): Monthly. The PPI is a measure of the average level of wholesale prices charged by producers and is published in the third or fourth week of the following month.

---

investment spending,[1] the total planned spending by business firms on new machines, factories, and other capital goods, plus planned spending on new homes; **government purchases**, spending by all levels of government (federal, provincial, and local) on goods and services (paper clips, computers, computer programming, missiles, government workers, and so on); and **net exports**, the net foreign spending on domestic goods and services, equal to exports minus imports. Using the symbols C for consumption expenditure, I for planned investment spending, G for government spending, and NX for net exports, we can write the following expression for aggregate demand Y^{ad}:

$$Y^{ad} = C + I + G + NX \tag{1}$$

Deriving the Aggregate Demand Curve

The first step to deriving the aggregate demand curve is to recognize that when the inflation rate rises ($\pi\uparrow$), the monetary authorities will raise the real interest rate ($r\uparrow$) in order to keep inflation from spiralling out of control. Next we can examine the effects of higher real interest rates on the individual components of aggregate demand. The resulting higher cost of financing purchases of new physical capital makes investment less profitable and causes planned investment spending to decline ($I\downarrow$). Because, as shown in Equation 1, planned investment spending is included

---

[1] Recall that economists restrict use of the word *investment* to the purchase of new physical capital, such as a new machine or a new house, that adds to spending on newly produced goods or services. This differs from everyday use of the term by noneconomists who use the word *investment* to describe purchases of common stocks or bonds, purchases that do not necessarily involve newly produced goods and services. But when economists speak of investment spending, they are referring to the purchase of new physical assets such as new machines or new houses—purchases that add to aggregate demand.

FIGURE 24-1 Leftward Shift in the Aggregate Demand Curve

The aggregate demand curve shifts to the left from AD_1 to AD_2 when there is an autonomous tightening of monetary policy ($\bar{r}\uparrow$), a decrease in government purchases ($\bar{G}\downarrow$), an increase in taxes ($\bar{T}\uparrow$), a decrease in net exports ($\overline{NX}\downarrow$), a decrease in autonomous consumption expenditure ($\bar{C}\downarrow$), a decrease in autonomous investment ($\bar{I}\downarrow$), or an increase in financial frictions ($\bar{f}\uparrow$).

in aggregate demand, the decline in planned investment spending causes aggregate demand to fall ($Y^{ad}\downarrow$). A higher inflation rate therefore leads to a lower level of the quantity of aggregate output demanded ($\pi\uparrow \Rightarrow Y^{ad}\downarrow$), and so the aggregate demand curve slopes down as in Figure 24-1. Schematically, we can write the mechanism just described as follows:[2]

$$\pi\uparrow \Rightarrow r\uparrow \Rightarrow I\downarrow \Rightarrow Y^{ad}\downarrow$$

Factors That Shift the Aggregate Demand Curve

Seven basic factors (often referred to as **demand shocks**) can shift the aggregate demand curve to a new position: (1) autonomous monetary policy, (2) government purchases, (3) taxes, (4) autonomous net exports, (5) autonomous consumption expenditure, (6) autonomous investment, and (7) financial frictions. As we examine each case, we ask what happens when each of these factors changes holding the inflation rate constant. As a study aid, Summary Table 24-1 summarizes the shifts in the aggregate demand curve from each of these seven factors.

1. *Autonomous monetary policy.* We have already noted that when current inflation rises, the central bank will raise the real interest rate to keep inflation from spiralling out of control. However, there are central bank movements in the real interest rate that are autonomous, denoted by $\bar{r}$, which are movements unrelated to the variables in the model, such as the current level of the inflation rate. When the Bank of Canada decides to increase this autonomous component of the real interest rate, $\bar{r}$, the higher real interest rate at any given inflation rate leads to a

---

[2]If you have already read Chapters 22 and 23, this discussion of aggregate demand is just a recap of the analysis in those chapters. Note that an additional mechanism for a downward-sloping aggregate demand curve operates through net exports, as discussed in Chapters 22 and 23.

TABLE 24-1   Factors That Shift the Aggregate Demand Curve

Factor	Change	Shift in Aggregate Demand Curve
Autonomous monetary policy, $\bar{r}$	↑	*(graph: π vs Y, AD_2 left of AD_1)*
Government purchases, $\overline{G}$	↑	*(graph: π vs Y, AD_1 left of AD_2)*
Taxes, $\overline{T}$	↑	*(graph: π vs Y, AD_2 left of AD_1)*
Autonomous net exports, $\overline{NX}$	↑	*(graph: π vs Y, AD_1 left of AD_2)*
Autonomous consumption expenditure, $\overline{C}$	↑	*(graph: π vs Y, AD_2 left of AD_1)*
Autonomous investment, $\overline{I}$	↑	*(graph: π vs Y, AD_1 left of AD_2)*
Financial frictions, $\overline{f}$	↑	*(graph: π vs Y, AD_2 left of AD_1)*

Note: Only increases (↑) in the factors are shown. The effect of decreases in the factors would be the opposite of those indicated in the "Shift" column.

higher cost of financing investment projects, which leads to a decline in investment spending and the quantity of aggregate demand, as the following schematic demonstrates.

$$\bar{r}\uparrow \Rightarrow I\downarrow \Rightarrow Y^{ad}\downarrow$$

Therefore, aggregate demand falls at any given inflation rate and the aggregate demand curve shifts to the left as in Figure 24-1.

2. *Government purchases.* An increase in government purchases at any given inflation rate adds directly to aggregate demand expenditure, and hence aggregate demand rises:

$$\overline{G}\uparrow \Rightarrow Y^{ad}\uparrow$$

Aggregate demand, therefore, rises at any given inflation rate and the aggregate demand curve shifts to the right as in Figure 24-2.

3. *Taxes.* At any given inflation rate, an increase in taxes lowers disposable income, which will lead to lower consumption expenditure and aggregate demand, so that aggregate demand falls:

$$\overline{T}\uparrow \Rightarrow C\downarrow \Rightarrow Y^{ad}\downarrow$$

Aggregate demand falls at any given inflation rate and the aggregate demand curve shifts to the left as in Figure 24-1.

4. *Autonomous net exports.* An autonomous increase in net exports at any given inflation rate adds directly to aggregate demand and so raises aggregate demand:

$$\overline{NX}\uparrow \Rightarrow Y^{ad}\uparrow$$

Aggregate demand rises at any given inflation rate and the aggregate demand curve shifts to the right as in Figure 24-2.

5. *Autonomous consumption expenditure.* When consumers become more optimistic, autonomous consumption expenditure rises and so they spend more at any given inflation rate. Aggregate demand therefore rises:

$$\overline{C}\uparrow \Rightarrow Y^{ad}\uparrow$$

Aggregate demand rises at any given inflation rate, and the aggregate demand curve shifts to the right as in Figure 24-2.

6. *Autonomous investment.* When businesses become more optimistic, autonomous investment rises and they spend more at any given inflation rate. Planned investment increases, and aggregate demand rises:

$$\overline{I}\uparrow \Rightarrow Y^{ad}\uparrow$$

Aggregate demand rises at any given inflation rate, and the aggregate demand curve shifts to the right as in Figure 24-2.

7. *Financial frictions.* The real cost of borrowing reflects not only the real interest rate on default-free debt instruments, r, but also financial frictions, denoted by $\overline{f}$, which are additions to the real cost of borrowing because of asymmetric information problems in financial markets that were described in Chapter 8. When financial frictions increase, the real cost of borrowing increases, so that planned investment spending falls at any given inflation rate and aggregate demand falls:

$$\overline{f}\uparrow \Rightarrow Y^{ad}\downarrow$$

Aggregate demand falls at any given inflation rate, and the aggregate demand curve shifts to the left as in Figure 24-1.

The conclusion from this analysis is as follows: ***aggregate demand increases at any given inflation rate, and the aggregate demand curve shifts to the right when there is (1) an autonomous easing of monetary policy ($\overline{r}\downarrow$), (2) an increase in government purchases ($\overline{G}\uparrow$), (3) a decrease in taxes ($\overline{T}\downarrow$), (4) an increase in***

FIGURE 24-2 Rightward Shift in the Aggregate Demand Curve

The aggregate demand curve shifts to the right from AD_1 to AD_2 when there is an autonomous easing of monetary policy ($\bar{r}\downarrow$), an increase in government purchases ($\overline{G}\uparrow$), a decrease in taxes ($\overline{T}\downarrow$), an increase in net exports ($\overline{NX}\uparrow$), an increase in autonomous consumption expenditure ($\overline{C}\uparrow$), an increase in autonomous investment ($\overline{I}\uparrow$), or a decrease in financial frictions ($\bar{f}\downarrow$).

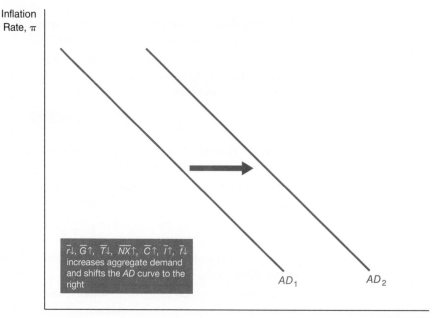

net exports $(\overline{NX}\uparrow)$, *(5) an increase in autonomous consumption expenditure $(\overline{C}\uparrow)$, (6) an increase in autonomous investment $\overline{I}\uparrow$, or (7) a decrease in financial frictions $(\bar{f}\downarrow)$. Conversely, the aggregate demand curve shifts to the left when any of these factors change in the opposite direction.*

Aggregate Supply

To complete our analysis we need to derive an **aggregate supply curve**, the relationship between the quantity of output supplied and the price level. In the typical supply and demand analysis, we have only one supply curve, but because prices and wages take time to adjust to their long-run level, the aggregate supply curve differs in the short and long runs. First, we examine the long-run aggregate supply curve. We then derive the short-run aggregate supply curve. Then we look at how both these curves shift over time and how the economy moves from the short run to the long run.

Long-Run Aggregate Supply Curve

The amount of output that can be produced in the economy in the long run is determined by the amount of capital in the economy, the amount of labour supplied at full employment, and the available technology. As discussed in Chapter 18, some unemployment cannot be helped because it is either frictional or structural. Thus at full employment, unemployment is not at zero, but is rather at a level above zero at which the demand for labour equals the supply of labour. This **natural rate of unemployment** is where the economy gravitates to in the long run. Many economists believe that the natural rate of unemployment is currently around 7%.

FIGURE 24-3 Long- and Short-Run Aggregate Supply Curves

The amount of aggregate output supplied at any given inflation rate is at potential output in the long run, so that the long-run aggregate supply curve *LRAS* is a vertical line at Y^P. The short-run aggregate supply curve, *AS*, is upward-sloping because as Y rises relative to Y^P, labour markets get tighter and inflation rises.

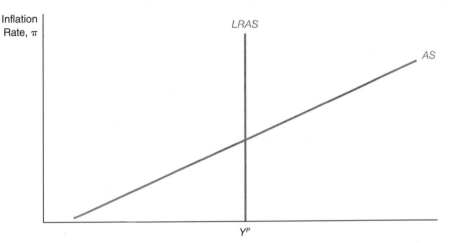

The level of aggregate output produced at the natural rate of unemployment is called the **natural rate of output** but is more often referred to as **potential output**: it is where the economy settles in the long run for any inflation rate. Hence the long-run aggregate supply curve $(LRAS)$ is vertical at potential output, denoted by Y^P, as drawn in Figure 24-3.

The long-run aggregate supply curve is vertical because potential output is independent of the price level and inflation rate. The reason for this is that in the long run the prices of goods and services (the price level) and the prices of the factors of production (most notably, the nominal wage rate) change in the same proportions, leaving the real wage rate constant at its full employment equilibrium. With no change in the real wage rate, employment remains constant and output remains constant at potential output, Y^P.

Short-Run Aggregate Supply Curve

The short-run aggregate supply curve is based on the intuition that three factors drive inflation: (1) expectations of inflation, (2) output gap, and (3) price (supply) shocks.

EXPECTED INFLATION, π^e Workers and firms care about wages in real terms—that is, in terms of the goods and services that wages can buy. When workers expect the price level to be rising, they will adjust nominal wages upward one-for-one with the rise in expected inflation, so that the real wage rate does not decrease. Because wages are the most important cost of producing goods and services, overall inflation will also rise one-for-one with increases in expected inflation.

OUTPUT GAP The **output gap** is defined as the difference between aggregate output and potential output, $Y - Y^P$. When output exceeds its potential level and the output gap is high, there is very little slack in the economy and workers will demand higher wages and firms will take the opportunity to raise prices. The result will be higher inflation. Conversely, when the output gap is negative, there will be a lot of slack in the economy and workers will accept smaller increases in wages and firms will need to lower prices to sell their goods, resulting in lower inflation. The short-run aggregate supply curve will therefore be upward-sloping, as is depicted in Figure 24-3, because the higher is aggregate output, the greater is the output gap, the less slack there is in the economy, and the higher inflation will be.

PRICE (SUPPLY) SHOCKS   **Supply shocks** occur when there are shocks to the supply of goods and services produced in the economy that translate into **price shocks**, that is, shifts in inflation that are independent of the amount of slack in the economy or expected inflation. For example, when supply of oil was restricted, as has occurred several times when wars have taken place in the Middle East, the resulting rise in the price of oil led firms to raise prices to reflect increased costs of production, thus driving up inflation. Energy price shocks can also occur when demand increases from developing countries like China, as occurred in 2007–2008 and again in 2011, again driving up inflation. Price shocks could also come from a rise in import prices or from **cost-push shocks**, in which workers push for wages higher than productivity gains, thereby driving up costs and inflation.

SHORT-RUN AGGREGATE SUPPLY CURVE   Putting all the analysis together results in a short-run aggregate supply curve that can be written as follows:

$$\pi = \pi^e + \gamma(Y - Y^P) + \rho$$
$$\text{Inflation} = \text{Expected} + \gamma \times \text{Output} + \text{Price} \qquad (2)$$
$$\text{Inflation} \qquad \qquad \text{Gap} \qquad \text{Shock}$$

where

$$\pi = \text{inflation,}$$
$$\pi^e = \text{expected inflation,}$$
$$Y - Y^P = \text{output gap,}$$
$$\gamma = \text{the sensitivity of inflation to the output gap,}$$
$$\rho = \text{price shock.}$$

The short-run aggregate supply curve in Equation 2 tells us that inflation is driven by three factors: (1) expectations of inflation, (2) output gaps, and (3) price shocks. Equation 2 also shows that the short-run aggregate supply curve is upward-sloping, as is shown in Figure 24-3, because a higher level of output Y means that the output gap, $Y - Y^P$, is higher, and this produces a higher level of inflation.

PRICE STICKINESS AND THE SHORT-RUN AGGREGATE SUPPLY CURVE   The short-run aggregate supply curve in Equation 2 implies that wages and prices are sticky, meaning that the aggregate price level adjusts slowly over time. The more flexible wages and prices are, the more they, and inflation, respond to deviations of output from potential output; that is, more flexible wages and prices imply that the absolute value of γ is higher, which implies that the short-run aggregate supply curve is steeper. If wages and prices are completely flexible, then γ becomes so large that the short-run aggregate supply curve is vertical, and it is identical to the long-run aggregate supply.

Shifts in Aggregate Supply Curves

Now that we have examined the long-run and short-run aggregate supply curves, we can look at why each of these curves shift.

FIGURE 24-4 Shift in the Long-Run Aggregate Supply Curve

The long-run aggregate supply curve shifts to the right from $LRAS_1$ to $LRAS_2$ when there is (1) an increase in the total amount of capital in the economy, (2) an increase in the total amount of labour supplied in the economy, (3) an increase in the available technology, or (4) a decline in the natural rate of unemployment. An opposite movement in these variables shifts the $LRAS$ curve to the left.

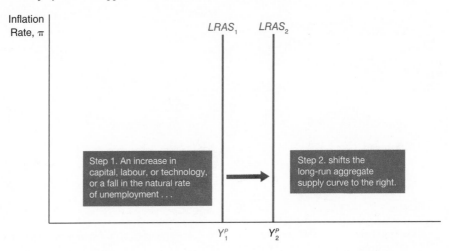

Shifts in the Long-Run Aggregate Supply Curve

The quantity of output supplied in the long run is determined by the three factors that cause potential output to change and thus shift the long-run aggregate supply curve: (1) the total amount of capital in the economy, (2) the total amount of labour supplied in the economy, and (3) the available technology that puts labour and capital together to produce goods and services. When any of these three factors increases, potential output rises, say, from Y_1^P to Y_2^P, and the long-run aggregate supply curve shifts to the right from $LRAS_1$ to $LRAS_2$, as in Figure 24-4.

Because all three of these factors typically grow fairly steadily over time, Y^P and the long-run aggregate supply curve will keep on shifting to the right at a steady pace. To keep things simple in diagrams later in this and following chapters, when Y^P is growing at a steady rate, we represent Y^P and the long-run aggregate supply curve as fixed.

Another source of shifts in the long-run aggregate supply curve is changes in the natural rate of unemployment. If the natural rate of unemployment declines, labour is being more heavily utilized, and so potential output will increase. A decline in the natural rate of unemployment thus shifts the long-run aggregate supply curve to the right from $LRAS_1$ to $LRAS_2$, as in Figure 24-4. A rise in the natural rate of unemployment would have the opposite effect, shifting the long-run aggregate supply curve to the left.

The conclusion from this analysis is as follows: ***the long-run aggregate supply curve shifts to the right when there is (1) an increase in the total amount of capital in the economy, (2) an increase in the total amount of labour supplied in the economy, (3) an increase in the available technology, or (4) a decline in the natural rate of unemployment. An opposite movement in these variables shifts the* LRAS *curve to the left.***

Shifts in the Short-Run Aggregate Supply Curve

The three terms on the right-hand side of Equation 2 for the short-run aggregate supply curve suggest that three factors can shift the short-run aggregate supply curve: (1) expected inflation, (2) price shocks, and (3) a persistent output gap. As a study aid, Summary Table 24-2 summarizes the shifts in the short-run aggregate supply curve from each of these three factors.

TABLE 24-2   Factors That Shift the Short-Run Aggregate Supply Curve

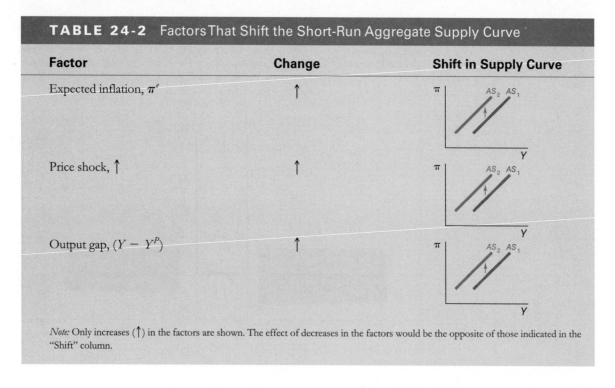

Factor	Change	Shift in Supply Curve
Expected inflation, π^e	↑	
Price shock, ↑	↑	
Output gap, $(Y - Y^P)$	↑	

Note: Only increases (↑) in the factors are shown. The effect of decreases in the factors would be the opposite of those indicated in the "Shift" column.

EXPECTED INFLATION   What if a newly appointed governor of the Bank of Canada does not think that inflation is costly and so is willing to tolerate an inflation rate that is two percentage points higher? Households and firms will then expect that the Bank of Canada will pursue policies that will let inflation rise by, say, two percentage points, in the future and will want to raise wages and prices by this amount. In such a situation, expected inflation will jump by two percentage points, and the short-run aggregate supply curve will shift upward and to the left from AS_1 to AS_2, as in Figure 24-5.

MyEconLab
Animation

FIGURE 24-5 Shift in the Short-Run Aggregate Supply Curve from Changes in Expected Inflation and Price Shocks

A rise in expected inflation or a positive price shock shifts the short-run aggregate supply curve upward from AS_1 to AS_2. (A decrease in expected inflation or a negative price shock would lead to a downward shift of the AS curve.)

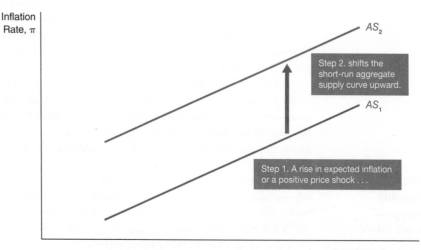

A rise in expected inflation causes the short-run aggregate supply curve to shift upward and to the left. Conversely, a decline in expected inflation causes the short-run aggregate supply curve to shift down and to the right. The larger is the change in expected inflation, the larger is the shift.

PRICE SHOCK   Suppose that energy prices suddenly shoot up because terrorists destroy a number of oil fields. This supply restriction (an unfavourable supply shock) causes the price shock term in Equation 2 to jump up, and so the short-run aggregate supply curve will shift up and to the left from AS_1 to AS_2, as in Figure 24-5. A favourable supply shock, which drives down prices, will have the opposite effect and cause the short-run aggregate supply curve to shift down and to the right. *Unfavourable supply shocks that drive up prices cause the short-run aggregate supply curve to shift up and to the left, while favourable supply shocks that lower prices cause the short-run aggregate supply curve to shift down and to the right.*

PERSISTENT OUTPUT GAP   We have already seen that a higher output gap leads to higher inflation, causing a movement along the short-run aggregate supply curve. We represent this movement from point 1 to point 2 on the initial short-run aggregate supply curve AS_1 in Figure 24-6. A persistent output gap, however, will cause the short-run aggregate supply curve to shift by affecting expected inflation. To see this, consider what happens if the aggregate output stays above potential output, $Y^2 > Y^P$, so the output gap remains persistently positive, say, at point 2 on the initial short-run aggregate supply curve, AS_1. Because inflation rises to π_2, expected

FIGURE 24-6   Shift in the Short-Run Aggregate Supply Curve from a Persistent Positive Output Gap

When output is above potential, the economy moves along the AS_1 curve from point 1 to point 2, and inflation rises to π_2. If output continues to remain above potential output, where the output gap is positive, the short-run aggregate supply curve shifts up to AS_2 and then to AS_3. The short-run aggregate supply curve stops shifting up when the economy reaches point 4 on the short-run aggregate supply curve, AS_4, where the output gap is zero.

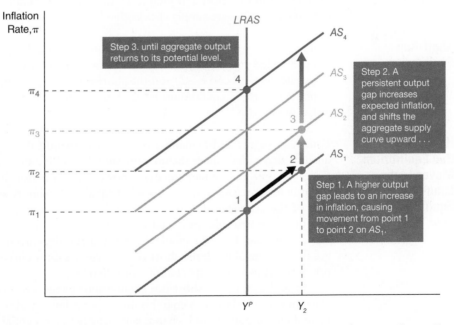

inflation will rise next period and so the short-run aggregate supply curve next period, AS_2, will then shift upward. If output remains above potential output at point 3, then inflation will rise further to π_3. As the vertical arrow indicates, the short-run aggregate supply curve will then shift upward to AS_3 next period.

When will the short-run aggregate supply curve stop rising? It will stop only when output returns to its potential level and the output gap disappears. Suppose this happens when inflation is at π_4 and aggregate output $Y = Y^P$. Because the output gap is zero, the aggregate supply curve drawn through point 4, AS_4, has no further reason to shift because inflation and expected inflation will stop rising.

The same reasoning indicates that if aggregate output is kept below potential for a period of time, $Y < Y^P$, then the short-run aggregate supply curve will shift downward and to the right. This downward shift of the aggregate supply curve will stop only when output returns to its potential level and the economy is back on the long-run aggregate supply curve.

Our analysis yields the following conclusion: ***when aggregate output is above potential output, so that a persistent positive output gap exists, the short-run aggregate supply curve shifts up and to the left. Conversely, when aggregate output falls below potential output, the short-run aggregate supply curve shifts down and to the right. Only when aggregate output returns to potential output does the short-run aggregate supply curve stop shifting***.

Equilibrium in Aggregate Demand and Supply Analysis

We can now put the aggregate demand and supply curves together to describe **general equilibrium** in the economy, when all markets are simultaneously in equilibrium at the point where the quantity of aggregate output demanded equals the quantity of aggregate output supplied. We represent general equilibrium graphically as the point where the aggregate demand curve intersects the aggregate supply curve. However, recall that we have two aggregate supply curves: one for the short run and one for the long run. Consequently, in the context of aggregate supply and demand analysis, there are short-run and long-run equilibriums. In this section, we illustrate equilibrium in the short and long runs. In following sections we examine aggregate demand and aggregate supply shocks that lead to changes in equilibrium.

Short-Run Equilibrium

Figure 24-7 illustrates a short-run equilibrium in which the quantity of aggregate output demanded equals the quantity of output supplied. In Figure 24-7, the short-run aggregate demand curve AD and the short-run aggregate supply curve AS intersect at point E with an equilibrium level of aggregate output at Y^* and an equilibrium inflation rate at π^*.

How the Short-Run Equilibrium Moves to the Long-Run Equilibrium over Time

Usually in supply and demand analysis, once we find the equilibrium at which the quantity demanded equals the quantity supplied, additional analysis is not needed. In *aggregate* supply and demand analysis, however, that is not the case. Even when the quantity of aggregate output demanded equals the quantity supplied at the intersection of the aggregate demand curve and the short-run aggregate supply curve, if output differs from its potential level ($Y^* \neq Y^P$), the short-run equilibrium will move over time. To understand why, recall that if the current level of inflation changes from its initial level, the short-run aggregate supply curve will shift as wages and prices adjust to a new expected rate of inflation.

We look at how the short-run equilibrium changes over time in response to two situations: when short-run equilibrium output is initially above potential output (the natural rate of output) and when it is initially below potential output.

MyEconLab
Animation

FIGURE 24-7 Short-Run Equilibrium

Short-run equilibrium occurs at point E at the intersection of the aggregate demand curve *AD* and the short-run aggregate supply curve *AS*.

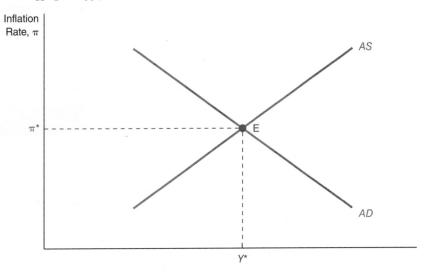

In panel (a) of Figure 24-8, the initial equilibrium occurs at point 1, the intersection of the aggregate demand curve *AD* and the initial short-run aggregate supply curve AS_1. The level of equilibrium output, Y_1, is greater than potential output Y^P, and there is excessive tightness in the labour market. Hence, the positive output gap at Y_1 drives wages up and causes firms to raise their prices at a more rapid rate. Inflation will then rise above the initial inflation rate, π_1. Hence, next period, firms and households adjust their expectations and expected inflation is higher. Wages and prices will then rise more rapidly, and the aggregate supply curve shifts up and to the left from AS_1 to AS_2.

The new short-run equilibrium at point 2 is a movement up the aggregate demand curve and output falls to Y_2. However, because aggregate output Y_2 is still above potential output Y^P, wages and prices increase at an even higher rate, so inflation again rises above its value last period. Expected inflation rises further, eventually shifting the aggregate supply curve up and to the left to AS_3. The economy reaches long-run equilibrium at point 3 on the vertical long-run aggregate supply curve (*LRAS*) at Y^P. Because output is at potential, there is no further pressure on inflation to rise and thus no further tendency for the aggregate supply curve to shift.

The movements in panel (a) indicate that the economy will not remain at a level of output higher than potential output over time. Specifically, the short-run aggregate supply curve will shift to the left, raise the inflation rate, and cause the economy (equilibrium) to move upward along the aggregate demand curve until it comes to rest at a point on the long-run aggregate supply curve (*LRAS*) at potential output Y^P.

In panel (b), at the initial equilibrium at point 1, output Y_1 is below the level of potential output. Because unemployment is now above its natural rate, there is excess slack in the labour markets. This slack at Y_1 decreases inflation, which decreases expected inflation and shifts the short-run aggregate supply curve in the next period down and to the right to AS_2.

The equilibrium will now move to point 2 and output rises to Y_2. However, because aggregate output Y_2 is still below potential, Y^P, inflation again declines from its value last period, shifting the aggregate supply curve down until it comes to rest

MyEconLab
Animation

FIGURE 24-8   Adjustment to Long-Run Equilibrium in Aggregate Supply and Demand
Analysis

In both panels, the initial short-run equilibrium is at point 1 at the intersection of *AD* and *AS*₁. In
panel (a), initial short-run equilibrium is above potential output, the long-run equilibrium, so the short-
run aggregate supply curve shifts upward until it reaches *AS*₃, where output returns to Y^P. In panel (b),
initial short-run equilibrium is below potential output, so the short-run aggregate supply curve shifts
down until output returns to Y^P. In both panels, the economy's self-correcting mechanism returns it
to the level of potential output.

(a) Initial short-run equilibrium above potential output

(b) Initial short-run equilibrium below potential output

MyEconLab
Animation

FIGURE 24-9 Positive Demand Shock

A positive demand shock shifts the aggregate demand curve upward from AD_1 to AD_2 and moves the economy from point 1 to point 2, resulting in higher inflation at π_2 and higher output of Y_2. Because output is greater than potential output and expected inflation increases, the short-run aggregate supply curve begins to shift up, eventually reaching AS_3. At point 3, the economy returns to long-run equilibrium, with output at Y^P and the inflation level rising to π_3.

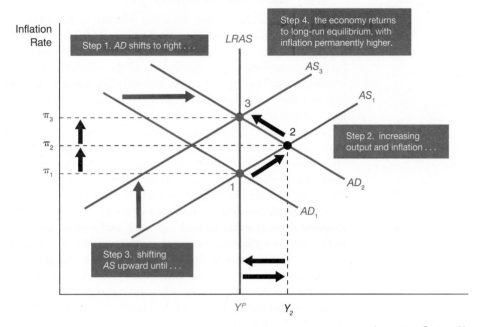

at AS_3. The economy (equilibrium) moves downward along the aggregate demand curve until it reaches the long-run equilibrium point 3, the intersection of the aggregate demand curve (AD) and the long-run aggregate supply curve ($LRAS$) at Y^P. Here, as in panel (a), the economy comes to rest when output has again returned to its potential level.

Self-Correcting Mechanism

Notice that in both panels of Figure 24-9, regardless of where output is initially, it returns eventually to potential output, a feature we call the **self-correcting mechanism**. The self-correcting mechanism occurs because the short-run aggregate supply curve shifts up or down to restore the economy to the long-run equilibrium at full employment (aggregate output at potential) over time.

Changes in Equilibrium: Aggregate Demand Shocks

With an understanding of the distinction between the short-run and long-run equilibria, you are now ready to analyze what happens when there are demand shocks, shocks that cause the aggregate demand curve to shift. Figure 24-9 depicts the effect of a rightward shift in the aggregate demand curve due to positive demand shocks caused by the following:

- An autonomous easing of monetary policy ($\bar{r}\downarrow$, a lowering of the real interest rate at any given inflation rate)
- An increase in government purchases ($\overline{G}\uparrow$)

- A decrease in taxes ($\overline{T}\downarrow$)
- An increase in net exports ($\overline{NX}\uparrow$)
- An increase in autonomous consumption expenditure ($\overline{C}\uparrow$)
- An increase in autonomous investment ($\overline{I}\uparrow$)
- A decrease in financial frictions ($\bar{f}\downarrow$)

Figure 24-9 shows the economy initially in long-run equilibrium at point 1, where the initial aggregate demand curve AD_1 intersects the short-run aggregate supply AS_1 curve at Y^P and the inflation rate at π_1. Suppose that consumers and businesses become more optimistic and the resulting increases in autonomous consumption and investment create a positive demand shock that shifts the aggregate demand curve to the right to AD_2. The economy moves up the short-run aggregate supply curve AS_1 to point 2, and both output and inflation rise to Y^2 and π_2, respectively. However, the economy will not remain at point 2 in the long run, because output at Y_2 is above potential output. Expected inflation will rise, and the short-run aggregate supply curve will eventually shift upward to AS_3. The economy (equilibrium) thus moves up the AD_2 curve from point 2 to point 3, which is the point of long-run equilibrium where inflation equals π_3 and output returns to Y^P. *Although the initial short-run effect of the rightward shift in the aggregate demand curve is a rise in both inflation and output, the ultimate long-run effect is only a rise in inflation because output returns to its initial level at Y^P.*[3]

We now turn to applying the aggregate demand and supply model to demand shocks, as a payoff for our hard work constructing the model. Throughout the remainder of this chapter, we will apply aggregate supply and demand analysis to a number of business cycle episodes, both in Canada and in foreign countries, over the past 40 years. To simplify our analysis, we always assume in all examples that aggregate output is initially at the level of potential output.

APPLICATION

The Bank of Canada Disinflation, 1981–1985

In the early 1980s, inflation in Canada had spun out of control and the inflation rate exceeded 12%. The Bank of Canada was determined to get inflation down. By early 1981, the Bank of Canada had raised short-term interest rates to over 20%, which led to a sharp increase in real interest rates. The Bank of Canada was indeed successful in bringing inflation down, as panel (b) of Figure 24-10 indicates, with the inflation rate falling from an average of 12.5% in 1981 to an average of 3.9% in 1985. The decline in inflation came at a high cost: in 1981–1982, the economy experienced the worst recession since World War II, with the unemployment rate increasing to over 12% in 1983.

---

[3]Note the analysis here assumes that each of these positive demand shocks occurs holding everything else constant, the usual *ceteris paribus* assumption that is standard in supply and demand analysis. Specifically this means that the central bank is assumed to not be responding to demand shocks. In the next chapter, we relax this assumption and allow monetary policymakers to respond to these shocks. As we will see, if monetary policymakers want to keep inflation from rising as a result of a positive demand shock, they will respond by autonomously tightening monetary policy.

FIGURE 24-10   The Bank of Canada Disinflation

Panel (a) shows that the Bank of Canada's actions to decrease inflation were successful but costly: the autonomous monetary policy tightening caused a negative demand shock that decreased aggregate demand and in turn inflation, resulting in soaring unemployment rates. The data in panel (b) support this analysis: note the decline in the inflation rate from 12.5% in 1981 to 3.9% in 1985, while the unemployment rate increased as high as 12% in 1983.

(a) Aggregate Demand and Aggregate Supply Analysis

(b) Unemployment and Inflation, 1981–1985

Year	Unemployment Rate (%)	Inflation (Year to Year) (%)
1981	7.6	12.5
1982	11.0	10.8
1983	11.9	5.8
1984	11.3	4.3
1985	10.5	3.9

Source: IMF International Financial Statistics and Statistics Canada CANSIM II series V2062815.

This outcome is exactly what our aggregate demand and supply analysis predicts. The autonomous tightening of monetary policy decreased aggregate demand and shifted the aggregate demand curve to the left from AD_1 to AD_2, as we show in panel (a) of Figure 24-10. The economy moved to point 2, indicating that unemployment would rise and inflation would fall. With unemployment above the natural rate and output below potential, the short-run aggregate supply curve shifted downward and to the right to AS_3. The economy moved toward long-run equilibrium at point 3, with inflation continuing to fall, output rising back to potential output, and the unemployment rate moving toward its natural rate level. Figure 24-10 panel (b) shows that by 1985 the unemployment rate had fallen (although not a lot) and the inflation rate was 3.9%, just as our aggregate demand and supply analysis predicts.

APPLICATION

Negative Demand Shocks in the United States, 2001–2004

In 2000, the U.S. economy was expanding when it was hit by a series of negative shocks to aggregate demand.

1. The "tech bubble" burst in March 2000, and the stock market fell sharply.
2. The September 11, 2001, terrorist attacks weakened both consumer and business confidence.

FIGURE 24-11 Negative Demand Shocks to the U.S. Economy, 2001–2004

Panel (a) shows that the negative demand shocks from 2001–2004 decreased consumption expenditure and investment, shifting the aggregate demand curve to the left from AD_1 to AD_2. The economy moved to point 2, where output fell, unemployment rose, and inflation declined. The large negative output gap when output was less than potential caused the short-run aggregate supply curve to begin falling to AS_3. The economy moved toward point 3, where output would return to potential: inflation declined further to π_3, and unemployment fell back again to its natural rate level of around 5%. The data in panel (b) support this analysis, with inflation declining to around 2% and the unemployment rate dropping back to 5.5% by 2004.

(b) Unemployment and Inflation, 2000–2004

Year	Unemployment Rate (%)	Inflation (Year to Year) (%)
2000	4.0	3.4
2001	4.7	2.8
2002	5.8	1.6
2003	6.0	2.3
2004	5.5	2.7

Source: Economic Report of the President.

3. The Enron bankruptcy in late 2001 and other corporate accounting scandals in 2002 revealed that corporate financial data were not to be trusted. Interest rates on corporate bonds rose as a result, making it more expensive for corporations to finance their investments.

All these negative demand shocks led to a decline in household and business spending, decreasing aggregate demand and shifting the aggregate demand curve to the left from AD_1 to AD_2 in panel (a) of Figure 24-11. At point 2, as our aggregate demand and supply analysis predicts, unemployment rose and inflation fell. Panel (b) of Figure 24-11 shows that the unemployment rate, which had been at 4% in 2000, rose to 6% in 2003, while the annual rate of inflation fell from 3.4% in 2000 to 1.6% in 2002. With unemployment above the natural rate (estimated to be around 5%) and output below potential, the short-run aggregate supply curve shifted downward to AS_3, as we show in panel (a) of Figure 24-11. The economy moved to point 3, with inflation falling, output rising back to potential output, and the unemployment rate returning to its natural rate level. By 2004, the self-correcting mechanism feature of aggregate demand and supply analysis began to come into play, with the unemployment rate dropping back to 5.5% (see panel (b) of Figure 24-11).

Changes in Equilibrium: Aggregate Supply (Price) Shocks

The aggregate supply curve can shift from temporary supply (price) shocks in which the long-run aggregate supply curve does not shift, or from permanent supply shocks in which the long-run aggregate supply curve does shift. We look at these two types of supply shocks in turn.

Temporary Supply Shocks

In our discussion of the short-run aggregate supply curve earlier in the chapter, we showed that inflation will rise independently of tightness in the labour markets or of increases in expected inflation when there is a temporary supply shock, such as a change in the supply of oil that causes prices to rise. When the temporary shock involves a restriction in supply, we refer to this type of supply shock as a *negative (or unfavourable) supply shock*, and it results in a rise in commodity prices. Examples of temporary negative supply shocks are a disruption in oil supplies, a rise in import prices when a currency declines in value, or a cost-push shock from workers pushing for higher wages that outpace productivity growth, driving up costs and inflation. When the supply shock involves an increase in supply, it is called a *positive (or favourable) supply shock*. Temporary positive supply shocks can come from a particularly good harvest or a fall in import prices.

To see how a temporary supply shock affects the economy using our aggregate supply and demand analysis, we start by assuming that the economy has output at its potential level of Y^P and inflation at π_1 at point 1 in Figure 24-12. Suppose that a temporary negative supply shock occurs because of a war in the Middle East. When the negative supply shock hits the economy and oil prices rise, the price shock term ρ causes inflation to rise above π_1, and the short-run aggregate supply curve shifts up and to the left from AS_1 to AS_2.

The economy will move up the aggregate demand curve from point 1 to point 2, where inflation rises above π_1 but aggregate output *falls* below Y^P. We call a

MyEconLab
Animation

FIGURE 24-12 Temporary Negative Supply Shock

A temporary negative supply shock shifts the short-run aggregate supply curve from AS_1 to AS_2 and the economy moves from point 1 to point 2, where inflation increases to π_2 and output declines to Y_2. Because output is less than potential, the negative output gap lowers inflation and the short-run aggregate supply curve begins to shift back down, eventually returning to AS_1, where the economy is again at the initial long-run equilibrium at point 1.

situation of rising inflation but a falling level of aggregate output, as pictured in Figure 24-12, **stagflation** (a combination of the words *stagnation* and *inflation*). Because the supply shock is temporary, productive capacity in the economy does not change, and so Y^P and the long-run aggregate supply curve *LRAS* remains stationary. At point 2, output is therefore below its potential level at Y_2, so inflation falls and shifts the short-run aggregate supply curve back down to where it was initially at AS_1. The economy (equilibrium) slides down the aggregate demand curve AD_1 (assuming that the aggregate demand curve remains in the same position) and returns to the long-run equilibrium at point 1 where output is again at Y^P and inflation is at π_1.

Although a temporary negative supply shock leads to an upward and leftward shift in the short-run aggregate supply curve, which raises inflation and lowers output initially, the ultimate long-run effect is that output and inflation are unchanged.

A favourable (positive) supply shock—say, an excellent harvest of wheat in the Prairie provinces—moves all the curves in Figure 24-12 in the opposite direction and so has the opposite effects. *A temporary positive supply shock shifts the short-run aggregate supply curve downward and to the right, leading initially to a fall in inflation and a rise in output. In the long run, however, output and inflation will be unchanged (holding the aggregate demand curve constant).*

We now will once again apply the aggregate demand and supply model, this time to temporary supply shocks to the Canadian economy. We begin with negative supply shocks in 1973–1975 and 1978–1980. (Recall that we assume that aggregate output is initially at its potential level.)

APPLICATION

Negative Supply Shocks, 1973–1975 and 1978–1980

In 1973, the Canadian and world economies were hit by a series of negative supply shocks:

1. As a result of the oil embargo stemming from the Arab–Israeli war of 1973, the Organization of Petroleum Exporting Countries (OPEC) engineered a quadrupling of oil prices by restricting oil production.

2. A series of crop failures throughout the world led to a sharp increase in food prices.

These events shifted the short-run aggregate supply curve sharply upward and to the left from AS_1 to AS_2 in panel (a) of Figure 24-13, and the economy moved to

FIGURE 24-13 Negative Supply Shocks, 1973–1975 and 1978–1980

Panel (a) shows that the temporary negative supply shocks in 1973 and 1979 led to an upward shift in the short-run aggregate supply curve from AS_1 to AS_2. The economy moved to point 2, where output fell, and both unemployment and inflation rose. The data in panel (b) support this analysis.

(b) Unemployment and Inflation, 1973–1975 and 1978–1980

Year	Unemployment Rate (%)	Inflation (Year to Year) (%)
1973	5.6	9.4
1974	5.3	14.6
1975	6.9	10.3
1978	8.3	6.5
1979	7.4	9.5
1980	7.5	10.9

Source: IMF International Financial Statistics and Statistics Canada CANSIM II series V2062815.

point 2. As the aggregate demand and supply diagram in Figure 24-13 predicts, both inflation and unemployment rose as per panel (b) of Figure 24-13.

The 1978–1980 period was almost an exact replay of the 1973–1975 period. By 1978, the economy had just about fully recovered from the 1973–1975 supply shocks, when poor harvests and a doubling of oil prices (as a result of the overthrow of the Shah of Iran) again led to another sharp upward and leftward shift of the short-run aggregate supply curve in 1979. The pattern predicted by Figure 24-13 played itself out again—inflation and unemployment both shot upward.

Permanent Supply Shocks and Real Business Cycle Theory

But what if the supply shock is not temporary? A permanent negative supply shock—such as an increase in ill-advised regulations that causes the economy to be less efficient, thereby reducing supply—would decrease potential output from, say, Y_1^P to Y_2^P and shift the long-run aggregate supply curve to the left from $LRAS_1$ to $LRAS_2$ in Figure 24-14.

Because the permanent supply shock will result in higher prices, there will be an immediate rise in inflation, and so the short-run aggregate supply curve will shift up and to the left from AS_1 to AS_2. Although output at point 2 has fallen to Y_2, it is still above Y_2^P: the positive output gap means that the aggregate supply curve will shift up and to the left. It continues to do so until it reaches AS_3 at the intersection with the aggregate demand curve AD and the long-run aggregate supply curve $LRAS_2$. Now because output is at Y_2^P at point 3, the output gap is zero and at an inflation rate of π_3 no further upward pressure on inflation occurs.

FIGURE 24-14 Permanent Negative Supply Shock

A permanent negative supply shock leads initially to a decline in output and a rise in inflation. In the long run, it leads to a permanent decline in output and a permanent rise in inflation, as indicated by point 3, where inflation has risen to π_3 and output has fallen to Y_2^P.

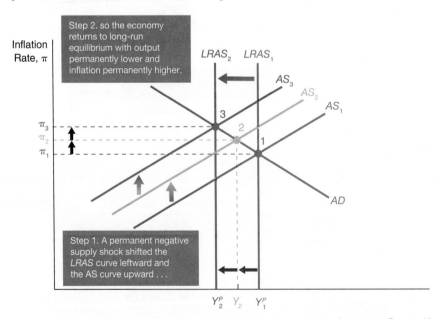

One group of economists, led by Edward Prescott of Arizona State University, believes that business cycle fluctuations result from permanent supply shocks alone, and their theory of aggregate economic fluctuations is called **real business cycle theory**. This theory views shocks to tastes (workers' willingness to work, for example) and technology (productivity) as the major driving forces behind short-run fluctuations in the business cycle, because these shocks lead to substantial short-run fluctuations in Y^P. Shifts in the aggregate demand curve, perhaps as a result of changes in monetary policy, by contrast, are not viewed as being particularly important to aggregate output fluctuations. Because real business cycle theory views most business cycle fluctuations as resulting from fluctuations in the level of potential output, it does not see much need for policies to eliminate high unemployment. Real business cycle theory is highly controversial and is the subject of intensive research.

Figure 24-14 generates the following result when we hold the aggregate demand curve constant: *a permanent negative supply shock leads initially to both a decline in output and a rise in inflation. However, in contrast to a temporary supply shock, in the long run the negative supply shock, which results in a fall in potential output, leads to a permanent decline in output and a permanent rise in inflation.*[4]

The opposite conclusion follows from a positive supply shock, say, because of the development of new technology that raises productivity. *A permanent positive supply shock lowers inflation and raises output both in the short run and in the long run.*

To this point, we have assumed that potential output Y^P and hence the long-run aggregate supply curve are given. However, over time, the potential level of output increases as a result of economic growth. If the productive capacity of the economy is growing at a steady rate of 3% per year, for example, every year Y^P will grow by 3% and the long-run aggregate supply curve at Y^P will shift to the right by 3%. To simplify the analysis, when Y^P grows at a steady rate, we represent Y^P and the long-run aggregate supply curve as fixed in the aggregate demand and supply diagrams. Keep in mind, however, that the level of aggregate output pictured in these diagrams is actually best thought of as the level of aggregate output relative to its normal rate of growth (trend).

The 1995–1999 period serves as an illustration of permanent positive supply shocks, as the following Application indicates.

APPLICATION

Positive Supply Shocks, 1995–1999

In February 1994, the Bank of Canada began to raise interest rates. It believed the economy would be reaching potential output and the natural rate of unemployment in 1995, and it might become overheated thereafter, with output climbing above potential and inflation rising. As we can see in panel (b) of Figure 24-15, however, the economy continued to grow rapidly, with the unemployment rate falling to below 7% in 1997. Also, inflation declined to around 1% in 1998, although the Bank of Canada was targeting the inflation rate at 2%.

---

[4]The results on the effect of permanent supply shocks assume that monetary policy is not changing, so that the aggregate demand curve remains unchanged. Monetary policymakers, however, might want to shift the aggregate demand curve to keep inflation at the same level. For example, see the following chapter.

FIGURE 24-15 Positive Supply Shocks, 1995–1999

Panel (a) shows that the positive supply shocks from the rise in productivity from the computer revolution led to a rightward shift in the long-run aggregate supply curve from $LRAS_1$ to $LRAS_2$ and a downward shift in the short-run aggregate supply curve from AS_1 to AS_2. The economy moved to point 2, where aggregate output rose, and unemployment and inflation fell. The data in panel (b) support this analysis: note that the unemployment rate fell from 9.4% in 1995 to 7.5% in 1999, while the inflation rate fell from 2.0% in 1995 to 1.0% in 1998.

(a) Aggregate Demand and Aggregate Supply Analysis

Step 2. and leads to a permanent rise in output and a permanent decrease in inflation.

Step 1. A permanent positive supply shock shifts *LRAS* rightward and *AS* downward . . .

(b) Unemployment and Inflation, 1995–1999

Year	Unemployment Rate (%)	Inflation (Year to Year) (%)
1995	9.4	2.0
1996	9.6	2.0
1997	8.5	2.0
1998	8.2	1.0
1999	7.5	2.0

Can aggregate demand and supply analysis explain what happened? One permanent positive supply shock hit the economy in the late 1990s. In particular, the computer revolution finally began to impact productivity favourably, raising the potential growth rate of the economy (which journalists dubbed the "new economy"). In addition, demographic factors, such as an increase in the relative number of older workers who are less likely to be unemployed, led to a fall in the natural rate of unemployment. These factors led to a rightward shift in the long-run aggregate supply curve to $LRAS_2$ and a downward and rightward shift in the short-run aggregate supply curve from AS_1 to AS_2, as shown in panel (a) of Figure 24-15. Aggregate output rose, and unemployment fell, while inflation also declined.

Conclusions   Aggregate demand and supply analysis yields the following conclusions:[5]

1. A shift in the aggregate demand curve—caused by changes in autonomous monetary policy (changes in the real interest rate at any given inflation rate), government purchases, taxes, autonomous net exports, autonomous consumption expenditure, autonomous investment or financial frictions—affects output only in the short run and has no effect in the long run. Furthermore, the initial change in inflation is lower than the long-run change in inflation when the short-run aggregate supply curve has fully adjusted.

2. A temporary supply shock affects output and inflation only in the short run and has no effect in the long run (holding the aggregate demand curve constant).

3. A permanent supply shock affects output and inflation both in the short and in the long run.

4. The economy has a self-correcting mechanism that returns it to potential output and the natural rate of unemployment over time.

AD/AS Analysis of Foreign Business Cycle Episodes

Our aggregate demand and supply analysis also can help us understand business cycle episodes in foreign countries. Here we look at three: the experience of the United States with both negative supply and demand shocks during the 2007–2009 global financial crisis, the business cycle experience of the United Kingdom during the 2007–2009 financial crisis, and the quite different experience of China during the same period.

APPLICATION

The United States and the 2007–2009 Financial Crisis

At the beginning of 2007, higher demand for oil from rapidly growing developing countries like China and India and slowing of production in places like Mexico, Russia, and Nigeria drove up oil prices sharply from around the $60 per barrel level. By the end of 2007, oil prices had risen to $100 per barrel and reached a peak of over $140 in July 2008. The run-up of oil prices, along with increases in other commodity prices, led to a negative supply shock that shifted the short-run aggregate supply curve in panel (a) of Figure 24-16 sharply upward from AS_1 to AS_2. To make matters worse, a financial crisis hit the economy starting in August 2007, causing a sharp increase in financial frictions, which led to contraction in both household and business spending (discussed in Chapter 9). This negative demand shock shifted the aggregate demand curve to the left from AD_1 to AD_2 in panel (a) of Figure 24-16 and moved the economy to point 2. These shocks led to a rise in the unemployment rate, a rise in the inflation rate, and a decline in output, as point 2 indicates. As our aggregate demand and supply analysis predicts, this perfect storm of negative shocks led to a recession starting in December 2007, with the unemployment rate rising from the 4.6% level in 2006 and 2007 to 5.5% by June 2008, and with the inflation rate rising from 2.5% in 2006 to 5% in June 2008 (see panel (b) of Figure 24-16).

---

[5]The aggregate demand and supply analysis can also be used to understand the effects of macroeconomic shocks on asset prices. This analysis can be found in the second Web Appendix for this chapter that is on the Companion Website at MyEconLab.

FIGURE 24-16 Negative Supply and Demand Shocks in the United States and the 2007–2009 Crisis

Panel (a) shows that the negative price shock from the rise in the price of oil shifted the short-run aggregate supply curve up from AS_1 to AS_2, while a negative demand shock from the financial crisis led to a sharp contraction in spending, resulting in the aggregate demand curve moving from AD_1 to AD_2. The economy thus moved to point 2, where a sharp contraction occurred in aggregate output, which fell to Y_2, and a rise in unemployment, while inflation rose to π_2. The fall in oil prices shifted the short-run aggregate supply curve back down to AS_1, while the deepening financial crisis shifted the aggregate demand curve to AD_3. As a result, the economy moved to point 3, where inflation fell to π_3 and output to Y_3. The data in panel (b) support this analysis: note that unemployment in the United States rose from 4.6% in 2006 to 5.5% in June 2008, while inflation rose from 2.5% to 5.0%. Then in the aftermath of the financial crisis and the decline of oil prices, by the end of 2009 U.S. unemployment rate rose to 10%, while inflation fell to 2.8%.

(a) Aggregate Demand and Aggregate Supply Analysis

(b) Unemployment and Inflation During the Perfect Storm of 2007–2009

Year	Unemployment Rate (%)	Inflation (Year to Year) (%)
2006	4.6	2.5
2007	4.6	4.1
2008, June	5.5	5.0
2008, Dec.	7.2	0.1
2009, June	9.5	−1.2
2009, Dec.	10.0	2.8

Source: Economic Report of the President.

After July 2008, oil prices fell sharply, shifting short-run aggregate supply back downward to AS_1. However, in the fall of 2008, the financial crisis entered a particularly virulent phase following the bankruptcy of Lehman Brothers, decreasing aggregate demand sharply to AD_3. As a result, the economy moved to point 3, with the unemployment rate rising to 10% by the end of 2009, while the inflation rate fell to 2.8% (see panel (b) of Figure 24-16).

APPLICATION

The United Kingdom and the 2007–2009 Financial Crisis

As in the United States, the rise in the price of oil in 2007 led to a negative supply shock. In Figure 24-17 panel (a), the short-run aggregate supply curve shifted up from AS_1 to AS_2 in the United Kingdom. The financial crisis did not at first have

FIGURE 24-17 U.K. Financial Crisis, 2007–2009

Panel (a) shows that a supply shock in 2007 from rising oil prices shifted the short-run aggregate supply curve up and to the left from AS_1 to AS_2 in the United Kingdom. The economy moved to point 2. With output below potential and oil prices falling after July 2008, the short-run aggregate supply curve began to shift down to AS_1. A negative demand shock following the escalating financial crisis after the Lehman Brothers bankruptcy shifted the aggregate demand curve to the left to AD_2. The economy now moved to point 3, where output fell to Y_3, unemployment rose, and inflation decreased to π_3. The data in panel (b) support this analysis: note that the unemployment rate increased from 5.4% in 2006 to 7.8% in December 2009, while the inflation rate rose from 2.3% to 3.9% and then fell to 2.1% over this same time period.

(a) Aggregate Demand and Aggregate Supply Analysis

(b) Unemployment and Inflation, 2006–2009

Year	Unemployment Rate (%)	Inflation (Year to Year) (%)
2006	5.4	2.3
2007	5.3	2.3
2008, June	5.3	3.4
2008, Dec.	6.4	3.9
2009, June	7.8	2.1
2009, Dec.	7.8	2.1

Source: Office of National Statistics, UK. www.statistics.gov.uk/statbase/tsdtimezone.asp.

a large impact on spending, so the aggregate demand curve did not shift and equilibrium instead moved from point 1 to point 2 on AD_1. The aggregate demand and supply framework indicates that inflation would rise, which is what occurred (see the increase in the inflation rate from 2.3% in 2007 to 3.9% in December 2008 in panel (b) of Figure 24-17). With output below potential and oil prices falling after July 2008, the short-run aggregate supply curve shifted down to AS_1. At the same time, the financial crisis after the Lehman Brothers bankruptcy impacted spending worldwide, causing a negative demand shock that shifted the aggregate demand curve to the left to AD_2. The economy now moved to point 3, with a further fall in output, a rise in unemployment, and a fall in inflation. As the aggregate demand and supply analysis predicts, the U.K. unemployment rate rose to 7.8% by the end of 2009, with the inflation rate falling to 2.1%.

APPLICATION

China and the 2007–2009 Financial Crisis

The financial crisis that began in August 2007 at first had very little impact on China.[6] When the financial crisis escalated in the United States in the fall of 2008 with the collapse of Lehman Brothers, all this changed. China's economy had been driven by extremely strong exports, which up until September of 2008 had been growing at over a 20% annual rate. Starting in October 2008, Chinese exports collapsed, falling at around a 20% annual rate through August 2009.

The negative demand shock from the collapse of exports led to a decline in aggregate demand, shifting the aggregate demand curve to AD_2 and moving the economy from point 1 to point 2 in Figure 24-18 panel (a). As aggregate demand and supply analysis indicates, China's economic growth slowed from over 11% in the first half of 2008 to under 5% in the second half, while inflation declined from 7.9% to 4.4%, and then became negative thereafter (see panel (b) of Figure 24-18).

Instead of relying solely on the economy's self-correcting mechanism, the Chinese government proposed a massive fiscal stimulus package of $580 billion in 2008, which at 12.5% of GDP was three times larger than the U.S. fiscal stimulus package relative to GDP. In addition, the People's Bank of China, the central bank, began taking measures to autonomously ease monetary policy. These decisive actions shifted the aggregate demand curve back to AD_1 and the Chinese economy very quickly moved back to point 1. The Chinese economy thus weathered the financial crisis remarkably well, with output growth rising rapidly in 2009 and inflation becoming positive thereafter.

---

[6]Note that just as in the rest of the world, China experienced an increase in energy prices that initially shifted up the short-run aggregate supply curve. Hence, as in the U.K., in 2007 the Chinese economy experienced a rise in inflation and a slight slowing of growth. This is not depicted in Figure 24-18 as it was in Figure 24-17 because doing so would have made Figure 24-18 too complex.

FIGURE 24-18 China and the Financial Crisis, 2007–2009

Panel (a) shows that the collapse of Chinese exports starting in 2008 led to a negative demand shock that shifted the aggregate demand curve to AD_2, moving the economy to point 2, where output growth fell below potential and inflation declined. A massive fiscal stimulus package and autonomous easing of monetary policy shifted the aggregate demand curve back to AD_1, and the economy very quickly moved back to long-run equilibrium at point 1. The data in panel (b) support this analysis: note that output growth slowed but then bounced back again, and inflation began to fall at a less rapid rate.

(a) Aggregate Demand and Aggregate Supply Analysis

Step 1. A negative demand shock shifted *AD* leftward . . .

Step 4. and restored long-run equilibrium values for inflation and output.

Step 3. A fiscal stimulus package increased *AD* . . .

Step 2. decreasing output and lowering inflation.

(b) Chinese Output Growth and Inflation, 2006–2009

Year	Output Growth (%)	Inflation (Year to Year) (%)
2006	11.8	1.5
2007	12.4	4.8
2008, June	11.2	7.9
2008, Dec.	4.4	3.9
2009, June	11.1	−1.1
2009, Dec.	10.4	−0.3

Source: International Monetary Fund. 2010. International Financial Statistics. Country Tables, February. http://www. imfstatistics.org/IMF/imfbrowser.aspx?docList=pdfs&path=ct%2f20100201%2fct_pdf%2f20100121_CHN.pdf.

MyEconLab MyEconLab is an online homework and tutorial system that puts you in control of your own learning with study and practice tools directly correlated to this chapter's content. Visit MyEconLab to explore the following resources:

- The Questions and Applied Problems are all available in the Study Plan on MyEconLab for further practice. You will also find the answers to all of the Questions and Applied Problems in the Student Resources section of your MyEconLab.

- Visit the Student Resources section of MyEconLab to access the following appendices for this chapter: Appendix 24.1: The Effects of Macroeconomic Shocks on Asset Prices; Appendix 24.2: Aggregate Demand and Supply: A Numerical Example; Appendix 24.3: The Algebra of the Aggregate Demand and Supply Model; Appendix 24.4: The Taylor Principle and Inflation Stability.

MyEconLab also features Additional Readings, Videos, Glossary Flashcards, Audio Chapter Summaries, Economics News Feeds, Animations, and many additional tools to help you master key concepts from the text.

SUMMARY

1. The aggregate demand curve indicates the quantity of aggregate output demanded at each inflation rate, and it is downward sloping. The primary sources of shifts in the aggregate demand curve are (1) autonomous monetary policy, (2) government purchases, (3) taxes, (4) net exports, (5) autonomous consumption expenditure, (6) autonomous investment, and (7) financial frictions.

2. The long-run aggregate supply curve is vertical at potential output. The long-run aggregate supply curve shifts when technology changes, when there are long-run changes to the amount of labour or capital, or when the natural rate of unemployment changes. The short-run aggregate supply curve slopes upward because inflation rises as output rises relative to potential output. The short-run supply curve shifts when there are price shocks, changes in expected inflation, or persistent output gaps.

3. Equilibrium in the short run occurs at the point where the aggregate demand curve intersects the short-run aggregate supply curve. Although this is where the economy heads temporarily, the self-correcting mechanism leads the economy to settle permanently at the long-run equilibrium where aggregate output is at its potential. Shifts in either the aggregate demand curve or the short-run aggregate supply curve can produce changes in aggregate output and inflation.

4. A positive demand shock shifts the aggregate demand curve to the right and initially leads to a rise in both inflation and output. However, in the long run it leads only to a rise in inflation, because output returns to its initial level at Y^P.

5. A temporary positive supply shock leads to a downward and rightward shift in the short-run aggregate supply curve, which lowers inflation and raises output initially. However, in the long run, output and inflation are unchanged. A permanent positive supply shock leads initially to both a rise in output and a decline in inflation. However, in contrast to a temporary supply shock, in the long run the permanent positive supply shock, which results in a rise in potential output, leads to a permanent rise in output and a permanent decline in inflation.

6. Aggregate supply and demand analysis is also just as useful for analyzing foreign business cycle episodes as it is for domestic business cycle episodes.

KEY TERMS

aggregate demand curve, p.571

aggregate supply curve, p. 576

consumption expenditure, p. 571

cost-push shocks, p. 578

demand shocks, p. 573

equilibrium, p. 571

general equilibrium, p. 582

government purchases, p. 572

natural rate of output, p. 577

natural rate of unemployment, p. 576

net exports, p. 572

output gap, p. 577

planned investment spending, p. 571

potential output, p. 577

price shocks, p. 578

real business cycle theory, p. 593

self-correcting mechanism, p. 585

stagflation, p. 590

supply shocks, p. 578

QUESTIONS

1. Explain why the aggregate demand curve slopes downward and the short-run aggregate supply curve slopes upward.

2. Identify changes in three factors that will shift the aggregate demand curve to the right and changes in three different factors that will shift the aggregate demand curve to the left.

3. "The depreciation of the Canadian dollar from December 2008 to December 2009 had a positive effect on aggregate demand in the United States." Is this statement true, false, or uncertain? Explain your answer.

4. What determines the unemployment rate when output is at potential?

5. As the labour force becomes more productive over time, how does that affect the long-run aggregate supply curve?

6. Why are central banks so concerned about inflation expectations?

7. "If prices and wages are perfectly flexible, then $\gamma = 0$, and changes in aggregate demand have a smaller effect on output." Is this statement true, false, or uncertain? Explain your answer.

8. What factors shift the short-run aggregate supply curve? Do any of these factors shift the long-run aggregate supply curve? Why?

9. If large budget deficits cause the public to think that there will be higher inflation in the future, what is likely to happen to the short-run aggregate supply curve when budget deficits rise?

10. Internet sites that allow people to post their resumés reduce the cost of a job search. How do you think the Internet has affected the natural rate of unemployment?

11. When aggregate output is below the natural rate of output, what will happen to the inflation rate over time if the aggregate demand curve remains unchanged? Why?

12. Suppose that the public believes that a newly announced anti-inflation program will work and so lowers its expectations of future inflation. What will happen to aggregate output and the inflation rate in the short run?

13. If the unemployment rate is above the natural rate of unemployment, holding other factors constant, what will happen to inflation and output?

14. What happens to inflation and output in the short run and the long run when government spending increases?

15. What factors led to a decrease in both the unemployment rate and the inflation rate in the 1990s?

16. Are there any "good" supply shocks?

17. Why did the Federal Reserve pursue inherently recessionary policies in the early 1980s?

18. In what ways is the Bank of Canada disinflation considered a success? What are the negative aspects of it?

19. Why did China fare much better than the United States and the United Kingdom during the 2007–2009 financial crisis?

APPLIED PROBLEMS

20. Using an aggregate demand and supply graph, show and describe the effects in both the short run and the long run of the following:

    a. A temporary negative supply shock.
    b. A permanent negative supply shock.

21. Many of the resources devoted to the fiscal stimulus packages by governments around the world during the global financial crisis encouraged investment in research and development of new technologies (e.g., more fuel-efficient cars, wind and solar power) and infrastructure investment (roads, bridges, and transportation networks). Assuming this policy results in a positive productivity change for the economy, what does aggregate demand and supply analysis predict in terms of inflation and output? Use a graph to demonstrate.

22. Predict the effect of an increase in sales taxes on both the aggregate supply and demand curves, showing the effects on output and inflation. Use a graph of aggregate supply and demand to demonstrate.

23. Suppose the inflation rate remains relatively constant, and output decreases and the unemployment rate increases. Using an aggregate demand and supply graph, show how this is possible.

24. Classify each of the following as a supply or demand shock. Use a graph to show the effects on inflation and output in the short run and the long run.

    a. Financial frictions increase.
    b. Households and firms become more optimistic about the economy.
    c. Favourable weather produces a record crop of wheat and corn in the Prairie provinces.
    d. Steel workers go on strike for four weeks.

25. During the first half of 2010, Bank of Canada officials discussed the possibility of increasing interest rates as a way of fighting potential increases in expected inflation. If the public came to expect higher inflation rates in the future, what would be the effect on the short-run aggregate supply curve? Show your answer, using an aggregate demand and supply graph.

WEB EXERCISES

1. Go to **www.bankofcanada.ca** and follow the link to employment statistics. What has happened to the unemployment rate since the end of the Great Recession in July 2009?

2. As the CPI inflation rate in Canada fell close to 1% at the beginning of 2009, Bank of Canada policymakers were beginning to be concerned about deflation. Go to **www.bankofcanada.ca**, and follow the link to the inflation statistics.

   a. What happened to the inflation rate since then?
   b. Does deflation still appear to be a threat?

CHAPTER 25

Monetary Policy Theory

LEARNING OBJECTIVES

After studying this chapter you should be able to

1. examine the role of monetary policy in creating inflation and stabilizing the economy
2. address the question of whether monetary policy should be activist or passive

PREVIEW
Between November 2007 and April 2009, the Bank of Canada lowered the target for its policy interest rate, the overnight interest rate, from 4.5% all the way down to 0.25% and continued to keep it around 1% for years afterwards. Why did the Bank of Canada lower interest rates this aggressively and continue to keep them so low?

Could this monetary policy easing spark undesirable inflation? Many commentators in the media thought so. Starting in the early 1960s, when the inflation rate hovered between 1% and 2%, the economy has suffered from higher and more variable rates of inflation. By 1974, it reached the double-digit level. After moderating somewhat during the 1976–1978 period, it shot close to 13% in 1981, slowed to around 4% from 1984 to 1988, declined further to less than 2% in the early 1990s, and then climbed to above 4% in 2003. Inflation has become a major concern of politicians and the public, and how to control it frequently dominates the discussion of economic policy.

In this chapter, we use the aggregate demand–aggregate supply (AD/AS) framework developed in Chapter 24 to develop a theory of monetary policy. Specifically, we will examine the role of monetary policy in creating inflation and stabilizing the economy. We apply the theory to three big questions: what are the roots of inflation? Does stabilizing inflation stabilize output? Should policy be *activist*—by responding aggressively to fluctuations in economic activity—or passive and *nonactivist*?

Response of Monetary Policy to Shocks

As we saw in Chapter 18, the central goal of central banks is price stability: that is, they try to maintain inflation, π, close to a target level (π^T), referred to as an **inflation target**, that is slightly above zero. Most central banks, like the Bank of Canada, set

π^T between 1% and 3%. An alternative way to think about how the central bank pursues price stability is that monetary policy should try to minimize the difference between inflation and the inflation target $(\pi - \pi^T)$, which we refer to as the **inflation gap**.

In Chapter 18, we learned that central banks also care about stabilizing economic activity. Because economic activity can be sustained only at potential output, this objective of monetary policy can be described as saying that monetary policymakers want to have aggregate output close to its potential level, Y^P. Another way of saying this is that central banks want to minimize the difference between aggregate output and potential output $(Y - Y^P)$, i.e., the output gap. In our analysis of aggregate demand and supply in Chapter 24, we examined three categories of economic shocks—demand shocks, temporary supply shocks, and permanent supply shocks—and the consequences of each on inflation and output. In this section, we describe a central bank's policy responses, given its objectives, to each of these shocks. In the case of both demand shocks and permanent supply shocks, policymakers can simultaneously pursue price stability and stability in economic activity. Following a temporary supply shock, however, policymakers can achieve either price stability or economic activity stability, but not both. This trade-off poses a thorny dilemma especially for central banks with dual mandates, like the Federal Reserve in the United States.

Response to an Aggregate Demand Shock

We begin by considering the effects of an aggregate demand shock, such as the disruption to financial markets starting in August 2007 that increased financial frictions and caused both consumer and business spending to fall. The economy is initially at point 1, where output is at Y^P and inflation is at π^T. The negative demand shock decreases aggregate demand, shifting AD_1 in Figure 25-1 to the left to AD_2. Policymakers can respond to this shock in two possible ways.

FIGURE 25-1 Aggregate Demand Shock: No Policy Response

An aggregate demand shock shifts the aggregate demand curve leftward from AD_1 to AD_2 and moves the economy from point 1 to point 2, where aggregate output falls to Y_2 while inflation falls to π_2. With output below potential, the short-run aggregate supply curve shifts down to AS_3, and the economy moves to point 3, where output is back at Y^P, but inflation has fallen to π_3.

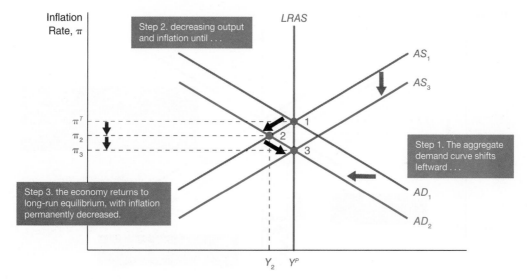

NO POLICY RESPONSE   Because the central bank does not respond by changing the autonomous component of monetary policy, the aggregate demand curve remains at AD_2 and so the economy goes to the intersection of AS_1 and AD_2. Here, aggregate output falls to Y_2, below potential output Y^P, and inflation falls to π_2, below the inflation target of π^T. With output below potential, slack begins to develop in the labour and product markets, lowering inflation. The short-run aggregate supply curve will shift down and to the right to AS_3, and the economy will move to point 3. Output will again be back at its potential level, while inflation will fall to a lower level of π_3. At first glance, this outcome looks favourable—inflation is lower and output is back at its potential. But aggregate output will remain below potential for some time, and if inflation was initially at its target level, the fall in inflation is undesirable for reasons outlined in both Chapter 9 and Chapter 18.

POLICY STABILIZES ECONOMIC ACTIVITY AND INFLATION IN THE SHORT RUN
Policymakers can eliminate both the output gap and the inflation gap in the short run by pursuing policies to increase aggregate demand to its initial level and return the economy to its preshock state. The central bank does this by autonomously easing monetary policy by cutting the real interest rate at any given inflation rate. This action stimulates investment spending and increases the quantity of aggregate output demanded at any given inflation rate, thereby shifting the AD curve to the right. As a result, the aggregate demand curve shifts from AD_2 back to AD_1 in Figure 25-2, and the economy returns to point 1. (The Federal Reserve in the United States took exactly these steps by lowering the federal funds rate from 5% to $\frac{1}{4}$% to zero over 15 months starting in September 2007.)

Our analysis of this monetary policy response shows that *in the case of aggregate demand shocks, there is no tradeoff between the pursuit of price stability and economic*

FIGURE 25-2 Aggregate Demand Shock: Policy Stabilizes Output and Inflation in the Short Run

An aggregate demand shock shifts the aggregate demand curve leftward from AD_1 to AD_2 and moves the economy from point 1 to point 2, where aggregate output falls to Y_2 while inflation falls to π_2. An autonomous easing of monetary policy lowers the real interest rate at any given inflation rate and shifts the AD curve back to AD_1. Aggregate output returns to potential at point 1 and inflation returns to its target level.

activity stability. A focus on stabilizing inflation leads to exactly the right monetary policy response to stabilize economic activity. No conflict exists between the dual objectives of stabilizing inflation and economic activity, which Olivier Blanchard (formerly of MIT, but now at the International Monetary Fund) referred to as the **divine coincidence**.

APPLICATION

Quantitative (Credit) Easing in Response to the Global Financial Crisis

We have seen that monetary policymakers can counter aggregate demand shocks and stabilize output and inflation by lowering the real interest rate. However, sometimes the negative aggregate demand shock is so large that at some point the central bank cannot lower the real interest rate further because the nominal interest rate hits a floor of zero, as occurred after the Lehman Brothers bankruptcy in late 2008. In this situation when the zero-lower-bound problem arises, the central bank must turn to nonconventional monetary policy of the type that has been discussed in Chapter 17. Although these nonconventional monetary policy measures involve liquidity provision and asset purchases, which result in an expansion of the central bank balance sheet and so are typically referred to as *quantitative easing*, they are more accurately characterized as *credit easing*. How did quantitative (credit) easing work to stabilize output and inflation during the global financial crisis?

As we saw in Chapter 9, after the Lehman Brothers collapse, the real cost of borrowing to both households and businesses shot up because financial frictions rose dramatically ($\bar{f}\uparrow$). The higher real cost of borrowing led to a decline in consumption expenditure and planned investment spending, thereby causing a sharp contraction in aggregate demand and a leftward shift of the aggregate demand curve to AD_2, as in Figure 25-2. Although the Federal Reserve autonomously lowered the federal funds rate to the zero lower bound, this was insufficient to shift the aggregate demand curve back to AD_1. By engaging in asset purchases and liquidity provision, the Fed was able to reduce financial frictions ($\bar{f}\downarrow$) and lower the real cost of borrowing to households and businesses. The result was that the aggregate demand curve did shift out to the right as shown in Figure 25-2, thereby avoiding deflation and boosting economic activity so that the economy did not enter a depression, as in the 1930s. However, the negative aggregate demand shock to the economy from the global financial crisis was so great that the Fed's quantitative (credit) easing was insufficient to overcome it, and the Fed was unable to shift the aggregate demand curve all the way back to AD_1. Hence, despite the Federal Reserve's efforts, the economy still suffered a severe recession, with inflation in the United States below the 2% level.

Response to a Permanent Supply Shock

We illustrate a permanent supply shock in Figure 25-3. Again the economy starts out at point 1, where aggregate output is at the natural rate Y_1^P and inflation is at π^T. Suppose the economy suffers a permanent negative supply shock because an increase in regulations permanently reduces the level of potential output. Potential output falls from Y_1^P to Y_3^P, and the long-run aggregate supply curve shifts leftward

FIGURE 25-3 Permanent Supply Shock: No Policy Response

A permanent negative supply shock decreases potential output from Y_1^P to Y_3^P, and the long-run aggregate supply curve shifts to the left from $LRAS_1$ to $LRAS_3$, while the short-run aggregate supply curve shifts upward from AS_1 to AS_2. The economy moves to point 2, with inflation rising to π_2 and output falling to Y_2. Because aggregate output is still above potential, the short-run aggregate supply curve would keep on shifting until the output gap is zero when it reached AS_3. The economy moves to point 3, where inflation rises to π_3 while output falls to Y_3^P.

from $LRAS_1$ to $LRAS_3$. The permanent supply shock triggers a price shock that shifts the short-run aggregate supply curve upward from AS_1 to AS_2. Two possible policy responses to this permanent supply shock are possible.

NO POLICY RESPONSE If policymakers leave autonomous monetary policy unchanged, the economy will move to point 2, with inflation rising to π_2 and output falling to Y_2. Because this level of output is still higher than potential output, Y_3^P, the short-run aggregate supply curve keeps shifting up and to the left until it reaches AS_3, where it intersects AD_1 on $LRAS_3$. The economy moves to point 3, eliminating the output gap but leaving inflation higher at π_3 and output lower at Y_3^P.

POLICY STABILIZES INFLATION According to Figure 25-4, monetary authorities can keep inflation at the target inflation rate and stabilize inflation by decreasing aggregate demand. The goal is to shift the aggregate demand curve leftward to AD_3, where it intersects the long-run aggregate supply curve $LRAS_3$ at the target inflation rate of π^T. To shift the aggregate demand to AD_3, the monetary authorities would autonomously tighten monetary policy by increasing the real interest rate at any given inflation rate, thus causing investment spending to fall and lowering aggregate demand at any given inflation rate. The economy thus goes to point 3, where the output gap is zero and inflation is at the target level of π^T.

Here again, keeping the inflation gap at zero leads to a zero output gap, so stabilizing inflation has stabilized economic activity. ***The divine coincidence still remains***

FIGURE 25-4   Permanent Supply Shock: Policy Stabilizes Inflation

A permanent negative supply shock decreases potential output from Y_1^P to Y_3^P, and the long-run aggregate supply curve shifts to the left from $LRAS_1$ to $LRAS_3$, while the short-run aggregate supply curve shifts upward from AS_1 to AS_2. An autonomous tightening of monetary policy shifts the aggregate demand curve to the left to AD_3, thereby keeping the inflation rate π^T at point 3.

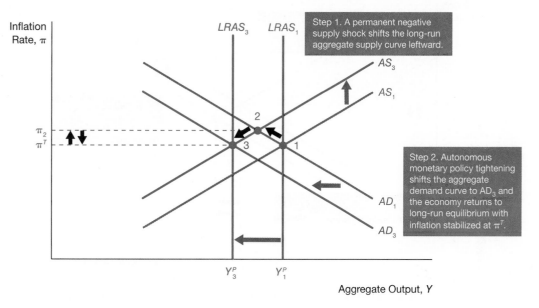

true when a permanent supply shock occurs: there is no tradeoff between the dual objectives of stabilizing inflation and economic activity.

Response to a Temporary Supply Shock

When a supply shock is temporary, such as when the price of oil surges because of political unrest in the Middle East or because of an act of god, such as a devastating hurricane, the divine coincidence does not always hold. Policymakers face a short-run tradeoff between stabilizing inflation and economic activity. To illustrate, we start the economy at point 1 in Figure 25-5, where aggregate output is at the natural rate Y^P and inflation is at π^T. The negative supply shock, say, a rise in the price of oil, shifts the short-run aggregate supply curve up and to the left from AS_1 to AS_2 but leaves the long-run aggregate supply curve unchanged because the shock is temporary. The economy moves to point 2, with inflation rising to π_2 and output falling to Y_2. Policymakers can respond to the temporary supply shock in three possible ways.

NO POLICY RESPONSE   One policy choice is not to make an autonomous change in monetary policy, so the aggregate demand curve does not shift. Since aggregate output is less than potential output Y^P, eventually the short-run aggregate supply curve will shift back down to the right, returning to AS_1. The economy will return to point 1 in Figure 25-5 and close both the output and inflation gaps, as output and inflation return to the initial levels of Y^P and π^T. Both inflation and economic activity stabilize over time. ***In the long run, there is no tradeoff between the two objectives, and the divine coincidence holds.*** While we wait for the long run, however, the economy will undergo a painful period of reduced output and higher inflation rates. This opens the door to monetary policy to try to stabilize economic activity or inflation in the short run.

FIGURE 25-5 Response to a Temporary Aggregate Supply Shock: No Policy Response

A temporary negative supply shock shifts the short-run aggregate supply curve upward from AS_1 to AS_2, moving the economy to point 2, with inflation rising to π_2 and output falling to Y_2. If the autonomous monetary policy remains unchanged, the short-run aggregate supply curve will shift back down and to the right in the long run, eventually returning to AS_1, and the economy moves back to point 1.

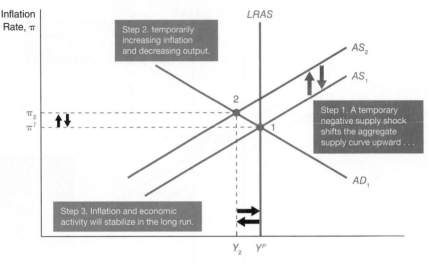

POLICY STABILIZES INFLATION IN THE SHORT RUN A second policy choice for monetary authorities is to keep inflation at the target level of π^T in the short run by autonomously tightening monetary policy and raising the real interest rate at any given inflation rate. Doing so would cause investment spending and aggregate demand to fall at each inflation rate, shifting the aggregate demand curve to the left to AD_3 in Figure 25-6. The economy now moves to point 3, where the aggregate demand curve, AD_3, intersects the short-run aggregate supply curve AS_2 at an inflation rate of π^T. Because output is below potential at point 3, the slack in the economy shifts the short-run aggregate supply curve back down to AS_1. To keep the inflation rate at π^T, the monetary authorities will need to move the short-run aggregate demand curve back to AD_1 by reversing the autonomous tightening and eventually, the economy will return to point 1.

As Figure 25-6 illustrates, stabilizing inflation reduces aggregate output to Y_3 in the short run, and only over time will output return to potential output at Y^P. *Stabilizing inflation in response to a temporary supply shock has led to a larger deviation of aggregate output from potential, so this action has not stabilized economic activity.*

POLICY STABILIZES ECONOMIC ACTIVITY IN THE SHORT RUN A third policy is for monetary policymakers to stabilize economic activity rather than inflation in the short run by increasing aggregate demand. According to Figure 25-7, now they would shift the aggregate demand curve to the right to AD_3, where it intersects the short-run aggregate supply curve AS_2 and the long-run aggregate supply at point 3. To do this, they would have to autonomously ease monetary policy by lowering the real interest rate at any given inflation rate. At point 3, the output gap returns to zero, so monetary policy has stabilized economic activity. However, inflation has risen to π_3, which is greater than π^T, so inflation has not been stabilized. *Stabilizing economic activity in response to a temporary supply shock results in a rise in inflation, so inflation has not been stabilized.*

FIGURE 25-6 Response to a Temporary Aggregate Supply Shock: Short-Run Inflation Stabilization

A temporary negative supply shock shifts the short-run aggregate supply curve from AS_1 to AS_2, moving the economy to point 2, with inflation rising to π_2 and output falling to Y_2. Autonomous tightening of monetary policy shifts the aggregate demand curve to the left to AD_3, and the economy moves to point 3, where inflation is at π^T. With output below potential at point 3, the short-run aggregate supply curve shifts back to AS_1, and to keep the inflation rate at π^T, the autonomous tightening of monetary policy is reversed, shifting the aggregate demand curve back to AD_1 and the economy back to point 1.

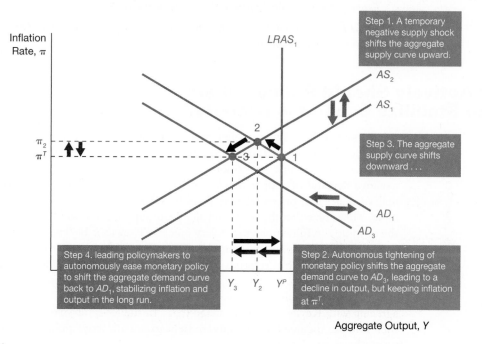

FIGURE 25-7 Response to a Temporary Aggregate Supply Shock: Short-Run Output Stabilization

A temporary negative supply shock shifts the short-run aggregate supply curve from AS_1 to AS_2, moving the economy to point 2, with inflation rising to π_2 and output falling to Y_2. To stabilize output, autonomous monetary policy easing shifts the aggregate demand curve rightward to AD_3. At point 3, the monetary policy action has stabilized economic activity, but at π_3 inflation is greater than π^T.

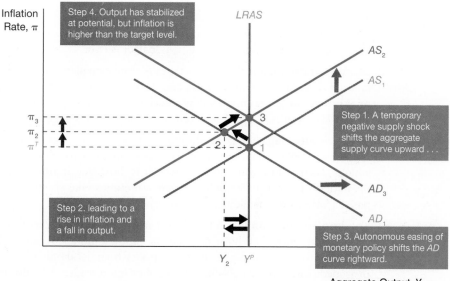

The Bottom Line: The Relationship Between Stabilizing Inflation and Stabilizing Economic Activity

We can draw the following conclusions from this analysis:

1. *If most shocks to the economy are aggregate demand shocks or permanent aggregate supply shocks, then policy that stabilizes inflation will also stabilize economic activity, even in the short run.*

2. *If temporary supply shocks are more common, then a central bank must choose between the two stabilization objectives in the short run.*

3. *In the long run there is no conflict between stabilizing inflation and economic activity in response to shocks.*

How Actively Should Policymakers Try to Stabilize Economic Activity?

All economists have similar policy goals (to promote high employment and price stability), yet they often disagree on the best approach to achieve those goals. Suppose policymakers confront an economy that has high unemployment resulting from a negative demand or supply shock that has reduced aggregate output. **Nonactivists** believe wages and prices are very flexible, so the self-correcting mechanism is very rapid. They argue that the short-run aggregate supply curve will shift down, returning the economy to full employment very quickly. They thus believe government action is unnecessary to eliminate unemployment. **Activists**, many of whom are followers of Keynes and are thus referred to as **Keynesians**, regard the self-correcting mechanism through wage and price adjustment as very slow because wages and prices are sticky. As a result, they believe it takes a very long time to reach the long run, agreeing with Keynes's famous adage that "In the long run, we are all dead." They therefore see the need for the government to pursue active policy to eliminate high unemployment when it develops.

Lags and Policy Implementation

If policymakers could shift the aggregate demand curve instantaneously, activist policies could be used to immediately move the economy to the full-employment level, as we have seen in the previous section. However, several types of lags prevent this immediate shift from occurring, and there are differences in the length of these lags for monetary versus fiscal policy.

1. The **data lag** is the time it takes for policymakers to obtain data indicating what is happening in the economy. Accurate data on GDP, for example, are not available until several months after a given quarter is over.

2. The **recognition lag** is the time it takes for policymakers to be sure of what the data are signalling about the future course of the economy. For example, to minimize errors, the government will not declare the economy to be in recession until at least six months after it has determined that one has begun.

3. The **legislative lag** represents the time it takes to pass legislation to implement a particular policy. The legislative lag does not exist for most monetary policy actions, such as lowering interest rates. It is, however, important for the implementation of fiscal policy, when it can sometimes take six months to a year to pass legislation to change taxes or government purchases.

4. The **implementation lag** is the time it takes for policymakers to change policy instruments once they have decided on the new policy. Again, this lag is less important for the conduct of monetary policy than fiscal policy because the Bank of Canada can immediately change its policy interest rate. Actually implementing

fiscal policy may take substantial time, however; for example, getting government agencies to change their spending habits takes time, as does changing tax tables.

5. The **effectiveness lag** is the time it takes for the policy actually to have an impact on the economy. The effectiveness lag is both long (often a year or longer) and variable (that is, there is substantial uncertainty about how long this lag is).

The existence of all these lags makes the policymakers' job far more difficult and therefore weakens the case for activism. When unemployment is high, activist policy to shift the aggregate demand curve rightward to restore the economy to full employment may not produce desirable outcomes. Indeed, if the policy lags described above are very long, then by the time the aggregate demand curve shifts to the right, the self-correcting mechanism may have already returned the economy to full employment, so when the activist policy kicks in it may cause output to rise above potential, leading to a rise in inflation. In the situation where policy lags are longer than the time it takes the self-correcting mechanism to work, a policy of nonactivism may produce better outcomes.

The activist/nonactivist debate came to the fore when the Obama administration advocated a fiscal stimulus package early in its administration in 2009 (see the FYI box The Activist/Nonactivist Debate over the Obama Fiscal Stimulus Package in the United States). In Chapter 26, we will return to the issue of how active policy should be, when we look at the role expectations play in monetary policy.

FYI

The Activist/Nonactivist Debate over the Obama Fiscal Stimulus Package in the United States

When President Obama entered office in January 2009, he faced a very serious recession, with unemployment over 7% and rising rapidly. Although policymakers had been using monetary policy aggressively to stabilize the economy, many activists argued that the government needed to do more by implementing a massive fiscal stimulus package. They argued that monetary policy, which had already lowered the federal funds rate to close to zero and so could not lower nominal interest rates further, would be unable to increase aggregate demand to the full-employment level. On the other hand, nonactivists opposed the fiscal stimulus package, arguing that fiscal stimulus would take too long to work because of long implementation lags. They cautioned that if the fiscal stimulus kicked in after the economy had already recovered, it could lead to increased volatility in inflation and economic activity.

The economics profession is split over the desirability of fiscal stimulus. Approximately 200 economists who supported fiscal stimulus in the United States signed a petition published in *The Wall Street Journal* and *The New York Times* on January 28, 2009. An opposing petition, also signed by about 200 economists, appeared on February 8. The Obama administration came down squarely on the side of the activists and proposed the American Recovery and Reinvestment Act of 2009, a $787 billion fiscal stimulus package that the U.S. Congress passed on February 13, 2009. Even after the fact, the desirability of the 2009 stimulus package is hotly debated, with some indicating it helped stabilize the economy while others believe it was not effective.

Inflation: Always and Everywhere a Monetary Phenomenon

Milton Friedman is famous for his adage that in the long run "Inflation is always and everywhere a monetary phenomenon." Here we will see that this adage is supported by our aggregate demand and supply analysis because it shows that monetary policy-makers can target any inflation rate in the long run by shifting the aggregate demand curve with autonomous monetary policy. To illustrate, look at Figure 25-8, where the economy is at point 1, with aggregate output at potential output Y^P and inflation at an initial inflation target of π_1^T.

Suppose the central bank believes this inflation target is too low and chooses to raise it to π_3^T. It eases monetary policy autonomously by lowering the real interest rate at any given inflation rate, thereby increasing investment spending and aggregate demand. In Figure 25-8, the aggregate demand curve shifts to AD_3. The economy would then move to point 2 at the intersection of AD_3 and AS_1, with inflation rising to π_2. Because aggregate output is above potential output $Y_2 > Y^P$, the short-run aggregate supply curve would shift up and to the left, eventually stopping at AS_3, with the economy moving to point 3, where inflation is at the higher target level of π_3^T and the output gap is back at zero.

The analysis in Figure 25-8 demonstrates the following key points:

1. *The monetary authorities can target any inflation rate in the long run with autonomous monetary policy adjustments.*

2. *Potential output—and therefore the quantity of aggregate output produced in the long run—is independent of monetary policy.*

FIGURE 25-8 A Rise in the Inflation Target

To raise the inflation target to π_3^T, the central bank undertakes an autonomous monetary policy easing, of lowering the real interest rate at any given inflation rate, thereby shifting the aggregate demand curve rightward to AD_3. The economy would then move to point 2 and the short-run aggregate supply curve would shift up and to the left, eventually stopping at AS_3, moving the economy to point 3, with the output gap at zero and inflation at π_3^T.

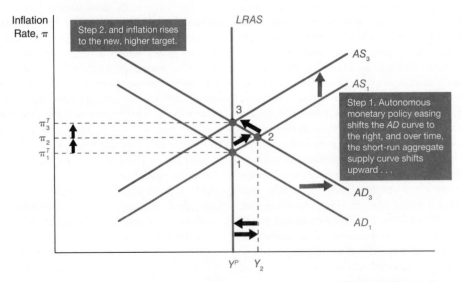

Causes of Inflationary Monetary Policy

If everyone agrees that high inflation is bad for an economy, why do we see so much of it? Do governments pursue inflationary monetary policies intentionally? We have seen that monetary authorities can set the inflation rate in the long run, so it must be that in trying to achieve other goals, governments end up with overly expansionary monetary policy and high inflation. In this section, we will examine the government policies that are the most common sources of inflation.

High Employment Targets and Inflation

The primary goal of most governments is high employment, and the pursuit of this goal can bring high inflation. For example, the U.S. government is committed by law (the Employment Act of 1946 and the Humphrey-Hawkins Act of 1978) to engage in activist policy to promote high employment. Both laws require a commitment to a high level of employment consistent with stable inflation—yet in practice the U.S. government and the Federal Reserve have often pursued a high employment target with little concern about the inflationary consequences of policies.

Two types of inflation can result from an activist stabilization policy to promote high employment:

1. **Cost-push inflation** results either from a temporary negative supply shock or a push by workers for wage hikes beyond what productivity gains can justify.

2. **Demand-pull inflation** results from policymakers' pursuing policies that increase aggregate demand.

We will now use aggregate demand and supply analysis to examine the effect of a high employment target on both types of inflation.

COST-PUSH INFLATION Consider the economy in Figure 25-9, which is initially at point 1, the intersection of the aggregate demand curve AD_1 and the short-run aggregate supply curve AS_1. Suppose workers succeed in pushing for higher wages, either because they want to increase their real wages (wages in terms of the goods and services they can buy) above what is justified by productivity gains, or because they expect inflation to be high and wish their wages to keep up with it. This cost-push shock, which acts like a temporary negative supply shock, raises the inflation rate and shifts the short-run aggregate supply curve up and to the left to AS_2. If the central bank takes no action to change the equilibrium interest rate and the monetary policy curve remains unchanged, the economy would move to point $2'$ at the intersection of the new short-run aggregate supply curve AS_2 and the aggregate demand curve AD_1. Output would decline to Y' below potential output and the inflation rate would rise to $\pi_{2'}$, leading to an increase in unemployment.

In contrast, activist policymakers with a high employment target would implement policies, such as a cut in taxes, an increase in government purchases, or an autonomous easing of monetary policy, to increase aggregate demand. These policies would shift the aggregate demand curve in Figure 25-9 to $AD_{2'}$, quickly returning the economy to potential output at point 2 and increasing the inflation rate to π_2. The workers fare quite well, earning both higher wages and government protection against excessive unemployment.

The workers' success might encourage them to seek even higher wages. In addition, other workers might now realize that their wages have fallen relative to their fellow workers, leading them to seek wage increases. As a result, another temporary negative supply shock would occur that would cause the short-run aggregate supply curve in Figure 25-9 to shift up and to the left again, to AS_3. Unemployment develops again when we move to point $3'$, prompting activist policies once again to

MyEconLab
Animation

FIGURE 25-9 Cost-Push Inflation

A cost-push shock (which acts like a temporary negative supply shock) shifts the short-run aggregate supply curve up and to the left to AS_2, and the economy moves to point 2'. To keep aggregate output at Y^P and lower the unemployment rate, policymakers shift the aggregate demand curve to AD_2 so that the economy will return quickly to potential output at point 2 and an inflation rate of π_2. Further upward and leftward shifts of the short-run aggregate supply curve to AS_3 and so on cause the policy-makers to keep on increasing aggregate demand, leading to a continuing increase in inflation—a cost-push inflation.

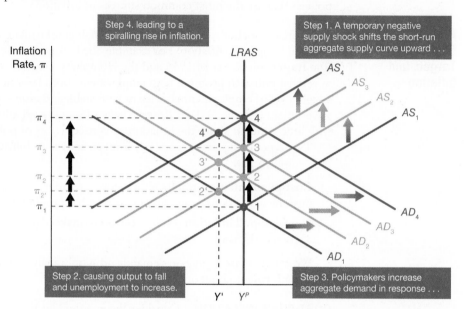

shift the aggregate demand curve rightward to AD_3 and return the economy to full employment at a higher inflation rate of π_3. If this process continues, the result will be a continuing increase in inflation—a cost-push inflation.

DEMAND-PULL INFLATION   The goal of high employment can lead to inflationary fiscal and monetary policy in another way. Even at full employment (the natural rate of unemployment), some unemployment is always present because of frictions in the labour market that complicate the matching of unemployed workers with employers. Consequently, the unemployment rate when employment is full will be greater than zero. When policymakers mistakenly underestimate the natural rate of unemployment and so set a target for unemployment that is too low (i.e., less than the natural rate of unemployment), they set the stage for expansionary monetary policy that produces inflation.

Figure 25-10 shows how this scenario can unfold, using an aggregate supply and demand analysis. If policymakers have set a 4% unemployment target that is below the 5% natural rate of unemployment, they will be trying to achieve an output target greater than potential output. We mark this target level of output in Figure 25-10 as Y^T. Suppose that we are initially at point 1: The economy is at potential output but below the target level of output Y^T. To hit the unemployment target of 4%, policymakers must enact policies such as expansionary fiscal policy or an autonomous easing of monetary policy to increase aggregate demand. The aggregate demand curve

FIGURE 25-10 Demand-Pull Inflation

Too low an unemployment target (too high an output target of Y^T) causes the government to increase aggregate demand, shifting the AD curve rightward from AD_1 to AD_2 to AD_3 and so on. Because the unemployment rate is below the natural rate level, wages will rise and the short-run aggregate supply curve will shift up and leftward from AS_1 to AS_2 to AS_3 and so on. The result is a continuing rise in inflation known as a demand-pull inflation.

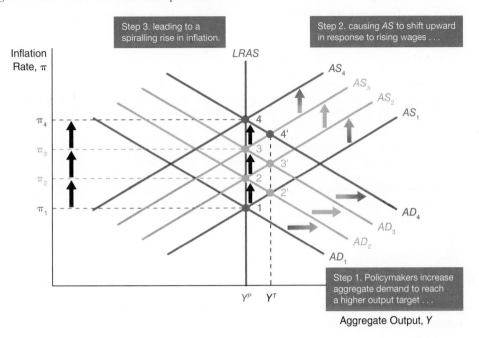

in Figure 25-10 shifts to the right until it reaches AD_2 and the economy moves to point $2'$, where output is at Y^T and policymakers have achieved the 4% unemployment rate goal—but there is more to the story. At Y^T, the 4% unemployment rate is below the natural rate level, and output is above potential, causing wages to rise. The short-run aggregate supply curve will shift up and to the left, eventually to AS_2, moving the economy from point $2'$ to point 2, where it is back at potential output but at a higher inflation rate of π_2. We could stop there, but because unemployment is again higher than the target level, policymakers would once more shift the aggregate demand curve rightward to AD_3 to hit the output target at point $3'$—and the whole process would continue to drive the economy to point 3 and beyond. The overall result is a steadily rising inflation rate.

Pursuing too low an unemployment rate target or, equivalently, too high an output target thus leads to inflationary monetary or fiscal policy. Policymakers fail on two counts: they have not achieved their unemployment target and have caused higher inflation. If, however, the target rate of unemployment is below the natural rate, the process we see in Figure 25-10 will be well under way before they realize their mistake.

COST-PUSH VERSUS DEMAND-PULL INFLATION When inflation occurs, how do we know whether it is demand-pull inflation or cost-push inflation? We would normally expect to see demand-pull inflation when unemployment is below the natural rate level, and cost-push inflation when unemployment is above the natural rate level. Unfortunately, economists and policymakers still struggle with measuring the natural rate of unemployment. Complicating matters further, a cost-push inflation can be initiated by a demand-pull inflation, blurring the distinction. When a demand-pull inflation produces higher inflation rates, expected inflation will eventually rise and cause workers to demand higher wages (cost-push inflation) so that their real wages do not fall. Finally, expansionary monetary and fiscal policies produce both kinds of inflation, so we cannot distinguish between them on this basis.

SUMMARY

1. For aggregate demand shocks and permanent supply shocks, the price stability and economic activity stability objectives are consistent: stabilizing inflation stabilizes economic activity even in the short run. For temporary supply shocks, however, there is a tradeoff between stabilizing inflation and stabilizing economic activity in the short run. In the long run, no conflict arises between stabilizing inflation and economic activity.

2. Activists regard the self-correcting mechanism through wage and price adjustment as very slow and hence see the need for the government to pursue active, accommodating policy to address high unemployment when it develops. Nonactivists, by contrast, believe that the self-correcting mechanism is fast and therefore advocate that the government avoid active policy to eliminate unemployment.

3. Milton Friedman's view that in the long run inflation is always and everywhere a monetary phenomenon is borne out by aggregate demand and supply analysis: it shows that monetary policymakers can target any inflation rate in the long run they want through autonomous monetary policy, which adjusts the equilibrium real interest rate using the overnight interest rate policy tool to change the level of aggregate demand.

4. Two types of inflation can result from an activist stabilization policy to promote high employment: cost-push inflation, which occurs because of negative supply shocks or a push by workers to get higher wages than is justified by productivity gains, and demand-pull inflation, which results when policymakers pursue high output and employment targets through policies that increase aggregate demand.

KEY TERMS

activists, p. 610
cost-push inflation, p. 613
data lag, p. 610
demand-pull inflation, p. 613
divine coincidence, p. 605

effectiveness lag, p. 611
implementation lag, p. 610
inflation gap, p. 603
inflation target, p. 602
Keynesians, p. 610

legislative lag, p. 610
nonactivists, p. 610
recognition lag, p. 610

QUESTIONS

1. What does it mean for the inflation gap to be negative?

2. "If autonomous spending falls, the central bank should lower its inflation target in order to stabilize inflation." Is this statement true, false, or uncertain? Explain your answer.

3. For each of the following shocks, describe how monetary policymakers would respond (if at all) to stabilize economic activity. Assume the economy starts at a long-run equilibrium.
   a. Consumers reduce autonomous consumption.
   b. Financial frictions decrease.
   c. Government spending increases.
   d. Taxes increase.
   e. The domestic currency appreciates.

4. During the global financial crisis, how were central banks around the world able to help offset the sharp increase in financial frictions, without the ability to lower interest rates further? Did it work?

5. Why does the divine coincidence simplify the job of policy making?

6. Why do negative supply shocks pose a dilemma for policymakers?

7. In what way is a permanent negative supply shock worse than a temporary negative supply shock?

8. Suppose three economies are hit with the same negative supply shock. In country A, inflation initially rises and output falls; then inflation rises more and output increases. In country B, inflation initially rises and output falls; then both inflation and output fall. In country C, inflation initially rises and output falls; then inflation falls and output eventually increases. What type of stabilization approach did each country take?

9. "Policymakers would never respond by stabilizing a temporary positive supply shock." Is this statement true, false, or uncertain? Explain your answer.

10. The fact that it takes a long time for firms to bring new plant and equipment on line is an illustration of the concept related to what policy problem?

11. If someone told you, "policymakers couldn't vote themselves out of a phone booth," what type of policy lag is he or she referring to?

12. Is stabilization policy more likely to be conducted with monetary policy or fiscal policy? Why?

13. "If the data and recognition lags could be reduced, activist policy would more likely be beneficial to the economy." Is this statement true, false, or uncertain? Explain your answer.

14. Why do activists believe the economy's self-correcting mechanism is slow?

15. If the economy's self-correcting mechanism works slowly, should the government necessarily pursue discretionary policy to eliminate unemployment? Why or why not?

16. Suppose one could measure the welfare gains derived from eliminating output (and unemployment) fluctuations in the economy. Assuming these gains are relatively small for the average individual, how do you think this conclusion would affect the activist/nonactivist debate?

17. Given a relatively steep and a relatively flat short-run aggregate supply curve, which one supports the case for nonactivist policy? Why?

18. "Because government policymakers do not consider inflation desirable, their policies cannot be the source of inflation." Is this statement true, false, or uncertain? Explain your answer.

19. How can monetary authorities target any inflation rate they want to?

20. What will happen if policymakers erroneously believe that the natural rate of unemployment is 7%, when it is actually 5%, and pursue stabilization policy?

21. How can demand-pull inflation lead to cost-push inflation?

APPLIED PROBLEMS

22. Suppose the government decides to decrease government expenditures as a means to cut the existing government budget deficit.
    a. Using a graph of aggregate demand and supply, show what the effect would be in the short run. Describe the effects on inflation and output.
    b. What would be the effect on the real interest rate, inflation rate, and output level if the Bank of Canada decides to stabilize the inflation rate?

23. Use a graph of aggregate demand and supply to demonstrate how lags in the policy process can result in undesirable fluctuations in output and inflation.

24. As monetary policymakers care more about inflation stabilization, the slope of the aggregate demand curve becomes flatter. How does the resulting change in the slope of the aggregate demand curve help stabilize inflation when the economy is hit with a temporary negative supply shock? How does this affect output? Use a graph of aggregate demand and supply to demonstrate.

25. Many developing countries suffer from graft and endemic corruption. How does this help explain why these economies have typically high inflation and economic stagnation? Use a graph of aggregate demand and supply to demonstrate.

WEB EXERCISES

1. It can be an interesting exercise to compare the purchasing power of the dollar over different periods in history. Go to **www.bankofcanada.ca/rates** and scroll down to the link to the inflation calculator. Use this calculator to compute the following:

   a. If a new house cost $10 000 in 1950, what would it have cost in 2012?
   b. From (a), what is the percent change in the price of the house from 1950 to 2012?
   c. What is the average annual rate of inflation?

CHAPTER 26

The Role of Expectations in Monetary Policy

LEARNING OBJECTIVES

After studying this chapter you should be able to

1. describe the Lucas critique of policy evaluation
2. recount the impact of rational expectations on policy-making models

PREVIEW

After World War II, economists, armed with models like the ones we developed in Chapter 22–25, felt that discretionary policies could reduce the severity of business cycle fluctuations without creating inflation. In the 1960s and 1970s, these economists got their chance to put their policies into practice, but the results were not what they had anticipated. The economic record for that period is not a happy one: Inflation accelerated, the rate often climbing above 10%, while unemployment figures deteriorated from those of the 1950s.[1]

In the 1970s and 1980s, economists, including Nobel Prize winners Robert Lucas of the University of Chicago and Thomas Sargent, now at New York University, used the rational expectations theory discussed in Chapter 7 to examine why discretionary policies appear to have performed so poorly. Their analysis cast doubt on whether macroeconomic models can be used to evaluate the potential effects of policy and on whether policy can be effective when the public *expects* that it will be implemented. Because the analysis of Lucas and Sargent has such strong implications for the way policy should be conducted, it has been labelled the *rational expectations revolution*.[2]

This chapter examines the analysis behind the rational expectations revolution. We start first with the Lucas critique, which indicates that because expectations are important in economic behaviour, it may be quite difficult to predict what the

---

[1]Some of the deterioration can be attributed to supply shocks in 1973–1975 and 1978–1980.
[2]Other economists who have been active in promoting the rational expectations revolution are Robert Barro of Harvard University, Bennett McCallum of Carnegie-Mellon University, Nobel Prize winner Edward Prescott of Arizona State, and Neil Wallace of Pennsylvania State University.

outcome of a discretionary policy will be. We then discuss the effect of rational expectations on the aggregate demand and supply analysis developed in Chapter 24 and explore how this theoretical breakthrough has shaped current policy-making models and debates.

Lucas Critique of Policy Evaluation

Economists have long used **macroeconometric models** to forecast economic activity and to evaluate the potential effects of policy options. In essence, the models are collections of equations that describe statistical relationships among many economic variables. Economists can feed data into such models, which then churn out a forecast or prediction.

In his famous paper "Econometric Policy Evaluation: A Critique," Robert Lucas spurred the rational expectations revolution by presenting a devastating argument against the use of macroeconometric models used at the time for evaluating policy.[3]

Econometric Policy Evaluation

To understand Lucas's argument, we must first understand how econometric policy evaluation is done. Say, for example, that the Bank of Canada wants to evaluate the potential effects of changes in the overnight interest rate from the existing level of 5%. Using conventional methods, the Bank economists would feed different overnight rate options—say, 4% and 6%—into a computer version of the model. The model would then predict how unemployment and inflation would change under the different scenarios. Then, the policymakers would select the policy with the most desirable outcomes.

Relying on rational expectations theory, Lucas identified faulty reasoning in this approach if the model does not incorporate rational expectations, as was true for macroeconometric models used by policymakers at the time: when policies change, public expectations will shift as well. For example, if the Bank of Canada raises the overnight interest rate to 6%, this action might change the way the public forms expectations about where interest rates will be in the future. Those changing expectations, as we've seen, can have a real effect on economic behaviour and outcomes. Yet econometric models that do not incorporate rational expectations ignore any effects of changing expectations, and thus are unreliable for evaluating policy options.

APPLICATION

The Term Structure of Interest Rates

Let's now apply Lucas's argument to a concrete example involving only one equation typically found in econometric models: the term structure equation. The equation relates the long-term interest rate to current and past values of the short-term interest rate. It is one of the most important equations in macroeconometric models because the long-term interest rate, not the short-term rate, is the one believed to have the larger impact on aggregate demand.

In Chapter 6, we learned that the long-term interest rate is related to an average of expected future short-term interest rates. Suppose that in the past, when the short-term rate rose, it quickly fell back down again; that is, any increase was temporary. Because rational expectations theory suggests that any rise in the short-term

---

[3]*Carnegie-Rochester Conference Series on Public Policy* 1 (1976): 19–46.

interest rate is expected to be only temporary, a rise should have only a minimal effect on the average of expected future short-term rates. It will cause the long-term interest rate to rise by a negligible amount. The term structure relationship estimated using past data will then show only a weak effect on the long-term interest rate of changes in the short-term rate.

Suppose the Bank of Canada wants to evaluate what will happen to the economy if it pursues a policy that is likely to raise the short-term interest rate from a current level of 3% to a permanently higher level of 5%. The term structure equation that has been estimated using past data will indicate that just a small change in the long-term interest rate will occur. However, if the public recognizes that the short-term rate is rising to a permanently higher level, rational expectations theory indicates that people will no longer expect a rise in the short-term rate to be temporary. Instead, when they see the interest rate rise to 5%, they will expect the average of future short-term interest rates to rise substantially, and so the long-term interest rate will rise greatly, not minimally as the estimated term structure equation suggests. You can see that evaluating the likely outcome of the change in Bank of Canada policy with an econometric model can be highly misleading.

The term structure application demonstrates another aspect of the Lucas critique. The effects of a particular policy depend critically on the public's expectations about the policy. If the public expects the rise in the short-term interest rate to be merely temporary, the response of long-term interest rates, as we have seen, will be negligible. If, however, the public expects the rise to be more permanent, the response of long-term rates will be far greater. *The Lucas critique points out not only that conventional econometric models cannot be used for policy evaluation, but also that the public's expectations about a policy will influence the response to that policy.*

The term structure equation discussed here is only one of many equations in econometric models to which the Lucas critique applies. In fact, Lucas uses the examples of consumption and investment equations in his paper. One attractive feature of the term structure example is that it deals with expectations in a financial market, a sector of the economy for which the theory and empirical evidence supporting rational expectations are much stronger. The Lucas critique should also apply, however, to sectors of the economy for which rational expectations theory is more controversial, because the basic principle of the Lucas critique is not that expectations are always rational but rather that the formation of expectations changes when the behaviour of a forecasted variable changes. This less stringent principle is supported by the evidence in sectors of the economy other than financial markets.

Policy Conduct: Rules or Discretion?

The Lucas critique exposed the need for new policy models that reflected the insights of rational expectations theory. Here, we explore the implications of the critique on a long-running debate among economists: whether monetary policymakers should have the flexibility to adapt their policy to a changing situation, or whether they should adopt **rules**, binding plans that specify how policy will respond (or not respond) to particular data such as unemployment and inflation.

Discretion and the Time-Inconsistency Problem

Policymakers operate with **discretion** when they make no commitment to future actions, but instead make what they believe in that moment to be the right policy decision for the situation. Empowering policymakers to shape policy on the fly introduces complexities. The *time-inconsistency problem* we discussed in Chapter 18 reveals the potential limitations of discretionary policy. Recall that the time-inconsistency problem is the tendency to deviate from good long-run plans when making short-run decisions. Policymakers are always tempted to pursue a policy that is more expansionary than firms or people expect because such a policy would boost economic output (and lower unemployment) in the short run. The best policy, however, is *not* to pursue expansionary policy, because decisions about wages and prices reflect workers' and firms' expectations about policy (an implication of the rational expectations revolution). When workers and firms see a central bank, for example, pursuing discretionary expansionary policy, they will recognize that this is likely to lead to higher inflation in the future. They will therefore raise their expectations about inflation, driving wages and prices up. The rise in wages and prices will lead to higher inflation, but may not result in higher output on average.

Policymakers will have better inflation performance in the long run if they do not try to surprise people with an unexpectedly expansionary policy, but instead keep inflation under control. One way to do this is to abandon discretion and adopt rules to govern policy making.

Types of Rules

In contrast to discretion, rules are essentially automatic. One famous type of rule, advocated by Milton Friedman and his followers who are known as **monetarists**, is the **constant-money-growth-rate rule**, in which the money supply is kept growing at a constant rate regardless of the state of the economy. Other monetarists such as Bennett McCallum and Alan Meltzer have proposed variants of this rule that allow the rate of money supply growth to be adjusted for shifts in velocity, which has often been found to be unstable in the short run. Rules of this type are nonactivist because they do not react to economic activity. Monetarists advocate rules of this type because they believe that money is the sole source of fluctuations in aggregate demand and because they believe that long and variable lags in the effects of monetary policy will lead to greater volatility in economic activity and inflation if policy actively responds to unemployment (as discussed in Chapter 25).

Activist rules, in contrast, specify that monetary policy should react to the level of output as well as to inflation. The most famous rule of this type is the *Taylor rule,* which we discussed in Chapter 18. It specifies that the Bank of Canada should set its overnight rate target by a formula that considers both the output gap $(Y - Y^P)$ and the inflation gap $(\pi - \pi^T)$.

The Case for Rules

As our discussion of the time-inconsistency problem suggests, discretionary monetary policy can lead to poor economic outcomes. If monetary policymakers operate with discretion, they will be tempted to pursue overly expansionary monetary policies to boost employment in the short run but generate higher inflation (and no higher employment) in the long run. A commitment to a policy rule like the Taylor rule or the constant-money-growth-rate rule solves the time-inconsistency problem because policymakers have to follow a set plan that does not allow them to exercise discretion and try to exploit the short-run tradeoff between inflation and employment. By binding their hands with a policy rule, policymakers can achieve desirable long-run outcomes.

Another argument for rules is that policymakers and politicians cannot be trusted. Milton Friedman and Anna Schwartz's monumental work, *A Monetary History of the United States,*[4] documents numerous instances in which the Federal Reserve made serious policy errors, with the worst occurring during the Great Depression,

---

[4]Milton Friedman and Anna Jacobson Schwartz, *A Monetary History of the United States, 1867–1960* (Princeton, NJ: Princeton University Press, 1963).

when the Fed just stood by and let the banking system and the economy collapse. The politicians who make fiscal policy are also not to be trusted because they have strong incentives to pursue policies that help them win the next election. They are therefore more likely to focus on increasing employment in the short run without worrying that their actions might lead to higher inflation further down the road. Their advocacy for expansionary policies can then lead to the so-called **political business cycle**, in which fiscal and monetary policy is expansionary right before elections, with higher inflation following later. (For an example, see the FYI box The Political Business Cycle and Richard Nixon.)

FYI

The Political Business Cycle and Richard Nixon

You might know that former U.S. president Richard Nixon and his aides took some extraordinary actions to ensure a landslide victory in the 1972 U.S. presidential election, such as breaking into the offices of political rivals at the Watergate Hotel. Less well known are similar actions on the economic front ahead of the election. The Nixon administration imposed wage and price controls on the economy, which temporarily lowered the inflation rate before the election. After the election, those same moves helped lead to a surge in inflation. Nixon also pursued expansionary fiscal policy by cutting taxes. And it has been rumoured that the chairman of the Federal Reserve, Arthur Burns, succumbed to direct pressure from Nixon to maintain low interest rates through election day. The aftermath was ugly. The economy overheated and inflation rose to over 10% by the late 1970s, which was abetted by the negative supply shocks during that period.

The Nixon episode led economists and political scientists to theorize that politicians would take steps to make themselves look good during election years. Specifically, the theory went, they would take steps to stimulate the economy before the election, leading to a boom and low unemployment that would increase their electoral chances. Unfortunately, the result of these actions would be higher inflation down the road, which then would require contractionary policies to get inflation under control later, with a resulting recession in the future. The resulting ups and downs of the economy would then be the result of politics and so could be characterized as a political business cycle. Although the Nixon episode in the United States provided support for the existence of a political business cycle, research has not come to a definitive answer regarding whether this phenomenon is a general one.[*]

*The paper that launched research on the political business cycle was William Nordhaus, "The Political Business Cycle," *Review of Economic Studies* 42 (1975): 169–190.

The Case for Discretion

Although policy rules have important advantages, they do have serious drawbacks. First, rules can be too rigid because they cannot foresee every contingency. For example, almost no one could have predicted that problems in one small part of the financial system, subprime mortgage lending, would lead to the worst financial crisis in over 70 years, with such devastating effects on the economy. The unprecedented steps that the central banks around the world took during this crisis to prevent it from causing a depression (described in Chapters 9 and 17) could not have been written into a policy rule ahead of time. Being able to act flexibly using discretion can thus be key to a successful monetary policy.

The second problem with policy rules is that they do not easily incorporate the use of judgment. Monetary policy is as much an art as a science. Monetary policy-makers need to look at a wide range of information in order to decide on the best course for monetary policy, and some of this information is not easily quantifiable.

Judgment is thus an essential element of good monetary policy, and it is very hard to write it into a rule. Only with discretion can monetary policy bring judgment to bear.

Third, no one really knows what the true model of the economy is, and so any policy rule that is based on a particular model will prove to be wrong if the model is not correct. Discretion avoids the straightjacket that would lock in the wrong policy if the model that was used to derive the policy rule proved to be incorrect.

Fourth, even if the model were correct, structural changes in the economy would lead to changes in the coefficients of the model. The Lucas critique, which points out that changes in policies can change the coefficients in macroeconometric models, is just one example. Another is that the relationship of monetary aggregates, like M1+ and M2+, to aggregate spending broke down in the 1980s as a result of financial innovation. Following a rule based on a constant growth rate of one of these aggregates would have produced bad outcomes. Indeed, this is what happened in the case of Switzerland in the late 1980s and early 1990s, when adherence to a rule using the growth rate of monetary aggregates led to a surge in inflation (discussed in the Global box The Demise of Monetary Targeting in Switzerland). Discretion enables policymakers to change policy settings when an economy undergoes structural changes.

GLOBAL

The Demise of Monetary Targeting in Switzerland

In 1975 the Swiss National Bank (Switzerland's central bank) adopted monetary targeting in which it announced a growth rate target for the monetary aggregate M1. From 1980 on, the Swiss switched their growth rate target to an even narrower monetary aggregate, the monetary base. Although monetary targeting was quite successful in Switzerland for many years, it ran into serious problems with the introduction of a new interbank payment system, the Swiss Interbank Clearing (SIC), and a wide-ranging revision of commercial banks' liquidity requirements in 1988. These structural changes caused a severe drop in banks' desired holdings of deposits at the Swiss National Bank, which were the major component of the monetary base. A smaller amount of the monetary base was now needed relative to aggregate spending, altering the relationship between the two, and so the 2% target growth rate for the monetary base was far too expansionary. Inflation subsequently rose to over 5%, well above that of other European countries.

High inflation rates horrified the Swiss, who have always prided themselves on maintaining a low-inflation environment even when the rest of Europe did not. These problems with monetary targeting led the Swiss to abandon it in the 1990s and adopt a much more flexible framework for the conduct of monetary policy.[*]

*For a further discussion of monetary targeting in Switzerland, see Chapter 4 of Ben S. Bernanke, Thomas Laubach, Frederic S. Mishkin, and Adam S. Posen, *Inflation Targeting: Lessons from the International Experience* (Princeton, NJ: Princeton University Press, 1999).

Constrained Discretion

The distinction between rules and discretion has strongly influenced academic debates about monetary policy for many decades. But the distinction may be too stark. As we have seen, both rules and discretion are subject to problems, and so the dichotomy between rules and discretion may be too simple to capture the realities that macroeconomic policymakers face. Discretion can be a matter of degree. Discretion can be a relatively undisciplined approach that leads to policies that change with the personal views of policymakers or with the direction of political winds. Or it might operate within a more clearly articulated framework, in which the general objectives and tactics of the policymakers—although not their specific actions—are committed to in advance. Ben Bernanke, now chairman of the Federal Reserve, along with one of the authors of this textbook, came up with a name for this type of framework, **constrained discretion**.[5] Constrained discretion imposes a conceptual structure and inherent discipline on policymakers, but without eliminating all flexibility. It combines some of the advantages ascribed to rules with those ascribed to discretion.

The Role of Credibility and a Nominal Anchor

An important way to constrain discretion is, as was earlier discussed in Chapter 18, by committing to a *nominal anchor*, a nominal variable—such as the inflation rate, the money supply, or an exchange rate— that ties down the price level or inflation to achieve price stability. For example, as discussed in Chapter 18, if a central bank has an explicit target for the inflation rate, say, 2%, and takes steps to achieve this target, then the inflation target becomes a nominal anchor. Alternatively, a government could commit to a fixed exchange rate between its currency and a sound currency like the dollar and use this as its nominal anchor. If the commitment to a nominal anchor has **credibility**—that is, it is believed by the public—it has important benefits.

Benefits of a Credible Nominal Anchor

First, a credible nominal anchor has elements of a behaviour rule. Just as rules help to prevent the time-inconsistency problem in parenting by helping adults to resist pursuing the discretionary policy of giving in, a nominal anchor can help overcome the time-inconsistency problem by providing an expected constraint on discretionary policy. For example, if monetary policymakers commit to a nominal anchor of achieving a specific inflation objective, say, a 2% inflation rate, then they know that they will be subject to public scrutiny and criticism if they miss this objective or pursue policies that are clearly inconsistent with this objective, such as an interest rate target that is too low. To avoid embarrassment and possible punishment, they will be less tempted to pursue overly expansionary, discretionary policies in the short run that will be inconsistent with their commitment to the nominal anchor.

Second, a credible commitment to a nominal anchor will help to anchor inflation expectations, which leads to smaller fluctuations in inflation. It thus contributes to price stability, but also helps stabilize aggregate output. Credibility of a commitment to a nominal anchor is therefore a critical element in enabling monetary policy to achieve both of its objectives, price stability and stabilizing economic activity. In other words, credibility of a nominal anchor helps make monetary policy more efficient.

We will use the aggregate demand and supply framework to show analytically why a credible nominal anchor helps produce this desirable outcome. First we will look at the effectiveness of stabilization policy when it is responding to an aggregate demand shock, and then we will do the same when it is responding to an aggregate supply shock. We will also look at the benefits of credibility for anti-inflation policy.

Credibility and Aggregate Demand Shocks

We now examine the importance of credibility in the short run when positive and negative demand shocks are present.

---

[5]See Ben S. Bernanke and Frederic S. Mishkin, "Inflation Targeting: A New Framework for Monetary Policy?" *Journal of Economic Perspectives* 11 (Spring 1997): 97–116.

POSITIVE AGGREGATE DEMAND SHOCK   Let's first look at what happens in the short run when a positive aggregate demand shock occurs. For example, suppose businesses suddenly get new information that makes them more optimistic about the future, and so they increase their investment spending. As a result of this positive demand shock, in panel (a) of Figure 26-1 the aggregate demand curve shifts to the right from AD_1 to AD_2, moving the economy from point 1 to point 2. Aggregate output rises to Y_2 and inflation rises above the inflation target of π^T to π_2. As we saw in Chapter 25, the appropriate response to stabilize inflation and economic activity is to tighten monetary policy and shift the short-run aggregate demand curve back down to AD_1 in order to move the economy back to point 1. However, because of the long lags until monetary policy has an effect on aggregate demand, it will take some time before the short-run aggregate demand curve shifts back to AD_1.

Now let's look at what happens to the short-run aggregate supply curve. Recall from Chapter 24 that the short-run aggregate supply curve is as follows:

$$\pi \quad = \quad \pi^e \quad + \quad \gamma(Y - Y^P) \quad + \rho$$

Inflation = Expected Inflation + γ × Output Gap + Price Shock

If the commitment to the nominal anchor is credible, then the public's expected inflation π^e will remain unchanged and the short-run aggregate supply curve will remain at AS_1. Inflation will therefore not go higher than π_2, and over time, as the short-run aggregate demand curve shifts back down to AD_1, inflation will fall back down to the inflation target of π^T.

But what if monetary policy is not credible? The public would worry that the monetary authorities are willing to accept a higher inflation rate than π^T and are not willing to drive the short-run aggregate demand curve back to AD_1 quickly. In this case, the weak credibility of the monetary authorities will cause expected inflation π^e to rise and so the short-run aggregate supply curve will rise, shifting from AS_1 to AS_3 and sending the economy to point 3 in the short run, where inflation has risen further to π_3. Even if the monetary authorities tighten monetary policy and return the aggregate demand curve to AD_1, the damage is done: inflation has risen more than it would have if the central bank had credibility. Our aggregate demand and supply analysis thus yields the following conclusion: ***monetary policy credibility has the benefit of stabilizing inflation in the short run when faced with positive demand shocks.***

NEGATIVE DEMAND SHOCK   Panel (b) of Figure 26-1 illustrates a negative demand shock. For example, suppose consumer confidence dips and consumer spending declines. The aggregate demand curve shifts left from AD_1 to AD_2, and the economy moves to point 2 in the short run where aggregate output has fallen to Y_2, which is below potential output Y^P, and inflation has fallen to π_2, below the target level of π^T. To stabilize output and inflation, the central bank eases monetary policy to move the aggregate demand curve back to AD_1. If the central bank has high credibility, expected inflation will remain unchanged, the short-run aggregate supply curve will remain at AS_1, and the economy will return to point 1.

However, what if the central bank's credibility is weak? When the public sees an easing of monetary policy, it might become concerned that the central bank is losing its commitment to the nominal anchor and will pursue inflationary policy in the future. In this situation, inflation expectations might increase, and so the short-run aggregate supply curve will rise to AS_3, sending the economy to point 3, where aggregate output has fallen even further to Y_3. Weak credibility causes a negative demand shock to produce an even greater contraction in economic activity in the short run. We have the following additional result: ***monetary policy credibility has the benefit of stabilizing economic activity in the short run when faced with negative demand shocks.***

FIGURE 26-1   Credibility and Aggregate Demand Shocks

In panel (a), the positive aggregate demand shock shifts the aggregate demand curve to the right from AD_1 to AD_2, moving the economy from point 1 to point 2. If monetary policy is not credible, expected inflation will rise and so the short-run aggregate supply curve will rise and shift to the left to AS_3, sending the economy to point 3, where inflation has risen further to π_3. In panel (b) the negative aggregate demand shock shifts the aggregate demand curve left from AD_1 to AD_2, and the economy moves to point 2. If monetary policy is not credible, inflation expectations might rise and the short-run aggregate supply curve will rise and shift to the left to AS_3, sending the economy to point 3, where aggregate output has fallen even further to Y_3.

(a) Positive Aggregate Demand Shocks

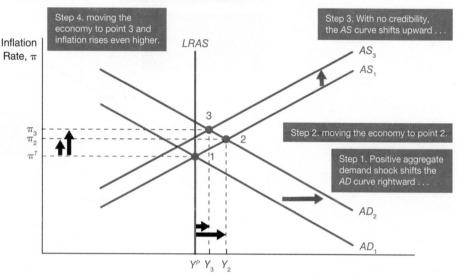

(b) Negative Aggregate Demand Shocks

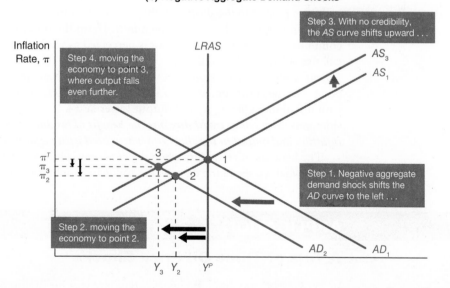

Credibility and Aggregate Supply Shocks

Now let's look at what happens in Figure 26-2 if a negative aggregate supply shock occurs. If energy prices increase, the short-run aggregate supply curve shifts up and to the left. How much the aggregate supply curve will shift, however, depends on the

FIGURE 26-2   Credibility and Aggregate Supply Shocks

If the credibility of monetary policy is high, the negative aggregate supply shock shifts the short-run aggregate supply curve only to AS_2 and the economy moves to point 2, where the rise in inflation to π_2 will then be minor, while the fall in output to Y_2 will also be minor. If credibility is weak, then inflation expectations will rise substantially and the upward shift of the short-run aggregate supply curve will be much larger, moving it up and to the left to AS_3. The economy will move to point 3, with worse outcomes on both inflation and output, that is, with inflation higher at π^3 and output lower at Y_3.

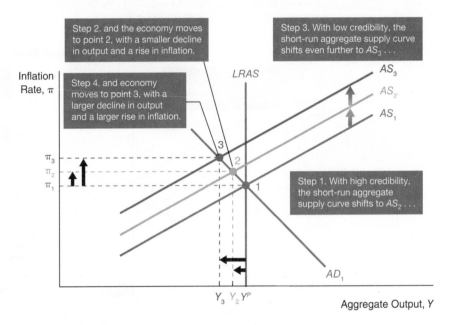

amount of credibility the monetary authorities have. If the credibility of the nominal anchor is strong, inflation expectations will not rise, so the upward and leftward shift of the short-run aggregate supply curve to AS_2 will be small. When the economy moves to point 2 in the short run, the rise in inflation to π_2 will then be minor, while the fall in output to Y_2 will also be minor. If, on the other hand, the central bank's commitment to the nominal anchor is perceived as weak, then inflation expectations will rise substantially and the upward shift to the left of the short-run aggregate supply curve will be much larger, moving it up to AS_3. Now the economy will move to point 3 in the short run, with worse outcomes on both inflation and output, that is, with inflation higher at π_3 and output lower at Y_3. We reach the following conclusion: ***monetary policy credibility has the benefit of producing better outcomes on both inflation and output in the short run when faced with negative supply shocks.***

The benefits of credibility when the economy is hit by negative supply shocks are exactly what we see in the data, as the following application illustrates.

APPLICATION

A Tale of Three Oil Price Shocks

In 1973, 1979, and 2007, the world economy was hit by three major negative supply shocks when the price of oil rose sharply; and yet in the first two episodes the inflation rate in Canada rose sharply, while in the most recent episode it rose much less, as we can see in panel (a) of Figure 26-3. In the case of the first two episodes,

FIGURE 26-3 Inflation and Unemployment 1970–2011

In the 1973 and 1979 oil shock episodes, inflation was initially high and the Bank of Canada's commitment to a nominal anchor was weak, whereas in the 2007 episode, inflation was initially low and the Bank of Canada's credibility was high. The result was that inflation and unemployment rose more in the first two episodes than in the last episode, with unemployment rising sharply in the third episode only after the 2007–2009 crisis took a disastrous turn in October 2008.

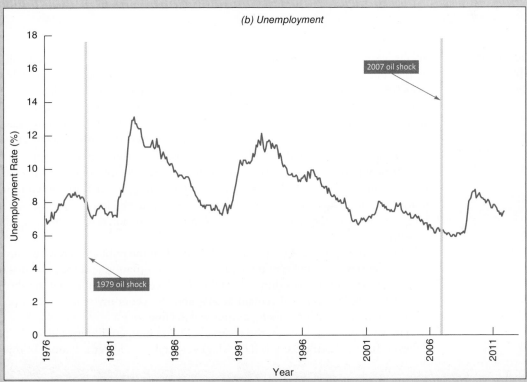

monetary policy credibility was extremely weak because the Bank of Canada had been unable to keep inflation under control, which had resulted in high inflation. In contrast, when the third oil price shock hit in 2007–2008, inflation had been low and stable for quite a period of time, so the Bank of Canada had more credibility that it would keep inflation under control. One reason that has been offered to explain why the last oil price shock appears to have had a smaller effect on inflation in the recent episode is that monetary policy has been more credible. Our aggregate demand and supply analysis provides the reasoning behind this view.

In the first two episodes where the commitment to a nominal anchor and credibility were weak, the oil price shocks would have produced a surge in inflation expectations and a large upward and leftward shift in the short-run aggregate supply curve to AS_3 in Figure 26-2. Thus, the aggregate demand and supply analysis predicts there would be a sharp contraction in economic activity and a sharp rise in inflation. This is exactly what we see in panels (a) and (b) of Figure 26-3, although the unemployment rate series in panel (b) starts in 1976. The economic contractions were very severe, with unemployment rising to almost 13% in the aftermath of the 1979 oil price shock (during the 1981–1982 recession). In addition, inflation shot up to around double-digit levels.

In the 2007–2008 episode, the outcome was quite different. Through greater policy credibility established over many years, inflation expectations remained grounded when the oil price shock occurred. As a result, the short-run aggregate supply curve shifted up and to the left much less, to only AS_2 in Figure 26-2. The aggregate demand and supply analysis predicts that there would be a much smaller increase in inflation from the negative supply shock, while the contraction in economic activity would also be less. Indeed, this is what transpired up until the global financial crisis entered its virulent phase in the fall of 2008. Inflation rose by much less than in the previous episodes, while the economy held up fairly well until the financial crisis took a disastrous turn in October 2008. Only then did the economy go into a tailspin, but it is clear that this was not the result of the negative supply shock. Inflation actually fell quite dramatically, indicating that a massive negative demand shock was the source of the sharp contraction in economic activity.

Credibility and Anti-Inflation Policy

So far we have examined the benefits of credibility when the economy is buffeted by demand and supply shocks. By the end of the 1970s, the high inflation rate (then over 10%) helped shift the primary concern of policymakers to the reduction of inflation. What role does credibility play in the effectiveness of anti-inflation policies? The aggregate demand and supply diagram in Figure 26-4 will help us answer this question.

Suppose that the economy has settled into a sustained 10% inflation rate at point 1, with the aggregate demand curve at AD_1 and the short-run aggregate supply curve at AS_1. Now suppose that a new Bank of Canada governor is appointed who decides that inflation must be stopped. He convinces the Governing Council to tighten monetary policy so that the aggregate demand curve is shifted to the left to AD_4, which in the long run will move the economy to point 4 and slow inflation down to the 2% inflation objective.

If the central bank has very little credibility, then the public will not be convinced that the central bank will stay the course to reduce inflation and they will not revise their inflation expectations down from the 10% level. The result is that the short-run aggregate supply curve will remain at AS_1 and the economy will move to point 2. Although inflation will fall to π_2, output will decline to Y_2.

However, what if, instead, the central bank has high credibility and so the public believes that the central bank will do whatever it takes to lower inflation. In this case,

FIGURE 26-4 Credibility and Anti-Inflation Policy

Anti-inflation policy shifts the aggregate demand curve to the left from AD_1 to AD_2. If the central bank lacks credibility, the short-run aggregate supply curve remains at AS_1 and the economy moves to point 2, where output falls to Y_2 and inflation falls to π_2. If the central bank has credibility, then expected inflation declines and the short-run aggregate supply curve shifts down to AS_3. The economy moves to point 3, where output has fallen by less, to Y_3, and inflation has fallen by more, to π_3. Eventually the economy moves to point 4, but with credibility, the anti-inflation policy is more effective, lowering inflation faster and at less cost in terms of output.

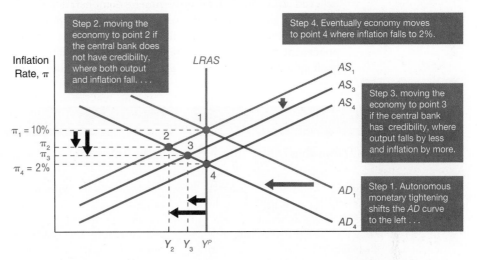

expectations of inflation will fall and the short-run aggregate supply curve will fall to AS_3 and the economy will move to point 3. Inflation will then fall even further, to π_3, and output will decline by less, to Y_3. Indeed, in the extreme case, in which the central bank is perfectly credible, there is even a possibility that inflation expectations will immediately decline to the 2% level and then the short-run aggregate supply curve would shift all the way down to AS_4. In this case, the economy would immediately move to point 4, where inflation has declined to the 2% inflation objective, and yet output would remain at Y^P. In this case, the anti-inflation policy would be costless because it would not require any loss of output. Although this last scenario is unlikely, we have shown the following result: ***the greater is the credibility of the central bank as an inflation fighter, the more rapid will be the decline in inflation and the lower will be the loss of output to achieve the inflation objective.***

Evidence that credibility plays an important role in successful anti-inflation policies is provided by the dramatic end of the Bolivian hyperinflation in 1985 (see the Global box). But establishing credibility is easier said than done. You might think that an announcement by policymakers at the Bank of Canada that they plan to pursue an anti-inflation policy might do the trick. The public would expect this policy and would act accordingly. However, that conclusion implies that the public will believe the policymakers' announcement. Unfortunately, that is not how the real world works.

The history of Bank of Canada policymaking suggests that the Bank of Canada has not always done what it set out to do. In the early 1970s, the Bank of Canada accommodated inflationary shocks by raising the rate of growth of monetary aggregates, thereby forming expectations of rising inflation. When in 1975 the Bank of Canada adopted a gradual anti-inflation policy, the public had no reason to believe in such a policy. Such episodes reduced the credibility of the Bank of Canada in the eyes of the public and, as Figure 26-4 predicts, the resulting lack of credibility had serious consequences. The reduction of inflation that occurred from 1981 to 1984 was bought at a very high cost; the 1981–1982 recession that helped bring the inflation rate down was one of the most severe recessions in the post–World War II period.

The government can play an important role in establishing the credibility of anti-inflation policy. We have seen that large budget deficits may help stimulate inflationary monetary policy, and when the government and the central bank announce that they will pursue a restrictive anti-inflation policy, it is less likely that they will be believed *unless* the federal government demonstrates fiscal responsibility. Another way to say this is to use the old adage "Actions speak louder than words." When the government takes actions that will help the central bank adhere to anti-inflation policy, the policy will be more credible. Unfortunately, this lesson has sometimes been ignored by politicians in the Canada and in other countries.

GLOBAL

Ending the Bolivian Hyperinflation: A Successful Anti-Inflation Program

The most remarkable anti-inflation program in recent times was implemented in Bolivia. In the first half of 1985, Bolivia's inflation rate was running at 20 000% and rising. Indeed, the inflation rate was so high that the price of a movie ticket often rose while people waited in line to buy it. In August 1985, Bolivia's new president announced his anti-inflation program, the New Economic Policy. To rein in money growth and establish credibility, the new government took drastic actions to slash the budget deficit by shutting down many state-owned enterprises, eliminating subsidies, freezing public-sector salaries, and collecting a new wealth tax. The finance ministry was put on a new footing; the budget was balanced on a day-by-day basis. Without exceptions, the finance minister would not authorize spending in excess of the amount of tax revenue that had been collected the day before. The Bolivian inflation was stopped in its tracks within one month, and the output loss was minor (less than 5% of GDP).

Certain hyperinflations before World War II were also ended with small losses of output, using policies similar to Bolivia's,* and a more recent anti-inflation program in Israel that also involved substantial reductions in budget deficits sharply reduced inflation without any clear loss of output. Without doubt, credible anti-inflation policies can be highly successful in eliminating inflation.

*For an excellent discussion of the end of four hyperinflations in the 1920s, see Thomas Sargent, "The Ends of Four Big Inflations," in *Inflation: Causes and Consequences*, ed. Robert E. Hall (Chicago: University of Chicago Press, 1982), 41–98.

APPLICATION

Credibility and the Bank of Canada's Victory over Inflation

In the period from 1965 through the 1970s, policymakers in Canada had little credibility as inflation fighters—a well-deserved reputation, as they pursued discretionary accommodating policy to achieve high employment. The outcome was not a happy one. Inflation soared to double-digit levels, while the unemployment rate remained high. To wring inflation out of the system, the Bank of Canada under Governor Gerald Bouey put the economy through two back-to-back recessions in 1980 and 1981–1982. Only after the 1981–1982 recession—the most severe in the postwar period, with unemployment above the 10% level—did Bouey establish credibility for the Bank of Canada's anti-inflation policy. By the end of 1983, inflation was running at a rate of less than 5%.

From November 1982 to January 1988, the primary objective of the Bank of Canada was price stability in the longer term and inflation containment in the shorter term. This policy, however, was carried out without intermediate targets or a specified path to the longer-term goal. In January 1988, John Crow, the governor of the Bank of Canada, announced that the Bank would subsequently pursue an objective of price stability. One indication of the Bank of Canada's credibility came in 1991 when the Bank's governor and the minister of finance jointly announced a series of declining inflation targets, with a band of plus and minus one percentage point around them. The targets were 3% by the end of 1992, falling to 2% by the end of 1995, to remain within a range of 1% to 3% thereafter. The 1% to 3% target range for inflation has recently been renewed (in November 2011), to apply until the end of 2016.

This has convinced the public and the markets that if inflation reared its head, the Bank of Canada would pursue a nonaccommodating policy of quashing it. Workers and firms have not raised wages and prices, which would have led to both inflation and unemployment. The success of the Bank of Canada's anti-inflation policy has been continuing to date—the inflation rate has been running at a rate of less than 3%. The Bank of Canada's triumph over inflation has been achieved, because it obtained credibility the hard way: it earned it.

Approaches to Establishing Central Bank Credibility

Our analysis has demonstrated that a credible nominal anchor that anchors inflation expectations is a key element to the success of monetary policy. But how do you achieve this credibility? We have already discussed several approaches in earlier chapters. One approach, discussed in Chapter 18, is through continued success at keeping inflation under control through concerted policy actions. Another approach that has been growing in popularity in recent years is *inflation targeting*, also discussed in Chapter 18, which involves public announcement of a medium-term numerical target for inflation and a commitment to achieve it. Another nominal anchor that some countries have successfully used to keep inflation under control is for a country to peg its exchange rate to an anchor country that already has a strong nominal anchor. We discussed this strategy, sometimes called *exchange-rate targeting*, in Chapter 20. Another approach to increasing central bank credibility is to give it more independence from the political process, discussed in Chapter 15. One additional approach, not discussed in earlier chapters but discussed below, is to appoint "conservative" central bankers.

Appoint "Conservative" Central Bankers

Kenneth Rogoff of Harvard University suggested that another way to establish central bank credibility is for the government to appoint central bankers who have a strong aversion to inflation.[6] He characterized these central bankers as "conservative," although a better description would be "tough" or "hawkish on inflation."

---

[6]Rogoff, "The Optimal Degree of Commitment to an Intermediary Monetary Target," *Quarterly Journal of Economics* (November 1985): 169–189.

When the public sees an appointment of a "conservative" central banker, it will expect that he or she will be less tempted to pursue expansionary monetary policy to exploit the short-run tradeoff between inflation and unemployment and will do whatever it takes to keep inflation under control. As a result, inflation expectations and realized inflation are likely to be more stable, with the benefits outlined previously.

The problem with this approach to solving credibility problems is that it is not clear that it will continue to work over time. If a central banker has more "conservative" preferences than the public, why won't the public demand that central bankers who are more in tune with their preferences be appointed? After all, in a democratic society, government officials are supposed to represent the will of the people.

MyEconLab

MyEconLab is an online homework and tutorial system that puts you in control of your own learning with study and practice tools directly correlated to this chapter's content. Visit MyEconLab to explore the following resources:

- The Questions and Applied Problems are all available in the Study Plan on MyEconLab for further practice. You will also find the answers to all of the Questions and Applied Problems in the Student Resources section of your MyEconLab.

MyEconLab also features Additional Readings, Videos, Glossary Flashcards, Audio Chapter Summaries, Economics News Feeds, Animations, and many additional tools to help you master key concepts from the text.

SUMMARY

1. The simple principle (derived from rational expectations theory) that how expectations are formed changes when the behaviour of forecasted variables changes led to the famous Lucas critique of econometric policy evaluation. Lucas argued that when policy changes, how expectations are formed changes; hence the relationships in an econometric model will change. An econometric model that has been estimated on the basis of past data will no longer be the correct model for evaluating the effects of this policy change and may prove to be highly misleading. The Lucas critique also points out that the effects of a particular policy depend critically on the public's expectations about the policy.

2. Advocates of rules to conduct monetary policy believe that rules solve the time-inconsistency problem because policymakers have to follow a set plan that enables them to stick to the plan and achieve desirable long-run outcomes. Advocates of discretion believe that rules are way too rigid because they cannot foresee every contingency and do not allow the use of judgment. Constrained discretion imposes a conceptual structure and its inherent discipline on policymakers, but it does so without eliminating all flexibility, so that it combines some of the advantages ascribed to rules with those ascribed to discretion.

3. An important way to constrain discretion is by committing to a credible, nominal anchor, a nominal variable, such as the inflation rate, the money supply, or an exchange rate, that ties down the price level or inflation to achieve price stability. A credible nominal anchor helps solve the time-inconsistency problem and anchor inflation expectations. Credibility has the benefit of stabilizing both output and inflation fluctuations and also enables anti-inflation policies to lower inflation at a lower cost in terms of lost output.

4. Approaches to establishing credibility include implementing actual policies to keep inflation low, inflation targeting, exchange-rate targeting, and the promotion of central bank independence. Another approach to establishing central bank credibility is the appointment of a "conservative" central banker who is hawkish on controlling inflation.

KEY TERMS

QUESTIONS

1. What does the Lucas critique say about the limitations of our current understanding of the way the economy works?

2. "The Lucas critique by itself casts doubt on the ability of discretionary stabilization policy to be beneficial." Is this statement true, false, or uncertain? Explain your answer.

3. Suppose an econometric model based on past data predicts a small decrease in domestic investment when the Bank of Canada increases the overnight interest rate. Assume that the Bank is considering an increase in the overnight rate target to fight inflation and promote a low inflation environment that promotes investment and economic growth.

    a. Discuss the implications of the econometric model's predictions if individuals interpret the increase in the overnight rate target as a sign that the Bank will keep inflation at low levels in the long run.

    b. What would be Lucas's critique of this model?

4. If the public expects the Bank of Canada to pursue a policy that is likely to raise short-term interest rates permanently to 12%, but the Bank does not go through with this policy change, what will happen to long-term interest rates? Explain your answer.

5. In what sense can greater central bank independence make the time-inconsistency problem worse?

6. What are the arguments for and against policy rules?

7. If, in a surprise victory, a new parliament is elected that the public believes will pursue inflationary policy, predict what might happen to the level of output and inflation even before the new parliament comes into power.

8. Many economists are worried that a high level of budget deficits may lead to inflationary monetary policies in the future. Could these budget deficits have an effect on the current rate of inflation?

9. In some countries, the government chooses the head of the central bank. The same government can fire the head of the central bank and replace him at any time. Explain the implications of such a situation for the conduct of monetary policy. Do you think the central bank will follow a monetary policy rule, or engage in discretionary policy?

10. What are the benefits and costs of sticking to a set of rules in each of the following cases? How do each of these situations relate to the conduct of economic policy?

    a. Going on a diet.
    b. Raising children.

11. How does the case of Switzerland's monetary targeting strategy demonstrate the case against monetary policy rules?

12. How is *constrained discretion* different from *discretion* in monetary policy? How are the outcomes likely to be different?

13. In general, how does credibility (or lack thereof) affect the aggregate supply curve?

14. As part of its response to the global financial crisis, the Federal Reserve in the United States lowered the federal funds rate target to nearly zero by December 2008 and nearly tripled the monetary base between 2008 and 2011, a considerable easing of monetary policy. However, survey-based measures of 5- to 10-year inflation expectations remained low through most of this period. Comment on the Fed's credibility to fight inflation.

15. "The more credible the policymakers who pursue an anti-inflation policy, the more successful that policy will be." Is this statement true, false, or uncertain? Explain your answer.

16. Why did the oil price shocks of the 1970s affect the economy differently than the oil price shocks in 2007?

17. Central banks that engage in inflation targeting usually announce the inflation target and time period for which that target will be relevant. In addition, central bank officials are held accountable for their actions (e.g., they could be fired if the target is not reached), which is also public information. Explain why transparency is such a fundamental ingredient of inflation targeting.

18. Suppose the statistical office of a country does a poor job in measuring inflation and reports an annualized inflation rate of 4% for a few months, while the true inflation rate has been around 2.5%. What would happen to the central bank's credibility if it is engaged in inflation targeting and its target was 2%, plus or minus 0.5%?

19. What are the purposes of inflation targeting and how does this monetary policy strategy achieve them?

20. How can establishing an exchange-rate target bring credibility to a country with a poor record of inflation stabilization?

21. What does it mean to be a "conservative" central banker?

APPLIED PROBLEMS

22. Suppose the central bank is following a constant money growth rule, and the economy is hit with a severe economic downturn. Use an aggregate supply and demand graph to show what the possible effects would be. How does this situation reflect on the credibility of the central bank if it maintains the money growth rule? How does this reflect on its credibility if it abandons the money growth rule to respond to the downturn?

23. Suppose country A has a central bank with full credibility, and country B has a central bank with no credibility. How does the credibility of each country affect the speed of adjustment of the aggregate supply curve to policy announcements? How does this affect output stability? Use an aggregate supply and demand diagram to demonstrate.

24. Suppose two countries have identical aggregate demand curves and potential levels of output, and γ is the same. Assume that in 2013, both countries are hit with the same negative supply shock. Given the table of values below for inflation in each country, what can you say, if anything, about the credibility of each country's central bank? Explain your answer.

	Country A	Country B
2012	3.0%	3.0%
2013	3.8%	5.5%
2014	3.5%	5.0%
2015	3.2%	4.3%
2016	3.0%	3.8%

25. How does a credible nominal anchor help improve the economic outcomes that result from a positive aggregate demand shock? How does it help if a negative aggregate supply shock occurs? Use graphs of aggregate supply and demand to demonstrate.

WEB EXERCISES

1. Robert Lucas won the Nobel Prize in economics. Go to **www.nobelprize.org/nobel_prizes/economics/** and locate the press release on Robert Lucas. What was his Nobel Prize awarded for? When was it awarded?

CHAPTER 27

Transmission Mechanisms of Monetary Policy

LEARNING OBJECTIVES

After studying this chapter you should be able to

1. understand the mechanisms though which monetary policy affects the economy (the interest-rate and exchange-rate channels, Tobin's q theory, and the credit view channels)

2. understand the link between monetary theory and the financial system

PREVIEW

Since 1980, the Canadian economy has been on a roller coaster, with output, unemployment, and inflation undergoing drastic fluctuations. At the start of the 1980s, inflation was running at double-digit levels, and the recession of 1980 was followed by one of the shortest economic expansions on record. After a year, the economy plunged into the 1981–1982 recession, with the unemployment rate climbing to over 10%, and only then did the inflation rate begin to come down to below the 5% level.

For several years following 1984, the Canadian economy enjoyed robust growth, with the inflation rate falling to around 3% and the unemployment rate to around 8% by early 1990. With the Iraqi invasion of Kuwait in the summer of 1990 and the collapse of consumer confidence in the United State, the Canadian economy again plunged into recession. Subsequent growth in the economy was sluggish at first but eventually sped up, lowering the unemployment rate to below 7%. However, with the onset of the global financial crisis, the economy entered a recession in December of 2007, with the unemployment rate rising to over 8.5%. Only in June of 2009 did the economy start to recover, making the recession of 2007–2009 the longest recession since World War II. In light of large fluctuations in aggregate output (reflected in the unemployment rate) and inflation, and the economic instability that accompanies them, policymakers face the following dilemma: what policy or policies, if any, should be implemented to reduce fluctuations in output and inflation in the future?

To answer this question, monetary policymakers must have an accurate assessment of the timing and effect of their policies on the economy. To make this assessment, they need to understand the mechanisms through which monetary policy affects the economy. In this chapter, we examine the transmission mechanisms of monetary policy and evaluate the empirical evidence on them to better understand the role that monetary policy plays in the economy. We will see that these monetary transmission mechanisms emphasize the link between the financial system (which we studied in the first three parts of this book) and monetary theory, the subject of this part.

Transmission Mechanisms of Monetary Policy

In this section we examine the ways in which monetary policy affects aggregate demand and the economy, which are referred to as **transmission mechanisms of monetary policy**. We start with interest-rate channels, because they are the key monetary transmission mechanism in the *AD/AS* model developed in Chapters 22, 23, and 24 and applied to monetary policy in Chapters 25 and 24.

Traditional Interest-Rate Channels

The traditional view of the monetary transmission mechanism can be characterized by the following schematic, which shows the effect of an easing of monetary policy by lowering the real interest rate:

$$r\downarrow \Rightarrow I\uparrow \Rightarrow Y^{ad}\uparrow \tag{1}$$

where an easing of monetary policy leads to a fall in real interest rates ($r\downarrow$), which in turn lowers the real cost of borrowing, causing a rise in investment spending ($I\uparrow$), thereby leading to an increase in aggregate demand ($Y^{ad}\uparrow$).

Although Keynes originally emphasized this channel as operating through businesses' decisions about investment spending, the search for new monetary transmission mechanisms recognized that consumers' decisions about housing and **consumer durable expenditure** (spending by consumers on durable items such as automobiles and refrigerators) also are investment decisions. Thus the interest-rate channel of monetary transmission outlined in Equation 1 applies equally to consumer spending, in which I also represents residential housing and consumer durable expenditure.

An important feature of the interest-rate transmission mechanism is its emphasis on the *real* (rather than the nominal) interest rate as the rate that affects consumer and business decisions. In addition, it is often the real *long-term* interest rate (not the real short-term interest rate) that is viewed as having the major impact on spending. How is it that changes in the short-term nominal interest rate induced by a central bank result in a corresponding change in the real interest rate on both short- and long-term bonds? We have already seen that the key is the phenomenon of *sticky prices*, the fact that the aggregate price level adjusts slowly over time, so that expansionary monetary policy, which lowers the short-term nominal interest rate, also lowers the short-term real interest rate. The expectations hypothesis of the term structure described in Chapter 6, which states that the long-term interest rate is an average of expected future short-term interest rates, suggests that a lower real short-term interest rate, as long as it persists, leads to a fall in the real long-term interest rate. These lower real interest rates then lead to rises in business fixed investment, residential housing investment, inventory investment, and consumer durable expenditure, all of which produce the rise in aggregate demand.

That the real interest rate rather than the nominal rate affects spending provides an important mechanism for how monetary policy can stimulate the economy, even if nominal interest rates hit a floor of zero during a deflationary episode. With nominal interest rates at a floor of zero, a commitment to future expansionary monetary policy can raise expected inflation ($\pi^{e}\uparrow$), thereby lowering the real interest rate,

$(r = i - \pi^e \downarrow)$ even when the nominal interest rate is fixed at zero, and stimulating spending through the interest-rate channel:

$$\pi^e \uparrow \Rightarrow r \downarrow \Rightarrow I \Rightarrow Y^{ad} \uparrow \tag{2}$$

This mechanism thus indicates that monetary policy can still be effective even when nominal interest rates have already been driven down to zero by the monetary authorities. Indeed, this mechanism explains why the Bank of Canada and other central banks resorted to the nonconventional monetary policy during the global financial crisis of committing to keep their policy rates at (or near) zero for an extended period of time. By so doing, central banks were trying to keep inflation expectations from falling in order to make sure that real interest rates remained low to stimulate the economy. In addition, the commitment to keep interest rates low for an extended period of time would help lower long-term interest rates, which would also induce greater spending.

Some economists, such as John Taylor of Stanford University, take the position that strong empirical evidence exists for substantial interest-rate effects on consumer and investment spending through the real cost of borrowing, making the interest-rate monetary transmission mechanism a strong one. His position is highly controversial, and many researchers, including Ben Bernanke, now the chairman of the Federal Reserve, and Mark Gertler of New York University, believe that the empirical evidence does not support strong interest-rate effects operating through the real cost of borrowing.[1] Indeed, these researchers see the empirical failure of traditional interest-rate monetary transmission mechanisms as having provided the stimulus for the search for other transmission mechanisms of monetary policy.

These other transmission mechanisms fall into two basic categories: those operating through asset prices other than interest rates and those operating through asymmetric information effects on credit markets (the **credit view**). (These mechanisms are summarized in the schematic diagram in Figure 27-1.)

Other Asset Price Channels

One drawback of the aggregate demand analysis in previous chapters is that it focuses on only one asset price, the interest rate, rather than on many asset prices. In addition to bond prices, two other asset prices receive substantial attention as channels for monetary policy effects: foreign exchange rates and the prices of equities (stocks).

EXCHANGE RATE EFFECTS ON NET EXPORTS   With the growing internationalization of economies throughout the world and the advent of flexible exchange rates, more attention has been paid to how monetary policy affects exchange rates, which in turn affect net exports and aggregate demand.

This channel also involves interest-rate effects, because, as we saw in Chapter 19, when domestic real interest rates fall, domestic dollar assets become less attractive relative to assets denominated in foreign currencies. As a result, the value of dollar assets relative to other currency assets falls, and the dollar depreciates (denoted by $E \downarrow$). The lower value of the domestic currency makes domestic goods cheaper than foreign goods, thereby causing a rise in net exports ($NX \uparrow$) and hence in aggregate demand ($Y^{ad} \uparrow$). The schematic for the monetary transmission mechanism that operates through the exchange rate is

$$r \downarrow \Rightarrow E \downarrow \Rightarrow NX \uparrow \Rightarrow Y^{ad} \uparrow \tag{3}$$

---

[1]See John Taylor, "The Monetary Transmission Mechanism: An Empirical Framework," *Journal of Economic Perspectives* 9 (Fall 1995): 11–26, and Ben Bernanke and Mark Gertler, "Inside the Black Box: The Credit Channel of Monetary Policy Transmission," *Journal of Economic Perspectives* 9 (Fall 1995): 27–48.

FIGURE 27-1   The Link Between Monetary Policy and Aggregate Demand: Monetary Transmission Mechanisms

This figure shows the different channels through which monetary policy affects aggregate demand.

TOBIN'S *q* THEORY   Nobel Prize winner James Tobin developed a theory, referred to as *Tobin's q theory*, that explains how monetary policy can affect the economy through its effects on the valuation of equities (stock). Tobin defines *q* as the market value of firms divided by the replacement cost of capital. If *q* is high, the market price of firms is high relative to the replacement cost of capital, and new plant and equipment capital is cheap relative to the market value of firms. Companies can then issue stock and get a high price for it relative to the cost of the facilities and equipment they are buying. Investment spending will rise, because firms can buy a lot of new investment goods with only a small issue of stock.

Conversely, when *q* is low, firms will not purchase *new* investment goods because the market value of firms is low relative to the cost of capital. If companies want to acquire capital when *q* is low, they can buy another firm cheaply and acquire old capital instead. Investment spending, the purchase of new investment goods, will then be very low. Tobin's *q* theory gives a good explanation for the extremely low rate of investment spending during the Great Depression. In that period, stock prices collapsed, and by 1933, stocks were worth only one-tenth of their value in late 1929; *q* fell to unprecedented low levels.

The crux of this discussion is that a link exists between Tobin's *q* and investment spending. But how might monetary policy affect stock prices? Quite simply, lower real interest rates on bonds mean that the expected return on this alternative to stocks fall. This makes stocks more attractive relative to bonds, so demand for them increases and raises their price.[2] Combining this with the fact that higher stock prices (P_s) will lead to a higher *q*, and thus higher investment spending *I*, leads to the following transmission mechanism of monetary policy:

$$r\downarrow \Rightarrow P_s\uparrow \Rightarrow q\uparrow \Rightarrow I\uparrow \Rightarrow Y^{ad}\uparrow \qquad (4)$$

WEALTH EFFECT   In their search for new monetary transmission mechanisms, researchers also looked at how consumers' balance sheets might affect their spending decisions. Franco Modigliani was the first to take this tack, using his famous life cycle hypothesis of consumption. **Consumption** is spending by consumers on nondurable goods and services.[3] It differs from *consumer expenditure* in that it does not include spending on consumer durables. The basic premise of Modigliani's theory is that consumers smooth out their consumption over time. Therefore, what determines consumption spending is the lifetime resources of consumers, not just today's income.

An important component of consumers' lifetime resources is their financial wealth, a major part of which is common stocks. When stock prices rise, the value of financial wealth increases, thereby increasing the lifetime resources of consumers, and consumption should rise. Considering that, as we have seen, monetary easing can lead to a rise in stock prices, we now have another monetary transmission mechanism:

$$r\downarrow \Rightarrow P_s\uparrow \Rightarrow \text{wealth}\uparrow \Rightarrow \text{consumption}\uparrow \Rightarrow Y^{ad}\uparrow \qquad (5)$$

Modigliani's research found this relationship to be an extremely powerful mechanism that adds substantially to the potency of monetary policy.

---

[2]An alternative way of looking at this transmission mechanism is to use the model discussed in Chapter 7 in which a decrease in the real interest rate lowers the required return on investments in stocks and so increases stock prices. Then the lower yield on stocks reduces the cost of financing investment spending through issuing equity. This way of looking at the link between stock prices and investment spending is formally equivalent to Tobin's *q* theory.

[3]Consumption also includes another small component, the services that a consumer receives from the ownership of housing and consumer durables.

The wealth and Tobin's q channels allow for a general definition of equity, so they can also be applied to the housing market, where housing is equity. An increase in house prices, which raises their prices relative to replacement cost, leads to a rise in Tobin's q for housing, thereby stimulating its production. Similarly, housing prices are extremely important components of wealth, so rises in these prices increase wealth, thereby raising consumption. Monetary expansion, which raises housing prices through the Tobin's q and wealth mechanisms described here, thus leads to a rise in aggregate demand.

Credit View

Dissatisfaction with the conventional stories that interest-rate effects explain the impact of monetary policy on expenditures on durable assets has led to a new explanation based on the problem of asymmetric information in financial markets that leads to financial frictions (see Chapter 8). This explanation, referred to as the *credit view*, proposes that two types of monetary transmission channels arise as a result of financial frictions in credit markets: those that operate through effects on bank lending and those that operate through effects on firms' and households' balance sheets.

BANK LENDING CHANNEL   The bank lending channel is based on the analysis in Chapter 8, which demonstrated that banks play a special role in the financial system because they are especially well suited to solve asymmetric information problems in credit markets. Because of banks' special role, certain borrowers will not have access to the credit markets unless they borrow from banks. As long as there is no perfect substitutability of retail bank deposits with other sources of funds, the bank lending channel of monetary transmission operates as follows: expansionary monetary policy, which increases bank reserves and bank deposits, raises the quantity of bank loans available. Because many borrowers are dependent on bank loans to finance their activities, this increase in loans will cause investment (and possibly consumer) spending to rise. Schematically, the monetary policy effect is

$$\text{Bank reserves} \uparrow \Rightarrow \text{bank deposits} \uparrow \Rightarrow \text{bank loans} \uparrow \Rightarrow I \uparrow \Rightarrow Y^{ad} \uparrow \qquad (6)$$

An important implication of the credit view is that monetary policy will have a greater effect on expenditure by smaller firms, which are more dependent on bank loans, than it will on large firms, who can get funds directly through stock and bond markets (and not only through banks).

BALANCE SHEET CHANNEL   Even though the bank lending channel may be declining in importance, it is by no means clear that this is the case for the other credit channel, the balance sheet channel. Like the bank lending channel, the balance sheet channel arises from the presence of financial frictions in credit markets. In Chapter 8, we saw that the lower the net worth of business firms, the more severe the adverse selection and moral hazard problems in lending to these firms. Lower net worth means that lenders in effect have less collateral for their loans, so their potential losses from adverse selection are higher. A decline in net worth, which raises the adverse selection problem, thus leads to decreased lending to finance investment spending. The lower net worth of businesses also increases the moral hazard problem because it means that owners have a lower equity stake in their firms, giving them more incentive to engage in risky investment projects. Because taking on riskier investment projects makes it more likely that lenders will not be paid back, a decrease in businesses' net worth leads to a reduction in lending and hence in investment spending.

Monetary policy can affect firms' balance sheets in several ways. Easing of monetary policy, which causes a rise in stock prices $(P_s \uparrow)$ along the lines described earlier, raises the net worth of firms and so leads to higher investment spending $(I \uparrow)$

and aggregate demand ($Y^{ad}\uparrow$) because of the decrease in adverse selection and moral hazard problems. This leads to the following schematic for one balance sheet channel of monetary transmission:

$$r\downarrow \Rightarrow P_s\uparrow \Rightarrow \text{firms' net worth}\uparrow \Rightarrow \text{adverse selection}\downarrow,$$
$$\text{moral hazard}\downarrow \Rightarrow \text{lending}\uparrow \Rightarrow I\uparrow \Rightarrow Y^{ad}\uparrow \qquad (7)$$

CASH FLOW CHANNEL   Another balance sheet channel operates by affecting cash flow, the difference between firms' cash receipts and cash expenditures. An easing of monetary policy, which lowers nominal interest rates, also causes an improvement in firms' balance sheets because it raises cash flow. The rise in cash flow increases the liquidity of the firm (or household) and thus makes it easier for lenders to know whether the firm (or household) will be able to pay its bills. The result is that adverse selection and moral hazard problems become less severe, leading to an increase in lending and economic activity. The following schematic describes this additional balance sheet channel:

$$i\downarrow \Rightarrow \text{firms' cash flow}\uparrow \Rightarrow \text{adverse selection}\downarrow,$$
$$\text{moral hazard}\downarrow \Rightarrow \text{lending}\uparrow \Rightarrow I\uparrow \Rightarrow Y^{ad}\uparrow \qquad (8)$$

An important feature of this transmission mechanism is that *nominal* interest rates affect firms' cash flow. Thus this interest-rate mechanism differs from the traditional interest-rate mechanism discussed earlier, in which the real interest rate affects investment. Furthermore, the short-term interest rate plays a special role in this transmission mechanism, because interest payments on short-term (rather than long-term) debt typically have the greatest impact on the cash flow of households and firms.

A related mechanism involving adverse selection through which expansionary monetary policy that lowers interest rates can stimulate aggregate demand involves the credit-rationing phenomenon. As discussed in Chapter 13, credit rationing occurs in cases where borrowers are denied loans even when they are willing to pay a higher interest rate. This happens because individuals and firms with the riskiest investment projects are exactly the ones who are willing to pay the highest interest rates, for if the high-risk investment succeeds, they will be the primary beneficiaries. Thus higher interest rates increase the adverse selection problem, and lower interest rates reduce it. When expansionary monetary policy lowers interest rates, risk-prone borrowers make up a lower fraction of those demanding loans, so lenders are more willing to lend, raising both investment and aggregate demand, along the lines of parts of the schematic in Equation 8.

UNANTICIPATED PRICE LEVEL CHANNEL   A third balance sheet channel operates through monetary policy effects on the general price level. Because in industrialized countries debt payments are contractually fixed in nominal terms, an unanticipated rise in the price level lowers the value of firms' liabilities in real terms (decreases the burden of the debt) but should not lower the real value of the firms' assets. An easing of monetary policy, which raises inflation and hence leads to an unanticipated rise in the price level ($P\uparrow$) therefore raises real net worth, which lowers adverse selection and moral hazard problems, thereby leading to a rise in investment spending and aggregate demand, as in the following schematic:

$$r\downarrow \Rightarrow \pi\uparrow \Rightarrow \text{unanticipated } P\uparrow \Rightarrow \text{firms' real net worth}\uparrow$$
$$\Rightarrow \text{adverse selection }\downarrow, \text{moral hazard}\downarrow \Rightarrow \text{lending}\uparrow \Rightarrow I\uparrow \Rightarrow Y^{ad}\uparrow \qquad (9)$$

The view that unanticipated movements in the price level affect aggregate demand has a long tradition in economics: it is the key feature in the debt-deflation view of the Great Depression outlined in Chapter 9.

HOUSEHOLD LIQUIDITY EFFECTS   Although most literature on the credit channel focuses on spending by businesses, the credit view should apply equally well to consumer spending, particularly on consumer durables and housing. Declines in bank lending induced by a monetary contraction should cause a decline in durables and housing purchases by consumers who do not have access to other sources of credit. Similarly, increases in interest rates cause a deterioration in household balance sheets, because consumers' cash flow is adversely affected.

Another way of looking at how the balance sheet channel may operate through consumers is to consider liquidity effects on consumer durable and housing expenditures, which were found to be important factors during the Great Depression (see the FYI box Consumers' Balance Sheets and the Great Depression). In the liquidity effects view, balance sheet effects work through their impact on consumers' desire to spend rather than on lenders' desire to lend. Because of asymmetric information about their quality, consumer durables and housing are very illiquid assets. If, as a result of a bad income shock, consumers needed to sell their consumer durables or housing to raise money, they would expect a big loss because they could not get the full value of these assets in a distress sale. (This is just a manifestation of the lemons problem described in Chapter 8.) In contrast, if consumers held financial assets (such as money in the bank, stocks, or bonds), they could easily sell them quickly for their full market value and raise the cash. Hence, if consumers expect a higher likelihood of finding themselves in financial distress, they would rather hold fewer illiquid consumer durable or housing assets and more liquid financial assets.

A consumer's balance sheet should be an important influence on his or her estimate of the likelihood of suffering financial distress. Specifically, when consumers have a large amount of financial assets relative to their debts, their estimate of the probability of financial distress is low, and they will be more willing to purchase consumer durables or housing. When stock prices rise, the value of financial assets increases as well; consumer durable expenditure will also rise because consumers have a more secure financial position and a lower estimate of the likelihood of suffering financial distress. This leads to another transmission mechanism for monetary policy, operating through the link between money and stock prices:

$$r\downarrow \Rightarrow P_s\uparrow \Rightarrow \text{value of households' financial assets}\uparrow$$
$$\Rightarrow \text{likelihood of financial distress}\downarrow \qquad (10)$$
$$\Rightarrow \text{consumer durable and housing expenditure}\uparrow \Rightarrow Y^{ad}\uparrow$$

FYI

Consumers' Balance Sheets and the Great Depression

The years between 1929 and 1933 witnessed the worst deterioration in consumers' balance sheets ever seen in the United States. The stock market crash in 1929, which caused a slump that lasted until 1933, reduced the value of consumers' wealth by $737 billion (in 2000 dollars), and as expected, consumption dropped sharply (by over $100 billion). Because of the decline in the price level in that period, the level of real debt consumers owed also increased sharply (by over 20%). Consequently, the value of financial assets relative to the amount of debt declined sharply, increasing the likelihood of financial distress. Not surprisingly, spending on consumer durables and housing fell precipitously: from 1929 to 1933, consumer durable expenditure in the United States declined by over 50%, while expenditure on housing declined by 80%.[*]

[*]For further discussion of the effect of consumers' balance sheets on spending during the Great Depression, see Frederic S. Mishkin, "The Household Balance Sheet and the Great Depression," *Journal of Economic History* 38 (1978): 918–937.

The illiquidity of consumer durable and housing assets provides another reason why a monetary easing, which lowers interest rates and thereby raises cash flow to consumers, leads to a rise in spending on consumer durables and housing. A rise in consumer cash flow decreases the likelihood of financial distress, which increases the desire of consumers to hold durable goods or housing, thus increasing spending on them and hence aggregate demand. The only difference between this view of cash flow effects and that outlined in Equation 8 is that it is not the willingness of lenders to lend to consumers that causes expenditure to rise, but the willingness of consumers to spend.

Why Are Credit Channels Likely to Be Important?

There are three reasons to believe that credit channels are important monetary transmission mechanisms. First, a large body of evidence on the behaviour of individual firms supports the view that financial frictions of the type crucial to the operation of credit channels do affect firms' employment and spending decisions. Second, evidence shows that small firms (which are more likely to be credit-constrained) are hurt more by tight monetary policy than large firms, which are unlikely to be credit-constrained. Third, and maybe most compelling, the asymmetric information view of financial frictions at the core of the credit channel analysis is a theoretical construct that has proved useful in explaining many other important phenomena, such as why many of our financial institutions exist, why our financial system has the structure that it has, and why financial crises are so damaging to the economy (topics discussed in Chapters 8 and 9). The best support for a theory is its demonstrated usefulness in a wide range of applications. By this standard, the asymmetric information theory supporting the existence of credit channels as an important monetary transmission mechanism has much to recommend it.

APPLICATION

The Great Recession

With the advent of the financial crisis in the summer of 2007, the Bank of Canada and many other central banks around the world began a very aggressive easing of monetary policy. For example, the Federal Reserve dropped the target federal funds rate from $5\frac{1}{4}\%$ to $\frac{1}{4}\%$ to 0% over a 15-month period from September 2007 to December 2008. At first, it appeared that the Fed's actions would keep the growth slowdown mild and prevent a recession. However, the U.S. economy proved to be weaker than the Fed or private forecasters expected, with the most severe recession in the post–World War II period beginning in December 2007. Why did the U.S. economy become so weak despite this unusually rapid reduction in the Fed's policy instrument?

The subprime meltdown led to negative effects on the economy from many of the channels we have outlined above. The rising level of subprime mortgage defaults, which led to a decline in the value of mortgage-backed securities and CDOs, resulted in large losses on the balance sheets of financial institutions. With weaker balance sheets, these financial institutions began to deleverage and cut back on their lending. With no one else to collect information and make loans, adverse selection and moral hazard problems, and hence financial frictions, increased in credit markets, leading to a slowdown of the economy. Credit spreads also went through the roof, with the increase in uncertainty from failures of so many financial markets. The decline in the stock market and housing prices also weakened the economy, because it lowered household wealth. The decrease in household wealth led to restrained consumer spending and weaker investment, because of the resulting drop in Tobin's q.

With all these channels operating, it is no surprise that despite the Fed's aggressive lowering of the federal funds rate, the U.S. economy still took a big hit.

Lessons for Monetary Policy

What useful implications for central banks' conduct of monetary policy can we draw from the analysis in this chapter? Four basic lessons can be learned.

1. *It is dangerous always to associate the easing or the tightening of monetary policy with a fall or a rise in short-term nominal interest rates.* Because most central banks use short-term nominal interest rates—typically, the interbank rate—as the key operating instrument for monetary policy, the danger exists that central banks and the public will focus too much on short-term nominal interest rates as an indicator of the stance of monetary policy. Indeed, it is quite common to see statements that always associate monetary tightenings with a rise in the interbank rate and monetary easings with a decline in the rate. We do not make this mistake in the analysis in this book because we have been careful to associate monetary easing or tightening with changes in *real* and not *nominal* interest rates.

2. *Other asset prices besides those on short-term debt instruments contain important information about the stance of monetary policy because they are important elements in various monetary policy transmission mechanisms.* As we have seen in this chapter, economists have come a long way in understanding that other asset prices besides interest rates have major effects on aggregate demand. As we saw in Figure 27-1, other asset prices, such as stock prices, foreign exchange rates, and housing prices, play an important role in monetary transmission mechanisms. Furthermore, the discussion of such additional channels as those operating through the exchange rate, Tobin's *q*, and wealth effects provides additional reasons why other asset prices play such an important role in monetary transmission mechanisms. Although economists strongly disagree among themselves about which channels of monetary transmission are the most important—not surprising, given that economists, particularly those in academia, always like to disagree—they do concur that other asset prices play an important role in the way monetary policy affects the economy.

   The view that other asset prices besides short-term interest rates matter has important implications for monetary policy. When we try to assess the stance of policy, it is critical that we look at other asset prices in addition to short-term interest rates. For example, if short-term interest rates are low or even zero and yet stock prices are low, housing prices are low, and the value of the domestic currency is high, monetary policy is clearly tight, not easy.

3. *Monetary policy can be effective in reviving a weak economy even if short-term interest rates are already near zero.* We have recently entered a world where inflation is not always the norm. Japan, for example, recently experienced a period of deflation when the price level was actually falling. In the United States, the federal funds rate hit a floor of zero by the end of 2008. One common view is that when a central bank has driven down short-term nominal interest rates to nearly zero, the monetary policy can do nothing more to stimulate the economy. The transmission mechanisms of monetary policy described here indicate that this view is false. As our discussion of the factors that affect the monetary base in Chapter 16 indicated, expansionary monetary policy to increase liquidity in the economy can be conducted with open market purchases, which do not have to be solely in short-term government securities. For example, purchases of private securities, as the Bank of Canada did in 2009, can reduce financial frictions by lowering credit spreads and stimulating investment spending. In addition, a commitment to future expansionary monetary policy helps revive the economy by raising general price-level expectations and by reflating other asset prices, which

then stimulate aggregate demand through the channels outlined here. Policies of this type are the nonconventional monetary policies we discussed in Chapter 17. Nonconventional monetary policy can be a potent force for reviving economies that are undergoing deflation and have short-term interest rates near zero. Indeed, as we saw in Chapter 9, aggressive nonconventional monetary policy during the recent financial crisis helped prevent the Great Recession from turning into a Great Depression and also helped the economy avoid a deflationary episode as occurred during the Great Depression era.

4. ***Avoiding unanticipated fluctuations in the price level is an important objective of monetary policy, thus providing a rationale for price stability as the primary long-run goal for monetary policy.*** As we saw in Chapter 18, central banks in recent years have been placing greater emphasis on price stability as the primary long-run goal for monetary policy. Several rationales have been proposed for this goal, including the undesirable effects of uncertainty about the future price level on business decisions and hence on productivity, distortions associated with the interaction of nominal contracts and the tax system with inflation, and increased social conflict stemming from inflation. The discussion here of monetary transmission mechanisms provides an additional reason why price stability is so important. As we have seen, unanticipated movements in the price level can cause unanticipated fluctuations in output, an undesirable outcome. Particularly important in this regard is the knowledge that, as we saw in Chapter 9, price deflation can be an important factor leading to a prolonged financial crisis, as occurred during the Great Depression. An understanding of the monetary transmission mechanisms thus makes it clear that the goal of price stability is desirable, because it reduces uncertainty about the future price level. Thus the price stability goal implies that a negative inflation rate is at least as undesirable as too high an inflation rate. Indeed, because of the threat of financial crises, central banks must work very hard to prevent price deflation.

APPLICATION

Applying the Monetary Policy Lessons to Japan

Until 1990, it looked as if Japan might overtake the United States in per capita income. Since then, the Japanese economy has been stagnating, with deflation and low growth. As a result, Japanese living standards have been falling further and further behind those in the United States. Many economists take the view that Japanese monetary policy is in part to blame for the poor performance of the Japanese economy. Could applying the four lessons outlined in the previous section have helped Japanese monetary policy perform better?

The first lesson suggests that it is dangerous to think that declines in interest rates always mean that monetary policy has been easing. In the mid-1990s, when short-term interest rates began to decline, falling to nearly zero in the late 1990s and early 2000s, the monetary authorities in Japan took the view that monetary policy was sufficiently expansionary. Now it is widely recognized that this view was incorrect, because the falling and eventually negative inflation rates in Japan meant that real interest rates were actually quite high and that monetary policy was tight, not easy. If the monetary authorities in Japan had followed the advice of the first lesson, they might have pursued a more expansionary monetary policy, which would have helped boost the economy.

The second lesson suggests that monetary policymakers should pay attention to other asset prices in assessing the stance of monetary policy. At the same time interest rates were falling in Japan, stock and real estate prices were collapsing, thus providing another indication that Japanese monetary policy was not easy. Recognizing the second lesson might have led Japanese monetary policymakers to recognize sooner that they needed a more expansionary monetary policy.

The third lesson indicates that monetary policy can still be effective even if short-term interest rates are near zero. Officials at the Bank of Japan have frequently claimed that they have been helpless in stimulating the economy, because short-term interest rates had fallen to nearly zero. Recognizing that monetary policy can still be effective even when interest rates are near zero, as the third lesson suggests, would have helped them to take monetary policy actions that would have stimulated aggregate demand by raising other asset prices and inflationary expectations.

The fourth lesson indicates that unanticipated fluctuations in the price level should be avoided. If the Japanese monetary authorities had adhered to this lesson, they might have recognized that allowing deflation to occur could be very damaging to the economy and would be inconsistent with the goal of price stability. Indeed, critics of the Bank of Japan have suggested that the bank should announce an inflation target to promote the price stability objective, but the bank has resisted this suggestion.

Heeding the advice from the four lessons in the previous section might have led to a far more successful conduct of monetary policy in Japan in recent years.

MyEconLab

MyEconLab is an online homework and tutorial system that puts you in control of your own learning with study and practice tools directly correlated to this chapter's content. Visit MyEconLab to explore the following resources:

- The Questions and Applied Problems are all available in the Study Plan on MyEconLab for further practice. You will also find the answers to all of the Questions and Applied Problems in the Student Resources section of your MyEconLab.
- Visit the Student Resources section of MyEconLab to access the following appendix for this chapter: Appendix 27.1: Evaluating Empirical Evidence: The Debate over the Importance of Money in Economic Fluctuations.

MyEconLab also features Additional Readings, Videos, Glossary Flashcards, Audio Chapter Summaries, Economics News Feeds, Animations, and many additional tools to help you master key concepts from the text.

SUMMARY

MyEcon
Audio Sum

1. The transmission mechanisms of monetary policy include traditional interest-rate channels that operate through the real cost of borrowing and affect investment; other asset price channels such as exchange rate effects, Tobin's q theory, and wealth effects; and the credit view channels—the bank lending channel, the balance sheet channel, the cash flow channel, the unanticipated price level channel, and household liquidity effects.

2. Four lessons for monetary policy can be drawn from this chapter: (a) it is dangerous always to associate monetary policy easing or tightening with a fall or a rise in short-term nominal interest rates; (b) other asset prices besides those on short-term debt instruments contain important information about the stance of monetary policy because they are important elements in the monetary policy transmission mechanisms; (c) monetary policy can be effective in reviving a weak economy even if short-term interest rates are already near zero; and (d) avoiding unanticipated fluctuations in the price level is an important objective of monetary policy, thus providing a rationale for price stability as the primary long-run goal for monetary policy.

KEY TERMS

consumer durable expenditure, p. 638

consumption, p. 641

credit view, p. 638

transmission mechanisms of monetary policy, p. 638

QUESTIONS

1. In 2009, in the wake of the global financial crisis when interest rates were at their lowest, the governments around the world instituted programs designed in part to stimulate new spending on automobiles and major appliances. What does this say about views of the health of the interest rate channel during that time?

2. "Considering that consumption is nearly 2/3 of total GDP, this means that the interest rate, wealth, and household liquidity channels are the most important monetary policy channels in Canada." Is this statement true, false, or uncertain? Explain your answer.

3. How can the interest rate channel still function when short-term nominal interest rates are at the zero lower bound?

4. Lars Svensson, a deputy governor of the Swedish central bank, proclaimed that when an economy is at risk of falling into deflation, central bankers should be "responsibly irresponsible" with monetary expansion. What does this mean, and how does it relate to the monetary transmission mechanism?

5. Describe an advantage and a disadvantage to monetary policy of having so many different channels through which monetary policy can operate.

6. "If countries fix their exchange rate, the exchange rate channel of monetary policy does not exist." Is this statement true, false, or uncertain? Explain your answer.

7. In the 2007–2009 recession, the value of common stocks in real terms fell almost 50%. How might this decline in the stock market have affected aggregate demand and thus contributed to the severity of this recession? Be specific about the mechanisms through which the stock market decline affected the economy.

8. "The costs of financing investment are related only to interest rates; therefore, the only way that monetary policy can affect investment spending is through its effects on interest rates." Is this statement true, false, or uncertain? Explain your answer.

9. Predict what will happen to stock prices after a monetary easing. Explain your prediction.

10. From mid-2008 to early 2009, the S&P/TSX Industrial Average declined sharply, while real interest rates were low or were falling. What does this suggest would have happened to investment?

11. Economist Franco Modigliani found that the most important transmission mechanisms of monetary policy involve consumer expenditure. Describe how at least two of these mechanisms work.

12. In the late 1990s, the stock market was rising rapidly, the U.S. economy was growing, and the Federal Reserve kept interest rates relatively low. Comment on how this policy stance would affect the economy as it relates to the Tobin q transmission mechanisms.

13. During and after the global financial crisis, the Bank of Canada reduced the overnight interest rate to nearly zero. At the same time, the stock market fell dramatically and housing market values declined. Comment on the effectiveness of monetary policy in this period through the wealth channel.

14. During and after the global financial crisis, the Bank of Canada provided banks with large amounts of liquidity. Banks' excess reserves increased sharply, while credit extended to households and firms decreased sharply. Comment on the effectiveness of the bank lending channel during this time.

15. Why does the credit view imply that monetary policy has a greater effect on small businesses rather than large firms?

16. Why might the bank lending channel be less effective than it once was?

17. One of the classic features of the global financial crisis is the failure of high-profile investment banks and financial firms, such as Lehman Brothers, Bear Stearns, and AIG in the United States. These firms experienced sharp contractions in the value of their balance sheets due to risky asset holdings. Comment on how this would affect the U.S. economy, as it relates to the balance sheet channel.

18. If adverse selection and moral hazard increase, how does this affect the ability of monetary policy to address economic downturns?

19. How does the Great Depression demonstrate the unanticipated price level channel?

20. How are the wealth effect and household liquidity effect similar? How are they different?

21. Following the global financial crisis, mortgage rates reached record low levels in 2011.

    a. What effect should this have, according to the household liquidity effect channel?

    b. During the same time, most banks raised their credit standards significantly, making it much more difficult to qualify for home loans and refinance existing loans. How does this alter your answer to part (a)?

22. What evidence exists to support the credit view of monetary policy?

23. "A decrease in short-term nominal interest rates necessarily implies a stance of monetary easing." Is this statement true, false, or uncertain? Explain your answer.

24. How does the case of Japan support the "four lessons for monetary policy"?

APPLIED PROBLEMS

25. Suppose the economy is in recession, and monetary policymakers lower interest rates to stabilize the economy. Use an aggregate supply and demand diagram to demonstrate the effects of a monetary easing when the transmission mechanisms are functioning normally, and when the transmission mechanisms are weak, such as during a deep downturn or when significant financial frictions are present.

WEB EXERCISES

1. Go to **www.martincapital.com** and click on "U.S. Financial Data" and then "U.S. Financial Charts," then on "Fed Funds Target" to find data showing real interest rates and nominal interest rates. When do the nominal and real interest rates give a very different picture about the tightness of monetary policy? How might this have led monetary policymakers to make mistakes if they focused entirely on nominal interest rates?

2. Go to **www.econlib.org/library/Enc1/Recessions. html** and review the material reported on recessions.

   a. What is the formal definition of a recession?
   b. What are the problems with the definition?

GLOSSARY

activists Economists who regard the self-correcting mechanism through wage and price adjustment as very slow because wages and prices are sticky and so see the need to pursue active policy to eliminate high unemployment when it develops. **610**

adaptive expectations Expectations of a variable based on an average of past values of the variable. **144**

adverse selection The problem created by asymmetric information before a transaction occurs: the people who are the most undesirable from the other party's point of view are the ones who are most likely to want to engage in the financial transaction. **35**

agency theory The analysis of how asymmetric information problems affect economic behaviour. **154**

aggregate demand The total quantity of output demanded in the economy at different price levels. **542**

aggregate demand curve A relationship between the price level and the quantity of aggregate output demanded when the goods and money markets are in equilibrium. **562, 571**

aggregate income The total income of factors of production (land, labour, capital) in the economy. **18**

aggregate output The total production of final goods and services in the economy. **7**

aggregate price level The average price of goods and services in an economy. **8**

aggregate supply curve The relationship between the quantity of output supplied and the price level. **576**

American option An option that can be exercised at any time up to the expiration date of the contract. **334**

anchor currency A currency to which other countries' currencies are pegged. **497**

"animal spirits" Waves of optimism and pessimism that affect consumers' and businesses' willingness to spend. **544**

annuities Financial contracts under which a customer pays an annual premium in exchange for a future stream of annual payments beginning at a set age (say, 65) and ending when the person dies. **272**

appreciation Increase in a currency's value. **11, 471**

arbitrage Elimination of a riskless profit opportunity in a market. **149, 327**

asset A financial claim or piece of property that is a store of value. **3**

asset management The acquisition of assets that have a low rate of default and diversification of asset holdings to increase profits. **300**

asset market approach An approach to determine asset prices using stocks of assets rather than flows. **90**

asset-price bubbles Increases in asset prices in the stock and real estate markets that are driven well above their fundamental economic values by investor psychology. **184, 450**

asset transformation The process of turning risky assets into safer assets for investors by creating and selling assets with risk characteristics that people are comfortable with and then using the funds acquired by selling these assets to purchase other assets that may have far more risk. **34**

asymmetric information The unequal knowledge that each party to a transaction has about the other party. **34**

at the money (trading at par) option Option whose exercise price is just equal to the current asset price. **336**

audits Certification by accounting firms that a business is adhering to standard business principles. **167**

automated banking machine (ABM) One location that provides an automated teller machine (ATM), an Internet connection to the bank's website, and a telephone link to customer service. **275**

automated teller machine (ATM) An electronic machine that provides banking services 24 hours a day. **245**

autonomous consumption expenditure The amount of consumer expenditure that is independent of disposable income. **543**

autonomous easing of monetary policy Lowering real interest rates at any given inflation rate. **561**

autonomous investment A component of planned investment spending that is completely exogenous and so is unexplained by the variables in a model. **544**

autonomous net exports The level of net exports that is treated as exogenous (outside the model). **456**

autonomous spending Exogenous spending that is unrelated to variables in the model such as output or real interest rate. **553**

autonomous tightening of monetary policy Raising real interest rates at any given inflation rate. **561**

balance of payments A bookkeeping system for recording all payments that have a direct bearing on the movement of funds between a country and foreign countries. **496**

balance-of-payments crisis A foreign exchange crisis stemming from problems in a country's balance of payments. **506**

balance sheet A list of the assets and liabilities of a bank (or firm) that balances: Total assets equal total liabilities plus capital. **294**

Bank Act Reform The legislation that took effect in October of 2001 regarding the policy framework of the Canadian financial services sector. **263**

bank failure A situation in which a bank cannot satisfy its obligations to pay its depositors and other creditors and so goes out of business. **211**

bank holding companies Companies that own one or more banks. **255**

Bank of Canada (the Bank) Canada's central bank. **10**

bank panic The simultaneous failure of many banks, as during a financial crisis. **184**

bank rate The interest rate the Bank of Canada charges to members of the Canadian Payments Association. **302, 377**

banker's risk The risk of not holding enough reserves to make immediate and larger than normal cash payments to liability holders. **296**

banks Financial institutions that accept money deposits and make loans (such as commercial banks, trust and mortgage loan companies, and credit unions and *caisses populaires*). **6**

base money The sum of the Bank of Canada's monetary liabilities (notes outstanding and bank settlement balances) and coins outstanding. Also called *monetary base*. **356**

Basel Accord An agreement that required that banks hold as capital at least 8% of their risk-weighted assets. **215**

Basel Committee on Banking Supervision An international committee of bank supervisors that meets under the auspices of the Bank for International Settlements in Basel, Switzerland. **215**

basis point One one-hundredth of a percentage point. **116**

bearer deposit notes CDs and GICs that can be traded and are in bearer form, meaning that whoever holds the instrument at maturity receives the principal and interest. **26**

behavioural finance A subfield of finance that applies concepts from other social sciences such as anthropology, sociology, and, particularly, psychology to understand the behaviour of securities prices. **154**

Board of Directors A board with 15 members (including the governor) that is responsible for the management of the Bank of Canada. **355**

Board of Governors of the Federal Reserve System A board with seven governors (including the chairman) that plays an essential role in decision making within the Federal Reserve System. **366**

bond A debt security that promises to make payments periodically for a specified period of time. **3**

borrowed reserves The loans the central bank makes to deposit-based financial institutions. **383**

branches Additional offices of banks that conduct banking operations. **239**

Bretton Woods system The international monetary system in use from 1945 to 1971 in which exchange rates were fixed and the U.S. dollar was freely convertible into gold (by foreign governments and central banks only). **498**

brokerage firms Firms that participate in securities markets as brokers, dealers, and investment bankers. **283**

brokers Agents for investors; they match buyers with sellers. **24**

bubble A situation in which the price of an asset differs from its fundamental market value. **153**

budget deficit The excess of government expenditure over tax revenues. **10**

budget surplus The excess of tax revenues over government expenditures. **10**

business cycles The upward and downward movement of aggregate output produced in the economy. **7**

call (redemption) A redemption feature allowing issues to be "called" on specified notice. **29**

call option An option contract that provides the right to buy a security at a specified price. **335**

call premium Price of a call option. **335**

Canada bonds (Canadas) Securities issued by the Government of Canada. **30**

capital account An account that describes the flow of capital between a country and other countries. **496**

capital adequacy management A bank's decision about the amount of capital it should maintain and then acquisition of the needed capital. **300**

capital buyout fund A private equity fund that makes investments in established businesses. **287**

capital controls Restrictions on the free movement of capital across borders. **501**

capital market A financial market in which longer-term debt (generally with original maturity of greater than one year) and equity instruments are traded. **25**

capital mobility A situation in which foreigners can easily purchase a country's assets and the country's residents can easily purchase foreign assets. **491**

carried interest A share of the profit paid to a private equity fund. **288**

cash flow The difference between cash receipts and cash expenditures. **202**

cash flows Cash payments to the holder of a security. **138**

central bank The government agency that oversees the banking system and is responsible for the amount of money and credit supplied in the economy; in Canada, the Bank of Canada. **10, 238**

central bank independence Advocates of central bank independence find that inflation performance is found to be the best for countries with the most independent central banks. **365**

closed-end fund A mutual fund in which a fixed number of nonredeemable shares are sold at an initial offering, then traded in the over-the-counter market like common stock. **284**

coinsurance A situation in which only a portion of losses are covered by insurance, so that the insured suffers a percentage of the losses along with the insurance agency. **277**

collateral Property that is pledged to the lender to guarantee payment in the event that the borrower is unable to make debt payments. **163**

commodity money Money made up of precious metals or another valuable commodity. **50**

common stock A security that is a claim on the earnings and assets of a company. **3**

compensating balance A required minimum amount of funds that a firm receiving a loan must keep in a chequing account at the lending bank. **310**

conditional statements The central bank's intervention in the formation of public expectations about future interest rates through public statements; also called *forward guidance*. **425**

conflicts of interest A manifestation of the moral hazard problem, particularly when a financial institution provides multiple services and the potentially competing interests of those services may lead to a concealment of information or dissemination of misleading information. **36**

consol A perpetual bond with no maturity date and no repayment of principal that periodically makes fixed coupon payments. Also called *perpetuity.* **70**

constant-money-growth-rate rule A policy rule advocated by monetarists whereby the central bank keeps the money supply growing at a constant rate. **622**

constrained discretion A framework in which the general objectives and tactics of policymakers—but not specific actions—are committed to in advance; this imposes a conceptual structure and inherent discipline on policymakers without eliminating all flexibility. **625**

consumer durable expenditure Spending by consumers on durable items such as automobiles and household appliances. **638**

consumption Spending by consumers on nondurable goods and services (including services related to the ownership of homes and consumer durables). **641**

consumption expenditure The total demand for consumer goods and services. **542, 571**

consumption function The relationship between disposable income and consumer expenditure. **542**

cost-push inflation Inflation that occurs because of the push by workers to obtain higher wages. **613**

cost-push shocks Price shocks in which workers push for wages higher than productivity gains, thereby driving up costs and inflation. **578**

costly state verification Monitoring a firm's activities, an expensive process in both time and money. **172**

coupon bond A credit market instrument that pays the owner a fixed interest payment every year until the maturity date, when a specified final amount is repaid. **65**

coupon rate The dollar amount of the yearly coupon payment expressed as a percentage of the face value of a coupon bond. **65**

credibility A commitment to policy actions that is believed by the public. **625**

credit boom A lending spree when financial institutions expand their lending at a rapid pace. **182**

credit default swaps (CDS) Financial insurance contracts that provide payments to holders of bonds if they default. **273**

credit derivatives Derivatives that have payoffs to previously issued securities, but ones that bear credit risk. **345**

credit easing Altering the composition of the central bank's balance sheet in order to improve the functioning of particular segments of the credit markets. **374**

credit-linked note A type of credit derivative that combines a bond and a credit option. **346**

credit options Options in which, for a fee, the purchaser has the right to get profits that are tied either to the price of an underlying risky security or to an interest rate. **345**

credit-rating agencies Investment advisory firms that rate the quality of corporate and government bonds in terms of the probability of default. **114**

credit rationing A lender's refusal to make loans even though borrowers are willing to pay the stated interest rate or even a higher rate or restriction of the size of loans made to less than the full amount sought. **311**

credit risk The risk arising from the possibility that the borrower will default. **300**

credit spread The difference between the interest rate on loans to households and businesses and the interest rate on completely safe assets that are sure to be paid off, such as Canada bonds. **187**

credit swap A transaction in which risky payments on loans are swapped for each other. **346**

credit view Monetary transmission mechanisms operating through asymmetric information effects on credit markets. **638**

currency Paper money (such as bills) and coins. **46**

currency board A monetary regime in which the domestic currency is backed 100% by a foreign currency (say, dollars) and in which the note-issuing authority, whether the central bank or the government, establishes a fixed exchange rate to this foreign currency and stands ready to exchange domestic currency at this rate whenever the public requests it. **517**

currency mismatch When emerging market economies denominate many debt contracts in foreign currency, while their assets are denominated in domestic currency. **203**

currency swap The exchange of a set of payments in one currency for a set of payments in another currency. **342**

current account An account that shows international transactions involving currently produced goods and services. **496**

current yield An approximation of the yield to maturity that equals the yearly coupon payment divided by the price of a coupon bond. **71**

data lag The time it takes for policymakers to obtain data indicating what is happening to the economy. **611**

dealers People who link buyers with sellers by buying and selling securities at stated prices. **24**

debt deflation A situation in which a substantial decline in the price level sets in, leading to a further deterioration in firms' net worth because of the increased burden of indebtedness. **185**

deductible The fixed amount by which the insured party's loss is reduced when a claim is paid off.

default A situation in which the party issuing a debt instrument is unable to make interest payments or pay off the amount owed when the instrument matures. **26**

default-free bonds Bonds with no default risk, such as Canada bonds. **118**

defined-benefit plan A pension plan in which benefits are set in advance. **278**

defined-contribution plan A pension plan in which benefits are determined by the contributions into the plan and their earnings. **278**

deleveraging When financial institutions cut back on their lending because they have less capital. **182**

demand curve A curve depicting the relationship between quantity demanded and price when all other economic variables are held constant. **87**

demand for money The quantity of money that people want to hold.   **527**

demand shocks Shocks that can shift the aggregate demand curve, including changes in the money supply, changes in government expenditure and taxes, changes in net exports, changes in consumer and business spending, and financial frictions.   **573**

demand-pull inflation Inflation that results when policy-makers pursue policies that shift the aggregate demand curve.   **613**

demutualization The process of converting a life insur-ance company into a stock company.   **271**

deposit facility The central bank's standing facility in which banks are paid a fixed interest rate that is less than the policy rate; in Canada, 25 basis points below the policy rate.   **434**

deposit outflows Losses of deposits when depositors make withdrawals or demand payment.   **300**

deposit rate ceiling Restriction on the maximum interest rate payable on deposits.   **248**

depreciation Decrease in a currency's value.   **11, 471**

desired reserve ratio The fraction of deposits that banks desire to keep as reserves.   **296, 377**

desired reserves Reserves that are held to meet the banks' desire that for every dollar of deposits, a certain fraction should be kept as reserves.   **296, 377**

devaluation Resetting of the fixed value of a currency at a lower level.   **501**

direct clearers Members of the Canadian Payments Association who participate directly in the Automated Clearing Settlement System (ACSS) and maintain a settle-ment account at the Bank of Canada.   **405**

discount bond A credit market instrument that is bought at a price below its face value and whose face value is repaid at the maturity date; it does not make any interest pay-ments. Also called a *zero-coupon bond.*   **65**

discount rate The interest rate that the Federal Reserve charges banks on discount loans.   **419**

discount window lending The Federal Reserve facility at which discount loans are made to banks.   **429**

discretion When policymakers make decisions they believe to be the right policies at the moment for a given situation.   **621**

disintermediation A reduction in the flow of funds into the banking system that causes the amount of financial intermediation to decline.   **248**

disposable income Total income available for spending, equal to aggregate income minus taxes.   **542**

diversification Investing in a collection (portfolio) of assets whose returns do not always move together, with the result that overall risk is lower than for individual assets.   **34**

dividends Periodic payments made by equities to share-holders.   **24, 138**

divine coincidence Phrase coined by Olivier Blanchard, referring to the situation in which a policy to stabilize inflation is also the right policy to stabilize economic activity—with no conflict between them.   **605**

dollarization The adoption of a sound currency, like the U.S. dollar, as a country's money.   **518**

dominated assets Assets such as currency and chequable assets which earn lower returns than other assets which are just as safe.   **535**

drawdowns Transfers of government deposits from the government's accounts with the direct clearers to the government's account with the Bank of Canada.   **418**

dual banking system The system in the United States in which banks supervised by the federal government and banks supervised by the states operate side by side.   **239**

dual mandate A central bank mandate that features two co-equal objectives: price stability and maximum employment.   **442**

duration analysis A measurement of the sensitivity of the market value of a bank's assets and liabilities to changes in interest rates.   **313**

e-cash Electronic money that is used on the Internet to purchase goods or services.   **52**

e-finance A new means of delivering financial services electronically.   **6**

economies of scale The reduction in transaction costs per dollar of transaction as the size (scale) of transactions increases.   **34**

economies of scope The ability to use one resource to pro-vide many different products and services.   **36**

effectiveness lag The time it takes for a policy to actually have an impact on the economy.   **611**

efficient market hypothesis The application of the theory of rational expectations to financial markets.   **146**

electoral business cycles Persistent cyclical patterns of key policy and target variables across electoral terms.   **363**

electronic money (e-money) Money that exists only in electronic form and substitutes for cash as well.   **51**

emerging market economies Economies in an earlier stage of market development that have recently opened up to the flow of goods, services, and capital from the rest of the world.   **199**

endowment insurance See *permanent life insurance.*   **272**

equation of exchange The equation $MV = PY$, which relates nominal income to the quantity of money.   **526**

equilibrium Condition that determines quantities and prices.   **571**

equities Claims to share in the net income and assets of a corporation (such as common stock).   **24**

equity capital See *net worth.*   **170**

equity multiplier (EM) The amount of assets per dollar of equity capital.   **306**

Eurobonds Bonds denominated in a currency other than that of the country in which they are sold.   **31**

Eurocurrencies A variant of the Eurobond; foreign curren-cies deposited in banks outside the home country.   **31**

Eurodollars U.S. dollars that are deposited in foreign banks outside the United States or in foreign branches of U.S. banks. **31**

European option An option that can be exercised only at the expiration date of the contract. **334**

European System of Central Banks (ESCB) Refers to the European Central Bank and the national central banks of all European Union (EU) member countries; when all EU member countries adopt the euro, the Eurosystem and the European System of Central Banks will become one entity. **369**

Eurosystem Refers to the European Central Bank and the national central banks of the countries that have adopted the euro. **369**

excess demand A situation in which quantity demanded is greater than quantity supplied. **78**

excess reserves Reserves in excess of desired reserves. **377**

excess supply A situation in which quantity supplied is greater than quantity demanded. **89**

Exchange Fund Account The fund that holds Canada's official foreign exchange assets. **357**

exchange rate The price of one currency stated in terms of another currency. **470, 545**

exchange-rate peg Fixing the value of the domestic currency to the value of another currency, so the exchange rate is fixed. **513**

exchange-rate targeting See *exchange-rate peg.* **513**

exchanges Secondary markets in which buyers and sellers of securities (or their agents or brokers) meet in one central location to conduct trades. **25**

exercise price (strike price) The price at which the purchaser of an option has the right to buy or sell the underlying financial instrument. **335**

exogenous Independent of variables in the model. **543**

expectations theory The proposition that the interest rate on a long-term bond will equal the average of the short-term interest rates that people expect to occur over the life of the long-term bond. **120**

expected return The return on an asset expected over the next period. **85**

face value A specified final amount paid to the owner of a coupon bond at the maturity date. Also called *par value.* **65**

fair-value accounting See *mark-to-market accounting.* **219**

fallen angels Investment-grade securities whose rating has fallen to junk levels. **115**

federal funds rate The interest rate on overnight loans of deposits at the Federal Reserve. **368, 429**

Federal Open Market Committee (FOMC) The committee that makes decisions regarding the conduct of open market operations; composed of the seven members of the Board of Governors of the Federal Reserve System, the president of the Federal Reserve Bank of New York, and the presidents of four other Federal Reserve banks on a rotating basis. **366**

Federal Reserve banks The 12 district banks in the Federal Reserve System. **366**

Federal Reserve System (the Fed) The central banking authority responsible for monetary policy in the United States. **366**

fiat money Paper currency decreed by a government as legal tender but not convertible into coins or precious metal. **50**

finance paper Short-term secured promissory notes issued by sales finance companies. **27**

financial crisis A major disruption in financial markets that is characterized by sharp declines in asset prices and the failures of many financial and nonfinancial firms. **5, 182**

financial derivatives Instruments that have payoffs that are linked to previously issued securities, used as risk reduction tools. **244, 323**

financial engineering The process of researching and developing new financial products and services that would meet customer needs and prove profitable. **188, 243**

financial frictions Asymmetric information problems that act as a barrier to efficient allocation of capital. **182**

financial futures A futures contract in which the standardized commodity is a particular type of financial instrument. **326**

financial futures option An option in which the underlying instrument is a futures contract. Also called a *futures option.* **334**

financial globalization The process of economies opening up to flows of capital and financial firms from other nations. **199**

financial innovation When an economy introduces new types of financial products. **6, 182**

financial intermediaries Institutions (such as banks, insurance companies, mutual funds, pension funds, and finance companies) that borrow funds from people who have saved and then make loans to others. **5**

financial intermediation The process of indirect finance whereby financial intermediaries link lender-savers and borrower-spenders. **33**

financial liberalization The elimination or restrictions on financial markets. **182**

financial markets Markets in which funds are transferred from people who have a surplus of available funds to people who have a shortage of available funds. **2**

financial panic The widespread collapse of financial markets and intermediaries in an economy. **41**

financial supervision (prudential supervision) Overseeing who operates financial institutions and how they are operated. **216**

fire sales Forced, rapid sales of assets to raise needed funds. **184**

fiscal policy Policy that involves decisions about government spending and taxation. **10**

Fisher effect The outcome that when expected inflation occurs, interest rates will rise; named after economist Irving Fisher. **86**

fixed exchange rate regime A regime in which central banks buy and sell their own currencies to keep their exchange rates fixed at a certain level. **497**

fixed investment Spending by firms on equipment (computers, airplanes) and structures (factories, office buildings) and planned spending on residential housing.   **543**

fixed-payment loan A credit market instrument that provides a borrower with an amount of money that is repaid by making a fixed payment periodically (usually monthly) for a set number of years.   **65**

float Cash items in process of collection at the Bank of Canada minus deferred-availability cash items.   **53, 383**

floating exchange rate regime An exchange rate regime in which the value of currencies are allowed to fluctuate against one another.   **498**

foreign bonds Bonds sold in a foreign country and denominated in that country's currency.   **30**

foreign exchange intervention An international financial transaction in which a central bank buys or sells currency to influence foreign exchange rates.   **492**

foreign exchange market The market in which exchange rates are determined.   **11, 470**

foreign exchange rate See *exchange rate*.   **11**

forward contract An agreement by two parties to engage in a financial transaction at a future (forward) point in time.   **324**

forward exchange rate The exchange rate for a forward transaction.   **471**

forward rate The interest rate predicted by pure expectations theory of the term structure of interest rates to prevail in the future.   **131**

forward transaction A transaction that involves the exchange of bank deposits denominated in different currencies at some specified future date.   **471**

four-pillar approach Regulation of the banking industry by institution (banking, brokerage, trusts, and insurance), versus regulation by function.   **167**

free banking A system that permits the organization of a bank by any group that meets certain established criteria concerning the amount of equity capital and maintenance of reserves.   **239**

free-rider problem The problem that occurs when people who do not pay for information take advantage of the information that other people have paid for.   **167**

fully funded Describing a pension plan in which the contributions to the plan and their earnings over the years are sufficient to pay out the defined benefits when they come due.   **278**

fundamental economic values Values of assets based on realistic expectations of their future income streams.   **184**

futures contract A contract in which the seller agrees to provide a certain standardized commodity to the buyer on a specific future date at an agreed-on price.   **244**

gap analysis A measurement of the sensitivity of bank profits to changes in interest rates, calculated by subtracting the amount of rate-sensitive liabilities from the amount of rate-sensitive assets.   **312**

general equilibrium When all markets are simultaneously in equilibrium at the point where the quantity of aggregate output demanded equals the quantity of aggregate output supplied.   **582**

generalized dividend model Calculates that the price of stock is determined only by the present value of the dividends.   **139**

globalization The growing integration and interdependence of national economies.   **468**

goal independence The ability of the central bank to set the goals of monetary policy.   **358**

gold standard A fixed exchange rate regime under which a currency is directly convertible into gold.   **240, 498**

Gordon growth model A simplified model to compute the value of a stock by assuming constant dividend growth.   **139**

Governing Council A council with six members (including the governor) that is responsible for the management of the Bank of Canada.   **355**

government budget constraint The requirement that the government budget deficit equal the sum of the change in the monetary base and the change in government bonds held by the public.   **531**

government purchases Spending by all levels of government (federal, provincial, and local) on goods and services.   **542, 572**

government-sponsored enterprises (GSEs) In the United States, federally sponsored agencies that function as private corporations with close ties to the government.   **288**

gross domestic product (GDP) The value of all final goods and services produced in the economy during the course of a year.   **18**

group life insurance Insurance sold to a group of people under a single policy.   **271**

haircuts The excess amount of collateral above the amount of the loan.   **193**

hedge To protect oneself against risk.   **244, 323**

hedge fund A special type of mutual fund that engages in "market-neutral strategies."   **285**

hierarchical mandate A mandate for the central bank that puts the goal of price stability first, but as long as it is achieved other goals can be pursued.   **442**

high-powered money The monetary base.   **377**

hyperinflation An extreme inflation in which the inflation rate exceeds 50% per month.   **50, 532**

implementation lag The time it takes for policymakers to change policy instruments once they have decided on a new policy.   **611**

impossible trinity Another term for the policy trilemma, in which a country cannot pursue the following three policies at the same time: free capital mobility, a fixed exchange rate, and an independent monetary policy.   **501**

in-the-money option Option that would be profitable to exercise.   **336**

incentive-compatible Having the incentives of both parties to a contract in alignment.   **174**

income The flow of earnings.   **47**

indebtedness In describing a country, the total amount it has borrowed from banks.   **262**

indexed bond A bond whose interest and principal payments are adjusted for changes in the price level, and whose interest rate thus provides a direct measure of a real interest rate.   **80**

individual life insurance Insurance sold one policy at a time.   **271**

inflation The condition of a continually rising price level.   **8**

inflation gap The difference between inflation and the inflation target.   **603**

inflation hedges Alternative assets whose real returns are less affected than that of money when inflation varies.   **535**

inflation rate The rate of change of the price level, usually measured as a percentage change per year.   **8**

inflation target A central bank target for the inflation rate.   **602**

inflation targeting A monetary policy strategy that involves public announcement of a medium-term numerical target for inflation.   **443**

initial public offering (IPO) A stock whose firm is issuing it for the first time.   **282**

institutional investors Institutional investors—mutual funds and pension funds—are important players in Canadian financial markets; they are also the predominant players in the stock markets, with over 70% of the total daily volume in the stock market due to their trading.   **284**

instrument independence The ability of the central bank to set monetary policy instruments.   **358**

interbank deposits Deposits made at other banks.   **296**

interest parity condition The observation that the domestic interest rate equals the foreign interest rate plus the expected appreciation in the foreign currency.   **489**

interest rate The cost of borrowing or the price paid for the rental of funds (usually expressed as a percentage per year).   **3**

interest-rate forward contract A forward contract that is linked to a debt instrument.   **324**

interest-rate futures contract A futures contract that is linked to a debt instrument. It is similar to an interest-rate forward contract.   **326**

interest-rate risk The possible reduction in returns associated with changes in interest rates.   **77, 300**

interest-rate swap A financial contract that allows one party to exchange (swap) a set of interest payments for another set of interest payments owned by another party.   **342**

intermediate target Any of a number of variables, such as monetary aggregates or interest rates, that have a direct effect on employment and the price level and that the Fed seeks to influence.   **454**

intermediate-term With reference to a debt instrument, having a maturity of between one and ten years.   **24**

International Monetary Fund (IMF) The international organization created by the Bretton Woods agreement whose objective is to promote the growth of world trade by making loans to countries experiencing balance-of-payments difficulties.   **498**

international policy coordination Agreements among countries to enact policies cooperatively.   **468**

international reserves Central bank holdings of assets denominated in foreign currencies.   **492**

intrinsic value The value of an option at expiration.   **336**

inventory investment Spending by firms on additional holdings of raw materials, parts, and finished goods.   **543**

inverted yield curve A yield curve that is downward-sloping.   **118**

investment banks Firms that assist in the initial sale of securities in the primary market.   **24**

IS curve The relationship that describes the combinations of aggregate output and interest rates for which the total quantity of goods produced equals the total quantity demanded (goods market equilibrium).   **548**

items in transit (bank float) Items in the process of collection.   **296**

junk bonds Bonds with ratings below Baa (or BBB) that have a high default risk.   **115**

Keynesian A follower of John Maynard Keynes who believes that movements in the price level and aggregate output are driven by changes not only in the money supply but also in government spending and fiscal policy and who does not regard the economy as inherently stable.   **610**

large, complex banking organizations (LCBOs) Large companies that provide banking as well as many other financial services.   **256**

Large Value Transfer System (LVTS) An electronic, net settlement system for the transfer of large-value payments.   **404**

law of one price The principle that if two countries produce an identical good, the price of this good should be the same throughout the world no matter which country produces it.   **473**

legislative lag The time it takes to pass legislation to implement a particular policy.   **611**

lender of last resort Provider of reserves to financial institutions when no one else would provide them to prevent a financial crisis.   **242, 402**

leverage cycle A feedback loop from a boom in issuing credit, leading to higher asset prices, resulting in higher capital buffers at financial institutions, which supports further lending, which raises prices further, etc.; in the bust, asset prices fall, leading to a cut in lending, a decline in asset prices, and so on.   **220**

leverage ratio A bank's capital divided by its assets.   **215**

leveraged buyout (LBO) A purchase of a publicly traded firm by buying all of its shares, while financing the purchase by increasing the leverage (debt) of the firm.   **287**

liabilities IOUs or debts.   **22**

liability management The acquisition of funds at low cost to increase profits.   **300**

liquid Easily converted into cash.   **24**

liquidity The relative ease and speed with which an asset can be converted into cash.   **49, 85**

liquidity management The decisions made by a bank to maintain sufficient liquid assets to meet the bank's obligations to depositors.   **300**

liquidity preference framework A model developed by John Maynard Keynes that predicts the equilibrium interest rate on the basis of the supply of and demand for money. **99**

liquidity preference theory John Maynard Keynes's theory of the demand for money. **533**

liquidity premium theory The theory that the interest rate on a long-term bond will equal an average of short-term interest rates expected to occur over the life of the long-term bond plus a positive term (liquidity) premium. **124**

liquidity services Services financial intermediaries provide to their customers to make it easier for them to conduct their transactions. **34**

liquidity trap A case of ultrasensitivity of the demand for money to interest rates in which conventional monetary policy has no direct effect on aggregate spending because a change in the money supply has no effect on the interest rate. **536, 567**

load funds Open-end mutual funds sold by salespeople who receive a commission that is paid at the time of purchase and is immediately subtracted from the redemption value of the shares. **284**

loan commitment A bank's commitment (for a specified future period of time) to provide a firm with loans up to a given amount at an interest rate that is tied to some market interest rate. **310**

loan sale The sale under a contract (also called a *secondary loan participation*) of all or part of the cash stream from a specific loan, thereby removing the loan from the bank's balance sheet. **317**

long in a call Purchase of a call option. **335**

long in a put Purchase of a put option. **336**

long position A contractual obligation to take delivery of an underlying financial instrument. **323**

long-term With reference to a debt instrument, having a maturity of 10 years or more. **24**

longer-term refinancing operations A category of open market operations by the European Central Bank that are similar to the U.S. Fed's outright purchases or sales of securities. **434**

LVTS participants Members of the Canadian Payments Association (CPA) who participate in the LVTS and maintain a settlement account at the Bank of Canada. **404**

M1 A measure of money that includes currency, traveller's cheques, and chequable deposits. **53**

M1+ Includes currency, personal chequing accounts, and current accounts, plus other assets that have cheque-writing features—all chequable notice deposits at chartered banks, TMLs, and CUCPs. **53**

M1++ M1, plus all nonchequable notice deposits at chartered banks, TMLs, and CUCPs. **53**

M2 Adds to M1 money market deposit accounts, money market mutual fund shares, smalldenomination time deposits, savings deposits, overnight repurchase agreements, and overnight Eurodollars. **53**

M2+ Includes M2 plus deposits at near banks, life insurance company annuities, and money market mutual funds. **53**

M2++ Adds to M2 Canada Savings Bonds and non-money market mutual funds. **53**

M3 Adds to M2 large-denomination time deposits, long-term repurchase agreements, and institutional money market fund shares. **55**

macro hedge A hedge of interest-rate risk for a financial institution's entire portfolio. **328**

macroeconomic models Models to forecast the effects of policy on economic activity that use collections of equations that describe statistical relationships among many economic variables. **620**

macroprudential supervision Supervision that focuses on the safety and soundness of the financial system in the aggregate. **220**

main refinancing operations Weekly reverse transactions (purchase or sale of eligible assets under repurchase agreements or credit operations against eligible assets as collateral) that are reversed within two weeks and are the primary monetary policy tool of the European Central Bank. **533**

managed float regime An exchange rate regime in which countries attempt to influence their exchange rates by buying and selling currencies (also called a *dirty float*). **498**

management of expectations Term coined by Michael Woodford that refers to the commitment of the central bank to keeping the federal funds rate at near zero for an extended period in order to cause the long-term interest rate to fall. **425**

margin requirement A sum of money that must be kept in an account (the margin account) at a brokerage firm. **332**

marginal lending facility The European Central Bank's standing lending facility in which banks can borrow (against eligible collateral) overnight loans from the national central bank at a rate 100 basis points above the target financing rate. **434**

marginal lending rate The interest rate charged by the European Central Bank for borrowing at its marginal lending facility. **434**

marginal propensity to consume The slope of the consumption function line that measures the change in consumer expenditure resulting from an additional dollar of disposable income. **543**

mark-to-market accounting An accounting method in which assets are valued in the balance sheets at what they would sell for in the market. **219**

marked to market Repriced and settled in the margin account at the end of every trading day to reflect any change in the value of the future contract. **331**

market equilibrium A situation occurring when the quantity that people are willing to buy (demand) equals the quantity that people are willing to sell (supply). **89**

market fundamentals Items that have a direct impact on future income streams of a security. **153**

maturity Time to the expiration date (maturity date) of a debt instrument. **24**

medium of exchange Anything that is used to pay for goods and services. **47**

micro hedge A hedge for a specific asset. **328**

microprudential supervision Supervision that focuses on the safety and soundness of individual financial institutions. **220**

monetarism A theory that emphasizes the importance of money in the economy, but opposes the use of discretionary stabilization policy. **463**

monetarist A follower of Milton Friedman who sees changes in the money supply as the primary source of movements in the price level and aggregate output and who views the economy as inherently stable. **622**

monetary aggregates The measures of the money supply used by the central bank (M1, M2, and M3). **53**

monetary base See *base money*. **376**

monetary conditions Determined by the level of short-term interest rates and the exchange rate of the Canadian dollar. **512**

monetary policy The management of the money supply and interest rates. **10**

monetary policy (*MP*) curve The relationship between the real interest rate the central bank sets and the inflation rate. **559**

monetary theory The theory that relates changes in the quantity of money to changes in economic activity. **7, 525**

monetizing the debt A method of financing government spending whereby the government debt issued to finance government spending is removed from the hands of the public and is replaced by high-powered money instead. Also called *printing money*. **532**

money (money supply) Anything that is generally accepted in payment for goods or services or in the repayment of debts. **6**

money centre banks Large banks in key financial centres (New York, Chicago, San Francisco). **304**

money market A financial market in which only short-term debt instruments (generally those with original maturity of less than one year) are traded. **25**

money multiplier A ratio that relates the change in the money supply to a given change in the monetary base. **391**

money supply The quantity of money. **8**

monoline insurance companies Insurance companies that specialize in credit insurance alone. **273**

moral hazard The risk that one party to a transaction will engage in behaviour that is undesirable from the other party's point of view. **35**

mortgage-backed securities Securities that cheaply bundle and quantify the default risk of the underlying high-risk mortgages. **29, 188**

mortgages Loans to households or firms to purchase housing, land, or other real structures, in which the structure or land itself serves as collateral for the loans. **29**

multilateral netting The LVTS process by which only the net credit or debit position of each participant vis-à-vis all other participants is calculated for settlement, thereby reducing the need for a large amount of settlement balances. **405**

multiple deposit creation The process whereby, when the central bank supplies the banking system with $1 of additional reserves, deposits increase by a multiple of this amount. **384**

municipal bonds (municipals) Bonds issued by cities and other government entities to raise money for public purposes, such as building schools, highways, hospitals, and other special projects. **30**

NAIRU (nonaccelerating inflation rate of unemployment) The rate of unemployment when demand for labour equals supply, consequently eliminating the tendency for the inflation rate to change. **458**

national banks Federally chartered banks in the United States. **239**

natural rate of output The level of aggregate output produced at the natural rate of unemployment at which there is no tendency for wages or prices to change. **441, 577**

natural rate of unemployment The rate of unemployment consistent with full employment at which the demand for labour equals the supply of labour. **440, 576**

net exports Net foreign spending on domestic goods and services, equal to exports minus imports. **542, 572**

net worth The difference between a firm's assets (what it owns or is owed) and its liabilities (what it owes). Also called *equity capital*. **170**

no-load funds Mutual funds sold directly to the public on which no sales commissions are charged. **284**

nominal anchor A nominal variable such as the inflation rate, an exchange rate, or the money supply that monetary policymakers use to tie down the price level. **439**

nominal interest rate An interest rate that does not take inflation into account. **70**

nonactivists Economists who believe wages and prices are very flexible, so the self-correcting mechanism is very rapid; they thus do not see the need to pursue policies to return the economy to full employment. **610**

nonaccelerating inflation rate of unemployment See *NAIRU*. **458**

nonborrowed monetary base The monetary base minus discount loans (borrowed reserves). **383**

nonconventional monetary policy tools Non-interest rate tools central banks use to stimulate the economy: liquidity provision, asset purchases, and commitment to future monetary policy actions. **425**

notional principal The amount on which interest is being paid in a swap arrangement. **343**

off-balance-sheet activities Bank activities that involve trading financial instruments and the generation of income from fees and loan sales, all of which affect bank profits but are not visible on bank balance sheets. **215**

official reserve transactions balance The current account balance plus items in the capital account. **496**

open-end fund A mutual fund from which shares can be redeemed at any time at a price that is tied to the asset value of the fund. **284**

open interest The number of contracts outstanding. **329**

open market buyback operations The Bank of Canada's buying or selling of bonds in the open market. **357**

open market operations The central bank's buying or selling of bonds in the open market. **377**

open market purchase A purchase of bonds by the central bank. **378**

open market sale A sale of bonds by the central bank. **378**

operating band The Bank's operational objective is to keep the overnight rate within an operating band of 25 basis points. **406**

operating instrument A variable that is very responsive to the central bank's tools and indicates the stance of monetary policy (also called *a policy instrument*). **454**

opportunity cost The amount of interest (expected return) sacrificed by not holding an alternative asset. **100**

optimal forecast The best guess of the future using all available information. **144**

option A contract that gives the purchaser the option (right) to buy or sell the underlying financial instrument at a specified price, called the exercise price or strike price, within a specific period of time (the term to expiration). **334**

originate-to-distribute model A business model in which the mortgage is originated by a separate party, typically a mortgage broker, and then distributed to an investor as an underlying asset in a security. **192**

out-of-the-money option An option that would not be profitable to exercise. **336**

output gap The difference between aggregate output and potential output. **577**

over-the-counter (OTC) market A secondary market in which dealers at different locations who have an inventory of securities stand ready to buy and sell securities "over the counter" to anyone who comes to them and is willing to accept their prices. **25**

overdraft loans Borrowings from the Bank of Canada. Also called *advances*. **295**

overnight cash rate The interest rate for very-short-term interbank loans in the euro area. **433**

overnight interest rate (reference rate) The interest rate at which participants borrow and lend overnight funds to each other in the money market. **405**

overnight rate The interest rate on overnight (one-day) securities. **403**

partisan business cycles Systematic and permanent differences in macroeconomic outcomes that differ by political party. **363**

payment technology Methods of payment that include credit cards and electronic payments. **533**

payments system The method of conducting transactions in the economy. **50**

permanent life insurance An insurance policy that has a constant premium throughout the life of the policy. **272**

perpetuity See *consol*. **70**

personal pension plans RRSPs that provide tax-sheltered, self-financed retirement funds. **280**

Phillips curve theory A theory suggesting that changes in inflation are influenced by the state of the economy relative to its production capacity, as well as to other factors. **459**

planned expenditure The total amount of spending on domestically produced goods and services that households, businesses, the government, and foreigners want to make. **542**

planned investment spending Total planned spending by businesses on new physical capital (e.g., machines, computers, apartment buildings) plus planned spending on new homes. **542, 571**

policy instrument A variable that is very responsive to the central bank's tools and indicates the stance of monetary policy (also called an *operating instrument*). **454**

policy rate The target for the Bank of Canada's overnight interest rate. **405**

policy trilemma Situation in which a country cannot pursue the following three policies at the same time: free capital mobility, a fixed exchange rate, and an independent monetary policy. **501**

political business cycle A business cycle caused by expansionary policies before an election. **363, 623**

portfolio A collection or group of assets. **34**

potential output The level of aggregate output produced at the natural rate of unemployment (also called *natural rate of output*). **441, 577**

preferred habitat theory A theory that is closely related to liquidity premium theory, in which the interest rate on a long-term bond equals an average of short-term interest rates expected to occur over the life of the long-term bond plus a positive term premium. **125**

premium The amount paid for an option contract. **334**

present discounted value See *present value*. **62**

present value Today's value of a payment to be received in the future when the interest rate is *i*. Also called *present discounted value*. **62**

price earnings ratio (PE) The ratio of a stock's price to its earnings per share. **141**

price shocks Shifts in inflation that are independent of the amount of slack in the economy or expected inflation. **578**

price stability Low and stable inflation. **438**

primary dealers Government securities dealers, operating out of private firms or commercial banks, with whom the central bank's open market desk trades. **415**

primary market A financial market in which new issues of a security are sold to initial buyers. **24**

principal–agent problem A moral hazard problem that occurs when the managers in control (the agents) act in their own interest rather than in the interest of the owners (the principals) due to different sets of incentives. **171**

printing money See *monetizing the debt*. **532**

private equity fund A fund that makes long-term investments in companies that are not traded in public markets. **287**

private pension plans Voluntary, employer-sponsored plans, with the contributions usually shared between employer and employee. **279**

provincial bonds (provincials) Bonds issued by Canada's provincial governments. **30**

prudential supervision See *financial supervision*. **216**

put option An option contract that provides the right to sell a security at a specified price. **336**

put premium Price of a put option. **336**

quantity theory of money The theory that nominal income is determined solely by movements in the quantity of money. **527**

quantitative easing An expansion of the central bank's balance sheet. **425**

quotas Restrictions on the quantity of foreign goods that can be imported. **473**

random walk The unpredictable movements in the price of a security.

rate of capital gain The change in a security's price relative to the initial purchase price. **75**

rate of return See *return*. **74**

rational expectations Expectations that reflect optimal forecasts (the best guess of the future) using all available information. **144**

real business cycle theory A theory that views real shocks to tastes and technology as the major driving force behind short-run business cycle fluctuations. **593**

real exchange rate The rate at which domestic goods can be exchanged for foreign goods; i.e., the price of domestic relative to foreign goods denominated in domestic currency. **474**

real interest rate The interest rate adjusted for expected changes in the price level (inflation) so that it more accurately reflects the true cost of borrowing. **78**

real money balances The quantity of money in real terms. **534**

real terms Terms reflecting actual goods and services one can buy. **78**

recession A period when aggregate output is declining. **7**

recognition lag The time it takes for policymakers to be sure of what the data are signalling about the future course of the economy. **611**

redeposits Transfers of government deposits from the Bank of Canada to direct clearers. **418**

registered bonds Bonds recorded on the books of a company in the name of the owner. They can be transferred to someone else only with the owner's endorsement. **29**

Regulation Q The regulation under which the Federal Reserve System had the power to set maximum interest rates that banks can pay on time deposits. **248**

regulatory arbitrage A process in which banks keep on their books assets that have the same risk-based capital requirement but are relatively risky, such as a loan to a company with a very low credit rating, while taking off their books low-risk assets, such as a loan to a company with a very high credit rating. **215**

regulatory forbearance Regulators' refraining from exercising their right to put an insolvent bank out of business. **215**

reinsurance An allocation of the portion of the insurance risk to another company in exchange for a portion of the insurance premium. **273**

repo See *special Purchase and Resale Agreements*. **415**

repurchase agreement (repo) An arrangement whereby the central bank, or another party, purchases securities with the understanding that the seller will repurchase them in a short period of time, usually less than a week. **193**

reserve currency A currency, such as the U.S. dollar, that is used by other countries to denominate the assets they hold as international reserves. **499**

reserves Banks' settlement balances with the Bank of Canada plus currency that is physically held by banks (vault cash). **296, 377**

residual claimant The right as a shareholder to receive whatever remains after all other claims against the firm's assets have been satisfied. **138**

restrictive covenants Provisions that restrict and specify certain activities that a borrower can engage in. **163**

return The payments to the owner of a security plus the change in the security's value, expressed as a fraction of its purchase price. More precisely called the rate of return. **74**

return on assets (ROA) Net profit after taxes per dollar of assets. **305**

return on equity (ROE) Net profit after taxes per dollar of equity capital. **305**

revaluation Resetting of the fixed value of a currency at a higher level. **501**

reverse repo See *Sale and Repurchase Agreements*. **415**

reverse transactions Purchase or sale of eligible assets by the central bank under repurchase agreements or credit operations against eligible assets as collateral that are reversed within two weeks. **433**

reverses Banks' holdings of deposits in accounts with the central bank plus currency that is physically held by banks (vault cash). **415**

risk The degree of uncertainty associated with the return on an asset. **34, 85**

risk of default See *default*. **113**

risk premium The spread between the interest rate on bonds with default risk and the interest rate on default-free bonds. **112**

risk sharing The process of creating and selling assets with risk characteristics that people are comfortable with and then using the funds acquired by selling these assets to purchase other assets that may have far more risk. **34**

risk structure of interest rates The relationship among the interest rates on various bonds with the same term to maturity. **112**

rules Binding plans that specify how policy will respond (or not respond) to particular data such as unemployment and inflation. **621**

Sale and Repurchase Agreements (SRAs) The Bank of Canada's sale of government securities to primary dealers with an agreement to repurchase them one business day later. **451**

Schedule I banks Comprised of the Big Six, together with the Laurentian Bank of Canada, the Canadian Western Bank, and another 14 domestic banks. **252**

Schedule II banks Comprised of 55 banks, including a number of domestic Schedule II banks and foreign bank subsidiaries.   **252**

Schedule III banks Foreign banks allowed to branch directly into Canada, under certain restrictions.   **252**

seasoned issue A stock issued for sale for which prior issues currently sell in the market.   **282**

secondary market A financial market in which securities that have previously been issued (and are thus second-hand) can be resold.   **24**

secondary reserves Short-term government securities held by banks.   **296**

secured debt Debt guaranteed by collateral.   **163**

securitization The process of transforming illiquid financial assets into marketable capital market instruments.   **188, 247**

security A claim on the borrower's future income that is sold by the borrower to the lender. Also called a *financial instrument*.   **3**

segmented markets theory A theory of term structure that sees markets for different-maturity bonds as completely separated and segmented such that the interest rate for bonds of a given maturity is determined solely by supply of and demand for bonds of that maturity.   **123**

seigniorage The revenue a government receives by issuing money.   **240, 519**

self-correcting mechanism A characteristic of the economy that causes output to return eventually to the natural rate level regardless of where it is initially.   **585**

settlement balances Deposits held by directly clearing members of the Canadian Payments Association at the Bank of Canada. They are also known as *clearing balances*.   **295, 377**

shadow banking system A system in which bank lending is replaced by lending via the securities market.   **192, 242**

shareholders Those who hold stock in a corporation.   **138**

short in a call Sale of a call option.   **335**

short in a put Sale of a put option.   **336**

short position A contractual obligation to deliver an underlying financial instrument.   **323**

short sales Borrowing stock from brokers and then selling the stock in the market, with the hope that a profit will be earned by buying the stock back again ("covering the short") after it has fallen in price.   **154**

short-term With reference to a debt instrument, having a maturity of one year or less.   **24**

simple deposit multiplier The multiple increase in deposits generated from an increase in the banking system's reserves in a simple model in which the behaviour of depositors and banks plays no role.   **387**

simple loan A credit market instrument providing the borrower with an amount of funds that must be repaid to the lender at the maturity date along with an additional payment (interest).   **62**

smart card A stored-value card that contains a computer chip that lets it be loaded with digital cash from the owner's bank account whenever needed.   **52**

sovereign debt Government debt issued in a foreign currency.   **196**

sovereign debt crisis A rise in interest rates faced by a government due to fear that it will default.   **196**

sovereign loans Loans to foreign governments and their agencies in the less developed countries.   **262**

sovereign wealth fund A state-owned investment fund that invests in foreign assets.   **284**

special Purchase and Resale Agreements (sPRAs) The Bank of Canada's purchase of government securities from primary dealers with an agreement to resell them one business day later.   **415**

specials See *term Purchase and Resale Agreements (PRAs)* and *Sale and Repurchase Agreements (SRAs)*.   **415**

special drawing rights (SDRs) An IMF-issued paper substitute for gold that functions as international reserves.   **504**

specialist A dealer-broker operating in an exchange who maintains orderly trading of the securities for which he or she is responsible.   **283**

speculative attack A situation in which speculators engage in massive sales of a currency.   **202**

spot exchange rate The exchange rate for a spot transaction.   **471**

spot rate The interest rate at a given moment.   **131**

spot transaction The predominant type of exchange rate transaction, involving the immediate exchange of bank deposits denominated in different currencies.   **471**

stagflation A situation of rising inflation but a falling level of aggregate output.   **590**

standing lending facility A lending facility in which healthy banks are allowed to borrow all they want from a central bank.   **421**

standing liquidity facilities Refers to the Bank of Canada standing ready to lend to or borrow from a participant to bring their settlement balances to zero at the end of the banking day.   **407**

state banks State-chartered banks in the United States.   **239**

state-owned banks Banks that are owned by governments.   **177**

sterilized foreign exchange intervention A foreign exchange intervention with an offsetting open market operation that leaves the monetary base unchanged.   **494**

stock A security that is a claim on the earnings and assets of a company.   **3**

stock market risk The risk associated with fluctuations in stock prices.   **333**

stock option An option on an individual stock.   **334**

store of value A repository of purchasing power over time.   **49**

stress tests Tests of financial institutions that calculate losses and the need for more capital under dire scenarios.   **218**

structured credit products Securities that are derived from cash flows of underlying assets and are tailored to have particular risk characteristics that appeal to investors with different preferences.   **188**

subprime mortgages Mortgages for borrowers with less than stellar credit records.   **188**

supply curve A curve depicting the relationship between quantity supplied and price when all other economic variables are held constant. **88**

supply shock Any change in technology or the supply of raw materials that can shift the aggregate supply curve. **578**

swap A financial contract that obligates one party to exchange (swap) a set of payments it owns for a set of payments owned by another party. **342**

sweep account An arrangement in which any balances above a certain amount in a corporation's chequing account at the end of a business day are "swept out" of the account and invested in overnight repos that pay the corporation interest. **249**

systemic risk The risk to the entire payments system due to the inability of one financial institution to fulfill its payment obligations in a timely fashion. **404**

systemically important financial institutions (SIFIs) Firms designated as systemically important that are subject to additional oversight and regulation. **233**

T-account A simplified balance sheet with lines in the form of a T that lists only the changes that occur in balance sheet items starting from some initial balance sheet position. **297**

target financing rate The European Central Bank's target for the overnight cash rate, the interest rate for very-short-term interbank loans in the euro area. **433**

tariffs Taxes on imported goods. **576**

Taylor principle The principle that the monetary authorities should raise nominal interest rates by more than the increase in the inflation rate. **457, 559**

Taylor rule Economist John Taylor's monetary policy rule that explains how the federal funds rate target is set. **457**

temporary life insurance An insurance policy with a premium that is matched every year to the amount needed to insure against death during the period of the term. **272**

term deposit receipts (term notes) Deposit instruments requiring a minimum investment at a predetermined interest rate for a stated term. **27**

term Purchase and Resale Agreements (PRAs) The Bank of Canada's purchase of government securities from primary dealers with an agreement to resell then at a specified future date. **428**

term repo See *term Purchase and Resale Agreements (PRAs)*. **428**

term structure of interest rates The relationship among interest rates on bonds with different terms to maturity. **112**

theory of efficient capital markets See efficient market hypothesis. **146**

theory of portfolio choice A theory of how much of an asset people want to hold in their portfolio, with the amounts determined by wealth, expected returns, risk, and liquidity. **86**

theory of purchasing power parity (PPP) The theory that exchange rates between any two currencies will adjust to reflect changes in the price levels of the two countries. **476**

time-inconsistency problem The problem that occurs when monetary policymakers conduct monetary policy in a discretionary way and pursue expansionary policies that are attractive in the short run but lead to bad long-run outcomes. **439**

trade balance The difference between merchandise exports and imports. **496**

transaction costs The time and money spent trying to exchange financial assets, goods, or services. **33**

transmission mechanisms of monetary policy The channels through which the money supply affects economic activity. **638**

Troubled Asset Relief Plan (TARP) Provision of the Bush administration's Economic Recovery Act of 2008 that authorized the Treasury to spend $700 billion to purchase subprime mortgage assets from troubled financial institutions or to inject capital into these institutions. **196**

trustee The representative of a person or corporation. **258**

underfunded Describing a pension plan in which the contributions and their earnings are not sufficient to pay out the defined benefits when they come due. **278**

underwriting Purchasing securities from a corporation at a predetermined price and then reselling them in the market. **24**

underwriters Investment banks that guarantee prices on securities to corporations and then sell the securities to the public. **282**

unemployment rate The percentage of the labour force not working. **7**

unexploited profit opportunity A situation in which an investor can earn a higher than normal return. **149**

unit of account Anything used to measure value in an economy. **48**

unsecured debt Debt not guaranteed by collateral. **163**

unsterilized foreign exchange intervention A foreign exchange intervention in which a central bank allows the purchase or sale of domestic currency to affect the monetary base. **493**

value at risk (VaR) Calculations that measure the size of the loss on a trading portfolio that might happen 1% of the time over a short period—say two weeks. **218**

vault cash Currency that is physically held by banks and stored in vaults overnight. **296**

velocity of money The rate of turnover of money; the average number of times per year that a dollar is spent in buying the total amount of final goods and services produced in the economy. **526**

venture capital fund A financial intermediary that pools the resources of its partners and uses the funds to help entrepreneurs start up new businesses. **287**

virtual bank A bank that has no building but rather exists only in cyberspace. **245**

wealth All resources owned by an individual, including all assets. **47, 85**

World Bank The International Bank for Reconstruction and Development, an international organization that provides long-term loans to assist developing countries in building dams, roads, and other physical capital that would contribute to their economic development.   **498**

World Trade Organization (WTO) An organization head-quartered in Geneva, Switzerland, that monitors rules for the conduct of trade between countries (tariffs and quotas).   **498**

yield curve A plot of the interest rates for particular types of bonds with different terms to maturity.   **118**

yield to maturity The interest rate that equates the present value of payments received from a credit market instrument with its value today.   **66**

zero-coupon bond See *discount bond*.   **65**

zero-lower-bound problem The liquidity trap a central bank faces when the short-term nominal interest rate is zero or near zero.   **425**

INDEX

Italicized *t* refers to tables, *f* refers to figures, and *b* refers to boxed material.